April 22–26, 2017
L'Aquila, Italy

Association for
Computing Machinery

Advancing Computing as a Science & Profession

ICPE'17

Proceedings of the 2017 ACM/SPEC International Conference on Performance Engineering

Sponsored by:

ACM SIGMETRICS, ACM SIGSOFT, & SPEC

Supported by:

Novatec, University of L'Aquila, & L'Aquila City Council

Association for
Computing Machinery

Advancing Computing as a Science & Profession

The Association for Computing Machinery
2 Penn Plaza, Suite 701
New York, New York 10121-0701

ISBN: 978-1-4503-4404-3 (Digital)

ISBN: 978-1-4503-5454-7 (Print)

Additional copies may be ordered prepaid from:

ACM Order Department
PO Box 30777
New York, NY 10087-0777, USA

Phone: 1-800-342-6626 (USA and Canada)
+1-212-626-0500 (Global)
Fax: +1-212-944-1318
E-mail: acmhelp@acm.org
Hours of Operation: 8:30 am – 4:30 pm ET

Printed in the USA

ICPE 2017 General Chairs' Welcome

It is with great pleasure we welcome you to the 8th ACM/SPEC International Conference on Performance Engineering (ICPE), and to the historical town of L'Aquila. Laid out within medieval walls upon a hillside in the middle of a narrow valley, tall snow-capped mountains of the Gran Sasso massif flank the town. A maze of narrow streets, lined with Baroque and Renaissance buildings and churches, open onto elegant piazzas. Home to the University of L'Aquila, it is a lively college town and, as such, has many cultural institutions.

This year ICPE continues its tradition of representing the premier forum for the integration of theory and practice in the field of performance engineering, while founding its roots into the ACM Workshop on Software Performance (WOSP since 1998) and the SPEC International Performance Engineering Workshop (SIPEW since 2008). It brings together researchers and industry practitioners to share ideas, discuss challenges, and present results of both work-in-progress and state-of-the-art research on performance engineering of software and systems.

Stemming from roots, ICPE 2017 is the fruit of a great team work.

Firstly, many thanks go to the Program Co-Chairs, Anne Koziolek and Evgenia Smirni, for the enormous effort they have put in attracting an excellent Research Program Committee, and in keeping the high-quality of papers with an exciting research track. The Industrial Chair, Meikel Poess, has done a very good job in selecting, along with the Industry Program Committee, an interesting set of industry research papers. The conference program has been enriched by a large and various set of workshops, thanks to the dedication of Hanspeter Mössenböck and Catia Trubiani, our Workshop Chairs, by an interesting mix of tutorials resulting from the thoughtful effort of Valeria Cardellini, our Tutorial Chair, and by a stimulating selection of posters and demos made by Lubomir Bulej, our Poster and Demo Chair. Moreover, we were delighted to attract three excellent keynote speakers: Thomas Wuerthinger (Oracle Labs), Francesco Quaglia (University of Rome La Sapienza) and Arif Merchant (Google).

The whole Organizing Committee has been invaluable in running a smooth process, and in particular we acknowledge the efforts of: André van Hoorn, for his dedicated job as Finance Chair; Petr Tuma and Murray Woodside, our Award Chairs, for running the award process; Davide Arcelli, for putting together the proceedings and managing the registration process, as our Publication and Registration Chair; our Publicity Chairs, Diego Perez and Andrea Rosà, for a broad, accurate and timely advertisement of the conference across traditional and novel publicity channels; Cathy Sandifer first, and thereafter Daniele Di Pompeo, our Web Chairs, for their continuous and timely updates to the web site. A special thank goes to Antinisca Di Marco for handling the multitude of local arrangements.

Our sincere thanks go to SPEC and ACM, through SIGSOFT and SIGMETRICS, for their continuous support. We are also thankful to Novatec, our corporate supporter, and to University of L'Aquila and L'Aquila City Council, our local supporters.

On behalf of the whole organizing committee, we welcome you to L'Aquila and hope you will enjoy the conference and the city.

Walter Binder
University of Lugano, Switzerland
ICPE 2017 General Co-Chair

Vittorio Cortellessa
University of L'Aquila, Italy
ICPE 2017 General Co-Chair

ICPE 2017 Program Chairs' Welcome

Welcome to the *8th ACM/SPEC International Conference on Performance Engineering (ICPE)*, taking place in L'Aquila, Italy, in April 22-26, 2017. The goal of ICPE is to integrate theory and practice in the field of performance engineering by providing a forum for sharing ideas and experiences between industry and academia. ICPE grew out of the ACM Workshop on Software Performance (WOSP Est. 1998) and the SPEC International Performance Engineering Workshop (SIPEW Est. 2008). It is a great pleasure to introduce the exciting program for this year's conference in which researchers and practitioners present their latest research, newest innovations, and vision for the future of performance engineering.

We received 83 high quality submissions across the Research, Industry/Experience and Work-In-progress/Vision tracks. The Research Track attracted 65 submissions with 24 papers (22 full, 2 short) accepted for presentation. In the Work-In-Progress/Vision Track 14 out of 25 contributions were selected and the Industry/Experience track attracted 18 submissions of which 5 were accepted for presentation. Each paper received at least three reviews from program committee members. Four best paper award candidates were also selected. The best paper is to be announced during the ICPE 2017 social event, after all four papers are presented at the conference.

We are excited to also present three keynote talks as part of the technical program.

- *Micro-Benchmarking Considered Harmful; When the Whole is Faster or Slower Than the Sum of its Parts,* by Thomas Wuerthinger (Oracle Labs)
- *Performance is Also a Matter of Where You Live,* by Francesco Quaglia (University of Rome La Sapienza)
- *Autonomic storage management at scale*, by Arif Merchant (Google)

In addition, the program includes five tutorials, a poster and demo track, the SPEC Distinguished Dissertation Award, and eight interesting workshops on Autonomous Control for Performance and Reliability Trade-offs in Internet of Services (ACPROSS), on Performance Analysis of Big Data Systems (PABS), on Challenges in Performance Methods for Software Development (WOSP-C), on Energy-aware Simulation (ENERGY-SIM), on Load Testing and Benchmarking of Software Systems (LTB), on Monitoring in Large-Scale Software Systems (MoLS), on Education and Practice of Performance Engineering (WEPPE), and on Quality-aware DevOps (QUDOS).

The program covers traditional ICPE topics such as design for performance and problem diagnosis, online performance management, analytic models, empirical studies, model building, and benchmarking, as well as application of performance engineering theory and techniques to several practical fields, including distributed systems, cloud computing, storage, energy, big data, virtualized systems, and hardware.

We thank all the authors who submitted their innovative work to ICPE this year. In addition, we thank all the program committee members and external reviewers for volunteering their time for the benefit of the ICPE community and their hard work in providing quality reviews. Finally, we thank all ICPE participants as we rely on you to make this event interactive, engaging, and thought-provoking for everyone involved.

Anne Koziolek
Technical Program co-Chair, Karlsruhe Institute of Technology, Germany

Evgenia Smirni
Technical Program co-Chair, College of William & Mary, USA

Meikel Poess
Industry Program Chair, Oracle Corporation, USA

Table of Contents

ICPE 2017 Conference Organization ix

ICPE 2017 Sponsors & Supporters xii

Keynote Address I

- **Micro-Benchmarking Considered Harmful** 1
  Thomas Wuerthinger *(Oracle Labs)*

Session 1: Memory and Hardware Impact

- **A Comprehensive Java Benchmark Study on Memory and Garbage Collection Behavior of DaCapo, DaCapo Scala, and SPECjvm2008** 3
  Philipp Lengauer, Verena Bitto, Hanspeter Mössenböck, Markus Weninger *(Johannes Kepler University)*
- **An Incremental Methodology for Energy Measurement and Modeling** 15
  Abdelhafid Mazouz, David C. Wong, David Kuck *(Intel Corporation)*, William Jalby *(UVSQ/ECR)*
- **Detecting Memory-Boundedness with Hardware Performance Counters** 27
  Daniel Molka, Robert Schöne, Daniel Hackenberg,
  Wolfgang E. Nagel *(Center for Information Services and High Performance Computing)*
- **Transferring Performance Prediction Models Across Different Hardware Platforms** 39
  Pavel Valov, Jean-Christophe Petkovich *(University of Waterloo)*,
  Jianmei Guo *(East China University of Science and Technology)*,
  Sebastian Fischmeister, Krzysztof Czarnecki *(University of Waterloo)*
- **Using Libception to Understand and Improve HTTP Streaming Video Server Throughput** 51
  Tyler Szepesi, Benjamin Cassell, Tim Brecht *(University of Waterloo)*, Derek Eager *(University of Saskatchewan)*,
  Jim Summers, Bernard Wong *(University of Waterloo)*

Session 2: Online Performance Management

- **An Empirical Analysis of Amazon EC2 Spot Instance Features Affecting Cost-effective Resource Procurement** 63
  Cheng Wang, Qianlin Liang, Bhuvan Urgaonkar *(Pennsylvania State University)*
- **An Experimental Performance Evaluation of Autoscaling Policies for Complex Workflows** 75
  Alexey Ilyushkin *(Delft University of Technology)*, Ahmed Ali-Eldin *(Umeå University)*,
  Nikolas Herbst *(University of Würzburg)*, Alessandro V. Papadopoulos *(Mälardalen University)*,
  Bogdan Ghit, Dick Epema, Alexandru Iosup *(Delft University of Technology)*
- **Dynamic Memory Partitioning for Cloud Caches with Heterogeneous Backends** 87
  Cristina L. Abad, Andres G. Abad, Luis E. Lucio *(Escuela Superior Politecnica del Litoral)*
- **Latency Aware Elastic Switching-based Stream Processing Over Compressed Data Streams** 91
  Sajith Ravindra, Miyuru Dayarathna *(WSO2, Inc.)*, Sanath Jayasena *(University of Moratuwa)*
- **On Moving Averages, Histograms and Time-Dependent Rates for Online Measurement** 103
  Michael Menth, Frederik Hauser *(University of Tuebingen)*

Session 3: Model Building

- **AutoPerf: Automated Load Testing and Resource Usage Profiling of Multi-Tier Internet Applications** 115
  Varsha Apte, T.V.S. Viswanath, Devidas Gawali, Akhilesh Kommireddy,
  Anshul Gupta *(Indian Institute of Technology - Bombay)*

- **Deriving Parameters for Open and Closed QN Models of Operational Systems through Black Box Optimization** ... 127
  Mahmoud Awad, Daniel A. Menascé *(George Mason University)*
- **HyperStar2: Easy Distribution Fitting of Correlated Data** ... 139
  Zhihao Shang, Tianhui Meng, Katinka Wolter *(Free University of Berlin)*
- **IRIS: Iterative and Intelligent Experiment Selection** ... 143
  Raoufehsadat Hashemian *(University of Calgary)*, Niklas Carlsson *(Linköping University)*, Diwakar Krishnamurthy, Martin Arlitt *(University of Calgary)*

Posters and Demonstrations Session

- **Autopilot: Enabling Easy Benchmarking of Workload Energy Efficiency** ... 155
  Jóakim von Kistowski, Maximilian Deffner *(University of Würzburg)*, Jeremy A. Arnold *(IBM Corporation)*, Klaus-Dieter Lange *(Hewlett-Packard Enterprise)*, John Beckett *(Dell Inc.)*, Samuel Kounev *(University of Würzburg)*
- **Accelerating Java Streams with a Data Analytics Hardware Accelerator** ... 157
  Karthik Ganesan, Ahmed Khawaja, Luyang Wang, Shrinivas Joshi, Michelle Szucs, Melina Demertzi, Yao-Min Chen *(Oracle Corp.)*
- **Technology Migration Challenges in a Big Data Architecture Stack** ... 159
  Rekha Singhal, Shruti Kunde *(TCS Innovation Labs)*
- **Time Bands: A Software Approach for Timing Analysis on Resource Constrained Systems** ... 161
  Giacomo Valente, Marco Rotondi, Vittoriano Muttillo *(TCS Innovation Labs)*
- **Open Source In-Memory Data Grid Systems: Benchmarking Hazelcast and Infinispan** ... 163
  Haytham Salhi, Feras Odeh, Rabee Nasser, Adel Taweel *(Birzeit University)*
- **SQL Query Volume Performance Estimation Tool** ... 165
  Rekha Singhal, Chetan Phalak *(TCS Research)*
- **(h|g)opper: Performance History Mining and Analysis** ... 167
  Christoph Laaber, Philipp Leitner *(University of Zurich)*
- **Generalized Synchronizations and Capacity Constraints for Java Modelling Tools** ... 169
  Giuliano Casale *(Imperial College London)*, Mattia Cazzoli *(Politecnico di Milano)*, Shuai Jiang, Vitor S. Lopes *(Imperial College London)*, Giuseppe Serazzi *(Politecnico di Milano)*, Lulai Zhu *(Imperial College London)*
- **PerfExt++: Performance Extrapolation of IO Intensive Workloads** ... 171
  Dheeraj Chahal, Mukund Kumar, Manoj Karunakaran Nambiar *(Tata Consultancy Services)*
- **DESiDE: Discrete Event Simulation Developers Environment** ... 173
  Beeny Mathew, Dheeraj Chahal *(Tata Consultancy Services)*
- **Demo: Time Series Online Measurement for Python (TSOMpy)** ... 175
  Michael Menth, Frederik Hauser *(University of Tuebingen)*

Keynote Address II

- **Performance is Also a Matter of Where You Live** ... 177
  Francesco Quaglia *(Sapienza University of Rome)*

Session 4: Industry and Experience

- **A Performance-centric Approach for Complex Decision Support** ... 179
  Ate Penders *(Thales Research & Technology)*, Ana Lucia Varbanescu *(University of Amsterdam)*, Gregor Pavlin *(Thales Research & Technology)*, Henk Sips *(Delft University of Technology)*
- **CloudPerf: A Performance Test Framework for Distributed and Dynamic Multi-Tenant Environments** ... 189
  Nicolas Michael, Nitin Ramannavar, Yixiao Shen, Sheetal Patil, Jan-Lung Sung *(Oracle Inc.)*
- **Cost-Efficient and Reliable Reporting of Highly Bursty Video Game Crash Data** ... 201
  Drew Zagieboylo, Kazi A. Zaman *(Electronic Arts)*

- **Technique for Detecting Early-Warning Signals of Performance Deterioration in Large Scale Software Systems** 213
  Raghu Ramakrishnan *(Tata Consultancy Services)*, Arvinder Kaur *(Guru Gobind Singh Indraprastha University)*
- **HPC Supported Mission-Critical Cloud Architecture** 223
  Tae Joon Jun, Myong Hwan Yoo, Daeyoung Kim *(Korea Advanced Institute of Science and Technology)*, Kyu Tae Cho, Seung Young Lee *(LIG Nex1 Corporation)*, Kyuoke Yeun *(Agency of Defense Development)*

Session 5: Analytic Models

- **A Tool Supporting the Analytical Evaluation of Service Level Agreements** 233
  Falko Bause, Peter Buchholz, Johannes May *(TU Dortmund)*
- **Analytic Models of Checkpointing for Concurrent Component-Based Software Systems** 245
  Noor Bajunaid, Daniel A. Menascé *(George Mason University)*
- **Practical Implication of Analytical Models for SSD Write Amplification** 257
  Changhyun Park *(Hanyang University)*, Seongjin Lee *(Gyeongsang National University)*, Youjip Won *(Hanyang University)*, Soohan Ahn *(The University of Seoul)*
- **Schedulability and Memory Interference Analysis of Multicore Preemptive Real-time Systems** 263
  Jalil Boudjadar, Simin Nadjm-Tehrani *(Linköping University)*
- **Timeliness Evaluation of Intermittent Mobile Connectivity over Pub/Sub Systems** 275
  Georgios Bouloukakis, Nikolaos Georgantas *(Inria Paris)*, Ajay Kattepur *(TCS Research & Innovation)*, Valérie Issarny *(Inria Paris)*

Session 6: Benchmarking

- **Conducting Repeatable Experiments in Highly Variable Cloud Computing Environments** 287
  Ali Abedi, Tim Brecht *(University of Waterloo)*
- **HTAPBench: Hybrid Transactional and Analytical Processing Benchmark** 293
  Fábio Coelho, João Paulo *(INESC TEC & Universidade do Minho)*, Ricardo Vilaça *(LeanXcale SL)*, José Pereira, Rui Oliveira *(INESC TEC & Universidade do Minho)*
- **TARUC: A Topology-Aware Resource Usability and Contention Benchmark** 305
  Gavin Baker *(Sandia National Laboratory)*, Chris Lupo *(California Polytechnic State University)*
- **Cloning IO Intensive Workloads Using Synthetic Benchmark** 317
  Dheeraj Chahal, Manoj Nambiar *(TCS Innovation Labs)*

Keynote Address III

- **Autonomic Storage Management at Scale** 321
  Arif Merchant *(Google, Inc.)*

Session 7: Design for Performance and Problem Diagnosis

- **An Efficient Performance-Driven Approach for HW/SW Co-Design** 323
  Daniele Di Pompeo *(University of L'Aquila)*, Emilio Incerto *(Gran Sasso Science Institute)*, Vittoriano Muttillo, Luigi Pomante, Giacomo Valenete *(University of L'Aquila)*
- **DuckTracks: Path-based Object Allocation Tracking** 327
  Stefan Fitzek, Philipp Lengauer, Hanspeter Mössenböck *(Johannes Kepler University)*
- **Efficient Sampling-based Lock Contention Profiling for Java** 331
  Andreas Schörgenhumer, Peter Hofer, David Gnedt, Hanspeter Mössenböck *(Johannes Kepler University)*
- **Identifying Derived Performance Requirements of System Components from Explicit Customer- and Application- Facing Performance Requirements** 335
  André B. Bondi *(Software Performance and Scalability Consulting LLC)*

- **Many Flies in One Swat: Automated Categorization of Performance Problem Diagnosis Results** 341
  Tobias Angerstein, Dušan Okanović *(University of Stuttgart)*, Christoph Heger *(NovaTec Consulting GmbH)*, André van Hoorn *(University of Stuttgart)*, Aleksandar Kovačević *(University of Novi Sad)*, Thomas Kluge *(NovaTec Consulting GmbH)*
- **Performance Analysis of Applications in the Context of Architectural Rooflines** 345
  Boyana Norris, Wyatt Spear, Allen Malony *(University of Oregon)*
- **Performance and Dependability Evaluation of Distributed Event-based Systems: A Dynamic Code-injection Approach** 349
  Saleh Mohamed, Matthew Forshaw, Nigel Thomas *(Newcastle University)*, Andrew Dinn *(Red Hat UK Ltd)*
- **Predicting Power Consumption of High-Memory-Bandwidth Workloads** 353
  Norbert Schmitt, Jóakim von Kistowski, Samuel Kounev *(Universität Würzburg)*
- **User-centered Offline Analysis of Memory Monitoring Data** 357
  Markus Weninger, Philipp Lengauer, Hanspeter Mössenböck *(Johannes Kepler University)*

Session 8: Empirical Studies

- **An Empirical Study of Computation-Intensive Loops for Identifying and Classifying Loop Kernels: Full Research Paper** 361
  Masatomo Hashimoto, Masaaki Terai, Toshiyuki Maeda, Kazuo Minami *(RIKEN Advanced Institute for Computational Science)*
- **An Exploratory Study of the State of Practice of Performance Testing in Java-Based Open Source Projects** 373
  Philipp Leitner *(University of Zurich)*, Cor-Paul Bezemer *(Queen's University)*
- **Collaborative Computing for Heterogeneous Integrated Systems** 385
  Li-Wen Chang *(University of Illinois at Urbana-Champaign)*, Juan Gómez-Luna *(Universidad de Córdoba)*, Izzat El Hajj, Sitao Huang, Deming Chen, Wen-mei Hwu *(University of Illinois at Urbana-Champaign)*
- **Empirical Study of Usage and Performance of Java Collections** 389
  Diego Costa, Artur Andrzejak, Janos Seboek *(Heidelberg University)*, David Lo *(Singapore Management University)*
- **Unit Testing Performance in Java Projects: Are We There Yet?** 401
  Petr Stefan, Vojtěch Horký *(Charles University)*, Lubomír Bulej *(Charles University & Università della Svizzera italiana)*, Petr Tůma *(Charles University)*
- **Agile Scalability Requirements** 413
  Gunnar Brataas, Tor Erlend Fægri *(SINTEF Digital)*

Tutorials

- **ICPE 2017 Tutorials Chair's Welcome** 417
  Valeria Cardellini *(University of Rome Tor Vergata)*
- **Software Performance Analytics in the Cloud** 419
  Kingsum Chow, Wanyi Zhu *(Alibaba Inc)*
- **SPEC Cloud ™ IaaS 2016 Benchmark** 423
  Salman Bast, Marcio Silva *(IBM Research)*, Nicholas Wakou *(Dell)*
- **Design and Evaluation of a Proactive, Application-Aware Auto-Scaler: Tutorial Paper** 425
  André Bauer, Nikolas Herbst, Samuel Kounev *(University of Würzburg)*
- **Application Performance Management: State of the Art and Challenges for the Future** 429
  Christoph Heger *(NovaTec Consulting GmbH)*, André van Hoorn *(University of Stuttgart)*, Mario Mann *(NovaTec Consulting GmbH)*, Dušan Okanović *(University of Stuttgart)*
- **An Introduction to Systems and Control Theory for Computer Scientists and Engineers** 433
  Alberto Leva *(Politecnico di Milano)*

Author Index 437

ICPE 2017 Conference Organization

General Chairs: Walter Binder *(Università della Svizzera Italiana, Switzerland)*
Vittorio Cortellessa *(Università dell'Aquila, Italy)*

Research Program Chairs: Anne Koziolek *(Karlsruhe Institute of Technology, Germany)*
Evgenia Smirni *(College of Williama and Mary, USA)*

Industry Program Chair: Meikel Poess *(Oracle, USA)*

Tutorials Chair: Valeria Cardellini *(Università di Roma Torvergata, Italy)*

Workshops Chairs: Hanspeter Mössenböck *(Johannes Kepler Universität Linz, Austria)*
Catia Trubiani *(Gran Sasso Science Institute, Italy)*

Demos and Posters Chair: Lubomir Bulej *(Charles University, Czech Republic)*

Awards Chairs: Petr Tuma *(Charles University, Czech Republic)*
Murray Woodside *(Carleton University, Canada)*

Proceedings & Registrations Chair: Davide Arcelli *(Università dell'Aquila, Italy)*

Finance Chair: André van Hoorn *(University of Stuttgart, Germany)*

Publicity Chairs: Andrea Rosà *(Università della Svizzera Italiana, Switzerland)*
Diego Perez *(Politecnico di Milano, Italy)*

Web Chairs: Daniele Di Pompeo *(Università dell'Aquila, Italy)*
Cathy Sandifer *(SPEC, USA)*

Local Organization Chair: Antinisca Di Marco *(Università dell'Aquila, Italy)*

Steering Committee: Andre B. Bondi (Co-Chair) (*Software Performance & Scalability Consulting LLC, USA)*
Samuel Kounev (Co-Chair) (*University of Würzburg, Germany)*
Meikel Poess (Secretary) (*Oracle Corporation, CA, USA)*
J. Nelson Amaral (*University of Alberta, Canada)*
Vittorio Cortellessa (*University of L'Aquila, Italy)*
Klaus-Dieter Lange (*Hewlett-Packard Enterprise, USA)*
Raffaela Mirandola (*Politecnico di Milano, Italy)*
Jerry Rolia
Alexandru Iosup (*Delft University of Technology, Netherlands)*
Bran Selic *(Simula Research Laboratory, Norway)*
Peter Tůma (*Charles University, Czech Republic)*
Murray Woodside (*Carleton University, Canada)*

Program Committee (Research Track, Work-in-Progress & Vision Track):

Amy Apon *(Clemson University)*
Martin Arlitt *(HP Labs and University of Calgary)*
Alberto Avritzer *(Sonatype Performance Engineering)*
Steffen Becker *(University of Technology Chemnitz)*
Robert Birke *(IBM Zurich Research Laboratory)*
Andre B. Bondi *(Software Performance and Scalability Consulting)*
Niklas Carlsson *(Linkoping University)*
Lydia Chen *(IBM Research)*
Lucy Cherkasova *(HPLabs)*
Vittoria de Nitto Personè *(Università di Roma Tor Vergata)*
Antinisca Di Marco *(Università dell'Aquila)*
Wilhelm Hasselbring *(Kiel University)*
Alexandru Iosup *(Delft University of Technology)*
Evangelia Kalyvianaki *(City University London)*
Samuel Kounev *(University of Wuerzburg)*
Heiko Koziolek *(ABB Corporate Research)*
Diwakar Krishnamurthy *(University of Calgary)*
Patrick P. C. Lee *(The Chinese University of Hong Kong)*
Catalina M.Lladó *(Universitat Illes Balears)*
Lei Lu *(VMware)*
Andrea Marin *(University of Venice)*
Daniel Menasce *(George Mason University)*
Daniel Sadoc Menasché *(Federal University of Rio de Janeiro)*
José Merseguer *(Universidad de Zaragoza)*
Ningfang Mi *(Northeastern University)*
Raffaela Mirandola *(Politecnico di Milano)*
Manoj Nambiar *(Tata Consultancy Services)*
Dorina Petriu *(Carleton University)*
Denys Poshyvanyk *(College of William and Mary)*
Ralf Reussner *(Karlsruhe Institute of Technology)*
Alma Riska *(Network Appliances)*
Jerry Rolia
Rekha Singhal *(Tata Consultancy Services)*
Mirco Tribastone *(IMT Institute for Advanced Studies Lucca)*
Catia Trubiani *(Gran Sasso Science Institute)*
Petr Tuma *(Charles University)*
Ana Lucia Varbanescu *(University of Amsterdam)*
Enrico Vicario *(University of Florence)*
Katinka Wolter *(Freie Universitaet zu Berlin)*
Murray Woodside *(Carleton University)*
Feng Yan *(University of Nevada-Reno)*
Xiaoyun Zhu *(Futurewei Technologies, Inc.)*

Program Committee (Industry Track):

Jeremy Arnold *(IBM)*
Andy Bond *(Red Hat)*
Klaus-Dieter Lange *(HPE)*
Raghu Nambiar *(Cisco)*
Dmitry Potapov *(Oracle)*
Tilmann Rabl *(Bankmark)*
Da Qi Ren *(Huawei R&D)*
Cloyce Spradling *(Oracle)*
Mike Tricker *(Microsoft)*

Additional reviewers:

André Bauer
Prateek Bhatnagar
Marco Biagi
Erik Burger
Axel Busch
Valeria Cardellini
Laura Carnevali
Sara Fioravanti
Markus Frank
Nikolas Roman Herbst
Marcus Hilbrich
Pushpa Hj
Emilio Incerto
Joseph Kanjirakkattu
Debish Kassa
Andrew Keithly
Heiko Klare
Greg Kopczynski
Karthik Kulkarni
Philipp Merkle
Armin Moebius
Kevin Moran
Danny Nasr
Fulvio Patara
Navaneeth Rameshan
Jose Ignacio Requeno
Rajesh Shroff
Christian Stier
Robert Underwood
Srinivasan Varadarajan Sahasranamam
Hector Vazquez
Jóakim von Kistowski
Jürgen Walter
Zhengyu Yang
Yi Yao
Jinzhong Zhang
Huichao Zhao
Christian Zirkelbach

ICPE 2017 Sponsors & Supporters

Sponsors:

Supporter:

Institutional Supporters:

UNIVERSITÀ DEGLI STUDI DE L'AQUILA

Comune dell'Aquila

Micro-Benchmarking Considered Harmful

Thomas Wuerthinger
Oracle Labs
Zurich, Switzerland
thomas.wuerthingerl@oracle.com

ABSTRACT

Measuring the time spent on small individual fractions of program code is a common technique for analysing performance behavior and detecting performance bottlenecks. The benefits of the approach include a detailed individual attribution of performance and understandable feedback loops when experimenting with different code versions. There are however severe pitfalls when following this approach that can lead to vastly misleading results. Modern dynamic compilers use complex optimisation techniques that take a large part of the program into account. There can be therefore unexpected side-effects when combining different code snippets or even when running a presumably unrelated part of the code. This talk will present performance paradoxes with examples from the domain of dynamic compilation of Java programs. Furthermore, it will discuss an alternative approach to modelling code performance characteristics that takes the challenges of complex optimising compilers into account.

CCS Concepts/ACM Classifiers

• Software and its engineering ~ Dynamic compilers

Author Keywords

Compilers; benchmarking; performance; compiler optimisations; dynamic compilation;

ICPE'17, April 22–26, 2017, L'Aquila, Italy.
ACM ISBN 978-1-4503-4404-3/17/04.
http://dx.doi.org/10.1145/3030207.3053656

BIOGRAPHY

Thomas Wuerthinger is a Senior Research Director at Oracle Labs leading programming language implementation teams for languages including Java, JavaScript, Ruby, and R. He is the architect of the Graal compiler and the Truffle self-optimising runtime system. Previously, he worked on the Crankshaft optimising compiler of V8 at Google, and the Maxine research virtual machine at Sun Microsystems. He received a PhD degree from JKU Linz for his research about dynamic code evolution.

A Comprehensive Java Benchmark Study on Memory and Garbage Collection Behavior of DaCapo, DaCapo Scala, and SPECjvm2008

Philipp Lengauer[1] Verena Bitto[2] Hanspeter Mössenböck[1] Markus Weninger[2]

[1]Institute for System Software
Johannes Kepler University Linz, Austria
philipp.lengauer@jku.at

[2]Christian Doppler Laboratory MEVSS
Johannes Kepler University Linz, Austria
verena.bitto@jku.at

ABSTRACT

Benchmark suites are an indispensable part of scientific research to compare different approaches against each another. The diversity of benchmarks is an important asset to evaluate novel approaches for effectiveness and weaknesses. In this paper, we describe the memory characteristics and the GC behavior of commonly used Java benchmarks, i.e., the DaCapo benchmark suite, the DaCapo Scala benchmark suite and the SPECjvm2008 benchmark suite. The paper can serve as a useful guide to select benchmarks in accordance with desired application characteristics on modern virtual machines as well as with different compilers and garbage collectors. It also helps to put results that are based on these benchmarks into perspective. Additionally, we compare Java's current default collector to the G1 GC.

Categories and Subject Descriptors

[**General and reference**]: Evaluation; [**General and reference**]: Performance

Keywords

Java, Benchmarks, Memory Behavior, GC Behavior, DaCapo, DaCapo Scala, SPECjvm2008

1. INTRODUCTION

Benchmarks are a state-of-the-art method to determine the quality of virtual machines, compiler optimizations, garbage collection algorithms, and monitoring tools in terms of performance. Results of such measurements are used, for example, to argue the superiority of one garbage collection algorithm over another, to demonstrate the benefits of a new optimization technique, or to evaluate the overhead of a new monitoring method.

ICPE'17, April 22-26, 2017, L'Aquila, Italy

 ISBN 978-1-4503-4404-3/17/04... $15.00

DOI: http://dx.doi.org/10.1145/3030207.3030211

Considerable effort has been put into building benchmark suites to represent diverse and real-world applications. The most widely used Java benchmark suites are DaCapo[1] introduced by Blackburn et al. [2], DaCapo Scala[2] introduced by Sewe et al. [7], SPECjvm2008[3] analyzed by Shiv et al. [8] and SPECjbb[4]. Unfortunately, those benchmarks either lack a detailed analysis of their comprising applications or their respective analysis is out of date. Since memory management, compilers, and GC algorithms have evolved since the introduction of those benchmarks, their actual behavior in modern systems is undocumented.

However, when reporting performance measurements, the selection of benchmarks is paramount to be able to report descriptive and comprehensive results. Moreover, interpreting results is difficult if one is unaware of the significant properties of the benchmarks at hand, especially if exceptional or unexpected behavior must be explained. Consequently, researchers tediously reexamine benchmarks to find properties that might explain observed behavior.

The goal and contribution of this work is to provide a description of commonly used benchmarks in terms of memory behavior and garbage collection behavior. We do not want to encourage cherry-picking benchmarks but rather enable researchers and reviewers to better evaluate the work of others. We will show important properties of popular Java benchmarks, as well as curiosities one should be aware of when using them and when evaluating other work based on these benchmarks. Furthermore, we split the benchmarks into categories, depending on observed properties, such as allocated memory, survivor ratios, live sizes, and garbage collection times under different virtual machine configurations. We selected DaCapo, DaCapo Scala and SPECjvm2008 because they are the most popular Java benchmark suites, they are free to use, and they are open source, which makes them ideal for scientific evaluations.

Since the observer effect in state-of-the-art monitoring approaches distorts the application behavior significantly (cf. Bitto et al. [1] for detailed analysis on the observer effect in memory and GC monitoring), we will base our analysis on AntTracks, a memory monitoring tool that is accurate at the

[1]http://www.dacapobench.org/
[2]http://www.dacapo.scalabench.org/
[3]https://www.spec.org/jvm2008/
[4]https://www.spec.org/jbb2015/

object-level and imposing only very low run-time overhead, first introduced by Lengauer et al. [6].

This paper is structured as follows: In Section 2 we describe our research methodology. Section 3 shows different metrics with respect to an application's allocation behavior and garbage collection behavior per benchmark suite. Section 4 presents related work, while Section 5 concludes this paper.

2. METHODOLOGY

This section describes the research methodology, i.e., the benchmarks we used and their configuration, the hardware setup, as well as the method of measurement.

Benchmarks.

Figure 1 shows all benchmarks of the DaCapo (version 9.12), DaCapo Scala (version 0.1.0-20120216.103539-3) and SPECjvm2008 benchmark suite, i.e., all benchmarks we will examine in this paper. It also shows the input used, the number of warmups performed before measurement, and the live size of every benchmark. The live size is defined as the maximum number of bytes alive at any given point in time throughout the execution of the benchmark. The input size is either identified by name (for DaCapo and DaCapo Scala) or by the number of operations (for SPECjvm2008, based on the concurrent lagom workload). The number of warmups, i.e., the number of times we executed the benchmark before measuring results, is ideally 20, however, we increased or decreased the warmups of specific benchmarks based on the input. We chose 20 (modified according to the input size) as the baseline for the warmups because the DaCapo suite's built-in mechanism automatically detects a steady state after at most this amount of warmups. Furthermore, we needed to increase the number of warmups until JIT-compilation and GC ergonomics also stabilized. As most benchmarks completely stabilized (i.e., DaCapo built-in convergence, JIT-compilation, GC ergonomics, and heap space resizing) after a similar number of warmups (close to 20, or a factor thereof depending on the input size), we chose 20 as a round number of wamups for all benchmarks. This number also prooved useful for the SPECjvm benchmarks built-in warmup mechanism runs for the same amount of time (the SPECjvm warmup mechanism is based on time rather than iterations). Some DaCapo and DaCapo Scala benchmarks have *huge* and *gargantuan* workloads, which we used to put more pressure on the memory system. In these cases we were able to decrease the number of warmups. Other benchmarks do not have large loads, or the large and default loads crash on Java 8 (because they rely on internal classes that do not exist any longer). In these cases we used the biggest functioning workload, and increased the number of warmups accordingly. The live size has been determined by finding the lowest maximum heap setting with which the benchmarks will execute without an `OutOfMemoryError`. This live size was determined by trial and error, i.e., binary searching the lowest possible heap setting with the `Xmx` flag with 1KB granularity. We will use a multiple of the live size to determine a realistic heap limit.

Setup.

All measurements were run on an Intel® Core(TM) i7-4770 CPU @ 3.40GHz x 4 (8 Threads) on 64-bit with 32 GB RAM and a Samsung SSD 840 PRO Series (DXM03B0Q), running Ubuntu Wily Werewolf 15.10 with the Kernel Linux 4.2.0-25-generic. All unnecessary services were disabled in order not to distort the experiments.

	Benchmark	Warmups	Input	Live[MB]
DaCapo	avrora	20	large	7.49
	batik	80	small	24.74
	eclipse	80	small	14.26
	fop	40	default	29.57
	h2	10	huge	1300.67
	jython	20	large	27.93
	luindex	40	default	5.03
	lusearch	20	large	2.64
	pmd	20	large	38.06
	sunflow	20	large	11.06
	tomcat	10	huge	17.02
	tradebeans	10	huge	278.42
	tradesoap	10	huge	110.81
	xalan	20	large	5.16
DaCapo Scala	actors	5	gargantuan	17.02
	apparat	5	gargantuan	66.68
	factorie	5	gargantuan	558.27
	kiama	40	default	6.45
	scalac	20	large	71.86
	scaladoc	20	large	68.44
	scalap	20	large	5.76
	scalariform	10	huge	19.15
	scalaxb	10	huge	109.06
	tmt	10	huge	39.22
SPECjvm2008	compiler.compiler	20	160ops	229.10
	compiler.sunflow	20	160ops	144.32
	compress	20	40ops	85.20
	crypto.aes	20	16ops	41.75
	crypto.rsa	20	120ops	3.19
	crypto.signverify	20	96ops	18.32
	derby	20	240ops	435.10
	mpegaudio	20	40ops	4.49
	scimark.fft.large	20	8ops	612.17
	scimark.fft.small	20	80ops	16.46
	scimark.lu.large	20	8ops	583.21
	scimark.lu.small	20	96ops	10.78
	scimark.monte_carlo	20	72ops	2.93
	scimark.sor.large	20	8ops	294.84
	scimark.sor.small	20	65ops	6.70
	scimark.sparse.large	20	8ops	446.93
	scimark.sparse.small	20	16ops	11.45
	serial	20	200ops	367.17
	sunflow	20	120ops	19.26
	xml.transform	20	56ops	35.12
	xml.validation	20	320ops	92.79

Figure 1: Benchmarks and their respective warmups, inputs (the name of the input for DaCapo and DaCapo Scala, and the number of operations for SPECjvm2008), and live sizes.

Measurement.

All numbers reported in this paper represent the steady-state performance of 50 runs, based on Georges et al. [4, 5]. Every benchmark has been warmed up before measurement to stabilize caches as well as JIT optimization. Consequently, we report peak performance only, i.e., we exclude all warmup runs and present the best value of the 50 measurements, whereupon the best run is defined as the measurment with the minimal run time. Also, we forced a garbage collection before every measurement to collect leftovers from previous warmups. This collection is not included in the measurement (because it would not occur naturally would we not force it).

In order to record global performance numbers, such as run time, compilation time, as well as garbage collection frequency and time, we used a custom agent hooking into the VM using the Java Virtual Machine Tool Interface (JVMTI) in combination with benchmark-specific mechanisms (DaCapo Callbacks and SPECjvm2008 Analyzers). We were very careful not to enable any capabilities in the VM that would change the VM's behavior.

To make more detailed measurements, we used AntTracks (version 20160101), a special HotSpot-based VM (based on OpenJDK 8u102), that records a trace of memory events almost without changing the VM's behavior. Based on the generated trace, we extracted metrics such as allocated objects, survivor ratios and top allocation sites.

AntTracks is able to record memory traces almost without changing the original behavior because it is implemented, compared to other state-of-the-art tools, directly into the VM and uses a very efficient trace format. It does not have to deal with heavy-weight instrumentation that impedes escape analysis and it also does not have to introduce `WeakReferences` for finalizers to detect object deallocations. The VM and especially the GC's are modified to efficiently generate a very compact event trace, omitting everything that can be reconstructed offline. A dedicated offline tool then postprocesses the trace and reconstructs everything that has been omitted. Moreover, the trace is complete, i.e., it does not miss a single object allocation of internal GC operation. Thus, the only disruption that might occur is a small overall overhead around 4%.

3. STUDY

The following sections describe the memory and garbage collection behavior of the benchmarks with a heap that is limited to three times the respective live size (adaptive heap limit). For evaluating the garbage collection behavior we used the *ParallelOld GC*, the current default collector in the HotSpot^{TM} VM. Figures for the concurrent *G1 GC*, the designated default collector in Java SE 9 allowing the handling of big heaps more efficiently, can be found in the appendix.

3.1 Allocation Behavior

This section examines the allocation behavior of every benchmark in detail. As allocations are only marginally influenced by the GC, we report only the results with an adaptive heap and the ParallelOld GC.

Figure 2 shows the basic allocation behavior of all examined benchmarks. It presents the number of allocations of every benchmark (final measurement iteration only, VM startup and warmups excluded), in number of objects as well as in bytes. The table also shows the number of objects and the amount of memory allocated per second, as well as the average object layout, i.e., the average object size, the percentage of array objects and their average length.

Total Allocations.

Measuring the total number of allocations (per iteration) shows us that factorie, serial, tmt, sunflow (SPECjvm2008) and derby are the 5 most allocation-intensive benchmarks. They allocate up to $5.7 * 10^9$ objects in a single iteration, which puts significant pressure on the GC. Looking at the amount of memory being allocated, the 5 most memory-intensive benchmarks are again factorie, serial, sunflow, derby, and tmt. Please note, that factorie and sunflow (SPECjvm2008) allocate up to 137GB and 134GB of memory respectively.

This metric is of particular interest when developing new allocation algorithms or instrumentation-based memory monitoring tools. Memory monitoring tools often instrument every `new` instruction to record allocations. They collect information such as the type, size, or length in case of an array. As these tools want to distort the application's behavior as little as possible in order to present the user with accurate analyses, benchmarks exhibiting a high number of allocations are interesting to use as a baseline for overhead measurements.

Allocation Rate.

Measuring object allocations per second (i.e., the number of objects allocated within one iteration divided by the run time of that iteration), the 5 most intensive benchmarks are derby, serial, tmt, factorie, and xml.transform (please note, that there are several other benchmarks that are only slightly below) with up to $3 * 10^7$ new objects per second. This number will have a direct impact on the garbage collection frequency (cf. Section 3.3). Looking at the amount of memory allocated every second, the most intensive benchmarks are derby, serial, sunflow (SPECjvm2008), tmt, and xml.transform.

Similarly to the total number of allocations, this metric is of interest for VM implementors and monitoring tool developers alike. Moreover, the allocation rate will have a significant impact if the underlying hardware is not fast enough, i.e., memory monitoring tools may write their data to disk. In addition, this metric is of interest for GC developers because a high allocation rate will lead to a high GC frequency. Also, the allocation rate may be a vital basic information for manually tuning GC parameters, i.e., to minimize the overall GC time or to keep the maximum pause time below a predefined threshold.

Object Layout.

In contrast to the total number of allocations, the largest objects are allocated by the scimark.fft.large benchmark. However, since all scimark benchmarks have a short run time and a small allocation rate in common, their actual pressure on the memory is low. The ratios of instances and arrays vary widely, ranging from 3.2 % arrays in the case of sunflow (SPECjvm2008) to up to 97.5 % in the case of mpegaudio.

Compared to the DaCapo benchmark suite and the DaCapo Scala benchmark suite, the SPECjvm2008 benchmarks show a much higher average array length in general. This is due to the fact, that many benchmarks work on either big input data (e.g., compress, crypto.*, and mpegaudio) or on big matrices (e.g., scimark.*), and, consequently, create many big arrays.

	Benchmark	Allocations				Object layout		
		[10^3]	[MB]	[10^3 / sec]	[MB / sec]	Avg obj size [b]	Array rate [%]	Avg array length
DaCapo	avrora	6,710.1	204.4	828.5	25.2	30.5	31.8	12.1
	batik	462.3	32.4	2,454.0	171.9	70.0	38.6	112.3
	eclipse	676.6	0.0	6,346.7	0.0	61.8	49.1	120.6
	fop	2,511.8	106.8	14,435.4	613.9	42.5	35.1	19.8
	h2	388,081.9	14,838.3	2,498.6	95.5	38.2	38.5	10.8
	jython	180,707.2	7,837.1	18,653.8	809.0	43.4	32.1	58.4
	luindex	217.4	10.6	618.4	30.3	48.9	38.0	182.7
	lusearch	21,904.6	2,270.3	4,565.7	473.2	103.6	44.0	553.0
	pmd	15,660.6	565.4	11,231.9	405.5	36.1	40.3	25.4
	sunflow	138,674.2	6,254.3	24,670.7	1,112.7	45.1	3.4	10.5
	tomcat	177,454.6	9,509.6	5,724.9	306.8	53.6	48.1	106.0
	tradebeans	925,570.5	38,817.5	15,678.1	657.5	40.0	40.0	14.3
	tradesoap	944,162.7	45,057.8	15,178.5	724.4	47.7	36.5	92.2
	xalan	103,069.1	4,989.3	5,614.9	271.8	48.4	40.3	60.9
DaCapo Scala	actors	245,235.3	6,002.2	15,843.8	387.8	24.5	3.9	6.8
	apparat	399,087.3	12,837.0	4,433.0	142.6	32.2	24.9	16.3
	factorie	5,716,589.7	137,521.8	37,494.4	902.0	24.1	5.4	3.9
	kiama	11,384.6	0.0	25,885.9	0.0	35.0	27.4	22.5
	scalac	42,252.8	1,335.0	13,752.4	434.5	31.6	18.9	21.5
	scaladoc	38,065.2	1,471.3	14,958.0	578.2	38.7	30.6	34.8
	scalap	3,454.1	87.4	16,201.3	409.7	25.3	12.3	39.2
	scalariform	50,745.1	1,259.1	21,352.9	529.8	24.8	17.6	7.3
	scalaxb	99,651.5	2,464.6	8,419.4	208.2	24.7	4.6	107.8
	tmt	2,663,579.5	65,294.7	54,697.7	1,340.9	24.5	0.8	62.4
SPECjvm2008	compiler.compiler	471,781.5	15,712.4	19,408.0	646.4	33.3	13.0	41.7
	compiler.sunflow	1,195,208.0	42,073.5	17,498.7	616.0	35.2	16.9	42.3
	compress	36.7	64.9	6.3	11.2	1,767.8	40.8	15,220.5
	crypto.aes	73.9	368.2	8.8	43.8	4,979.5	63.6	61,137.9
	crypto.rsa	32,880.1	2,081.6	2,583.7	163.6	63.3	59.6	26.7
	crypto.signverify	4,009.0	867.1	383.3	82.9	216.3	65.9	1,598.2
	derby	2,001,219.7	77,974.7	86,931.7	3,387.2	39.0	20.6	14.9
	mpegaudio	561.1	279.8	54.2	27.0	498.7	97.5	3,916.1
	scimark.fft.large	1.1	72.6	0.1	9.2	66,335.2	45.6	157,485.6
	scimark.fft.small	87.1	355.5	11.1	45.4	4,080.7	66.9	6,382.7
	scimark.lu.large	34.5	68.5	1.0	1.9	1,985.1	98.3	2,060.3
	scimark.lu.small	4,023.3	875.1	309.2	67.3	217.5	99.1	222.6
	scimark.monte_carlo	13.4	1.5	1.4	0.2	108.1	41.3	748.4
	scimark.sor.large	17.8	34.2	2.5	4.9	1,916.6	96.9	2,021.2
	scimark.sor.small	11.4	1.6	1.7	0.2	141.5	70.1	477.0
	scimark.sparse.large	1.1	53.9	0.1	4.8	50,820.6	48.6	141,717.1
	scimark.sparse.small	6.2	38.1	1.9	11.4	6,154.3	66.0	12,441.3
	serial	3,361,406.2	134,122.4	64,576.1	2,576.6	39.9	48.6	16.2
	sunflow	2,047,771.6	93,002.4	29,547.1	1,341.9	45.4	3.2	9.7
	xml.transform	253,054.8	9,716.2	30,966.1	1,189.0	38.4	39.1	38.6
	xml.validation	807,942.9	27,876.6	30,325.7	1,046.3	34.5	33.5	12.9

Figure 2: Allocations total and per second as well as the average object layout (size, array rate, array length)

3.2 Allocating Subsystems

Figure 3 shows the percentage of objects allocated by VM-internal code (e.g., native code or filler objects for keeping the heap unfragmented), of objects allocated by interpreted code (i.e., code that has not been deemed worth compiling yet), of objects allocated by C1-compiled code (i.e., code that has been compiled by the client compiler), and of objects allocated by C2-compiled code (i.e., code that has been compiled by the server compiler). It also shows the overall compile time ratio, i.e., the time the application spent on compiling in relation to the overall run time.

Allocating Code.

When executing a method for the first time, the VM starts interpreting the code without applying any optimizations. During interpretation, statistics about the method are recorded, e.g., execution counters, branch frequencies, and value ranges for variables. Using these statistics, the method will eventually be compiled by the client compiler. This compiler applies some optimizations and also inserts code to continue recording statistics about executions. Finally, if the method is used often enough, it will be compiled by the server compiler. The server compiler will apply more aggressive optimizations and makes assumptions based on observations made by the interpreter or by the client-compiled code. Should an assumption turn out to be wrong, the compiled code will be discarded and the VM will fall back to the interpreter for this method and start over recording new statistics. Eventually, the VM will retry compilation.

Looking at how much of the allocating code is compiled can tell us how well the benchmark is warmed up because we do not want the VM to execute unoptimized methods or to spend time on compiling while we are measuring. Our measurements show that all benchmarks except some of the SPECjvm2008 scimark.* benchmarks have been properly warmed up with our configuration.

The scimark benchmarks perform mathematical computations that are not very allocation intensive. They consist of small amounts of code operating only on primitive matrices as data structures if any. Consequently, they have an unusually big memory-to-object ratio. Moreover, as they have many long-running methods doing number crunching in loops, it takes some time until they reach an execution frequency that is high enough for triggering compilation. However, because they have neither a lot of total allocations nor a large allocation rate, they are not very useful for examining allocation behavior anyway.

The lusearch benchmark reports 13.7% VM-internal allocations due to the unlucky use of Exceptions in normal control flow. Creating an object of type `Throwable` (superclass of all exceptions and errors) results in a call to the native method **`fillInStackTrace`**. This method walks the stack, creates several `Object`, `short`, and `int` arrays containing the objects, methods, and the corresponding bci offsets on the stack, and finally puts those arrays in the `Throwable` object. The lusearch benchmark allocates more than 99.9% of all VM-internally allocated objects by filling the stack trace of an unnecessary exception, the rest are mostly application domain objects created by cloning. Figure 4 shows the stack of an exception used to indicate the end of a character-based stream.

Like lusearch, the pmd benchmark allocates about 90% of all VM-internal objects by filling the stack trace of an

Suite	Benchmark	Allocated by [%] VM	Int.	C1	C2	Comp. [%]
DaCapo	avrora	1.1	0.0	0.5	98.3	0.11
DaCapo	batik	0.6	0.1	1.8	97.5	1.06
DaCapo	eclipse	4.6	0.0	2.4	93.0	0.00
DaCapo	fop	0.2	0.1	0.9	98.9	24.48
DaCapo	h2	1.0	0.0	0.0	99.0	3.64
DaCapo	jython	2.1	0.0	0.0	97.9	0.85
DaCapo	luindex	1.6	0.3	0.8	97.3	0.70
DaCapo	lusearch	13.7	0.0	0.1	86.2	0.12
DaCapo	pmd	11.6	0.0	0.1	88.3	2.91
DaCapo	sunflow	0.2	0.0	0.0	99.8	0.01
DaCapo	tomcat	1.8	0.0	0.5	97.7	6.80
DaCapo	tradebeans	0.5	0.0	0.0	99.5	3.33
DaCapo	tradesoap	0.4	0.0	0.0	99.6	0.25
DaCapo	xalan	1.8	0.0	0.0	98.2	0.01
DaCapo Scala	actors	0.2	0.0	0.0	99.7	0.39
DaCapo Scala	apparat	0.1	0.0	0.1	99.8	0.37
DaCapo Scala	factorie	0.0	0.0	0.0	100.0	0.18
DaCapo Scala	kiama	0.0	0.0	0.3	99.7	9.37
DaCapo Scala	scalac	0.1	0.3	0.6	99.0	23.59
DaCapo Scala	scaladoc	0.2	0.0	0.7	99.1	13.09
DaCapo Scala	scalap	0.1	0.0	0.6	99.3	10.14
DaCapo Scala	scalariform	0.0	0.0	0.5	99.5	4.72
DaCapo Scala	scalaxb	0.0	0.0	0.1	99.9	1.54
DaCapo Scala	tmt	0.0	0.0	0.0	100.0	0.02
SPECjvm2008	compiler.compiler	0.1	0.0	0.0	99.9	0.11
SPECjvm2008	compiler.sunflow	0.2	0.0	0.0	99.8	0.00
SPECjvm2008	compress	1.4	0.3	29.4	68.9	0.05
SPECjvm2008	crypto.aes	4.3	0.3	8.9	86.5	0.08
SPECjvm2008	crypto.rsa	2.6	0.0	0.0	97.4	0.07
SPECjvm2008	crypto.signverify	1.9	0.0	0.1	98.0	0.01
SPECjvm2008	derby	0.0	0.0	0.0	100.0	0.06
SPECjvm2008	mpegaudio	5.1	0.0	1.3	93.6	0.12
SPECjvm2008	scimark.fft.large	4.9	39.1	42.3	13.7	0.05
SPECjvm2008	scimark.fft.small	5.8	0.2	4.2	89.8	0.11
SPECjvm2008	scimark.lu.large	2.0	48.7	1.4	48.0	0.03
SPECjvm2008	scimark.lu.small	20.0	0.0	0.1	70.6	0.05
SPECjvm2008	scimark.monte_carlo	1.6	1.0	34.7	62.7	0.09
SPECjvm2008	scimark.sor.large	2.7	94.3	2.1	0.8	0.42
SPECjvm2008	scimark.sor.small	8.1	18.9	30.8	42.2	0.01
SPECjvm2008	scimark.sparse.large	9.0	38.5	31.3	21.2	0.02
SPECjvm2008	scimark.sparse.small	20.3	5.2	21.6	53.0	7.23
SPECjvm2008	serial	0.0	0.0	0.0	100.0	0.00
SPECjvm2008	sunflow	0.2	0.0	0.0	99.8	0.02
SPECjvm2008	xml.transform	0.1	0.0	0.0	99.9	0.36
SPECjvm2008	xml.validation	0.6	0.0	0.0	99.4	0.02

Figure 3: Objects allocated by VM-internal code, interpreted code, C1 compiled code, or by C2 compiled code respectively (green: 1st top allocator, yellow: 2nd top allocator, red: 3rd top allocator), as well as the time spent compiling in relation to the overall run time

```
java.lang.Throwable.fillInStackTrace():16
java.lang.Throwable.<init>():24
java.lang.Exception.<init>():2
java.io.IOException.<init>():2
org.apache.lucene.queryParser.
    FastCharStream.refill():156
org.apache.lucene.queryParser.
    FastCharStream.readChar():12
org.apache.lucene.queryParser.
    FastCharStream.BeginToken():9
org.apache.lucene.queryParser.
    QueryParserTokenManager.getNextToken()
    :7
...
```

Figure 4: Stack of an exception used to steer control flow in the lusearch benchmark, resulting in about 2,629,000 objects for representing the stack traces

exception. The other 10% of VM-internal allocations are `Strings` and the corresponding `char[]` that are used to look up classes using an `URLClassLoader`. Figures 5 and 6 show the stack of an exception when using the `URLClassLoader`.

```
java.lang.Throwable.fillInStackTrace():16
java.lang.Throwable.<init>():24
java.lang.Exception.<init>():3
java.lang.ReflectiveOperationException.<
    init>():3
java.lang.ClassNotFoundException.<init>()
    :3
java.net.URLClassLoader.findClass():41
java.lang.ClassLoader.loadClass():70
org.dacapo.harness.DacapoClassLoader.
    loadClass():24
java.lang.ClassLoader.loadClass():38
java.lang.ClassLoader.loadClass():3
net.sourceforge.pmd.typeresolution.
    ClassTypeResolver.processOnDemand():56
```

Figure 5: Stack of an exception used to steer control flow in the pmd benchmark, resulting in 1,598,438 objects for representing the stack traces

```
java.lang.ClassLoader.findLoadedClass():12
java.lang.ClassLoader.loadClass():10
sun.misc.Launcher$AppClassLoader.loadClass
    ():81
java.lang.ClassLoader.loadClass():38
org.dacapo.harness.DacapoClassLoader.
    loadClass():24
java.lang.ClassLoader.loadClass():3
net.sourceforge.pmd.symboltable.
    ScopeAndDeclarationFinder.
    createClassScope():23
```

Figure 6: Stack of class loading by the `URLClassLoader`, resulting in 193,682 objects for looking up a class by name

Compile time.

The JIT compile time ratio (i.e., the summed up compile time of all compilation threads within an iteration divided by the cpu time of that iteration) shows that, if the application has been warmed up properly, the compile time is negligible in most benchmarks. Some benchmarks, however, i.e., fop, scalac, and scalap, show a high compilation time although almost all allocations are already executed by compiled code. This indicates, that these benchmarks should probably be warmed up better if run time performance is measured. However, in these cases we stuck to the selected methodology to be still comparable.

3.3 Garbage Collection

This section examines the garbage collection behavior of every benchmark in detail. For comparability we provide figures for a heap limited to three times the benchmark's live size (see Figure 7). For a fixed heap size of 1GB and for a heap that is unlimited, please refer to Figures 9 and 10 in the Appendix.

Figure 7 shows the garbage collection count, the total garbage collection time, and the average pause time for the ParallelOld GC and the G1 GC. All metrics are split into values for *minor* (-) and *major* (+) collections. In a major collection, the entire heap is collected, whereas a minor collection collects only parts of the heap (the young generation in case of the ParallelOld GC, any subset of regions in case of the G1 GC).

GC Count.

The benchmarks differ widely in terms of GC count, from scimark.fft.large without any collection, to lusearch with 7041 collections. Only some benchmarks perform major collections with the ParallelOld GC.

In general, there is an easy-to-see 97% correlation (linear Pearson correlation) between the number of collections (minor and major) of the ParallelOld GC and the G1 GC. However, the G1 GC usually performs less collections than the ParallelOld GC with only a few exceptions, i.e., compiler.sunflow, crypto.rsa, scimark.fft.small, scimark.lu.*, scimark.sor.large, and serial. This is due to the fact, that G1 can select which heap regions to collect. Consequently, G1 selects regions with a lot of garbage, resulting in more memory being freed. Moreover, G1 can include regions of the old generation in a minor collection, whereas the ParallelOld GC can collect the old generation only with a major collection. This behavior can reduce floating garbage (old dead objects keeping young objects alive) significantly.

In contrast to the ParallelOld GC, where a major collection normally occurs after some minor collections, the G1 GC uses major collection only as an emergency action. For this reason, G1 major collections are so rare and occur only in 4 benchmarks, i.e., lusearch, xalan, scimark.fft.small, and scimark.lu.small. These benchmarks have a very small live set, and consequently a very low heap limit. This shows that G1, although performing well in most cases, is not built to handle small heaps efficiently.

For evaluating garbage collection algorithms which depend on the number of live objects, only allocation-intensive benchmarks with short-living objects are advisable, e.g., tmt and serial. Allocation-intense benchmarks with long-living objects, e.g., derby, are recommendable to test the performance of compaction algorithms, e.g., Mark & Compact.

This metric is interesting to test monitoring tools and GCs which introduce overhead per collection. Especially considering stop-the-world GCs may introduce a significant

Suite	Benchmark	ParallelOld GC Count [#] -	ParallelOld GC Count [#] +	ParallelOld GC Time [%] -	ParallelOld GC Time [%] +	ParallelOld GC Pause [ms] -	ParallelOld GC Pause [ms] +	ParallelOld GC YR [%]	G1 GC Count [#] -	G1 GC Count [#] +	G1 GC Time [%] -	G1 GC Time [%] +	G1 GC Pause [ms] -	G1 GC Pause [ms] +	G1 GC YR [%]
DaCapo	avrora	68	0	1.5	-	1	-	50	48	0	0.7	-	1	-	76
	batik	10	0	11.7	-	2	-	49	3	0	6.5	-	3	-	89
	eclipse	1	0	1.8	-	2	-	531	2	0	3.4	-	2	-	376
	fop	10	0	24.1	-	4	-	58	5	0	12.1	-	3	-	112
	h2	28	0	5.4	-	300	-	94	28	0	1.4	-	81	-	129
	jython	468	0	11.3	-	2	-	111	255	0	5.8	-	2	-	231
	luindex	11	0	7.5	-	2	-	37	5	0	2.3	-	1	-	91
	lusearch	6,979	62	56.0	12.7	0	9	36	4,748	1,431	23.9	64.2	0	7	82
	pmd	50	0	17.8	-	4	-	66	20	0	5.5	-	3	-	137
	sunflow	771	8	15.9	1.6	1	11	53	559	0	12.5	-	1	-	129
	tomcat	1,234	0	4.4	-	1	-	114	680	0	1.9	-	0	-	293
	tradebeans	178	1	14.2	1.0	47	590	49	105	0	5.0	-	29	-	103
	tradesoap	961	12	46.0	4.9	29	254	50	981	0	25.4	-	14	-	93
	xalan	4,607	422	45.8	30.5	1	13	31	3,369	337	32.7	29.8	1	13	50
DaCapo Scala	actors	388	1	1.9	0.0	0	14	53	264	0	1.2	-	0	-	143
	apparat	259	0	1.7	-	6	-	73	148	0	0.8	-	4	-	148
	factorie	272	0	41.1	-	253	-	180	171	0	1.4	-	9	-	100
	kiama	28	0	43.9	-	6	-	59	23	0	22.0	-	3	-	69
	scalac	46	0	25.2	-	16	-	112	22	0	7.4	-	9	-	146
	scaladoc	53	0	26.8	-	12	-	138	26	0	7.6	-	6	-	149
	scalap	40	0	31.6	-	1	-	90	13	0	12.7	-	1	-	276
	scalariform	127	0	21.0	-	3	-	124	48	0	6.8	-	3	-	204
	scalaxb	50	0	2.2	-	5	-	176	35	0	1.2	-	4	-	160
	tmt	2,326	0	4.5	-	0	-	100	1,597	0	3.7	-	1	-	123
SPECjvm2008	compiler.compiler	155	11	50.2	10.9	78	243	41	119	0	32.7	-	54	-	95
	compiler.sunflow	612	54	49.4	13.9	55	175	43	638	0	40.9	-	35	-	68
	compress	14	0	0.1	-	0	-	49	4	0	0.0	-	1	-	177
	crypto.aes	163	2	2.8	0.2	1	8	49	64	0	2.6	-	3	-	6
	crypto.rsa	1,047	2	3.6	0.1	0	7	35	1,078	0	3.7	-	0	-	171
	crypto.signverify	715	32	7.0	2.2	1	7	39	407	0	5.0	-	1	-	21
	derby	181	0	3.5	-	4	-	95	103	0	1.4	-	3	-	184
	mpegaudio	683	7	2.8	0.4	0	6	46	458	0	2.2	-	0	-	109
	scimark.fft.large	0	0	-	-	-	-	-	1	0	0.0	-	1	-	0
	scimark.fft.small	322	0	2.5	-	0	-	100	381	1	4.4	0.0	0	6	15
	scimark.lu.large	2	0	0.1	-	33	-	191	13	0	0.2	-	7	-	54
	scimark.lu.small	1,738	377	14.5	20.1	1	6	34	2,353	44	16.4	2.6	0	8	45
	scimark.monte_carlo	3	0	0.0	-	0	-	115	1	0	0.0	-	1	-	261
	scimark.sor.large	2	0	0.4	-	17	-	190	12	0	0.7	-	4	-	39
	scimark.sor.small	3	0	0.0	-	0	-	74	4	0	0.0	-	1	-	77
	scimark.sparse.large	3	0	0.5	-	20	-	127	1	0	0.0	-	1	-	0
	scimark.sparse.small	70	2	1.4	0.3	0	6	34	45	0	1.4	-	1	-	74
	serial	384	0	0.9	-	1	-	128	1,156	0	1.6	-	0	-	47
	sunflow	5,500	40	10.2	1.0	1	18	51	3,929	0	10.2	-	1	-	132
	xml.transform	562	9	13.1	3.0	1	27	50	333	0	7.8	-	1	-	126
	xml.validation	608	27	23.2	13.8	10	136	51	442	0	16.3	-	9	-	68

Figure 7: GC count, GC time relative to the total run time (green: less than 5%, yellow: less than 15%, red: more than 15%), and average pause time for minor (-) and major (+) GCs for the ParallelOld GC and the G1 GC respectively (green: less than 10ms, yellow: less than 100ms, red: more than 100ms)

overhead when all application threads need to be suspended repeatedly. Also, this metric can be used to tune the GC behavior.

GC Time.

The GC time, i.e., the percentage the application spends on garbage collection relative to its entire run time, depends on the number of collections as well as on the length of every collection. For G1, which marks concurrently, this metric only includes the time the application was paused (the G1 GC is not fully concurrent but pauses the application to move objects). The measurements show that a benchmark can easily spend more than 50% of its total run time on garbage collection. This illustrates that, even if memory performance is not one's primary concern, it must be dealt with.

Again, the G1 GC performs better in most cases with the same exceptions as for the GC count. Especially, in some cases with a high GC time, the G1 performs a lot better (e.g., factorie 41% vs 1.4%).

Obviously, this metric is of interest for GC developers for optimizing garbage collection algorithms. Also, memory monitoring tools that rely on detecting deallocations with the help of `WeakReferences` or finalizers can make good use of benchmarks with a high GC time. As `WeakReferences` and finalizers introduce a lot of additional work for the GC, benchmarks with an already high GC time will be interesting for overhead measurements.

GC Pauses.

The length of a GC pause depends on the complexity of the underlying collection algorithm. The ParallelOld GC and the G1 GC use different algorithms for minor and major collections respectively.

The complexity of a minor collection (in the ParallelOld GC as well as in the G1 GC) mostly depends on the number of live objects residing in the collected regions, as they must be evacuated to the survivor space or promoted to the old generation. The complexity of a major collection (in the ParallelOld GC as well as in the G1 GC) depends on the total number of objects, as both algorithms walk the entire heap to compact live objects towards its beginning.

On average, the minor pause time of the G1 GC is only 71% of the pause time of the ParallelOld GC. In addition, G1 has less spikes in the pause times (e.g., the h2 benchmark has an average pause time of 300ms with the ParallelOld GC, and only 81ms with the G1 GC) . This is mostly due to the fact that G1 can select which regions to collect and consequently can control its pause time as well as the amount of memory that will be freed.

Also, the G1 GC has less and shorter major GCs because a major GC is seen as an emergency that is to be avoided at any cost. The most extreme example is the tradebeans benchmark with a major GC pause time of 590ms in the ParallelOldGC and no major collection in the G1 GC.

Long GC pauses impede the application's availablity. For example, UI applications will need to react within at most half a second on user-input so that the user is not hindered. Similarly, server applications also must react within some time interval to client requests. Long GC pauses will effectively freeze applications. Thus, more concurrent GC algorithms emerge trying to minimize GC pauses, some even try to guarantee a maximum pause time. Benchmarks with long GC pauses are ideal to test these algorithms.

Young Generation Ratio.

The young generation ratio shows the maximum amount of memory before a collection in the young generation in relation to the maximum amount of memory before a collection in the old generation. A value below 100% indicates that the young generation is only a fraction of the old generation, whereas a value larger than 100% indicates that the young generation was bigger. This ratio shows us, whether the GC is able to handle most objects as young objects or if it has to keep a lot of them in the old generation.

Please note, that scimark.fft.large has no such ratio, as there was no collection and the VM consequently did not have the chance to adjust the generation sizes. Also, benchmarks without a major collection might have not yet reached the full capacity of the old generation. Consequently, the ratio is a *high estimate* in those cases.

It is interesting to see, that the ParallelOld GC and the G1 GC do not always agree on what generation is dominant (i.e., whether the young generation ratio is below or above 100%). In general, the young generation is bigger in the G1 GC. Thus, the G1 GC keeps potentially dead objects longer in the young generation compared to the ParallelOld GC.

This metric tells us what part of the garbage collection algorithms are under more pressure and enables focused testing and debugging for new collection algorithms.

3.4 Object References

Figure 8 examines the object pointers that were recorded by AntTracks during garbage collections. Since AntTracks records pointers only during a collection, the recorded pointers depend on the number of garbage collections (initially introduced in Figure 7). While usually the average number of pointers per object is monadic, DaCapo xalan and luindex, DaCapo Scala factorie and kiama, as well as SPECjvm serial stand out in terms of this metric. All these benchmarks make use of few, but very large arrays to store objects. This results in a high average pointer ratio. The DaCapo database h2 is especially useful for all kind of pointer-related measurements due to its high amount of pointers.

4. RELATED WORK

In 2006, Backburn et al. released the DaCapo benchmark suite. At the same time, they published an analysis paper (Blackburn et al. [2]), where they compared their benchmark suite against SPECjvm98 and a modified version of SPECjbb2000. For doing so, they evaluated the DaCapo benchmark suite across different architectures and JVMs. However, 10 years later, Java, JVMs and their components have changed significantly. When they published their paper, the used the Jikes RVM version 2.4.4+. In version 2.9 the Jikes RVM has been substantially rewritten to support Java SE 5. Moreover some benchmarks of the initial release have been completely removed in 2009. New benchmarks, such as avrora, h2, sunflow, are therefore not covered in the paper at all.

In 2006, the DaCapo Scala benchmark suite has been released. In 2011, Sewe et al. [7] analyzed this suite, with a primary focus on the design of the applications. Moreover, they demonstrated the main difference between Java

	Benchmark	Object Pointers (ParallelOld GC) GCs [#]	Ptrs / GC [#]	Avg ptrs / object [#]	Null rate [%]	Old-to-young rate [%]
DaCapo	avrora	68.4	157,143.4	5.1	12.7	6.4
	batik	10.0	161,875.6	4.3	43.1	3.8
	eclipse	1.0	77,906.3	3.0	40.5	4.8
	fop	10.0	351,025.9	3.5	45.4	1.0
	h2	27.6	37,958,744.0	5.8	28.8	8.9
	jython	468.4	1,674.8	3.8	34.6	15.9
	luindex	11.0	83,738.7	14.8	79.1	5.4
	lusearch	7,041.0	11,497.7	9.0	79.0	9.1
	pmd	50.4	443,487.8	3.6	44.9	5.5
	sunflow	774.5	80,871.7	3.3	45.0	15.4
	tomcat	1,234.3	33,188.4	4.9	67.2	15.0
	tradebeans	179.2	4,809,331.3	6.9	50.1	6.7
	tradesoap	973.2	885,545.1	8.3	54.3	6.9
	xalan	5,028.0	339,669.5	26.3	93.2	4.3
	actors	387.5	9,185.8	2.7	25.9	13.8
	apparat	259.8	324,520.0	2.4	23.5	8.1
	factorie	271.9	10,287,986.8	27.8	59.0	9.5
	kiama	28.5	822,980.2	13.0	49.5	6.2
	scalac	45.9	1,623,276.1	5.5	31.3	6.9
	scaladoc	53.0	1,133,381.0	6.1	40.7	6.5
	scalap	40.3	87,220.5	2.8	33.9	6.7
	scalariform	127.8	149,652.0	2.3	8.9	13.3
	scalaxb	48.5	189,187.9	1.5	8.8	0.2
	tmt	2,325.5	7,510.2	3.7	24.5	9.8
SPECjvm2008	compiler.compiler	165.6	8,521,325.4	3.4	28.5	12.2
	compiler.sunflow	665.9	5,843,973.8	3.3	27.7	10.1
	compress	14.1	1,290.0	3.2	43.2	4.3
	crypto.aes	165.6	2,083.5	2.9	45.3	3.1
	crypto.rsa	1,048.6	1,069.7	2.5	40.2	6.9
	crypto.signverify	752.5	5,589.5	2.7	44.1	1.0
	derby	181.0	445,557.6	8.2	15.1	13.6
	mpegaudio	691.0	1,776.3	2.2	38.1	5.0
	scimark.fft.large	0.0	-			
	scimark.fft.small	322.6	240.7	2.1	46.8	19.8
	scimark.lu.large	2.0	24,170.5	1.3	24.5	0.2
	scimark.lu.small	2,116.4	24,004.2	2.4	38.9	0.4
	scimark.monte_carlo	3.0	1,293.0	3.3	46.2	7.3
	scimark.sor.large	2.0	16,820.6	1.8	42.9	0.4
	scimark.sor.small	3.0	3,231.7	1.9	25.6	4.4
	scimark.sparse.large	2.8	906.1	3.6	51.0	5.4
	scimark.sparse.small	71.8	3,257.0	2.7	45.7	1.0
	serial	384.4	51,066.1	10.6	82.8	6.3
	sunflow	5,540.5	88,540.0	4.2	34.5	15.6
	xml.transform	571.3	138,410.2	4.2	54.4	4.4
	xml.validation	638.4	1,201,517.9	3.8	41.8	0.9

Figure 8: Object pointers per GC of all benchmarks

and Scala code. However, they did not provide information regarding memory, pointer, or garbage collection behavior.

The SPECjvm2008 benchmark suite has been evaluated in 2009 by Shiv et al. [8]. While on the one hand they provide a detailed description of all benchmarks, they also present performance numbers for different hardware and software setups. They used Sun's Hotspot JVM (Java SE 6) to perform their evaluations. Though they do not explicitly state the kind of collector they used, we assume from their description that they already used the ParallelGC. While they also present numbers for allocations and garbage collections, their evaluation focuses on hardware-related performance issues, e.g., performance counters on processors, the effect of SMT (simultaneous multi threading). Therefore, their evaluation does not provide insights into the applications' memory behavior, e.g., in terms of allocations, pointers and GC impact.

Dieckmann et al. [3] published a study on the SPECjvm98 benchmark suite in 1998. For their evaluation they used Sun's Hotspot JVM (Java SE 5) and a tracing algorithm to log all memory-related information. However, their monitoring tool performs additional garbage collections and therefore clearly distorts memory behavior. Apart from that, they provide a detailed analysis of heap sizes, object lifetimes and object layout, as well as object references.

5. CONCLUSION

In this paper, we described the memory characteristics and the GC behavior of common Java benchmark suites, i.e., the DaCapo benchmark suite, the DaCapo Scala benchmark suite and the SPECjvm2008 benchmark suite. We showed what benchmarks are best suited when looking for benchmarks with a large total amount of allocations, a high allocation rate, many large objects and large arrays, a high GC count, a high overall GC time, high GC pauses, many young or many old objects, as well as a high pointer density per object. We also showed some curiosities, for example that even though all benchmarks have been warmed up according to the instructions of the respective publishers, the scimark benchmarks allocate most of their objects in code that has not been fully compiled yet, and that the lusearch and pmd benchmarks steer a large part of their normal control flow via exceptions. We want to emphasize that we do not encourage cherry picking benchmarks. However, both researchers and reviewers need to understand whether a selected benchmark meets the characteristics one is trying to test or benchmark.

All tests were applied under modern, state-of-the-art processors, virtual machines, garbage collection algorithms and compilers. We based our analysis on AntTracks, a memory monitoring tool which aims to not distort memory behavior by using a lightweight, VM-internal logging approach.

By revealing internals and curiosities of commonly used benchmarks, this paper provides a basis for explaining outliers in measurement. It can be further used for selecting benchmarks with specific memory characteristics.

6. ACKNOWLEDGEMENTS

This work was supported by the Christian Doppler Forschungsgesellschaft, and by Dynatrace Austria GmbH.

References

[1] V. Bitto and P. Lengauer. Building custom, efficient, and accurate memory monitoring tools for java applications. In *Proceedings of the 7th ACM/SPEC on International Conference on Performance Engineering*, ICPE '16, pages 321–324, New York, NY, USA, 2016. ACM.

[2] S. M. Blackburn, R. Garner, C. Hoffmann, A. M. Khang, K. S. McKinley, R. Bentzur, A. Diwan, D. Feinberg, D. Frampton, S. Z. Guyer, M. Hirzel, A. Hosking, M. Jump, H. Lee, J. E. B. Moss, A. Phansalkar, D. Stefanović, T. VanDrunen, D. von Dincklage, and B. Wiedermann. The DaCapo Benchmarks: Java Benchmarking Development and Analysis. In *Proc. of the Annual ACM SIGPLAN Conf. on Object-oriented Programming Systems, Languages, and Applications*, pages 169–190, 2006.

[3] S. Dieckmann and U. Hoelzle. A study of the allocation behavior of the specjvm98 java benchmarks. Technical report, Santa Barbara, CA, USA, 1998.

[4] A. Georges, D. Buytaert, and L. Eeckhout. Statistically rigorous java performance evaluation. In *Proceedings of the 22Nd Annual ACM SIGPLAN Conference on Object-oriented Programming Systems and Applications*, OOPSLA '07, pages 57–76, New York, NY, USA, 2007. ACM.

[5] A. Georges, L. Eeckhout, and D. Buytaert. Java performance evaluation through rigorous replay compilation. In *Proceedings of the 23rd ACM SIGPLAN Conference on Object-oriented Programming Systems Languages and Applications*, OOPSLA '08, pages 367–384, New York, NY, USA, 2008. ACM.

[6] P. Lengauer, V. Bitto, and H. Mössenböck. Accurate and efficient object tracing for java applications. In *Proc. of the 6th ACM/SPEC Int'l. Conf. on Performance Engineering*, ICPE '15, pages 51–62, 2015.

[7] A. Sewe, M. Mezini, A. Sarimbekov, and W. Binder. Da capo con scala: Design and analysis of a scala benchmark suite for the java virtual machine. In *Proceedings of the 2011 ACM International Conference on Object Oriented Programming Systems Languages and Applications*, OOPSLA '11, pages 657–676, 2011.

[8] K. Shiv, K. Chow, Y. Wang, and D. Petrochenko. Specjvm2008 performance characterization. In *Proceedings of the 2009 SPEC Benchmark Workshop on Computer Performance Evaluation and Benchmarking*, pages 17–35, Berlin, Heidelberg, 2009. Springer-Verlag.

APPENDIX

In this section, we provide additional data we did not discuss in the main sections. Figure 9 and Figure 10 show the same experiment as discussed in Section 3.3, but with a fixed 1GB heap size and an unlimited heap respectively.

	Benchmark	ParallelOld GC Count [#]		ParallelOld GC Time [%]		ParallelOld GC Pause [ms]		ParallelOld GC YR [%]	G1 GC Count [#]		G1 GC Time [%]		G1 GC Pause [ms]		G1 GC YR [%]
		-	+	-	+	-	+		-	+	-	+	-	+	
DaCapo	avrora	1	0	0.0	-	6	-	9,597	13	0	0.4	-	2	-	223
DaCapo	batik	0	0	-	-	-	-	147	0	0	-	-	-	-	131
DaCapo	eclipse	0	0	-	-	-	-	771	2	0	3.4	-	2	-	398
DaCapo	fop	0	0	-	-	-	-	2,891	3	0	6.8	-	3	-	545
DaCapo	h2	oom	oom	oom	oom	oom	oom	oom	296	6	6.7	6.8	43	21,888	16
DaCapo	jython	35	0	1.0	-	2	-	1,588	38	0	1.0	-	2	-	1,839
DaCapo	luindex	0	0	-	-	-	-	604	1	0	1.0	-	3	-	184
DaCapo	lusearch	31	0	3.6	-	1	-	16,592	33	0	4.1	-	1	-	20,528
DaCapo	pmd	3	0	3.7	-	14	-	1,448	7	0	3.2	-	5	-	622
DaCapo	sunflow	18	0	1.1	-	2	-	6,593	34	0	1.8	-	2	-	2,458
DaCapo	tomcat	55	0	0.4	-	2	-	2,045	49	0	0.4	-	2	-	3,821
DaCapo	tradebeans	138	0	11.8	-	54	-	54	92	0	3.2	-	21	-	149
DaCapo	tradesoap	301	0	45.0	-	82	-	123	216	0	25.1	-	53	-	125
DaCapo	xalan	27	0	3.0	-	3	-	8,715	37	0	2.3	-	2	-	3,041
DaCapo Scala	actors	35	0	0.2	-	1	-	6,058	72	0	0.4	-	0	-	342
DaCapo Scala	apparat	50	0	1.1	-	19	-	519	50	0	0.5	-	8	-	396
DaCapo Scala	factorie	421	0	51.9	-	256	-	117	267	1	1.4	0.8	6	978	66
DaCapo Scala	kiama	1	0	3.9	-	9	-	581	2	0	2.4	-	3	-	504
DaCapo Scala	scalac	6	0	9.9	-	41	-	10,076	10	0	4.4	-	11	-	885
DaCapo Scala	scaladoc	8	0	13.9	-	3	-	10,891	10	0	5.1	-	10	-	986
DaCapo Scala	scalap	0	0	-	-	-	-	5,815	4	0	3.2	-	1	-	2,210
DaCapo Scala	scalariform	6	0	0.9	-	2	-	11,451	16	0	2.4	-	3	-	12,931
DaCapo Scala	scalaxb	13	0	1.1	-	10	-	14,787	23	0	0.9	-	4	-	219
DaCapo Scala	tmt	312	0	0.8	-	1	-	378	495	0	1.4	-	1	-	456
SPECjvm2008	compiler.compiler	96	5	51.2	6.5	115	284	41	57	0	27.0	-	77	-	126
SPECjvm2008	compiler.sunflow	226	7	41.3	3.0	78	183	45	97	0	10.5	-	31	-	152
SPECjvm2008	compress	2	0	0.0	-	1	-	278	4	0	0.0	-	1	-	177
SPECjvm2008	crypto.aes	9	0	0.2	-	2	-	1,587	7	0	1.4	-	16	-	1
SPECjvm2008	crypto.rsa	22	0	0.1	-	0	-	2,916	718	0	2.5	-	0	-	150
SPECjvm2008	crypto.signverify	24	0	0.4	-	1	-	2,886	31	0	3.1	-	8	-	11
SPECjvm2008	derby	220	0	3.8	-	5	-	78	144	0	1.6	-	2	-	133
SPECjvm2008	mpegaudio	14	0	0.1	-	0	-	3,911	98	0	0.8	-	0	-	479
SPECjvm2008	scimark.fft.large	1	1	0.5	0.2	47	18	71	1	0	0.0	-	0	-	1
SPECjvm2008	scimark.fft.small	18	0	0.2	-	1	-	2,373	9	0	2.0	-	15	-	1
SPECjvm2008	scimark.lu.large	4	0	0.2	-	24	-	65	15	0	0.3	-	7	-	24
SPECjvm2008	scimark.lu.small	20	0	0.6	-	1	-	2,529	35	0	1.1	-	1	-	1,226
SPECjvm2008	scimark.monte_carlo	0	0	-	-	-	-	1,337	2	0	0.0	-	1	-	144
SPECjvm2008	scimark.sor.large	2	0	0.5	-	20	-	187	12	0	0.7	-	4	-	42
SPECjvm2008	scimark.sor.small	0	0	-	-	-	-	1,409	5	0	0.0	-	1	-	82
SPECjvm2008	scimark.sparse.large	4	0	0.5	-	16	-	90	1	0	0.0	-	1	-	1
SPECjvm2008	scimark.sparse.small	1	0	-	-	0	-	7,780	42	0	1.6	-	1	-	80
SPECjvm2008	serial	387	0	0.9	-	1	-	125	955	0	1.4	-	0	-	56
SPECjvm2008	sunflow	274	1	5.1	0.0	10	21	49	363	0	2.0	-	3	-	2,776
SPECjvm2008	xml.transform	42	0	2.3	-	3	-	209	49	0	2.0	-	2	-	1,867
SPECjvm2008	xml.validation	136	4	22.4	2.6	34	139	48	71	0	10.6	-	31	-	138

Figure 9: GC count, GC time relative to the total run time (green: less than 5%, yellow: less than 15%, red: more than 15%), and average pause time for minor (-) and major (+) GCs for the ParallelOld GC and the G1 GC respectively (green: less than 10ms, yellow: less than 100ms, red: more than 100ms) (heap limited to 1GB)

Suite	Benchmark	ParallelOld GC							G1 GC						
		Count [#]		Time [%]		Pause [ms]		YR [%]	Count [#]		Time [%]		Pause [ms]		YR [%]
		-	+	-	+	-	+		-	+	-	+	-	+	
DaCapo	avrora	2	0	0.1	-	6	-	7,251	37	0	0.7	-	1	-	179
	batik	0	0	-	-	-	-	120	0	0	-	-	-	-	113
	eclipse	0	0	-	-	-	-	719	2	0	4.0	-	2	-	406
	fop	0	0	-	-	-	-	2,828	3	0	6.7	-	3	-	772
	h2	8	0	1.7	-	353	-	264	16	0	1.1	-	116	-	112
	jython	20	0	0.6	-	2	-	2,457	31	0	0.9	-	2	-	2,453
	luindex	0	0	-	-	-	-	539	2	0	2.1	-	3	-	245
	lusearch	10	0	2.7	-	2	-	38,857	37	0	3.4	-	1	-	15,363
	pmd	3	0	3.6	-	14	-	1,409	5	0	2.4	-	6	-	1,336
	sunflow	15	0	1.0	-	2	-	8,567	26	0	1.4	-	2	-	4,697
	tomcat	61	0	0.5	-	2	-	1,721	14	0	0.2	-	5	-	29,220
	tradebeans	10	0	3.3	-	197	-	1,320	90	0	2.8	-	20	-	152
	tradesoap	13	0	41.8	-	1,680	-	754	64	0	14.6	-	193	-	61
	xalan	11	0	2.3	-	6	-	25,235	21	0	0.1	-	3	-	25,056
DaCapo Scala	actors	44	0	0.3	-	1	-	1,680	68	0	0.3	-	0	-	3,418
	apparat	22	0	0.5	-	21	-	9,099	31	0	0.3	-	11	-	7,080
	factorie	17	0	5.9	-	381	-	1,787	44	0	1.2	-	33	-	604
	kiama	1	0	3.5	-	9	-	518	2	0	1.8	-	2	-	496
	scalac	3	0	5.6	-	45	-	15,515	10	0	4.0	-	10	-	3,269
	scaladoc	3	0	6.3	-	41	-	21,921	7	0	4.0	-	12	-	2,699
	scalap	0	0	-	-	-	-	5,686	3	0	3.9	-	2	-	4,169
	scalariform	8	0	1.5	-	3	-	9,271	14	0	1.9	-	2	-	13,395
	scalaxb	16	0	1.3	-	10	-	2,034	19	0	0.7	-	4	-	462
	tmt	271	0	0.7	-	1	-	695	220	0	0.7	-	1	-	1,517
SPECjvm2008	compiler.compiler	2	0	1.9	-	93	-	9,525	11	0	6.6	-	69	-	967
	compiler.sunflow	6	0	1.2	-	51	-	14,019	23	0	2.3	-	28	-	3,877
	compress	1	0	0.0	-	1	-	373	4	0	0.0	-	0	-	175
	crypto.aes	3	0	0.1	-	2	-	14,930	17	0	0.3	-	1	-	6,812
	crypto.rsa	11	0	0.0	-	0	-	4,906	301	0	1.4	-	0	-	381
	crypto.signverify	10	0	0.1	-	1	-	8,820	34	0	0.5	-	1	-	2,803
	derby	8	0	0.6	-	16	-	2,516	33	0	0.5	-	4	-	802
	mpegaudio	7	0	0.0	-	0	-	6,605	249	0	1.5	-	0	-	251
	scimark.fft.large	0	0	-	-	-	-	17,221	1	0	0.0	-	1	-	3
	scimark.fft.small	7	0	0.1	-	1	-	9,910	341	0	2.8	-	0	-	302
	scimark.lu.large	0	0	-	-	-	-	25,817	12	0	0.3	-	11	-	70
	scimark.lu.small	7	0	0.2	-	1	-	21,669	25	0	0.8	-	2	-	3,125
	scimark.monte_carlo	0	0	-	-	-	-	1,163	0	0	-	-	-	-	0
	scimark.sor.large	0	0	-	-	-	-	11,629	11	0	1.4	-	9	-	22
	scimark.sor.small	0	0	-	-	-	-	1,214	1	0	0.0	-	3	-	438
	scimark.sparse.large	0	0	-	-	-	-	13,222	3	0	0.0	-	3	-	6
	scimark.sparse.small	1	0	0.0	-	1	-	6,805	34	0	1.1	-	0	-	448
	serial	263	0	0.7	-	1	-	307	804	0	1.1	-	0	-	94
	sunflow	81	0	0.7	-	5	-	1,570	265	0	1.4	-	3	-	2,808
	xml.transform	1	0	0.1	-	5	-	43,979	18	0	0.7	-	2	-	6,853
	xml.validation	4	0	1.3	-	55	-	9,426	22	0	2.4	-	21	-	1,442

Figure 10: GC count, GC time relative to the total run time (green: less than 5%, yellow: less than 15%, red: more than 15%), and average pause time for minor (-) and major (+) GCs for the ParallelOld GC and the G1 GC respectively (green: less than 10ms, yellow: less than 100ms, red: more than 100ms) (heap unlimited)

An Incremental Methodology for Energy Measurement and Modeling

Abdelhafid Mazouz*
Intel Corporation
Champaign, IL, USA
first.last@gmail.com

David C. Wong
Intel Corporation
Austin, TX, USA
first.c.last.@intel.com

David Kuck
Intel Corporation
Austin, TX, USA
first.last@intel.com

William Jalby
UVSQ/ECR
Versailles, France
first.last@uvsq.fr

ABSTRACT

This paper presents an empirical approach to measuring and modeling the energy consumption of multicore processors. The modeling approach allows us to find a breakdown of the energy consumption among a set of key hardware components, also called HW nodes. We explicitly model the front-end and the back-end in terms of the number of instructions executed. We also model the L1, L2 and L3 caches. Furthermore, we explicitly model the static and dynamic energy consumed by the the uncore and core components. From a software perspective, our methodology allows us to correlate energy to the executed code, which helps find opportunities for code optimization and tuning.

We use binary analysis and hardware counters for performance characterization. Although, we use the on-chip counters (RAPL) for energy measurement, our methodology does not rely on a specific method for energy measurement. Thus, it is portable and easy to deploy in various computing environments. We validate our energy model using two Intel processors with a set of HPC codelets, where data sizes are varied to come from the L1, L2 and L3 caches and show 3% average modeling error. We present a comprehensive analysis and show energy consumption differences between kernels and relate those differences to the algorithms that are implemented. Finally, we discuss how vectorization leads to energy savings compared to non-vectorized codes.

CCS Concepts

•Computing methodologies → **Modeling methodologies; •Hardware** → **Power and energy; •Computer systems organization** → *Multicore architectures;*

*Abdelhafid Mazouz contributed to this work as an Intel employee. He is now at Bull/Atos.

ICPE'17, April 22-26, 2017, L'Aquila, Italy

DOI: http://dx.doi.org/10.1145/3030207.3030224

Keywords

Energy modeling; Performance evaluation, RAPL

1. INTRODUCTION

Power or energy models are widely used in the context of dynamic power management and DVFS controllers [1, 3, 22]. They can serve as a tool to dynamically find hardware (HW) parameters that are best suited for a given workload in a computing system. Accurate power and energy modeling of HW are also important components for software (SW) development tools and HW/SW codesign tools [11, 12]. Generally, one needs a model in which power or energy is related to the amount of each HW resource used in a given computation. We define HW resources (called HW nodes) as HW components that can enhance the overall performance. This allows expression of system or subsystem power or energy as the sum of individual HW node contributions, so for each computation the contributions of each node can be understood. This paper gives a general procedure for generating such models by iteratively refining high-level measurements down to lower-level HW details, and in the limit to individual operations and instructions.

Our methodology is portable, as we rely on HW counters for performance and energy measurement, which are available on most modern general purpose processors. In this paper, we apply our methodology to estimate energy consumption for multicore processors. We use the *Running Average Power Limit* [5, 10] (RAPL) interfaces for energy measurement and estimation. As we focus on Intel microprocessors, such HW interfaces are provided to estimate the core and uncore energy. Although errors are observed in such HW estimates [9, 16], it allows us to deploy and apply our methodology in various computing environments without the need for physical HW probes. If physical HW probes or an accurate high-level simulator were available for such, our methodology could be applied directly to those physical energy measurements. The general procedure incrementally produces as much detail as can be isolated by microbenchmark measurements and HW counters. The two key parameters in our model are static power and dynamic energy consumption. We give lumped static power estimates for core and uncore, as well as dynamic energy contribution down to low-level nodes.

The paper discusses our overall methodology and validation of the model, as well as some observations about the results. These include comparisons of two HSW microprocessors, comparison of numerical codelets, and relative energy consumption of scalar, SSE and AVX vector versions of each codelet. This allows one to understand problems with a HW design, e.g. which nodes are most important to improve in a new system for a given workload. Also, the results can be used in SW development tools to understand what changes to make to each codelet to improve its overall energy or performance/energy ratio for an existing system.

The main contributions of the paper are:

1. A way of separating static and dynamic power at the level of the core and uncore:
   (a) Using clock modulation [10] to estimate static power of the core. Unlike DVFS, clock modulation allows us to vary frequency while voltage is kept constant.
   (b) Using multicore runs to estimate uncore static power. This allows us to vary the number of active vs non-active cores. When all cores are non active (deep `C-States` [10]), their voltage is set to zero, exposing the uncore power consumption.
2. A general iterative model that starts with high-level energy and performance measurements and derives lower level node energy information by a series of micro-benchmarking steps:
   (a) Dynamic energy breakdown among all key HW nodes, including those impacting performance.
   (b) Multi-step methodology allowing isolation of the energy contribution of all modeled HW nodes.
3. Energy comparison:
   (a) Low level analysis of energy consumption by different codelets.
   (b) Instruction set comparison.
   (c) Architectural comparison.

This paper is organized as follows. Section 2 presents our experimental setup and measurement methodology. Section 3 motivates our energy modeling work. Section 4 describes the different steps of our energy modeling methodology. Section 5 presents our experimental results. Section 6 presents some background on energy modeling. Finally, Section 7 gives our conclusions/perspective.

2. EXPERIMENTAL SETUP

2.1 Hardware platforms

For our evaluation, we use two Intel test platforms, one is a server machine and the other is a workstation/client. The two machines exhibit differences in terms of the maximal supported clock frequency and the size of the L3 cache.

- **Haswell** client machine (`HSW-CL`). The machine consists of a single `Xeon` E3-1270 v3 processor. The processor has 4 cores running at 3.5 GHz maximal non-turbo frequency. The four cores share an L3 cache of 8 MB. In each core, the L1 instruction cache size is 32 KB, the L1 data cache size is 32KB and L2 cache is 256KB. The process technology is 22 nm.
- **Haswell** server machine (`HSW-SE`). The machine consists of a single `Xeon` E5-2630 v3 processor. The processor has 8 cores running at 2.4 GHz maximal non-turbo frequency. The eight cores share an L3 cache of 20 MB. In each core, the L1 instruction cache size is 32 KB, the L1 data cache size is 32KB and L2 cache size is 256KB. The process technology is 22 nm.

2.2 Measurement methodology

To ensure the predictability and the reproducibility of our results [17], we turned off Hyper-Threading (HT) and Turbo-boost (TB) in all our experiments. We also fixed the CPU frequency in each processor to the maximal non-Turbo frequency using the Linux *user space* governor. Consequently, we prevent the OS/HW from changing the frequency at runtime. Because prefetch can help or hinder performance across codelets, for simplicity, we only run experiments with prefetch off. While turning on Hyper-Threading and HW prefetch does not limit the applicability of our methodology, turning on Turbo-boost on can be a challenge for any modeling methodology as voltage and frequency are dynamically varied by the HW depending on various runtime parameters without being fully exposed to the OS and applications. Though our modeling approach includes multicore training runs, this paper presents only unicore validation results and leaves multicore validation for future work.

To build the energy model, we created a set of dedicated assembly micro-benchmarks to stress various HW components. As for model validation, We run a set of kernels that we call codelets. They are extracted from numerical recipes (NR) [19, 20], where many families of algorithms are represented: Linear Algebraic Equations, Eigensystems, Fast Fourier Transform and Partial Differential Equations. All the codelets were carefully selected and they cover a wide range of performance and code structure characteristics [19]: single, double and mixed precision data, non-vectorized, partially vectorized and fully vectorized, 1D and 2D loops, 1D and 2D arrays, unit stride and non-unit stride memory accesses. There are also scalar, vector-vector, matrix-vector and matrix-matrix types of computations. For each codelet, we can control the data sizes, so we picked data sizes that fit the L1, L2 and L3 caches.

The codelets were compiled using the `Intel Icc` compiler version 15.0.0. In order to study the relationship between vectorized code and energy efficiency, we created three versions of each codelet whenever possible.

- **Scalar SSE** (`SC`). Each codelet is compiled using the `-O3 -xSSE4.2 -no-vec` flag. The compiler generates pure scalar code using SSE4.2 instructions (the `-no-vec` is necessary for codelets where the compiler can generate vector code by default).
- **Vector SSE** (`SSE`). Each codelet is compiled using the `-O3 -xSSE4.2` flag. The compiler generates vectorized code using the `SSE4.2` instruction set.
- **Vector AVX** (`AVX2`) Each codelet is compiled using the `-O3 -xcore-avx2` flag. The compiler generates vectorized code using the `AVX2` instruction set.

There are 26 NR codelets, 19 are vectorizable and 7 are purely scalar. As we can use the `-no-vec` flag, we can generate a total of 26 `SC`,19 `SSE`, 19 `AVX2` codelets. So we used a total of 64 codelets in our experiments.

For energy measurements, we use the RAPL [10] interfaces present in each of our processors. They are a set of non-architectural HW counters[1] used for power management like power limiting. Depending on the platform type (client or server), these interfaces are organized into multiple domains: the package (PKG), the cores (PP0), the graphics (PP1) and the memory domain (DRAM). In our paper, we use only the energy measurement capability of RAPL and focus on the PKG domain. The PKG domain estimates energy for all the chip including all cores and uncore components. While we rely on RAPL, our methodology is not bound to such interfaces. If physical HW probes for energy measurement were available, then our methodology could be applied directly to those physical energy measurements.

We use multiple metrics to express performance, power and energy. We express performance rate as computational capacity C[operations/second] (we also use flop in place of operation), power as W[Watts], and energy as E[Joules], E[Watt-hour]. As we deal with fine grained codelets, we also express E in milli-Joules (mJ) or nano-Joules (nJ). The quality of a computation (a codelet running on an architecture) can be expressed in many ways and we use the quality metrics: C, C/W and C/E [4, 7]. C/W expresses a traditional HW metric $C/W[operations/energy] = O/E$, and C/E is a traditional system-level metric expressed as C/E[perf/operating cost]. While traditional metrics are sometimes the reciprocals of these, we prefer graphs in which higher is better.

3. MOTIVATION

Unlike many research efforts [1, 3, 22], we focus on energy modeling instead of power because energy exhibits much more variation than power. We focus on energy because its dynamic range is much greater than the power range (numerically), as shown in Figure 1. Figure 1 illustrates why we consider energy instead of power. It also shows similarity and monotonic order of total energy E and power W measurements of all NR codelets regardless of the instruction set. While this data is related to measurements on `HSW-CL`, the same conclusions result from measurements on `HSW-SE`.

Figure 1 shows that while E has an approximate range of 45X, power has only an approximate range of 1.4X between the observed minimal and maximal power consumption values. Although, these codelets were run with data sizes chosen to come from the L3 cache, one may think that it is unfair to compare energy values of different codes as these codelets implement various algorithms with various operation counts. To tackle this issue, Figure 2 compares normalized energy values against performance numbers for all NR codelets. We make clear distinction between codelets that belong to each instruction set category: `SC`, `SSE` and `AVX`. On one side, the y-axis reports the E/O metric which represents the energy necessary to perform one floating point operation. In fact, $E/O = W/C$, so energy per operation is equivalent to the ratio of power by performance. The x-axis shows performance C and it is expressed in terms of GFlops.

These normalized metrics allow comparing multiple codelets. Figure 2 also shows that there is wide range between $E/O = W/C$ values on one hand, and C values on the other one. In fact, W/C exhibits a 60 X range and C exhibits an 80 X range. Furthermore, the hyperbolas fitted to each instruction set show less than 1 watt separating the `SC`, `SSE` and `AVX2` instruction sets (see equation numerators in Figure 2), where the `SSE` curve is slightly above `SC`, and `AVX2` is slightly above `SSE`. This suggests that an energy model more easily exhibits codelet differences than a power model.

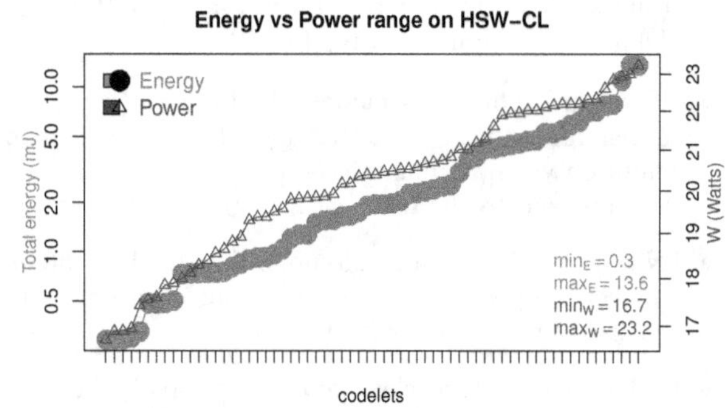

Figure 1: Energy and power range per codelet on `HSW-CL` of 64 NR codelets in rank order

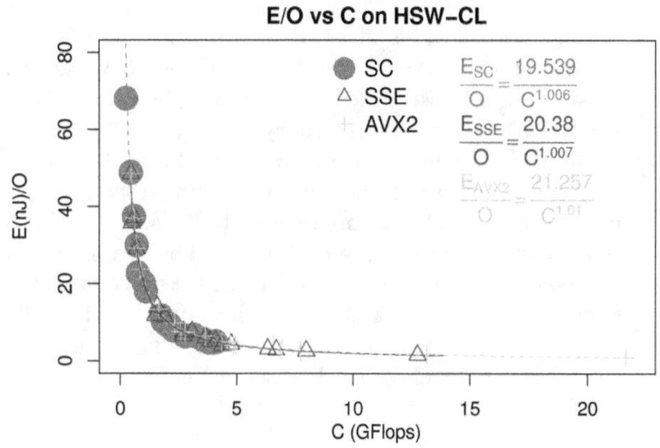

Figure 2: Comparison of normalized energy to performance per codelet on `HSW-CL`

4. ENERGY CONSUMPTION ESTIMATION

The idea behind our modeling approach is to identify key HW components that impact performance and lead to observable energy consumption. Once these HW nodes are identified, it is possible to associate energy weights proportionally to their usage. The profiling information about HW node usage can be obtained using static and dynamic analysis. Static analysis is performed on the extracted assembly code using the MAQAO [15] framework. It allows us to obtain metrics about the mix of instructions that are executed. Dynamic analysis relies on hardware performance counters and allows us to collect the memory traffic while executing a code. Memory traffic can be defined as the cache line movement between the L1 and L2 caches on one hand, and between the L2 and L3 caches on the other hand.

4.1 Modeled HW nodes

We consider that a CPU consists of a set of cores, each with private L1 and L2 caches and an uncore component.

[1] Also referred to as MSR.

The uncore is shared between all the cores and it includes the L3 cache. Moreover, each core consists of a front-end for instruction decoding and a back-end for instruction execution. As we target HPC codes composed of multiple loop-nests, we can classify the modeled HW nodes into four main categories: floating-point execution units (FPU), integer execution units (INT), front-end (FE) and memory (Caches), all modeling the dynamic energy of a CPU.

- **FE** nodes. This class models the front-end stage. It consists of a single node that models the energy consumption when issuing micro-ops or instructions from the front-end to the back-end.
- **INT** node. This is a single node that models the energy consumption when executing integer instructions, e.g. used in the control flow of loops.
- **FPU** nodes. This class represents mostly floating-point operations that are executed in the back-end (dispatch). The modeled nodes/operations are `ADD`, `MUL`, `DIV` and `FMA`. For all of these, a distinction is made in terms of the number of bytes processed by each instruction, e.g. we model ADD32, ADD64, ADD128 and ADD256. This class has a total of 17 nodes.
- **Cache** nodes. This class models memory traffic between the core and the hierarchy of memory caches. First, we model `L1` nodes representing the energy consumption of executing memory loads (`LD`) and stores `ST` in the L1 cache. There are four `LD` and four `ST` nodes; each captures the energy consumed when varying the data width of operations (32, 64, 128 or 256 bits). Next, are the `L2` and `L3` node. The former models the energy consumption for the data movement between the L1 and L2 caches. The latter models the energy consumption of cache line movement between the L2 and L3 caches. Both account for read and write traffic.

Besides the nodes that model the dynamic energy, we also explicitly model the static energy that is consumed in the uncore and in the core. The static energy of the core is a single quantity that accounts for the OoO engine, FE logic, execution units, plus the L1 and L2 caches. The static energy of the uncore on the other hand covers the L3, IMC and other components.

4.2 Modeling methodology

To precisely isolate the energy contribution of each modeled HW node, we rely on an incremental methodology. As depicted in Figure 3, we distinguish two main steps: 1) static energy (E^{static}) estimation and 2) dynamic energy ($E^{dynamic}$) estimation. Consequently, we express the total energy using Equation 1.

$$E_{CPU}^{total} = E_{CPU}^{static} + E_{CPU}^{dynamic} \tag{1}$$

For the static energy, we first model the static energy of the uncore E_{uncore}^{static}, then we model the static energy of each active core E_{core}^{static}. For a given codelet, dynamic energy consumption represents the aggregate energy of all the HW nodes that are stressed while running that codelet. As discussed in Section 4.1, we consider FE, INT, FPU and cache nodes to model the dynamic energy of a CPU.

All of the steps we follow rely on a set of dedicated micro-benchmarks written in assembly code to stress the various HW components that we want to model. Using this methodology, we believe that we can find a breakdown of the energy consumption of any workload, regardless of the measurement method . For example, we use the RAPL interface to measure total energy consumption, but energy measurements using physical probes or simulation numbers could be used.

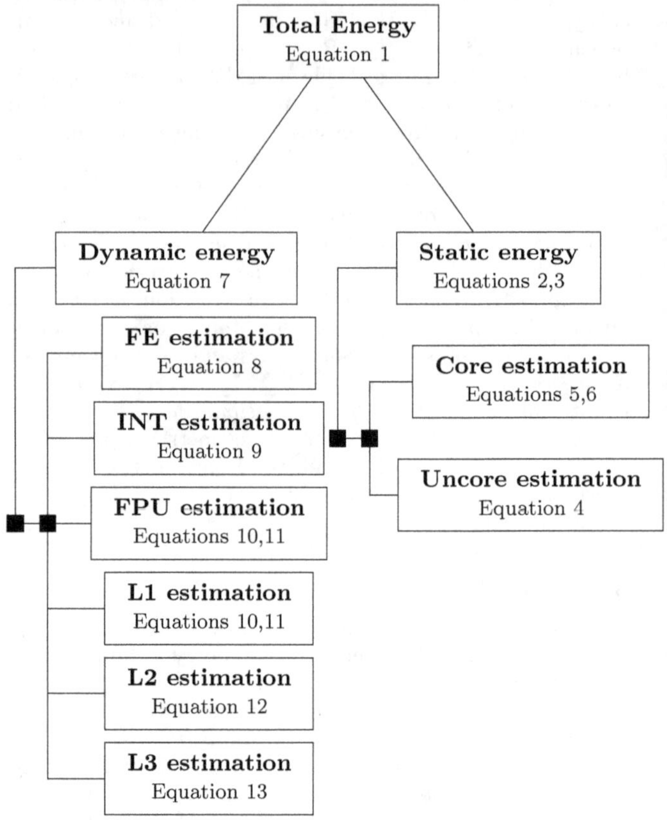

Figure 3: Energy modeling diagram

4.2.1 *Static energy estimation*

Instead of estimating directly the static energy, which is workload dependent, we estimate the static power W_{CPU}^{static}. W_{CPU}^{static} of a multicore processor is modeled using Equation 2. The static energy of a workload can be computed as the product of the static power W_{CPU}^{static} and the measured time duration T of the workload (Equation 3)

$$W_{CPU}^{static} = ActiveCores \times W_{core}^{static} + W_{uncore}^{static} \tag{2}$$

$$E_{CPU}^{static} = W_{CPU}^{static} \times T \tag{3}$$

While we rely on varying the number of active cores to estimate the static power of the uncore, we rely on the duty cycle modulation [10] feature to estimate the static power of the core. Duty cycle modulation also called `T`-states[2] is a mechanism for active power management available on Intel processors starting from `Pentium 4`. It is a throttling mechanism used to modulate processor core frequency, mainly for

[2]T-states refer also to thermal states.

thermal management techniques. Duty cycle modulation allows processor power and temperature reduction by lowering core activity to some predefined level.

Static power of the uncore. To estimate W_{uncore}^{static}, we run a pure floating-point code (no memory accesses). By excluding memory accesses, we avoid having dynamic power consumed by L1, L2 or L3 accesses. Consequently, the total power consumed by the chip consists of W_{uncore}^{static}, W_{core}^{static} and $W_{core}^{dynamic}$. We can then measure the total power consumption of the chip while varying the number of active cores that run the same FP code simultaneously. We model the static power of the uncore using Equation 4. W_{uncore}^{static} is estimated as the intercept of the simple linear regression when the number of active cores equals 0.

$$W_{CPU}^{total} = ActiveCores \times (W_{core}^{dynamic} + W_{core}^{static}) + W_{uncore}^{static} \quad (4)$$

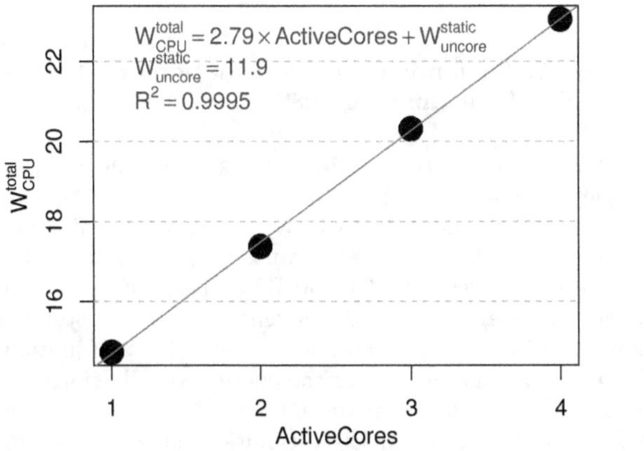

Figure 4: Estimation of uncore static power on HSW-CL

Figure 4 reports the static power of the uncore on the HSW-CL machine when the number of active cores is varied from 1 to 4. We assume that when C-States [10] is enabled and no workloads assigned to the cores (not active), they enter into deep sleep states where voltage is set to 0. We then consider that since all the cores are turned off, the measured power consumption is due to the uncore component. So we define that power as the uncore static power.

Static power of the core. Once we estimate the power consumption of the uncore, the second step is to model the static power of the core. We consider that the static power of the core includes all the core logic plus the static power of the L1 and L2 caches. We make two main assumptions. First, to avoid any measurement noise related to memory operations, we use pure FP micro-benchmarks. Second, we run a copy of our designed FP micro-benchmark on all the available cores on the machine simultaneously, to ensure that no core enters deep sleep states that may lead to wrong conclusions about the static power estimation.

If we run codes that do not have memory requests, then the total power of a CPU can be modeled using Equation 5. For a fixed voltage V, $\beta(V) = W_{CPU}^{static}$ (Equation 5). While $\beta(V)$ expresses the static power of all active cores plus the static power of the uncore as a function of V, $\alpha(V) \times F$ expresses the dynamic power of the core in terms of V and F. This means that in order to estimate $W_{core}^{static}(V)$, we need to fix V and vary F such that $W_{core}^{dynamic}(F, V) = 0$. In the context of our test machines, changing CPU frequency[3] leads to V and F being varied simultaneously. To overcome this limitation, we use clock modulation to control the effective frequency F_{eff} while keeping the voltage constant.

$$W_{CPU}^{total} = \alpha(V) \times F_{eff} + \beta(V) \quad (5)$$

From Equation 5, if $F_{eff} = 0$, then no dynamic power is consumed by the CPU. This means that $W_{CPU}^{total} = \beta(V) = W_{CPU}^{static}$. From Equation 2, we can compute the static power of each active core using Equation 6. Figure 5 shows an example of how W_{core}^{static} is estimated on the HSW-CL machine.

$$W_{core}^{static} = \frac{W_{CPU}^{static} - W_{uncore}^{static}}{ActiveCores} \quad (6)$$

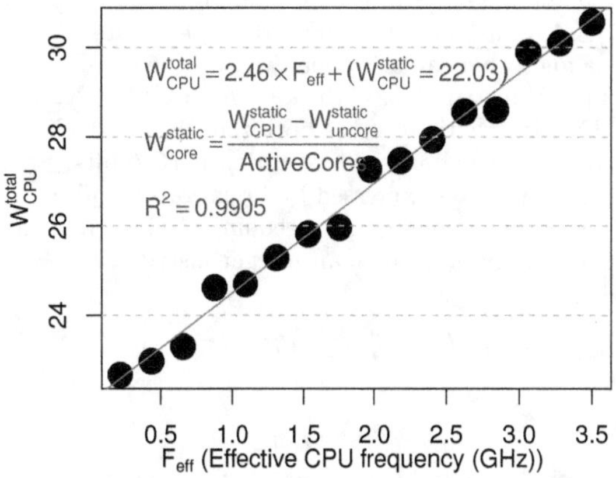

Figure 5: Estimation of core static power on HSW-CL

Table 1 reports estimated uncore static power values and static power of each individual core on both HSW machines.

Static power	HSWE3 (3.5GHz)	HSWEP (2.4GHz)
Uncore (nJ/Cycle)	3.42	6.55
Uncore (Watt)	11.97	15.72
Per core (nJ/Cycle)	0.72	0.79
Per core (Watt)	2.52	1.89

Table 1: Static power estimated values on the HSW-CL and HSW-SE machines. Values are expressed in terms of nano-Joules/Cycle and in terms of Watts

4.2.2 *Dynamic energy estimation*

After estimating static power of each active core and static power of the uncore, we focus on modeling the total dynamic energy. It consists of the sum of energy consumption of all the HW nodes (N) that we consider as impacting performance. Equation 7 summarizes the dynamic energy of a CPU. Energy consumption of each individual node is proportional to its usage/activity. For example, instruction/FPU

[3] CPU frequency change is also called a DVFS pair change.

nodes are modeled in terms of the number of instructions that are executed.

$$E_{CPU}^{dynamic} = \sum_{node}^{N} E_{node}^{dynamic} \tag{7}$$

FE and INT nodes estimation. Our first step in modeling dynamic energy consumption is to estimate 1) the FE and the INT nodes. The former models the energy consumption in the FE ($E_{FE}^{dynamic}$) in terms of the number of instructions that are issued to the back-end I_{FE}. The second models the energy consumption ($E_{INT}^{dynamic}$) of executing any number of integer loop-control instructions I_{INT}.

We use Equations 8 and 9 to estimate the energy consumption of the FE and INT components. To evaluate $E_{FE}^{dynamic}$, we create micro-benchmarks where we vary the number of non-operation instructions. Such instructions allow us to isolate the behavior of the FE issue stage. While these instructions are issued by the FE and retired/committed by the back-end, they are not dispatched to execution units/ports. We emulate non-operations by running a set of **XCHG %AX,%AX** instructions. Similarly, to evaluate $E_{INT}^{dynamic}$, we use a micro-benchmark where we vary the number of executed integer instructions of the kind **ADD %RAX,%RCX**. These INT instructions stress both the FE and back-end as they are dispatched and use execution ports/units. Solving the linear regression expressed by Equations 8 and 9, allows us to compute the energy for decoding a single instruction e_{FE}, and energy to execute an integer instruction e_{INT}.

$$E_{FE}^{dynamic} = e_{FE} \times I_{FE} \tag{8}$$

$$E_{INT}^{dynamic} = e_{INT} \times I_{INT} \tag{9}$$

LD, ST and FP nodes estimation. At this level, we focus on estimating the dynamic energy of executing multiple floating-point and memory (load and store) operations that hit the L1 cache. We cover the cases of operations using 32, 64, 128 and 256 bits data width. For each desired data width, we use a set of micro-benchmarks where various levels of instruction mixes are created. While it is possible to create a specific micro-benchmark for each instruction for which we want to estimate energy, our observations show that having a mix of instructions allows us to accurately estimate the cost of various instructions. In fact, using mixed instruction micro-benchmarks helps to capture the complex interactions arising from the Out-of-Order execution engine.

For each family of instructions that use a certain portion of the available width, we solve systems expressed by Equation 10. For each instruction $I \in$ {LD, ST, MUL, ADD, DIV, FMA} with a width $w \in \{32, 64, 128, 256\}$, we can express its energy by Equation 11.

$$E_{FPU}^{dynamic} = \sum_{I} \sum_{w} E_{I,w}^{dynamic} \tag{10}$$

$$E_{I,w}^{dynamic} = e_{I,w} \times NbInst_{I,w} \tag{11}$$

L2 energy estimation. Workloads with memory accesses that miss L1 but are L2 hits require modeling these L2 accesses explicitly. To this end, we designed micro-benchmarks composed of a set of strided (64 byte granularity) memory loads and stores. Each access triggers a distinct cache line movement between the L1 and the L2 caches $MemTr_{L2}$, defined as the memory traffic between the L1 and L2 caches.

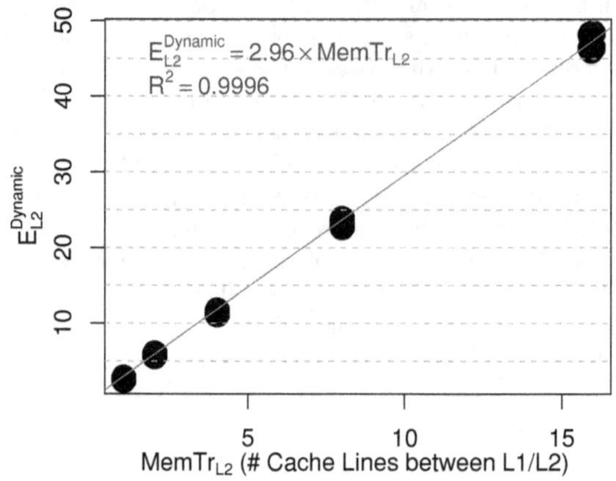

Figure 6: Dynamic energy estimation of L2 accesses per microbenchmark on HSW-CL

Once we measure the total energy and the number of requests to L2, it is possible to solve a linear regression represented by Equation 12, where e_{L2} represents the energy consumption regression variable for moving a single cache line between the L1 and L2 caches. Since the micro-benchmarks are composed of memory loads and stores plus loop-control integer instructions, the LHS of Equation 12 is formed by summing over the energy contributions of FE, INT and L1 nodes from the RHS of Equation 7. Figure 6 shows the L2 access energy estimation on HSW-CL when we vary $MemTr_{L2}$, the number of cache line requests to the L2 from the L1 cache.

$$E_{L2}^{dynamic} = e_{L2} \times MemTr_{L2} \tag{12}$$

L3 energy estimation. The final step in processor dynamic energy consumption focuses on L3 memory access hits. For model training purposes, we use the same micro-benchmarks as for the L2 training, but we choose data sizes to trigger distinct cache line requests to L3, so all the memory accesses will miss L1 and L2 but will hit L3.

To model the energy consumption for cache line movement between the L2 and L3 caches, we define such traffic as $MemTr_{L3}$. We vary the number of distinct cache line requests to L3 while measuring total energy and solve the linear regression (Equation 13) to compute e_{L3} which is the energy necessary to move one cache line between the L2 and L3 caches. As in L2 modeling, the LHS of Equation 13 is formed by summing over the energy contribution of FE, INT, L1 and L2 nodes from the RHS of Equation 7. Figure 7 shows the L3 access energy estimation on HSW-CL when we vary $MemTr_{L3}$, the number of cache line requests to L3, where all the accesses are L1 and L2 misses.

$$E_{L3} = e_{L3} \times MemTr_{L3} \tag{13}$$

Energy coefficient for modeled machines. By applying this methodology, it is possible to assign energy consumption to individual HW node usage. Table 2 reports the

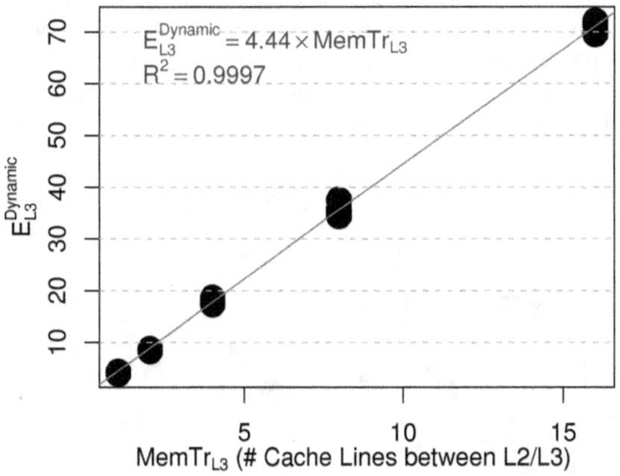

Figure 7: Dynamic energy estimation of L3 accesses per microbenchmark on HSW-CL

energy coefficient of the various HW nodes that we model on both the HSW-CL and HSW-SE machines.

Energy (nJ)/ HW node	HSWE3 (3.5GHz)	HSWEP (2.4GHz)
FE (nJ/Inst)	0.11	0.08
INT (nJ/Inst)	0.14	0.13
ADD (SS/SD) 32/64 (nJ/Inst)	0.33	0.33
ADD (PS/PD) 128 (nJ/Inst)	0.33	0.33
ADD (PS/PD) 256 (nJ/Inst)	0.60	0.45
MUL (SS/SD) 32/64 (nJ/Inst)	0.16	0.13
MUL (PS/PD) 128 (nJ/Inst)	0.30	0.15
MUL (PS/PD) 256 (nJ/Inst)	0.33	0.25
DIV (SS) 32 (nJ/Inst)	3.76	4.19
DIV (SD) 64 (nJ/Inst)	5.59	5.46
DIV (PS) 128 (nJ/Inst)	5.21	4.80
DIV (PD) 128 (nJ/Inst)	6.32	6.15
DIV (PS) 256 (nJ/Inst)	11.83	11.20
DIV (PD) 256 (nJ/Inst)	14.09	17.05
FMA (PS/PD) 256 (nJ/Inst)	0.70	0.63
LD/L1 (SS/SD) 32/64 (nJ/Inst)	0.30	0.15
LD/L1 (PS/PD) 128 (nJ/Inst)	0.33	0.18
LD/L1 (PS/PD) 256 (nJ/Inst)	0.45	0.34
ST/L1 (SS/SD) 32/64 (nJ/Inst)	0.69	0.69
ST/L1 (PS/PD) 128 (nJ/Inst)	0.69	0.69
ST/L1 (PS/PD) 256 (nJ/Inst)	0.78	0.69
L2 (Read/Write) (nJ/64 bytes)	2.96	2.12
L3 (Read/Write) (nJ/64 bytes)	4.59	4.70

Table 2: Energy coefficients expressed in nano-Joule

5. VALIDATION AND RESULTS

We evaluated the accuracy of our energy model using the NR codelets with data sizes chosen to run from L1, L2 and the caches. All of our experimental results were obtained by turning the HW prefetcher off. As the range of errors of all codelets is similar regardless of the data sizes that are chosen, this paper discusses only results of L3 data sizes due to lack of space. As we assume uniform consumption among cores, the presented numbers express unicore run results on multicore systems.

5.1 Energy model error prediction analysis

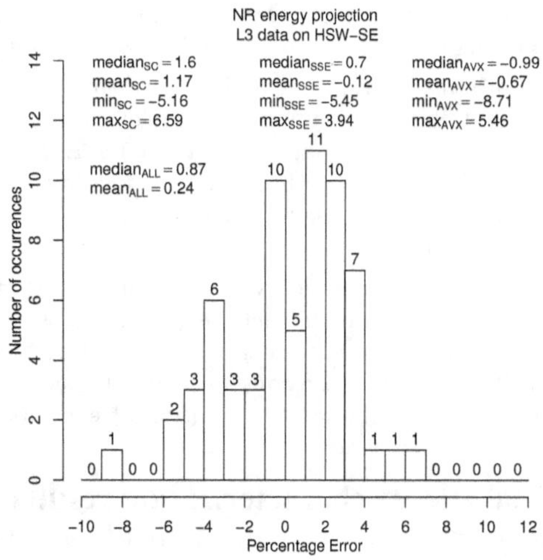

Figure 8: Energy prediction errors when running SC, SSE and AVX2 codelets out of L3 on HSW-SE

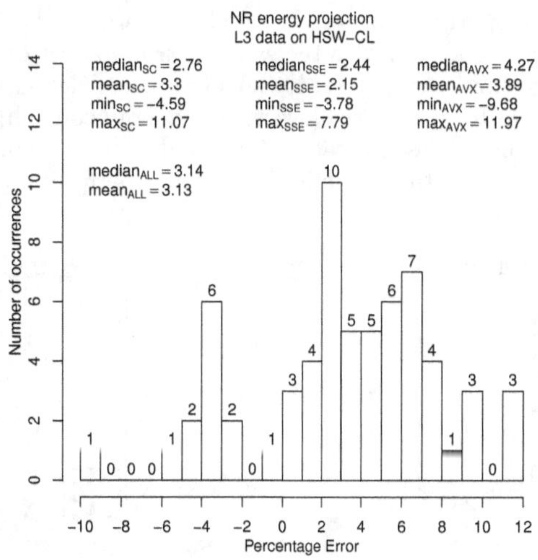

Figure 9: Energy prediction errors when running SC, SSE and AVX2 codelets out of L3 on HSW-CL

Figures 8 and 9 summarize the errors observed when comparing energy measurement to energy values computed by our model for HSW-SE and HSW-CL respectively. Though both histograms report all the error independently of the used instruction set, we also show median, average, minimal and maximal errors of the SC, SSE and AVX2 codelets. We can make the following observations.

1. When errors are greater than 0, the model underestimates energy consumption, otherwise, the model overestimates energy consumption. While the errors are evenly split around the 0% error point on HSW-SE, they are evenly split around the 3% point on HSW-CL.

2. While the proportion of codelets for which energy is overestimated is less than 20% on HSW-CL, that proportion is less than 44% on HSW-SE though overestimation does not exceed 5% in most cases.
3. On both machines, prediction accuracy varies little across instruction sets. Observed minimal and maximal errors fall in the same range for SC, SSE and AVX2.
4. On both machines, the model overestimates energy consumption for the same set of codelets, which we can split into two sub groups: 1) unit stride and 2) non-unit stride codelets. All codelets belonging to these sub groups share the same memory access and computation patterns.
5. For this study, while energy underestimation is mainly due to non-modeled instructions (like single to double precision conversion instructions), we believe that energy overestimation is a consequence of the complexity of isolating the energy consumption of each modeled HW node independently.

5.2 Total energy characterization results

We can use the energy model in multiple ways. In this paper, we limit our study to analyze the energy consumption of different codelets on one hand, and differences in energy between different instruction sets on the other hand.

As our codelets were compiled to generate a scalar (SC) and two vector versions (SSE and AVX2), we study the energy efficiency of codelets using the quality metrics of Section 2. Figure 10 reports the average total CPU energy E, C/E and C/W for all codelets with the same instruction set on both test platforms. As expected, the more a codelet uses the available vector width, the lower is the energy consumption, and the higher are the ratios C/E and C/W. Figure 10 confirms that vectorization leads to higher performance and lower energy.

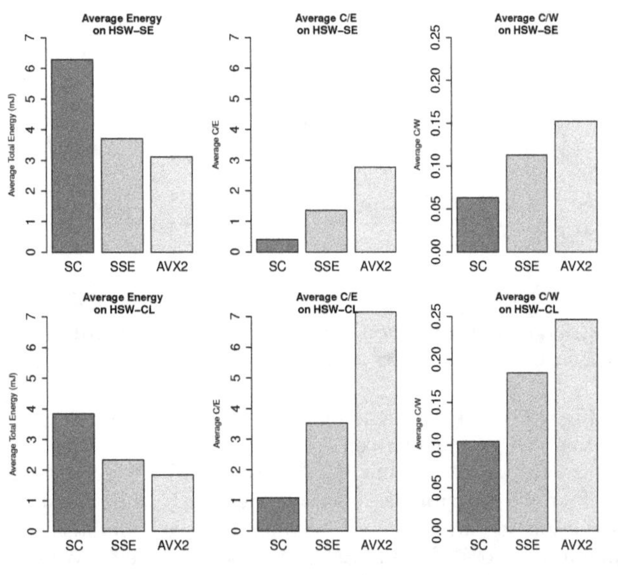

Figure 10: Average total energy (lower is better), C/E (higher is better) and C/W (higher is better) metrics across instruction sets on the HSW-SE and HSW-CL

Looking at C/E and C/W per codelet and per instruction set in Figures 11 and 12 shows that according to the C/E metric, almost all SSE codelets outperform SC versions by a factor between 2 to 10X. Similarly, except for few codelets, AVX2 outperforms SSE by up to 3X. Though the magnitudes differ, we also observe the same trend in the C/W metric, and all codelets behave similarly on both machines.

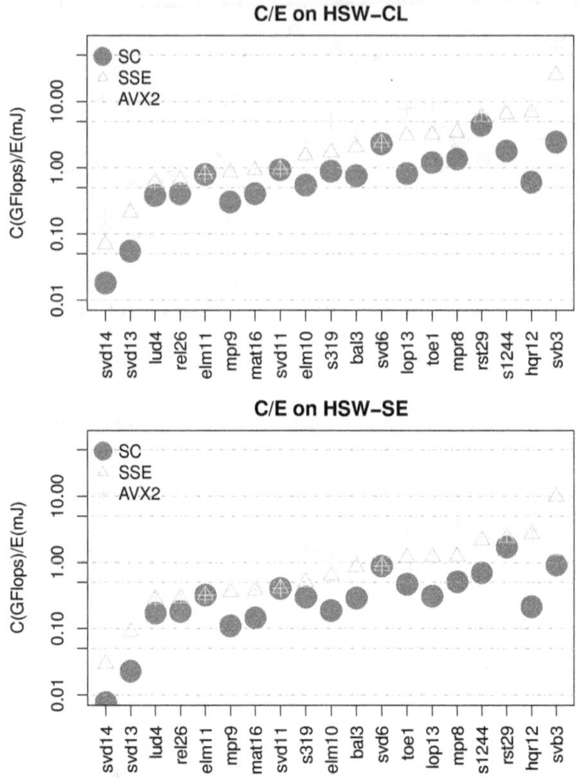

Figure 11: C/E per codelet and per instruction set on the HSW-SE and HSW-CL

As the analysis of C/E and C/W leads to the same overall observations, we focus on C/E and analyze the source of variation between codelets. To do so, we consider SSE codes running on HSW-CL. Figure 13 shows the C/E values for each codelet sorted in increasing order. It also shows corresponding C and E values using multiple y-axes.

Table 3 compares the details of 6 codelets selected from Figure 13 for their diversity, arranged in increasing C/E order (over a range of 300X). While high C/E represents an attractive system metric, specific C and E values may vary widely. The table shows a range of 32X for performance and 110X for energy. Table 3 also shows the origin of variations in C and E values. The total amount of arithmetic (flop count), and the performance limiters (one or more nodes whose performance enhancements will enhance total system performance for a given codelet) contribute to performance as does memory activity. While all data sizes were chosen to run from L3, the energy contributions give another view of the HW nodes. Energy comparisons relative to these 6 codelets and absolute node energy relative to a given codelet are shown in the last two columns. Relative and absolute energy contributions of each node are also highlighted in Figure 14.

Svd13 has the lowest C/E value, which clearly arises from both poor performance and high energy because of its dom-

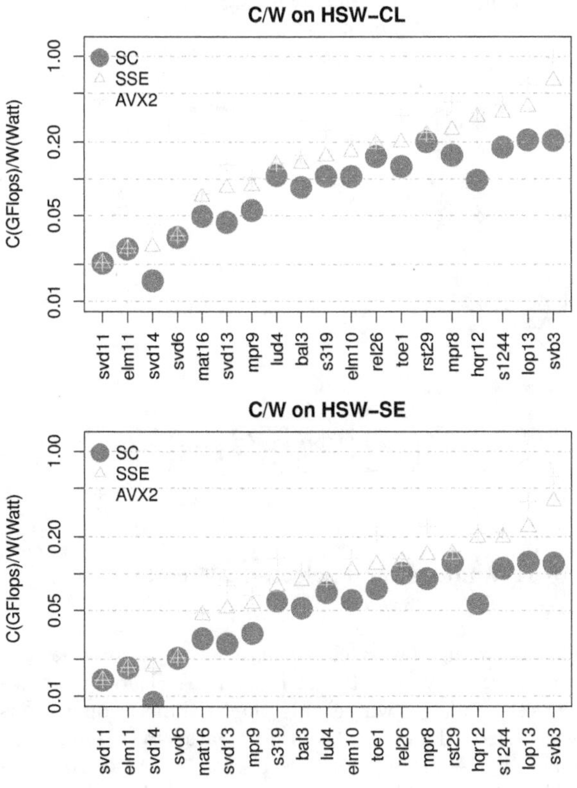

Figure 12: C/W per codelet and per instruction set on HSW-SE and HSW-CL

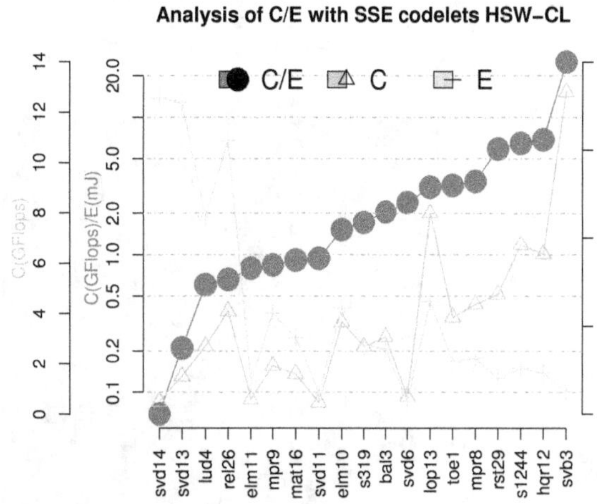

Figure 13: Computed C/E, C and total E for SSE codes running on the HSW-CL machine

Codelet	C/E	Perf (C)	MFlops	Perf limiter	E	E high rel to codelets	Dyn E high rel to nodes
Svd13	0.2	1.5	0.6	Divide	7.1	Static uncore, FPU	FPU, L3
Relax	0.7	4.1	1.2	PRF, some /	6.2	L2, FPU	L2, FPU
Svd11	0.9	0.5	0.01	LFB, LDA	0.5	L2, L3	L3
Toepl	3.2	3.9	0.24	LM	1.2	L3	L3
Rstrct	5.9	4.8	0.19	PRF	0.8	L1, FE	L3
Svb3	25.4	12.8	0.32	LM	0.5	L3,FE	L3

Table 3: Energy and performance comparison of 6 SSE codelets selected from the C/E range

ination by division. In fact its relative static energy dominates that of the other codelets, as shown in Table 3 and Figure 14. Relative to other nodes dynamic energy, the FPU (division dominated) and L3 consume most energy.

At the other extreme, svb3 has the highest C/E and performance and low energy. svb3 implements a matrix-vector multiply using single precision elements. Its performance is limited by the RS (reservation station) and LM (load matrix). Relative to other codelets, its energy is dominated by L3 and to some extent the FE. Relative to other nodes, its dynamic energy is quite balanced, though L3 energy is slightly higher.

Rstrct is another codelet with high C/E and performance, and relatively low energy. *rstrct* is a finite difference operator stencil that does red/black computation (stride 2 in 2 dimensions), so indexing covers only $\frac{1}{4}$ of the total data per iteration, reducing it from *relax* (also a finite difference operator but using a divide). Performance is limited by the PRF (physical register file) driven by its arithmetic. Its relative energy is dominated by L1 and the front-end, which must process many arithmetic instructions, relative to other codelets. Its dynamic energy is quite well balanced across cache levels and FE.

The other 3 codelets fall in the middle with diverse characteristics. One to note is *svd11* which has the poorest performance due to poor memory behavior, indicated by LFB (line fill buffer) as its performance limiter. It is a 2d array indexed to stride by the array size, which drives the cache energy up.

Because the uncore is shared across many cores on chip, the percentage of dynamic energy will actually increase by a factor proportional to the number of cores used for a multicore run.

5.3 Vectorization analysis results

It is a common belief that vectorization is most likely to lead to better performance and energy savings. Figure 15 shows energy consumption of SC, SSE and AVX2. Codelets are sorted relative to increasing order of SC energy. While the y-axis on the left side reports energy values, the y-axis on the right side reports the ratio of energy between SC to SSE, between SC to AVX2 and between SSE to AVX2.

Clearly, vectorization causes important variations in energy reductions. We observe both extremes, nearly no effect and high energy savings (about 4X). Moreover, as we reported in Figure 10, Figure 15 shows that AVX2 and SSE codelets are 2.2X and 1.6X more energy efficient on average than SC codelets. However, it shows as far as L3 data is concerned that AVX2 codelets are more energy efficient than SSE ones by only 1.3X.

To highlight the HW nodes that benefit most from vectorization in terms of energy, consider the codelets discussed in Table 3. As these codelets exhibit a wide range in E, they are good candidates to illustrate energy efficiency due to vectorization. Table 4 shows the absolute energy contribution

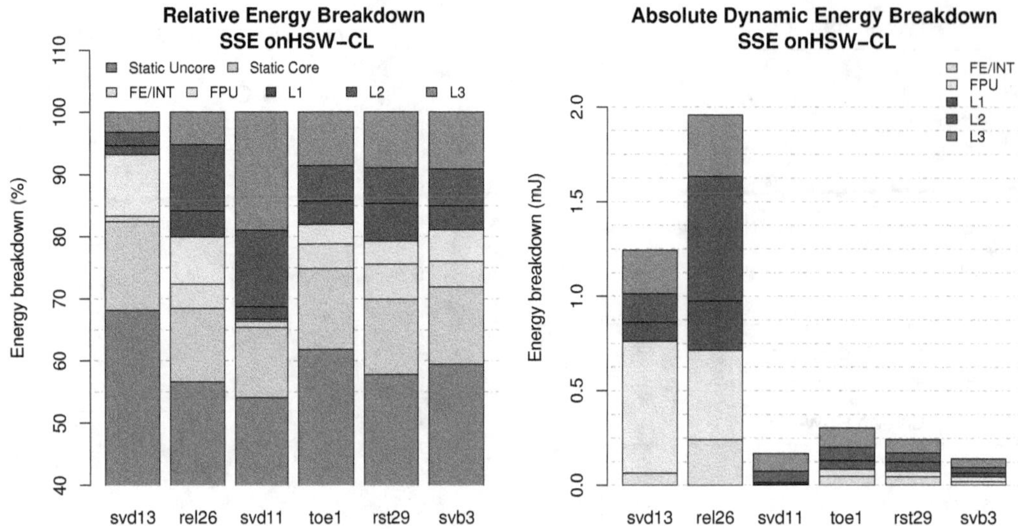

Figure 14: Relative and absolute energy contribution of HW nodes on 6 selected SSE codelets.

of HW nodes for each of the selected codelets on the HSW-CL machine. Energy breakdown information is provided for each of SC, SSE and AVX2 versions of each selected codelet.

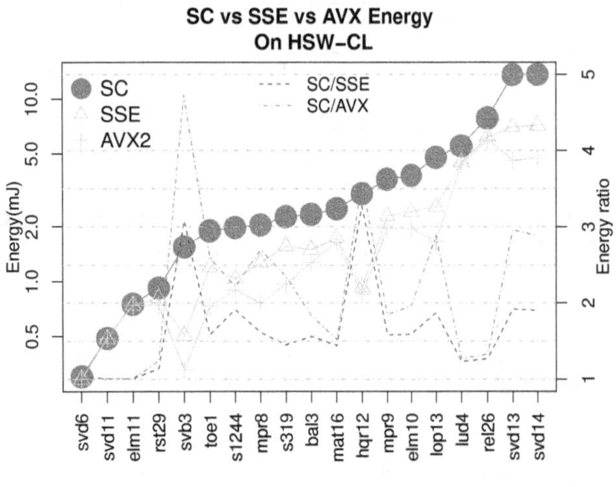

Figure 15: Comparing total E of SC, SSE and AVX codes on the HSW-CL machine

Overall, analyzing the energy breakdown of the 6 codelets allows us to see that except for **svd11**, both static and dynamic energy are reduced when going from scalar to vectorized codelet. As far as dynamic energy is concerned, Table 4 shows that the dynamic energy of the L2 and L3 caches remains unchanged regardless of the instruction set. This is true as the memory traffic between the L1 and L2 caches and the memory traffic between the L2 and L3 caches remains the same (the same number of cache lines is required to do the computations). In practice, most energy savings are due to the FE, FPU and the L1. This can be explained easily by the fact that these nodes correlate very well with the number of instructions that are executed and vectorized codelets usually lead to lower numbers of instructions than scalar codelets, so energy is reduced accordingly.

Svd11 is among the codelets where vectorization does not lead to energy savings. **Svd11** is an LDA (leading dimension access) codelet, where only the arithmetic operations are vectorized. Therefore, it is dominated by memory operations. Since the data size is chosen to come from the L3 cache, its dynamic energy is dominated by L2 and L3 accesses. Consequently, partial vectorization brings neither performance nor energy savings. **relax** and **rstrct** (like **svd11**) have a non-negligible number of scalar memory operations, but unlike **svd11**, these stencil codes also have vectorized memory operations. Consequently, vectorization brings only unimportant energy improvements.

One of the codelets that benefits most from vectorization is **svb3**, a matrix-vector multiply codelet with unit stride memory accesses. Though its 2D data fits the L3 cache, the vector part fits in the L1. So only the matrix elements need to be brought to the L1. Moreover, as the matrix and the vector are single precision floating-point elements, **SSE** and **AVX2** versions are able to process 4 and 8 elements in each vector, respectively. This leads to the observed energy savings. Though **AVX2** instructions have twice the width of **SSE** instructions, energy saved on this codelet does not reflect that. In fact, the vectorized version of **svb3** is RS and LM performance limited. Consequently, **SC** to **AVX2** energy savings are only slightly higher than those of **SC** to **SSE**.

Vectorization is also effective on **toep1**. However, unlike **svb3**, **toep1** uses double precision elements instead of single. Finally, even a high energy consumption codelet like **svd13** benefits from vectorization. In fact, as the L1, FPU and FE energy drop to almost half, its static energy is also reduced in the same proportion due to time reductions from vectorization.

6. RELATED WORK

The need for dynamic power management techniques [1, 3, 22] or HW design trade-offs [13] has motivated many research efforts to develop power and energy models for processors. These models can be classified in terms of whether they rely on some performance metrics (hardware performance counters) or rely on cycle-accurate/RTL simulators.

Codelet	Static E			FE			FPU			L1			L2			L3			Total Dynamic		
	SC	SSE	AVX	SC	SSE	AVX	SC	SSE	AVX	SC	SSE	AVX	SC	SSE	AVX	SC	SSE	AVX	SC	SSE	AVX
Svd13	11.7	5.83	3.35	.13	.07	.05	1.22	.70	.74	.20	.10	.06	.15	.15	.15	.23	.23	.23	1.93	1.24	1.23
Relax	5.49	4.25	3.99	.26	.24	.29	.83	.47	.44	.29	.26	.23	.70	.66	.67	.32	.32	.32	2.40	1.96	1.95
Svd11	.32	.32	.32	.01	.00	.01	.00	.00	.00	.01	.01	.01	.06	.06	.06	.09	.09	.09	.17	.17	.17
Toep1	1.52	.90	.50	.05	.05	.02	.06	.04	.02	.10	.05	.02	.07	.07	.07	.10	.10	.10	.38	.30	.23
Rstrct	.66	.57	.52	.03	.05	.04	.05	.03	.02	.06	.05	.04	.05	.05	.05	.07	.07	.07	.26	.24	.22
Svb3	1.21	.36	.21	.06	.02	.01	.08	.03	.02	.12	.02	.01	.03	.03	.03	.05	.05	.05	.34	.14	.11

Table 4: Absolute energy breakdown (mJ) of 6 selected codelets on `HSW-CL` machine

Architecture-level simulators like McPAT or CACTI-P [13, 14] can provide detailed and accurate information about energy or power consumption of modern multicore processors. However, simulation speed can be a limitation for software tuning and optimization.

To drive power management policies at runtime, many power models were built using hardware performance counters. Similar to our work, the idea is to associate energy weights to activity factors computed using hardware counters that correlate the most with performance. Such approaches are developed in [3, 22] and applied in the context of DVFS controllers to adjust CPU frequency to the demand on the machine. Though useful, these techniques do not provide an accurate distribution of energy among the different HW components or associate energy consumption with code characteristics. As these models rely on general linear regressions, some power or energy coefficients have negative slopes which are meaningless from a physics point of view. Consequently, it is hard to understand and estimate the amount of power or energy that micro-architectural components consume.

Bertran et al. [1] discuss an incremental methodology to build a power model to isolate the power consumption of main CPU components. The proposed model does not make explicit separation between the static and dynamic power consumption. Goel et al. [6] propose a methodology that explicitly separates between dynamic and static power consumption. However, the methodology they follow requires some special boards (overclocked CPU for the gaming community) to model the static power. Such custom HW allows explicit voltage tuning for core and uncore components.

McCullough et al.[18] compare the effectiveness of various power modeling techniques for system components. Like us, they turned off Turbo-Boost and HT. They conclude that CPU power-models can lead to non-negligible prediction errors due to hidden states, and advice to not rely on these models. We agree that parameters that are not explicitly exposed by HW may lead to prediction errors, but unlike their tested modeling techniques, an incremental approach can help isolating the energy contribution of various components compared to single linear or non-linear regressions.

Sahoa et al. [21] discuss a methodology where energy consumption is estimated in terms of the mix of vector instructions that are executed on the Xeon Phi processor. In fact, no separation between the various operations is made as the cost of a multiply can be very different from the one for an add operation. Unlike these previous research efforts, we correlate energy consumption to software characteristics like the different instruction sets that the hardware supports. We also make an explicit distinction between static and dynamic energy. This methodology allows us to be more fine grained when associating energy to the generated code.

Other research efforts focused on studying energy efficiency of different HW. Czechowski et al. [4] discuss energy and power improvement for various generations of Intel processors. Gupta et al. [8] study energy efficiency of the uncore component compared to the core component. All these studies focus on hardware and do not provide insight on how effective the HW can be for a particular code.

From a software tuning perspective, Cebrián et al. [2] discuss energy savings due to vectorization using two benchmarks. While they show and confirm that vectorization improves performance while decreasing energy consumption, they do not show which the components benefit the most from vectorization. Thanks to our methodology, we can give a detailed breakdown of energy consumption and drive software tuning to generate better code.

7. CONCLUSION

In this paper, we presented a methodology to build linear energy models for multicore processors. Our method starts with high-level energy and performance measurement and drives low-level energy breakdown information among a set of HW nodes. Also, our methodology presents a new way of separating static and dynamic power at the level of the core and the uncore, using the clock modulation feature and a series of multicore runs. Thus, our approach has the ability to associate the energy consumption of various HW nodes to the quality of the generated code, helping developers in the process of code optimization and tuning.

Using a set of codelets, our experimental evaluation shows an average error of 3%, regardless of the test machine, data size (footprint) or the instruction set we use. These results show that our methodology can be the basis of tools to analyze the energy efficiency of hardware and the quality of the analyzed code. We show that while total static energy can be as high as 80%, the static energy of the uncore component can contribute up to 70% (Figure 14). Our numbers suggest that this requires much attention as it is a good candidate for energy consumption reduction.

Using a set of quality metrics, we analyze differences between various codelets and show that HW nodes consuming most energy correlate well with performance limiters. In fact, our method allows us to link energy consumption to the various algorithms that are implemented in the codelets we use. We can also show and explain why vectorization using the `AVX2` and `SSE` instruction sets leads to higher performance and lower energy consumption. Though few codelets have similar energy consumption regardless of the instruction set, the general trend shows that `AVX2` is more energy efficient than `SC` or `SSE`.

Our work has been limited to multicore systems in throughput mode, with prefetch, HT, and Turbo-boost disabled. We plan to extend the model to deal with prefetch and HT on. Since Turbo-boost has hidden HW state activities, controlled measurement and modeling are probably too difficult to do with low, predictable errors. We do plan to extend our methodology to parallel workloads on multicore systems, and to accelerator-like systems.

8. REFERENCES

[1] R. Bertran, M. Gonzalez, X. Martorell, N. Navarro, and E. Ayguade. Decomposable and responsive power models for multicore processors using performance counters. In *Proceedings of the 24th ACM International Conference on Supercomputing*, ICS '10, pages 147–158, New York, NY, USA, 2010. ACM.

[2] J. M. Cebrián, L. Natvig, and J. C. Meyer. Performance and energy impact of parallelization and vectorization techniques in modern microprocessors. *Computing*, 96(12):1179–1193, Dec. 2014.

[3] M. Curtis-Maury, F. Blagojevic, C. D. Antonopoulos, and D. S. Nikolopoulos. Prediction-based power-performance adaptation of multithreaded scientific codes. *IEEE Transactions on Parallel and Distributed Systems*, 19(10):1396–1410, Oct 2008.

[4] K. Czechowski, V. W. Lee, E. Grochowski, R. Ronen, R. Singhal, R. Vuduc, and P. Dubey. Improving the energy efficiency of big cores. *SIGARCH Comput. Archit. News*, 42(3):493–504, June 2014.

[5] H. David, E. Gorbatov, U. R. Hanebutte, R. Khanna, and C. Le. Rapl: Memory power estimation and capping. In *Proceedings of the 16th ACM/IEEE International Symposium on Low Power Electronics and Design*, ISLPED '10, pages 189–194, New York, NY, USA, 2010. ACM.

[6] B. Goel and S. A. McKee. A methodology for modeling dynamic and static power consumption for multicore processors. In *2016 IEEE International Parallel and Distributed Processing Symposium (IPDPS)*, pages 273–282, May 2016.

[7] R. Gonzalez and M. Horowitz. Energy dissipation in general purpose processors. In *Low Power Electronics, 1995., IEEE Symposium on*, pages 12–13. IEEE, 1995.

[8] V. Gupta, P. Brett, D. Koufaty, D. Reddy, S. Hahn, K. Schwan, and G. Srinivasa. The forgotten 'uncore': On the energy-efficiency of heterogeneous cores. In *Proceedings of the 2012 USENIX Conference on Annual Technical Conference*, USENIX ATC'12, pages 34–34, Berkeley, CA, USA, 2012. USENIX Association.

[9] D. Hackenberg, T. Ilsche, R. Schone, D. Molka, M. Schmidt, and W. E. Nagel. Power measurement techniques on standard compute nodes: A quantitative comparison. *2013 IEEE International Symposium on Performance Analysis of Systems and Software (ISPASS)*, 0:194–204, 2013.

[10] Intel Corporation. Intel 64 and IA-32 architectures software developer's manual: System programming guide, September 2016.

[11] W. Jalby, D. C. Wong, D. J. Kuck, J. Acquaviva, and J. C. Beyler. Measuring computer performance. In M. W. Berry, K. A. Gallivan, E. Gallopoulos, A. Grama, and B. Philippe, editors, *High-Performance Scientific Computing - Algorithms and Applications.*, pages 75–95. Springer, 2012.

[12] D. J. Kuck. *Computational Capacity Based Codesign of Computer Systems*, pages 45–73. Springer London, London, 2012.

[13] S. Li, J. H. Ahn, R. D. Strong, J. B. Brockman, D. M. Tullsen, and N. P. Jouppi. Mcpat: An integrated power, area, and timing modeling framework for multicore and manycore architectures. In *Proceedings of the 42Nd Annual IEEE/ACM International Symposium on Microarchitecture*, MICRO 42, pages 469–480, New York, NY, USA, 2009. ACM.

[14] S. Li, K. Chen, J. H. Ahn, J. B. Brockman, and N. P. Jouppi. Cacti-p: Architecture-level modeling for sram-based structures with advanced leakage reduction techniques. In *Proceedings of the International Conference on Computer-Aided Design*, ICCAD '11, pages 694–701, Piscataway, NJ, USA, 2011. IEEE Press.

[15] MAQAO. Maqao project, 2016.

[16] A. Mazouz, B. Pradelle, and W. Jalby. Statistical validation methodology of cpu power probes. In *Revised Selected Papers, Part I, of the Euro-Par 2014 International Workshops on Parallel Processing - Volume 8805*, pages 487–498, New York, NY, USA, 2014. Springer-Verlag New York, Inc.

[17] A. Mazouz, S. A. A. Touati, and D. Barthou. Study of variations of native program execution times on multi-core architectures. In L. Barolli, F. Xhafa, S. Vitabile, and H. Hsu, editors, *CISIS 2010, The Fourth International Conference on Complex, Intelligent and Software Intensive Systems, Krakow, Poland, 15-18 February 2010*, pages 919–924. IEEE Computer Society, 2010.

[18] J. C. McCullough, Y. Agarwal, J. Chandrashekar, S. Kuppuswamy, A. C. Snoeren, and R. K. Gupta. Evaluating the effectiveness of model-based power characterization. In *Proceedings of the 2011 USENIX Conference on USENIX Annual Technical Conference*, USENIXATC'11, pages 12–12, Berkeley, CA, USA, 2011. USENIX Association.

[19] J. Noudohouenou, V. Palomares, W. Jalby, D. C. Wong, D. J. Kuck, and J. C. Beyler. Simsys: A performance simulation framework. In *Proceedings of the 2013 Workshop on Rapid Simulation and Performance Evaluation: Methods and Tools*, RAPIDO '13, pages 1:1–1:8, New York, NY, USA, 2013. ACM.

[20] W. H. Press, S. A. Teukolsky, W. T. Vetterling, and B. P. Flannery. *Numerical Recipes in C (2Nd Ed.): The Art of Scientific Computing.* Cambridge University Press, New York, NY, USA, 1992.

[21] Y. S. Shao and D. M. Brooks. Energy characterization and instruction-level energy model of intel's xeon phi processor. In *International Symposium on Low Power Electronics and Design (ISLPED), Beijing, China, September 4-6, 2013*, pages 389–394, 2013.

[22] V. Spiliopoulos, A. Sembrant, and S. Kaxiras. Power-sleuth: A tool for investigating your program's power behavior. In *2012 IEEE 20th International Symposium on Modeling, Analysis and Simulation of Computer and Telecommunication Systems*, pages 241–250, Aug 2012.

Detecting Memory-Boundedness with Hardware Performance Counters

Daniel Molka Robert Schöne Daniel Hackenberg

Wolfgang E. Nagel

Center for Information Services and High Performance Computing
Zellescher Weg 12-14, Dresden, Germany
{daniel.molka, robert.schoene, daniel.hackenberg, wolfgang.nagel}@tu-dresden.de

ABSTRACT

Modern processors incorporate several performance monitoring units, which can be used to count events that occur within different components of the processor. They provide access to information on hardware resource usage and can therefore be used to detect performance bottlenecks. Thus, many performance measurement tools are able to record them complementary to information about the application behavior. However, the exact meaning of the supported hardware events is often incomprehensible due to the system complexity and partially lacking or even inaccurate documentation. For most events it is also not documented whether a certain rate indicates a saturated resource usage. Therefore, it is usually difficult to draw conclusions on the performance impact from the observed event rates. In this paper, we evaluate whether hardware performance counters can be used to measure the capacity utilization within the memory hierarchy and estimate the impact of memory accesses on the achieved performance. The presented approach is based on a small selection of micro-benchmarks that constantly stress individual components in the memory subsystem, ranging from caches to main memory. These workloads are used to identify hardware performance counters that provide good estimates for the utilization of individual components in the memory hierarchy. However, since access latencies can be interleaved with computing instructions, a high utilization of the memory hierarchy does not necessarily result in low performance. We therefore also investigate which stall counters provide good estimates for the number of cycles that are actually spent waiting for the memory hierarchy.

Keywords

hardware performance counters, benchmarking, performance analysis

ICPE'17, April 22 - 26, 2017, L'Aquila, Italy

ISBN 978-1-4503-4404-3/17/04 . . . $15.00

DOI: *http://dx.doi.org/10.1145/3030207.3030223*

1. INTRODUCTION

High performance computing (HPC) is an indispensable tool that is required to obtain new insights in many scientific disciplines. While HPC systems are getting more and more powerful from year to year, scientific applications typically are not able to fully utilize this potential. Utilization levels of 10% and lower are not uncommon [19].

Modern microprocessors feature multiple levels of cache—small and fast buffers for frequently accessed data—that improve the performance of memory accesses. Still, memory access latencies often account for a significant portion of the average cycles per instruction [4]. Since caches and the memory interface can be shared between multiple cores of a processor, the contention of shared resources can limit the scalability of parallel applications. Moreover, the physical memory is typically distributed among multiple processors of a system, leading to varying performance depending on the distance to the accessed data. These non-uniform memory access (NUMA) characteristics influence the performance and scalability of parallel applications [15]. The performance of memory accesses is also affected by the cache coherence protocols [18]. Overall, the complexity of contemporary computer systems results in various potential bottlenecks that can cause application performance penalties.

Our understanding of the application performance can be improved by determining the limitations that are caused by the various components of the memory hierarchy. This can be achieved with the help of performance monitoring units (PMUs), which are included in many modern processors. Using PMUs to detect memory related performance issues is common practice [5, 13, 25, 26]; [10, Appendix B.3]. However, the available events are often specific to a certain processor generation and their meaning is not always obvious. Two things are required to decide if the observed performance counter event rates are significant: The attribution of events to the utilization of individual components, and reference values for peak event rates.

In this paper we contribute a portable approach for the identification of hardware performance events that can be used to detect performance problems that are caused by memory accesses. We describe a method to derive metrics for the utilization of individual components in the memory subsystem and the memory-boundedness of applications. The applicability of our methodology is demonstrated on a contemporary dual-socket server system.

2. BACKGROUND AND RELATED WORK

Figure 1 depicts the basic structure of contemporary multi-processor systems. Typically each core has dedicated level-one caches. Per-core level-two caches also are a widely-used feature. In contrast, last level cache and memory interface are typically shared by multiple cores. Each level in the memory hierarchy has different characteristics. The level-one caches support high data rates and have very low latencies. However, their capacity is very low. Each further level in the memory hierarchy provides higher capacities along with lower data rates and higher latencies. The compute nodes of HPC systems often contain multiple processors in order to increase the compute power and memory capacity. However, the communication via the processor interconnects results in a higher latency for remote cache and memory accesses and the data rates of the links are limited [17].

Caches are transparent for the software, i.e., they are no directly addressable memory. Instead, caches contain duplicates of small blocks from main memory. Which data is placed in the caches is determined by the hardware at runtime based on the observed memory accesses. The used heuristics include keeping data that has already been accessed in cache in anticipation of further accesses to the same locations as well as various techniques that recognize regular access patterns and prefetch data that will probably be accessed soon. Furthermore, multiple copies of the same memory location can exist concurrently in different caches. Cache coherence protocols ensure that writes performed by one core eventually become visible to all cores in order to maintain the impression of a single copy. However, this often requires that cached data is invalidated. Due to the inherent unpredictability of the replacement, prefetch, and coherence mechanisms it is virtually impossible to determine the cache usage of an application using static code analysis.

Caches significantly reduce the average memory latency. However, time consuming main memory accesses are not avoided entirely and cache accesses, especially in case of large last level caches, also have considerable latencies. Therefore, processors used in HPC (excluding accelerators) typically have well-developed out-of-order execution capabilities to fill the remaining waiting times with useful work. Furthermore, the load-store units comprise multiple load and store buffers in order to facilitate multiple concurrently outstanding requests instead of processing memory accesses one after another. A sufficient number of concurrently outstanding requests is a prerequisite for achieving high data rates [14]. The caches typically support multiple outstanding misses as well to avoid being blocked by a single cache miss. The ability to continue the program execution while memory accesses are pending can significantly improve the performance. However, this and the overlapping of multiple accesses further complicates the assessment of memory related performance losses as only a fraction of the individual access latencies causes delays in the execution.

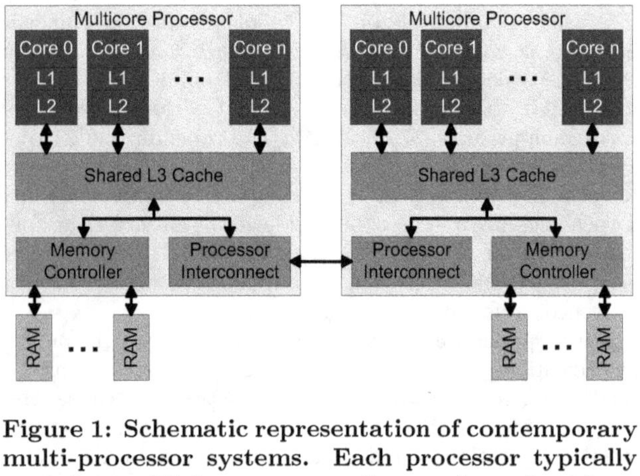

Figure 1: Schematic representation of contemporary multi-processor systems. Each processor typically contains multiple cores as well as various shared resources. The processors are typically connected to each other via point-to-point connections.

The achievable application performance can be limited by various components. Performance monitoring units (PMUs) that collect information about the usage of these components are included in many contemporary processors [2, Section 2.7]; [11, Vol. 3, Section 18.1]. Typically, each core has a number of dedicated PMUs that can be used to count events from this core, e.g., the number of executed instructions. Multi-core processors often implement additional PMUs that monitor shared resources [2, Section 2.7.2]; [8]. Typically, each PMU contains two registers, the control register and the performance monitoring counter (PMC) register. The former is used to *specify* the events that are recorded, the latter incorporates an *accumulator* that is incremented with every occurrence of an event. A widely-used tool for recording performance counter data is the Performance API (PAPI) [24], which defines a standardized interface for accessing PMUs of various processor architectures. Many performance measurement tools, e.g., *HPCToolkit* [1], and *Score-P* [12], use it to record performance counters in addition to information about the application behavior.

PMUs are primarily intended for verification purposes [27]. However, they can be used to detect performance issues as well [10, Appendix B]. This has also been studied extensively by the scientific community: Eranian [5] shows that PMUs can in principle be used to detect performance problems, although no systematic analysis of the available events is included in his study. Treibig et al. [25] describe common bottlenecks of specific applications and how they can be detected with PMUs. Their approach requires events that correctly represent the bandwidth utilization in order to diagnose memory related performance problems. Levinthal [13] and Yasin [26] present procedures that identify bottlenecks in the memory hierarchy using PMUs. However, their studies do not include any verification whether the PMUs count the selected events accurately. Yoo et al. [27] use micro-benchmarks to correlate known performance pathologies, e.g., performing random accesses on large data sets, with PMU events on Westmere-EP and Sandy Bridge HE test systems. The approach does not only allow to detect potential performance issues, it also categorizes them. However, it is inherently limited to the known types of problems. While also relying on micro-benchmarks, our approach is different as we focus on the potential bottlenecks in the hardware instead of unfavorable properties of the software. Palomares lists PMC events that correlate to cache and memory traffic in [20, Table 5.3]. However, the given events do not distinguish read and write accesses. Furthermore, the listed DRAM events for the Sandy Bridge, Ivy Bridge, and Haswell architectures only measure the DRAM accesses per package. In our work, we also investigate if the core PMUs can be used to measure the bandwidth usage of individual cores.

3. METHODOLOGY

Each component in the memory hierarchy can limit the achievable application performance, either due to limited bandwidths or due to access latencies that stall the execution. Therefore, the utilization level of the available bandwidths as well as the percentage of cycles that is spent waiting for the memory hierarchy are good indicators for memory related performance problems. In this section we describe how these metrics can be derived from performance counters. Performance counters are architecture specific, i.e., the evaluation of their significance has to be repeated for every new micro-architecture. Therefore, we propose a portable approach based on a small selection of micro-benchmarks. We demonstrate its applicability on a dual socket Haswell-EP system. A similar study for the Sandy Bridge micro-architecture is presented in [16, Section 5.3].

3.1 Bandwidth Utilization

Memory intensive applications with sequential or otherwise regular memory access patterns are typically bandwidth-bound. As the required memory addresses are predictable, there are enough concurrent requests to fill the load or store buffers and the request queues for accesses to lower levels in the memory hierarchy. This leads to a high utilization of the data paths. The bandwidth utilizations within the memory subsystem are easy to understand metrics that indicate if the application behaves as expected.

In order to determine the utilization level for each component, one needs to know the respective peak bandwidth as well as the bandwidth usage of the application. A component's theoretical peak bandwidth can be calculated by multiplying the width of the corresponding data paths with the data rates (operating frequencies), which are typically documented by the hardware vendors. However, the practically achievable bandwidths can be significantly lower [17]. Micro-benchmarks that stress individual components provide much better reference values for the achievable performance. The achieved bandwidth usage of applications needs to be recorded at runtime. Performance monitoring units provide information about the utilization of various components. However, they typically count accesses to certain levels in the memory hierarchy or packages that are transferred between processors instead of directly measuring the used bandwidth. The amount of data that is transferred per reported event is not necessarily known. Furthermore, prefetchers can request data before it is actually accessed, which may disguise memory accesses. Therefore, it can be difficult to judge if the observed event rates, e.g., for cache misses, are indicative of a performance problem.

Our methodology requires bandwidth benchmarks that perform sequential read and write accesses, use configurable data set sizes, and support NUMA-aware memory allocation. Such benchmarks can be used to identify performance counters that correlate with the utilization of individual components and determine their respective maximal event rates, which represent an utilization of 100 %. The proposed workflow comprises the following steps:

1. Identify events that show high event rates if data is transferred between the core and the L1 cache. Load and store instructions with multiple widths are used in this step to test if the usage of SIMD instructions can be recognized.
2. For each further level in the memory hierarchy: identify events that show high event rates if data is read from or written back there. This step is performed using the widest load and store instructions that are available. It is important to identify events that consider the read for ownership (RFO) requests in case of writes in order to capture all transfers to the L1 cache.
3. Allocate memory from another NUMA node in order to identify events that show high event rates if data is located in remote memory.
4. Determine the overlap between the identified counters, i.e., check if events that correlate well with the number of accesses to a certain location include other accesses as well. If possible, use additional PMU events to compensate the overlap in order to measure the number of accesses independently for every location.
5. Derive upper bounds for the event rates of the identified counters based on the measured performance and the observed number of events per memory access.

There are per core limits for the achievable bandwidths for each level in the memory hierarchy as well as limited aggregate bandwidths for the shared resources [22]. Therefore, the analysis is performed once using a single core and once using all cores that share a resource in order to determine the respective upper bounds for the associated hardware performance counters.

3.2 Memory Related Stalls

Applications with irregular memory access patterns, e.g., dereferencing chains of pointers when traversing linked lists or trees, may not generate enough concurrently outstanding requests to fully utilize the data paths. Nevertheless, such applications are clearly limited by the performance of memory accesses as well. Therefore, considering the bandwidth utilization is not sufficient to detect all memory related performance issues. However, multiplying the number of accesses to each location with the respective latency would overestimate the total waiting time in the majority of cases. Furthermore, a high bandwidth utilization is not necessarily a performance problem. As long as the out-of-order engine can keep the execution units busy with useful work, using all the available bandwidth does not pose a bottleneck. Therefore, we also search for performance counters that measure memory related waiting times, i.e., periods without any useful computation, in order to quantify the performance impact of memory accesses.

A low instruction throughput without being bandwidth bound indicates that there are high latency operations. This can however be caused by slow arithmetic instructions like *div* or *sqrt* as well as high memory accesses latencies. Fortunately, performance counters for various types of stall cycles also are a widely-used feature in contemporary processors. With our methodology it is possible to check if memory related stalls can be distinguished from other stall reasons with the existing PMU events. Furthermore, it can be checked if stalls that are caused by high access latencies and stalls between consequtive data transfers in bandwidth limited scenarios can be differentiated.

Our methodology requires a pointer-chasing benchmark that supports configurable data set sizes. This benchmark needs to be modified in order to be able to distinguish memory related stalls from other stall reasons. In a first modification, independent arithmetic instructions have to be added between the memory accesses. In another modified version, the arithmetic operations have to be added in a way that results in a single dependency chain that comprises all operations, e.g., by repeated additions of 0 or multiplications by 1. The workflow to identify meaningful counters for memory related stall cycles comprises the following steps:

1. Use standard latency benchmark to identify stall counters that comprise all latency related stalls
2. Use modified pointer-chaising benchmarks to check if there are counters that distinguish memory related stalls from other stall reasons. In case of independent operations between the loads the runtime stays constant. A suitable counter for memory related stalls needs to deduct the cycles that perform computations from the reported number of stalls. If there is a single dependency chain, it should report the same values as for the unmodified latency benchmark.
3. Check if there are additional counters that correlate with the number of total stall cycles reported for the bandwidth benchmarks but do not cover the stalls during the latency benchmark.

If useful counters are found in step two, they can be used to check if delays caused by memory accesses account for a significant portion of the runtime. Depending on the outcome of step three, the memory-bound fraction can possibly be subdivided into latency-bound and bandwidth-bound parts.

3.3 Benchmarks

We use *x86-membench* [16, Chapter 3], which is particularly suitable to stress individual components in the memory subsystem of systems with 64 bit x86 processors. Furthermore, x86-membench can record hardware performance counters in addition to the latency and bandwidth measurements via an integrated PAPI instrumentation. The constant workloads in combination with the integrated hardware monitoring are used to identify performance counters that provide good estimates for the utilization of the individual components.

The correlation of hardware performance counters with the utilization of the memory hierarchy is evaluated using the load and store variants of *x86-membench's* throughput kernel [16, Section 3.5.4]. These benchmarks measure the achievable bandwidths for different levels in the memory hierarchy by repeatedly accessing a buffer. The size of the buffer determines the level in the memory hierarchy that is evaluated. Memory can be allocated from specific NUMA nodes. In order to determine suitable performance counters for the bandwidth that is consumed per core the throughput benchmark has to be configured as follows[1]:

- BENCHIT_KERNEL_CPU_LIST is set to "0", which restricts the measurement to CPU 0.
- A CPU from another processor that is directly connected to the processor that contains CPU 0 is entered in BENCHIT_KERNEL_MEM_BIND.
- BENCHIT_KERNEL_MIN is set to 50% of the L1 data cache size or lower.
- BENCHIT_KERNEL_MAX is set to at least ten times the LLC size.
- BENCHIT_KERNEL_ALLOC is initially set to "L" (localalloc) in order to evaluate the local memory hierarchy. It is changed to "B" (bind-to-core) in order to examine remote memory accesses.
- BENCHIT_KERNEL_INSTRUCTION is configured to perform loads or stores with different widths as required, e.g., "avx_load_pd" for 256 bit loads.

In order to investigate shared resources in multi-core processors, the benchmark configuration is changed as follows:

- All CPUs that belong to the first socket are entered in BENCHIT_KERNEL_CPU_LIST.
- BENCHIT_KERNEL_MEM_BIND contains all CPUs from another socket that is directly connected to the first socket.

The counter that most accurately represents the delay caused by memory accesses can be identified with a slightly adapted version of *x86-membench's* latency benchmark [16, Section 3.5.1]. This benchmark repeatedly dereferences a pointer in the register *RBX*. It represents a worst case scenario with only one outstanding memory request at a time, a hardly predictable access pattern, and no other instructions between the memory accesses. In order to investigate the effect of overlapping memory accesses and computation on the number of reported stall cycles, arithmetic instructions are added between the loads. There are two versions of the modified latency benchmark—one that adds multiplications without data dependencies to the workload and one with multiplications that are part of the dependency chain [16, Section 5.3.2]. In the former case the added multiplications use different registers (R8 – R15) and can therefore be reordered around the memory accesses. In the latter case the pointer itself is repeatedly multiplied by 1. Since all operations form a single dependency chain, they cannot be reordered. The parameters have to be configured as follows:

- one CPU from every processor is entered in BENCHIT_KERNEL_CPU_LIST
- settings for BENCHIT_KERNEL_MIN and BENCHIT_KERNEL_MAX are identical to the bandwidth measurements
- BENCHIT_KERNEL_ALLOC is set to "L" (localalloc)

4. EVALUATION OF HASWELL-EP

We conduct our experiments on a Bull SAS bullx R421 E4 system, which is described in Table 1. As depicted in Figure 2, each processor contains twelve cores with dedicated L1

Table 1: Dual socket Haswell-EP test system

Processors	2x Intel Xeon E5-2680 v3
Cores / threads	2x 12 / 2x 24
Core clock	2.5 GHz (2.1 GHz AVX freq. [9])
Uncore clock	up to 3.0 GHz
L1 / L2 cache	2x 32 KiB / 256 KiB per core
L3 cache	30 MiB per chip
Memory	128 GiB (8x 16 GiB) PC4-2133P-R
QPI speed	9.6 GT/s (38.4 GB/s)
Operating System	Ubuntu 16.04 LTS, kernel 4.4.0-21-generic

[1] defaults are used for the remaining parameters, see *https://fusionforge.zih.tu-dresden.de/plugins/mediawiki/wiki/benchit/index.php/X86membench*

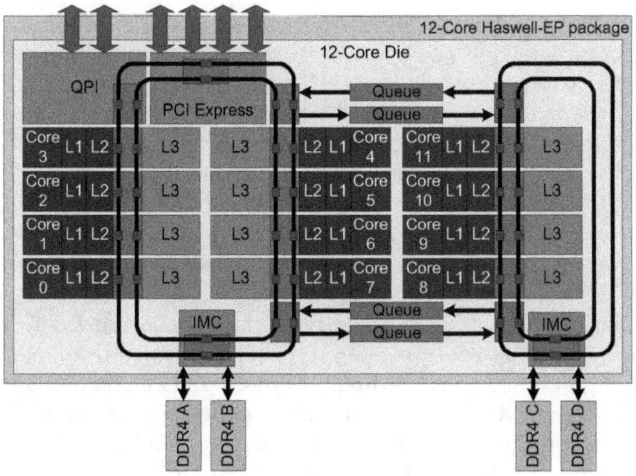

Figure 2: Xeon E5-2680 v3 package

and L2 caches as well as various shared resources. Each core has a dedicated performance monitoring unit that monitors the activity of the execution units, cache hits and misses, and so-called offcore requests, which supply data that is not found in the core's local L1 and L2 cache. Furthermore, there are multiple PMUs for the shared resources, which reside in the so-called *uncore* [8, Figure 1-2]. The L3 cache is partitioned into twelve slices. Each slice has a dedicated caching agent (CA) with an associated performance monitoring unit called C-Box. Memory accesses are monitored by the home agent (HA) counters that observe memory accesses on the coherence protocol level as well as the integrated memory (IMC) counters that record information related to the actual DRAM accesses. Since each processor contains two memory controllers, there are two HA and two IMC PMUs per processor. Data transfers between the processors are covered by the QPI counters—separately for each link.

We are using PAPI version 5.4.3 to access the PMUs. The recorded events are configured via x86-membench's BENCHIT_KERNEL_PAPI parameter. We use the event names as they are reported by the papi_native_avail command.

Haswell is an aggressive out-of-order micro-architecture [10, Section 2.2]. The large reorder window enables the processor cores to continue executing instructions while multiple outstanding memory requests are processed. However, main memory accesses that are not anticipated by the hardware prefetchers can take several hundreds of cycles and the bandwidths supported by the memory hierarchy are limited [18]. This eventually stalls the execution once a required resource, e.g., the load or store buffers, is fully used.

4.1 Bandwidth Usage of a Single Core

Since uncore counters record aggregate performance data that can hardly be attributed to actions of a single core, the evaluation is restricted to the core counters. However, there are still numerous memory related events.

The event *perf::L1-DCACHE-LOADS* counts all load instructions. This can be used to determine how many times the load ports are used. However, no distinction is made between loads of different widths. As long as the data set fits into the L1 cache, the number of reported *perf::L1-DCACHE-LOAD-MISSES* is close to zero. For larger data sets the number of events per load instruction depends on their width. One out of eight 64 bit loads generates a miss event. 128 bit loads cause a miss on every fourth access. In case of 256 bit wide loads every second load instruction misses the L1 cache. This means that the *perf::L1-DCACHE-LOAD-MISSES* increases by one for every cache line that is transferred to the L1 cache. Writes to lower cache levels also generate one load miss per cache line, i.e., RFO requests are included in the measurement. Therefore, the *perf::L1-DCACHE-LOAD-MISSES* provide a good estimate for the number of cache lines that are brought into the L1 cache. Analogous events for write accesses are available as well. The event *perf::L1-DCACHE-STORES* counts all write accesses. The event *perf::L1-DCACHE-STORE-MISSES* is not defined by the Linux kernel and is therefore not functional. However, the number of cache lines that are written back to lower levels of the memory hierarchy can be counted using the *L2_TRANS:L1D_WB*.

The remaining challenge is to find events that distinguish accesses to different memory hierarchy levels and local from remote memory accesses. As depicted in Figure 3, the *MEM_LOAD_UOPS_RETIRED* events are not suitable to determine the origin of the data in case of sequential loads. Half of the accesses hit the L1 cache or the line fill buffers (LFB). This can be explained by the fact that the benchmark performs two loads per cache line. Therefore, only every second access causes a data transfer from a lower level. The sum of the reported *L2_HIT*, *L3_HIT*, and *L3_MISS* events is equal to the number of *perf::L1-DCACHE-LOAD-MISSES*. However, the individual values do not correlate well with the number of cache lines that are delivered from the L2 cache, L3 cache, and main memory, respectively. The *L2_HIT* sub-event shows a non-negligible number of false positives if data is read from the L3 cache and main memory. Likewise, sequential memory accesses also cause a high number of *L3_HIT* events. Thus, using the *L3_MISS* events can severely underestimate the number of memory accesses. The discrepancy between the values reported by the performance counters and the actual number of accesses is presumably caused by the hardware prefetchers. Furthermore, reads that are caused by read for ownership (RFO) requests are not covered by *MEM_LOAD_UOPS_RE-TIRED*.

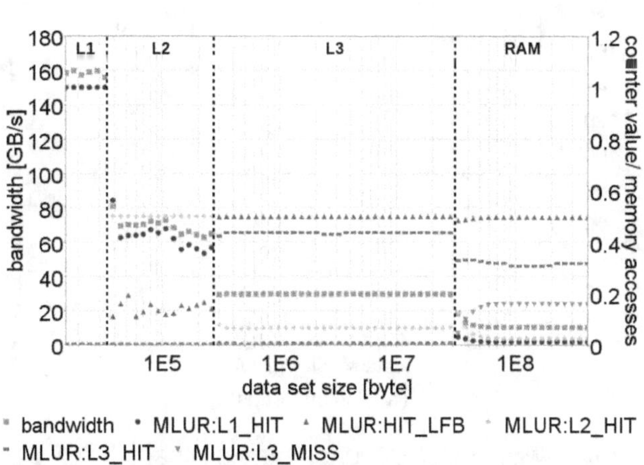

Figure 3: Date source according to MEM_LOAD_UOPS_RETIRED (MLUR) events: This event distinguishes load operations with respect to the origin of the accessed data. However, it does not correctly represent the number of data transfers from the individual levels in the memory hierarchy.

Figure 4 depicts performance counter readings that subdivide the L1 misses according to the data's prior location within the memory hierarchy. If the data is located in the L2 cache, loads cause *L2_TRANS:DEMAND_DATA_RD* and *L2_RQSTS:DEMAND_DATA_RD_HIT* events while stores generate *L2_TRANS:RFO* events. The event rates are close to the number of lines requested by the L1 cache as reported by *perf::L1-DCACHE-LOAD-MISSES*, i.e., approximately one event per accessed cache line is recorded. Surprisingly, the *L2_RQSTS:RFO_HIT* event does not record any RFO requests as long as all data fits into the L2 cache. In contrast, *L2_RQSTS:ALL_RFO* – *L2_RQSTS:RFO_MISS* correctly represents the number of RFOs that hit the L2 cache (not depicted). For data sets that exceed the L2 capacity the values reported by *L2_TRANS* and *L2_RQSTS* differ significantly. Apparently, the sub-events of L2_TRANS also capture accesses to lower levels of the memory hierarchy. However, the values are significantly higher than the corresponding number of misses in the L1 cache, especially in case of loads. This indicates that additional cache lines from the L2 cache are requested by the L1 cache's prefetchers while waiting for the data from lower cache levels. The L2_RQSTS readings seem to only consider cache lines that are actually delivered by the L2 cache. However, as it is the case for the *MEM_LOAD_UOPS_RETIRED* events, a significant number of false positives are reported when data is streamed from lower levels in the memory hierarchy.

The *OFFCORE_RESPONSE* events observe requests that miss in the L2 cache and provide numerous filters to isolate data transfers from a certain location. Events are specified in the following format: *OFFCORE_RESPONSE_{0|1}<request type><response type>* where the *response type* is either *ANY_RESPONSE* or *<supplier><snoop>*. The *request type* is set to *ANY_DATA:ANY_RFO* in order to include read only requests as well as the RFOs caused by stores. The *supplier* field in the *response type* can be used to distinguish L3 cache and main memory accesses. If it is set to *L3_HIT*, all L3 accesses that hit cache lines in state *Modified*, *Exclusive*, *Shared*, or *Forward* are considered. The number of cache lines requested from local main memory can be counted using *L3_MISS_LOCAL* as supplier. Remote accesses can be counted via *L3_MISS_REMOTE_HOP{0|1|2P}* (not depicted). The *SNP_ANY* setting used for the *snoop* field includes cache lines that are forwarded from other caches in the measurement (not relevant in the used benchmark). *SNP_MISS:SNP_NO_FWD: SNP_NOT_NEEDED* can help to exclude forwarded cache lines from the measurement. However, *SNP_ANY* is the most cautious choice for measuring the utilization since on-chip transfers include a L3 lookup. Furthermore, cache lines that are forwarded from caches in other processors are typically delivered from memory as well or involve a directory lookup in the home node.

If data is delivered by the L3 cache, there are as many *L3_HIT* events as there are *L1-DCACHE-LOAD-MISSES*. In contrast, the number of *L3_MISS_LOCAL* events does not match the number of L1 cache misses if data is delivered from main memory. Therefore, the proportion of main memory accesses is severely underestimated by the *OFFCORE_RESPONSE* events. However, the sum of the L3 hit and L3 miss events is very close to the number of L1 misses in both cases, so the number of cache line transfers from the uncore to each core can be measured quite accurately.

Figure 4(b) shows a write bandwidth measurement, but the recorded events only cover the read for ownership transfers that place the data in the L1 cache prior to the modification. Indicators for the write backs are depicted in Figure 5. The total number of cache lines that are written back from the L1 cache can be counted via the *L2_TRANS:L1D_WB* event. Write backs from the L2 cache to lower levels of the memory hierarchy are represented by the values reported by *L2_TRANS:L2_WB*. Core counter events that indicate the number of write backs to main memory have not been found.

Table 2 shows the bandwidths that can be achieved by a single thread for read and write accesses to the local memory hierarchy as well as remote memory. The measured bandwidths are used to calculate the resulting number of transfers per second. The maximal event rates are derived from the performance counter readings presented in this section.

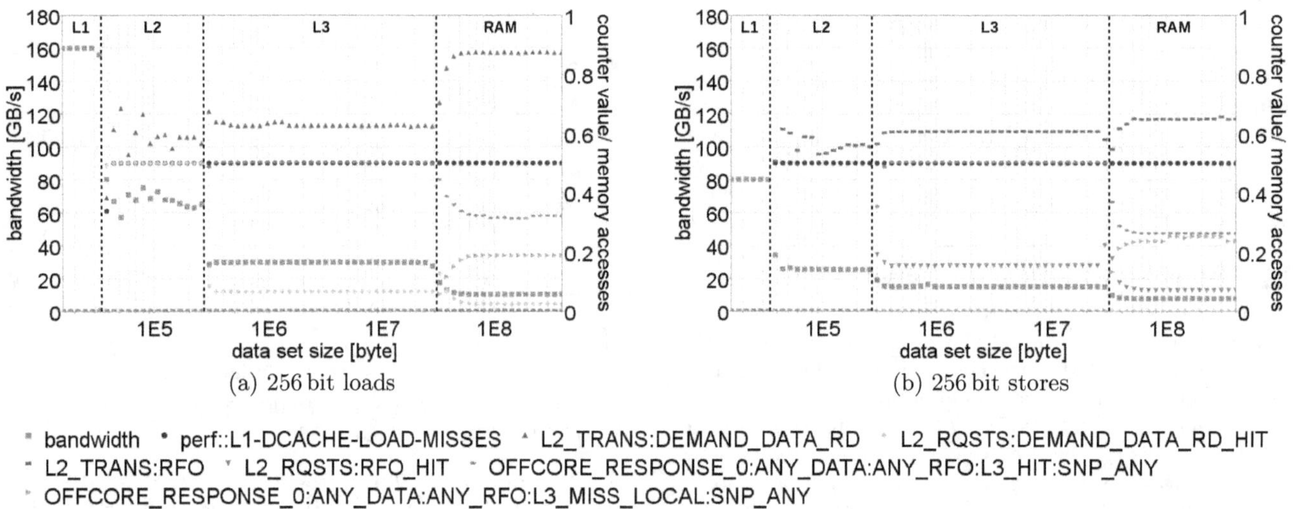

(a) 256 bit loads

(b) 256 bit stores

Figure 4: The Utilization of the L2 cache can be measured via the L2_TRANS and L2_RQSTS events. L3 cache and main memory accesses can be recorded using the OFFCORE_RESPONSE events. The correlation with the amount of accessed data is far from perfect. However, it is possible to gain important insight.

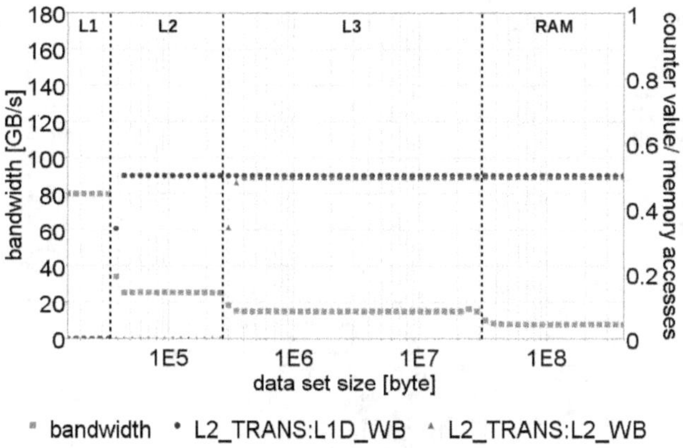

Figure 5: Write bandwidth (256 bit stores) and write back events: The L2_TRANS:L1D_WB and L2_TRANS:L2_WB events represent write backs from the L1 and L2 cache, respectively.

Most of them are identical to the number of transfers. Unfortunately, the number of transfers per second cannot be used to derive the bandwidth utilization of the L1 cache. With 64 bit instructions it is possible to reach the maximal event rates while using only 25% of the available bandwidth. However, this could still be defined as 100% load as all L1 load or store ports are active each cycle. The numbers reported by the *L2_TRANS:DEMAND_DATA_RD_HIT* and *L2_TRANS:RFO* events are higher than the actual number of requested cache lines that miss the L1 cache—presumably as some prefetcher requests are included as well. Furthermore, the *OFFCORE_RESPONSE* counters for L3 misses underestimate memory accesses. Nevertheless, the maximal event rates provide reference values for the 100% utilization of the corresponding components, which allows us to estimate the degree of capacity utilization for application runs.

4.2 Utilization of Shared Resources

The last level cache, the memory bandwidth, and the links between the processors are potential bottlenecks that may limit the application performance. In this section it is evaluated if the processor's uncore performance counters [8] can be used to measure the utilization of these shared resources. The uncore performance monitoring is implemented by multiple per-component performance monitoring units (also called "boxes") [8, Figure 1-2]. Uncore events are specified in the format: *hswep_unc_<comp>::<event name>* where *comp* selects a component, e.g. a L3 slice (C-Box), and the *event name* specifies the events that are counted. The *"hswep_unc_"* prefix is omitted here. *X86-membench* records performance counters only on one CPU and derives the event ratios by dividing the recorded number of events by the number of memory accesses performed by this CPU. This is sufficient for the collection of core counters since the workload is homogeneous, i.e., all cores would report very similar values. It also avoids conflicts between the CPUs if uncore counters are recorded as only a single CPU is accessing the uncore PMUs. However, in this case all events are attributed to a single CPU, which needs to be considered in the interpretation of the results. In case of the Xeon E5-2680 v3 processor the uncore is shared by twelve cores, i.e., the reported event ratios have to be divided by twelve to get the correct result.

Figure 6 depicts the correlation between accesses to different levels in the memory hierarchy and C-Box events. The *UNC_C_LLC_LOOKUP* and *UNC_C_TOR_INSERTS* events can be used to measure the aggregated L3 bandwidth. As shown in Figure 6(b), RFOs are not covered by the *UNC_C_LLC_LOOKUP:DATA_READ* event. Therefore, *UNC_C_LLC_LOOKUP:ANY* has to be used in order to capture all loads, although this event also includes stores and the event rates are higher than expected in case of L2 accesses as well as reads from the L3 cache. Furthermore, most main memory accesses are also counted as LLC lookups. The *UNC_C_LLC_LOOKUP:WRITE* events correlate well with the number of cache lines written to the L3 cache. *UNC_C_TOR_INSERTS* events also count L3 accesses. In contrast to *UNC_C_LLC_LOOKUP:ANY* events, the reads (*:OPC_DRD* and *:OPC_RFO*) also include all main memory accesses, which simplifies compensating for the overlap with the DRAM counters. Unfortunately, different types of *UNC_C_TOR_INSERTS* events cannot be counted concurrently.

Reads from and writes to the main memory can be observed via the *UNC_H_REQUESTS* events in the home agent PMUs, which report one event per accessed cache line. Writes can also be counted via *UNC_H_IMC_WRITES:FULL*, which explicitly excludes partial writes. The PMUs in the inte-

Table 2: Suitable indicators for bandwidth usage per core

access type		achievable bandwidth	million transfers/s	most appropriate indicator for bandwidth utilization (including transfers from lower levels)	maximal events/s
L1D	read	159.8 GB/s	4,993 (32 byte)	perf::L1-DCACHE-LOADS	4,993 million
	write	79.9 GB/s	2,496 (32 byte)	perf::L1-DCACHE-STORES	2,496 million
L2	read	75.0 GB/s	1,171 (64 byte)	L2_TRANS:DEMAND_DATA_RD + L2_TRANS:RFO	1,546 million
	write	25.5 GB/s	398 (64 byte)	L2_TRANS:L1D_WB	398 million
L3	read	29.9 GB/s	467 (64 byte)	*OCR_L3-HIT* + *OCR_L3-MISS-loc* + *OCR_L3-MISS-rem*	467 million
	write	15.0 GB/s	277 (64 byte)	L2_TRANS:L2_WB	277 million
local DRAM	read	10.4 GB/s	162 (64 byte)	*OCR_L3-MISS-loc*	61 million
	write	7.7 GB/s	120 (64 byte)	n/a	n/a
remote DRAM	read	8.0 GB/s	125 (64 byte)	*OCR_L3-MISS-rem*	63 million
	write	5.5 GB/s	85 (64 byte)	n/a	n/a

OCR_L3-HIT = OFFCORE_RESPONSE_{0|1}:ANY_DATA:ANY_RFO:L3_HIT:SNP_ANY
OCR_L3-MISS-loc = OFFCORE_RESPONSE_{0|1}:ANY_DATA:ANY_RFO:L3_MISS_LOCAL:SNP_ANY
OCR_L3-MISS-rem = OFFCORE_RESPONSE_{0|1}:ANY_DATA:ANY_RFO:L3_MISS_REMOTE_HOP0:L3_MISS_REMOTE_HOP1:L3_MISS_REMOTE_HOP2P:SNP_ANY

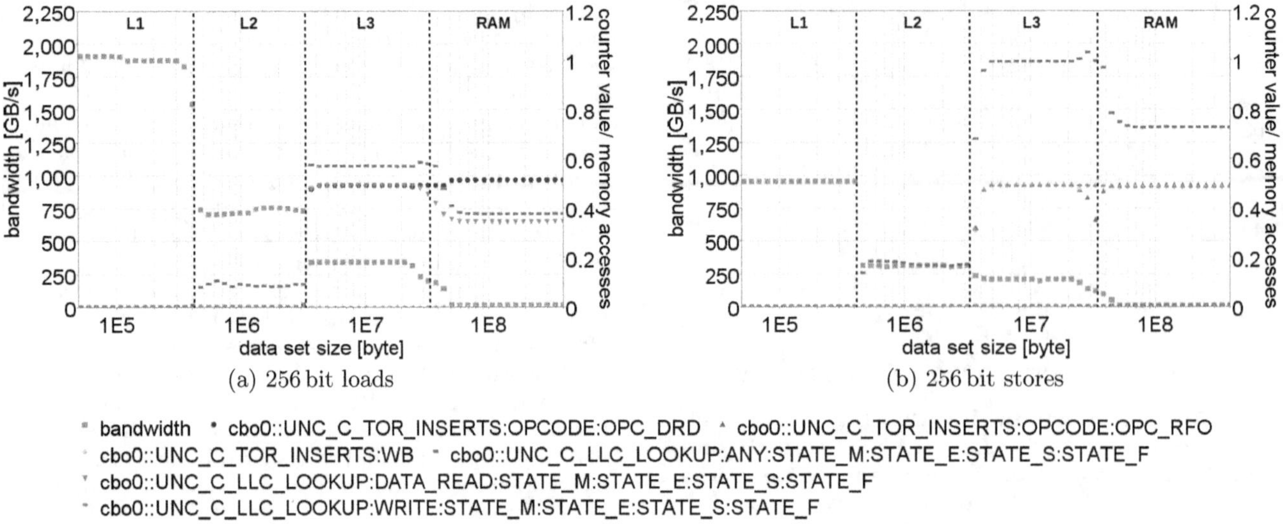

(a) 256 bit loads

(b) 256 bit stores

Figure 6: Last level cache counters: All C-Boxes report very similar results, i.e., the data is evenly distributed across the L3 slices. For the purpose of clarity only the results from a single C-Box are shown. This also compensates the incorrect attribution of events caused by twelve CPUs to a single CPU as only one twelfth of the events is considered. Thus, the shown event ratios are correct.

grated memory controller (IMC) record additional DRAM specific information (precharges, refreshes, ECC errors, etc.). However, the home agent events are sufficient to measure the bandwidth utilization per socket. The traffic between the sockets can be measured separately for each of the two QPI links. The *UNC_ Q_RXL_FLITS_G1:DRS_DATA* and *UNC_Q_TXL_FLITS_ G1:DRS_DATA* events observe incoming and outgoing traffic, respectively. These events record eight flits (flow control unit—the link layer's unit of transfer [7]) per cache line. This matches the expectation of 64 bit data per flit (80 bits including CRC and control [7]). It is also possible to count the snoop requests and response caused by the coherence protocol via the *:DRS_NONDATA* subevent.

Table 3 summarizes the results of this section. If the maximal event rates are reached the respective component is 100% occupied. In contrast to the core counters, the uncore counters recognize all cache lines that are read from or written to memory. Therefore, the bandwidth in GB/s can be derived from the recorded event rates with a high accuracy.

4.3 Memory Related Stalls

In this section, we analyze if the stall counters that are available on Intel Xeon E5 v3 processors correctly represent the fraction of time that is spent waiting for the memory hierarchy. Multiple events correlate well with the execution time of the latency measurements. A selection of the available events is depicted in Figure 7. The event *CYCLE_ACTIVITY:STALLS_LDM_PENDING* perfectly matches the measured latency. The same is true for the *:CYCLES_NO_EXECUTE* subevent as well as the *UOPS_{ISSUED, EXECUTED,RETIRED}:STALL_CYCLES* events (not depicted). However, the latency benchmark does not include any operations other than the memory accesses. Therefore, it is unclear if the various events comprise other stall reasons as well. The *CYCLE_ACTIVITY:STALLS_L1D_PENDING* and *:STALLS_L2_PENDING* events report fewer stall cycles as they do not include the L1 and L2 lookup, respectively.

Figure 8 shows how the performance counter readings change if arithmetic operations are added between the loads. If independent operations are added (see Figure 8(a)), the

Table 3: Indicators for bandwidth usage per processor: The maximal event rates for the *UNC_C_ events refer to the sum of the events reported by the twelve C-Boxes (hsw_unc_cbo*). Likewise, the *UNC_H_** and *UNC_Q_** refer to the sum of both home agent (hsw_unc_ha*) and QPI Boxes (hsw_unc_qpi*), respectively.**

resource	access type	peak bandwidth	million transfers/s	most appropriate indicator for bandwidth utilization	maximal events/s
L3 cache	read	342 GB/s	5,343 (64 byte)	UNC_C_TOR_INSERTS:OPCODE:OPC_DRD / OPC_RFO*	5,279 million
	write	209 GB/s	3,265 (64 byte)	UNC_C_LLC_LOOKUP:WRITE	3,212 million
memory controller	read	63.1 GB/s	985 (64 byte)	UNC_H_REQUESTS:READS	985 million
	write	25.8 GB/s	403 (64 byte)	UNC_H_IMC_WRITES:FULL	403 million
QPI links	read	16.3 GB/s	254 (64 byte)	UNC_Q_RXL_FLITS_G1:DRS_DATA	2,032 million
	write	11.0 GB/s	171 (64 byte)	UNC_Q_TXL_FLITS_G1:DRS_DATA	1,368 million

*: cannot be measured together since the same filter register is used [8, Table 2-40], alternatively: UNC_C_LLC_LOOKUP:ANY – UNC_C_LLC_LOOKUP:WRITE, but this does not include all DRAM accesses that pass through the L3 cache

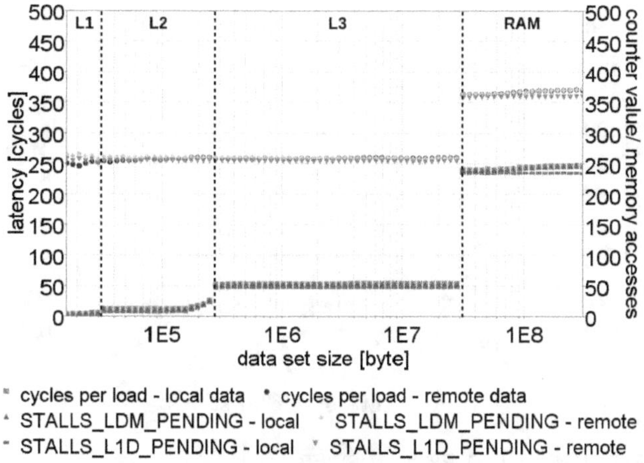

Figure 7: CYCLE_ACTIVITY events for latency benchmark: The pending loads and outstanding misses correlate well with the measured latency.

multiplications fill the gaps between the loads. Thus, the execution time remains constant if the latency is higher than the time required for the additional arithmetic operations. A useful indicator for the cycles lost due to memory accesses should only include the cycles that cannot be used for any other operations. This is the case for *CYCLE_ACTIVITY:CYCLES_NO_EXECUTE* and *:STALLS_LDM_PENDING*. They both report 29 instead of 53 cycles per memory access for data sets that fit into the L3 cache while the execution time is 53 cycles per load instruction with and without the multiplications. The 24 cycle reduction is identical to the number of operations added (throughput of 1 instruction per cycle [10, Table C-17]). If the multiplications are part of the dependency chain (see Figure 8(b))), the situation changes. In this case, the arithmetic operations depend on the result of their respective predecessor. Thus, the instruction latency (3 cycles [10, Table C-17]) also contributes to the execution time. These delays are clearly not caused by memory accesses and should therefore not be counted as memory related stalls. The results of an ideal memory stall counter would be identical to the latency measurements from Figure 7. However, such a counter does not exist. The *CYCLE_ACTIVITY:STALLS_LDM_PENDING / CYCLES_NO_EXECUTE* and *UOPS_ {ISSUED,EXECUTED,RETIRED}:STALL_CYCLES* events report an increased number of stall cycles in this scenario, i.e., they include the delays caused by data dependencies between the multiplications. Therefore, they have to be excluded as indicators for memory related stalls. Only the *STALLS_L1D_PENDING* event looks promising. For accesses to the local L2 and L3 cache, the reported number of stalls is very close to the measured latency. The values reported for local and remote memory accesses are reasonably close as well. However, accesses to the L1 cache are not included.

There are two flavors of memory-boundedness—latency bound and bandwidth bound. In the former case the data waited upon is required to continue execution, i.e., the following instructions have a data dependency from the requested data. In the latter case independent instructions are available, but the data paths are used to their capacity, which restricts the processing speed of memory accesses. It is important to distinguish both cases as there are different optimization strategies for them, e.g., adding prefetch instructions in latency bound code or introducing cache blocking in bandwidth bound programs. The out-of-order execution cores are decoupled from the memory hierarchy via load and store buffers [10, Section 2.2.4.1]. Furthermore, several request queues exist that handle outstanding requests at various levels in the memory hierarchy. Bandwidth bound applications—which issue many independent requests—tend to fully utilize the available request buffers. Therefore, a high utilization ratio of the request queues is an indicator for bandwidth-boundedness.

Figure 9 shows the event rates reported by several stall counters for bandwidth measurements. All stalls can be attributed to the memory accesses as the measurement routines do not include any other instructions. Therefore, the event *CYCLE_ACTIVITY:CYCLES_NO_EXECUTE* is used as a reference. The remaining events show no significant event rates for the latency measurement. Thus, they can be used to detect bandwidth-boundedness.

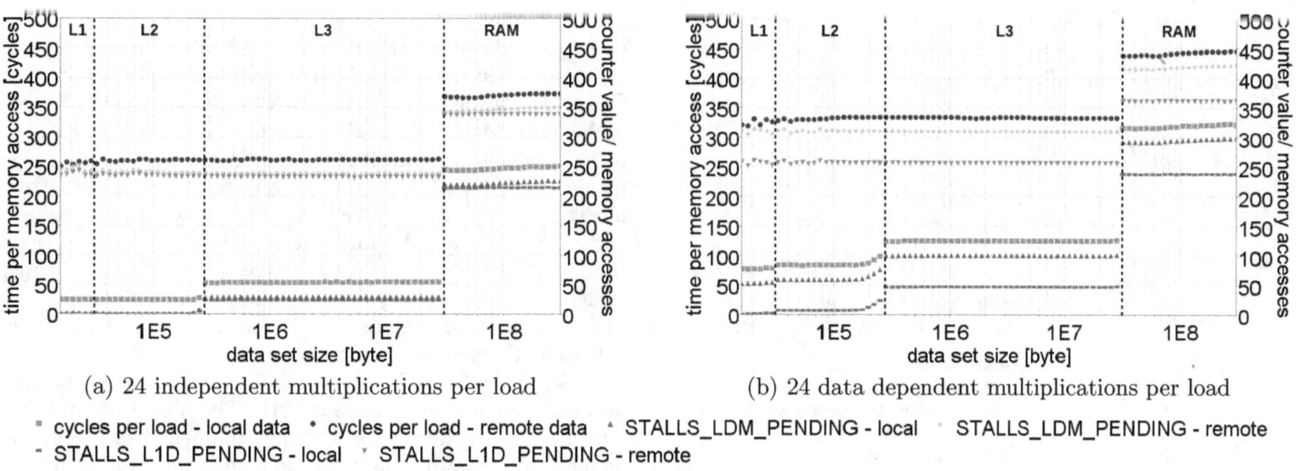

(a) 24 independent multiplications per load

(b) 24 data dependent multiplications per load

Figure 8: Correlation of stall cycles with adapted latency benchmark: Both events deduct the cycles required for performing the calculations from the reported number of stall cycles (left). However, the STALLS_LDM_PENDING event also includes delays caused by data dependencies (right).

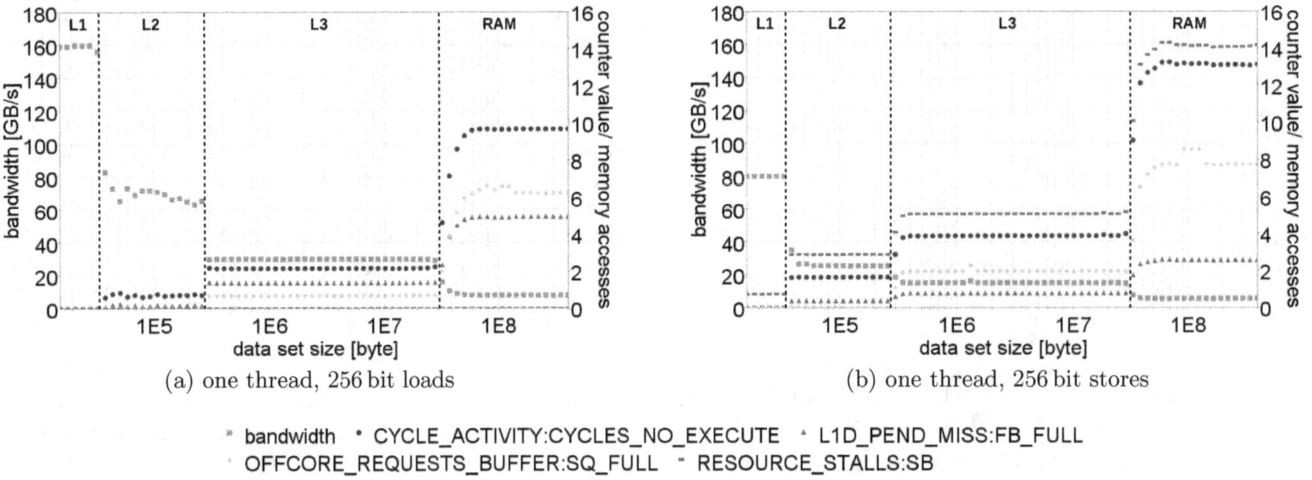

(a) one thread, 256 bit loads

(b) one thread, 256 bit stores

Figure 9: Indicators for bandwidth-boundedness: In contrast to latency-bound scenarios, bandwidth-bound applications issue multiple concurrent requests. Typically, the cores can issue requests faster than they can be serviced. The execution is stalled eventually when the required buffers are filled.

Unfortunately, none of the events count the number of stall cycles accurately. *L1D_ PEND_MISS:FB_FULL* and *OFFCORE_REQUESTS_BUF-FER:SQ_FULL* do not cover bandwidth bound accesses in the L2 cache, but show high event rates in case of misses in the L2 cache. Unfortunately, even their sum is lower than the total number of stall cycles caused by the resulting L3 and memory accesses. However, it is the best available estimate for bandwidth bound loads. The event *RESOURCE_STALLS:SB* does not capture load accesses but correlates well with the stall cycles caused by stores. Unfortunately, it also overlaps with *CYCLE_ACTIVITY:STALLS_ L1D_PENDING* in case of mixed memory accesses (not depicted). The event *CYCLE_ACTIVITY:STALLS_L1D_ PENDING*, for example, includes cycles that are stalled for other reasons if there are loads outstanding at the time.

Based on these observations presented above, the stall cycles can be decomposed as shown in Figure 10. The *memory bound* fraction is determined as the maximum of the load related (*CYCLE_ACTIVITY:STALLS_L1D_PENDING*) and the store related (*RESOURCE_STALLS:SB*) stall cycles due to the potential overlap in mixed workloads. However, this can lead to an underestimation of the memory-boundedness if a measurement interval includes discrete load bound and store bound phases. The *bandwidth bound* metric also uses the maximum as the events that capture loads also include RFOs caused by stores as depicted in Figure 9(b). The miss-prediction of branches is not considered here, i.e., "productive cycles" does not mean that the processed instructions are on the correct path. Ineffective speculation can be detected as described in [10, Appendix B.3.2]. Front-end stalls—including instruction cache misses—are also not covered by the approach presented here.

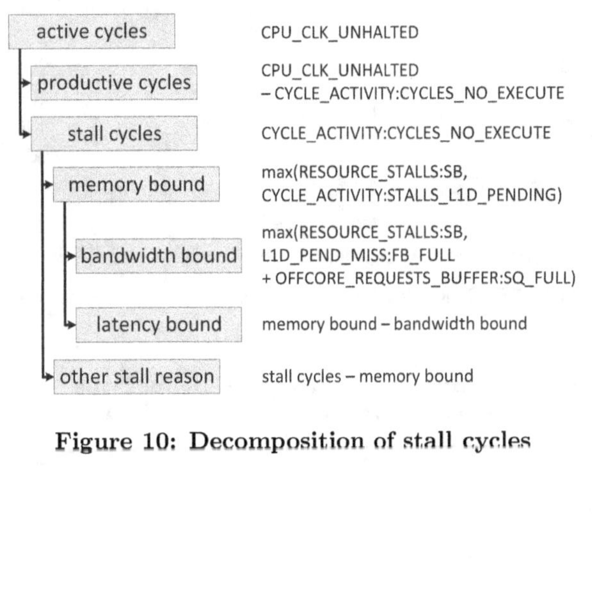

Figure 10: Decomposition of stall cycles

5. APPLICABILITY FOR ENERGY EFFICIENCY OPTIMIZATION

One possible application of the findings presented so far are energy efficiency optimizations. Researchers use the detection of memory boundedness to determine program phases where power-saving mechanisms can be used. Based on the assumption that the memory performance is not linked to the processor frequency, they use dynamic voltage and frequency scaling (DVFS) to slow down processor cores [23]. However, this approach is not viable for all processor architectures [22]. We used our model to optimize the OpenMP parallel NAS benchmark bt [3] in version 3.3.1.

We gather the metrics that are described in Figure 10 by using Score-P. A profile of the executed parallel regions is depicted in Figure 11(a). An excerpt of the trace is visualized in Figure 11(b). During the execution of the parallel regions defined in `add.f` and `rhs.f` the processor cores spend less than 50 % of their time in productive cycles. The remaining cycles are mostly stalls due to memory bandwidth limitation. Thus, these regions can be optimized using dynamic voltage and frequency scaling.

We used the Score-P substrate plugin interface to call the optimization library `libadapt` [21]. This library is able to optimize the hardware software environment based on predefined rules that are passed via a configuration file. In this file, we stated that the frequency should be reduced to 1300 MHz when the parallel region in `add.h` is started and that the frequency should be reset when the parallel region in `rhs.f` is left.

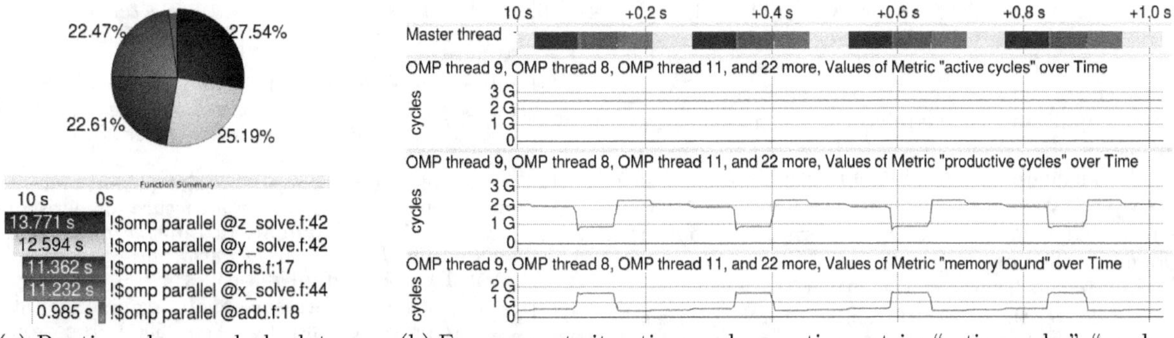

(a) Runtime share and absolute runtimes of parallel regions

(b) Four compute iterations and respective metrics "active cycles", "productive cycles", and "bandwidth bound cycles".

Figure 11: VAMPIR visualization of the OpenMP parallel NAS benchmark *bt* at reference frequency. The parallel regions in *add.f* and *rhs.f* have a high share of non-productive bandwidth bound cycles.

The resulting runtime profile and the recorded metrics are depicted in Figure 12. To verify the optimization results, we collect power consumption information from the test system using a ZES-ZIMMER LMG 450 power meter. This highly accurate device is attached to the power plug of the server and returns power consumption samples every 50 ms [6]. The average power consumption while executing the unoptimized version of the benchmark is 284 Watts. After reducing the frequency in the selected parallel regions, the overall average power consumption is reduced to 271 Watts, which is a reduction of 4.6 % based on the reference measurement. The runtime is increased by 0.2 %. However, the optimization only targets 25 % of the runtime and does not change the frequency of the uncore, which represents a significant share of the overall power consumption of the processor. Thus, the potential for energy efficiency optimizations with DVFS is limited for the given application.

6. CONCLUSIONS

Knowing the maximal achievable performance of individual components in the memory hierarchy is an essential prerequisite to detect memory related performance issues. In order to determine the impact of the memory hierarchy on the achieved application performance, the waiting times caused by memory accesses have to be measured at runtime. This creates several challenges: While the performance degradation due to resource limitations is often reflected by certain hardware events, raw performance counter values are usually difficult to understand. Furthermore, modern processors support numerous events that monitor memory accesses. Selecting the relevant ones is not a trivial task. The fact that many events do not work as one might expect further complicates the performance analysis task.

To tackle these challenges, we present a portable methodology that derives meaningful metrics for the resource utilization from hardware performance counters. The practically achievable bandwidths (e.g., via QPI) can be lower than the theoretical peak performance. Thus, even if suitable events for measuring the achieved bandwidth do exist, the resource utilization can be severely underestimated if the theoretical peak performance is used as a reference. We therefore base our utilization metrics on the achievable bandwidth, which we measure with highly optimized microbenchmarks. Furthermore, we present a novel approach to verify if the various stall events that can be counted by the core PMUs are able to distinguish memory related stall cycles from other stall reasons. We also describe how events that differentiate bandwidth bound and latency bound stall cycles can be identified.

We demonstrate the applicability of the approach on a Haswell-EP based system. We show that the available core counters can be used as indicator for a high utilization, but are not very useful for accurately measuring the bandwidth usage of shared resources. In contrast, the uncore counters provide events that measure the bandwidth usage quite ac-

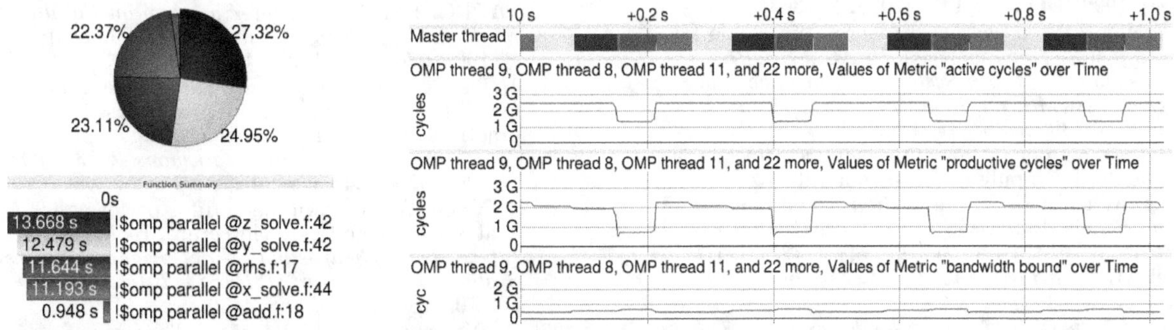

(a) Runtime share and absolute runtimes of parallel regions

(b) Four compute iterations and respective metrics "active cycles", "productive cycles", and "bandwidth bound cycles".

Figure 12: DVFS optimization of *add.f* and *rhs.f* where a frequency of 1300 MHz is applied. The overall cycles and the number of bandwidth bound cycles are reduced by approx. 50 % during these functions.

curately. We show that the CYCLE_ACTIVITY:STALLS _LDM_PENDING event, which is intended to detect memory related stalls, also includes stalls that are caused by data dependencies between register-only operations. It is therefore not applicable to reliably detect memory bound program phases. Based on our verified set of performance counters, the adequate combination of multiple counter values and a visualization of the performance counter data, we demonstrate that complex memory performance problems can be found by the non-expert user.

As our experiments have shown, some performance counter events do not deliver the expected results. Therefore, it cannot be recommended to rely on performance counter readings without validating that they correlate with the characteristic that should be measured. *X86-membench* is ideally suited to perform such validations. The presented workflow is portable to other architectures. However, our benchmarks only support the x86 instruction set at the moment. The results obtained on one architecture cannot easily be transferred to other architectures as the set of available events as well as their definition and functionality can be different. Analyzing a new processor architecture currently is a time consuming task with many manual steps. The automatic detection of (potentially) useful counters and the generation of the corresponding metrics is subject to future work.

Acknowledgments

This work has been funded in a part by the European Union's Horizon 2020 program in the READEX project under grant agreement number 671657 and by the Bundesministerium für Bildung und Forschung via the research project Score-E (BMBF 01IH13001).

References

[1] L. Adhianto et al. Hpctoolkit: tools for performance analysis of optimized parallel programs. *Concurrency and Computation: Practice and Experience*, 2010. DOI: 10.1002/cpe.1553.

[2] AMD. *BIOS and Kernel Developer's Guide (BKDG) for AMD Family 15h Models 00h-0Fh Processors*, Jan 2013. Publication # 42301, Revision: 3.14.

[3] D. H. Bailey et. al. The nas parallel benchmarks—summary and preliminary results. In *ACM/IEEE Conference on Supercomputing*, 1991. DOI: 10.1145/125826.125925.

[4] L. A. Barroso et al. Memory system characterization of commercial workloads. *SIGARCH Comput. Archit. News*, 1998. DOI: 10.1145/279361.279363.

[5] S. Eranian. What can performance counters do for memory subsystem analysis? In *ACM SIGPLAN Workshop on Memory Systems Performance and Correctness (MSPC)*, 2008. DOI: 10.1145/1353522.1353531.

[6] D. Hackenberg et al. Power measurement techniques on standard compute nodes: A quantitative comparison. In *IEEE International Symposium on Performance Analysis of Systems and Software (ISPASS)*, 2013. DOI: 10.1109/ispass.2013.6557170.

[7] Intel. *An Introduction to the Intel® QuickPath Interconnect*, 1 2009.

[8] Intel. *Intel® Xeon® Processor E5 and E7 v3 Family Uncore Performance Monitoring Reference Manual*, 6 2015. Document Number: 331051-002.

[9] Intel. *Intel® Xeon® Processor E5 v3 Product Families - Specification Update*, 8 2015. Reference Number: 330785-009US, Revision 009.

[10] Intel. *Intel® 64 and IA-32 Architectures Optimization Reference Manual*, Jan 2016. Order Number: 248966-032.

[11] Intel. *Intel® 64 and IA-32 Architectures Software Developer's Manual, Combined Volumes 1, 2A, 2B, 2C, 3A, 3B and 3C*, Apr 2016. Order Number: 325462-058US.

[12] A. Knüpfer et al. Score-P: A joint performance measurement run-time infrastructure for periscope, scalasca, tau, and vampir. In *International Workshop on Parallel Tools for High Performance Computing*. 2012. DOI: 10.1007/978-3-642-31476-6_7.

[13] D. Levinthal. Performance analysis guide for Intel Core i7 processor and Intel Xeon 5500 processors. Technical report, Intel, 2009.

[14] J. D. Little. A proof for the queueing formula: $L = \lambda \cdot W$. *Operations Research*, 9(3), 1961.

[15] Z. Majo and T. R. Gross. Memory system performance in a numa multicore multiprocessor. In *International Conference on Systems and Storage (SYSTOR)*, 2011. DOI: 10.1145/1987816.1987832.

[16] D. Molka. *Performance Analysis of Complex Shared Memory Systems*. PhD thesis, Technische Universität Dresden, 2017.

[17] D. Molka et al. Main memory and cache performance of intel sandy bridge and amd bulldozer. In *Workshop on Memory Systems Performance and Correctness (MSPC)*, 2014. DOI: 10.1145/2618128.2618129.

[18] D. Molka et al. Cache coherence protocol and memory performance of the intel haswell-ep architecture. In *International Conference on Parallel Processing (ICPP)*, 2015. DOI: 10.1109/ICPP.2015.83.

[19] L. Oliker et. al. A performance evaluation of the cray x1 for scientific applications. In *High Performance Computing for Computational Science (VECPAR 2004)*. 2005. DOI: 10.1007/11403937_5.

[20] V. Palomares. *Combining static and dynamic approaches to model loop performance in HPC*. PhD thesis, Université de Versailles, 2015. https://tel.archives-ouvertes.fr/tel-01293040.

[21] R. Schöne and D. Molka. Integrating performance analysis and energy efficiency optimizations in a unified environment. *Computer Science - Research and Development*, 2014. DOI: 10.1007/s00450-013-0243-7.

[22] R. Schöne et al. Memory performance at reduced cpu clock speeds: an analysis of current x86_64 processors. In *USENIX conference on Power-Aware Computing and Systems (HotPower)*, 2012.

[23] V. Spiliopoulos et al. Green governors: A framework for continuously adaptive dvfs. In *International Green Computing Conference and Workshops (IGCC)*, 2011. DOI: 10.1109/IGCC.2011.6008552.

[24] D. Terpstra et al. Collecting performance data with PAPI-C. In *International Workshop on Parallel Tools for High Performance Computing*, 2009. DOI: 10.1007/978-3-642-11261-4_11.

[25] J. Treibig et al. Performance patterns and hardware metrics on modern multicore processors: Best practices for performance engineering. In *Euro-Par 2012: Parallel Processing Workshops*. 2013. DOI: 10.1007/978-3-642-36949-0_50.

[26] A. Yasin. A top-down method for performance analysis and counters architecture. In *IEEE International Symposium on Performance Analysis of Systems and Software (ISPASS)*, 2014. DOI: 10.1109/ISPASS.2014.6844459.

[27] W. Yoo et al. Adp: Automated diagnosis of performance pathologies using hardware events. In *Proceedings of the 12th ACM SIGMETRICS/ PERFORMANCE Joint International Conference on Measurement and Modeling of Computer Systems*, 2012. DOI: 10.1145/2254756.2254791.

Transferring Performance Prediction Models Across Different Hardware Platforms

Pavel Valov
University of Waterloo
200 University Avenue West
Waterloo, ON, Canada
pvalov@uwaterloo.ca

Jean-Christophe Petkovich
University of Waterloo
200 University Avenue West
Waterloo, ON, Canada
j2petkovich@uwaterloo.ca

Jianmei Guo*
East China University of Science and Technology
130 Meilong Road
Shanghai, China
gjm@ecust.edu.cn

Sebastian Fischmeister
University of Waterloo
200 University Avenue West
Waterloo, ON, Canada
sfischme@uwaterloo.ca

Krzysztof Czarnecki*
University of Waterloo
200 University Avenue West
Waterloo, ON, Canada
kczarnec@gsd.uwaterloo.ca

ABSTRACT

Many software systems provide configuration options relevant to users, which are often called features. Features influence functional properties of software systems as well as non-functional ones, such as performance and memory consumption. Researchers have successfully demonstrated the correlation between feature selection and performance. However, the generality of these performance models across different hardware platforms has not yet been evaluated.

We propose a technique for enhancing generality of performance models across different hardware environments using linear transformation. Empirical studies on three real-world software systems show that our approach is computationally efficient and can achieve high accuracy (less than 10% mean relative error) when predicting system performance across 23 different hardware platforms. Moreover, we investigate why the approach works by comparing performance distributions of systems and structure of performance models across different platforms.

CCS Concepts

•Software and its engineering → Software performance;

Keywords

Performance Modelling, Regression Trees, Model Transfer, Linear Transformation

*Corresponding authors

ICPE'17, April 22-26, 2017, L'Aquila, Italy
© 2017 ACM. ISBN 978-1-4503-4404-3/17/04...$15.00
DOI: http://dx.doi.org/10.1145/3030207.3030216

1. INTRODUCTION

Many software systems provide *configuration options*. These configuration options usually have a direct influence on the functional behaviour of target software systems. Some configuration options may impact systems' non-functional properties, such as response time, memory consumption and throughput. Configuration options that are relevant to users are usually called *features* [5], and a particular selection of features defines a system *configuration*.

Performance prediction of configurable software systems is a highly-researched topic [5, 6, 7, 8, 17, 18, 20, 21]. For example, Guo et al. [5] predicted a system configuration's performance by using regression trees based on small random samples of measured configurations. However, none of the previous work studied whether or not it is possible to transfer performance prediction models for configurable software systems across different hardware platforms.

The need for transferring performance prediction models occurs in many application scenarios. For example, a user of a software system performs a thorough performance benchmarking of the system and builds a performance prediction model for it. However, the prediction model is built only for the particular benchmarked machine. The performance prediction process on a different machine may not be able to directly reuse previous benchmarking results and prediction models. Modern Software as a Service (SaaS), Platform as a Service (PaaS) and other cloud-based industries face similar challenges. Based on a historical performance data collected for their software on one cluster, users want to know how to tune the performance of their software systems for a new cluster with a different hardware, or how to select the best hardware platform with which to build their cluster.

We investigate the problem of performance prediction model transfer. We make the following contributions:

- We propose an approach for transferring performance models of configurable software systems across platforms with different hardware settings. This approach (1) builds a performance prediction model based on a small random sample of configurations measured on one hardware platform and (2) transfers this model using linear transformation to other hardware platforms.

- We implement the proposed approach and demonstrate its generality using three real-world configurable software systems. Our empirical results show that for majority of model transfers our approach achieves a high prediction accuracy (less than 10% mean relative error). We also observe a decreasing trend of mean relative error with the increase of the training data for the performance prediction model or for the linear transformation model.
- We carry out a thorough exploratory analysis to understand why our approach works. We compare performance distributions and structure of performance prediction models across different hardware platforms and show that the more similar distributions and prediction models across different platforms, the better transfer results are. Moreover, we carry out a comparative analysis of our methodology for different configurable systems and assess time costs of our method.

Source code and data to reproduce our experiments are available online at https://bitbucket.org/valovp/icpe2017.

2. EXAMPLE AND NOTATION

Our objective is to enable the transfer of performance prediction results from one hardware platform to another. Consider purchasing a new hardware platform to encode large amounts of video using x264, which is a configurable application for encoding video streams in the H.264/MPEG-4 AVC compression format. Media encoding programs such as x264 usually have a large number of configurable features; tuning them has a significant impact on the quality of the video output and on the time necessary to encode it. In our example, we have measurements for 11 different configuration features, each with 2 individual settings. Obtaining these performance measurements with a video that takes a modest 15 minutes to encode requires 1536 hours of execution time. Rather than exhaustively measuring same configurations on a new unstudied platform, it would be better to reuse performance data from previous tuning experiments to predict the performance of configurations on this new platform.

To formalize the problem of performance prediction, we represent features of a configurable software system as a set of binary decision variables $F = \{f_1, f_2, \dots f_{N_f}\}$, where f_i represents a particular variable and N_f represents a total number of features of the configurable software system. Each configuration $\mathbf{c}$ of the system is a set of value assignments to N_f variables f_i. We denote the set of all valid configurations of the system by $\mathbf{C}$. Table 1 represents a sample of 10 configurations along with their measured performance values. Each row of the Table 1 represents a particular configuration of x264, while each column represents a particular feature of the system.

We define performance of a system as a total time required to execute a particular system benchmark. Performance of each configuration is expected to differ in a heterogeneous collection of machines that we denote by $M = \{m_1, m_2, \dots, m_{N_m}\}$, where m_i represents a particular machine or hardware platform and N_m represents the total number of machines in the collection. Each valid configuration, $\mathbf{c}$, of the software system has an actual performance value, $a_{\mathbf{c},m_i}$, on a machine m_i, a set of configurations, $\mathbf{C}$, has a set of actual performance values, $A_{\mathbf{C},m_i}$, on machine m_i. We define *training machine*, m_{trn}, as a machine that is used to build performance prediction models for a given configurable software system (e.g., x264). In a practical setting, training machine is one on which a particular software system is already well-studied and historical performance data for the system is acquired. We define *target machine*, m_{tgt}, as a machine to which performance prediction models must be transferred.

For example, we acquire a small random sample of configurations, $\mathbf{C}_S \subset \mathbf{C}$, along with their actual performance values, $A_{S,m_{trn}} \subset A_{\mathbf{C},m_{trn}}$, together forming sample, $S_{m_{trn}}$, on our training machine m_{trn}. Our goal is to predict the performance of all other configurations, $\mathbf{C} \setminus \mathbf{C}_S$, on machine m_{trn} based on this small random sample $S_{m_{trn}}$, and subsequently to predict the performance of the whole set of valid configurations $\mathbf{C}$ on all other machines in the collection M.

Table 1: Sample of 11 randomly-selected configurations of x264 system, along with their actual performance measurements on Machine №75

Conf.	Features											Perf. (s)
$\mathbf{c}_i$	f_1	f_2	f_3	f_4	f_5	f_6	f_7	f_8	f_9	f_{10}	f_{11}	$a_{\mathbf{c}_1,m_{75}}$
$\mathbf{c}_1$	0	0	1	1	1	0	1	0	0	0	1	52.01
$\mathbf{c}_2$	0	1	0	1	1	1	0	0	1	0	0	24.09
$\mathbf{c}_3$	1	0	0	0	1	1	0	0	0	0	1	58.13
$\mathbf{c}_4$	1	1	0	1	1	0	0	1	0	1	0	37.49
$\mathbf{c}_5$	0	0	1	0	1	1	0	0	0	0	1	75.89
$\mathbf{c}_6$	1	1	0	1	0	0	0	1	0	0	1	51.05
$\mathbf{c}_7$	1	1	1	0	0	1	0	0	0	0	1	82.15
$\mathbf{c}_8$	1	0	0	1	1	1	0	0	0	0	1	41.40
$\mathbf{c}_9$	1	0	0	1	0	0	0	1	1	0	0	23.16
$\mathbf{c}_{10}$	0	0	0	0	1	0	1	0	1	0	0	23.20
$\mathbf{c}_{11}$	0	0	1	0	1	0	1	0	1	0	0	28.95

3. TRANSFERRING PERFORMANCE PREDICTION MODELS

The overall process of transferring performance prediction models across different hardware platforms is sequential and can be separated into the following main steps: (1) training performance prediction model, (2) training linear transfer model, and (3) transferring prediction results.

3.1 Training The Performance Prediction Model

We used regression trees for building models of the performance effects of software features. We selected regression trees as our method of model construction as they have been extensively used for performance prediction of configurable software systems and demonstrated good results [5, 17, 18, 20]. The resulting prediction models can be graphically represented and readily understood by end users. Regression trees proved effective for a thorough exploratory analysis for our model transferring problem (see Section 4.5 for more detail).

We need to choose a method for sampling training data to build regression trees. Previous studies of feature performance modelling, Guo et al. [5] and Valov et al. [18], used small random samples of measured configurations to build prediction models. The use of random sampling in those works was motivated by the idea that in practice, available measured configurations of a system might not follow any particular feature-coverage criteria and would be essentially random. In our study we also use small random samples for prediction model building.

For the purpose of experiment reproducibility we provide datasets of measured configurations for each studied software system (for more details see Section 4.1.1). However, measuring the entire configuration space $\mathbf{C}$ of each software system under test was prohibitively expensive and couldn't be done in the time budget available (for more details see Section 4.1.2). Therefore, for each system we measured only a subset of valid configurations $\mathbf{C}_{exp} \subset \mathbf{C}$.

To choose which configurations should be included in $\mathbf{C}_{exp}$ we used experimental design techniques. Experimental design is an efficient procedure for obtaining experimental data that can be analysed to produce valid results [1]. Experimental design techniques can maximize information obtained by a practitioner for a given experimentation budget. Selection of a concrete design for a particular experiment depends on the goal of the experiment and the number of variables involved.

In our study we use "screening" experimental designs, where the goal is to "screen out" or select the main effects that influence the response variable (in our case system performance), such as *full factorial* and *fractional factorial* experimental designs. This is achieved by selecting the most "informative" configurations for a given system.

Full factorial design generates all possible combinations of all input variables, i.e., in our case this design generates all possible configurations of a given software system. This design is suitable only for systems with a small number of features, since it generates 2^{N_f} configurations for N_f binary features.

Fractional factorial design is more suitable for systems with a large number of features N_f. This design selects only a fraction of configurations generated by a full factorial design, thus saving experimentation effort. However, when using this design some information is inevitably lost, which causes *confounding* or inability to capture some higher-order feature interactions. *Resolution* of a fractional factorial design defines the level to which main effects or lower-order interactions are confounded with higher-order interactions, i.e., how well we can assess or model main effects and lower-order interactions. For example, fractional factorial design of resolution VI provides enough information to estimate main effects and two-factor feature interactions unconfounded by four-factor (or less) and three-factor (or less) interactions respectively, what is a very precise assessment.

Another question is how many configurations should we sample to build a precise performance prediction models? Valov et al. [18] used samples of sizes $T \times N_f$ to evaluate different performance prediction models, where T is a training coefficient which can take values in $\{1, \ldots, 5\}$, and N_f is the number of features available in the configurable software system under test. It was demonstrated [18] that measuring $3 \times N_f$ random configurations permitted construction of models with high performance prediction accuracy using regression trees for majority of studied systems. We use the same heuristic $T \times N_f$, where $T = \{3, 4, 5\}$. We found that this provides sufficient coverage of the feature space for construction of accurate performance prediction models.

We denote a regression tree model by a function RT trained using a small random sample of configurations $\mathbf{C}_S$ of size $T \times N_f$ and their actual performance values $A_{S,m_{trn}}$, measured on a training machine m_{trn}, which predicts the performance value $p_{\mathbf{c},m_{trn}}$ on the machine m_{trn} for a specified configuration $\mathbf{c}$:

$$RT(\mathbf{C}_S, A_{S,m_{trn}}, \mathbf{c}) = p_{\mathbf{c},m_{trn}} \tag{1}$$

Next, we must select a metric for assessing the prediction accuracy of the trained prediction model RT, and a validation method to prevent overfitting. We use *mean relative error (MRE)* as a metric for evaluating prediction accuracy. *Relative error (RE)* is the relative difference between an actual performance value $a_\mathbf{c}$ and a predicted performance value $p_\mathbf{c}$ for a particular configuration $\mathbf{c}$:

$$RE(\mathbf{c}) = \frac{a_\mathbf{c} - p_\mathbf{c}}{a_\mathbf{c}} \times 100\% \tag{2}$$

Mean relative error is the average of the relative errors calculated for each individual configuration $\mathbf{c}_i$ of a particular sample of configurations $\mathbf{C}_S$,

$$MRE(\mathbf{C}_S) = \frac{\sum_{i=1}^{N_c} RE(\mathbf{c}_i)}{N_c} \tag{3}$$

where N_c is a total number of configurations in the sample $\mathbf{C}_S$.

Finally, we must select a validation method. As mentioned previously, we use random samples of configurations $\mathbf{C}_S$ of a fixed size $T \times N_f$. These configurations are sampled from the set of measured configurations $\mathbf{C}_{exp}$. Since the size of the training sample $\mathbf{C}_S$ is fixed, a natural model validation strategy is *holdout validation*. This method separates all available data, $\mathbf{C}_{exp}$, into a training set, $\mathbf{C}_S$, and a testing set, $\mathbf{C}_{exp} \backslash \mathbf{C}_S$. We train a performance prediction model RT using the training set $\mathbf{C}_S$, and assess prediction accuracy of the model using MRE over the testing set: $MRE(\mathbf{C}_{exp} \setminus \mathbf{C}_S)$.

It is worth mentioning that in an industrial setting a different validation method might be required, i.e., when the cost of performance measuring is extremely high and it is not desirable to measure all $T \times N_f$ configurations upfront or simply to have an extra set of measured configurations available. Practitioner could start with a very small training sample $\mathbf{C}_S$ and progressively train their models until they are satisfied with its accuracy. An effective validation method for these low sample sizes is *leave-one-out cross-validation (LOOCV)*. *LOOCV* separates all available data $\mathbf{C}_S$ into two sets: a testing set, consisting of only one configuration $\mathbf{c}_i$, and a training set, consisting of all other configurations $\mathbf{C}_S \backslash \mathbf{c}_i$. A prediction model RT is then trained using $\mathbf{C}_S \backslash \mathbf{c}_i$ and assessed using relative error over $re_i = RE(\mathbf{c}_i)$. This process is repeated for all possible combinations of training sets and testing sets. The overall accuracy of the prediction model RT for the sample $\mathbf{C}_S$ can be assessed by averaging all individual relative errors: $\sum_{i=1}^{N_c} re_i / N_c$.

3.2 Training The Transfer Model

To reuse the previously generated performance prediction model built for m_{trn} for performance prediction on a target machine m_{tgt} a practitioner must train a transfer model. We use linear regression models as our transfer models since we found that they provide good approximations of the transfer function (see Section 4.5.3 for more details).

The samples we use for linear models training should contain configurations that are measured on both the m_{trn} and m_{tgt} hardware platforms. From the steps described in Section 3.1, we have a training sample, $\mathbf{C}_S$, of configurations measured on machine m_{trn} of size $T \times N_f$. Instead of measuring a completely new sample of configurations on both m_{trn} and m_{tgt} machines for training the linear model, we can measure the same configurations from $\mathbf{C}_S$ on the target machine m_{tgt}. In this way, we acquire a training sample $\mathbf{C}_S$ of size $T \times N_f$ measured on both m_{trn} and m_{tgt}.

However, measuring all $T \times N_f$ configurations on the target machine m_{tgt} may be prohibitively expensive. Instead, we measure only a subset of $\mathbf{C}_S$ on both machines $\mathbf{C}_{both} \subset \mathbf{C}_S$. We populate $\mathbf{C}_{both}$ by selecting at least five configurations from $\mathbf{C}_S$ using Sobol sampling [14] (see Section 4.6 for more details).

Using the sample $\mathbf{C}_{both}$ we can build a model to transfer performance prediction results from m_{trn} to m_{tgt}. We use simple linear regression model as a transfer model since it provides good approximation of transfer functions between different machines in our case study (see Section 4.5.3 for more details). This linear model L, given a performance value $p_{\mathbf{c},m_{trn}}$ for a configuration $\mathbf{c}$ on the machine m_{trn}, can predict performance value $p_{\mathbf{c},m_{tgt}}$ of $\mathbf{c}$ on the machine m_{tgt}:

$$L(p_{\mathbf{c},m_{trn}}) = \alpha + \beta \times p_{\mathbf{c},m_{trn}} = p_{\mathbf{c},m_{tgt}} \quad (4)$$

3.3 Transferring Prediction Results

In the previous steps we selected training and target machines (m_{trn} and m_{tgt}), built a performance prediction model RT based on a small sample $\mathbf{C}_S$ of configurations measured on m_{trn}, and built a linear transfer model L based on a small subsample $\mathbf{C}_{both} \subset \mathbf{C}_S$ of configurations measured on both m_{trn} and m_{tgt} machines. To transfer the prediction model RT to m_{tgt} we just need to transform the predictions of RT using the linear transfer model L. For example, we have a configuration $\mathbf{c}$ that is not measured neither on m_{trn} nor on m_{tgt} machines. To compute $p_{\mathbf{c},m_{tgt}}$ we can use the following equations:

$$p_{\mathbf{c},m_{trn}} = RT(\mathbf{C}_S, A_{S,m_{trn}}, \mathbf{c}) \quad (5)$$

Then we can use L to assess performance of $\mathbf{c}$ on m_{tgt}:

$$p_{\mathbf{c},m_{tgt}} = L(p_{\mathbf{c},m_{trn}}) \quad (6)$$

4. EVALUATION

In order to evaluate our approach, we address the following research questions through a set of experiments:

RQ1 How accurate are the transferred performance models created using the process described in Section 3? (Section 4.2)

RQ2 How does model accuracy vary between different configurable software systems? (Section 4.3)

RQ3 How fast is the process of transferring performance prediction models? (Section 4.4)

RQ4 Why does the proposed approach work or are the results accidental? (Section 4.5)

RQ5 What is an optimal way of building the linear transfer model? (Section 4.6)

Table 2: Summary of hardware platforms on which configurable software systems were measured; MID – Machine ID in DataMill cluster; NC – Number of CPUs; IS – Instruction set; CCR – CPU clock rate (MHz); RAM – RAM memory size (MB)

Systems			Machines				
XZ	x264	SQLite	MID	NC	IS	CCR	RAM
✓			73	2	i686	1733	1771
✓	✓	✓	75	2	i686	3200	977
✓			77	2	i686	2992	2024
✓			78	1	i686	1495	755
✓			79	4	x86_64	3291	7961
✓			80	8	x86_64	3401	7907
✓	✓		81	16	x86_64	2411	32193
	✓		87	1	i686	1595	249
	✓		88	1	i686	1700	978
		✓	90	2	i686	3200	977
	✓		91	1	i686	2400	1009
	✓	✓	97	2	i686	2992	873
	✓	✓	98	2	i686	2992	873
		✓	99	2	i686	2793	880
	✓		103	2	i686	3200	881
	✓		104	1	i686	1800	502
	✓	✓	105	2	i686	3200	881
	✓		106	2	i686	3192	494
		✓	125	4	x86_64	3301	7960
	✓		128	2	i686	2993	2024
		✓	130	2	i686	3198	880
		✓	146	2	i686	2998	872
		✓	157	36	x86_64	2301	15954

Table 3: Summary of measured systems; N_f – Number of features; NM – Number of machines on which systems were measured; NMC – Number of measured configurations

System	N_f	NM	NMC
XZ	7	7	154
x264	7	11	165
SQLite	5	10	32

4.1 Experimental Setup

4.1.1 Subject Systems

We measure the performance impact of several different features of 3 different software systems, XZ[16], x264[19], and SQLite[15]. These systems represent several common tasks performed by applications: compression of data, transformation of media, and interaction with a database. XZ is a compression utility for UNIX-like operating systems which uses LZMA2 compression. x264 is a library and utility for encoding video streams into the H.264/MPEG-4 AVC compression format. SQLite is a library and application that implements a file-oriented SQL database and is a popular choice for application file formats due to its flexibility.

Each feature that we varied was chosen either based on previous experiments in feature performance regression [5], or system documentation and preliminary experiments. For XZ, we measure performance effects from features such as varying the "extreme" parameter, varying the "sparse output file" option and applying constraints on memory usage. For x264, we measure performance effects from turning on and off different assembly optimizations, varying the "frame-lookahead", and varying partition search types. For SQLite, we measure performance effects from varying the "synchronous" option, varying the journalling strategy, and varying the amount of space available to mmap.

4.1.2 Subject Hardware Platforms

We carried out our system performance measurements on DataMill[11], a distributed heterogeneous performance evaluation platform. Each machine of DataMill was setup with identical software and executes Gentoo Linux (Kernel version 3.8.13). Only the DataMill worker software, a kernel, boot manager, and logging daemon were installed on each machine on top of the base set of Gentoo packages, resulting in a minimal set of software. Table 2 summarizes hardware configurations of DataMill machines used for our experiments.

Although we did have an exclusive access to DataMill machines, we only had a limited time to use DataMill itself since it is used by many research groups. Therefore we weren't able to measure each configurable system on the whole DataMill cluster, but only on a subset of machines. Table 2 shows which machines were used for measuring performance of different software systems.

Due to constraints on experiment bandwidth on DataMill, and differing support for features on certain platforms, some feature-configuration/hardware-platform combinations were not measured. Moreover, not all experiment trials terminated correctly; thus only a subset of desired configurations were measured across all machines. Table 3 provides a summary of available machines and measured configurations for each configurable system. The scripts used to perform the experiment trials are available on the DataMill website for the purposes of experiment reproduction.

4.1.3 Measurements and Sampling

For each software system, we analyse the effect of choosing training and target machine pairs and the effect of varying the size of the performance training sample $\mathbf{C}_S$ and the transfer training sample $\mathbf{C}_{both}$ on model accuracy. The sample $\mathbf{C}_S$ varies in $\{3 \times N_f, 4 \times N_f, 5 \times N_f\}$, and the sample $\mathbf{C}_{both}$ varies in $\{5, 10, 15\}$.

As mentioned in Section 4.1.2, we measured each studied configurable system on multiple platforms as shown in Table 2 and Table 3. However, due to space constraints for each system we present results only for a subset of four different training and target machines. The data we obtained from these machines is summarized in Tables 4, 8, and 6.

We examine each combination of the training machine m_{trn}, target machine m_{tgt}, and sampling sizes for both $|\mathbf{C}_S|$ and $|\mathbf{C}_{both}|$, in a full-factorial experiment design [2, 10]. For each configurable system we have 4 training machines, 4 target machines, 3 sizes of $\mathbf{C}_S$, and 3 sizes of $\mathbf{C}_{both}$, which produces a total of $4 \times 4 \times 3 \times 3 = 144$ different test cases. To acquire mean prediction relative error for each test case, we follow the model transferring process described in Section 3 for 100 different randomly sampled $\mathbf{C}_S$ and $\mathbf{C}_{both}$.

4.2 Experiment on Prediction Accuracy

To answer RQ1, we present the results of our transferred performance prediction models across different hardware plat-

Table 4: Mean Relative Error (%) of transferred performance models of XZ system, built using different sampling sizes on training and target machines

Target Machines	Sampling Sizes	Training Machines: Machine №75			Machine №78			Machine №80			Machine №81		
		Sampling Sizes			Sampling Sizes			Sampling Sizes			Sampling Sizes		
		$3N_f$	$4N_f$	$5N_f$	$3N_f$	$4N_f$	$5N_f$	$3N_f$	$4N_f$	$5N_f$	$3N_f$	$4N_f$	$5N_f$
75	5	5.8	2.0	1.4	9.5	5.4	5.0	8.0	5.2	4.5	6.8	4.1	3.4
75	10	5.2	2.1	1.1	7.2	4.6	3.8	8.1	5.0	4.7	6.9	3.8	3.7
75	15	5.7	2.3	1.7	6.8	4.3	3.3	8.8	5.4	4.4	7.3	4.0	3.1
78	5	8.5	5.7	4.9	6.6	3.0	1.6	9.9	7.3	6.7	8.7	6.9	6.1
78	10	6.6	5.0	3.8	6.5	3.0	1.5	8.1	5.4	4.6	7.7	4.5	3.6
78	15	7.3	3.6	3.6	8.4	3.3	1.8	7.9	5.4	4.6	7.2	4.2	3.9
80	5	10.2	6.9	5.8	11.9	9.6	9.4	9.5	4.8	1.6	10.6	3.8	3.4
80	10	8.2	6.3	5.5	10.6	6.8	5.6	8.2	2.0	1.9	7.1	3.4	2.7
80	15	10.4	6.5	5.1	11.0	6.4	5.6	8.5	4.3	2.3	7.2	3.8	2.6
81	5	9.0	5.9	4.3	11.5	8.2	7.1	9.7	3.6	3.1	7.9	4.1	1.6
81	10	8.9	5.1	4.2	8.7	5.2	4.5	8.8	3.4	2.8	6.5	4.2	1.9
81	15	8.6	5.0	4.0	10.1	5.1	4.5	9.6	3.2	2.6	10.0	2.9	1.5

Table 5: Mean Relative Error (%) of XZ system added by the transferring process

Target Machines	Sampling Sizes	Training Machines: Machine №75			Machine №78			Machine №80			Machine №81		
		Sampling Sizes			Sampling Sizes			Sampling Sizes			Sampling Sizes		
		$3N_f$	$4N_f$	$5N_f$	$3N_f$	$4N_f$	$5N_f$	$3N_f$	$4N_f$	$5N_f$	$3N_f$	$4N_f$	$5N_f$
75	5	0.1	0.0	0.0	5.0	4.5	4.3	5.1	4.0	4.1	4.1	3.0	2.9
75	10	0.1	0.0	0.0	4.3	3.5	3.4	4.5	4.2	4.1	3.5	3.0	3.0
75	15	0.1	0.0	0.0	3.8	3.0	2.9	4.7	3.9	3.7	3.8	3.2	2.7
78	5	5.0	4.3	4.1	0.1	0.0	0.0	6.6	6.1	6.2	5.7	5.4	5.3
78	10	4.1	3.3	2.9	0.0	0.0	0.0	4.4	4.2	3.8	3.7	3.2	2.9
78	15	3.7	2.7	2.6	0.1	0.0	0.0	4.5	3.9	3.8	3.7	3.0	2.9
80	5	5.6	4.6	4.7	8.4	8.1	8.0	0.0	0.0	0.0	3.0	2.6	2.3
80	10	5.2	4.8	4.6	7.2	4.6	4.5	0.1	0.0	0.0	2.8	2.2	2.0
80	15	4.9	4.4	4.4	5.6	4.5	4.6	0.1	0.0	0.0	3.9	2.0	1.9
81	5	5.1	3.6	3.6	7.2	7.5	7.0	3.6	2.7	2.6	0.1	0.0	0.0
81	10	5.1	4.3	3.8	4.6	3.8	3.8	3.3	2.3	2.2	0.1	0.0	0.0
81	15	4.6	3.3	3.4	4.4	3.9	3.8	3.1	2.4	2.1	0.1	0.0	0.0

Table 6: Mean Relative Error (%) of transferred performance models of SQLite system, built using different sampling sizes on training and target machines

Target Machines	Sampling Sizes	Training Machines: Machine №75			Machine №99			Machine №125			Machine №157		
		Sampling Sizes			Sampling Sizes			Sampling Sizes			Sampling Sizes		
		$3N_f$	$4N_f$	$5N_f$	$3N_f$	$4N_f$	$5N_f$	$3N_f$	$4N_f$	$5N_f$	$3N_f$	$4N_f$	$5N_f$
75	5	0.7	0.5	0.4	0.7	0.6	0.6	1.4	1.3	1.3	2.8	2.6	2.6
75	10	0.8	0.5	0.4	0.7	0.6	0.6	1.3	1.2	1.2	2.6	2.6	2.4
75	15	0.7	0.5	0.4	0.7	0.6	0.6	1.3	1.2	1.1	2.6	2.5	2.4
99	5	0.8	0.7	0.6	0.8	0.6	0.6	1.6	1.4	1.3	2.6	2.6	2.6
99	10	0.8	0.6	0.6	0.9	0.6	0.6	1.5	1.3	1.2	2.6	2.4	2.4
99	10	0.7	0.0	0.0	0.8	0.0	0.0	1.4	1.3	1.2	2.0	2.4	2.4
125	5	1.5	1.4	1.3	1.6	1.5	1.4	1.9	1.5	1.1	2.6	2.4	2.3
125	10	1.4	1.3	1.3	1.5	1.4	1.3	1.9	1.5	1.1	2.7	2.3	2.2
125	15	1.4	1.3	1.2	1.5	1.4	1.3	1.8	1.5	1.1	2.4	2.3	2.1
157	5	3.7	3.5	3.5	3.5	3.4	3.3	3.2	2.9	2.7	4.4	4.1	3.6
157	10	3.4	3.2	3.2	3.2	3.1	3.0	3.0	2.7	2.5	4.2	4.0	3.7
157	15	3.3	3.2	3.2	3.1	3.0	2.9	3.0	2.7	2.5	4.3	3.9	3.5

Table 7: Mean Relative Error (%) of SQLite system added by the transferring process

Target Machines	Sampling Sizes	Training Machines: Machine №75			Machine №99			Machine №125			Machine №157		
		Sampling Sizes			Sampling Sizes			Sampling Sizes			Sampling Sizes		
		$3N_f$	$4N_f$	$5N_f$	$3N_f$	$4N_f$	$5N_f$	$3N_f$	$4N_f$	$5N_f$	$3N_f$	$4N_f$	$5N_f$
75	5	0.0	0.0	0.0	0.6	0.5	0.4	1.1	1.1	1.0	2.6	2.5	2.5
75	10	0.0	0.0	0.0	0.5	0.4	0.4	1.2	1.1	1.0	2.4	2.4	2.4
75	15	0.0	0.0	0.0	0.5	0.5	0.4	1.1	1.0	1.0	2.4	2.3	2.3
99	5	0.6	0.6	0.5	0.0	0.0	0.0	1.3	1.2	1.1	2.6	2.5	2.4
99	10	0.6	0.5	0.5	0.1	0.0	0.0	1.1	1.1	1.0	2.4	2.3	2.2
99	15	0.6	0.5	0.5	0.0	0.0	0.0	1.2	1.0	0.9	2.2	2.1	2.1
125	5	1.3	1.1	1.1	1.4	1.4	1.3	0.0	0.0	0.0	2.3	2.1	2.0
125	10	1.2	1.2	1.1	1.3	1.3	1.3	0.0	0.0	0.0	2.1	2.0	1.9
125	15	1.3	1.2	1.1	1.4	1.2	1.2	0.0	0.0	0.0	2.2	2.1	2.0
157	5	2.9	2.7	2.7	2.8	3.0	2.8	2.7	2.7	2.4	0.0	0.0	0.0
157	10	2.8	2.6	2.5	2.8	2.6	2.6	2.4	2.4	2.3	0.0	0.0	0.0
157	15	2.8	2.7	2.5	2.8	2.6	2.5	2.6	2.3	2.2	0.0	0.0	0.0

Table 8: Mean ± Standard Deviation [Mean Confidence Interval] of the relative error (%) of transferred performance models of x264 system, built using different sampling sizes on training and target machines

Target Machines	Sampling Sizes	Training Machines: Machine №75, Sampling Sizes $3N_f$	Machine №75 $4N_f$	Machine №75 $5N_f$	Machine №81, Sampling Sizes $3N_f$	Machine №81 $4N_f$	Machine №81 $5N_f$	Machine №88, Sampling Sizes $3N_f$	Machine №88 $4N_f$	Machine №88 $5N_f$	Machine №103, Sampling Sizes $3N_f$	Machine №103 $4N_f$	Machine №103 $5N_f$
75	5	5.3±9.3 [5.2, 5.5]	3.2±7.0 [3.1, 3.4]	2.0±5.1 [1.9, 2.1]	13.5±10.2 [13.3, 13.6]	13.1±9.7 [12.9, 13.2]	13.0±9.3 [12.8, 13.1]	5.4±9.4 [5.3, 5.5]	3.5±6.3 [3.4, 3.6]	2.4±4.6 [2.3, 2.4]	5.2±8.4 [5.1, 5.4]	3.5±6.3 [3.4, 3.6]	2.4±4.1 [2.3, 2.5]
75	10	5.5±9.8 [5.3, 5.6]	3.2±7.1 [3.1, 3.3]	1.7±4.6 [1.7, 1.8]	12.8± 9.3 [12.6, 12.9]	12.3±8.8 [12.2, 12.5]	12.1±8.8 [12.0, 12.3]	5.0±8.5 [4.9, 5.1]	3.2±6.0 [3.1, 3.3]	2.3±4.8 [2.2, 2.4]	4.7±8.2 [4.6, 4.9]	3.1±5.8 [3.0, 3.2]	2.1±4.0 [2.1, 2.2]
75	15	5.4±9.5 [5.2, 5.6]	3.4±7.2 [3.2, 3.5]	2.0±5.2 [1.9, 2.1]	12.5± 9.1 [12.4, 12.7]	12.1±8.5 [12.0, 12.2]	12.0±8.4 [11.8, 12.1]	5.2±8.8 [5.0, 5.3]	3.3±6.4 [3.2, 3.4]	2.3±4.6 [2.3, 2.4]	4.8±8.3 [4.7, 5.0]	3.0±5.7 [3.0, 3.1]	2.1±4.0 [2.0, 2.1]
81	5	14.3±12.9 [14.1, 14.5]	13.2±10.6 [13.0, 13.4]	12.8±9.8 [12.7, 13.0]	6.0±7.5 [5.9, 6.1]	4.7±6.0 [4.6, 4.8]	3.7±5.3 [3.6, 3.8]	13.7±11.7 [13.5, 13.8]	12.9±10.1 [12.7, 13.0]	12.7±10.0 [12.6, 12.9]	13.6±11.2 [13.4, 13.8]	12.7±9.9 [12.6, 12.9]	12.3±9.2 [12.2, 12.5]
81	10	12.3±10.1 [12.2, 12.5]	11.4± 8.8 [11.3, 11.5]	11.0±8.4 [10.9, 11.2]	5.8±7.1 [5.7, 5.9]	4.7±6.2 [4.6, 4.8]	3.9±5.4 [3.8, 4.0]	12.1± 9.6 [11.9, 12.2]	11.4± 8.7 [11.2, 11.5]	11.0± 8.3 [10.9, 11.2]	11.9± 9.8 [11.7, 12.0]	11.2±8.8 [11.0, 11.3]	10.7±8.2 [10.6, 10.9]
81	15	11.7± 9.2 [11.6, 11.9]	11.0± 8.9 [10.9, 11.1]	10.6±8.1 [10.5, 10.7]	6.3±7.7 [6.1, 6.4]	4.7±6.1 [4.6, 4.8]	3.9±5.5 [3.8, 4.0]	12.2±10.1 [12.0, 12.3]	11.1± 8.5 [10.9, 11.2]	10.8± 7.9 [10.6, 10.9]	11.6± 9.1 [11.5, 11.7]	10.8±8.0 [10.6, 10.9]	10.6±8.0 [10.4, 10.7]
88	5	4.7±7.9 [4.6, 4.8]	3.3±5.8 [3.2, 3.4]	2.3±4.2 [2.2, 2.4]	13.7±10.1 [13.6, 13.9]	12.8±9.8 [12.6, 12.9]	12.4±8.9 [12.2, 12.5]	5.3± 9.2 [5.1, 5.4]	3.8±8.6 [3.6, 3.9]	2.2±5.6 [2.1, 2.3]	5.8±8.2 [5.6, 5.9]	3.9±5.8 [3.8, 4.0]	3.0±3.9 [2.9, 3.1]
88	10	5.0±9.0 [4.9, 5.2]	3.0±5.7 [2.9, 3.1]	2.2±4.2 [2.1, 2.2]	12.3± 9.0 [12.2, 12.5]	12.1±9.1 [11.9, 12.2]	11.8±8.6 [11.7, 12.0]	5.8±10.1 [5.6, 6.0]	3.5±7.3 [3.4, 3.7]	2.0±5.2 [1.9, 2.1]	5.2±8.1 [5.0, 5.3]	3.7±5.8 [3.6, 3.7]	2.8±4.2 [2.7, 2.9]
88	15	5.0±8.6 [4.8, 5.1]	3.3±6.3 [3.2, 3.4]	2.2±4.4 [2.1, 2.3]	12.2± 8.9 [12.1, 12.4]	11.7±8.6 [11.6, 11.9]	11.7±8.4 [11.6, 11.8]	5.4± 9.9 [5.3, 5.6]	3.5±7.2 [3.3, 3.6]	2.1±5.3 [2.0, 2.2]	5.1±8.1 [5.0, 5.2]	3.4±5.3 [3.3, 3.5]	2.7±4.0 [2.7, 2.8]
103	5	5.6±9.2 [5.5, 5.7]	3.6±6.2 [3.5, 3.7]	2.6±4.4 [2.5, 2.7]	14.4±11.0 [14.3, 14.6]	13.4±9.8 [13.3, 13.6]	13.2±9.4 [13.1, 13.4]	6.0±8.5 [5.9, 6.2]	4.5±6.8 [4.4, 4.6]	3.1±4.1 [3.1, 3.2]	5.9±10.1 [5.7, 6.1]	3.7±7.4 [3.6, 3.8]	2.1±5.0 [2.1, 2.2]
103	10	5.3±9.1 [5.1, 5.4]	3.3±6.3 [3.2, 3.4]	2.2±4.1 [2.2, 2.3]	13.2± 9.6 [13.1, 13.4]	12.6±9.0 [12.5, 12.8]	12.8±9.2 [12.7, 13.0]	5.9±9.2 [5.8, 6.1]	3.8±5.9 [3.7, 3.9]	3.1±4.5 [3.0, 3.1]	6.2±10.6 [6.0, 6.4]	3.2±6.6 [3.1, 3.3]	2.1±4.9 [2.0, 2.1]
103	15	5.3±8.9 [5.1, 5.4]	3.3±6.0 [3.2, 3.4]	2.3±4.3 [2.3, 2.4]	13.4±11.3 [13.2, 13.5]	12.8±9.2 [12.6, 12.9]	12.4±8.8 [12.3, 12.6]	5.6±9.0 [5.5, 5.8]	4.0±6.5 [3.9, 4.1]	2.9±4.8 [2.9, 3.0]	5.8± 9.6 [5.6, 6.0]	3.2±6.9 [3.1, 3.4]	2.4±5.7 [2.3, 2.5]

Table 9: Mean ± Standard Deviation of the time cost (ms) of building performance prediction and transferring models of x264 system, using different sampling sizes on training and target machines

Target Machines	Sampling Sizes	Training Machines: Machine №75, Sampling Sizes $3N_f$	Machine №75 $4N_f$	Machine №75 $5N_f$	Machine №81, Sampling Sizes $3N_f$	Machine №81 $4N_f$	Machine №81 $5N_f$	Machine №88, Sampling Sizes $3N_f$	Machine №88 $4N_f$	Machine №88 $5N_f$	Machine №103, Sampling Sizes $3N_f$	Machine №103 $4N_f$	Machine №103 $5N_f$
75	5	5.7±0.9	5.4±0.7	5.9±0.7	5.5±0.5	6.1±0.5	6.3±0.8	5.6±0.5	5.7±0.6	6.1±0.5	6.5±0.5	6.4±1.1	6.7±0.6
75	10	6.0±0.6	6.0±0.6	6.0±0.4	5.3±0.9	5.7±0.5	6.2±0.4	5.5±0.5	5.8±0.4	5.9±0.7	5.8±0.6	6.4±0.8	6.3±0.8
75	15	5.3±0.5	5.5±0.5	6.1±0.7	5.7±0.6	5.8±0.6	6.3±0.6	5.5±0.7	5.8±0.6	5.5±0.5	5.8±0.9	6.5±1.1	6.2±0.6
81	5	5.8±0.9	5.6±0.5	6.0±0.4	5.5±0.5	5.9±0.8	6.0±0.6	5.5±0.7	6.1±0.3	5.9±0.7	5.7±0.6	6.0±1.0	6.2±0.9
81	10	5.5±1.0	5.5±0.5	5.9±0.7	5.3±0.6	5.7±0.5	6.1±0.7	5.9±0.7	6.0±0.8	5.8±0.4	5.9±0.5	7.0±0.8	6.1±0.5
81	15	6.2±0.7	6.1±0.8	6.1±0.7	5.4±0.7	5.8±0.4	6.0±0.9	5.6±0.5	5.9±0.3	5.9±0.5	5.2±0.9	6.3±0.6	6.2±0.7
88	5	6.6±0.5	5.8±0.6	5.8±0.6	5.9±0.5	5.8±0.6	5.8±0.4	5.5±0.8	5.7±0.8	6.4±0.9	5.3±0.5	6.0±0.4	6.2±0.6
88	10	5.9±0.8	6.2±0.7	6.2±0.4	5.4±0.7	5.5±0.5	6.0±0.4	5.5±0.5	6.0±0.6	6.1±0.9	5.1±0.7	6.2±0.9	6.4±0.5
88	15	6.0±0.4	5.9±0.5	6.2±1.0	5.4±0.8	5.9±0.3	6.2±0.6	5.7±1.0	5.8±0.6	5.8±0.6	5.2±0.7	5.9±0.7	6.7±1.4
103	5	5.7±0.6	5.9±0.7	6.0±0.6	5.5±0.5	6.0±0.4	5.5±0.7	5.8±0.4	5.7±0.5	6.0±0.4	5.4±0.5	5.5±0.7	6.3±0.8
103	10	5.7±0.8	5.6±0.7	6.3±0.6	5.7±0.8	6.0±0.0	6.2±1.0	5.5±0.5	5.8±0.6	6.3±0.8	5.2±0.9	5.8±0.7	6.5±0.9
103	15	5.6±0.7	5.9±0.5	6.2±0.6	5.8±0.7	5.7±0.5	6.4±0.9	5.7±0.8	6.0±0.6	6.4±0.9	5.6±0.8	6.0±0.8	6.2±0.7

Table 10: Mean Relative Error (%) of x264 system added by the transferring process

Target Machines	Sampling Sizes	Training Machines: Machine №75, Sampling Sizes $3N_f$	Machine №75 $4N_f$	Machine №75 $5N_f$	Machine №81, Sampling Sizes $3N_f$	Machine №81 $4N_f$	Machine №81 $5N_f$	Machine №88, Sampling Sizes $3N_f$	Machine №88 $4N_f$	Machine №88 $5N_f$	Machine №103, Sampling Sizes $3N_f$	Machine №103 $4N_f$	Machine №103 $5N_f$
75	5	0.3	0.2	0.1	12.4	11.9	12.0	2.3	2.0	1.6	2.5	2.1	1.6
75	10	0.2	0.2	0.1	11.7	11.5	11.6	1.9	1.9	1.6	2.6	1.9	1.5
75	15	0.1	0.2	0.1	11.8	11.4	11.7	2.3	1.8	1.6	2.9	1.8	1.5
81	5	11.8	11.0	11.0	0.2	0.1	0.1	11.5	11.0	11.1	11.5	10.8	10.7
81	10	10.1	9.4	9.7	0.2	0.1	0.1	10.1	9.5	9.5	10.2	9.3	9.2
81	15	9.9	9.3	9.3	0.2	0.2	0.1	9.5	9.6	9.3	9.9	9.4	9.1
88	5	2.3	2.1	1.6	12.3	12.0	11.7	0.2	0.1	0.1	3.8	2.8	2.5
88	10	2.6	1.9	1.8	11.5	11.4	11.5	0.4	0.1	0.1	3.0	2.5	2.2
88	15	2.1	1.7	1.5	11.1	11.4	11.3	0.3	0.2	0.1	3.3	2.7	2.2
103	5	2.6	1.9	1.8	12.9	12.3	12.3	3.8	2.9	2.3	0.3	0.1	0.1
103	10	2.6	1.8	1.4	12.1	11.7	11.8	3.3	2.5	2.2	0.2	0.2	0.1
103	15	2.6	1.7	1.4	11.8	11.8	11.9	3.1	2.3	2.1	0.1	0.2	0.1

forms (Table 4, Table 6, Table 8). As we can see from the results, the majority of training and target machine pairs have strong monotonically decreasing trends in their mean relative error with the increase in training sample size from $3 \times N_f$ to $5 \times N_f$. This follows the intuition that more training data results in more accurate performance prediction models.

We can also observe sharp decrease in the mean relative error when the sampling size increases from 5 to 15 configurations. This is expected, as again, more training data generally leads to better model accuracy. However, this trend is not always monotonic and in some special cases doesn't hold at all. These observations agree with our analysis of learning curves of linear transformation models performed in Section 4.6. From Figure 4 and Figure 5 we can see that even samples as small as 5 configurations can provide very good approximations of the linear transfer model due to the simplicity of linear models. However, when training with small sample sizes (in our experience, on the interval [5, 20]) the linear transfer model may get stuck in a local cost-minimum where the generated model may be biased. This is the reason for the non-monotonically decreasing error we observe in Tables 4, 6, and 8.

Table 8 shows not only mean values of the relative errors from our models, but also standard deviations and confidence intervals at the 95% confidence level. From Table 8 we can see that although our mean relative error is often small, the standard deviations we measure are relatively large and can exceed the mean in absolute value. However, confidence intervals for the mean value, calculated using bootstrapping [2, 10], are narrow and are almost always less than or equal to 0.5% of the mean relative error.

The data obtained from our experiments $\mathbf{C}_{exp}$, described in Section 3.1, is sufficient to capture feature interactions up to order three. However, we built prediction models RT using only small samples $\mathbf{C}_S \subset \mathbf{C}_{exp}$. Therefore, although sample $\mathbf{C}_S$ may permit making a good approximation of its corresponding performance distribution, its possible that our performance models, $RT_1, RT_2, \ldots, RT_n$, simply cannot capture all feature interactions that are captured by $\mathbf{C}_{exp}$. This creates a situation where RT produces precise performance predictions for the majority of tested configurations $\mathbf{C}_{exp} \setminus \mathbf{C}_S$ (less that 1% relative error), but for some configurations, which contain uncaptured feature interactions, RT can produce very inaccurate predictions (with more than 50% relative error). This is why we see low mean relative errors, high standard deviations (because of the small set of very large outliers), and very narrow confidence intervals (since it is hard for bootstrapping to capture these outliers).

We can assess accuracy of transferred performance models from a slightly different perspective. We can evaluate how much worse are transferred models compared to "native" models, generated specifically for a target hardware platform. To achieve that, for each performance model trained on m_{trn} and transferred to m_{tgt}, we generate a "native" performance model using the same set of configurations which were measured on m_{tgt}. Then we calculate mean relative error of the native model and subtract it from the mean relative error of the transferred model, thus assessing how much we lose in accuracy when transferring a model from a different platform. Results of this assessment are presented in Table 5, Table 7 and Table 10. One can notice that added mean relative error, when transferring prediction models to the same machine, has a non-zero value. This is caused by the fact that implementation of CART that we use in our study is not exactly deterministic and in some special cases it might generate slightly different prediction models from the same training data. This causes different predictions by these models and thus non-zero difference of mean relative prediction error.

In summary, prediction accuracy generally improves with increasing sampling sizes on training and target machines. However, the proposed approach relies on good sampling strategies for generating the training data $\mathbf{C}_S$ such that it captures necessary feature interactions. This may cause problems in a practical setting where the training sample $\mathbf{C}_S$ might not follow any feature-coverage criteria. We suggest using experimental design for generating samples of configurations for measurement on target machines as they will maximize the amount of information available in the training sample $\mathbf{C}_S$.

4.3 Experiment on System Comparison

To answer RQ2 we compare Tables 6 and 8. As we can see from these tables the mean relative errors for x264 are much higher than those of SQLite. The same process of performance model transfer produces different prediction accuracy for different configurable systems. This is not unexpected as we can generally expect that different systems will have varying levels of predictability in the performance effects of their features, and in the performance effects of the interactions between features. In the case of x264, many features, such as the size of the window used for a filter, or the number of passes used for encoding, have compounding effects with other features. Configurable features of x264 have many complex interactions that can geometrically increase or decrease its encoding performance. Furthermore, for special cases like video encoders, many chipsets include on-board hardware decoding support, further complicating accurate

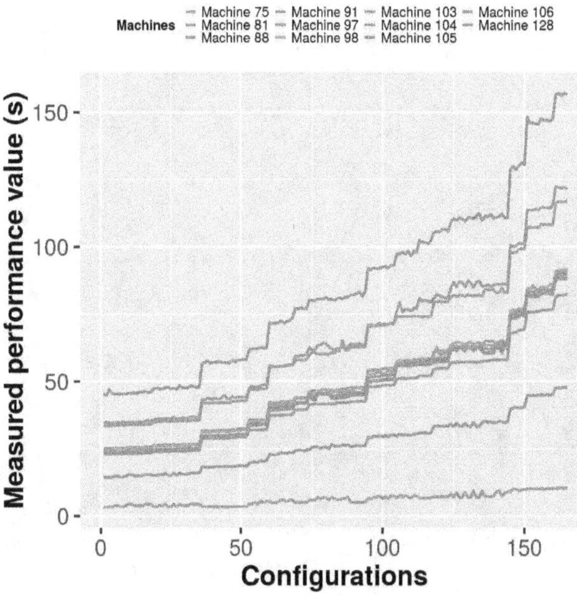

Figure 1: Performance distributions of x264 deployed on different machines

prediction of feature performance across different hardware platforms. On the other hand, simpler software systems like SQLite have far fewer features and many that do not interact significantly, it is much simpler to predict as a result.

4.4 Experiment on Time Cost

Toward answering RQ3, Table 9 shows the execution time of building both performance prediction models RT and performance transfer models L for different training sample sizes $|\mathbf{C}_S|$ and $|\mathbf{C}_{both}|$. We can see from this table that the amount of training time necessary for building both prediction and transfer models is a small fraction of the time necessary to benchmark individual configurations, let alone exhaustively exploring all feature setting combinations in $\mathbf{C}$ on even a modest sized benchmark of a given software system. For comparison, Table 1 shows examples of the amount of time necessary for benchmarking individual configurations of x264.

4.5 Exploratory Analysis

Toward answering RQ4, we conduct a thorough analysis of our methodology. We investigate the performance distributions of configurable systems deployed on multiple hardware platforms, compare the structure of performance models trained on different hardware platforms, and show that linear models are effective approximations for performance transfer models. Therefore we show that the accuracy of our results is not accidental or a result of over-fit, and provide explanations of why our approach works.

4.5.1 Analysis of Performance Distributions

To assess the feasibility of transferring performance models of systems between different hardware platforms, we analyzed the similarity of their performance distributions. Studied systems have many features, thus their feature spaces are highly multidimensional and difficult to represent in a man-

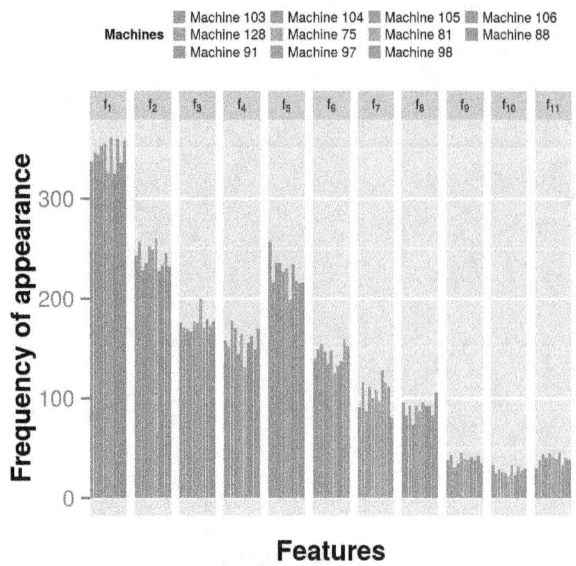

Figure 2: Feature distributions of regression trees trained for performance prediction of x264 on different machines

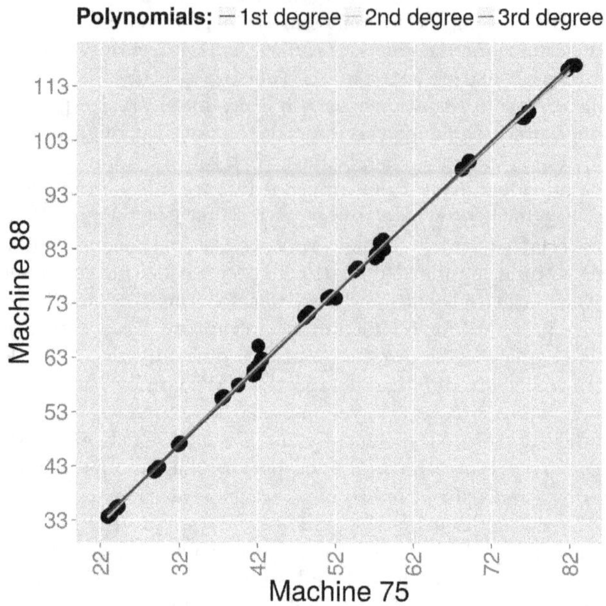

Figure 3: Transformation between performance distributions of x264 system deployed on Machine №75 and Machine №88

ner readily interpretable by the human eye. To visualise the performance distributions of our systems, we take a sample of the configurations that we measure and sort them by the performance of one of the benchmarked hardware platforms.

Figure 1 presents performance distributions of x264 deployed on different hardware platforms. We can see that almost all distributions have very similar shapes, although different in absolute values. Though it is only a cursory analysis of the similarity of the performance distributions of our systems across machines, it does give us confidence that even simple polynomial transformations between these distributions could give us good predictions between hardware platforms. There is a clear pattern indicating that configurations retain their relative performance profile across different hardware platforms, i.e., configuration with low relative performance on one platform, will have low relative performance on another platform.

4.5.2 Comparison Analysis of Regression Trees

Regression trees are built by recursively partitioning training dataset into subsets using dataset features. Therefore, features used for dataset partitioning play a major part in defining the structure of a regression tree. Listing all features used in the nodes of a regression tree can be used as a metric for comparing the structure of two different regression trees. Thus by using this metric we can assess the similarity of two regression trees built for the same configurable system, but deployed on different hardware platforms.

Following this logic, we built a feature distribution of regression trees trained for performance prediction of a system deployed on different platforms. From Figure 2, we can see that the distributions of features used by trees on different hardware platforms are very similar to each other. From this we can conclude that the structure of the trees themselves are similar across the different hardware platforms we use in our experiments. Therefore it should be possible for us to train a regression tree for performance prediction of a configurable system on one platform and reuse this tree, with small modifications, on another platform.

4.5.3 Analysis of Distributions Transformations

To select a method for transferring prediction models across different platforms we investigated *transfer models* between training and target machine distributions. We used visualizations of the relationships between training and target machine performance distributions to guide the selection of the models used for transfer. An example of the visualizations we used is shown in Figure 3. The x-axis corresponds to a configuration's performance on the training platform, while the y-axis corresponds to that same configuration's performance on the target platform.

By exploring several possible transfer models for all systems in our case study, we found that a polynomial regression model provides a good approximations of the transfer function between machines. To evaluate our hypothesis, we fitted three polynomial models to the transformation data: 1st, 2nd and 3rd degree polynomials. For all those software systems and hardware platforms that we tested, we found that a 1st degree polynomial provides an excellent fit of our transformation data, while 2nd and 3rd degree polynomials appear to cause overfitting and unnecessary complications of the transfer model.

4.5.4 Summary

We believe that our proposed process of performance model transfer achieved high prediction accuracy as a result of several main factors. Firstly, the studied configurable systems have very similar performance distributions when deployed on different hardware platforms. Secondly, the transfer function between these distributions is simple and can be easily approximated using a linear model. Finally, the prediction models trained on the studied software systems have very similar structure when built independently on different platforms. All of these factors together allowed us to use simple and robust methods for performance prediction and model transfer, which resulted in high accuracy achieved by our proposed approach.

4.6 Building Linear Transfer Models

To answer RQ5 we performed a thorough analysis of transfer model building process and tried to answer several important questions. (1) Is it possible to measure only a subset of $\mathbf{C}_S$ on both machines $\mathbf{C}_{both} \subset \mathbf{C}_S$ and build a reliable linear transfer model? (2) Which sampling method to use for $\mathbf{C}_{both}$ to achieve acceptable results faster? (3) Is it possible to figure out a minimum amount of configurations to measure on both m_{trn} and m_{tgt} machines? (4) What is the amount of measured configurations after which additional measurements are not necessary? Toward answering these questions, we decided to analyse the learning curves of the linear transfer models.

We evaluated three different methods of sampling $\mathbf{C}_{both}$: Walker's alias sampling [13], stratified sampling [12] and Sobol sampling [14]. *Walker's alias sampling* [13] is a random sampling method which is the default sampling strategy in the R programming language. Walker's alias sampling is an example of a classical pseudo-random sampling method that generates new samples according to a specified probability distribution. *Stratified sampling* [12] is a random sampling method that exhaustively divides a sampled population into mutually exclusive subsets of observations before performing actual sampling. This allows to cover the sampled population more evenly, which in some cases significantly improves representation of the whole population by a sample. *Sobol sampling* [14] is an example of a quasi-random sampling method. Sobol sampling is similar to pseudo-random sampling, as it generates new samples with respect to a given probability distribution, however quasi-random methods are specifically designed to cover a sampled population more uniformly than pseudo random strategies.

To generate a linear transfer model between the performance distributions of machines m_{trn} and m_{tgt}, we build a training dataset using all available configurations $\mathbf{C}_{exp}$. An example of this training data and the resulting linear transfer model is shown in Figure 3.

The algorithm we used for building learning curves for linear transfer models is as follows:

1. Initialize $\mathbf{C}_{both}$ by randomly sampling a configuration from $\mathbf{C}_{exp}$.

2. Randomly sample another configuration from the set $\mathbf{C}_{exp} \setminus \mathbf{C}_{both}$ and add it to the training sample $\mathbf{C}_{both}$.

3. Build a linear model L based on the sample $\mathbf{C}_{both}$.

4. Assess how well L approximates transformation by using *mean squared error (MSE)* over the full set of configurations $\mathbf{C}_{exp}$.

5. If the set $\mathbf{C}_{exp} \setminus \mathbf{C}_{both}$ is non-empty go to the Step 2. Otherwise, build the learning curve of L by combining mean squared errors for different sizes of $\mathbf{C}_{both}$.

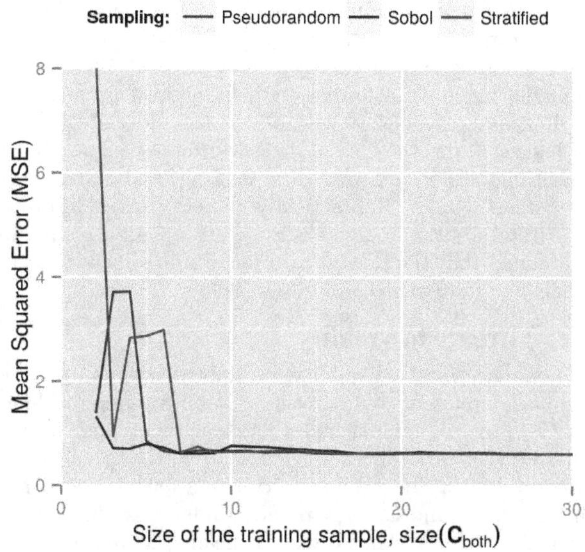

Figure 4: Learning curves of a linear transformation between performance distributions of x264 system on Machine №75 and Machine №88

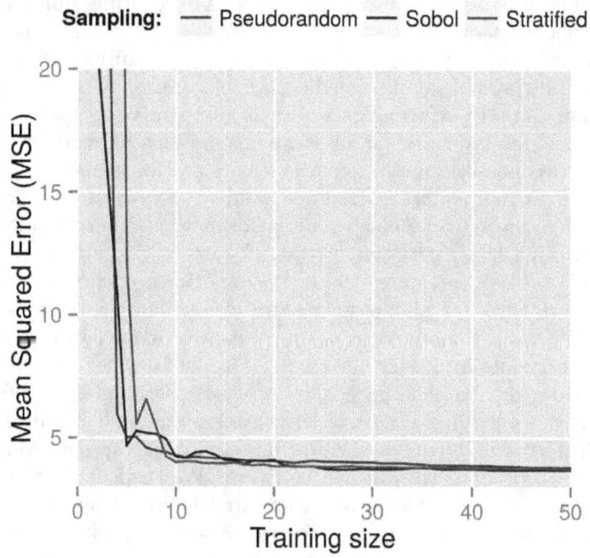

Figure 5: Average learning curve of a linear transformation between performance distributions of x264 system

Figure 4 represents the learning curve of a linear model approximating the transfer function between the performance distributions of Machine №75 and Machine №88 when running the x264 software system. Figure 5 shows the average learning curve of a linear transformation between performance distributions of individual machines running the x264 software system.

We gained several key insights through analysis of our averaged learning curves for all studied configurable software systems and learning curves for all combinations of training and target machines. Firstly, it is possible to measure only a small sample of configurations $\mathbf{C}_{both} \subset \mathbf{C}_S$ to build a reliable linear transformation between two performance distributions. Secondly, we noticed that for all systems, the biggest improvement in the performance of our linear transfer models occurs when $size(\mathbf{C}_{both}) \in [2, 10]$. However, when $size(\mathbf{C}_{both}) > 20$ practically no performance improvement from additional samples is observed. As a result, we recommend that the size interval for training linear transfer models be set to $size(\mathbf{C}_{both}) \in [10, 20]$.

4.7 Threats to validity

To enhance internal validity, we implemented automated random sampling of configurations $\mathbf{C}_S$ on training machines and $\mathbf{C}_{both}$ on target machines. As was mentioned in Section 4.1.3, $\mathbf{C}_S$ varies in $\{3 \times N_f, 4 \times N_f, 5 \times N_f\}$, and $\mathbf{C}_{both}$ varies in $\{5, 10, 15\}$. For each combination of these sampling sizes, $\mathbf{C}_S$ and $\mathbf{C}_{both}$ were independently and randomly sampled ten times. Thus resulting mean relative errors presented in Tables 4, 8, 6 are averaged over ten independent transferring experiments. This allowed us to avoid bias caused by selecting training data for prediction and transfer models.

An obvious threat to external validity is that the results are derived from experiments on a limited number of software systems and a limited range of hardware. To reduce the threat we benchmarked three configurable systems with different sizes, number of features and covering different application domains. All of the studied systems are used in real-world settings. When benchmarking subject configurable systems we measured each configuration three times. Thus actual performance values in our study are averages over three independent measurements. This allowed us to address possible measurement error in our experiment.

To further enhance external validity, we measured each system on multiple hardware platforms with different number of CPUs, instruction sets, clock rates and memory sizes (see Table 2 for more details). We performed transferring experiments for all possible pairs of machines with differing hardware configurations and presented a subset of these experiments in Tables 4, 8, 6, 9.

However, we acknowledge that our experiments investigated a very limited set of software systems and hardware platforms and current results might not extrapolate very well to other hardware and software. We suspect that our approach might not work when transferring performance prediction model of a software system that is specifically designed for a particular hardware configuration. For example, some software systems might use hardware acceleration, like GPUs, for it's tasks. If such a system is deployed on a hardware that doesn't have a dedicated GPU, it's performance distribution might appear completely distorted. Thus linear transformation might not provide a good approximation of a transfer model. This hypothesis should be investigated in future work.

5. RELATED WORK

Performance prediction of configurable software systems is a highly researched topic. Researches investigate which models are best suited for predicting system performance, which strategies can be used for tuning these models, and how to minimize the amount of measured configurations necessary for model training.

Guo et al. [5] proposed a variability-aware approach for performance prediction of configurable software systems based on small random samples of measured configurations. To reveal a correlation between a selection of configuration options and system performance, the authors use CART. They perform a case study of the proposed approach using six configurable software systems with different application domains, implementation languages, configuration spaces and sizes. This study shows that the proposed approach on average achieves prediction accuracy of 94%, when using small samples for CART prediction model training. Finally, the authors show that the approach achieves the best results when a training sample has a similar performance distribution as the whole population of configurations.

Valov et al. [18] extended the work of Guo et al. [5], by carrying out an empirical comparison of regression methods for the problem of variability-aware performance prediction. They compare prediction accuracy of four methods: CART, Bagging, Random Forest and SVM. For each method the authors generate multiple parameter settings, by using Sobol sampling, and select parameters that provided the best, the average and the worst prediction accuracy for each method. By analysing prediction accuracy of methods for combinations of different parameter settings, target configurable software systems and training sampling sizes, they assess which methods provide the best prediction most of the time, i.e. which method is the most robust one. Results showed Bagging to be the most robust technique for performance prediction, even when allowing an interval for selecting the best performance accuracy.

Westermann et al. [20] proposed an approach for automatic, measurement-based method for inferring performance prediction functions. To minimize the amount of measurements, they developed three algorithms that iteratively select new data points if necessary. To build actual performance prediction functions, the authors use four different regression and interpolation methods: MARS, CART, GP, and Kriging. To validate built prediction functions, they use three different strategies. They provide a framework for evaluation of function building methods for performance prediction and for evaluation of different combinations of function building methods and parameter tuning strategies. Finally, they evaluated the methodology for performance prediction in two industrial case studies.

Hutter et al. [7, 8] performed a comprehensive study of methods for configurable algorithms runtime prediction. Authors propose new methods for performance prediction based on random forests and approximate Gaussian processes. Moreover, authors show how methods of survival analysis can be used for improving random forest technique to better handle incomplete performance measurements. With respect to the actual domain of algorithms which performance is predicted, authors investigated satisfiability (SAT), travelling salesperson (TSP) and mixed integer programming (MIP) problems and inferred new probing and timing features for them. Finally, authors present a comprehensive evaluation of different performance prediction methods including ridge regression and it's variants, neural networks, regression trees, Gaussian processes and random forests.

Our work is similar to the aforementioned ones [5, 7, 8, 18, 20], since we also use CART for building performance prediction models. However, we do not perform a comparison of different regression methods, parameter tuning techniques or sampling strategies. Instead, we concentrate on transferring generated performance prediction models to different hardware environments.

System performance prediction across different hardware platforms is a highly researched topic as well. Researches investigate different methodologies for cross-platform performance prediction and ways for collecting necessary performance data.

Thereska et al. [17] proposed an approach for performance modelling of complex popular applications such as Microsoft's Office suite and Visual Studio. All explored applications were specifically instrumented to export their current state as well as all necessary performance relevant metrics. Moreover, all explored applications were deployed on multiple machines, thus allowing them to monitor how each particular application with different configurations behaves in various hardware platforms. To predict performance of a system on a particular hardware platform, the authors (1) select configuration options (both software and hardware) that influences a chosen performance metric the most, (2) use similarity search to select hardware platforms with similar hardware configuration, (3) return distribution of possible performance metric values from a number of similar configurations as the result.

Hoste et al. [6] proposed an approach for performance prediction of a given software application on a set of hardware platforms, to find out which platform provides the best performance for the given application. Authors propose a set of special applications, called a benchmark suite, that have their microarchitecture-independent characteristics and performance values measured. Using this measured benchmark suite, authors build a data transformation matrix that is used to transform applications performance characteristics and values into points in so-called benchmark space. Benchmark space is populated by applications from the benchmark suite and by the target application which performance needs to be predicted. Finally, performance prediction of the target application is carried out by taking weighted average of performance values of neighbouring applications in the benchmark space.

Although Thereska et al. [17] and Hoste et al. [6] propose methodologies for performance prediction of configurable software systems across different hardware platforms, they are completely different from ours. In the current work we build a prediction model for one hardware platform and transfer it to another using a linear model. On the contrary, Thereska uses similarity search on the collected performance data and Hoste uses transformation to a specially designed benchmark space and neighbourhood search to predict system performance on the target platform.

6. CONCLUSION AND FUTURE WORK

We proposed an approach for transferring performance prediction models of configurable software systems across different hardware platforms. We performed a rigorous exploratory analysis of the proposed methodology, including: performance distributions comparison, regression models structure comparison, linear transformation analysis, and comparison of different sampling strategies. We observed a high correlation between performance distributions similarity and high prediction accuracy of our method. We showed that similarity of performance distributions is correlated with structure of performance prediction models. We demonstrated that linear model provides a good approximation of transformation between performance distributions of a system deployed in different hardware environments and showed that it is possible to build a reliable linear transfer model using a small sample of measured configurations $\mathbf{C}_{both}$, where $size(\mathbf{C}_{both}) \in [5, 10]$.

We performed a thorough quantitative analysis of our methodology. We showed that our approach achieves high accuracy (less than 10% mean relative error) for majority of prediction model transfers. Moreover, we observe a decreasing tendency of prediction error with increase of the training data for prediction or linear transfer models. Finally, we demonstrated that time required for building both performance prediction and linear transfer models is negligible (less than 10 ms) compared to time budget required for acquiring configuration measurements.

In future work we plan to test our approach on more configurable systems. All systems, that we've explored so far, demonstrate very similar performance distributions across a wide range of heterogeneous hardware environments. However, if a software system is specifically developed or tuned for a particular hardware configuration or architecture, it might exhibit a dramatically different performance distribution when deployed on a completely different hardware platform. We intend to find and analyse these systems in order to improve generality of our methodology. This might require using a different performance prediction model or using a more complex transformation between performance distributions.

We plan to extend our approach by varying not only configuration options of studied systems, but also systems' workload during benchmarking. We suspect that variations in system workload might influence transferability of system's performance prediction model by distorting system's performance distribution across different hardware environments.

Another direction of future work might be enhancing our approach using queuing networks. A large body of work has been aggregated on theory and application of queueing networks to performance modelling and prediction of configurable software and hardware systems. Balsamo et al. [3] and Cortellessa et al. [4] propose approaches for automatic derivation of performance models, based on different types of queueing networks, from UML-based designs of software systems. Kowal et al. [9] propose a queueing-networks-based approach for performance modelling and prediction of families of systems (e.g. software product lines or complex configurable software systems) by approximating performance models using ordinary differential equations and symbolically analysing them. All this work can be used to completely or partially abstract studied systems as queueing networks thus improving performance prediction across different hardware environments.

7. ACKNOWLEDGEMENTS

We thank anonymous reviewers for their comments, corrections and ideas provided. This work was partially supported by Natural Sciences and Engineering Research Council of Canada, Pratt & Whitney Canada, and Shanghai Municipal Natural Science Foundation (No. 17ZR1406900).

8. REFERENCES

[1] NIST/SEMATECH e-Handbook of Statistical Methods. http://www.itl.nist.gov/div898/handbook/.

[2] J. Antony. *Design of Experiments for Engineers and Scientists.* Butterworth-Heinemann, 2003.

[3] S. Balsamo and M. Marzolla. Performance Evaluation of UML Software Architectures with Multiclass Queueing Network Models. In *Proceedings of the 5th International Workshop on Software and Performance.* ACM, 2005.

[4] V. Cortellessa and R. Mirandola. PRIMA-UML: a performance validation incremental methodology on early UML diagrams. *Science of Computer Programming*, July 2002.

[5] J. Guo, K. Czarnecki, S. Apel, N. Siegmund, and A. Wasowski. Variability-aware performance prediction: A statistical learning approach. In *Proc. ASE.* IEEE, 2013.

[6] K. Hoste, A. Phansalkar, L. Eeckhout, A. Georges, L. K. John, and K. De Bosschere. Performance prediction based on inherent program similarity. In *Proceedings of the 15th International Conference on Parallel Architectures and Compilation Techniques*, PACT '06, pages 114–122, New York, NY, USA, 2006. ACM.

[7] F. Hutter, L. Xu, H. H. Hoos, and K. Leyton-Brown. Algorithm runtime prediction: Methods & evaluation. *Artificial Intelligence*, 206(0):79–111, Jan. 2014.

[8] F. Hutter, L. Xu, H. H. Hoos, and K. Leyton-Brown. Algorithm runtime prediction: Methods & evaluation (extended abstract). In *Proceedings of the 24th International Joint Conference on Artificial Intelligence (IJCAI)*, July 2015.

[9] M. Kowal, M. Tschaikowski, M. Tribastone, and I. Schaefer. Scaling Size and Parameter Spaces in Variability-Aware Software Performance Models (T). In *2015 30th IEEE/ACM International Conference on Automated Software Engineering (ASE).* IEEE, 2015.

[10] D. Montgomery. *Design and Analysis of Experiments.* John Wiley & Sons, 2008.

[11] J. C. Petkovich, A. Oliveira, Y. Zhang, T. Reidemeister, and S. Fischmeister. DataMill: A Distributed Heterogeneous Infrastructure For Robust Experimentation. *Software: Practice and Experience*, pages n/a–n/a, 2015.

[12] W. H. Press, S. A. Teukolsky, W. T. Vetterling, and B. P. Flannery. *Numerical Recipes in C (2nd Ed.): The Art of Scientific Computing.* Cambridge Univ. Press, 1992.

[13] B. D. Ripley. *Stochastic simulation*, volume 316. John Wiley & Sons, 2009.

[14] I. Sobol and Y. Levitan. A pseudo-random number generator for personal computers. *Computers and Mathematics with Applications*, 37(4–5):33–40, 1999.

[15] SQLite. SQLite. https://www.sqlite.org/. Accessed April. 15th, 2016.

[16] The Tukaani Project. XZ Utils. http://tukaani.org/xz/. Accessed April. 17th, 2016.

[17] E. Thereska, B. Doebel, A. X. Zheng, and P. Nobel. Practical performance models for complex, popular applications. *SIGMETRICS Perform. Eval. Rev.*, 38(1):1–12, June 2010.

[18] P. Valov, J. Guo, and K. Czarnecki. Empirical comparison of regression methods for variability-aware performance prediction. In *Proceedings of the 19th International Conference on Software Product Line*, SPLC '15, pages 186–190, New York, NY, USA, 2015. ACM.

[19] VideoLAN Organization. x264, the best H.264/AVC encoder. http://www.videolan.org/developers/x264.html. Accessed April. 15th, 2016.

[20] D. Westermann, J. Happe, R. Krebs, and R. Farahbod. Automated inference of goal-oriented performance prediction functions. In *Proceedings of the 27th IEEE/ACM International Conference on Automated Software Engineering*, ASE 2012, pages 190–199, New York, NY, USA, 2012. ACM.

[21] Y. Zhang, J. Guo, E. Blais, and K. Czarnecki. Performance prediction of configurable software systems by fourier learning. In *Proceedings of the International Conference on Automated Software Engineering (ASE)*, 2015.

Using Libception to Understand and Improve HTTP Streaming Video Server Throughput

Tyler Szepesi
University of Waterloo
Waterloo, ON, Canada
stszepes@cs.uwaterloo.ca

Benjamin Cassell
University of Waterloo
Waterloo, ON, Canada
becassel@cs.uwaterloo.ca

Tim Brecht
University of Waterloo
Waterloo, ON, Canada
brecht@cs.uwaterloo.ca

Derek Eager
University of Saskatchewan
Saskatoon, SK, Canada
eager@cs.usask.ca

Jim Summers
University of Waterloo
Waterloo, ON, Canada
jasummer@cs.uwaterloo.ca

Bernard Wong
University of Waterloo
Waterloo, ON, Canada
bernard@cs.uwaterloo.ca

Abstract

Video streaming applications generate a large fraction of Internet traffic. Much of this content is delivered over HTTP using standard web servers. Unlike other types of web workloads, HTTP video streaming workloads are typically disk bound, and therefore an important problem is that of optimizing disk access.

In this paper we design, implement and evaluate Libception, an application-level shim library that implements techniques for improving disk I/O efficiency. Web servers can achieve the benefits of these techniques simply by linking with Libception, without the need to modify source code. In contrast to making kernel changes or attempting to optimize kernel tuning, Libception provides a portable and relatively simple setting in which techniques for optimizing I/O in HTTP video streaming servers can be implemented and evaluated.

We report experimental results evaluating the efficacy of the aggressive prefetching and disk I/O serialization techniques currently implemented in Libception, for three web servers (Apache, nginx and the userver) and two operating systems (FreeBSD, Linux). We find that on FreeBSD, video streaming throughput with all three web servers can be doubled by linking with Libception. On Linux, performance similar to that provided with Libception was eventually obtained by examining the kernel source to understand and tune kernel parameters. With the default kernel parameter settings, however, and regardless of which Linux disk scheduler is selected, we find that use of Libception can approximately double throughput. We find that both aggressive prefetching and serialization are necessary to achieve these benefits.

ICPE'17, April 22 - 26, 2017, L'Aquila, Italy

ISBN 978-1-4503-4404-3/17/04. . . $15.00

DOI: http://dx.doi.org/10.1145/3030207.3030231

1. INTRODUCTION

Video streaming over HTTP is now the largest contributor to Internet traffic. The catalogue of available content from popular video streaming services has also been growing rapidly, and although memory caching and SSD can be effective for the most popular content, HTTP streaming video server workloads are often disk-bound [13]. Techniques for improving disk throughput in such systems are therefore of considerable interest.

There has been much past work on improving disk access efficiency. In the context of HTTP video streaming, however, there are two complicating factors. First, unlike early video streaming systems, HTTP-based video streaming is pull-based: the server responds to client requests for video chunks, rather than pushing video data to the client at some server-determined rate. Second, contemporary servers may be highly concurrent, responding to video chunk requests from hundreds or thousands of clients concurrently.

A well-known approach to making disk access more efficient for applications that access files sequentially is to perform larger reads, by prefetching data before it has been requested. In prior work we observed that the *serialization* of reads may also be important in some contexts [33, 34]. In particular, we found that a modification to a web server (the userver) to both aggressively prefetch, by performing large reads, *and* to serialize its reads, yielded large performance improvements on FreeBSD. Requests are serialized by not permitting new `read` or `sendfile` system calls for data from video files for one client until the previous request (from another client) has completed. Serialization can be beneficial if the operating system breaks large reads into smaller I/O buffer-sized reads, and if sequences of these smaller reads from concurrently-issued large read requests can get interleaved inside the operating system. This prior work did not investigate whether the approach of combining aggressive prefetching with serialization could yield similarly large benefits for other web servers or on other operating systems.

Implementing techniques for improving disk access efficiency inside the application requires detailed knowledge of the application code, and must be repeated for each application of interest. This could be quite difficult for applications with large code bases like Apache and nginx. On the other hand, a kernel implementation is operating system specific, requires detailed knowledge of the relevant pieces of kernel code, and has the additional problem of potential adverse impacts on other types of applications.

In this paper, we address the problem of improving disk access efficiency in HTTP video streaming servers by developing an application-level shim library in which applicable techniques can be implemented. We then apply this library to evaluate the performance improvements provided by aggressive prefetching and serialization, for the widely used Apache and nginx web servers as well as the userver, and two operating systems (FreeBSD, Linux).

Our contributions are as follows:

- We design and implement Libception, a portable, application-level shim library that implements techniques for improving disk I/O efficiency. We demonstrate that web servers can achieve the benefits of these techniques simply by linking with Libception, without the need for source code changes. Comparing a web server that we had modified to incorporate the techniques directly, and the unmodified server linked with Libception, we find essentially identical performance.
- We show that the aggressive prefetching and disk I/O serialization techniques currently implemented in Libception can approximately double the peak HTTP video streaming throughput of a variety of web servers (Apache, nginx, and the userver), both on FreeBSD, and on Linux when using the default kernel parameter settings, regardless of which Linux disk scheduler is chosen.
- We apply Libception to address the question of whether aggressive prefetching by itself is sufficient on Linux, or whether combining aggressive prefetching with serialization provides substantial further performance benefits. We find that combining the techniques yields substantially better performance than aggressive prefetching (or serialization) alone.
- We discover that there is great scope for improving HTTP video streaming performance on Linux, when not using Libception, by tuning kernel parameters. In particular, by tuning parameters to improve both prefetching and serialization, we find that peak throughput can be more than doubled, yielding peak throughput slightly higher than that obtained with Libception. In contrast, when using Libception, kernel parameter tuning yields only marginal additional improvements.

2. BACKGROUND AND RELATED WORK

HTTP streaming video workloads are typically disk-bound due to the large size of video files and the tendency of the popularity distributions of these files to have a very long tail (meaning the large majority of content is accessed infrequently) [13]. There are three general techniques for improving the bottleneck of disk performance: file caching, disk scheduling and prefetching. Our research is primarily interested in the effects of request scheduling and prefetching. File caching plays a significant role in improving server throughput for our workload, but competes with prefetching for system memory resources [5]. For the purposes of our experiments, we simply use the kernel file caching algorithm as-is.

In the following sections we describe prior work for disk scheduling and prefetching, and discuss how the results apply to an HTTP streaming video workload. We also specifically discuss handling concurrent I/O streams, because the bulk of the research into scheduling and prefetching assumes a single-threaded workload (which is not consistent with our workload).

2.1 Block I/O Scheduling

Block I/O schedulers play a major role in most modern operating systems, and typically act as a layer between user I/O requests and requests to block device drivers. As of kernel version 2.6.33, Linux provides three different default options for scheduling block I/O devices: NOOP, deadline, and completely fair queuing (CFQ). All three schedulers attempt to take advantage of different aspects of temporal and spatial locality between requests in order to yield higher throughput for disk-bound workloads.

The NOOP scheduler is the least complicated of the Linux schedulers. It provides a simple first-in-first-out (FIFO) queue for requests, and also performs basic request merging [2]. The deadline scheduler maintains sector-sorted read and write queues, as well as queues which are organized by expiration times. The deadline scheduler gives priority to expired requests in the secondary queues, and otherwise batches requests from the sector-sorted queues. It is tailored towards workloads that require latency guarantees on I/O requests [2]. CFQ divides access to the disk into time slices which are allocated between groups of per-process request queues and sized by process priority. CFQ idles shortly on empty queues whose time-slices have not expired, even if other queues contain outstanding requests [2].

Linux previously offered an anticipatory scheduler (AS), which was introduced as a means to eliminate "deceptive idleness". Deceptive idleness occurs when processes leave a small data processing gap between I/O requests. During this time, naive schedulers may switch to servicing other processes, introducing seeks that can degrade system performance [11]. The abilities of AS are mostly a subset of CFQ, and as such AS was removed in version 2.6.33 of the Linux kernel [3].

The schedulers built into the Linux kernel are necessarily designed to handle a wide range of workloads. However, there are characteristics of streaming video workloads that can be exploited by specialized scheduling algorithms. There are many studies, aimed at broadcast streaming scenarios in which servers push data to clients, where scheduling is used as a means to maximize throughput [29, 9, 7]. These studies contain valuable insights, but are not directly applicable to HTTP streaming video servers, where clients individually pull requests from the server. As we will demonstrate experimentally, the choice of block I/O scheduler is not very important for HTTP streaming video workloads. Regardless of which scheduler is chosen, significant throughput benefits are gained from the use of other techniques to improve I/O.

2.2 Prefetching

Prefetching is a well-studied technique, and refers to reading data from the disk into memory before it is actually requested by the user. This allows subsequent read requests to return immediately instead of blocking on disk operations. Prior research has shown the effectiveness of using prefetching as a means of off-setting latency and CPU stalls [22, 6,

36]. Papathanasiou and Scott demonstrated that aggressive prefetching (prefetching far beyond what is requested by the user) can be used to offset request latency [20]. However, latency of disk access is not a significant concern for HTTP streaming video workloads. Clients use buffering to cope with potentially high network latencies, so lower latencies incurred by disk I/O are unlikely to affect the quality of service experienced by end users.

Instead, HTTP streaming video would benefit from using prefetching as a vehicle for increasing disk throughput. Examples of systems that have studied prefetching within this context are DiskSeen, a system that modifies the Linux kernel to introduce history-aware prefetching into the operating system [12], and libprefetch, which uses both kernel and application modifications to provide application-directed prefetching [35]. Unlike previous work, our research considers disk request serialization in combination with highly aggressive prefetching, and does not require code changes at the user level nor in the kernel.

Prefetching is commonly performed at the hardware level, in addition to the software level. We refer to prefetching done by the disk itself as "lookahead". Ruemmler and Wilkes demonstrated that lookahead could improve read times by up to 42% on Unix-based systems [27], and subsequently showed that effective use of on-disk caches for lookahead can yield optimal results for sequential workloads by eliminating unnecessary rotational delays [26].

An important issue in prefetching concerns how much data to request with each read operation. A larger prefetch amortizes the overhead cost of a disk access over more bytes of data but can have adverse consequences, such as the eviction of useful data from the cache. Panagiotakis, et al. [19] demonstrate that using a large fixed prefetch size to service 100 sequential streams improves throughput by up to 4 times compared to not prefetching. Li, et al. [14] provide a 2-competitive algorithm that uses hard drive performance specifications to determine a prefetch size. In prior work, we found that the best prefetch size depends on both available system resources and specific workload characteristics [32]. We provide an automated algorithm for dynamically determining a good prefetch size [32], and we demonstrate that it is possible to further increase the efficiency of servicing a streaming video workload by exploiting knowledge of specific workload characteristics to implement a prefetch algorithm [31]. For this paper, we implement a simple prefetch algorithm in Libception that uses fixed-size prefetches, with a default size of 2 MB (we experiment with different fixed prefetch sizes in Sections 5.4 and 5.5). In the future, for use in a production server or for different workloads, we could implement an automated workload-specific prefetch algorithm in Libception.

2.3 Concurrent I/O Streams

It is important to consider the trade-off between reading from disk efficiently using large prefetches and servicing concurrent disk requests fairly. Panagiotakis et. al demonstrated rapid degradation of I/O throughput as additional I/O streams are introduced across a variety of Linux schedulers [19].

The Argon system [37] focused on meeting service-level agreements by using disk-head time-slicing to ensure minimum levels of throughput to competing applications. Unlike Argon's target workload, HTTP streaming video workloads only require that clients avoid re-buffering (it is not uncommon for clients to buffer about 5 – 30 seconds of video [1, 4]). Because HTTP streaming clients are insensitive to disk latency, there is scope to reduce fairness between individual clients in exchange for higher disk throughput.

We will demonstrate that, by using request serialization in combination with aggressive prefetching, we can achieve significantly higher HTTP streaming video server throughput than if we were to allow the system to process the I/O requests in parallel.

3. DESIGN AND IMPLEMENTATION

We developed a library shim, Libception, that provides applications with the necessary capabilities for both I/O serialization and aggressive prefetching without the need for source code or kernel modifications.

Our library is portable, operates in user space, and has been tested on FreeBSD, Linux and Mac OS X. It is comprised of two components: The first component is Deception, a dynamically linked shared object which inserts itself between the application and libc calls. Deception intercepts I/O requests from the application and forwards them to the system's second component, Reception. Reception is a server process that runs separately from applications using Deception. Reception receives, services, and responds to requests generated by applications using Deception (including prefetching data when necessary). Figure 1 shows a high-level overview of the components of Libception.

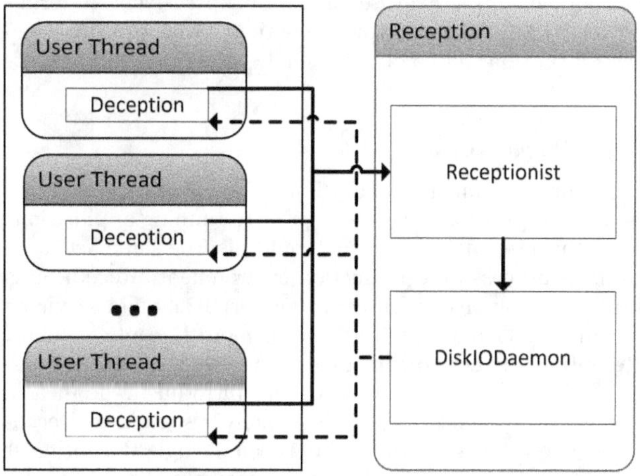

Figure 1: Libception design

3.1 Deception

Deception is the primary interface for communication between user applications and the Libception library. It is implemented as a shared object that is dynamically linked at launch-time by the application that wishes to make use of it (for example by using the `LD_PRELOAD` environment variable on most Unix-based operating systems). Once loaded, Deception begins silently intercepting calls to a variety of libc I/O-related functions including `open`, `read` and `sendfile`. This technique allows applications to take advantage of the Libception library's benefits without requiring any source code modifications. Furthermore, because Deception is implemented in user space, it requires no changes to the underlying operating system.

Most calls to Deception perform several validity checks, and then determine whether or not the application's I/O request is already resident in the system's file cache. This is done by using the system calls `mmap` and `mincore` to check all memory blocks of the request (excluding blocks that would be prefetched if the request went to disk). If a request is found to be contained entirely in memory, Deception passes the call to the original libc function (which returns without needing to go to disk). Otherwise, disk I/O is required, and a Libception I/O request is constructed and sent to Reception using Unix sockets (which duplicates any necessary file descriptors).

Should a disk read be necessary, Deception waits on a response from Reception before it proceeds. To ensure transparency, Deception always finishes by executing the application's original libc call and returning to it the appropriate return codes (even if a parameter input fails sanity checks). This allows Deception to run invisibly, without affecting the guarantees of the API for the associated libc call. This in turn means that the application can expect the same control and user-functionality for libc I/O calls that it would be afforded if Libception was not being employed.

Some additional non-I/O libc functions are also intercepted by Deception (such as `getpid` and `fork`). These functions are intercepted for functionality purposes, do not communicate with the Reception layer, and are also invisible to the user (as they terminate by making the original libc calls as well). All initialization for Deception is handled transparently at launch by GCC constructor functions and all cleanup is likewise handled unobtrusively at termination by GCC deconstructor functions which are run when the Libception shared object is loaded and unloaded, respectively.

3.2 Reception

In our experiments, Reception is launched as a separate user space process by the user, prior to running applications with the Deception shim. It could also be launched as a daemon process in a production environment. Reception is primarily responsible for accepting, serializing and servicing incoming I/O requests from one or more Deception shims. Reception furthermore modifies requests as necessary (for example, by enlarging read sizes to introduce readahead), executes the prefetch itself, and finally responds to Deception. These tasks are divided between a single Receptionist thread, and one or more DiskIODaemon threads.

The Receptionist thread acts as a server, accepting requests over Unix sockets. I/O requests received by the Receptionist thread are sorted by device, and are placed in one of multiple queues to be serviced by the appropriate DiskIODaemon thread. The Receptionist server thread also may delegate requests to a separate maintenance thread that performs utility tasks, such as statistics collection and aggregation.

DiskIODaemon threads are responsible for performing I/O for different devices. By default, Reception runs in a single DiskIODaemon mode, with all requests being serviced sequentially in the system by one thread. Alternatively, the user may set Reception to create individual DiskIODaemon threads for individual devices in the system. In this case, the Receptionist de-multiplexes incoming I/O requests to the DiskIODaemon threads based on the underlying device for the file descriptor in the request.

Regardless of which mode is selected, DiskIODaemon threads each use their own lock-protected request queue, which is filled by the Receptionist, and drained by the DiskIODaemon thread. Only one request is removed from this queue at a time by the DiskIODaemon thread, ensuring that I/O to whichever device it is servicing is serialized. As requests are pulled from this queue, they are expanded to include any necessary prefetch information, and are then sent to disk. Once finished servicing the request, the DiskIODaemon thread sends a message to the Deception shim that made the request, allowing it to unblock and proceed.

Libception additionally contains options that allow it to perform prefetch-free serialization, serialization-free prefetching, and simple request tracking without either serialization or prefetching (useful, for instance, in latency profiling or other statistics gathering). Serialization-only mode indicates to Libception not to extend reads provided by the user and is identical to prefetching with a prefetch size of zero. Prefetch-only mode transfers the burden of extending and performing requests from Reception to Deception. In this mode, instead of communicating with Reception, Deception shims simply immediately extend their requests and perform application-side `pread` calls before completing the original I/O request.

4. EXPERIMENTAL METHODOLOGY

We used the methodology described in [33] to generate experimental workloads and benchmarks. Our workload represents a large number of HTTP streaming video clients requesting videos with characteristics similar to requests for YouTube videos in 2011. We use a small number of client machines to generate traffic simulating thousands of concurrent sessions. Each session represents an end user viewing video. The video selected for each session is chosen using a Zipf distribution with an α value of 0.8. This video is watched for some fraction of its duration. It is an important characteristic of video workloads that users do not typically watch to the end of a video, so this property is reflected in our workloads: The percentage of a video that any given user requests is in line with the watching patterns of a typical YouTube-like workload.

Another important characteristic of our workload is that the network is not the primary bottleneck. Netflix, for example, uses Open Connect Appliance (OCA) servers that have operational throughputs between 9 Gbps and 36 Gbps [16], but are provisioned with up to 40 Gbps of network capacity [18]. Instead, the workload is heavily disk-bound. This can be seen in the findings of our recent work characterizing the properties of a Netflix video workload [31]. Video providers maintain a large catalogue of content in order to appeal to a broad audience. Netflix, for instance, has a catalogue which is approximately 2 Petabytes in size [31]. Large video libraries have long tails [13], meaning they contain a large amount of infrequently viewed content. Cost effective storage is achieved by storing videos on large, inexpensive HDDs and the infrequent access means that the data being requested must be serviced from disk.

Videos are stored on the server hard drives by storing each video in a separate file. We stored data for a video in a single file rather than multiple chunks because we found this approach is more efficient in prior experiments [34]. The disk is populated with 20,000 video files which have an average duration of 265 seconds, with a similar distribution as

YouTube videos [8]. The files represent videos with a fixed bit rate of 420 kbps. This bit rate was chosen based on information available at the time of creation of the benchmark [10]. With these duration and bit rate characteristics, our average file size is 13 MB.

Each client session consists of a sequence of requests for 10 second intervals of video data, which are 0.5 MB in size. The first three requests in a session are made as quickly as the server can deliver the results, then subsequent requests are made on a fixed 10 second interval. This represents the filling of a playout buffer at the beginning of a session, followed by requests to refill the buffer as it is consumed at the bit rate of the video. This is a simplified model of a pull-based video client; it does not attempt to represent user actions like pausing the video, skipping to different points in the playback, or changing the quality level of the video. These actions were rare in the YouTube workload we modelled, but our methodology is flexible enough that we could represent these actions for workloads where they are significant.

The average duration of a video session is 160 seconds, using a distribution derived from real-world measurements. During experiments, video sessions are started at a chosen rate, using a Poisson distribution for session initiation. Experiments consist of 14,400 sessions, with a maximum of about 650 concurrent sessions. A total of 118 GB of video data is requested from 6581 different videos. Each video is viewed 2.2 times on average and 67.8% of videos are requested a single time during the experiment.

The clients monitor the service time for each request, and if it takes longer than 10 seconds to completely receive the data from a request, the client terminates the session and stops making further requests. For our experiments, we are interested in determining the highest aggregate client request rate that can be serviced, so that we can compare different web servers and configurations. To determine this rate, the *maximum failure-free rate*, we conduct a number of benchmark runs with a range of different aggregate rates of requests. From this, we determine the highest rate that results in fewer than 0.3% session failures. This value was chosen to permit clients to perform a small but very limited amount of re-buffering.

The clients are connected to the server over a local area network with high bandwidth and low delay. To better represent the conditions available to real-world users, we use dummynet [23], which allows us to simulate different network types. We throttle 50% of client sessions in the workload to 3.5 Mbps, and the other 50% of client sessions to 10.0 Mbps, in order to represent a mix of end-user cable and DSL access speeds. Furthermore, we add 50 ms of delay to the network in each direction in order to model more realistic wide-area network conditions.

The equipment and environment we use to conduct our experiments were selected to ensure that network and processor resources are not a limiting factor in the experiments. We use two server machines, one for FreeBSD experiments and the other for Linux experiments. Both are HP DL380 G5 systems which contain two four-core Intel E5400 2.8 GHz processors and 8 GB of RAM. The Linux system uses Ubuntu 12.04 with a Linux 3.2.0 kernel, and a Western Digital Red (WDC WD10EFRX) 1.0 TB 5,400 RPM 3.5 inch SATA3 disk to store video files (chosen for its combination of relatively high throughput and low power consumption). The FreeBSD system uses FreeBSD 8.0 and stores videos on an HP 146 GB 10,000 RPM 2.5 inch SAS disk. We use FreeBSD 8.0 so we can try to match the performance obtained previously with a modified web server [33]. Video files accessed during experiments are stored on a separate disk from the operating system.

Four client machines are used to generate the load of thousands of viewers on the servers. Each of these systems contains either dual 2.4 or dual 2.8 GHz Xeon processors and 2 GB or 3 GB of memory. Client machines run Ubuntu 10.04 on top of version 2.6.32-30 of the Linux kernel. They also use a version of httperf [15] that was modified locally to support new features in a workload generation module named wsesslog. These modifications also allow the clients to track additional statistics. All clients are connected to the server via multiple 1 Gbps network links through multiple 24-port switches, helping to further ensure that the network is not a bottleneck.

5. PERFORMANCE EVALUATION

We now evaluate the maximum failure free throughput (often referred to henceforth as throughput) of the Apache, nginx, and userver web servers while utilizing Libception on FreeBSD and Linux servers. In all cases, we have tuned the web server to the best of our ability so that it provides the greatest maximum failure free throughput. Unless otherwise specified, the prefetch size used by Libception is 2 MB (we examine other sizes in Sections 5.4 and 5.5).

5.1 Evaluation on FreeBSD

In previous work [33, 34] we demonstrated how modifications to the userver web server to perform asynchronous serialized aggressive prefetching (ASAP) within the application significantly increased server throughput when servicing streaming video workloads. Unfortunately, these benefits rely on modifying the web server to use the `SF_NODISKIO` option [25] to the `sendfile` system call which is only available on FreeBSD. This flag causes `sendfile` calls that would block on disk I/O to instead return EBUSY.

The basic architecture of the userver using ASAP is to have a separate thread which performs large disk reads (thus implementing asynchronous, serialized, aggressive prefetching). This was relatively straightforward in the userver because it integrates well with its event-driven architecture and we were very familiar with the relatively small code base of the userver.

In this section we are interested in providing similar benefits to the more widely used Apache and nginx web servers without directly modifying either application. Note that nginx running on FreeBSD is of interest because the servers in the Netflix Open Connect Content Delivery Network use nginx on FreeBSD [17]. This is particularly relevant because Netflix currently accounts for a large fraction of peak Internet traffic in the United States [28].

We avoid making code modifications to the web servers because they each have a much larger code base than the userver and because Apache uses a significantly different software architecture (thread-per connection) [21]. Additionally, we want to determine if Libception can improve web server performance without using the non-portable `SF_NODISKIO` option to the `sendfile` system call.

Figure 2 shows the maximum failure free throughput obtained when using each of the Apache (labelled "A"), nginx (labelled "N") and userver (labelled "U") web servers. Throughput is shown without Libception (labelled "Vanilla"), when using Libception (labelled "Libception"), and for the modified version of the userver that uses the SF_NODISKIO option (labelled "ASAP"). Additionally, this graph shows both the disk throughput and the web server throughput as observed by all of the client machines.

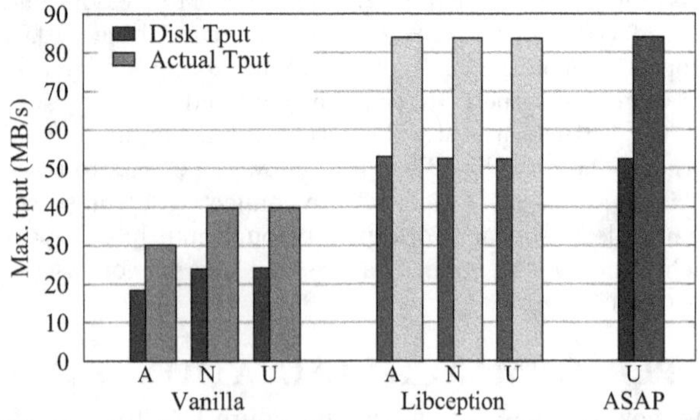

Figure 2: FreeBSD throughput without and with Libception and with ASAP

These results show that Libception is able to more than double disk throughput and total server throughput for all three web servers. As well, when using Libception, the maximum failure free throughput obtained by each server is equal to that obtained by the modified ASAP userver. This is despite Libception's use of `mincore` prior to each call to `sendfile` (rather than relying on the non-portable SF_NODISKIO option) to determine whether or not data needs to be prefetched before calling `sendfile`. Although previous work reports that `mincore` call overhead can be significant [24], these video server workloads are disk-bound and can therefore easily tolerate the increase in CPU overhead.

It is worth pointing out that, in these experiments, not all of the data that is requested needs to be read from disk. For example, two clients requesting the same video content in quick succession will only require the data to be read from disk one time. Therefore, the difference between the total server throughput and the disk throughput is due to file system cache hits.

To the best of our knowledge, the version of FreeBSD used for these experiments does not provide any options to control the block I/O scheduler. There were also relatively few options available to influence kernel prefetching decisions and we were not able to significantly improve throughput using kernel parameters.

5.2 Evaluation on Linux

As noted previously, one of the key goals of Libception is to provide improved throughput for HTTP video web servers using techniques that are portable across different Unix-based operating systems. As a result, we now examine the performance of Apache, nginx and the userver on Linux. Recall that the disks used on the FreeBSD and Linux systems are different so we can not compare performance across the different operating systems.

Figure 3 shows the disk throughput and maximum failure free throughput obtained using each of the different web servers on Linux running with and without Libception. As was the case for FreeBSD, Libception again provides significant improvements in disk and server throughput. On Linux server throughput is increased by a factor of about 2.5 times when using Libception.

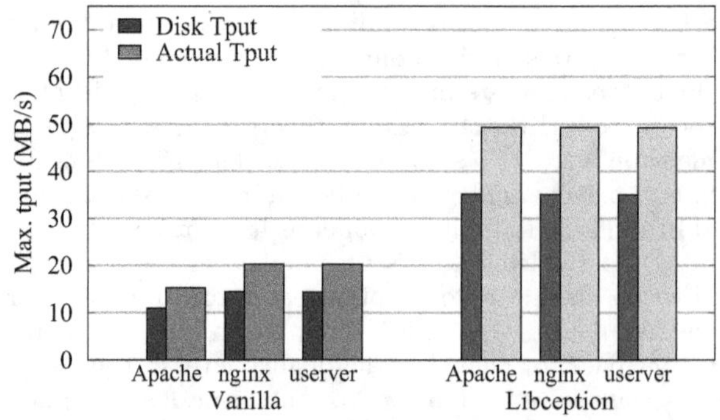

Figure 3: Linux throughput without and with Libception

To our surprise, despite years of research on prefetching techniques in operating systems, these applications and workloads do not appear to perform very well on either FreeBSD or Linux.

5.3 Evaluating Linux Block I/O Schedulers

The default Linux configuration on our system uses the CFQ block I/O scheduler [2]. We expected that the anticipatory nature of the Linux CFQ scheduler might be well-suited to this workload. Because web servers simultaneously process requests from thousands of clients, we expected that blocks from different requests might provide reordering opportunities that could be exploited by CFQ to improve disk and server throughput. For completeness we now examine the performance of all web servers with each of the three block I/O schedulers available in Linux. Figure 4 shows the throughput obtained without Libception while using the CFQ (labelled "C"), deadline (labelled "D") and NOOP (labelled "N") schedulers. Figure 5 shows the results obtained using the same schedulers but this time while using Libception.

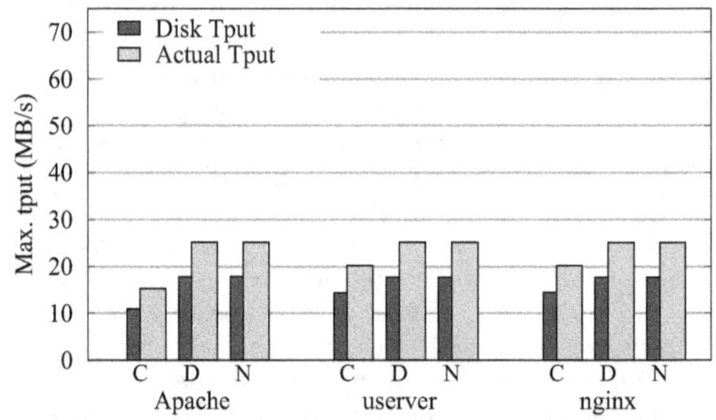

Figure 4: Servers without Libception using different block I/O schedulers

Interestingly, Figure 4 shows that without Libception the server throughput is slightly higher with the deadline and NOOP schedulers than with the CFQ scheduler. On the other hand, when using Libception (see Figure 5) all web servers obtain the same maximum failure free throughput of nearly 50 MB/second regardless of the block I/O scheduler used. We believe that this is because Libception is serializing all of the reads that go to disk and as a result the schedulers only ever see a single outstanding request, which leaves no room for scheduling policies to make a difference. Note that we have spent some time attempting to adjust the parameters designed to control the behaviour of the deadline and CFQ block I/O schedulers. We did not see throughput improvements when compared with the default values.

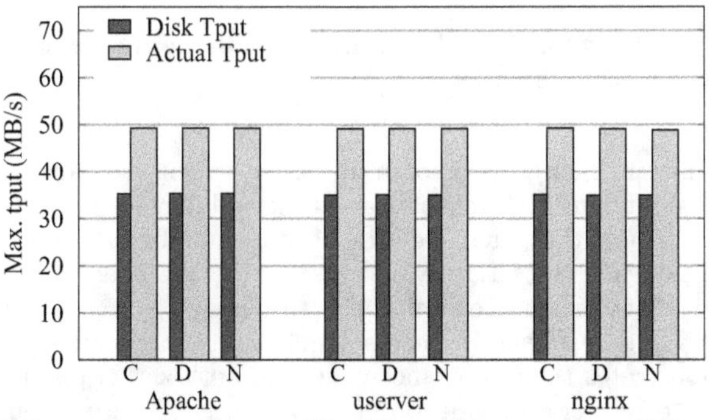

Figure 5: Servers with Libception using different block I/O schedulers

In summary, the different schedulers do not significantly improve web server throughput on this workload. More importantly, Libception provides significant increases in throughput that are not possible using the block I/O scheduling algorithms.

5.4 Evaluation Insights

In this section we first conduct a sequence of experiments designed to understand the relative importance of the prefetching and serialization components of Libception. For the remainder of the paper we focus solely on the nginx server and the CFQ block I/O scheduler. We chose nginx because it is used by Netflix for serving HTTP video streaming workloads. We chose CFQ because it is the default block I/O scheduler on our Linux server and because the schedulers did not significantly affect performance when using Libception (see Figure 5).

Figure 6 shows the maximum failure free throughput obtained using nginx without Libception (labelled "Vanilla"), with Libception using only serialization (labelled "Serialized"), with Libception using only prefetching (labelled "Prefetching"), and with Libception using both serialization and prefetching (labelled "Libception"). As can be seen in this figure, serialization alone actually reduces throughput. We believe that this is primarily due to the relatively small size of reads that the application performs. These small reads, in conjunction with serialization, result in small requests being issued one at a time, which causes very poor performance. On the other hand, using prefetching without serialization does significantly increase both disk and server throughput when compared with the "Vanilla" server. Finally, by combining both aggressive prefetching and serialization, a further increase of approximately 25% beyond that of prefetching is alone is achieved. These experiments demonstrate that, while aggressive prefetches are essential, the full potential of Libception is not realized unless the requests to the disk are serialized.

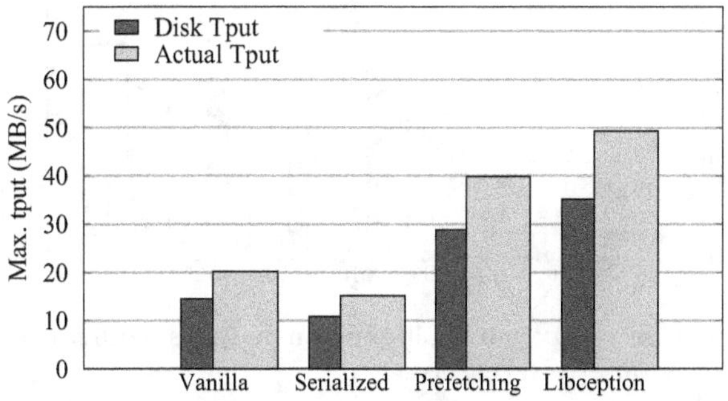

Figure 6: nginx Vanilla, and nginx with Libception using serialization only, prefetching only, and both

In previous work [33, 34] and in all experiments in this paper up to this point, the prefetch size was set to 2 MB. We now examine a range of prefetch sizes and study the impact on the throughput of nginx while using Libception with prefetching but without serialization (see Figure 7) and with both prefetching and serialization (see Figure 8)

Figure 7 shows that, without serialization, throughput does not improve until a prefetch size of 2 MB or greater is used. It also demonstrates that prefetch sizes of 3 and 4 MB provide slightly better throughput than a prefetch size of 2 MB.

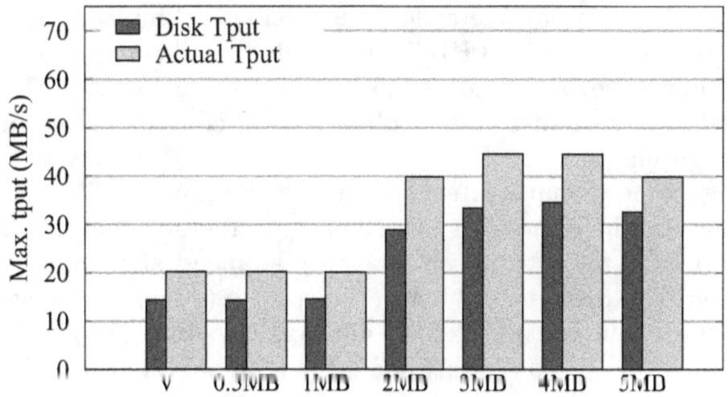

Figure 7: nginx with Libception using various prefetch sizes (no serialization)

Figure 8 shows that when using Libception, with both serialization and prefetching, small prefetch reads actually slightly reduce server throughput. However a prefetch size of 1 MB does significantly improve server throughput, which is not the case when prefetching is used without serialization. When using both serialization and prefetching, throughput peaks with prefetch sizes of 2 – 4 MB, and also shows that serialization provides additional benefits (about 10%) when compared with prefetching alone.

5.5 Using Insights to Improve Linux

We now use the insights obtained from the previous section to modify Linux kernel parameters in an attempt to improve the performance of nginx when running on Linux without the use of Libception. The question being examined

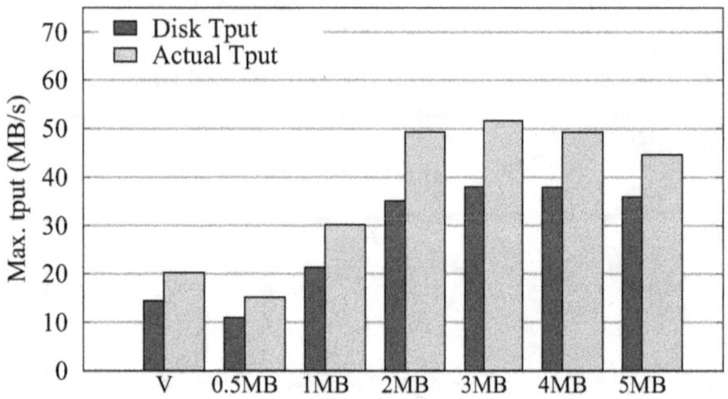

Figure 8: nginx with Libception using serialization and various prefetch sizes

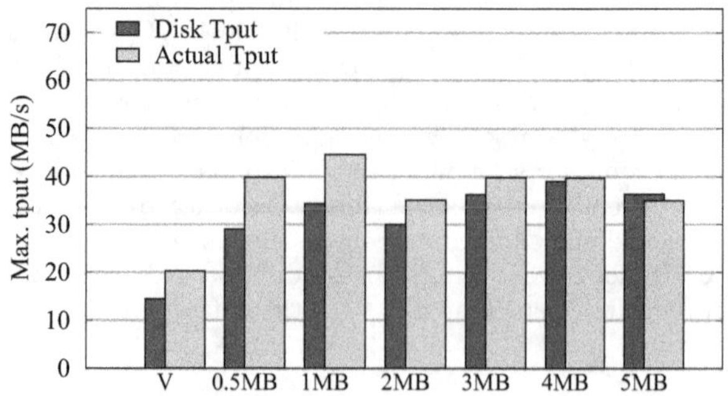

Figure 9: nginx without Libception using various `read_ahead_kb` sizes

is: can we find and tune appropriate Linux kernel parameters in order to obtain throughput that equals that obtained using Libception?

It was not too difficult to find a Linux kernel parameter that we were able to adjust to increase the amount of data being read from disk by the kernel. When obtaining data from disk the Linux kernel may (depending on several factors the details of which aren't relevant to this discussion) extend the read beyond what the user has requested. Roughly speaking, a readahead size is tracked per file and under proper conditions grows for each successive read. However, the maximum readahead size for all files on a device is limited by the kernel parameter `read_ahead_kb`, which can be set differently for each device. The default setting for this parameter for the version of Linux used in our experiments is 128 KB. This is quite small compared to the aggressive prefetches we use in Libception (e.g., 2 MB in many cases) in order to obtain significant increases in throughput.

Figure 9 demonstrates how the throughput of nginx changes as the value of the readahead parameter is increased. As an example of how we set the readahead size to 1024 KB on disk drive used to store video files (`/dev/sdb1`), we use the command `blockdev -setra 1024 /dev/sdb1`. As can be seen in this graph, `read_ahead_kb` values of 0.5 MB and 1 MB provide significant improvements over the default value of 128 KB (labelled "V" for Vanilla). Larger values for `read_ahead_kb` do not perform as well as 1 MB. While throughput obtained with 1 MB is about 45 MB/second it is not as high as that obtained using Libception (50 MB/second). Understanding why this is the case involved significantly more work.

Although the size of the prefetch for files were actually reaching the limit imposed by `read_ahead_kb`, using the Linux `blktrace` facility we were able to determine that requests to the disk were being limited to 512 KB. We believe that, as a result, some requests for reads to different files were being interleaved (this is similar to the Libception case where prefetching is used but serialization is not).

By examining the Linux kernel source we were eventually able to determine that another kernel parameter was placing further limits on the size of reads. This value `/sys/block/sdb/queue/max_sectors_kb` (for the disk `/dev/sdb`) uses the default size of 512 KB. We expect that the default values for these two limits (`read_ahead_kb` and `max_sectors_kb`) are chosen in order to ensure fairness across different disk requests and to keep latencies low.

To ensure that `max_sectors_kb` does not limit the size of disk reads we set its value to 16 MB. We then adjust `read_ahead_kb` and examine the throughput obtained by nginx. Figure 10 shows the results of these experiments and demonstrates the importance of setting both kernel parameters to proper values in order to obtain good throughput on this workload. In this case a `read_ahead_kb` size of 1 or 2 MB, now results in throughput of about 58 MB/second, which is slightly better than that obtained using Libception.

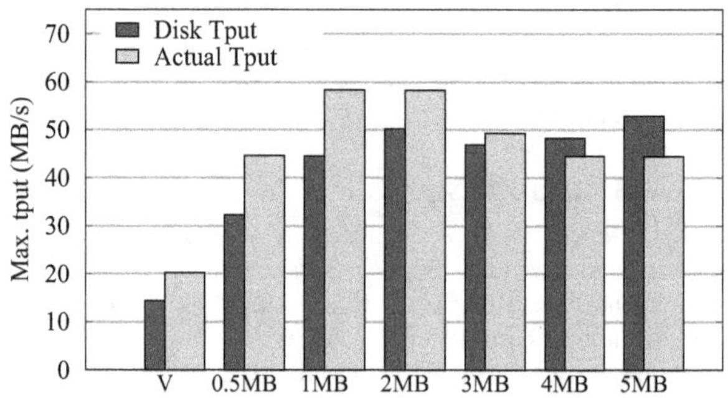

Figure 10: nginx without Libception using various `read_ahead_kb` sizes, with `max_sectors_kb` = 16 MB

Figure 11 now shows results obtained using Libception in addition to using modified Linux kernel parameters. In this case `max_sectors_kb` is set to 16 MB to ensure that it does not limit read sizes and the Libception prefetch size and `read_ahead_kb` are adjusted together using the values shown along the x-axis of the graphs. The column labelled "V" is showing the vanilla case where nginx runs without Libception and the default kernel parameter values are used. Although these results show a slight improvement in maximum failure free throughput when compared with just using Libception, they are still lower than adjusting the kernel parameters alone and not using Libception.

We observe that for some configurations of the experiments conducted in this section, the disk throughput exceeds the total server throughput. In these cases data that is being prefetched is actually being evicted before it is requested by and sent to the client. This means that, for the amount of memory in the current system, prefetching has become too

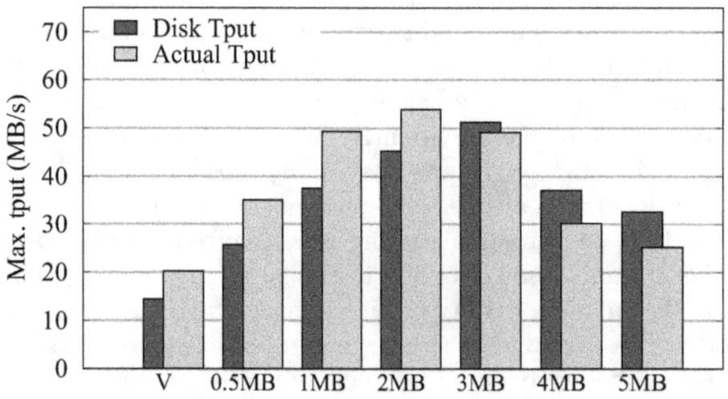

Figure 11: nginx with Libception using various prefetch and read_ahead_kb sizes, with max_sectors_kb = 16 MB

aggressive and is causing evictions. We expect that in these cases, increasing the amount of memory in the system will likely increase total server throughput because there will be less memory pressure created by aggressive prefetching. It seems that, in HTTP video streaming workloads, it may be more important to have memory acting as a buffer for large aggressive prefetching (in order to obtain high disk throughput) than as a file system cache.

5.6 Evaluating Latencies

When servicing HTTP video server workloads, server throughput is strongly influenced by disk throughput. This is because video services like YouTube and Netflix have large numbers of videos that are viewed infrequently (i.e., the popularity distribution of videos has a long tail). In order to improve disk throughput Libception prefetches relatively large amounts of data and serializes access to each disk. This naturally increases disk throughput while potentially increasing latencies for some requests. The potential for increased latencies should be relatively harmless when servicing video server workloads because clients are designed to be able to tolerate fairly significant latencies by using a play out buffer. The play out buffer is filled before play begins and is used to seamlessly continue playing the video even during periods where the client may experience latencies due to the network or HTTP server. For example, a client with a 10 second play out buffer can tolerate nearly 10 seconds of latency for some requests. As long as the data being requested arrives (and can be decoded before) within 10 seconds of when it is requested, the user will not experience any problems.

Before delving into further empirical analysis, it is important to note that all of our results place an implicit bound on latency. Client timeouts occur when a request has not received a corresponding response after 10 seconds. This latency includes the time to transmit the request, service the request at the server, and transmit the response. Therefore, if a client completes a session without errors, all of the latencies must have been acceptable.

In order to better understand the latencies incurred by using Libception and the aggressive tunings of Linux kernel parameters that support high server throughput, we now examine the latencies experienced by server processes. We use an existing system call tracing facility that exists in the userver to record the time required for every call to **sendfile** in memory and print those times to disk after the server has finished servicing all requests. While client-side latency measurement would give an indication of end-user quality of experience, latency measurement at the server simplifies the collection process. Furthermore, as noted in Section 4, in our workload the network does not serve as a bottleneck. Therefore, server-side latencies should be reflective of client-side latencies, minus network transfer time.

Figure 12 shows the cumulative distribution function of **sendfile** call times without Libception and with default kernel parameters (labelled "Vanilla"), with Libception, and with the aggressive kernel parameter tunings. The "Vanilla" and "Libception" lines are created using data from one run with the userver using the configuration that obtains the highest error free rate (i.e., the two userver configurations used in Figure 3). The "Aggressive Kernel Params" line was created by setting **read_ahead_kb** to 2 MB and **max_sectors_kb** to 16 MB and using the same request rate as used for the configuration of nginx shown in Figure 10.

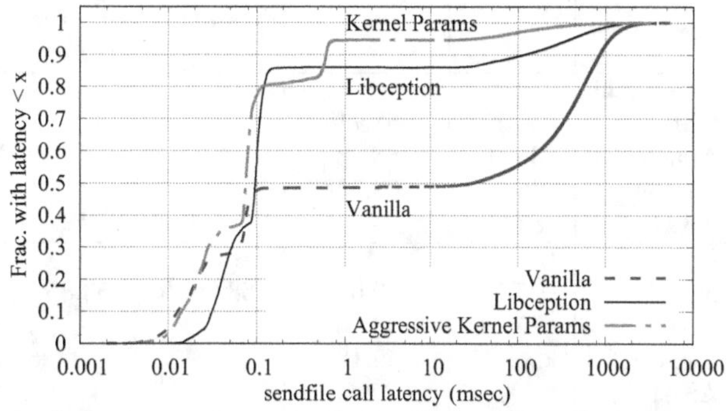

Figure 12: userver sendfile latency CDF

Figure 12 shows that Libception has the smallest density of requests that are serviced in the lowest range of latencies (i.e., below 0.1 ms). This is due to the extra overhead incurred from the **mincore** system call, which is used to determine if the data being requested is in memory or if it should be prefetched from disk. In cases where the data is already in memory, the lowest latencies are achieved by calling **sendfile** directly. For requests where the desired data is not in memory at the time of the **sendfile** call, the "Vanilla" configuration results in a blocking call to **sendfile** because the data being requested needs to be read from disk. When a disk read occurs using either Libception or aggressively tuned kernel parameters, the application-initiated read is serialized and increased in size (to 2 MB in this case) to implement prefetching. Although this incurs some overhead for that individual request, subsequent reads will often be served directly from the file system cache with comparatively low latencies. The net result is a significant reduction in latencies for a large number of **sendfile** calls. While about 49% of **sendfile** calls take less than 1 ms under the "Vanilla" configuration, about 85% of **sendfile** calls take less than 1 ms for the Libception configuration, and about 95% of **sendfile** calls take less than 1 ms for the aggressive kernel parameters configuration.

The key observation from this experiment is that, although one might expect latencies to increase because of large serialized prefetches, for this workload they actually decrease for a large number of data requests.

5.7 Evaluation Summary

Table 1 summarizes the main results from our experiments. Entries marked with an asterisk are not possible to obtain (e.g., the ASAP userver requires an option to `sendfile` that is only available on FreeBSD so it can't be run on Linux). Entries marked with "–" are not included due to space and/or because they are unlikely to provide new insights. On FreeBSD, the use of Libception more than doubled the peak server throughput for Apache, nginx and userver. We were not able to improve the poor performance achieved by these web servers without Libception by tuning FreeBSD kernel parameters. Comparing the results for the userver modified to directly incorporate aggressive prefetching and serialization (ASAP) shows that the overhead of implementing these techniques in a shim library, rather than directly, is negligible for our HTTP video streaming workload (on FreeBSD the throughput obtained with Libception for all servers matches that obtained with ASAP).

	Default	Libception	Kernel Tuning	Libception + Kernel Tuning
FreeBSD				
nginx	39.75	83.71	*	*
Apache	30.10	83.88	*	*
userver	39.74	83.56	*	*
ASAP	83.99	–	*	*
Linux				
nginx	25.11	49.06	58.29	53.85
Apache	25.18	49.26	–	–
userver	25.16	49.18	–	–
ASAP	*	*	*	*

Table 1: Summary of Results: Throughput in MB/sec.

These FreeBSD results raise the question of whether they might reflect some deficiency in the block I/O scheduler in that system. This prompted us to take a careful look at performance on Linux, which supports three different block I/O schedulers. We found that use of Libception approximately doubled the peak server throughput on Linux, for all three web servers, regardless of the choice of block I/O scheduler. However, using our insights from Libception as a guide and in some cases examining the Linux kernel source code, we were able to discover kernel parameters that we could tune to obtain slightly better performance than that with Libception. In contrast to Libception which is highly portable, we could not run our modified version of the userver on Linux since it makes use of a system call option that is not available on that system. Finally, a potential concern might be that these throughput improvements have significant cost with respect to latency, but as shown in Section 5.6 this does not appear to be the case.

6. DISCUSSION

Perhaps surprisingly, our results show that, without Libception, none of the web servers we investigated yield good performance for HTTP video streaming workloads, on either FreeBSD, or Linux with default kernel parameter settings. This finding suggests that web server implementations are still optimized for more traditional web workloads, despite the rapid growth of HTTP video streaming. Also, web server developers might assume that, after many years of research and development, prefetching (or readahead) in operating systems, to efficiently use a magnetic disk is a "solved problem", but evidently this is not the case. Although with Linux, it was eventually possible to achieve good performance after kernel parameter tuning, it is noteworthy that such manual tuning was required. For services like Netflix and YouTube, due to the large amounts of video available, the wide variety of bit rates at which each video is encoded, and because of the large number of videos that are viewed infrequently, it is not economically viable to store it all on SSDs. As a result, obtaining good performance when servicing video from disks is still important in these settings. We have found Libception to be a relatively simple and portable platform for implementing and evaluating techniques for improving disk I/O efficiency. In particular, using Libception we were able to readily evaluate the benefits of aggressive prefetching and I/O serialization for HTTP video streaming workloads, using multiple web servers and operating systems.

As demonstrated in Section 5.4 and Section 5.5, selecting a prefetch size which is too small results in low disk throughput. Likewise, selecting a prefetch size which is too large leads to a drop in system throughput. As a result obtaining peak server throughput requires choosing the most appropriate prefetch size. In previous work we have demonstrated how the best prefetch size and the benefits obtained from prefetching are sensitive to workload and system properties [32]. We show how the best prefetch size can be affected by the amount of available system memory, the distribution of the popularity of videos requested, hard drive characteristics, and the bit rates of files being served.

In order to avoid having to exhaustively and repeatedly determine the best prefetch size when workload or system characteristics change, we have designed an algorithm for dynamically and automatically adjusting the prefetch size with the goal of obtaining peak server throughput [32]. We demonstrate that a gradient descent algorithm, which minimizes a score based on a combination of disk transfer times and file system cache miss ratio, is effective at selecting prefetching sizes that result in high server throughput. This adaptive algorithm results in throughputs that rival those obtained by exhaustive manual tuning across a variety of different workload and system characteristics. We believe that such a strategy could be added to Libception, allowing it to continue providing high throughput while also eliminating the need to manually set a prefetch size.

In more recent work [30, 31] we have analyzed log files of HTTP requests to characterize the workloads of two different types of production Netflix servers. We use simulation to show that workload-specific adjustments can be used to increase server throughput. However, some of these improvements require knowledge of request streams and other information about the workload that may be difficult to infer in Libception. An interesting question is how much information can be provided to Libception, without requiring changes to web server code and whether or not it such changes can compete with the performance that can be obtained by directly modifying the web server. We intend to explore such questions in future work.

7. CONCLUSIONS

HTTP video streaming has become an important class of web server workloads. Such workloads have quite different characteristics than the web server workloads that have been the focus of most prior work on web server performance. In particular, the requests to HTTP video streaming servers are for large chunks of data commonly stored on disk, so these servers are frequently disk-bound.

In this work, we have designed, implemented and evaluated Libception, an application-level shim library incorporating techniques for improving disk access efficiency. HTTP video streaming servers can achieve the benefits of these techniques simply by linking with Libception, without the need for any source code modification. Experiments with three web servers (Apache, nginx and the userver) and two operating systems (FreeBSD and Linux) showed that with the aggressive prefetching and disk I/O serialization techniques currently implemented in Libception, peak server throughput can be doubled. Only on Linux with kernel parameters tuned for this workload was it possible to achieve performance competitive with Libception. We believe that Libception could be fruitfully applied to investigate other techniques for improving HTTP video streaming performance, and possibly for improving the performance of other disk-intensive applications.

Acknowledgments

Brecht, Eager, and Wong thank the Natural Sciences and Engineering Research Council (NSERC) of Canada for partial support for this project through Discovery Grants. Brecht has also received an NSERC Discovery Accelerator Supplement in support of this work. Cassell, Summers and Szepesi were partially supported by NSERC graduate scholarships and Cassell and Summers were partially supported by a University of Waterloo Cheriton Scholarship. The authors would also like to thank the anonymous reviewers for their comments.

8. REFERENCES

[1] Adhikari, V. K., Guo, Y., Hao, F., Varvello, M., Hilt, V., Steiner, M., and Zhang, Z.-L. Unreeling Netflix: Understanding and improving multi-CDN movie delivery. In *Proc. IEEE International Conference on Computer Communications (INFOCOM)* (2012), pp. 1620–1628.

[2] Axboe, J. Linux block IO – present and future. In *Proc. Ottawa Linux Symposium (OLS)* (2004), pp. 51–61.

[3] Axboe, J. Linux kernel Git commit. http://git.kernel.org/cgit/linux/kernel/git/torvalds/linux.git/commit/?id=492af6350a5ccf087e4964104a276ed358811458, 2009.

[4] Begen, A., Akgul, T., and Baugher, M. Watching video over the web: Part 1: Streaming protocols. *IEEE Internet Computing 15*, 2 (2011), 54–63.

[5] Butt, A. R., Gniady, C., and Hu, Y. C. The performance impact of kernel prefetching on buffer cache replacement algorithms. In *Proc. ACM SIGMETRICS International Conference on Measurement and Modeling of Computer Systems* (2005), pp. 157–168.

[6] Cao, P., Felten, E. W., Karlin, A. R., and Li, K. Implementation and performance of integrated application-controlled file caching, prefetching, and disk scheduling. *ACM Transactions on Computer Systems (TOCS) 14*, 4 (1996), 311–343.

[7] Dhage, S. N., Patil, S. K., and Meshram, B. B. Survey on: Interactive video-on-demand (VoD) systems. In *Proc. IEEE International Conference on Circuits, Systems Communication and Information Technology Applications (CSCITA)* (2014), pp. 435–440.

[8] Finamore, A., Mellia, M., Munafò, M. M., Torres, R., and Rao, S. G. YouTube everywhere: Impact of device and infrastructure synergies on user experience. In *Proc. ACM SIGCOMM Internet Measurement Conference (IMC)* (2011), pp. 345–360.

[9] Ghose, D., and Kim, H. J. Scheduling video streams in video-on-demand systems: A survey. *Springer Multimedia Tools and Applications 11*, 2 (2000), 167–195.

[10] Gill, P., Arlitt, M., Li, Z., and Mahanti, A. Youtube traffic characterization: a view from the edge. In *Proc. ACM SIGCOMM Internet Measurement Conference (IMC)* (2007), pp. 15–28.

[11] Iyer, S., and Druschel, P. Anticipatory scheduling: A disk scheduling framework to overcome deceptive idleness in synchronous I/O. In *ACM Symposium on Operating Systems Principles (SOSP)* (2001), pp. 117–130.

[12] Jiang, S., Ding, X., Xu, Y., and Davis, K. A prefetching scheme exploiting both data layout and access history on disk. *ACM Transactions on Storage (TOS) 9*, 3 (2013), 10:1–10:23.

[13] Kasbekar, M. On efficient delivery of web content. GreenMetrics Keynote Talk, 2010.

[14] Li, C., Shen, K., and Papathanasiou, A. E. Competitive prefetching for concurrent sequential I/O. In *Proc. ACM European Conference on Computer Systems (EuroSys)* (2007), pp. 189–202.

[15] Mosberger, D., and Jin, T. httperf – a tool for measuring web server performance. *ACM SIGMETRICS Performance Evaluation Review (PER) 26*, 3 (1998), 31–37.

[16] Netflix. Appliance hardware. https://openconnect.netflix.com/en_gb/hardware, 2017.

[17] Netflix. Appliance software. https://openconnect.netflix.com/en_gb/software, 2017.

[18] Netflix. Requirements for deploying embedded appliances. https://openconnect.netflix.com/en_gb/requirements-for-deploying, 2017.

[19] Panagiotakis, G., Flouris, M. D., and Bilas, A. Reducing disk I/O performance sensitivity for large numbers of sequential streams. In *Proc. IEEE International Conference on Distributed Computing Systems (ICDCS)* (2009), pp. 22–31.

[20] Papathanasiou, A. E., and Scott, M. L. Aggressive prefetching: An idea whose time has come. In *Proc. USENIX Workshop on Hot Topics in Operating Systems (HotOS)* (2005).

[21] Pariag, D., Brecht, T., Harji, A., Buhr, P., Shukla, A., and Cheriton, D. R. Comparing the

performance of web server architectures. In *Proc. ACM European Conference on Computer Systems (EuroSys)* (2007), pp. 231–243.

[22] Patterson, R. H., Gibson, G. A., Ginting, E., Stodolsky, D., and Zelenka, J. Informed prefetching and caching. In *Proc. ACM Symposium on Operating Systems Principles (SOSP)* (1995), pp. 79–95.

[23] Rizzo, L. Dummynet: a simple approach to the evaluation of network protocols. *ACM SIGCOMM Computer Communication Review (CCR) 27*, 1 (1997), 31–41.

[24] Ruan, Y., and Pai, V. S. Making the "Box" transparent: System call performance as a first-class result. In *Proc. USENIX Annual Technical Conference (ATC)* (2004).

[25] Ruan, Y., and Pai, V. S. Understanding and addressing blocking-induced network server latency. In *Proc. USENIX Annual Technical Conference (ATC)* (2006).

[26] Ruemmler, C., , and Wilkes, J. An introduction to disk drive modeling. *IEEE Computer 27*, 3 (1994), 17–28.

[27] Ruemmler, C., and Wilkes, J. UNIX disk access patterns. In *Proc. USENIX Winter Conference* (1993), pp. 405–420.

[28] Sandvine. Global Internet phenomena report, 2012.

[29] Steinmetz, R. Multimedia file systems survey: Approaches for continuous media disk scheduling. *Elsevier Computer Communications 18*, 3 (1995), 133–144.

[30] Summers, J. *Understanding and Efficiently Servicing HTTP Streaming Video Workloads.* PhD thesis, University of Waterloo, 2016. https://uwspace.uwaterloo.ca/handle/10012/10956.

[31] Summers, J., Brecht, T., Eager, D., and Gutarin, A. Characterizing the workload of a Netflix streaming video server. In *Proc. IEEE International Symposium on Workload Characterization (IISWC)* (2016).

[32] Summers, J., Brecht, T., Eager, D., Szepesi, T., Cassell, B., and Wong, B. Automated control of aggressive prefetching for HTTP streaming video servers. In *Proc. ACM International Conference on Systems and Storage (SYSTOR)* (2014), pp. 5:1–5:11.

[33] Summers, J., Brecht, T., Eager, D., and Wong, B. Methodologies for generating HTTP streaming video workloads to evaluate web server performance. In *Proc. ACM International Systems and Storage Conference (SYSTOR)* (2012), pp. 2:1–2:12.

[34] Summers, J., Brecht, T., Eager, D., and Wong, B. To chunk or not to chunk: Implications for HTTP streaming video server performance. In *Proc. ACM International Workshop on Network and Operating System Support for Digital Audio and Video (NOSSDAV)* (2012), pp. 15–20.

[35] VanDeBogart, S., Frost, C., and Kohler, E. Reducing seek overhead with application-directed prefetching. In *Proc. USENIX Annual Technical Conference (ATC)* (2009).

[36] Varki, E., Hubbe, A., and Merchant, A. Improve prefetch performance by splitting the cache replacement queue. In *Proc. IEEE International Conference on Advanced Infocomm Technology (ICAIT)* (2012), pp. 98–108.

[37] Wachs, M., Xu, L., Kanevsky, A., and Ganger, G. R. Exertion-based billing for cloud storage access. In *Proc. USENIX Workshop on Hot Topics in Cloud Computing (HotCloud)* (2011).

An Empirical Analysis of Amazon EC2 Spot Instance Features Affecting Cost-effective Resource Procurement

Cheng Wang, Qianlin Liang, Bhuvan Urgaonkar
Pennsylvania State University
{cxw967,qxl5068,bhuvan}@cse.psu.edu

ABSTRACT

Many cost-conscious public cloud workloads ("tenants") are turning to Amazon EC2's spot instances because, on average, these instances offer significantly lower prices (up to 10 times lower) than on-demand and reserved instances of comparable advertized resource capacities. To use spot instances effectively, a tenant must carefully weigh the lower costs of these instances against their poorer availability. Towards this, we empirically study four features of EC2 spot instance operation that a cost-conscious tenant may find useful to model. Using extensive evaluation based on both historical and current spot instance data, we show shortcomings in the state-of-the-art modeling of these features that we overcome. Our analysis reveals many novel properties of spot instance operation some of which offer predictive value while others do not. Using these insights, we design predictors for our features that offer a balance between computational efficiency (allowing for online resource procurement) and cost-efficacy. We explore "case studies" wherein we implement prototypes of dynamic spot instance procurement advised by our predictors for two types of workloads. Compared to the state-of-the-art, our approach achieves (i) comparable cost but much better performance (fewer bid failures) for a latency-sensitive in-memory Memcached cache, and (ii) an additional 18% cost-savings with comparable (if not better than) performance for a delay-tolerant batch workload.

Keywords

Spot instance features, resource procurement

1. INTRODUCTION

Amazon EC2 has been offering *spot instances* [5] since 2009 and a large segment of its "tenant" workloads has come to embrace these [22]. The appeal of spot instances lies in their low prices - up to 1/10 that of *on-demand* instances of equivalent capacities. Unlike an on-demand instance, whose price changes slowly (over months or years), a spot instance has a highly dynamic price that may change as frequently as once every few minutes[1].

From a tenant's point of view, an EC2 spot instance is a virtual machine (VM) that is cheaper than its on-demand or reserved counterpart but appears to have poorer availability. In order to use spot instances effectively, a tenant must be able to model well relevant aspects of their operation: After submitting a bid, how long does it take for an instance to be ready for use? What is the expected lifetime of an instance? What would the costs be during its lifetime? What is the probability of simultaneous bid failures if the tenant places bids across spot markets? Finally, the tenant must combine these predictions with its application-specific trade-offs to devise online instance procurement algorithms[2]. Whereas such online procurement ("control") algorithms have been extensively researched recently (see Section 2.2), we find significant shortcomings in modeling and prediction of key features of spot operation that these algorithms rely upon. Overcoming these shortcomings is the goal of this study.

Research Contributions:

- We consider four key features that we think a tenant should model: (i) lifetime of an instance, (ii) average spot price during lifetime, (iii) simultaneous revocations, and (iv) startup delay. In particular, for (i) and (ii), we show that the most commonly used prediction approach (based on cumulative distribution of spot prices) fails to capture the tenant's service contiguity, and design quantitative models and computationally efficient predictors (Section 3.1). For (iii), we find that the existing approach (based on correlations of spot price traces from different markets) overlooks the tenant's bids in its prediction and thus may fail to reflect the actual likelihood of simultaneous revocations, which our technique captures well (Section 3.2). Finally, our study provides valuable first-hand data and insightful results for evaluating the predictability of (iv) (Section 3.3), which is usually ignored by prior work, and the predictive power of "effective capacity" for spot prices (Section 3.4).
- We evaluate the efficacy of our modeling and prediction in two ways. First, by using extensive real-world data, we demonstrate that our proposed models and predictors outperform the baseline approaches which are commonly used in prior work (Section 3). Second, we take two real-world case studies and adapt resource procurement algorithms from related work to demon-

[1]Although it may seem surprising to some, spot prices are known to exceed on-demand prices, sometimes significantly - see several examples in Figure 2. We surmise that this may be part of mechanisms employed by EC2 to shed increasing load on its servers hosting spot instances. Others have also reported that EC2 spot pricing seems to have elements beyond simply reflecting supply-demand relationships [1].

[2]These trade-offs would be between costs, on the one hand, and overheads of possible revocations (either in the form of fault-tolerance mechanisms or loss of performance/correctness), on the other.

ICPE'17, April 22-26, 2017, L'Aquila, Italy

DOI: http://dx.doi.org/10.1145/3030207.3030210

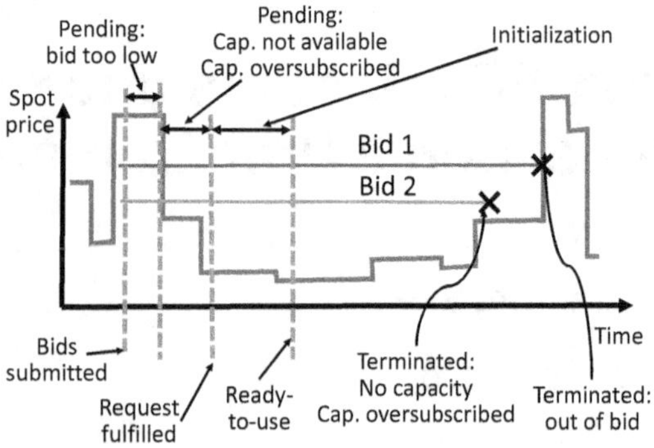

Figure 1: Illustration of spot instance operation using two hypothetical bids (Bid 1 and Bid 2).

strate how the tenants could leverage our models and predictors for cost-effective operations, as well as the improvements in performance and/or costs[3] (Section 4). Our approach offers (i) comparable cost but much better performance (fewer bid failures and lower tail latency) for a latency-sensitive in-memory Memcached workload, and (ii) an additional 18% cost-savings with comparable performance for a delay-tolerant batch workload.

- Our study reveals several novel insights about spot operation with implications for tenant control. Amongst our salient findings are: (i) Whereas raw spot prices are best considered non-stationary, most of our features exhibit short-term *temporal locality* (borrowing a phrase from caching and memory management) that can be leveraged for prediction. (ii) Exploiting spatial locality simply via cross-correlation of spot prices across markets could be misleading; it is important that the modeling of simultaneous revocations be conditioned on specific bid values. (iii) We do not find significant statistical correlation between effective capacity measurements and spot price, indicating the evolution of spot price likely depends on a spatially coarse (e.g., data center or availability zone wide) load metric.

Outline: In Section 2, we discuss the lifecycle of a spot instance and related work. In Section 3, we identify the key features and present our models and predictions. In Section 4, we provide real-world case studies to show the efficacy of our approaches. We conclude in Section 5.

2. BACKGROUND

2.1 Life of a Spot Instance

We show the key events in the life of a spot instance in Figure 1; more details can be found in [24]. We assume that Bid 1 and Bid 2 (with the former being higher) are placed at the time shown. After a tenant submits a bid, there can be a period during which its bid is strictly less than the spot price. It is quite well-known that during such a period, the tenant's request for an instance is not granted (EC2 shows the status of the tenant's request as "pending: bid too low.") It is less well-known, however, that there may sometimes be an additional delay [4] with the request status being "pending: capacity not available" or "pending: capacity oversubscribed" *even after* the spot price has fallen below the bid. According to EC2, this happens if the spot market does not have available capacity or capacity is oversubscribed. After the request is "fulfilled," EC2 launches a spot instance and "initializes" it with the tenant-specified configuration, after which the instance is "ready to use."

In Fig. 1, both the bids are fulfilled at the same time resulting in the two instances becoming ready to use at the same time. The following two ways for an instance to terminate are well-known: (i) the tenant may use the instance till its needs are met and then voluntarily terminate the instance, or (ii) the bid may fall below the spot price that would cause EC2 to revoke the instance (shown for Bid 1 with a status of "terminated: out of bid"). A third less well-known way for an instance to terminate, however, is one shown occurring for Bid 2 wherein the instance is reclaimed by EC2 allegedly due to capacity scarcity (with a status of "terminated: out of capacity" or "terminated: oversubscribed"). Startup delays or involuntary terminations due to alleged capacity scarcity are aspects of spot instance operation that bring additional complexity into their usage but have not been considered in related work.

When an instance is revoked by EC2, the tenant loses all its local state (contents of main memory and local disks of the instance). EC2 does issue a warning to the tenant before revoking a spot instance (2 minutes prior to revocation). The tenant may choose to use this warning period to save some or all of that instance's local state. Finally, it must be noted the tenant is billed based on the spot price during the instance's lifetime (and *not based on its bid*).

2.2 Related Work

Spot Price Modeling/Prediction: Prior work on spot price modeling/prediction ranges from relatively simple ones (in terms of the amount of historical data employed as well as the computational complexity of the model), e.g., auto-regressive models [1,30,36] or empirically measured cumulative distributions of key parameters [6,10,15,19,20,26,27], to more complex ones, e.g., employing Markovian models [14,17,21,35], including adapting model parameters over time. Simple regressive models might fail to provide insights on how the spot price might evolve in the long run since it could change at a minute's granularity. Models based on empirical distributions, although offering an improved treatment of longer term properties than regressive models, usually discard valuable temporal information about the continuity of the spot price staying below different bid values. Therefore, they may fail to capture well the continuity of service availability, which is of great concern particularly for long-lived and "stateful" applications. We refer to such approaches as "CDF-based" (short for cumulative density function based) and discuss the details of their limitations in Section 3.1. To our knowledge, one exception to the above models is [21] wherein the "sojourn time" of a spot instance procured via a particular bid is modeled and predicted via a Semi-Markov chain. However, tenant control based on such multidimensional models would likely suffer scalability limitations when considering multiple spot markets with multiple bids for better availability and profitability.

Prior work models concerns arising from simultaneous revocation of spot instances across markets via cross-correlations or correlation coefficients of *raw* spot price traces [26,27]. In Section 3.2, we argue why this can be misleading and why it is important to consider simultaneous revocations conditioned on specific bid values. Finally, related work has ignored the startup delay of spot instances (which can be longer than that of on-demand instances) and its implications for control design and operation. The only one exception

[3] All our code and data is available at [18]. Our code includes both trace analysis and control implementation of tenant-side instance procurement on EC2.

[4] There may in fact be even more reasons of delay. We discount these since these are mostly due to issues with the tenant's configuration. E.g., the tenant may tell EC2 to launch a set of spot instance only if it can launch them all (a.k.a. launch group); the bid status would be "launch-group-constraints" if EC2 cannot launch all at the same time.

is [13]. Even this, however, focuses on the boot time of instances which is only part of the overall startup delay.

Cost-effective resource procurement with spot instances. A large body of related work provides cost-effective solutions for tenant-side procurement ("control") of spot instances, combined with on-demand and/or reserved instances, for different workloads or applications, e.g., delay-tolerance batch jobs [6, 12, 14, 17, 21, 26, 28, 35], video streaming [8], data caching [34]. On the one hand, for tractability reasons, the prior work usually resorts to the aforementioned simple spot price prediction techniques in their resource procurement, which do not capture well the key feature we identify in our work, e.g., the continuity of service availability and simultaneous revocations across spot markets. Several fault-tolerance mechanisms have been explored to deal with bid failures, e.g., checkpointing, live-migration, replication, which are complementary to our work and can be incorporated with the key features we identify to provide better performance. EC2 itself provides a facility called Spot Fleet [23] for tenant procurement. However, the default bidding strategies are either evenly spread the spot requests across pools, which may not be cost-effective, or only choose the pool with the lowest spot price which may suffer from simultaneous bid failures.

3. USEFUL SPOT FEATURES

We describe *four* spot instance features that we think a tenant should focus on. For each, we present a quantitative representation (a "model") and offer intuition for why it might be useful in online resource procurement ("control"). A key idea cross-cutting our models is to express our features as quantities that are *conditioned on specific bids* chosen out of a small set of pre-selected values. For each feature, we explore one or more of the following properties that might be intuitively appealing for their potential in offering predictive value:

- *Temporal Locality:* Does historical data offer useful hints about future evolution of this feature? If so, what is the right amount of historical data to consider?
- *Spatial Locality:* How does the evolution of this feature in a market relate to that in others in the same vs. different availability zones or geographic regions?
- *Capacity Measurements:* Do effective capacity measurements [32] have any predictive value? That is, do such measurements serve as faithful indicators of changes in spot prices or availability capacity in the concerned marketplace?

Using lessons learnt from this exercise, we design computationally efficient predictors for our features. Finally, we evaluate our predictors on a large set of spot price marketplaces. Figure 2 shows 90-day long spot price timeseries for 16 marketplaces for which we present such evaluation in this paper. We also plot the moving average and standard deviation of spot prices over a two-day sliding window in the same figures. These measurements show high variations especially in spot markets with frequent spikes, e.g., c3.2xlarge in us-west-1a and suggest that *raw* spot prices are best considered (highly) non-stationarity making questionable the efficacy of approaches in existing work (e.g., [1, 30, 36]) that rely on modeling them directly (i.e., implicitly assuming temporal locality in raw prices). A key finding of our work (elaborated upon throughout the rest of this section) is that while assuming temporal locality in raw spot prices may not be reasonable, the features we identify (and which we find useful for control) do indeed show short-term temporal locality.

3.1 Features 1 & 2: Lifetime and Average Price during Lifetime

We present our first two features together due to significant connections between their modeling and prediction.

A tenant would like a spot instance to be available for long enough to serve its needs. That is, it would be interested in the following question: how long is a successful bid going to last? To answer this, our first feature is concerned with the *lifetime* of a spot instance, which we define as the duration between when it becomes ready to use till its termination[5]. An effective model for this feature should not overestimate this quantity - doing so may render a control scheme overly optimistic in its estimation of the cost vs. performance trade-off. On the other hand, underestimating it may lead to higher than desired costs. Based on Section 2.1, a spot instance could be terminated due to either bid failure ("terminated: out of bid") or non-bid failure ("terminated: not enough capacity" or "terminated: capacity oversubscribed"). We find the latter to be a rare event in today's EC2 spot markets. Therefore, in what follows, we ignore time to non-bid failure and only focus on time to bid failure in our analysis. It should be pointed out that in an alternate spot market (e.g., in a future cloud with higher data center utilization and/or one using alternate resource management policies [11]), such terminations may not be non-negligible. Modeling of spot instance lifetime in such environments would be made especially complex because these two types of terminations may themselves not be independent (due to possible dependence through load on the data center).

Our second feature is the *average spot price during an instance's lifetime*. Since spot prices tend to be significantly smaller than on-demand prices (of equally-sized instances) during periods when a bid is successful, and since EC2 charges a tenant based on the spot price during such periods (but not the bid), attempting to predict spot prices accurately is of little value. A visual inspection of the 90-day spot prices in Figure 2 and how these prices compare with a bid that equals to the on-demand price clarifies this[6]. In particular, it suffices that we predict the average spot price during such periods with reasonable accuracy (since that is what will determine our costs).

Limitation of Prior Work: As discussed in Section 2.2, prior studies that rely on CDF-based modeling (even if dynamically updated) of spot price to predict instance lifetime may not be able to capture well service contiguity. We illustrate their pitfalls using Figure 3 via three

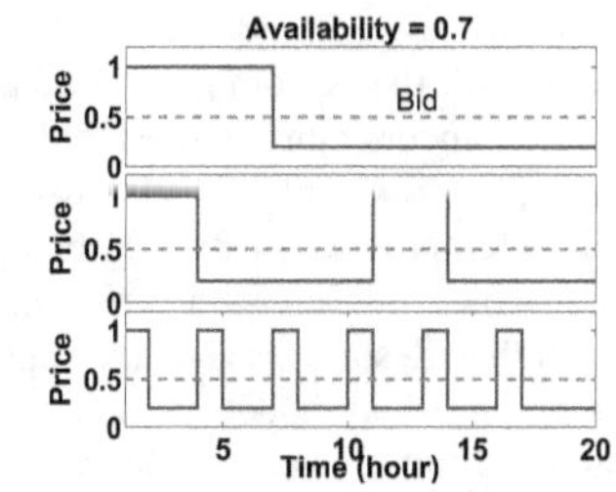

Figure 3: Pitfalls of CDF-based approaches used in prior work.

[5]Clearly, the lifetime defined in this manner could depend intimately on the time when a bid is placed. We do not consider this complexity in our work because it is conceptually simple to extend our characterization for this. E.g., we could carry out our analysis separately for each hour of the day (or another appropriate time duration).

[6]Although it may seem surprising to some, spot prices are known to exceed on-demand prices, sometimes significantly - see several examples in Figure 2. We surmise that this may be part of mechanisms employed by EC2 to shed increasing load on its servers hosting spot instances. Others have also reported that EC2 spot pricing seems to have elements beyond simply reflecting supply-demand relationships [1].

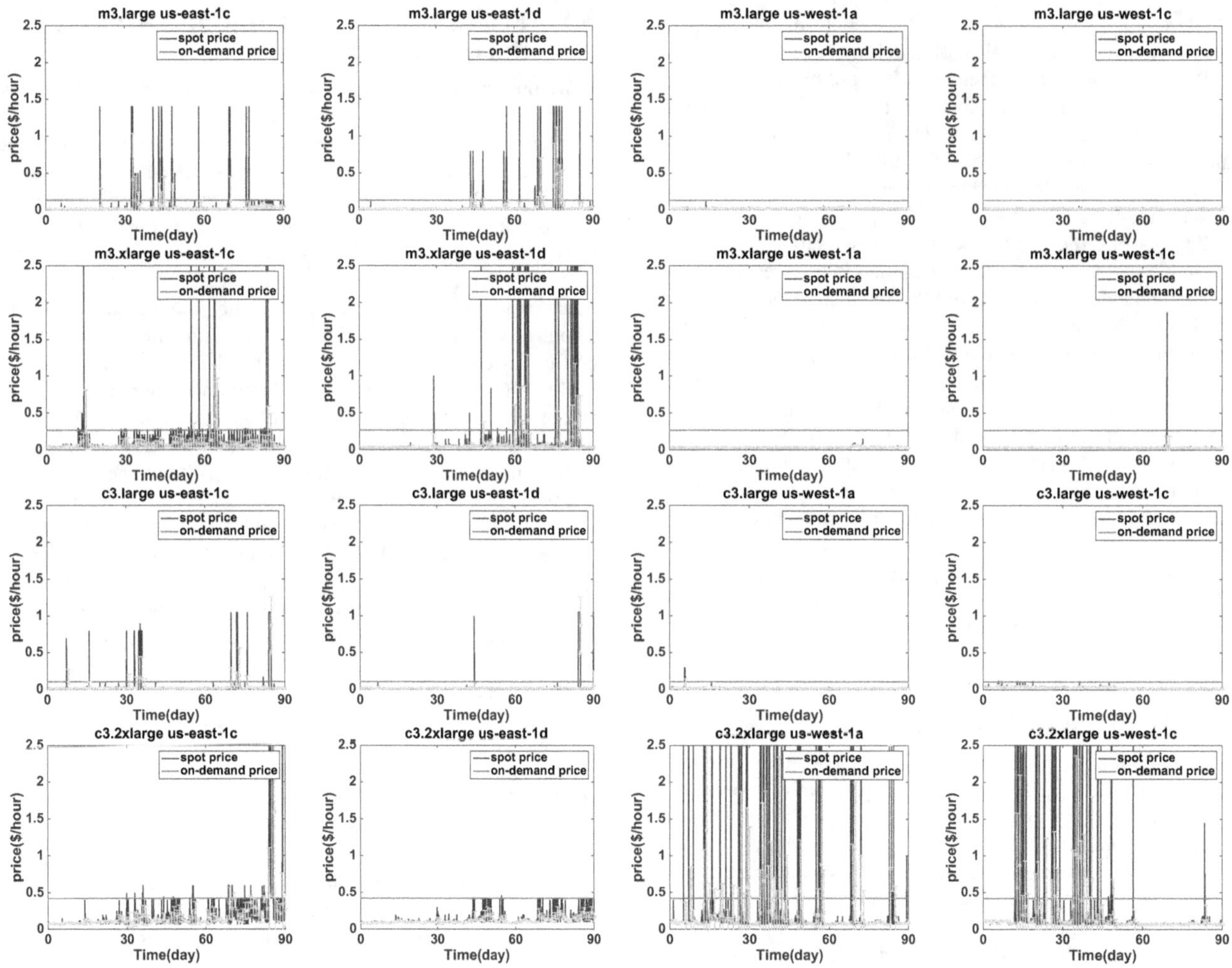

Figure 2: Sample spot price timeseries collected during the 90-day period (2015/07/08 to 2015/10/06) and are chosen due to their very different properties. The green "*" and error bars represent moving average and standard deviations over 2-day interval.

synthetic traces. Although all traces have availability of 0.7 under the same bid, the bottom trace is clearly much worse than the top one since it incurs more frequent bid failures, which the CDF-based approaches would fail to distinguish. With such a model a tenant might be tempted to use spot instances more aggressively than he should, which might cause performance degradation due to more frequent than desired service interruption. On the other hand, more complex statistical models usually result in control that suffer from scalability limitations (the "curses of dimensionality" of Dynamic Programming based approaches).

Models and Temporal Locality-based Prediction: For both these features, we find that effective models are offered by viewing them as random variables informed by empirically measured probability distributions in the recent past. A key requirement for such modeling to be effective lies in choosing the right amount of historical data as we describe momentarily. First, we introduce the definitions for the random variables we choose. We model as a random variable $L(b)$ the length of a *contiguous* period during which the spot price is less than or equal to a bid b. In other words, $L(b)$ captures the upper bound of the lifetime of a spot instance using bid b. We denote as $\bar{p}(b) = E[p_t|L(b)]$ a random variable for the average spot price p_t during a period when the bid b is successful [7], which serves to estimate the cost of a spot instance procured by placing a bid b. We set $L(b)$ and $\bar{p}(b)$ to 0 during the period when the bid fails. Figure 4 illustrates $L(b)$ and $\bar{p}(b)$.

Our prediction techniques assume temporal locality over a recent sliding time window (H most recent time slots, e.g., days) for making predictions of $L(b)$ and $\bar{p}(b)$. H must be chosen such that temporal locality[8] indeed holds for these quantities. Large $L(b)$ and small $\bar{p}(b)$ imply long service continuity and low costs, thereby encouraging the use of spot instances using bid b. We use a small percentile (e.g., 5th) of the recently constructed distribution of $L(b)$ - denoted as $\hat{L}(b)$ - as our prediction in the ongoing horizon. The reasoning behind this choice is that if the statistical properties of $L(b)$ do not change much over H, we expect that with a very high probability, bid b would be successful for at least $\hat{L}(b)$ time units. We use average of $\bar{p}(b)$ during the relevant H as its predictor (denoted as $\hat{\bar{p}}(b)$). Note that our approach would result in a control formulation wherein the number of state/control variables grows

[7]We are overloading the term $L(b)$ to mean a contiguous duration when bid b is successful as well as its length. We are avoiding additional notational complexity since the distinction is very clear based on context.

[8]By temporal locality, we mean that over relatively short time-scales (a day to a few days), the key features tend to change little, whereas over longer time-scales (weeks to months), they might undergo more substantial changes.

linearly with the number of (market,bid) pairs, whereas the Semi-Markov model-based approach discussed in Section 2.2 has to discretize all state and control variables including spot prices from different markets, bids, sojourn time (from minutes to hours), and other application-specific variables, which results in optimization problems that suffer from scalability limitations.

Evaluation of Our Predictors: To evaluate our predictors, we introduce the following assessment metrics. We say that an *over-estimation* of $L(b)$ has occurred when $\hat{L}(b) > L(b)$. This represents a scenario wherein the tenant was likely overly ambitious in using spot instances. We further define $L(b)$ *over-estimation rate* as the fraction of $L(b)$ predictions that result in over-estimation, denoted as $f(b)$. The assessment metric for $\hat{\bar{p}}(b)$ should capture the extent of its deviation from actual values. Therefore, we compute $\xi(b) = (\bar{p}(b) - \hat{\bar{p}}(b))/\bar{p}(b)$ and define as *relative deviation* of $\bar{p}(b)$ the mean value of $\xi(b)$ for all occurrences of $\bar{p}(b)$ in the relevant H. Lower values are better for both $f(b)$ and $\xi(b)$. We focus on the right choice of history window size (for model training), which turns out to be dependent on both the market and the bid. None of the prior works (to our knowledge) have analyzed these idiosyncracies.

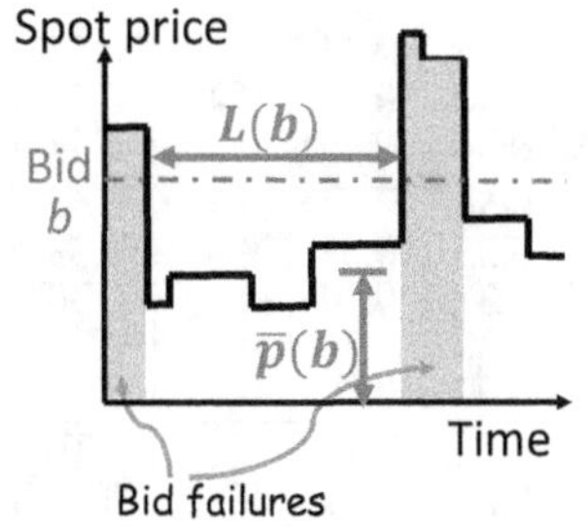

Figure 4: Illustration of features 1 and 2: lifetime of a spot instance and average spot price during lifetime.

Setup: We vary instance types, markets, bids, history window size H and show the assessment metrics f ($L(b)$ over-estimation rate) and ξ ($\bar{p}(b)$ relative deviation) in Table 1. The 90-day spot price traces are chosen from Figure 2, with bid b picked from $\{0.5d, d, 2d, 5d, 10d\}$, where d is the corresponding on-demand price[9]. As a *baseline* approach, we also present the above metrics based on predictions of $L(b)$ and $\bar{p}(b)$ by using the empirical cumulative density function (CDF) of spot prices within H (updated dynamically), denoted as "CDF-based." For this baseline, $\hat{L}(b) = H \cdot Prob(p_t \leq b)$ and $\hat{\bar{p}}(b) = E[p_t | p_t \leq b]$. This baseline represents approaches commonly considered in related work.

Validation of Predictor Efficacy: Under most of (market, bid) pairs, the best (lowest) f and ξ are below 10%, which we consider a reasonable demonstration of the efficacy of our predictors. We do see a small number of exceptions. E.g., for c3.large-c, even if we use 5th percentile as prediction for $L(b)$, f and ξ are much higher than those from other markets. It might be better not to use this market temporarily until we observe better predictability.

The "Right Choice" for History Window Size: We find that (i) the best choice of H varies across markets and bids, implying the necessity for considering different markets separately when determining history window size, instead of blindly choosing a single window size for all markets, and (ii) changing bid values may not affect f and ξ much (e.g., m3.large-c), possibly due to the fact that the $L(b)$ and $\bar{p}(b)$ do not vary much when spot price exceeds bid.

More generally, we find that the evolution of $L(b)$ is often not smooth, and regression-based models (one natural alternative to our approach) may not work well. Again, accurate prediction of $L(b)$ may not be necessary as discussed before. Our choice of prediction with 5th percentile of $L(b)$ tends to be conservative such that higher probability of service contiguity can be achieved. If the application can tolerate more frequent service interruptions, higher percentiles or more aggressive prediction techniques could be used.

Insights and implications: (i) There exists short-term temporal locality in $L(b)$ and $\bar{p}(b)$ and the history window size can be leveraged to improve the quality of prediction, (ii) modeling of these features should be conditioned on specific bids; (iii) our approach outperforms CDF-based approaches by offering smaller over-estimation rate of $L(b)$ and less relative deviation from the actual $\bar{p}(b)$.

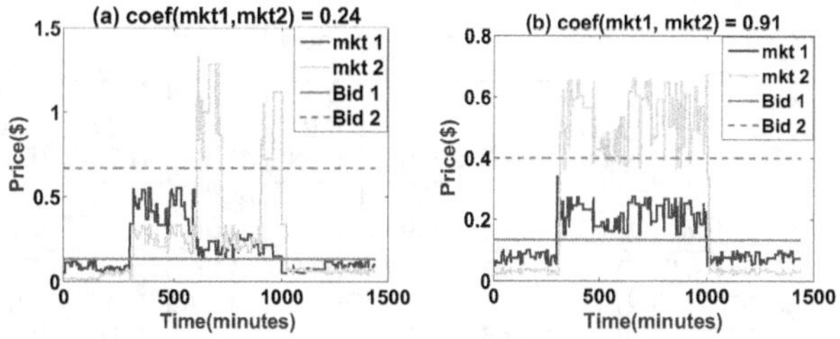

Figure 5: Synthetic examples with simultaneous revocations related to bids. "coef" is correlation coefficient.

3.2 Feature 3: Simultaneous Revocations

Limitations of Prior Work: When placing bids for multiple instances, a tenant may wish to avoid picking spot markets with "high" likelihood of simultaneous revocations (the spot instances may be terminated simultaneously due to coincident bid failures). Prior works, e.g., [20, 26], suggest bidding across markets where there are no significant statistical correlations among the "raw" historical spot price traces (referred to as the correlation coefficient-, or coef-based approach). However, such raw correlations might be misleading. To appreciate this, let us consider illustrative examples in Figure 5. We generate synthetic spot prices for two markets: (a) the cross-correlation between the two markets' spot prices is low and (b) the cross-correlation is high. In (a) the tenant might be tempted to use both markets whereas in (b) it may not want to use the two markets together at all, if its decision is only based on the raw correlation. However, it is obvious that the bid failures from the two markets are highly correlated under bid 1 but not under bid 2. Therefore, it may be imprudent for the tenants to make decisions solely based on the raw correlations without considering the actual bids. More specifically, what the tenant really needs are measurements of simultaneous revocations *conditioned on bids*. Furthermore, the statistical correlation of bid failures across markets may not be very informative for decision-making regarding bid placement. Instead, a tenant might find it more beneficial to learn the absolute time durations of simultaneous revocations, i.e., the total amount of time that a bid fails in two markets within the history window.

Model and Temporal Locality-based Prediction: Based on these insights, a more informative metric that we propose is based on characterizing simultaneous revocations conditioned on pre-specified bids. Under a given bid, we denote as A and B the sets of time periods when the bid fails in two spot markets under comparison[10], respectively. Denote as $T(A)$ and $T(B)$ the corresponding lengths/sizes of A and B. $T(A \cap B)$ and $T(A \cup B)$ represent

[9]This is based on the discussions from [20, 26] and our observations that high spot price values are usually around multiples of on-demand prices. Although spot price stays below the on-demand price most of the time as shown in Figure 2, the tenants may still bid at a price that is higher than the on-demand price, in order to reduce bid failures and achieve better performance.

[10]Our analysis can be easily generalized to compare more than two markets.

	Bid	$f(b)$				$\xi(b)$				$f(b)$ CDF-based				$\xi(b)$ CDF-based			
H		7	14	21	28	7	14	21	28	7	14	21	28	7	14	21	28
m3.large-c	$0.5d$	0.12	0.12	0.13	0.14	0.08	0.08	0.08	0.09	0.29	0.28	0.28	0.30	0.14	0.14	0.15	0.16
	$1d$	0.07	0.08	0.08	0.09	0.07	0.07	0.10	0.11	0.09	0.09	0.08	0.09	0.11	0.12	0.12	0.14
	$2d$	0.02	0.03	0.03	0.03	0.09	0.10	0.10	0.11	0.02	0.03	0.01	0.02	0.11	0.12	0.13	0.14
	$5d$	0.02	0.03	0.03	0.03	0.09	0.10	0.10	0.11	0.02	0.03	0.01	0.02	0.11	0.12	0.13	0.14
	$10d$	0.02	0.03	0.03	0.03	0.09	0.10	0.10	0.11	0.02	0.03	0.01	0.02	0.11	0.12	0.13	0.14
m3.large-d	$0.5d$	0.10	0.07	0.07	0.08	0.06	0.06	0.08	0.07	0.62	0.60	0.61	0.65	0.23	0.23	0.24	0.25
	$1d$	0.10	0.06	0.07	0.07	0.07	0.07	0.09	0.09	0.50	0.50	0.53	0.56	0.22	0.23	0.23	0.24
	$2d$	0.10	0.08	0.09	0.10	0.10	0.10	0.11	0.12	0.45	0.44	0.47	0.51	0.22	0.22	0.23	0.24
	$5d$	0.13	0.12	0.14	0.16	0.09	0.12	0.12	0.13	0.40	0.39	0.42	0.45	0.23	0.23	0.24	0.25
	$10d$	0.07	0.08	0.08	0.09	0.19	0.19	0.17	0.17	0.34	0.32	0.34	0.37	0.25	0.25	0.25	0.27
c3.large-c	$0.5d$	0.10	0.09	0.08	0.08	0.06	0.07	0.13	0.00	0.56	0.52	0.49	0.52	0.21	0.21	0.22	0.22
	$1d$	0.12	0.17	0.19	0.20	0.11	0.16	0.19	0.21	0.33	0.32	0.32	0.33	0.25	0.25	0.26	0.26
	$2d$	0.14	0.18	0.19	0.21	0.11	0.16	0.19	0.21	0.31	0.30	0.29	0.30	0.25	0.26	0.26	0.26
	$5d$	0.14	0.17	0.18	0.20	0.13	0.16	0.18	0.19	0.30	0.29	0.28	0.30	0.26	0.26	0.27	0.27
	$10d$	0.00	0.00	0.00	0.00	0.87	0.76	0.73	0.70	0.00	0.00	0.00	0.00	0.84	0.72	0.68	0.63
c3.large-d	$0.5d$	0.10	0.08	0.09	0.10	0.06	0.06	0.07	0.07	0.16	0.15	0.17	0.19	0.11	0.11	0.12	0.13
	$1d$	0.06	0.06	0.07	0.09	0.07	0.11	0.11	0.10	0.08	0.09	0.10	0.11	0.10	0.10	0.10	0.11
	$2d$	0.06	0.06	0.07	0.08	0.07	0.10	0.10	0.10	0.06	0.06	0.08	0.09	0.10	0.10	0.10	0.11
	$5d$	0.06	0.06	0.07	0.08	0.07	0.10	0.10	0.10	0.06	0.06	0.08	0.09	0.10	0.10	0.10	0.11
	$10d$	0.00	0.00	0.00	0.00	0.34	0.22	0.18	0.16	0.00	0.00	0.00	0.00	0.40	0.26	0.22	0.20

Table 1: The assessment metrics $f(b)$ and $\xi(b)$ under different bid values and history window sizes (H in days). The shaded cells represent the best window size that minimizes $f(b)$ and $\xi(b)$. "-c" and "-d" represent the markets. We round up the results and only show two digits after the decimal point due to space limit. "CDF-based" $f(b)$ and $\xi(b)$ are computed based on predictions of $L(b)$ and $\bar{p}(b)$ using CDF of spot prices.

	H	3	7	14	21	28
c3.2xl	$0.5d$	0.1778	0.1563	0.1286	0.1426	0.1270
	d	0.1353	0.1129	0.0894	0.1008	0.0971
	$5d$	0.0789	0.0799	0.0842	0.0952	0.0892
c3.l	$0.5d$	0.0242	0.0126	0.0000	0.0000	0.0000
	d	0.0141	0.0000	0.0000	0.0000	0.0000
	$5d$	0.0000	0.0000	0.0000	0.0000	0.0000

Table 2: Under-estimation rate of simultaneous revocations. We vary the history window H (days) and only show a subset of results here; the simultaneous revocation is computed for (us-west-1a, us-west-1c) for each instance type. The shaded cells represent the best H.

the time durations of coincident bid failures and total bid failures, respectively. $\frac{T(A \cap B)}{T(A \cup B)}$ reflects the probability that the bid fails in both markets when the bid already fails at one market. It is informative to look at both the durations of bid failures (e.g., $T(A)$) and $\frac{T(A \cap B)}{T(A \cup B)}$ when comparing markets. E.g., even if $T(A)$ and/or $T(B)$ are relatively small compared with the history window size, if $\frac{T(A \cap B)}{T(A \cup B)}$ is high, which implies markets (A,B) almost always fail together under the given bid, it may be better not to place bids in markets (A,B) simultaneously. On the other hand, even if both $\frac{T(A \cap B)}{T(A \cup B)}$ and $T(A \cap B)$ are small, we may use neither A nor B if $L(b)$ is also small in both markets. Tenants can combine such metrics with predicted $L(b)$ and $\bar{p}(b)$ to get a better understanding of simultaneous revocations for cost analysis.

Again, we find temporal locality useful for predicting simultaneous revocations. Similar to prediction of average price during lifetime, we use the measured simultaneous revocations from a history window H as prediction for the near future. We vary the history window and explore the temporal locality. Our assessment metric is the rate of *under-estimation to the actual simultaneous revocations*: the fraction of simultaneous revocation predictions that result in under-estimation. From Table 2, we find that (i) the under-estimation rate is low in general, implying good temporal locality for prediction, (ii) history window size matters for different spot markets under different bids and (iii) the under-estimation rate could be 0, implying few bid failures in such markets under the particular bid. A tenant can use such information to de-correlate bid failures in his dynamic resource procurement.

Spatial Locality: Since EC2 regions and availability zones are geo-distributed, some naturally appealing ideas for improving the (market,bid) selection are: Is there any spatial locality in spot prices? Are markets spread across regions/availability zones un-correlated? Are such effects affected by bids? We show our measurements on simultaneous revocations across multiple regions, availability zones and instance types in Table 3. We have several observations: (i) Increasing bid may de-correlate bid failures: even if spot prices of two markets always jump simultaneously, they don't usually reach the same high spot price. When the bid increases, one of the markets may experience less bid failures whereas the other remains unaffected (possibly because the bid is not high enough). (ii) Increasing bid may also increase the extent to which simultaneous revocation occurs, e.g., as the total failure time $T(A \cup B)$ decreases in markets (c,d) of c3.large (highlighted in Table 3), the fraction of time that concurrent bid failure occurs becomes less. (iii) Since the properties of simultaneous revocations highly depend on markets and bids (and possibly also history window size), simply comparing the raw statistical correlations of multiple markets' spot prices may not suffice and might even lead to *faulty* decision making. It is crucially important to take into account the impact of bid values. (iv) Although the EC2 regions and availability zones are created for other types of failures, e.g., infrastructure failure, they unintentionally also amount to similar effects for spot bid failures.

Additionally, if we look at the simultaneous revocations across instance types but fix the availability zone (Table 4), we observe that in general the spot prices across different instance types are not highly correlated; even for the pair (c3.large, c3.2xlarge) that has the highest "coef", $\frac{T(A \cap B)}{T(A \cup B)}$ is still quite low under all bids. Such observation encourages the tenant to spread its bids across different instance types. However, although both $T(A)$ and $T(B)$ decrease

	Bid		0.5d				d				5d			
		coef	A	B	$A \cap B$	$\frac{A \cap B}{A \cup B}$	A	B	$A \cap B$	$\frac{A \cap B}{A \cup B}$	A	B	$A \cap B$	$\frac{A \cap B}{A \cup B}$
m3.large	b,c	0.0968	2590	1347	607	0.1823	1386	35	6	0.0042	900	6	6	0.0067
	c,d	0.1102	1347	2391	58	0.0158	35	1730	24	0.0138	6	1489	0	0
	d,e	0.0594	2391	10204	727	0.0613	1730	4517	329	0.0556	1489	0	0	0
	b,c'	0.0748	2590	0	0	0	1386	0	0	0	900	0	0	0
	c,a'	-0.0120	1347	7	0	0	35	0	0	0	6	0	0	0
	a',c'	-0.0846	0	0	0	0	0	0	0	0	0	0	0	0
m3.xlarge	b,c	0.2268	13314	103	54	0.0040	7050	0	0	0	376	0	0	0
	c,d	0.2109	103	3408	32	0.0092	0	1070	0	0	0	774	0	0
	d,e	0.0859	3408	279	5	0.0014	1070	9	0	0	774	9	0	0
	b,c'	0.0027	13314	84	0	0	7050	50	0	0	376	4	0	0
	c,a'	0.2001	103	5	0	0	0	0	0	0	0	0	0	0
	a',c'	0.1462	5	84	0	0	0	50	0	0	0	4	0	0
c3.large	b,c	0.6614	1459	3725	1121	0.2759	1103	2340	976	0.3956	1059	2274	921	0.3818
	c,d	0.7728	3725	1408	1211	0.3088	2340	1200	1189	0.5057	2274	1194	1184	0.5184
	d,e	0.4177	1408	298	251	0.1725	1200	284	238	0.1910	1194	279	233	0.1879
	b,c'	-0.0766	1459	2487	60	0.0154	1103	470	0	0	1059	0	0	0
	c,a'	-0.0158	3725	565	51	0.0120	2340	470	0	0	2274	0	0	0
	a',c'	0.3268	565	2487	335	0.1233	470	124	22	0.0385	0	0	0	0
c3.2xlarge	b,c	0.1456	6291	22998	5036	0.2076	1589	3917	946	0.2075	511	1152	18	0.0109
	c,d	0.3704	22998	8039	6272	0.2533	3917	14	0	0	1152	0	0	0
	d,e	0.3315	8039	7115	2350	0.1935	14	756	0	0	0	0	0	0
	b,c'	-0.0238	6291	7593	144	0.0105	1589	4011	8	0.0014	511	2899	0	0
	c,a'	0.0125	22998	9727	1915	0.0622	3917	7233	301	0.0277	1152	5047	20	0.0032
	a',c'	0.3680	9727	7593	4407	0.3413	7233	4011	2609	0.3021	5047	2899	1504	0.2335

Table 3: Simultaneous revocations across different pairs of markets (b,c,d,e) from region us-east and (a',c') from region us-west under different bids. The measurements are in minutes. The $T(.)$ operator is omitted for space. "coef" is the coefficient of variation of two price traces. We set $\frac{A \cap B}{A \cup B} = 0$ when $A \cup B = 0$, which we interpret as no bid failures.

as we increase the bid from $0.5d$ to d for (m3.large,m3.xlarge), we notice that $\frac{T(A \cap B)}{T(A \cup B)}$ increases from 0.0044 to 0.1304, which re-emphasizes our key finding that analysis of simultaneous revocations should take into account the bids instead of blindly looking at the "coef" as done by the prior work.

Heuristic for Efficiently Finding Marketplaces with Low Likelihood of Simultaneous Bid Failures: One possible way to exploit the observed spatial locality is through clustering of candidates formed by (market, bid) pairs. For example, similar to the k-means clustering [7], we can interpret our model of simultaneous revocations ($\frac{T(A \cap B)}{T(A \cup B)}$) as the distance between two candidates. Then standard clustering algorithms can be applied to create clusters of candidates wherein candidates in the same cluster have higher probability of simultaneous bid failures. A tenant can simply spread its choice of (market, bid) across clusters to reduce correlated bid failures[11].

Insights and implications: (i) Temporal locality can be employed for predicting simultaneous revocations. (ii) Modeling and prediction of simultaneous revocations should take into account bids; only looking at the raw cross-correlation may lead to faulty understanding/prediction of simultaneous bid failures. (iii) There is spatial locality of spot bid failures across regions, availability zones and different instance types, which can better help the tenant de-correlate bid failures.

3.3 Feature 4: Time to Start

Time to start is an important feature for tenant's resource procurement. For example, during unexpected flash crowds, if the tenant wants to allocate new spot instance but finds that the spot bid status is still *pending* after a long waiting time, the application performance might be severely degraded. EC2's official documentation only provides rough estimates of maximum instance boot times (corresponding to the duration labeled "Initialization" in Figure 1) which range from 1 to 5 min [4]. However, recall from Figure 1 that there can be additional contributors to spot instance startup delay of two types: (i) a period when the bid is lower than the spot price and (ii) a period (even after the spot price has become lower than the bid) during which EC2 makes the tenant wait (allegedly) due to a lack of capacity at its end.

Limitations of Prior Work: To the best of our knowledge, this feature has been ignored by related work. The only research work that explores a limited aspect of this issue is [13], which focuses only on instance boot up times. For spot instance, they observe no significant correlation between spot price and time-to-start; however, they do not explore/report the temporal locality and the predictive property of time-to-start.

Model and Temporal Locality-based Prediction: Of course, (i) depends on the bid placed by the tenant - a higher bid will exceed the spot price sooner than a lower bid. We find that for relatively high bids (greater than or equal to the price of the comparable on-demand instance), this type of delay can be ignored for all practical purposes. However, for lower bids (that certain cost-conscious tenants may prefer), we do not find any patterns that can be generalized readily for useful prediction.

To see the predictability of (ii), we choose instance types and several spot markets across different time zones and bid spot instances every 5 min over two days. The bids are uniformly chosen from $\{\frac{1}{4}d, \frac{1}{2}d, \frac{3}{4}d, d, 2d, 5d, 10d, max\}$, wherein d is the on-demand price and max is the maximum bid allowed. We report a subset of our results in Figure 6. In some cases (top and middle traces shown in Figure 6(a)) we find time-of-day like behavior or small variance around a fixed value. This seems to depend very much on the market with no other obvious predictive indicators

[11]Picking instances from multiple marketplaces (especially those geographically distributed) is of course more complex. E.g., there may be concerns related to communication between instances over a WAN or issues of proximity to tenants that we can not consider in our work [33]. An actual decision-making would need to consider these against the issues that we do model here.

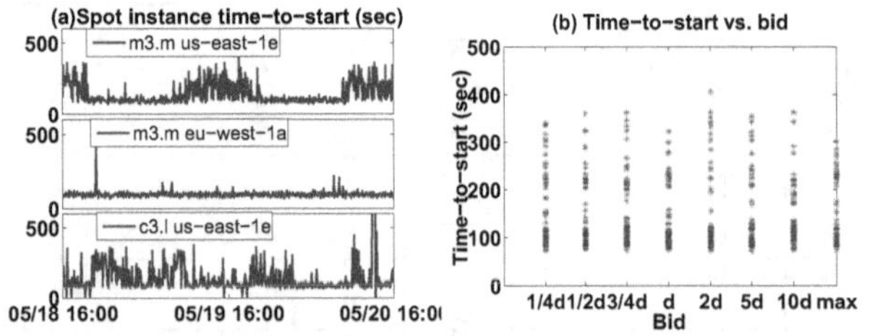

Figure 6: (a) Spot instance time-to-start. (b) Spot instance time-to-start vs. bids. We request one instance every 5 min across two days from 2016/05/18 16:00 to 2016/05/20 16:00 with bids uniformly chosen from $\{\frac{1}{4}d, \frac{1}{2}d, \frac{3}{4}d, d, 2d, 5d, 10d, max\}$, wherein d is the on-demand price and max is the maximum bid allowed. The time-to-start is set to 0 if bid is less than spot price. The largest two values in the bottom trace of (a) are 2800+ seconds.

(e.g., more in a particular region or availability zone or instance type, etc.) In such marketplaces, a tenant may be able to exploit such predictability. In others, however, a tenant may have to resort to working with worst-case values. For example, in the bottom trace in Figure 6(a), the largest two samples are greater than 2800 seconds.

We also explore the relationship between time-to-start vs. bid. Intuitively, higher bids should give the tenant higher priority for resource procurement, thus shorter time-to-start, since EC2 might make more profit by serving higher bids first. However, we do not observe a statistically significant correlation between time-to-start and different bid values (Figure 6(b)).

Insights and implications: It is important to model this feature, which has not been addressed in related work. However, we do not find generally useful evidence for temporal locality like we do for our features 1-3. Therefore, tenants may be forced to work conservatively with this feature, e.g., allowing for a large delay just to be safe based on high percentiles of previous observations.

3.4 Do Effective Capacity Measurements Provide Predictive Power?

EC2 claims that the spot price is set based on its supply/demand relationship [3]. Therefore, a natural thought is: Can we further improve the predictability of spot prices if we can somehow infer the current resource demand vs. capacity status in the spot pool? For example, when there are too many tenants' spot requests and the spot pool becomes "congested," it is highly possible that the "effective" capacity, as opposed to the advertized capacity, perceived by the tenant could be lower or have higher variations (reflected by degraded application performance) than when the spot pool has enough unused capacity. In particular, we have the following hypotheses: (i) Is there any predictive power in effective capacity vs. spot price? (ii) Is there any predictive power in effective capacity vs. sudden revocations? Such relationships, if observed, can be exploited by the tenants to improve their prediction of spot prices (or of features 1-3).

To test our hypotheses, we conduct experiments on several EC2 spot markets wherein we record effective capacity variations based on application performance measurements from commonly-used micro-benchmarks. Due to space limit, we only show a subset of our measurement results in Figure 7. As illustrated by the scatter plots of normalized performance vs. spot price, we do not observe enough predictive power in dynamic effective capacity (reflected by the varying performance measurements) for spot prices. We further infer that the evolvement of spot prices may not be reflected by local congestion signals, or that even when there is not enough capacity (implied by the peak price periods) EC2 would rather kick off spot instances by raising the spot prices instead of sacrificing capacity/performance.

We do not see significant performance/capacity difference across on-demand and spot instances with the same resource configuration. Our interpretation is that EC2 might have provided the same guarantee of performance and capacity isolations for both on-demand and spot instances. However, when the on-demand resource pool lacks capacity, EC2 might revoke spot instances to make room for the more profitable on-demand instances. We leave more comprehensive and extensive comparison studies of on-demand vs. spot instance to our future work.

4. CASE STUDIES

The goal of our case studies is **not** to devise fundamentally novel resource procurement (i.e., "control") algorithms. Recall from Section 2 that such control algorithms have received a lot of attention recently for a variety of workload types. Instead, we are interested in evaluating the cost/performance improvements that our modeling and prediction techniques can offer to this existing body of work. Given this, we adapt control algorithms in related work to use our modeling and prediction for two real-world applications: (i) an in-memory Memcached-based data store, and (ii) a homegrown synthetic batch processing workload. Both these workloads possess the following property making the use of spot instances suitable for them: *the failure of an instance may only degrade their performance but does not affect their correctness.* In both cases, our control formulations attempt to minimize operational costs while maintaining specified application-level performance guarantees using a combination of spot and on-demand instances.

4.1 Case Study I: In-memory Data Store

We consider the problem of cost-effective operation for a Memcached-based (a popular in-memory key-value data store [16]) caching tier within a larger data storage application. As a typical mode of operation for such an application, we assume that the entire working set needs to be kept in memory for satisfactory performance. When a spot instance assigned to the caching tier is lost due to a bid failure, the back-end database serves misses. When servicing misses, the requested data be inserted into caching tier and stale data is evicted based on an LRU policy when there is not enough memory capacity.

Control Design: We formulate an online optimization problem that exploits predictability within the workload (request arrival rate $\hat{\lambda}_t$ and working set size $\hat{M}_t$) and spot price features ($L(b)$ and $\bar{p}(b)$)) to determine: (i) how many and which on-demand and spot instances to procure/de-allocate and (ii) how to partition the overall working set (itself dynamic) among on-demand and spot instances. Implicit in this decision-making are the markets from which to pick spot instances and the bids to place. Alternative approaches, such as data replication across multiple markets [34], are complementary to our work.

We view on-demand instances as special spot markets with $L(b) = \infty$ and $\bar{p}(b)$ equal to the corresponding on-demand price. This allows us to conveniently represent all different markets in a unified way. Denote as $s \in S$ a spot market, as b a bid picked from B_s (a set of pre-selected bid values depending on the market s). Denote as N_t^{sb} and $\tilde{N}_t^{sb}$ the existing number of instances and extra instances to procure/de-allocate from market s under bid b at the beginning of time-slot t, respectively. Denote as x_t^{sb} the fraction of working set kept in market s under bid b. Denote as m^s and c^s the amount of RAM and number of vCPUs for instance in market s.

	Bid	0.5d				d				5d			
	coef	A	B	$A \cap B$	$\frac{A \cap B}{A \cup B}$	A	B	$A \cap B$	$\frac{A \cap B}{A \cup B}$	A	B	$A \cap B$	$\frac{A \cap B}{A \cup B}$
m3.l, m3.xl	0.1357	1046	328	6	0.0044	24	28	6	0.1304	6	0	0	0
m3.l, c3.l	0.0146	1566	3631	11	0.0021	987	2335	3	0.0009	6	2274	0	0
m3.l, c3.2xl	0.1939	35	41898	29	0.0007	6	17538	0	0	6	1167	0	0
m3.xl, c3.l	0.1153	431	3348	0	0	28	2317	0	0	0	1552	0	0
m3.xl, c3.2xl	0.2870	60	29769	56	0.0019	0	15715	0	0	0	1158	0	0
c3.l, c3.2xl	0.3214	2327	45478	1987	0.0434	2306	18261	1492	0.0782	0	1167	0	0

Table 4: Simultaneous revocations across different instance types in us-east-1c.

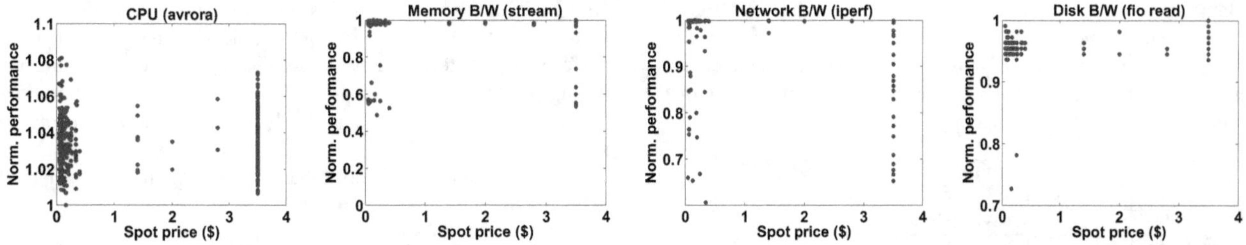

Figure 7: Scatter plots of 24-hour micro-benchmark performance measurements on a single r3.xlarge instance vs. spot price from us-east-1d. avrora is a CPU-intensive benchmark [2]; STREAM [25], iperf [9] and fio [9] are commonly used benchmarks that measure the bandwidths of memory, network and disk I/O. The performance measurements are normalized w.r.t. the best performance samples in the experiments. The spot price varies from $\frac{1}{7}$ to 10 times the on-demand price.

We present our optimization formulation as follows:

$$\min_{\tilde{N}_t^{sb}, x_t^{sb}} \sum_{s \in S} \sum_{b \in B_s} [\hat{\bar{p}}_t^s(b)(N_t^{sb} + \tilde{N}_t^{sb})T + \frac{\alpha x_t^{sb} \hat{M}_t}{\hat{L}^s(b)} T$$
$$+ \beta \max\{0, -\tilde{N}_t^{sb}\}]$$
$$\text{s.t.} \sum_{s \in S} \sum_{b \in B_s} x_t^{sb} = 1$$
$$\sum_{s \in S'} x_t^{sb} \geq \xi, \quad S' = \{\text{OD}\}$$
$$x_t^{sb} \hat{M}_t \leq (N_t^{sb} + \tilde{N}_t^{sb}) m^s, \quad \forall s \in S, b \in B_s$$
$$\phi(\hat{\lambda}_t x_t^{sb}, (N_t^{sb} + \tilde{N}_t^{sb}) c^s) \leq l^{TGT} \quad \forall s \in S, b \in B_s$$

where $\{\text{OD}\}$ is the set of on-demand instance types. In the objective function, the first term represents the resource costs which depend on the predicted average spot price $\hat{\bar{p}}_t^s(b)$ during the optimization window T; the second term is the bid failure penalty, a decreasing function of the predicted $L(b)$ in a spot market, implying a certain "loss rate;" the last term reflects the resource deallocation penalty that depresses performance oscillation due to overly frequent workload re-balancing among markets. α, β reflect the weights of each term in the objective. The first constraint leads to a full partition of the working set and the second constraint forces at least ξ percent of the working set should be placed on on-demand instances to ensure service availability if all spot markets fail. We use the third constraint to guarantee enough RAM capacity in each market to hold its portion of the working set. Finally, the last constraint enforces an application-specific latency target l^{TGT} wherein $\phi(\hat{\lambda}_t x_t^{sb}, (N_t^{sb} + \tilde{N}_t^{sb}) c^s)$ is a function capturing the relationship between latency, arrival rates and the number of vCPUs. $\phi(.)$ can be obtained by various techniques, e.g., regression using empirical measurements.

We update the predictions of $L(b)$ and $\bar{p}(b)$ with history window H identified to be appropriate for the chosen markets in Section 3, and solve our optimization problem once every hour. In case of bid failures, we start new on-demand instances with the same capacity as the failed instances and redirect the requests accordingly. More details about our control design can be found in our technical report [31].

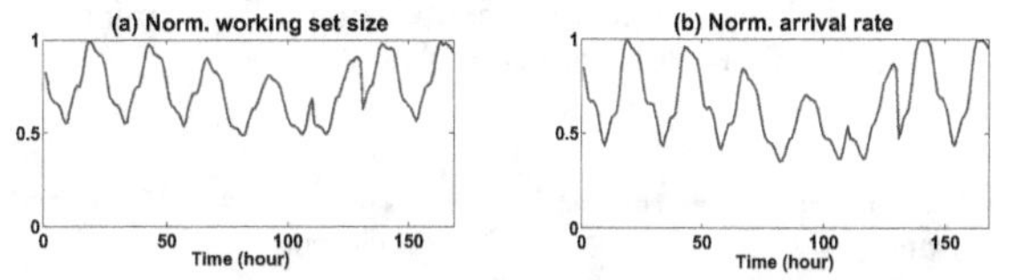

Figure 8: Normalized working set size and request arrival rates from Wikipedia access trace [29]. Normalization is done against the maximum value in each trace.

Experiment Design: We assume that our tenant uses a single spot instance type across two availability zones with bids of $b = d, 5d$ (denoted as b_1, b_2 respectively) in each zone where d is the on-demand price. We evaluate our approach using a variety of 90-day spot price traces taken from Figure 2. We generate our workload by scaling the dynamic arrival rates λ_t and working set size M_t from Wikipedia access trace [29] (Figure 8). We find that both λ_t and M_t can be well captured via AR(2) models with R-Squared equal to 0.99 and 0.94, respectively.

Baselines: Denote as "PROP" our proposed online approach. We further create two baselines to compare against: (i) "BL-OD": all data are stored on on-demand instances (no bidding). (ii) "BL-CDF": Predicting $L(b)$ and $\bar{p}(b)$ via the CDF-based approach (cf. Section 3). In all baselines, the workload partition on spot instances across markets under different bids is determined by the same online optimizer.

Trace-driven Simulation: We conduct experiments with a variety of spot price traces and show the cost-saving (against BL-OD) and performance (reflected by data loss due to bid failures) under different strategies in Table 5 and Figure 9. First, we observe that in the region us-west where the spot prices are quite low and bid failures are rare events, PROP and BL-CDF have almost the same cost-savings (up to 72%) and same number of failures, which is because the spot prices in these cases have good temporal locality. Second, we find that in region us-east where the spot prices fluctuate a lot and bid failures occur quite often, PROP offers less but still comparable cost-savings compared to BL-CDF. Recall our discussion in Section 2.2 and Figure 3 that the CDF-based approach make the tenant tempted to use spot instance more aggressively even if there are short-lived but frequent spikes in spot prices, thereby achieving lower costs than PROP. However, this comes at the expenses of much more bid failures. Third, not only does PROP lead to less bid failures, it also has much less data loss during each bid failure than BL-CDF. As Figure 9 shows, BL-CDF has 13 and 22 times of 90% data loss (out of working set) in the two cases whereas PROP only has 5 and 1 times at the same data loss level, respectively. This is possibly because PROP's prediction of the key features are closer to the actual values, which further demonstrates better temporal locality than the CDF-based approach.

	m3.l		m3.xl		c3.l		c3.2xl	
	e	w	e	w	e	w	e	w
Cost savings (%)								
BL-CDF	67	72	51	59	62	68	42	46
PROP	58	72	45	59	61	68	42	26
Number of bid failures								
BL-CDF	23	0	28	1	3	0	9	49
PROP	13	0	10	0	4	0	2	6

Table 5: Cost savings of different strategies compared against BL-OD. 'e' and 'w' represent experiments using all spot price traces from us-east and us-west, respectively.

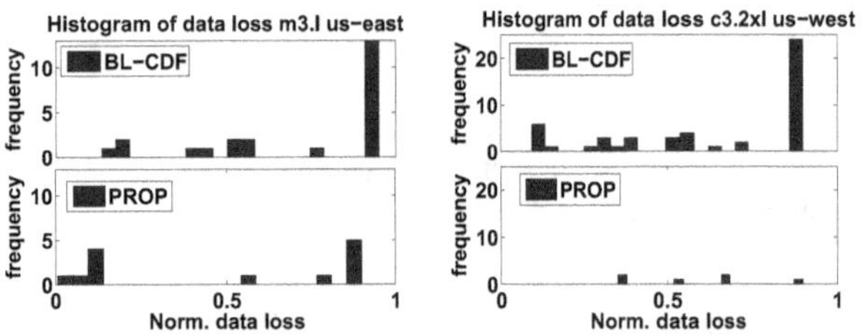

Figure 9: Histograms of data loss (norm. against actual working set size) during bid failures.

Experiments with Prototype on EC2: To explore operation in the real world (especially, application performance that may be affected by factors that our simulations may not capture), we conduct experiments with Memcached on our prototype system on EC2 using a 24-hour subset from the workload trace in Figure 8, and 24-hour spot price traces taken from m3.large in us-east (Figure 10(a)). Three bid failures occur under Bid 1 in us-east-1d. For BL-CDF, the third failure is avoided after it updates prediction of $L(b)$ and $\bar{p}(b)$. PROP does not incur any bid failures.

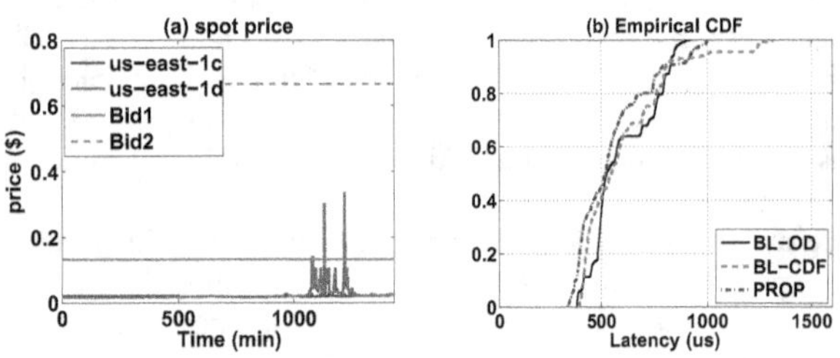

Figure 10: (a) 24-hour spot price of m3.large from two markets with Bid1= d and Bid2= $5d$. (b) The CDF of latencies.

We show the application performance under different strategies in Figure 10(b). We find that the three strategies offer comparable performance up to 90%ile latencies. Below 90%ile, sometimes BL-CDF and PROP could outperform BL-OD since they could use more spot instances to serve the requests without incurring higher costs than BL-OD. Beyond 90%ile, BL-OD offers the best performance possibly because it does not spread working set among multiple markets which depresses the latency oscillation due to working set re-partition. Meanwhile, Prop is able to beat BL-CDF and gets closer to BL-OD (however with much less costs) whereas BL-CDF has worse performance due to bid failures.

Key Insights: PROP offers less but still comparable cost-savings with BL-CDF. However, PROP is able to achieve much better performance in terms of both less bid failures and less data loss during bid failures, particularly in markets with higher variations. Since in-memory data store is usually considered as a performance-sensitive/latency-critical application, the tenant may desire "always-on"/"service contiguity" more than cost saving and prefer PROP to BL-CDF.

4.2 Case Study II: Batch Processing

We leverage a fault-tolerance mechanism, replicating computation, to optimize the cost vs. performance trade-off for a tenant running delay-tolerant batch jobs.

Algorithm Design: When a batch job arrives, we put a "primary copy" of it on a spot instance and a "backup copy" on an on-demand instance. Jobs on the spot instances are guaranteed to have enough resource capacity (regular capacity) for their normal execution, whereas the on-demand instance capacities are over-subscribed so that the backup copies only get a small portion out of their own regular capacities. Therefore, primary copies would finish sooner than backup copies. Since spot instances are in general much cheaper than on-demand instances and the on-demand capacities are over-subscribed, the expected costs would be much lower than if we run the jobs only on on-demand instances and with over-subscription. If the spot instance is not revoked by the time when the primary copy finishes, we terminate the backup copy to save costs and make more room for new jobs; otherwise, we boost the performance of the backup copies whose primary copies have failed by allowing them to use more resources temporarily.

By default, we place one primary copy per vCPU in the primary pool (spot) but at most four backup copies per vCPU in the backup pool (on-demand). As an initial step towards a more comprehensive solution, we apply a simple yet effective strategy for **primary copy placement**: Upon the arrival of a new job j, find all the valid (market, bid) pairs that satisfy $\hat{L}(b) \geq \hat{l}_j$ as candidates, wherein $\hat{l}_j$ is the predicted execution time of job j if given regular capacity; then randomly choose a candidate with $\bar{p}(b)$ less than or equal to the n-th smallest $\bar{p}(b)$ to execute the primary copy. For **backup copy placement**, we compute an *index* for each instance in the backup pool which is a function (e.g., summation) of the probability of simultaneous revocations of each existing job on that instance vs. the new job; then we choose the instance with the lowest index value, which indicates less probability of simultaneous revocations and probably offers more capacity headroom for the backup copy of the new job for performance boosting when unexpected bid failure occurs. If the lowest index exceeds a certain threshold, a new on-demand instance will be allocated. We leave more details and advanced performance enhancements to our technical report [31].

Experimental Setup: We use m3.xlarge (4 vCPUs) across us-east-1c (s_1) and us-east-1d (s_2) with bids $b_1 = d, b_2 = 5d$ where d is the on-demand price. We mark four markets: s_1b_1, s_1b_2, s_2b_1 and s_2b_2. The three-month price traces are shown in Figure 2. We use an exponential distribution to generate the inter-arrival time of jobs, with $\lambda = 10$ jobs per hour. The lengths of the jobs are uniformly selected from the range $[30, 300]$ (minutes). The jobs are CPU-intensive, with little memory I/O and no network traffic.

Our Baselines: We create BL-OD which does not use spot instances and runs one job per vCPU on on-demand instances without replication. To compute the index for a pair of jobs (existing vs. new), we use the summation of probabilities of simultaneous revocations, which is calculated via $\frac{T(A \cap B)}{T(A \cup B)}$ for our approach PROP, and via "coefficient of variation" for another baseline BL-COEF (mimicking the approach used by prior work [20, 26]).

Trace-driven Simulation: We conduct trace-driven simulation using the three-month spot price traces to demonstrate the long-term benefit of our proposed approach. Figure 11 shows the cost break-down and CDF of job execution time under different strategies.

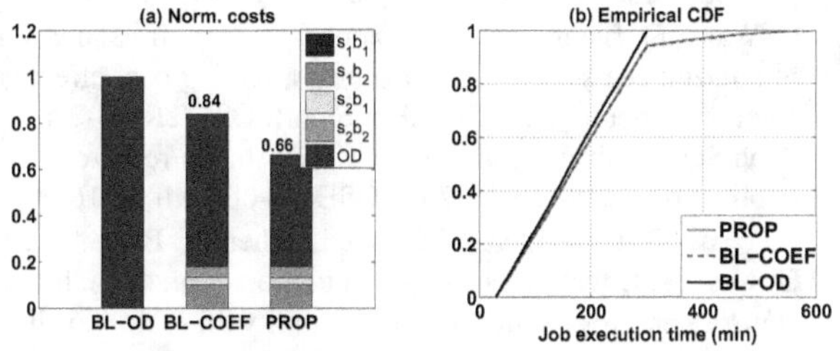

Figure 11: (a) Cost break-down and (b) CDF of job execution time. The CDFs of BL-CDF and PROP overlap.

We have several observations. First, PROP saves as much as 33.7% and 17.7% costs compared to BL-OD and BL-COEF (Figure 11(a)), respectively. This is because BL-OD only uses on-demand instances which are expensive and BL-COEF does not compute probability of simultaneous revocations conditioned on bids, thereby determining the backup placement conservatively and using more on-demand instances. For example, if two jobs' primary copies are in the same spot market but under different bids, BL-COEF would consider them to fail simultaneously with probability of 1, which may not be true if spot price falls between the two bids and only one of the jobs fails. Second, from Figure 11(b), we find that BL-OD offers best performance since there is no bid failure. BL-COEF and PROP has almost the same CDF of job execution time, implying PROP captures the simultaneous revocations well and provides similar capacity headroom for performance boosting when failures occur compared to the conservative BL-COEF.

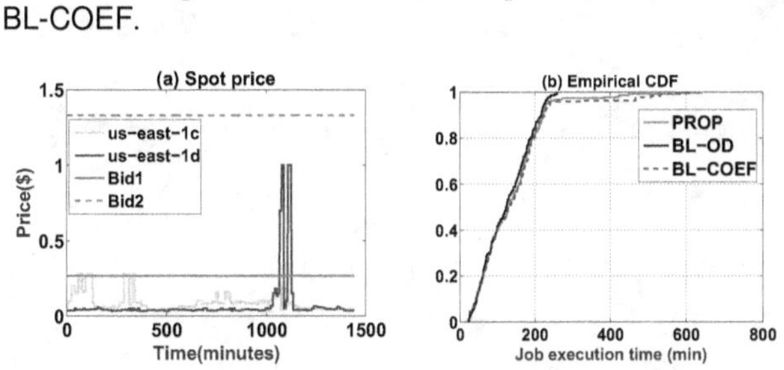

Figure 12: (a) 24-hour spot price of m3.xlarge from two markets with Bid1= d and Bid2= $5d$ (d: on-demand price). (b) The CDF of job execution time under different strategies.

Experiments with Prototype on EC2: To demonstrate the efficacy of our proposed approach in a real-world setting, we deploy a prototype system on EC2 with 24-hour spot price traces of m3.xlarge (Figure 12(a)) and conduct realtime experiments. A bid failure occurs at around 1100-th minute under Bid 1. Since the predicted $L(b)$ is smaller for us-east-1c, two markets s_1b_1 and s_1b_2 (both in us-east-1c) are excluded by our algorithm in this experiment.

We show the performance under different strategies in Figure 12(b). We observe that the relative performance of all strategies are similar from trace-driven simulation to the real-world experiment. However, we notice that the performance of PROP is better (though not much) than BL-COEF for jobs that are affected by bid failures. This is possibly because BL-COEF is not only conservative but may also be misleading: even if the "coef" is low for two spot markets, the probability of simultaneous revocation could become high depending on the specific bids.

Key insights: For batch jobs that can tolerate bid failure-induced delay, our approach can save more costs by applying simultaneous revocation features while still providing comparable (if not better than) performance with the traditional approach which neglects the impact of bids.

5. CONCLUSION

In this paper, we identified four key features of spot instance operation that a tenant should model. Using extensive empirical evaluation based on both historical and current spot instance data, we showed shortcomings in the state-of-the-art that our model and prediction overcome. We further demonstrated the efficacy of our proposed approaches using two real-world case studies via both trace-driven simulation and system prototyping on EC2.

6. ACKNOWLEDGEMENT

This research was supported, in part, by NSF CAREER 0953541 grant and an IBM faculty partnership award. We gratefully acknowledge this support as well as the reviewers' feedback.

7. REFERENCES

[1] O. A. Ben-Yehuda, M. Ben-Yehuda, A. Schuster, and D. Tsafrir. Deconstructing amazon ec2 spot instance pricing. In *Proc. of CloudCom'11*, 2011.

[2] Avrora, 2016. http://dacapobench.org/benchmarks.html.

[3] Building price-aware applications using ec2 spot instances, 2015. https://aws.amazon.com/blogs/aws/category/ec2-spot-instances/.

[4] Ec2 boot time, 2016. http://docs.aws.amazon.com/AWSEC2/latest/UserGuide/ComponentsAMIs.html.

[5] EC2 spot, 2016. http://aws.amazon.com/ec2/spot-instances/.

[6] Y. Gong, B. He, and A. C. Zhou. Monetary cost optimizations for mpi-based hpc applications on amazon clouds: Checkpoints and replicated execution. In *Proc. of the SC'15*, 2015.

[7] J. A. Hartigan and M. A. Wong. Algorithm as 136: A k-means clustering algorithm. *Journal of the Royal Statistical Society. Series C (Applied Statistics)*, 28(1):100–108, 1979.

[8] J. He, Y. Wen, J. Huang, and D. Wu. On the cost–qoe tradeoff for cloud-based video streaming under amazon ec2's pricing models. *Circuits and Systems for Video Technology, IEEE Transactions on*, 2014.

[9] iPerf, 2016. https://iperf.fr/iperf-download.php.

[10] B. Javadi, R. Thulasiramy, and R. Buyya. Statistical modeling of spot instance prices in public cloud environments. In *Proc. of UCC'11*, 2011.

[11] G. Kesidis, B. Urgaonkar, N. Nasiriani, and C. Wang. Neutrality in future public clouds: Implications and

challenges. In *HotCloud'16*, 2016.

[12] S. Khatua and N. Mukherjee. Application-centric resource provisioning for amazon ec2 spot instances. In *Euro-Par 2013 Parallel Processing*. 2013.

[13] M. Mao and M. Humphrey. A performance study on the vm startup time in the cloud. In *Proc. of IEEE CLOUD'12*, 2012.

[14] A. Marathe, R. Harris, D. Lowenthal, B. R. de Supinski, B. Rountree, and M. Schulz. Exploiting redundancy for cost-effective, time-constrained execution of hpc applications on amazon ec2. In *HPDC'14*, 2014.

[15] M. Mattess, C. Vecchiola, and R. Buyya. Managing peak loads by leasing cloud infrastructure services from a spot market. In *Proc. of HPCC'10*, 2010.

[16] Memcached, 2016. https://memcached.org/.

[17] I. Menache, O. Shamir, and N. Jain. On-demand, spot, or both: Dynamic resource allocation for executing batch jobs in the cloud. In *Proc. of ICAC'14*, 2014.

[18] Spot characterization code and data, 2016. https://github.com/patiner/spot_characterization.git.

[19] P. Sharma, D. Irwin, and P. Shenoy. How not to bid the cloud. In *Proc. of HotCloud'16*, 2016.

[20] P. Sharma, S. Lee, T. Guo, D. Irwin, and P. Shenoy. Spotcheck: Designing a derivative iaas cloud on the spot market. In *Proc. of EuroSys'15*, 2015.

[21] Y. Song, M. Zafer, and K. Lee. Optimal bidding in spot instance market. In *INFOCOM'12*, 2012.

[22] Spot instance: featured customer testimonials, 2015. https://aws.amazon.com/ec2/spot/testimonials/.

[23] Spot fleet, 2016. http://docs.aws.amazon.com/AWSEC2/latest/UserGuide/spot-fleet.html.

[24] Spot bid status, 2016. http://docs.aws.amazon.com/AWSEC2/latest/UserGuide/spot-bid-status.html.

[25] STREAM, 2016. http://www.cs.virginia.edu/stream/.

[26] S. Subramanya, T. Guo, P. Sharma, D. Irwin, and P. Shenoy. Spoton: A batch computing service for the spot market. In *Proc. of SoCC'15*, 2015.

[27] S. Subramanya, A. Rizk, and D. Irwin. Cloud spot markets are not sustainable: The case for transient guarantees. In *Proc. of HotCloud'16*, 2016.

[28] S. Tang, J. Yuan, and X.-Y. Li. Towards optimal bidding strategy for amazon ec2 cloud spot instance. In *Proc. of IEEE CLOUD'12*, 2012.

[29] G. Urdaneta, G. Pierre, and M. Van Steen. Wikipedia workload analysis for decentralized hosting. *Elsevier Computer Networks*, 53(11), 2009.

[30] R. M. Wallace, V. Turchenko, M. Sheikhalishahi, I. Turchenko, V. Shults, J. L. Vazquez-Poletti, and L. Grandinetti. Applications of neural-based spot market prediction for cloud computing. In *IDAACS'13*, 2013.

[31] C. Wang, Q. Liang, and B. Urgaonkar. An empirical analysis of amazon ec2 spot instance features affecting cost-effective resource procurement. Technical report, CSE TR-16-006, Penn State University. http://www.cse.psu.edu/research/publications/tech-reports/2016/CSE-16-006.pdf, 2016.

[32] C. Wang, B. Urganokar, A. Gupta, L. Chen, R. Birke, and G. Kesidis. Effective capacity modulation as an explicit control knob for public cloud profitability. In *ICAC'16*, 2016.

[33] Z. Wu, M. Butkiewicz, D. Perkins, E. Katz-Bassett, and H. V. Madhyastha. Spanstore: Cost-effective geo-replicated storage spanning multiple cloud services. In *Proc. of SOSP'13*, 2013.

[34] Z. Xu, C. Stewart, N. Deng, and X. Wang. Blending on-demand and spot instances to lower costs for in-memory storage. In *Proc. of IEEE Infocom'16*, 2016.

[35] M. Zafer, Y. Song, and K.-W. Lee. Optimal bids for spot vms in a cloud for deadline constrained jobs. In *Cloud'12*, 2012.

[36] H. Zhao, M. Pan, X. Liu, X. Li, and Y. Fang. Optimal resource rental planning for elastic applications in cloud market. In *Proc. of IPDPS'12*, 2012.

An Experimental Performance Evaluation of Autoscaling Policies for Complex Workflows

Alexey Ilyushkin[1], Ahmed Ali-Eldin[2], Nikolas Herbst[3], Alessandro V. Papadopoulos[4], Bogdan Ghiț[1], Dick Epema[1], Alexandru Iosup[1]

[1]Delft University of Technology, the Netherlands [2]Umeå University, Sweden
[3]University of Würzburg, Germany [4]Mälardalen University, Sweden

{a.s.ilyushkin, b.i.ghit, d.h.j.epema, a.iosup}@tudelft.nl, ahmeda@cs.umu.se, nikolas.herbst@uni-wuerzburg.de, alessandro.papadopoulos@mdh.se

ABSTRACT

Simplifying the task of resource management and scheduling for customers, while still delivering complex Quality-of-Service (QoS), is key to cloud computing. Many autoscaling policies have been proposed in the past decade to decide on behalf of cloud customers when and how to provision resources to a cloud application utilizing cloud elasticity features. However, in prior work, when a new policy is proposed, it is seldom compared to the state-of-the-art, and is often compared only to static provisioning using a predefined QoS target. This reduces the ability of cloud customers and of cloud operators to choose and deploy an autoscaling policy. In our work, we conduct an *experimental* performance evaluation of autoscaling policies, using as application model workflows, a commonly used formalism for automating resource management for applications with well-defined yet complex structure. We present a detailed comparative study of general state-of-the-art autoscaling policies, along with two new workflow-specific policies. To understand the performance differences between the 7 policies, we conduct various forms of pairwise and group comparisons. We report both individual and aggregated metrics. Our results highlight the trade-offs between the suggested policies, and thus enable a better understanding of the current state-of-the-art.

1. INTRODUCTION

Cloud computing is a model of outsourcing IT services on demand, pay-per-use. To make this model useful for a variety of customers, cloud operators have to simplify the process of obtaining and managing a useful supply of services. To this end, cloud operators make available to their customers various autoscaling policies (*autoscalers, AS*), which are essentially parametrized cloud-scheduling algorithms that dynamically regulate the amount of resources allocated to a cloud application based on the load demand and the Quality-of-Service (QoS) requirements typically set by the customer. Many autoscalers already exist, both general autoscalers for request-response applications [5, 9, 43, 16, 34] and autoscalers for more task- and structure-oriented applications such as workflows [7, 14, 10, 37, 12]. The selection of an appropriate autoscaling policy is crucial, as a good choice can lead to significant performance and financial benefits for cloud customers, and to improved flexibility and ability to meet QoS requirements for cloud operators. Selecting among the proposed autoscalers is not easy, as no method currently exists to systematically evaluate and compare autoscalers. To alleviate this problem, in this work we propose and use the first systematic method to evaluate and compare experimentally the performance of autoscalers for workflow-based workloads running in cloud settings.

The lack of a method for comparing autoscalers derives in our view from scientific and industry practice. For the past decade, much academic work has focused on building basic mechanisms and autoscalers for specific applications, and thus there was little related work to compare to, and the threshold for publication has been kept low to develop the community. In industry, much attention has been put on building cloud infrastructures that enable autoscaling as a mechanism, and relatively less on providing good libraries of autoscalers for customers to choose from. (The authors' own prior work reflects this situation [21, 36].) However, for the past two years a collaboration started within SPEC Research's Cloud Group that highlighted the need for deeper, systematic work in the evaluation and comparison of autoscalers, raising questions such as *How to evaluate the performance of individual autoscalers?*, and *How to compare autoscalers?*

Among the many application types, our focus on workflow-based workloads is motivated by two aspects. First, we are motivated by the increasing popularity [39, 40] of workflows for science and engineering [1, 25, 27], big data [28], and business applications [41], and by the ability of workflows to express complex applications whose interconnected tasks can be managed automatically on behalf of cloud customers [24]. Second, although generic autoscalers focus mainly on QoS aspects, such as throughput, response-time and cost constraints, state-of-the-art autoscalers can also take into account application structure [31]. *How does the performance of generic and of workflow-specific autoscalers differ?*

Modern workflows have different structures, sizes, task types, run-time properties, and performance requirements, and thus raise specific and important challenges in assessing the performance of autoscalers: *How does the performance of generic and of workflow-specific autoscalers depend on workflow-based workload characteristics?*

ICPE'17, April 22–26, 2017, L'Aquila, Italy

DOI: http://dx.doi.org/10.1145/3030207.3030214

Towards addressing the aforementioned questions, our contribution is three-fold:

1. We design a comprehensive method for evaluating and comparing autoscalers (Sections 2–4). Our method includes a model for elastic cloud platforms (Section 2), identifying a set of relevant metrics for assessing autoscaler performance (Section 3), and a taxonomy and survey of exemplary general and workflow-specific autoscalers (Section 4).
2. Using the method, we comprehensively and experimentally quantify the performance of 7 generic and workflow-specific autoscalers, for more than 10 metrics (Section 5). We show the differences between various policy types, analyze parametrization effects, evaluate the influence of workload characteristics on individual performance metrics, and explain the reasons for the performance variability we observe in practice.
3. We also compare the autoscalers systematically (Section 6), through 3 main approaches: a pair-wise comparison specific to round-robin tournaments, a comparison of fractional differences between each system and an ideal system derived from the experimental results, and a head-to-head comparison of several aggregated metrics.

2. A MODEL FOR ELASTIC CLOUD PLATFORMS

The autoscaling problem is an incarnation of the dynamic provisioning problem that has been studied in the literature for over a decade [8]. While in essence trying to solve the problem of how much capacity to provision given a certain QoS, most state-of-the-art algorithms published make different assumptions on the underlying environment, mode of operation, or workload used. It is thus important to identify the key requirements of all algorithms, and establish a fair cloud system for comparison.

2.1 Requirements

In order to improve the QoS and decrease costs of a running application, an ideal autoscaler proactively predicts and provisions resources such that: a) there is always enough capacity to handle the workload with no under-provisioning; b) the cost is kept minimal by reducing the number of resources not used at any given time, thus reducing over-provisioning; and c) the autoscaler does not cause consistency and/or stability issues in the running applications.

Since there are no perfect predictors, no ideal autoscaler exists. There is thus a need to have better understanding of the capabilities of the various available autoscalers in comparison to each other. For our work, we classify the autoscaling algorithms in two major groups: general and workflow-specific. Examples of general autoscalers include algorithms for allocating virtual machines (VMs) in data-centers, or algorithms for spawning web-server instances, etc. They are general because they mostly take their decisions using only external properties of the controlled system, e.g., workload arrival rates, or the output from the system, e.g., response time. In contrast, workflow-specific autoscalers base their decisions on detailed knowledge about the running workflow structure, job dependencies, and expected runtimes of each task [32]. In most cases, the autoscaler is integrated with the task scheduler [31].

While many autoscaling algorithms targeting different use case scenarios have been proposed in the literature, they are rarely compared to previously published work. In addition, they are usually tested on a limited set of relatively short traces. Most autoscaling-related papers seldom go beyond meeting some predefined metrics, e.g., with respect to response time or throughput. While the performance of most autoscalers is very dependent on how they are configured, this configuration is rarely discussed. Thus, to the best of our knowledge, there are no major comparative studies that analyse the performance of various autoscalers in realistic environments with complex applications. Our study aims to fill this gap by evaluating a set of algorithms in realistic setting.

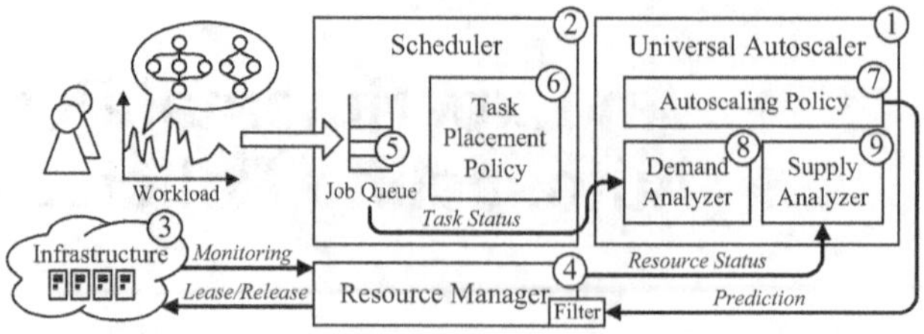

Figure 1: Elastic cloud platform.

2.2 Architecture Overview

Keeping the diversity of used cloud applications and underlying computing architectures in mind, we setup an elastic cloud platform architecture (Figure 1) which allows for comparable experiments by providing relatively equal conditions for different autoscaling algorithms and different workloads. The equal size of the virtual computing environment, which is agnostic to the used application type, is the major common property of the system in our model. We believe that the selected architecture of the proposed unified elastic cloud platform properly reflects the approaches used in modern commercial solutions.

The core of our system is the autoscaling service (Component 1 in Figure 1) that runs independently as a REST service. The experimental testbed consists of a scheduler (2) and a virtual infrastructure service (3) which maintains a set of computing resources. A resource manager (4) monitors the infrastructure and controls the resource provisioning. Users submit their complex jobs directly to the scheduler which maintains a single job queue (5). The tasks from the queued jobs are mapped on the computing resources in accordance to the task placement policy (6). The scheduler periodically calls the autoscaling service providing it with monitoring data from the last time period. We refer to this period as the *autoscaling interval*. In contrast, in event-based autoscaling the autoscaler is invoked on every change in the demand curve. However, we do not use the event-based autoscaling approach because it can be derived from the interval-based autoscaling with rather short autoscaling interval. Additionally, the event-based autoscaling would make the experimental setup more complex and would require to incorporate extra processing logic into the scheduler.

The autoscaling service implements an autoscaling policy (7) and has a demand analyzer (8) which uses information about running and queued jobs to compute the momentary demand value. The supply analyzer (9) computes the momentary supply value by analyzing the status of computing resources. The autoscaling service responds to the scheduler with the predicted number of resources which should be allocated or deallocated. Before applying the prediction, the resource manager filters it trimming the obtained value by the maximal number of available resources. To avoid error accumulation, the autoscaling interval is usually chosen so that the provisioning actions made during the autoscaling interval has already taken effect. Thus it is guaranteed that the provisioning time is always shorter than the autoscaling interval. In case when the provisioning time is longer than the autoscaling interval, the resource manager should apply the prediction only partially considering the number of "straggling" resources. In practice, it means that the resource manager should consider booting VMs as fully provisioned resources.

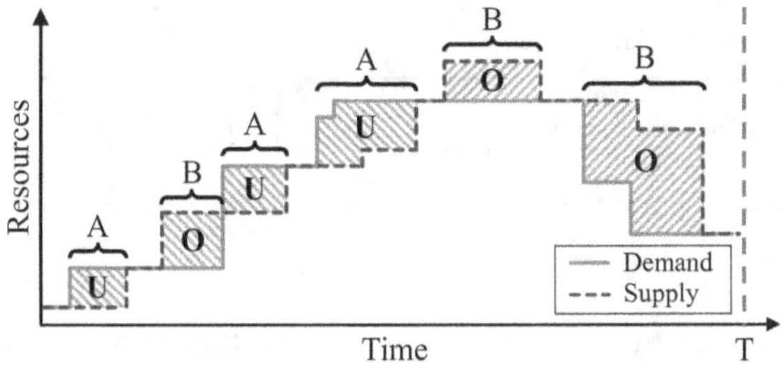

Figure 2: The supply and demand curves illustrating the under- and over-provisioning periods (A and B) quantified in the number of resources (areas U and O).

2.3 Workflows as Main Applications

For our experiments, we use complex workflows as a workload for our system. A *workflow* is a set of tasks with precedence constraints among them. Alternatively it can be represented in the form of a Directed Acyclic Graph (DAG). Each workflow task can start its execution when all of its input constraints are satisfied (e.g., when the input files are ready). Each task can have multiple inputs and multiple outputs. The precedence constraints make workflow scheduling non-work-conserving as there may be idle processors in the system while there are no waiting tasks with all their dependencies satisfied. This property is one of the reasons we selected workflows for our experiments, since it puts the considered autoscaling algorithms in more stringent conditions. Additionally, depending on the DAG structure, workflows can also reflect the behavior of other popular jobs types such as web-requests, bags-of-tasks or parallel applications. One whole workflow in our setup is considered as a job. The *size* of a workflow is defined as the number of tasks it has. We focus on workflows which only consist of tasks requiring a single processor core.

3. PERFORMANCE METRICS FOR ASSESSING AUTOSCALERS

We use both system- and user-oriented evaluation metrics to assess the performance of the autoscalers. The system-oriented metrics quantify over-provisioning, under-provisioning, and stability of the provisioning. Notably, some of these metrics have been endorsed by the Research Group of the Standard Performance Evaluation Corporation (SPEC) [21]. The user-oriented metrics are aimed to assess the impact of autoscaler usage on the speed of workflow execution.

3.1 Supply and Demand

All the considered system-oriented metrics are based on the analysis of discrete supply and demand curves. The resource *demand* induced by a load is understood as the minimal amount of resources required for fulfilling a given performance-related service level objective (SLO). In the context of workflows, we define the momentary demand as the number of eligible and running tasks in all the queued workflows, as in our model a resource can only process one task at a time. Accordingly, the *supply* is the monitored number of provisioned resources that are either idle, booting or processing tasks. Figure 2 shows an example of the two curves. If demand exceeds supply, there is a shortage of available resources (under-provisioning) denoted by intervals A and areas U in the figure. In contrast, over-provisioning is denoted by intervals B and areas O.

3.2 Accuracy

Let the resource demand at a given time t be d_t, and the resource supply s_t. The *under-provisioning accuracy* metric a_U is defined as the average fraction by which the demand exceeds the supply:

$$a_U := \frac{1}{T \cdot R} \sum_{t=1}^{T} (d_t - s_t)^+ \Delta t,$$

where T is the time horizon of the experiment expressed in time steps, R is the total number of resources available in the current experimental setup, $(x)^+ := \max(x, 0)$ is the positive part of x, and Δt is the time elapsed between two subsequent measurements. Analogously, we define the *over-provisioning accuracy* a_O as:

$$a_O := \frac{1}{T \cdot R} \sum_{t=1}^{T} (s_t - d_t)^+ \Delta t.$$

Figure 2 shows an intuition of the meaning of the provided accuracy metrics. Under-provisioning accuracy a_U is equivalent to summing the areas U where the resource demand exceeds the supply normalized by the duration of the measurement period T. Similarly, the over-provisioning accuracy metric a_O is based on the sum of areas O where the resource supply exceeds the demand.

It is also possible to normalize the metrics by the actual resource demand, obtaining therefore a normalized, and more fair indicator. In particular, the two metrics can be modified as:

$$\bar{a}_U := \frac{1}{T} \sum_{t=1}^{T} \frac{(d_t - s_t)^+}{\max(d_t, \varepsilon)} \Delta t,$$

$$\bar{a}_O := \frac{1}{T} \sum_{t=1}^{T} \frac{(s_t - d_t)^+}{\max(d_t, \varepsilon)} \Delta t,$$

with $\varepsilon > 0$; in our setting we selected $\varepsilon = 1$. The normalized metrics are particularly useful when the resource demand has a large variance over time, and it can assume both large and small values. In fact, under-provisioning of 1 resource unit when 2 resource units are requested is much more harmful than under-provisioning 1 resource unit when 1000 resource units are requested. Therefore, this type of normalization allows a more fair evaluation of the obtainable performance.

Since under-provisioning results in violating SLOs, a customer might want to use a platform that minimizes under-provisioning. Thus, the challenge is to ensure that enough resources are provided at any point in time, but at the same time distinguish themselves from competitors by minimizing the amount of over-provisioned resources. Considering this, the defined separate accuracy metrics for over- and under-provisioning allow providers to better communicate their autoscaling capabilities and customers to select the provider or autoscaling algorithm that best matches their needs.

In the context of workflows, over-provisioning accuracy can also be represented in the number of idle resources (i.e. the resources which were excessively provisioned and currently are not utilized). In ideal situation when an autoscaler perfectly follows the demand curve, there should be no idle resources as the system will always have enough eligible tasks to run. Thus we present an additional over-provisioning accuracy metric m_U which is equal to the average number of idle resources during the experiment time:

$$m_U := \frac{1}{T \cdot R} \sum_{t=1}^{T} u_t \Delta t,$$

where u_t is the number of idle resources at time t.

3.3 Wrong-Provisioning Timeshare

The timing aspect of elasticity is characterized from the viewpoint of the *wrong-provisioning timeshare* on the one hand, and from the viewpoint of the induced *instability* accounting for superfluous or missed adaptations on the other hand [20].

The accuracy metrics allow no reasoning as to whether the average amount of under-/over-provisioned resources results from a few big deviations between demand and supply or if it is rather caused by a constant small deviation. To address this, the following two metrics are designed to provide insights about the fraction of time in which under- or over-provisioning occurs.

As visualized in Figure 2, the following metrics t_U and t_O are computed by summing the total amount of time spent in an under- A or over-provisioned B state normalized by the duration of the measurement period. Letting sign (x) be the sign function of x, the overall timeshare spent in under- or over-provisioned states can be computed as:

$$t_U := \frac{1}{T}\sum_{t=1}^{T}(\text{sign}\,(d_t - s_t))^{+}\Delta t,$$

$$t_O := \frac{1}{T}\sum_{t=1}^{T}(\text{sign}\,(s_t - d_t))^{+}\Delta t.$$

3.4 Instability

Although the accuracy and timeshare metrics characterize important aspects of elasticity, platforms can still behave differently while producing the same metric values for accuracy and wrong-provisioning timeshare. The *instability* metric k captures this instability and inertia of elasticity mechanisms. A low stability increases adaptation overheads and costs (e.g., in case of instance-hour-based pricing), whereas a high level of inertia results in a decreased SLO compliance.

Letting $\Delta d_t := d_t - d_{t-1}$, and $\Delta s_t := s_t - s_{t-1}$, the *instability* metric k which shows the fraction of time the supply and demand curves move in opposite directions is defined as:

$$k := \frac{1}{T-1}\sum_{t=2}^{T}\min((\text{sign}\,(\Delta s_t) - \text{sign}\,(\Delta d_t))^{+}, 1)\Delta t.$$

Similarly, we define a complementary metric k' which captures the moments when the curves move towards each other:

$$k' := \frac{1}{T-1}\sum_{t=2}^{T}\min((\text{sign}\,(\Delta d_t) - \text{sign}\,(\Delta s_t))^{+}, 1)\Delta t.$$

If supply follows demand perfectly then both instability metrics are equal to zero.

3.5 User-Oriented Metrics

To assess the autoscaling policies from the user perspective, we employ the (average) elastic slowdown, which is defined in steps in the following way.

The *wait time* T_w of a workflow is the time between its arrival and the start of its first task. The *execution time* T_e of a workflow is the sum of the runtimes of all its tasks. The *makespan* T_m of a workflow is the time between the start of its first task until the completion of its last task. The *response time* T_r of a workflow is the sum of its wait time and its makespan: $T_r = T_w + T_m$. The *slowdown* S of a workflow is its response time (in a busy system, when the workflow runs simultaneously with other workflows) normalized by its makespan T'_m in an empty system of the same size (when the workflow has exclusive access to all the resources): $S = T_r \ / \ T'_m$. The *elastic slowdown* S_e of a workflow is its response time in a system which uses an autoscaler (where the workflow runs simultaneously with other workflows) normalized by its response time T'_r in a system of the same size without an autoscaler (where the workflow runs simultaneously with the same set of other workflows and where a certain amount of resources is constantly allocated): $S_e = T_r \ / \ T'_r$. In ideal situation, where jobs do not experience slowdown due to the use of an autoscaler, the optimal value for S_e is 1. When S_e is less than 1, then a workflow accelerates from the use of an autoscaler. We define the *average number of resources* $\overline{V}$ the system utilized during the experiment to compute the *gain* of using an autoscaler. We also calculate the *average task throughput* $\overline{T}$ which is defined as the number of tasks processed per time unit (e.g., second, minute or hour).

Source of Information	Timeliness of Information	
	Long-term	**Current/Recent**
Server (General)	Hist, Reg, ConPaaS	React, Adapt
Job (WF-specific)	Plan	Token

Table 1: The two-dimensional taxonomy of the considered autoscalers.

4. AUTOSCALING POLICIES

For evaluation, we select five representative general autoscalers and propose two workflow-specific autoscalers. We classify them using a taxonomy along two dimensions and summarize the survey of common autoscaling policies across these dimensions in Table 1. The taxonomy allows us to ensure the proper coverage of the design space. We identify four groups of autoscalers, which differ in the way they treat the workload information. The first group consists of general autoscalers Hist, Reg, and ConPaaS which require server-specific information and use historical data to make their predictions. The second group consists of React and Adapt autoscalers which also require server-specific information for their operation but they do not use history to make autoscaling decisions. The last two groups use job-specific information (e.g., structure of a workflow) and also differ in a way they deal with the historical data: Plan needs detailed per-task information while Token needs far less historical data and only requires a runtime estimate for the whole job. Further, we present all the autoscalers in more detail. When introducing each autoscaler we additionally indicate in the title of the section to which dimensions of the taxonomy it belongs.

4.1 General Autoscaling Policies

As different autoscalers exhibit varying performance, five existing general autoscalers have been selected. By a general autoscaler, we refer to autoscalers that have been published for more general workloads including multi-tier applications, but that are not designed particularly for workflow applications. The five autoscalers can be used on a wide range of scenarios with no human tuning. We implement four state-of-the-art autoscalers that fall in this criteria. In addition, we acquire the source codes of one open-source state-of-the-art autoscaler. The selected methods have been published in the following years 2008 [43] (with an earlier version published in 2005 [42]), 2009 [9], 2011 [23], 2012 [5, 3], and 2014 [16]. This is a representative set of the development of cloud autoscalers design across the past 10 years.

4.1.1 General Autoscalers for Workflows

All of the chosen general autoscalers have been designed to control performance metrics that are still less commonly used for workflow applications, namely, request response time, and throughput. The reason is that historically, workflow applications were rather big or were submitted in batches [40]. However, emerging workflow types which require quick system reaction and the usage of workflows in the areas in which they were less popular, e.g., for

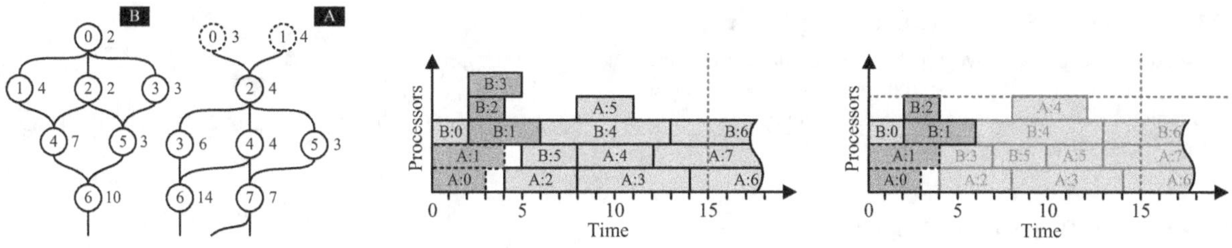

(a) Job queue. (b) Unlimited partial plan. (c) Limited partial plan.

Figure 3: The Plan autoscaling algorithm.

complex web requests, making the use of general autoscalers more promising.

The autoscalers aimed to control the response time are designed such that they try to infer a relationship between the response time, request arrival rates, and the average number of requests that can be served per VM per unit time. Then, based on the number of request arrivals, infer a suitable amount of resources. This technique is widely used in the literature [18, 29] due to the non-linearity in the relationship between the response time and allocated resources.

A similarity does exist though between workflows and other cloud workloads. A task in a workflow job can be considered as a long running request. The number of tasks becoming eligible can be considered as the request arrival rate for workflows. Therefore, we have adapted the general autoscalers to perform the scaling based on the number of task arrivals per unit time.

4.1.2 The React Policy (Server, Current)

Chieu et al. [9] present a dynamic scaling algorithm for automated provisioning of VM resources based on the number of concurrent users, the number of active connections, the number of requests per second, and the average response time per request. The algorithm first determines the current web application instances with active sessions above or below a given utilization. If the number of overloaded instances is greater than a predefined threshold, new web application instances are provisioned, started, and then added to the front-end load-balancer. If two instances are underutilized with at least one instance having no active session, the idle instance is removed from the load-balancer and shutdown from the system. In each case the technique *React*s to the workload change. For the rest of the paper, we refer to this technique as *React*. The authors introduce the scaling algorithm but provide no experiments to show the performance of the proposed autoscaler. The main reason we are including this algorithm in the analysis is that this algorithm is the baseline algorithm in our opinion since it is one of the simplest possible workload predictors. We have implemented this autoscaler for our experiments.

4.1.3 The Adapt Policy (Server, Recent)

Ali-Eldin et al. [5, 3] propose an autonomous elasticity controller that changes the number of VMs allocated to a service based on both monitored load changes and predictions of future load. We refer to this technique as *Adapt*. The predictions are based on the rate of change of the request arrival rate, i.e., the slope of the workload, and aims at detecting the envelope of the workload. The designed controller *Adapt*s to sudden load changes and prevents premature release of resources, reducing oscillations in the resource provisioning. *Adapt* tries to improve the performance in terms of number of delayed requests, and the average number of queued requests, at the cost of some resource over-provisioning. The algorithm was tested using a simulated environment using a non-scaled version of the FIFA 1998 worldcup server traces, traces from a Google cluster and traces from Wikipedia.

4.1.4 The Hist Policy (Server, Long-term)

Urgaonkar et al. [43] propose a provisioning technique for multi-tier Internet applications. The proposed methodology adopts a queuing model to determine how many resources to allocate in each tier of the application. A predictive technique based on building *Hist*ograms of historical request arrival rates is used to determine the amount of resources to provision at an hourly time scale. Reactive provisioning is used to correct errors in the long-term predictions or to react to unanticipated flash crowds. The authors also propose a novel datacenter architecture that uses Virtual Machine (VM) monitors to reduce provisioning overheads. The technique is shown to be able to improve responsiveness of the system, also in the case of a flash crowd. We refer to this technique as *Hist*. The authors test their approach using two open source applications, RUBIS which is an implementation of the core functionality of an auctioning site, and Rubbos a bulletin-board application modeled after an online news forum. The testing is performed using 13 VMs running on Xen. Traces from the FIFA 1998 worldcup servers are scaled in time and intensity and used in the experiments. We have implemented this autoscaler for our experiments.

4.1.5 The Reg Policy (Server, Long-term)

Iqbal et al. propose a regression-based autoscaler (hereafter called *Reg*) [23]. The autoscaler has a reactive component for scale-up decisions and a predictive component for scale-down decisions. When the capacity is less than the load, a scale-up decision is taken and new VMs are added to the service in a way similar to *React*. For scale-down, the predictive component uses a second order regression to predict future load. The regression model is recomputed using the complete history of the workload when a new measurement is available. If current load is less than the provisioned capacity, a scale-down decision is taken using the regression model. This autoscaler was performing badly in our experiments due to two factors; first, building a regression model for the full history of measurements for every new monitoring data point is a time consuming task. Second, distant past history becomes less relevant as time proceeds. After contacting the authors, we have modified the algorithm such that the regression model is evaluated for only the past 60 monitoring data points.

4.1.6 The ConPaaS Policy (Server, Long-term)

ConPaaS, proposed by Fernandez et al. [16]. The algorithm scales a web application in response to changes in throughput at fixed intervals of 10 minutes. The predictor forecasts the future service demand using standard time series analysis techniques, e.g., Linear Regression, Auto Regressive Moving Average (ARMA), etc. The code for this autoscaler is open source. We downloaded the authors' implementation.

4.2 Workflow-Specific Autoscaling Policies

In this section, we present two workflow-specific autoscalers designed by us. Their designs are inspired by previous work in this field and adapted to our situation. The presented autoscalers differ in a way they use workflow structural information and task runtime estimates.

4.2.1 The Plan Policy (Job, Long-term)

This autoscaler makes predictions by constructing and analyzing a partial execution *Plan* of a workflow. Thus it uses the workflow structure and workflow task runtime estimates. The idea is partially based on static workflow schedulers [2]. On each call, the policy constructs a partial execution plan considering both workflows with running tasks and workflows waiting in the queue. The maximal number of processors which are used by this plan is returned as a prediction. The time duration of the plan is limited by the autoscaling interval. The plan is two-dimensional, where one dimension is time and another dimension is processors (VMs).

The policy employs the same task placement strategy as the scheduler. In our case, the jobs from the main job queue are processed in first-come, first-served (FCFS) order and the tasks are prioritized in ascending order of their identifier (each task of a workflow is supposed to be assigned with a unique numeric identifier). For already running tasks, the runtimes are calculated as a remaining time to their completion. The algorithm operates as follows. On each call it initializes an empty plan with start time 0. Then it sequentially tries to add tasks in the plan in such as their starting times are minimal. The algorithm adds a task to the plan only if it is eligible or its parents are already in the plan. The plan construction lasts until there are no tasks which can be added in the plan or until the minimal possible task start time equals or exceeds the planning threshold (which is equal to the autoscaling interval), or until the processor limit is reached. If the processor limit is reached then this is returned as the prediction. Otherwise, the prediction is calculated as the maximal number of processors ever used by the plan within the planning interval.

Figure 3 shows an example of the operation of the algorithm. In Figure 3a we show the job queue at the moment when the autoscaler is called. The queue contains two workflows A and B, where A is at the head of the queue. Each workflow task is represented by a circle with an identifier within it and runtime in time units on the right. Tasks A:0 and A:1 are already running, finished tasks are not shown. The autoscaling interval (a threshold) is equal to 15 time units and is represented by a vertical red dashed line. Figure 3b shows an example of an unlimited plan where the processor limit is not reached. In this case the maximal number of processors used within the 15 time units interval is 5 which equals to the number of green rectangles in the figure (A:0, A:1, B:1, B:2, B:3). Figure 3c shows a plan where the number of available processors is limited by 4 (the horizontal red dashed line). In this case, the algorithm stops constructing the plan after placing task B:2 and returns the prediction, which simply equals to the maximal number of available processors (i.e., 4).

4.2.2 The Token Policy (Job, Recent)

The *Token* policy uses structural information of a DAG and does not directly consider task runtimes to make predictions and instead requires an estimated execution time of the whole workflow. It uses tokens to estimate the *Level of Parallelism* (LoP) of a workflow [22] by simulating an execution "wave" through a DAG. The operation of the algorithm is illustrated in Figure 4. The algorithm processes the workflows in the queue in the FCFS order. In the beginning, the algorithm picks a workflow from the queue and places tokens in all

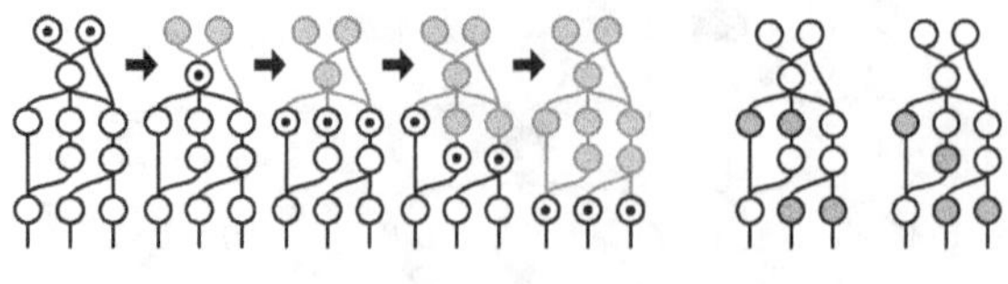

(a) Token propagation steps. (b) Two real LoPs.

Figure 4: The token-based LoP approximation.

of its entry tasks. Then in successive steps it moves these tokens to all the nodes all of whose parents already hold a token or were earlier tokenized. After each step, the number of tokenized nodes is recorded. For each workflow, the number of propagation steps is limited by a certain depth δ, which is defined as $\delta = (\Delta t \cdot N)/L$, where Δt is the autoscaling interval, N is the number of tasks on the critical path of the workflow, and L is the total duration of the tasks on the critical path of the workflow. Thus, the intuition is to evaluate the number of "waves" of tasks (future eligible sets) that will finish during the autoscaling interval. When δ or the final task of a workflow is reached, the largest recorded number of tokenized nodes is the approximated LoP value. The algorithm stops when the prediction value exceeds the maximal total number of available processors or when the end of the queue is reached. The final prediction is the sum of all of the separate approximated LoPs of the considered workflows.

The token-based algorithm does not guarantee the correct estimation of the LoP. The quality of the estimation depends on the DAG structure. In Figure 4a the estimated LoP of 3 is lower than the maximal possible LoP of 4 in Figure 4b. However, in our previous work [22], we showed that this method provides meaningful results for popular workflow structures.

5. EXPERIMENTAL EVALUATION

In this section, we present the workloads and the configuration of the cloud infrastructure we use for the experimental evaluation of the unified cloud system introduced in Section 2. To design our workloads, we use a set of representative scientific workflows. We take an experimental approach to evaluate chosen autoscaling algorithms with an extensive set of experiments in a virtualized environment deployed on our multi-cluster system.

5.1 Setup of Workflow-based Workloads

We choose three popular scientific workflows from different fields, namely Montage, LIGO, and SIPHT. The main reason for our choice is the existence of validated models for these workflow types. Montage [25] is used to build a mosaic image of the sky on the basis of smaller images obtained from different telescopes. LIGO [1] is used by the Laser Interferometer Gravitational-Wave Observatory (LIGO) to detect gravitational waves. And SIPHT [27] is a bioinformatics workflow used to discover bacterial regulatory RNAs.

We generate synthetic workflows using a workflow generator by Bharathi et al. [26, 6]. Each workflow is represented by a set of task executables and a set of input files. We use two workloads: a primary Workload 1 and a secondary Workload 2 each consisted of 200 workflows of different sizes in range from 30 to 600. Each workload contains an equal mixture of all of the three considered workflow types. As with many other workloads in computer systems, in practice, workflows are usually small, but very large ones may exist too [35]. Therefore, in our experiments we distinguish small, medium, and large workflows, which constitute fractions of 75%, 20%, and 5% of the workload. The size of the small, the medium, and the large workflows is uniformly distributed on the intervals [30, 39], [40, 199], and [200, 600], respectively. The distribution of the

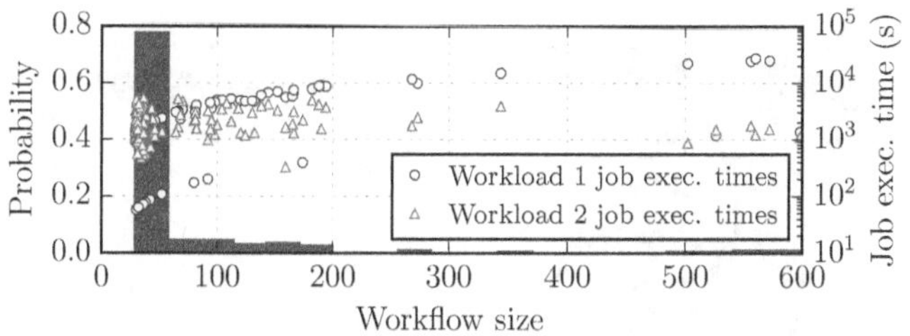

Figure 5: The distribution of job sizes in the workloads (histogram, left vertical axis) and the dependency between the job size and its execution time (glyphs, right vertical axis). The right vertical axis is in log scale.

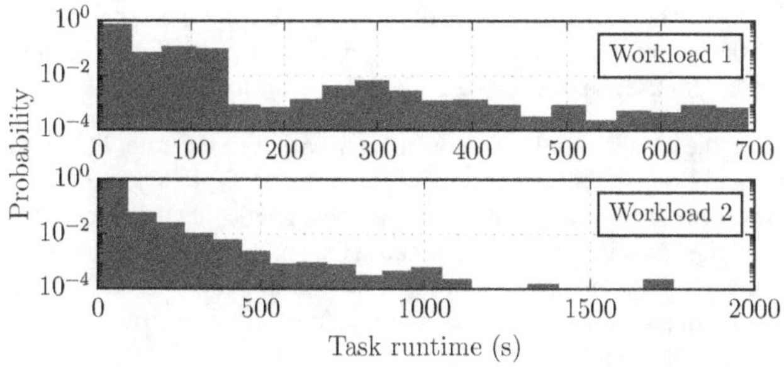

Figure 6: The distribution of task runtimes in the workloads (the horizontal axes have different scales, and the vertical axes are in log scale).

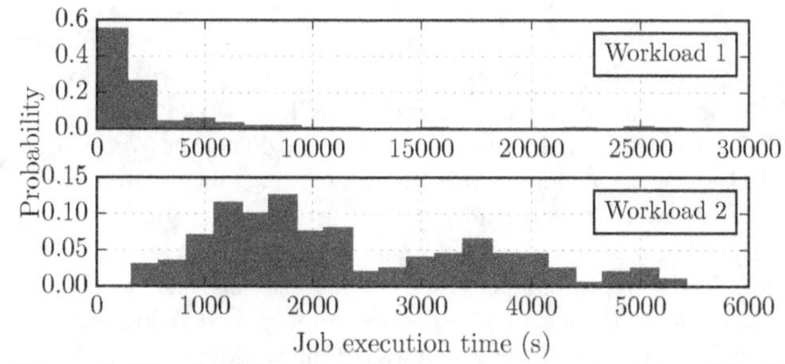

Figure 7: The distribution of job execution times in the workloads (all the axes have different scales).

job sizes in the workloads is presented in Figure 5. Figure 6 shows the distribution of task runtimes. Figure 7 shows the distribution of job execution times T_e in the workloads. For Workload 1, we use the original job execution time distribution from the Bharathi generator. For Workload 2, we keep the same job structures as in Workload 1 but change the job execution times using a two-stage hyper-Gamma distribution derived from the model presented in [30]. The shape and scale parameters (α, β) for each Gamma distribution are set to (5.0, 323.73) and (45.0, 88.291), respectively. Their proportions in the overall distribution are 0.7 and 0.3. Table 2 summarizes the properties of both workloads.

5.2 Setup of the Private Cloud Deployment

To schedule and execute workflows, we use the experimental setup in Figure 1 (Section 2). The KOALA scheduler is used for scheduling workflow tasks [15] on the DAS-4[1] cluster deployed at TU Delft. Our cluster consists of 32 nodes interconnected through QDR InfiniBand with 8-core 2.4GHz CPU and 24GB of RAM each. As a cloud middleware, OpenNebula is used to manage VM deployment, and configuration.

[1]http://www.cs.vu.nl/das4

Property	Workload 1	Workload 2
Mean task runtime	33.52 s	33.29 s
Median task runtime	2.15 s	2.65 s
SD of task runtime	65.40 s	87.19 s
Mean job execution time	2,325 s	2,309 s
Median job execution time	1,357 s	1,939 s
SD of job execution time	3,859 s	1,219 s
Total task runtime	465,095 s	461,921 s
Mean workflow size	69 tasks	
Median workflow size	35 tasks	
SD of workflow size	98 tasks	
Total task number	13,876 tasks	

Table 2: Statistical characteristics of the workloads. SD stands for standard deviation.

The execution environment for a single workflow consists of a single head VM and multiple worker VMs. The head VM uses a single CPU core and 4GB of RAM, while each worker VM uses a single core and 1GB of RAM. Tasks are then scheduled on the VMs. The workload generator with the workflow runners run on a dedicated node. The workflow runner coordinates the workflow execution by following the task placement commands from the scheduler. The runner is also responsible for copying files (task executables, input and output files) to and from the VMs in the virtual cluster. For data storage and transfer, we use a Network File System (NFS). This implies that if the head VM and worker VM are located on the same physical node, the data transfer time between them is negligible. In other cases, data transfer delays occur.

Compared to the job execution time, file transfer delays and the scheduling overhead are negligible. All tasks write their intermediate results directly to the shared storage to reduce data transfer delays for all workflows. A task can then run as soon as all of its dependencies are satisfied. Additionally, the runner copies all input files for a workflow to the virtual cluster before starting the execution. Thus, the impact from the file transfer delay between tasks on the system performance is negligible. Tasks are scheduled using *greedy backfilling* as it has been shown to perform well when task execution times are unknown a priori [22]. During the experiment only the autoscaler has the access to the information about job execution times and task runtimes.

5.3 Experiment Configuration

To configure the general autoscalers we use the average number of tasks a single resource (VM) is able to process per autoscaling interval (hereafter called *service rate*). The autoscaling interval, or the time between two autoscaling actions, is set to 30 seconds for all of our experiments.

We test with three different configurations in our experiments, where we change the value of the service rate parameter or the VM provisioning latency. The service rate in a request-response system is usually the average number of requests that can be served per VM. This parameter is either estimated online, e.g., using an analytical model to relate response time, as the one used in Hist [42], or offline [18, 13]. For a task-based workload, there are multiple options including using the mean task service time, the median task service time, or something in between.

In the first configuration, we assume that a VM serves on average 1 task per autoscaling interval, i.e., 2 tasks per minute. We derive this value by rounding to the nearest integer the service rate calculated based on the mean task runtime in the workloads (Table 2). This service rate allows us to perform additional comparison between general and workflow-specific autoscalers as the demand curves have the same dimension. In the second configuration, we use the median task runtime of Workload 1 which gives a service rate equal to 14 (also rounding to the nearest integer) tasks per autoscaling interval, i.e., 28 tasks per minute. The general autoscalers using the second configuration are marked with a star (⋆) symbol. While in the first two configurations we guarantee that all the provisioned VMs are booted at the moment when the autoscaler is invoked, in the third configuration the VM booting time of 45 s exceeds the autoscaling interval of 30 s. This configuration is also used to test workflow-specific autoscalers. The autoscalers using the third configuration are marked with a diamond (⋄).

For all the configurations and for both workloads the workload player periodically submits workflows to KOALA to impose the average load on the system about 40%. The workflows submitted to the system arrive according to a Poisson process. The mean inter-arrival interval is 117.77 s which results into arrival rate of 30.57 jobs per hour. Thus, the minimal duration of each experiment is approximately 6.5 h. If the autoscaler tends to under-provision resources or the provisioning time in the system is rather large then the experiment can take longer. We choose this relatively low utilization level on purpose to decrease the number of situations when the demand exceeds the maximum possible supply ceiling. Additionally, as workflow scheduling is non-work-conserving the system can saturate even at low utilizations. Thus, low utilization allows us to see better the dynamic behavior of the autoscalers by minimizing the number of extreme cases.

5.4 Experimental Results

The main findings from our experiments are the following:

1. Workflow-specific autoscalers perform slightly better than general-autoscalers but require more detailed job information.
2. General autoscalers show comparable performance but their parametrization is crucial.
3. Autoscalers reduce operational costs but slow down the jobs.
4. Long VM booting times negatively affect the performance.
5. No autoscaler outperforms all other autoscalers with all configurations and/or metrics.

5.4.1 *Analysis of Elasticity Metrics*

To better show the trade-offs between the autoscalers, we use the metrics described in Section 3. While calculating the system-oriented metrics, we excluded the periods where the demand curve exceeds the maximal available resource limit of 50 VMs. Since all the system-oriented metrics are normalized by the time of the experiment this approach does not bias the results.

The aggregated metrics for all the experimental configurations are presented in Table 3 and Table 4. Considering the cases where VMs are booting faster than the autoscaling interval, Table 3 shows that the autoscalers under-provision between 1% (using Hist) and 8% (using Adapt) less resources from the demand needs. Hist's superior under-provisioning with respect to others comes at the cost of on average provisioning 7 times the actual demand, compared to 27% over-provisioning for Adapt.

The policies with longer booting VMs in Table 3 show slightly different results compared to the runs with faster booting VMs. Both React$^{\diamond}$ and Plan$^{\diamond}$ tend to under-provision more when the VM provisioning time is longer. The job slowdowns are also higher. We picked only these two policies to have one from each group of autoscalers. Thus, we can conclude that longer provisioning times decrease the number of available resources for the workload. We can also notice that the average number of idle VMs decreases for React$^{\diamond}$ as the tasks more fully utilize provisioned VMs. m_U does not change for Plan$^{\diamond}$ as it over-provisions less.

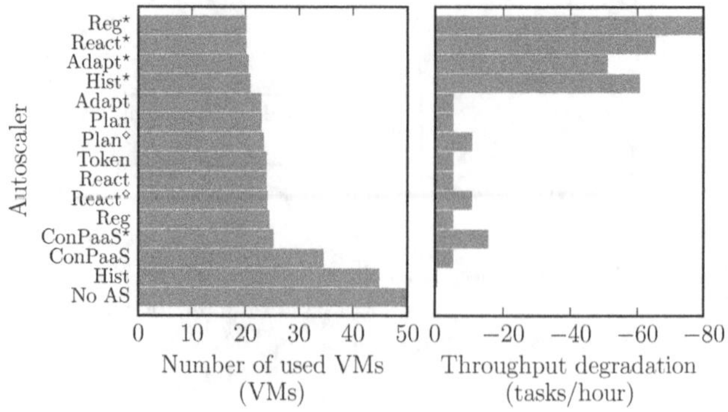

Figure 8: The average number of used VMs during the experiment and the average throughput degradation (compared with the no autoscaler case). All results are given for Workload 1.

For the general policies configured with service rate 1.0 and for workflow-specific policies in Table 3 and Table 4 job elastic slowdowns show low variability. We can conclude that the resources either significantly over-provisioned (Hist and ConPaaS) or already provisioned resources are running at low utilization (React, Adapt, Reg, Plan, and Token). The non-zero values of m_U metric in these cases confirm our assumption.

5.4.2 *The Influence of Different Workloads*

The difference is also visible between the workloads. While Workload 1 has the majority of short jobs, Workload 2 has a more equal distribution of job execution times and thus less bursty. Elastic job slowdowns in both tables confirm this tendency. For Workload 2 they slightly increase (the Plan policy in Table 4 is an exception) while going from small to large job sizes. We do not run Workload 2 with service rate different from 1.0 as we expect that the trend will be the same as for Workload 1.

The system-oriented metrics do not vary much between the workloads. For example, compare React in Table 3 with React in Table 4. Only Hist over-provisions less while running with Workload 2 as can be explained by lower burstiness of the workload.

5.4.3 *The Dynamics of Autoscaling*

Figure 9 shows the system dynamics for each autoscaling policy while executing Workload 1. Some of the autoscalers have a tendency to over-provision resources (Hist and ConPaaS). The other policies appear to be following the demand curve more or less closely. Note, that the demand curve has different shape for each autoscaler as the autoscaling properties affect the order in which workflow tasks become eligible.

The workflow-specific Plan policy follows the demand curve quite good and shows results similar to general autoscalers React, Adapt, and Reg running with service rate of 1.0. However, if policy follows the demand too close that increases job slowdowns. The Token policy, due to its specifics, needs to guess more while predicting the future demand and thus tends to over-provision a bit more.

5.4.4 *The Influence of Service Rate Parameter on the Autoscaling Dynamics*

The most noticeable differences in the results are between general autoscalers running with service rate 1.0 and with service rate 14.0. Figure 10 shows the selection of general autoscalers running with the same workload as in Figure 9. The demand curves in these two figures look very different, as well as the supply curve does not follow the demand curve so close anymore. We do not show ConPaaS in Figure 10 as it has similar supply pattern as for service

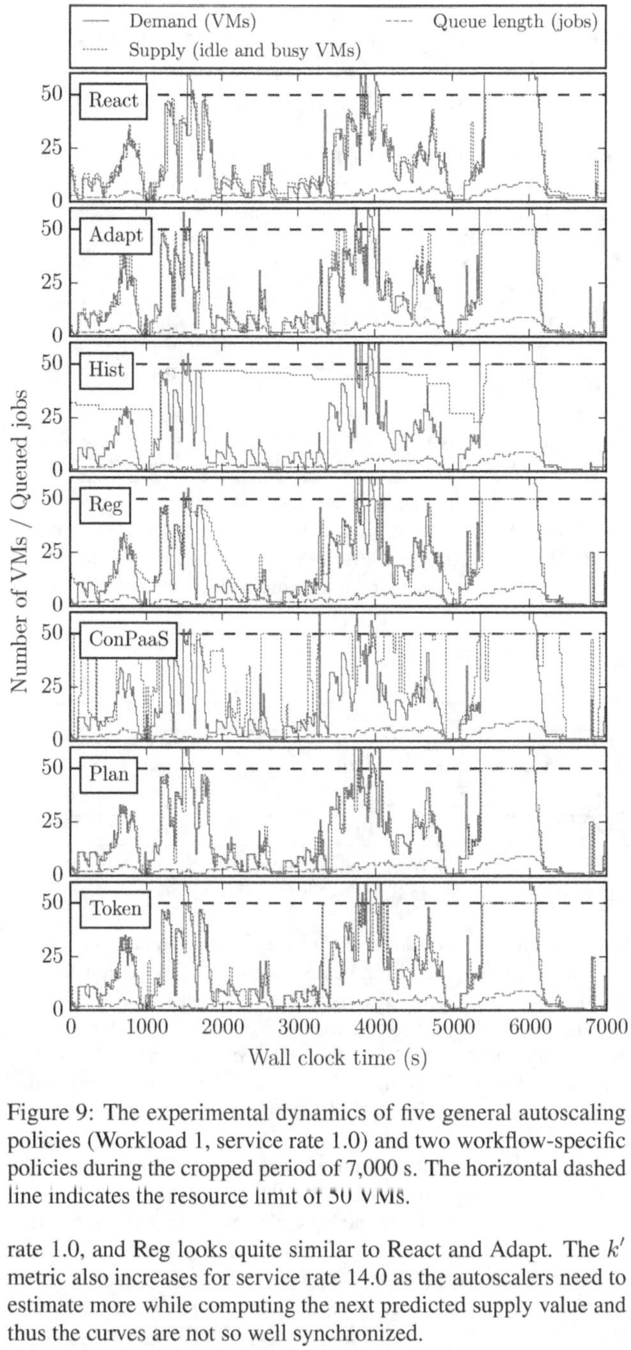

Figure 9: The experimental dynamics of five general autoscaling policies (Workload 1, service rate 1.0) and two workflow-specific policies during the cropped period of 7,000 s. The horizontal dashed line indicates the resource limit of 50 VMs.

rate 1.0, and Reg looks quite similar to React and Adapt. The k' metric also increases for service rate 14.0 as the autoscalers need to estimate more while computing the next predicted supply value and thus the curves are not so well synchronized.

5.4.5 *The Trade-off Between Operational Cost and Performance*

Here we study the influence of the number of used VMs on the throughput. We evaluate only two user-oriented metrics: the throughput degradation in tasks per hour compared with the no autoscaler case and the number of used resources (VMs). The values of these metrics are plotted in Figure 8. For example, for React the throughput degradation of –24 tasks per hour contributes only to 1.16% of the hourly throughput. In Figure 8, we can see that $\overline{T}$ is definitely affected by the $\overline{V}$. The variation of $\overline{T}$ depends on the properties of the workload such as task durations, the total number of tasks in the workload, and the number of tasks per job.

From these results we can conclude the following. Hist over-provisions quite a lot and achieves low throughput degradation.

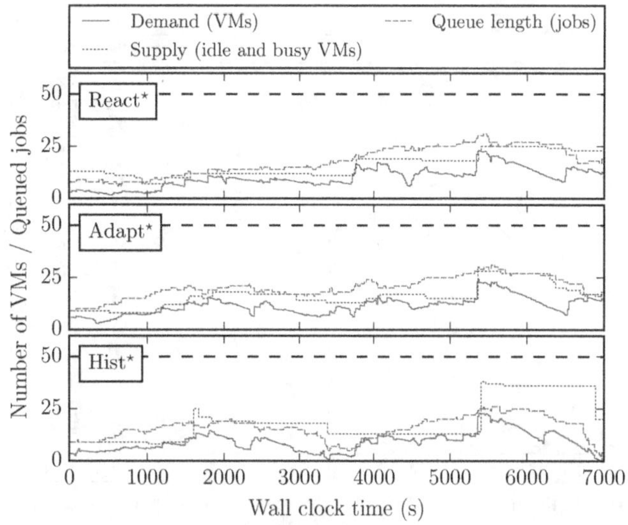

Figure 10: The experimental dynamics of three selected autoscaling policies (Workload 1, service rate 14.0) during the cropped interval of 7,000 s. The horizontal dashed line indicates the resource limit of 50 VMs.

ConPaaS also over-provisions but the throughput is not much affected because its supply curve is very volatile. ConPaaS* over-provisions less than ConPaaS as it "supposes" that the system needs less active VMs to process the same workload. Accordingly, the throughput degradation for ConPaaS* is also bigger. Reg, React, Token, Plan, and Adapt show almost similar results for service rate 1.0. Plan and Token policies show good balance between the number of used VMs and the throughput. Parametrization with the service rate of 14.0 (based on the median task runtime) decreases the performance by allocating less VMs. We can also see that longer booting VMs (React$^{\diamond}$ and Plan$^{\diamond}$) negatively affect the throughput.

6. WHICH POLICY IS THE BEST?

At first glance, considering all the computed metrics and all the autoscalers it is hard to distinguish the winners. Comparing only $\overline{V}$ and $\overline{T}$ metrics could be insufficient. Definitely, there is no single best and the final choice of a policy depends on many factors: application choice, optimization goals, etc. Thus, it is necessary to establish a procedure to allow the comparison of autoscalers in such a multilateral evaluation. For all the assessments presented in this section we use the set of experiments with Workload 1 as the most comprehensive. To include all the computed metrics into consideration we utilize two raking methods based on pairwise and fractional difference comparisons. Additionally, we aggregate elasticity and user metrics using an approach from our previous work.

6.1 Pairwise Comparison

In this section, we rank the autoscalers using the pairwise comparison method [11]. In this method, for each algorithm we pairwise compare the value of each metric with the value of the same metric of all the other autoscalers. We consider system metrics (a_U, a_O), (t_U, t_O), (k, k'), and user metrics S_e, $\overline{V}$, and $\overline{T}$. We do not consider $\overline{a}_U$ and $\overline{a}_O$, as well as m_U due to redundancy with the selected accuracy metrics. For all the metrics except $\overline{T}$, smaller value is better. In case when smaller value is better, for a pair of two autoscalers A and B, autoscaler A accumulates one point if the value of its certain metric is lower than the value of the same metric of autoscaler B. In case when bigger is better, autoscaler B gets the

Type	AS	a_U %	a_O %	$\overline{a}_U$ %	$\overline{a}_O$ %	t_U %	t_O %	k %	k' %	m_U %	S_e frac.	S_e (S) frac.	S_e (M) frac.	S_e (L) frac.	$\overline{T}$ tasks/h	$\overline{V}$ VMs
General	React	2	6	5	50	15	84	20	32	7	1.23	1.24	1.20	1.21	2,071	23.89
	React$^\diamond$	6	5	13	40	32	64	21	32	6	1.57	1.60	1.52	1.33	2,066	24.01
	Adapt	4	4	8	27	23	51	21	34	5	1.28	1.32	1.20	1.15	2,071	22.86
	Hist	1	60	1	737	2	97	**17**	43	60	**1.05**	**1.05**	**1.04**	**1.02**	**2,076**	44.81
	Reg	3	8	6	51	17	51	20	**31**	8	1.29	1.32	1.20	1.11	2,071	24.42
	ConPaaS	2	33	5	273	11	76	20	40	34	1.18	1.22	1.07	1.06	2,071	34.50
	React*	**0**	19	**0**	179	2	98	19	64	**0**	17.32	20.69	8.76	4.06	2,011	20.13
	Adapt*	**0**	16	1	150	4	96	19	63	**0**	20.06	23.25	12.26	6.08	2,026	20.49
	Hist*	**0**	25	1	463	5	95	20	60	1	12.93	15.30	7.00	3.24	2,016	20.87
	Reg*	**0**	12	1	78	5	94	20	62	**0**	25.57	30.04	14.38	7.22	1,997	**20.11**
	ConPaaS*	**0**	44	1	1092	**1**	98	21	45	7	2.11	2.12	2.26	1.25	2,061	25.15
WF-specific	Plan	3	4	7	19	20	41	20	**31**	4	1.30	1.32	1.28	1.18	2,071	22.93
	Plan$^\diamond$	8	**3**	17	**16**	38	**35**	21	32	4	1.64	1.72	1.44	1.38	2,066	23.31
	Token	3	6	7	35	16	53	20	33	7	1.25	1.28	1.20	1.20	2,071	23.88
None	No AS	0	73	0	869	0	100	17	43	73	1.00	1.00	1.00	1.00	2,076	50.00

Table 3: Calculated metrics for the main set of experiments with all the considered autoscalers and Workload 1. The diamond symbol ($\diamond$) marks the experiments where the VM booting time is longer than the autoscaling interval and service rate parameter is set to 1.0. The star symbol ($\star$) marks general autoscalers configured with service rate 14.0. All the other general autoscalers are configured with service rate 1.0. The metric S_e as well presented for small (S), medium (M), and large (L) job sizes. Best values in each column are highlighted in bold, except the No AS case.

Type	AS	a_U %	a_O %	$\overline{a}_U$ %	$\overline{a}_O$ %	t_U %	t_O %	k %	k' %	m_U %	S_e frac.	S_e (S) frac.	S_e (M) frac.	S_e (L) frac.	$\overline{T}$ tasks/h	$\overline{V}$ VMs
General	React	2	7	4	36	17	81	21	**32**	7	1.11	1.08	1.19	1.21	**1,905**	22.83
	Hist	**1**	46	**1**	338	**5**	94	**19**	41	46	**1.05**	**1.03**	**1.10**	**1.16**	**1,905**	40.82
WF-specific	Plan	3	**4**	6	**11**	22	**39**	21	**32**	**4**	1.16	1.13	1.24	1.28	**1,905**	**21.89**
None	No AS	0	66	0	563	0	100	19	41	66	1.00	1.00	1.00	1.00	1,910	50.00

Table 4: Calculated metrics for the additional set of experiments with selected autoscalers and Workload 2. The metric S_e as well presented for small (S), medium (M), and large (L) job sizes. Best values in each column are highlighted in bold, except the No AS case.

point. If both values are equal then both autoscalers get half point each. The results of the comparison are given in Table 5. The bigger the number of points the better.

6.2 Fractional Difference Comparison

In this section, we rank the autoscalers using the fractional difference method comparing all the autoscalers with an ideal case. For ideal case we construct an empirical ideal system that achieves the best performance for all the metrics we consider. Note, this system does not exist in practice. Thus, the ideal system is a system which compiles all the optimal values from Table 3 including the No Autoscaler case. For each metric m_i we compute its best value b_i which is either minimum or maximum value from the set of metric's values, depending on the metric (e.g., among our metrics only for $\overline{T}$ the biggest value is the best). For each autoscaler the score p for the metric j is computed as following:

$$p_j := \sum_{i=1}^{M} \frac{|m_i - b_i|}{\max(b_i, \varepsilon)},$$

where M is the total number of considered metrics, and $\varepsilon > 0$, which is here set to $\varepsilon = 1$. The final score of an autoscaler is the average of all the individual p_j scores. The final score shows the fraction by which the autoscaler differs from the empirically established ideal system. Thus, the smaller the final score the better. The results of the comparison are given in Table 5.

6.3 Aggregated Elasticity and User Metrics

In this section, we aggregate both elasticity and user metrics as proposed by Fleming et al. [17]. As commonly done in the benchmarking domain, we select a baseline as reference to compute speedup ratios and then average the speedups using an unweighted geometric mean. We choose as baseline the metric results with no active autoscaler. We group the elasticity metrics based on the covered aspects into three groups: accuracy (a_U, a_O), wrong provisioning timeshare (t_U, t_O), and instability (k, k'). We do not consider a_U and a_O, and m_U metrics. In addition, we compute a ratio based on the user metrics $\overline{V}$ (average number of VMs), the elastic slowdown S_e and the average throughput $\overline{T}$ to represent a balance between user-experienced performance and resource consumption. An overall ratio combines the user and elasticity ratios with the geometric mean. The resulting ranking is presented in Table 5. Using the described metric aggregation approach, the workflow-specific autoscaler Plan outperforms the generic ones. The Token policy is ranked on the same level as the generic Adapt and React policies. Hist and ConPaaS perform slightly better than without an autoscaler in this context. Strong impact on the autoscalers has the service rate parameter, a smaller impact can be observed for the experiments with longer provisioning time ($\diamond$).

7. THREATS TO VALIDITY

The limitations of the study are mainly expressed in the constrained number of considered job types and autoscalers. Improvements can be achieved by adding extra workloads with different characteristics to ideally consider wider spectrum of major job types that benefit from autoscaling. For example, data analytics workflows, streaming workflow applications, and workflows requiring quick reaction time [44]. Additionally, it is possible to report the job slowdown per workflow type. To make the study more appli-

AS	Pairwise points	Fractional frac.	Elasticity frac.	User frac.	Overall frac.
React	73.5	**2.23**	2.20	**1.19**	1.62
React$^{\diamond}$	51.0	4.50	1.99	1.10	1.48
Adapt	66.0	3.17	2.38	**1.19**	1.69
Hist	70.0	2.83	1.07	1.02	1.04
Reg	69.5	2.53	2.26	1.17	1.62
ConPaaS	62.0	2.84	1.34	1.07	1.20
React*	57.0	2.96	1.41	0.52	0.85
Adapt*	60.0	3.37	1.49	0.49	0.86
Hist*	55.0	3.02	1.30	0.56	0.86
Reg*	56.0	3.94	1.65	0.45	0.87
ConPaaS*	44.5	2.06	1.15	0.98	1.06
Plan	**78.5**	2.68	**2.72**	**1.19**	**1.80**
Plan$^{\diamond}$	59.0	5.23	2.18	1.09	1.54
Token	71.0	2.36	2.37	**1.19**	1.68
No AS	72.0	3.01	1.00	1.00	1.00

Table 5: The pairwise and fractional comparison, the aggregated elasticity and user metrics. The winners in each category (except No AS) are highlighted in bold.

cable to cloud environments, one can extend the set of workflow-related autoscalers with algorithms which consider job deadlines and costs [32, 10].

One of the interesting aspects is related to possible meanings of metric values. In fact our metrics are application-agnostic but their interpretation is not. In this sense, they can be seen as a raw metrics which, however, in a proper service-level agreement, can be assigned with certain thresholds and interpretation.

The experimental setup used in this paper could also be improved. Despite the fact that our private OpenNebula environment is rather representative, the number of concurrent users in Amazon EC2 and Microsoft Azure is much higher than in our case. Thus, it would be beneficial to consider public clouds to capture possible performance effects which could arise there. In addition, avoiding interval-based autoscaling in real setups could improve the quality of predictions by reacting to changes in the demand more quickly. We parametrize general autoscalers (computed service rate parameter) using the statistical properties of the whole workload as we have an access to this information. However, in the case when the workload properties are unknown different demand estimation methods can be used [38]. We do not analyze CPU utilization and RAM usage as for the considered workloads CPU and RAM information has low value as we primarily assign one task per VM and focus on performance characteristics from the perspective of job execution times.

8. RELATED WORK

Our work provides the first comprehensive comparative experimental study of autoscaling for workflows. We are unaware of any similar study in terms of the methodology taken, the number of policies compared, the number of performance metrics, and the size of experiments run. The importance of comparing different autoscaling algorithms has been recently discussed in the literature but mostly from a theoretical point of view [29, 36]. One exception is a tool that tries to utilise the differences between different autoscaling policies to achieve better QoS for customers by selecting a policy based on the workload [4]. That work, nevertheless, does not include any experimental comparison or deep analysis between the performance of the autoscalers as we do in our work.

The problem of scaling workflows has been studied in the literature with a focus on designing new autoscaling policies. Malawski et al. [31] discuss the scheduling problem of ensembles of scientific workflows in clouds while considering cost- and deadline-constraints. Mao et al. [33] optimize the performance of cloud workflows within budget constraints. They propose two algorithms, namely, *scheduling-first* and *scaling-first*. Cushing et al. [10] deal with prediction-based autoscaling of scientific data-centric workflows. Buyn et al. [7] try to achieve cost-optimized provisioning of elastic resources for workflow applications. They use the *Balanced Time Scheduling (BTS)* algorithm to calculate the minimal required number of resources which will allow to execute the workflow within a given deadline. Dörnemann et al. [14] consider scheduling of Business Process Execution Language (BPEL) workflows in Amazon's elastic computing cloud. Their main findings include the methods to automatically schedule workflow tasks to underutilized hosts and to provide additional hosts in peak situations. The proposed load balancer uses the overall system load to take scaling decisions in contrast to other systems where the throughput is more important. Heinis et al. [19] propose a design and evaluate the performance of a workflow execution engine with self-tuning capabilities. The engine is purely reactive and does not employ workload prediction. It has an autonomic controller to automatically reconfigure itself to adjust to the changes in the resource demand.

9. CONCLUSION AND ONGOING WORK

The ability to select autoscalers is beneficial for customers and operators of cloud computing, because it enables simple control over cloud elasticity and thus facilitates an on-demand, pay-per-view delivery of IT services. In this work, we have proposed a comprehensive method for comparing autoscalers when running workflow-based workloads in cloud environments. Our method includes a model for elastic cloud platforms, a set of over 10 relevant metrics for evaluating autoscalers, a taxonomy and survey of exemplary general and workflow-specific autoscalers, and experimental and analysis steps to conduct the comparison.

Using our method, we have evaluated 7 generic and workflow-specific autoscalers, and several autoscaler variants, when used to control the capacity for a workflow-based workload running in a realistic cloud environment. Our results across the diverse metrics highlight the trade-offs of using the different autoscalers. At the best of our knowledge, the efficiency of general autoscalers was previously unknown for workflows. We show that although workflow-specific autoscalers have the privilege of knowing the workflow structure in advance, it is possible for properly configured general autoscalers to achieve similar performance. Our results demonstrate that a correct parametrization of general autoscalers is very important. In our case, the service rate parameter is not the only one to affect the performance of general autoscalers. In particular, VM booting times and the choice of the autoscaling interval are also crucial, as many general autoscalers are designed to stably operate when VM booting times do not exceed a certain threshold. Finding optimal values for parameters could be even impossible (as they could be implementation-related) and will probably require more experiments.

Remarkably, our workflow-specific Plan autoscaler wins 4 out of 5 competitions while providing a good balance between operational costs and performance. The correct choice of an autoscaler is important but significantly depends on the application type. Thus, no single universal solution exists. In such a situation, the multilateral ranking methods which we use gain more importance.

For the future, we plan to extend this work to consider other application models, such as request-response services and media streaming workloads, and to conduct through the SPEC Research Group vendor-driven experiments.

10. REFERENCES

[1] B. Abbott et al. Search for Gravitational Waves from Binary Inspirals in S3 and S4 LIGO Data. *Physical Review D*, 77:062002, 2008.

[2] S. Abrishami, M. Naghibzadeh, and D. H. J. Epema. Cost-Driven Scheduling of Grid Workflows using Partial Critical Paths. *IEEE TPDS*, 23:1400–1414, 2012.

[3] A. Ali-Eldin et al. Efficient Provisioning of Bursty Scientific Workloads on the Cloud using Adaptive Elasticity Control. In *ScienceCloud Workshop*, 2012.

[4] A. Ali-Eldin et al. Workload Classification for Efficient Auto-Scaling of Cloud Resources. Technical report, Umeå University, Lund University, 2013.

[5] A. Ali-Eldin, J. Tordsson, and E. Elmroth. An Adaptive Hybrid Elasticity Controller for Cloud Infrastructures. In *IEEE NOMS*, 2012.

[6] S. Bharathi et al. Characterization of Scientific Workflows. In *WORKS Workshop*, 2008.

[7] E.-K. Byun et al. Cost Optimized Provisioning of Elastic Resources for Application Workflows. *FGCS*, 27:1011–1026, 2011.

[8] J. S. Chase et al. Managing Energy and Server Resources in Hosting Centers. In *ACM SIGOPS*, 2001.

[9] T. Chieu et al. Dynamic Scaling of Web Applications in a Virtualized Cloud Computing Environment. In *IEEE ICEBE*, 2009.

[10] R. Cushing et al. Prediction-Based Auto-Scaling of Scientific Workflows. In *MGC Workshop*, 2011.

[11] H. A. David. Ranking from Unbalanced Paired-Comparison Data. *Biometrika*, 74:432–436, 1987.

[12] E. De Coninck et al. Dynamic Auto-Scaling and Scheduling of Deadline Constrained Service Workloads on IaaS Clouds. *JSS*, 118:101–114, 2016.

[13] C. Delimitrou and C. Kozyrakis. Quasar: Resource-Efficient and QoS-Aware Cluster Management. *ACM SIGPLAN Notices*, 49:127–144, 2014.

[14] T. Dornemann, E. Juhnke, and B. Freisleben. On-Demand Resource Provisioning for BPEL Workflows using Amazon's Elastic Compute Cloud. In *9th IEEE/ACM CCGrid*, 2009.

[15] L. Fei et al. KOALA-C: A Task Allocator for Integrated Multicluster and Multicloud Environments. In *IEEE Cluster*, 2014.

[16] H. Fernandez, G. Pierre, and T. Kielmann. Autoscaling Web Applications in Heterogeneous Cloud Infrastructures. In *IEEE IC2E*, 2014.

[17] P. J. Fleming and J. J. Wallace. How Not to Lie with Statistics: The Correct Way to Summarize Benchmark Results. *ACM Communications*, 29:218–221, 1986.

[18] A. Gandhi et al. Autoscale: Dynamic, Robust Capacity Management for Multi-Tier Data Centers. *ACM TOCS*, 30, 2012.

[19] T. Heinis et al. Design and Evaluation of an Autonomic Workflow Engine. In *IEEE ICAC*, 2005.

[20] N. Herbst et al. BUNGEE: An Elasticity Benchmark for Self-adaptive IaaS Cloud Environments. In *SEAMS*, 2015.

[21] N. Herbst et al. Ready for Rain? A View from SPEC Research on the Future of Cloud Metrics. Technical report, SPEC Research Group, Cloud Working Group, 2016.

[22] A. Ilyushkin, B. Ghit, and D. Epema. Scheduling Workloads of Workflows with Unknown Task Runtimes. In *IEEE/ACM CCGrid*, 2015.

[23] W. Iqbal et al. Adaptive Resource Provisioning for Read Intensive Multi-Tier Applications in the Cloud. *FGCS*, 27:871–879, 2011.

[24] M. Islam et al. Oozie: Towards a Scalable Workflow Management System for Hadoop. In *ACM SIGMOD Workshop SWEET*, 2012.

[25] J. C. Jacob et al. Montage: An Astronomical Image Mosaicking Toolkit. *Astrophysics Source Code Library*, 1:10036, 2010.

[26] G. Juve et al. Synthetic Workflow Generators. https://github.com/pegasus-isi/WorkflowGenerator.

[27] J. Livny. Bioinformatic Discovery of Bacterial Regulatory RNAs Using SIPHT. In *Bacterial Regulatory RNA*. 2012.

[28] D. Logothetis et al. Stateful Bulk Processing for Incremental Analytics. In *SoCC*, 2010.

[29] T. Lorido-Botran et al. A Review of Auto-Scaling Techniques for Elastic Applications in Cloud Environments. *Journal of Grid Computing*, 12:559–592, 2014.

[30] U. Lublin and D. G. Feitelson. The Workload on Parallel Supercomputers: Modeling the Characteristics of Rigid Jobs. *JPDC*, 63:1105–1122, 2003.

[31] M. Malawski et al. Cost-and Deadline-Constrained Provisioning for Scientific Workflow Ensembles in IaaS Clouds. In *IEEE SC*, 2012.

[32] M. Mao and M. Humphrey. Auto-Scaling to Minimize Cost and Meet Application Deadlines in Cloud Workflows. In *SC*, 2011.

[33] M. Mao and M. Humphrey. Scaling and Scheduling to Maximize Application Performance within Budget Constraints in Cloud Workflows. In *IEEE IPDPS*, 2013.

[34] A. Naskos et al. Dependable Horizontal Scaling Based on Probabilistic Model Checking. In *IEEE/ACM CCGrid*, 2015.

[35] S. Ostermann et al. On the Characteristics of Grid Workflows. In *CoreGRID Integration Workshop*, 2008.

[36] A. V. Papadopoulos et al. PEAS: A Performance Evaluation Framework for Auto-Scaling Strategies in Cloud Applications. Tail Response Time Modeling and Control for Interactive Cloud Services. *ACM TOMPECS*, 2016.

[37] M. Pundir et al. Supporting On-demand Elasticity in Distributed Graph Processing. In *IEEE IC2E*, 2016.

[38] S. Spinner et al. Evaluating Approaches to Resource Demand Estimation. *Performance Evaluation*, 92:51 – 71, 2015.

[39] D. Talia. Toward Cloud-based Big-data Analytics. *IEEE Computer Science*, pages 98–101, 2013.

[40] I. J. Taylor et al. *Workflows for e-Science: Scientific Workflows for Grids*. Springer, 2014.

[41] S. Tilloo. Running Arbitrary DAG-based Workflows in the Cloud. http://www.ebaytechblog.com/2016/04/05/running-arbitrary-dag-based-workflows-in-the-cloud.

[42] B. Urgaonkar et al. An Analytical Model for Multi-Tier Internet Services and its Applications. In *ACM SIGMETRICS*, 2005.

[43] B. Urgaonkar et al. Agile Dynamic Provisioning of Multi-Tier Internet Applications. *ACM TAAS*, 3:1:1–1:39, 2008.

[44] N. Vydyanathan et al. A Duplication Based Algorithm for Optimizing Latency under Throughput Constraints for Streaming Workflows. In *ICPP*, 2008.

Dynamic Memory Partitioning for Cloud Caches with Heterogeneous Backends

Cristina L. Abad, Andres G. Abad and Luis E. Lucio
Escuela Superior Politecnica del Litoral, ESPOL. Guayaquil, Ecuador.
{cabadr,agabad,lelucio}@espol.edu.ec

ABSTRACT

Software caches, implemented with in-memory key-value stores, are important components of cloud architectures. In a common scenario, one server may serve requests from several applications with different workloads, each supported by a different backend (database or storage system); these applications compete for an allocation of the total memory. We present a model for dynamic memory partitioning for cloud caches with heterogeneous backends. Our work differs from recent work for cloud caches in that we consider: (1) the effect of having backends with different performance profiles, and (2) the cost of re-partitioning the memory. We discuss implementation issues that must be addressed, including the need for on-line and lightweight mechanisms for estimating the miss rate curves (MRCs) and ways to solve the non-convex optimization problem; specifically, we propose a probabilistic adaptive search algorithm that can be used for discontinuous, non-differentiable, or non-convex MRCs.

1. INTRODUCTION

Providers use caches to reduce latency and serve content faster, which in turn leads to increased sales and user engagement. For example, a 100ms latency penalty can lead to a 1% sales loss for Amazon, and an additional 400ms delay in search responses can reduce search volume by 0.74% [6]. For this reason, software caches—implemented with in-memory key-value stores like Redis and Memcached—have become important components of cloud architectures.

Software caches are simple, built to serve requests at a high-throughput, with minimum latency. Beyond their eviction policies, like Least Recently Used (LRU), they do not have any additional intelligence, making them unable to adapt to workload changes or application demands [3].

In this paper, we consider the case of a single organization that has multiple application workloads to cache. For example, consider a dynamic website that has four workloads to cache: SQL results, dynamic HTML pages, user profiles and user avatars. Each of these workloads can be served by a different Redis instance—in a multi-instance architecture—or by a single Memcached instance—in a multi-tenant architecture. Figure 1 illustrates these architectures. In this scenario, a challenge is how to efficiently share the limited memory resource between the applications. This is currently done statically [3], relying on empirical human expertise and offline workload analysis.

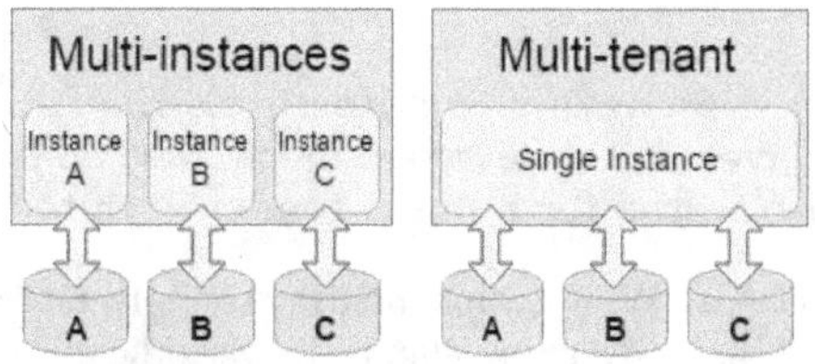

Figure 1: Multi-instance vs. multi-tenant cloud cache deployments; Redis favors the architecture on the left while Memcached, the one on the right.

We propose a model that can be used to dynamically configure memory allocations based on the observed workloads so that the overall system utility is maximized. Our work differs from recent work in memory partitioning for cloud caches [2, 3, 7, 5] in that we consider: (1) the effect of having backends with different performance profiles, and (2) the cost of re-partitioning the memory between applications.

Unlike recent work that has used the cache hit rate as the utility function to maximize [2, 3, 7, 5], we seek to minimize the overall expected access time of objects in the system; this includes the time to access the cache on a hit, and the time to access the backend on a miss. In addition, and given that different backends may be able to support different throughput, we include restrictions for the maximum throughput supported by each backend.

The cache re-partitioning cost, measured in increased latency while the memory is being reassigned, has not been considered by recent work either. The reason for this is that these solutions [2, 3, 7, 5] have been tailored for the multi-tenant architecture, encouraged by Memcached, for which the re-partitioning cost is negligible compared to the cost of re-assigning memory between different software instances[1].

We model these requirements and constraints as an optimization problem, whose utility function could be non-convex (as has been observed in real deployments [3]). We propose a probabilistic adaptive search algorithm that can be used for discontinuous, non-differentiable, or non-convex

[1]We ran experiments and confirmed our hypothesis that reassigning memory between instances incurred in a non-negligible cost; our results are reported in Section 3.

ICPE'17, April 22-26, 2017, L'Aquila, Italy

DOI: http://dx.doi.org/10.1145/3030207.3030237

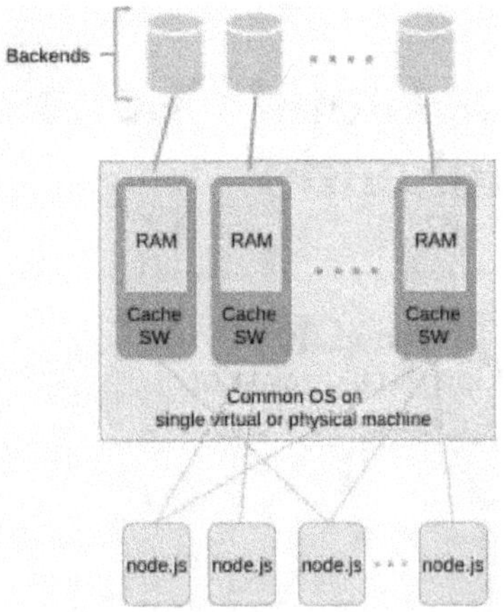

Figure 2: Motivating architecture: multi-instance caching layer with heterogeneous backends. Our model also works for a multi-tenant architecture.

utility functions. We are implementing the solver as a service that can be used by many clients to periodically calculate their optimal partitioning. The miss rate curves (MRCs)—the variable component of our utility functions—will be profiled by our service to determine the best way to solve the problem (LP-solver, hill climbing or our algorithm).

Finally, we discuss the implementation issues that should be addressed to implement our model, including the need for on-line mechanisms for estimating the MRCs, how to do so without adding latency to cache requests, among others.

2. THE CACHE PARTITIONING PROBLEM

We consider a system where a single virtual or physical machine hosts n instances of a software cache like Redis, each serving a different application workload (see Figure 2). These applications compete for the allocation of the total memory M. Our model also works for a multi-tenant architecture, as long as the different applications sharing the cache belong to the same organization (as discussed later in this section). For a solution that considers competing applications possibly trying to game the system, see [5].

In case of a cache miss, each application i is served by a backend with a maximum request throughput T_i. For example, a database server used to construct user profiles may have a lower throughput than a server that generates user identity avatars based on client IP (like Github's identicon).

Our model considers memory as the only shared resource, ignoring the sharing of CPU. In-memory key-value stores are memory- and not CPU-bound. This has been reported by Redis, and observed in caching-as-a-service providers as well as in large Memcached deployments [3].

The goal is *Pareto efficiency*: Fully utilize the memory, compute the ideal memory allocation $\mathbf{m} = [m_1, \ldots, m_n]$ and achieve the highest overall utility, given individual utility functions U_i's and total memory constraint M. This can be expressed as optimization problem:

$$\begin{aligned} \underset{\mathbf{m}}{\text{maximize}} \quad & \mathcal{F}(\mathbf{m}) = \sum_{i=1}^{n} w_i U_i(m_i) \\ \text{subject to} \quad & \sum_{i=1}^{n} m_i \le M, \\ & m_i \ge \underline{m}_i, i = 1, ..., n, \end{aligned} \tag{1}$$

where $U_i(m_i)$ is the utility function of application i as a function of its assigned memory m_i, and w_i is the weight assigned to i; this lets us indicate that one application is more (or less) important. If all the weights are equal, then all applications are equally important. $\underline{m}_i$ is the minimum memory assignment for application i.

We assume a non-adversarial model in which the applications are not trying to game the system. This is a reasonable assumption when all the applications belong to the same cloud client. Given that we consider a non-adversarial model, we do not seek *strategy proofness* [5]. Some application could be able to issue workloads that lead to a higher memory assignment to said application, but this would be at the cost of reduced overall system performance.

2.1 Backend-agnostic utility function

If we ignore the differences between the performance profiles of the backends, then the utility function can be expressed as the product of the application hit rate and the frequency of requests issued during some period:

$$U_i(m_i) = f_i \times h_i(m_i), \tag{2}$$

where $h_i(m_i)$ is the hit rate of application i as a function of assignment m_i, and f_i is the frequency of requests of i.

Recent work on on-line and lightweight miss rate curve (MRC) estimation [10, 9, 4] can be used to estimate the hit rate curve of each application, h_i, at a low cost. In Section 3 we discuss the overhead associated with these methods.

2.2 Backend performance

A limitation of the utility function described in (2) is that it optimizes the hit rate, regardless of whether an application may require a higher hit rate or tolerate a lower one. In practice, improving the hit rate of one application may not be as equally useful as improving the hit rate of another application, due to differences in the performance profiles of the corresponding backends. For example, all other things being equal, if one of the applications has a slow backend (e.g., if it processes complex SQL queries), increasing the hit rate of the cache serving that application is more useful than increasing the hit rate of a cache in front of a faster backend (e.g., a NoSQL database storing user profiles).

Instead of the hit rate, we use the *effective access time (EAT)* of an application as its utility function. The EAT_i is the time that it takes, on average, to access an object in application i. If we define cd_i as the time to access an object in the caching system and bd_i as the time to access an object in the backend system (including the time to process a cache miss), then the utility function to maximize is:

$$\begin{aligned} & U_i(m_i) = -f_i \times EAT_i(m_i), \text{ where} \\ & EAT_i(m_i) = h_i(m_i) \times cd_i + [1 - h_i(m_i)] \times bd_i. \end{aligned} \tag{3}$$

2.3 Solving the optimization problem

Consider optimization problem (1)[2]. If functions U_i's are all quasi-linear (as assumed in [2]) the resulting optimization problem can be solved by solving a sequence of feasibility problems, with a guaranteed precision of ϵ after $\lceil \log_2 R/\epsilon \rceil$ iterations, where R is the length of the search interval. If

[2]Our discussion henceforth applies to any of the utility functions in this paper.

functions U_i's are all concave, we have a convex optimization problem easily solved with off-the-shelf solvers. When functions U_i's are: discontinuous, non-differentiable, or non-convex, alternative approaches are required due to a lack of gradient or the presence of local optima.

One alternative is to use probabilistic search approaches, in which a generative model is used to generate candidate points in the search of an optimum. An adaptive mechanism may be added to the generative model to improve the performance of the sequentially generated candidates.

Let $\mathbf{x} = [x_1, \ldots, x_n]$ with $x_i = (m_i - \underline{m}_i)/(M - \sum_i \underline{m}_i)$, satisfying $\sum_i x_i = 1$ and $0 < x_i < 1$. We assume that the variability of $\mathbf{x}$ can be well modeled by a Dirichlet[3] distribution $Dir(\mathbf{x}|\alpha)$, with parameter vector $\alpha = [\alpha_1, \ldots, \alpha_n]$. Then, we define:

$$\tilde{\mathcal{F}}(\mathbf{x}) = \mathcal{F}\left((M - \sum_i \underline{m}_i)\mathbf{x} + \underline{\mathbf{m}}_i\right), \tag{5}$$

where $\underline{\mathbf{m}}_i = [\underline{m}_1, \ldots, \underline{m}_n]$.

We propose the following general approach, inspired in evolutionary strategies, for solving problem (1) in the case of non-convex and non-quasi-linear functions U_i's. We begin by setting α_i to $1/n$, for all i. We then generate K points $\mathbf{x}_k^\star|\alpha \sim Dir(\mathbf{x}|\alpha)$ for $k = 1, \ldots, K$. Note that points generated in this way satisfy all restrictions of problem (1).

Using points in set $\{\mathbf{x}_k^\star\}_{k=1}^K$ we construct the following prior mixture density for α:

$$g(\alpha; \{\mathbf{x}_k^\star\}) = \frac{1}{Z} \sum_{\mathbf{x} \in \{\mathbf{x}_k^\star\}} \phi_{\mathbf{x}}(\alpha), \tag{6}$$

where Z is a normalization constant and $\phi_{\mathbf{x}}$ is a non-negative function with finite mass concentrated around $\mathbf{x}$ (e.g., a *radial basis function* centered at $\mathbf{x}$). We proceed by sampling α from g and generating points $\mathbf{x}|\alpha_\gamma \sim Dir(\mathbf{x}|\alpha_\gamma)$, where α_γ is the vector with elements $\gamma\alpha_i$ for $\gamma > 1$. Note that, while random variables $\mathbf{x}|\alpha$ and $\mathbf{x}|\alpha_\gamma$ have the same expected value, γ has the effect of reducing the variance of $\mathbf{x}|\alpha_\gamma$ by a factor of γ^{-1}.

The above generative procedure corresponds to the following bayesian hierarchical structure:

$$\begin{aligned} \alpha &\sim G(\alpha; \{\mathbf{x}_k^\star\}) \text{ and} \\ \mathbf{x}|\alpha_\gamma &\sim Dir(\mathbf{x}|\alpha_\gamma), \end{aligned} \tag{7}$$

where G is the distribution function corresponding to mixture density g.

Our method proceeds by alternatively generating parameters α—the exploration stage—and generating J points $\mathbf{x}$'s conditioned on α_γ—the exploitation stage. The prior distribution for α is then updated using the K best cumulatively-observed points $\mathbf{x}_k^\star$'s and the procedure is repeated until a satisfactory solution is found.

Algorithm 1 provides the details of the proposed procedure. It rests to define how to choose $\gamma^{(j)}$ within the inner loop. The idea is to increase its value at each iteration to reduce the variance of α_γ and guarantee its convergence.

[3]The Dirichlet distribution $Dir(\mathbf{x}|\alpha)$ has a density function:

$$f(\mathbf{x}|\alpha) = \frac{\Gamma(\sum_{i=1}^n \alpha_i)}{\prod_{i=1}^n \Gamma(\alpha_i)} \prod_{i=1}^n x_i^{\alpha_i - 1}, \tag{4}$$

expected value $\mathbb{E}[x_i] = \alpha_i/A$ and variance $\mathbb{V}[x_i] = \alpha_i(A - \alpha_i)/(A^2(A+1))$, where $A = \sum_i \alpha_i$.

Algorithm 1: Probabilistic adaptive search

Input: Functions U_i's; number K of points to use; number J of rounds; function $\phi_{\mathbf{x}}$

Output: Best point $\mathbf{x}^*$, such that $\tilde{\mathcal{F}}(\mathbf{x}^*) \geq \mathbf{x}$ for every point $\mathbf{x}$ generated

$\alpha_i := 1/n$ for $i = 1 \ldots, n$
Generate $\mathbf{x}_k^\star|\alpha \sim Dir(\mathbf{x}|\alpha)$ for $k = 1, \ldots, K$
repeat
  Generate $\alpha \sim G(\alpha; \{\mathbf{x}_k^\star\})$
  for $j = 1, \ldots, J$ **do**
    Generate $\mathbf{x}|\alpha_{\gamma^{(j)}} \sim Dir(\mathbf{x}|\alpha_{\gamma^{(j)}})$
    if $\tilde{\mathcal{F}}(\mathbf{x}) > \min_k \{\tilde{\mathcal{F}}(\mathbf{x}_k^\star)\}$ **then**
      $\{\mathbf{x}_k^\star\} := \mathbf{x} \cup \{\mathbf{x}_k^\star\} \setminus \arg\min_{\mathbf{x} \in \{\mathbf{x}_k^\star\}} \tilde{\mathcal{F}}(\mathbf{x})$
until *Satisfactory solution* $\mathbf{x}^\star = \arg\max_{\mathbf{x} \in \{\mathbf{x}_k^\star\}} \tilde{\mathcal{F}}(\mathbf{x})$ *is found;*
return $\mathbf{x}^\star$

2.4 Backend constraints

One may also want to add a backend's maximum throughput, T_i, to the problem formulation; increasing the hit rate is a way to ensure that T_i is not exceeded. This can be expressed as a non-linear constraint:

$$f_i \times [1 - h_i(m_i)] \leq T_i, i = 1, ..., n. \tag{8}$$

However, adding this constraint complicates the probabilistic search: We can reject solutions that do not satisfy the constraint requirements, but this would increase the convergence time. An alternative approach is to incorporate this constraint in the EAT_i formula in (3): When a backend's constraint is exceeded, requests get queued up and the time to access an object in the backend system, bd_i, increases.

2.5 Dynamic partitioning

As the optimal allocation may change over time, the optimal assignment should be recalculated periodically. We must consider the cost of re-partitioning the memory: While the cache instance adapts to the new partition size (e.g., by evicting keys if it is to use less memory than before), it may incur in a penalty of a reduced throughput.

Let $\mathbf{m}^{(t)}$ be a feasible solution to problem (1) at time t. The cost of going from a solution $\mathbf{m}^{(t-1)}$ to solution $\mathbf{m}^{(t)}$ will be represented by non-negative function $C(\mathbf{m}^{(t-1)}, \mathbf{m}^{(t)})$. We do not assume C to be symmetric in its arguments since allocating and deallocating memory may have different operational costs (our preliminary experiments confirm this to be the case; results in Section 3). Cost function C is incorporated to the objective function of (1) at time t as:

$$\mathcal{F}^{(t)}(\mathbf{m}) = \sum_{i=1}^{n^{(t)}} w_i^{(t)} U_i^{(t)}(m_i) - C(\mathbf{m}^{\star,(t-1)}, \mathbf{m}), \tag{9}$$

where $\mathbf{m}^{\star,(t-1)}$ is the chosen solution to (1) at time $t-1$.

We propose the use of a cost function of the form:

$$C(\mathbf{m}^{(t-1)}, \mathbf{m}^{(t)}) = \sum_{i=1}^{n} \beta_i(m_i^{(t-1)} - m_i^{(t)}), \tag{10}$$

where:
$$\beta_i = \begin{cases} \beta_i^+ & \text{if } m_i^{(t-1)} \leq m_i^{(t)}; \\ -\beta_i^- & \text{else.} \end{cases} \quad (11)$$

Thus, we assume a cost (proportional to the memory size) of β_i^+ for allocating and β_i^- for deallocating.

Objective function (9) can be directly handled by the adaptive search approach described above. For solvers that cannot handle the proposed cost function directly, we cast the following equivalent optimization problem:

$$\begin{aligned} \underset{\mathbf{m},\eta^+,\eta^-}{\text{maximize}} \quad & \mathcal{F}^{(t)}(\mathbf{m},\eta^+,\eta^-) = \sum_{i=1}^{n} w_i U_i^{(t)}(m_i) \\ & \quad - \sum_{i=1}^{n} \beta_i^{+,(t)}\eta_i^+ - \sum_{i=1}^{n} \beta_i^{-,(t)}\eta_i^- \\ \text{subject to} \quad & m_i^{\star,(t-1)} - m_i \leq \eta_i^+, \text{for all } i \qquad (12) \\ & - m_i^{\star,(t-1)} + m_i \leq \eta_i^-, \text{for all } i \\ & \sum_{i=1}^{n} m_i \leq M, \\ & m_i - \underline{m}_i^{(t)}, \eta_i^+, \eta_i^- \geq 0, \text{for all } i, \end{aligned}$$

which preserves convexity and quasi-linearity from (1).

3. IMPLEMENTATION ISSUES

We are working on using our model to implement a dynamic memory partitioning tool for Redis. In the process, we need to solve the following problems.

Workload monitoring and hit rate curve estimation: The goal is to implement a very lightweight monitoring mechanism to construct hit rate curves with very little space and time overhead. For our Redis monitoring module we plan on adapting SHARDS [9], a novel algorithm that can construct approximate miss rate curves by sampling a small percentage of requests and has a small memory footprint. For example, it can process as much as 17 million requests per second and build curves with $< 2.6\%$ error, with a constant memory footprint (authors report excellent accuracy in 1 MB footprint for very large workloads [9]). To avoid slowing down cache requests, we are implementing the workload profiler as an asynchronous module with a lock-free buffer using the Disruptor pattern, originally developed for a high-performance financial exchange [8].

Cost of re-sizing the memory: We ran simple tests in which we deallocated 350 MB from one Redis instance and reassigned this RAM to another instance. We report the results averaged across 3 experimental runs: In our tests, deallocating memory from an instance took 28.6 seconds, while adding RAM took 2.4 seconds. During this period, the Redis instance stopped serving requests. Our model considers this cost, which may vary from system to system. Our plan is to implement a profiler that measures the re-sizing cost and can be used to automatically configure our tool.

Solving the optimization problem: Miss rate curves (MRCs) can have performance cliffs [3] which complicate the task of solving the optimization problem. Optimal allocation is NP-complete with non-convex MRCs [1] so no efficient solution is known. In the past, others have tackled the problem as follows: (1) For concave or near concave MRCs, Dynacache [2] applies convex piece-wise fitting and solves the problem with an LP-solver; (2) Cliffhanger [3] modified Memcached's LRU so that up to one performance cliff is removed using shadow queues, an approach inspired by Talus [1]; it then uses a gradient-based algorithm (hill-climbing) to optimize the allocation; since the full MRC curve is never built, the allocation is iteratively optimized, an approach that makes sense when reallocating memory is cheap, but inadequate for the problem being solved in this paper; finally, (3) others [7, 5] have simply proposed solutions that only work for concave MRCs; however, real measurements have revealed that this assumption may not hold [3]. We plan to implement the solver as a cloud service that could be used by many cloud clients to periodically calculate their optimal memory partitioning. The miss rate curves (MRCs) will be profiled by our service to determine the best way to solve the problem at hand: LP-solver, gradient-based method (with or without convex hull elimination) or probabilistic adaptive search. We also plan to explore the option of iterating between methods to speed up convergence.

4. CONCLUSIONS AND FUTURE WORK

We studied the problem of dynamic memory partitioning of cloud caches and modeled it as an optimization problem. Our formulation considers the effect of having back-ends with different performance profiles, as well as the cost of re-partitioning the memory. We proposed a probabilistic search algorithm that can be used when the utility functions are non-convex (which may be the case in our problem).

We are currently working on implementing our proposed approach as follows: (1) A miss rate curve profiling tool for Redis, leveraging recent high-performance solutions like SHARDS and LMAX's Disruptor pattern; (2) a profiling tool for Redis that can learn the cost of re-partitioning the memory between Redis instances; and (3) a partitioner-as-a-service tool that will implement several ways to solve the optimization problem and profile the utility function to choose the most appropriate one depending on the actual workload.

Acknowledgements. This work was partly funded by a Google Faculty Research Award.

5. REFERENCES

[1] Beckmann and Sanchez. Talus: A simple way to remove cliffs in cache performance. In *HPCA*, 2015.

[2] Cidon, Eisenman, Alizadeh, and Katti. Dynacache: Dynamic cloud caching. In *HotCloud*, 2015.

[3] Cidon, Eisenman, et al. Cliffhanger: Scaling performance cliffs in web memory caches. In *NSDI*, 2016.

[4] Hu, Wang, Zhou, Luo, et al. Kinetic modeling of data eviction in cache. In *Usenix ATC*, 2016.

[5] Pu, Li, Zaharia, Ghodsi, and Stoica. Fairride: Near-optimal, fair cache sharing. In *NSDI*, 2016.

[6] Singla, Chandrasekaran, Godfrey, and Maggs. The Internet at the speed of light. In *HotNets*, 2014.

[7] Stefanovici, Thereska, O'Shea, Schroeder, et al. Software-defined caching: Managing caches in multi-tenant data centers. In *SOCC*, 2015.

[8] Thompson et al. Disruptor: High performance alternative to bounded queues for exchanging data between concurrent threads. *LMAX Tech. Rep.*, 2011.

[9] Waldspurger, Park, Garthwaite, and Ahmad. Efficient MRC construction with SHARDS. In *Usenix FAST*, 2015.

[10] Wires, Ingram, Drudi, et al. Characterizing storage workloads with counter stacks. In *OSDI*, 2014.

Latency Aware Elastic Switching-based Stream Processing Over Compressed Data Streams

Sajith Ravindra[1], Miyuru Dayarathna[1,2], Sanath Jayasena[2]
[1]WSO2, Inc., [2]Dept of Computer Science & Engineering, University of Moratuwa
sajithr@wso2.com, miyurud@wso2.com, sanath@cse.mrt.ac.lk

ABSTRACT

Elastic scaling of event stream processing systems has gained significant attention recently due to the prevalence of cloud computing technologies. We investigate on the complexities associated with elastic scaling of an event processing system in a private/public cloud scenario. We develop an Elastic Switching Mechanism (ESM) which reduces the overall average latency of event processing jobs by significant amount considering the cost of operating the system. ESM is augmented with adaptive compressing of upstream data. The ESM conducts one of the two types of switching where either part of the data is sent to the public cloud (data switching) or a selected query is sent to the public cloud (query switching) based on the characteristics of the query. We model the operation of the ESM as the function of two binary switching functions. We show that our elastic switching mechanism with compression is capable of handling out-of-order events more efficiently compared to techniques which does not involve compression. We used two application benchmarks called EmailProcessor and a Social Networking Benchmark (SNB2016) to conduct multiple experiments to evaluate the effectiveness of our approach. In a single query deployment with EmailProcessor benchmark we observed that our elastic switching mechanism provides 1.24 seconds average latency improvement per processed event which is 16.70% improvement compared to private cloud only deployment. When presented the option of scaling EmailProcessor with four public cloud VMs ESM further reduced the average latency by 37.55% compared to the single public cloud VM. In a multi-query deployment with both EmailProcessor and SNB2016 we obtained a reduction of average latency of both the queries by 39.61 seconds which is a decrease of 7% of overall latency. These performance figures indicate that our elastic switching mechanism with compressed data streams can effectively reduce the average elapsed time of stream processing happening in private/public clouds.

CCS Concepts

•**Information systems** → **Data stream mining;** *Computing platforms;* •**Networks** → **Cloud computing;**

ICPE'17, April 22-26, 2017, L'Aquila, Italy
© 2017 ACM. ISBN 978-1-4503-4404-3/17/04. . . $15.00
DOI: http://dx.doi.org/10.1145/3030207.3030227

Keywords

Event-based systems, Elastic data stream processing, cloud computing, compressed event processing, data compression, IaSS, Software Performance Engineering, System sizing and capacity planning

1. INTRODUCTION

Data stream processing is a paradigm where streams of data are processed to extract useful insights of real world events. Multiple different recent applications of stream processing could be found in the areas of health informatics [1], telecommunications [26], electric grids [12], transportation [15][16], etc. A number of stream processing systems have been introduced in recent times to operate in a variety of software/hardware environments. Most of them are intended to operate in single cloud environments while others operate in multiple clouds. WSO2 CEP [28] server is an example stream processing engine which is designed to operate in multiple clouds.

Infrastructure as a Service (IaaS) service model provides physical and virtual hardware which can be provisioned and decommissioned via a self-service interface [9]. This includes resources such as servers, storage, and networking infrastructure. IaaS provides an environment which is very similar to resources which IT departments within organizations handle.

Data stream processing applications which usually get deployed in private clouds (i.e., private compute clusters) often face resource limitation while their operation due to unexpected loads [2][7]. Multiple approaches exist for mitigating resource limitation issues such as elastically scaling into an external cluster, load shedding, approximate query processing, etc. However, most of them have multiple limitations such as not considering the possible optimizations of the use of network resources, low accuracy of the results produced, and the cost associated with such approaches. Efficient use of compression techniques for optimizing the use of network connection between private and public clouds (IaaS) is one such area which has not been investigated in detail yet.

In this paper we discuss about elastic scaling in a private/public cloud scenario with compressed data streams. We design and implement an Elastic Switching Mechanism (ESM) over private/public cloud system. We use data field compression technique on top of this switching mechanism for compressing the data sent from private cloud to public cloud. We discuss the importance of data switching (sending part of data to public cloud) vs query switching (sending entire query) in the context of ESM. We use two real world data stream processing benchmarks called EmailProcessor and Social Network Benchmark (SNB2016) during the evaluation of the proposed approach. Using multiple experiments on real-world system setup with the two stream processing benchmarks we demonstrate the effectiveness of our approach for elastic switching-based stream processing using compressed data streams. In a single query deployment with EmailProcessor benchmark we observed that our elastic scaling technique provides 1.24 seconds average latency improvement per processed event which is 16.70% improvement compared to private cloud only deployment. When presented the option of scaling EmailProcessor with four public cloud VMs ESM further reduced the average latency by 37.55% compared to the single public cloud VM. In a multi-query deployment with both EmailProcessor and SNB2016 we obtained a reduction of average latency of both the queries by 39.61 seconds which is a decrease of 7% of overall latency. Specifically the contributions of our work can be listed as follows.

- *Elastic Switching Mechanism (ESM)* - We design and develop a mechanism for conducting elastic scaling of stream processing queries over private/public cloud.
- *Switching at Different Granularities* - We describe means of conducting adaptive switching at different granularities based on the semantics of stream processing queries. Specifically we describe the scenarios of data switching and query switching.
- *Compression with Out-of-order* - We handle out-of-order introduced due to switching with the public cloud. We show our compression technique improved the quality of out-of-order event handling.
- *Evaluation* - We evaluate the proposed approaches by implementing them on real world systems.

The paper is organized as follows. Next, we provide related work in Section 2. An overview for the stream processing software and the benchmarks used in this study are given in Section 3. We provide the details of system design and implementation of the ESM in Section 4. We discuss about the use of data stream compression in ESM in Section 5. Furthermore, we discuss techniques for handling out-of-order introduced by elastic switching in Section 6. The evaluation details are provided in Section 7. We provide the conclusions in Section 8.

2. RELATED WORK

There have been multiple previous work on elastic scaling of event processing systems in cloud environments.

Kleiminger *et al.* studied on implementing a distributed stream processor system based on MapReduce on top of a cloud IaaS to allow it to scale up/down elastically [19]. The main use case of their work was to implement financial algorithms on their framework. They explored how a local stream processor can be deployed in cloud infrastructure to scale to keep up with the expected latency constraints. They mainly talk about two load balancing strategies to achieve this. First one is always-on (load balanced between local and cloud) and second one is adaptive load balancing (move to cloud when the capacity is not enough in local node).

Cloud computing allows for realizing an elastic stream computing service, by dynamically adjusting used resources to the current conditions. Waldemar *et al.* discussed how elastic computing of data streams can be achieved on top of Cloud computing [14]. Features particularly interesting for elastic stream processing in the Cloud includes handling of stream imperfections, guaranteed data safety and delivery, and automatic partitioning and scaling of applications. Load shedding is a well-studied mechanism for reducing the system load by dropping certain events from the stream. Deferred processing of data that cannot be immediately handled are stored for later processing. The assumption of deferred processing is that the overload is limited in time. They mentioned that the most obvious form of elasticity is to scale with the input data rate and the complexity of operations (acquiring new resources when needed, and releasing resources when possible). However, most operators in stream computing are stateful and cannot be easily split up or migrated (e.g., window queries need to store the past sequence of events). In ESM we handle this type of queries by query switching.

Stormy is a system developed to evaluate the "stream processing as service" concept [21]. The idea was to build a distributed stream processing service using techniques used in cloud data storage systems. Stormy is built with scalability, elasticity and multi-tenancy in mind to fit in the cloud environment. They have used distributed hash tables (DHT) to build their solution. They have used DHTs to distribute the queries among multiple nodes and to route events from one query to another. Stormy intent to build a public streaming service where users can add new streams on demand; that is, register and share queries, and instantly run their stream for as long as they want. One of the main limitations in Stormy is it assumes that a query can be completely executed on one node. Stormy is unable to deal with streams for which the incoming event rate exceeds the capacity of a node which is an issue which we address in our work.

Cervino *et al.* tries to solve the problem of providing a resource provisioning mechanism to overcome inherent deficiencies of cloud infrastructure [2]. They have conducted some experiments on Amazon EC2 to investigate the problems that might affect badly on a stream processing system. They have come up with an algorithm to scale up/down the number of VMs(or EC2 instances) based solely on input stream rate. The goal is to keep the system with a given latency and throughput for varying loads by adaptively provisioning VMs for streaming system to scale up/down. In contrast to [21] Cervino *et al.*'s work is focused on running a big query efficiently which is decomposed to smaller quarries which can run on different VMs. However, none of the above mentioned works have investigated on reducing the amount of data sent to public clouds in such elastic scheduling scenarios. In this work we address this issue.

Data stream compression has been studied in the field of data mining. Cuzzocrea *et al.* has conducted a research on a lossy compression method for efficient OLAP [4] over data streams. Their compression method exploits semantics of the reference application and drives the compression process by means of the "degree of interestingness". The goal of this work was to develop a methodology and required data structures to enable summarization of the incoming data stream in order to finally make the usage of advanced analysis/mining tools over data streams more effective and efficient. However, the proposed methodology trades off accuracy and precision for the reduced size.

Jeffery *et al.* has tried to address shortcomings of RFID (Radio-frequency identification) data streams by cleaning the data streams using smoothing filters, they have proposed a middleware layer between the sensors and the application which process data streams. This middleware is responsible for making physical device issues transparent to the higher level application by correcting them at the middleware. The layer/middleware is referred to as "Metaphysical data independenc"(MDI) in their work [18].

Work done in [18] is utilized in [8] to clean and compress data generated by RFID tags deployed in a book store. In this work the data stream is compressed by removing redundant data. They have taken application and deployment semantics into account to develop an efficient data compression method for that specific domain. The MDI layer presented in [18] is customized by adding application specific compression algorithms and they claim that results in better performance than employing the generic method suggested in [18]. Yanming Nie *et al.* have done a research on inference and compression over RFID data streams [3][24]. They have developed online compression method. The compression of the data stream is mainly achieved by identifying and discarding redundant data.

Multiple work have recently been conducted on privacy preserving data stream mining. Privacy of patient health information has been serious issue in recent times [25]. Fully Homomorphic Encryption (FHE) has been introduced as a solution [10]. FHE is an advanced encryption techniques that allows data to be stored and processed in encrypted form. This provides cloud service providers the opportunity for hosting and processing data without even knowing what the data is. However, current FHE techniques are computationally expensive needing excessive space for keys and cypher texts. However, it has been shown with some experiments done with HElib [11] (an FHE library) that it is practical to implement some basic applications such as streaming sensor data to the cloud and comparing the values to a threshold. We plan to extend this work to the domain of FHE in future.

3. OVERVIEW OF STREAM PROCESSING SOFTWARE

In this section we provide brief description of WSO2 CEP which is the stream processing engine used for implementing the elastic switching mechanism. Furthermore, we provide a short introductions to the EmailProcessor and SNB2016 benchmarks used for the experiments.

3.1 Overview of WSO2 CEP

WSO2 Complex Event Processor (WSO2 CEP) is a lightweight, easy-to-use, stream processing engine. It is available as an open source software under the Apache Software License v2.0 [28]. WSO2 CEP lets users provide queries using an SQL like query language in order to get notifications on interesting realtime events, where it will listen to incoming data streams and generate new events when the conditions given in those queries are met by correlating the incoming data streams.

WSO2 CEP uses a SQL like Event Query language to describe queries. For example, the following query detects the number of taxis dropped-off in each cell in the last 15 minutes [16].

```
from Trip#window.time(15 min)
select count(medallion) as count
group by cellId
insert into OutputStream
```

Listing 1: Example CEP query.

When WSO2 CEP receives a query, it builds a graph of processors to represent the query where each processor is an operator like filter, join, pattern, etc. Input events are injected to the graph, where they propagate through the graph and generate results at the leaf nodes. Processing can be done using a single thread or using multiple threads, where in the latter case we use LMAX Disruptor [27] to exchange events between threads. More details of the WSO2 CEP is available from [28].

3.2 EmailProcessor Benchmark

EmailProcessor is an application benchmark originally designed by Nabi *et al.* [23]. The benchmark is designed around the canonical Enron email data set which is described in [20]. The data set consisted of 517,417 emails with a mean body size of 1.8KB, the largest being 1.92MB. The dataset we used had undergone an offline cleaning and staging phase where all the emails were serialized and stored within a single file with the help of Apache Avro. In our benchmark implementation[1] the data injector read emails from the Avro file, deserialized them and sent to Q1 for filtering. Q1 dropped emails that did not originate from an address ending with `@enron.com`. Furthermore, it removed all email addresses that did not end with `@enron.com` from To, CC, and BCC fields. Q2 modified each and every email by obfuscating the names of three individuals:Kenneth Lay, Jeffrey Skilling, and Andrew Fastow in the email body by replacing their names with Person1, Person2, and Person3 respectively. Q3 operator gathered metrics of each email such as number of characters, words, and paragraphs in the email body. This information is sent to Q5 which aggregated such metrics from multiple Q3 operators in a running window. The processed emails were sent from Q3 to Q4, which were compressed in Avro format and written to `/dev/null` which effectively get discarded. The correct benchmark implementation filters out 89,230 unwanted emails and outputs 42,8187 emails. The architecture of the EmailProcessor benchmark is shown in Figure 1. The choice of EmailProcessor for the experiments was mainly because it does not involve any shared state and it introduced the workload spikes we wanted during the experiments providing good example of real world work load.

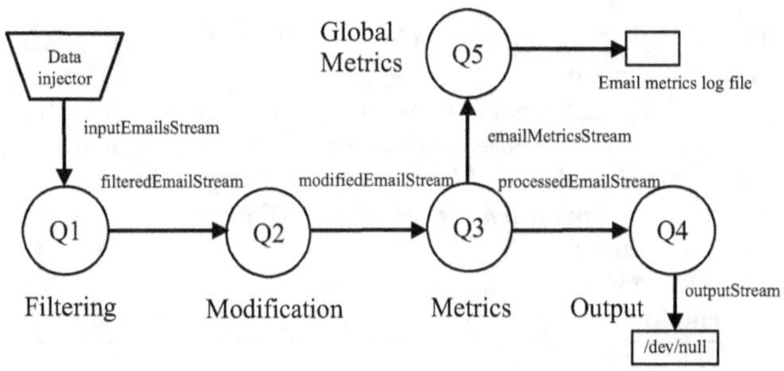

Figure 1: Email Processor

3.3 Social Network Benchmark (SNB2016)

The second application benchmark we used is a version of the DEBS 2016 Grand Challenge which we name as SNB2016 [17] (See Figure 2). SNB2016 is focused on conducting real time streaming analytics on an evolving social network graph. There are four different input streams for SNB2016 Posts, Comments, Friendships, and Likes. The modified version of the benchmark [2] we used in this paper conducts identification of the posts that currently trigger the most activity.

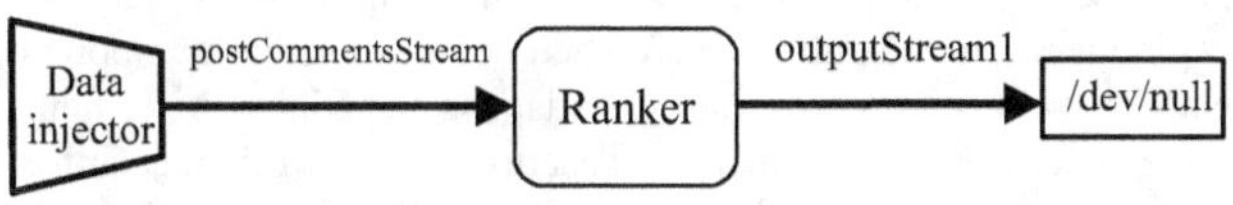

Figure 2: Social Network Benchmark 2016 (SNB2016)

The benchmark calculates the top-3 scoring active posts. An active post P's total score is computed as the sum of its own score and

[1]https://github.com/miyurud/EmailProcessor_Siddhi
[2]https://github.com/miyurud/debs2016

the score of all of its related comments. New posts and new comments each has an initial score of 10 which decreases by 1 each time another 24 hours passes since the post's/comment's creation. The data set used in our experiments consisted of 8,585,497 posts with an average event size of 0.018 Bytes while there were 24,485,315 comments each of 82.09 Bytes. The application logic involved in calculating the top-3 active posts is described in Algorithm 1.

Algorithm 1 Ranker: Find Top 3 Posts

```
postMap ← {}
commentPostMap ← {}
timeWindow ← {}
postScoreMap ← {}
for all event in stream do
    if event.isPost then
        postMap.add(event, postScoreMap)
        timeWindow.update(event.time, postScoreMap)
        timeWindow.addPost(event, postScoreMap)
        if postScoreMap.topThreeChanged then
            print(postScoreMap.topThree)
        end if
    else
        if event.isCommentToPost then
            commentPostMap.update(event)
        else
            commentPostMap.getParent(event).update()
        end if
        timeWindow.update(event.time, postScoreMap)
        timeWindow.addComment(event, postScoreMap)
        if postScoreMap.topThreeChanged then
            print(postScoreMap.topThree)
        end if
    end if
end for
```

As shown in Algorithm 1, the Ranker component of the SNB2016 involves accessing a shared time window as well as accessing a shared map data structure called *commentPostMap*. This is an example scenario for a stream processing application which involves shared state. It requires all the events to be sent via the Ranker component.

4. ELASTIC SWITCHING MECHANISM

In this work we present a mechanism for latency aware elastic scaling in private/public cloud scenario. The proposed approach has been implemented on a mechanism called Elastic Switching Mechanism (ESM). The ESM system architecture and two of its application scenarios are shown in Figures 3 and 5.

The ESM is designed to operate between the boundaries of the private and the public clouds. Copies of the same stream processing engine is run in the public cloud when needed. Profiler component gathers the system performance statistics. Scheduler implements the elastic scheduling functions based on the performance information provided by the Receiver. The OOH (Out-of-order handler) component does the reordering when Out-of-order handling has been enforced for a particular stream application. The operations of the ESM is dependent on the Quality of Service (QoS) specification provided by the user.

In our current implementation we use a predefined average latency value as the QoS parameter. Latency is the time spent by an event within the data stream processing system. We use average latency per event as the performance metric since additional latency gets introduced in the case of switching to public cloud. Furthermore, we use the average value rather than 95th percentile value because we want to account for the entire data set sent to public cloud. We had measured 95th percentile average latencies in several performance experiments of ESM and found that 95th latencies obtained from elastic scaling leads to better latency numbers than what is reported in this paper. However, to consider the 5% of the events which are outliers as well as to maintain the simplicity of the presentation we use average latency rather than percentiles. Note that we conduct full processing of stream processing data rather than conducting approximate processing by neglecting high latency events.

Publisher is the component which emits the data stream to public cloud. Data stream compression logic is implemented in the Compresser component. When the data stream sent to the public cloud with compression is enabled it is intercepted by a compression handler component deployed in the public cloud. Compression handler decompresses certain compressed fields as indicated by the preconfigured settings.

The normal mode of operation where the ESM operates within the specified QoS constraints is shown in Figure 3 (a). In this mode the amount of resources in the private cloud is sufficient to maintain user specified QoS. Hence the Stream processing job(s) executes only in the stream processing engine running in the private cloud. Note that at a particular time several stream processing jobs can run in parallel within the stream processing engine (denoted by $Q_1 ... Q_n$ in Figures 3 and 5).

An example for the elastic mode of operation of the ESM is shown in Figure 3 (b). When the scheduler decides that private cloud's resources are insufficient to maintain the QoS specifications, it starts a VM and instantiates a stream processing engine in public cloud. The decision of moving part of the data (data switching) or the entire input data stream (query switching) is dependent on the semantics of the stream processing application. It is indicated to the scheduler via a preconfigured settings. The scheduler starts/migrates the stream processing job which needs to be run in the public cloud based on this preconfigured settings.

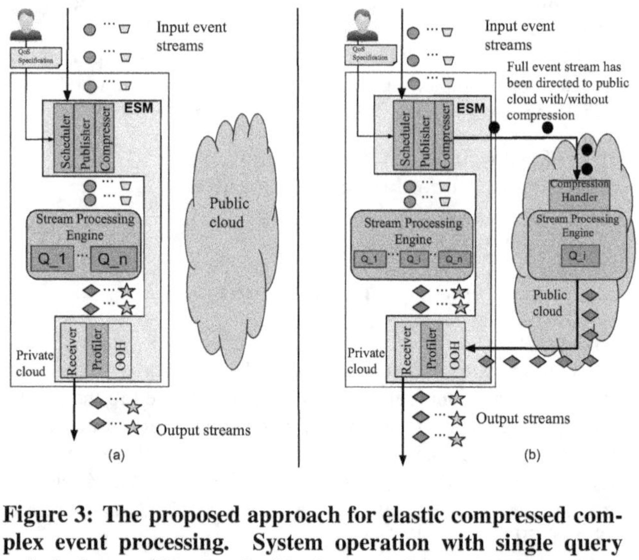

Figure 3: The proposed approach for elastic compressed complex event processing. System operation with single query switched to public cloud with data switching. (a) The private cloud only mode of operation. (b) The hybrid cloud mode of operation with data switching and compression.

The ESM ranks the stream processing jobs/data to be moved to the public cloud based on the difference of their current average latency and the user specified QoS. The ESM switches these jobs one after the other based on the assigned rank until the results of such switching provides QoS gains. Note that the Figures 3 and 5 indicate different input streams and output streams using different symbols for the sake of clarity of the presentation. Furthermore, the notation used in our paper is explained in Table 1.

4.1 Switching Functions

During the operation of the ESM there are three key switching decisions to be made. First, the public cloud needs to be initialized. The required number of VMs needs to be started and the corresponding stream processing engine needs to be instantiated. In our approach the decision of starting VMs in public cloud in time period t is made considering the average latency threshold observed at the Publisher in the previous time slot $t-1$ (i.e., $L_{t-1} > L_s$). Instantiating VMs is the costliest decision to be made during the system's operation. If N number of VMs each having cost C billed hourly basis are instantiated, irrespective of whether VMs are used for 10 minutes or 50 minutes, a total cost of NC will be incurred. Hence in ESM we start VMs one after the other systematically in such a way that the total cost of VMs can be kept at minimum.

Second, once the VMs get instantiated in the public cloud the decision of when to switch the incoming data stream and which portion to switch is another important decision. As mentioned previously which portion of the data to switch only matters in the case of data switching. In such occasion ESM starts sending data to public cloud when the average latency of the output stream exceeds L_d. When the average latency plummets less than L_d we keep sending data only to private cloud. It should be noted that we maintain the invariant $L_s > L_d$ since L_s is the threshold which makes the costliest operation. After making the decision at the L_s latency level, since the VM is already running in public cloud, sending data to public cloud can be conducted even at a lower latency such as L_d since sending data does not incur a significant cost as with the switching decision taken at L_s. The elastic switching process of data switching of a single stream processing job can be expressed as two binary functions $\phi_{VM}(t)$ and $\phi_{data}(t)$,

$$\phi_{VM}(t) = \begin{cases} 1, L_{t-1} \geq L_s, \tau \textit{ has elapsed.} \\ 0, D_{t-1} < D_s, L_{t-1} < L_p & \text{Otherwise,} \end{cases} \quad (1)$$

$$\phi_{data}(t) = \begin{cases} 1, \phi_{VM}(t-1) = 1, L_{t-1} \geq L_d, L_s > L_d \\ 0, & \text{Otherwise,} \end{cases} \quad (2)$$

where ϕ_{VM} is the function for a single VM and ϕ_{data} is the function for transferring data from private cloud to public cloud. t is the time period for which the values of the binary functions needs to be calculated. A time period of τ has to be elapsed in order for the VM startup process to trigger. D_s is the threshold for total amount of data received by the VM from private cloud. Once the data switching process starts, the QoS value of the stream processing job is measured via latency of the private cloud. The same binary switching function ϕ_{VM} is used for spawning multiple other VMs in the public cloud until the desired QoS latency (L_{QoS}) is achieved for that particular stream processing job.

Finally, once the VMs are instantiated, they need to be checked whether to continue or not once their rental period ends. In the above example, if the VMs are not shutdown before the one hour period elapses another NC amount will be billed by the public cloud. On the otherhand if the need of starting the VM in the public cloud arises just after the VM being shutdown it also incurs considerable time and cost to bring the VM back online. Hence deciding when to shutdown is as important as starting a VM. In our elastic stream processing model we make the decision of when not to continue use of a VM by tracking the amount of data received by the VM ($D_{t-1} = D_s$) during the last operating window $t-1$ and the average latency value recorded by the Publisher running in the private cloud (L_p) during $t-1$. At least D_s amount of data has to be sent to public cloud in order to keep the VM for the next billing session without shutting it down. When the billing period reaches, the switching model evaluates if still the latency is higher than L_p. If the current latency is less than L_p then switching model checks if the number of events sent to public cloud is greater than D_s. The L_p and D_s parameters help the switching model to shutdown underutilized VMs and to retain well utilized VM for next session.

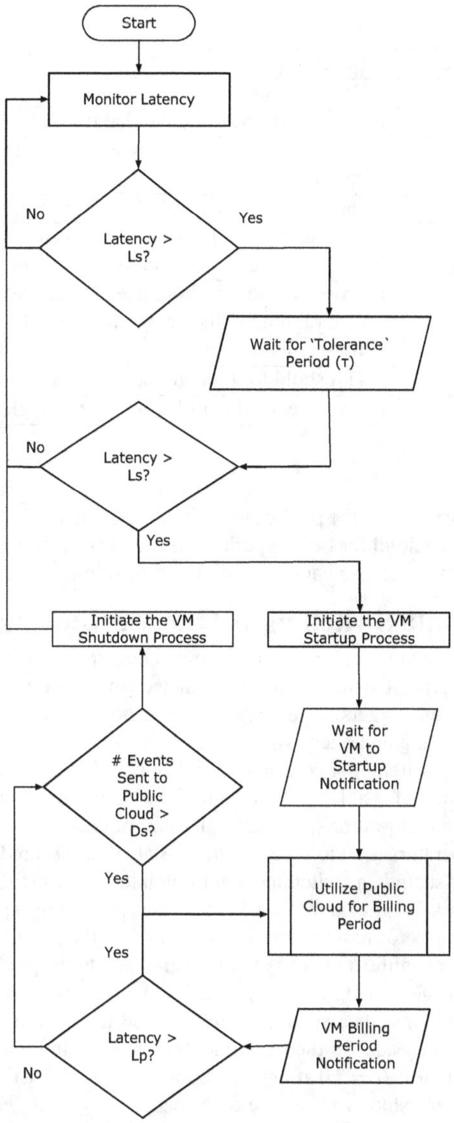

Figure 4: State transition diagram depicting the process of operating a single VM in the public cloud.

The state-transition diagram in Figure 4 describes the process of

Table 1: Notation.

Notation	Description
t	Unit time slot
L_t	Average latency measured at the Receiver component of the ESM during the time slot t
L_s	VM Startup threshold latency. When the average latency exceeds this value the ESM decides to initiate the VM start up process.
L_d	Data switching threshold latency. When $L > L_d$, the ESM starts sending data to public cloud.
τ	Tolerance period. After the unit timeslot (t) elapses, the ESM waits additional τ period before it initiates the VM startup process. In the current implementation of the ESM τ is set equal to t.
L_p	Private cloud threshold latency. At least L_p amount of latency needs to be present in the private cloud for a VM to be kept running in the next unit time slot.
D_t	Total amount of data received by the VM from private cloud during the time slot t
D_s	Threshold for total amount of data received by the VM from private cloud during the time slot t
L_{QoS}	User specified QoS Latency for a single specific stream job.

operating a VM in the public cloud. The rectangle marked as "Utilize Public Cloud for Billing period" indicates the entire process of data/query switching happening in that time frame.

4.2 Data Switching vs Query Switching

An important aspect of our elastic switching mechanism is deciding what type of switching to be conducted when the binary switching function triggers. There are mainly two types of switching as data switching and query switching.

In data switching a portion of the data is switched to the public cloud. This is feasible only if the queries used in stream processing application allows for split-merge (fission) of data items [6]. If the query operators need to access a shared state (i.e., a shared memory location) such data switching is not possible. The EmailProcessor benchmark is an example for such stream processing application which allows for fission. Elastic switching into the public cloud introduces a significant latency to the events sent to the public cloud. Hence in the context of data switching we send only R percentage of the input data stream to public cloud to avoid unnecessary latency overheads. In the experiments conducted in this paper we selected to use $R = 10$ after conducting multiple experiments with different R values with all the other parameters fixed. For example, we run the same experiment multiple times in each round with different R values such as 1,2,4,8,10,12,14,20, etc.

On the otherhand there are certain queries which require the entire set of input events to be passed through the operators to produce correct results (i.e., need to access shared state). For example, for the correct operation of SNB2016 benchmark, the entire event stream needs to be passed through the query operators of its Ranker component. Aggregation of results is another example. Hence in such situations data switching cannot be performed. Instead the whole stream processing application needs to be migrated to the public cloud. As indicated by the bent arrow, Q_i has been completely transferred from the private cloud to public cloud.

5. EVENT STREAM COMPRESSION

Several key techniques exist for compressing event streams before they are sent to the public cloud. First technique is Compression by Field Trimming (i.e., query parameter tuning) where the input queries are adjusted and tuned in such away that only the required set of fields are sent to the public cloud. The second technique is by field compression where large data items of an event gets compressed using a compression algorithm. In this paper we implement only the former technique while we discuss the field compression for the sake of completeness of the discussion.

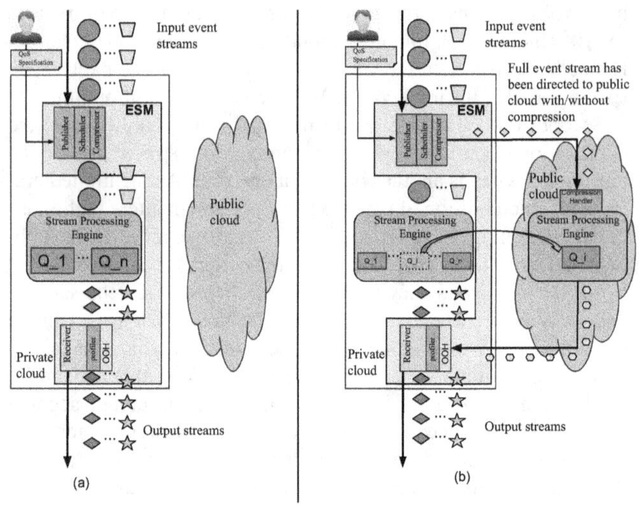

Figure 5: System operation with single query switched to public cloud with query switching. (a) The private cloud only mode of operation. (b) The hybrid cloud mode of operation with query switching without compression.

5.1 Compression by Field Trimming

Query transformation is a technique which converts a given stream processing query into another form which effectively gives the same results when executed by the event processor engine [6].

The query transformation technique involves static analysis of the query and deciding which fields can be omitted by looking at the query. If a certain field is not used in the query we can drop that particular event from the data stream, and thereby reduce the amount of data sent through the wire. For example, lets consider the example in Figure 6. In the query shown on top only 3 fields out of 8 fields available in the data stream is included in the output. Therefore, by looking at the output it can be concluded it is safe to omit sending non-used fields that are not in the output. In this particular example we can omit sending iij_timestamp, fromAddress, bccAddresses, subject, and regexstr fields.

5.2 Data Field Compression

In the data field compression technique, the contents of pre-selected set of data fields are compressed using Gzip compression algorithm. The selection of the fields to be compressed is done via offline profiling. Once the fields to be compressed are selected,

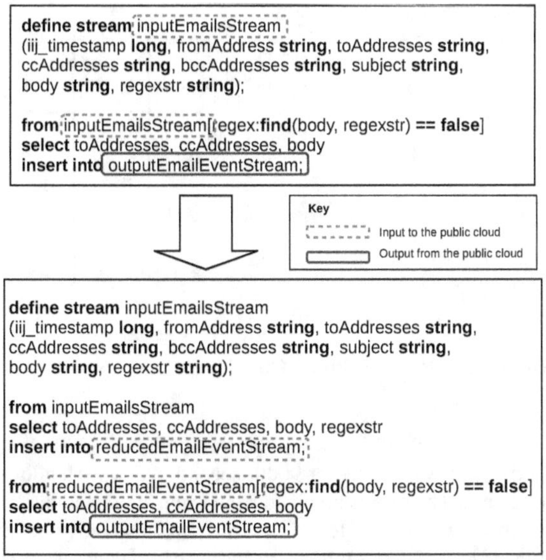

Figure 6: An example of query transformation based event stream compression.

they are configured in the elastic switching mechanism through a configuration file. While one could argue that involvement of an additional step of compression may increase average latency per event, our experiments in real world environment has shown this is not the case.

6. OUT-OF-ORDER EVENTS HANDLING

Certain stream processing applications are sensitive for out-of-order events [22]. There are two ways in which out-of-order events could get introduced to the output stream from elastic stream processing system. First, due to the switching activity with public cloud which is unavoidable in an stream processing system. Second, out-of-order events can already be present in the input stream for the stream processing system. From multiple experiments conducted on the above two scenarios we observed that the out-of-ordering introduced by switching into public cloud far outperforms the out-of-ordering which could occur naturally in the input stream. For example, the effect of out-of-ordering introduced by the input stream to become a significant factor compared to the out-of-order introduced due to switching to the public cloud, we found that at least about 60% of the events in the input stream needs to be arriving out-of-order. This is uncommon in many stream processing scenarios. Hence in this paper we ignore the out-of-order which is naturally present in the input streams.

There are four main techniques of disorder handling: Buffer-based, Punctuation-based, Speculation-based, and Approximation-based. In this paper we discuss the use of a buffer for reordering out-of-order events which are gathered from both the private and public clouds. We allow user to specify as a parameter whether the event stream output from the stream processing system needs to handle out-of-order events or not. We use buffer-based technique called reordering which essentially reorders events at the output and periodically flushes the reordered events to the output stream.

We implement out-of-order event handling at the receiver of the stream processing system. We detect whether there are any out-of-order event in the input stream. If found we send those out-of-order events to private cloud to avoid further delays of processing the events. We have found that this technique gives higher quality output compared to a scenario of buffer-based reordering which does not send events to public cloud at all.

7. EVALUATION

The evaluations described in this paper were conducted on 2 physical computers and on 4 Virtual Machines deployed in a compute cluster of WSO2. Two physical computers were used in all the experiments described in Sections 7.1 to 7.4. One of the computers was used as the public cloud and the other computer as the private cloud. The public cloud computer was running on Intel® Core i5® M560, 2.67 GHz. Each VM had 4 cores, 3072KB L2 cache and 32KB L1(d/i) caches. The public cloud computer had 4GB RAM. The private cloud computer was a 64-bit Genuine Intel® Core™ i7-4800MQ CPU which operates at 2.70GHz, 8 cores, 8 hardware threads. The sizes of the L1(d/i), L2, and L3 caches of this computer were 32KB, 256KB, and 6144KB respectively. We used Oracle JDK 1.8.0_101 and WSO2 CEP Server 4.0.0 during the experiments. The private and public clouds were connected via a wireless network. We used NetEm network emulator [13] to simulate 70ms latency which is present between two data centers operating in the East and the West coasts of the United States [5].

Each VM out of the 4 VMs were running 64-bit Intel® Xeon E312xx (Sandy Bridge) which operate at 2.70GHz. Each VM had one CPU socket, with 2 cores. The sizes of the L1(d/i), L2, and L3 caches were 32KB, 32KB, and 4096KB respectively. Each VM had 4GB RAM with one 40GB hard disk. Each VM was installed with Linux Ubuntu (kernel 3.13.0-36-generic).

Note that the ESM's source code has been released under open-source license[3][4].

7.1 Elastic Switching Without Event Stream Compression

In the first round of the experiments we evaluated the performance benefits of our elastic scaling mechanism. We used EmailProcessor benchmark for this purpose and one computer was used as the public cloud while the private cloud was running in another computer. We conducted performance experiments to measure how effective would our stream processing system be in reducing the overall average latency of processing P number of input events. We use average latency as the performance metric because in an elastic scaling system event processing latency acts as an indicator of system performance. The results present in this paper are taken single round experiments. The input data rate variation of the EmailProcessor benchmark during the experiments is shown in Figure 7. This indicates that the workload distribution had significant variations. VM rental period was set to 1 minute to reduce the time taken during the experiments while VM setup period was set to 10 seconds. In our current implementation we do initiate the full stream processing job in the public cloud during an elastic scaling operation. The latency thresholds L_s and L_d were set as 12,000 and 10,000 milliseconds respectively.

Figure 8 indicates the latency distribution of running the EmailProcessor benchmark both without switching to public cloud and with switching to public cloud. It can be observed that there are two significant spikes in the workload distribution. Figure 8 shows the average latency variation of the private cloud without switching and with switching scenarios. The four dotted vertical lines on Figure 8 indicates the points in the timeline where VM start/VM

[3]https://github.com/sajithshn/event-publisher

[4]https://github.com/sajithshn/statistics-collector

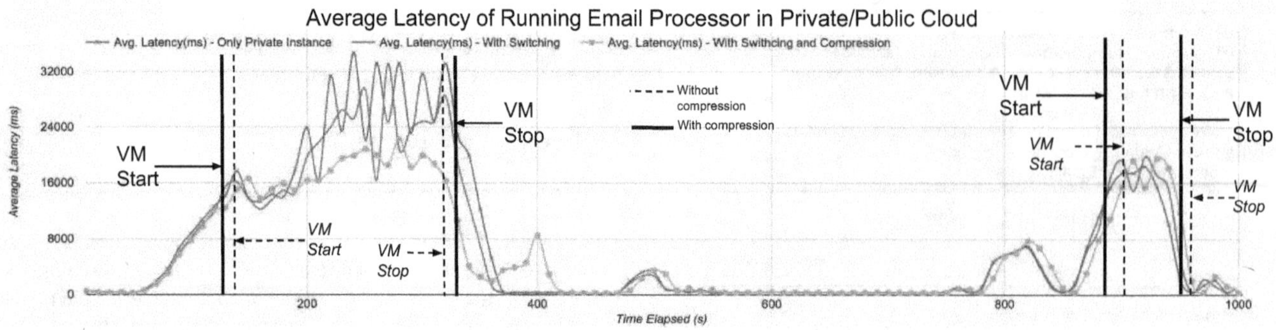

Figure 8: Average Latency of Running EmailProcessor in Private/Public Cloud

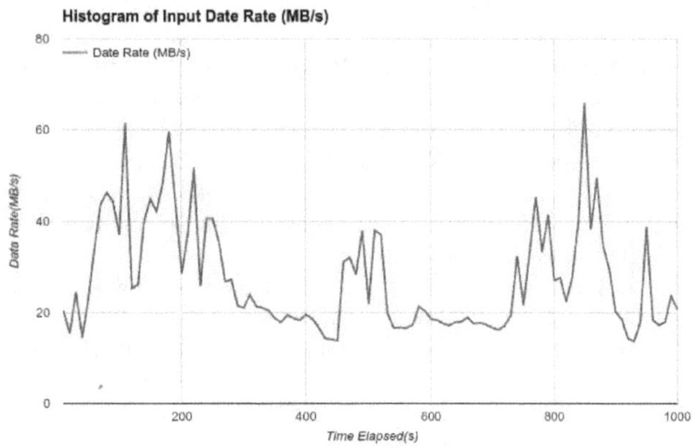

Figure 7: Input data rate variation

shutdown operations has been initiated. Elastic scaling system instantiates the VM in the public cloud at 130th second. When wall clock is 340 seconds, the VM is shutdown. The benchmark is run only in the private cloud in the time range between 340 seconds and 890 seconds. At 890 seconds the VM instantiation process starts again. The VM shutsdown when wall clock time is 950 seconds. The results give notable results with an improvement of the average latency of 0.581 seconds in hybrid cloud (i.e., with switching) which is 7.84% improvement compared to private cloud only deployment. The 7.84% improvement of the average latency was calculated by taking the average values of the data points corresponding to the "Avg. Latency(ms) - Only Private Instance" and "Avg. Latency(ms) - With Switching" curves. The difference of the two averages was 0.581 seconds which was 7.84% improvement compared to "Avg. Latency(ms) - Only Private Instance" case. Note that we do not plot when actually the data stream gets switched to/from the public cloud to maintain the simplicity of the charts. Furthermore, the elastic switching reduces the load average of the system operation. This can be observed from Figure 8.

7.2 Elastic Switching with Event Stream Compression

Next, we applied event stream compression on top of the elastic switching operations of the ESM. The results are shown in Figure 8. The four vertical continuous lines indicates where the VM start/shutdown has been initiated with this round of experiments. It can be observed a significant latency gain has been made with use of event stream compression on the events sent to the public cloud. ESM instantiates the VM in the public cloud at 140th second. The VM is shutdown when the wall clock was 330 seconds. Again the VM was started at 900th second and was shutdown at 960th second. The results obtained from event stream compression was impressive compared to the naive private cloud only operation. ESM provided 1.24 seconds per event average latency gain compared to the private cloud only operation. This is a 16.70% latency improvement. Furthermore, event stream compression provides us 8.86% more performance gain compared to elastic switching which does not involve compression.

7.3 Elastic Switching in the Presence of Multiple Queries

Next, we run multiple queries simultaneously in the private cloud and elastically scale one of the queries to the public cloud when the load in the private cloud exceeds specified QoS constraints. Another objectives of this experiment was to investigate on the performance variation happen when query switching has been conducted with the ESM.

Figure 9 (a) indicates how average latency variation occurs in both EmailProcessor and SNB2016 benchmarks when deployed only in the private cloud. Figure 9 (b) shows how latency variation happens when only SNB2016 has been deployed in the public cloud. Note that in this case we completely take SNB2016 out from private cloud and deploy it in the public cloud while EmailProcessor continues to run as it is in the private cloud. Similar to the previous experiment we have marked the switching points in Figure 9 (b). In this experiment ESM has started the VM in the public cloud at 220th second while the VM was shutdown at 340th second. Again the VM has been started at 960th second and shutdown at 980th second.

It can be observed that our elastic scaling mechanism successfully reduces the average latency of the SNB2016. Although migration of the SNB2016 to public cloud completely has resulted in slight increase of average latency of SNB2016 by 34.89 seconds (7.58% increase), the performance benefits of elastic scaling far outweighs that drawback. Specifically the elastic scaling of SNB2016 reduces the average latency of EmailProcessor by 74.47 seconds which is 15.75% improvement in average latency of the EmailProcessor. Overall the elastic scaling reduces the average latency of both the queries by 39.61 seconds which is a decrease of the overall average latency by 7%. Note that we do not investigate on load average variation in this experiment because we have only one query compared to the non-switching scenario.

7.4 Effect of Elastic Switching with Reordering

Elastic scaling into a public cloud in general introduces disor-

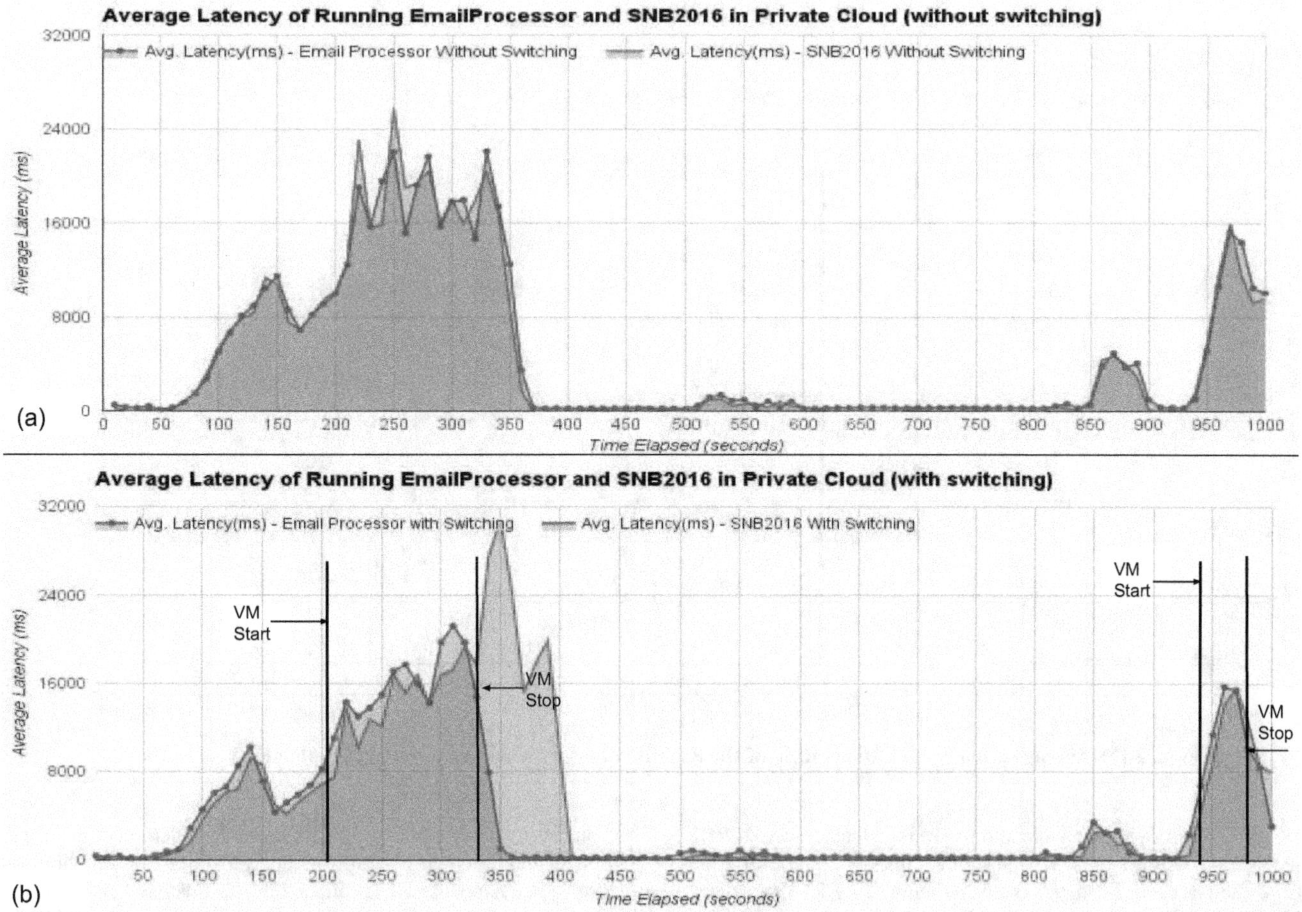

Figure 9: Evaluation of the effectiveness of the ESM in the presence of multiple queries. (a) Latency variation for EmailProcessor and SNB2016 where both benchmarks run on private cloud. (b) Latency variation for hybrid cloud operation where SNB2016 getting deployed in the public cloud.

der to an event stream. In this experiment we use a buffer in the Receiver component of ESM to gather events sent from both public and private clouds and sort them. A timer is used to flush events periodically. The results of running EmailProcessor benchmark with data switching with/without compression is shown in Figure 10.

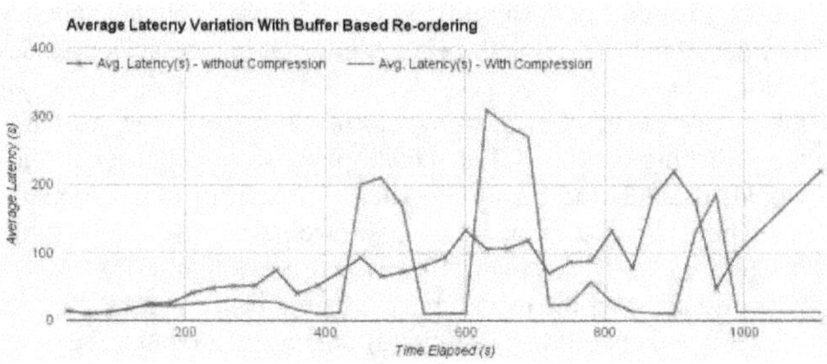

Figure 10: Effect of reordering on the average latency of the event streams output by ESM.

The experiment results on Figure 10 indicated that buffer-based reordering with compression provides 16 seconds average latency improvement compared to conducting the same reordering on a scenario without compression. Use of data stream compression introduced 19.44% latency improvement when compression has been used. Furthermore, we observed that out-of-order events percentage at the Receiver was 45.40% when reordering was conducted on elastic data stream without compression. However, reordering on the elastic data stream with compression reduced the percentage of out-of-order events further by 7% to 38.4%. These results indicates that our data stream compression based ESM can better handle out-of-order events which are produced in general on naive elastic scaling mechanisms.

7.5 Elastic Switching with Multiple Public Cloud VMs

Experiments described till this point were conducted only using single VM instance in public cloud. In this experiment we demonstrate the ability of conducting elastic scaling on multiple VMs. Each VM was configured to run on separate computer. The scaling experiments were conducted with maximum four VMs on four physical computers running in the public cloud. We observed that although we added more VMs (and physical computers) to the public cloud the switching mechanism did not start more VMs other than four due to the system conditions did not satisfy the conditions of the binary switching function $\phi_{VM}(t)$. The results of this experiment are shown in Figure 11.

It can be observed from Figure 11 that overall average latency reduces significantly when two public cloud VMs were used than sin-

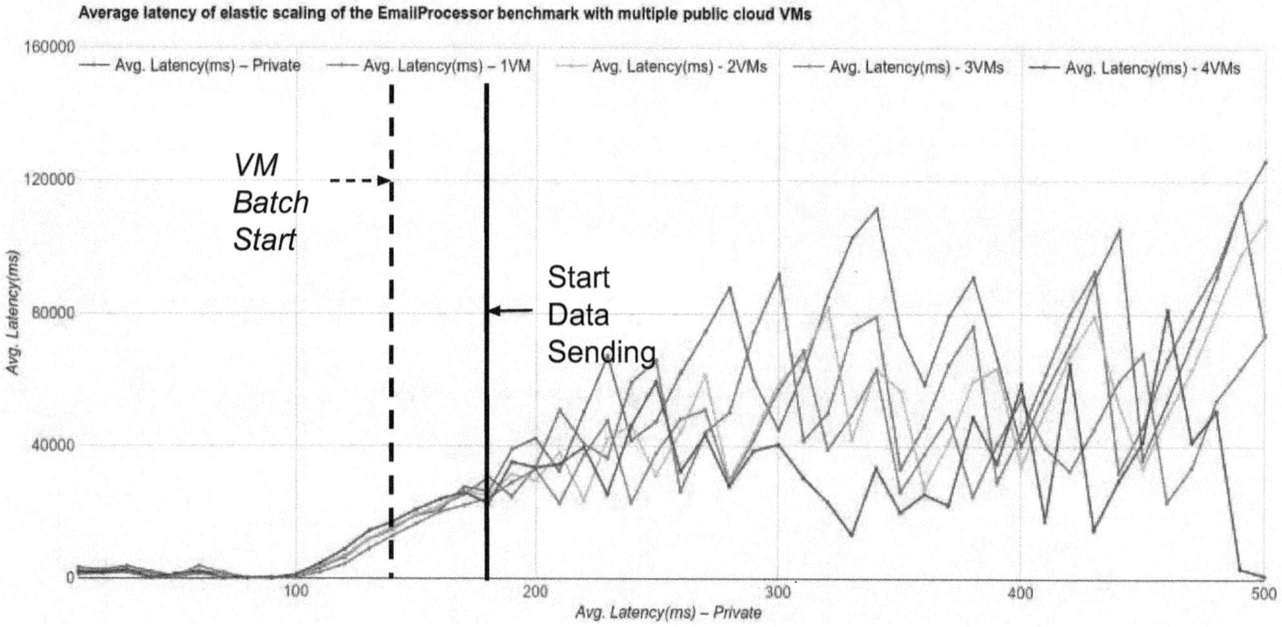

Figure 11: Average latency of elastic scaling of the EmailProcessor benchmark with multiple public cloud VMs

gle VM. The naive private cloud only average latency was 129.32 seconds. When a single VM on public cloud was started by the ESM the per event latency was further reduced by 53.33 seconds. This was a 15.1% average latency improvement compared to private cloud only deployment. However, when the ESM was configured to use maximum 2 VMs the overall average latency was reduced to 110.78 seconds which is a reduction of 18.54 seconds (22.8%) compared to the private cloud only deployment. Introduction of 3rd and 4th public cloud VMs resulted in further reductions in average latency by 36% and 47% compared to the private cloud only mode. Compared to the single public cloud VM, the 4 public cloud VMs further reduce the latency by 37.55%. These results indicate that ESM is capable of elastically scaling to multiple public cloud VMs and Scaling introduces significant performance gains. Note that the results shown on Figure 11 does not include the scenarios of VM shutdown since the motivation of the experiment was to indicate that the proposed ESM can reduce the overall latency further to considerable extent when additional VMs were added in the public cloud.

7.6 Discussion

The above five different experiments indicate the effectiveness of our elastic stream processing mechanism in lowering the average latency of data stream processing. In this paper our focus was on stream processing jobs which get deployed in public cloud completely during such elastic scaling scenario. Elastic scaling of a portion of the stream processing job is an important area. For example, the last three query operators of the EmailProcessor benchmark (Q_3, Q_4, and Q_5) can be transferred to public cloud while the first two operators (Q_1 and Q_2) could still remain in the private cloud.

We have demonstrated how effective it is to use compression along with elastic switching to handle out-of-order events which gets produced due to the use of public cloud. However, a limitation of our current implementation is that out-of-order event handling implementation could not turn off the VM once the switching to public cloud happens. This is due to the added latency of the buffer based re-ordering. We are working on to fix this issue.

We have used average latency as the user specified QoS metric in the current implementation because latency is one of the most important performance metrics in an elastic stream processing mechanism. However, we plan to investigate on use of other metrics such as throughput, system load average, etc. as parameters for switching process in future. We need to consider higher percentiles when there are a large number of outlier values in a dataset. We see two potential uses of higher percentile latencies in relation to ESM. First, for the switching function where the decision for switching needs to be taken. Because there are less number of events with outlier latencies in the private cloud mode of operation there is no significant difference in the use of average latency or a percentile such as 95th percentile for taking the switching decision. The switching decision is influenced only by the latency of the private cloud. Hence we opt to use average latency to make the switching decision. The second place where higher latencies would matter is measuring the latency benefit of elastic scaling. Switching to public cloud inherently introduces events with outlier latencies to the event stream. However, the benefit of ESM realizes when we consider the overall picture using the average latency. In hybrid cloud (public+private cloud) operation, although there are few outlier events with large latencies, their effect is subdued by the overall average latency reduction achieved by elastic switching. Hence, for measuring the elastic scaling benefit of using ESM we used the reduction of average latency but not the reduction of higher percentiles such as 95th percentile.

It should be noted that the ESM presented in this paper reorders events only at the output of the streaming pipeline. This assumes that the operations conducted within the elastic stream processing pipeline (i.e., the public cloud portion of the stream processing pipeline) are not sensitive for the order of the events.

We used two application benchmarks which we believe are good example applications for stream processing. However, there are other different types of applications which involve complex operations which we plan to conduct in future. Event pattern matching, event sequence matching, sliding window operations, etc. are some examples for such applications.

8. CONCLUSIONS

In this paper we present an elastic switching mechanism (ESM) for elastic scaling of data stream processing systems. ESM leverages public cloud to augment a private cloud when the private cloud is overloaded. We implement the proposed approach on WSO2 Complex Event Processsor (WSO2 CEP). We have tested the feasibility of our approach by using two application benchmarks (i.e., queries) called EmailProcessor and SNB2016. We observe that in both data switching and query switching elastic scaling scenarios our elastic switching mechanism provides performance benefits in terms of latency reductions. In the case of the data switching scenario with single public cloud VM instance we obtained 16.7% improvement of average latency compared to private cloud only operation. The proposed compressed stream processing approach achieves 8.86% performance gain compared to naive elastic switching. In another experiment which involves query switching we obtained 7% improvement of overall average latency. Furthermore, we demonstrated that our data field compression based ESM could effectively produce lesser out-of-order events by 7% compared to a scheme which does not involve data stream compression. Moreover, when presented the option of scaling EmailProcessor with four public cloud VMs ESM further reduced the average latency by 37.55% compared to the single public cloud VM. These performance figures indicate that our elastic scaling mechanism can effectively reduce the average elapsed time spent on stream data processing.

Currently we do switch entire query to public cloud in the case of query switching. In future we plan to migrate only portions of the queries which will lead for better control of the elastic switching process. We also plan to investigate and implement Fully Homomorphic Encryption based ESM which will be useful for implementing stream processing applications which involve sensitive data such as processing health records. Furthermore, we plan to add microbenchmarks for different components in the ESM as well as use more elaborate performance models which may consider multiple aspects such as immediate saturation of the latencies. While a network emulator has been used to simulate latency between two distant data centers, we plan to conduct experiments in real cloud environments in future.

9. REFERENCES

[1] M. Blount, M. Ebling, J. Eklund, A. James, C. McGregor, N. Percival, K. Smith, and D. Sow. Real-time analysis for intensive care: Development and deployment of the artemis analytic system. *Engineering in Medicine and Biology Magazine, IEEE*, 29(2):110–118, March 2010.

[2] J. Cervino, E. Kalyvianaki, J. Salvachua, and P. Pietzuch. Adaptive provisioning of stream processing systems in the cloud. In *Data Engineering Workshops (ICDEW), 2012 IEEE 28th International Conference on*, pages 295–301, April 2012.

[3] R. Cocci, T. Tran, Y. Diao, and P. Shenoy. Efficient data interpretation and compression over rfid streams. In *2008 IEEE 24th International Conference on Data Engineering*, pages 1445–1447, April 2008.

[4] A. Cuzzocrea and S. Chakravarthy. Event-based lossy compression for effective and efficient {OLAP} over data streams. *Data & Knowledge Engineering*, 69(7):678 – 708, 2010. Advanced Knowledge-based Systems.

[5] Datapath. Datapath.io. URL: http://console.datapath.io/map, 2016.

[6] M. Dayarathna and T. Suzumura. Automatic optimization of stream programs via source program operator graph transformations. *Distributed and Parallel Databases*, 31(4):543–599, 2013.

[7] M. Dayarathna and T. Suzumura. *A Mechanism for Stream Program Performance Recovery in Resource Limited Compute Clusters*, pages 164–178. Springer Berlin Heidelberg, Berlin, Heidelberg, 2013.

[8] N. Dindar, Ã. Balkesen, K. Kromwijk, and N. Tatbul. Event processing support for cross-reality environments. *IEEE Pervasive Computing*, 8(3):34–41, July 2009.

[9] C. Fehling, F. Leymann, R. Retter, W. Schupeck, and P. Arbitter. *Cloud Computing Fundamentals*, pages 21–78. Springer Vienna, Vienna, 2014.

[10] C. Gentry. Fully homomorphic encryption using ideal lattices. In *Proceedings of the Forty-first Annual ACM Symposium on Theory of Computing*, STOC '09, pages 169–178, New York, NY, USA, 2009. ACM.

[11] S. Halevi and V. Shoup. *Algorithms in HElib*, pages 554–571. Springer Berlin Heidelberg, Berlin, Heidelberg, 2014.

[12] J. Hazra, K. Das, D. P. Seetharam, and A. Singhee. Stream computing based synchrophasor application for power grids. In *Proceedings of the First International Workshop on High Performance Computing, Networking and Analytics for the Power Grid*, HiPCNA-PG '11, pages 43–50, New York, NY, USA, 2011. ACM.

[13] S. Hemminger. Network emulation with netem. 2005.

[14] W. Hummer, B. Satzger, and S. Dustdar. Elastic stream processing in the cloud. *Wiley Interdisciplinary Reviews: Data Mining and Knowledge Discovery*, 3(5):333–345, 2013.

[15] T. Hunter, T. Das, M. Zaharia, P. Abbeel, and A. Bayen. Large-scale estimation in cyberphysical systems using streaming data: A case study with arterial traffic estimation. *Automation Science and Engineering, IEEE Transactions on*, 10(4):884–898, Oct 2013.

[16] S. Jayasekara, S. Perera, M. Dayarathna, and S. Suhothayan. Continuous analytics on geospatial data streams with wso2 complex event processor. In *Proceedings of the 9th ACM International Conference on Distributed Event-Based Systems*, DEBS '15, pages 277–284, New York, NY, USA, 2015. ACM.

[17] M. Jayasinghe, A. Jayawardena, B. Rupasinghe, M. Dayarathna, S. Perera, S. Suhothayan, and I. Perera. Continuous analytics on graph data streams using wso2 complex event processor. In *Proceedings of the 10th ACM International Conference on Distributed and Event-based Systems*, DEBS '16, pages 301–308, New York, NY, USA, 2016. ACM.

[18] S. R. Jeffery, M. J. Franklin, and M. Garofalakis. An adaptive rfid middleware for supporting metaphysical data independence. *The VLDB Journal*, 17(2):265–289, 2008.

[19] W. Kleiminger, E. Kalyvianaki, and P. Pietzuch. Balancing load in stream processing with the cloud. In *Data Engineering Workshops (ICDEW), 2011 IEEE 27th International Conference on*, pages 16–21, April 2011.

[20] B. Klimt and Y. Yang. Introducing the enron corpus. In *CEAS 2004 - First Conference on Email and Anti-Spam, July 30-31, 2004, Mountain View, California, USA*, 2004.

[21] S. Loesing, M. Hentschel, T. Kraska, and D. Kossmann. Stormy: An elastic and highly available streaming service in the cloud. In *Proceedings of the 2012 Joint EDBT/ICDT Workshops*, EDBT-ICDT '12, pages 55–60, New York, NY, USA, 2012. ACM.

[22] C. Mutschler and M. Philippsen. Distributed low-latency out-of-order event processing for high data rate sensor streams. In *Parallel Distributed Processing (IPDPS), 2013 IEEE 27th International Symposium on*, pages 1133–1144, May 2013.

[23] Z. Nabi, E. Bouillet, A. Bainbridge, and C. Thomas. Of streams and storms. *IBM White Paper*, 2014.

[24] Y. Nie, R. Cocci, Z. Cao, Y. Diao, and P. Shenoy. Spire: Efficient data inference and compression over rfid streams. *IEEE Transactions on Knowledge and Data Engineering*, 24(1):141–155, Jan 2012.

[25] A. Page, O. Kocabas, S. Ames, M. Venkitasubramaniam, and T. Soyata. Cloud-based secure health monitoring: Optimizing fully-homomorphic encryption for streaming algorithms. In *2014 IEEE Globecom Workshops (GC Wkshps)*, pages 48–52, Dec 2014.

[26] B. Theeten, I. Bedini, P. Cogan, A. Sala, and T. Cucinotta. Towards the optimization of a parallel streaming engine for telco applications. *Bell Labs Technical Journal*, 18(4):181–197, 2014.

[27] M. Thompson, D. Farley, M. Barker, P. Gee, and A. Stewart. High performance alternative to bounded queues for exchanging data between concurrent threads. *technical paper, LMAX Exchange*, 2011.

[28] WSO2. Wso2 complex event processor. URL: http://wso2.com/products/complex-event-processor/, 2016.

On Moving Averages, Histograms and Time-Dependent Rates for Online Measurement

Michael Menth and Frederik Hauser
Department of Computer Science
University of Tuebingen, Germany
{menth, frederik.hauser}@uni-tuebingen.de

ABSTRACT

Moving averages (MAs) are often used in adaptive systems to monitor the state during operation. Their output is used as input for control purposes. There are multiple methods with different ability, complexity, and parameters. We propose a framework for the definition of MAs and develop performance criteria, e.g., the concept of memory, that allow to parameterize different methods in a comparable way. Moreover, we identify deficiencies of frequently used methods and propose corrections. We extend MAs to moving histograms which facilitate the approximation of time-dependent quantiles. We further extend the framework to rate measurement, discuss various approaches, and propose a novel method which reveals excellent properties. The proposed concepts help to visualize time-dependent data and to simplify design, parametrization, and evaluation of technical control systems.

1. INTRODUCTION

Moving averages (MAs), moving histograms, and time-dependent rates calculate time-dependent statistics from time series while giving more importance to recent than to old samples. The exponential MA (EMA) is a simple example:

$$A_i = a \cdot A_{i-1} + (1-a) \cdot X_i. \quad (1)$$

X_i is the size of an observed sample at time i and A_i is the time-dependent average at that time. The smoothing parameter a is often set to $a = 0.9$, but there is only little insight in literature about appropriate configuration.

On the one hand, the above mentioned methods are helpful to track and visualize the behavior of technical systems over time. On the other hand, they are used for control purposes by adaptive systems to observe their state and react appropriately. A prominent example is TCP [1] which estimates the current roundtrip time (RTT) by exponential smoothing of individual RTT samples. As another example, we currently develop an automatic bypass for a rate-constraint firewall using software-defined networking (SDN). The firewall is attached to a border switch which steers all in- and outgoing traffic through the firewall. Traffic leaving the firewall is monitored by exporting every n^{th} packet to the SDN controller using sFlow. The controller calculates a time-dependent rate over a relatively short time scale to detect congestion when a rate threshold is exceeded. Then, the controller bypasses sampled flows around the firewall through installation of appropriate flow rules on the switch. As the switch can support only a limited number of rules, the installation rate may be high if congestion occurs rather seldom, and should be low otherwise. To that end, we track congestion using a MA over a relatively long time scale and use its value for computation of a suitable offloading rate.

In this paper, we consider multiple MA methods with different parameters. We define some metrics for MAs that relate to time scale. The memory is most important and helps to set the parameters of the different methods such that their output behaves similarly. MAs are mostly applied under the assumption that samples are equidistantly spaced in time (evenly spaced time series). However, in practice unevenly spaced time series may also occur. Therefore, we adapt well-known MA methods such that the time between samples has influence on calculated average values. We show that EMA has a strong bias towards the first observed sample X_0 and propose a method for an unbiased EMA (UEMA). We demonstrate that EMA's existing extension for unevenly spaced time series (TEMA) is even persistently biased and suggest an unbiased TEMA (UTEMA). A challenge for the application of MAs is the tradeoff between accuracy and timeliness: MAs require a large memory to produce accurate estimates for mean values which is desired under the assumption of a stationary process. However, they need a short memory to quickly reveal changed behavior of a non-stationary process. We illustrate this tradeoff and give recommendations for appropriate parametrization. We propose moving histograms (MHs) as a straightforward extension of MAs including an efficient implementation. They allow approximation of time-dependent quantiles. Time-dependent rates should reflect the recent intensity of a sample process. We define time-dependent rate measurement (TDRM) as an extension of MAs. The time scale of TDRM can be controlled by the memory of the underlying MA. We review and compare existing TDRM methods and suggest TDRM-UTEMA as a novel method which exhibits desired properties.

The authors acknowledge the funding by the Deutsche Forschungsgemeinschaft (DFG) under grant ME2727/2-1.

ICPE'17, April 22-26, 2017, L'Aquila, Italy

DOI: http://dx.doi.org/10.1145/3030207.3030212

We believe that this rather elementary work contributes to a more informed usage of MAs, MHs, and TDRM. It focuses on online measurement, i.e., only the past of the process is known at measurement time. In contrast, offline measurement can consider a complete time series as input and smooth values or determine rates by leveraging both past and future samples around an observation point. While this work considers time series in the time domain, there is a large body of related work for time series analysis in the frequency domain [2].

The paper is structured as follows. Section 2 shows that MAs are used in various fields with different applications. Section 3 provides a novel framework to define MAs, suggests novel metrics to characterize MA properties, in particular the memory, reviews well-known MA approaches, and proposes new methods. Section 4 studies the impact of memory on the accuracy and timeliness of UEMA. MAs are extended towards MHs in Section 5. An extension for TDRM is proposed in Section 6: existing methods and a novel one are presented and compared. Section 7 concludes this work.

2. RELATED WORK

Though exponential smoothing is a standard technique for scientific work, it is hard to track back its roots in scientific literature. Books about fundamental statistics like [3] present only unweighted (simple) and weighted moving averages. However, we did not find an overview of general MA concepts and their properties. MAs are known under a broad range of different terms, e.g., they are also referred to as smoothing or filtering methods. Eckner describes simple and exponential moving averages as well as rolling operators [4] for the purpose of smoothing. The work in [5] presents similar concepts for the specific requirements of unevenly spaced time series. Autoregressive MAs and variants are discussed to model stochastic processes for the purpose of forecasting which is different from our application which is the calculation of an average value for the current observation point.

MAs are often applied in networking. Three different modifications of EMA (low pass, gradient adaptive, and retrospective) for bandwidth estimation are presented in [6]. Conga [7] is a distributed congestion-aware load balancing mechanism for datacenters. It leverages a discounting rate estimator which is similar to EMA. CSFQ [8] aims at providing fair bandwidth allocation. Exponential averaging with variable weights is used to estimate flow arrival rates. The active queue management PIE [9] is designed to control latency and jitter in the Internet. Its departure rate estimation uses exponential smoothing. TCP's smoothed roundtrip time (SRTT) mechanism computes the retransmission timeout in data communication with exponential averaging [1]. In [10] we presented a rate measurement method based on exponential smoothing. It was leveraged by the authors in [11] for time-decaying Bloom filters. Furthermore, we introduced the concept of moving histograms in [12] to calculate time-dependent quantiles.

MAs also have application in other areas. A simple window-based moving average is used in [13] for detection of the end of the transient phase of a stochastic process. To that end, a symmetric moving window is applied as low-pass filter to a time series, extracting its long-term trend. Exponential smoothing is widely used in the context of operations research and financial analyses for trend forecasting (e.g. [14]). The Holt-Winters forecasting procedure [15] uses three degrees of smoothing to extract level, trend, and seasonal components in time series. In quality control, exponential smoothing with optimized weights is used for the generation of control charts which detect exceedance or shortfall of critical boundaries [16, 17].

3. MOVING AVERAGES (MA)

We consider MAs for samples observed with evenly and unevenly spaced time series. For both cases, we propose a general definition of MAs. We introduce several performance metrics to characterize properties of MAs. We consider specific MAs and express their properties depending on their parameters. We point out differences among presented MAs, show that widely used exponential moving averages for evenly and unevenly spaced time series have an initial or even persistent bias, and propose unbiased variants.

3.1 MAs for Evenly Spaced Time Series

Let $(X_i)_{0 \leq i < \infty}$ be an evenly spaced time series with samples of size X_i and Δt time between consecutive samples (inter-sample time). We define a MA A_j for observation point j by

$$S_j = \sum_{0 \leq i \leq j} g_i(i-j) \cdot X_i \quad (2)$$

$$N_j = \sum_{0 \leq i \leq j} g_i(i-j) \quad (3)$$

$$A_j = \begin{cases} \frac{S_j}{N_j} & N_j > 0 \\ 0 & \text{otherwise.} \end{cases} \quad (4)$$

The sample-specific discrete weight functions $g_i(.)$ are characteristic for special types of MAs. They are used to compute a weighted sample sum S_j and weighted sample number N_j. Thereby, the weight functions $g_i(.)$ may reduce the impact of samples X_i on the MA that are distant from the observation point j. For most MA types, the weight $g_i(0)$ for the most recent sample takes the maximum $g_i^{max} = \max_k(g_i(k))$. The function decreases monotonously towards negative and positive arguments whereby only negative arguments are considered for online measurement. The fraction of the weighted sample sum and the weighted sample number yields the MA A_j if the number N_j is positive. Otherwise, we define the MA to be zero.

3.1.1 Metrics

If the weight functions $g_i(.)$ for samples X_i do not differ, their subscript as well as those of the following metrics may be omitted.

The contribution C_i quantifies how much a sample X_i contributes to all average values A_j. It can be calculated by

$$C_i = \sum_{-\infty < k \leq 0} g_i(k) \cdot \Delta t. \quad (5)$$

If contributions C_i differ, the MA has a bias to towards samples with larger contributions.

The memory M_i quantifies the average duration over which a sample X_i contributes to average values A_j. It considers fractional contributions relative to the maximum sample weight g_i^{max} and can be derived as

$$M_i = \frac{C_i}{g_i^{max}}. \quad (6)$$

Essentially, the memory reflects the time scale over which samples are averaged. If weight functions $g_i(.)$ differ among samples, they may – but do not need to – yield different contributions C_i and memory M_i.

The memory depends on the inter-sample time Δt which must be taken into account when applying MAs in practice. A MA may be used to track the transmission delay of packets on a communication line. Transmission of packets with 1500 bytes yields inter-sample times of $\Delta t = 12$ ms and $\Delta t = 0.012$ ms on a 1 Mb/s and 1 Gb/s link, respectively. Irrespective of the specific type of MA, the resulting memory differs by three orders of magnitude if MAs are applied with identical parametrization. If the timely dynamics of the measured averages should be comparable, the parameters of the MAs need to be adapted to the specific inter-sample time Δt so that the MAs exhibit the same memory for all considered processes.

The delay D_i quantifies the average age of all contributions of a sample X_i to all average values A_j. It is computed by

$$D_i = \sum_{-\infty<k\leq 0} (|k| \cdot \Delta t) \cdot \frac{(g_i(k) \cdot \Delta t)}{C_i}. \quad (7)$$

Shifting a MA's weight function by j to $g_i^*(k) = g_i(k+j)$ for $k \leq -j$ and $g_i^*(k) = 0$ for $k > -j$ leads to another MA with the same memory but a larger delay.

3.1.2 *Cumulative Mean (CumMean)*

CumMean is defined by

$$A_j = \frac{1}{j+1} \cdot \sum_{0\leq i\leq j} X_i. \quad (8)$$

It fits the Definitions (2) – (4) for homogeneous weights $g(k) = 1$, $-\infty < k \leq 0$. Thus, each sample exhibits a contribution, delay, and memory of $M = D = C = \infty \cdot \Delta t$. Figure 1(a) visualizes the evolution of the CumMean for the evenly spaced time series $(X_0, ..., X_{11}) = (1, 1, 0, 1, 1, 1, 0, 1, 0, 0, 0, 0)$. The impact of recent samples diminishes with increasing time index because all past samples equally contribute to CumMean's average. Therefore, CumMean does not focus on the recent evolution of the observed process and cannot provide appropriate feedback for self-adapting systems.

3.1.3 *Window Moving Average (WMA)*

WMA, also known as simple moving average (SMA) [4], essentially computes the arithmetic mean of the last w samples whereby w is an integer. The weighted sample sum is

$$S_j = \sum_{max(0,j-w+1)\leq i\leq j} X_i \quad (9)$$

and the weighted sample number is $N_j = min(w, j+1)$. This fits the Definitions (2) – (4) for weights

$$g(k) = \begin{cases} 1 & -w < k \leq 0 \\ 0 & \text{otherwise} \end{cases}. \quad (10)$$

Contribution and memory are $C = M = w \cdot \Delta t$ and delay is $D = \frac{(w-1)\cdot\Delta t}{2} = \frac{M}{2} - \frac{\Delta t}{2}$.

Figure 1(a) visualizes the evolution of WMA-based averages for the above introduced sample series. It yields an average value of $A_{11} = 0$ because it disregards past samples outside its window. Furthermore, it yields $A_5 = 0.75$ and $A_6 = 0.75$ although the observed '1' are younger in A_5 than in A_6. This is due to the fact that all samples within a WMA's window are equally weighted.

3.1.4 *Disjoint Windows Moving Average (DWMA)*

DWMA partitions a time series into sets of consecutive and disjoint windows $\mathcal{W}_k = \{k \cdot w \leq i < (k+1) \cdot w\}$ with w time indices each. At the end of such a window, the arithmetic mean of the samples falling in this window is taken as current average until the next measurement value is available. This can be denoted by

$$S_j = \begin{cases} 0 & j < w-1 \\ \sum_{i\in\mathcal{W}_{(\lfloor\frac{j+1}{w}\rfloor-1)}} X_i & \text{otherwise} \end{cases} \quad (11)$$

and $N_j = w$. It fits the Definitions (2) – (4) for sample-specific weights

$$g_i(k) = \begin{cases} 1 & \begin{cases} (i \mod w) - (2\cdot w - 1) \\ < k \leq \\ (i \mod w) - (w-1) \end{cases} \\ 0 & \text{otherwise.} \end{cases} \quad (12)$$

Thus, contribution and memory are $C = M = w \cdot \Delta t$. The sample-specific delay is $D_i = \frac{w-1}{2} \cdot \Delta t + ((w-1) - (i \mod w)) \cdot \Delta t$ and the average delay is $\overline{D} = (w-1) \cdot \Delta t = M - \Delta t$.

Figure 1(a) shows the evolution of DWMA. For the first $w-1$ observation points, there is no actual average value available. Due to its increased delay, DWMA clearly lags behind WMA and it is coarser.

3.1.5 *Unbiased Exponential Moving Average (UEMA)*

We propose UEMA as a novel algorithm using the weight function

$$g(k) = a^{-k} \quad (13)$$

and the Definitions (2) – (4) for the computation of the average values. The underlying geometric model enables an elegant, recursive calculation:

$$S_j = \begin{cases} X_j & j = 0 \\ a \cdot S_{j-1} + X_j & j > 0 \end{cases} \quad (14)$$

$$N_j = \begin{cases} 1 & j = 0 \\ a \cdot N_{j-1} + 1 & j > 0 \end{cases}. \quad (15)$$

UEMA has a contribution and memory of $C = M = \frac{\Delta t}{1-a}$, and a delay of $D = \frac{a\cdot\Delta t}{1-a}$ for all samples, i.e., $D = a \cdot M$. Figure 1(a) compares the evolution of UEMA with the one of WMA for the same memory $M = 4 \cdot \Delta t$. While WMA disregards samples that lie outside its window and yields $A_{11} = 0$, UEMA respects the full past of the process and yields $A_{11} = 0.21$. WMA also disregards the position of samples within its window. In contrast, UEMA is sensitive to that and yields $A_5 = 0.87$ (observed 0 in WMA's window is old) and $A_6 = 0.62$ (observed 0 in WMA's window is young).

Figure 1(b) illustrates the impact of UEMA's memory on the evolution of the MA. The MA is more inert for larger memory, i.e., for a larger smoothing factor a.

3.1.6 *Exponential Moving Average (EMA)*

EMA, also known as Exponentially Weighted MA (EWMA) or exponential smoothing, calculates its weighted sum S_j as

$$S_j = \begin{cases} X_0 & j = 0 \\ a \cdot S_{i-1} + (1-a) \cdot X_j & j > 0 \end{cases} \quad (16)$$

and the weighted number of samples is $N_j = 1$. Thus, S_j already computes A_j (see Equation (1)). These formulae fit

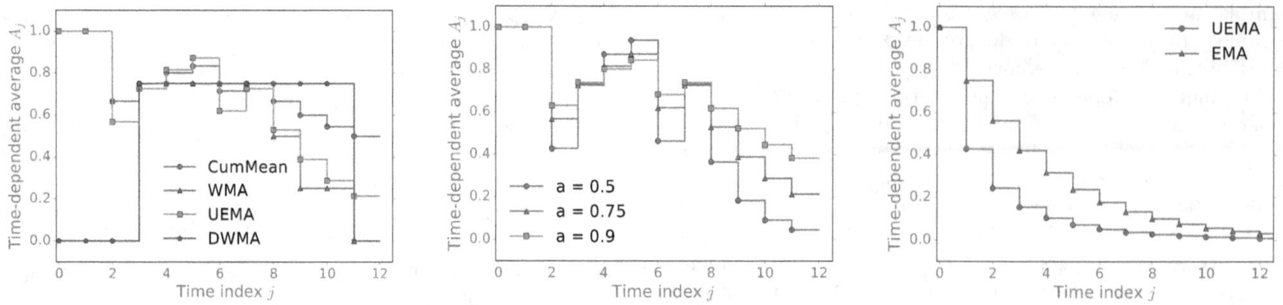

(a) CumMean ($M = \infty$), WMA, DWMA (both with $w = 4$, $M = 4 \cdot \Delta t$), and UEMA ($a = \frac{3}{4}$, $M = 4 \cdot \Delta t$) for time series $(X_0, ..., X_{11}) = (1, 1, 0, 1, 1, 1, 0, 1, 0, 0, 0, 0)$.

(b) Comparison of UEMA for $a \in \{\frac{1}{2}, \frac{3}{4}, \frac{9}{10}\}$ ($M \in \{2 \cdot \Delta t, 4 \cdot \Delta t, 10 \cdot \Delta t\}$) for time series $(X_0, ..., X_{11}) = (1, 1, 0, 1, 1, 1, 0, 1, 0, 0, 0, 0)$.

(c) EMA and UEMA with $a = 0.75$ ($M = 4 \cdot \Delta t$) for time series $(X_0, ..., X_{11}) = (1, 0, 0, 0, 0, 0, 0, 0, 0, 0, 0, 0)$: EMA has an initial bias.

Figure 1: Timely evolution of MAs for evenly spaced time series.

the Definitions (2) – (4) for sample-specific weights

$$g_i(k) = \begin{cases} a^{-k} & i = 0 \\ (1-a) \cdot a^{-k} & \text{otherwise} \end{cases}. \quad (17)$$

The two different weight functions yield the same memory $M = \frac{\Delta t}{1-a}$ and delay of $D = \frac{a \cdot \Delta t}{1-a}$ which equal those of UEMA. However, the contribution of X_0 is $C_0 = \frac{\Delta t}{1-a}$ while the one of all other samples is $C_i = \Delta t$. This causes a bias towards X_0 in the time series of the resulting MA A_j. To illustrate this effect, Figure 1(c) compares the resulting averages for EMA and UEMA for consecutive samples $(X_0, ..., X_{11}) = (1, 0, 0, 0, 0, 0, 0, 0, 0, 0, 0, 0)$. EMA and UEMA are both configured with $a = 0.75$, i.e., $M = 4 \cdot \Delta t$. The difference between the two curves is the bias induced by EMA's larger contribution of X_0. As the bias vanishes over time, EMA may be used if accuracy for initial values A_j does not matter. This may be advantageous as EMA is slightly simpler than UEMA. While EMA is already applied in many technical systems and research papers, UEMA is a novel method proposed in this work.

3.2 MAs for Unevenly Spaced Time Series

Let $(X_i)_{t_i \in \mathcal{T}, 0 \leq i < \infty}$ be an unevenly spaced time series of samples with different size X_i. Figure 2(a) contrasts two examples to an evenly spaced time series.

MAs for unevenly spaced time series respect the time structure of samples such that the impact of a sample on resulting average values diminishes over time instead with progressing time index. We define a MA A_t for observation point t by

$$S_t = \sum_{\{i: t_i \leq t\}} g_i(t_i - t) \cdot X_i \quad (18)$$

$$N_t = \sum_{\{i: t_i \leq t\}} g_i(t_i - t) \quad (19)$$

$$A_t = \begin{cases} \frac{S_t}{N_t} & N_t > 0 \\ 0 & \text{otherwise} \end{cases}. \quad (20)$$

Definitions (18) – (20) are analogous to Definitions (2) – (4) but account for the fact that sample times are now continuous. Therefore, the sample-specific weight functions $g_i(.)$ are also continuous.

3.2.1 *Metrics*

The metrics are also analogous to those of MAs for evenly spaced time series. The contribution C_i of sample X_i can be calculated as

$$C_i = \int_{-\infty}^{0} g_i(t) dt \quad (21)$$

and the memory is

$$M_i = \frac{C_i}{g_i^{max}} \quad (22)$$

with $g_i^{max} = \max_{-\infty < t \leq 0}(g_i(t))$. The delay is

$$D_i = \frac{\int_{-\infty}^{0} |t| \cdot g(t) dt}{C_i}. \quad (23)$$

3.2.2 *Time Window Moving Average (TWMA)*

TWMA computes the average of the samples within a recent time window of duration W. Let $\mathcal{W}_t = \{i : t_i \in (t - W; t]\}$ be the index set of samples arriving within that window at time t. Average values for TWMA can be computed by $N_t = |\mathcal{W}_t|$ and

$$S_t = \begin{cases} 0 & |\mathcal{W}_t| = 0 \\ \sum_{i \in \mathcal{W}_t} X_i & \text{otherwise} \end{cases}. \quad (24)$$

This fits the Definitions (18) – (20) for the weight function

$$g(t) = \begin{cases} 1 & -W < t \leq 0 \\ 0 & \text{otherwise} \end{cases}. \quad (25)$$

Contribution and memory are $C = M = W$ and the delay is $D = \frac{W}{2} = \frac{M}{2}$. The resulting MA A_t returns to zero if the last sample is older than W, which may be an undesired property. We omit illustrations of TWMA due to space limitations.

3.2.3 *Disjoint Time Windows Moving Average (DTWMA)*

DTWMA partitions the time axis into consecutive measurement intervals of duration W, computes the arithmetic mean of samples observed within a measurement interval at its end, and uses this average value until the next average value is available. Let $\mathcal{W}_k = \{i : t_i \in (k \cdot W; (k+1) \cdot W]\}$ be the index set of samples arriving within window number k since measurement start at time $t = 0$. Average values for DTWMA are computed by $N_t = |\mathcal{W}_{(\lceil \frac{t}{W} \rceil - 1)}|$ and

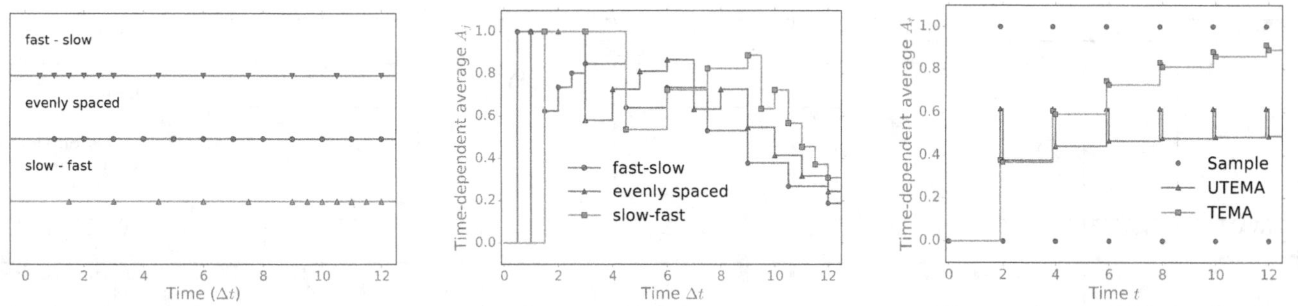

(a) Three considered arrival times: samples first arrive fast and then slowly, vice-versa, and at constant speed.

(b) UTEMA with $\beta = \frac{1}{4\cdot\Delta t}$ $(M = 4\cdot\Delta t)$ for time series $(1,1,0,1,1,1,0,1,0,0,0,0)$ and the arrival times in Figure 2(a).

(c) TEMA and UTEMA with $\beta = \frac{1}{\Delta t}$ $(M = 1\cdot\Delta t)$: TEMA exhibits an initial and a persistent bias. Sample arrivals and sizes are represented by dots.

Figure 2: Timely evolution of MAs for unevenly spaced time series.

$$S_t = \begin{cases} 0 & t < W \vee |\mathcal{W}_{(\lceil \frac{t}{W}\rceil -1)}| = 0 \\ \sum_{i\in\mathcal{W}_{(\lceil \frac{t}{W}\rceil -1)}} X_i & \text{otherwise} \end{cases}. \quad (26)$$

These equations fit Definitions (18) – (20) for sample-specific weight functions

$$g_i(t) = \begin{cases} 1 & \begin{cases} t_i - (\lceil \frac{t_j}{W}\rceil + 1)\cdot W \\ < t \leq \\ t_i - \lceil \frac{t_j}{W}\rceil \cdot W \end{cases} \\ 0 & \text{otherwise} \end{cases}. \quad (27)$$

Thus, contribution and memory are $C_i = M_i = W$. The sample-specific delay is $D_i = (\lceil \frac{t_i}{W}\rceil \cdot W - t_i) + \frac{W}{2}$ and the average delay is $\overline{D} = W$. The MA A_t returns to zero after a measurement interval without any samples. We omit illustrations of DTWMA due to space limitations.

3.2.4 Unbiased Time-Exponential Moving Average (UTEMA)

We propose UTEMA as a novel MA method which uses the exponential weight function

$$g(t) = e^{\beta\cdot t} \quad (28)$$

in Definitions (18) – (20). The underlying exponential model allows for recursive equations:

$$S_t = \begin{cases} 0 & t < t_0 \\ X_0 & t = t_0 \\ e^{-\beta\cdot(t-t_{i-1})}\cdot S_{t_{i-1}} + X_i & t = t_i \\ e^{-\beta\cdot(t-t_i)}\cdot S_{t_i} & t_i < t < t_{i+1} \end{cases} \quad (29)$$

$$N_t = \begin{cases} 0 & t < t_0 \\ 1 & t = t_0 \\ e^{-\beta\cdot(t-t_{i-1})}\cdot N_{t_{i-1}} + 1 & t = t_i \\ e^{-\beta\cdot(t-t_i)}\cdot N_{t_i} & t_i < t < t_{i+1} \end{cases}. \quad (30)$$

UTEMA has a contribution, memory, and delay of $C = M = D = \frac{1}{\beta}$.

Figure 2(b) shows that UTEMA respects the time structure of the sample processes given in Figure 2(a). If samples first arrive fast and then slowly, UTEMA yields a lower average $A_{t=12\cdot\Delta t}$ at the end of the observation interval than for the evenly spaced time series because observed '1' are older. Likewise, if samples first arrive slowly and then fast, UTEMA leads to a larger $A_{t=12\cdot\Delta t}$ than for the evenly spaced time series because observed '1' are younger. When UEMA is applied for one of the unevenly spaced time series, it yields UTEMA's average values for the evenly spaced time series.

UEMA can provide exactly the same average values for an evenly spaced time series as UTEMA if its smoothing factor is set such that it yields the same weights for integral multiples of Δt, i.e., $a = e^{-\beta\cdot\Delta t}$. Figure 3 compares such weight functions of UTEMA and UEMA with a smoothing rate of $\beta = \frac{0.25}{\Delta t}$ and smoothing factor of $a = 0.7788$, respectively. The memory for UTEMA is $M = 4\cdot\Delta t$ while the one for UEMA is $M = 4.52\cdot\Delta t$. The discrepancy is due to the fact that UTEMA's weight function $g_{UTEMA}(t)$ interpolates only the lower corners of UEMA's weights $g_{UEMA}(k)$ and, therefore, leads to a lower integral value. This difference converges to $\frac{\Delta t}{2}$ for large memory M.

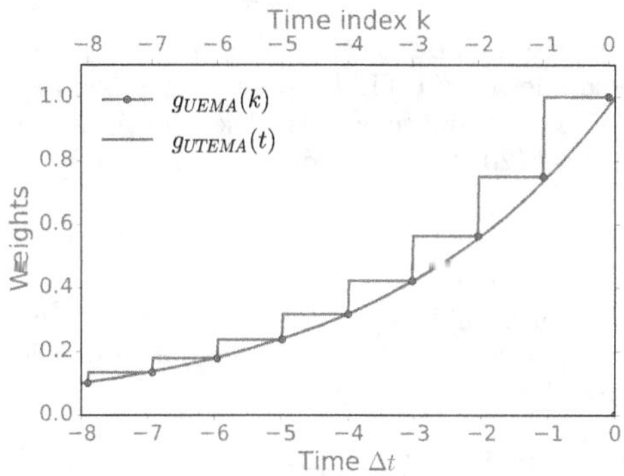

Figure 3: Weight functions for UEMA and UTEMA configured such that they reveal equal weights for integral multiples of Δt ($a = 0.7788$ and $\beta = \frac{0.25}{\Delta t}$, respectively). UTEMA yields a lower memory because its weight function $g_{UTEMA}(t)$ interpolates only the lower corners of UEMA's step function $g_{UEMA}(k)$.

The difference between UTEMA's average curves for evenly and unevenly spaced time series quantifies the error caused by UEMA. Its practical significance depends on the time scale of interest because the difference decreases for increasing memory M. If the time structure of the observed process is essential, UTEMA is a good alternative to UEMA and also to TWMA which does not respect the time struc-

Table 1: Considered MAs including properties.

Method	Param.	Contribution C	Memory M	Delay D	Delay D dep. on M	Comments
MAs for evenly spaced time series						
CumMean	Δt	∞	∞	∞	∞	Does not discount old samples.
WMA	$w, \Delta t$	$w \cdot \Delta t$	$w \cdot \Delta t$	$\frac{(w-1)\cdot\Delta t}{2}$	$\frac{M}{2} - \frac{\Delta t}{2}$	Does not account for samples outside window and sample position within window.
DWMA	$w, \Delta t$	$w \cdot \Delta t$	$w \cdot \Delta t$	$(w-1) \cdot \Delta t$ (avg.)	$M - \Delta t$ (avg.)	Like WMA, additional delay
UEMA	$a, \Delta t$	$\frac{\Delta t}{1-a}$	$\frac{\Delta t}{1-a}$	$\frac{a \cdot \Delta t}{1-a}$	$a \cdot M$	Method proposed in this work
EMA	$a, \Delta t$	$\frac{\Delta t}{1-a}$, Δt	$\frac{\Delta t}{1-a}$	$\frac{a \cdot \Delta t}{1-a}$	$a \cdot M$	Bias towards X_0
MAs for unevenly spaced time series						
TWMA	W	W	W	$\frac{W}{2}$	$\frac{M}{2}$	May return to zero (invalid value).
DTWMA	W	W	W	W (avg.)	M (avg.)	Like TWMA, additional delay
UTEMA	β	$\frac{1}{\beta}$	$\frac{1}{\beta}$	$\frac{1}{\beta}$	M	Method proposed in this work
TEMA	β	$\frac{1}{\beta}$ for X_0, $\frac{1-e^{-\beta\cdot(t_i-t_{i-1})}}{\beta}$ for X_i	$\frac{1}{\beta}$	$\frac{1}{\beta}$	M	Bias towards X_0 and other samples

ture within its measurement window and may return to zero in the absence of sufficiently young samples.

For UTEMA, the half-life time may be used as another metric. It can be computed by $H = \frac{\ln(2)}{\beta}$, but it is not applicable to most other MA variants.

3.2.5 *Time-Exponential Moving Average (TEMA)*

TEMA is sometimes used as adaptation of EMA to unevenly spaced time series [4]. Its sample sum is computed by

$$S_t = \begin{cases} 0 & t < t_0 \\ X_0 & t = t_0 \\ e^{-\beta\cdot(t_i-t_{i-1})} \cdot S_{t_{i-1}} + & t_i \le t < t_{i+1} \\ (1-e^{-\beta\cdot(t_i-t_{i-1})}) \cdot X_i & \end{cases}. \quad (31)$$

and its weighted number of samples is $N_j = 1$. Thus, TEMA is hardly simpler than UTEMA since it also requires the calculation of exponential functions. The equations fit the Definitions (18) – (20) for the sample-specific weight functions

$$g_i(t) = \begin{cases} e^{\beta\cdot t} & i = 0 \\ (1-e^{-\beta\cdot(t_i-t_{i-1})}) \cdot e^{\beta\cdot t} & i > 0 \end{cases}. \quad (32)$$

While EMA has only two different sample-specific weight functions, those of TEMA may all be different. The contributions are also sample-specific:

$$C_i = \begin{cases} \frac{1}{\beta} & i = 0 \\ \frac{1-e^{-\beta\cdot(t_i-t_{i-1})}}{\beta} & i > 0 \end{cases}. \quad (33)$$

Nevertheless, the weight functions of all samples reveal the same memory $M = \frac{1}{\beta}$ which equals the one of UTEMA. TEMA's bias towards some samples is more severe than the one of EMA because it does not vanish over time. Its impact is illustrated in Figure 2(c). Sample sizes are 0 after a short inter-sample time of $0.1 \cdot \Delta t$ and 1 after a long inter-sample time of $1.9 \cdot \Delta t$. While UTEMA yields average values converge to 0.5 most of the time, TEMA's average values continuously increase as large samples have a larger contribution than small samples in this process. We also simulated a Poisson arrival process over $10^6 \cdot \Delta t$ time with rate $\lambda = \frac{1}{\Delta t}$ and set the sample size X_i to the value of the preceding inter-arrival time divided by Δt. We averaged the obtained time-dependent average values over time. UTEMA yields 1.11, 1.05, and 1.02 for $M \in \{\Delta t, 4 \cdot \Delta t, 10 \cdot \Delta t, 25 \cdot \Delta t\}$ while corresponding values for TEMA are 1.80, 1.91, and 1.96. Thus, the bias is significant and even increases with larger memory.

3.3 Summary

Table 1 summarizes properties of considered MAs.

4. ANALYSIS OF UEMA

We illustrate the impact of UEMA's memory on the accuracy and timeliness of obtained averages. Accuracy addresses the deviation of UEMA's computed average from the true mean μ of an observed stationary sample process $(X_i)_{0 \le i < \infty}$. Timeliness addresses UEMA's ability to early reflect changes regarding μ in the observed process.

Table 2: Averaged squared deviation of computed averages A_i from the known sample mean μ.

	σ^2					
$M(\Delta t)$	1	3	10	30	100	300
3	0.1999	0.5997	1.9990	5.9969	19.9896	59.9687
10	0.0527	0.1580	0.5266	1.5798	5.2655	15.7966
30	0.0170	0.0511	0.1734	0.5112	1.7039	5.1116
100	0.0051	0.0152	0.0508	0.1525	0.5082	1.5246
300	0.0017	0.0051	0.0171	0.0514	0.1712	0.5136
1000	0.0005	0.0016	0.0053	0.0158	0.0527	0.1580
CumMean	0.0000	0.0000	0.0001	0.0004	0.0012	0.0036

4.1 Impact of Memory on Accuracy

We generate $n = 10^6$ normally distributed random variables X_i with mean $\mu = 0$ and variance $\sigma^2 \in \{1, 3, 10, 30, 100, 300\}$ and track them by UEMA with a memory of $M \in \{3, 10, 30, 100, 300, 1000\} \cdot \Delta t$. Table 2 shows the arithmetic mean of the squared deviations of the averages from the observed random variable's mean μ: $dev^2(n) = \frac{1}{n} \cdot \sum_{0 \le i < n}(A_i - \mu)^2$. The accuracy of the estimate depends on the variance of the observed process and UEMA's memory. It can be explained as follows. According to Equations (2) – (4) and (13), UEMA's average value A_j is the sum S_j of weighted, independent random variables multiplied by the scalar value $\frac{1}{N_j}$. Therefore, the variance of A_j can be calculated as

$$VAR[A] = \frac{\sum_{0 \le i < \infty} a^{2 \cdot i} \cdot \sigma^2}{(\sum_{0 \le i < \infty} a^i)^2} = \frac{(1-a)^2}{1-a^2} \cdot \sigma^2 = \frac{\sigma^2}{2 \cdot \frac{M}{\Delta t} - 1} \quad (34)$$

which explains the observation in our experiment.

Equation (34) helps to find a minimum smoothing factor a if the variance σ^2 of the samples is roughly known. We assume that the averaged values A_j are distributed according to a normal distribution. With $E[A] = \mu$ and $VAR[A] = \frac{1-a}{1+a} \cdot \sigma^2$ we define $Y = \frac{A-\mu}{\sqrt{\frac{1-a}{1+a} \cdot \sigma^2}}$ which is distributed according to a standard normal distribution[2]. Therefore, we get

$$P(-z_{1-\frac{\alpha}{2}} \le Y \le z_{1-\frac{\alpha}{2}}) = 1 - \alpha \quad (35)$$

$$P(\mu - \delta(a,\alpha) \le A \le \mu + \delta(a,\alpha)) = 1 - \alpha \quad (36)$$

with $z_{1-\frac{\alpha}{2}}$ being the $(1-\frac{\alpha}{2})$-quantile of the standard normal distribution and $\delta(a,\alpha) = z_{1-\frac{\alpha}{2}} \cdot \sqrt{\frac{1-a}{1+a} \cdot \sigma^2}$. We conclude that A deviates at most δ from the true mean μ with probability $1-\alpha$. This derivation helps to understand the accuracy of UEMA depending on a, but cannot calculate the accuracy when random variables with unknown variance σ^2 are observed. A solution is to assume orders of magnitude for σ^2.

We use this derivation to choose a lower bound $a_{min}(\alpha, \varepsilon)$ for a such that a maximum error ε can be achieved with probability $1-\alpha$:

$$a_{min}(\alpha, \varepsilon) \ge \frac{1 - \left(\frac{\varepsilon}{\sigma \cdot z_{1-\frac{\alpha}{2}}}\right)^2}{1 + \left(\frac{\varepsilon}{\sigma \cdot z_{1-\frac{\alpha}{2}}}\right)^2}. \quad (37)$$

Table 3 illustrates the accuracy of that approach for 10^7 normally distributed random variables and compares it with a standard smoothing factor of $a = 0.9$.

Table 3: Percentage ρ of UEMA averages deviating at most $\varepsilon = 1$ from the actual mean $\mu = 0$ depending on smoothing factor a. Smoothing factor a_{min} is chosen for $\alpha = 0.1$ ($z_{1-\frac{\alpha}{2}} = 1.645$) according to Equation (37).

σ^2	1	3	10	30	100	300
$a_{min}(\alpha, \epsilon)$	0.4579	0.7795	0.9283	0.9755	0.9926	0.9975
$\rho(a_{min}(\alpha, \epsilon))$	0.8990	0.8989	0.8990	0.8902	0.8991	0.9001
$\rho(a = 0.9)$	1.0000	0.9881	0.8319	0.5740	0.3371	0.1987

Equation (37) helps to estimate probabilities with a certain accuracy. Probabilities p can be determined by counting $X = 1$ if a sample fulfills a certain condition, and $X = 0$ otherwise. This yields a Bernoulli process with variance $\sigma^2 = (1-p) \cdot p \le 0.25$ which may be used to determine an appropriate smoothing factor. Thus, $a_{min} = 0.99971$ may be used to estimate probabilities with accuracy of $\varepsilon = 0.01$ and error probability of $\alpha = 0.1$.

4.2 Impact of Memory on Timeliness

To illustrate the ability of UEMA to reveal changed process behavior, we simulate $n+1 = 10001$ samples of normally distributed random variables X_i. The mean of X_i increases over time and is set to $E[X_i] = \frac{i}{n}$, $0 \le i \le n$ while the variance $\sigma^2 = 1$ remains stable. We performed this experiment $n_{runs} = 10000$ times to calculate average $\overline{A_i}$ and the empirical variance $S^2(A_i)$ of the average values A_i. Table 4 shows these values estimated after $i \in \{3333, 6666, 10000\}$ steps by UEMA for different memory and for CumMean.

Table 4: Samples with increasing expectations $E[X_i]$. Average ($\overline{A_i}$ and empirical variance $S^2(A_i)$ of average values A_i for UEMA with different memory and for CumMean (CM).

i	3333		6666		10000	
$M(\Delta t)$	$\overline{A_i}$	$S^2(A_i)$	$\overline{A_i}$	$S^2(A_i)$	$\overline{A_i}$	$S^2(A_i)$
1	0.3355	0.9987	0.6773	1.0051	0.9886	1.0128
3	0.3297	0.1983	0.6680	0.2021	0.9949	0.2022
10	0.3320	0.0533	0.6648	0.0530	0.9975	0.0521
30	0.3305	0.0174	0.6623	0.0169	0.9964	0.0166
100	0.3233	0.0052	0.6557	0.0051	0.9899	0.0049
300	0.3032	0.0017	0.6361	0.0017	0.9702	0.0016
1000	0.2458	0.0005	0.5672	0.0005	0.9901	0.0005
3000	0.1972	0.0003	0.4475	0.0002	0.7370	0.0002
10000	0.1762	0.0003	0.3701	0.0002	0.5820	0.0001
CM	0.1670	0.0003	0.3334	0.0002	0.5001	0.0001
$E[X_i]$	0.3333	-	0.6666	-	1.0000	-

The table shows that the averaged averages $\overline{A_i}$ approximate the configured expectations $E[X_i]$ well for small memory and clearly underestimate them for larger memory. Best values are obtained in this specific experiment for a memory of at most $M = 100 \cdot \Delta t$. We also observe that the sample variance $S^2(A_i)$ depends on the memory M but not on the index i. The latter is due to the fact that all X_i have the same variance σ^2 so that the expectation of the sample variance can be approximated by $VAR[A_i] = \frac{1}{2 \cdot \frac{M}{\delta t} - 1} \cdot \sigma^2$ which is well approximated by the values in the table. As A_i computed with small memory, e.g., $M = 10 \cdot \Delta t$ or smaller, reveal a large variance, they often deviate from their average $\overline{A_i}$ and are only little reliable. Thus, there is a tradeoff between accuracy and timeliness that can be controlled by UEMA's memory.

To guarantee timeliness of computed averages, the smoothing factor a must be low enough. The last m samples contribute an overall weight of $\sum_{0 \le i < m} a^i = \frac{1-a^m}{1-a}$ to the average while the average contains an overall weight of at most $\sum_{0 \le i < \infty} a^i = \frac{1}{1-a}$. To limit the influence of samples older than m time steps to a fraction γ, $\frac{1-a^m}{1-a} \ge \frac{1-\gamma}{1-a}$ must hold, i.e., $a \le \sqrt[m]{\gamma}$ must be met. Conversely, for a given a, the impact of samples older than $\lceil \frac{\ln(\gamma)}{\ln(a)} \rceil$ time steps is limited to γ.

5 MOVING HISTOGRAMS (MH)

A histogram partitions the sample range into k intervals and associates with each of them a counter $bin(i)$, $0 \le i < k$. We denote their lower and upper bound by $l(i)$ and $u(i)$. We define that the lower bound is part of the preceding interval and that the upper bound is part of the considered interval. Left- and rightmost intervals are extended towards $\pm\infty$. All bins are initialized with zero. At sample arrival, the corresponding bin of a cumulative histogram (CumHist) is incremented by 1. The relative frequency for samples in a certain interval i can be calculated by

$$h(i) = \frac{bin(i)}{\sum_{0 \le j < k} bin(j)}. \quad (38)$$

While other relative frequencies such as $h(X \le x)$ can also be determined by MAs, histograms allow the approximation of quantiles. The p-quantile Q_p is the infimum of values x for which $P(X \le x) \le p$ holds. Histograms can approximate it by

$$\widehat{Q_p} = u(i) : \sum_{0 \le j < i} h(j) < p \le \sum_{0 \le j \le i} h(j). \quad (39)$$

[2]The approach taken is similar but not equal to the estimation of confidence intervals for the mean of independent samples. In our case, consecutive average values A_j are highly correlated so that the variance cannot be derived from samples. We solve that problem by assuming an appropriate value for σ^2.

We adapt the concept of MAs to histograms. Moving histograms (MHs) can provide time-dependent quantiles. We presented an application in [12]. In the following, we discuss MHs on the base of UEMA and UTEMA.

5.1 MHs for Evenly Spaced Time Series

We present the unbiased exponential moving histogram (UEMH) which extends UEMA. When a new sample arrives, all bins are devaluated by the smoothing factor a. Afterwards, the bin associated with the new sample is incremented by 1. Thereby, the contribution of older samples to the histogram decreases. Relative frequencies are determined according to Equation (38). A single bin corresponds to UEMA's S_j and the sum of all bins to UEMA's N_j. Properties like contribution C, memory M, and delay D of UEMA also apply.

This straightforward adaptation requires high multiplication effort. As an alternative, devaluation may be omitted and $\frac{1}{a^i}$ may be used as increment for sample X_i instead of 1. This causes numerical instability as $\frac{1}{a^i}$ rises exponentially. A compromise is to avoid that increments exceed a value η. To that end, we devaluate bins only after $n_{dev} = \lceil\frac{-\ln(\eta)}{\ln(a)}\rceil$ steps by a factor $\frac{1}{a^{n_{dev}}}$ and choose $a^{i \bmod n_{dev}}$ as increment for X_i.

5.2 MHs for Unevenly Spaced Time Series

The unbiased time-exponential moving histogram (UTEMH) extends UTEMA. In contrast to UEMH, bins are devaluated by $e^{-\beta\cdot(t_i-t_{i-1})}$ instead of a when X_i arrives. Similarly, increments of size $e^{\beta\cdot(t_i-t_0)}$ may be used instead of $\frac{1}{a^i}$ to avoid devaluation of all bins. To avoid numerical problems, bins are devaluated after $t_{dev} = \frac{\ln(\eta)}{\beta}$ time by $e^{-\beta\cdot t_{dev}}$ and increments $e^{\beta\cdot((t_i-t_0) \bmod t_{dev})}$ are chosen.

Table 5: 10%-quantiles of UEMH with different memory and cumulative histogram (CH) for samples with increasing expectations $E[X_i]$.

i	3333		6666		10000	
$M(\Delta t)$	$\overline{Q_{10\%,i}}$	$\widehat{Q_{10\%,i}}$	$\overline{Q_{10\%,i}}$	$\widehat{Q_{10\%,i}}$	$\overline{Q_{10\%,i}}$	$\widehat{Q_{10\%,i}}$
1	-0.27	-0.89	-0.06	-0.58	+0.18	-0.36
3	-0.75	-0.92	-0.43	-0.55	-0.09	-0.29
10	-0.89	-0.92	-0.53	-0.55	-0.25	-0.26
30	-0.90	-0.92	-0.57	-0.57	-0.29	-0.28
100	-0.93	-0.94	-0.60	-0.60	-0.29	-0.29
300	-0.97	-0.97	-0.63	-0.63	-0.31	-0.31
1000	-1.03	-1.03	-0.71	-0.71	-0.38	-0.39
3000	-1.08	-1.08	-0.85	-0.85	-0.57	-0.58
10000	-1.11	-1.11	-0.93	-0.39	-0.75	-0.75
CH	-1.12	-1.11	-0.97	-0.97	-0.83	-0.83
$Q_{10\%,i}$	-0.949		-0.615		-0.282	

5.3 Timeliness of UEMH and CumHist

We illustrate the timeliness of UEMH with different memory M and cumulative histograms. We perform the same experiment as in Section 4.2 and set up histograms with equal-size ranges between −3 and 1 of width 0.1. Table 5 shows estimates of 10%-quantiles after i samples. They are computed as average values $\overline{Q_{10\%,i}}$ of 10%-quantiles gained from $n_{runs} = 100$ runs or as 10%-quantiles $\widehat{Q_{10\%,i}}$ based on the aggregated histogram information after sample i from all the n_{runs} different runs which is closer to the true value of the 10% quantile due to reduced variance. However, we see that both methods yield very similar results for $M = 30\cdot\Delta t$ or larger. The analytical values are given on the bottom of the table. They are well approximated by both methods with memories between 30 and $300\cdot\Delta t$. The 10% quantiles derived from a single run significantly fluctuate, but the values for $\overline{Q_{10\%,i}}$ show that they yield the right values on average. The quantiles estimated with cumulative histograms increase only slowly over time and clearly underestimate the analytical values. Smaller memory for UEMH cannot hold enough data for sufficiently accurate calculation of quantiles. MHs with larger memory are too much influenced by older samples which were generated with lower mean and cause lower estimates. Thus, there is also a tradeoff between timeliness and accuracy for MHs.

6. TIME-DEPENDENT RATE MEASUREMENT (TDRM)

A rate denotes an average number of samples per time, possibly weighted by their size. A time-dependent rate reflects mainly the recent past of the observed process. We present various techniques for TDRM and provide a comparison. Among the considered methods, TDRM-UTEMA is new and excels through timeliness, ease of configuration, and the fact that its measured rates are continuous with regard to configured memory.

6.1 TDRM Methods

We suggest a framework for the definition of TDRM methods and present five different instantiations.

6.1.1 A Framework for TDRM Methods

A time-dependent rate R_t at time t may be determined by

$$R_t = \begin{cases} \frac{S_t}{T_t} & T_t > 0 \\ 0 & \text{otherwise} \end{cases} \quad (40)$$

$$T_t = \int_0^t g(\tau - t)d\tau \quad (41)$$

where S_t is the weighted sample sum, taken from some MA method, and T_t is the weighted measurement interval which is computed analogously to S_t. Measured rates depend on a time scale which is the duration over which samples are considered for rate computation. In the presented definition the time scale is inherited from the memory M of the applied MA method. Also the concepts contribution C and delay D are inherited.

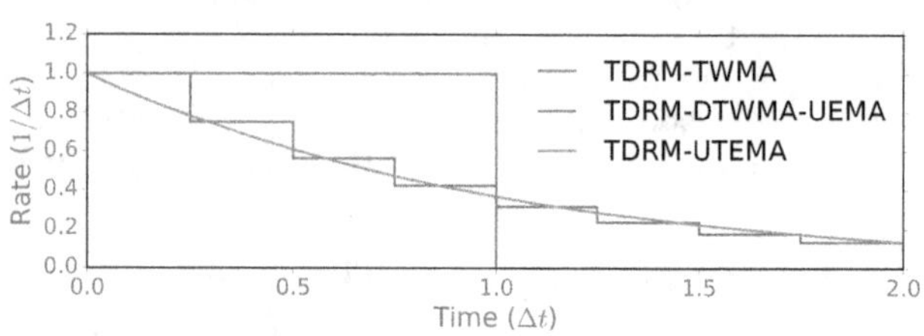

Figure 4: Rate impulses for TDRM-{TWMA, DTWMA-UEMA, UTEMA} with $t \to \infty$ used for calculation of T_t.

6.1.2 TDRM with Time Window Moving Average (TDRM-TWMA)

TDRM-TWMA calculates the sample sum S_t according to Equation (24). The corresponding weighted measurement interval is $T_t = \min(t, W)$ under the assumption that the measurement process starts at $t = 0$. The memory is

$M = W$ and the delay is $D = \frac{W}{2} = \frac{M}{2}$. As S_t may be zero, measured rates may be zero. TDRM-TWMA requires temporary storage of the samples within the measurement window and a timer indicating when the next sample leaves it. Therefore, the computation memory needed for TDRM-TWMA scales with the configured memory M and the rate of the process to be measured.

Figure 4 visualizes rate impulses for different TDRM methods. TDRM-TWMA generates a rate $\frac{1}{M}$ over a duration M for every observed sample of unit size. This rate can be considered as an impulse and the superposition of impulses from all measured samples (scaled by their size) yields the measured rate. The figure depicts rate impulses for various TDRM methods. They have the same memory M but contribute with a different time-dependent rate impulse to an overall measured rate. The impulses have an integral of 1 as $t \to \infty$ is assumed for computation of T_t. Superposition of such impulses ensures that the average of the overall measured rate approximates the sum of the observed sample sizes divided by the duration of the observation interval.

6.1.3 *TDRM with Disjoint Time Windows Moving Average (TDRM-DTWMA)*

TDRM-DTWMA computes rates for disjoint time windows of duration W. It uses the weighted sum S_t for DTWMA in Equation (26) and $T_t = W$. Memory is $M = W$ and average delay is $\overline{D} = M$. As S_t may be zero, measured rates may be zero. In contrast to TDRM-TWMA, TDRM-DTWMA does not necessarily require storage of samples. It yields the same rate impulse like TDRM-TWMA, but the impulse for a sample may become visible only in the next measurement window.

6.1.4 *TDRM with DTWMA and (U)EMA (TDRM-DTWMA-(U)EMA)*

TDRM-DTWMA-(U)EMA calculates rates according to TDRM-DTWMA and smoothes them with (U)EMA. It is used in [9] for dequeue rate estimation and requires two parameters: the window size W and the smoothing parameter a. The resulting memory is $M = \frac{W}{1-a}$ and the average delay is $\overline{D} = \frac{W}{2} + \frac{a \cdot W}{1-a} + \frac{W}{2} = M$. An advantage of this method over TDRM-DTWMA is that the effect of measured samples becomes visible after at most W instead of M time. Furthermore, samples contribute with vanishing degree to all future measured rates instead of only to the measured rate of the following measurement window.

The rate impulse starts with rate $\frac{1-a}{W} = \frac{1}{M}$ and is reduced by a factor of a for consecutive measurement intervals of duration W. Again, the rate impulse of a sample may become visible only at the beginning of the next measurement interval. This takes at most $W = M \cdot (1-a)$ time and makes TDRM-DTWMA-(U)EMA react faster than TDRM-DTWMA although they both exhibit the same average delay. Unlike TDRM-DTWMA-EMA, TDRM-DTWMA-UEMA does not suffer from a bias towards the measured rate of the first measurement window.

6.1.5 *TDRM with UTEMA (TDRM-UTEMA)*

TDRM-UTEMA leverages the weighted sum S_t of UTEMA according to Equation (29) and uses the weighted time

$$T_t = \int_0^t e^{-\beta\cdot(t-\tau)} d\tau = \frac{1}{\beta} \cdot (1 - e^{-\beta\cdot t}). \tag{42}$$

The memory and delay of TDRM-UTEMA are $M = D = \frac{1}{\beta}$. The rate impulse of TDRM-UTEMA is an exponentially decreasing function. In Figure 4 it is visualized for $T_t = \frac{1}{\beta}$, i.e., idealized for $t \to \infty$, and resembles the rate impulse of TDRM-DTWMA-UEMA. In fact, TDRM-UTEMA can be viewed as the limit of TDRM-DTWMA-UEMA for decreasing window sizes W.

The advantage of TDRM-UTEMA over TDRM-DTWMA-UEMA is its immediate reaction and the need for only a single parameter β. The advantage of TDRM-DTWMA-UEMA is its computational efficiency as it does not require the computation of exponential functions.

6.1.6 *TDRM with UTEMA and Continuous Packet Arrivals (TDRM-UTEMA-CPA)*

In [8], the following recursion formula has been applied for online rate computation:

$$R_{t_i} = \begin{cases} \frac{X_0}{t_0} & i = 0 \\ e^{-\beta\cdot(t_i - t_{i-1})} \cdot R_{t_{i-1}} + \\ (1 - e^{-\beta\cdot(t_i - t_{i-1})}) \cdot \frac{X_i}{t_i - t_{i-1}} & \text{otherwise} . \end{cases} \tag{43}$$

The start of the measurement period is at $t = 0$. Later in this section we show that this recursive formula essentially implements TDRM-UTEMA with the assumption that packets continuously arrive during their preceding inter-arrival time instead of arriving instantly at their actual arrival time.

6.2 Comparison of TDRM Methods

We first visualize the results of TDRM-{TWMA, DTWMA, DTWMA-UEMA, UTEMA} for burst arrivals with equal inter-arrival times. Then we measure a Poisson arrival process using different memory. Finally, we show that TDRM-UTEMA-CPA can be derived from TDRM-UTEMA and point out its shortcomings.

6.2.1 *Measuring a Burst*

The bottom line of Figure 5 shows a burst of equal-size packets arriving with equal inter-arrival times at a rate of $\lambda = \frac{1}{\Delta t}$. Before and after the burst the arrival rate is zero. The figure illustrates the measured rates for the above mentioned TDRM methods, each configured with a memory of $M = 10 \cdot \Delta t$.

TDRM-TWMA produces a step function that first linearly increases, reaches a measured rate of $\frac{1}{\Delta t}$ after $M = 10 \cdot \Delta t$ time, stays constant for a while, then linearly decreases, and reaches zero again after M time. The method exhibits a high timeliness as the rate increases shortly after the arrival of the first packet and returns to zero shortly after the arrival of the last packet.

TDRM-DTWMA reveals a positive rate only with the start of the next measurement window after the arrival of the first packet and captures the full rate only one measurement window later. The end of the burst is reflected late by TDRM-DTWMA's measured rate.

TDRM-DTWMA-UEMA also yields a step function. Its measured rate reflects the beginning of the burst earlier than TDRM-DTWMA since it uses a shorter measurement window. However, it takes some time to approach the full observed rate of $\frac{1}{\Delta t}$ because it does not completely forget about the past when no packets arrived. In a similar way, the measured rate geometrically decreases after the arrival of the last

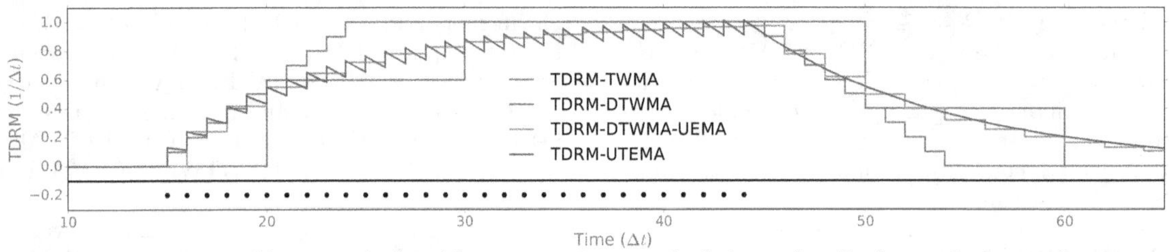

Figure 5: Rate measurement of burst arrivals with constant inter-arrival times Δt. Packet arrivals are shown on the bottom of the figure. The TDRM methods are configured with a memory of $M = 10 \cdot \Delta t$. TDRM-DTWMA-UEMA uses a window of $W = 2 \cdot \Delta t$ and $a = \frac{4}{5}$.

packet. Therefore, it takes long to approach zero. We used a measurement window of $W = 2 \cdot \Delta t$ for the rate curve in the figure. A measurement window of $W = 2.5 \cdot \Delta t$ alternately covers 2 or 3 arrivals which imposes an oscillating behavior on the obtained rates although the observed process has constant rate. This is a general, undesired artifact of window-based TDRM methods.

The rate measured by TDRM-UTEMA jumps with every packet arrival and exponentially decreases in the absence of new samples. Therefore, its shape at large resembles the one measured by TDRM-DTWMA-UEMA, but TDRM-UTEMA does not exibit the above mentioned artefact.

6.2.2 *Measuring a Poisson Process*

We consider a Poisson arrival process with an arrival rate of $\lambda = \frac{1}{\Delta t}$ and equal-size samples over a duration of $10^6 \cdot \Delta t$. A cutout between $40 \cdot \Delta t$ and $240 \cdot \Delta t$ is illustrated in Figure 6(a). Figures 6(b)–6(e) illustrate time-dependent rates of this process measured by TDRM-{TWMA, DTWMA, DTWMA-UEMA, UTEMA} with a memory of $M = 20 \cdot \Delta t$ and $M = 40 \cdot \Delta t$ as well as the rate difference between these curves.

TDRM-TWMA's measured rate in Figure 6(b) is a step function and changes whenever a new sample arrives or an old sample leaves the measurement window. Frequently arriving samples cause rising or high rates while frequently leaving samples cause falling or low rates. The curves measured with the longer memory of $M = 40 \cdot \Delta t$ are influenced by the same arriving samples but different leaving samples compared to the curves measured with shorter memory. Therefore, the memory has a clear and non-continuous impact on measured TDRM-TWMA's rates. The resulting rate difference is also shown in the figure. We calculate the average absolute rate difference and denote it by R^{abs}_{diff}. It is given in the captions of the figures and it is relatively high for TDRM-TWMA. The variance of TDRM-TWMA's rate curves is rather high because it computes the rate only from the small number of samples within its measurement window. To quantify this observation, we compute the coefficients of variation $c_{var}(M)$ of the rate curves and also report them in the captions of the figures.

The rate curves for TDRM-DTWMA in Figure 6(c) suffer from the same problems as TDRM-TWMA which is quantified by R^{abs}_{diff} and $c_{var}(M)$. They behave similarly as those for TDRM-TWMA but are clearly delayed. Some low (high) values of TDRM-TWMA are suppressed, e.g., between $t = 160 \cdot \Delta t$ and $t = 180 \cdot \Delta t$ because TDRM-DTWMA's few discrete measurement windows comprise both low- and high-frequent arrivals.

We consider TDRM-DTWMA-UEMA configured with a window of size $5 \cdot \Delta t$. Its rates are reported in Figure 6(d) and are represented by step functions. TDRM-DTWMA-UEMA's rates measured with $M = 20 \cdot \Delta t$ and $M = 40 \cdot \Delta t$ exhibit significantly less difference compared to TDRM-TWMA and TDRM-DTWMA because TDRM-DTWMA-UEMA is continuous with regard to the configured memory. The measured rates reveal a lower coefficient of variation because their calculation takes all previous samples into account.

Rates measured by TDRM-UTEMA are illustrated in Figure 6(e). They jump at each packet arrival and exponentially decrease in between. They are very similar to those measured by TDRM-DTWMA-UEMA which exhibit geometric decay in the absence of samples. TDRM-UTEMA's rates are also continuous with regard to memory. TDRM-UTEMA exhibits the least average difference R^{abs}_{diff} between rates measured with different memory. Its rate computation also respects all past samples and its rates reveal the least variance among all TDRM methods.

The variance of measured rates decreases for all TDRM methods with increasing memory. However, the variance for TDRM-TWMA and TDRM with $M = 40 \cdot \Delta t$ is about as large as the variance for TDRM-DTWMA-UEMA and TDRM-UTEMA with $M = 20 \cdot \Delta t$.

6.2.3 *Comparison of TDRM-UTEMA-CPA and TDRM-UTEMA*

We derive the recursion formula in Equation (43) to point out its connection with TDRM-UTEMA. We assume that packets X_i continuously arrive with rate $\frac{X_i}{t_i - t_{i-1}}$ during their preceding inter-arrival time and partial packets are already devaluated with passing time τ by $e^{-\beta \cdot (t_i - \tau)}$, similar to Equation (29). As a result, the remaining packet size at t_i is the modified sample size

$$X_i^* = \int_{t_{i-1}}^{t_i} \frac{X_i}{t_i - t_{i-1}} \cdot e^{-\beta \cdot (t_i - \tau)} d\tau = \frac{X_i}{\beta \cdot (t_i - t_{i-1})} \cdot (1 - e^{-\beta \cdot (t_i - t_{i-1})}). \quad (44)$$

An exception is the first modified sample whose size is computed as $X_0^* = \frac{X_0}{\beta \cdot t_0}$. Application of TDRM-UTEMA to these modified samples yields TDRM-UTEMA-CPA's recursion formula in Equation (43). More specifically, the sample sum in Equation (29) is computed based on X_i^* instead of X_i and $T_t = \frac{1}{\beta}$ is taken as weighted time which is exact for $t \to \infty$. Therefore, TDRM-UTEMA-CPA has only an initial bias due to the different computation of X_0^*, but does not exhibit a persistent bias due to its consistency with TDRM-UTEMA. This is not obvious because Equation (43) looks at first sight like an application of TEMA to short-term rates

(a) Cutout of the observed Poisson arrival process with arrival rate $\lambda = \frac{1}{\Delta t}$.

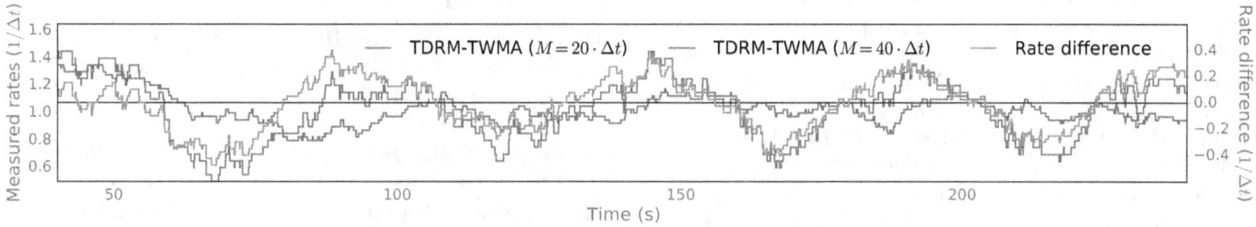

(b) TDRM-TWMA: $R^{abs}_{diff} = 0.126$, $c_{var}(20 \cdot \Delta t) = 0.224$, $c_{var}(40 \cdot \Delta t) = 0.158$

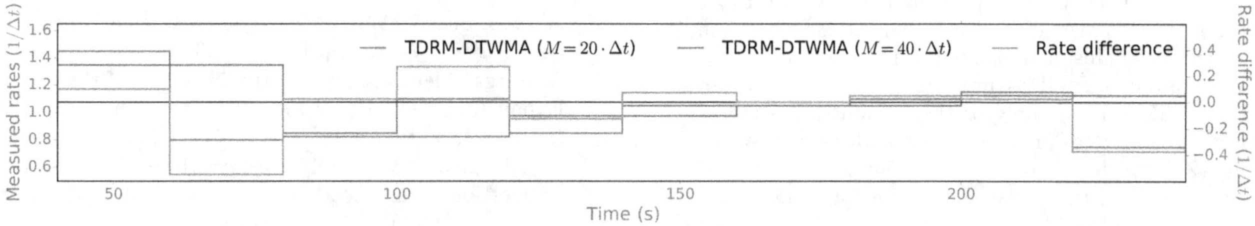

(c) TDRM-DTWMA: $R^{abs}_{diff} = 0.172$, $c_{var}(20 \cdot \Delta t) = 0.223$, $c_{var}(40 \cdot \Delta t) = 0.159$

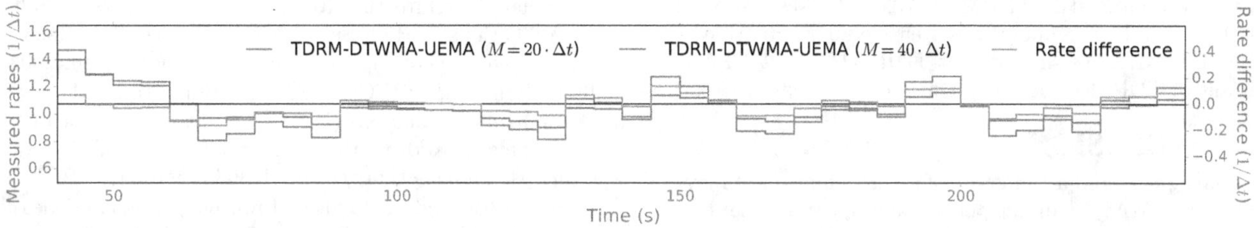

(d) TDRM-DTWMA-UEMA: $R^{abs}_{diff} = 0.059$, $c_{var}(20 \cdot \Delta t) = 0.169$, $c_{var}(40 \cdot \Delta t) = 0.116$

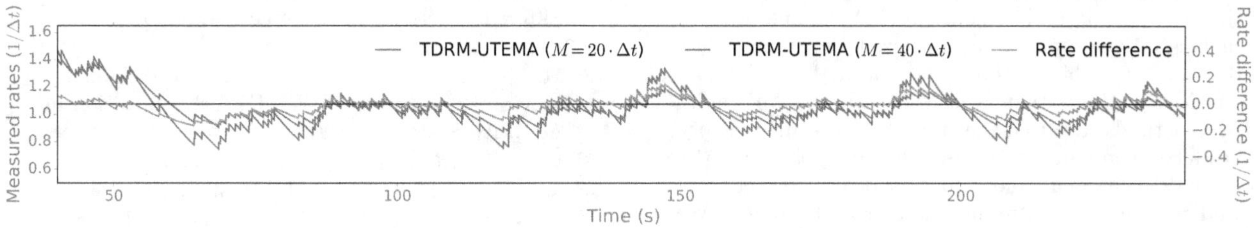

(e) TDRM-UTEMA: $R^{abs}_{diff} = 0.052$, $c_{var}(20 \cdot \Delta t) = 0.158$, $c_{var}(40 \cdot \Delta t) = 0.112$

Figure 6: Poisson arrival process and time-dependent rates measured by various TDRM methods with $M = 20 \cdot \Delta t$ and $M = 40 \cdot \Delta t$; coefficient of variations (c_{var}) of and average deviations R^{abs}_{diff} between the two curves are given in the captions.

$R^*_i = \frac{X_i}{t_i - t_{i-1}}$ computed at each packet arrival, and TEMA exhibits both an initial and a persistent bias.

After the initial bias towards X^*_0 has vanished, TDRM-UTEMA-CPA yields rates for arrival instants that are slightly lower than those of TDRM-UTEMA. While TDRM-UTEMA yields a piecewise exponentially decaying function, TDRM-UTEMA-CPA updates rates only at arrival instants and leads to a step function. The missing decay during inter-arrival times can overestimate rates over time. To quantify this effect, we measured the rates of a Poisson process ($c_{var} = 1.0$) and an arrival process whose inter-arrival times have a coefficient of variation of $c_{var} = 2.0$. The processes have an arrival rate of $\lambda = \frac{1}{\Delta t}$ and take $10^6 \cdot \Delta t$ time. Table 6 shows average rates measured by TDRM-UTEMA and TDRM-UTEMA-CPA with a memory of $M \in \{10, 100\} \cdot \Delta t$. TDRM-UTEMA does not overestimate rates while the overestimation through TDRM-UTEMA-CPA is significant for short memory M and the arrival process with highly varying inter-arrival times.

Table 6: Average rates measured by TDRM-{UTEMA,UTEMA-CPA}.

	$c_{var}(A) = 1.0$		$c_{var}(A) = 2.0$	
Memory M	$10 \cdot \Delta t$	$100 \cdot \Delta t$	$10 \cdot \Delta t$	$100 \cdot \Delta t$
TDRM-UTEMA	1.000	1.000	1.000	1.000
TDRM-UTEMA-CPA	1.048	1.005	1.186	1.020

6.3 Summary

We have proposed a framework for TDRM. We considered four methods from literature and a novel one: TDRM-UTEMA. Only TDRM-TWMA and TDRM-UTEMA immediately reflect rate changes in measured time-dependent rates. In contrast, TDRM-DTWMA and TDRM-DTWMA-UEMA take some time until rate changes become visible. Thereby, TDRM-DTWMA-UEMA uses shorter measurement windows than TDRM-DTWMA and exponential smoothing so that it can react faster to rate increases than TDRM-DTWMA. For small measurement windows, rates measured by TDRM-DTWMA-UEMA converge to those measured by TDRM-UTEMA. While TDRM-TWMA and TDRM-DTWMA yield measurement curves with high variance, TDRM-UTEMA and TDRM-DTWMA-UEMA exhibit clearly lower variance when being configured with the same memory because they average over all past samples. While time-dependent rates measured by TDRM-DTWMA-UEMA and TDRM-UTEMA are continuous with regard to configured memory, rates measured by TDRM-TWMA and TDRM-DTWMA significantly depend on the configured memory. This makes TDRM-TWMA and TDRM-DTWMA more difficult to interpret and use. The novel TDRM-UTEMA is the only of these studied methods (1) whose measured rates are continuous with regard to memory and (2) immediately react to rate changes, (3) which can be configured by a single parameter, and (4) which cannot not produce window-based artifacts. Therefore, its measured rates depend least on the chosen memory. Nevertheless, the two-parametric TDRM-DTWMA-UEMA can possibly serve as a less computation-intensive approximation of TDRM-UTEMA. We showed that TDRM-UTEMA-CPA is a variant of TDRM-UTEMA but may overestimate rates.

7. CONCLUSION

We have presented a framework for the definition of moving averages (MAs) including performance metrics like memory and delay. We presented several MA variants for evenly and unevenly spaced time series, showed that they fit well into that framework, and demonstrated that some of them have a bias. We proposed the unbiased exponential MA (UEMA) and the unbiased time-exponential MA (UTEMA) as novel MA methods that avoid such a bias. We configured MA methods such that they revealed the same memory and produced comparable results. Our analysis of UEMA showed that the memory allows for a tradeoff between accuracy and timeliness when mean values are determined. We also suggested some equations that help to choose appropriate smoothing parameters when UEMA should provide average values with a certain accuracy. We discussed moving histograms (MHs) as an extension of MAs and showed how they may be used to determine quantiles. Finally, we extended the framework to time-dependent rate measurement (TDRM). We embedded four existing TDRM methods in that framework and suggested TDRM-UTEMA as a novel method that excels by its timeliness, ease of configuration, and by the fact that its measured rates continuously depend on the configured memory. We performed experiments to illustrate and compare these TDRM methods and pointed out their pros and cons.

We presented a demo of all methods discussed in this work at [18] and made the source code available at [19].

This work focused on online measurement, i.e., on the assumption that future samples of the measured process are unknown. It has applicability in self-adaptive systems. The work may be extended to offline measurement so that time series can be smoothed while taking both past and future samples into account when calculating averages, histograms, or time-dependent rates.

8. REFERENCES

[1] Information Sciences Institute, "RFC793: Transmission Control Protocol," September 1981.

[2] G. Jenkins and D. Watts, *Spectral analysis and its applications.* Holden-Day, 1968.

[3] R. M. Chiulli, *Quantitative Analysis: An Introduction.* CRC Press, 1999.

[4] A. Eckner, "Algorithms for Unevenly Spaced Time Series: Moving Averages and Other Rolling Operators," Apr. 2012.

[5] E. Zivot and J. Wang, *Modelling Financial Time Series with S-Plus.* Springer, 2006.

[6] L. Burgstahler et al., "New Modifications of the Exponential Moving Average Algorithm for Bandwidth Estimation," in *ITC Specialist Sem.*, 2002.

[7] M. Alizadeh *et al.*, "CONGA: Distributed Congestion-Aware Load Balancing for Datacenters," in *ACM SIGCOMM*, Chicago, IL, USA, Aug. 2014.

[8] I. Stoica et al., "Core-Stateless Fair Queueing: A Scalable Architecture to Approximate Fair Bandwidth Allocations in High-Speed Networks," *IEEE/ACM Transactions on Networking*, vol. 11, no. 1, Feb. 2003.

[9] R. Pan *et al.*, "RFC8033: Proportional Integral Controller Enhanced (PIE): A Lightweight Control Scheme to Address the Bufferbloat Problem," https://tools.ietf.org/html/rfc8033, Feb. 2017.

[10] R. Martin and M. Menth, "Improving the Timeliness of Rate Measurements," in *GI/ITG MMB*, 2004.

[11] G. Bianchi et al., "On-Demand Time-Decaying Bloom Filters for Telemarketer Detection," *ACM CCR*, vol. 41, no. 5, Oct. 2011.

[12] M. Menth et al., "Time-Exponentially Weighted Moving Histograms (TEWMH) for Application in Adaptive Systems," in *IEEE Globecom*, 2006.

[13] W. D. Kelton and A. M. Law, *Simulation Modeling and Analysis.* McGraw Hill Boston, 2000.

[14] R. G. Brown and R. F. Meyer, "The Fundamental Theorem of Exponential Smoothing," *Operations Research*, vol. 9, no. 5, pp. 673–685, 1961.

[15] C. Chatfield *et al.*, "The Holt-Winters Forecasting Procedure," *Appl. Statistics*, vol. 27, no. 3, 1978.

[16] S. J. Hunter, "The Exponentially Weighted Moving Average," *Jrnl. of Quality Techn.*, vol. 4, no. 18, 1986.

[17] P. E. Maravelakis *et al.*, "An EWMA Chart for Monitoring the Process Standard Deviation when Parameters are Estimated," *Comp. Statistics & Data Analysis*, vol. 53, no. 7, 2009.

[18] M. Menth and F. Hauser, "Demo: Time Series Online Measurement for Python (TSOMpy)," in *ACM/SPEC International Conference on Performance Engineering (ICPE)*, L'Aquila, Italy, Apr. 2017.

[19] ——, "TSOMpy – Time Series Online Measurement for Python," https://www.github.com/uni-tue-kn/TSOMpy, 2017.

AutoPerf: Automated Load Testing and Resource Usage Profiling of Multi-Tier Internet Applications

Varsha Apte* T. V. S. Viswanath Devidas Gawali Akhilesh Kommireddy Anshul Gupta
Computer Science and Engineering Department
Indian Institute of Technology - Bombay
Powai, Mumbai 400 076, India

ABSTRACT

A multi-tier Internet server application needs to be analyzed for its performance before it is released. Performance analysis is usually done by (a) load testing of the application on a testbed and (b) building a performance model of the application. While there are a plethora of Web load-generator tools available, there are two problems with these tools: one, the tests have to be configured manually, which can lead to a time-consuming trial-and-error process until the desired performance charts in the appropriate load ranges are obtained; and two, the load generator tools do not produce output that is directly useful for creating a performance *model* of the application. In this paper, we present *AutoPerf*, a load generator tool designed to meet two distinct goals, named *capacity analysis* and *profiling*. The goal of capacity analysis is to run a comprehensive load test on a Web application, in an appropriately chosen range, at a minimal number of load levels, while still producing an accurate graph of throughput and response time vs load levels. The goal of profiling is to generate a detailed *server resource usage profile per request type*, without instrumenting the application code. This data (e.g. CPU execution time by Web server for one request) is crucial for parameterizing performance models of the application. AutoPerf intelligently plans and configures its load tests by using analytical results from queuing theory along with some heuristics. Results show that AutoPerf is able to run performance tests very efficiently while still producing an accurate chart of performance metrics.

CCS Concepts

•**General and reference** → **Performance;** *Measurement; Experimentation;* •**Software and its engineering** → **Software performance;**

*This work was supported by Tata Consultancy Services under the aegis of the TCS-IIT Bombay Research Cell.

ICPE'17, April 22-26, 2017, L'Aquila, Italy
© 2017 ACM. ISBN 978-1-4503-4404-3/17/04...$15.00
DOI: http://dx.doi.org/10.1145/3030207.3030222

Keywords

Performance, Load generators, Profilers, Capacity analysis

1. INTRODUCTION

A multi-tier server system that supports a typical Internet application is usually subjected to *load testing* before its release. Load testing involves the synthetic generation of requests on the application deployed in a *testbed* at certain *load level* so that its performance under that load level can be measured. This load level is usually the *number of users* who are simultaneously engaged in a *session* with the application. A typical load test suite consists of experiments conducted at gradually increasing load levels until the application reaches *saturation*. Thus the primary purpose of load testing is to determine the *capacity* of this application on the testbed platform, usually in terms of the number of users of the type being emulated, that it can support.

Load testing is carried out using one of several *load generator tools* that are available freely or commercially [7]. These tools generally take as input a session description (list of URLs that a user accesses in a session), the user *think time*, and a test plan which typically specifies a starting load level, an increment and an ending load level. For each load level, the tools also need inputs such as warm-up time and overall test duration.

The important outcomes of such a load test are the graph of *throughput vs load level* and the graph of *response time vs load level*. The capacity of an application maybe determined either as the level after which throughput stops increasing, or by the level after which a response time target is exceeded. The nature of the throughput and response time curves is also of interest to a performance analyst so as to understand the behaviour of the application.

Load testing in this manner may require several iterations before the test is properly configured. For example, the range of load levels could be wrong - that is, the highest load level turns out to be too low with respect to application capacity, or the lowest load level could be too high with respect to the capacity. In both cases, if the performance-tester is not well-trained, performance tests could be misinterpreted, or it may take a long time and other resources to figure out and run the load test in the correct range.

The time duration of the load test is another parameter that can go wrong. It could be too short, in which case one may not get steady-state values of the performance metrics at each load level, or it could be too long, in which case the overall test may take a long time.

Another major pitfall of load testing, is running into *client bottleneck* - that is, the load generating client process itself reaches the maximum number of requests that *it* can generate on the local client resources. In our experience this is the most common cause of mis-interpretation of results. Typical server capacity is very high for modern servers, so a highly scalable load generator is required to "load" such servers. Sometimes the capacity of the application to serve requests exceeds the capacity of the load generator clients to issue requests. In such a case, when throughput flattens out, if a performance analyst is not an expert, the capacity of the *client* may get reported as the capacity of the server.

In this paper, we present *AutoPerf* - an automated load testing tool for *multi-tier* Web applications. AutoPerf requires no specification of load level ranges or test duration or warm-up time for performing a capacity analysis test suite that results in throughput and response time charts as a function of load levels. AutoPerf produces this chart with a minimal number of load tests, and ensures that the metrics represent steady-state values. Furthermore AutoPerf uses a platform-independent heuristic to be self-aware of its own bottlenecking, and reports such bottlenecking to the user.

The key to making AutoPerf work intelligently is to run *profiler agents* on each of the servers, which send server profiling data to the load testing controller which runs on the load generating client. The AutoPerf controller incorporates several intelligent mechanisms, some of which make use of the profiling data and apply well-known results from queuing theory, to run the load test efficiently. We summarize the novel mechanisms being used in AutoPerf in the following:

- *Minimal configuration*: The input provided to Autoperf just consists of the description of the URLs to be fired, a probabilistic user session in terms of these URLs, user think time, the IP addresses of the servers, and the identifiers of the server processes. No other configuration such as range of user load levels or duration of a test is required. It auto-determines parameters such as:
  - *Minimum Load Level*: AutoPerf ensures that load tests at an unnecessarily low load level are not run. It uses profiling data sent from the server to determine the load level that will utilize the bottleneck CPU to some minimum configured level and sets that as the minimum of the range.
  - *Maximum load level detection*: For CPU intensive applications, AutoPerf determines the maximum load level at which load tests need to be performed by using the CPU service demand at each tier, which is used in the *Kleinrock saturation heuristic for queuing networks* [9]. Thus, it works for a multi-tier application. For non-CPU intensive applications, where this heuristic can overestimate the maximum load level, AutoPerf detects such overload using a heuristic based on the "power of a queue", and breaks out of tests at that load level.
  - *Intermediate load levels*: In between the minimum and the maximum load levels, AutoPerf runs load tests at an "optimal" number of load levels - that is, it intelligently selects load levels in such a way that the "actual" shape of the curve is seen, yet load testing is not done at fine intervals.
  - *Auto-setting the duration at a load level*: AutoPerf auto-detects whether "steady state" has been achieved at any particular load level and terminates the test at a load level when the average values of performance metrics have converged.
- *Client bottleneck detection*: AutoPerf uses a novel indicator of client bottlenecking - if the *achieved* think time as estimated using Little's Law is much larger as compared with the configured think time, AutoPerf concludes that there is a client bottleneck. This is a more reliable indicator of client bottleneck than client CPU utilization.
- *Resource demand profile per request, per tier, per resource*: AutoPerf can be run in *profiling mode*, where it takes as input a list of URLs whose resource demands need to be profiled, and the load level at which they need to be profiled. It runs the suite of tests required to give the following per-request resource demands for each URL, at each tier: CPU ms per request per server process, Network bytes read and written per request per host, disk bytes read and written per request per host. This type of data is crucial for *extrapolating* results from load tests to scenarios for which tests have not been carried out, by using models that need such inputs.

The rest of the paper is as follows: Section 2 presents the detailed design of AutoPerf and Section 3 presents experiments conducted to validate and evaluate AutoPerf's mechanisms. Section 4 discusses related tools and methodologies and Section 5 concludes the paper.

2. AUTOPERF DESIGN

One of AutoPerf's main goals is to automatically run a suite of load tests on a typical multi-tier Web application, so that graphs such as Throughput vs Number of Users, and Response Time vs Number of Users as shown in Figure 3 are generated without having to manually give inputs such as minimum load level, maximum load level, step size, duration of one load level, etc. We call this the *capacity analysis* mode of running Autoperf. Thus, AutoPerf was designed with the goal of producing the "curve" of these metrics vs load levels, up to saturation and a little beyond, with only the input from the user that is absolutely required to produce these curves.

Autoperf's second goal is to calculate resource demands such as CPU ms per request at each server process on each host, disk bytes read and written per host per request, and network bytes read and written per host, per request. We call this the *profiling* mode of running Autoperf.

The key components in AutoPerf architecture that support these goals are *profilers* that run on the server hosts.

Thus, AutoPerf's input specification (given in the form of an XML file) consists of only two required blocks: one containing the URLs and session description, and one naming the hosts (IP addresses) and server processes names which are possible bottlenecks in the Web application, which should be profiled for their resource demands. AutoPerf accepts user session description in the form of a probabilistic

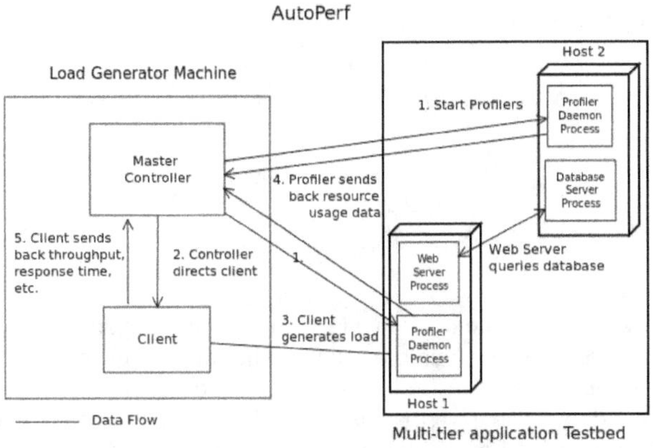

Figure 1: AutoPerf Architecture

navigation graph i.e. the navigation probability from one URL to the next, called a *Customer Behaviour Model Graph (CBMG)* [10] and the think time between getting a response and issuing the next request.

Apart from these inputs, there are some configuration parameters such as error thresholds and maximum number of requests or profiler reading thresholds that AutoPerf uses in its automation mechanisms, which are specified in a separate configuration file (*config.properties*). However, unless the user is an "advanced user", this file need not be edited for running a typical test.[1] In the rest of this section we describe the architecture and algorithms that achieve this automation.

2.1 AutoPerf Architecture and Algorithms

Figure 1 shows an overview of AutoPerf's architecture.

AutoPerf consists of two main modules: *Profilers* and the *Master Controller.* Profilers are daemon processes that run on the host machines on which server processes are running. A profiler is responsible for accumulating resource usage information for a particular process. Thus AutoPerf requires one profiler per server process. Profilers are instantiated before generation of load. Profilers start and stop collecting measurements when they receive instruction from the Master-Controller. The profilers which are currently build for Linux systems, use existing Linux measurement utilities such as *ps, vmstat* and *netstat* to sample and send these values to the controller.

The master in itself has two main components: controller and client (which generates load on the application).

In *capacity analysis* mode, AutoPerf has to determine two main settings using these components:

- The *load levels* (number of users) at which tests should be run. This involves determining the minimum load level, the maximum load level, and a *minimal* set of intermediate load levels such that a faithful throughput vs load level curve is produced, from low throughput, to saturation throughput.
- The *duration* of each load test. The throughput and response time that we obtain from each load test is expected to be at *steady state*, so AutoPerf needs to ensure that adequate "warm up" has happened. Furthermore, AutoPerf uses the CPU service demand of a request at each server in its load level selection algorithm, thus the duration of the test should be such that an accurate estimate of this parameter is obtained.

[1]AutoPerf does offer a "manual override" option, where we can specify the exact load levels at which to run load tests at, and the duration of each such test.

Before a capacity analysis run begins, the controller first simply initializes the profilers. Then, it starts its load level selection mechanism, which determines the load level and instructs the client to generate load (HTTP requests) at that load level. After a load test at a particular level starts, the Controller instructs the client to continue to generate load until *throughput convergence* has been achieved (this is a simple check based on the difference between consecutive time-averaged values of throughput falling under a certain threshold). At this point, the client stops sending throughput and response time measurements to the controller, but continues to generate load on the server for the purpose of calculating the *CPU service demand* per request. The controller now directs the profilers to start *profiling* the server.

The controller now starts receiving *cumulative service demand* measurements from the profilers (cumulative CPU ms used by each server process specified in the input file, network bytes per host, and disk bytes per host). It uses this and client-side request counts to estimate the average service demand per request for various server resources. Load generation continues further until *CPU service demand convergence* check has been satisfied. Note that in capacity analysis mode, this service demand is a *weighted average* of CPU service demands of the various requests in the specified session.

Now the controller uses this average service demand to estimate the minimum and the maximum load levels.

We note here that many of the mechanisms related to determining load levels in AutoPerf are currently centered around *CPU service demand per request* of the server processes. This is because AutoPerf is primarily built for typical transactional Web applications that tend to be heavier in their CPU usage. However, AutoPerf uses a different set of algorithms, not dependent on CPU service demand for determining these parameters when the bottleneck tier is not CPU-intensive.

In the following subsections, we describe the details of the various mechanisms for automated load-testing and profiling that are built into AutoPerf. Since the CPU service demand estimation is at the core of many other algorithms we describe that algorithm first.

2.1.1 Estimation of CPU service demand per request

The profiler agent deployed at the server periodically (every 1 second) sends the cumulative service time of the server process to the autoperf master. In Unix-based systems, it gathers this value using "ps" utility. The master keeps track of number of URLs $n_{urls}(t)$ processed till time t. Then, the service time estimate at any point of time t is calculated as:

$$\tau_{p,CPU}(t) = \frac{S_{p,CPU}(t)}{n_{urls}(t)}$$

where $S_{p,CPU}(t), n_{urls}(t)$ and $\tau_{p,CPU}(t)$ are the cumulative CPU execution time of the process p till time t, the number of URLs completed in this load test till time t and the CPU service demand estimate at process p at time t.

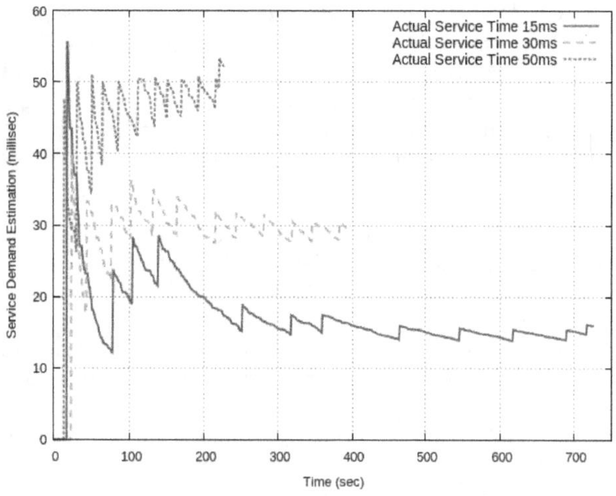

Figure 2: Service Demand Convergence Algorithm

While this basic method is obvious and straightforward, there is a challenge of *granularity* in this. The ps utility has a granularity of 1 second. Thus the cumulative service demand sent from the server is rounded off to the nearest integer value. Thus the service time estimate curve is a saw tooth curve (Figure 2) because until one second worth of execution time time is not accumulated, the cumulative execution time value $S_{p,CPU}(t)$ does not increment. The decreasing trend in the graph is when $S_{p,CPU}(t)$ remains the same but $n_{urls}(t)$ increases. The "jump" is when there is an increment of one second in $S_{p,CPU}(t)$. Thus, since the CPU service demand estimate keeps changing, a mechanism is required to check whether the value has converged.

The convergence detection has to avoid some pitfalls - because of the saw-tooth nature of the curve, we cannot use a routine check of the percentage difference between consecutive estimates decreasing below a threshold - since this method can easily lead to a false convergence detection just before a "jump" in the curve.

One way would be to detect convergence when the relative jump magnitude itself goes under a certain threshold. However it can be shown that, the relative jump magnitudes are not necessarily monotonically decreasing. Thus, we could again falsely detect a local convergence. To overcome this, we use an additional check of detecting a *global* convergence of the jump sizes, and only then check for *local* convergence of the service demand estimates.

Suppose consecutive readings of the profiler are $S_{p,CPU}(t)$ seconds of cumulative CPU service demand, with $n_{urls}(t)$ URLs completed, and $S_{p,CPU}(t+1)$ seconds of cumulative CPU service demand, with $n_{urls}(t+1)$ URLs completed. Suppose there is a jump in the service demand estimate; i.e.

$$\frac{S_{p,CPU}(t)}{n_{urls}(t)} < \frac{S_{p,CPU}(t+1)}{n_{urls}(t+1)}$$

The jump magnitude as a percent of the previous estimate is

$$\Delta\tau_{p,CPU} = \frac{\left(\frac{S_{p,CPU}(t+1)}{n_{urls}(t+1)} - \frac{S_{p,CPU}(t)}{n_{urls}(t)}\right) \times 100}{\frac{S_{p,CPU}(t)}{n_{urls}(t)}}$$

Since $n_{url}(t+1) > n_{url}(t)$

$$\frac{S_{p,CPU}(t+1)}{n_{url}(t+1)} < \frac{S_{p,CPU}(t+1)}{n_{url}(t)}.$$

Thus

$$\Delta\tau < \frac{\left(\frac{S_{p,CPU}(t+1)}{n_{url}(t)} - \frac{S_{p,CPU}(t)}{n_{urls}(t)}\right) \times 100}{\frac{S_{p,CPU}(t)}{n_{urls}(t)}}$$

Now, suppose the host on which the process p is running has N cores. It is obvious that the maximum possible difference between $S_{p,CPU}(t)$ and $S_{p,CPU}(t+1)$ on this server is N seconds (in the extreme case that all N cores are busy with the process p for the one second between t and $t+1$).

$$\Delta\tau = \frac{(S_{p,CPU}(t+1) - S_{p,CPU}(t)) \times 100}{S_{p,CPU}(t)} < \frac{N \times 100}{S_{p,CPU(t)}}$$

Thus a strict "global" convergence check can be that

$$\frac{N \times 100}{S_{p,CPU}(t)} < \epsilon \tag{1}$$

since this implies that $\Delta\tau < \epsilon$ where ϵ is a pre-configured threshold. Note that once this inequality is satisfied for t, it will be satisfied for all future values $u > t$ since $S_{p,CPU}(t)$ is monotonically increasing with t. Thus, this indicates a global convergence of jump sizes.

While this condition works well, we find that it is overly strict and convergence detection can take a long time. This is because at low load, accumulating an $S_{p,cpu}$ value that is large enough so that the "maximum" possible percentage difference goes below a threshold can take a long time. Instead we use a heuristic to arrive at an "expected" difference. Consider a load test at a user level L, the running average response time $R(L)$ and a thinktime γ. The expected number of URLs completed in one second is given by the expected throughput of requests. For a closed system the throughput is given by

$$\Delta(L) = \frac{L}{\gamma + R(L)}$$

Given this, we can argue that at most each of these requests could have kept one core busy for the entire second, in the one second profiler interval. Thus, the consecutive busy time values ($S_{p,CPU}(t+1)$ and $S_{p,CPU}(t)$) can then be expected to be separated by $\Delta(L)$. For a server with N active cores, we redefine $\triangle S$ as

$$\triangle S = \min(\Delta(L), N)$$

When the load level and thus the throughput is low, and N is high, we expect that the difference will be $\Delta(L)$. In our modified global convergence check we replace the N in Equation 1 by $\triangle S$. We flag global convergence as achieved when

$$\frac{\triangle S \times 100}{S_{p,CPU}(t)} < \epsilon.$$

After global convergence is achieved, a simple "local" convergence check is made where the variation in the values of a moving window of consecutive service demand estimates is calculated (maximum value - average value in the window). Local convergence is flagged as achieved when this difference goes below a configured threshold.

While this approach eventually does result in a good estimate of the average service demand, it may still sometimes take prohibitively long time for the service demand to converge, if the execution time is very small, the load level is low, and the think times large. This results in a low rate of requests being sent, which in turn results in the cumulative CPU execution time not increasing fast enough. Thus the profiler may keep reporting zero cumulative CPU time for a long time (5-6 hours in an experiment that we ran).

To address this problem, we use the following heuristic to break out of the service demand estimation loop: after a certain max number (p_{max}) of profiler readings have been received, if the maximum of the cumulative CPU execution times reported for all the server processes is still zero, we assume that the cumulative processing time on a bottleneck server was some value S_{low}, which is currently set to a value less than 0.5 seconds (since ps has 1-second granularity). If this break happens at time t, the CPU service demand is then estimated as

$$\tau_{p,CPU}(t) = \min\left(\frac{S_{low}}{n_{urls}(t)}, R(L)\right). \quad (2)$$

Here we use $R(L)$ as the estimate of bottleneck service demand at low load, if it is the lower of the two estimates. If the load test results in such "timing out" it sets a flag which indicates that "load level is too low", which indicates to the Controller that it should keep searching for the correct "minimum" load level at which to run a load test.

There is another case that has to be considered: this is where the maximum cumulative CPU execution time among all the server processes reported is positive, but a few server processes report zero cumulative CPU execution time, even after p_{max} readings. In this case, we set an "ignore" flag for each of these server processes, which indicates that the controller will not wait for convergence of service demand for these processes. Figure 2 shows three examples of varying service demands, estimated fairly accurately by AutoPerf.

2.1.2 The Load Level Selection Algorithm

AutoPerf's load level selection mechanism is designed to solve two distinct problems:

- Figuring out the range - i.e., the *maximum* and the *minimum* load levels that the load tests should be run for. The maximum level should ideally be the one where the application achieved its maximum throughput. However, we have designed AutoPerf so that it generates load just a little beyond this maximum. We set the minimum to whatever keeps the bottleneck server CPU busy at least ρ_{min} fraction of time, where ρ_{min} is a configurable tool parameter whose default value is 0.1.
- Once the range is known, *minimizing* the number of load levels in between the minimum and the maximum, at which a load test is run while still generating a precise graph of throughput vs load levels.

Determining the minimum load level

Our goal is to set the minumum load level to that which achieves a certain minimum CPU utilization ρ_{min} on the "bottleneck" CPU server. For this, AutoPerf needs an estimate of the CPU service demand per request on this bottleneck server. AutoPerf starts its capacity analysis experiments at minimum load level 1. As described in the above section, if the loadtest "times out" with a "load level too low" flag set, the controller uses the service demand estimate from that run to estimate the minimum load level N_{min} it should run at, by using Utilization law as follows:

$$\frac{Nmin}{R(N_{min}) + \gamma} \times \tau_{p,CPU}(N_{min}) = \rho_{min} \times n_{cores}$$

$$N_{min}(L) = \frac{R(N_{min}) + \gamma}{\tau_{p,CPU}(N_{min})} \times \rho_{min} \times n_{cores}$$

$$N_{min}(L) \approx \frac{R(L) + \gamma}{\tau_{p,CPU}(L)} \times \rho_{min} \times n_{cores}$$

where $R(N_{min})$ and $\tau_{p,CPU}(N_{min})$ are estimated by $R(L)$ and $\tau_{p,CPU}(L)$ respectively. Note that we assume here that no other system resource bottlenecks before the bottleneck CPU reaches ρ_{min} utilization.

Determining the maximum load level - CPU intensive application

AutoPerf uses Kleinrock's saturation number formula [9] as a heuristic to estimate the maximum number of users the server system can support. It can be shown that a closed queuing network with M queuing stations, where expected service demand at station i is τ_i, and average user think time is γ, can support approximately N_{max} number of users, where

$$N_{max}(L) = \frac{\gamma + \sum_{i=1}^{M} \tau_i(L)}{\tau_b(L)} \times n_{cores}^{b} \quad (3)$$

where $\tau_i(L)$ is the CPU service demand at tier i at load level L, and $\tau_b(L) = \max_i \tau_i(L)$ is the *bottleneck CPU service demand* at load level L and n_{cores}^{b} is the number of CPU cores at the bottleneck tier.

Thus, at the end of a load test at load level L, AutoPerf estimates all the service demands $\tau_i(L)$, based on measurement data sent by the profilers, and calculates the $N_{max}(L)$ using the above formula. Note that this estimate can keep changing after each test at different load levels, since the service demand estimates may keep changing.

The problem with the suggested method is that the result is valid only when the application has CPU bottleneck. When CPU is not the bottleneck, the N_{max} value determined by using CPU service demand is an overestimate, and results in AutoPerf running load tests beyond the *saturation* region, in the *overloaded* region of the capacity of a server system. We have a mechanism to detect this situation. We will first describe AutoPerf's basic load level selection algorithm, and then present the overload detection mechanism.

Minimizing the number of tests carried out

AutoPerf tries to minimize the number of experiments required to produce a "smooth" graph of throughput vs number of users. It does this by using a simple approach where the throughput curve is approximated by a linear segments. A recursive algorithm, is called after load tests at the two endpoints of a range L_{min} to L_{max} have been carried out. When called for this range, it firsts runs a load test at load level $L_{mid} = \frac{L_{min}+L_{max}}{2}$. Let $\Lambda(L)$ denote the throughput measured at load level L. Then if

$$\Lambda(L_{mid}) \approx \frac{\Lambda(L_{min}) + \Lambda(L_{max})}{2}$$

then no more load tests are required for this region. If not, then the algorithm is recursively called for ranges (L_{min}, L_{mid}) and (L_{mid}, L_{max}). After running tests in the minimum to maximum range, AutoPerf runs tests at every load level from the estimated maximum to a level slightly beyond this maximum.

In summary, AutoPerf first starts at Load level 1, and then uses the minimum Load level selection algorithm to ramp up to the minimum load level (N_{min}). Using the CPU service demand estimates from the load tests run so far, it estimates the maximum load level N_{max} of this application. The recursive algorithm is called with this N_{min} and N_{max} as its L_{min} to L_{max} range. Note that since CPU service demand estimates are constantly updated, we may have a new estimate of N'_{max} at the end of this run. In this case, the recursive algorithm is called again in the (N_{max}, N'_{max}) range.

Determining the maximum Load Level - non CPU intensive application

The above algorithm works fine when CPU is indeed the bottleneck resource of this server system. However, when this is not the case, the N_{max} estimate can turn out to be much higher than the actual capacity of the system. When experiments are run in the overloaded range of a server, the throughput values can be highly unstable, resulting in a jagged curve (see Figure 4) and the algorithm that is attempting to find the linear segments to fit this jagged curve can take a long time to terminate. Thus, we need a mechanism to detect that (a) the load levels seem to be in overload region and (b) the experiments seem to be stuck in a jagged part of the curve.

We use a state-machine based approach to address this. The state machine detects whether the current series of experiments are in a "high load" region (load near saturation) and further whether they are in an "overload" region (load beyond saturation and system unstable).

The heuristic we use to detect "high load" uses the metric of *power of a queuing system* ($P(L)$) [9] which is given by

$$P(L) = \frac{\Lambda(L)}{R(L)}$$

This is combined metric which helps us determine the ideal load level at which a queue provides good throughput - too low would result in low throughput, and thus low power, and too high would result in high response time and thus low power. As load tests are done, we keep track of the current maximum power (P_{max}) and the load at which that was achieved ($L_{P_{max}}$) and the current maximum throughput (Δ_{max}) and the corresponding load ($L_{\Delta_{max}}$). The state machine starts in a normal load state (state 0). If the following conditions are detected at load level L:

$$P(L) < P_{max} \text{ and } L > L_{P_{max}}$$
$$\Delta(L) < \Delta_{max} \text{ and } L > L_{\Delta_{max}}$$

then the state machine moves to the next state (+1), which indicates possible unstable state. The conditions essentially tell us that the load level L is an "overloaded" load level, since both Power and throughput at that level are lower, even though the load level is higher than those levels at which these metrics had higher values. If this happens K_{ovld} consecutive times, this indicates being "stuck" in the jagged part of the curve and an overload state is confirmed. Otherwise, the state machine moves back to the normal load state.

If overload state is confirmed, we terminate the experiment run and report the summary of results. Note that because of the way the recursive algorithm described earlier progresses, where the left side of the range is called first, we can assume that when we are in the saturated region of the curve, the tests corresponding to the load levels to the left of this region have already been carried out.

2.1.3 Client Bottleneck Detection

One of the biggest pitfalls of closed loop load testing is that often it is the load generating *clients* that are bottlenecking. Thus as we see in later the experiments in Figure 5, the throughput flattening could indicate either a client bottleneck, or server bottleneck. We have developed a heuristic independent of the hardware on which AutoPerf is run, to detect client bottleneck. At the end of a run at a load level, the think time achieved in the experiment is calculated using Little's law for closed loop systems [9] as follows:

$$\gamma_{achieved} = \frac{L}{\Lambda(L)} - R(L)$$

and is compared to the think time value provided as input. Our claim is that if the achieved think time is much higher than configured think time, this indicates that the tasks related to generating the requests in a load generating client were queuing for resources and not issuing requests in a timely manner. This indicates a client-side bottleneck. In AutoPerf, if achieved think time is higher than the configured think time by a given threshold, we declare a warning to the user on the screen. This alerts the user in case the throughput is flattening out, that it could be due to client capacity limit, rather than server capacity limit.

2.1.4 AutoPerf Profiling Mode

In this mode, the purpose of running an experiment is not to find saturation throughput of an application. Instead, the user specifies a list of URLs that (s)he would like to *profile*, i.e. find per-request resource demands for. AutoPerf profiles requests by generating load of only one type of request. E.g. if a "login" request has to be profiled, AutoPerf issues only logins, and uses the CPU service demand convergence algorithms to output an accurate estimate of this parameter for all the server processes being profiled. It also calculates disk bytes read and written per host per request, and network bytes read and written per host per request. Note that if in a session based application a request requires, say, a "login" before it can be executed, this can be specified to AutoPerf. AutoPerf executes the "pre-requisite" requests before it profiles the subsequent requests.

3. EXPERIMENTAL EVALUATION

In this section we present results of experiments done to evaluate the various automated mechanisms built into AutoPerf. We also evaluate the scalability of AutoPerf itself, since the ability to generate high load is one of the most important requirements of a load generator tool. We do this by comparing AutoPerf with popular load generator tools such as Tsung [15] and JMeter [5]. On the server end, we evaluate AutoPerf under various scenarios such as a very high capacity ("infinte server") system, server system with CPU bottleneck, server system with non-CPU bottleneck, and under a well-known benchmark called "DellDVD", in which we validate AutoPerf's mechanisms while using a probabilistic navigation graph.

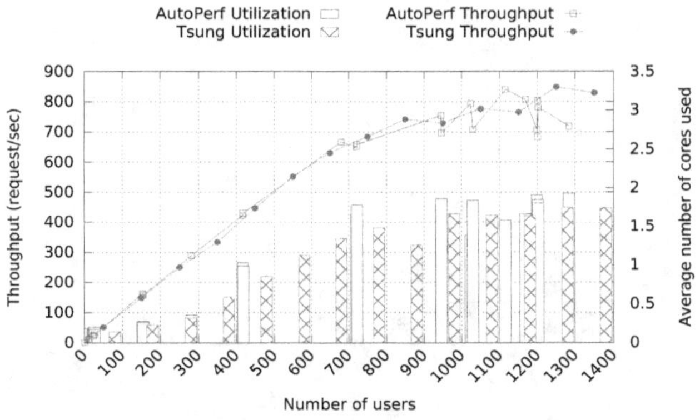

(a) Throughout and Web Server CPU Utilization

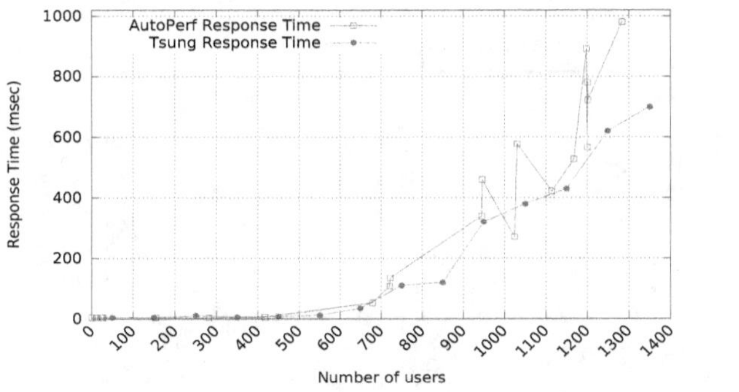

(b) Response Time

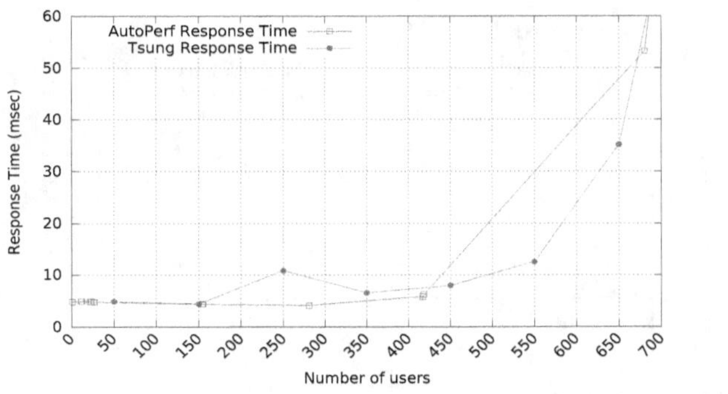

(c) Response Time Before Saturation

Figure 3: Correctness validation - CPU bottleneck with AutoPerf-Capacity Analysis mode and Tsung

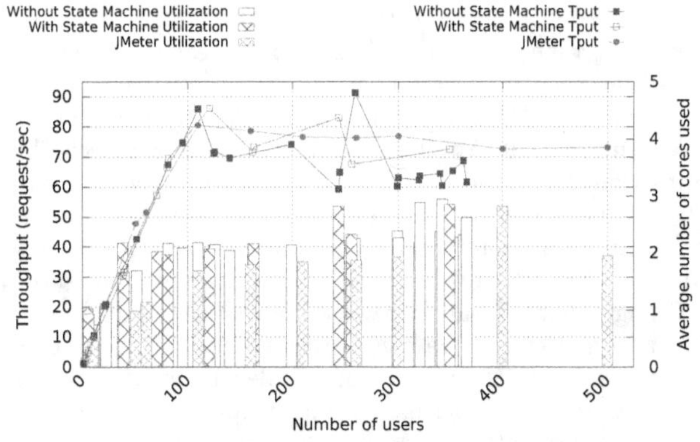

(a) Throughout and Web Server CPU Utilization

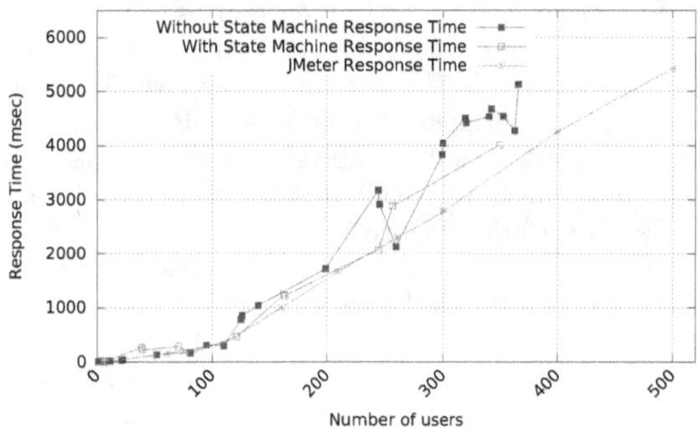

(b) Response Time

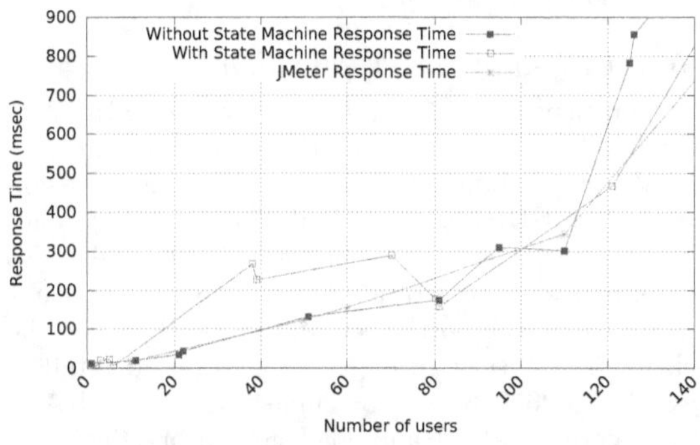

(c) Response Time Before Saturation

Figure 4: Correctness validation - non CPU bottleneck with AutoPerf-Capacity analysis mode and JMeter

3.1 Accuracy of AutoPerf's mechanisms

To validate AutoPerf's ability to faithfully recreate a throughput and response time graph that a correctly but manually configured tool would produce, we run it in "capacity analysis" mode to automatically run load tests for two types of applications: CPU intensive, and non-CPU intensive and compare the results with existing load generators Jmeter [5] and Tsung [15].

3.1.1 CPU intensive Application

The application we used here is *DellDVD*. This is a two-tier DVD store application with a Web server tier and a database server tier. The testbed consisted of a 16 core Intel(R) Xeon(R) CPU E5-2650 v2 with 16GB RAM, with only *two* cores enabled which hosted the Web server and an Intel(R) Core(TM) i5 CPU 650 host having 4 cores as the database server. The DellDVD database was populated with 5000 users. The client was a 16 core AMD Opteron(TM) Processor 6212 machine with 16GB RAM. The client and servers were connected by a 1 Gbps switched network. In the user sessions, each user navigated probabilistically between four DellDVD URLs, with a think time of 1 second. We ran AutoPerf in capacity analysis mode for this application, and compared it with running Tsung with DellDVD request probabilities that corresponded to AutoPerf's CBMG values, with the same think time, in a range of 50-750 users in steps of 50. The duration of each load level was set to 180 seconds. We verified manually that this time duration was giving steady-state results.

Figures 3 shows the comparison between the throughput and response time graphs produced by AutoPerf and Tsung respectively. Figure 3a also shows the Web server CPU utilization. We see that the CPU utilization (shown in the units of average number of busy cores) reaches 2, which shows that the Web server CPU is the bottleneck in this application (the DB server CPU had very low utilization).

We can see that AutoPerf is able to largely match the graphs that Tsung produced, thus basic correctness of AutoPerf measurements is validated. Note that all the parameters such as minimum and maximum load levels, and test duration, were arbitrarily chosen and manually configured for Tsung, whereas AutoPerf would have determined everything automatically. We can see that AutoPerf is able to correctly estimate the maximum load level and achieves its goal of performing experiments until throughput saturates. Note that this would have required the service demand convergence algorithm to work properly. Its minimal intermediate load levels selection algorithm reproduces the shape of the manual curve faithfully. At the low load end we can see that AutoPerf searches for the minimum load level for some time. Thus, this experiment validates AutoPerf's saturation number based maximum load level heuristic for systems with a CPU bottleneck, and validates its minimal intermediate load levels selection algorithm. It also confirms that in every load test run, AutoPerf is giving steady state results close to Tsung's thus validating its warm-up detection mechanism.

AutoPerf finished this capacity analysis run in 832 seconds (14 mins) while Tsung finished in 45 minutes. Thus, AutoPerf took much lesser time than Tsung and still gave almost the same results.

3.1.2 Non CPU-intensive Application

In this experiment we used a simple php script on the Web server, which was writing random characters onto the disk to behave like a I/O bound application. The user session consists of just this URL with a think time of one second. The server side script uses an exclusive lock mechanism, so only one user can write at a time. Thus, the writes are serialized and represent the bottleneck and the CPU is not the bottleneck. The Web server tier was hosted on an Intel(R) Xeon(R) CPU E5-2650 16-core machine with 16 GB RAM, with 4 CPU cores enabled and load generator client was hosted on Intel(R) Core(TM) CPU i7-4790 8-core machine with 8 GB RAM. The client and the servers were connected by 1 Gbps switched network.

Figure 4 shows AutoPerf experiments with the power and throughput heuristic-based state machine enabled and disabled respectively. Figure 4a also shows the bottleneck (Web server) CPU utilization in units of average number of busy cores. We can see the the cores were not fully busy even when throughput of the application flattened, thus the CPU is indeed not the bottleneck in this application. Without the state machine, AutoPerf carries out many experiments in the overloaded region. With the state machine enabled, AutoPerf was able to detect the situation when the experiments got "stuck" in the jagged area in the overloaded region of the curve, and ran the capacity analysis at fewer load levels to generate the curve in Figure 4.

3.2 Scalability Analysis

For these experiments the application used is a Web server serving a simple blank HTML file. This was done so that we had a server with very large capacity, that would exceed the capacity of all the load generators, and therefore would reveal *their* capacity. We call this server the "infinite server". These experiments are divided into three progressive parts: i) First, where each load generator simply fires one static URL at the server; ii) the second, where the load generators create dynamic URLs which have name-value pairs where the values are read from a file and iii) dynamic URL with name-value pairs read from a file with a probabilistic URL generation where possible. AutoPerf does this using a CBMG, and Tsung takes unconditional URL probabilities as input. This allows us to characterize the load generator scalability when it has to do varying degrees of work. We expect

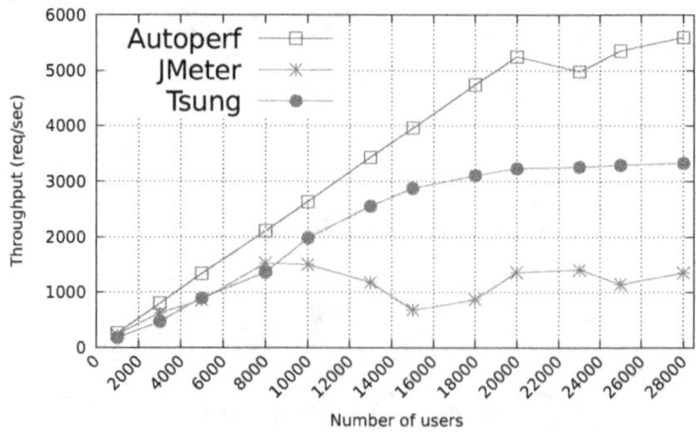

(a) Throughput vs Load Level

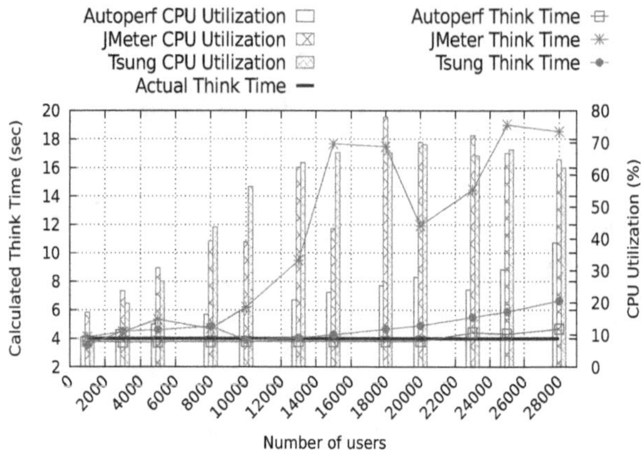

(b) Achieved Think Time and Client CPU Utilization

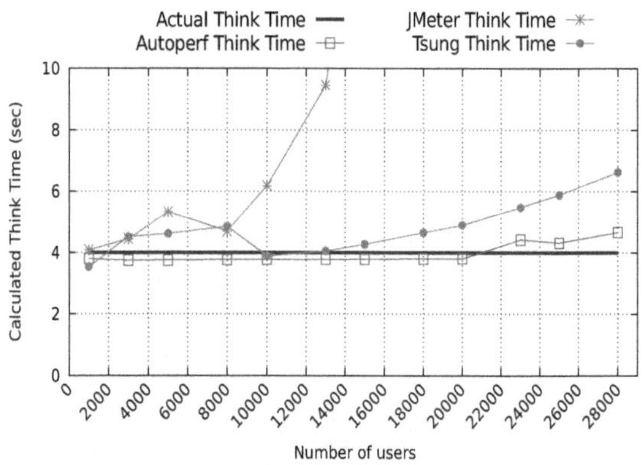

(c) Achieved Think Time

Figure 5: Experiments for scalability with AutoPerf, Tsung and JMeter with "Infinite server" and configured think time 4 sec, single URL of blank HTML file

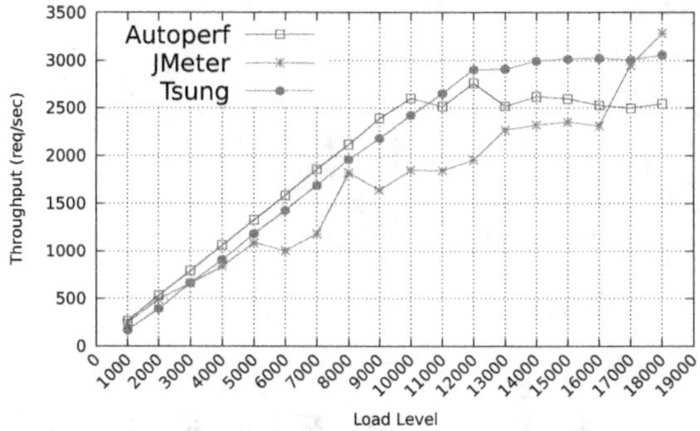

(a) Throughput vs Load Level

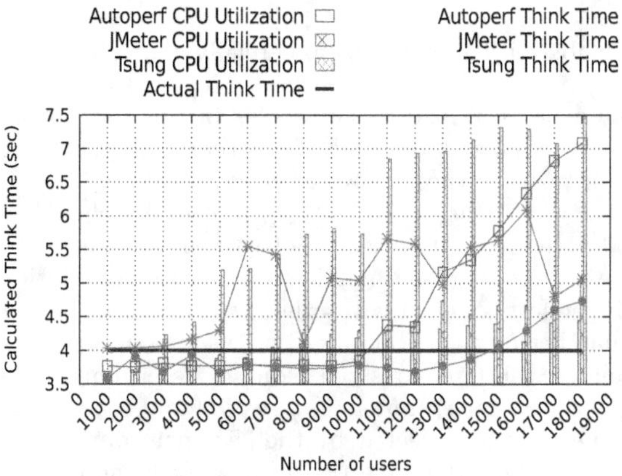

(b) Achieved Think Time and Client CPU Utilization

Figure 6: Experiments for scalability with AutoPerf, Tsung and JMeter with "Infinite server" and configured think time 4 sec, Reading Name-Value pairs from a file

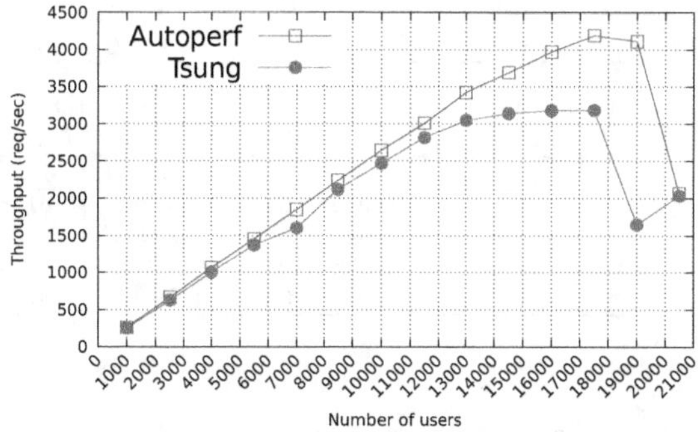

(a) Throughput vs Load Level

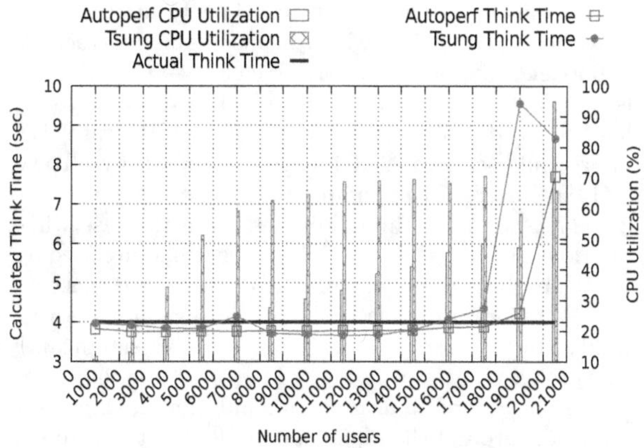

(b) Achieved Think Time and Client CPU Utilization

Figure 7: Experiments for scalability with AutoPerf, Tsung and JMeter with "Infinite server" and configured think time 4 sec, Name-values from file with probabilistic URL generation

the static URL firing to be least client resource-intensive and (ii) and (iii) to be more client resource intensive.

The client machine used was 4 core AMD Opteron(TM) Processor 6212 (max Frequency 2.6 GHz). We had 10GB of memory allocated to java heap size for the runs. The server machine was 24 core Intel(R) Xeon(R) CPU E5-26200 (max Frequency: 2 GHz). The power governor settings at both the client side and the server side were set to performance. The apache2 version 2.2.22 was deployed on the server. The prefork module was enabled with MaxClient value set to 100000. We ran the experiments at various load levels from 1000 to almost 20000 users. Each test at a load level was for one minute.

Figures 5, 6 and 7 show the results of the experiments done with tools AutoPerf, JMeter and Tsung with configured think time of 4 seconds and for the three respective workload scenarios described earlier.

Figure 5a shows the throughput vs load level graphs for each of these load generators for the static single URL case. Note again that since the server is of "infinite" capacity, these graphs show us the *load generator* capacities. For this particular case, AutoPerf achives the highest maximum throughput at user load level of 20,000 with a request throughput of approximately 5000 requests/second. Tsung also bottlenecks at 20,000 users with a maximum throughput of about 3000 requests/second. Jmeter does most poorly in this experiment, bottlenecking at 8000 users, with a maximum throughput of just 1500 requests/second. Figure 5b shows the load generator ("client") CPU utilization and also the "calculated" think time for the three load generators, which we claim is the actual *achieved* think time by applying Little's Law to this closed loop system. Since Jmeter's achieved think time values dominated this graph, Figure 5c shows the think time at a zoomed in scale so that AuoPerf's and Tsung's achieved think time values can be observed properly. As discussed in Section 2.1.3, we claim that the bottlenecking of closed loop load generators can be detected in terms of this achieved think time. We observe that around the load level at which each load generator starts bottlenecking and throughput starts flattening out, the achieved think time also start inflating as compared to the configured think time of 4 seconds. Jmeter displays a rather inconsistent value of achieved think time for lower load levels also, however AutoPerf and Tsung show think time inflation around the level that their througputs flatten. However, it is important to note that *client CPU utilization* in all cases remains below 70%, which by *does not* indicate exhaustion of local CPU resources and would not have indicated client bottlenecking. Thus, think time inflation is a much more reliable indicator of client bottlenecking, or some other misbehavior of the load generator tool.

Figure 6a shows the same comparison for the scenario of reading name-value pairs from a file. In this case, Tsung

Table 1: Request resource demand of web and DB tier after profiling of an application using AutoPerf

Transaction	Service Demand (ms)		N/W Packets Read(KB)		N/W Packets Written		Disk Blocks Read		Disk Blocks Written	
	Apache	MySQL	Apache	MySQL	Apache	MySQL	Apache	MySQL	Apache	MySQL
Login	0.5875	0.4197	343930	161480	364076	124637	0	8	2236	631
SearchActor	1.5443	0.0922	202556	69400	233046	53424	4	0	4264	162
SearchCategory	2.4188	0.0568	176440	43245	182050	33375	0	0	292	139
SearchTitle	1.5952	0.0948	190662	63798	218086	49193	0	0	492	146

achieves the highest throughput, but AutoPerf is not too far behind. Jmeter again displays the most unstable curve. Figure 6b shows the achieved think time vs load level for the three load generators, which again is able to track the client bottlenecking fairly closely. We can see that the load levels at which the clients bottlenecked were lower for all the load generators than those for the static URL case. E.g. AutoPerf could scale to 20,000 users with the static URL vs about 14,000 users with dynamic URL generation.

Figure 7a shows the throughput graph in the case where AutoPerf is using a CBMG, and Tsung is using direct equivalent URL probabilities. Jmeter is not included in this comparison as it does not have probabilistic session generation capability. In this scenario, AutoPerf achieves significantly higher throughput than Tsung. The corresponding think time graph in Figure 7b again shows inflation in think time at high loads, around the same load levels that the throughputs were flattening out, even when the client CPU was not bottlenecking. Surprisingly enough, AutoPerf scales to 18,000 users with 4200 requests/second throughput in this (more resource intensive) case as opposed to 14,000 users with 2500 requests/second in the previous case. At this point we do not have a good explanation for this anomaly.

We conclude from these experiments that AutoPerf scalability is in a similar range or in some cases better than existing high-capacity load generators. Our experiments also confirm our think time heuristic for client bottleneck detection in closed loop load tests. We believe this is a powerful check that every load testing exercise should do to ensure that the client is behaving as it has been configured to behave, and eliminate the possibility that the throughput capacity determined in a load test, is of the *client* rather than the server.

3.3 AutoPerf Profiling Mode results

AutoPerf can be used to determine the per request resource demands at each tier, for each type of request in a multi-tier system. Table 1 shows the profiling results for four profiled request types in DellDVD at the Web tier and the Database tier. We note that doing this task manually for each request for each tier is extremely tedious and would require huge amount of manpower resources.

AutoPerf is the only tool that we know of that can produce this result. These results expand the use of AutoPerf greatly, from an efficient capacity analysis tool, to a tool that can be used in a pipeline of measurement and modeling tools to *predict* the performance of an application using *models*. For example, per request service demands are a critical input required for parameterizing queuing models of such systems [6].

4. BACKGROUND AND RELATED WORK

Performance tests can be carried out on multi-tier Web applications using one of a very large number *load testing* tools available either free or commercially [7]. Jiang and Hassan [8] present a comprehensive survey and classification of all aspects of load testing tools. In this section, we discuss a few popular tools, and a few other tools that have comparable goals to those of AutoPerf.

One of the most used load testing tool is Apache JMeter [5]. JMeter is a GUI-based tool written in Java. The JMeter test plan for a web application consist of a session of HTTP requests defined with other workload parameters such as number of users, running time, user ramp up time, think time etc. JMeter fires the requests deterministically in a sequential manner, completes a session and collects the result. The reports collected by the "listener component" of JMeter show standard metrics such as total number of request generated, average response time, throughput etc. The JMeter architecture depends on plugins which allow it to be extended to offer many additional features. E.g. a plugin for JMeter server agent is available, which can be used to monitor the server and report server metrics such as CPU usage, memory and disk statistics, etc.

Tsung is another feature-rich tool which provides great flexibility in defining the test environment (client and server configuration), user behaviour and load distribution. The test plan for a Web application consist of sessions configured with a probability value, where each session is composed of transactions and each transaction consists of a group of HTTP requests. Each virtual user chooses a session based on the probability value and fires URLs accordingly. Tsung runs for a predefined time and provides average response time and highest server throughput achieved for all requests, transactions as well as each session defined in an XML file which is given as input. It also retrieves server activities i.e. CPU activity, load average and memory usage by communicating to server agents or monitoring through Munin or SNMP.

There are numerous of other load generator tools that can be found on the Internet [7], however JMeter and Tsung are among the most feature-rich. However, these tools are also essentially built to be manually driven by a performance tester, who by trial and error can figure out the correct range in which to run the tests for, and the duration of the test. When the server capacity is not known, this can be a time and resource intensive process. The application in this testbed could have very high capacity - say 10,000 users and the analyst could spend a lot of time running tests in a low range. On the other hand, the tester could run tests in too high a range, and keep getting only saturation results.

Finally the range could be correct, but the step size could be unnecessarily small, or too large.

The duration of the test is another pitfall. Assuming that steady-state results are desired, the test could be run for too short a duration, resulting in non-representative results, or it could be run for too long a duration, which will result in too much time for the overall experiment. If the tester is not a trained performance engineer, such errors could result in misinterpretation of the application performance.

Some existing methodologies have been proposed that address this problem. The CLIF benchmarking service [14] automatically determines the saturation level and aims to never run an experiment at a level higher than server capacity. CLIF uses response time at the single user load test as an indicator of the service time at the server, and models the server as an $M/M/K$ queue, where the algorithm tries to guess the number of servers K. It uses a specified "fineness factor" to determine the number of load levels at which the load tests should be run in the range between single user and saturation level. CLIF can also "scale itself" when it detects that its own CPU usage is exceeding a certain threshold, and use new virtual machines to generate additional load.

A methodology which also addresses the problem of static and manual setting of load testing parameters was proposed by Shivam et al [13] in the context of NFS server benchmarking. They propose various mechanisms such as binary search for "searching" for the saturation load level. They determine the duration and number of repetitions of load tests using statistical techniques of confidence determination. The primary goal of their work though, is "mapping response surfaces" - i.e. generating the performance surface as a function of workload, server configuration and amount of resources available.

BenchLab [4] is a load testing framework that addresses the problem of making load tests much more "realistic". It uses real web browsers to emulate users with automated load injection tool, uses traces to replay realistic workload and uses cloud resources to place clients in geographically distributed locations. There is minimal interaction between these clients.

Rain [2] is load generation toolkit that can generate "open" load, closed load as well as a mix. It is also the only other tool we know that accepts a probabilistic navigation graph to describe a user session. It can also generate time-varying load.

While the above tools and methodologies address some of the problems in efficient running of load tests, they still have some drawbacks. Tsung, JMeter, BenchLab, Rain and a host of other load generator tools are clearly not made for automated load testing runs. While CLIF does automate saturation detection, it is not clear how CLIF's response time heuristic works in the case of multi-tier applications - where response time is not equal to the bottleneck server's service time, and in the case when service demand changes with load levels - which is very often the case with real-life applications. While Shivam et al's methodology [13] addresses many issues raised here, their goal is different from our goal of generating throughput and response time vs load level curves for multi-tier Web applications.

A second very important need that is not met by any existing tool that we know of is that of collecting data that can be used to parameterize *performance models* of an application. While a load test reveals important characteristics of an application, performance modeling is an important step after performance testing, which requires very different quantitative inputs. Queuing models are parameterized by *service demands* of each different class of requests. The service demand is the resource usage requirement of *one request* at any server resource. Queuing models are used so that performance can be predicted for different request mixes, and different server platforms. Collection of service demands requires very different kinds of test and measurement.

There are some methodologies proposed to address the problem of measuring CPU service demand. Several make use of request logs and utilization data from production systems to estimate the CPU service demand per request type, using Utilization Law [3, 11, 16]. Some estimate the service demand by measuring response times and throughputs [1]. However, to our knowledge no existing *load testing tool* provides this information, and none gives per-request resource demands for resources other than the CPU.

5. SUMMARY AND CONCLUSIONS

In this paper, we presented an intelligent load generator and resource usage profiling tool AutoPerf, which completely takes the tedium of trial-and-error out of the process of load testing of multi-tier Web applications. It additionally offers a unique feature not offered by any other load testing tool - that of discovering *service demands of individual requests* at various server resources. This is immensely useful in creating performance models of multi-tier applications.

AutoPerf does this by working symbiotically with the theory of queuing systems - it uses some simple results such as Utilization Law, Little's Law, the Saturation Number Heuristic, the "power of the queue" metric to inform its load testing process so that it can be run automatically with very little configuration, and is self-aware of its own bottlenecking. On the other hand, it produces measurement data that can be used to parameterize queuing models of the application.

Out results showed that AutoPerf can run an efficient load test that produces throughput and response time graphs that are very close to those produced by a conservatively configured load test - i.e. one with a fine step size and a long test duration.

There are several directions we plan to expand AutoPerf in, in the future. Firstly, the self-bottleneck detection can be trivially employed to have AutoPerf auto-scale to use a bank of client load generator machines, if one machine is bottlenecking. This work is in progress. Further currently, AutoPerf only reports server-side resource usage profiles. We can build an additional capability of AutoPerf carrying out *diagnosis* regarding performance bottlenecks using these server-side measurements. We also plan to enhance AutoPerf so that it explores server-side configurations that improve performance. Lastly, while a tool *VirtPerf* [12] was built using AutoPerf, for performance benchmarking of virtualized applications, it needs to be enhanced so that it can provide additional parameters required to create performance models of applications on virtual machines.

6. REFERENCES

[1] M. Awad and D. A. Menascé. On the predictive properties of performance models derived through input-output relationships. In *European Workshop on*

Performance Engineering, pages 89–103. Springer, 2014.

[2] A. Beitch, B. Liu, T. Yung, R. Griffith, A. Fox, and D. A. Patterson. Rain: A workload generation toolkit for cloud computing applications. Technical Report UCB/EECS-2010-14, EECS Department, University of California, Berkeley, Feb 2010.

[3] G. Casale, P. Cremonesi, and R. Turrin. Robust workload estimation in queueing network performance models. In *Parallel, Distributed and Network-Based Processing, 2008. PDP 2008. 16th Euromicro Conference on*, pages 183–187. IEEE, 2008.

[4] E. Cecchet, V. Udayabhanu, T. Wood, and P. Shenoy. Benchlab: an open testbed for realistic benchmarking of web applications. In *Proceedings of the 2nd USENIX conference on Web application development*, pages 4–4. USENIX Association, 2011.

[5] H. H. Emily. *Apache JMeter: A practical beginner's guide to automated testing and performance measurement for your websites.* Packt Publishing Limited, Birmingham, 2008.

[6] D. Gawali and V. Apte. The m3 (measure-measure-model) tool-chain for performance prediction of multi-tier applications. In *Proceedings of the 2nd International Workshop on Quality-Aware DevOps*, pages 30–35. ACM, 2016.

[7] R. Hower. Web site test tools and site management tools. http://www.softwareqatest.com/qatweb1.html#LOAD.

[8] Z. M. Jiang and A. E. Hassan. A survey on load testing of large-scale software systems. *IEEE Transactions on Software Engineering*, 41(11), Nov 2015.

[9] L. Kleinrock. *Queueing systems, volume II: Computer applications.* Wiley interscience, 1976.

[10] D. A. Menasce, V. A. Almeida, L. W. Dowdy, and L. Dowdy. *Performance by design: computer capacity planning by example.* Prentice Hall Professional, 2004.

[11] G. Pacifici, W. Segmuller, M. Spreitzer, and A. Tantawi. Cpu demand for web serving: Measurement analysis and dynamic estimation. *Performance Evaluation*, 65(6):531–553, 2008.

[12] P. Patil, P. Kulkarni, and U. Bellur. Virtperf: a performance profiling tool for virtualized environments. In *Cloud Computing (CLOUD), 2011 IEEE International Conference on*, pages 57–64. IEEE, 2011.

[13] P. Shivam, V. Marupadi, J. S. Chase, T. Subramaniam, and S. Babu. Cutting corners: Workbench automation for server benchmarking. In *Proc. USENIX Annual Technical Conference*, pages 241–254, 2008.

[14] A. Tchana, B. Dillenseger, N. De Palma, X. Etchevers, J.-M. Vincent, N. Salmi, and A. Harbaoui. Self-scalable benchmarking as a service with automatic saturation detection. In *Proc. Middleware 2013*, pages 389–404. Springer, 2013.

[15] Tsung is an open-source multi-protocol distributed load testing tool. http://tsung.erlang-projects.org/.

[16] Q. Zhang, L. Cherkasova, and E. Smirni. A regression-based analytic model for dynamic resource provisioning of multi-tier applications. In *Autonomic Computing, 2007. ICAC'07. Fourth International Conference on*, pages 27–27. IEEE, 2007.

Deriving Parameters for Open and Closed QN Models of Operational Systems Through Black Box Optimization

Mahmoud Awad
Computer Science Department
George Mason University
Fairfax, VA, 22030, USA
mawad1@gmu.edu

Daniel A. Menascé
Computer Science Department
George Mason University
Fairfax, VA, 22030, USA
menasce@gmu.edu

ABSTRACT

Black-box modeling techniques are used when modeling computer systems with unknown internal structure or behavior and/or when it is not feasible or too time consuming to monitor a running computer system. The main challenge in these situations lies in estimating values for the parameters of these models, especially the values of service demands at the various devices for each transaction class. These estimates have to be compliant with the input-output relationships observed through measurements. This means that solving a model of the system with the estimated parameters should yield the same outputs (e.g., response times) for the same inputs (e.g., arrival rates or concurrency level). This paper presents a method for automatically estimating service demands for open, closed, single and multiclass queuing networks (QN). The method is based on casting the estimation problem as a non-linear optimization problem. However, because the solution of closed QNs does not have a closed form, we need to resort to black-box optimization techniques. The parameter estimation method presented here is part of *iModel*, a framework for automatically deriving performance models of systems whose detailed characteristics (structure and behavior) are unknown. Other portions of the framework were discussed in detail in previous publications by the authors. This paper illustrates the ideas through several numerical examples and then applies them to a multi-tiered operational system running OFBiz. The estimated service demands closely satisfy the input-output relationships at various workload intensity levels and can be used for prediction purposes.

CCS Concepts

•**Mathematics of computing → Queueing theory;** Cluster analysis; Nonlinear equations; •**Applied computing →** *Operations research;*

ICPE '17, April 22–26, 2017, L'Aquila, Italy.

DOI: http://dx.doi.org/10.1145/3030207.3030208

Keywords

queuing network models; parameter estimation; non-linear optimization; black-box optimization; MVA; AMVA

1. INTRODUCTION

In our previous work, we described a framework called *iModel* for the dynamic derivation of analytical performance models in autonomic computing environments [1, 2, 3]. This work is very important in autonomic computing systems that rely on performance models to dynamically adjust their configurations and system resources to respond to changing workload demands. Our framework infers a system model (queues and interconnections) and a workload model, which are combined to produce an analytical performance model.

The system model is identified using reverse engineering techniques to determine the architectural pattern that best matches the system. The workload model is identified by collecting and analyzing the system and application logs. These logs represent the system's observable behavior, such as arrival rates, system's concurrency level, and response times. Depending on how much can be harvested from the system and application logs, *iModel* determines the best overall analytical model to select (black-box, white-box or the right level of gray in between).

Understanding and analyzing user behavior and identifying user-system interaction patterns is an active research problem in workload modeling. However, the majority of the literature in this area focuses on workload prediction and proactive resource allocation, which are also natural outcomes of our research in automated system model derivation. In [11], the authors presented an on-line workload classification mechanism for optimized forecasting method selection. Based on the level of overhead (noise level) presented in the various time-series-based workload classification methods, the proposed mechanism dynamically selects the appropriate method using a decision tree. The decision tree takes into account user specified forecasting objectives. The authors in [10] proposed a trace-based approach for capacity management. Workload pattern analysis uses a pattern recognition step and quality and classification step, which measure the difference between the current workload and the pattern, computed as the average absolute error. The authors also presented a process for generating a synthetic trace to represent future workload demands. In [14], the authors presented an approach for finding and characterizing workload patterns from data traces and predicting future workload patterns across virtual machines.

In our framework, user-system interaction patterns are

used to produce Customer Behavior Model Graphs (CBMG) [19] and Client-Server Interaction Diagrams (CSID) [19], which are necessary in determining the characteristics of the workload model as well as the system model. These interaction patterns are also necessary to determine whether the system should be modeled as a closed or open QN.

A key aspect of automatically deriving a performance model is the determination of its parameters, which are divided into workload intensity parameters and service demands for each transaction class at each queue. The process of automatically characterizing the workload in *iModel* has been addressed by the authors in a previous publication. Automatically deriving the values of service demands in a non-intrusive way is the goal of this paper. A first attempt at that was presented by the authors in [2]. That approach treated the computer system as a black box and estimated the service demands by solving a non-linear optimization problem in which the service demands are the decision variables.

The approach in [2] dealt with open Queuing Network (QN) only and relied on the fact that open QNs have a closed form expression for their solution. The method described in [2] had another drawback, namely, it required regular calibrations because it relied on a single measured input-output relationship per class. This paper extends that approach in two important ways: (1) service demands for both open and closed QNs are estimated using a black box optimization approach [8], i.e., a method in which the objective function and maybe some of the constraints do not have a closed form expression but just an algorithmic way (e.g., Mean Value Analysis or Approximate Mean Value Analysis) of computing the value of the function and/or constraint. (2) the need for calibration is vastly reduced because the method relies on a set of measured input-output points per class and not on a single one as in [2].

The rest of the paper is organized as follows. Section 2 presents some background on system modeling and our proposed approach. Section 3 provides a high-level description of *iModel* to provide the context of the contribution of this paper. Section 4 describes our service demand estimation method in detail. The closed QN method is described in sub-section 4.1 and the open QN method in sub-section 4.2. Section 5 describes the implementation details of the testbed used for validation and shows the results of our experiments using OFBiz, JMeter, and the ELK stack. Section 6 discusses some related work. Finally, Section 7 includes concluding remarks and discusses some of our future plans related to the automatic derivation of system performance models.

2. BACKGROUND

Computer system modeling requires a certain level of understanding of the application and system architecture and behavior of the system being modeled. Just as important is the understanding of how the users interact with the system in terms of workload and patterns of use. When all such details are available to performance engineers, it becomes possible to employ white-box modeling techniques in which detailed and precise models are developed, parameterized, and tested.

When modeling existing operational systems, such information may not be available or easy to gather, possibly because of the system complexity or the inability to conduct detailed analysis of the software architecture and behavior. In such cases, performance engineers resort to black-box or gray-box modeling depending on how much can be gleaned from system documentation, system log traces or from interviews with software developers and system architects.

Black-box modeling is used when none of the internal system details are known (or they are intentionally abstracted) and focuses on the interfaces between system components. Gray-box modeling can be used when white-box modeling is costly or unnecessary while the black-box model is inaccurate or fails to adequately represent the real system.

When modeling an operational system, where few internal details are available, one might resort to reverse engineering techniques, where source code is recovered and analyzed to determine the application behavior and its impact on the hardware resources. Another approach is to analyze system logs and audit traces in order to understand the application's architecture and behavior. Reverse engineering the source code is intrusive and assumes having proper access to the application executables and permission to reverse engineer them. However, system log and audit trace analysis -although less accurate- is less intrusive while providing more insight into the system internals than black-box modeling.

The problem we address in this paper is the ability to derive analytic models of an operational system given only experimental (testing environment runs) or system logs of the system's production environment.

3. THE IMODEL FRAMEWORK

Our framework, *iModel*, aims at automating the process of building an analytic model of an operational system. The automation engine of *iModel* parses and analyzes the system's configuration and log files in order to arrive at the best fit workload model and system model. *iModel* includes a knowledge base of well-known single-queue and queuing network (QN) analytic models with their mathematical formulas or algorithmic solution and parameters. The automation engine determines the best optimization technique and tool to solve the analytic model depending on the system's architecture and observed behavior inferred from the log files. The three main components of *iModel* are:

1. Workload Model Analyzer, which analyzes the user behavior recorded in the various system and application logs in order to develop Customer Behavior Model Graphs (CBMG) [19] and Client-Server Interaction Diagrams (CSID) [19]. CBMGs are used to model the interactions between the user and the system and CSIDs are used to model the interaction between system components, and, as a result, derive the system workload.

2. Performance Model Analyzer, which is the focus of this paper, determines the possible system architecture and application components and their interconnections (communications) by analyzing configuration and log files. Details of this step can be found in [1].

3. Performance Model Repository, which is used to find the best-fit analytic model that matches the system physical characteristics and user behavior. The model is solved using the Performance Model Analyzer's execution engine using solvers that are parameterized using the workload model and the model definition in

the repository (metrics and input parameters and their data types and constraint definitions).

Figure 1 shows the workflow of *iModel*, explained in detail in [1]. The focus of this paper is on steps 7 and 8, in which the model execution engine parameterizes the model using the method described in this paper and solves it.

4. AUTOMATIC DERIVATION OF SERVICE DEMANDS FOR QNS

The problem we address in this paper is that of deriving service demands for a QN model of an *operational* system from measured response times and workload intensity values. We show in this section how that can be done when the goal is to model the operational system as a closed QN and as an open QN. In the case of a closed QN model, the workload intensity is given by the customer population (i.e., average number of customers in the system) and in the case of open QNs by average arrival rates. It is important to emphasize that the fundamental assumption throughout our discussion is that the systems we are interested are in production and cannot be stopped for experimentation purposes nor can they be subject to intrusive measurement techniques. We only rely on data commonly available by system logs generated by such systems.

In general, we can say that a QN model computes the average response R_r for class r transactions through a function f_r described below

$$R_r = f_r(\mathbf{D}, \vec{W}) \tag{1}$$

where $\mathbf{D}$, shown below, is the matrix of service demands where $D_{i,r}$ is the average service demand of class r ($r = 1, \cdots, R$) transactions at queue i ($i = 1, \cdots, K$). The service demand of a transaction at a queue is the total service time of the transaction at the queue and does not include waiting time at the queue.

$$\mathbf{D} = \begin{pmatrix} D_{1,1} & D_{1,2} & \cdots & D_{1,r} & \cdots & D_{1,R} \\ D_{2,1} & D_{2,2} & \cdots & D_{2,r} & \cdots & D_{2,R} \\ \vdots & \vdots & \vdots & \vdots & \vdots & \vdots \\ D_{i,1} & D_{i,2} & \cdots & D_{i,r} & \cdots & D_{i,R} \\ \vdots & \vdots & \vdots & \vdots & \vdots & \vdots \\ D_{K,1} & D_{K,2} & \cdots & D_{K,r} & \cdots & D_{K,R} \end{pmatrix} \tag{2}$$

The vector $\vec{W} = (w_1, \cdots, w_r, \cdots, w_R)$ is the vector of workload intensities per class. In the case of open QNs, $w_r = \lambda_r$, which is the average arrival rate of class r transactions. In the case of closed QNs, $w_r = N_r$, i.e., the customer population for class r (i.e., the concurrency level of class r).

The techniques described in this section are used to derive the matrix of service demands $\mathbf{D}$ given a series of values of response times R_r and the workload intensity levels for which they were obtained. Numerical examples discussed in this section show how response times can be successfully predicted by an analytic model when the workload intensity values are different from the ones used to derive the service demands. In other words, the parameterized model has predictive capability.

4.1 Closed QNs

In this subsection, we show how we can derive the service demands that can be used to build a closed QN model of an operational system for which we assume that we can measure the response time and throughput of transactions submitted to the system.

To illustrate our ideas, we start with a single-class closed QN and then we generalize for multiple classes. In the single-class case, the matrix of service demands $\mathbf{D}$ becomes the vector $\vec{D} = (D_1, \cdots, D_i, \cdots, D_K)$ of service demands.

Consider that time is divided into M intervals $t_1, t_2, \cdots, t_j, \cdots, t_M$ all of duration τ, that R^a_j is the average response time of the transactions that completed during interval j and that C^a_j is the number of transactions that completed during that interval. Thus, according to Little's Law [16], the average number of transactions in the system during interval t_j is $n_j = R^a_j \times X^a_j$ where the throughput X^a_j during interval t_j is C^a_j / τ. The superscript a is used throughout the paper to indicate actual values, i.e., values obtained through measurements of the system as opposed to values predicted by a model.

Let f described below be a function that computes the computer system's average response time $R(n)$ when the average number of transactions in the system is equal to n. Besides n, the function takes as a parameter the vector $\vec{D} = (D_1, \cdots, D_i, \cdots, D_K)$ of service demands for the K queues in the QN. As indicated above, service demands do not include waiting time and therefore are independent of the system's load, represented by n.

$$R(n) = f(\vec{D}, n). \tag{3}$$

There is no closed form equation for the function f, only computational algorithms such as Mean Value Analysis (MVA) and Approximate Mean Value Analysis (AMVA) [20, 18].

Our problem can then be be formalized as follows. Given the sequence $\{(n_1, R^a_1), \cdots, (n_j, R^a_j), \cdots, (n_M, R^a_M)\}$ find the vector of service demands $\vec{D}$. For each interval j we can define the error ξ_j as

$$\xi_j = R(n_j) - R^a_j = f(\vec{D}, n_j) - R^a_j. \tag{4}$$

Equation (4) indicates the diference between the response time computed by function f for a concurrency level equal to n_j given service demands $\vec{D}$ and the actual response time R^a_j measured during that interval. We can find $\vec{D}$ by solving the following optimization problem.

$$\begin{aligned} \text{Minimize} \quad & \sum_{j=1}^{M} \xi_j^2 \\ \text{s.t.} \quad & \sum_{j=1}^{M} \xi_j = 0 \\ D_i \; & \geq \; 0 \;\; i = 1, \cdots K \\ \sum_{i=1}^{K} D_i \; & \leq \; \min_{j=1,\cdots,M} \{R^a_j\}. \end{aligned} \tag{5}$$

The decision variables for the above problem are the service demands in $\vec{D}$, the objective function to be minimized is the sum of square errors, the first constraint forces the sum of the errors to be equal to zero, the second constraint

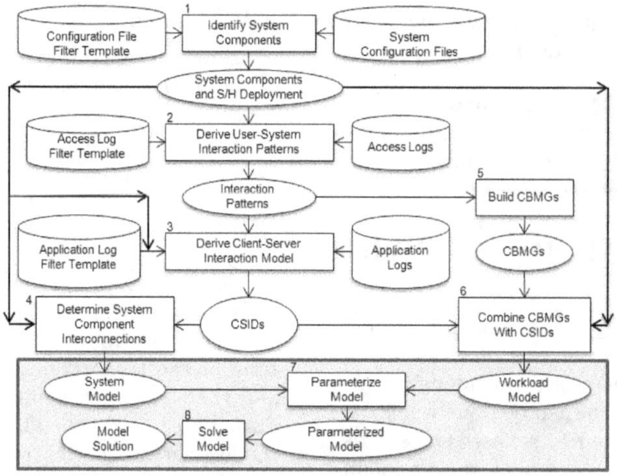

Figure 1: ***iModel*** **Flowchart**

indicates that the service demands cannot be negative, and the last constraint says that the sum of the service demands is the lowest possible value for the response time, i.e., the response time when there is no congestion.

This is a non-linear optimization problem that does not have a closed form solution for the objective function nor for its first constraint. Thus, we resort to black-box optimization methods.

Solving the optimization problem above for the data in Table 1 using Excel's Generalized Reduced Gradient (GRG) non-Linear solver provides the following values for service demands: $D_1 = 1.512$ sec, $D_2 = 1.781$ sec, and $D_3 = 2.008$ sec. It is important to note that the errors are all exactly equal to zero even though we do not have a constraint that requires that.

To check if the above service demands provide predictive capabilities, we solve an MVA model using these service demands for $n = 7$ and 11 and obtain the following response time values: 16.291 sec and 23.850 sec, respectively.

Table 1: Sequence of values of n_j, R_j^a, and X_j^a.

n_j	R_j^a (in sec)	X_j^a
2	7.09	0.2821
4	10.71	0.3736
5	12.53	0.3991
6	14.36	0.4177
8	18.06	0.4430
9	19.92	0.4518
10	21.79	0.4589

Figure 2 shows measured response times as a function of the concurrency level according to Table 1 (black triangles) and the two points, for $n = 7$ and 11 (unfilled squares). As it can be seen, the points computed by a model that uses the service demands estimated by our method match the curve obtained through measurements.

Figure 3 shows the measured throughput as a function of the concurrency level according to Table 1 (black triangles) and the two points, for $n = 7$ and 11 (unfilled squares) predicted by a closed QN model that uses the derived service demands resulting from the solution of the optimization

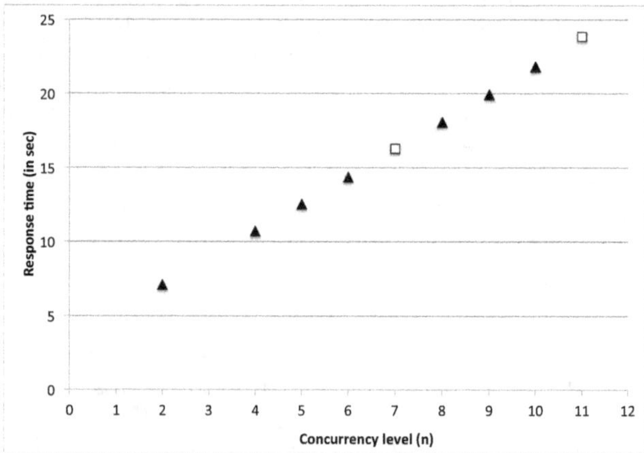

Figure 2: Response time (in sec) vs. concurrency level. Triangles: measured response time. Squares: predicted by a model.

problem described above. As it can be seen and as expected, the points computed by the QN model that uses the service demands estimated by our method match the curve obtained through measurements.

As another example of the power of the technique described here, we present another example in which the system is balanced (i.e., the service demands are the same for all devices). The graph in Fig. 4 shows throughput values measured from a system (black triangles) for concurrency levels equal to 2, 4, 6, 8, 9, 11, and 14. Applying our method yielded the following demands: $D_1 = 1.503$ sec, $D_2 = 1.501$ sec, and $D_3 = 1.496$ sec. The squares in the figure show the throughputs obtained by using a closed QN model that takes as inputs the service demands obtained by solving the optimization model. The figure shows that the throughput values obtained for concurrency levels equal to 1, 3, 5, 7, 10, and 13 (i.e., values not used in solving the optimization model) match exactly what they should be.

We now provide the algorithm that can be used to compute the average response time R_j^a, the average concurrency level n_j, and the throughput X_j^a for the intervals t_j from an

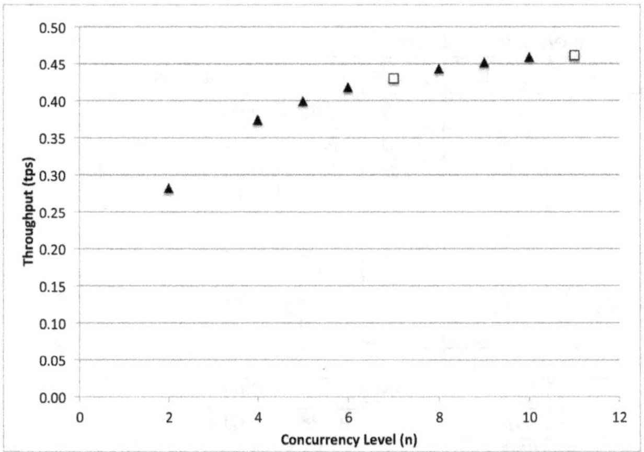

Figure 3: Throughput (in tps) vs. concurrency level. Triangles: measured throughput. Squares: predicted by a model.

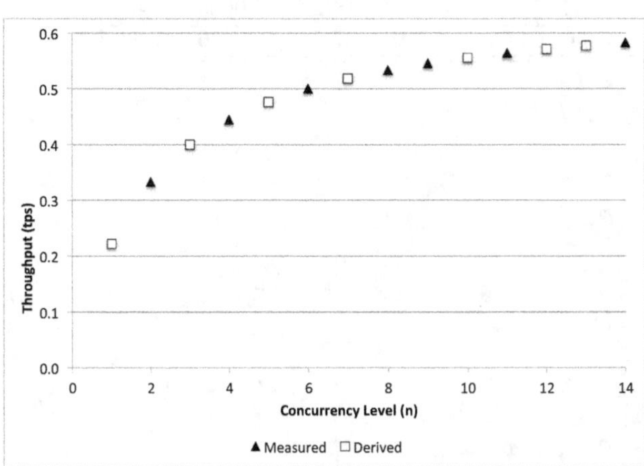

Figure 4: Throughput (in tps) vs. concurrency level for a balanced system. Triangles: measured throughput. Squares: predicted by the model.

operational system. We describe the algorithm for a single class case (i.e., similar transactions) but assume that while a system is in operation, its workload intensity and, consequently, the response time and throughputs will vary over time. The generalization for multiple classes is straightforward by segregating transactions based on their type (as indicated in operational logs, most of the time by the URL). The goal of the algorithm below is to determine time intervals during which there is very little variability (within a given tolerance η) in the average concurrency level n_j during the interval. Assume that an operational log of the operational system contains one entry per completed transaction. Entry i is of the type (t_i, R_i) where t_i is the timestamp of the entry and R_i is the response of the transaction that finished at time t_i.

Step 1: initialization TotalRespTime $\leftarrow$ 0; StartTime $\leftarrow$ 0; $n_j^{\text{prev}} \leftarrow 0$; $i \leftarrow 0$;

Step 2: accumulate response time $i \leftarrow i + 1$; TotalRespTime $\leftarrow$ TotalRespTime + R_i;

Step 3: compute concurrency level (see [18])

$$n_j^{\text{curr}} \leftarrow \text{TotalRespTime}/(t_i - \text{StartTime}) \quad (6)$$

Step 4: check tolerance If $\mid n_j^{\text{curr}} - n_j^{\text{prev}} \mid / n_j^{\text{curr}} > \eta$ then $n_j^{\text{prev}} \leftarrow n_j^{\text{curr}}$ and go to Step 2;

Step 5: outputs $n_j \leftarrow n_j^{\text{curr}}$; $R_j^a \leftarrow$ TotalRespTime$/i$; $X_j^a = i/(t_i - \text{StartTime})$.

An example of the execution of the algorithm above is given in Table 2 that was generated from snippets of an actual analysis of the log of a real operational system. The table shows two identified intervals, one including entries numbered 29-36 and the other for entries numbered 46-54. The average concurrency level for the first interval shown in the table is 5.32 and is equal to 7.36 for the second. Their coefficients of variation are 0.05 and 0.09, respectively, i.e., very small. The average response times are 8.3 sec and 12.4 sec, respectivey, in these intervals.

Having presented the problem description for a single-class closed QN case, we generalize the problem for multiple classes. The equations below are an obvious generalization of equations (3)-(5).

$$R_r(\vec{N}) = f_r(\mathbf{D}, \vec{N}) \quad (7)$$

$$\xi_{j,r} = R_r(\vec{N}_j) - R_{j,r}^a = f_r(\mathbf{D}, \vec{N}_j) - R_{j,r}^a \quad (8)$$

where $\vec{N}_j$ is the population vector observed at interval t_j and the optimization problem is

$$\begin{aligned} \text{Minimize} \quad & \sum_{r=1}^{R}\sum_{j=1}^{M} \xi_{j,r}^2 & (9) \\ \text{s.t.} \quad & \sum_{r=1}^{R}\sum_{j=1}^{M} \xi_{j,r} = 0 \\ D_{i,r} \quad & \geq \quad 0 \;\; i = 1, \cdots K \text{ and } r = 1, \cdots, R \\ \sum_{i=1}^{K} D_{i,r} \quad & < \quad \min_{j=1,\cdots,M} \{R_{j,r}^a\} \quad r = 1, \cdots, R. \end{aligned}$$

where $f_r(\mathbf{D}, \vec{N})$ is computed using AMVA [18].

4.2 Open QNs

Similarly to the closed QN case, time is divided into intervals $t_1, \cdots, t_j, \cdots, t_M$. For each interval t_j, we can measure the average response time per class, $R_{j,r}^a$, and the average arrival rate $\lambda_{j,r}^a$ per class.

The equations above are easily transformed into the open QN case by changing the workload intensity vector from $\vec{N}$ into the vector of arrival rates $\vec{\lambda} = (\lambda_1, \cdots, \lambda_r, \cdots, \lambda_R)$. We added a last constraint to the optimization problem to guarantee that the utilization $U_i = \sum_{r=1}^{R} \lambda_r \times D_{i,r}$ of device i for all devices $i = 1, \cdots, K$ is less than one.

$$R_r(\vec{\lambda}) = f_r(\mathbf{D}, \vec{\lambda}) \quad (10)$$

$$\xi_{j,r} = R_r(\vec{\lambda}_j) - R_{j,r}^a = f_r(\mathbf{D}, \vec{\lambda}_j) - R_{j,r}^a \quad (11)$$

Table 2: Example of interval computation based on real data for $\eta = 0.005$

i	Completion time (t_i)	Response time (sec) (R_i)	TotalRespTime	n_j^{curr}	n_j^{prev}	Error	$\bar{n}_j^{\text{curr}}$
29	27.52	13.23 0	132.872	4.83	4.62	0.0431	-
30	27.63	3.336	136.208	4.93	4.83	0.0207	-
31	29.06	18.77	154.978	5.33	4.93	0.0755	-
32	28.95	3.663	158.641	5.48	5.33	0.0267	-
33	30.3	4.01	162.651	5.37	5.48	0.0207	-
34	30.49	3.197	165.848	5.44	5.37	0.0132	-
35	32.6	16.311	182.159	5.59	5.44	0.0264	-
36	33.39	4.102	186.261	5.58	5.59	0.0017	5.32
-	-	-	-	-	-	-	-
46	41.42	5.129	260.197	6.28	6.39	0.0164	-
47	41.85	6.563	266.76	6.37	6.28	0.0144	-
48	42.19	29.899	296.659	7.03	6.37	0.0936	-
49	42.28	4.993	301.652	7.13	7.03	0.0144	-
50	42.10	22.807	324.459	7.71	7.13	0.0744	-
51	44.10	29.812	354.271	8.03	7.71	0.0405	-
52	43.87	5.583	359.854	8.20	8.03	0.0206	-
53	47.01	3.722	363.576	7.73	8.20	0.0606	-
54	47.33	3.038	366.614	7.75	7.73	0.0016	7.36

where $\vec{\lambda}_j$ is the vector of arrival rates at interval t_j and the optimization problem is

$$\begin{aligned}
\text{Minimize} \quad & \sum_{r=1}^{R}\sum_{j=1}^{M} \xi_{j,r}^2 & (12)\\
\text{s.t.} \quad & \sum_{r=1}^{R}\sum_{j=1}^{M} \xi_{j,r} = 0 \\
D_{i,r} \;\; & \geq \;\; 0 \quad i = 1, \cdots K \text{ and } r = 1, \cdots, R \\
\sum_{i=1}^{K} D_{i,r} \;\; & \leq \;\; \min_{j=1,\cdots,M} \{R_{j,r}^a\} \quad r = 1, \cdots, R. \\
U_i = \sum_{r=1}^{R} \lambda_r \times D_{i,r} \;\; & < \;\; 1 \quad i = 1, \cdots, K.
\end{aligned}$$

In the case of open QNs, the function $f_r(\mathbf{D}, \vec{\lambda})$ is computed through the following well-known closed-form equation [18].

$$f_r(\mathbf{D}, \vec{\lambda}) = R_r(\vec{\lambda}) = \sum_{i=1}^{K} \frac{D_{i,r}}{1 - \sum_{r=1}^{R} \lambda_r \times D_{i,r}}. \qquad (13)$$

Figure 5 shows an example in which the (arrival rate, response time) pairs shown by the solid triangles were used to solve the optimization problem described in Eq. (12) for an open QN. The solution to this problem yields the following set of service demands: $D_1 = 2.30$ sec, $D_2 = 1.60$ sec, $D_3 = 1.60$ sec, and $D_4 = 1.58$ sec. We then used a single class open QN model to compute the response times for the following values of the arrival rate (in tps), which were not used as input to solve the optimization problem: 0.04, 0.10, 0.14, 0.16, 0.22, 0.26, 0.30, 0.32, 0.36, 0.40, and 0.41. The values of the response times predicted by the model are plotted in Fig. 5 as unfilled triangles. As the figure illustrates, the predicted values match perfectly with the curve that underlies the measured points.

We now show an example with two classes and three de-

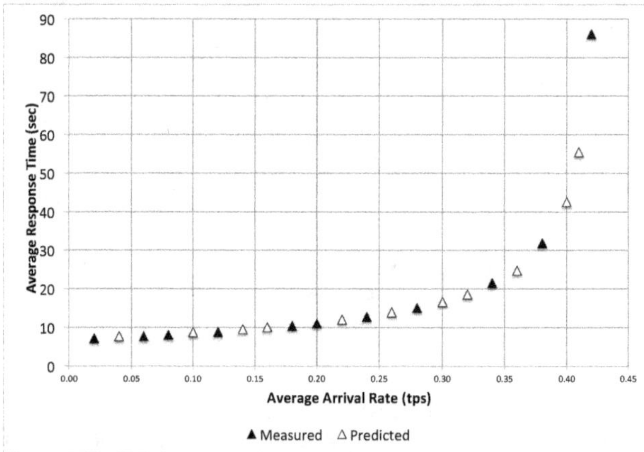

Figure 5: Average response time (in sec) vs. average arrival rate (in tps). Solid triangles: measured response times. Unfilled triangles: predicted by a model.

vices. Table 3 shows the measured arrival rates and measured response times per class for six measurement intervals.

Table 4 shows the matrix of service demands that resulted from the solution of the optimization problem above.

Figures 6 and 7 use solid markers (triangles and squares) to show the average response times for classes 1 and 2, respectively, for the six intervals shown in Table 3. Additionally, the unfilled markers in these figures show response time values predicted for the average arrival rates shown in Table 5 and computed by Eq. (13). The two predicted values in each figure do not show a perfect continuity because the values of the arrival rates for all classes impact all other classes through the utilization of all devices (see denominator of Eq. (13)). Nevertheless, since the arrival rates for which the prediction is shown in Table 5 are within the arrival rates for two successive intervals, one can see how the

Table 3: Measured arrival rates (in tps) and average response times (in sec) per class.

	Class 1		Class 2	
Interval	$\lambda^a_{j,1}$ (tps)	$R^a_{j,1}$ (sec)	$\lambda^a_{j,1}$ (tps)	$R^a_{j,2}$ (sec)
t_1	0.030	3.300	0.015	2.827
t_2	0.050	3.475	0.045	2.977
t_3	0.100	3.832	0.080	3.282
t_4	0.300	5.792	0.150	4.910
t_5	0.350	7.375	0.220	6.241
t_6	0.450	13.992	0.320	11.656

Table 4: Derived service demands (sec).

Queue	Class 1	Class 2
CPU	1.00	0.80
Disk 1	1.25	0.80
Disk 2	0.90	1.10

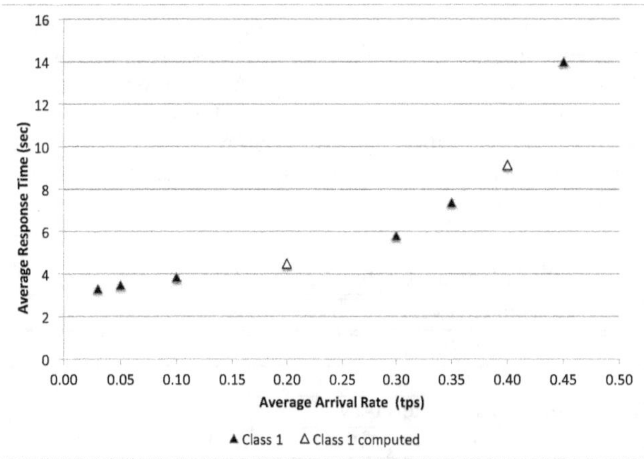

Figure 6: Average response time (in sec) for class 1 vs. average arrival rate (in tps). Solid triangles: measured response time. Unfilled triangles: predicted by a model.

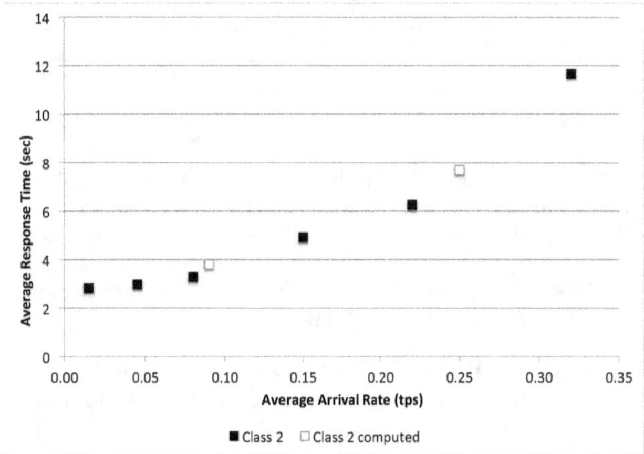

Figure 7: Average response time (in sec) for class 2 vs. average arrival rate (in tps). Solid squares: measured response time. Unfilled squares: predicted by a model.

predicted values fall within the measured values. For example, the first pair of arrival rates for which predictions are shown in Table 5 is 0.2 tps and 0.09 tps for classes 1 and 2, respectively. In both cases, these arrival rates fall within those of intervals t_3 and t_4. The corresponding predicted response times also fall between the measured response times for these intervals.

5. EXPERIMENTAL VALIDATION

This section presents a validation of the method described in this paper on an experimental testbed. Our implementation used a number of supporting tools and technologies, including Apache OFBiz (ofbiz.apache.org) and Apache JMeter (jmeter.apache.org) for running the experiment, and LogStash (www.elastic.co) for parsing system logs. We used jMetal (see http://jmetal.sourceforge.net) as the optimization framework for solving the non-linear optimization problem. This framework allows one to use various optimization algorithms. After experimenting with several, we settled on MOEA, which is an open-source evolutionary computation library for Java that specializes in multi-objective optimization. We also used an in-house implementation of the Approximate Mean Value Analysis (AMVA) algorithm.

Apache OFBiz^{TM} is an open source ERP (Enterprise Resource Planning) system from Apache. Logstash, which is part of the ELK stack (Elasticsearch, Logstash, and Kibana,) is an open source tool used to collect, organize, and parse various system logs and uses templates defined using regular expressions to describe the log structure and parse its contents. The output of Logstash is stored in Elasticsearch, which is a document store and a search server, where documents are stored in JSON format (Java Script Object Notation).

Apache JMeter is an open source tool used to record, generate, and run multiple workloads. It uses different techniques for spawning processes representing system users, and it has many extensions for recording experiment results in various formats.

Table 5: Computed average response times (in sec) per class.

Class 1		Class 2	
λ_1 (tps)	R_1 (sec)	λ_1 (tps)	R_2 (sec)
0.20	4.466	0.09	3.805
0.40	9.132	0.25	7.680

5.1 Experimental Conditions and Assumptions

Our testbed uses Ubuntu Linux servers to host the OFBiz ERP software suite, which was installed on a Tomcat 7.0 application server, and to host the MySQL database supporting the OFBiz suite. Apache JMeter was used to record and run a test plan that simulates different groups of users performing the business function Order Entry.

Table 6 shows the Order Entry sequence of steps, called workflow heretofore, performed by the users and captured by JMeter. Most of the workflow steps are interactive, such as login (step 2) and initorderentry (step 6). Other steps are performed by the system and do not require think time, such as image loading and search lookahead, as in steps 4, 5 and 8, where the system performs multiple AJAX (Asynchronous JavaScript And XML) requests while the user is typing a customer name or product name. Steps 4, 5, 8 and 9 are repeated multiple times for a total of 21 transactions in a workflow.

Table 6: Order Entry Workflow

no.	Workflow Step
1	/ordermgr/main
2	/ordermgr/login
3	/ordermgr/orderentry
4	/ordermgr/LookupUserLoginAndPartyDetails (2)
5	/ordermgr/LookupCustomerName (3 times)
6	/ordermgr/initorderentry
7	/ordermgr/setOrderCurrencyAgreementShipDates
8	/ordermgr/LookupProduct (4 times)
9	/ordermgr/additem (2 times)
10	/images/GZ-1001/small.png
11	/images/GZ-9290/small.png
12	/ordermgr/quickcheckout
13	/ordermgr/updateCheckoutOptions/quickcheckout
14	/ordermgr/checkout

We used JMeter to run the workflow shown in Table 6 using 5, 10, 15, 20, 22, 25, 27, 30, 32, 35, 40 and 45 users, called threads heretofore, under the following conditions:

1. Response time is defined as the time it takes to perform all 21 steps of the workflow.
2. JMeter's "Ramp-Up Period" is set to 30 seconds, which is the time JMeter takes to ramp up to the full number of threads.
3. JMeter's "Delay Thread Creation Until Needed" is set to true to eliminate the overhead of starting all threads at the beginning of the experiment.
4. JMeter's Loop Count is set to 10, which means that, for each experiment, threads ran 10 times consecutively. For example, an experiment with 10 users means the workflow in Table 6 ran 100 times producing 2100 transactions.
5. Experiment ramp-up and ramp-down times. In order to capture measurements during the system's steady state, we defined the measurement start time, T1, and end time, T2, for each experiment as follows:

   T1 = maximum start time of all workflows for all threads.

   T2 = minimum end time of all workflows for all threads.

   For each of the 10 experiments, all threads that started or ended prior to T1 or after T2 were removed from the final measurements. By doing that, we eliminated all partial workflows that might skew the average response time or average throughput given our definition of response time.
6. Think time between workflow steps uses a uniform random timer between 0 and 3 seconds. The random think time is only used between interactive steps. For example, think time is added between all steps except steps 10 and 11 (image loading) and between the multiple AJAX calls of steps 5 and 8 (LookupCustomerName and LookupProduct).

To validate our method we performed the following steps:

Step 1 - Measurements Perform several measurements on a system running the OFBiz ERP software suite for several intervals to obtain the throughput and response time. The results of our measurements are reported in Table 7 for intervals t_1-t_{12}. Each line shows the number of clients generating requests in each interval. The number of workflows generated in each interval varied from 42 to 362 excluding the ramp-up and ramp-down times (actual total workflows varied from 50 to 450.) We used Little's Law [16] to obtain the concurrency level n_j for each interval t_j as the product of the measured throughput and the measured response time (i.e., $n_j = X_j^a \times R_j^a$). Figure 8 shows the average response time per workflow execution and Fig. 9 shows the average throughput in workflows per second (wps).

Table 7: Apache OFBiz Results

Interval	X_j^a (in wps)	R_j^a (in sec)	n_j
t1 (5 users)	0.130	4.406 ± 0.145	0.575
t2 (10 users)	0.255	4.481 ± 0.149	1.141
t3 (15 users)	0.389	4.602 ± 0.149	1.788
t4 (20 users)	0.516	5.234 ± 0.123	2.700
t5 (22 users)	0.565	5.337 ± 0.141	3.016
t6 (25 users)	0.622	5.751 ± 0.398	3.574
t7 (27 users)	0.659	6.722 ± 0.168	4.427
t8 (30 users)	0.738	7.193 ± 0.191	5.307
t9 (32 users)	0.746	8.430 ± 0.225	6.286
t10 (35 users)	0.773	10.077 ± 0.257	7.785
t11 (40 users)	0.805	15.002 ± 0.372	12.076
t12 (45 users)	0.806	20.462 ± 0.465	16.497

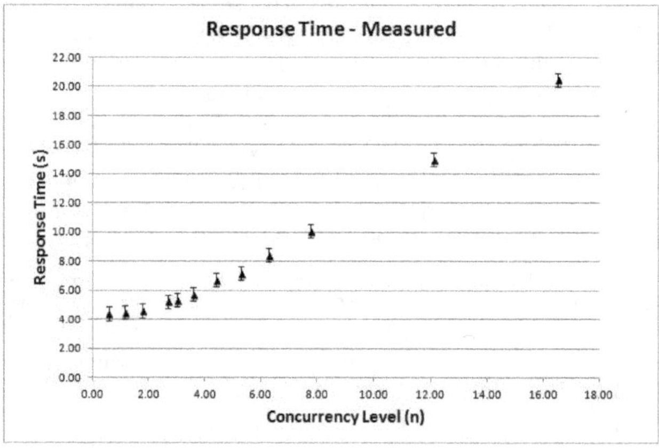

Figure 8: Average response time (in sec) vs. concurrency level.

Step 2 - Estimating Service Demands Apply the optimization technique described in the previous sections to estimate the service demands for the closed QN

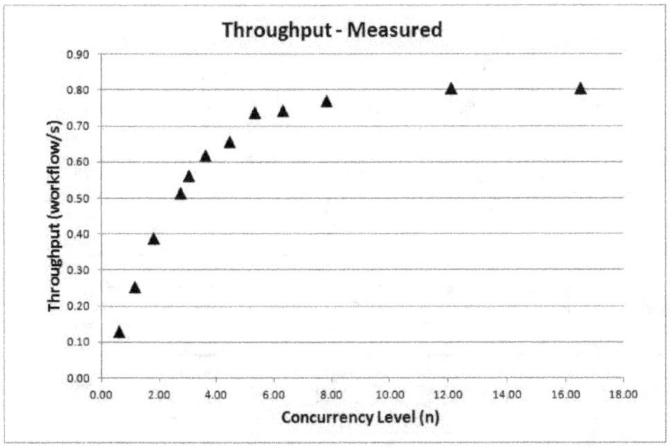

Figure 9: Average throughput (in wps) vs. concurrency level.

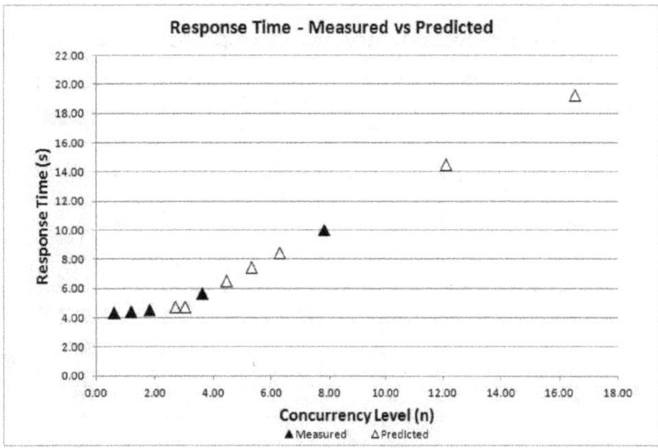

Figure 10: Response time (in sec) vs. concurrency level. Solid Triangles: measured response time. Unfilled Triangles: predicted by a model.

model that represents the experimental testbed. In our example, we built a closed QN model with three queues representing the Web server, the application server, and the database server. The service demands derived by solving the optimization model, using as inputs the data for intervals t_1, t_2, t_3, t_6 and t_{10} are 0.937 sec, 1.114 sec and 1.002 sec, respectively. Because the concurrency levels for those five intervals are not integer, we used Approximate MVA, which uses the Bard-Schweitzer approximation to solve closed QNs with non-integer concurrency levels [22].

Step 3 - Prediction Using the closed QN model with the service demands obtained in step 2, compute the throughput and response time for concurrency levels not used in step 2. See the X^{model} and R^{model} columns for intervals t_4, t_5, t_7, t_8, t_9, t_{11} and t_{12} in Table 8.

Step 4 -Validation Compare the response time values predicted by the model in step 3 with measured response times for the same concurrency levels. If the values are relatively close (i.e., on the order of 10% difference), the service demand estimation process is validated and the resulting closed QN model can be considered to have predictive power. As it can be seen in the last two columns of Table 8, the percent absolute error defined as $100 \times (measurement - model)/measurement$ for intervals t_4, t_5, t_7, t_8, t_9, t_{11} and t_{12} is small (less than 10% and—in most cases—less than 5%), which indicates that the derived model has predictive power for concurrency levels not used in the derivation of the service demands. It is important to note that the largest errors occurred for small concurrency levels (2.7 and 3.0 workflows) due to the fact that we used AMVA, which does not provide a good approximation for low concurrency levels. Also, production systems rarely operate at such low concurrency levels.

Figure 10 shows five measured response times as a function of the concurrency level according to Table 8 (see black triangles) and the seven points t_4, t_5, t_7, t_8, t_9, t_{11} and t_{12} (white triangles). As it can be seen, the points computed by a model that uses the service demands estimated by our method match the curve obtained through measurements.

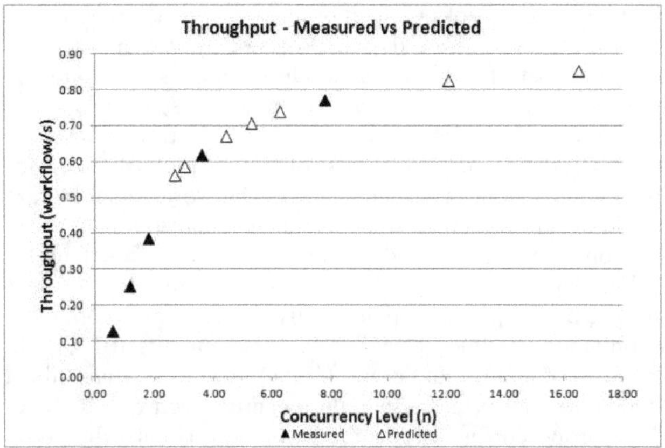

Figure 11: Throughput (in workloads per sec) vs. concurrency level. Solid Triangles: measured response time. Unfilled Triangles: predicted by a model.

Figure 11 shows the measured throughput as a function of the concurrency level according to Table 8 (see black triangles) and the seven points t_4, t_5, t_7, t_8, t_9, t_{11} and t_{12} (white triangles) predicted by a closed QN model that uses the derived service demands resulting from the solution of the optimization problem described above. As it can be seen and as expected, the points computed by the QN model that uses the service demands estimated by our method match the curve obtained through measurements.

6. RELATED WORK

We have already referenced before our own prior work [1, 2, 3]. In this section we discus related prior work by others. Some of the prior work that tackled the parameterization of analytical models includes [5, 6, 7], where the problem of estimating known model parameters is treated as an optimization problem that is solved using derivative-free optimization. The objective function to be optimized is based on the distance between the observed measurements and the corresponding points derived from the model. The authors point out that the main problem is determining how to cou-

Table 8: Validation with experimental results obtained using OFBiz Order Entry transactions.

Period	No. Users	X_j (in Wps)	R_j^a (in sec)	n_j	X^{model} (in Wps)	R^{model} (in sec)	% Rel. Error Throughput	% Rel. Error Resp. Time
t_1	5	0.130	4.406 ± 0.145	0.575	NA	NA	NA	NA
t_2	10	0.255	4.481 ± 0.149	1.141	NA	NA	NA	NA
t_3	15	0.389	4.602 ± 0.149	1.788	NA	NA	NA	NA
t_6	25	0.622	5.751 ± 0.398	3.574	NA	NA	NA	NA
t_{10}	35	0.773	10.077 ± 0.257	7.785	NA	NA	NA	NA
Comparison between measurements and model predicted results								
t_4	20	0.516	5.234 ± 0.123	2.700	0.56	4.80	-9%	8%
t_5	22	0.565	5.337 ± 0.141	3.016	0.59	4.84	-4%	9%
t_7	27	0.659	6.722 ± 0.168	4.427	0.67	6.58	-2%	2%
t_8	30	0.738	7.193 ± 0.191	5.307	0.71	7.49	4%	-4%
t_9	32	0.746	8.430 ± 0.225	6.286	0.74	8.51	1%	-1%
t_{11}	40	0.805	15.002 ± 0.372	12.076	0.83	14.60	-3%	3%
t_{12}	45	0.806	20.462 ± 0.465	16.497	0.85	19.32	-6%	6%

ple these two sets of points in order to arrive at an objective function to be minimized. The proposed approach is applied to a small set of single-queue models, whereas our approach applies to single and multiclass open and closed QNs.

The work in [4] used Kalman filters to estimate resource service demands for the purpose of system performance testing. The authors attempted to find the workload mix that would eventually saturate a certain system resource in a test environment in order to determine the system's bottlenecks.

The work in [15, 25, 26] addressed the problem of estimating model parameters in highly dynamic autonomic environments in which Service Level Agreements (SLAs) (in the form of Quality of Service (QoS)) have to be maintained while offering optimal use of data center resources. The authors proposed the use of a model-based estimator based on Extended Kalman Filters, where the current state depends on prior knowledge of previous states. Our approach, on the other hand, relies on solving an optimization problem where only current input and output values are known.

Menascé tackled the issue of model parameterization for open QNs when some input parameters are already known [17]. The author proposed a closed-form solution to the case when a single service demand value is unknown, and a constrained non-linear optimization solution when a feasible set of service demands are unknown. However, that work did not propose a solution when none of the service demands are known a priori.

In [9], the authors introduced a method for performance parameter estimation using Kalman filters and Layered Queuing Models. They used a clustering algorithm to determine the optimal number of classes such that the LQN closely tracks the behavior of the real system.

In [21], the authors presented three service demand estimation methods (RPS, MLPS and MINPS) for multi-threaded applications. RPS is used in single-processor systems, MLPS is used in multi-processor systems and MINPS consolidates both methods. Both RPS and MLPS methods over-estimate the service demand in the type of workload they handle. MINPS runs both methods and chooses the method that produces the smaller estimated mean service time.

In [24], the authors presented a survey of service demand estimation techniques, such as Kalman filter, optimization, machine learning, and linear regression. The authors introduced a classification scheme based on the input parameters, output metrics and the ability of the estimation technique to tolerate input data anomalies. In order to evaluate the accuracy of the various estimation techniques, the authors generated two data sets; one using an M/M/1 queuing simulator, and another using a real system. MATLAB functions were used to implement the estimation techniques, such as least-squares regression and constrained non-linear optimization. The accuracy of the estimation technique was assessed using the mean relative demand error, relative utilization error or relative response time error. The results presented in the paper show how service demand estimation accuracy is impacted by the length of sampling interval, number of samples, number of workload classes, load level, delays during processing and execution time. The experimental results presented in the paper are meant to help performance engineers decide which estimation technique to use given the impact of variations in sampling intervals, workload classes and execution time on the accuracy of the technique's service demand results. An example of the results is that estimation techniques that rely on response time measurements are not as negatively impacted by missing workload classes as techniques that rely on utilization measurements.

The work in [13] proposes an approach based on queuing networks to represent system configurations. They use symbolic analysis and satisfiability modulo theory (SMT) to find a model that fits continuous changes in run-time conditions.

In[12], the authors used the previously introduced Descartes Modeling Language (DML) to illustrate how self-aware systems can manage their resources using a closed-feedback loop (MAPE-K control loop). Their proposed online performance prediction process takes into consideration the system's performance objectives, constraints and overhead. Online performance prediction is achieved by answering performance queries that specify the performance metrics desired and the constraints and overhead that would impact the adaptation plan selection. Performance queries are implemented using a declarative (and expressive) query language. Using the DML instance of the system and the performance query, the performance prediction process produces a model that is either fine grained, coarse grained or black-box and—eventually—solves the model, thereby producing performance query results. The framework uses a number of solving techniques to solve the generated model, including bound analysis techniques based on Little's law and utilization law, LQN solver for solving LQN's and a combination of QNs and Colored Generalized Stochastic Petri Nets. The experimental results show how parameterizing the model at lower load levels (20% CPU utilization) can be used to predict the system's performance at higher load levels within 5% error in resource utilization and 20% error in mean response time.

7. CONCLUDING REMARKS AND FUTURE WORK

This paper presented and validated a method to automatically derive service demand parameters of open and closed multiclass queuing network models. The input to the method is a set of measured response times for different levels of workload intensity (arrival rates or concurrency levels). Then, a non-linear optimization problem is setup where the objective function is the sum of square errors between the measured response times and the response times computed by the QN model. The problem is that there is no closed form expression for response times for closed QNs. To overcome this problem we resorted to black box optimization techniques. We validated our method by setting up an experimental testbed to run the OFBiz suite. We then took measurements, derived the service demands using the method presented in this paper and then used the automatically parameterized model to predict the response time for non-measured workload intensity levels.

The method described in this paper can be applied to situations in which the machines are multi-core. This can be done by using Seidmann's approximation [23] in which a service center with a single queue and m servers (e.g., m cores) each with service demand D can be replaced in the QN by a single server queue with service demand D/m followed by a delay server with service demand $D(m-1)/m$. The use of this approximation transforms an open or closed QN with multiserver queues into one with only single server queues.

8. ACKNOWLEDGMENTS

This work was partially supported by the AFOSR grant FA9550-16-1-0030. The authors thank Ms. Noor Bajunaid for having developed the Java code for the implementation of AMVA.

9. REFERENCES

[1] Awad, M. and Menascé, D.A., "Performance Model Derivation of Operational Systems Through Log Analysis," IEEE Intl. Symp. Modeling, Analysis and Simulation of Computer Systems and Telecommunication Systems (MASCOTS 2016), Imperial College, London, UK, Sept. 19-21, 2016.

[2] Awad, M. and Menascé, D.A., "On the Predictive Properties of Performance Models Derived Through Input-Output Relationships", Proc. European Performance Engineering Workshop (EPEW 2014), Venice, Italy, 2014.

[3] Awad, M. and Menascé, D.A., "Dynamic Derivation of Analytical Performance Models in Autonomic Computing Environments", Proc. Computer Measurement Group Conf. Performance and Capacity, Atlanta, GA, 2014.

[4] Barna, C., Litoiu, M., Ghanbari, H., "Autonomic load-testing framework," Proc. 8th ACM Intl. Conf. Autonomic Computing, Karlsruhe, Germany, 2011, pp. 91–100.

[5] Begin, T., Brandwajn, A., Baynat, B., Wolfinger, B.E., Fdida, S., "Towards an automatic modeling tool for observed system behavior," Formal Methods and Stochastic Models for Performance Evaluation, pp. 200–212. Springer Berlin Heidelberg (2007)

[6] Begin, T., Brandwajn, A., Baynat, B., Wolfinger, B. E., Fdida, S., "High-level approach to modeling of observed system behavior," ACM SIGMETRICS Performance Evaluation Review, 35(3), 34–36 (2007)

[7] Begin, T., Baynat, B., Sourd, F., Brandwajn, A., "A DFO technique to calibrate queuing models," Computers & Operations Research, 37, no. 2, 2010, pp. 273–281.

[8] Durillo,J.J. and Nebro, A.J., "jMetal: a Java Framework for Multi-Objective Optimization," Advances in Engineering Software, 42(2011), pp. 760-771.

[9] Ghanbari, H., Barna, C., Litoiu, M., Woodside, M., Zheng, T., Wong, J., Iszlai, G., "Tracking Adaptive Performance Models Using Dynamic Clustering of User Classes," Proc. 2nd ACM/SPEC Intl. Conf. Performance Engineering, Karlsruhe, Germany, March 14-16, 2011.

[10] Gmach, D., J. Rolia, L. Cherkasova, and A. Kemper. "Workload Analysis and Demand Prediction of Enterprise Data Center Applications," Proc. 2007 IEEE 10th Intl. Symp. Workload Characterization (IISWC '07), Boston, MA, Sept. 27-29, 2007.

[11] Herbst, N.R., N. Huber, S. Kounev, and E. Amrehn. "Self-adaptive workload classification and forecasting for proactive resource provisioning." Proc. 4th ACM/SPEC Intl. Conf. Performance Engineering (ICPE '13), Prague, Czech Republic, April 21-24, 2013.

[12] Huber, N., F. Brosig, S. Spinner, S. Kounev, and M. Bahr, "Model-Based Self-Aware Performance and Resource Management Using the Descartes Modeling Language," to appear in the IEEE Tr. Software Engineering, DOI 10.1109/TSE.2016.2613863

[13] Incerto, E., M. Tribastone, and C. Trubiani, "Symbolic Performance Adaptations" Proc. 11th Intl. Symp. Software Engineering for Adaptive and Self-Managing Systems (SEAMS 2016), May 16-17, 2016, Austin, TX.

[14] Khan A., X. Yan, S. Tao and N. Anerousis, "Workload characterization and prediction in the cloud: A multiple time series approach," 2012 IEEE Network Operations and Management Symposium, Maui, HI, 2012

[15] Litoiu, M., Woodside, M., Zheng, T., "Hierarchical model-based autonomic control of software systems," ACM SIGSOFT Software Engineering Notes, Vol. 30, No. 4, pp. 1–7 (2005)

[16] Little, J.D.C., "A Proof for the Queuing Formula: L = λ W," Operations Research. 9 (3), 1961, pp 383–387.

[17] Menascé, D., "Computing Missing Service Demand Parameters for Performance Models," Proc.

Thirty-fourth Intl. Computer Measurement Group Conf., Las Vegas, NV, Dec. 7-12, 2008, pp. 7–12.

[18] Menascé, D.A., Almeida, V.A.F., and Dowdy, L., "Performance by Design: Computer Capacity Planning By Example." Prentice Hall, 2004.

[19] Menascé, D.A. and Almeida, V.A.F., "Scaling for E-Business: technologies, models, performance, and capacity planning," Prentice Hall, 2000.

[20] Reiser, M. and Lavenberg, S. S. "Mean-Value Analysis of Closed Multichain Queuing Networks," J. ACM., 27(2), April 1980, pp. 313–322.

[21] Pérez, J.F., Pacheco-Sanchez, S., Casale, G., "An Offline Demand Estimation Method for Multi-Threaded Applications," Proc. 2013 IEEE 21st Intl. Symp. Modeling, Analysis and Simulation of Computer and Telecommunication Systems (pp. 21-30), IEEE Computer Society, 2013.

[22] Schweitzer, P. "Approximate analysis of multiclass closed networks of queues." Proc. Intl. Conf. Stochastic Control and Optimization, 1979.

[23] Seidmann, A., P. Schweitzer, and S. Shalev-Oren, "Computerized Closed Queueing Network Models of Flexible Manufacturing," Large Scale System J., North Holland, Vol. 12, 1987, pp. 91–107.

[24] Spinner S., G. Casale, F. Brosig, and S. Kounev., "Evaluating Approaches to Resource Demand Estimation," Performance Evaluation, 92:51 - 71, October 2015, Elsevier B.V.

[25] Woodside, M., Zheng, T., Litoiu, M., "The use of optimal filters to track parameters of performance models," Second Intl. Conf. Quantitative Evaluation of Systems, Torino, Italy, Sept. 19-22, 2005, pp. 74–83.

[26] Zheng, T., Yang, J., Woodside, M., Litoiu, M., Iszlai, G. "Tracking time-varying parameters in software systems with extended Kalman filters," Proc. 2005 Conf. of the Centre for Advanced Studies on Collaborative Research, 2005, pp. 334–345.

HyperStar2: Easy Distribution Fitting of Correlated Data

Zhihao Shang, Tianhui Meng and Katinka Wolter
Department of Mathematics and Computer Science
Freie Universität Berlin
Takustr.9, Berlin, Germany
{zhihao.shang, tianhui.meng and katinka.wolter}@fu-berlin.de

ABSTRACT

In this paper, we present HyperStar2, a tool for fitting Markov Arrival Processes (MAPs) to empirical data. HyperStar2 uses a two-step approach, where the first step is cluster-based fitting of phase-type distributions and the second step is the construction of a correlation matrix. In the first step, we use the cluster-based algorithm for Hyper-Erlang distribution fitting from HyperStar [1]. Based on the Hyper-Erlang fitting result and the clusters of samples, in the second step we construct the correlation matrix.

The tool targets engineers and scientists who need distribution fitting for non-standard distributions but have little interest in the underlying theory. Therefore the tool has a GUI that offers graphical presentation of the data, the fitted distribution and the empirical as well as theoretical autocorrelation. We discuss the use of HyperStar2 in common application scenarios and the fitting algorithms behind it.

We provide some numerical examples, which show the abilities and limits of the fitting tool. We find that HyperStar2 can fit distributions very well but for some autocorrelation structures ProFiDo provides better results for autocorrelation.

CCS Concepts

•**Mathematics of computing** → **Markov processes;**

Keywords

probability distribution fitting, phase-type fitting, MAP fitting, tool description

1. INTRODUCTION

Markovian Arrival Processes (MAPs) play an important role in the field of performance evaluation. MAPs have a long history in stochastic modeling [2] and are powerful modelling tools. MAPs, in theory, allow the representation of almost all relevant stochastic behaviors that are observed in practice. MAPs were proposed in [3] and are widely used for probabilistic analysis of communication network traffic and stochastic modeling [4]. To capture empirical behavior by MAPs, the parameters of a MAP have to be fitted according to some trace resulting from observations. The most general approach is to find a MAP that maximizes the likelihood according to the available traces. The EM algorithm [5] can be used for this purpose and many specific variants of the algorithm for MAP fitting are available [6]. There are also some MAP fitting methods based on the two-phase approach [7], which suggested splitting the task into two phases: fitting of the inter-arrival times in the first phase by a PH fitting method and fitting the correlation in the second phase. However, it is still an open question what are the statistics that capture the correlation structure of the trace the best.

In recent years, several tools have been proposed [8, 9] that provide good fitting results. But only users with deep understanding of the underlying concepts of the distributions and the applied algorithms can use them well. The motivation of our work is to develop a user-friendly tool which allows for intuitive user interaction and provides direct user feed-back. Using HyperStar2 requires no knowledge of the underlying mathematics or theoretical foundations. The tool is used by working directly with the empirical data.

In this paper, we discuss our cluster-based approach to MAP fitting, implemented as HyperStar2, a tool with a graphical user interface where the user can mark density peaks of the empirical data to support the clustering algorithm and improve fitting results. The rest of this paper is structured as follows: We first introduce some basic concepts of PH distributions and MAPs in section 2. We describe our cluster-based fitting approach in section 3. Section 4 gives an overview of our implementation of the HyperStar2 tool. We evaluate the tool in section 5 by numerical experiments. Section 6 concludes the paper with an outlook on future work.

ICPE'17, April 22 - 26, 2017, L'Aquila, Italy

ISBN 978-1-4503-4404-3/17/04. . . $15.00

DOI: http://dx.doi.org/10.1145/3030207.3030243

2. MATHEMATICAL BACKGROUND

A Hyper-Erlang distribution is a mixture of Erlang distributions. We consider a Hyper-Erlang distribution that consists of M independent Erlang distributions weighted with initial probabilities $\alpha_1, \alpha_2, ..., \alpha_M$, where $0 < \alpha_m \leq 1$. The number of phases in the mth Erlang distribution is denoted with r_m and the rate parameter of the mth Erlang distribution is denoted λ_m. The Hyper-Erlang distribution is commonly represented by a vector-matrix tuple $(\alpha, \mathbf{Q})$, where α is the vector of initial probabilities and $\mathbf{Q}$ is the generator matrix. They are presented in (1) and (2).

$$\alpha = (\alpha_1, \alpha_2, ..., \alpha_M) \tag{1}$$

$$\mathbf{Q} = \begin{pmatrix} \mathbf{Q}_1 & 0 & & \\ 0 & \mathbf{Q}_2 & \ddots & \\ & \ddots & \ddots & 0 \\ & & 0 & \mathbf{Q}_m \end{pmatrix} \tag{2}$$

where $\mathbf{Q}_m$ is the generator matrix of the mth Erlang distribution.

An essential feature of Hyper-Erlang distribution is that an observation belongs to Erlang branch m always with probability α_m. This creates no correlation in the Hyper-Erlang distribution. To reflect correlation of samples, a MAP should be used instead of a Hyper-Erlang distribution.

A MAP of order n is usually defined by two $n \times n$ matrices $(\mathbf{D}_0, \mathbf{D}_1)$. Matrix $\mathbf{D}_0$ contains the rates of internal transition rates without an arrival and matrix $\mathbf{D}_1$ describes the transition rates with an arrival. And $\mathbf{D} = \mathbf{D}_0 + \mathbf{D}_1$ is an irreducible generator of the background n-state continuous-time Markov chain (CTMC). Let φ be the steady-state probability vector of the background CTMC, then φ is the solution of the linear system $\varphi\mathbf{D} = 0, \varphi\mathbf{1}^T = 1$, where $\mathbf{1}$ is a row vector of ones of the appropriate dimension. The pdf of a MAP is

$$f(t) = \pi e^{\mathbf{D}_0 t}(-\mathbf{D}_0\mathbf{1}) \tag{3}$$

and the lag-k correlation is computed as

$$\rho_k = \frac{\lambda^2\pi(-\mathbf{D}_0)^{-1}P^k(-\mathbf{D}_0)^{-1}\mathbf{1} - 1}{2\lambda^2\pi(-\mathbf{D}_0)^{-1}(-\mathbf{D}_0)^{-1}\mathbf{1} - 1} \tag{4}$$

3. THE FITTING ALGORITHM

In this section we discuss the theoretical aspects of the fitting algorithm. The main idea of the algorithm is to construct the $\mathbf{D}_0$ and $\mathbf{D}_1$ matrices separately. So there are two steps in our MAP fitting algorithm. The first step is using a cluster-based algorithm to fit the samples with a Hyper-Erlang distribution. We use the generator matrix of the Hyper-Erlang distribution as $\mathbf{D}_0$ matrix. After performing the cluster-based fitting, we have the Hyper-Erlang distribution and M clusters. The matrix $\mathbf{D}_1$ is constructed by analysing the sample transitions between clusters and assigning the relative switching frequency between two clusters to the respective transition probability.

3.1 Constructing the $\mathbf{D}_0$ matrix

The cluster-based fitting algorithm consists of clustering and refinement. In the clustering step, the samples are clustered using the k-means alorithm and each cluster is fitted with an Erlang distribution. We use a probabilistic re-assignment strategy for the cluster refinement. The refinement is repeated iteratively until either the parameters in each Erlang distribution do no longer change or a maximal number of iterations has been exceeded. More details can be found in our earlier work [1].

3.2 Constructing the $\mathbf{D}_1$ matrix

For a Hyper-Erlang distribution, the phase distribution after an arrival is always α. For a MAP, the phase distribution after an arrival depends on the phase immediately before that arrival and $\mathbf{D}_1$ describes the transitions rate between phases, which are states of a CTMC.

Our approach is to analyse the relative frequency of transitions between clusters, and constructing the $\mathbf{D}_1$ based on the transition frequencies. When an arrival occurs, let $\eta_{(i,j)}$ be the probability that the next phase is j given the current phase is i. We can obtain the element of $\mathbf{D}_1$ at row i column j by scaling $\eta_{(i,j)}$ with a proper factor because $\mathbf{D}_1$ and $\eta_{(i,j)}$ describe the same thing using different notation. In our MAP fitting algorithm, we construct $\mathbf{D}_1$ based on the relative frequency of transitions between clusters.

After Hyper-Erlang fitting, a generator matrix $\mathbf{Q}$ for the Hyper-Erlang distribution is obtained. If there are k_i phases in the Erlang distribution of cluster i it follows that $\mathbf{D}_0$ is a $K \times K$ matrix, where $K = \sum_{i=1}^{M} k_i$. Because the matrix $\mathbf{D}_0$ is associated with transitions without arrivals and we use a generator matrix of a Hyper-Erlang distribution in our MAP fitting algorithm, transitions with arrivals only happen between Erlang branches. Every Erlang branch is associated to a sample cluster and we analyze transitions between clusters to obtain the transitions between Erlang branches that are associated with arrivals. Let $\mathbf{CS}$ be a $K \times K$ zero matrix and $\mathbf{CS}_{(r,c)}$ be the element at row r column c. We use matrix $\mathbf{CS}$ to count the transitions between clusters.

Let B_i be the first phase of the ith Erlang distribution and E_i the last phase of the ith Erlang distribution. We can get

$$B_i = \sum_{a=1}^{i-1} k_a + 1 \qquad E_i = \sum_{a=1}^{i} k_a. \tag{5}$$

If a sample belongs to the ith cluster and the next sample belongs to the jth cluster, where i may be equal to j, we update the counter as below:

$$\mathbf{C}S_{(E_i,B_j)} = \mathbf{CS}_{(E_i,B_j)} + 1. \tag{6}$$

We can set $\mathbf{D}_1^{'}$ to the probability matrix for sample transitions.

$$\mathbf{D}_1^{'} = \frac{1}{n-1}\mathbf{CS}. \tag{7}$$

Let $\mathbf{D}_{1(r,c)}^{'}$ be the element of $\mathbf{D}_1^{'}$ at position (r, c). Hence $\mathbf{D}_{1(r,c)}^{'}$ is the probability that the sample generating process transits from state r to state c. We assume $\mathbf{D}_{1(r,c)}^{'}$ equals the probability that transitions occur between states in the MAP. To get $\mathbf{D}_1$, we must convert the probability in $\mathbf{D}_1^{'}$ to state transition rates by scaling every element in $\mathbf{D}_1^{'}$ with a suitable factor. Let $\mathbf{F}$ be the matrix of factors and $\mathbf{D}_1$ is the Hadamard product of $\mathbf{D}_1^{'}$ and $\mathbf{F}$.

$$\mathbf{D}_1 = \mathbf{D}_1^{'} \circ \mathbf{F}. \tag{8}$$

The matrix $\mathbf{D}_0 + \mathbf{D}_1$ is an irreducible generator of a CTMC, so

$$(\mathbf{D}_0 + \mathbf{D}_1)\mathbf{1} = \mathbf{0}, \tag{9}$$

where $\mathbf{0}$ is a row vector of zeros of the appropriate dimension.

Let $\mathbf{D}_{1(r,c)}$ be the element of $\mathbf{D}_1$ at row r column c. Combining (8) and (9), then we can get

$$\mathbf{D}_{1(r,c)} = \begin{cases} -\frac{\mathbf{D}_{0(r)}}{\mathbf{D}_{1(r)}^{'}}\mathbf{D}_{1(r,c)}^{'} & \text{if } \mathbf{D}_{1(r)}^{'} \neq 0 \\ 0 & \text{if } \mathbf{D}_{1(r)}^{'} = 0 \end{cases} \tag{10}$$

where

$$\mathbf{D}_{0(r)} = \sum_{c=1}^{K} \mathbf{D}_{0(r,c)} \qquad \mathbf{D}^{'}_{1(r)} = \sum_{c=1}^{K} \mathbf{D}^{'}_{1(r,c)} \tag{11}$$

4. IMPLEMENTATION

We implemented the fitting method in the tool HyperStar2. In earlier work [1] we found that the human user can very often detect clusters much better than a fully automatic algorithm by marking the peaks in the distribution as relevant values in the observations.

For most cases, users do not have to set the parameters and HyperStar2 can provide good fitting results with the default values after simply clicking the *Fit* button. If the user is not satisfied with the fitting result, the peaks on the histogram can be marked in the GUI. The density peaks are used as the initial centers of the K-means algorithm. There are also fitting parameters that can be set to improve the fitting result. Table 1 lists some important fitting parameters to control the behaviour of the fitting algorithm. The tool can export the result after completion of the fitting procedure. It can only export plain text for now. Among our the future work is the export of scripts that can generate samples from the fitted MAP in some simulators.

Table 1: Fitting parameters

Parameter	Description(default value)
fitter	distribution to be fitted (MAP)
branch	number of branch to be fitted (6)
reassignment	maximum number of iterations (20)
shuffles	number of reassignments in a iteration (2)

5. EVALUATION

In this section we demonstrate the fitting properties of HyperStar2 by analysing some examples. We fit distributions and evaluate the goodness of fit by comparing the empirical and the theoretical probability density function as well as the lag-k correlation. We also compare our result with the results from ProFiDo [8], which we found to be a very versatile fitting tool. Computation of error measures is also among our future work.

We show two examples that demonstrate the advantages and disadvantages of our tool. We first generated samples from a given MAP and then study how well HyperStar2 is able to approximate this distribution. We use samples that contain obvious peaks in the first example. There are not many samples in the overlap area between clusters. Therefore, it is clear which cluster a sample falls into and the estimate of the relative frequency of transitions between clusters in the sample sequence is highly accurate. In this case the algorithm provides a good correlation fit. In the second example, the samples do not contain as obvious peaks. Hence, there are many samples in the overlap area between clusters. These samples may be assigned to different clusters. The assignment may not impact the density fitting very much, but we suspect that it impairs the autocorrelation fitting as the estimate of relative frequencies of changes between clusters in the sample sequence has much more uncertainty.

The *branch* parameter indicates into how many clusters the data is splitted. This is a very import parameter in our algorithm as it impacts the fitting result severely. So we show fitting results with different numbers of *branches* in the two examples.

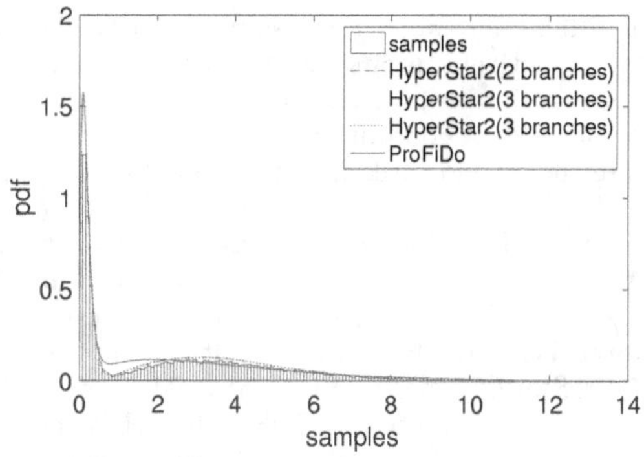

Figure 1: pdf of the first example

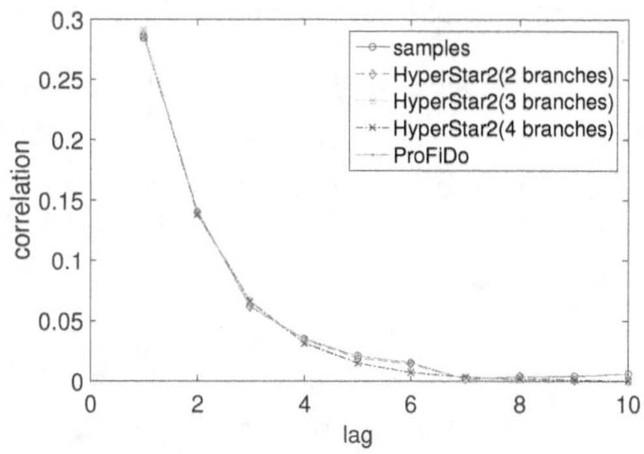

Figure 2: correlation of the first example

The first example uses a 6-state MAP with the following matrices. Using this generator there are two states that contribute strongly to the dynamics of the model, while the remaining four states are less influential. This can also be seen in Figure 1, where the empirical density has two peaks.

$$\mathbf{D}_0 = \begin{pmatrix} -10 & 10 & 0 & 0 & 0 & 0 \\ 0 & -10 & 0 & 0 & 0 & 0 \\ 0 & 0 & -1 & 1 & 0 & 0 \\ 0 & 0 & 0 & -1 & 1 & 0 \\ 0 & 0 & 0 & 0 & -1 & 1 \\ 0 & 0 & 0 & 0 & 0 & -1 \end{pmatrix}$$

$$\mathbf{D}_1 = \begin{pmatrix} 0 & 0 & 0 & 0 & 0 & 0 \\ 7 & 0 & 3 & 0 & 0 & 0 \\ 0 & 0 & 0 & 0 & 0 & 0 \\ 0 & 0 & 0 & 0 & 0 & 0 \\ 0 & 0 & 0 & 0 & 0 & 0 \\ 0.3 & 0 & 0 & 0.7 & 0 & 0 \end{pmatrix}$$

The first data set consists of 25000 samples generated from this MAP. We fit the samples using HyperStar2 and ProFiDo. Setting the *branch* parameter to 2, which means the algorithm splits the data into 2 clusters and there are 2 Erlang branches in the Hyper-Erlang distribution. Fig. 1 shows the histogram of samples and the densities of the fitted distributions. The solid line represents the pdf of the result from ProFiDo. The other three lines represent the pdf of results from HyperStar2 using different parameter settings. The red line shows the 2-branch result from HyperStar2, the yellow and blue lines show the results for 3 branches and 4 branches respectively. From Fig. 1 we observe that HyperStar2 fits this data set very well with 2, 3 or 4 branches. ProFiDo provides a good fit of the density but is not able to capture the second peak and the gap between the peaks as precisely.

Fig. 2 shows the autocorrelation function of the resulting MAP. As expected, the autocorrelation function is fitted well by both tools. The figure indicates that the result with 2 Erlang branches is the best of the results we have computed using HyperStar2. It is as good as the result from ProFiDo.

But for different numbers of Erlang branches the results are not as good. The 3-branch and 4-branch results for the density are not as good as 2-branch result, but they are also very close to the samples' autocorrelation.

In the second example, we approximate the following MAP:

$$\mathbf{D}_0 = \begin{pmatrix} -0.2 & 0.2 & 0 & 0 & 0 & 0 \\ 0 & -0.2 & 0.2 & 0 & 0 & 0 \\ 0 & 0 & -0.2 & 0 & 0 & 0 \\ 0 & 0 & 0 & -0.5 & 0.5 & 0 \\ 0 & 0 & 0 & 0 & -0.5 & 0.5 \\ 0 & 0 & 0 & 0 & 0 & -0.5 \end{pmatrix}$$

$$\mathbf{D}_1 = \begin{pmatrix} 0 & 0 & 0 & 0 & 0 & 0 \\ 0 & 0 & 0 & 0 & 0 & 0 \\ 0.16 & 0 & 0 & 0.04 & 0 & 0 \\ 0 & 0 & 0 & 0 & 0 & 0 \\ 0 & 0 & 0 & 0 & 0 & 0 \\ 0.02 & 0 & 0 & 0.03 & 0 & 0 \end{pmatrix}$$

We again generated 25000 samples from this MAP and fitted them with HyperStar2 and ProFiDo.

We used 2, 4 and 6 *branches*. It is not easy to see the peaks in this, so we did not mark any peak on the histogram. Fig. 3 and Fig. 4 show the fitting results.

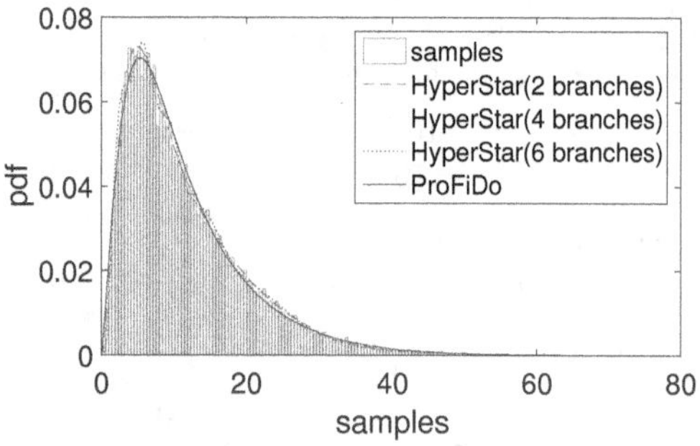

Figure 3: Probability density of the second example

Fig. 3 shows that both ProFiDo and HyperStar2 can fit the distribution very well. Although there are 2 Hyper-Erlang branches in the original MAP, HyperStar2 can still provide a good fit with 4, or 6 branches.

From Fig. 4, we can see that ProFiDo fits the correlation better than HyperStar2. But the distribution fit of HyperStar2 is still better than that of ProFiDo. We assume that HyperStar2 is less suited to capture relatively small autocorrelation, which means that clusters have a strong overlap. High autocorrelation typically shows as strongly distinct clusters and those are captured much better by HyperStar2 than less distinct clusters.

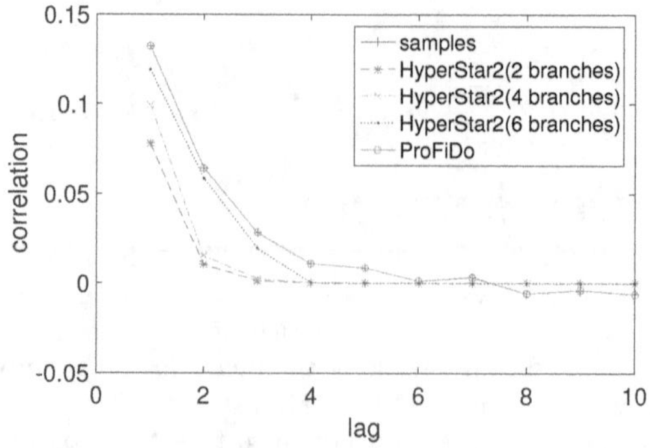

Figure 4: Correlation of the second example

6. CONCLUSION AND FUTURE WORK

In this paper we have presented HyperStar2, a fitting tool for correlated data and the algorithms behind it. We have shown that HyperStar2 can capture the shape of a distribution very well, but autocorrelation is not in all cases represented as well as done by ProFiDo. Numerical examples show that the tool can fit empirical data with MAPs very well. In the future, we will improve the accuracy of autocorrelation fitting and provide the user with metrics for the goodness-of-fit.

7. REFERENCES

[1] Philipp Reinecke, Tilman Krauß, and Katinka Wolter. Cluster-based fitting of phase-type distributions to empirical data. *Computers & Mathematics with Applications*, 64(12):3840–3851, 2012.

[2] Marcel F Neuts. Matrix-geometric solutions in stochastic models, volume 2 of johns hopkins series in the mathematical sciences, 1981.

[3] David M Lucantoni, Kathleen S Meier-Hellstern, and Marcel F Neuts. A single-server queue with server vacations and a class of non-renewal arrival processes. *Advances in Applied Probability*, pages 676–705, 1990.

[4] Alma Riska, Mark Squillante, Shun-Zheng Yu, Zhen Liu, and L Zhang. Matrix-analytic analysis of a map/ph/1 queue fitted to web server data. *Matrix-Analytic Methods; Theory and Applications*, pages 333–356, 2002.

[5] Peter Buchholz. An em-algorithm for map fitting from real traffic data. In *International Conference on Modelling Techniques and Tools for Computer Performance Evaluation*, pages 218–236. Springer, 2003.

[6] Lothar Breuer. An em algorithm for batch markovian arrival processes and its comparison to a simpler estimation procedure. *Annals of Operations Research*, 112(1-4):123–138, 2002.

[7] Peter Buchholz and Andriy Panchenko. A two-step em algorithm for map fitting. In *International Symposium on Computer and Information Sciences*, pages 217–227. Springer, 2004.

[8] Falko Bause, Peter Buchholz, and Jan Kriege. Profido-the processes fitting toolkit dortmund. In *Quantitative Evaluation of Systems (QEST), 2010 Seventh International Conference on the*, pages 87–96. IEEE, 2010.

[9] Giuliano Casale, Eddy Z Zhang, and Evgenia Smirni. Kpc-toolbox: Simple yet effective trace fitting using markovian arrival processes. In *Quantitative Evaluation of Systems, 2008. QEST'08. Fifth International Conference on*, pages 83–92. IEEE, 2008.

IRIS: Iterative and Intelligent Experiment Selection

Raoufehsadat Hashemian
University of Calgary
Calgary, AB, Canada
rhashem@ucalgary.ca

Niklas Carlsson
Linköping University
Linköping, Sweden
niklas.carlsson@liu.se

Diwakar Krishnamurthy
University of Calgary
Calgary, AB, Canada
dkrishna@ucalgary.ca

Martin Arlitt
University of Calgary
Calgary, AB, Canada
martin.arlitt@ucalgary.ca

ABSTRACT

Benchmarking is a widely-used technique to quantify the performance of software systems. However, the design and implementation of a benchmarking study can face several challenges. In particular, the time required to perform a benchmarking study can quickly spiral out of control, owing to the number of distinct variables to systematically examine. In this paper, we propose **IRIS**, an **I**te**R**ative and **I**ntelligent Experiment **S**election methodology, to maximize the information gain while minimizing the duration of the benchmarking process. IRIS selects the region to place the next experiment point based on the variability of both dependent, i.e., response, and independent variables in that region. It aims to identify a performance function that minimizes the response variable prediction error for a constant and limited experimentation budget. We evaluate IRIS for a wide selection of experimental, simulated and synthetic systems with one, two and three independent variables. Considering a limited experimentation budget, the results show IRIS is able to reduce the performance function prediction error up to 4.3 times compared to equal distance experiment point selection. Moreover, we show that the error reduction can further improve through system-specific parameter tuning. Analysis of the error distributions obtained with IRIS reveals that the technique is particularly effective in regions where the response variable is sensitive to changes in the independent variables.

Categories and Subject Descriptors

System performance [**Performance benchmarking**]: Controlled Experimentation

Keywords

Experiment selection, Benchmarking, performance function, Kriging

ICPE'17, April 22-26, 2017, L'Aquila, Italy
© 2017 ACM. ISBN 978-1-4503-4404-3/17/04...$15.00
DOI: http://dx.doi.org/10.1145/3030207.3030225

1. INTRODUCTION

Careful performance benchmarking is important to understand how computer systems will operate under different loads and configurations. Benchmark results are often used to optimize a system's configuration or to prepare a capacity plan, and must therefore be accurate. However, creating and modifying testbeds to accurately characterize applications under different configurations and workloads is often time consuming and expensive. As an example, a previous benchmarking study on interactive Web applications deployed on multicore hardware [6] required around 1,800 experiments to examine six independent variables in a full factorial setup, even with three of the variable being binary.

At a high level, careful performance benchmarking involves quantifying the performance impact that different system configurations and workload parameters, i.e., independent variables, have on various system performance metrics, i.e., response variables. To capture these relationships, i.e., the underlying performance function of the system under test, it is important to determine (i) where in the independent variable space to place experimental measurement points, and (ii) how to estimate the underlying function that relate these variables, given a set of such experimental points. Most prior work in this area have been focused on the second question, typically by comparing the accuracy of different function prediction techniques and their abilities to build statistically inferred models or interpolated functions of system performance [17] [3] [5]. In contrast, we focus on where in the independent variable space to place experimental measurement points, to achieve a desirable accuracy in a cost-effective manner.

In particular, we present **IRIS**, an **I**te**R**ative and **I**ntelligent Experiment **S**election methodology which reduces the number of experimental points needed for good performance function prediction and evaluate its effectiveness when applied to a variety of performance functions. IRIS allows us to focus on regions of greater interest more quickly and efficiently. Furthermore, in contrast to most existing experiment selection techniques, IRIS is iterative and in each step places new test points where they are expected to provide maximum information about the underlying performance relationships.]

To illustrate the value of careful, iterative point selection, consider a system in which the independent variable is the user population of a Web server and the response variable is the server's response time. A naive benchmarking approach

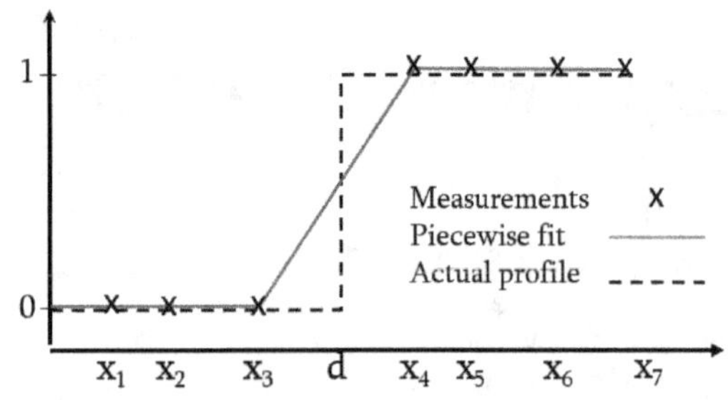

Figure 1: Sample point toy example.

would perform experiments for user population sizes evenly split over the expected range of population sizes. The problem with this approach is that the response time may be relatively constant for a wide range of (smaller) user populations, but may increase dramatically for a small range of (larger) user population sizes, for which the system utilization approaches one. The naive approach places unnecessary points in the flat region of the independent variable space, where performance function estimation is easy. A more efficient approach would instead place additional points in the region that sees the most change, and where it is more difficult to estimate performance accurately. If the approximate shape of the underlying performance function is known or can be quickly (and adaptively) learned, a more intelligent sampling strategy, based on the current knowledge and estimates of the underlying shape, can instead redistribute experimental points to the region with the bigger changes in the response variable. This can in turn allow for better tracking of the performance function and result in more accurate benchmarking. IRIS leverages this observation.

This paper makes three main contributions. First, we introduce the IRIS technique for performance benchmarking. IRIS carefully adapts the experimental sample points selection based on the current knowledge learned through existing system models and the results obtained from prior experiments. To capture the importance of these aspects, IRIS allows the user to determine the weight given to the initial point selection, e.g., based on offline system models, relative to the iterative point selection process. IRIS uses a single tuning parameter α that weights the desire to evenly cover the full independent variable space and placing particular focus on regions with larger changes in the response variable.

Second, we evaluate IRIS using several experimental, simulation based, and synthetic datasets for systems with up to three independent variables. These datasets represent a wide range of system performance functions, allowing us to provide insights into parameter tuning under different types of performance behaviours. The results show that IRIS can significantly outperform baseline approaches based on equal distance point selection. In particular, considering scenarios with limited experimentation budget, we measure up to 4.3 times error reduction for the systems with one independent variable and 2.8 times error reduction for the systems with multiple independent variables. Moreover, IRIS does not cause a significant degradation in prediction accuracy for any of the eight cases we examine.

Third, we perform an in-depth analysis of different aspects that impact the effectiveness of IRIS. In particular, we focus on the criteria behind the selection of tuning parameters, the effect of using an educated guess about the performance function for the initialization of IRIS, the individual effect of iterative versus weight based point selection, and the impact of IRIS on the prediction error distribution. Our analysis provides insights into how to best use IRIS to obtain the ideal trade-off between prediction accuracy and the number of experiments needed.

The remainder of this paper is organized as follows. Section 2 introduces IRIS and describes its behaviour under different dimensions of independent variables. Section 3 explains our evaluation process. Section 4 compares IRIS with baseline approaches for different systems. Section 5 presents results that further characterize the behaviour of IRIS. Section 6 discusses related work. Section 7 concludes the paper.

2. IRIS

2.1 Motivation

When using measurements to estimate the performance function for an underlying system, not all measurement points are of the same value. Some measurements provide little new information about the system, while other points may be very important to improve the overall accuracy of the performance function. To illustrate this point, consider the simple toy example illustrated in Figure 1. Here, the measured response variable y_j is sampled from an underlying step function $f_d(x)$, which is 1 when the independent variable x is greater than d, and 0 otherwise. Furthermore, assume that we use a piecewise linear function between the measurement points (x_j, y_j) to estimate the underlying function. In this case, the two measurement points closest to either side of the step at $x = d$ have the greatest impact on the accuracy of the model, whereas any points that are on the horizontally flat regions, i.e., between points with the same $y = f_d(x)$ value; either all $y = 0$ or all $y = 1$, provide no additional information.

Taking the above toy example one step further, let us consider the case where we have an initial set $\mathcal{S}$ of measurement points, and we want to use additional experiments to determine more precisely where the step takes place. In this case, assuming that we have at least one point on either side of the step, a sensible algorithm would be to use a binary search, in which a measurement is added at the midpoint $x' = \frac{x_a + x_b}{2}$ between the two points $x_a = \max_{j \in \mathcal{S}}(x_j | y_j = 0)$ and $x_b = \min_{j \in \mathcal{S}}(x_j | y_j = 1)$ closest to and on either side of the step. This procedure is then repeated until the maximum error $(x_b - x_a)$ of the current estimate of the x-value of the step is less than some desired maximum error or until we have reached our measurement point budget; in which case the error is minimized, given a certain point budget.

In addition to showing that not all points have the same value, this example also shows that the accuracy of the model can be significantly improved by adapting where the measurements are placed based on the current knowledge of the system. For example, a naive solution that spreads all measurement points evenly across the full measurement region would require exponentially more measurement points to achieve the same accuracy of where the step is located. To see this, note that the error of the binary search (above) reduces as $O(2^{-|\mathcal{S}|})$, whereas the maximum error when spreading all points evenly is proportional to $O(\frac{1}{|\mathcal{S}|})$.

While real systems typically have more than one point of interest and typically involve more than one independent variable, this example clearly shows that (i) there are significant advantages to selecting measurement points carefully when building a performance function of the underlying system, and (ii) there are advantages to making use of past measurements when selecting future measurement points. In the following, we describe how IRIS generalizes the approach illustrated on the above toy example to multiple independent variables (dimensions) and more general relationships between the response variable and the independent variables. Considering a limited point budget to keep the duration of the benchmarking exercise from spiraling out of control, IRIS carefully places measurement points based on the current knowledge of the system, to maximize the information gain and achieve the overall goal of providing the best possible performance function for the system. Equivalently, when the accuracy of the performance function can be explicitly evaluated, the same technique can easily be used to solve the (equivalent) problem of minimizing the number of measurements needed to achieve a given accuracy.

2.2 Methodology Overview

Our solution is simple and intuitive. It splits the point selection process into two phases. First, an *initial point selection* phase is used to obtain an initial sample point set $\mathcal{S}_i$, with $N_i = |\mathcal{S}_i|$ sample points. In the simplest case, these points are evenly spread across the independent variable space. This is possible even with very limited system knowledge. However, we can typically do better than this. For example, a user with a large number of initial measurements can leverage a queuing model or other system knowledge to carefully select points in regions of particular interest. While step functions around which a user may want to place points such as in the toy example are rare in real systems, most systems have known regions, e.g., high-utilization regions, with larger response time differences than in other regions. Later in this section, we describe how a queuing model can be used to carefully select the initial points to target some of these regions. In general, however, the initial point selection phase is only used to obtain an initial set of sample points and initialize the identification of region(s) of interest.

Second, an *iterative refinement* phase is used to identify the regions of most interest and to iteratively refine the measurement point selection. For this phase, we assume that we have $N \geq N_i$ current sample measurements and a total sample point budget N_t. During each of the remaining $(N_t - N)$ iterations, a new sample point is placed so as to greedily improve the accuracy of the performance function. More specifically, in each step, the independent variable space is divided into regions, e.g., the x-axis segments between the sample points in our toy example, and a weighted gain G_j is calculated for each region based on the variation in the response variable and the size of the region. The intuition here is that regions with bigger weighted gains are better candidates to add measurement points. At the end of each iteration, a new sample point is always added to the centroid (defined in Section 2.3) of the region with the biggest weighted gain. Section 2.3 provides the technical details on how regions are defined in multiple dimensions, and how the weighted gains are calculated for problems with different dimensionality using the current set of sample points.

2.3 Multi-dimensional Weighted Gains

To determine the region that may most benefit from an additional measurement point, we calculate a weighted gain for each region. To weight the importance of regions with large variations in the response variable y with the desire to have sufficient points in larger regions with smaller variations in the response variable, we calculate the gain factor G_j of region j as the product

$$G_j = A_j^{\alpha} \times R_j^{1-\alpha}, \tag{1}$$

where A_j is the normalized size[1] of region j, R_j is a normalized measure of the maximum observed difference in the response variable, and α ($0 \leq \alpha \leq 1$) is a parameter that weights the importance of these two factors. With smaller α values, IRIS gives higher importance to placing experiments in regions where there are likely to be larger changes in the response variable.

One independent variable: First consider cases with a single independent variable x. In this case, the size A_j of region j is equal to the difference in x-values between neighbouring measurement points and the response spread factor R_j is equal to the absolute difference in y-values between neighbouring measurement points. For example, assuming an ordered list of N measurement points for which $x_j \leq x_{j+1}$, we can now calculate the two factors as $A_j = x_{j+1} - x_j$ and $R_j = |y_{j+1} - y_j|$, for each of the $N-1$ regions. Referring back to the toy example, we note that the gain G_j of equation (1) would only be non-zero for the region that we would like to split into two regions, as long as $\alpha < 1$. This process ensures that we focus on the region of most interest.

For more general systems, there typically are multiple regions with non-zero gain. In these cases, our approach will greedily add a new point in the region with the greatest weighted gain. Since each new measurement point splits a region into multiple smaller regions, both A_j and R_j will be smaller for this region, effectively increasing the relative weight given to other regions, which may yet need to be split to reach a desired accuracy.

Two independent variables: In this case, the experiment candidates are selected from candidate regions in a two-dimensional plane. Here, each candidate region is defined as a triangle, with the corners of the triangle corresponding to close-by measurement points from the current sample set. For our triangulation, we use Delaunay triangulation [2]. Delaunay triangulations are relatively easy to calculate, guarantee a unique planar triangulation of the independent variable space, and generalize to multiple dimensions. By maximizing the minimum angle of all the angles of the triangles, Delaunay triangulations also provide triangles consisting of points with high proximity. This is important in our context, as we will select regions that will be further split.

For our gain calculation, the size factor A_j is calculated as the area of each triangle and the response difference factor R_j is calculated as the maximum absolute difference between the three corners of the triangle. For point selection, we consistently add an additional measurement point at the

[1]In the 1D case the size of a region is defined as a length, in the 2D case it is defined as an area, and in higher dimensions it is defined as a volume.

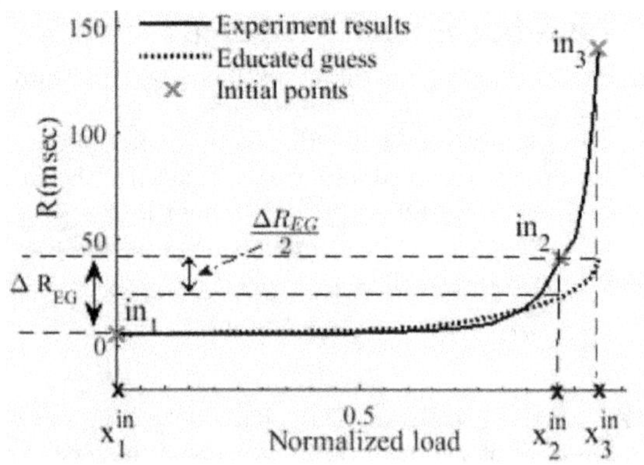

Figure 2: Initial point selection phase.

centroid of the region with the largest gain, where the centroid is used to capture the center point of each triangle.

Many independent variables: To further generalize the above Delaunay triangulation approach to the case when there are $K > 2$ independent variables to examine, we define each region as a convex hull of $K + 1$ points in the K-dimensional space. Similar to the two-dimensional case, the use of Delaunay triangulation ensures that the circum-hypersphere of any triangle does not contain any interior points. For each region, the size factor A_j is calculated as the volume of each K-dimensional triangle and the response difference factor R_j is calculated as the maximum absolute difference between any pair of the the response variables as observed at the corners of the triangle. Finally, we again define the centroid as the center point of the hypersphere and place an additional measurement point at this centroid.

2.4 Detailed Demonstration

We now demonstrate the two phases of our methodology by applying the algorithm to a simple experimental dataset, focusing on a single independent variable. The system under study is a multicore Web server. The goal is to measure the user experienced response time, i.e., the response variable, as a function of the number of concurrent users or load, i.e., the independent variable. To understand the actual system function, we have previously conducted extensive experimentation, in which we measured the response time for a large number of experiments with equally spaced load values [7]. We normalize the load to be a number between 0 and 1. In Figure 2, the curve named "Experiment Results" shows the measured response time values as a function of normalized load.

(*i*) **Initial point selection:** In this phase, an educated guess is used to determine an initial set of N_i sample points. System models can help us identify reasonable estimates of the regions of interest and provide us with initial boundaries of those regions. A simple way to come up with such an educated guess is to run experiments for boundary values and use linear interpolation. An alternative method to place the initial points would be to use performance bound analysis [9] to determine the values for the upper and lower bounds of the response variable and the corresponding values of the independent variables. A more advanced approach would be to use a queuing model or other approximate models of the system to estimate the response variable in the desired range of independent variables. Such models or educated guesses of the underlying performance function can then be used to place the N_i initial points so as to cover variations in both the independent and response variables. In general, this can be done by splitting the parameter range so that the maximum (expected) gain G_j of any of the resulting regions is minimized. For our discussion here, we will assume a single independent variable x and $\alpha = 0$ for the initial point selection. In this case, the points x_j^{in} are placed so that they split the (expected) y-range of the $N_i - 1$ intervals evenly.

Figure 2 depicts the initial point selection phase for our sample system. The plot shows the actual performance function of the system, i.e., the curve named "experiment results", the educated guess, and the initially selected points. As mentioned earlier, the system under study is a multicore web server. The educated guess is obtained from a layered queuing model [14] of the system, with model parameters determined using estimated demands of hardware, software, and network resources. Due to inaccuracy of the demand estimation process, the final model has more than 100% errors in some regions. However, the model is still useful for determining the initial points. For this example, we start with three initial points ($N_i = 3$), labeled in_1, in_2, and in_3 in the figure.

Let's look closer at the initial point selection. First, based on the educated guess (EG), the value of response variable, $R_{EG}(x)$, varies for a range of ΔR_{EG}. We divide this y-range into two equal intervals by adding a single point in the middle of the y-interval at $\frac{\Delta R_{EG}}{2}$. Given the expected points x_1^{in} and x_3^{in} with the minimum and maximum load of interest, the second initial point is selected as $x_2^{in} = R_{EG}^{-1}(R_{EG}(x_1^{in}) + \frac{\Delta R_{EG}}{2})$, where $R_{EG}(x_1^{in})$ is the expected response time for the low load case and $R_{EG}^{-1}()$ is the inverse function of $R_{EG}()$. Finally, experiments are conducted to determine the actual values of the response variables, y_j^{in}, as shown by the red crosses in Figure 2.

The best number of initial points depends on the shape of the educated guess and the properties of the system under study. In general, since the initial point selection is performed with $\alpha = 0$, the systems that benefit from a smaller value of α can benefit the most from the initial point selection phase. In Section 5.3, we present an example of how the initial point selection phase can influence the overall error reduction achieved through IRIS.

(*ii*) **Iterative point selection:** There are two input parameters for this phase of the algorithm: (i) a sample point budget (N_t), which is the maximum number of experiments we can run, and (ii) the factor α that weights the importance of independent and response variables in selecting the next point. In this section, we assume that both parameters are known prior to the start of the iterative phase.

Having selected an initial point set, an ordered list of already measured (x_j, y_j) points are available, where initially $1 \leq j \leq N_i$. With this as the base case, the algorithm then calculates the gain factor G_j, using equation (1), for all intervals. The centroid of the interval corresponding to the maximum G_j is selected as the next point to be examined. After the first iteration, the list of available points grows to $N_i + 1$ points. The iterative phase continues until the number of available points reaches the N_t limit.

We next demonstrate the point selection process for our example system considering different values of α. Figures 3(a) to 3(c) show the actual performance functions reflecting the experiment data as well as the selected points for $\alpha = 0$, $\alpha = 0.5$, and $\alpha = 1$. For ease of comparison,

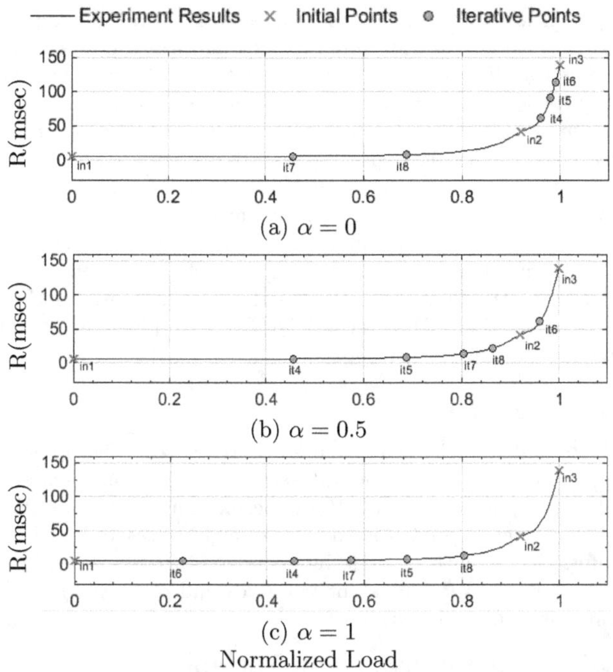

Figure 3: Iterative point selection phase.

in all cases, we have used the same $N_i = 3$ initial points shown with red crosses and a total sample point budget of $N_t = 8$ shown as green circles. In Figure 3(a), where $\alpha = 0$, the first iteratively selected point, labeled as *it*4 to indicate that it is added during the iterative phase and is the 4th selected point, is selected in the right-most interval since it has the maximum value of R_j of the different candidate intervals, and the interval with maximum R_j is always prioritized when $\alpha = 0$. After this point is added to the set, the algorithm examines three intervals in the second iteration. Again, the next point, *it*5, is selected as the centroid of the right-most interval. The iterative phase continues until the number of selected points reaches N_t.

Considering the changes in the position of selected points from Figure 3(a) for $\alpha = 0$ to 3(c) for $\alpha = 1$, we note that as the α values increases, the selected points are more spread along the x-axis. This illustrates how the α parameter can be used as a tuning knob to put more or less emphasis on the regions with higher changes on the response variables. For example, with $\alpha = 1$ the interval with the largest x-range difference (A_j) is always split, and with $\alpha = 0$ the interval with the largest y-range difference (R_j) is always split.

3. EVALUATION METHODOLOGY

For the purpose of evaluation, we have applied IRIS to several systems with different characteristics. This section provides details of the general evaluation process. In particular, we outline a common baseline protocol against which we compare our technique, describe the input parameters, and explain evaluation metrics and the techniques we used to estimate the performance function.

3.1 Equal Distance Point Selection

A common way of selecting the values of independent variables to perform benchmarking studies is through *equal distance* (EQD) point selection. With this approach, the possible range of each independent variable is divided into $N-1$ equally sized intervals. Assuming D dimensions, each dimension d ($1 \leq d \leq D$) divided into $N_d - 1$ intervals, this approach results in $\prod_{j=1}^{D} N_j$ evenly spread experiment points.

A major drawback of EQD is the cost of adding additional points to achieve a desirable accuracy. As a simple example, consider a system with a single independent variable, where the initial estimate of the required number of points is five. Now assume that after running the experiments for five equally distanced points and applying a function estimation technique, the accuracy of the estimated function is not desirable. If there is additional budget available for adding more experiment points, and one wants to spend the additional points through the EQD approach, there are two ways to proceed. First, one can replace the three middle points with four new points that are equally spaced. Second, one can add a single point in the middle of each interval. In both cases, four new experiment points are required to increase the accuracy of the predicted function while still maintaining the equal distance property. Therefore, one requires nine points for identifying the performance function at this stage. These examples describe cases where the available point budget is spent in multiple rounds of EQD. We refer to this approach as *multi-stage* EQD.

We also consider a penalty-free version in which any previously performed measurements not used, as in the first of the above approaches, are ignored. This corresponds to the optimistic case when we always guess the correct number of sample points to use from the start and place all the point budget in a single round of EQD. We refer to this optimistic approach as *single-stage* EQD.

In our case studies, we compare both *multi-stage* EQD and *single-stage* EQD with IRIS, emphasizing that *single-stage* EQD is optimistic in most cases. For the systems with a single variable, the number of equally distanced points is set to N_t. For the cases with more than one independent variable, we consider all combinations of number of intervals in different directions that lead to a total of N_t points.

3.2 IRIS Parameters

As described in Section 2.4, there are four main input parameters for IRIS: (i) an educated guess of the expected performance function, (ii) the number of initial points N_i, (iii) the weight tuning gain parameter α, and (iv) the total sample point budget N_t. In the case studies presented in Section 4, we keep the first three inputs constant to facilitate a direct comparison. For the evaluation, we typically assume minimum knowledge about the system and try to minimize the effect of the initial point selection. In particular, we assume that the educated guess is simply a linear relationship between the independent and response variables and use $N_i = 3^D$, where D is the number of dimensions. Hence, for the single dimensional case we have $N_i = 3$. Section 4 considers the performance using default settings, before Section 5 evaluates the effect of tuning these parameters on the final results. For each case study, we explore a range of N_t values. The minimum of this range depends on the dimensionality of the system. The maximum is determined as the point budget beyond which there is no significant improvement in the prediction errors from the performance functions estimated by all the techniques.

For each case study, five values of α $(0, 0.25, 0.5, 0.75$, and $\alpha = 1-\epsilon)$ are examined for a wide range of N_t values. Recall that $\alpha = 0$ leads the algorithm to only consider the change in the response variable R_j. Conversely, $\alpha = 1$ considers the other extreme and only considers the area A_j of each region in the gain calculations. Selecting $\alpha = 1 - \epsilon$ ensures that in case IRIS encounters equal areas, it selects the region with maximum variability in the response variable R_j.[2]

3.3 Evaluation Metrics

All methods are compared based on their relative accuracy for fixed numbers of point budgets. To calculate the accuracy metric we use the following three steps for each dataset and algorithm considered.

1. Run the algorithm: The output of this step is the set of selected points. Each point is a set of values for the independent variables and the corresponding response variable obtained from the experiment dataset.

2. Estimate the performance function: The set of points selected in the previous step is fed to a function estimation technique to estimate the performance function. The prediction for each point x_j obtained from this function is referred to as $R_{PRD}(x_j)$. The function estimation techniques we consider are explained in Section 3.4.

3. Calculate the Average Absolute Error (AAE): At this step, the values predicted by the performance function are compared with their corresponding experimentally measured values for all the available points in the experiment dataset. The AAE is calculated as follows:

$$AAE = \frac{\sum_{j=1}^{n} |R_{PRD}(x_j) - R(x_j)|}{\sum_{j=1}^{n} R(x_j)} \cdot 100, \qquad (2)$$

   where n is the number of input points in the experiment dataset. For our evaluation, we consider constrained experiment budgets; i.e., $N_t << n$.

For head-to-head comparisons, we repeat the same process with the two EQD point selection approaches in step 1. For each dataset, the process is repeated for a range of point budgets (N_t). Finally, to quantify the effectiveness of IRIS compared to the EQD baselines, we define the *Error Reduction* (ER) ratio as:

$$ER = \frac{(\overline{AAE}_{baseline} - \overline{AAE}_{IRIS})}{\overline{AAE}_{IRIS}}, \qquad (3)$$

where the $\overline{AAE}$ is the average of all AAE values measured for setups with different point budgets (N_t). To calculate $\overline{AAE}$, we only consider N_t's that are common between the IRIS and baseline methods.[3] Note that the baseline method can be any of the two EQD approaches.

3.4 Function Estimation Techniques

In this study, we used two function estimation techniques, namely, the commonly used *Cubic Spline* interpolation technique for one-dimensional systems and *Kriging* for multi-dimensional systems. The Cubic Splines method can also be applied for multi-dimensional systems. However, it requires a grid of points in all dimensions to perform the interpolation. Recall that IRIS is based on scattered and iterative point selection. Therefore, we select the *Kriging* [4] technique as it is better equipped to handle scattered point selection in multi-dimensional scenarios. Previous studies [17] have also confirmed the applicability of Kriging for estimating performance functions. Kriging has several variants such as simple Kriging, ordinary Kriging and universal Kriging. We select the ordinary Kriging approach as it requires no initial information about the trend of the estimated performance function. We use the UQLab [15] implementation of Kriging for MATLAB.

[2]We use $\epsilon = 0.001$ for all the datasets.

[3]Due to the stepwise nature of *multi-stage* EQD approach, only a subset of point budget values are possible with this approach.

4. RESULTS

To evaluate the effectiveness of IRIS, we perform several case studies based on datasets collected through experiments, simulations, or synthetic performance functions. We evaluate the approach for a total of eight datasets based on four systems with a single independent variable, three systems with two independent variables and one system with three independent variables.

4.1 Single Independent Variable

We consider four systems with vastly different shapes of the underlying performance functions. Each dataset consists of a family of performance functions with similar high-level characteristics but different properties, e.g., different sizes of the flat regions. This allows us to determine the relationship between the tuning parameters, in particular α, and the properties of the performance function, as we will elaborate later in Section 5.1. The plots in Figure 4 show the normalized response variable (y) as a function of the normalized independent variable (x) for all four families of performance functions considered. Note that both the independent and response variables are normalized by rescaling to the range of $[0, 1]$.

The performance functions of the first dataset, shown in Figure 4(a), are the results of a simulation study of a closed system with two resources and two user classes. The independent variable (x-axis) is the service time for resource one while the response variable (y-axis) is the response time of the class that poses the largest service demand on that resource. Each curve $C1$, $C2$ and $C3$ in Figure 4(a) are the results of simulations for various combinations of populations for the two classes. Further discussions about the analysis of the system's behavior can be found in Chapter 7 of the textbook by Lazowska *et al.* [9]. These *s-shaped* curves represent cases where the response variable is initially constant then has a sharp increment before entering a saturation mode.

The second dataset, shown in Figure 4(b), is collected from the experimental system described in Section 2.4. Here, a large number of concurrent web requests are served using a multicore server, and the primary performance trade-off of interest is the impact that the normalized load, i.e., normalized number of concurrent users per core, has on the mean response time. We refer to this system as the *load-response time* dataset. The curves, $C1$, $C2$ and $C3$ show the actual experimental results for this system with two, four and eight processor cores, respectively. The three curves differ in terms of the extent of the flat region as well as the rate at which the response time increases with load. The main characteristics of this system is that the response variable

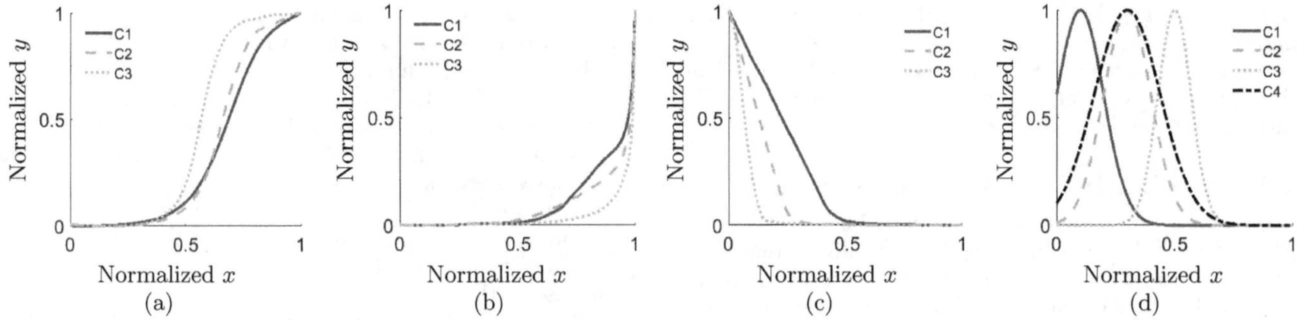

Figure 4: 1D systems: (a) S-shaped, (b) Load-response time, (c) Hockey stick, and (d) Bell-shaped.

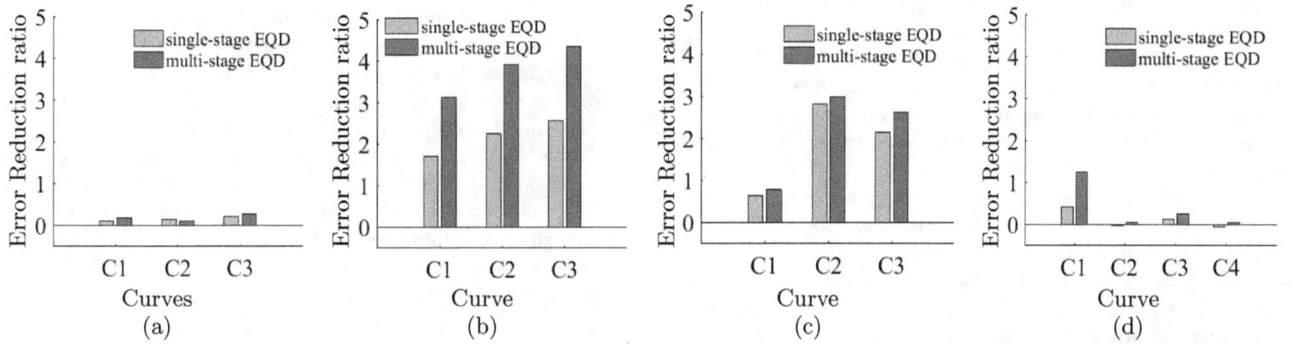

Figure 5: ER ratios for 1D systems: (a) S-shaped, (b) Load-response time, (c) Hockey stick, and (d) Bell-shaped.

increases sharply for a small range of the independent variable.

Third, we consider a group of performance functions generated by simulating a closed queuing model with three resources. The goal of this simulation is to identify the impact of user think time on the average response time. The results of this study are depicted in Figure 4(c). We refer to this family of curves as *hockey stick* as they have a section with constant slope as well as a flat region. The combinations of the resource demand values used in the simulation results in three curves that are different in terms of the extent of the flat region. Similar to the load-response time system, this dataset contains a region where the response variable does not change significantly with the independent variable. However, in contrast to the load-response time system, the increase in the response variable is only gradual in the hockey stick dataset.

The last dataset, shown in Figure 4(d), includes a group of *bell-shaped* synthetic functions representing normal distributions. We change the mean and standard deviation to vary the position of the maximum response and the width of the bell in the four curves. Compared to the previous datasets, the bell shapes display both an increase and decrease in the response variable over the range of the independent variable.

Figures 5(a) to 5(d) show the Error Reduction (ER) ratio for IRIS compared to the two EQD baselines. We again note that the *single-stage* EQD is highly optimistic in most cases, is not always feasible, but provides the most competitive baseline comparison in one dimensional cases. A negative ER value implies that IRIS causes a larger AAE compared to the baseline method. The ER ratios in Figure 5 are calculated for $\alpha = 0.5$. We will discuss the effect of other values of α in Section 5.1.

Figure 5 reveals that IRIS leads to a positive ER ratio for a vast majority of cases. Figure 5(a) for the s-shaped dataset suggests that our approach led to a maximum of $ER = 0.3$, which is equivalent to a 30% error reduction. The maximum ER value is measured for the curve with the steepest slope and the largest flat region. IRIS yields dramatic gains for the load-response time dataset. As shown in Figure 5(b), IRIS leads to an ER of 4.3 and 2.3 compared to *multi-stage* and *single-stage EQDs*, respectively. The results also reveal that the ER ratio increases as we move from $C1$ with the smallest flat region to $C3$ with the largest flat region. A similar trend is observable for the hockey stick dataset, as shown in Figure 5(c). For this system, the ER ratios are slightly less than the load-response time dataset. Finally, the results for the bell-shaped curves, as depicted in Figure 5(c), reveal a few cases where IRIS with $\alpha = 0.5$ sees slightly worse performance than *single-stage* EQD, i.e., negative ER values. However, in general, IRIS improves the accuracy for the bell-shaped curves as well. In particular, for C1 it reduces errors by as much 130%. It should also be noted that IRIS allows incremental point selection, allowing the technique to be used iteratively until meeting a desired accuracy or stopping criteria. In contrast, single-stage EQD is optimistic in that it always "guesses" the correct number of sample points.

Overall, these results show that IRIS can result in up to 2.3 times improvement in terms of AAE, compared to the *single-stage* EQD. The improvements are even higher relative to *multi-stage* EQD. Moreover, the maximum achievable improvement depends on the shape of the system's actual performance function. Selecting the value of α based on the expected system behaviour can further increase the ER ratio, as we will discuss in Section 5.1.

4.2 Multiple Independent Variables

In this section we consider datasets with multiple independent variables. The first three datasets are systems with two independent variables while the last one is a simulation system with three independent variables. Figure 6 shows the systems with two independent variables. Similar to the single variable systems, each dataset consists of surfaces with similar high-level characteristics that differ in specific properties such as the area of the flat surface or the slope.

The system functions of the first dataset, shown in Figure 6(a), are the results of a simulation study of a closed system with two resources and two user classes [9]. The first and second independent variables (x_1 and x_2) are the service times for resource one and two, respectively. The response variable (y) is the response time of the class that poses the large service demand on resource two. Each surface represents the results of the simulation for a combination of populations for the two classes. The focus of our analysis is on the s-shaped surfaces of the response variable that is almost constant with respect to x_1 and is initially constant then has a sharp increment and then enters a saturation mode with respect to x_2.

The second dataset, depicted in Figure 6(b), is a load-response time dataset with two load parameters as independent variables. In this case the system functions are collected from simulating an open queuing model with an m server resource and two user classes. The request arrival rate for each user class is considered as an independent variable and the average response time over all classes of users as the response variable. The surfaces $S1$ to $S3$ are the results of running the simulation for $m = 1$, $m = 2$ and $m = 4$.

The last dataset, shown in Figure 6(c), represents a group of three synthetic Gaussian surfaces with different means and standard deviations. Similar to the single variable bell-shaped system, this dataset is selected to examine surfaces with a maximum point in the middle of the range of independent variables. $S1$ and $S2$ have similar maximum points but differ in terms of the radius of the bell. $S3$ has a similar radius with $S2$ but a different position for the maximum point.

Figures 7(a) to 7(c) show the ER ratios calculated for the systems with multiple independent variables. Note that IRIS provides a positive ER ratio when applied to all three systems. The maximum ER ratio was measured for the s-shaped dataset, as shown in Figure 7(a). From Figure 7(b), the ER ratios for the load-response time dataset are between 0.5-0.7 (50%-70%) and 0.3-0.4 (30%-40%) relative to *multi-stage* EQD and *single-stage* EQD, respectively. While the ratios are all positive, they are lower compared to the s-shaped dataset. This can be explained by the large size of the flat region in this dataset. In Section 5.4, we will discuss a better criteria to evaluate the effect of applying IRIS for datasets with large flat regions. Finally, applying IRIS results in considerable error reductions for the bell-shaped surfaces, as depicted in Figure 7(c). Comparing the results for $S1$ and $S2$, the ER ratio is larger for the wider surface $S1$. It is also larger for the symmetric curves $S1$ and $S2$ compared to $S3$. We explore the relationship between properties of the bell-shaped surfaces and the effectiveness of IRIS in more detail in Section 5.1.

Next, we apply IRIS to a dataset with 3 independent variables. This dataset is obtained from the results of a simulation study of a closed system with two resources and two user classes presented in Chapter 7 of the textbook by Lazowska *et al.* [9]. The example illustrates a case where the combination of service demand values for the two classes on the two resources results in the response time of class one to increase as the service time for resource two decreases. We used this remarkable behaviour to create a surface with a hump-shaped maximum point in the middle of the parameter plane. The service time of resource two and the ratio of class populations for the two classes are selected as the first and second independent variables. We extend the parameter space to the third dimension by running the simulation for a range of user populations. The final system is different from the previous systems in that it simultaneously displays bell-shaped, s-shaped and the load-response behaviours.

Table 1 shows the ER ratios for various values of α when compared with *multi-stage* and *single-stage* EQD baselines. The results show that except for the $\alpha = 0$ case and relative to the highly infeasible *single-stage* EQD case, all the ER ratios are positive and vary between $0.21 < ER < 2.79$. The largest error reduction was achieved with $\alpha = 1 - \epsilon$.

Table 1: ER ratios for 3D system.

α	*multi-stage* EQD	*single-stage* EQD
0	0.21	-0.28
0.25	1.75	0.63
0.5	1.99	0.77
0.75	2.76	1.22
$1-\epsilon$	2.79	1.24

5. DISCUSSION

This section provides additional experiments to illustrate various properties of IRIS. We first investigate the best choice of the tuning parameter α based on the expected shape of the system's actual performance function. Second, we isolate the effect of the iterative point selection to further understand this component's contribution to the improvements seen with IRIS. Third, we show how a partially accurate educated guess about the system under study can improve the ER ratio. Finally, we perform an in-depth analysis of the error distribution to identify the regions of the independent variable space that benefit the most from applying IRIS.

5.1 Tuning the Gain Parameter

The results presented in Section 4 show that IRIS is able to reduce the AAE for a vast majority of system functions with $\alpha = 0.5$. We now investigate how the initial knowledge about shape of the system function can be used to select an even better α. To quantify the effect of α on the AAE, we apply IRIS to the one-dimensional and two-dimensional datasets for a range of gain parameter α values, $0 < \alpha < 1$.

In general, we find that α should be small when the underlying function has a convex knee, e.g., the load-response time

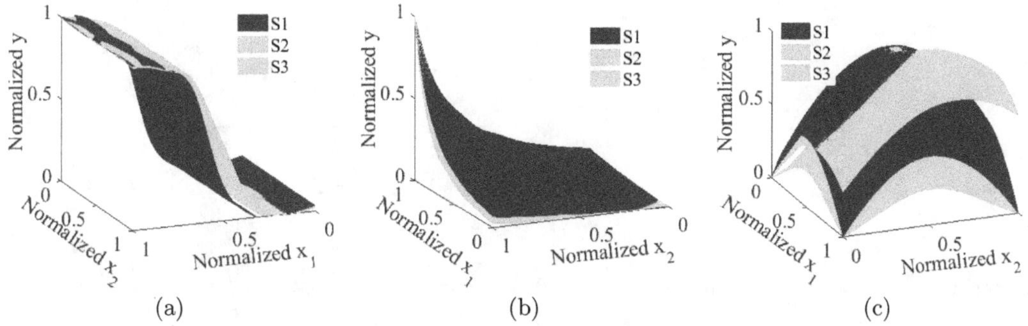

Figure 6: 2D systems: (a) S-shaped, (b) Load-response time, and (c) Bell-shaped.

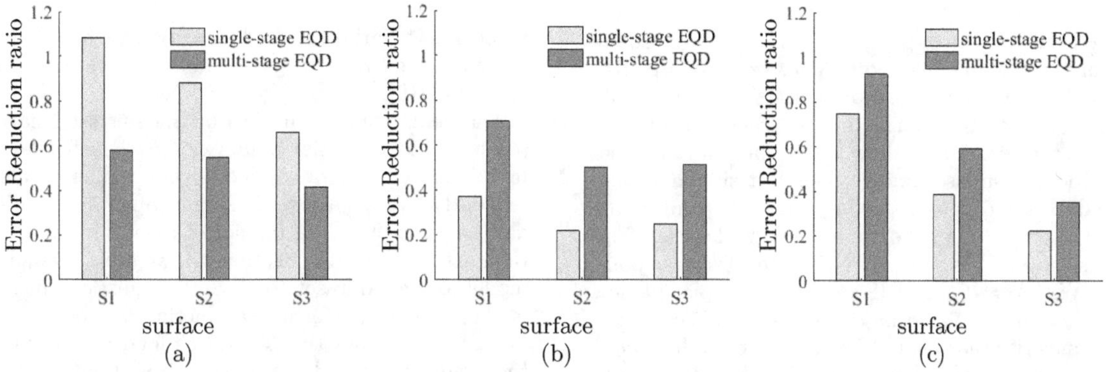

Figure 7: ER ratios for 2D systems: (a) S-shaped, (b) Load-response time, and (c) Bell-shaped.

or hockey stick systems, and should be larger in the rarer cases when the system has a symmetric maximum point, e.g., the bell-shaped systems. The results for one example of each type are illustrated in Figures 8 and Figures 9 for the one-dimensional and two-dimensional systems, respectively.

Figure 8(a) shows the AAE as a function of the α parameter for the load response time dataset. Here, larger values of α, say above 0.6, result in a larger AAE. This behaviour is expected, considering the shape of the three curves in this dataset, and confirms our intuition that greater weight should be given to the region with large changes in the response time (i.e., the R_j term in equation 1). Using a large α value for this dataset is sub-optimal since it places too many points in the flat low-load region. Instead, using smaller α values appears desirable as this allows more points to be placed closer to the region of most interest.

In contrast, from Figure 8(b), for the bell-shaped dataset the optimal α depends on the position of the maximum point as well as the size of the flat region. More specifically, for curves $C2$ and $C4$ with a more symmetric shape and smaller flat regions, the higher values of α result in lower errors. In contrast, for $C1$ and $C3$ with the larger flat region, setting $\alpha < 0.8$ can minimize the AAE. The difference between the two systems shows the value of careful selection of the α parameter. For systems where the existing system knowledge suggests that there is a convex sharp knee we may want to pick a smaller α, and in the rarer cases in which the system knowledge suggests a concave and symmetric maximum point we may want to select a larger α.

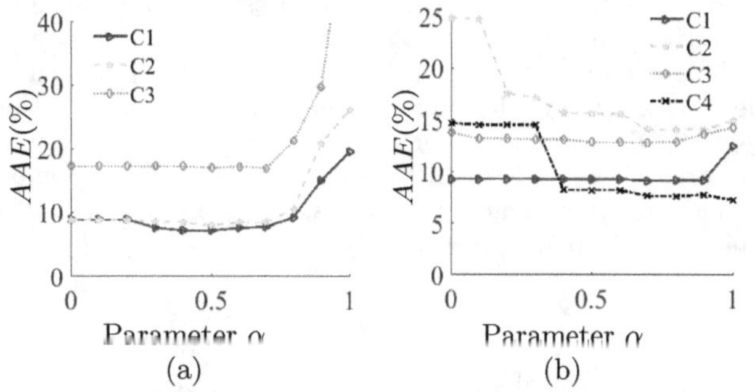

Figure 8: Effect of α on AAE for 1D systems: (a) Load-response time, and (b) Bell-shaped.

The two-dimensional results shown in Figures 9(a) and 9(b) confirm that these observations extend to multiple dimensions. For the load response time dataset, the surfaces have a large flat region that can suffer from setting α to lower values. Therefore, as shown in Figure 9(a), an intermediate α (say $\alpha = 0.5$) is best in this case. For the three bell-shaped surfaces without flat regions, the optimal setting is $\alpha = 1$.

5.2 Effect of Iterative Point Selection

As mentioned in Section 2, IRIS aims to improve prediction accuracy by applying two main modifications compared to EQD point selection: (i) selecting the points iteratively, and (ii) selecting the position of the next point based on

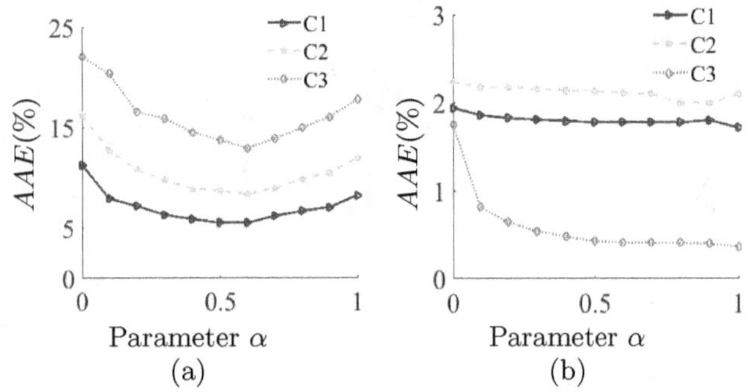

Figure 9: Effect of α on AAE for 2D systems: (a) Load-response time, and (b) Bell-shaped.

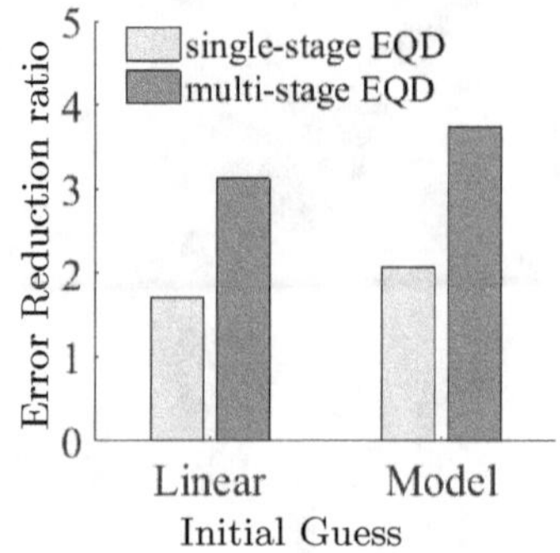

Figure 11: Linear guess vs. model based guess.

the observed changes in the response variable. To isolate the effect of the first modification alone, we evaluate IRIS with $\alpha = 1 - \epsilon$, in which case points are spread as evenly as possible ignoring the changes in the response variable. Due to space constraints, we show results only for the one-dimensional load-response time systems but similar results are observed for the other systems as well. We calculate the average AAE across all of the curves in this dataset. Figure 10 shows the AAE as a function of the total sample point budget N_t. With $\alpha = 1 - \epsilon$, IRIS would always place a new point at the midpoint of the largest current interval. It is therefore no surprise that the IRIS result matches the *single-stage* EQD results for the cases when N_t = 5, 9,and 17. In all these cases the distances between the points selected by IRIS should be equal. For the other N_t cases, IRIS leads to significantly lower AAE compared to both *multi-stage* and *single-stage* EQD. This emphasizes the importance of iterative point selection.

The results also confirm that IRIS can achieve a desired level of accuracy with a smaller point budget compared to both EQD baselines. For instance, considering a desired accuracy level of 40%, IRIS needs to spend $N_t = 6$ points, while the *single-stage* and *multi-stage* EQD need $N_t = 9$ and $N_t = 19$ points, respectively.

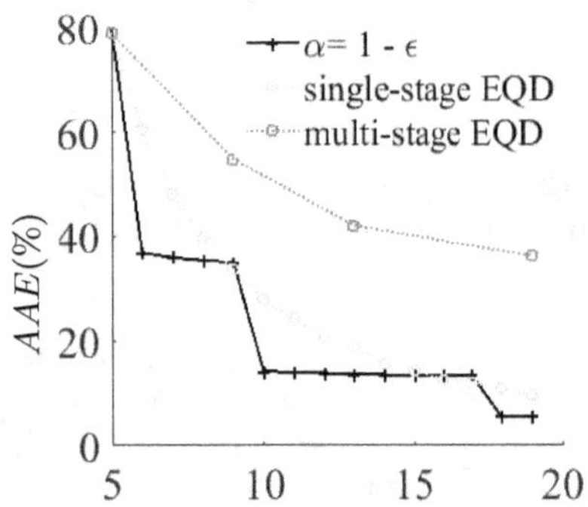

Figure 10: Effect of iterative point selection.

5.3 Effect of Initial Point Selection

In the results presented in Section 4, we tried to minimize the effect of the initial point selection by assuming that there is limited knowledge about the system under study. Specifically, we assume linear relationships between response and independent variables. In this section we show the effect of using a more educated guess about the system in the initial phase of IRIS.

The demonstration in Section 2.4 suggests that a careful selection of the initial points can be beneficial for system functions that generally benefit from smaller α values. Consequently, we consider the single dimension load-response dataset to explore the impact of careful initial point selection. As mentioned in Section 2.4, we use a layered queueing model for this dataset to obtain a realistic, educated guess of the system's performance function.

Figure 11 shows the ER ratios for the linear guess, i.e., the results presented in Section 4.1, and our educated guess based on the model. For example, considering *single-stage* EQD, selecting the initial points based on the model's educated guess can increase the ER ratio by around 17% over a linear initial guess. Similar results are obtained for other curves in this dataset as well as all surfaces of the load-response time dataset with two independent variables.

5.4 Error Distributions

In Section 4, we compared IRIS against the two baseline algorithms considering the differences between their "average" prediction errors (AAE). The results reveal that while applying IRIS can lead to a significant error reduction in most cases, the ER ratio improvements are more moderate for a subset of datasets. For instance, applying IRIS to the load-response time dataset with two dimensions results in relatively modest ER ratios between 0.3 to 0.7, depending on the surface. This may seem counter-intuitive given the sharp and convex knee point in the surfaces of this dataset. Our hypothesis is that for this case the AAE metric is biased towards the prediction errors for the large flat regions of the surfaces since the metric gives the same weight to all points in the two dimensional plane. Therfore, it does not capture the fact that the knee point may be of greater interest to practitioners, where IRIS can significantly outperform the EQD techniques. We confirm this hypothesis by analyzing the distribution of prediction errors throughout the two-dimensional space.

Figures 12(a), 12(b), and 12(c), show the colour map of error values when predicting surface $S3$ of the load-response time dataset for IRIS with $\alpha = 0.5$, *single-stage* EQD, and *multi-stage* EQD, respectively. The contour lines in the graphs show the values of the response variable in that surface. The figures show that with IRIS the error values for a large area of the independent variable space, corresponding

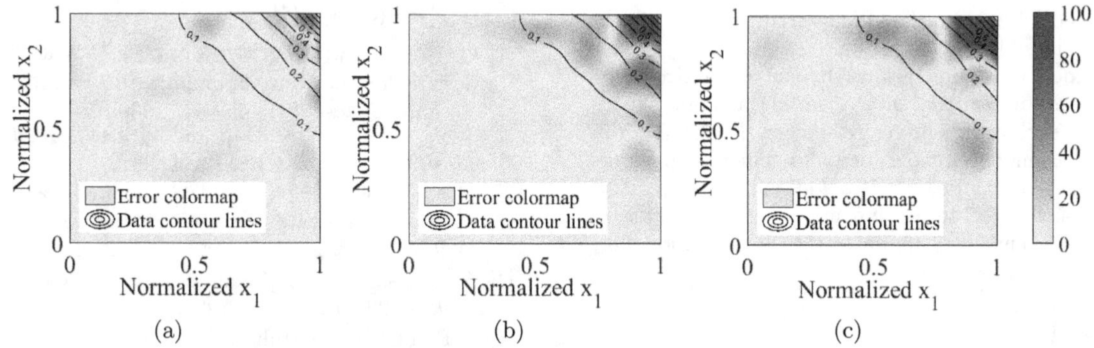

Figure 12: Color map of errors: (a) IRIS with $\alpha = 0.5$, (b) *single-stage* EQD and (c) *multi-stage* EQD.

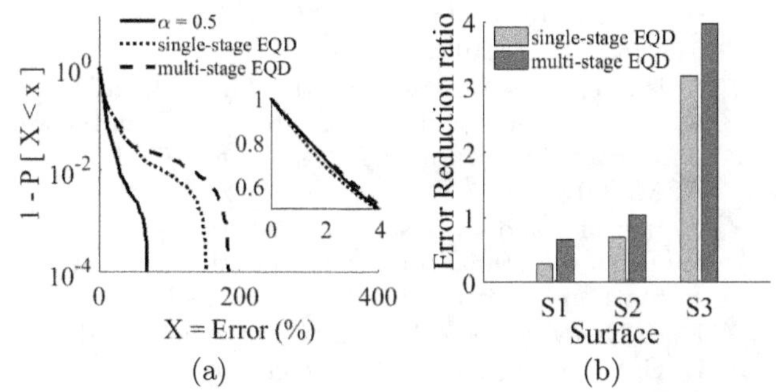

Figure 13: (a) ccdf of errors and (b) ER ratios for $0.1 < R < 0.4$.

to $0 < R < 0.1$, are somewhat higher compared to the *single-stage* EQD as indicated by the larger dark areas. However, the error values for a smaller area of the space, corresponding to $0.1 < R < 1$, are significantly lower compared to the *single-stage* EQD. A similar trend is observed for *multi-stage* EQD. Recall that for $S3$ IRIS achieves ER ratios of 0.4 and 0.2, over the *multi-stage* EQD and *single-stage* EQD, respectively. This implies that despite the slightly higher error values in the large flat area IRIS still improves the average errors by up to 40%.

These observations are further quantified by illustrating the complementary cumulative distribution function (ccdf) of errors as depicted in Figure 13(a). The main plot in this figure indicates that the baselines have significantly heavier tails than IRIS. Considering $1-P[X<x] < 10^{-1}$, errors are three to four times higher for the two baselines. In contrast, a closer look at the small, zoomed plot reveals that up to the 50th percentile of error, i.e., smaller error values in the flat region, the error values are slightly higher for IRIS compared to the two baselines.

These results reveal that IRIS is more successful in reducing prediction errors for the area of the knee point where the response time increases sharply for a small change in the load. In most scenarios practitioners are interested in the behaviour of the underlying system for this particular range of the response variable. We now calculate the effectiveness of IRIS when predicting the system function in this region of interest. Figure 13(b) shows the ER ratios for the three surfaces while only considering $0.1 < R < 0.4$ as the desirable range of response times. For this region, the ER ratio for IRIS is up to 6 times higher comparing the ER ratios in Figures 13(b) and 7(b) for the full region. This again demonstrate the high accuracy of IRIS in the regions often of most interest.

6. RELATED WORK

Experiment design techniques focus on identifying the independent variables that most influence the response variable [1, 12]. Typically, an initial set of experiments is conducted and used to estimate a regression model that relates the response variable to individual independent variables, as well as to interactions between the independent variables. Insights from the model are then used to eliminate independent variables that do not significantly influence the response variable from subsequent experiments. IRIS complements experiment design techniques. In particular, given the identified independent variables of interest, IRIS can help with the placement of experiment points.

Response Surface Methodology (RSM) [11, 10] is a technique to identify the independent variable settings at which the response variable attains the optimum, i.e., minimum or maximum, value. An experiment design phase is first carried out to establish an initial model of the response variable as a function of the independent variables. This model is then used to approximately determine the region that contains the optimal response. Next, more experiments are conducted in this region, aiming to refine the initial model. Finally, the refined model is used to estimate the independent variable settings that cause the optimal response. Jamshidi *et al.* [8] also propose a technique similar to RSM to identify optimum configuration settings for applications. In contrast to IRIS, RSM-based techniques are focus on a particular region and are not designed for identifying a performance function that spans the entire independent variable space.

Similar to IRIS, Reussner *et al.* [13] propose an experimentation technique that seeks to continually improve performance prediction accuracy for a suite of Message Passing Interface (MPI) benchmarks. Their technique iteratively estimates regions where the performance function has the highest errors and conducts additional experiments in those regions to reduce these errors. In contrast to IRIS, this technique focuses only on MPI benchmarking. Furthermore, unlike IRIS, it can only consider one independent variable at a time when refining the performance function.

Courtois and Woodside [3] and Westermann *et al.* [16] propose similar iterative experiment selection techniques for building a regression model based performance function. While these techniques can consider more than one independent variable at a time, they require multiple experiment points to be placed in each iteration so as to quantify the errors of the model in various regions. In contrast, IRIS carries out experiments more sparingly by adding a single experiment point in each iteration. As we show in Section 5.2, this can facilitate using fewer experiments to achieve a given degree of accuracy. Furthermore, IRIS does not rely on a model but instead uses actual measurements to drive its point selection. Consequently, it eliminates the effect of modelling errors on the point selection.

7. CONCLUSIONS

This paper presents an iterative and intelligent experimentation technique called IRIS. The main objective of IRIS is to obtain the best possible insights on a system's performance for a given experimentation budget. Given an initial experimentation plan based on an educated guess, IRIS iteratively and intelligently adds further experiments in regions of the independent variable space where the independent variables have the most effect on the response variable. IRIS exposes a single tunable gain parameter α that allows an experimenter to trade off the desire to evenly cover the independent variable space and placing particular focus on regions with larger changes in the response variable.

Extensive experiments involving systems with single and multiple dimensions show that IRIS significantly outperforms baseline techniques that rely on equal distance point selection for a vast majority of cases. Moreover, there was no significant degradation in accuracy for other cases. For a given experimentation budget, performance functions estimated based on experiments suggested by IRIS can yield average prediction errors for the response variable that are lower by up to a factor of 4.3. Furthermore, due to the iterative nature of IRIS, fewer experiments are needed to achieve a desired level of response variable prediction accuracy. IRIS parameterized with lower values of α, e.g., $\alpha = 0.5$, are particularly effective in improving system performance predictions in regions that practitioners typically find interesting, e.g., the "knee" regions where response times can change considerably. The gains from IRIS when considering only such regions is up to 6 times more than that when considering all regions.

A sensitivity analysis of α settings shows that in general α should be small when the underlying system performance function has a convex knee and should be larger in the rarer cases when the system has a symmetric maximum point. Our analysis also shows that gains from IRIS can increase even more if the initial educated guess leverages domain knowledge or approximate performance models of the system under study. We note that IRIS takes negligible time to make its point selection decisions.

Future work will focus on applying IRIS to systems with higher dimensionality. We will also focus on leveraging our insights regarding the relationship between α and the system performance function to dynamically optimize the value of α during experimentation. Finally, we will also explore further the impact of the initial guess on prediction accuracy.

8. REFERENCES

[1] G. E. Box and D. W. Behnken. Some new three level designs for the study of quantitative variables. *Technometrics*, 2(4):455–475, 1960.

[2] S.-W. Cheng, T. K. Dey, and J. Shewchuk. *Delaunay Mesh Generation*. CRC Press, 2012.

[3] M. Courtois and M. Woodside. Using regression splines for software performance analysis. In *Proc. of WOSP '00*, pages 105–114. ACM, 2000.

[4] N. Cressie. The origins of kriging. *Mathematical geology*, 22(3):239–252, 1990.

[5] J. H. Friedman. Multivariate adaptive regression splines. *The Annals of Statistics*, pages 1–67, 1991.

[6] R. Hashemian, D. Krishnamurthy, and M. Arlitt. Overcoming web server benchmarking challenges in the multi-core era. In *Proc. of ICST '12*, pages 648–653. IEEE, 2012.

[7] R. Hashemian, D. Krishnamurthy, M. Arlitt, and N. Carlsson. Improving the scalability of a multi-core web server. In *Proc. of ICPE '13*, pages 161–172. ACM, 2013.

[8] P. Jamshidi and G. Casale. An uncertainty-aware approach to optimal configuration of stream processing systems. *arXiv preprint arXiv:1606.06543*, 2016.

[9] E. D. Lazowska, J. Zahorjan, G. S. Graham, and K. C. Sevcik. *Quantitative System Performance: Computer System Analysis Using Queueing Network Models*. Prentice-Hall, Inc., 1984.

[10] K. Molka and G. Casale. Experiments or simulation? a characterization of evaluation methods for in-memory databases. In *Proc. of CNSM '15*, pages 201–209. IEEE, 2015.

[11] R. H. Myers, D. C. Montgomery, and C. M. Anderson-Cook. *Response Surface Methodology: Process and Product Optimization using Designed Experiments*, volume 705. John Wiley & Sons, 2009.

[12] R. L. Plackett and J. P. Burman. The design of optimum multifactorial experiments. *Biometrika*, pages 305–325, 1946.

[13] R. Reussner, P. Sanders, L. Prechelt, and M. Müller. SKaMPI: A detailed, accurate MPI benchmark. In *Recent Advances in Parallel Virtual Machine and Message Passing Interface*, pages 52–59. Springer, 1998.

[14] J. A. Rolia and K. C. Sevcik. The method of layers. *IEEE Transactions on Software Engineering*, 21(8):689–700, 1995.

[15] Uqlab: The framework for uncertainty quantification. http://www.uqlab.com/.

[16] D. Westermann, J. Happe, R. Krebs, and R. Farahbod. Automated inference of goal-oriented performance prediction functions. In *Proc. of ASE '12*, pages 190–199. ACM/IEEE, 2012.

[17] D. Westermann, R. Krebs, and J. Happe. Efficient experiment selection in automated software performance evaluations. In *Computer Performance Engineering*, pages 325–339. Springer, 2011.

Autopilot: Enabling easy Benchmarking of Workload Energy Efficiency (Demo Paper)

Jóakim v. Kistowski
University of Würzburg
joakim.kistowski@uni-wuerzburg.de

Maximilian Deffner
University of Würzburg
maximilian.deffner@stud-mail.uni-wuerzburg.de

Jeremy A. Arnold
IBM Corporation
arnoldje@us.ibm.com

Klaus-Dieter Lange
Hewlett-Packard Enterprise
klaus.lange@hpe.com

John Beckett
Dell Inc.
john_beckett@dell.com

Samuel Kounev
University of Würzburg
samuel.kounev@uni-wuerzburg.de

ABSTRACT

Benchmarking of energy efficiency is important as it helps researchers, customers, and developers to evaluate and compare the energy efficiency of software and hardware solutions. Developing and deploying energy-efficiency benchmarking workloads are challenging tasks, as work must be able to be executed in a power measurement environment using an energy-efficiency measurement methodology. The existing SPEC Chauffeur Worklet Development Kit (WDK) enables the development and use of custom workloads (called worklets) within a standardized power measurement methodology. However, it features no integration in development environments, making building and deployment of workloads challenging. We address this challenge by proposing Autopilot, a plugin for the Eclipse IDE. Autopilot enables fast and easy building and deployment of a workload under development on a system for testing. It also enables benchmark execution directly from the development environment.

Keywords

SPEC, Workloads, Energy Efficiency, Load level, Deployment, Development

1. INTRODUCTION

Server energy-efficiency benchmarking helps researchers, customers, and developers to evaluate and compare the efficiency of hardware and software. Which in turn enables better decision making and leads to greater overall energy efficiency. However, benchmarks must meet a number of quality criteria in order to deliver usable results: They must be relevant, reproducible, fair, verifiable, and usable [3]. Consequently, developing energy-efficiency benchmarks is challenging. Energy-efficiency benchmarks, specifically, must meet these criteria and must also be able to be run in a power measurement environment. This includes a need for discrete power and temperature measurement equipment and stable environmental conditions.

Measurement device requirements and a general benchmarking methodology for energy efficiency measurements are specified in the SPEC Power and Performance Benchmarking Methodology [2]. The SPEC Chauffeur WDK [1] supports this methodology. It is a framework and development kit that manages benchmark configuration, calibration, execution, and data collection. It allows for the development of custom workloads (called worklets) to be executed and benchmarked. A developer using the Chauffeur WDK can focus on the specific benchmarking workload only, leaving other benchmarking considerations to the framework.

The Chauffeur WDK rapidly speeds up the development of energy-efficiency benchmarks. However, worklet building, deployment, and configuration remain a time-consuming process, as multiple executables must be deployed, configured, and started separately. Similarly, log files must be collected from all running instances for analysis of program behavior. To alleviate this, we introduce Autopilot. Autopilot is a plug-in for the Eclipse development environment that automates worklet building, deployment, and configuration. It also offers a graphical user interface that enables execution of benchmarks in development directly within the development environment. It displays measurement results to the developer and provides comparison features that allow for investigation of the impact recent changes in development have had on software energy efficiency.

We envision Autopilot's use in two scenarios: Autopilot's core scenario is its use for development of worklets for energy-efficiency benchmarking. In addition, it may also be used to test the energy efficiency of application software during its development.

ICPE'17 April 22-26, 2017, L'Aquila, Italy

ACM ISBN 978-1-4503-4404-3/17/04.

DOI: http://dx.doi.org/10.1145/3030207.3053667

2. USAGE SCENARIOS

Autopilot allows for quick and easy energy-efficiency testing of software during development. It features an automated building and deployment system, as well as graphical user interfaces for test execution, result interpretation and comparison directly in the Eclipse IDE. We envision two primary usage scenarios for this functionality:

1. **Development of Benchmarking Workloads**: Autopliot can be used to create and test benchmarking

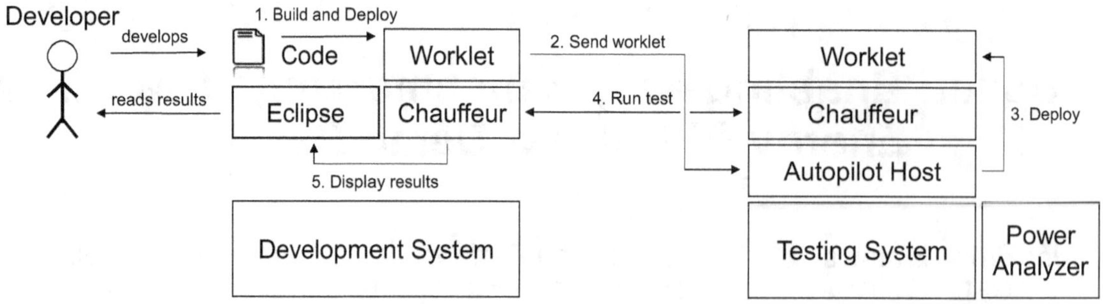

Figure 1: Autopilot workflow

worklets for the Chauffeur WDK. In contrast to traditional development for Chauffeur, Autopilot enables easier building, deployment, and testing. Worklets can be quickly tested and improved during development, ensuring that their power consumption characteristics behave as desired.

2. **Efficiency Testing of Software in Development**: Autopilot may also be used to test software or software components that are not specifically created to serve as energy efficiency benchmarks. As energy efficiency of software becomes a growing concern, its testing during development may help to improve the energy-efficiency of the final software.

3. AUTOPILOT WORKFLOW

Autopilot is intended to be used during the development phase of software creation. At each point in time at which the software under development is in an executable state Autopilot may be used to build, deploy and test the energy efficiency of the software under development. Autopilot also offers features enabling comparison of the performance, power consumption, and energy efficiency of test results. This way, a developer or tester can check the changes a recent change in the software has had on the energy efficiency.

The developer uses a graphical user interface in the Eclipse environment to initiate a test. This user interface is also used to configure the test. It prompts the user for few pieces of information required to execute the test, which includes the IP address of the testing system, test duration, and power analyzer information. Additionally, the user may choose to enter additional information, such as number of test load levels and warmup durations.

After initiating a test, Autopilot performs the following actions (as depicted in Fig. 1):

1. **Build and Deploy**: The project code is built and packaged into a Java .jar file using ANT scripts, as is common for Chauffeur WDK projects. It is also deployed on the developer system, which serves as experiment director for the test.
2. **Send worklet**: The packaged worklet is transferred to the testing system, where it is received by the Autopilot Host.
3. **Deploy**: The Autopilot Host deploys the worklet into the Chauffeur Host that runs on the testing system.
4. **Run test**: Chauffeur components on the development and testing systems are triggered to begin test execution, as configured by the user.
5. **Display results**: Results are forwarded from Chauffeur to Eclipse to be displayed to the user. Autopilot offers comparisons between different test runs, showing absolute and relative changes in power consumption, throughput, and energy efficiency between different versions of the software under test.

We expect tests to be configured to run for a short duration so that they may be run at a high frequency during development. This also means that development tests are usually not configured as full benchmark tests would be (i.e., they run at shorter durations, fewer load levels, shorter warm up phases). To support this scenario, Autopilot features a simple and advanced configuration mode. The simple mode features few configuration options and is intended to be used for quick testing during development. The advanced mode features more options and allows setting of interval durations and execution options that may be necessary for more complex or specialized workloads.

Of course, worklets developed using Autopilot are still normal worklets that can be used in any Chauffeur environment. Specifically, this means that the Jar file built by Autopilot, as well as the generated configuration files, can be moved to any other Chauffeur execution instance and executed from there.

4. CONCLUSIONS

This paper introduces Autopilot, an Eclipse plug-in that aides in development of energy-efficiency benchmarking worklets for the Chauffeur WDK framework. Autopilot automates the process of building and deploying a worklet in development for testing. It provides graphical user interface for test execution from the development environment and for result comparison.

Autopilot's measurement results can be used to improve energy efficiency of software under development. In addition, Autopilot simplifies development and testing of benchmarking loads, making testing and deploying easier than in conventional development.

5. REFERENCES

[1] SPEC Chauffeur WDK. http://spec.org/chauffeur-wdk/.

[2] SPEC Power and Performance Benchmark Methodology. http://spec.org/power/docs/SPEC-Power_and_Performance_Methodology.pdf.

[3] J. von Kistowski, J. A. Arnold, K. Huppler, K.-D. Lange, J. L. Henning, and P. Cao. How to Build a Benchmark. In *Proceedings of the 6th ACM/SPEC International Conference on Performance Engineering (ICPE 2015)*, ICPE '15, New York, NY, USA, February 2015. ACM.

Accelerating Java Streams With A Data Analytics Hardware Accelerator

Karthik Ganesan
karthik.ganesan@oracle.com

Ahmed Khawaja
ahmed.khawaja@oracle.com

Luyang Wang
luyang.wang@oracle.com

Shrinivas Joshi
shrinivas.joshi@oracle.com

Michelle Szucs
michelle.szucs@oracle.com

Melina Demertzi
melina.demertzi@oracle.com

Yao-Min Chen
yaomin.chen@oracle.com

Oracle Corp., USA

ABSTRACT

In this paper, we demonstrate how new technology from Oracle can be utilized to provide big data analytics acceleration in a streamlined fashion. Specifically, our approach leverages the acceleration capabilities of the Data Analytics Accelerator (DAX) unit provided by Oracle's T7/M7/S7 SPARC processors and the Java Stream API to seamlessly accelerate Java applications by up to 20X, while using drastically fewer resources.

Keywords

Java; hardware accelerator; data analytics; big data

1. INTRODUCTION

With the ever increasing importance of data analytics, we need approaches that allow us to process large amounts of data efficiently and in a programmer-friendly manner. The Java Virtual Machine (JVM) and the Java language have been foundational in the execution of many big data analytics applications and frameworks. One of the features in the Java language which allows the grouping and fast processing of large data is the Java collections framework (JCF) and the Java Stream API [3].

In this paper, we develop a standalone Java library that offloads the Java Stream API to the DAX on Oracle's T7/M7/S7 SPARC systems to achieve high-performance data analytics while using drastically fewer compute resources.

2. JAVA 8 STREAM API

The Stream API [3] was introduced in Java 8. One of its key capabilities is to process data in collections, such as an SQL query, to simplify data processing. Using this API, we can write very abstract query-like code without going into the details of iterating over the collection elements.

For instance, consider a Java method (Figure 1) which iterates through an array of daily high temperature data and counts the number of days that temperature exceeded 90 degrees Fahrenheit (F). This traditional implementation would typically be compiled into serial code ignoring the large amount of data parallelism [1] in this logic and result in very long execution times. An experienced developer could parallelize this code manually resulting in better performance at much increased programmer effort.

```
private static int Hotdays_count_nonStreamWay (int[]
      TemperatureArray) {
         int count = 0;
         for (int val : TemperatureArray) {
                if (val > 90) count++;
         }
         return count;
}
```

Figure 1: Java method to count no. of days temperature > 90F

The same logic could be implemented using Java 8 Stream, as illustrated in Figure 2, in a less error-prone way and in fewer lines of code. With Stream, we can explicitly specify whether an operation is data-parallel by using the construct called *parallel*(). With this hint, the Stream library automatically creates multiple threads to process the data in parallel, which results in better performance on a multithreaded or multicore system.

```
private static int Hotdays_count_StreamWay (int[]
      TemperatureArray) {
         return DaxIntStream.of(TemperatureArray).parallel().
               filter(t->t>90).count();
}
```

Figure 2: Stream API to count no. of days temperature > 90F

While a thread-parallel implementation brings many performance benefits, it still suffers from some overhead in terms of thread creation and resource utilization. A hardware accelerator targeted to speed up stream-style code can be more performant than a thread-parallel implementation and get the work done with dramatically fewer resources on the chip.

3. DAX FOR STREAM ACCELERATION

The DAX co-processor, seen in Figure 3 on Oracle's T7/M7/S7 systems provides hardware acceleration for query-like operations and it is a great match for accelerating Stream functions. DAX can perform specialized functions (including Scan, Select, Extract, Fill, and Translate) at blindingly fast speeds. Therefore, if DAX is exposed to Java through the Stream API, we can achieve significant acceleration of multiple data analytics frameworks written in Java and other JVM languages, such as Scala, with minimal effort from the developer side. For instance, we can call the Stream API from a program running on Apache Spark and get all the

ICPE'17 April 22-26, 2017, L'Aquila, Italy

ACM ISBN 978-1-4503-4404-3/17/04.

DOI: http://dx.doi.org/10.1145/3030207.3053664

benefits that DAX provides without the need of re-writing the application from scratch for a specific platform or an accelerator. The use of Stream API in the code is seamless, but for best performance, needs to be written adhering to certain patterns. Currently, the API supports offloading of IntStream. Acceleration for other streams and object-based streams is possible and left for future work. Best practice documents are available online [2].

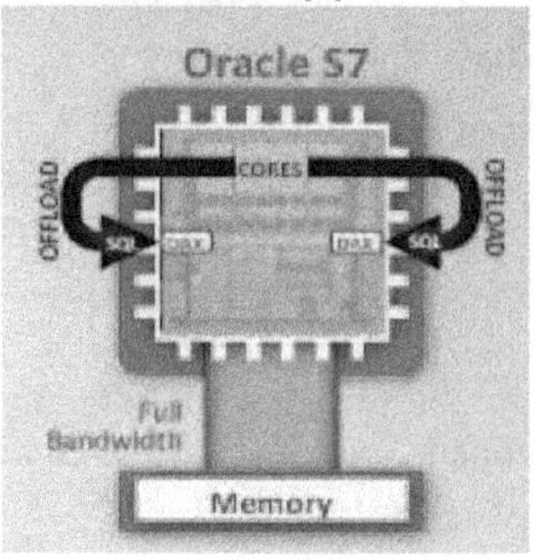

Figure 3: High-level view of a SPARC S7

4. STANDALONE LIBRARY

We create a standalone library available on Oracle Software in Silicon Developer Cloud [4] with the same interface as that of the standard Stream API with offloads to DAX. Table 1 shows the Stream operations offloaded to DAX and their correspondence to DAX primitives. The filter function returns a stream consisting of the elements matching the given predicate passed to this function. The map(ternary) is a special usage of map function that returns an integer array of zeroes and ones after applying a given predicate specified as a boolean ternary operator. Based on this mapping to DAX primitives, an existing code that uses Stream API can take advantage of the library and experience significant performance improvement without any source code changes, except for a minor change of adding an import statement and using DaxIntStream instead of IntStream.

Stream Operation	DAX Primitive
DaxIntStream.filter	Scan and Select
DaxIntStream.allMatch	Scan
DaxIntStream.anyMatch	Scan
DaxIntStream.noneMatch	Scan
DaxIntStream.filter.count	Scan
DaxIntStream.filter.toArray	Scan and Select
DaxIntStream.map(ternary).toArray	Scan, Select, and Extract

Table 1: Mapping of Stream operations to DAX primitives

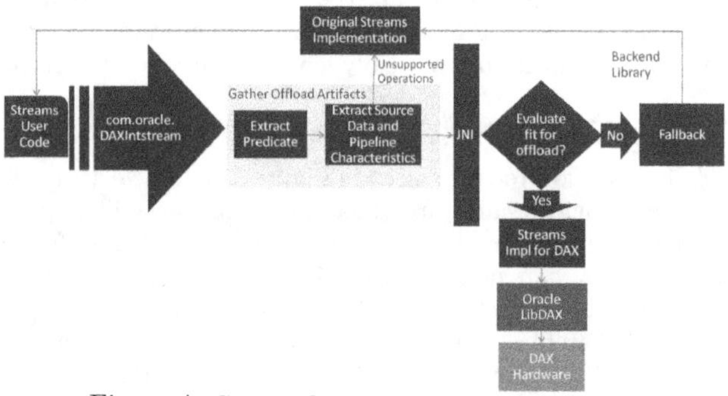

Figure 4: Control flow in the system architecure

The flowchart in Figure 4 shows the control flow in the system architecture. First, the offload artifacts are gathered in terms of predicate, pipeline characteristics, and the source

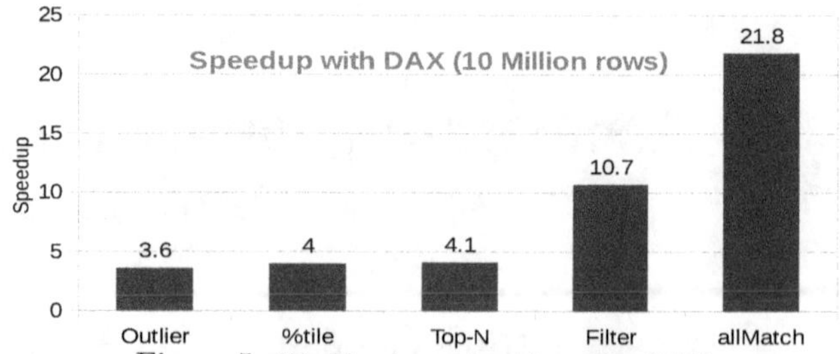

Figure 5: Workloads sped up by using DAX

data. The offload artifacts are checked against a few quick rules to determine if offloading is possible. If the offload artifacts are not conducive to offloading, the execution falls back to the traditional stream implementation. If the offload artifacts are conducive to offloading, the JNI gateway is invoked with the offload artifacts. Runtime decisions are made regarding whether to run an operation on the DAX coprocessor or on the core based on detailed heuristics that determine profitability in the back-end library. Only the streams marked as parallel are offloaded to DAX.

5. USE CASES

The analytics use cases that involve SQL-style Java, such as weather analysis, top-N integers, cube building, outlier detection, percentile calculators, and the K-Nearest Neighbor (KNN) algorithm benefit the most from our approach.

The standalone library for offloading stream functions to DAX achieves up to 22 times faster execution of Java-based analytics applications at significantly lower resource utilization. In addition to the performance benefits seen by acceleration on DAX, we free resources on the cores to be used for other operations. This results in less resource consumption and cooler datacenters. Furthermore, because the DAX hardware is exposed through an existing Java API, we can write platform-agnostic Java code that gets automatically offloaded to DAX "under the hood" on a SPARC platform.

The chart in Figure 5 shows the potential of this technology in speeding up some of the workloads we have experimented with. As part of a demo, we will showcase live demonstration of the speedups from using this technology to do fraud detection for an online retailer.

6. CONCLUSION

In this paper, we demonstrate how a new technology from Oracle can be used to accelerate big data analytics. We develop a standalone library that uses the Java Stream API and the DAX provided by Oracle's T7/M7/S7 SPARC processors to achieve high performance (up to 22X faster than Java-based analytics applications) while using drastically fewer compute resources.

7. REFERENCES

[1] M. J. Flynn. Some Computer Organizations and Their Effectiveness. *IEEE Trans. Comput.*, 21(9):948–960, Sept. 1972.

[2] K. Ganesan. Accelerating Java Streams with the SPARC Data Analytics Accelerator. https://community.oracle.com/docs/DOC-1006352.

[3] Java 8. Interface Stream. https://docs.oracle.com/javase/8/docs/api/java/util/stream/Stream.html, 2016.

[4] Oracle. Software in Silicon Developer Cloud. http://swisdev.oracle.com, 2016.

Technology Migration Challenges in a Big Data Architecture Stack

Rekha Singhal
TCS Research
Mumbai, India.
rekha.singhal@tcs.com

Shruti Kunde
TCS Research
Mumbai, India.
shruti.kunde@tcs.com

ABSTRACT

Application and/or data migration is a result of limitations in existing system architecture to handle new requirements and the availability of newer, more efficient technology. In any big data architecture, technology migration is staggered across multiple levels and poses functional (related to components of the architecture and underlying infrastructure) and non-functional (QoS) challenges such as availability, reliability and performance guarantees in the target architecture. In this paper, (1) we outline a big data architecture stack and identify research problems arising out of the technology migration in this scenario (2) we propose a smart rule engine system which facilitates the decision making process for the technology to be used at different layers in the architecture during migration.

Keywords

Big data, Migration, Performance

1. INTRODUCTION

Application or data migration [3] generally results owing to the introduction of more efficient, cost effective technology. Migration impacts the overall system architecture from various perspectives. (1) **The business impact** defines the business processes and re-architects organizational needs (2) **The cost impact**, outlines the total cost of ownership (3) **The technology impact**, defines impact on the application performance, software stack, hardware and data storage. Technology migration is triggered due to reasons such as change in business demands or functions, availability of new types of data, scalability, platform consolidation, limitation of existing technology, increase in workload and increase in total cost of ownership (TCO).

The ultimate aim of technology migration is to improve the overall system performance and TCO to ensure scalability and reliability over time, while meeting new types of data processing needs. The foremost challenge is to detect which application component(s) need to be migrated

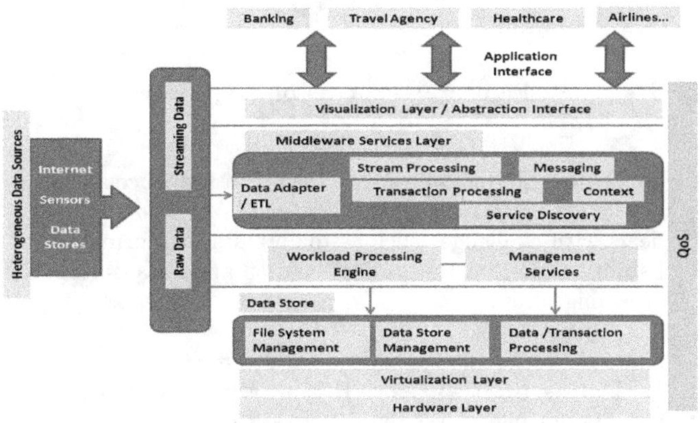

Figure 1: Big Data Architecture

and then to decide the architecture, comprising big data processing platforms, for migration while ensuring performance and security during physical technology migration to newer platforms. The big data architecture we envision (Figure 1) is composed of multiple layers such as data acquisition layer, data messaging layer (Kafka, RabbitMQ, ZeroMQ [2]), stream data processing layer (Storm, Redis), data storage layer (relational, columnar), parallel data processing engine (Ignite, Memsql, Hbase, Hadoop), SQL query processing engine (Phoenix, Shark, Hive) and data visualization layer (elastic search, data visualization tools [1]). Each layer has various implementations available commercially as well as in open source [4]. The challenge lies in choosing the *most appropriate* component at each layer to guarantee *performance* to end users with growing data and workload size across all application components. Here, *performance* becomes a multi-objective function of latency, throughput, energy, reliability and total cost of ownership.

2. MIGRATION PROCESS AND CHALLENGES

A migration process (Figure 2) happens only when a business experiences degradation in performance or increase in TCO. Some significant questions arising are - Should all or only critical components of a system migrate? What does the target architecture for components to be migrated look like? This decision making phase for (1) finalizing the technology in the big data architecture (2) satisfying the required performance and TCO objectives for migration, is referred to as the *Analysis Phase.* The actual (or physical) migration involves preparing the *migration plan* (How to migrate

ICPE'17 April 22-26, 2017, L'Aquila, Italy

ACM ISBN 978-1-4503-4404-3/17/04.

DOI: http://dx.doi.org/10.1145/3030207.3053670

Table 1: Rule Grammar

Constructs	Objects	Operations	Operators
IF, THEN, AND, OR	Event/Data properties, Performance metrics	Assert, Set, Average, Min, Max	$\geq, \leq, =, <, >, \neq,$

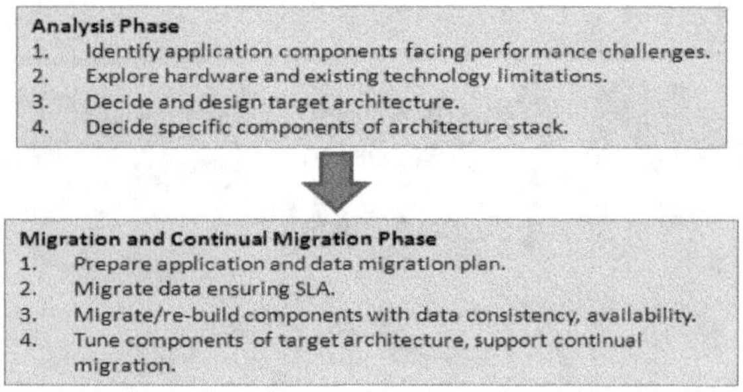

Figure 2: Process of Migration

application/ data while guaranteeing performance and security?) is the *Migration and Continual Migration Phase.* It deals with challenges such as maintaining performance, reliability and correctness of application and data during and after migration.

Some of the research issues we tackle are :
1. Define multi-objective function based on desirable cost, performance, reliability, growth of data and users in the system.
2. Identifying workload characteristics based on the application domain such as the load (arrival rate/size of requests), format of input data (streaming, continuous queries, raw data), data volume, data delivery semantics (exactly once, at most once, at least once) and message ordering.
3. Identifying relevant benchmarks or building new ones for evaluating performance and availability of applications deployed on the stack (Figure 1). Benchmarks should be able to handle a mix of different types of workloads such on-line transaction, business intelligence (adhoc and interactive queries), reporting, exploratory, continuous queries and queries on streaming data.
4. Multi objective performance and capacity planning models to guarantee QoS on the target architecture in terms of workload throughput, average latency for large scale systems (data, cluster, workload), availability and reliability using measurements conducted during POC (Proof of Concept) on small scale systems.

3. SMART RULE BASE

We propose a smart rule engine system (Figure 3), which will store rules formulated using the rule grammar outlined in Table 1. The rules are created by experts based on a literature survey (survey snapshot in Table 2), practitioner experiences and by benchmarking big data architecture stack. The benchmarking results enable the decision making process for matching performance guarantees required in the target architecture, while the state of the art study, facilitates feature set matching. The rule engine incorporates the intelligence to determine compatibility of the technologies that will be recommended at different layers in the big data architecture stack and to make a holistic recommendation based on the overall target architecture during the

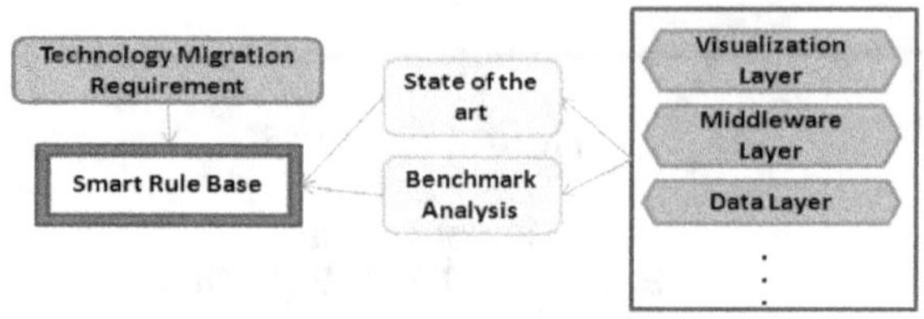

Figure 3: Smart Rule Engine System

Table 2: State of the art (A snapshot)

Query Engine	Cluster Size	Data Size	WorkLoad Type	Scalability
Shark	5+1 nodes, 68GB, 8 cores	5GB-525GB	Scan 10 sec, Agg 10min	Cluster sca till 4
Impala	5+1 nodes	5GB-525GB	Scan 40 sec 12hr-30min, Agg 5-10min	Performance bad on nodes

migration process. The rule engine is designed to be flexible and will evolve over a period of time to incorporate new experiences and thus provide improved recommendations.

4. CONCLUSIONS

In this paper we have presented a framework of a big data architecture stack, while highlighting the challenges involved in technology migration at each layer. We also propose a solution in the form of a smart rule engine system, which facilitates the decision making process of selecting the appropriate technology at various layers in the target architecture. Advances in newer technologies, performance guarantees and heterogeneous nature of incoming data, have all given rise to several non-trivial research challenges in the area of performance, which have been addressed in this paper. We conclude with an underlying need for having an auto migration process in which the system can continually learn, decide and migrate to a target big data architecture.

5. REFERENCES

[1] Open Souce Visualization Tools. `https://opensource.com/life/15/6/eight-open-source-data-visualization-tools/`.

[2] Performance Evaluation of Messaging Brokers. `http://www.eharmony.com/engineering/in-pursuit-of-messaging-brokers/`.

[3] Z. Bian, K. Wang, Z. Wang, G. Munce, I. Cremer, W. Zhou, Q. Chen, and G. Xu. Simulating big data clusters for system planning, evaluation and optimization. In *Proceedings of 43rd International Conference on Parallel Processing*, 2014.

[4] S. Mazumder. *Big Data Tools and Platforms.* Springer, 2016.

Time Bands: A Software Approach for Timing Analysis on Resource Constrained Systems

Giacomo Valente
DISIM
Via Vetoio, 1
L'Aquila, Italy
giacomo.valente@graduate.univaq.it

Marco Rotondi
DISIM
Via Vetoio, 1
L'Aquila, Italy
marco.rotz@gmail.com

Vittoriano Muttillo
DISIM
Via Vetoio, 1
L'Aquila, Italy
vittoriano.muttillo@graduate.univaq.it

ABSTRACT

Timing analysis of embedded systems is an operation performed when there are tasks that have to execute with a well precise deadline, and need to be scheduled, such as those on real-time systems. The diffusion of embedded systems to different kind of application areas is driving platforms toward heterogeneous multi-core architectures, that require a timing analysis done by using measurement based techniques. Measurements collection, when done via an instrumentation of the application, can cause an overhead in the execution time, footprint and necessary space to store data, that can affect the behaviour of the system. In such a scenario, this work proposes a framework that allows a user to quickly perform instrumentation choices, by using a concept named Time Band, and to have a direct feedback about the impact of its choices on some performance parameters. Time Band is then applied to Rapitime, a diffused timing analysis tool, and first tests have been done on IA-32 and PowerPC architectures, showing the advantages of different techniques the can be applied to realize the framework.

Keywords

Timing analysis, Resource constrained systems, Embedded Systems, WCET

1. INTRODUCTION

The analysis of a system from the point of view of timing, named timing analysis, relates to the set of operations performed to collect information about its timing performance. *Worst Case Execution Time* (WCET), *Worst Case Response Time* (WCRT) and *High-Watermark Execution Time* (HWET) are three parameters used in different contexts, for example in real-time systems design and general embedded systems development. Several tools have been developed in order to support timing analysis, each one targeting one or more of the representative times indicated above.

ICPE'17 April 22-26, 2017, L'Aquila, Italy

ACM ISBN 978-1-4503-4404-3/17/04.

DOI: http://dx.doi.org/10.1145/3030207.3053665

Such tools rely on different techniques to make evaluation or estimation, for example *static analysis* or *measurement based* ones. In this context, the latter have gained a strong attention in the last years [5], mainly because the static analysis generally requires a model of the processor that could be not available or too complex, in particular when considering the complex architectures (e.g. multi-core) recently adopted also in the embedded systems domain. On the contrary, the measurement based analysis helps to support the calculation of representative times by keeping into account the real target behaviour. In this context, *Rapitime* [3] represents a tool that performs a measurement based analysis: it makes use of measurements taken from the system at runtime, and joins them with a static description of the application, in order to delineate the worst case path that leads to WCET. The measures are constituted of timestamps related to execution of the code, taken after a source code instrumentation phase and using *Instrumentation Points* (Ipoints) inserted in the application: the level of instrumentation can be selected by the designer. However, since in the embedded systems domain resources can be very limited, the use of Ipoints can easily lead to a meaningful overhead, mainly related to *Timestamp Acquisition* (TA) and their *Storage*, the two operations required by the instrumentation action. So, this overhead can distort the real behaviour of the system and, more in general, can drive to the variation of other features such as *Memory Footprint* (MFP) and *Execution time* (ET), and also provide a certain *Storage Impact* (SI). For such a reason, there is the need for a solution that offers a direct feedback, among the possible instrumentation strategies, about the impact on the parameters that characterize the application (MFP, ET, and SI) and the level of accuracy that can be obtained. Moreover, such a solution should provide, while satisfying typical embedded systems non-functional requirements (e.g. MFP, ET, and SI), a set of timestamps sufficient to provide the required monitoring action (a feature called "monitorability"). In this context, this work provides the preliminary vision of a framework, and related techniques/tools, that, starting from measurement based timing analysis tools, offers this kind of solution.

2. PROPOSED APPROACH

The work proposes a framework that supports the designer for timing analysis on embedded systems. Specifically, it offers a direct feedback among instrumentation choices, their impact on the parameters that characterize an application (MFP, ET and SI) and the level of accuracy. The work is presented basing on *Rapitime* tool. A new concept, named *Time Band*, is proposed: it refers to a source code instrumentation with different detail degrees. For each Time Band, a proper instrumentation will be obtained, that gives some information and causes certain overhead. Basing on this concept, the user will have the possibility to use the framework in two ways: the first by inserting information about platform and application (such as allowed ET overhead, MFP increase and SI), defining the type of measure required, and waiting for an automatic generated configuration suitable for his constraints; the second by acting directly on Time bands selection and code segments in order to drive the instrumentation and, consequently, the accuracy and the overhead. In order to identify a good instrumentation solution, and to address the problem of overhead limitation, a *runtime variable configuration* is proposed, with implementation in four versions using four different techniques reported in the poster.

3. RUNTIME VARIABLE CONFIGURATION

Four techniques are proposed to support the identification of an instrumentation solution able to fit monitorability and non functional requirements. In the following, a timestamp is considered as an instance of an Ipoint, while N is supposed to be the total number of Ipoints that are inserted in the code. The techniques are the following ones: (i) *Conditional*, (ii) *Function Pointer*, (iii) *Assembly Nop* and (iv) *Function Copy*.

In the first one, a *conditional* expression checks if an Ipoint is enabled by using an array of size N called *enabled_Ipoints*: if yes, the timestamp is stored. A considerable overhead has been observed, also when all Ipoints are disabled: this is mainly due to the added instructions for conditional checks.

The second technique is similar to conditional but it uses function pointers. Two functions are considered: *store_timestamp* and *do_nothing*; the latter has the same signature of the former, but it has an empty body. *enabled_Ipoints* is a function pointer array that points to *store_timestamp* if Ipoint is enabled, otherwise it points to *do_nothing*.

In the third technique, the *Nop* assembler instruction is considered: *Nop* is a common word to indicate no operation. After code instrumentation, it is possible to substitute all calls to *store_timestamp* with *Nops* and then restore only the desired ones. This solution shows a problem: on the tested IA-32 architecture, an overhead on ET similar to those obtained with a function call has been noted. This overhead is architecture dependent. Therefore, this way can be investigated only in the case the architecture provides a very low overhead.

In the last technique, named *Function Copy*, every function has a copy. The original one is not instrumented, named *function_name_NO_INSTR* while the copy, *function_name_INSTR*, yes: a function pointer is used to switch between these two ones.

4. VALIDATION

Some validation activities have been performed by inserting the different techniques in the *cjpeg* application, a program to compress an image file in JPEG format, taken from *MiBench* benchmark suite [4]. These first activities are related to the evaluation of the impact of the techniques on the original program: they have been done considering only empty instrumentation. Experiments have been performed on two platforms: the first is a laptop with a Linux 64-bit OS running on Intel Core i7-2630QM processor with 4 GB RAM memory, while the second a PowerPC G4 architecture[1] with 512 MB RAM memory, where execution has been simulated by using QEMU [2]. Results are reported in Table 1. *Original* row is the original application, *Time Full* refers to the application instrumented with the *Time Full* profile of *Rapitime*, that offers the maximum level of accuracy, but also the maximum ET, MFP and SI overhead, and the four following rows represent the four different techniques to perform the *runtime variable configuration* proposed approach. The PPC Nop implementation is scheduled for a future work because the assembly is different than x86.

Table 1: Empty instrumentation measures

	Intel		PowerPC	
Technique	**ET (%)**	**MFP (%)**	**ET (%)**	**MFP (%)**
Original	0	0	0	0
Time full	400	23	763	45
Conditional	41	62	118	90
Function pointer	80	63	407	91
Nop	40	23	-	-
Function copy	6	123	10	109

5. ACKNOWLEDGMENTS

This work has been supported by Rapita Systems LTD.

6. REFERENCES

[1] Powerpc. https://www-01.ibm.com/chips/techlib/techlib.nsf/productfamilies/PowerPC/. Accessed: 2016-12-22.

[2] Qemu homepage. http://wiki.qemu.org/Main_Page. Accessed: 2016-12-22.

[3] Rapitime. https://www.rapitasystems.com/products/rapitime. Accessed: 2016-12-22.

[4] M. R. Guthaus, J. S. Ringenberg, D. Ernst, T. M. Austin, and R. B. B. T. Mudge. Mibench: A free, commercially representative embedded benchmark suite. In *Proceedings of the Fourth Annual IEEE International Workshop on Workload Characterization. WWC-4 (Cat. No.01EX538)*, pages 3–14, Dec 2001.

[5] R. Wilhelm, J. Engblom, A. Ermedahl, N. Holsti, S. Thesing, D. Whalley, G. Bernat, C. Ferdinand, R. Heckmann, T. Mitra, F. Mueller, I. Paut, P. Puschner, J. Staschulat, P. Stenstrom. The worst-case execution-time problem — overview of methods and survey of tools. *ACM Trans. Embed. Comput. Syst.*, 7(3):36:1–36:53, May 2008.

Open Source In-Memory Data Grid Systems: Benchmarking Hazelcast and Infinispan

Haytham Salhi
hsalhi89@gmail.com
Faculty of Engineering and Technology
Birzeit University, Palestine

Feras Odeh
ferasodh@gmail.com
Faculty of Engineering and Technology
Birzeit University, Palestine

Rabee Nasser
rabinasser@gmail.com
Faculty of Engineering and Technology
Birzeit University, Palestine

Adel Taweel
ataweel@birzeit.edu
Department of Computer Science, Faculty of Engineering and Technology
Birzeit University, Palestine

ABSTRACT

In this paper, we studied the performance of two popular open source distributed cache systems (Hazelcast and Infinispan) indifferently. The conducted performance analysis shows that Infinispan outperforms Hazelcast in the simple data retrieval scenarios as well as most of SQL-like queries scenarios, whereas Hazelcast outperforms Infinispan in SQL-like queries for small data sizes.

Keywords

Benchmarking, Hazelcast, Infinispan

1. INTRODUCTION

In computing, a cache is a software component that stores portions of datasets which would otherwise either take a long time to calculate, process, or originate from an underlying backend system [8]. A cache system could be used either to decrease application latencies or gain additional performance [8].

In this paper, the performance of Hazelcast (version 3.6.1) and Infinispan (version 8.1.2.Final) was studied, with specific focus on two key factors: *number of concurrent clients* and *size of processed data*. The study focused on the data retrieval aspects, that they are the most common operations in the use cases of distributed caches. Yardstick was used as a primary benchmarking framework [5], however, an additional mechanism was also developed, to benchmark distributed caches, to enable capturing the varying number of clients and data sizes to ensure proper synchronization of run-times.

Other benchmarking tools have been considered, which some have been specially extended to produce metrics for database operations within transactions to detect anomalies from workload processing, e.g. "Yahoo! Cloud Serving Benchmark" (YSCB) [6, 4] extended to YSCB+T [7]. However, Yardstick [5] has been chosen because it provides a more extensible feature-rich open source framework to develop and customize. Also Yardstick provides benchmarks that are relatively easier and faster to develop than other frameworks, e.g. Java Microbenchamrking Harness (JMH) [2], Radar Gun [3], and YSCB [6, 4]. The results show that there is a clear relationship between the performance of data retrieval operations and the number of concurrent clients and size of data.

ICPE'17 April 22-26, 2017, L'Aquila, Italy

ACM ISBN 978-1-4503-4404-3/17/04.

DOI: http://dx.doi.org/10.1145/3030207.3053671

2. FACTORS OF INTEREST

The performance of a distributed cache system depends on several different factors. Since the dependent variable of interest is *the performance of data retrieval operations*, in this experiment, we are particularly concerned with the effect of two key independent variables as follows: *(1) Number of concurrent clients:* ***1, 2, 4, 8, 16, 32, 64, and 128.*** *(2) Data sizes:* **100, 1000, 10000, 100,000, and 1,000,000**. The developed benchmarks and shell scripts, used in this experiment, can be found on our public Github[1] repository.

3. BENCHMARKING RESULTS

Figures 1 and 2 draw obtained results, each representing the behaviour of performance for each of the two studied systems. The Y-axis represents the throughput (ops/sec), while the X-axis shows the number of concurrent clients.

For *get* query, as shown in Figure 1, the throughput of Infinispan is generally better than Hazelcast. However, for *SQL-like* queries, which are more complex than the primitive *get* query, the throughput of both systems is significantly smaller compared to the case for *get* query. There is a significant drop in throughput for both systems for changes in data size from 100 to 100000. The results also show that the effect of the number of concurrent clients becomes less significant for larger data sizes.

[1]https://github.com/ferasodh/Distributed-Caches-Benchmarking-Experiment

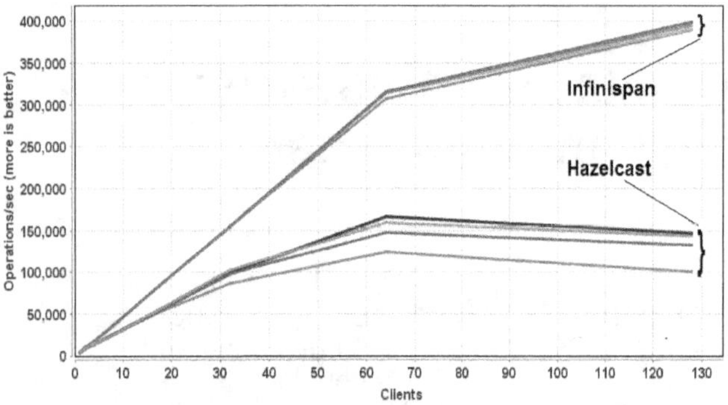

Figure 1: Behaviour of *get* operation performance in term of throughput (ops/sec) as a function of number of clients (each colour represents a data size; as shown the larger the data size the smaller the average throughput).

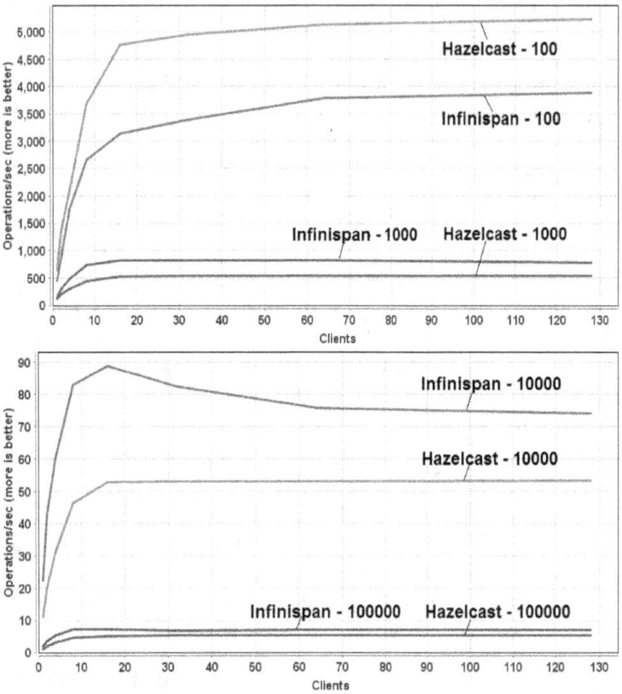

Figure 2: General behaviour of *SQL-like* performance in term of throughput (ops/sec) as a function of number of clients for all data sizes.

4. DISCUSSION

There are several factors that affect the performance of Infinispan and Hazelcast that could be reasons for performance bottlenecks. Some of these factors are discussed below:

- **Data serialization:** For each request a cache system processes, nearly 20% of the processing time is spent in serialization and deserialization in most configurations [1], which can be computationally expensive.

- **In-memory objects format:** In Hazelcast, the default format is the binary format. However, this format is not efficient if the application is processing large number of SQL-like queries, where then serialization and deserialization happen on the server side [9].

- **Indexing** is one of the most significant factors in query performance. Although single-attribute indexes were added to both systems, the engine for Infinispan, which is based on hibernate search and Apache Lucene, is more optimized than Hazelcast default indexing mechanism, thus may have resulted in improved performance.

5. CONCLUSION AND FUTURE WORK

The above results show that studying performance analysis of cache systems with dynamically varying number of concurrent clients and data sizes is critical in determining a more accurate performance readings. Measuring performance with static independent variable or factors may provide misleading results, particularly in systems where cache is a critical part of a system function or design. These require building benchmarking tools that consider such dynamically changing variables to reflect and replicate real-life usage of systems.

In addition, the results show that Infinispan (version 8.1.2.Final) outperforms Hazelcast (version 3.6.1) in all the tested cases except in SQL-like queries with small data sizes. They show also that the concurrent clients, where each client opens its own connection, has a considerable impact on the performance of *get* and *SQL-like* queries. The data size, on the other hand, has very small impact on the performance of *get* query but large impact on the performance of *SQL-like* queries.

Further, based on the mechanism followed in this experiment, a more integrated benchmarking framework, as proposed above, needs to be developed which takes into account the varying number of concurrent clients and data sizes for distributed caches. To test more accurately, future work may include developing new techniques that improves the performance with respect to data representation and communication protocols.

6. REFERENCES

[1] Infinispan. http://www.aosabook.org/en/posa/infinispan.html#fn10. Accessed on: 25/06/2016.

[2] Jmh - java microbenchmark harness. http://tutorials.jenkov.com/java-performance/jmh.html. Accessed on: 28/05/2016.

[3] Radargun documentation. https://github.com/radargun/radargun/wiki. Accessed on: 28/05/2016.

[4] Yahoo! cloud serving benchmark. https://github.com/brianfrankcooper/YCSB/wiki. Accessed on: 28/05/2016.

[5] Yardstick - benchmarking framework. https://github.com/yardstick-benchmarks/yardstick. Accessed on: 28/05/2016.

[6] Cooper, B. F., Silberstein, A., Tam, E., Ramakrishnan, R., and Sears, R. Benchmarking cloud serving systems with ycsb. In *Proceedings of the 1st ACM symposium on Cloud computing* (2010), ACM, pp. 143–154.

[7] Dey, A., Fekete, A., Nambiar, R., and Röhm, U. Ycsb+t: Benchmarking web-scale transactional databases. In *Proceedings of Data Engineering Workshops (ICDEW), 2014 IEEE 30th International Conference on* (2014), IEEE, pp. 223–230.

[8] Engelbert, C. White paper: Caching strategies. Tech. rep., Hazelcast Company.

[9] Evans, B. White paper: An architect's view of hazelcast. Tech. rep., Hazelcast Company.

SQL Query Volume Performance Estimation Tool(DEMO)

Rekha Singhal
TCS Research
Mumbai, India.
rekha.singhal@tcs.com

Chetan Phalak
TCS Research
Mumbai, India.
chetan1.phalak@tcs.com

ABSTRACT

Typically, applications are tested on small data size for both functional and non functional requirements. However, in production environment, the applications, having SQL queries, may experience performance violations due to increase in data volume. There is need to have tool which could test SQL query performance for large data sizes without elongating application testing phase. In this paper, we have presented a tool for estimating SQL query execution time for large data sizes without actually generating and loading the large volume of data. The model behind the working of the tool has been validated with TPC-H benchmarks and industry applications to predict within 10% average prediction error. The tool is built using underlying popular open source project CoDD with better project management and user interfaces.

1. INTRODUCTION

Most of the reporting and analytic applications constituting SQL queries may experience performance degradation in production environment. One of the prime reason is the increase in the data volume in production system whereas, the application was tested on small data size during its development. A naive approach to ensure performance assurance is to generate large data size, load it in the database and execute application's SQL queries to check the performance violations. However, this increases the cost to deployment by elongating the application testing phase and huge investment in building large size infrastructure in testing environment. There is a need to have tool which could estimate a SQL query execution time in testing phase for large data size without actually generating and loading the large volume of data. In this paper we have presented a tool which could estimate a SQL query (or set of SQL queries) execution time for large data sizes in relational databases without elongating testing cycle time significantly. The tool may be used by an application developer in testing environment to estimate a SQL query execution time in isolation

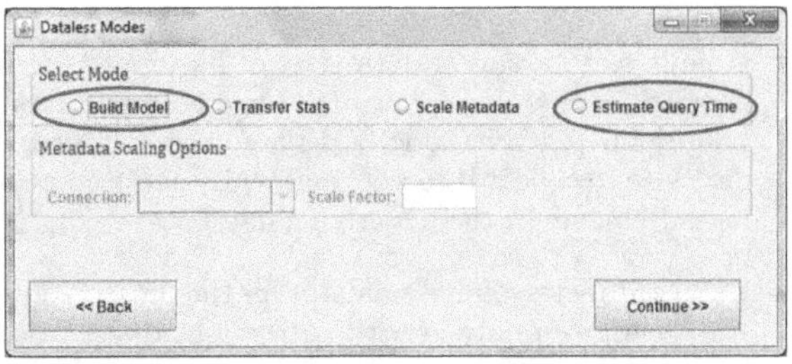

Figure 1: Extension to CoDD for SQL Query Performance Estimation

for large data volume without actually generating it in the same environment. Currently, model is built assuming serial execution of SQL query execution plan, however, work has been done on extending it for parallel execution as well. The model behind the working of the tool has been validated for TPC-H benchmarks and industrial applications to predict within 10% average prediction error [4]. The output of model and tool for a given SQL query and projected data size is shown in Fig 2. The tool has provision for application project management to manage the testing of different application components for different data sizes. The tool has automated various processes of building and applying the model for SQL query performance estimation. The tool supports database volume extrapolation across different types of relational databases such as Postgres and Oracle. Our tool is an extension of popular open source project Constructing Dataless Database (CoDD) [1] as shown in Fig 1. The paper is organized as follows. Section 2 presents in brief the model used by the tool for estimating SQL execution time for large data sizes. Section 3 talks about the tool in detail including its features and implementation. Finally the paper is concluded in Section 4.

2. SQL QUERY VOLUME PERFORMANCE MODEL

The model for estimating a SQL execution time for large data volume has following steps.

- Define elementary steps in a SQL query execution plan as shown in Fig 2. Build models for estimating time taken by each elementary step, as function of the input(s) data size, in the testing environment- IO model is built as function of data size for estimating data access time using Full scan, Index scan, Primary Index and Secondary Index scan [3]. Operator Model

ICPE'17 April 22-26, 2017, L'Aquila, Italy

ACM ISBN 978-1-4503-4404-3/17/04
DOI: http://dx.doi.org/10.1145/3030207.3053663

ID	Operation	Name	Rows	Bytes	Cost	
0	Select		102 M	27G	105 M	2422.03
1	Nested Loop					2422.03
2	Nested Loop		102 M	27G	105 M	
3	Table Access Full	Supplier	1280 K	175 M	7314	3.54
4	Index Range Scan	Partsupp_sk	80		2	
5	Table Access by Index ROWID	Partsupp	80	11520	83	630.37

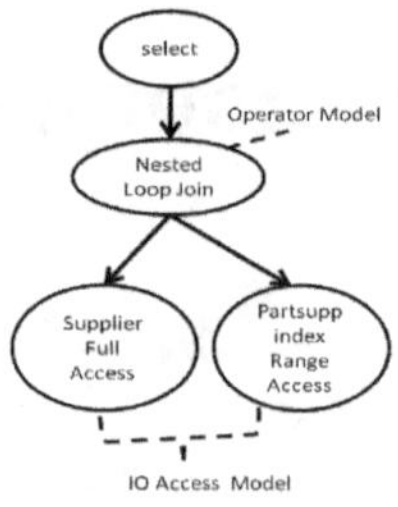

Figure 2: SQL query Execution Plan with Estimated Execution Time and Elementary Steps

is built as function of data sizes of its inputs for Aggregate, Hash Join, Sort, Sort Merge Join and Nested Loop join [4]. Synthetic SQLs are executed on small data size to collect IO access and SQL operator specific measurements in the underlying database.

- Build database volume emulator for the projected data size with given data growth patterns across relational tables [2, 1].

- For each SQL query- Get the SQL query execution plan from DB volume emulator.Map the SQL execution plan to set of the defined elementary steps. Estimate input(s) data size for each elementary step i.e. cardinality [4]. Predict the SQL query execution time as summation of estimated execution time of each of its elementary steps.

3. TOOL ARCHITECTURE

The tool is divided into two components GUI and Core engine as shown in Fig 3. User connects to GUI to provide inputs required for tool execution and receive output generated by tool. Core engine connects to databases to set and fetch required content. GUI consists of three subcomponents- 'Repository' which store environment access credentials, model's synthetic SQL queries and scripts for building model(s), 'Session handler' manages user's session with core engine and 'Output screen' where user gets output of the tool. Core engine is set of four engines. 'Model builder' generates small size database, build model and stores model parameters in 'Repository'. 'Replicator' creates content less replica of testing DB schema, which is called as emulated schema. 'Statistics Extrapolator' takes scale factor as input and extrapolates the emulated schema statistics by the scale factor. 'SQL response time estimator' estimates execution time of set of SQL queries received from the user and sends the output to GUI for user.

3.1 Features

User Interaction: The tool facilitates easy interface for interaction with the tool such as Add/remove/open projects workspace, Enter environment credentials, selective table(s) volume emulation and different ways of input/output

Platform Independent: The tool is fully developed in java and distributed in form of jar (java archive) file. All components of tool including GUI screens, four types of engines and database connectors are developed in java. Tool package also contains other supporting files placed in repository. This repository contains only text files and jar files. All these facts make the tool platform independent.

Project Management: The provision of separate project workspace for different kind of databases or different schemas of one database helps user to easily distinguish and organize the various types of work in cohesive unit. Workspaces are very helpful in cases of complex scenarios when user need to maintain lots of emulated DBs with variant properties or configuration for different components of a large application.

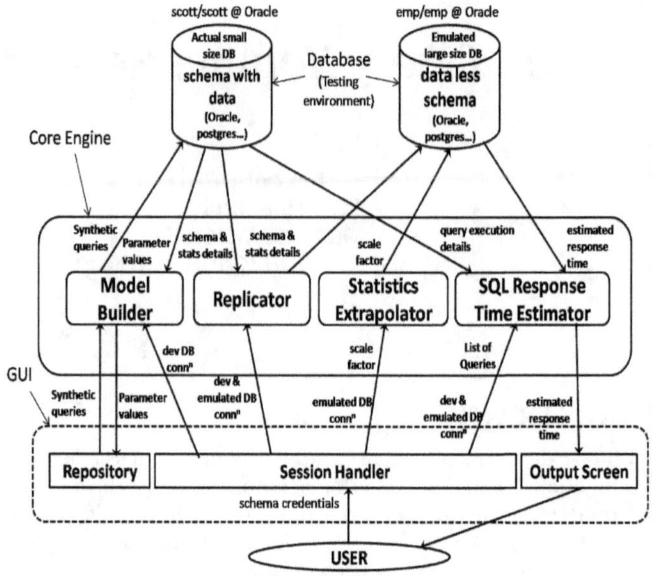

Figure 3: SQL Query Volume Performance Estimation Tool Architecture

4. CONCLUSIONS

In this paper, we have presented a tool architecture for estimating a SQL query (or set of SQL queries) execution time for large data volume in application testing environment. The tool is based on model which can emulate large data volume using database statistics and estimate SQL query execution time using IO access and Operator models as function of emulated data sizes [4]. The presented tool is an extensive extension of open source database volume emulator CoDD [1]. The tool supports project management, platform independence, database independence and GUI interface.

5. REFERENCES

[1] I. N. Rakshit S. Trivedi and J. R. Haritsa. Codd: Constructing dataless databases. In *In Proceedings of DBTest*, 2012.

[2] R. Singhal and M. Nambiar. Extrapolation of sql query elapsed response time at application development stage. In *In Proceedings of INDICON IEEE Proceedings*, 2012.

[3] R. Singhal and M. Nambiar. Measurement based model to study the effect of increase in data size on query response time. In *In Proceedings of Peformance and Capacity CMG*, 2013.

[4] R. Singhal and M. Nambiar. Predicting sql query execution time for large data volume. In *In Proceedings of IDEAS ACM Proceedings*, 2016.

(h|g)opper: Performance History Mining and Analysis

Christoph Laaber
Department of Informatics
University of Zurich
Switzerland
laaber@ifi.uzh.ch

Philipp Leitner
Department of Informatics
University of Zurich
Switzerland
leitner@ifi.uzh.ch

ABSTRACT

Performance changes of software systems, and especially performance regressions, have a tremendous impact on users of that system. Historical data can help developers to reason about how performance has changed over the course of a software's lifetime. In this demo paper we present two tools: *hopper* to mine historical performance metrics based on benchmarks and unit tests, and *gopper* to analyse the data with respect to performance changes.

1. INTRODUCTION

Performance is an important factor when building and maintaining software systems. Therefore performance changes - either regressions or improvements - are of interest to software developers. Nevertheless performance changes, in particular regressions, are often not recognized for a long time [2]. While application performance management tools such as NewRelic[1] provide monitoring capabilities of deployed systems, performance testing presents the developer early feedback about a system's performance. However, performance testing is not as well understood among developers as unit testing is [3]. Statistical methods such as t-tests and change point analysis provide the means for detecting performance changes. A different approach to looking at performance test results is applying a cost model to detect potential performance regressions [1].

Reasoning about performance changes over a software's lifetime might give developers insight into which kind of changes led to a particular change. Ideally developers can deduct which changes can possibly introduce performance changes and use that information to their advantage.

This demo paper introduces two command-line tools for mining historical performance data based on tests and analysing the acquired results with respect to performance changes. Both, *hopper*[2] and *gopper*[3] are available online.

[1]https://newrelic.com
[2]https://github.com/sealuzh/hopper
[3]https://github.com/sealuzh/gopper

ICPE'17 April 22-26, 2017, L'Aquila, Italy

ACM ISBN 978-1-4503-4404-3/17/04.
DOI: http://dx.doi.org/10.1145/3030207.3053662

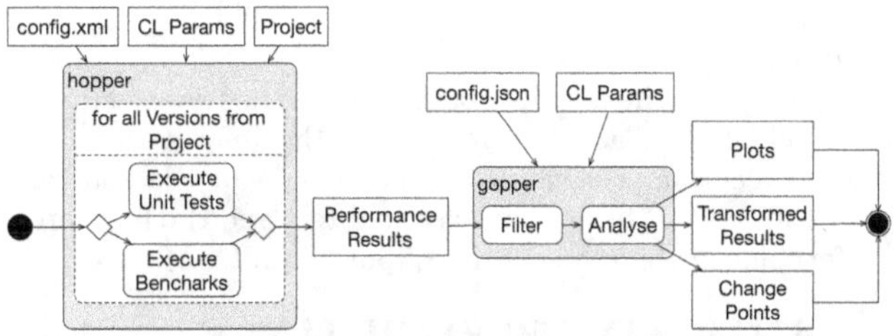

Figure 1: Sample Workflow

2. MINING PERFORMANCE DATA

Figure 1 depicts an example workflow for mining and analysing historical performance data, similar in idea to the methods used in previous research [1]. The first stage - on the left in Figure 1 - of the presented tool chain is *hopper*, a tool to extract historical performance data of Java software projects. *hopper* (i) walks through the history of a project version by version, (ii) retrieves performance metrics by executing tests for each version, and (iii) stores these results in a file. The supported types of applications are described along three dimension: build-system, version-type, and test-type. Maven (MVN)-based projects are supported with version-types based on git commits and Maven versions. Gradle-based projects are only supported with git commit version-types. *hopper* can currently execute two types of tests: Java Microbenchmarking Harness (JMH) performance benchmarks[4], and JUnit tests.

Input

As input, *hopper* takes a configuration file, a set of parameters and a project (as part of the config-file). The config-file defines the name and location of the project, test-type-specific parameters and which version range the mining should be applied to. Program parameters specify config and output file path, which test-type to execute, which version-type and which build-system to use. In addition more fine-grained options are available, such as (i) whether versions that did not change executable code are skipped, (ii) execution of every x^{th} version, (iii) whether the versions are incrementally build, and (iv) if only a subset of all tests should be executed.

The bash command in Listing 1 executes the unit tests of protostuff [5] for every 5th chronological git version. A config-file similar to the one in Listing 2 is required. It declares a version range from `277eded` to `5bbf909`. The tag `execs` specifies the number of test executions per version. For executing benchmarks, the tags `jmh_root` for the JMH tests

[4]http://openjdk.java.net/projects/code-tools/jmh/
[5]https://github.com/protostuff/protostuff

Listing 1: *hopper* Bash Command

```
python ./Hopper.py -f /tmp/config.xml \
    -o /tmp/results.cvs -t unit -b commits \
    --skip 5
```

Listing 2: *hopper* Config-File

```
<historian type="MvnCommitWalker">
  <project name="protostuff" dir="/tmp/ps">
    <junit><execs>20</execs></junit>
    <versions>
      <start>277eded</start>
      <end>5bbf909</end>
    </versions>
  </project>
</historian>
```

and `jmh_arguments` for the JMH command line arguments (e.g. warmup/measurememt, forks) are required.

Output.

`hopper` saves the metrics obtained from the test executions to a CSV-file. Each line represents the information of a single execution, consisting of the version of the software (e.g. the commit hash), the executed test and the measured performance metric (e.g. throughput or runtime).

3. ANALYSING PERFORMANCE DATA

The second stage - on the right in Figure 1 - deals with data transformation and analysis with respect to performance changes.

Subprograms.

gopper currently implements six subprograms: (i) `merge` - merging multiple performance metric files into a single file, (ii) `filter` - filtering test results by minimum mean value, minimum median value and/or minimum versions, (iii) `analyse` - analysing test results for performance changes with either Bayesian Change Point Analysis or Welch's t-test, (iv) `toCangePoints` - transforming test results to change points, (v) `plot` - plotting test result data with (if available) their change points, and (vi) `save` - saving the transformations and change points to files.

Input.

Input to `gopper` is a config-file and a non-empty list of subprograms. The config-file defines: (i) `"In"` - the input file(s), (ii) `"Out"` - the output files for the transformed test results, identified change points and printed plots, (iii) `"Analyse"` - the analysis function and their parameters for analysing performance changes between consecutive project versions, and (iv) `Transform` - the transformation functions and their parameters for filtering test results.

Listings 4 and 3 show a simple example that use the result from stage 1 (see Figure 1: Performance Results), filter those where the mean value is below 0.01, calculate the change points, plot the test results (see Figure 2), and save the transformed test results and change points.

Output.

Three kinds of output are supported by *gopper*: plots, test results and change points. Plots are either time series with a single performance value per version (e.g. unit test execution times), or box plots with multiple values per version (e.g. throughput benchmarks). The plot in Figure 2 shows the performance results for one particular unit test. On the y-axis we see the execution time in seconds and the x-axis shows the different versions from older (left side) to newer (right side). The analysis function (t-test) discovered a change point between version 714e618 and 1dfc05f, which

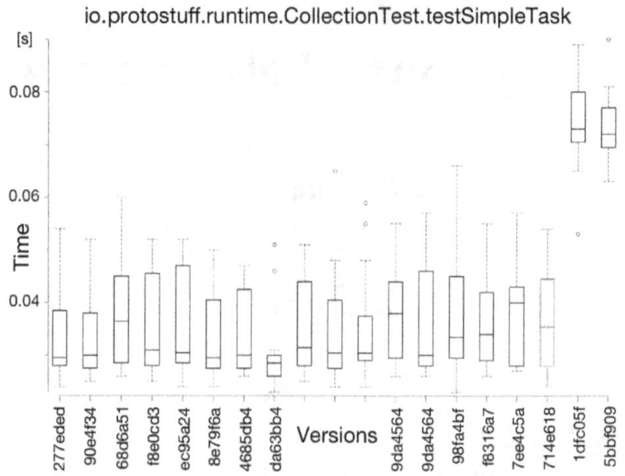

Figure 2: Unit Test Execution Plot with one Change Point

Listing 3: *gopper* Bash Command

```
gopper -c /tmp/config.json \
        filter analyse toChangePoints plot save
```

Listing 4: *gopper* Config-File

```
{ "In": ["/tmp/results.csv"],
  "Out": {
    "TestResults": ["/tmp/results_altered.csv"],
    "ChangePoints": ["/tmp/cps.json"],
    "Plot": "/tmp/plots" },
  "Analyse": {
    "Name": "ttest",
    "Params": [0.99, true] },
  "Transform": [{
    "Name": "minMean",
    "Params": [0.01] }]}
```

is marked in red in the plot. Furthermore `gopper` supports saving the transformed input file in the same format (CSV) as `hopper` and a JSON file that shows the change points detected with the corresponding tests it occurred in.

4. CONCLUSION AND FUTURE WORK

hopper calculates performance metrics based on repeated execution of tests over the history of a system. As a second step *gopper* takes that data, analyses it, and plots the results. For the future, we want to add Infrastructure-as-Code (e.g. Docker, Chef) scripts to ease the installation process. The robustness of the statistical tests needs some additional work, such that reported change points are more reliable. Moreover we want to focus on reproducible results in virtual environments, such that parallelization of test executions on e.g. cloud instances is possible.

5. REFERENCES

[1] Juan Pablo Sandoval Alcocer, Alexandre Bergel, and Marco Tulio Valente. "Learning from Source Code History to Identify Performance Failures". In: *Proceedings of the 7th ACM/SPEC International Conference on Performance Engineering (ICPE)*. 2016, pp. 37–48.

[2] Christoph Heger, Jens Happe, and Roozbeh Farahbod. "Automated Root Cause Isolation of Performance Regressions during Software Development". In: *Proceedings of the 4th ACM/SPEC International Conference on Performance Engineering (ICPE)*. 2013, pp. 27–38.

[3] Philipp Leitner and Cor-Paul Bezemer. "An Exploratory Study of the State of Practice of Performance Testing in Java-Based Open Source Projects". In: *Proceedings of the 8th ACM/SPEC International Conference on Performance Engineering (ICPE)*. 2017.

Generalized Synchronizations and Capacity Constraints for Java Modelling Tools

Giuliano Casale
Imperial College London, UK
g.casale@imperial.ac.uk

Mattia Cazzoli
Politecnico di Milano, Italy
mattia.cazzoli@mail.polimi.it

Shuai Jiang
Imperial College London, UK
shuai.jiang14@imperial.ac.uk

Vitor S. Lopes
Imperial College London, UK
v.soares-lopes@imperial.ac.uk

Giuseppe Serazzi
Politecnico di Milano, Italy
giuseppe.serazzi@polimi.it

Lulai Zhu*
Imperial College London, UK
lulai.zhu15@imperial.ac.uk

ABSTRACT

Java Modelling Tools (JMT) is a suite of performance evaluation tools based on queueing network models. Recently *JSIMgraph*, the JMT discrete-event simulation tool, has been extended to express features of current computing systems such as Big data applications. The goal of this demonstration is to showcase novel support in JMT for fork-join synchronization, dynamic scaling of parallelism levels, memory and group capacity constraints.

Keywords

Queueing network, simulation, synchronization, JMT

1. INTRODUCTION

Java Modelling Tools (JMT) is an integrated framework of tools for performance evaluation of computer systems based on queueing network models [1]. This features primarily discrete-event simulation and mean value analysis algorithms, among others. In the most recent releases (JMT 0.9.4 and 1.0.0) we have substantially extended the expressiveness of the simulation models in *JSIMgraph*, JMT's queueing network simulator, in order to simplify the modelling of complex systems with advanced synchronization types and more flexible capacity constraints. While still classifiable as queueing networks, the resulting models extend the types of nodes that are typically considered in queueing network theory. Moreover, certain components that facilitate the modelling of specific technologies such as Hadoop/MapReduce have been added to JMT.

1.1 Advanced Synchronization Strategies

JSIMgraph has supported since several years the definition of fork-join subsystems. Two simulation components, the *Fork* and the *Join* nodes, disassemble a job into tasks then re-assemble them in the original job, respectively. More precisely, once a job enters a Fork, it generates an identical user-customizable number of tasks to each output link. Later on, the Join node waits for all such tasks to arrive in order to merge them back in the original job. An extension of this mechanism was provided with two main goals: i) allow the customization of the number of tasks sent on each individual link outgoing from the Fork node; ii) allow flexibility in the synchronization policy adopted at the Join node.

*The authors thank Phumin Phuangjaisri and Marco Gribaudo for contributions and helpful discussions. This research has been partially funded by the European Union's Horizon 2020 research and innovation programme under grant agreement No. 644869 (DICE).

ICPE'17 April 22-26, 2017, L'Aquila, Italy

ACM ISBN 978-1-4503-4404-3/17/04.

DOI: http://dx.doi.org/10.1145/3030207.3053666

1.1.1 Advanced Fork Strategies

The new *Branch Probabilities Fork Strategy* enables the user to specify the probability that the k-th outgoing link from the Fork node will receive one or more tasks. For each link, the user may also specify the distribution of the number of tasks sent on that link for each forked job. A different set of probabilities can be specified for each job class. Such fine-grained settings allows to precisely control the generation of synchronized batches going from a source (the fork) to processing systems.

The *Random Subset Fork Strategy* allows users to specify the probability that the Fork sends tasks to k outgoing branches, which will be then chosen randomly among the n available output branches of the Fork. This abstraction may be useful, for instance, to represent systems where work is replicated across a subset of servers to mitigate the risk of contention.

Two additional fork strategies, called *Class Switch* and *Multi-Branch Class Switch* strategies, allow *JSIMgraph* to instantaneously change the class of all the sibling tasks, differentiating it from the class of the job from which they were forked. In the Multi-Branch case, a different mix of classes can be generated on each outgoing link of the Fork.

1.1.2 Advanced Join Strategies

The standard join strategy waits for all the forked tasks to wait at the same join node prior to merge them all and output the original job. Novel variants of this policy are the *Quorum* strategy, which allows Join nodes to wait only k out of n forked tasks prior to re-assembling the original job, ignoring the subsequent arrivals of other tasks from the same job, and the *Guard* policy which further refines this notion by allowing to wait for a specific mix of jobs, where a mix is a given combination of job classes.

1.1.3 Semaphore Synchronization

The *Semaphore* is a new *JSIMgraph* node inspired by the *slow start* mechanism present in Hadoop/MapReduce (HMR). In HMR a job is sequentially processed in map and reduce phases. A number of key-value pairs are produced at the end of the map phase, then sorted and shuffled, and finally delivered to the reducers. With slow start, the reducers can reduce network contention by starting to collect some of the produced key-value pairs before the map phase is concluded. This mechanism is triggered when a certain *percentage* of the total number of mappers has completed.

Assuming to represent key-value pairs as forked tasks of an high-level HMR job, one may attempt to model slow start using a Quorum strategy, where k out of n key-value pairs are transferred to the reduce phase. This is however incorrect since the Quorum strategy would ignore the remaining $n - k$ tasks, removing them from the simulation once they reach the Join node. Thus the first k tasks would be merged into a job circulating *outside* the Fork-Join section sent to the reducers, whereas $n - k$ valid tasks are still cycling *inside* the section while finishing service at the mappers.

The Semaphore instead provides a node that temporarily *blocks* a set of tasks inside a Fork-Join subsystem. For each forked job the Semaphore will wait for exactly k tasks. Once they have all entered the Semaphore, they will be released *as tasks*, i.e., without any Join. Any subsequent task forked from the the same job that arrives to the Semaphore is not delayed.

1.1.4 Scaler

The *Scaler* is a new *JSIMgraph* node motivated by the problem of modelling the Directed Acyclic Graph (DAG) used to model Apache Spark jobs. Spark jobs comprise a series of operators on data, arranged according to a DAG. DAGs are split into map and reduce stages that are then scheduled for execution.

The DAG structure of Spark jobs can be captured by JMT: a network of queues normally represents the processing elements, whereas the degree of parallelism in each stage and the synchronisation between stages may be controlled using the advanced Fork-Join policies. However, it is foreseeable that large DAGs where stages see frequent changes in the parallelism level of the application may become cumbersome to model.

The Scaler addresses this design issue by providing in a single element a Join followed by a Fork. Hence, the Scaler receives k tasks and outputs n tasks. The advantage of the Scaler is to offer in a single element the ability to change parallelism level from k to n, instead of having to include separate Join and Fork elements, which would complicate the graphical representation of the model and slow down the simulation.

1.2 Advanced Capacity Constraints

A finite capacity region (FCR) is a subnetwork with constraints on the number of jobs that can be inside it at any given time. Such limits can refer to the total number of jobs in the network, or to the jobs of specific classes, or both. This has been a standard element of JMT since the early releases, which can be used to model features such as resource pooling and software limits to thread parallelism. However, in practice it is often the case that also memory is a limiting factor in deciding whether to schedule a thread by a software system or not. Moreover, constraints may exist only to prevent only certain specific mixes of classes to run altogether. The latest version of JMT supports these extensions.

1.2.1 Memory Capacity Constraints

A memory constraint associates to each class a *memory weight*. Each FCR has a total *memory capacity* M which is temporarily depleted by jobs that enter the FCR. If the kth job inside the FCR carries a memory weight m_k, then the available memory is $M - \sum_k m_k$. A new job is admitted to the FCR only if it satisfies all finite capacity constraints and its memory requirement fits in the available memory. Note that the notion of memory is here entirely

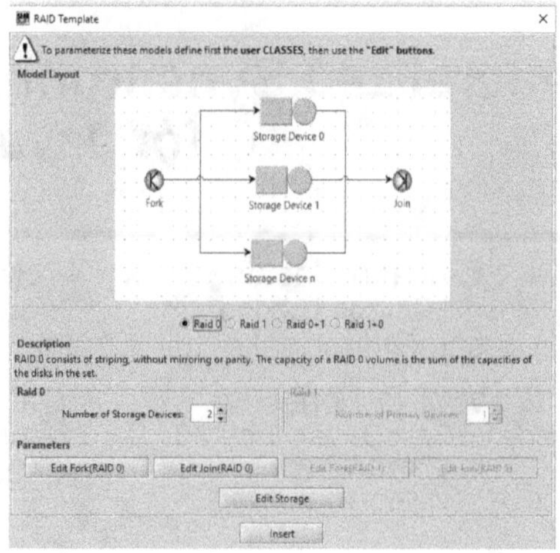

Figure 1: JSIMgraph template: RAID disk modelling

deterministic, as JMT does not support yet the definition of a time-varying memory weight. Clearly, this new feature can help in modelling the memory behavior of software systems. A new metric, called *FCR Memory Weight*, provides the current memory value of $\sum_k m_k$, i.e., the currently allocated memory inside the FCR.

1.2.2 Group Capacity Constraints

As mentioned, a FCR constraints the total and per-class number of jobs inside the region. However, it is possible that in some cases the user wants to constraint certain groups of jobs belgoning to a subset of classes. For example, one could set that if a group is formed by two classes A and B and a capacity constraint is set to 5 jobs, then the sum of A and B jobs inside the FCR must not exceed 5 at any time. This feature is helpful in particular for cases where a single class A is split into multiple classes $A_0, A_1, \ldots$ by means of a *ClassSwitch* simulation element. By listing the said classes in a group, a constraint can be put in place effectively limiting the parallelism of class A without having to change all classes A_i back into A, prior to entering the FCR.

1.3 Templates

Templates are a new feature for *JSIMgraph.* They are downloadable modules used to automate the sequence of operations required to create a complex simulation model for a specific technology. They can be dynamically retrieved either from the official server from servers run by third parties who want to enrich the JMT functionalities. Currently, the offered templates range from creation of three-tier application models, to modelling of RAIDs and the CEPH storage system. A user interface allows to browse a tree of the available templates, as shown in Figure 1.

2. REFERENCES

[1] M. Bertoli, G. Casale, and G. Serazzi. Java modelling tools: an open source suite for queueing network modelling and workload analysis. In *Proc. of QEST*, 119–120. IEEE, 2006.

[2] M. Bertoli, G. Casale, and G. Serazzi. The jmt simulator for performance evaluation of non-product-form queueing networks. In *Proc. of the 40th Annual Simulation Symposium (ANSS)*, 3–10, 2007.

PerfExt^{++}: Performance Extrapolation of IO Intensive Workloads

Dheeraj Chahal Mukund Kumar Manoj Nambiar

{d.chahal|mukund.k@tcs.com|m.nambiar}@tcs.com
TCS Innovation Labs
Mumbai, India

ABSTRACT

We present a tool, PerfExt^{++}, for cross platform performance extrapolation of IO intensive workloads. The tool is based on *trace and replay* mechanism and has the capability to record and replay the temporal and spatial characteristics of IO workloads. We show the design and implementation of PerfExt^{++}, which requires minimal intervention from the user to predict and extrapolate performance metrics across platforms.

Keywords

Performance prediction; IO traces; extrapolation

1. INTRODUCTION

Application migration is inevitable when it outgrows the storage resources allocated to it. The migration process involves moving the application from source system containing low-end storage devices having high utilization and latency to a newer target system with better storage devices like high-end hard disk drives (HDDs) or solid state drives (SSDs). The application migration is a non-trivial and time consuming process as it requires performance characterization of the application on potential target systems.

Trace and replay is a preferred technique as it does not require deploying the actual application or database on the target system as performance is dependent on the access pattern than actual data. Traces are portable and deterministic in nature and hence prove to be a better technique than modeling techniques in some situations [1]. However, trace collection tools like *strace* or *blktrace* slowdown the execution of application hence result in overhead at large workloads or concurrencies (no. of users). One solution is to collect application traces only at low concurrencies and then extrapolate for larger concurrencies.

Our contribution is a tool called PerfExt^{++} that can be used for performance prediction of IO intensive applications across multiple target systems containing advanced storage devices. The tool captures traces at low concurrencies on the source system and replays on target systems. The performance data of traces on target system is extrapolated for higher concurrencies. Moreover, the approach followed in the tool does not require deploying applications or databases on target systems.

The extrapolation using PerfExt^{++} is based on the assumption that there are no software bottlenecks in the application of interest and the first bottleneck arises due to the hardware resource limitations.

ICPE'17 April 22-26, 2017, L'Aquila, Italy

ACM ISBN 978-1-4503-4404-3/17/04.

DOI: http://dx.doi.org/10.1145/3030207.3053669

2. OUR APPROACH

Our approach consists of three important steps :

1) Systematically collecting the traces of an IO intensive application for varying concurrencies on the source system.

2) Replaying the collected straces on the target systems and collecting the performance data.

3) Extrapolating the performance data for larger concurrencies on the target system.

These three steps are implemented in PerfExt^{++} as below:

2.1 Trace Collection

The IO trace of the application is captured using the *strace* utility available in linux systems. Trace contains all IO system calls: *read(), write(), pread(), pwrite(), open(), close(), fsync(), lseek()*. To capture the trace of an application on database server, our tool filters all the thread IDs initiated by MySQL and *strace* is attached to each of these thread IDs. A trace file is generated corresponding to each thread ID. All the trace files are merged and sorted based on timestamp value of each system call to maintain the same order of execution while replaying. IO traces are collected for multiple concurrency levels.

2.2 Trace Replay

Once the trace collection is over, the tool copies all the database and trace files to a temporary directory on the target system. Any reference to a database file in the trace is replaced with the path to temporary directory on the target system. Traces collected on the source system are replayed on the target system using IOreplay [3] and performance data is recorded for each trace replay. Using the timestamp value associated with system call in the trace, we ensure that IO calls are executed at the same time interval as in the original system so that workload is replicated correctly on the target system.

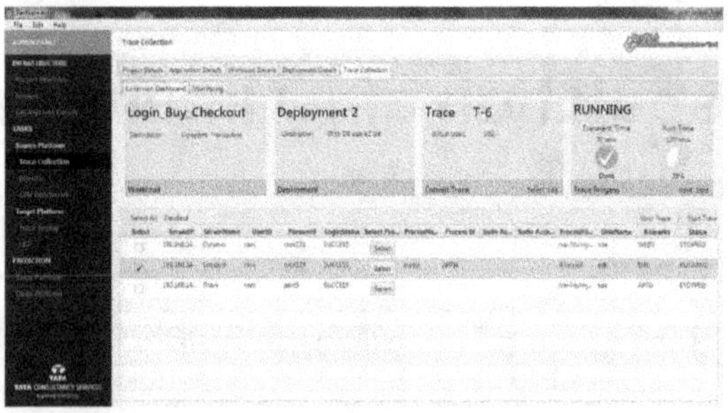

(a) Trace collection view of GUI

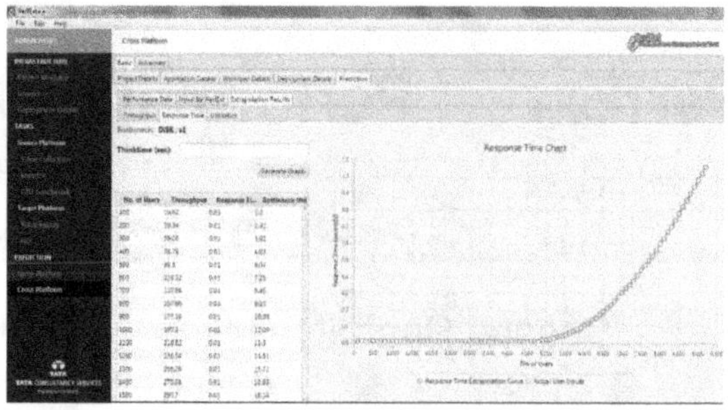

(b) Response time and bottleneck resource prediction

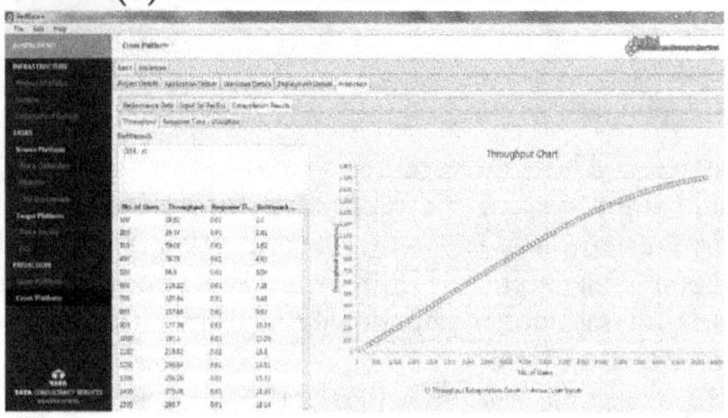

(c) Throughput and bottleneck resource prediction

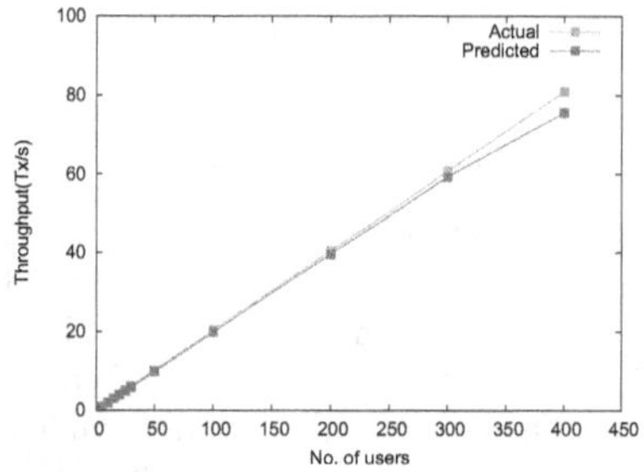

(d) Throughput prediction on SSD for TPCC

Figure 1: PerfExt^{++} GUI showing trace collection view, extrapolated performance metrics and comparison of predicted and actual throughput on SSD for TPCC application.

2.3 Performance Extrapolation

For extrapolating the performance data of an application from small number of users to a large number of users, we use previously developed tool called PerfExt [2]. PerfExt takes perfromance data from trace runs on the target system as input for a small number of users in terms of throughput and resource utilization. Linear regression and S-curve technique is used to predict the throughput. PerfExt has been tested successfully with a number of sample multi-tier applications and is able to provide accuracy of about 90% in throughput and utilization metrics. PerfExt has been integrated with PerfExt^{++}, which has cross platform prediction capabilities.

3. PerfExt^{++}: SALIENT FEATURES

PerfExt^{++} GUI (Figure 1a) allows user to create a project and add or create applications for the project.The workload details which are essentially the transactions or mix of transactions can be mapped to the applications created for a project. Current deployment infrastructure details and target infrastructure details like server IPs (web, application, database etc.), user credentials, storage sub systems of the source and the target system being used by the application of interest are requested from the user. User can map different workloads to the physical servers. PerfExt^{++} can be used to collect traces of a particular workload by attaching to processes running on the source system (Figure 1a). Traces are archived in the repository on the source system. Collected IO profile traces are then replayed on target systems using trace replay feature and performance data is collected. The tool also provides an interface to monitor resource utilization in real-time while traces are running. Both cross-platform and same platform predictions are possible using embedded extrapolation tool PerfExt. GUI displays extrapolated performance metrics including response time, throughput, resource utilization (CPU, Disk) on multiple servers in a tabular as well as graphical representation (Figure 1b and 1c).

4. EVALUATION

PerfExt^{++} has been evaluated successfully for application migration studies of TPCC[1], JPetStore[2] and TCS client applications from low-end HDD to high-end HDD, high-end HDD to SSDs etc. Figures 1b and 1c shows prediction of response time for JPetStore application respectively on high-end HDD using trace from low-end HDD. Figure 1d shows comparison of predicted and actual throughput on SSD using trace from HDD.

5. REFERENCES

[1] D. Chahal, R. Virk, and M. Nambiar. Performance extrapolation of io intensive workloads: Work in progress. In *Proceedings of the 7th ACM/SPEC on International Conference on Performance Engineering*, ICPE '16, pages 105–108, New York, NY, USA, 2016. ACM.

[2] S. Duttagupta and R. Mansharamani. Extrapolation tool for load testing results. In *Performance Evaluation of Computer Telecommunication Systems (SPECTS) 2011 International Symposium on*, pages 69–76, June 2011.

[3] ioreplay. http://code.google.com/p/ioapps/wiki/ ioreplay,2016.{Online;accessed-2016-08-06}.

[1] http://www.tpc.org/tpcc/

[2] https://github.com/mybatis/jpetstore-6

DESiDE:Discrete Event Simulation Developers Environment

Benny Mathew

Dheeraj Chahal

{benny1.m|d.chahal}@tcs.com
TCS Innovation Labs
Mumbai, India

ABSTRACT

Performance prediction of an application early in its Systems Development Life Cycle (SDLC) is essential due to stringent application performance Service Level Agreements (SLAs). Accurate sizing during requirement analysis phase helps in meeting application SLAs and also in reducing expensive performance tuning efforts, hardware upgrades and redesign after the application has been developed and migrated to production environment. There is growing need to use scientific and accurate application performance prediction techniques to reduce cost and increase profitability. We present our tool called DESiDE that uses systematic profiling of components of previously developed applications to accurately size infrastructure for new application during requirement or design phase using discrete event simulation.

Keywords

Performance prediction; discrete event simulations

1. INTRODUCTION

Often it is required to estimate the total cost of implementing an IT solution at the time of requirement analysis. Cost of the required infrastructure is one of the factors that contribute to the overall cost of the solution. Estimating infrastructure cost accurately when the solution artifacts are not ready is a challenging task. Infrastructure requirements are bound by application performance SLAs. Hence application performance modeling is essential and inevitable during the requirement gathering phase.

There exists performance prediction tools like TeamQuest's Predictor [1] and Netuitive [2]. These tools can be used only after the system goes live. Some other products like OPNET [3] have built in models of web, application and database servers. However technical architects find it difficult to relate their application requirements to default options provided in these products.

Roy et al. [3] proposed a technique to break down existing applications into components and carry out performance testing of each of these components followed by analytical approach to predict performance of new applications using the data available from these components.

Another popular approach is use of discrete event simulation (DES) for prediction instead of analytical approach so that systems can be modeled with higher complexity. There are many freeware and open source tools for DES like JMT [2] and OMNET [4]. These tools have enough APIs required for DES but sometimes there is a need to manipulate the dependent libraries to perform complex modeling e.g. dynamic addition and removal of a resource and all its scheduled events, time of day and day of week aware simulations, metrics like 90 percentile wait times, application code implementation in the simulator etc.

We address these limitations and enhances the capabilities of the existing DES tools in our tool called DESiDE. DESiDE also has capabilities to carry out several *what-if* studies such as how much benefit can be derived by improving infrastructure specifications or if the workload is expected to change in future, how that is going to affect the application performance.

2. DESIDE ARCHITECTURE AND FEATURES

DESiDE Architecture is as shown in Figure 1. It comprises of 4 layers. The interface layer helps connect to different input/output modes like XML, Excel (through Apache-POI library) and databases. The Simulation Model layer comprising of built-in as well as user created resource and entity models. DESiDE has a few built-in models that can be reused or extended. The built-in server model has attributes like number of CPUs, speed factor and queuing discipline. The supported queuing disciplines are FIFO, LIFO, SIRO (Service in Random Order), priority, pre-emptive priority and processor sharing. The built-in load generator model is used to model workloads in terms of transactions and inter-arrival times.

The Core Simulation Layer provides libraries to manage, run and collect statistics required discrete event simulations. The random variate library supports rich set of continuous

[1]www.teamquest.com

[2]www.netuitive.com

[3]http://www.opnet.com

[4]https://omnetpp.org/

ICPE'17 April 22-26, 2017, L'Aquila, Italy

ACM ISBN 978-1-4503-4404-3/17/04.

DOI: http://dx.doi.org/10.1145/3030207.3053672

and discrete distributions that help to model random behavior of the system. This is particularly useful to model inter-arrival times, service time, packet size and error conditions. The inherent variation in demand can also be defined in terms of one of the available distributions. Load dependent demand is also supported in DESiDE using linear, quadratic, cubic and quartic curve fitting functions defined in random variate library. The flow between servers is specified using entity flow APIs provided by the routing library. If there are more than one destination resource, the routing library provides four options: probabilistic, RR (Round Robin), SNF (Shortest Number), and named resource. In the named resource option, the source server itself specifies the destination server. The future event library contains the list of scheduled events and controls the simulation. Metrics library not only computes mean, variance but also reports the confidence level.
The CERN's COLT [5] library provides random number generation and various mathematical libraries that can be used by end-user to build resource models.

3. MODELING IT SYSTEMS USING DESIDE

3.1 Modeling IT Servers

We first build resource models representing each tier of an IT system by extending the built-in server models and creating models of web server, application server and database server.

3.2 Component Based Modeling of Workload

We then build a component repository using various reference IT applications. Transactions of each reference application are broken down into smaller components. Service demand of each component is then measured with respect to CPU, memory, disk and network utilization. Modeling transactions at such granular level promotes reusability. This means that new transactions can be modelled just by reusing existing components. These components with their measured demand are stored in a component repository for reuse.

3.3 Simulating IT Systems

Once the server models are ready (section 3.1) and the component repository(section 3.2) is populated with demand data from many representative applications, we can use them to predict performance of an application that is still in design stage. Transactions of the new application are modeled using component repository. The application complexity factor is used to adjust the difference in complexity of the application and the component used from the repository for modeling. Likewise, server speed factor is used to adjust relative speed of the target server as compared to the server on which measurements were taken.

4. EVALUATION

As an example we show the evaluation of JPetStore [1] application. We modeled three JPetStore transactions Tx1, Tx2 and Tx3 in DESiDE using components from component library and simulated the same with the page sequence and percentage of transaction mix as described below.
Tx1: HomePage->Searchpage->SearchAction (50%)
Tx2: HomePage->CategoryPage->SelectCategory (30%)
Tx3: HomePage->LoginPage->LoginAction (20%)
The performance comparison of experimental and simulation data using DESiDE is as shown in the Figure 2.

[5]https://dst.lbl.gov/ACSSoftware/colt/

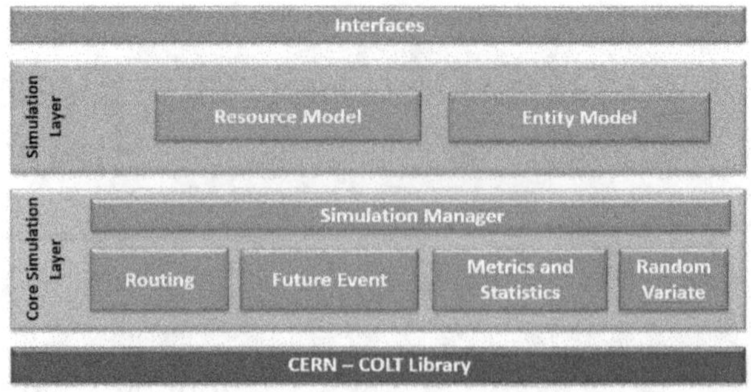

Figure 1: DESiDE Architecture

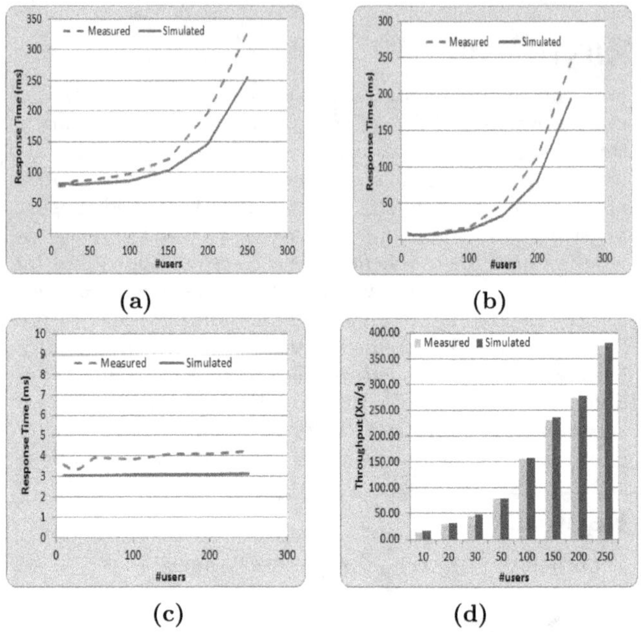

Figure 2: Measured vs simulation (a) Response time of Tx1 (b) Response time of Tx2 (c) Response time of Tx3 (d) Throughput

5. REFERENCES

[1] iBATIS JPetStore. http://sourceforge.net/projects/ibatisjpetstore/.

[2] M. Bertoli, G. Casale, and G. Serazzi. JMT: Performance Engineering Tools for System Modeling. *SIGMETRICS Perform. Eval. Rev.*, 36(4):10–15, Mar. 2009.

[3] N. Roy, A. Dubey, A. Gokhale, and L. Dowdy. A capacity planning process for performance assurance of component-based distributed systems. In *Proceedings of the 2Nd ACM/SPEC International Conference on Performance Engineering*, ICPE '11, pages 259–270, New York, NY, USA, 2011. ACM.

Demo: Time Series Online Measurement for Python (TSOMpy)

Michael Menth and Frederik Hauser
Department of Computer Science
University of Tuebingen, Germany
{menth, frederik.hauser}@uni-tuebingen.de

ABSTRACT

TSOMpy is a Python library for online measurement of time series, i.e., it provides functions to calculate moving averages, moving histograms, and time-dependent rates. The demo illustrates various methods for these concepts and points out their differences. The tool can be used to apply online measurement to time series randomly generated according to specified stochastic processes or to own data sets. The library furthermore allows the reproduction of the tables and figures presented in [1].

1. INTRODUCTION

Adaptive systems monitor their states and use these measurement values for control purposes. Mostly, neither the last observation value nor long-term averages are of interest, but averages of observations over the recent past are needed. We address this issue by online measurement that includes moving averages (MA), moving histograms (MH), and time-dependent rate measurement (TDRM). With online measurement only past samples can be used since future samples are not yet available. In [1], we proposed a framework for the definition of MAs, MHs, and TDRMs. We pointed out shortcomings of existing methods and suggested improvements.

We developed a library for time series online measurement in Python (TSOMpy) implementing all investigated methods of [1] including test and plot functions. The proposed demo illustrates the use of TSOMpy, reproduces the experiments and their visualizations in [1], and allows to apply the various MA, MH, and TDRM methods to configurable stochastic processes and own sample traces.

We implemented TSOMpy in Python because this programming language is most suitable for rapid prototyping and it is one of the most widely used programming language in statistics and data science today. It allows programmers to produce readable code through plain syntactical concepts, and profits from a wealth of available external community-based libraries that can be easily used. Python is an interpreted programming language supporting, e.g., the object-oriented, the procedural, and the functional programming paradigms. We use Python in version 3.5.0 and limited the dependency on external libraries to matplotlib [2] for data visualization.

The source code of TSOMpy will be published under a GPLv3 license on Github [2].

The authors acknowledge the funding by the Deutsche Forschungsgemeinschaft (DFG) under grant ME2727/2-1.

ICPE'17 April 22-26, 2017, L'Aquila, Italy

ACM ISBN 978-1-4503-4404-3/17/04
DOI: http://dx.doi.org/10.1145/3030207.3053673

2. RELATED WORK

General averages like CumSum or (biased) exponential MAs (EMA) are simple and quickly programmed or available as functions in many programming languages or external libraries. One example is the qcc package [3] for the R programming language. The Python community also provides numerous external libraries for basic online measurement: Numpy [4] supports a method for a customizable, weighted average. Pandas [5] includes implementations for CumSum and the (biased) EMA. Other libraries provide CumSum and (biased) EMA for analysis of stock market data [6] or implement the window-based moving average (WMA) [7]. However, we could not find packages implementing advanced online measurement methods like unbiased EMA, time-dependent MAs, time-dependent MHs, novel TDRM methods, and allow their evaluation and comparison. Therefore, we developed the TSOMpy library.

3. CONCEPT

TSOMpy allows the generation of time series according to stochastic processes or alternatively read time series from CSV files. It implements the online measurement methods presented in [1] and allows their application to the time series with a graphical user interface. Additional functions reproduce the tables and figures shown in [1]. In the following, we explain the time series generation offered by TSOMpy. We give an overview of the implemented online measurement methods including class structures and challenges for their illustration.

3.1 Generation and Import of Time Series

Evenly spaced time series can be represented by a vector of values which are associated with evenly spaced time instants whose inter-sample time is a basic time unit Δt. In contrast, unevenly spaced time series consist of both a vector of values and a vector of time instants with possibly different, non-zero inter-sample times. TSOMpy supports generation of constant, equally, exponentially, normally, Gamma-, and

Table 1: Class names of online measurement methods and their full names with reference to their descriptions in [1].

Class name	Full method's name
MAs (for evenly-spaced time series)	
CumMean	Cumulative Mean (3.1.2)
WMA	Window MA (3.1.3)
DWMA	Disjoint Windows MA (3.1.4)
UEMA	Unbiased Exponential MA (3.1.5)
EMA	Exponential MA (3.1.6)
Time-dependent MAs (for unevenly-spaced time series)	
TWMA	Time Window MA (3.2.2)
DTWMA	Disjoint Time Windows MA (3.2.3)
UTEMA	Unbiased Time-Exponential MA (3.2.4)
TEMA	Time-Exponential MA (3.2.5)
MHs (for evenly-spaced time series)	
MH_CumMean	MH with CumMean (5.1)
MH_WMA	MH with WMA (not considered in [1])
MH_DWMA	MH with DWMA (not considered in [1])
MH_UEMA	MH with UEMA (5.1)
MH_EMA	MH with EMA (not considered in [1])
Time-dependent MHs (for unevenly-spaced time series)	
TDMH_TWMA	TDMH with TWMA (not considered in [1])
TDMH_DTWMA	TDMH with DTWMA (not considered in [1])
TDMH_UTEMA	TDMH with UTEMA (5.2)
TDMH_TEMA	TDMH with TEMA (not considered in [1])
Time-dependent RMs (for unevenly-spaced time series)	
TDRM_TWMA	TDRM with Time Window MA (6.1.2)
TDRM_DTWMA	TDRM with DTWMA (6.1.3)
TDRM_DTWMA_UEMA	TDRM with DTWMA and UEMA (6.1.4)
TDRM_UTEMA	TDRM with UTEMA (6.1.5)
TDRM_UTEMA_CPA	TDRM with UTEMA and Continuous Packet Arrivals (6.1.6)

Pareto-distributed values and also values created according to an autoregressive process. It offers constant, equally, exponentially, Gamma-, and Pareto-distributed inter-sample times for the time vectors. The distributions can be configured with appropriate parameters. Both time and value vectors can be imported from CSV files. It is possible to combine imported time or value vectors with generated counterparts.

3.2 Online Measurement Methods

Table 1 lists all implemented online measurement methods. Normal MAs and MHs are applicable only to evenly spaced time series while time-dependent MAs (TDMA) and MHs (TDMH) are extended for application to unevenly spaced time series. TDRM methods are applied only to unevenly spaced time series. They can also be applied to mere time vectors with a constant value vector or to a value vector combined with an evenly spaced time vector.

We used an object-oriented class hierarchy for the implementation of all online measurement methods. Normal MA methods inherit from "MovingAverage", TDMA methods inherit from "TimeDependentMovingAverage", MH methods inherit from "MovingHistogram", and TDMH methods inherit from "TimeDependentMovingHistogram". "TimeDepenentRateMeasurement" inherits from "TimeDependentMovingAverage" and TDRM methods inherit from both "TimeDependentMovingRate" and possibly from some specific TDMA method.

Some TDRM methods produce step curves with jumps at sample instants and drops some constant time afterwards. Others lead to curves with jumps at sample instants and continuously decreasing phases in between. Illustrations are provided in [1]. TSOMpy produces such curves and offers functions to calculate variance, differences, and accumulates.

4. DEMONSTRATION

The demonstration explains various online measurement methods and points out their differences using visualization and quantitative metrics.

The module *TsomDemo* includes classes demonstrating the usage of TSOMpy, e.g., the reproduction of the tables and figures in [1] with the same or different parameters. It also provides a user interface to apply the online measurement methods to imported data or to specified random data. In addition to visualization, calculated averages and rates can be exported as CSV for further investigation, e.g., in a statistical software tool like R. TSOMpy includes functions that may be used by other processes to calculate the proposed metrics and to visualize them.

5. CONCLUSION

TSOMpy is a Python library for time series online measurement. The associated tool and the demo illustrate various algorithms for the moving averages (MA), moving histograms (MH), and time-dependent rate measurement (TDRM) presented in [1]. Moreover, it reproduces the results presented in the tables and figures of that paper and allows the community to evaluate the proposed online measurement methods with own experiments and data. On the one hand, the tool may serve educational purposes and be used for the processing of research data. On the other hand, the functions provided by the library may directly be integrated in control algorithms of adaptive systems.

6. REFERENCES

[1] M. Menth and F. Hauser, "On Moving Averages, Histograms and Time-Dependent Rates for Online Measurement," in *ACM/SPEC ICPE*, 2017.

[2] ——, "TSOMpy – Time Series Online Measurement in Python," https://www.github.com/uni-tue-kn/TSOMpy, 2017.

[3] L. Scrucca. (2014, Oct.) Cran: Quality control charts (qcc). [Online]. Available: https://cran.r-project.org/web/packages/qcc/

[4] N. Developers. (2016, May) Numpy. [Online]. Available: http://www.numpy.org/

[5] T. P. D. Team. (2016, Dec.) Python data analysis library. [Online]. Available: http://pandas.pydata.org/

[6] C. Zhuang. (2016, Nov.) Python package index: Stockstats 0.2.0. [Online]. Available: https://pypi.python.org/pypi/stockstats

[7] S. Reifschneider. (2011, Nov.) Github repository: Python-movingaverage. [Online]. Available: https://github.com/linsomniac/python-movingaverage

Performance is Also a Matter of Where You Live

Francesco Quaglia
Sapienza University of Rome, Italy
Via Ariosto 25 - 00185
quaglia@dis.uniroma1.it

ABSTRACT

Nowadays, a plethora of techniques and methods are available to optimize the runtime behavior of complex applications, ranging from modeling/prediction tools to the employment of recognized patterns and/or knowledge-bases on the expected performance under specific workloads. However, in common scenarios, the ultimate applications' behavior may depend on features that are scarcely predictable or difficult to be taken into account when designing the applications and their own runtime optimizers. Among them, we mention the actual structure of the underlying hardware and/or virtualized platforms, as well as specific runtime dynamics such as thread correlation on data and synchronization---not much the average behavior, rather punctual effects. We believe that the environment where applications live, like operating systems and user-space runtime libraries, play a central role in coping with these features. We similarly believe that such environments must be re-staged so as to be actually effective in pursuing the performance optimization goal. In this talk, we discuss specific guidelines to re-stage the environments, based on a real experience, and we point as well to challenges that are still untackled and deserve attention by the research community.

CCS Concepts/ACM Classifiers

• Software and its engineering~Operating systems • Software and its engineering~Software performance

Author Keywords

Software Environments, Operating Systems, Performance and Energy Efficiency

BIOGRAPHY

Francesco Quaglia received the Laurea degree (MS level) in Electronic Engineering in 1995 and the PhD degree in Computer Engineering in 1999 from the University of Rome "La Sapienza.". From summer 1999 to summer 2000 he held an appointment as a Researcher at the Italian National Research Council (CNR).

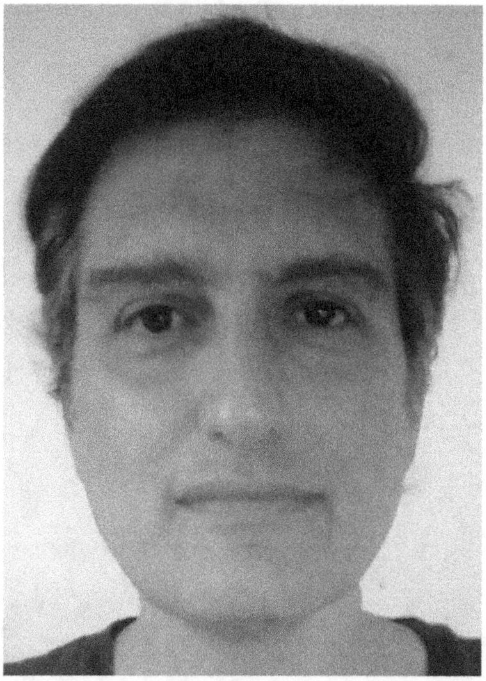

Since January 2005 he works as an Associate Professor at the School of Engineering of the University of Rome "La Sapienza," where he has previously worked as an Assistant Professor since September 2000 to December 2004. His main research interests are in the areas of high performance computing, dependable computing, transactional systems, operating systems, automatic code parallelization, performance analysis and optimization. Currently, he is the director of the HPDCS (High Performance and Dependable Computing Systems) Research Lab at the University of Rome "La Sapienza.".

ICPE'17, April 22–26, 2017, L'Aquila, Italy.
ACM ISBN 978-1-4503-4404-3/17/04.
http://dx.doi.org/10.1145/3030207.3053655

A Performance-centric Approach for Complex Decisions Support

Ate Penders
Thales Research&Technology,
Delft University of Technology
ate.penders@d-cis.nl

Ana Lucia Varbanescu
University of Amsterdam
a.l.varbanescu@uva.nl

Gregor Pavlin
Thales Research&Technology
gregor.pavlin@d-cis.nl

Henk Sips
Delft University of Technology
h.j.sips@tudelft.nl

ABSTRACT

Many situations in the security domain require decision-making based on complex data, i.e., many variables which need to be taken into account before adequate decisions can be made. For example, in a surveillance scenario, the size and complexity of the area of interest, the mix of objects, and the unexpected behavior of suspects are just a few examples of complex variables to be analyzed in the process. Existing decision support systems provide some analysis, but are typically limited in the complexity they can handle. Therefore, users end up with simplified models which often suffer in the accuracy of their decisions and, ultimately, may lead to incorrect decisions. In this work, we present a framework that can scale to cope with the complexity and time requirements of real-world scenarios, while remaining flexible to handle the ad-hoc adaptation to the situation. We discuss the challenges and solutions for such a scalable and flexible system, and validate it using a target tracking scenario in urban environments of different sizes.

1. INTRODUCTION

Border security, maritime security, wildlife protection, or search & rescue operations are examples of critical applications in the security domain. Situation assessment in the security domain requires unstructured (big) data and complex processes to be combined for decision making, which in turn should lead to one or more simple and concrete actions and orders, like "apprehend suspect" or "ignore, false alarm". Ideally, this translation of complex processes and data into actions is performed by a (semi-)automated system for decision support.

The data in all applications in the security domain come from some form of surveillance. The resources used for surveillance (i.e., the sensors) and their availability are dependent on the application: with border security, the pres-

ICPE'17, April 22 - 26, 2017, L'Aquila, Italy
Industrial Paper

ISBN 978-1-4503-4404-3/17/04, , $15.00
DOI: http://dx.doi.org/10.1145/3030207.3044532

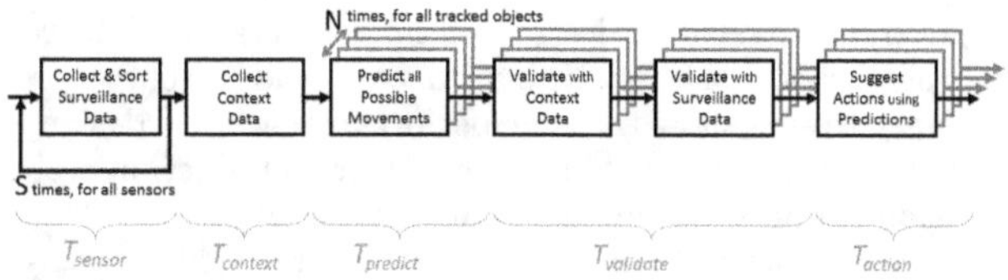

Figure 1: The pipeline of processes in a surveillance system, from extracting the surveillance data from each of the S sensors to the suggested actions based on the predicted movement of the N target objects. This pipeline is executed for every time step.

ence of security cameras can be expected, while search & rescue operations often depend on human surveillance or cell towers. Regardless of these differences, in all cases, the data read from many relevant sensors, of different kinds, must be combined. Reading relevant surveillance data is an essential part of situation assessment. Furthermore, the data is unstructured, heterogeneous, and can be very large in size. A first critical task of the system is extracting and filtering the surveillance data relevant for the decision making process.

The filtered set of surveillance data is used for further analysis. For example, it can be used to create situation awareness by using tracking algorithms that collect data of specific objects over time and predict the most likely next position of these objects. Such prediction is a complex and time consuming task, requiring both historical data of the object, if available, and information on the context of the surroundings in which the object moves (e.g. road maps, traffic information, road blockages) [8]. Therefore, the second critical task of a decision support system is the complex and time consuming analysis process (or group of processes), where the filtered set of surveillance data is used to generate relevant information about the target object (e.g., its destination), eventually leading to one or more concrete actions.

Figure 1 presents the sequence of the components required for a decision support system for object tracking. The system, which collects data from S sensors to track N objects, is organized as a pipeline of processes, and suggests an action per object, based on the surveillance data collected at a specific time. The pipeline is executed at each time step; ideally, a decision had been reached in all previous time steps before a new step begins, a condition that limits the possible frequency of the system. We note there are two iterative blocks in the system. The first one iterates over the number of available surveillance processes (S) to collect all the surveillance data that can later be used by the tracking processes; the second one is performing the tracking process and action suggestion for each of the N tracked objects. Thus, the time step of the system is at least T_{seq}, defined in Equation 1; by design, the performance of the decision system is limited by the time-to-decision, T_{seq}.

$$T_{seq} = T_{context} + S \cdot T_{sensor} + N \cdot (T_{predict} + T_{validate} + T_{action}) \quad (1)$$

The overarching goal of our work is to provide flexible, high-performance decision systems. Therefore, we propose a first generic framework for security applications, which can adapt to the type of surveillance resources and decision-making scenarios, while still providing fast decisions. Specifically, our main requirements for the framework are: (1) minimize the time per step, and (2) scale with *both* the number of sensors and decisions to be made. We present in this paper our framework's design and implementation, followed by the performance analysis of a case-study. These preliminary results show that our performance-centric design is flexible and scalable, holding promise for a production-ready decision support system for security applications.

The remainder of this paper is structured as follows. In Section 2 we introduce a motivating scenario to demonstrate the requirements of a real surveillance application. In Section 4 we present the common challenges of decision making in security domain applications. We follow-up with the design and implementation of our framework, as presented in Sections 5 and 6, respectively. Section 7 discusses the usage of the framework, in Section 8 the framework is validated, while Section 9 discusses our preliminary results. We conclude the paper in Section 10.

2. MOTIVATING SCENARIO

Situation assessment is a combination of knowledge about the environment, the whereabouts of the target (in case of tracking), how the former affects the latter, and viceversa. All this knowledge is specific to the desired type of assessment, making support systems difficult to generalize.

Target tracking in urban environments is one example of complex decision making, representative in many aspects for various situations in the security domain. Across this paper, we use target tracking as a practical example to illustrate the baseline requirements for a decision support system.

In the scenario of target tracking in urban environments, we are interested in the apprehension of the target by means of blocking streets. The situation assessment therefore should give insight in the required number of blockages, the impact blocking the streets has on the "normal" traffic, and the availability of law enforcement in the area. The scenario is a combination of separate complex processes: (1) prediction of target movement, (2) traffic monitoring, (3) minimal blockage determination, (4) impact estimation, and (5) law enforcement localization.

Each one of these five process may consist of one or more (sub)processes. For example, the prediction of target movement has a prediction model that uses the last known position and direction to predict the next likely position; observations from sensors are used to improve and validate previous predictions, as well as adjust current predictions; finally, the environmental context (e.g., road maps), is also used to improve and validate predictions.

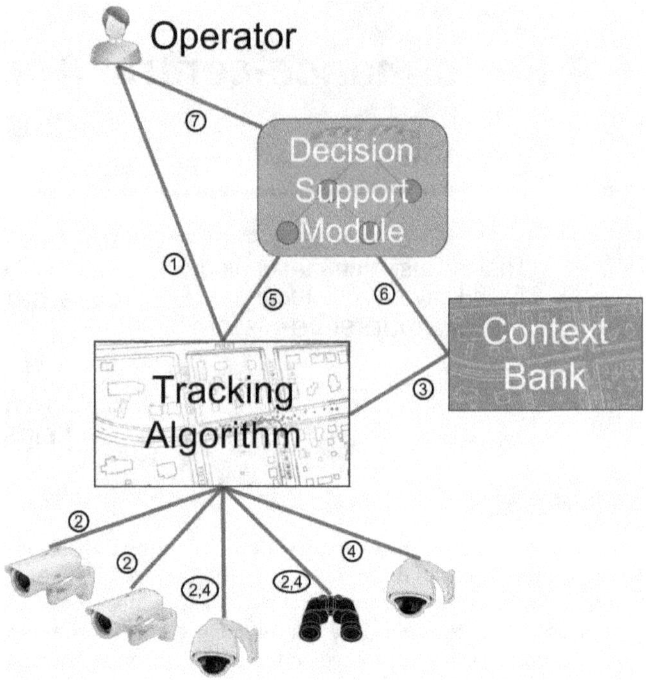

Figure 2: A scenario for target tracking in urban environments: (1) initiate tracking, (2) request sensors in area, (3) validate prediction based on context, (4) new sensor for updated area, (5) report predictions, (6) use context for decision proposal, and (7) suggest action.

Target tracking is typically initialized by an operator, an officer who gets the order to follow and apprehend a suspicious person or vehicle. This request triggers the start of a tracking process, which in turn triggers requests to sensors (e.g., license plate recognition cameras) in a specific area. The tracking algorithm, for example a particle filter [5][9], periodically predicts all possible next positions. The prediction is validated (and adjusted) when the sensors detect the object of interest. In urban environments, but also in other situations, the prediction can be further improved based on knowledge about the context (e.g. road maps, traffic, construction): the target tracker sends its prediction to a context bank, which adjusts the likelihood of these predictions based on a database of context information. Based on the updated prediction the tracker will update its request to sensors[1]. New predictions are reported to the operator and/or a decision support module. The decision support module is in place to assist the operator in providing suggested actions for apprehending the target. The target tracking terminates when a decision is made by the operator or the target is lost (i.e. no observations are done by any sensor for a long period of time, hence the predictions have very low probability). Figure 2 shows a graphical illustration of the described scenario.

3. RELATED WORK

A decision support system requires a large collection of (different) processes able to handle and manage the het-

[1]The last position of the target with a radius of the maximum traveling distance between two time-steps of the tracking algorithm plus some margin.

erogeneous and unstructured surveillance data coming from different (types of) sensors. Ultimately, all these data feed a set of predictor processes.

As described in [3], decision support systems for situation assessment scenarios have to be adaptive because (1) the data-to-decision interval is very short, and (2) the evolution of the situation is usually unpredictable. Thus, the set of predictors interested in particular data will change between iterations, due to the dynamic behavior of target objects. Usually, a prediction process interested in surveillance data from a sensor in one iteration, may not be interested in surveillance data from the same sensor in the next iteration, because its target object moved out of range. This dynamic binding and un-binding of processes requires a flexible environment for both expressing *and* analysing the scenarios.

In such a rich environment of heterogeneous processes with dynamic interconnections, a message passing system [2] ensures flexibility and scalability, while employing parallel processing can improve performance. Therefore, in building our decision support framework, we got inspired by actor-based systems [1][4][10], i.e., systems of concurrently executing objects (i.e. actors) that communicate exclusively via asynchronous messages. Each actor buffers the messages it receives in a mailbox and processes them sequentially, one at a time [7]. Where the components in the process chain of Figure 1 can each be represented by an actor, using asynchronous communication avoids unnecessary stalls due to differences in execution time of the various components.

Our design focuses on generality, flexibility, and performance, hence our goal to implement this approach into a framework. To the best of our knowledge, ours is the first framework for decision-support in the security domain which combines heterogeneous processes, actor-based systems, and parallelism, to provide *high performance* in terms of both *speed* and *scalability*.

4. CHALLENGES AND APPROACH

The usability of decision support frameworks in real-life situations is often hindered by their performance, as they become too complex to cope with decision taking in due time. Our goal is to address this challenge at a structural level, aiming to improve the per-step performance of data collection, analysis, and decision making by design.

Consequently, we impose the processing time of the decision taking pipeline (Figure 1) to be within given time constraints, as seen in Equation 2, where T^* is the maximum period between observations.

$$T_{seq} \leq T^* \quad (2)$$

Note that the actual time constraints are entirely dependent on the situation. For example, for our target tracking in an urban environment, if we want to track a car driving at an average speed of 30 km/h and the data processing takes 10 minutes (that is, $T_{seq} = 10min$), the car could move 5 km away from the last known position, making any suspect apprehension unfeasible. When the execution time is reduced to $T_{seq} \leq 2min$, the car only moves 1 km, making it still possible for law enforcement to apply the suggested action, and reducing the unpleasant consequences in the area. In a scenario of wildlife tracking, the average speed of moving objects is closer to 5 km/h, making the range of movement in 10 minutes roughly 800 meters; this is an acceptable range. However, because the density of sensors covering the area is likely to be much lower than in a city, chances are high to miss the few available sensors. Again, reducing T_{seq} is desired to decrease the chance of missing the important sensor observations and with it increase the likelihood of success.

It is difficult to determine an acceptable threshold for the interval of observation. In our experience so far, this threshold is a combination of situation specific variables, like average speed of the target object and density of the sensors in the area, and possible/desirable decisions. Therefore, building a framework where performance and scalability are addressed by design, and can be further tuned by using a better computational solution, is the right way forward.

When analyzing the pipeline for decision support, we identify two types of tasks that are both time consuming and involve large sets of data, and therefore may hinder processing speed:

- sorting and filtering surveillance data, and
- analyze the surveillance data and produce relevant target information.

For large-scale scenarios, like decision support for security domains usually are, T_{seq} (see Equation 2) is rapidly increasing since both S and N tend to grow. As increasing T^* is not really an option for real-life situations, we conclude that a sequential solution will not scale. Instead, we must reduce T_{seq}.

To reduce the processing time of the data collection and filtering, we distribute the workload, i.e., we move the sorting and filtering closer to the physical location of the sensors, allowing this iterative process to be done in parallel by the sensors. This is possible because each sensor operates independently, so the communication to and from the sensors can be asynchronous. Distribution also allows us to efficiently handle the dynamics in the scenario by connecting and disconnecting to the relevant sensors and only using the data that is relevant for the current situation. The distribution improves performance, but introduces a new challenge: resource discovery - i.e., determining which are the relevant sensors. We address this additional challenge in the next section.

For the task of analyzing surveillance data and producing target information, synchronization between parts of the analysis process is required, making it less suitable for a distributed approach. Instead we apply parallelism to speedup the task itself. For example, a tracking algorithm that needs to predict the most likely next position of the object must consider multiple options, for each option a number of steps evaluate the options to determine its likelihood and finally the different options are compared against each other. In between the different steps (e.g. create new potential option, is this option possible or block by construction, use surveillance data to determine the current direction and compare against this option) some or more synchronization is required but the different options can be evaluated in parallel. Figure 3 shows the setup of the process chain that uses the distribution of the S sensors and a distribution for the N active object tracking. Note that, for simplicity, this figure does not show the parallel design of the analysis steps.

To summarize, with the new processing pipeline based on parallel processing, Equation 2 is rewritten as Equation 3. Where time indicator $T_{communication}$ is the cost of moving the process blocks to distributed or parallel nodes, introducing more communication and communication over longer distances.

$$\max(\max_{S}(T_{sensor}), T_{context}, \max_{N}(T_{predict})) + \max_{N}(T_{validate} + T_{action}) + T_{communication} \leq T^{*} \quad (3)$$

Our work focuses on designing and implementing a generic decision support framework able to handle such a hybrid solution of distribution combined with parallel computing for surveillance situations. In the following sections, we discuss the framework's requirements and specifications, its architecture, and present a first implementation able to integrate and interpret the data from the active sensors towards recommending a decision.

5. FRAMEWORK DESIGN

Figure 3 presents the architecture of the proposed framework. To allow our framework to run efficiently, we must make sure that modules operate without fast processes suffering long idle times due to slower processes. Therefore, our framework uses asynchronous communication in a data-flow like model: as soon as the data is available, it is further communicated to the processing pipeline. With independent sensors, the lack of ordering due to asynchronous communications poses no challenges to consistency. Further, to handle the dynamic nature of decision support systems and the distribution of work, resource discovery and dynamic (dis)connecting of resources is required (illustrated by the solid and dashed lines in Figure 3).

5.1 Resource discovery and Dynamic (dis)connecting of resources

The challenge of resource discovery is solved by introducing a *yellow pages service*. As the name suggests, this service acts the same as a lookup table to find addresses of the available processes grouped on their type. When a process X (e.g. a tracking process) needs data from a different type of process Y (e.g. sensor), X will use the yellow pages to discover and localize the instances of Y and use the addresses information to establish a communication link.

It is expected that the system will have many more sensor processes available than the ones the tracking process is actually interested in (i.e., those that are in the area of interest). In our tracking example, a tracking algorithm is interested in sensor data of red cars, but data from a sensor 300 miles from the current position is irrelevant at this moment. As the tracked object moves over time, previously irrelevant sensors can suddenly become relevant and vice versa, meaning that the tracking algorithm needs to be able to connect and disconnect to relevant sensors on demand.

Filtering and selection of available sensor processes based on the interest of the tracking process is called *negotiation*, and it is designed to avoid unnecessary communication: a data request message is sent to all sensors, but those sensors outside the area of interest will simply ignore it and send no response. Negotiation is an instance of the more generic mechanism of dynamic, on-demand activation and deactivation of connections, which allows different processes to connect and disconnect via asynchronous message passing.

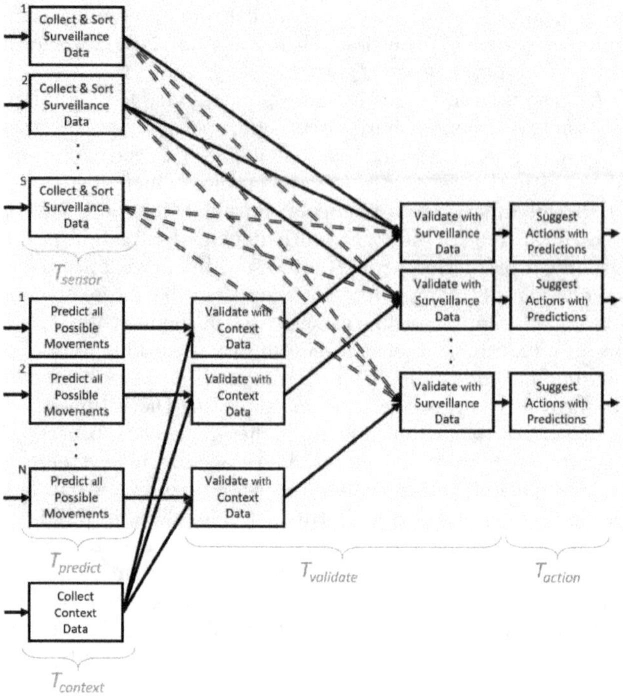

Figure 3: The multiple pipelines of processes in a surveillance system, using our framework. The collection of surveillance data can run in parallel with the execution of the prediction step; afterwards, only the relevant sensors are connected to the validation step. These pipelines are executed for every time step.

5.2 Distinguish information flows

As the system is designed to scale with the number of requests, keeping track of the origins of a request and its own flow of information through multiple processes (i.e. distinguish information flows) is another very important feature that has to be handled by the framework. In the tracking example, a request to follow a black van is a completely different flow than that of tracking a red car, and the estimated next position of the red car is of no relevance to the operator interested in the black van. Therefore, each process needs some notion of *task management*: each request from a process will trigger a new task (or replace a task) in the current process, and any result produced in this task is therefore directly linked the request.

To summarize, our framework consists of a yellow pages service that allows the initial resource filtering based on a given set of features (i.e., type), a negotiation mechanism that reduces the list of producers to only the relevant ones (given a specific scenario), and a task manager that allows information flows cross paths without interference (see Figure 4).

6. IMPLEMENTATION

Our proposed framework is based on the principles of the Dynamic Process Integration Framework (DPIF) [6] – a framework that allows modular algorithms to connect and allow human experts to interact with one or more of the modules – adapted to high-performance situations, that allows us to find resources using a service oriented approach.

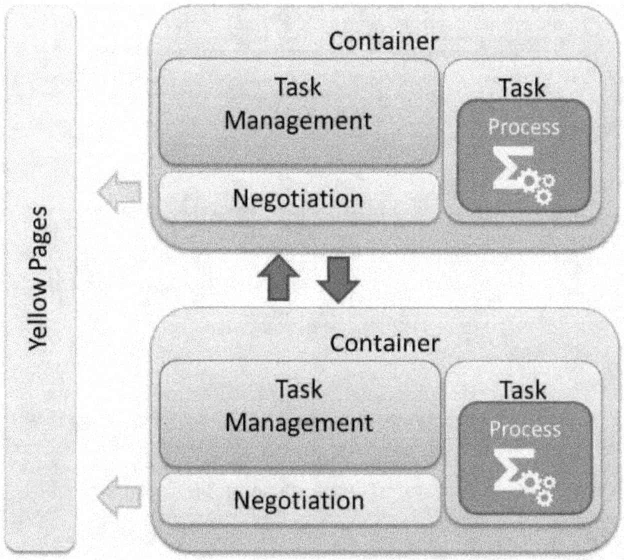

Figure 4: Overview of the framework design. Each process (A, B and C) is connected to a task; processes negotiate before establishing a connection to exchange information asynchronously through Akka messaging. The Yellow Pages helps discovering and locating other processes; the task management ensures separation of the information flows from and to a process.

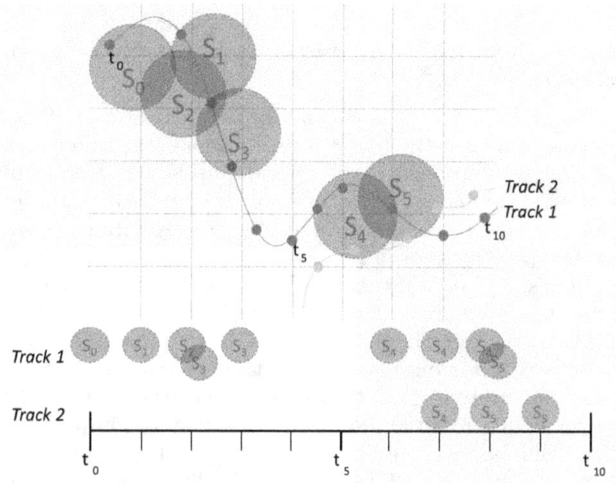

Figure 5: Two target objects move over time in the area of interest (the red and yellow dots). There are five sensors, $S1-S5$, and the task management ensures a clean separation of information flows as two different target objects cross paths and need different data from the same sensors.

For the communication between process blocks we use Akka[2], an actor-based middleware [1] that supports asynchronous communication [10], a feature we require to make the large variety of (types of) processes inter-operable without creating serious performance bottlenecks. Using an actor-based middleware allows us to represent each process block as an actor or group of actors, where actors use asynchronous communication among themselves. For example, a validation process gathers movement prediction, surveillance data, and context data from various resources and pushes its validated predictions to the next step in the process chain. The validation process can be represented by a group of actors, validating, in parallel, all different predictions of the target movement.

For process blocks to discover and be discovered by resources they have to be aware of their process types and the required types of input resources [6]. The process type is registered at the yellow pages service along with the address of the actor performing this type of process. Other processes that require data from this process type as input can now lookup the entries in the yellow pages and use the addresses to establish a communication link to these actors to create an information flow.

The yellow pages service running in the system is globally accessible and allows resource discovery with simple search requests. The retrieved addresses from the yellow pages can be used to establish a peer-to-peer communication between processes. In the initial design of the framework, the yellow pages is a central service, but future designs will support a distributed and fault-tolerant service.

6.1 Information Flows

Since process types and their required inputs are not situation specific, and the request from within a situation assessment is, additional filtering is required on top of the basic search provided by the yellow pages, namely negotiation. After a list of potential information suppliers is requested from the yellow pages, the requester sends its criteria (e.g. location, maximum response time) to participate in the information flow to the suppliers. The suppliers will match the criteria against their own settings and decide if they can participate in the proposed information flow, by replying with a accept or reject. The requester now has a set of relevant suppliers and can continue with his specific task. This negotiation procedure is a process running separately from the actual algorithm to reduce interference.

Arrangements to work together on a specific topic for a specific situation (*contracts*) established in time step t may or may not be useful in the next time step $t+1$, depending on the algorithm and the situation. As an extension to the above described negotiation procedure, reevaluating active contracts allows an updated set of criteria to keep the list of suppliers up to date with respect to relevance. In other words, when the process decides that the criteria for the input data have changed, the negotiation procedure is repeated; existing contract are reevaluated and potential new information suppliers are considered. The negotiation allows the system to only connect to the relevant resources, reducing the communication links.

Filtering on the relevance of suppliers is an important step in the creation of information flows. However, since security domains tend to cover large areas it is unlikely for a single information flow to be active in the entire system. With multiple information flows, their communication paths are expected to cross every now and then. By introducing task management, we keep track of the active tasks of every actor, where a task is a wrapper around a local instance of the process that is part of a specific information flow. Any received data is routed by the task management to the correct task, the task in turn needs to transfer the data to the correct part of the process. As illustrated in Figure 5: object one on *Track 1* is covered by sensors S_1 - S_5; as object 2

[2]Akka's webpage: http://akka.io/.

on *Track 2* crosses the path of object 1, they can both use the data from the same sensors without mixing the actual information flows.

Since both the negotiation and the task management functionality are agnostic to that of the processes, the framework require each process to be wrapped inside a container of generic components (the orange box in Figure 4). The container exists of a task management, the negotiation, an interface with fixed set of process calls, and the yellow pages mechanism (the yellow box). Each process is required to implement a common interface, accessible by the task, with fixed structure to communicate with other processes, using primitives like request for input data, receive input data, and report output data. As the container is agnostic to the implementation of the process, a few configuration parameters, like input and output data formats used by the process (described in more detail in section 7), allow the framework to be adapted to many situations.

6.2 Scaling up

For large-scale scenarios, like decision support for security domains usually are, the framework has to be scalable to run hundreds or thousands of processes that are scattered across big areas (like a country's road network). Akka already has support for a large distributed setup, i.e., using multiple compute nodes for hosting and processing the actions of thousands of actors, as well as efficient asynchronous communication between actors.

Increasing the number of sensors, S, and/or the number of objects being tracked, N, leads to a proportional increase in the number of processes, and therefore actors. Scaling up the number of processes is relatively easy: once the yellow pages system contains the addresses of the actors running the desired process type, any process can exchange data on-demand with other processes. Our current implementation of the framework uses a central yellow pages service accessible by all running actors, this service can easily store tens of thousands of addresses, without any penalty on performance. Future implementations will have a distributed yellow pages, thus avoiding any potential bottleneck caused by quick developing scenarios, where a lot of processes require resource localization very often.

The components of the framework have a small footprint, and the communication over per process is small as well; however, the interaction of all these actors can pose scalability challenges to the system. Meaning, when $T_{communication}$ becomes the dominant factor in Equation 3, thus the communication overhead exceeds the computation times. To further reduce the framework's overhead, each actor runs its different tasks concurrently, by spawning more actors. The implementation of a process can apply a similar strategy when it requires a parallel solution, to improve performance.

In summary, our choice for Akka as a backbone of our framework, as well as the distribution of processes over actors, the simple, query-driven design of the yellow pages system, and the on-demand activation and deactivation of the inter-process links allow for smooth scaling up of the system. The use of parallel and distributed computing, as well as the concurrent design of processes, allows our framework to reach high performance.

```xml
<?xml version="1.0" encoding="UTF-8" standalone="yes"?>
<ns1:processdef xmlns:ns1="xml.process">
    <function name="License plate camera" outputCapability="LPC"
            autoCreateTaskOnStartup="false" className="sensor.MappedSensor">
        <variables>
            <outputRequest variableName="AreaOfInterest" variableType="datatypes.MapData" />
            <outputRequest  variableName="LicensePlate" variableType="java.lang.String" />
            <outputResponse variableName="Location" variableType="datatypes.MapData" />
            <outputResponse variableName="Timestamp" variableType="java.util.Date" />
            <outputResponse variableName="Certainty" variableType="java.lang.Double" />
        </variables>
        <arguments>
            <argument name="name">LPC1</argument>
            <argument name="location">POLYGON((103.87412301731814
            1.3587278034721435,103.86965264805309 1.3599333597062853,103.8663801000986l
            1.3632270035791627,103.86518225000309 1.3677262118682691,103.86638007125877
            1.3722254283670943,103.86965261921326 1.3755190886594102,103.87412301731814
            1.3767246531032713,103.87859341542303 1.3755190886594102,103.88186596337749
            1.3722254283670943,103.8830637846332 1.3677262118682691,103.88186593453769
            1.3632270035791627,103.87859338658319 1.3599333597062853,103.87412301731814
            1.3587278034721435))</argument>
            <argument name="socketHost">localhost</argument>
            <argument name="socketPort">3232</argument>
        </arguments>
    </function>
</ns1:processdef>
```

Figure 6: The process configuration file of a *Licence Plate Camera* that requires the target object's license plate *and* the area of interest (that will be used in the negotiation phase). Its response is a location, a timestamp and a certainty-of-observation value.

7. FEATURES AND USABILITY

To be applicable for a variety of decision support scenarios, our framework is designed to require little setting up effort for different scenarios. Because each process requires the same set of basic components – the means to find other resources and the actual communication to these resources, these components (described in section 5) do not have to be altered in any way. What the components do require is a *configuration of inputs and outputs.* In other words, the inputs and outputs define a resource type.

7.1 Configuration

The system configuration is the key element that allows the whole system to function, since it describes the *type* of resources in the system, and their potential interconnections (i.e. the output of a process is a potential input/resource for other processes). It further describes the format in which data is delivered by specifying the parameters of requests and answers; these parameters form a sort of standard of communication between processes, which ensures coherent data interpretation.

For example, at high level, a *Licence Plate Camera* component type is defined by a license plate and the coordinates of an area of interest as inputs, and the location of the license plate as output. Figure 6 shows an example of how the configuration file of the *Licence Plate Camera* surveillance process looks like. The license plate is stored in the *License-Plate* variable in the request for data, to be able to filter its surveillance data. The camera produces the observed location plus a value reflecting the certainty of the observation. The second value in the request (*AreaOfInterest*) can be used in the negotiation phase. Next to the variables, arguments can be passed to the process, like the position of a device and the procedure for connecting to it. Since a camera does not require any input resources, no variables of this type are shown in the example, but the configuration of input variables uses a syntax similar to that of the output variables.

7.2 Simulation

To test and evaluate the system, a simulator is used to mimic the real world. This simulator generates objects (vehicles in the case of the tracking scenario) that randomly

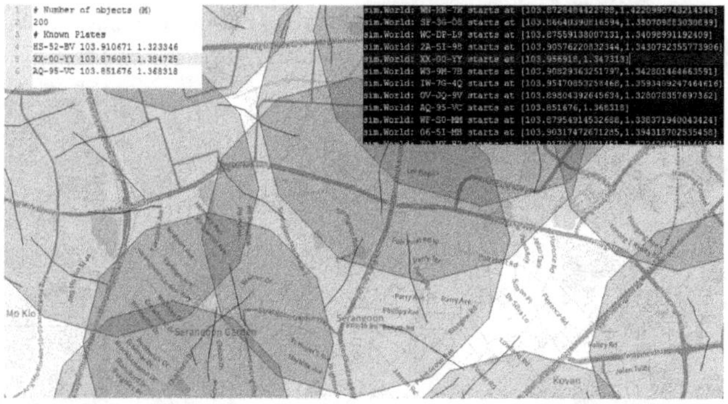

Figure 7: The simulation randomly generates M objects, except for a few "known" objects (top left). The objects (the blue lines) move through the world while the sensors (the red areas) periodically check the objects in their line of sight.

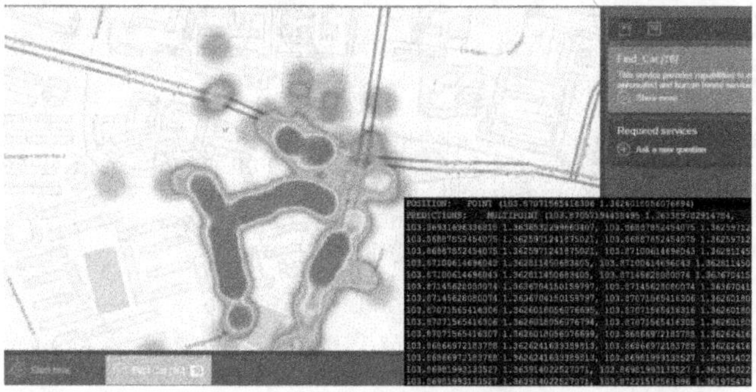

Figure 8: Screenshot of the operator view, showing the predicted next position of the requested car using a heat map.

move through an area, following context information in the form of a road map.

When starting the simulator, different parameters can be set - e.g., the number of objects in the environment and a set of objects with their starting positions. For example, vehicle with license plate *XX-00-YY* should start at position A. Next to this required vehicle, the simulator should fill the area with other random vehicles up to a total of N objects. With the use of context data (e.g. road maps, traffic information, obstruction due to construction) all N objects navigate through the environment using random choices of turns.

In the context of target tracking, each sensor connects to the simulator, requests all objects within its range, and applies its own filter on this subset of objects to try and find the objects it is asked to look for, similar to how it will operate in real-life situations. Figure 7 illustrates the simulated world, using the configuration from the top left corner of the image to generate 200 objects of which only 3 have a known starting position, the rest receive a randomly generated starting position and random license plate. Figure 8 shows an example how the result of the tracking system can be used to help the operator make a decision, by showing a heat map of the predicted movements based on the observed surveillance data. Where the heat map is constructed of a set of points, each with a likelihood of the target being there, displayed with a colour indicating the likelihood as warmth (red: very likely, blue: not likely).

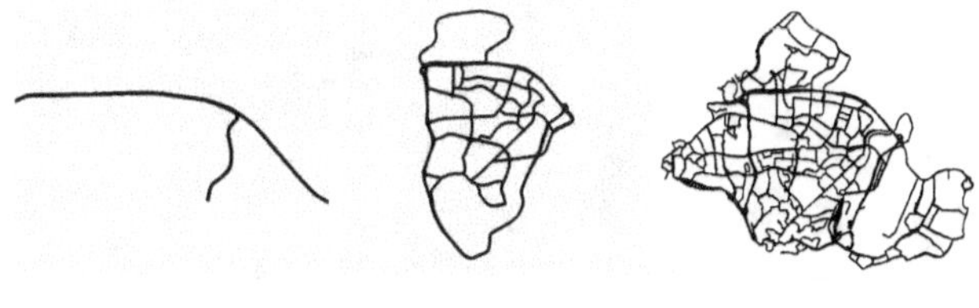

Figure 9: From left to right: a synthetic scenario with one junction, a more complex synthetic scenario, and a real life scenario of a small city.

For the setup of the simulator multiple information and configuration files are required: (1) files or database containing the context data, (2) the set of structured objects, and (3) some tuning parameters (e.g. number of noise objects, the frequency of updating the objects, the maximum speed of an object).

8. VALIDATION

For evaluation, we use the specific case-study of target tracking in urban environments and we focus on correctness. The idea for this validation is to change the environment (i.e. the road map) to a case that has known results - that is, it is either obvious or known in advance how the situation evolves and must be resolved. If correct, the simulator will match the ground truth in its behavior.

At the moment, no ground truth data is available (and generating it is another research problem in itself). Therefore, to validate the correct functionality of our simulator and system, we use synthetic scenarios. These synthetic scenarios are simplified environments - e.g., a main road with a single junction, were it splits into two side roads (left most image in Figure 9). In such cases, a full 1-to-1 comparison can be made between the expected results and those automatically calculated. When we observe that the tracker properly follows the car into the right direction, the communication between sensors, context bank and tracking algorithm is correct. As for the decision model, it should choose to close down the one side road and not both or the main road, to actually minimize the impact on normal traffic. Once these synthetic microtests are passed correctly, we further validate against realistic scenarios, which use real road maps and data (two examples are shown in Figure 9). In this case, validation is done by randomly sampling intermediate results and comparing them against the real-world and/or simulated results.

We note here that, the system we have built so far works correctly and fully automated for the simple microtests. Sample-based validation for larger synthetic cases is work in progress. Furthermore, we note that empirical validation cannot guarantee the full correctness of the system, but rather its compliance to the expected outcome for a large number of (simple) situations. For example, see Figure 10: the simulator correctly reads the data from the sensors and computes the predictions for the future position of the tracked object, but it can only take a clear decision in the situation on the left, not in the situation on the right.

We conclude that the simulator is accurate in following the targets on the map, which essentially proves that it is able to manage several processes and sensors correctly. We emphasize that this matches its goal to support decision

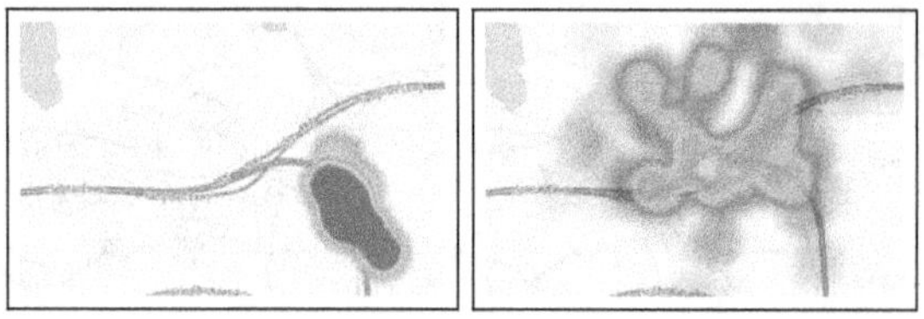

Figure 10: Left: the simulator correctly predicts the trajectory of the object (high intensity on the heat-map); a decision can be made to shut off the road before the junction. Right: the simulator detects the T-junction and predicts both rows as probable destinations. No single-road can be selected to be closed before the a new measurement is made.

making by providing the operator enough data to make an informed decision based on high-probability predictions.

9. PERFORMANCE ANALYSIS

For the framework to be applicable in the targeted security domains, scalability is mandatory. Therefore, we present a first attempt to analyze the scalability of the system.

Our metrics for scalability are processing time and information transfer time. Processing time is defined as the time between arrival of new information and the time an (updated) output is ready. For the transfer time, the definition is less straightforward, because it could involve more than a mere exchange of information from A to B. Thus, to transfer information in a situation where the processes are already connected, the transfer time equals the time to exchange the information (exchange cost). To transfer information when no connection exists, the transfer time includes both the time to find potential receivers and establish a connection (negotiation cost), and the actual sending of the information (exchange cost). We therefore define the transfer time as the sum of the negotiation cost and data exchange cost, where the negotiation cost for an established connection is zero.

For measuring the processing time of the system we ran experiments with varying numbers of sensors (S) and tracked target objects (N) between 1 to 30. In each experiment, we simulated the movement of 50 objects randomly through an urban environment (see the rightmost scenario in Figure 9) to provide the sensors with data. We position the sensors to cover the whole area, to ensure a known number of connections (meaning the negotiation has a known outcome namely all sensors will be connected).

Running an experiment with $S = 5, N = 5$ means that 5 objects (out of the total 50) are tracked during the whole experiment, and all 5 of the validation blocks receive information from each of the 5 sensors active in the system. Projecting this setup on the pipeline of Figure 3 we can calculate the number of transmitted messages for each new output, namely $S+4$ messages: from each sensor, the movement prediction and the context collection to the validation, in between the two validation blocks and one from validation to the action suggestion step. So in a setup of $S = 5, N = 5$ we have $5 \times (5 + 4) = 45$ messages for each iteration. For a large setup of $S = 30, N = 30$, we have 1020 messages each iteration. Based on these numbers we expect an exponential growth in communicotion time.

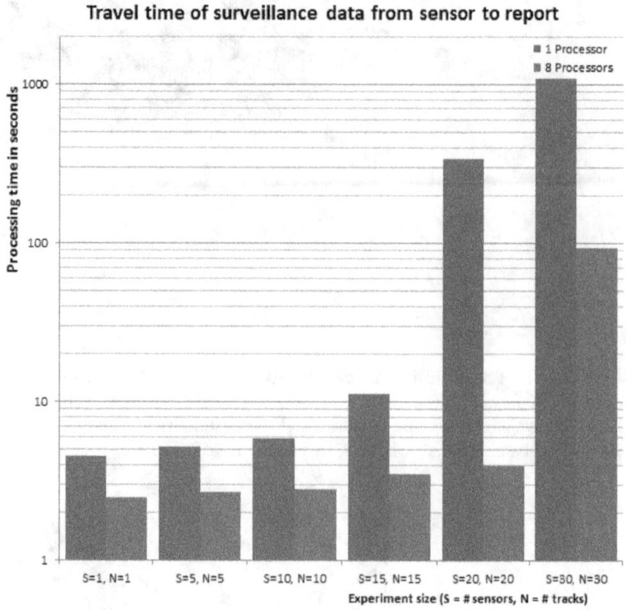

Figure 11: Processing time in seconds for target tracking – time from arrival of new surveillance data to the time a new output is ready, using 1 and 8 processors. Note the increasing number of sensors S and tracks N, where each sensor connects to all available tracks.

For the experiments we used two hardware configurations:

	Name	Clock Freq.	Processors
single-core	Intel Xeon CPU E5-2450	2.5GHz	1 core
multi-core	Intel Xeon CPU E5-2450	2.5GHz	8 cores

Figure 11 shows the median processing time of our simulation over 1000 iterations.

We observe that already with a single sensor and track the *multi-core configuration* (8 processors) outperforms the *single-core configuration* (1 processor), since the different blocks in the pipeline can now run in parallel allowing, for example, a next iteration to start before the previous finished. Furthermore between $S = 1, N = 1$ and $S = 20, N = 20$ the processing time increases with only 1.5 seconds against 336.5 seconds for the *1 processor* experiment. These performance numbers demonstrate that (a) performance is challenging for a system with relatively low density of objects, tracks, and sensors, and (b) that our proposed decision support system is able to make use of system parallelism. For the $S = 30, N = 30$ experiment, both hardware configurations show a huge increase in processing time, which is not surprising given the fact that we move from 480 to 1020 messages per iterations and the number of processing blocks in this setup adds up to 151 blocks. Clearly, although our system can still scale to cope with such data-intensive, complex cases, the time-to-decision can becomes unacceptable. To address this challenge, our current work focuses on increasing system efficiency through better parallelisation strategies.

We also note that gathering the results from the $S = 30, N = 30$ scenario on the *single-core configuration* was very difficult because only 25% of the iteration finished successfully, due to the lack of computation and/or memory resources. It is important to note that no such issues appeared when switching to the 8-core configuration. These results demonstrate *both* the importance of scalability for such decision support systems, and the ability of the proposed framework to automatically use more resources, when available.

10. CONCLUSION

In the security domain, many complex situations need to combine unstructured data and complex processes to effectively support the decisions of a human operator. Similar scenarios (with even larger variability and complexity) emerge today in the Internet-of-Things (IoT) domain.

In this work, we presented a generic, scalable framework for decision support in complex situations. Our contributions are: (1) identifying the functional and computational requirements of such a framework, (2) proposing a first architecture for this framework, (3) implementing a first functional prototype for semi-automated decision support, and (4) defining and testing validation scenarios for surveillance applications.

Our results so far are promising in terms of correctness and simple-case performance. Our immediate future work focuses on complex scenario implementation and testing, thus identifying and tackling the complex scalability challenges and boundaries for real situations. Furthermore, we currently investigate the applicability and the limitations of our framework for IoT applications.

11. REFERENCES

[1] C. Hewitt, P. Bishop and R. Steiger. *A Universal Modular ACTOR Formalism for Artificial Intelligence*, IJCAI, pp 235âĂŞ245, 1973.

[2] J. Burns, *A formal model for message passing systems*, Computer Science Department, Indiana University, 1980

[3] R. Sprangue, *A framework for the development of decision support systems*, MIS, pp 1-26, 1980

[4] G. Agha, *ACTOR: A Model of Concurrent Computation in Distributed Systems*, MIT Press series in artificial intelligence, 1986

[5] F. Gustafsson, F. Gunnarsson, N. Bergman, U. Forssell, J. Jansson, R. Karlsson and P. Nordlund, *Particle Filters for Positioning, Navigation, and Tracking* IEEE Transactions on Signal Processing, 50(2):425âĂŞ437, 2002.

[6] A.Penders, G. Pavlin and M. Kamermans, *A collaborative approach to construction of complex service oriented systems*, IDC, pp 55-66, 2010.

[7] S. Tasharof, P. Dinges and R. Johnson, *Why Do Scala Developers Mix the Actor Model with Other Concurrency Models?*, ECOOP, pp 302âĂŞ326, 2013.

[8] H. Koen, P. de Villiers, G. Pavlin, A. de Waal, P. de Oude and F. Mignet, *A framework for inferring predictive distributions of rhino poaching events through causal modelling*, Fusion, 2014.

[9] R. Claessens, A. de Waal, P. de Villiers, A. Penders, G. Pavlin and Karl Tuyls, *Multi-Agent Target Tracking using Particle Filters enhanced with Context Data*, AAMAS, 2015

[10] A. Rosà, L. Chen and W. Binder, *Profiling Actor Utilization and Communication in Akka*, Erlang, pp 24-32, 2016

CloudPerf: A Performance Test Framework for Distributed and Dynamic Multi-Tenant Environments

Nicolas Michael
nicolas.michael@oracle.com

Nitin Ramannavar
nitin.ramannavar@oracle.com

Yixiao Shen
yixiao.shen@oracle.com

Sheetal Patil
sheetal.patil@oracle.com

Jan-Lung Sung
janlung.sung@oracle.com

Oracle Inc.
4180 Network Circle
Santa Clara, California 95054

ABSTRACT

The evolution of cloud-computing imposes many challenges on performance testing and requires not only a different approach and methodology of performance evaluation and analysis, but also specialized tools and frameworks to support such work. In traditional performance testing, typically a single workload was run against a static test configuration. The main metrics derived from such experiments included throughput, response times, and system utilization at steady-state. While this may have been sufficient in the past, where in many cases a single application was run on dedicated hardware, this approach is no longer suitable for cloud-based deployments. Whether private or public cloud, such environments typically host a variety of applications on distributed shared hardware resources, simultaneously accessed by a large number of tenants running heterogeneous workloads. The number of tenants as well as their activity and resource needs dynamically change over time, and the cloud infrastructure reacts to this by reallocating existing or provisioning new resources. Besides metrics such as the number of tenants and overall resource utilization, performance testing in the cloud must be able to answer many more questions: How is the quality of service of a tenant impacted by the constantly changing activity of other tenants? How long does it take the cloud infrastructure to react to changes in demand, and what is the effect on tenants while it does so? How well are service level agreements met? What is the resource consumption of individual tenants? How can global performance metrics on application- and system-level in a distributed system be correlated to an individual tenant's perceived performance?

In this paper we present *CloudPerf*, a performance test framework specifically designed for distributed and dynamic multi-tenant environments, capable of answering all of the above questions, and more. CloudPerf consists of a distributed harness, a protocol-independent load generator and workload modeling framework, an extensible statistics framework with live-monitoring and post-analysis tools, interfaces for cloud deployment operations, and a rich set of both low-level as well as high-level workloads from different domains.

ICPE'17, April 22 - 26, 2017, L'Aquila, Italy

ISBN 978-1-4503-4404-3/17/04...$15.00

DOI: http://dx.doi.org/10.1145/3030207.3044530

CCS Concepts

•**Computing methodologies → Simulation environments; Simulation tools;**

Keywords

Performance testing; workload modeling; load generation; statistics collection; multi-tenancy; cloud

1. INTRODUCTION

Cloud providers offer on-demand infrastructure, platform, or software as a service (abbreviated IaaS, PaaS, and SaaS) to their users, called *tenants*, on a subscription-based payment model. Rather than purchasing hardware and software up-front and integrating, deploying and managing it in their own data center, tenants rely on the cloud provider for these tasks. In order to minimize their cost, cloud providers will try to maximize the number of supported tenants on their infrastructure by sharing physical resources among tenants. This is typically achieved by some form of virtualization on the hardware, operating system, platform, or application layer. While providers aim at maximizing the *overall* performance of their infrastructure, tenants are more concerned about their *individual* performance. This can easily create a conflict of interest, as the provider needs to restrict a tenant's resource consumption in order to host as many tenants as possible, while tenants may need more resources in order to achieve their desired performance objectives. Provider and tenant therefore often negotiate a service level agreement (SLA), in which the provider guarantees a certain minimum quality of service (QoS), sometimes combined with penalty payments if the SLA is not met. As the provider has little control over the workloads of its tenants, it can become challenging to fulfill their SLAs as workload characteristics of tenants may change at any point in time. A tenant on the other hand may complain if it suddenly experiences performance degradation due to a noisy neighbor although its own workload did not change.

Performance testing of cloud deployments is equally important for providers and tenants. Cloud service providers must be able to simulate realistic tenant behavior in order to optimize their infrastructure to best support a large number of tenants without violating their SLAs. Tenants must have certainty that the offered cloud services fulfill their requirements before moving their applications and workloads into the cloud. In order to support such tests, a performance test framework must be able to span potentially hundreds of nodes from which it collects data across all layers, including system-, platform- and application-level statistics. Rather than assuming a static infrastructure, it must support nodes to be added or removed from the system under test (SUT) at any time during a test run. To test the robustness of the infrastructure, it must be able to inject errors into the system to trigger application or node failures, and initiate operations such as the provisioning of new tenants or live-migration of a workload. It must be able to simulate the behavior of thousands of tenants running heterogeneous workloads, while controlling each tenant's workload individually to simulate their changes in load. Each tenant's throughput and response times must be measured separately to verify the fulfillment of SLAs. For metering and charge-back, it must also be possible to measure each tenant's resource consumption individually and correlate it to the tenant's behavior. Last but not least, such a framework must provide efficient ways to aggregate, post-process, report, analyze, and correlate the collected data across all nodes, layers, and tenants in configurable and comprehensive ways. While many existing performance test tools cover some of these requirements, we are not aware of any tool that addresses all of them.

In this paper we present *CloudPerf*, a performance test framework we have been developing at Oracle since 2012. The main design goals of CloudPerf were to create a distributed, dynamic, and extensible framework scalable to hundreds of nodes and thousands of tenants, with a protocol-independent load generator providing workload modeling abstractions for the implementation of arbitrary workloads, a statistics framework for live-monitoring, post-processing and analysis of workload and system statistics across all nodes, layers, and tenants, and integration with deployment operations in cloud environments. All necessary tasks from workload development, test deployment, test execution and statistics collection to test evaluation and analysis should be provided end-to-end under the umbrella of a single, tightly integrated framework.

The main contributions of this paper are:

- CloudPerf, a performance test framework for distributed and dynamic multi-tenant environments
- a detailed description of CloudPerf's architecture and components
- examples how CloudPerf can be used for performance testing of use-cases relevant to cloud deployments

The remainder of this paper is organized as follows: In section 2 we formulate requirements for cloud performance testing. In section 3 we describe the architecture and components of CloudPerf, and illustrate key features of CloudPerf in section 4. Related work is summarized in section 5, and we conclude with section 6.

2. REQUIREMENTS

Before designing and developing a performance test framework, requirements need to be formulated which the framework shall address. In this section, we gather requirements important for performance testing in cloud environments. This requirement list is certainly not exhaustive, but covers many central and relevant aspects and incorporates as well as exceeds requirements formulated by other researchers [7][10][11]. In sections 3 and 4, we then discuss how CloudPerf fulfills these requirements.

R 1 (SCALABILITY). *Scalability to hundreds of nodes, thousands of tenants, days of test duration, and virtually unlimited number of end users, transaction rates, and concurrent sessions.*

R 2 (ELASTICITY). *Support of elastic SUTs with nodes being added and removed from the SUT during a test run.*

R 3 (AVAILABILITY). *Support of destructive tests and accidental node deaths during a test.*

R 4 (GENERIC WORKLOAD MODELING). *Modeling abstractions for the implementation of arbitrary high-level as well as synthetic workloads using reusable building blocks.*

R 5 (PROTOCOL INDEPENDENCY). *Load generation independent of any protocol or application domain to allow implementation of workloads for any domain using the same framework and modeling abstractions.*

R 6 (DYNAMIC LOAD GENERATION). *Support of open and closed system load generation models for synthetic load generation with dynamic change of request rates, concurrency, and other workload parameters.*

R 7 (LOAD REPLAY). *Replay of captured workload profiles at configurable speed.*

R 8 (MULTI-TENANCY). *Support for mixed workloads and individual per-tenant control of any load generation or workload parameter.*

R 9 (FAULT INJECTION). *Injection of faults and execution of arbitrary actions during a test run to simulate or trigger errors and other operations.*

R 10 (CLOUD LIFE CYCLE OPERATIONS). *Triggering and measurement of deployment and other cloud management operations performed by the cloud provider such as provisioning or live-migration of tenants.*

R 11 (STATISTICS COLLECTION). *Collection of fine-grained load generation, system- and application-level statistics across all nodes and layers.*

R 12 (CONDITIONAL EVENTS). *Conditional execution of load changes, fault injection or management operations based on observed tenant or system behavior.*

R 13 (METRICS AND RESULTS). *Calculation of metrics and result verification using arbitrary statistics.*

R 14 (LIVE OBSERVABILITY AND INTERACTION). *Live observability of a test run including monitoring of any collected statistics during runtime as well as interactive intervention (such as change of load) during a run.*

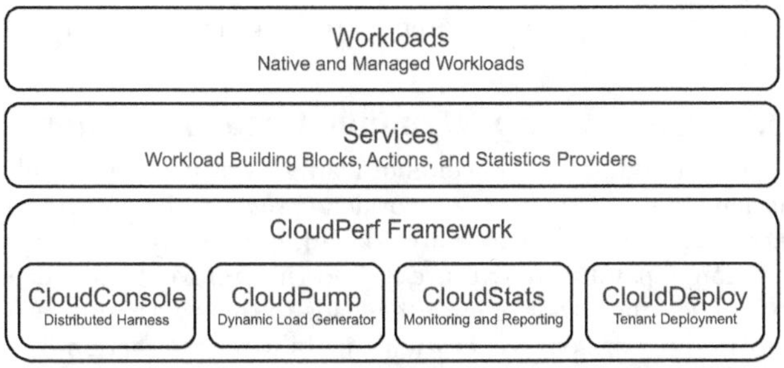

Figure 1: CloudPerf Framework Architecture

R 15 (TIME-BASED STATISTICS AGGREGATION). *Aggregation of statistics based on time intervals defined by load changes or other triggers to allow evaluation of statistics, metrics, and results across the entire test run as well as for each individual interval.*

R 16 (FLEXIBLE REPORTING). *Flexible report generation of statistics, metrics, and results using user-defined templates supporting arbitrary aggregation and correlation of statistics from any source. Report generation across multiple test runs for test comparison.*

R 17 (INTERACTIVE ANALYSIS). *Tools for interactive analysis and correlation of all collected statistics for troubleshooting and deep-dive analysis.*

R 18 (REPEATABILITY AND AUTOMATION). *Repeatable test execution using pre-configured events and interfaces for automated test submission.*

R 19 (EXTENSIBILITY AND REUSABILITY). *Well-defined APIs for high degree of reusability and extensibility, especially for statistics collection, workload development, and fault injection.*

R 20 (EASE OF USE). *Ease of use from workload development, test deployment, test execution, to test evaluation.*

3. ARCHITECTURE

Key objectives of CloudPerf were to design a scalable, extensible, flexible, and reusable framework for performance tests of all kinds, that provides as much as possible common functionality in the framework without limiting its use to any specific domain. In order to accomplish this, we have designed CloudPerf in a very generic way using abstractions that are common across nearly all workloads, statistics, or deployment types, and where necessary also allow to by-pass framework components to even cover those corner-cases not directly supported by our framework. CloudPerf is written in Java and therefore runs on any environment supported by Java.

CloudPerf is a modular software product comprised of individually developed and packaged *modules*. The CloudPerf *Framework* module consists of four core components, *CloudConsole*, *CloudPump*, *CloudStats*, and *CloudDeploy* complemented by a set of tools. The framework module is extended through *Service* and *Workload* modules (figure 1). The remainder of this sections describes the framework components, services, and workloads in detail.

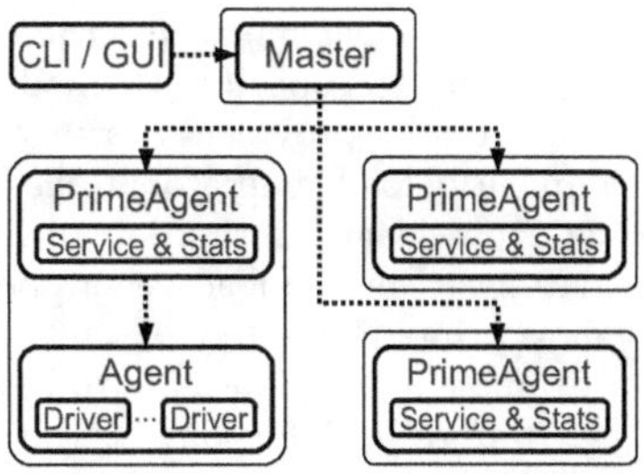

Figure 2: CloudPerf Process Architecture

3.1 CloudConsole: Distributed Harness

CloudConsole is a distributed harness which manages the overall test deployment, configuration, submission of test runs and events, communication between nodes, result gathering, and live polling of statistics.

3.1.1 Deployment and Process Model

A CloudPerf deployment is managed through a *Master* process running on a dedicated node, which serves as the single point of administration. From this node, the CloudPerf software is automatically installed or updated on all configured nodes of the test deployment. On each node of an installation, a *Prime Agent* process is started. The prime agent remains idle until being requested to participate in a run by the master. A test run may be submitted to all or just a subset of the provisioned prime agents, separating software distribution from test execution. Prime agents serve two main purposes (also simultaneously) during a test run, the collection of system statistics and the management of load generators. While statistics collection is done by the prime agents themselves, they spawn separate *Agent* processes to run the actual load generators (*Driver*) on selected nodes. A sample deployment is illustrated in figure 2.

Note that CloudPerf does not explicitly distinguish clients and SUT, but treats all nodes the same. Whether a node that runs a load generator is considered client or SUT is entirely the decision of the performance tester. CloudPerf also allows to run master, prime agent, and agents all on the same node for single-node deployments, and even supports to run them inside a single JVM for development purposes.

During a run, the master supervises all participating prime agents and polls statistics from them, which in turn supervise and poll statistics from all agents they have spawned. The inter-process communication is implemented through Java Remote Method Invocation using parallel threads to ensure scalability to hundreds of nodes (R1). Users can connect to the master using graphical (GUI) and command-line (CLI) tools to monitor and control test runs.

3.1.2 Run Configuration and Submission

A run is configured through a set of XML-based configuration files. The CloudPerf framework itself provides *framework* and *cloudpump* configuration files which specify framework parameters such as ports, JVM options, trace and debug settings, and basic load generator parameters. *Service developers* create *service* descriptions specifying resources offered by a service as well as reporting of service-provided statistics. *Workload developers* create *workload* descriptions specifying Java class names, transaction names and distributions, metrics, result checks, and arbitrary other parameters offered by workloads. A *deployment description* is created by a *performance tester*, who specifies the nodes to be used for a test run, the statistics providers to run, their configuration, the assignment of load generators to hosts, as well as workload-specific deployment information such as URLs of web servers or databases for the load generators to connect to. Wildcards allow prime agents to join a test run after run submission, for example if new nodes are to be dynamically created during a run (R2). Additionally, the performance tester creates a *run description*, in which the test flow is specified in form of load change events and actions, their timing and load parameters such as injection rates or concurrency. Finally, a *report template*, which is provided by the framework but may be customized by the performance tester, specifies the content of the generated performance report.

Configuration parameters can be overwritten by configuration files in the order described in this section, which for example allows a performance tester to override basic load generator or workload parameters in the deployment or run descriptions without modifying the load generator or workload configuration files. Except for the basic framework configuration, which is read by each prime agent during startup, all other configuration files are passed to the master through a GUI or CLI when submitting a test run. These files can therefore be edited in a single, centralized location. Performance testers can use a web-based user-interface (WebGUI) to generate deployment and run description files automatically rather than manually editing them (R20).

3.1.3 Events

Events can trigger load changes in load generators (see section 3.2) or execute *actions* inside prime agents. Actions are small pieces of Java code provided by services which allow the execution of arbitrary code on any host at any point in time. With actions it is possible to inject faults into the SUT by killing a process, panicking a host, or simulating memory shortages by consuming all available memory (R9). Actions can also trigger operations such as the creation of new VMs, adding of CPUs to a VM, or the migration of a tenant to another host (R10).

Events can be pre-configured in the run description, depend on the outcome of actions, triggered by conditions based on the evaluation of statistics (R12), or interactively submitted through GUIs and CLIs (R14).

3.1.4 Result Gathering

In order to minimize network bandwidth consumed by the harness, all captured statistics are kept locally on each node during runtime. At the end of a test run, each prime agent and agent perform a local post-processing of their statistics in parallel (R1) before sending them to the master. Once the master has received all statistics, it invokes the reporter for report generation.

3.1.5 Live Polling

Any collected statistics such as transaction throughput and response times or CPU utilization can be polled live during runtime. Clients like LiveView or CLIs (see section 3.7) can connect to the master during runtime to fetch and display live statistics from all nodes. This allows performance testers to monitor a test while it is running (R14) rather than waiting for a report to be generated after test completion.

3.2 CloudPump: Dynamic Load Generator

The fundamental concepts of load generation are entirely independent of the type of workload, yet workload developers often not just develop a workload, but also the load generation capability to execute it, and thus reinvent the wheel with every new tool. This often leads to tools with only very restricted workload generation capabilities (see section 5).

With CloudPerf we take a different approach and provide all load generation capability inside the framework decoupled from the individual workloads. Workload developers only need to implement the business logic of their workload, while all load generation functionality is provided by the framework. This not only simplifies workload implementation as developers can focus on the business logic, but also provides consistent and reusable load generation capabilities with identical characteristics across all workloads (R19). To achieve this, we have designed a workload implementation model providing abstractions common across all workloads (R4). The scheduling of requests is independent of the workload domain and communication protocols (R5) and supports dynamic load changes (R6), load replay (R7) as well as multi-tenancy with per-tenant load control and reporting (R8).

3.2.1 Workload Modeling

CloudPerf provides a generalized workload model through APIs and abstract classes. Workload and service developers use these modeling concepts to implement workloads and services. This section briefly describes the core concepts of our workload model.

Implemented by Service

Operation A reusable building block to perform a certain task (examples: HTTP GET, database prepared statement, network read, disk write)

Connection A communication channel on which to run an operation (examples: HTTP connection, JDBC connection, TCP connection)

Connection Pool A pool of connections or a connection factory to be used by clients to connect to a server

Connection Listener A listening endpoint of a server for incoming client connections

Implemented by Workload

Transaction A set of operations glued together by business logic (examples: add to shopping cart, place a new order, receive and reply)

Session A sequence of related transactions (scheduled with think or cycle time) executed in the same context on behalf of a common user (identified through a common user ID)

Context The state of a session

Load A vector of values describing a workload's magnitude and parameters (such as rate, concurrency, user range, and custom attributes)

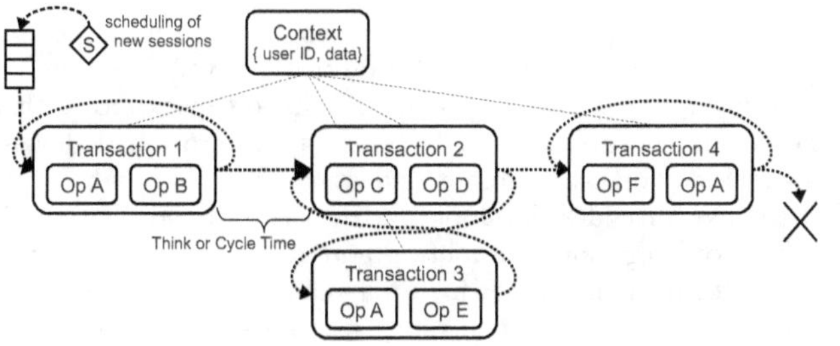

Figure 3: CloudPerf Workload Modeling

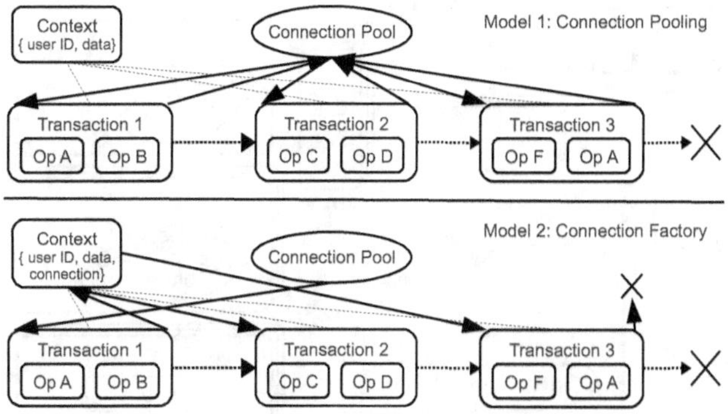

Figure 4: CloudPerf Connection Handling

Figure 3 illustrates a workload consisting of four transactions. In this example, a new session always begins with *Transaction 1* (initial transaction), which is scheduled by the framework's scheduler *(S)* according to a configured injection rate or concurrency (see section 3.2.2). The framework also creates a session context for this session and picks a user ID based on a configurable distribution. *Transaction 1* executes two operations *Op A* and *Op B* provided by a service, and then selects a subsequent transaction to run for this session and instructs the framework to schedule either *Transaction 2* or *Transaction 1* next. The scheduling of subsequent transactions may depend on the outcome of the current transaction or any other criteria and uses either think or cycle time to determine when to run the subsequent transaction. *Transaction 2* participates in the same session and therefore references the same session context through which data can be shared across transactions of the same session. Further state transitions eventually execute *Transaction 3* and *Transaction 4*, which may re-schedule itself or terminate the session.

If this example was a workload simulating the use of an online shop, *Transaction 1* could be a login transaction in which a user tries to login to their account, which is repeated until the login was successful. The user name could be derived from the user ID selected by the framework. *Transaction 2* could be a transaction in which the user browses a catalog of shopping items. In *Transaction 3*, the user may add an item to their shopping cart, and then continue browsing for more items in *Transaction 2*, until the user finally proceeds to *Transaction 4* in which the checkout and payment could be implemented. After successful payment, the session is completed. Operations could be HTTP GET and POST operations to load web pages from a web server and submit user input if this was a web workload, or prepared statements to be run against a database if this was a database workload. Any metadata such as web cookies, number of login attempts, or items already placed into the shopping cart, would be stored in the session context.

Figure 4 illustrates the use of connections. The first model depicts a classical connection pooling model in which connections are borrowed from a pool at the beginning of each transaction and returned back to the pool at the end of a transaction. In the second model, the connection pool is used as a factory: A new connection is created in the first transaction of the session and then stored in the session context. Subsequent transactions of this session use the previously created connection from the context, and the last transaction of the session closes the connection. CloudPerf makes no restrictions as to how many connections a session may create or borrow (as long as sufficient connections are available in the pool or the pool has not yet reached its maximum size). Also arbitrary combinations of the illustrated models are possible. For example, a session may store a borrowed connection in its session context or use both borrowed and newly created connections in the same session.

This model has proven to be very flexible for implementing any arbitrary workload. During workload design, developers will try to map a workload's elements onto the provided modeling abstractions in the most elegant way. Depending on the workload, some of these abstractions might not be applicable and will consequently not be used. For example, disk I/O workloads have no concept of connections. Other workloads consist only of unrelated events and do not require sessions. In those cases, operations may perform disk reads and writes without using connections, and sessions may consist of only a single transaction. User IDs chosen by the framework in uniform or non-uniform ways typically identify a range of data accessed by a workload (for example customer records in a database). A disk I/O workload without the concepts of users may instead use the user ID to decide the offset in a file for a read or write operation.

3.2.2 *Load Generation*

Load generation is implemented inside a *driver* provided by the CloudPerf framework. In a multi-tenant deployment, each individual tenant will typically be simulated by a dedicated driver. Mixed workloads will typically be run with one driver per workload and tenant. While drivers are highly performant[1], scale-out by instantiating multiple drivers per tenant provides virtually unlimited scalability for load generation (R1).

Figure 5 illustrates the main components of a CloudPerf driver. A *Scheduler Thread* creates *jobs* for new sessions at either a configurable injection rate (open system model) or based on a target rate of concurrent sessions to maintain (closed system model), and enqueues these jobs in a *Scheduling Queue*. An idle *Driver Thread* from a pool of threads dequeues the next job. If the job requires the start of a new session, it picks a random initial transaction from a transaction distribution table, creates a new session context, and executes the business logic of that transaction. If the transaction does not schedule a subsequent transaction, the driver

[1]A single driver can reliably schedule about 200,000 new sessions per second on Intel Westmere servers while just consuming a small fraction of CPU. Overall CPU consumption of a driver primarily depends on the implemented workload business logic.

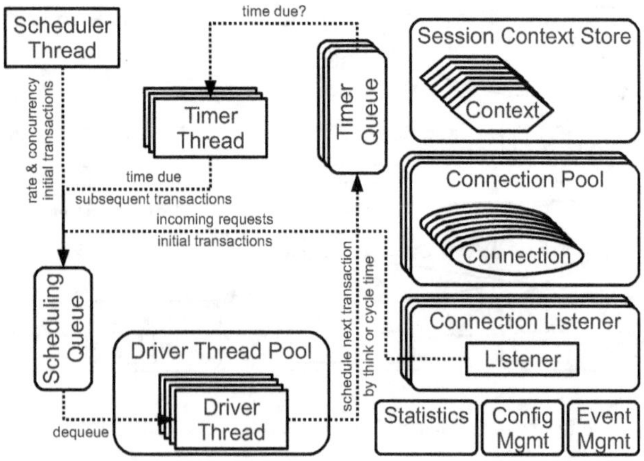

Figure 5: CloudPerf Driver Architecture

thread terminates the session after executing the transaction and deletes the session context. If the transaction has requested a subsequent transaction to be scheduled, the driver thread computes the due time of the subsequent transaction based on think or cycle time and inserts a job for the subsequent transaction into a *Timer Queue*[2]. For each timer queue, a *Timer Thread* dequeues jobs that have reached their scheduled time, and inserts them into the scheduling queue, where an idle driver thread will dequeue them and execute the scheduled subsequent transaction.

Note that subsequent transactions of the same session may execute on different driver threads and must therefore use the session context rather than thread-local variables to store session-related data. Driver threads are only used during execution of a transaction and then returned back to the pool. With this design, CloudPerf supports a virtually infinite number of concurrent sessions (only limited by the memory needs of the session contexts) where the number of driver threads only depends on the transaction rate and duration but not the think or cycle time or the number of concurrent sessions (R1).

The use of a scheduling queue decouples load injection from load processing and provides an open system model that simulates request-driven workloads much more accurately than closed system models[16]. Note that the scheduling queue only serves as a buffer and will be mostly empty if load processing keeps up with the injection rate. CloudPerf provides multiple options to handle overload, including the discarding of jobs when the scheduling queue is full and limits on the maximum queueing time for jobs in the queue (those jobs will be counted as failed transactions), which maintains an open system model also during overload.

Transactions may use connection pools provided by the driver as described in section 3.2.1. The driver maintains a configurable number of connections in each pool, specified through minimum and maximum size, and also supports resize operations during runtime, recreation of connections at configurable rates, and other features.

The driver captures statistics about transaction and operation throughput, success and failure rates, and response times including percentiles as well as resource usage of internal resources such as connection pool, driver thread pool, and scheduling queue length. User-defined timers and statistics counters can be used by service and workload developers for additional timing and statistics. Through APIs the driver provides developers with access to workload and other configuration parameters and reacts to events it receives from the master, which may cause it to change injection rates or target concurrency for the scheduler, resize a connection pool, change a workload parameter, or stop the workload.

For most workloads such as database and mid-tier workloads or CPU and storage micro-benchmarks, the driver will act as an initiator of requests. Through its *Connection Listener*, it can also act as a server, for example to implement client-server network micro-benchmarks. If the connection listener receives an incoming request, it will create a job for a new session and insert it into the scheduling queue, from which a driver thread will dequeue and execute it.

For synthetic workloads, requests are typically randomly generated based on a configurable distribution, injection rate, and concurrency. A random selection however, even if following a certain distribution, has limits and may not always be an accurate simulation of a given scenario. For example, a storage and its caching strategies may react differently to a synthetic random read/write mix than to the I/O profile of a real application, which generates specific sequences of read and write requests of a certain size on particular file descriptors. CloudPerf therefore also supports the replay of a previously captured profile in which the timing, type, and parameters of transactions are described in a text file. During load replay, the scheduler thread reads this profile and creates jobs for corresponding transactions accordingly. A configurable replay speed allows users to execute a profile faster or slower than it was captured (R7).

3.2.3 Load Changes and Dynamic Load

Load parameters can be changed at any time during a test run through load change events that are delivered to all or a select subset of drivers (R6). Drivers can increase or decrease injection rates, concurrency of sessions, replay speed, connection pool sizes, or any other workload parameters upon load change events. Changes in value can either be immediately or gradually applied over a configurable period of time.

To simulate constantly changing injection rates, CloudPerf also supports to configure load curves that continually adjust the injection rate based on a mathematical function with a certain period and magnitude such as a sine or gaussian function.

3.2.4 Mixed Workloads and Multi-Tenancy

Since two drivers share no resources (other than potentially the JVM or host they are deployed on), they act completely autonomously and can simulate individual tenants or workloads (R8). Each driver can have dedicated configuration and load parameters, run different workloads or transactions, and keeps its individual statistics to measure throughput and response times.

CloudPerf allows users to deploy an arbitrary number of drivers in an agent process, an arbitrary number of agent processes per host, and distribute agents across an arbitrary number of hosts. These deployment options enable Cloud-

[2]For better scalability, each driver maintains a set of timer queues, which are used in a round-robin fashion. Subsequent transactions with a think-time of 0 bypass the timer queues and are directly re-executed in the same driver thread.

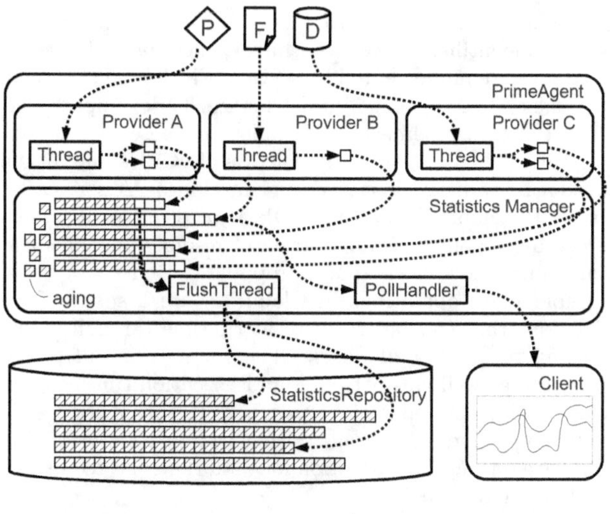

Figure 6: CloudPerf Statistics Framework

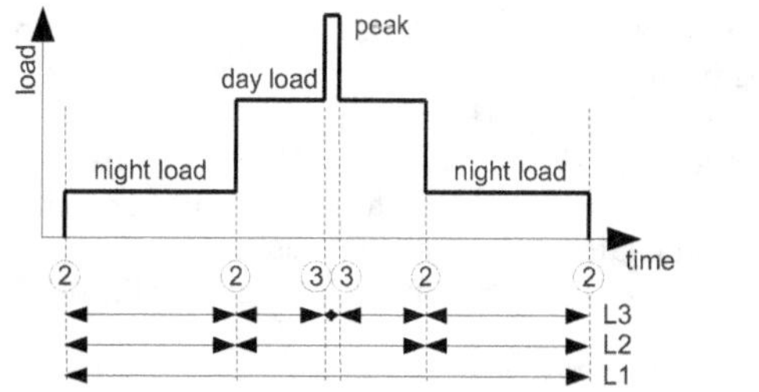

Figure 7: Time-Based Statistics Aggregation

Perf to scale to thousands of individually controlled and reported tenants running same or different workloads (R1).

3.3 CloudStats: Monitoring and Reporting

Monitoring and reporting are essential tasks of performance engineering and performance testing work. Most performance test tools are capable of capturing throughput and response time statistics for the load they generate, yet only few also capture comprehensive system-level or application statistics. The use of dedicated monitoring tools leaves the performance engineer with the task to integrate load generation and monitoring, which becomes increasingly challenging if load generation is not steady and load levels are changed throughout the test so that load changes need to be correlated in time with system statistics.

CloudPerf therefore natively integrates monitoring (R11) and reporting (R16) by providing an extensible and generic statistics framework (R19). This framework consists of a statistics repository in which all statistics are stored in a uniform way, and a set of pluggable statistics providers that capture data and add them into the repository, complemented by a GUI for live-monitoring, a customizable reporter for report generation, and other post-processing tools.

3.3.1 Data Organization and Repository

CloudPerf stores statistics in form of *series* which each consist of a sequence of *samples*. Each sample is a time-value pair. Series are created by statistics *providers* in a hierarchical namespace. The fully qualified name of a series consists of the provider name (*hostname*, *service*, *providername*, *providerid*) and the series name (*category*, *subcategory*, *series*).

Figure 6 illustrates the statistics framework architecture. Statistics providers are implemented by services and started on a host inside a prime agent. They register their series with the *statistics manager* which maintains the statistics repository and periodically flushes data to disk as it is being captured. Flushing also ensures that statistics data is not lost during destructive tests where nodes are crashed or rebooted during runs (R3). Recent samples are kept in memory to allow clients to poll for selective statistics, while old samples are aged out and purged from the statistic manager's cache to save memory. Statistics providers may use arbitrary ways to obtain their data such as the forking of a process (P) and reading of its output, tailing of a log file (F), connecting to an application like a database (D) and querying performance statistics, sampling of counters or registering for notifications. They may add samples to their series at arbitrary times and intervals.

3.3.2 Live Observability

Performance testing is usually an iterative process in which bottlenecks are eliminated and parameters adjusted until a workload or system behaves as desired. To facilitate such process better, CloudPerf provides a *LiveView* GUI for live observability of the system during runtime to allow performance testers to troubleshoot performance during the run rather than waiting for a report to be generated at the end (R14). LiveView uses CloudPerf's polling interface on the master to register for statistics series of interest and periodically poll latest samples. The master forwards these requests to all prime agents, which in turn forward them to all agents, and then aggregates the results before returning them back to the client. With statistics polling, any statistic collected on any node in a distributed environment can be observed and displayed live during runtime.

3.3.3 Conditions and Alerts

Conditions are rules based on mathematical expressions configured by a user for a certain set of statistics series on a node, which are evaluated by the statistics manager at runtime. When the configured expression evaluates to *true*, the statistics manager raises an alert, which triggers an action (delivered through an event) on any arbitrary host (R12). Performance testers can use this mechanism in many ways, for example to add VCPUs to a virtual machine if CPU utilization exceeds a threshold or to adjust load generation parameters based on the observed resource usage or response times.

3.3.4 Time-Based Statistics Aggregation

When load is dynamically changed throughout a test run, any statistical summary that only considers the run as a whole but does not distinguish its individual phases is of little value. Figure 7 illustrates a test run consisting of three major phases: a night-load, day-load, and night-load phase. During the day-load phase, a spike in traffic was simulated. Load change events in CloudPerf are tagged with a *level*, shown as a circled number in this figure. A level 1 event is automatically inserted at the very start and end of a test. Event timestamps determine the aggregation intervals for all captured statistics. Each aggregation interval is defined by two events of same or lower level. In the example, an L1 aggregation would represent statistics for the entire tests, while the L2 aggregation would distinguish night-load, day-load, and night-load phases, and the L3 aggregation would further break the day-load phase into the time period before, during, and after the peak. Statistic samples for all series are aggregated for each of these intervals (R15).

3.3.5 Customizable Reporting

At the end of a test run, all statistics captured by prime agents and agents are copied to the master's repository. The CloudPerf *reporter* then creates an HTML report for the test run. The content and format of the report is controlled through a customizable XML template (R16). It defines how statistics should be aggregated (for example, total throughput as the sum of the throughput of each individual driver, or disk servicing times as the average of all servicing times of disks of a particular host) and reported (in tabular form for each of the aggregation intervals, or plotted as a graph). The reporter makes no restrictions as to which series to aggregate or report and correlate in a common table or graph. Further report contents include captured system and configuration information, log files, and links to raw data. While the default report template satisfies most needs, users are encouraged to adapt it to fine-tune the reporting of their results to organize and summarize data in the most suitable form for their experiments.

The reporter can be manually rerun for previous tests to regenerate reports with different templates. Performance engineers often run series of tests in which selective parameters are varied to study their effects. To facilitate such analysis, the reporter can compare up to ten tests and create a comparative report in which data for multiple tests is reported side-by-side including relative differences of values.

Workload developers and performance testers can further specify *metrics* and *result checks* to compute higher-level metrics from the captured statistics or validate their values to determine whether a test should be considered successful or failed (R13). Metrics and result checks are either defined in XML or implemented as Java-callbacks for more complex evaluation. Services may also implement Key Performance Indicators (KPIs) which classify certain statistics or metrics into user-defined categories such as low, medium, and high.

3.4 CloudDeploy: Deployment Operations

Section 3.2 discussed the generation of user load. While the load profiles of users (or tenants) play a central role in cloud deployments, they are not the only activities that determine the overall performance of an environment. Administrative operations performed by the cloud service provider such as tenant deployment operations are equally important. CloudPerf provides the following abstractions for tenant deployment and management operations (R10):

Create Creation of a virtual resource

Start Starting of a virtual resource

Modify Modification of a virtual resource

Migrate Migration of a virtual resource

Stop Stopping of a virtual resource

Destroy Deletion of a virtual resource

Virtual resources describe the owning tenant, resource type and identifier, as well as arbitrary metadata. These abstractions are implemented by services which integrate them with the underlying cloud infrastructure. For example, a service for virtual machines could implement these abstractions as creation, boot, adding and deletion of vCPUs, migration, shutdown, and deletion of virtual machines. A service for Oracle Pluggable Databases (PDBs) could implement them as cloning, opening, configuration of resource management plans, migration, closing, and dropping of PDBs.

Deployment operations in CloudPerf are a special form of actions that can be triggered at runtime through events directed to any set of hosts. The framework will record their rate as well as start, end, and execution times to correlate deployment operations with performance metrics such as network bandwidth usage during VM creation or quality of service during live-migration for both the migrated as well as all other tenants.

3.5 Services

The CloudPerf framework is designed to be entirely agnostic of any particular product or domain. Services developed and packaged as individual modules adapt, map, and extend the framework capabilities to particular products and domains. They implement well-defined APIs and are relatively easy to develop (R19). Services provide:

Reusable workload building blocks such as connection pools and listeners, connections, and operations

Actions for performing deployment operations and other arbitrary tasks at runtime

Statistics providers for capturing of runtime statistics

Configuration gathering for capturing of system parameters

Precondition checks for validating a system configuration before a test run

Among the services we have developed are *HTTP*, *JDBC*, and *Network* services to provide the necessary building blocks for middleware, database, and network workloads. *Solaris* and *Linux* services provide OS-level statistics ranging from CPU utilization, memory usage, network and disk activity, and process statistics to hardware performance counters, NUMA and resource management statistics, and many more. A *GenericOS* service is capable of running generic scripts or tailing arbitrary log files and extracting data from them through configurable regular expressions. *Oracle*, *WebLogic* and *HotSpot* services capture detailed database, application server, and JVM statistics, and further services implement deployment operations for VMs and PDBs.

3.6 Workloads

As discussed before, the CloudPerf framework only provides generic modeling abstractions for workloads to implement workloads of any domain. The effort for the implementation of a new workload depends largely on the complexity of the workload and is often fairly low for simple workloads.

We have implemented numerous workloads ranging from high-level workloads to micro-benchmarks, and continue to add new ones. Our workloads include database OLTP workloads such as TPC-C, flight booking and the customizable

CRUD workload[14], DSS and analytical workloads such as a generic customizable DSS workload capable of running arbitrary queries and query streams and HTTP-based middleware workloads. Networking, disk, and scheduling workload provide powerful micro-benchmarks for multi-node and multi-tier networking tests, storage benchmarking, and optimization of operating system scheduling.

A generic *wrapper workload* is capable of wrapping existing workloads or commands to integrate them into CloudPerf and run them through the framework in a distributed environment without the need of porting or rewriting them. The concurrency of running commands can be changed any time through load change events, and regular expressions help to extract data from the output of these commands to feed it back into the statistics framework.

3.7 Tools

The CloudPerf framework includes several tools, many of which have been mentioned in previous sections already. The most important tools are:

Installer to install, update, and deinstall modules

DataLoader to populate a database, flat file, or other medium with test data

CLIs to restart master and prime agent processes, submit workloads and events, query the status of scheduled runs, and automate test submission (R18)

WebGUI to create deployment and run configuration files, submit workloads, and browse through results

LiveView to submit workloads, interactively change load, and monitor statistics during runtime (figure 9)

Reporter to create reports and compare test runs

StatsCollector for stand-alone statistics collection

StatsTool to export statistics from our repository for post-processing in spreadsheets or other tools

Performance Data Analyzer (PDA)[4] is not included but tightly integrated with the framework and supports interactive analysis and correlation of statistics (R17).

4. CLOUD PERFORMANCE TESTING

Section 3 described the architecture and key features of CloudPerf. In this section, we will illustrate on some examples how these features can be leveraged for performance testing in the cloud or other dynamic and distributed environments.

4.1 Test Series

In performance engineering it is very common to run test series in which a single parameter is changed from run to run to study its effect. Arguably most common are scaling tests in which either the injection rate or concurrency are increased. Though not directly related to cloud, such kind of experiments are greatly simplified by CloudPerf's ability to change load during a test. Rather than running a series of individual tests, CloudPerf enables performance engineers to run the entire test series in a single test run with multiple individually reported load steps where injection rate or concurrency are adjusted through load change events. This not only speeds-up test execution as lengthy ramp-up phases, pre- or post-processing steps can be avoided or greatly reduced, but also reduces the risk of accidental changes to the environment in between tests. Also workload parameters that alter the behavior of the workload can be changed through load change events. System and application parameters can be altered during a test through action events such as the *exec* action implemented in the Solaris and Linux services which executes any arbitrary command.

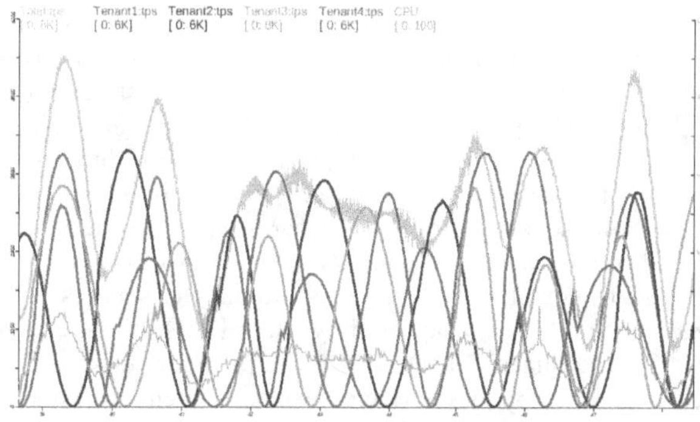

Figure 8: Dynamic Load Curves

4.2 Dynamic Load Curves

Performance at *steady-state* was and is widely used by performance testers to assess and report performance of an environment, yet it is a simplification which neglects the elastic aspects of shared deployments such as cloud. As infrastructure is shared among workloads or tenants, the elasticity of an environment - its ability to react to changes in demand - becomes an essential factor of its overall performance characteristics. Especially as cost considerations drive service providers to a higher degree of sharing, the risk of resource contention increases if tenants consume more resources than anticipated, be it network bandwidth, storage IOPS, or CPU cycles. The simulation of dynamic load curves is therefore a crucial feature of performance test frameworks for the cloud.

Figure 7 already illustrated how CloudPerf can be used to simulate different levels of activity such as day- or night-load phases as well as sudden load peaks through load change events. As discussed in section 3.2.3, tenants simulated by individual drivers can be controlled separately by directing load change events to selective drivers, creating potentially different load patters for each tenant.

Load change events however become impractical if load for a large number of tenants shall be constantly and individually adjusted. With the support of mathematical functions to generate per-tenant load curves with randomized period and magnitude, dynamic load patterns can be easily configured in CloudPerf even for hundreds of tenants (R6). Figure 8 shows a plot generated by CloudPerf for randomized sine load curves of four tenants.

4.3 Noisy Neighbors

Load change events and load curves are also ideal instruments to study the effects of noisy neighbors and the potential degradation of quality of service due to interference with other tenants. Such experiments can be conducted by keeping the injection rate for a primary tenant constant while increasing the rate of colocated tenants (neighbors) through load change events. The noisiness of a neighbor typically depends not just on its activity, but also its proximity to the primary tenant. The experiment can be further enhanced by changing the proximity of colocated tenants through action events, for example by changing the CPU binding of their virtual machines or containers from a different socket to the same socket or even same cores as the primary tenant. Throughput and response times of the primary tenant can then be correlated to other system metrics such as cache misses and stalls (also captured by CloudPerf) to assess their effect on the quality of service on the primary tenant.

Note that for request-driven workloads such experiments are much more meaningful with an open system load generation model than with a closed one. In an open system model, a fixed injection rate for the primary tenant will maintain its throughput as long as no resource is saturated even though its quality of service degrades. This degradation appears in form of increased response times, for example due to higher network, storage latencies, or cache misses as in the above sketched experiment, which can be directly compared to identical throughput of the tenant in isolation. In a closed system model, the quality of service degradation will manifest itself in a reduction in throughput for the primary tenant. In other words, the primary tenant would appear to be changing its behavior due to its noisy neighbors, which is typically not an adequate simulation of request-driven workloads where requests originate from external end-users and are fairly independent of response times unless they exceed critical thresholds.

4.4 Tenant Deployment and Node Addition

Not just the load of tenants constantly changes in cloud deployments, but also the number of hosted tenants. The time needed to provision a new tenant, the resource consumption of tenant provisioning, and the impact of tenant provisioning on the quality of service of other tenants are important performance attributes of cloud environments. As discussed in section 3.4, deployment operations in CloudPerf are implemented by services and may invoke cloud management software APIs to deploy or destroy tenants. At runtime, they are triggered through deployment events. Performance testers may use this to evaluate the cost of tenant deployment or the scalability of an environment as the number of tenants increases.

If new virtual machines are created for a tenant, a prime agent in that VM can be automatically started when the VM boots. It will then contact the master, which will lookup that prime agent's *role* and assign it a task, for example to collect statistics or start load generators. This way newly started hosts can join a running performance test and participate as if they had been there from the beginning, supporting dynamic changes of the SUT at runtime (R2).

4.5 Fault Injection and High Availability

Service availability is a key attribute of cloud offerings and is largely impacted by the robustness and fault tolerance of an environment as well as its ability and time needed to recover from failures. Stress testing in which faults are simulated is therefore besides performance testing another cornerstone of non-functional testing of cloud infrastructures. CloudPerf supports stress testing in many ways (R3).

Fault injection is enabled through actions, which execute arbitrary Java code and can be triggered on any host at any point in time through action events. Actions allow stress testers to kill processes, panic a host, change routing tables, offline CPUs, simulate memory shortages through allocation of large amounts of memory, and anything else that can be implemented in code.

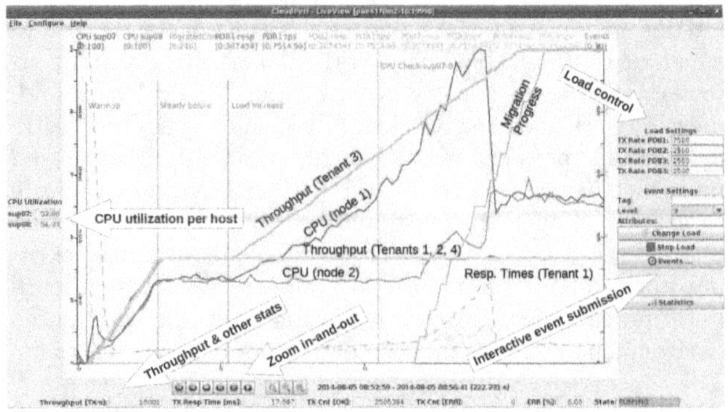

Figure 9: LiveView: Live Monitoring and Control

The open system load generation model of CloudPerf decouples load injection from its processing. If processing stalls, the driver's internal scheduling queue will run full. For stress testing both queue length as well as maximum queueing time can be limited so that requests are discarded if not handled within a specified time. CloudPerf reports both the duration of total service downtime (no single request serviced successfully) as well as request failure rates. Together with other statistics such as throughput, response times, and system statistics, those are reported separately for the period before the service failure (the time of the action event), during service downtime or degradation until the service is restored (identified through either conditions or other watchdogs that raise alerts upon restoration), and after full restoration of the service.

If services provide information about the state of connections, the framework's connection pool will automatically discard and re-establish failed connections. For database stress testing, CloudPerf's *JDBC* service also integrates the *Oracle Universal Connection Pool (UCP)* for advanced failover strategies of JDBC connections.

CloudPerf is also robust against failures of any monitored host on which a prime agent is running. Captured statistics are continuously flushed to disk to minimize data loss to a few seconds. On a rebooted host, a prime agent can resume statistics collection and re-join an existing test run.

4.6 Cloud Life Cycle Management

Conditions as described in section 3.3.3 can be used to monitor statistics values and trigger actions upon certain criteria, for example to add VCPUs to an overloaded VM or migrate a tenant off an overloaded host. Such experiments can be useful to design or prototype cloud management software decisions or improved migration algorithms.

In [14] we presented and evaluated a new methodology to migrate PDBs between nodes of a cluster which we tested and prototyped using CloudPerf. Figure 9 shows a screenshot of CloudPerf's LiveView GUI visualizing throughput and response times of four tenants as well as CPU utilization of two hosts during the runtime of a similar live migration experiment. Tenants 1 and 3 are deployed on node 1, while tenants 2 and 4 are deployed on node 2. After a warmup and steady-state phase, the load of tenant 3 is gradually increased through a load change event, slowly driving up CPU utilization on node 1 (sup07). A condition has been configured on node 1 to monitor CPU utilization and trigger an action to initiate live-migration of tenant 1 off the overloaded node once it exceeds a certain value. The screenshot shows response times of all four tenants as dashed lines, clearly indicating the response time increase of tenant 1 as it is being migrated from node 1 to node 2, as well as tenant 3 which suffers from high CPU utilization on node 1. Once tenant 1 has been migrated off the overloaded node 1, the CPU utilization for that node drops and utilization on both nodes is balanced. The bold horizontal overlayed curves in the middle of the graph show throughput for tenants 1, 2, and 4. Throughput for the migrated tenant 1 is steady throughout the migration without any downtime.

CloudPerf not only provides the necessary features for such complex experiments, but can even be used to prototype improved algorithms or to monitor system behavior live during test execution.

4.7 Multi-Tenancy

In [17] we used CloudPerf to compare the efficiency and scalability of two different database deployment models by deploying and simulating 252 tenants. Tenants were split into three groups (small, medium, large) of 84 tenants each with different database sizes and injection rates. The focus of our study was to determine the resource needs and resulting throughput and response times for tenants in both deployments. Using CloudPerf's services providing operating system and database observability, we captured CPU consumption, memory footprint, storage I/O, and database statistics such as waits and buffer cache misses per tenant group for each deployment. In another experiment, we deployed application server and database clusters, storage infrastructure and load generators for 29 tenants across a total of 128 nodes (R8).

The ability of CloudPerf to control this many tenants on a distributed infrastructure in a single test run and automate the correlation of statistics to tenants made these experiments feasible (R1).

4.8 Service Level Agreements

Cloud providers and tenants typically negotiate SLAs to specify guaranteed levels of performance, availability, and other attributes of the service. The fulfillment or violation of service levels can be validated for each test run by the CloudPerf reporter through result checks as described in 3.3.5. Test runs are then automatically marked as successful or failed based on the configured criteria (R13).

4.9 Scalability and Overhead

Testing all aspects of cloud demands highest scalability from a performance test framework. We designed CloudPerf such that its architecture scales to largest deployments by providing horizontal scalability of load generation, parallel and asynchronous message-based three-level communication between master, prime agents, and agents, node-local storage of statistics during runtime with parallel post-processing, and many other features. In our daily work, we have challenged the implementation of CloudPerf to live up to its architectural possibilities and resolved bottlenecks where we found them. At the time of writing, we have run experiments with up to 252 tenants, 128 hosts, on servers with 1 to 384 cores per host, 72 hours of runtime, up to half a million statistic series per host with hundred millions of samples, and hundreds of GB of result data per run (R1).

The overhead of the framework can be categorized into CPU, memory, network, and disk I/O consumption. The CPU cost of load generation primarily depends on the workload's business logic, while the overhead for scheduling and timing is typically below 5% for high-level workloads (micro-benchmarks with minimal business logic may have a higher overhead). CPU cost for statistics collection depends on the invoked commands or queried APIs. The framework itself only consumes minimal CPU cycles (typically less than 0.1% of a system). The memory footprint of prime agents depends on the number of sampled statistics and usually ranges from tens to hundreds of MB. Heartbeats and statistics polling only consume negligible network bandwidth. Flushing of statistics data is batched and only generates few disk writes.

5. RELATED WORK

Numerous performance test tools and frameworks have been developed over the years, each with a different purpose in mind. Some tools such as vdbench[6], iperf[20], or uperf[5] specialize in a particular micro-benchmark and only run this single workload. YCSB[9] and YCSB++[15] are targeting cloud, but also just execute a single workload. Others tools are broader and capable of running different workloads but limited to just one domain. For example, OLTPBench[10] and SwingBench[12] only run database workloads, Cloudstone[19] only runs web workloads. JMeter[1] has expanded beyond web workloads, but is limited to supported protocols. Faban[2] is merely a harness without built-in load generation and instead leaves driver implementation to the workload. None of them support multi-tenancy. MuTeBench[13] adds multi-tenant support to OLTPBench but only supports a static SUT. CloudBench[18] emphasizes on VM deployment and automation for performance comparison of infrastructure cloud providers, but does not provide workload modeling abstractions. CloudSim[8] is a simulation framework for cloud infrastructures without tenant load generation capabilities on its own. Rally[3] is designed to benchmark OpenStack only and neither supports other cloud management software nor tenant load generation.

Many of the above tools only support steady load execution of a single tenant and require a second instance of the tool be be started to simulate either a load increase of the first tenant or activity of a second tenant. This quickly becomes impractical when frequent load changes or hundreds of tenants shall be simulated. Most tools just support closed system load generation models in which a number of threads is created to execute requests either back-to-back or with a configurable think-time. Such a model only allows to configure the concurrency of load generation, but is incapable of maintaining a configured request rate. Partly open system models implemented in some tools use cycle-time to achieve a mostly deterministic request rate, but require a sometimes impractically large number of threads if the cycle-time is high, which dramatically limits the scalability of that model. In reality however, the request arrival rate is externally given for most request-driven applications, which can only be adequately simulated with an open system model.

With the exception of those tools that focus on VM deployments, all of the above tools require a static SUT that does not change throughout test execution. They also do not support destructive stress tests in which nodes crash or reboot.

6. CONCLUSIONS AND FUTURE WORK

We have presented CloudPerf, an extensible and versatile performance test framework. Its application ranges from synthetic micro-benchmarks to high-level web or database workloads. It can be used to run performance tests against stand-alone scale-up systems as well as distributed scale-out environments. With its workload modeling abstractions it provides a high level of reuse and decouples workload development from load generation. CloudPerf supports both open as well as closed system load generation models to adequately simulate any kind of workload such as request-driven OLTP workloads, analytical or batch workloads. Its load generation capabilities range from single-tenant steady-state to dynamically changing load steps, curves or spikes for hundreds of individually controlled tenants running identical or heterogeneous workloads. CloudPerf supports elastic infrastructures and changes in the SUT such as hosts leaving or joining a test, which allows testers to conduct stress tests in which hosts are panicked or rebooted or new hosts or VMs are dynamically provisioned during a run. The load generation features of CloudPerf are complemented by an extensible statistics framework, customizable reporting, and live-monitoring of tests to allow users to analyze and correlate performance-relevant statistics across all layers of the stack. CloudPerf can be used for more traditional test scenarios where the performance of an application, database, server, or storage is evaluated or optimized, but it especially plays out its strengths in distributed and dynamic multi-tenant environments — such as *cloud.*

CloudPerf's framework has proven very versatile for all our work so far. While we keep enhancing and improving it, our future efforts mostly focus on areas beyond the framework such as the development of new workloads and services and the application of data analysis techniques on the data we capture. Especially the integration with various cloud life cycle management software through CloudPerf services will be necessary to better test and optimize cloud management. Data analytics could be used at runtime to develop and validate models for predictive forecasting of SLA violations to automatically take corrective actions, or on test results stored in a central repository to assist software and hardware architecture and design decisions for next-generation products.

7. REFERENCES

[1] Apache jmeter. http://jmeter.apache.org/. Accessed: 2016-09-17.

[2] Faban. http://faban.org. Accessed: 2016-09-17.

[3] Openstack rally. https://wiki.openstack.org/wiki/Rally. Accessed: 2016-09-17.

[4] Performance data analyzer. http://pda.nmichael.de/. Accessed: 2016-09-17.

[5] uperf. http://www.uperf.org/. Accessed: 2016-09-17.

[6] vdbench. http://vdbench.sourceforge.net. Accessed: 2016-09-17.

[7] C. Binnig, D. Kossmann, T. Kraska, and S. Loesing. How is the weather tomorrow?: towards a benchmark for the cloud. In *Proceedings of the Second International Workshop on Testing Database Systems*, page 9. ACM, 2009.

[8] R. N. Calheiros, R. Ranjan, A. Beloglazov, C. A. De Rose, and R. Buyya. Cloudsim: a toolkit for modeling and simulation of cloud computing environments and evaluation of resource provisioning algorithms. *Software: Practice and Experience*, 41(1):23–50, 2011.

[9] B. F. Cooper, A. Silberstein, E. Tam, R. Ramakrishnan, and R. Sears. Benchmarking cloud serving systems with YCSB. In *Proceedings of the 1st ACM symposium on Cloud computing*, pages 143–154. ACM, 2010.

[10] D. E. Difallah, A. Pavlo, C. Curino, and P. Cudre-Mauroux. Oltp-bench: An extensible testbed for benchmarking relational databases. *Proceedings of the VLDB Endowment*, 7(4), 2013.

[11] E. Folkerts, A. Alexandrov, K. Sachs, A. Iosup, V. Markl, and C. Tosun. Benchmarking in the cloud: What it should, can, and cannot be. In *Technology Conference on Performance Evaluation and Benchmarking*, pages 173–188. Springer, 2012.

[12] D. Giles. Swingbench 2.2 reference and user guide.

[13] A. Göbel. Mutebench: Turning OLTP-Bench into a multi-tenancy database benchmark framework. In *CLOUD COMPUTING 2014, The Fifth International Conference on Cloud Computing, GRIDs, and Virtualization*, pages 84–87, 2014.

[14] N. Michael and Y. Shen. Downtime-free live migration in a multitenant database. In *Technology Conference on Performance Evaluation and Benchmarking*, pages 130–155. Springer, 2014.

[15] S. Patil, M. Polte, K. Ren, W. Tantisiriroj, L. Xiao, J. López, G. Gibson, A. Fuchs, and B. Rinaldi. Ycsb++: benchmarking and performance debugging advanced features in scalable table stores. In *Proceedings of the 2nd ACM Symposium on Cloud Computing*, page 9. ACM, 2011.

[16] B. Schroeder, A. Wierman, and M. Harchol-Balter. Open versus closed: A cautionary tale. In *NSDI*, volume 6, pages 18–18, 2006.

[17] Y. Shen and N. Michael. Oracle Multitenant on SuperCluster T5-8: Scalability study. Oracle White Paper, 2014.

[18] M. Silva, M. R. Hines, D. Gallo, Q. Liu, K. D. Ryu, and D. Da Silva. Cloudbench: experiment automation for cloud environments. In *Cloud Engineering (IC2E), 2013 IEEE International Conference on*, pages 302–311. IEEE, 2013.

[19] W. Sobel, S. Subramanyam, A. Sucharitakul, J. Nguyen, H. Wong, A. Klepchukov, S. Patil, A. Fox, and D. Patterson. Cloudstone: Multi-platform, multi-language benchmark and measurement tools for web 2.0. In *Proc. of CCA*, volume 8, 2008.

[20] A. Tirumala, F. Qin, J. Dugan, J. Ferguson, and K. Gibbs. Iperf: The TCP/UDP bandwidth measurement tool. 2005.

Cost-Efficient and Reliable Reporting of Highly Bursty Video Game Crash Data

Drew Zagieboylo
Electronic Arts
dzagieboylo@ea.com

Kazi A. Zaman
Electronic Arts
kzaman@ea.com

ABSTRACT

Video game crash events are characterized primarily by large media payloads and by highly bursty traffic patterns, with hundreds of thousands or millions of reports being issued in only a few minutes. These events are invaluable in quickly responding to game breaking issues that directly impact user experience. Even the slightest delay in capturing, processing and reporting these events can lead to user abandonment and significant financial cost.

A traditional standalone RESTful service, backed by a vertically scaled SQL database is neither a reliable nor cost-effective solution to this problem. An architecture that decouples capture and persistence and uses a horizontally scalable NoSQL database is not only easier to provision, but also uses fewer cpu and memory resources to provide the same end to end latency and throughput.

By replacing our RESTful implementation with one that takes advantage both of the aforementioned design and multi-tenant provisioning, we have reduced our dedicated cpu footprint by 63% and memory footprint by 59%. Additionally, we have decreased our data loss during spikes to essentially 0, maintained sub-second persistence latency and improved query latency in the average case by 54% with only a 3% sacrifice for worst case queries.

CCS Concepts

•**Computer systems organization** → **Cloud computing;** *Real-time system architecture;* Reliability; Maintainability and maintenance; •**Applied computing** → Media arts;

Keywords

Cloud Infrastructure, NoSQL, Reliability, Crash Reporting, Cost Efficiency

ICPE'17, April 22 - 26, 2017, L'Aquila, Italy

ISBN 978-1-4503-4404-3/17/04 . . . $15.00

DOI: http://dx.doi.org/10.1145/3030207.3044529

1. INTRODUCTION

Crash reporting is an invaluable system in the world of online gaming. As any software developer knows, the best tested code is not without bugs and even in the case where the code "works as expected" problems will arise due to the limitations of software and hardware infrastructure. Most games will experience their highest peak simultaneous users upon game or expansion release; this implies that any given game will likely be under its most demanding load when it has had the least amount of exposure to users (and therefore realistic testing). In such situations where bugs are not resolved expediently, there can be significant user backlash and abandonment [13]. Thus the crash reporting system (CRS) needs to be highly available and reliable; dropped crash reports and high query latencies limit the data available to developers and increase time to mitigation.

However, there are several challenges to implementing a CRS. One such challenge, which is common among many software applications, is the minimization of client overhead. Game clients cannot wait many seconds or minutes to submit crash reports, since submission time directly increases recovery time and user experience [14]. If a CRS is unresponsive due to the numerous clients trying to report simultaneously, the client is forced to disconnect and fails to submit the crash data or must submit at a significantly later date.

Another practical restriction is cost and scalability. As previously noted, many major problems are encountered at times with high peak simultaneous users, and often affect the vast majority of the current users; this in turn leads to an extremely bursty traffic pattern. The classic tradeoff between over and under provisioning (a.k.a. the tradeoff between cost and negative impact, respectively) applies quite starkly to this use case and needs to be closely considered. Lastly, crash reports that occur near simultaneously are often indistinguishable except for detailed stack traces and memory dumps. This makes keyed partitioning effectively useless for balancing resource usage during peak load. In such architectures, horizontal scaling of hardware resources can be effectively nullified and provisioning for peak load means adding memory and/or I/O bandwidth to a single machine.

In this paper, we describe how the New CRS is an improvement over the simplistic model of RESTful service for crash reporting. We address all of the aforementioned challenges, while comparing and contrasting other solutions that we considered. Our goals are specifically to reduce data loss, increase cost-efficiency (as measured by report throughput

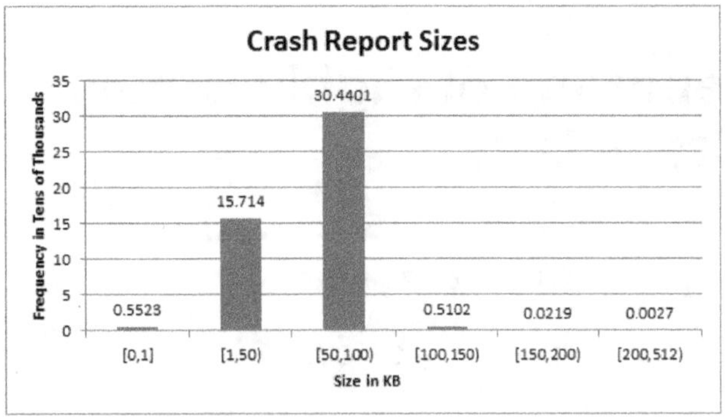

Figure 1: Sample of Reports from AAA Title Beta

per cpu and memory provisioned) and maintain or improve query latency. This paper will describe each of the architectural modifications and technology choices that we made in order to achieve this goal. For each component in the design, this paper will additionally detail both the performance benchmarks we ran during evaluation and the behavior of the sytem since its release to our production environment. Once evaluating the results of our efforts, this paper will explore further work that can be done to improve usability of the system, while still maintaining high throughput, reliability and scalability.

2. BACKGROUND

2.1 Crash Report Taxonomy

EA crash reports have a small number of required fields that help users to differentiate reports based on game, crash type, etc. Many game teams also opt to send detailed debugging data that notably includes any or all of the following: stack trace, screenshot, and heap memory dump. These blob fields represent the bulk of the data volume and are encoded in base64. For the purposes of this paper we will concern ourselves primarily with the following fields:

- *sku* - the game/game-platform combination on which the crash originated
- *submitTime* - the time at which the crash report became readable through the CRS
- *reportId* - an internal UUID assigned to each crash report by the CRS

In addition to crash reports, the CRS also accepts 'session' events, which simply represent a session beginning either for a game client or game server. These are always small since they contain the same required fields as reports but no media or large text fields.

2.2 Crash Report Workload Profile

Crash reports in the system have an approximately bimodal distribution of 'large' and 'small' reports. Large reports are those that include the media or blob text fields listed above, these range anywhere from 10 KB to 512KB. Small reports contain no media or large text fields (except for a stack trace) and range from several hundred bytes to about 5KB. The average size of all reports is 5KB, but that can be a misleading measurement due to the bimodal distribution mentioned above. For example Figure 1 represents the sizes of crash reports from a single EA game during its open beta; for this game the average report size is significantly higher, around 100 KB. The design and benchmarks listed later in this paper reflect this 100KB crash report profile in order to not only prepare for the worst case, but also to better future proof for the time when more game teams decide to provide large media in their crash reports.

The baseline submission load for the CRS is between 350 and 800 requests per second, depending on the time of day. Of those requests, approximately between 30 and 50 are crash reports and the remainder are session events. Based on the above average data size, we can extrapolate that our baseline data throughput for crashes is 250KB/s. Peaks approach 2500-3000 crash reports per second and are short lived. Figure 2 shows incoming report events per minute during the open beta for a AAA title. This depicts the unique characterization of large but short-lasting spikes of crash traffic.

Lastly, the CRS maintains crash report data for 90 days. The majority of this data is not queried with any frequency, as game developers are usually concerned with only the most recent crashes; nevertheless old data is retained to allow post mortems and other long term analysis. The primary implication of this fact is that our database needs to store approximately 2TB of data (excluding replication), while only a small fraction of that needs to be quickly accessible for fast read or update operations.

2.3 Crash Report Query Profile

On average there are approximately 10 concurrent queries per second. 99.0% of queries return fewer than 2000 crash reports and 99.9% of queries return fewer than 20000; the vast majority of queries return fewer than 100 reports. Again, due to the bimodal distribution of report sizes, this causes a vast range in query size from hundreds of KB to hundreds of MB. This paper will further discuss performance characteristics in the Benchmarking section.

2.4 Hardware Resources

We used Amazon Web Services' Elastic Cloud Computing to provision our hardware resources for this implementation. AWS EC2 allows us to add or remove hardware easily with various configurations. For this project we used m3.xlarge instances, running CentOS 6. M3.xlarge instances have 4 virtual cpus, 15 GB of RAM, approximately 100 MB/s of network bandwidth and 80 GB of ssd storage. For components that required additional storage, we attached Amazon Electronic Block Storage, which provided persistent virtual ssd drives [3].

M3.xlarge instances provide the maximum network bandwith per dollar of all AWS instance types. Flux7 has performed Amazon-recommended benchmarking with i-series I/O optimized instances and m3 instances; while i-series instances do provide higher bandwidth per instance, the dollar cost per MB/s of bandwidth per hour is $0.005456 for i2.8xlarge and $0.00266 for m3.xlarge on-demand instances [1]. No cheaper instance provides better bandwidth than the m3.xlarge, according to Amazon's network performance descriptions and these tests. In practice, we have also noticed a network cap of 100-130 MB/s for m3.xlarge instances, corroborating the findings of Flux7.

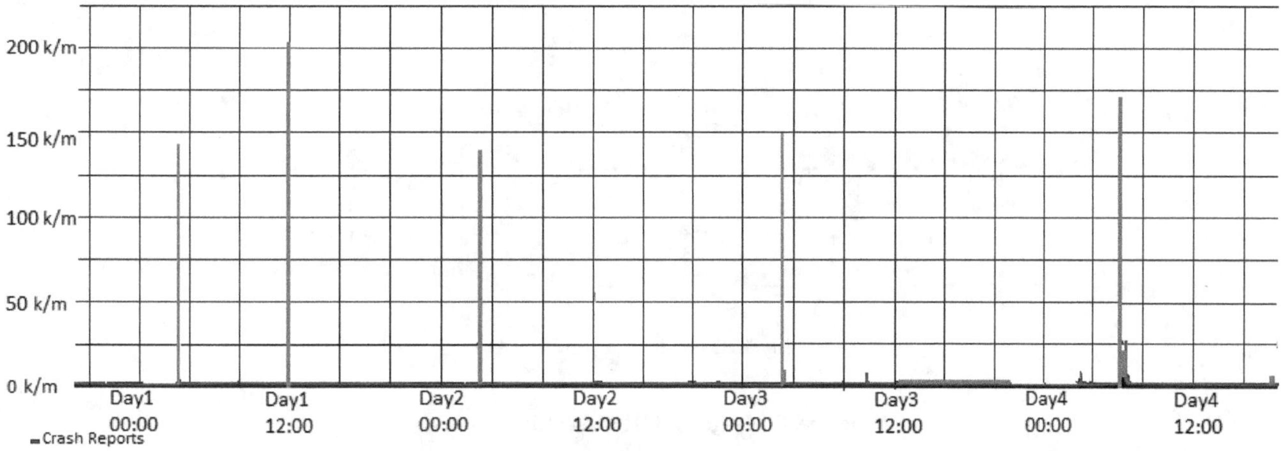

Figure 2: Incoming Crash Reports in Requests per Minute During Public Beta

3. PREVIOUS WORK

3.1 Other Research

While crash reporting has been researched previously, most work focuses on techniques for analyzing crash data. For example, there are many papers that describe processes for deduplicating crash reports based on memory and stack similarities [9, 14]. This paper seeks to fill a hole regarding infrastructural design and performance analysis. The CRS detailed in this paper provides the mechanism for information storage and retrieval, which is then used by downstream applications for bug detection.

3.2 Legacy CRS

In the introduction to this paper, we highlighted many of the challenges faced by a production scale crash reporting system. This section details how the Legacy CRS at EA handled some of those challenges and failed to account for others. The legacy implementation was a single-tiered capture and persistence service. Several servers, called collectors, in a company data center were load balanced behind a virtual IP to which clients could connect. After receiving client crash reports these collectors then wrote them into one of three MySQL databases. Other servers, called reporters, handled read requests; game developers used an API to connect to these servers to retrieve crash report data. Figure 3 depicts this design with game client connections on the left and game developer queries depicted on the right.

To avoid high client latencies in the event of a database outage or sluggishness, the collectors used an in-memory queue to buffer crash reports. Asynchronously, they were removed from the queue and then written to persistent storage. In order to increase write throughput and storage space, the application manually sharded data, based on crash report sku, to different MySQL database servers. Each MySQL server also had a matching slave server that was used by the reporters in order to prevent heavy read load from impacting write throughput.

3.2.1 Legacy CRS Shortcomings

While the above attempts to mitigate or solve performance and scale problems were improvements over a completely unintelligent RESTful service, they had some major flaws. First, the collectors maintained in-memory queues whose sizes were constrained by system memory; once the server ran out of heap space, the collector would crash and all reports in that queue were effectively discarded.

Next, there were also a few fundamental flaws with the data partitioning approach taken by the Legacy CRS. As previously mentioned, when a crash report spike occurs, it is usually due to a single game; this means that most reports will have the same one or two skus (one for each game platform that is affected). In this case, the data partitioning scheme listed here has no effect since utilization for one MySQL server will be maxed out, while the others lay mostly idle. Moreover there was no intelligent system for choosing how to map each sku to each database; two games that had higher than average crash rates could end up on the same server. This also lead to uneven MySQL utilization.

The Legacy CRS also had usability issues for game developers which arose due to the MySQL master-slave architecture. This design created an eventual consistency model for the reporters; data would be available for read at some undefined point after it had been written to the MySQL master (i.e. once the slave had replicated it). To make this situation more complicated, each MySQL master slave pair had its own independent 'lag'; there was no central way to measure inconsistency. During a crash spike, slave lag would increase significantly; querying the last five minutes worth of crashes would certainly result in an incomplete list of crash reports since some number of them had not yet been replicated from master to slave. Due to the indeterminate nature of the consistency there was no way for the API to compensate for this 'pseudo-missing' data.

Finally, since this entire system was built at an in-house data center, there was no ability to launch new application or database servers during a crash spike. It would take days to coordinate hardware provisioning and setup, rather than the minutes or hours needed to either horizontally or vertically scale any piece of the system.

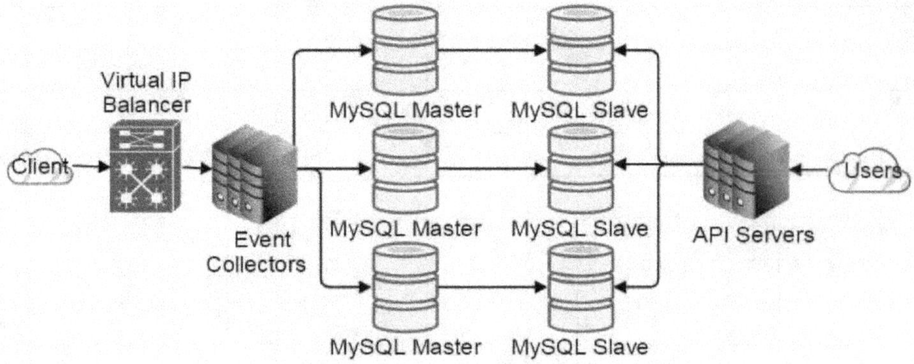

Figure 3: Legacy CRS Architecture

4. DESIGN OVERVIEW

4.1 Technologies

In this design we chose to use Kafka and Couchbase to implement the messaging and persistence layers of the design.

Kafka is a distributed message broker, which allows for highly scalable and redundant message publishing and consumption. Kafka performance is bounded primarily by network and disk I/O bandwidth; which is consumed via publishing, consumption and replication [4].

Couchbase is a horizontally scalable key-value store built on top of Memcached. The primary API is a simple GET-PUT interface, where the key is a string and the value is JSON document (although Couchbase does also support arbitrary binary data). Starting with Couchbase 4.0, it also offers document indexing and querying with an SQL called N1QL [8].

4.2 Persisting Crash Reports

When a game client or server experiences a crash, the following chain of events occurs:

1. Via HTTP, the client connects to a lightweight capture service and uploads the crash report.
2. While this connection is open, the capture service writes the report to Kafka and appends the report to a local file on disk.
3. Upon completion of these writes, the connection to the capture service is closed.
4. A consumer process reads the capture report from the Kafka queue.
5. The consumer persists the report to Couchbase.
6. The consumer updates a MySQL table that is used to indicate to the reporter that the crash data is available to be read.
7. The consumer updates a time-series counter (stored in MySQL) which tracks total sessions and crash incidents.[1]

Notably, the legacy collector has been refactored into two processes: capturing data via the http service and Kafka; and persisting data via a Kafka consumer. Additionally, crash report storage has been migrated from MySQL to Couchbase, while the pre-existing MySQL has been converted into index storage.

4.3 Querying Crash Reports

While these changes were made in order to increase write throughput and reliability, they also incurred some changes to the reporter. Since the crash reports are no longer stored in an rdbms, there needs to be a mechanism for translating user query filters (such as time range and sku) into a list of document keys. MySQL is used as an 'index' to map submitTime, reportId, and sku to a given document key. This generates the following set of actions when querying the CRS:

1. User connects to reporter and supplies query parameters.
2. Reporter executes a MySQL query to retrieve the relevant document keys.
3. Reporter retrieves all of the reports from Couchbase in parallel.
4. Reporter applies non-indexed query filters, serializes the reports and returns them to the user.

This design is highlighted in Figure 4, and is visually separted into the three phases of Capture, Persistence and Reporting.

5. REPORT CAPTURE SERVICE

5.1 Overview

The capture service is a taxonomy-independent and pre-existing EA application which has exactly one job: accept incoming HTTP payloads and persist them with very high fault tolerance and minimal latency. Prior to work on the new CRS, this service was already in use for the purpose of receiving and storing game telemetry. It makes data available for downstream processing by storing it on local log files

[1]Step (7) is taken wholesale from the Legacy CRS; the MySQL-stored time series metrics were not a significant concern when developing the New CRS and so that piece of the system was left untouched. While improvements could certainly be made there as well, it is not the focus of this paper and will be largely undiscussed.

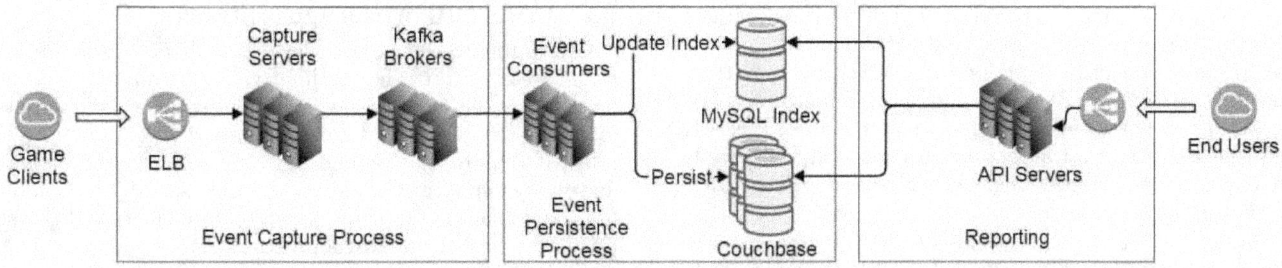

Figure 4: New CRS Architecture

and then rotating those files every 15 minutes to S3. From S3, scheduled ingestion processes pull the data into other locations in order to translate and process it.

The capture service runs on m3.xlarge EC2 instances and uses an Elastic Load Balancer to distribute work across servers.

Although this was a nearly ideal candidate for crash report capture, the batch processes involved in moving data to and from S3 had too much end to end latency. Users of the Legacy CRS expected near real time availability of crash reports, not multi-hour turn around times. To solve this, we replicated the legacy system of an in-memory queue by using a distributed messaging queue (i.e. Kafka). The capture service now also routes incoming data to a pre-configured Kafka topic based on the client URI; in this way crash reports are filtered out from other data streams and published to Kafka.

6. DATA PERSISTENCE

6.1 Crash Event Consumer

Once crash data has been stored safely in Kafka, it can at any time be consumed into a queryable data store. To accomplish this, we used the simple Kafka consumer api to build an application that reads the crash data stream, parses the events and writes them to Couchbase. This API allows the consumer to be a distributed application whose parallelism is limited primarily by the number of partitions in the Kafka topic from which it is reading. Adding or removing a new consumer instance will automatically rebalance the assignment of partitions to consumers, thus making hardware failure and horizontal scaling easy to handle. While the main purpose of the consumer is straightforward, there are a few practical considerations: how is the Couchbase document key generated; how are errors handled; and how does the MySQL index get updated.

6.1.1 Key Generation

The first and last points here are closely interrelated. In the Legacy CRS, each report was given a unique id by inserting a new row into a MySQL table with an auto-increment column; then the report was written to another table using that value as its reportId. This order of events creates data inconsistency; there is no order enforced on the stream of incoming reports and it becomes impossible to guarantee that a client has read all of the data that is actually present in the system. It follows that in the New CRS, the report is first written to Couchbase and then the MySQL index table is updated; however this means that the reportId is not generated until after the document is already stored in couchbase. Some other value must be used as a Couchbase key.

Here we take advantage of another feature of the capture service. It assigns a UUID to each event that it receives and attaches that in a header field of the published message. We have opted to use a hash of this UUID in order to uniquely generate each crash report key. This gives us the convenient side-effect that writing a report is idempotent; reprocessing or retrying will not generate undue duplicate entries and it does not require any extra logic to enforce. Importantly, we use a truncated hash of the UUID in order to reduce the memory overhead of storing a single report in Couchbase. The truncation to 16 bytes reduces the Couchbase key length by 20 bytes per document. Although it is not a necessary step, it is one that allows more data to be stored in memory in Couchbase and thus more data that can be queried at peak throughput.

6.1.2 Data Partitioning in Couchbase

As previously noted, the Legacy CRS had a hotspot issue caused by the difficulty of partitioning similar-looking crash reports. Couchbase partitions data randomly by hashing document keys, which leads to even usage across the cluster. Regardless of the key generation implementation, employing Couchbase as a storage engine removes the former hotspot bottlenecks.

6.1.3 Index Format

The MySQL index is represented as a single MySQL table with four columns, most of which are repeated from above:

- reportId - the ID used by clients to query a given report or range of reports
  - Primary key
- submitTime - the time at which the crash report became readable through the CRS
  - Partition key
- sku - the game/game-platform combination on which the crash originated
  - Indexed
- storageId - the couchbase document key

After writing a document to couchbase an entry is made into this table, where reportId is generated as an auto-increment value. This is the only bottleneck in the entire pipeline which cannot be horizontally scaled; luckily, it is a very fast operation. The average latency for this step is < 1 ms. However, the critical section must be shorter than these observed latencies since we have supported more than 250 index entries per second. We have not measured precisely the length of this critical section; ultimately it will dictate an upper bound on consumer throughput at 1/len(critical section) reports per second.

For any user queries which apply other filters (e.g. errorCode), the reporter application must scan all of the documents that fall in the specified time range for that sku; much like querying via an unindexed field in traditional rdbms. The cost to index a new field would be to alter this table to include a new column, scan every crash report and update that entry in the index table. This is a highly expensive operation and a notable drawback of this implementation; this paper will address this concern in the future work section.

6.1.4 Error Handling

The consumer needs to handle several different error cases: malformatted data, temporary infrastructure errors, and non-recoverable errors.

The first is the easiest case to handle but is quite frequent, especially in testing. The consumer simply drops data that it cannot parse or that is is missing any required fields. The benefit of using Couchbase for storage is that we can actually persist the entire payload, even if it has unexpected fields or fields with unexpected types; this minimizes our 'required' field list to include only fields which need to be indexed for querying. However, there is a significant downside to handling user errors asynchronously; the New CRS cannot respond to the client with debug information about why a particular report was dropped. In our integration environment, we have enabled payload inspection on the capture service to allow client to receive detailed 4XX errors, if they so choose; however this drastically reduces the throughput of a single capture instance and is not cost-effective for a production environment.

Temporary errors occur frequently in production cloud (and physical data center) environments. They include but are not limited to: temporary network outages, latency spikes and short failover periods during server hardware failure. They are also fairly straightforward to handle by ensuring that only idempotent operations be retried and that offsets are committed to Kafka only once the corresponding data has been persisted. To this end, the consumer will stop reading data from a Kafka partition if it encounters a temporary error during processing. Then it will repeatedly retry until the error is resolved. Since all operations other than index updates in the persistence process are idempotent (and a successfull index update indicates successful persistence) it is safe to simply retry the entire procedure.

Non-recoverable errors should be rare and require manual intervention to resolve. For example, a server might run out of disk space or memory due to a faulty configuration or simple accident, causing an error. The consumer handles these cases identically to temporary errors because it can be difficult to distinguish between them. System administrators are notified of such errors via email when any of the consumer threads are stuck in the retry state for an extended period of time. This configurable period effectively dictates the minimum time to detection for any serious issues.

6.2 Alternative Storage Options

Before finally settling on Couchbase as our database we considered several other technologies. Ultimately Couchbase won out for a few reasons: it provides some controls for multi-tenancy; it has competitive write throughput per node; it requires no complicated logic to horizontally scale and it is simple to configure and maintain. While it is often overlooked in benchmarks and white papers, this last point is critical to creating a practical production system. A difficult to optimize database leads to higher costs in both performance and developer-hours spent debugging esoteric issues. This section will introduce the competitors that we considered and will conclude with comparisons to couchbase.

6.2.1 SQL (MySQL)

The'least-effort' implementation for us would have been to leave the legacy MySQL system in-place, potentially modifying the data schema to improve write performance. As we've already described there are significant issues with this approach; primarily the inability to easily remove hotspots and extra overhead required to shard data intelligently. Therefore, to use MySQL as our database we could either simply accept the occasionally high latency spikes and unavailability of data or we could attempt to improve the sharding algorithm. The former was deemed unacceptable for obvious reasons.

To implement the latter would have required maintaining a dynamic mapping for each report to shard mapping (we would have to remove the sku-based sharding to avoid hotspots), in the form of a hash function. Additionally we would have had to implement replication, cluster expansion and failover algorithms; at this point we would already be implementing most of the features provided by NoSQL storage engines. For almost any realistic use case, this is not worth the labor cost or the likelihood of introducing bugs with complicated logic.

6.2.2 Document Store (MongoDB)

The leading open source document based storage engine is MongoDB. Document-oriented databases are essentially key-value stores that also provide additional 'relational' features based on object metadata. Ideally, this allows for high scalability while still providing a traditional SQL interface and query optimization via indexing (at least for MongoDB). However, several independent benchmarks show that both read latency and throughput for MongoDB are significantly worse than other NoSQL competitors, specifically due to architectural decisions that do not scale well, such as the single-instance MongoDB Router [12]. These benchmarks caused us to immediately discount MongoDB as too cost-inefficient for our peak provisioning.

6.2.3 Column Store (Cassandra)

The most promising alternative to Couchbase was a column store, Cassandra. Column-oriented databases provide the ability to read or write only specific data columns efficiently and have very flexible indexing and partitioning capabilities.

For our purpose, we considered Cassandra since it is a leading open source column store, with many vocal users. In some benchmarks, Cassandra outperforms Couchbase in terms of throughput per node and latency [7]. On the other hand, other benchmarks have shown Couchbase to provide better performance and additionally, the previous paper used an older version of couchbase which is known to have worse performance than the current 4.x versions [2]. In any case, both linear scaling properties and the per node performance of Cassandra and Couchbase are comparable. Further discussion of benchmarks can be found in the Benchmarking section.

For the purpose of productionalizing the new CRS, the major issue with Cassandra was cost in developer time. In order to achieve the reported performance for Cassandra with our use case, fairly extensive data modeling and system tuning would have been required.We executed our own load tests with YCSB and found that Cassandra ran into issues while inserting large records, which Couchbase did not have. This is certainly a problem that can be solved with intelligent schema design, but out of the box a simple cassandra 'table' would not support our needs for storing several terabytes of large rows.

Cassandra uses a hash of the 'partition key' (a set of columns from a row) to determine on which node data is located. This causes some challenges when you want to retrieve data based on a date range, since the data is distributed across the entire cluster and you cannot take advantage of Cassandra's ordered storage of data on disk. DataStax does offer several data models that enable time range queries, but they have limitations of row size that would quickly be overwhelmed by 100KB crash reports [11]. While it is certainly possible to implement time range queries on large data sets in Cassandra, it requires a non-trivial amount of effort that quickly racks up cost in terms of developer time.

In addition, there are many configuration options for Cassandra that in some cases drastically change performance characteristics. This is a useful feature, since it allows for so much control; however several of these configurations become scaling bottlenecks with no manifestation of problems until the bottleneck is reached [10, 5].

Cassandra is certainly a highly scalable NoSQL database that provides much flexibility, both in terms of system tuning and indexing options. For many use cases it is a highly desirable storage solution. Nevertheless, we decided to use Couchbase since there was no obvious benefit from Cassandra for our use case. Setting up and maintaining Couchbase is much simpler due to the minimal configuration requirements, both have comparable throughputs and latencies in the CRS scenario and the developer effort required to integrated Cassandra added undue complexity.

6.3 Alternative Indexing Strategies

Before settling on the MySQL-based indexing strategy listed above, we considered two other options: using Couchbase 4.x's built-in Global Secondary Indexes, and using Elasticsearch.

6.3.1 Couchbase Indexing

The primary draw for using Couchbase GSIs was to allow the reporting API to issue SQL queries to Couchbase directly and remove the MySQL dependency completely. GSIs provide partitioned indexes that allow queries to scan a subset of document keys based on the provided partition columns. We did not even consider using a primary index since that requires a full bucket scan which, after even minimal testing, was clearly not viable with our 500 million document dataset. The GSI model we considered involved building one GSI per sku, since every API query requires a sku filter. Ultimately, Couchbase indexing was impractical because enabling it made the cluster's responsiveness highly intermittent, the read throughput was significantly lower and it required manual management of index creation and replication.

When only one index was created for one sku with our production data, we saw repeated failures of couchbase processes. On all of the servers the indexing and key-value processes repeatedly crashed and restarted due to timeouts or out of memory errors. While Couchbase does allow for setting memory limits on the key-value and indexer processes, it does not for the 'projector' process that forwards data between the key-value data stream and the indexer. We saw that this process was using an inordinate amount of memory and causing the system to fail. The only recommended solution we could find was to allocate more hardware and memory. Since we have several hundred skus active in our system and this issue presented itself while indexing merely one, it was clearly not cost-effective to allocate enough hardware to sustain the Couchbase indexer.

Furthermore, we saw drastically slower read performance when using Couchbase's built-in N1QL query service. Although indexing did not impact write performance (outside of the aforementioned cluster instability), it performed markedly worse than the key-value api in read throughput. Using 5KB documents, a single server could sustain 4500 key-value read operations per second, while it could only support 2200 GSI-backed read operations per second via N1QL. While 'read throughput' is not a common term for read evaluation, it is notable in that it sets the lower limit of the query latency. If only 2200 operations per second are supported, then a query returning 10000 documents will take at least 4.5 seconds to complete. Using N1QL would double our hardware requirements to support the same worst-case latency for large queries.

Finally, using Couchbase GSIs was not even remotely practical from an administrative point of view. Couchbase does not have any support for automatic index creation or replication. We would need to monitor any new data coming in for new skus and initiate index creation at that point in time. Additionally, we would need to build replica indices in the case of node failover; N1QL does handle reading from the correct index in the case of failover, but Couchbase doesn't support the auto-generation of replicas. Index creation also requires a full bucket scan, which ends up taking hours to days of time and requires a large amount of disk space (about 5 * final index size) due to fragmentation that only gets cleaned up after creation is complete. The final implications of this were that we would have to build quite a large monitoring and automation system to ensure that all required indexes were always present and replicated; even then, the latency required to build new indexes means that data for new games would be un-queryable for some time.

6.3.2 Elasticsearch

Elasticsearch is open source software built on top of Lucene and provides a scalable full-text search engine [6]. Couchbase provides an Elasticsearch plugin which utilized Couchbase's cluster replication feature to load data into an Elasticsearch cluster. The primary issue with this model is that indexing occurs completely asynchronously; we cannot guar-

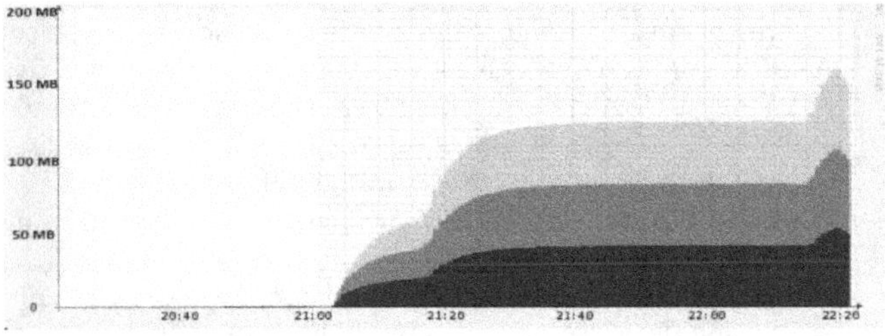

Figure 5: Incoming Network I/O Utilization of Kafka Servers (MB/s)

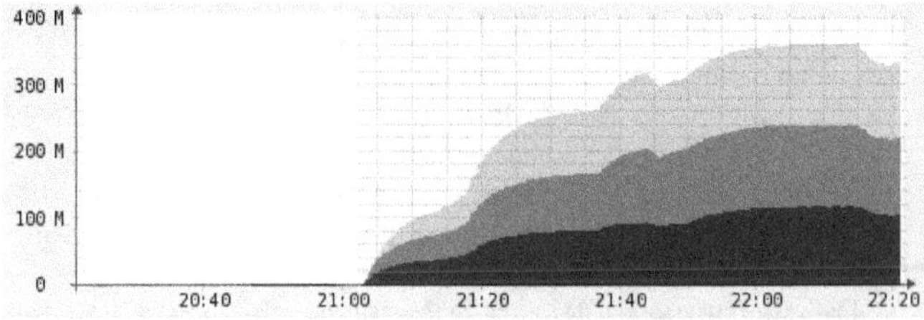

Figure 6: Outgoing Network I/O Utilization of Kafka Servers (MB/s)

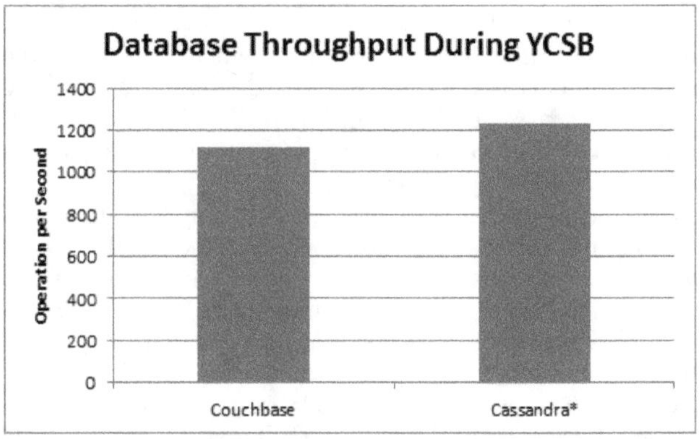

Figure 7: Couchbase vs. Cassandra Throughput with Worst-Case CRS Workload

antee what, if any, documents have been properly replicated to the Elasticsearch cluster. Consistency is one of the Legacy CRS concerns that we wished to address and so this eventual consistency model was too loose for the our current use case. We are investigating elasticsearch as a tool for enabling full text search on crash reports but that will be detailed in the 'Future Work' section of this paper.

7. BENCHMARKING

We executed synthetic benchmarks using sample data from our production environment and in some cases synthetic data that mirror production scenarios. We were most concerned with realistic benchmarks for the event capture process since insufficient scale for those would imply data loss; inaccurate provisioning of downstream components would only affect user experience. These benchmarks give us average case latencies and maximum throughputs that can be supported by a given amount of EC2 hardware. All tests were executed in a Virtual Private Cloud in AWS EC2, using m3.xlarge instances.

7.1 Capture Process

7.1.1 Methodology

For tests with production data we used several EC2 m3.xlarge instances to download past requests from S3 and replay them. We generously overprovisioned load generators to ensure they did not produce false bottlenecks. As mentioned previously, there are several data taxonomies which the capture service accepts; the following benchmark results describe isolated tests where only one data stream was replayed at a time.

7.1.2 Throughput

As you can see from the results in Table 1, for crash report payloads, the entire 100 MB/s network bandwidth was utilized, thus indicating that these tests measure accurate ceilings on throughput. With this model, we predicted that the capture service was capable of publishing approximately 1,800 crash reports or 15,000 session events per second to Kafka per server. We used this to estimate our production capture server requirements in the provisioning section.

7.1.3 Kafka

We used the same testing methodology to prove that Kafka is strictly network I/O bound in this environment; in addition we ran a consumer process that read data from Kafka to produce both read and write load. We used m3.xlarge instances for Kafka, with a three node setup and triplicate replication enabled. Figures 5 and 6 represent the three Kafka servers' inbound and outbound network usage over the course of the benchmarking test, respectively. These graphs represent the usage as we slowly increased the test traffic until we reached a peak steady state of approximately 90MB/s (or 30MB/s per Kafka broker) as seen in Figure 5. At this point, each broker was utilizing approximately 120 MB/s of total network bandwidth (which was derived by adding the values in Figures 5 and 6). When we attempted to increase the throughput (at time 22:15 in the aforementioned graphs), replication failures in the Kafka cluster began to occur, presumably due to the network I/O ceiling.

Since Kafka needs to use I/O to receive, replicate and send data, the 4:1 ratio of I/O usage to data volume makes natural sense. One part is used for receiving the data stream, two parts are used to generate the two other replicas and one part is used for client consumption.

7.2 Couchbase and Cassandra

Although there are many YCSB results for NoSQL databases, we executed our own since none of those tests use documents larger than 1KB. We used documents of size 100KB and ran the YCSB using m3.xlarge instances for both the clients and servers; these tests represent the performance using only a single server and without replication. Additionally, most other tests do not cover situations where data does not completely fit in memory; the above tests represent storing 50% of data in memory. We attempted to reflect a scenario where nearly no reads occured in memory; however when loading data into Cassandra we experienced many timeout errors that made this impossible. During the actual tests, this also caused timeouts on insert operations for Cassandra.

Table 1: Capture Service Benchmark

API	Throughput (Requests/s)	Average Latency (ms)	Network Usage (MB/s)	CPU Usage (%)
session events	15,000	16.0	34.9	98
crash reports	1800	33.3	108.2	98

Table 2: YCSB Latencies with 100KB Records

Database	Op	Min (ms)	Max(ms)	Avg(ms)
Couchbase	Read	0.80	138	7.45
Cassandra*	Read	0.80	562	18.7
Couchbase	Insert	2.6	365	11.3
Cassandra*	Insert	1.47	2000	6.80

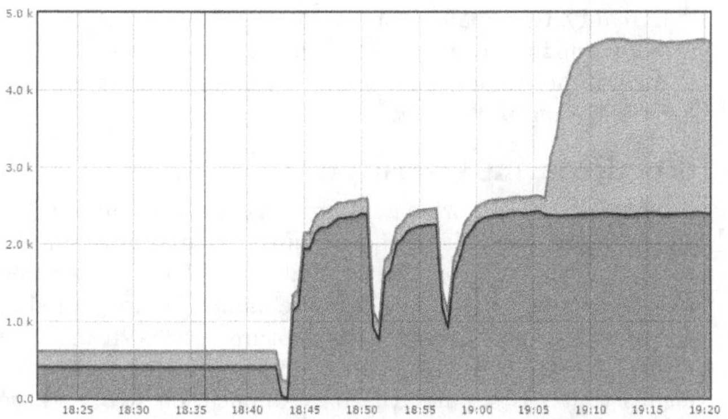

Figure 8: Session and Crash Events Persisted Per Second by Instance

For these tests, our goal was to determine if either database significantly outperformed the other. Table 2 shows that, in terms of latency Couchbase outperforms Cassandra on average for read operations and Cassandra outperforms Couchbase. The startlingly high 2,000 ms maximum latency for Cassandra, in conjunction with the aforementioned errors, indicated to us that Couchbase would perform more consistently out of the box. Figure 7 also shows that Cassandra executes approximately 100 more operations per second than Couchbase. Neither the differences in average latency or throughput signaled a clear winner to us; however, the fact that Couchbase provided more reliable performance became one of the deciding factors in this evaluation.

7.3 Consumer

7.3.1 Methodology

We ran two integration load tests with the consumer; one with normal CRS traffic and one with a data stream that consisted only of crash reports. The former represents the day-to-day throughput capability, while the second is a 'worst-case scenario' that could occur during a severe crash spike. For each load test, we preloaded a Kafka topic with several GB of production data to ensure that data availability in Kafka would not be a bottleneck.

For the normal data stream, we started a single m3.xlarge consumer instance, waited 10 minutes and then started a second instance; the results of that test can be seen starting at minute 19:00 in Figure 8. The earlier peaks in the graph represent starts and restarts of the consumer to confirm functionality prior to the load test and each color represents the throughput of one instance. Since we see equal throughput rates for both instances, both before and after starting a second, we can infer that the bottleneck to throughput during this test was indeed the consumer and not Kafka or Couchbase.

For the crash-only test we repeated the same procedure; Figure 9 only displays the throughput of a single consumer instance.

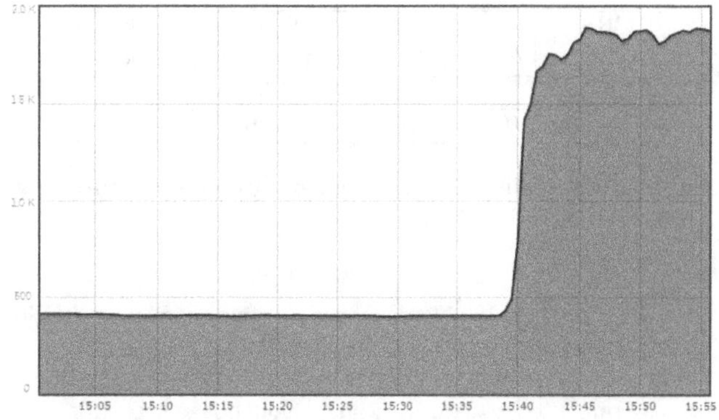

Figure 9: Crash Reports Persisted Per Second

7.3.2 Results

Figure 8 shows that the consumer can persist 2,300 events per second from the normal mix of event types. If all events are crash reports, each consumer can processt about 1,700 crash reports per second, which also translates to approximately 8.5 MB of data per second. This scales linearly with number of consumer instances until read parallelism from Kafka or write parallelism to Couchbase becomes a bottleneck.

7.4 Reporter

7.4.1 Methodology

To benchmark the reporter we ran multiple sets of tests for latency on both the Legacy and Couchbase-backed implementations. We varied both the size of the quries (measured in number of reports returned) and the number of concurrent queries. Network I/O is an uncontrolable factor for both systems, since clients operate in different network environments than either the Legacy data center or AWS. In order to account for these network disparities, we measured time to first byte (TTFB) responses. Each test was run 5 separate times and all latency results were averaged together. All queries were made using the same *sku*, which averaged reports of size 100 KB.

The Legacy Reporter was run on a single CentOS 6 machine, which has 16 cores and 42 GB of RAM. It was con-

CRS	1 Report	200 Reports	2,000 Reports	20,000 Reports
Legacy	0.10	0.20	1.42	2.76
New	0.17	0.51	2.34	25.0

Table 3: Latency for Reporter Queries of Varying Size - Simple Fields Only (sec)

CRS	1 Report	200 Reports	2,000 Reports	20,000 Reports
Legacy	0.14	1.73	4.57	23.9
New	0.17	0.51	2.26	24.7

Table 4: Latency for Reporter Queries of Varying Size - All Fields (sec)

nected to a MySQL 5.7 database, running on a CentOS6 machine with 24 cores and 94 GB of RAM.

The New Reporter was run on a single m3.xlarge instance. It was connected to two m3.xlarge Couchbase servers.

7.4.2 Results

Tables 3, 4 and 5 compare the latencies of queries, varying in size between 1 report returned and 20,000 reports returned (100KB to 2GB of data). Table 3 refers to queries which exclude fetching blob and media data from the reports; in this case the amount of data returned is only a few hundred bytes per report. Table 4 refers to normal queries, which return the full report data. Table 5 refers to when 10 concurrent queries were run of the specified size.

The Legacy MySQL implementation was by far superior if the API was required to only return the simple field set, since Couchbase requires fetching the entire document, even if only some fields are returned. In addition, the MySQL implementation was slightly better performing in the case where the queries were very large; however this was most likely due to the vastly superior hardware used in the Legacy Reporter.

The new implementation outstripped the legacy implementation in all situations where multiple queries were issued simultaneously and where a smaller number of reports were queried.This does suggest that client behavior needs to be modified, such that they issue many small queries in parallel. A *limit* and *offset* system such as that used in SQL has been incorporated into the reporting API to encourage such behavior.

It should be noted, that in the case where many MB of data are queried (such as with 2000 or more reports), I/O will be the dominant factor in latency. The average network bandwidth allocated per connection for the network between client and reporter is no more than 1 MB/s; as such the 25 or 29 seconds to query 2000 reports is dwarfed by the 100 seconds taken to transfer the data. However, this network bandwidth is limited per connection and not per server; issuing multiple small queries will help to alleviate this issue for clients and further reinforces the advantages of the new approach.

CRS	1 Report	200 Reports	2,000 Reports
Legacy	0.85	4.32	29.78
New	0.99	1.96	23.2

Table 5: Latency for Reporter Queries of Varying Size - 10 Concurent Queries (sec)

8. PROVISIONING AND COST

Based on the above performance metrics, the CRS use case needs 7 m3.xlarge instances and 1 m1.xlarge instance to process normal traffic volume: 1 capture server, 1 Kafka broker, 1 consumer, 1 reporter api server and 3 couchbase servers. In fact, for most of those services, the hardware will not be fully utilized.Additionally, one mysql master-slave pair is retained from the Legacy CRS; however it is likely overprovisioned for its new use and will be scaled down in the future to a small piece of hardware.

In reality, this small number of machines is not sufficient to provide a highly available and reliable service; neither does it include provisioning for data spikes nor does it account for replication of data in Kafka.

8.1 Reducing Overhead

The daily CRS workload is not massive; it is only during spike events when the traffic volume becomes a significant issue. We need to provision for that event since that is when reliability and scale is key, and we cannot entirely predict it ahead of time. However,the capture service, Kafka and Couchbase are are all multi-tenant in our ecosystem; this means that CRS is not the only application to use those resources. In general, the capture service and kafka are already provisioned with headroom to ensure no data loss for other taxonomies already. This headroom is already enough to handle 5-6 times the volume of normal CRS traffic. Since crash spikes are so short lived, and other data streams have much more predictable patterns, there is little risk that total usage will exceed this headroom. Either the crash spike will be processed before any other issues can occur, or there will be enough warning to provision more capture servers to compensate for the issue (rising traffic, cloud availability zone outage, etc.)

In this way, it is justified to claim that this design does not need to pay the costs of high availability; they are essentially one-time costs paid by the organization that become amortized across services.

9. PRODUCTION PERFORMANCE

The New CRS has been deployed on the aforementioned hardware and has been running as part of our production environment for several months. Not only has this project been a theoretical proof of concept, but it has withstood the test of several prominent game launches and open betas with minimal issue. The average time elapsed between crash submission and crash report availability is 600 ms and the 95th percentile for this latency is 950 ms. Specifically, Couchbase performs significantly better than anticipated, with a 3 ms average insert latency and supports 2,000 operations per second per server; the majority of the latency comes from publishing data to and consuming data from Kafka.

As far as dataloss, reports are dropped occasionally due to various temporary glitches. Figure 10 presents a view of all such events over the course of one month in terms of reports dropped per second from the real-time system. Very rarely do such glitches cause data loss of more than 10 events per

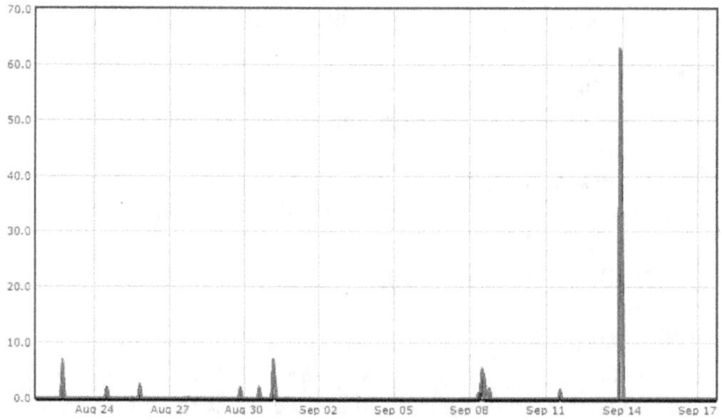

Figure 10: Events Dropped Per Second over 1 Month

second and all such issues are resolved within approximately 10 seconds. The largest spike of 62 events per second was caused by a hardware failure and bug which caused retries to be incorrectly attempted; this issue was caused merely by implementation, not a design flaw.

10. CONCLUSIONS

Overall, the New CRS improves or maintains data reliability, data availaibility and query responsiveness, while reducing cpu and memory usage.

10.1 Data Integrity

With the Legacy CRS, there were numerous incidents where we lost millions of of session events and tens of thousands of crash reports. While the Legacy CRS lacked the requisite monitoring to get exact figures, it would routinely lose millions of session events and hundreds of thousands of crash reports. With the new CRS, there is still occasional data loss; however it is mitigated to very small periods of time due to temporary errors that exceed the duration of capture service retries. Furthermore, none of that data is permanently lost, it is merely lost from the near-real time reporting of the CRS and is still reprocessable. This is very clearly an improvement over the Legacy CRS.

10.2 Latency

Next we can compare the query latency and end-to-end persistence latency of the Legacy and New CRS. The end-to-end latency is the total time elapsed between report capture and data being visible to the reporter api. For the Legacy CRS, it is on the order of 1 to 2 seconds in the normal case. The new CRS achieves a steady 550 ms average and 900 ms 95th percentile end-to-end latency. During load spikes, the end-to-end latency will rise if the provisioned consumer processes cannot meet the incoming crash rate. This is the tradeoff that we have made to ensure that data is eventually persisted[2].

For query latency, the load testing section above clearly demonstrates the general superiority of New CRS. The most common scenario in production is around 10 concurrent user queries, which average 20 to 100 reports in size; the New CRS responds to those queries with a 54% decrease in latency. In the case of very large queries, the New CRS did perform slightly worse with a 3% increase in query latency. However, the New CRS is arbitrarily horiztonally scalable and thus such poorly performing queries can be improved simply by splitting them into smaller concurrent queries.

10.3 Resource Usage

As mentioned above, the new CRS needs only provision 6 m3.xlarge instances and 1 m1.xlarge instance, thanks to amortizing the cost of high availability across other services. The Legacy CRS used 8 collection servers, 3 MySQL master-slave pairs and a single reporter server. All of these had varying specifications, which were invariably larger than the m1 and m3 instances provisioned in AWS. In total, the Legacy system used 208 CPUs and 710 GB of RAM: 48 cores and 100GB for collection; 144 cores and 564 GB for MySQL; and 16 cores and 46GB for reporting. The New CRS uses 80 cores and 308 GB of RAM: 8 cores and 30 GB for the capture process; 40 cores and 154 GB for data persistence; and 4 cores and 15 GB for reporting. This represents a 63% decrease in CPU usage and a 59% decrease in memory usage.

10.3.1 Other Costs

While it is less quantitative, the time spent to maintain these systems should also be taken into account. The New CRS is built on cloud infrastructure that survives without manual interaction even in the event of node failure. This also allows for much quicker turn around on server maintenance, scaling and configuration. Furthermore, we have found couchbase to be a very stable system that requires little configuration or headache to maintain, as long as its N1QL indexing is not enabled. It is difficult to put a price on these advantages, but they have certainly allowed us more rapid and reliable testing and provisioning of hardware than if we were still using a proprietary data center.

11. FUTURE WORK

At the moment, the reporting API is very bare and can only optimize queries based on time ranges. We would like to continue to investigate other methods for asynchronous indexing, either by building an in-house system using rdbms for index storage (as we have primitively implemented here) or by taking advantage of open source software such as Lucene and Elasticsearch. For either of these approaches our primary concerns are focused on enabling full-text search and creating an index service that scales both with the amount of incoming data and the number of index scan requests. Furthermore, there are more demands from game developers to increase payload size by including even more detailed stack traces, higher resolution images and/or short video clips. We seek to support these changes by evaluating the impact of storing even larger media files on Couchbase and how best to efficiently process such bulky reports, at protocol and infrastructure levels.

[2]For the current provisioning, a 5 minute crash spike reaching 3300 reports per second (over a 10X rate spike) will incur a worst case latency no more than 5 minutes.

12. REFERENCES

[1] F. 7. Benchmarking network performance of m1 and m3 instances, 2014.

[2] Altoros. The nosql technical comparison report, 2014.

[3] I. Amazon.com. Amazon web services, 2016.

[4] Apache. Apache kafka, 2016.

[5] S. Bisbee. Scale it to billions - what they don't tell you in the cassandra readme, 2015.

[6] E. Co. Elasticsearch, 2016.

[7] E. P. Corporation. Benchmarking top nosql databases, 2015.

[8] Couchbase. Couchbase, 2016.

[9] Y. Dang, R. Wu, H. Zhang, D. Zhang, and P. Nobel. Rebucket: A method for clustering duplicate crash reports based on call stack similarity. In *Proceedings of the 34th International Conference on Software Engineering*, ICSE '12, pages 1084–1093, Piscataway, NJ, USA, 2012. IEEE Press.

[10] Datastax. Cassandra configuration, 2016.

[11] Datastax. Getting started with time series data modeling, 2016.

[12] J. Klein, I. Gorton, N. Ernst, P. Donohoe, K. Pham, and C. Matser. Performance evaluation of nosql databases: A case study. In *Proceedings of the 1st Workshop on Performance Analysis of Big Data Systems*, PABS '15, pages 5–10, New York, NY, USA, 2015. ACM.

[13] I. B. Times. Battlefield 4: Bugs and issues lead to backlash, 2013.

[14] R. Wu. Diagnose crashing faults on production software. In *Proceedings of the 22Nd ACM SIGSOFT International Symposium on Foundations of Software Engineering*, FSE 2014, pages 771–774, New York, NY, USA, 2014. ACM.

Technique for Detecting Early-Warning Signals of Performance Deterioration in Large Scale Software Systems

Raghu Ramakrishnan*
Tata Consultancy Services
Noida, UP, INDIA
raghuramakrishnan71@gmail.com

Arvinder Kaur†
USICT, Guru Gobind Singh Indraprastha University
Dwarka, Delhi, INDIA
arvinder70@gmail.com

ABSTRACT

The detection of early-warning signals of performance deterioration can help technical support teams in taking swift remedial actions, thus ensuring rigor in production support operations of large scale software systems. Performance anomalies or deterioration, if left unattended, often result in system slowness and unavailability. In this paper, we presents a simple, intuitive and low-overhead technique for recognizing the early warning signs in near real time before they impact the system The technique is based on the inverse relationship which exists between throughput and average response time in a closed system. Because of this relationship, a significant increase in the average system response time causes an abrupt fall in system throughput. To identify such occurrences automatically, Individuals and Moving Range (XmR) control charts are used. We also provide a case study from a real-world production system, in which the technique has been successfully used. The use of this technique has reduced the occurrence of performance related incidents significantly in our daily operations. The technique is tool agnostic and can also be easily implemented in popular system monitoring tools by building custom extensions.

Keywords

System monitoring, performance anomaly, performance deterioration, Little's law, production systems, closed systems

*Raghu Ramakrishnan is Technology Head of Government Business in Tata Consultancy Services, Noida, INDIA. He is also pursuing research at USICT, Guru Gobind Singh Indraprastha University, Delhi, INDIA.

†Arvinder Kaur is Professor in University School of Information and Communication Technology, Guru Gobind Singh Indraprastha University, Delhi, India.

ICPE'17, April 22-26, 2017, L'Aquila, Italy

© 2017 ACM. ISBN 978-1-4503-4404-3/17/04. . . $15.00

DOI: http://dx.doi.org/10.1145/3030207.3044533

1. INTRODUCTION

Large scale, heterogeneous software systems are becoming pervasive in many areas. Such systems are usually not monolithic and may be made of a number of constituent systems working in an integrated manner to fulfil customer requirements. Monitoring the performance of critical software systems at run-time is an important activity carried out during the operations phase of the software life cycle. The main objective of performance monitoring is to be able to proactively identify performance related deterioration or anomalies much before they severely affect the end users. We can describe a performance anomaly in a software system as an unanticipated, undesirable degradation or deterioration in the performance of the system at run-time. Performance anomalies can severely impact services provided by the system to the customers, resulting in customer complaints, loss of business in the form of potential customers and penalties on account of violating contractual service level agreements. The availability of a functional system monitoring setup is an essential prerequisite for operational readiness and go-live of large scale software systems. System monitoring can be carried out at different levels of granularity like continuous monitoring, monitoring at predefined time (e.g. analyzing and reporting the system health at close of business) or post-hoc monitoring (e.g. reporting investigation results after occurrence of an event or incident in production). Early, continuous and near-real time detection of performance deterioration signals help Network Operations Center (NOC) teams to proactively carry out remediation actions, increasing the chances of avoiding system slowness or unavailability. NOC comprises of one or more command and control centers from where the production system is monitored to ensure its smooth functioning.

Open source and commercial available system monitoring tools, as they are commonly called in the IT industry have matured over time and established their place in IT monitoring landscape. The basic version of system monitoring tools collect a large number of performance counters or metrics from the components on which software systems are deployed (like physical servers, virtual machines, networks, storage, web server, application server, database servers) at predefined time intervals. Some of the monitoring tools can also be configured to collect and display metrics related to web services, like response time and throughput. The detection and alerting of performance deterioration in these system monitoring tools is mostly based on identifying performance counters which exceed static or dynamic threshold values set by administrators.

Often, the components of critical large scale software systems are configured for high availability using a N+M redundancy model. In an N+M model, N components required for full functioning have a minimum of M redundant components. For critical systems, it is important to note that the immediate priority on detecting a performance deterioration is to take actions for preventing or reducing any further impact on the Quality of Service (QoS) offered by the system. Root Cause Analysis (RCA) is is a secondary objective and is expected to follow later. The time available between the detection of a performance anomaly and it transformation to a major performance incident is very limited. Therefore, any technique designed to detect anomalous conditions that emerge during operations should not rely on triage and analysis of a large number of IT infrastructure performance counters. Our experience in the industry tells us that the common remediation actions carried out by support teams include killing and restarting application processes, servers, terminating expensive database queries and locks. If the components are redundant, they can be restarted one at a time to minimize downtime. The optimization or fixing of code, tuning of parameters, realigning resources, augmentation of compute, storage or network needed to overcome performance problems, is usually done on a short to medium term horizon.

Our extensive experience in the area of monitoring large scale software systems and running NOC operations indicates that ease of implementation, intuitiveness and low runtime overhead of an anomaly detection technique is a driving factor in its effectiveness and adoption. The paper describes a technique based on application services instead of a large number of IT infrastructure performance counters for identifying early-warning signals of performance deterioration, which we have been successfully using in production support of mission critical software systems for last few years. The technique has helped us to proactively undertake remediation activities and eliminate occurrences of high severity performance incidents. The technique, which initially relied on continuous visual inspection to match steep increase in average system response time with an abrupt decline in system throughput, was enhanced to have automated detection capabilities through the use of Individuals and Moving Range (XmR) control charts.

The contributions of this paper are:

- We propose a technique based on Little's Law and XmR control charts to identify early-warning signs of performance deterioration. The technique is simple, intuitive and has a low overhead.
- Software systems are usually deployed using a multi-tier architecture like presentation, application and data. The proposed technique is deployment tier agnostic i.e. it is equally applicable for all the tiers.
- We demonstrate that our technique can automatically detect early-warning signs of performance deterioration by evaluating its accuracy on a large software system used in industry.

The paper is organized as follows: Section 2 provides a motivating example driving this work. Section 3 explores the related work in this area. Section 4 describes our technique. Section 5 presents a reference implementation of the technique. Section 5 details real-world case study of performance anomaly detection during production support. Section 6 lists the threats to the validity of our work. Section 7 provides the conclusions and direction on future work.

2. MOTIVATING EXAMPLE

In this section, we describe an actual situation observed by the production support team while monitoring the performance of a large scale case management system. The system is used for processing application forms daily at various customer touch points. The system has a three tier deployment architecture: web, application and data tier. The web tier contains the presentation components, application tier contains web services and data tier hosts the database, document store. The throughput and average response time at each tier is calculated from the data collected from the web tier log, application tier log and database snapshot. The throughput is represented by the symbol X and the average response time is represented by the symbol R. For web and application tier, the standard web server logs are used. Throughput is the number of requests processed by the software system in a given time interval. Response time is the time elapsed between the software system receiving the request and the requests is processed. The terms response time and processing time are used interchangeably in this paper. The value of X and R are calculated every two minutes. Figures 1, 2 and 3 shows the value of X and R plotted against time. The total number of measurements is 270, conforming to a monitoring duration of nine hours. We now examine the graphs related to each tier in detail.

Web Tier: In Figure 1a, an abrupt increase in R is observed in monitoring intervals 229 to 234. The average processing time R changed from 0.47 s to 34.49 s. The increase is accompanied by a rapid decline in X in the same interval, as observed in Figure 1b. The throughput dropped from 2,215 to 58. Figures 1c and 1d show a magnified view of the monitoring intervals 226 to 237 for better understanding.

Application Tier: In Figure 2a, a steep increase in R is observed in monitoring intervals 229 to 234. The average processing time R changed from 0.36 s to 75.69 s. The increase is accompanied by a rapid decline in the throughput X in the same interval, as observed in Figure 2b. The throughput dropped from 2,431 to 173. The web and application tier show a similar pattern for throughput because the web tier uses the facade design pattern and makes a single call to composite web services in the application tier. However, the web services may internally invoke a number of database queries for completing a functionality. The same can be observed in the large value of X in Figure 3b. The maximum value of X is more than 188,000.

Data Tier: The average execution time for database queries collected from the database snapshot during normal operations, was between 10 ms to 20 ms. Figure 3a shows an increase in R to 0.099 s. The increase is accompanied by a rapid decline in the throughput X in the same interval, as observed in Figure 3b. The throughput dropped from 123,000 to 91,000.

The performance incident in this case, continued till the end of monitoring period 234. The root cause in this incident was a database query with an incorrect filter criteria returning a large number of records to the calling web service, leaving

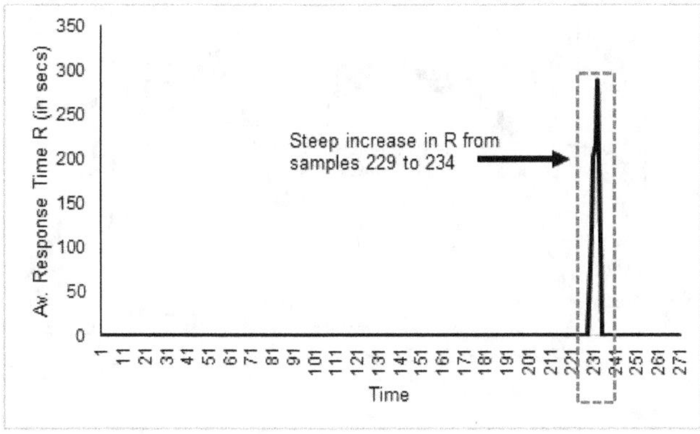

(a) R vs. time

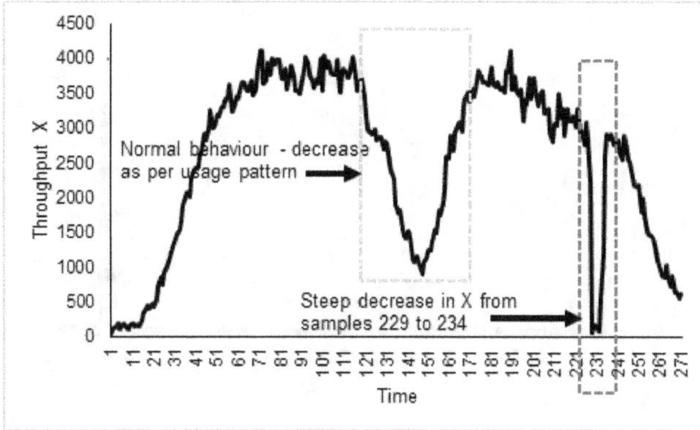

(b) X vs. time

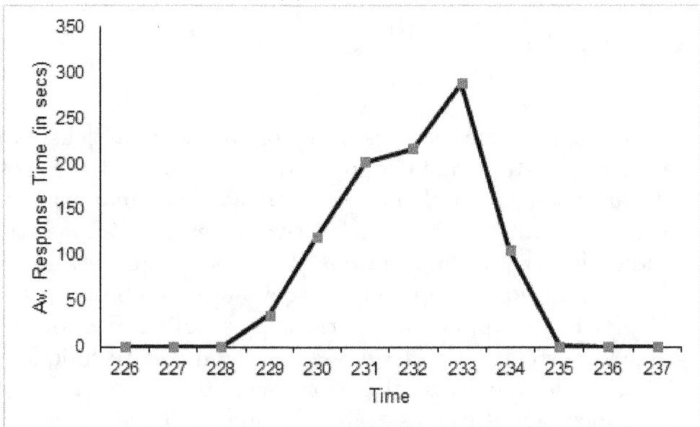

(c) R during performance deterioration

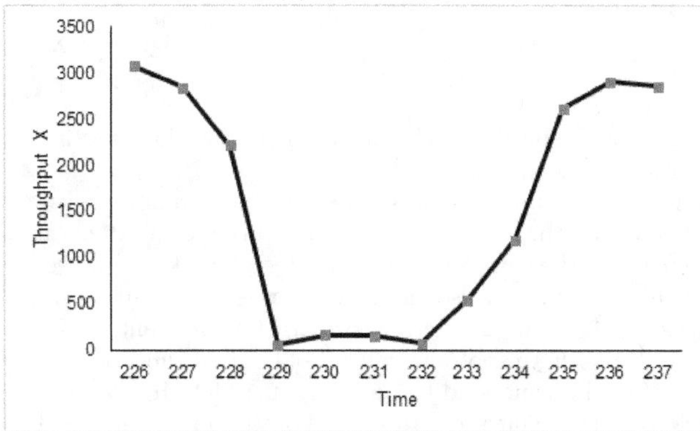

(d) X during performance deterioration

Figure 1: X and R for web tier

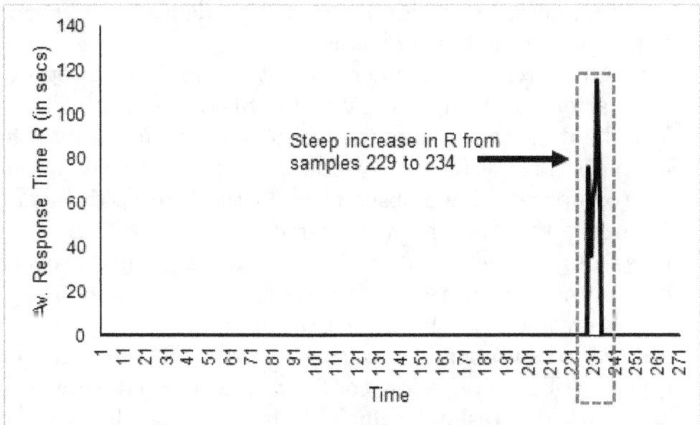

(a) R vs. time

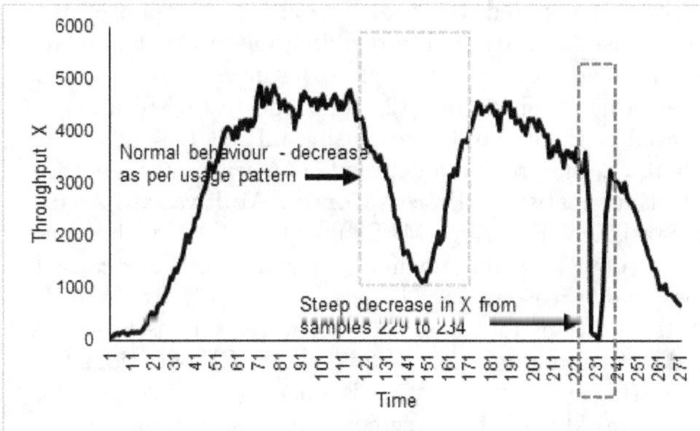

(b) X vs. time

Figure 2: X and R for application tier

the application server with no free memory. The threads which were currently executing web services in the application server stalled causing the calling web tier services to become extremely slow. The early-warning signals of an impending performance related incident are clearly seen in sampling period 229 and 230. The signals can be easily detected by continuous visual monitoring of the pair of R and X values, for each tier. While, using visual analysis, we can detect such patterns which point to a performance anomaly or abnormal performance behaviour, it is prone to misses. Our objective is to design a technique to detect such patterns automatically. Such a technique will enable generation of early warning alerts so that remediation can be quickly carried out.

3. RELATED WORK

In this section, we review the available work related to identifying performance related anomalies in software systems. The anomaly detection techniques can be classified as online or offline. Online techniques analyze monitoring data as it gets collected. Offline techniques analyze moni-

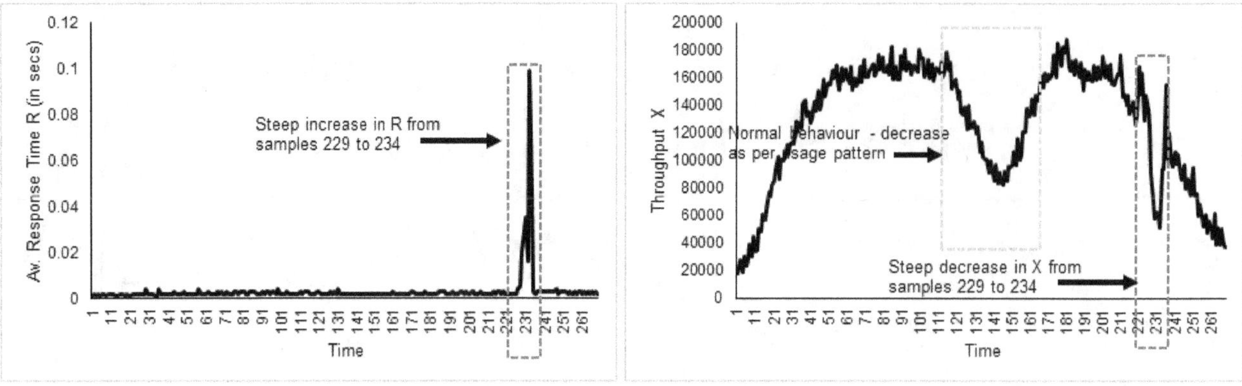

(a) R vs. time

(b) X vs. time

Figure 3: X and R for data tier

toring data at specified time e.g. at the end of load testing execution cycle, after business hours.

There are a number of techniques in literature for detecting anomalies during performance monitoring of production systems or at the completion of a load test. Malik et. al. recommend use of supervised and unsupervised learning techniques like K means clustering, principal component analysis, WRAPPER to spot anomalies in IT infrastructure metrics collected during load test execution [19][18][16][17]. For checking performance related regressions in a new release of a software, Nguyen et. al. use statistical control charts [21]. The control charts are based on IT infrastructure metrics like CPU utilization, memory utilization, network IO and disk IO. The distribution of response time from a given load test can be compared with the distribution of response time from a baseline test. If the distributions are not similar, then the load test results need to be investigated further for performance anomalies [12]. The load testing results are validated at the end of the test using Little's Law [20].

Frank et. al. provide a detailed comparison of Hypothesis Testing, Statistical Process Control, Multivariate Adaptive Statistical Filtering (MASF) and ANOVA techniques used for detecting abnormality in metrics that are caused by assignable reasons [7]. The use of control charts, MASF and its variations for monitoring software systems was proposed by Trubin et al. [24][25][26][27]. MASF partitions the time during which the system is operational, into hourly, daily or weekly reference segments to characterize repeatable or similar workload behavior experienced by a software system [8]. For example, the workload encountered by the system on Monday between 9:00 a.m. - 10:00 a.m. may be different from the workload between 10:00 a.m. - 11:00 a.m. Each segment is characterized by its mean and standard deviation. The number of reference sets can be further reduced using clustering techniques. The upper and lower limits are established for each reference at three standard deviations from the mean.

Foo et. al. propose the use of association rule mining technique on metrics from a baseline load test run to establish rules, with each rule containing a set of metrics which are correlated [11]. For example, a large number of requests may correlate with high CPU utilization. The violations of defined rules is taken as an early-warning sign of a performance anomaly. The use of predictive rules generated by an offline analysis of historical incident tickets and alerts in system monitoring is described in [23]. Satoshi et. al. use control charts with average, maximum, median and minimum statistic to proactively identify response time anomalies in web applications [13]. João Paulo et. al. define a framework comprising of aspect-oriented programming (AOP) based application performance data collection, statistical correlation and time-series alignment techniques to identify the incidence of performance anomalies [15]. Performance signatures established using failures which have occurred in the past can also be used to proactively determine anomalies [1, 5, 11]. Cherkasova et. al. propose an integrated framework comprising of a regression based transaction model and an application performance signature for enabling service providers to quickly identify and prevent performance related problems [9].

Open source and commercial system monitoring tools collect various performance data at defined intervals. The collected data is then compared to one or more threshold values for detecting performance issues. Thresholds can be simple (compare a single observation to the threshold), average (compare the average of most recent n observations to the threshold), successive (threshold is violated multiple consecutive times), occurrences (threshold is violated m times in n observations) or delta (of two observations separated by a specified number of observations violates the threshold) type [4]. The tools allow configuration of separate warning and critical threshold values. It is also possible to set the number of consecutive times a threshold must be violated for triggering an alert.For example, if CPU is 90% or more for over 3 times, an alert can be triggered. The threshold values can be defined for different times of the day or week to account for variations in workload profile. Apart from manually setting the thresholds, the tools also provide adaptive [6] or self-tuning [4] methods. In this case, the thresholds are statistically calculated periodically using historical data. The threshold values are based on statistic like percentile, a percentage of maximum value or a scaling factor of standard deviation.

System monitoring tools allow for searching for patterns and keywords in logs that may characterize a performance (or functional) issue. Some of the tools allow for deriving the health of a monitored entity based on the health of its constituents [3]. For example, we can define the overall hardware availability of a system to be dependent on the availability of all its server clusters. The availability of a server cluster may further depend on the availability of individual servers in the cluster.

Of all the above techniques, association rules and statistical process control charts appear to be the most intuitive for practitioners and easy to implement in commercial or open source system monitoring tools using custom extensions. However, association rules require thresholds to be set, which is dependent on the knowledge and experience of the practitioner. Similarly, a control chart can be used to monitor a single variable at a time, which restricts our ability to correlate multiple variables of interest. Through this work, an attempt has been made to correlate the monitoring done by two separate control charts: one for system throughput and the second for average system response time. The correlation is based on the inverse relationship between system throughput and average system response time as established by Little's Law [12],

4. PROPOSED TECHNIQUE

Software systems can be modeled using an open, closed or partly-open system model [22]. In a closed system model, a user submits a new request only when the response for the previously submitted request is received. This model is characterized by a fixed number of users. Load testing of software systems involving a fixed number of virtual users executing scripts containing data parametrization is an example of closed system behaviour. In an open system model, request submissions and completions are independent. Each arriving user submits a request, receives the response and then departs from the system. This model is characterized by the average arrival rate of users (λ).

In real-world, software systems are usually a mix of both open and closed models. Such systems are called as hybrid or partly-open systems as shown in Figure 4. Box 1 is the boundary of a partly-open system comprising of user arrivals, request-response interactions and departures. Box 2 is the boundary of a closed system containing only request-response interactions of users. The users arrive at and depart from the software system like in an open system. Prior to departing, users interact with the system multiple times. During every interaction, the user submits a request, waits to receive the response before submitting the next request. Partly-open systems can be treated as a closed system if the number of requests in user sessions are $\geq$ 10 [22]. So, for all practical purposes, we can model real-world software systems as closed systems.

For closed systems, Little's Law [14] establishes the relationship between the number of users in the system (N), throughput of the system (X), average response time (R) and average think time of the user (Z). The relationship is described by Equation (1). The terms X and R have been already introduced in section 2. Think time is the time spent by the user between consecutive interactions with the system like entering data in a form, viewing results of a previous request, navigating on the screen [28].

$$N = X(R + Z) \tag{1}$$

For closed systems, it can be intuitively argued that because N and Z do not change, X is inversely related to R [12]. For open systems, because N is not fixed, X and R are

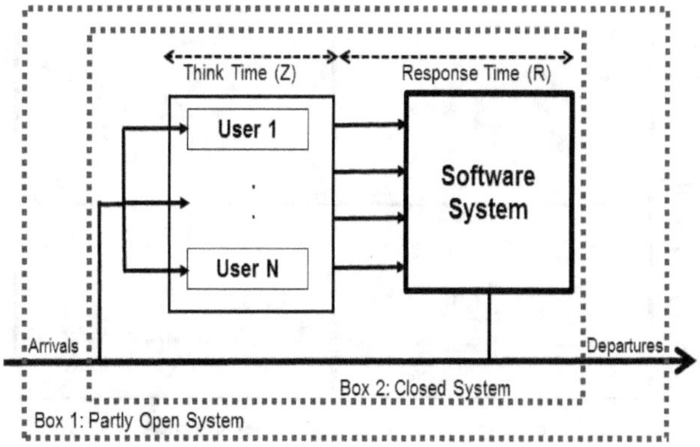

Figure 4: Partly open model representation of a software system

not correlated. For illustration, let us consider an interactive software system with 20 users, average think time of 5 sec and average response time of 15 sec. The throughput of the system calculated using Equation (1) is $\frac{20}{(15+5)} = 1$ request/sec. If the average response time increases by two times to 30 sec, the throughput of the system decreases to $\frac{20}{(30+5)} = 0.57$ request/sec. The increase in average response time by 100% leads to 43% decrease in throughput. Our experience shows that commonly used system monitoring tools in industry have no in-built support for establishing such correlation.

The proposed technique leverages the inverse relationship between X and R for identifying early-warning signals of performance deterioration in software systems. For this, we consider monitoring of software systems in production as a simplified process with two variables: throughput (X_S) and average response time (R_S). The subscript S denotes the monitoring interval. X_S is the number of requests completed in interval S. R_S is the sum of processing times of all requests completed in interval S divided by X_S. The value of X_S and R_S is calculated for requests processed during interval S. For example, a software system processed 400 requests in an interval of two minutes. The sum of the individual processing times of all the requests is calculated as 32 sec. Using this data, X_S and R_S are calculated as 400 and $\frac{32}{400} =$ 0.08 sec respectively. The value of X_S and R_S can increase or decrease from their values of the preceding monitoring interval (S-1). Figure 5 shows the four scenarios which can arise while comparing consecutive X_S and R_S values. Each scenario corresponds to one of the four quadrants. The X axis represents the behavior of X_S and the Y axis represents the behaviour of R_S.

As all pairs of X_S and R_S which fall in quadrant (1) may not be a real-warning signal, our objective is to devise a mechanism to distinguish signals from noise. For this, we will use the Individuals chart of an Individuals and Moving Range (XmR) statistical process control chart. The XmR chart is a set of two charts: X and mR. The mR chart shows the moving ranges of the variable of interest calculated using Equation (3) and the X or Individuals chart shows the individual values [10]. We use a two-point moving average. The Central Line (CL), Upper Control Limit (UCL) and Lower Control Limit (LCL) of the Individuals chart is calculated using Equations (4) to (6). The CL and UCL for correspond-

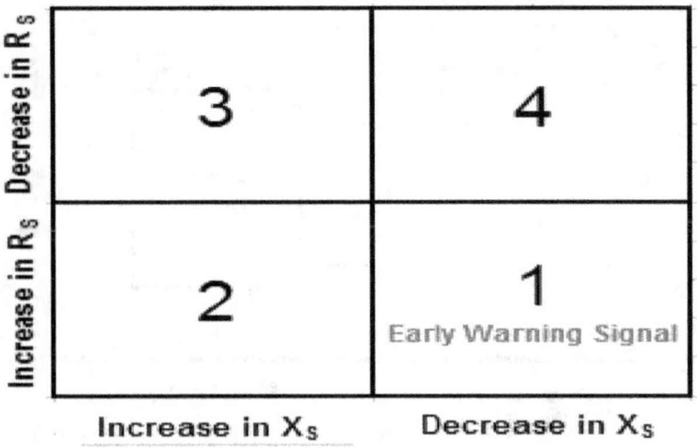

Figure 5: Scatter diagram showing the relationship between change in X_S and R_S

ing mR chart is calculated using Equations (7) and (8). X_i denotes the ith measurement. There is no LCL in the mR chart because the absolute difference between consecutive values is used. If there are n consecutive measurements, we have $r = n - 1$ two-point moving range values.

$$\bar{X} = \frac{1}{n}\sum_{i=1}^{n} X_i \tag{2}$$

$$\bar{mR} = \frac{1}{r}\sum_{i=1}^{r} mR_i, \quad \text{where} \quad mR_i = |X_{i+1} - X_i| \tag{3}$$

$$CL_I = \bar{X} \tag{4}$$

$$UCL_I = \bar{X} + 2.660 * \bar{mR} \tag{5}$$

$$LCL_I = \bar{X} - 2.660 * \bar{mR} \tag{6}$$

$$CL_{mR} = \bar{mR} \tag{7}$$

$$UCL_{mR} = 3.268 * \bar{mR} \tag{8}$$

To further increase the sensitivity in eliminating noise from signals, we recommend that practitioners establish control limits in accordance with the workload profile of the system to be monitored. In our case study, we have calculated control limits for every business hour of each weekday rather than having a single control limit for all business hours of the weekday. Therefore, we have separate control limits for Monday 9:00 a.m. to 10:00 a.m., 10:00 a.m. to 11:00 a.m., 11:00 a.m. to 12:00 p.m.,.., Friday 9:00 a.m. to 10:00 a.m., 10:00 a.m. to 11:00 a.m., 11:00 a.m. to 12:00 p.m.,..,Friday 4:00 p.m. to 5:00 p.m.. We define the following rule for identifying an early-warning signal.

Early-Warning Signal Rule

X_S is below LCL and R_S is above UCL in the Individuals (X) chart for a specified number of consecutive monitoring intervals.

5. REFERENCE IMPLEMENTATION

In the real-world case study described in section 6, we used the standard web server log entries generated by the presentation tier components and application tier components. The application tier components encapsulate processing logic in the form of web services. For the data tier, we used the database snapshot. Figure 6 shows a standard log entry. The %T and %D directive is used to log the processing time taken by a request in seconds and microseconds respectively [2]. The web server log is available by default in all web applications. We conducted several tests in a controlled environment and did not see any noticeable increase in the resource utilization on enabling the processing time directive (which may requires an additional function call internally). If a web server is not available, applications can be instrumented using techniques like AOP to write similar entries in a custom log file. In [15], the overhead introduced by using AOP for data collection is reported to be almost negligible.

Entry Time

```
10.0.10.19 - - [12/Oct/2013:11:08:00 +0530]
"GET /TestApp/SubmitData2.action HTTP/1.1" 200
12187 0 51273
```

Processing Time

Figure 6: A web server log entry

We want to highlight that the proposed technique is not application specific because it is not for collecting the performance data but for discovering useful insights from the collected data. The underlying data collection mechanism can be the more efficient Application Programming Interface (API), if software system provides such data via APIs.

A health sensing script is scheduled on each component to be monitored. The script processes the newly added entries in the last S minutes and calculates the value of X_S and R_S. The calculated values are then submitted to a central collection service for storage using an API. The dashboard of the central collection service displays the Individuals control charts and generates an alert in case the Early-Warning Signal Rule defined in section 4 is violated. The calculation of X_S and R_S incurs minimal computation overhead as it requires only sum, count and a single division, making it suitable for near real-time monitoring. We have empirically determined that for the system used in our case study, setting S to two minutes provides the correct balance of acceptable performance deterioration detection capability and compute overhead. In case of a multi-tier deployment, the health sensing script is deployed on each tier and the dashboard displays one entry for each of the tier. This allows us to drill down to the tier in which the performance deterioration originated.

6. REAL-WORLD CASE STUDY

The objective of this case study is to apply the proposed technique and validate its effectiveness. The study uses X_S and R_S data from the presentation tier of the system described in section 2.

First, we use data from a randomly selected month for setting control limits. Table 1 lists the statistics of the data. The data corresponds to the working days of the selected month, containing five Mondays, five Tuesdays, four Wednesdays, four Thursdays and four Fridays. Thus, Monday and Tuesday each have 1,200 observations whereas Wednesday, Thursday and Friday each have 960 observations. During this month, no incidents of slowness were reported by the end users.

Table 1: Statistics of data used for setting control limits

Statistics	Values
No of days	22
No of business hours per day	8
Monitoring interval (S)	120 secs
No of observations per hour	30
No of observations per day	240
Total no of observations	5,280

We use two Individuals charts, one for throughput and second for average response time. We determine the UCL and LCL for both the charts using Equations (4) to (6). The control limits of each chart are separately calculated for every weekday and business hour combination, resulting in 40 distinct control limits. Figures 7a and 7b show the control charts for one weekday.

Next, to evaluate the accuracy of our technique in identifying early-warning signals, we used our technique on data from another 23 days. During these days, four established incidents of slowness were documented. Table 2 lists the statistics of the data used in our validation. The data corresponds to five Mondays, four Tuesdays, four Wednesdays, five Thursdays and five Fridays. Thus, Thursday and Friday each have 1,200 observations whereas Tuesday and Wednesday each have 960 observations. Monday has 1,170 observations, as one Monday had only 210 observations. This is our test dataset.

Table 2: Statistics of data used in validation

Statistics	Values
No of days	23
Monitoring interval (S)	120 secs
Total no of observations	5,490
Total no of slowness incidents	4

To compare our technique with those used by practitioners, we also calculated the number of pairs of X_S and R_S in the second month which satisfied the following conditions.

- $X_S < X_{S-1}$ and $R_S > R_{S-1}$
- X_S has decreased and R_S has increased by a specified value ϵ
- Using the 3-sigma control limits in Early-Warning Signal Rule, calculated using Equations (11) and (12). The symbol σ denotes the standard deviation.

$$UCL = \bar{X} + 3\sigma \quad (9)$$

$$LCL = \bar{X} - 3\sigma \quad (10)$$

- X_S is less than the LCL of the Individuals chart.
- R_S is greater than the UCL of the Individuals chart.

Table 3 summarizes the results. The count of observations in rows 4 to 6 is less than 5,490 because for every 30 data values, there are 29 two point moving range values. The number of consecutive violations was set at 1 and 2. The value of ϵ was set at 0.05 and 0.10. We use precision and recall to evaluate the accuracy of our technique. If the identified signal is not substantiated by slowness reported by end users or analysis done by an expert, the signal is considered as a false signal. If an incidence of acknowledged slowness is not detected, then it is considered as a missed signal. The precision is calculated using Equation (11) and recall is calculated using Equation (12).

$$Precision = \frac{No\,of\,true\,signals}{No\,of\,signals\,detected\,by\,our\,technique} \quad (11)$$

$$Recall = \frac{No\,of\,true\,signals\,detected\,by\,our\,technique}{Actual\,no\,of\,early\,warning\,signals} \quad (12)$$

The results clearly confirm that our technique shows significant improvement (by reducing false alerts) than other techniques used by practitioners like independent monitoring of response time and/or throughput, using 3-sigma limits or exceeding a specified rate of change. Our technique has a recall of 100% (calculated using Equation (12)) i.e. we were able to spot all the four incidents. Out of the 32 early-warning signals our technique detected when the number of consecutive violations was set at 1, the number of signals corresponding to the four incidents was 21. Our technique has a precision of $\frac{21}{32}$ =65.63%. The precision improved significantly to $\frac{21}{21}$ =100% when the number of consecutive violations was taken as 2. In comparison, using 3-sigma limits we missed detecting any of the 21 signals. To improve alerting precision, we can tune the number of consecutive violations parameter. We conclude that our technique has helped in fulfilling the objective stated in section 2.

The reason for the commonly used 3-sigma thresholds, not performing well can be understood by comparing the value of σ and $\bar{mR}$. If σ is greater than $\bar{mR}$, then the tolerance limits established using Equations (11) and (12) are wider than tolerance limits established using Equations (5) and (6), leading to early-warning signals not being detected. For $\bar{X} = 1,934, \sigma = 563$ and $\bar{mR} = 183$, the 3-sigma UCL and LCL are 3,624 and 244 respectively. The UCL and LCL for Individuals chart are 2,420 to 1,447 respectively. Figure 8 shows the 3-sigma limits based control charts for the same weekday used in the Individuals charts of Figure 7.

For using control charts, it is not necessary to assume a specific distribution for the data. Tchebycheff's inequality states that for a stable process, at least $1 - \frac{1}{k^2}$ of the observations lie within k standard deviations of the mean of the observations [10]. Tchebycheff's inequality is applicable for any distribution. If k = 3, at least 88.9% of the observations, in the long duration, will lie within 3 standard deviations of the mean of the observations. The probability of false alarms in this case is 0.111. If observations are normally distributed, at least 99.73% of the observations, in the long duration, will lie within 3 standard deviations of the mean of the observations. In this case, the probability of false alarms is only 0.0027.

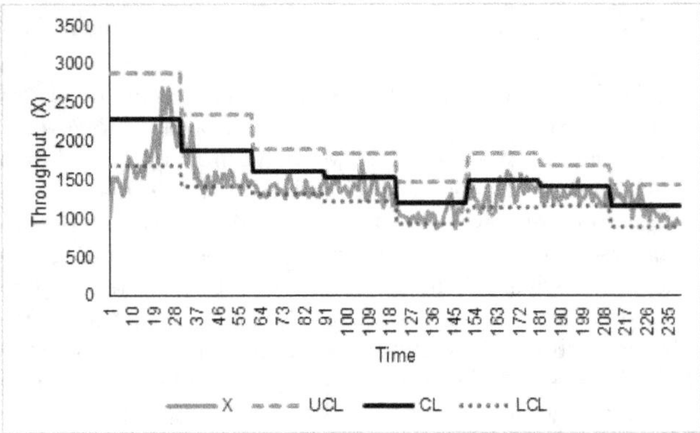

(a) Individuals chart for throughput

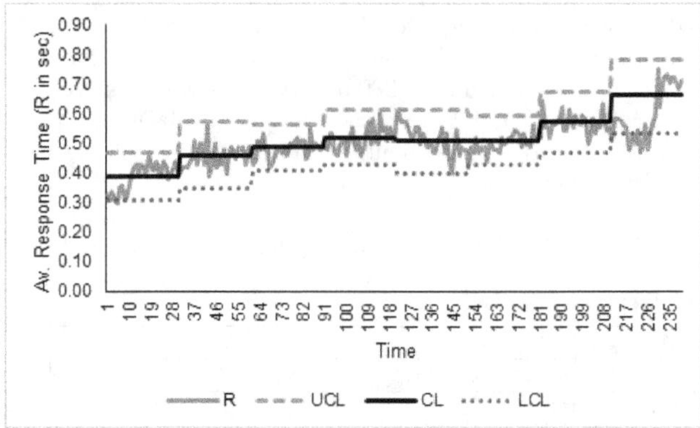

(b) Individuals chart for average response time

Figure 7: XmR Chart

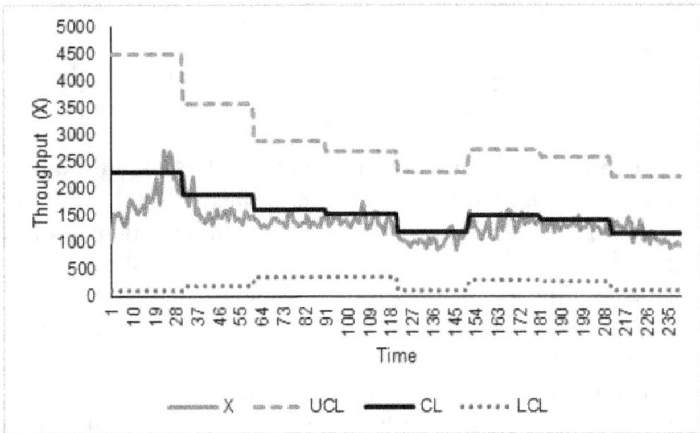

(a) 3-sigma control limits for throughput

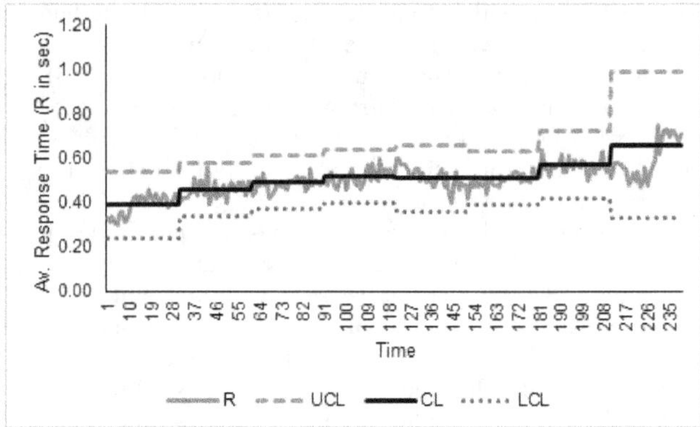

(b) 3-sigma control limits for average response time

Figure 8: Control Chart with 3-sigma limits

Table 3: Summary of results

Technique	**Warning Signals Detected**	**Normal Signals Detected**	**Total**
Individuals chart (consecutive violations=1)	32 (0.58%)	5,458 (99.42%)	5,490
Individuals chart (consecutive violations=2)	21 (0.38%)	5,469 (99.62%)	5,490
3-sigma control limits	0 (0%)	5,490 (100%)	5,490
X_S Down, R_S Up	1,572 (29.62%)	3,735 (70.38%)	5,307
X_S Down, R_S Up, $\epsilon = 0.05$	639 (12.04%)	4,668 (87.96%)	5,307
X_S Down, R_S Up, $\epsilon = 0.10$	214 (4.03%)	5,093 (95.97%)	5,307
X_S < LCL (of Individuals chart)	592 (10.78%)	4,898 (89.22%)	5,490
R_S > UCL (of Individuals chart)	156 (2.84%)	5,334 (97.16%)	5,490

7. THREATS TO VALIDITY

Internal Validity: The proposed technique uses data from an software system used in industry. The data is historical and may be influenced by the version of the software system corresponding to the time of data. The data reflects the real-world behaviour as it is also not possible to impose any kind of controls in a real-world system and may influence the accuracy of our findings. To reduce this threat, we have used performance data corresponding to one complete month.

External Validity: In the paper, we validate our approach using a mission critical software system from industry. To generalize our technique further, additional software systems from industry and publicly available e-commerce benchmarking applications like DellDVD [1] can be included. The monitoring interval used in this paper has been empirically determined and found to work well for the application used in the case study. The same cannot be generalized for all applications without more tests.

We plan to address the above limitations as an extension of this work in future.

8. CONCLUSION

The technique proposed by us has helped in institutionalizing a structured and systematic approach for system monitoring teams to proactively spot early-warning signs of performance related issues using two application metrics and take corrective action. This is a significant improvement over the existing system monitoring methods which is mostly silo-based in which different dimensions of IT infrastructure like server compute, storage, network, middleware and database are monitored in isolation and not linked to application service metrics like response time and throughput. It is often seen that software projects in industry acquire complex system monitoring tools but are unable to use them effectively in their daily operations because of the complexity and abundance of performance counters being monitored, level of expertise needed in setting realistic thresholds. The advantage of the proposed technique is its simplicity, intuitiveness, low implementation overhead and accuracy. The technique and its underlying concept complements and strengthens existing system monitoring tools typically used by practitioners in industry.

Our future work will include experiments on open source benchmark applications to further validate our model. We also intend to do a comprehensive study on the anomaly detection and alerting techniques provided by commercial and open source system monitoring tools like SCOM [4], OEM [6] and Nagios [5].

9. ACKNOWLEDGMENTS

We wish to thank Nidhi Dahiya, Vikash Vardhan, Gopal Sharma, Madhuri Kumari and other anonymous reviewers for their valuable feedback on improving this work.

10. REFERENCES

[1] Dell DVD Store Database Test Suite. http://linux.dell.com/dvdstore/. Online; accessed 21 February 2017.

[2] Logging control in w3c httpd. https://www.w3.org/Daemon/User/Config/Logging.htmlcommon-logfile-format. Online; accessed 25 September 2016.

[3] Microsoft System Center: Monitors and Rules. https://technet.microsoft.com/en-us/library/hh457603(v=sc.12).aspx. Online; accessed 23 February 2017.

[4] Microsoft System Center Operations Manager. https://technet.microsoft.com/library/hh205987.aspx. Online; accessed 21 February 2017.

[5] Nagios - The Industry Standard In IT Infrastructure Monitoring. https://www.nagios.org/. Online; accessed 21 February 2017.

[6] Oracle Enterprise Manager 12c. http://www.oracle.com/technetwork/oem/enterprise-manager/overview/index.html. Online; accessed 21 February 2017.

[7] F. M. Bereznay. Did something change? using statistical techniques to interpret service and resource metrics. In *Int. CMG Conference*, 2006.

[8] J. P. Buzen and A. W. Shum. Masf - multivariate adaptive statistical filtering. In *Int. CMG Conference*, pages 1–10. Computer Measurement Group, 1995.

[9] L. Cherkasova, K. Ozonat, N. Mi, J. Symons, and E. Smirni. Anomaly? application change? or workload change? towards automated detection of application performance anomaly and change. In *2008 IEEE International Conference on Dependable Systems and Networks With FTCS and DCC (DSN)*, pages 452–461, June 2008.

[10] W. A. Florac and A. D. Carleton. *Measuring the Software Process: Statistical Process Control for Software Process Improvement.* Addison-Wesley Longman Publishing Co., Inc., Boston, MA, USA, 1999.

[11] K. C. Foo, Z. M. Jiang, B. Adams, A. E. Hassan, Y. Zou, and P. Flora. Mining performance regression testing repositories for automated performance analysis. In *2010 10th International Conference on Quality Software*, pages 32–41, July 2010.

[12] M. Harchol-Balter. *Performance Modeling and Design of Computer Systems: Queueing Theory in Action.* Cambridge University Press, New York, NY, USA, 1st edition, 2013.

[13] S. Iwata and K. Kono. Narrowing down possible causes of performance anomaly in web applications. In *2010 European Dependable Computing Conference*, pages 185–190, April 2010.

[14] J. D. C. Little. A proof for the queuing formula: $L = \lambda w$. *Oper. Res.*, 9(3):383–387, June 1961.

[15] J. P. Magalhaes and L. M. Silva. Detection of performance anomalies in web-based applications. In *2010 Ninth IEEE International Symposium on Network Computing and Applications*, pages 60–67, July 2010.

[16] H. Malik, B. Adams, and A. E. Hassan. Pinpointing the subsystems responsible for the performance deviations in a load test. In *2010 IEEE 21st International Symposium on Software Reliability Engineering*, pages 201–210, Nov 2010.

[17] H. Malik, B. Adams, A. E. Hassan, P. Flora, and G. Hamann. Using load tests to automatically compare the subsystems of a large enterprise system. In *2010 IEEE 34th Annual Computer Software and Applications Conference*, pages 117–126, July 2010.

[18] H. Malik, H. Hemmati, and A. E. Hassan. Automatic detection of performance deviations in the load testing of large scale systems. In *2013 35th International Conference on Software Engineering (ICSE)*, pages 1012–1021, May 2013.

[19] H. Malik, Z. M. Jiang, B. Adams, A. E. Hassan, P. Flora, and G. Hamann. Automatic comparison of load tests to support the performance analysis of large enterprise systems. In *2010 14th European Conference on Software Maintenance and Reengineering*, pages 222–231, March 2010.

[20] R. K. Mansharamani, A. Khanapurkar, B. Mathew, and R. Subramanyan. Performance testing: Far from steady state. In *COMPSAC Workshops*, pages 341–346. IEEE Computer Society, 2010.

[21] T. H. Nguyen, B. Adams, Z. M. Jiang, A. E. Hassan, M. Nasser, and P. Flora. Automated detection of performance regressions using statistical process control techniques. In *Proceedings of the 3rd ACM/SPEC International Conference on Performance Engineering*, ICPE '12, pages 299–310, New York, NY, USA, 2012. ACM.

[22] B. Schroeder, A. Wierman, and M. Harchol-Balter. Open versus closed: A cautionary tale. In *Proceedings of the 3rd Conference on Networked Systems Design &*

Implementation - Volume 3, NSDI'06, pages 18–18, Berkeley, CA, USA, 2006. USENIX Association.

[23] L. Tang, T. Li, L. Shwartz, F. Pinel, and G. Y. Grabarnik. An integrated framework for optimizing automatic monitoring systems in large it infrastructures. In *Proceedings of the 19th ACM SIGKDD International Conference on Knowledge Discovery and Data Mining*, KDD '13, pages 1249–1257, New York, NY, USA, 2013. ACM.

[24] I. Trubin. Review of IT Control Chart. *Journal of Emerging Trends in Computing and Information Sciences*, 4(11):857–868, Dec. 2013.

[25] I. Trubin and V. C. Scmg. Capturing workload pathology by statistical exception detection system. In *Proceedings of the Computer Measurement Group*, 2005.

[26] I. A. Trubin. Global and Application Level Exception Detection System, Based on MASF Technique. In *28th International Computer Measurement Group Conference, December 8-13, 2002, Reno, Nevada, USA, Proceedings*, pages 557–566, 2002.

[27] I. A. Trubin and L. Merritt. "Mainframe Global and Workload Level Statistical Exception Detection System, Based on MASF". In *30th International Computer Measurement Group Conference, December 5-10, 2004, Las Vegas, Nevada, USA, Proceedings*, pages 671–678, 2004.

[28] T. Wilson. What were they thinking: Modeling think times for performance testing. 2011.

HPC Supported Mission-Critical Cloud Architecture

Tae Joon Jun, Myong Hwan Yoo, Daeyoung Kim
School of Computing, KAIST
Daejeon, Korea
{taejoon89, yoomhwan, kimd}@kaist.ac.kr

Kyu Tae Cho, Seung Young Lee
LIG Nex1 Corporation
Yongin, Korea
{kyutae.cho, seungyoung.lee}@lignex1.com

Kyuoke Yeun
Agency of Defense Development
Daejeon, Korea
koyeun@add.re.kr

ABSTRACT

Tactical Operations Center (TOC) system in military field is an advanced computer system composed of multiple servers and desktops to interlock internal/external weapon systems processing mission-critical applications in combat situation. However, the current TOC system has several limitations such as difficulty of integrating tactical weapon systems including missile launch system and radar system into the single TOC system due to the heterogeneity of HW and SW between systems, and an inefficient computing resource management for the weapon systems.

In this paper, we proposed a novel HPC supported mission-critical Cloud architecture as TOC for Surface-to-Air-Missile (SAM) system with OpenStack Cloud OS, Data Distribution Service (DDS), and GPU virtualization techniques. With this approach, our system provides elastic resource management over the weapon systems with virtual machines, integration of heterogeneous systems with different kinds of guest OS, real-time, reliable, and high-speed communication between the virtual machines and virtualized GPU resource over the virtual machines. Evaluation of our TOC system includes DDS performance measurement over 10Gbps Ethernet and QDR InfiniBand networks on the virtualized environment with OpenStack Cloud OS, and GPU virtualization performance evaluation with two different methods, PCI pass-through and remote-API. With the evaluation results, we conclude that our system provides reasonable performance in the combat situation compared to the previous TOC system while additionally supports scalable and elastic use of computing resource through the virtual machines.

CCS Concepts

•Networks → Cloud computing; •Applied computing → Military; •Computer systems organization → Heterogeneous (hybrid) systems; Dependable and fault-tolerant systems and networks;

ICPE'17, April 22-26, 2017, L'Aquila, Italy

DOI: http://dx.doi.org/10.1145/3030207.3044531

Keywords

Cloud Computing; Tactical Operations Center; Data Distribution Service; GPGPU;

1. INTRODUCTION

In the military field, multiple internal/external weapon systems such as radar system, early warning system, missile launch system, and satellite system are required for the SAM system in the combat situation. The TOC for SAM system is a composite computer system which controls above weapon systems for the SAM in the real combat situation. For example, the TOC for SAM system analyzes data from the radar tracking system while the missile launch system targets enemy forces in the combat situation. Fig. 1 shows an overview of the general TOC for SAM system.

However, the current TOC for SAM system has several limitations. Firstly, internal/external weapon systems are heterogeneous, mixing several operating systems, hardware requirements, programming languages, and development environments. Supporting an integrated control system for these heterogeneous systems with traditional server-client model is an inefficient approach and almost impossible to implement in real world. Secondly, the number of weapon systems used in the combat situation is different from time to time. For example, when the early warning system is in active state with the satellite and the radar systems, other

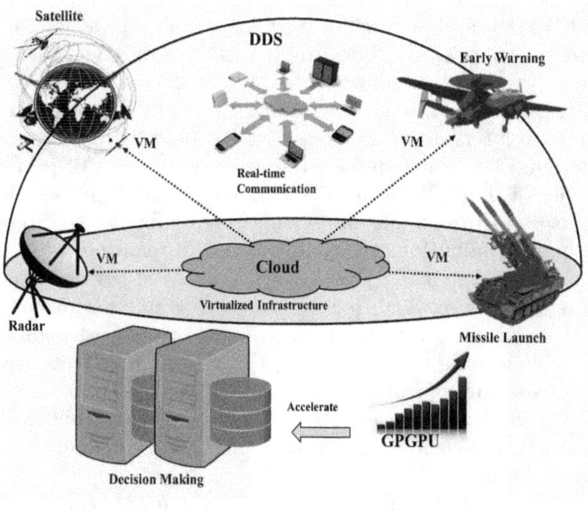

Figure 1: Overview of the TOC System

weapon systems such as air defense system and guided missile system may not be turned on. Providing computing resources to every weapon system is an extremely inefficient approach from the resource management view point. Finally, making decisions to control in the combat situation should be real-time and accurate. Communication between the weapon systems related to the SAM should be high-speed. In addition, analyzing combat data from the weapon systems should be accurate too.

In this paper, we proposed a novel HPC supported mission-critical Cloud architecture as TOC for SAM system with OpenStack Cloud OS [16], Data Distribution Service (DDS), and GPU virtualization techniques. To overcome the heterogeneous system problem, we used OpenStack open source cloud OS to provide virtualized infrastructure to the system. Every weapon system is loaded to the virtual machines created by OpenStack Cloud OS with different guest OS such as Windows and Linux. Cloud computing also enables the elastic use of computing resource for the weapon systems which overcomes the second problem stated above. DDS with high speed network, such as 10Gbps Ethernet and QDR InfiniBand, assures real-time communication between the weapon systems in the TOC system with the virtual machines. GPUs are used to accelerate algorithm that supports fast and accurate data analysis for the decision making. For example, Kalman filter algorithm for the radar tracking system can be written in GPGPU programming languages such as CUDA and OpenCL. GPU virtualization techniques including PCI pass-through and remote-API are used to provide virtualized GPU resources to the virtual machines. With DDS and GPU virtualization, our approach solves the third limitation stated above.

Evaluation of our TOC for SAM system processed in three different ways. First, we evaluated the DDS performance over two high speed networks, 10Gbps Ethernet and QDR Infiniband, in both non-virtualized and virtualized environments. Then, we experimented the DDS on the multiple virtual machines to check scalability of the DDS in the virtualized TOC system. Finally, we measured the performance of the real world GPU benchmark programs with two common GPU virtualization techniques, PCI pass-through and remote-API, on the virtual machines. From the evaluation, latency of the DDS over 10Gbps Ethernet with 1ms stable message interval shows average 5% faster than that of the QDR Infiniband. Between non-virtualized and virtualized environments, latency result with 1ms message interval time in the non-virtualized environment shows average 65% faster than that of the virtualized one. In case of 0.1ms message interval, we checked that the blocked messages at the publisher can significantly decreases the overall performance of the DDS in the TOC system. In addition, we also measured throughput, and standard error for the DDS performance evaluation. With the DDS performance results, we concluded that using DDS with the message period higher than 1ms can provide reliable and reasonable performance and scalability over the TOC system. In case of running GPU benchmark programs on the virtual machines with PCI pass-through and remote-API, execution time of the programs shows various results that are related to the characteristic of benchmark programs such as high memory copy proportion.

The paper is organized as follows. Section 2 provides background information and Section 3 covers the detail architecture of the system. Section 4 includes evaluation and experimental results of the system. Previous works related to our approach is provided in the Section 5. Conclusion of our work and future work are described in the Section 6.

2. BACKGROUND

2.1 OpenStack Cloud OS

OpenStack is an open source project for the cloud computing platform that began in 2010. The project was started by Rackspace Hosting and NASA. Currently, OpenStack Foundation manages the project and more than 500 companies are participated in the project, including AMD, Cisco, Dell, Google, IBM, Intel, Oracle, VMware, etc. Updated version of OpenStack platform is released around every six-months under the terms of the Apache License.

When classifying Cloud computing according to service and deployment models, OpenStack can be classified as an infrastructure as a service (IaaS) for public, private, and hybrid cloud. OpenStack is composed of several lower branches of projects including Nova, Glance, Keystone, Neutron, etc. Fig. 2 shows the conceptive architecture of OpenStack projects. Our interest in OpenStack for this paper is focused on compute and network services

2.2 Data Distribution Service

DDS is a publish/subscribe based machine-to-machine (M2M) standard, approved by the Object Management Group (OMG) , that enables real-time, high-speed, and scalable data communication between publishers and subscribers. Many of todayâĂŹs systems are heterogeneous, mixture of different hardware, operating systems, programming languages, and development environments. In case of our TOC system, the weapon systems are heterogeneous. For example, the missile launch system uses Windows based OS with Java applications while the early warning system uses Linux based OS with C++ applications. In this scenario, integrating these two systems requires standard middleware APIs such as DDS, CORBA, and JMS.

DDS is widely used in many kinds of systems such as aerospace, military, traffic control, simulation, and medical

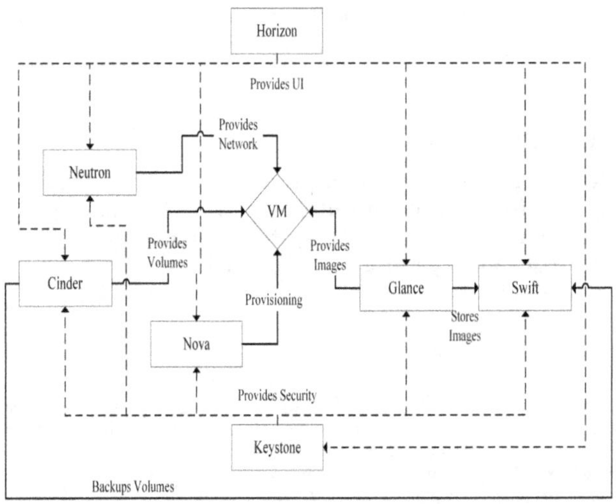

Figure 2: Conceptive architecture of OpenStack projects

system. Recently, there is a movement of adopting DDS to Internet of Things (IoT) system especially for Industrial Internet of Things (IIoT). RTI Corporation, which is DDS development Company, already participates in the Industrial Internet Consortium (IIC), and according to the market study conducted by Appinions in July 2014, RTI has been ranked the most influential industrial IoT Company [15]. This implies that DDS will take more important role in the IoT field.

2.3 GPU Virtualization

General Purpose computing on Graphic Processing Unit (GPGPU) is nowadays a common technique to boost up parallel applications that are traditionally processed by CPUs. GPGPU has been used in many scientific computing applications including molecular modeling, bioinformatics, financial computing, and digital signal processing. In particular, applications involving vector or matrix operations can gain large benefits from GPGPU programming. In our TOC system, algorithm for decision making, Montel Carlo simulation, and Kalman filter algorithm require GPGPU based system to support high-performance operational control in the combat situation. However, using GPUs in the virtual machine needs GPU virtualization techniques to support GPGPU programming on the guest OS. Currently, there are about three approaches for the GPU virtualization, PCI pass-through [10], remote-API, and hardware supported virtualization [4].

3. PROPOSED SYSTEM

Our TOC system has two major components, tactical and operational control system and weapon system. Tactical and operational control system includes combat control servers, tactical console servers, controller server, and data link servers. The combat control servers manage tactical and operational information and perform critical decision making during the combat situation. Tactical console servers provide visual information to the managers who command operational actions. Controller server is OpenStack controller server which manages the entire TOC system related to OpenStack components. Data link servers handle connection between internal/external weapon devices. Weapon system is a collage of multiple weapon device software such as missile launch and radar tracking software. Fig. 3 shows an overall architecture of the TOC system.

Every server in tactical and operational control system, except the controller server, is also a compute node of OpenStack Cloud platform. Each server has nova-compute, KVM hypervisor, and nova-network packages. With nova-compute and KVM hypervisor, the virtual machine is created in the target server. For example, weapon handling software which controls multiple weapons in combat situation is installed in virtual machine that placed at the combat control server. Every virtual machine in the TOC system communicates through DDS middleware. To support high speed data exchange between virtual machines, local network of the system is composed of 10Gbps Ethernet and QDR Infiniband network

3.1 Weapon System

Weapon system composed of multiple servers that are compute nodes of OpenStack. Weapon software related to SAM in the combat situation such as radar software, missile launch software, satellite software, and early warning software are installed in the virtual machines that are placed at servers. As same as the tactical and operational control system, DDS middleware is installed in the virtual machines.

3.2 Tactical and Operational Control System

Tactical and operational control system is the main component of the TOC for SAM system. The system manages the weapon systems and make control decision in the combat situation. Combat control servers are central part of the tactical and operational control system. Combat control software including sensor handling, air picturing, Threat Evaluation and Weapon Assignment (TEWA), weapon handling, weapon tactical, and basic utility software are installed in the virtual machines that placed at combat control servers. In addition, every server is also the compute node of OpenStack Cloud that nova-compute and nova-network are installed as OpenStack packages.

Some parts of combat control servers have special purpose virtual machines such as decision making in the combat situation, Kalman filtering for radar tracking, and Monte Carlo simulation to support probabilistic simulation. These servers have high-end GPUs to provide GPGPU features to the virtual machines and PCI pass-through and remote-API techniques are both implemented for the GPU virtualization. Tactical console servers include tactical multi-media interfaces (MMI) to support visualized monitoring over the TOC system and data link servers act as link handler between servers.

Controller server is a single server which manages the entire TOC system related to OpenStack features. Controller server has many OpenStack components such as keystone for authentication, glance for the guest OS image management, horizon for OpenStack dashboard support, heat for orchestration over the virtual machines, ceilometer for the server resource monitoring, and nova related packages for the virtual machine management. Because virtual machines are not created in this server, there is no KVM hypervisor. In addition, controller has only one network interface for an OpenStack management purpose while other servers have two network interfaces, one for OpenStack management and the other for data exchange between virtual machines. Every virtual machine in the tactical and operational system has DDS middleware to support high-speed and reliable communication between the virtual machines.

3.2.1 System Network

Neutron and nova-network are network services for OpenStack. In an earlier version of OpenStack, nova-network was the only network service for the virtual machine networking. From the OpenStack version Folsom, new network service project called Quantum has been released and from the version Havana, project name has changed to Neutron, which provides Software Defined Network (SDN) as a network service [1]. Despite of many difference between SDN and legacy network services, our interest for OpenStack network services focused on the floating IP range for the virtual machines. Legacy network, which is nova-network, assigns a fixed IP to the virtual machine. Main role of nova-network is to support Linux bridge network between the virtual network interface in the virtual machine and the physical network interface in the compute node. However, this fixed IP can only be used inside the Cloud system. To access

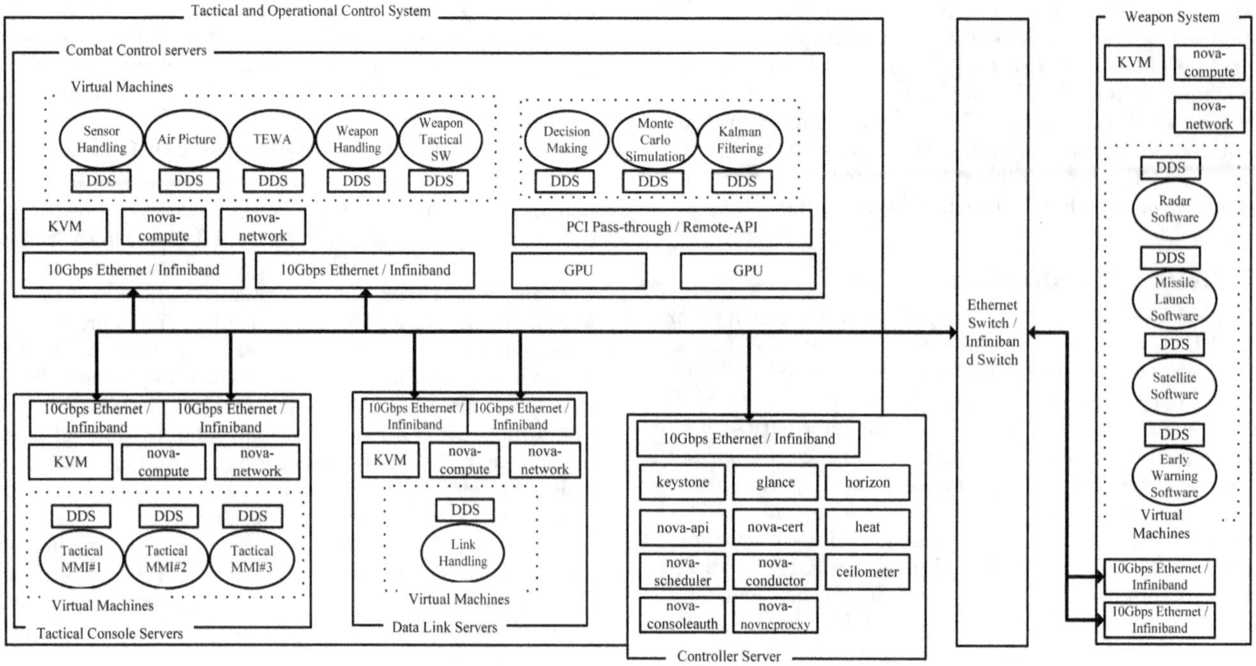

Figure 3: TOC System Architecture

the guest OS from the outside system, a floating IP should be assigned to the virtual machine. When nova-network is used, the range of floating IPs is same as that of the servers where OpenStack is installed. This limitation occurs a huge problem when the cloud system is composed of thousands of servers.

Neutron eliminates this limitation with SDN concept. When Neutron is used, network control software that was installed in the network devices are all programmed into the independent software. With Neutron, we can observe several new things such as ML2 plugin, L2 Agent, and OpenvSwitch that were not visible when nova-network is used. Because every network control software is configurable and programmable, the range of floating IPs is no longer limited by the range of the host servers. Although many of todayâĂŹs public cloud service deployed SDN for Cloud networking in the data center, using SDN for networking in private cloud service, like our TOC system, can be inefficient especially when the cloud system only requires small number of virtual machines, particularly less than 1,000.

3.2.2 Virtual Machine Communication

DDS middleware provides communication between the virtual machines. DDS is composed of Data-Centric Publish-Subscribe (DCPS) and Data Local Reconstruction Layer (DLRL) [17]. DCPS is the lower part of APIs layer that enables applications to communicate topic data with other applications. Meanwhile, DLRL is the upper part of the layer that allows integration between applications and DDS interfaces. Communication between applications are separated by the domain that applications with same domain only can exchange their data through the DDS. Fig. 4 shows overall architecture of DDS, especially includes DCPS entities. Topics are basic unit of data to be published and subscribed. Domain participants are entry points for data access. Publishers contain Data-writers to perform the write operation and subscribers have Data-reader to access data. There are two ways of accessing data through the subscriber, wait-based data access and listener-based data access. The wait-based approach blocks participant until data change occurs, which is a synchronous approach. However, the listener-based approach notifies participant whenever data changes, which is an asynchronous approach. These DCPS entities, topics, data-writers, data-readers, are configurable with quality of service (QoS) policies that consider deadline, resource limitation, reliability, durability, etc.

3.2.3 GPGPU Support

We used two different GPU virtualization techniques to support GPGPU for acceleration of the decision making. Firstly, PCI pass-through technique binds physical GPUs to the virtual machine through the hypervisor. This technique requires IOMMU support from CPU. Fig. 5 shows an architecture of the PCI pass-through for GPUs. Attaching GPUs to the guest OS requires following steps, removing GPUs from the hostâĂŹs PCI interface, binding GPUsâĂŹ vendor and device ID to the PCI stub driver, and assigning GPUs on the virtual machine creation time. In case of OpenStack, vendor and device ID of GPUs are defined in Nova configuration file with pci-passthrough-whitelist and pci-alias options. OpenStack also supports scheduling of GPUs with PCIPassthroughFilter option in nova-scheduler of the controller node [2]. When a virtual machine creation is requested, GPUs are pre-allocated to the virtual machine flavors and user can access GPUs from the guest OS as same as accessing from the host OS.

Advantage of PCI pass-through technique comes from the direct access of GPUs from the guest OS PCI interface. User can use every feature of GPUs from the guest OS as it was in the host OS, and the performance of GPU applications shows almost near performance as that of native GPU. However, there is a critical limitation which is a lack of scalability. GPUs that are bound to the virtual machine cannot be shared with other virtual machines which compromises inefficient use of GPU resources. Unlike CPUs, GPUs are used in small fraction of time compared to the idle time of CPUs. Increasing idle time of GPUs in an entire system is crucial, especially for the Cloud service provider due to the high cost of GPU resources. In case of Amazon EC2 public Cloud service, which is the most popular IaaS Cloud service today, virtual machine with GPUs are about one dollar per hour more expensive than the same flavor of virtual machine without GPUs [12]. In conclusion, sharing GPUs resource among virtual machines are an important issue in GPU the virtualization technique and this limitation brought remote-API virtualization technique.

Secondly, Remote-API technique allows using GPUs in remote host through the network. Main idea of remote-API techniques is capturing API calls from GPU applications, then send these API calls to BackEnd module in the host server side which has GPUs. After GPU driver and GPU execute API calls, the result returns back to GPU applications through network or loopback interface. Fig. 6 shows the general architecture of remote-API technique. When GPU application starts, FrontEnd module captures API calls with the wrapper library. Then FrontEnd module sends captured API calls to BackEnd module through the network interface. Because FrontEnd and BackEnd modules are separated, GPU application can be executed even there is no GPU in the host where the application is running. After BackEnd module receives API calls, it delivers API calls to GPU driver. When GPU finishes execution for API calls, the result returns back to FrontEnd module and to GPU application. Main advantage of remote-API technique is a separation of FrontEnd and BackEnd modules that enables GPU applications to use GPUs in the remote hosts. This helps an efficient use of GPU resources when the system is distributed and not all hosts have GPUs for computing resources. Primary target system of remote-API was a large distributed system with small number of GPUs so that the applications in every hosts can use GPUs logically through the network interface. Nowadays the virtualized system such as Cloud computing has huge interests in the remote-API technique. With remote-API, the virtual machine can access GPUs in the server host through the virtualized network interface.

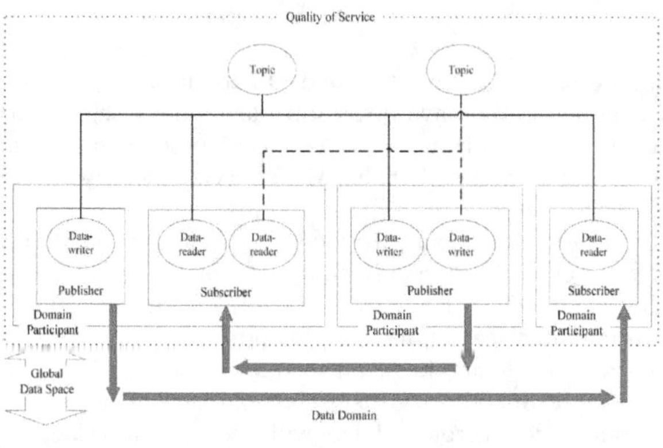

Figure 4: Overall Architecture of DDS

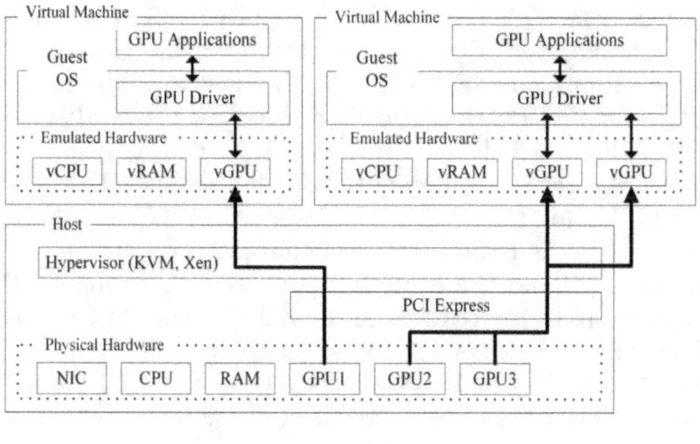

Figure 5: PCI Pass-through Architecture

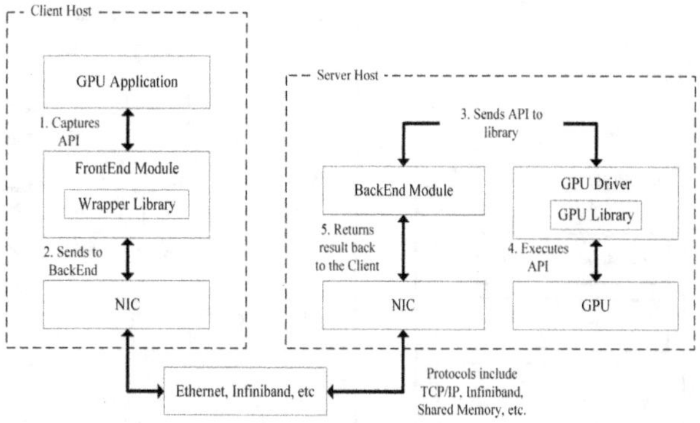

Figure 6: Remote-API Architecture

Our interest in GPU virtualization also focuses on the remote use of GPUs among the TOC system. However, because data communication between GPU application and GPU memory is processed through the network interface, performance of GPU applications highly depends on the network status. In addition, GPU driver is installed in the host server side, not in the client side, which limits GPU features from the client side OS due to the invisibility of GPU through the PCI-e interface. Despite the limitation of GPU features and performance issue, remote API is still attractive GPU virtualization technique that allows remote use of GPUs in the distributed system. There are several remote-API methods such as gVim [11], gVirtus [24], vCUDA [19], and rCUDA [20] [13]. As far as we know, rCUDA is the only updated remote-API technique which supports CUDA version 7.0. Table 1 describes difference between these remote-API techniques.

Table 1: Comparison between Remote-API methods

	gVim	**gVirtus**	**vCUDA**	**rCUDA**
Version	None (2009)	Beta3 (2011.11)	None (2012.6)	v15.07 (2015.7)
S/W Available	No	Yes	No	Yes
GPGPU Model	CUDA1.1	CUDA3.2 OpenCL1.1	CUDA3.2	CUDA7.0
Network Channel	XenStore	TCP/IP (vm-Socket)	VMRPC (Shared memory)	TCP/IP Infiniband

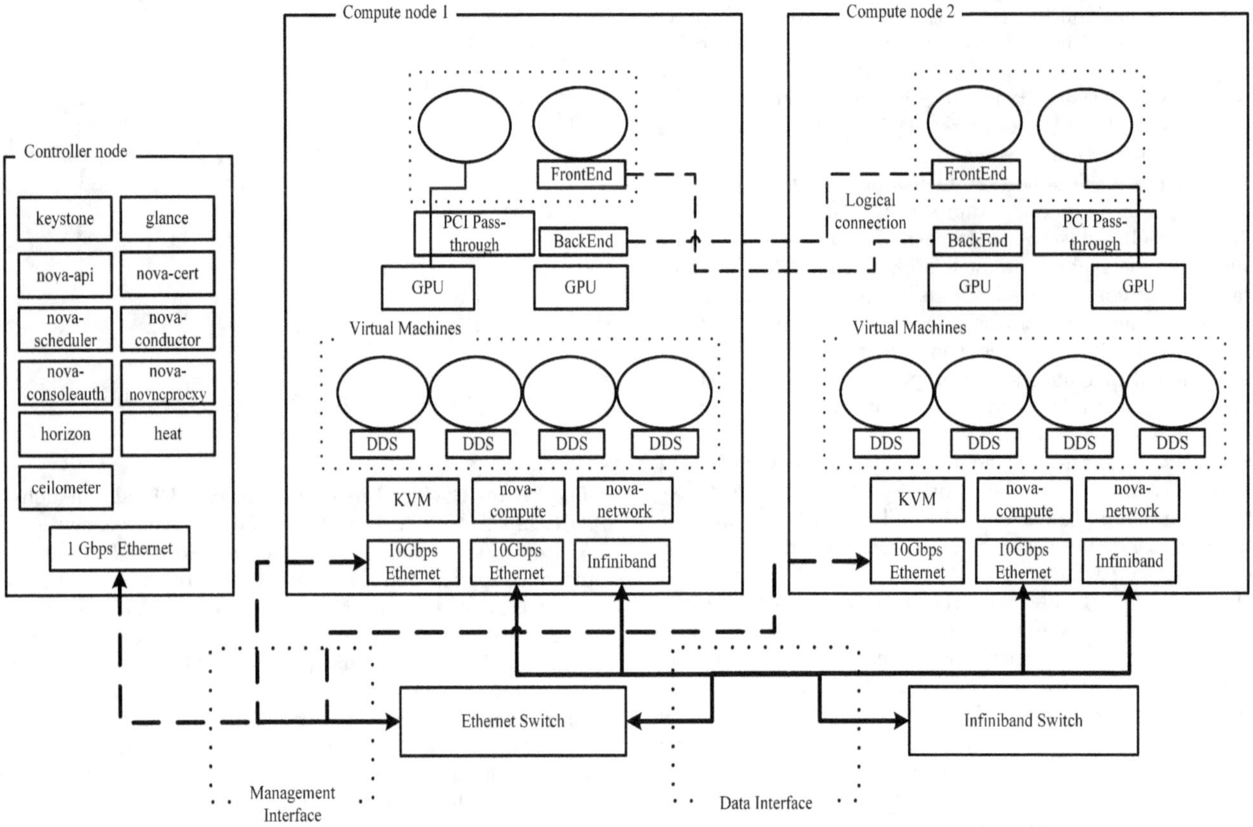

Figure 7: Experimentation System Architecture

4. EXPERIMENTAL EVALUATION

Our experiments are categorized into two different evaluation. First, we evaluate the performance of DDS middleware in virtualized and non-virtualized environments with 10Gpbs Ethernet and QDR Infiniband network. In addition, we evaluate the scalability of DDS middleware with eight virtual machines across two distributed servers. Second, we analyzed the performance of general GPU applications with two different GPU virtualization techniques, PCI pass-through and remote-API, on our experimentation system.

4.1 Experimental Setup

To evaluate the performance of the TOC system, we implemented another system for the experimentation. Due to the military security reason, it is forbidden to expose the actual TOC system specification to the public. So we implemented a reduced size TOC system for the research and experimental purpose. The system composed of one PC for the controller node and two servers for the compute nodes. The PC has Intel Core i7 CPU and 8GB RAM while each server has two Intel Xeon E5 CPUs, 64GB RAM, and two high-end NVIDIA Tesla K20 GPUs. Infiniband that we used for the experimentation is QDR Infiniband that theoretically shows 40Gbps bandwidth on Infiniband protocol while shows 10Gbps on IP over Infiniband (IPoIB) configuration. Ubuntu 14.04 is used in every host OS with Linux kernel version 3.19.0-26. Fig. 7 shows an overall architecture of the experimentation system. As same as the actual TOC system, we used OpenStack Cloud OS to support virtualized environment. We have one controller node with keystone, glance, nova, horizon, heat, and ceilometer installed and two compute nodes with KVM hypervisor, nova-compute, and nova-network.

For the management interface, used to deliver commands between OpenStack components, is composed of 1 Gbps Ethernet interface from the controller node and 10 Gbps Ethernet interfaces from compute nodes. Data interface provides data exchange between virtual machines. This is the most important interface to DDS middleware because the communication through DDS will use data interface. As result, data interface is composed of two high-speed networks, 10Gbps Ethernet and QDR Infiniband. However, nova-network does not support Infiniband protocols for the internal network interface, so we deployed Infiniband interface into a virtual Ethernet interface by using Ethernet on IP over Infiniband (E-IPoIB) [6]. Because of additional interface for the IPoIB, E-IPoIB shows lower bandwidth than that of IPoIB which is a theoretically up to 10Gbps.

In the system, each compute node has two NVIDIA Tesla K20 GPUs for the high performance GPGPU computing. One of GPUs is bound to the virtual machine through PCI pass-through and the other is bound through remote-API, especially rCUDA. rCUDA is the only remote-API method which supports recent CUDA version with other important GPGPU libraries such as CUBLAS, CUDNN, CUFFT, CURAND, and CUSPARSE. With rCUDA, the virtual machine can use GPUs in both compute nodes that are not bound to the specific virtual machines through PCI passthrough. When the virtual machine executes GPU applications, rCUDA uses management interface for API and data exchange between FrontEnd and BackEnd modules. For this reason, management interface of compute nodes can be either 10Gbps Ethernet or virtual Ethernet interface with E-IPoIB.

To measure the performance and scalability of DDS middleware, we used RTI Connext DDS Professional 5.1.0 [22] and RTI PerfTest 5.1.0.9 [21]. For the performance measurement, we set the following four different environments, non-virtualized 10Gbps Ethernet, non-virtualized QDR Infiniband with E-IPoIB, virtualized 10Gbps Ethernet, and virtualized QDR Infiniband with E-IPoIB. Virtualized environments are composed of m1.large type virtual machine in OpenStack Cloud which uses two virtual CPUs, 8GB RAM, and 80GB disk with an Ubuntu 14.04 for the guest OS. From DDS, each publisher sends 100,000 messages with message queue size 50, and message length from 1 byte to 10bytes with multicast option enabled. DDS performance is measured with average latency of single message, throughput of the subscriber, and standard error of latency in the single test.

To evaluate DDS more precisely, we set the interval time between messages sent from publisher to subscriber. For the latency driven evaluation, we set the interval time to 1ms to check the latency difference between 10Gbps and E-IPoIB QDR Infiniband. For the throughput driven evaluation, the interval time is set to 0.1ms to check the throughput difference between the two networks.

Scalability of DDS in virtual machines is measured through eight virtual machines that are separated into four each. Each compute node has up to four virtual machines and we measured the latency and throughput of publishers and subscribers with one-to-one to four-to-four matching.

For the performance measurement of GPU applications, we used Rodinia 3.0 benchmark suite [5] which is generally used to measure the performance of real-world applications written in GPGPU programming languages including CUDA and OpenCL. Within the Rodinia suite, we chose 8 GPU applications written in CUDA, Backprop, BFS, CFD, Hotspot, LUD, NN, NW, and Pathfinder. Table 2 shows description of GPU programs used in Rodinia suite.

Table 2: GPU Benchmark Program Description

Name	Description
Bacprop	Back Propagation which is a machine learning algorithm that used in neural network
BFS	Breadth-First-Search (BFS) is well known graph traversal algorithm
CFD	CFD is a volume solve program for 3D Euler equations for compressible flow
Hotspot	Hotspot is used to estimate the processor temperature
LUD	LU Decomposition is well known algorithms to solve linear equations
NN	K-nearest neighbors is popular algorithm in pattern recognition for classification and regression
NW	Needleman-Wunch is optimization method that used for DNA sequence alignments
Pathfinder	Pathfinder uses dynamic programming to find a path in 2D grid with the smallest accumulated weights

4.2 Evaluation Result

4.2.1 DDS performance evaluation results

Fig. 8 shows the performance evaluation results of DDS with 1ms message interval. In case of our TOC system, actual message interval period required in the system is between 100ms and 1000ms which is much slower than 1ms. As result, we concluded that testing with 1ms message interval is sufficient enough to show stable latency over the TOC system. From the Fig. 8a, average latency of DDS on 10Gbps Ethernet is 5% lower than that of E-IPoIB Infiniband. Between non-virtualized and virtualized, average latency in non-virtualized environments show 65% lower than that of virtualized one due to the increased number of layers from the virtualized network interface. From the Fig. 8b, throughput of subscriber linearly increases when data length of message gets higher which is reasonable result considering that messages are published with multicast option enabled. From the Fig. 8c, standard error of every test is below 10 which is stable enough in case of our TOC system requirement.

Fig. 9 shows the performance evaluation results of DDS with 0.1ms message interval. Compared to the 1ms interval message, 0.1ms interval drives the TOC system network throughput into the limitation. With the 0.1ms interval test, we purposed to check the negative effect of blocked messages over the entire TOC system. From the Fig. 9a, average latency of DDS in non-virtualized environment is 41% lower than that of virtualized one until the message length reaches 5 bytes. However, after the 6 bytes message length, average latency non-virtualized environments is 260% lower than that of virtualized one. The reason of this abnormal increase of latency results in virtualized environment is from the increased number of blocked messages. When the message queue of publisher is full, messages are blocked until the queue gets empty. The latency of this blocked message is over 30,000us which is about 100 times slower than the stable latency. Table 3 shows the maximum latency of 0.1ms interval time results. From the Table 4 and Fig. 9c, we can observe that standard error also dramatically increases when the messages are blocked. From the Fig. 9b, we can observe that throughput of virtualized environments reaches 1Gbps than decreases after message length of 5 bytes. The reason of this throughput limitation comes from virtio, which is I/O virtualization layer used in KVM hypervisor [23]. When virtio is used, there is only one queue for each network receive (Rx) and transmit (Tx) in the virtual machine. This default option limits network throughput of virtual machine around 1Gbps. However, we believe that it is not a reliable approach to increase the number of queues for Rx and Tx for the single virtual machine due to the load balance issue of traffics between virtual machines. We will re-discuss this problem in further research.

4.2.2 DDS scalability evaluation results

Fig. 10 shows the evaluation results of DDS scalability. To get a stable results, we configured interval time between messages to 1ms. From the Fig. 10a, latency of DDS gets lower when data length of the message increases. Between 10Gbps Ethernet network and E-IPoIB Infiniband network, E-IPoIB Infiniband shows lower latency until data length of the message reaches 5 bytes. However, from the 6 bytes, 10Gbps shows better latency than that of E-IPoIB Infiniband net-

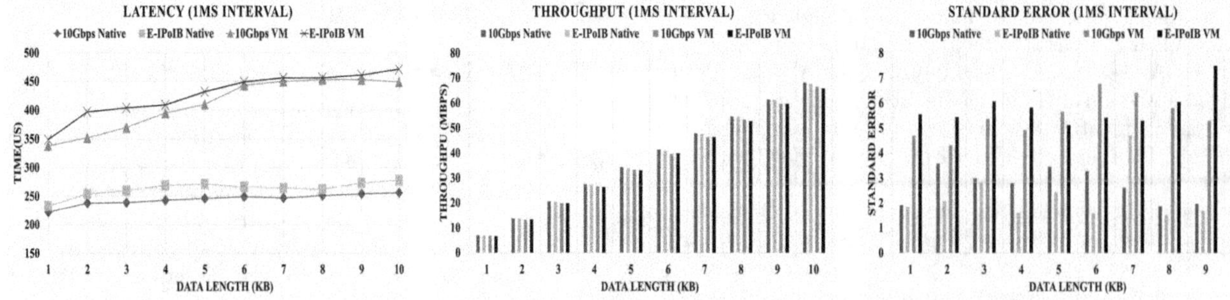

(a) Latency (b) Throughput (c) Standard Error

Figure 8: DDS Performance Evaluation Results with 1ms Message Interval

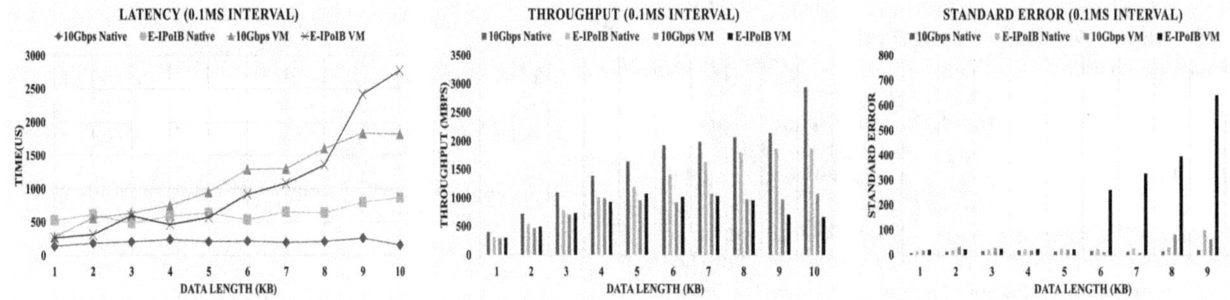

(a) Latency (b) Throughput (c) Standard Error

Figure 9: DDS Performance Evaluation Results with 0.1ms Message Interval

work. This result implies that DDS should be carefully configured considering the number of publisher and subscribers, and data length of the messages. From the Fig. 10b, we can also observe that the throughput of each subscriber increases when data length of messages gets higher. These results can be different when the multicast option for DDS is turned off. In this experimentation, we set the multicast option to get the best results from DDS and also it is a general approach to set multicast option when using DDS with multiple publishers and subscribers.

Table 3: Maximum Latency Result

Size(KB)	10Gbps Native	E-IPoIB Native	10Gbps VM	E-IPoIB VM
1	821	1024	2094	893
2	800	1597	3146	939
3	864	1169	2881	1320
4	889	1391	1984	1011
5	1025	1203	2477	1008
6	1217	1311	3943	32217
7	1155	1220	2397	32900
8	1213	1837	33461	33221
9	1238	31442	35500	33598
10	1128	31249	34901	33964

Table 4: Standard Error Result

Size(KB)	10Gbps Native	E-IPoIB Native	10Gbps VM	E-IPoIB VM
1	8.08	16.97	19	21.85
2	13.93	19.84	33.04	22.43
3	15.94	22.09	28.86	24.69
4	19.09	23.21	18.84	24.34
5	14.61	24.18	22.64	22.4
6	16.83	25.52	12.24	260.59
7	13.84	27.14	9.36	327.4
8	15.24	30.76	81.96	395.55
9	19.95	101.04	63.55	642.78
10	9.77	103.61	78.76	712.27

4.2.3 GPU benchmark programs evaluation results

Fig. 11 shows the performance evaluation results of GPU benchmark programs in Rodinia suite. Fig. 11a, shows normalized execution time based on the results of rCUDA using localhost GPUs through loopback interface. From the result, we can observe that PCI pass-through does not always show better performance than that of rCUDA. The reason of performance gap between PCI pass-through and rCUDA comes from pre-load of runtime libraries into the main memory. When rCUDA is used to execute GPU applications, the runtime library is a chunk of wrapper libraries which is pre-loaded on the main memory. Because whole library is already loaded, processing time of API calls is faster than that of original approach. However, this advantage is removed when there is a lot of memory copy between GPU application and GPU memory. From the Fig. 11b, proportion of execution time for the memory copy API calls in NW benchmark is higher than 80%. In result of NW benchmark, the average execution time of the NW benchmark using remote GPUs through the networks is 128% higher than result of using the local GPUs. In contrast, the average execution time of other 7 benchmarks using remote GPUs is only 7% higher than that of using local GPUs.

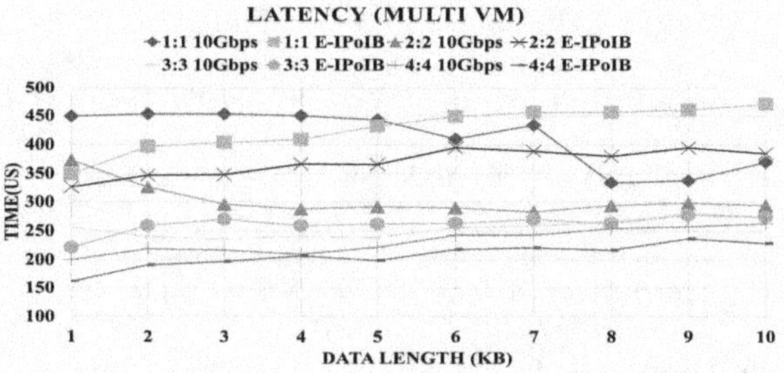

(a) Latency

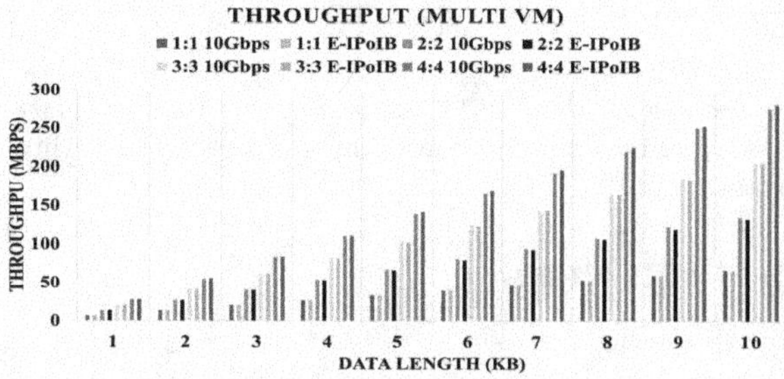

(b) Throughput

Figure 10: DDS Scalability Evaluation Results

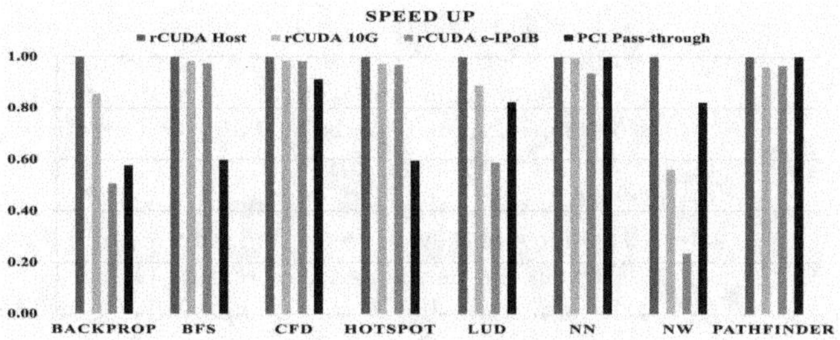

(a) Speed Up

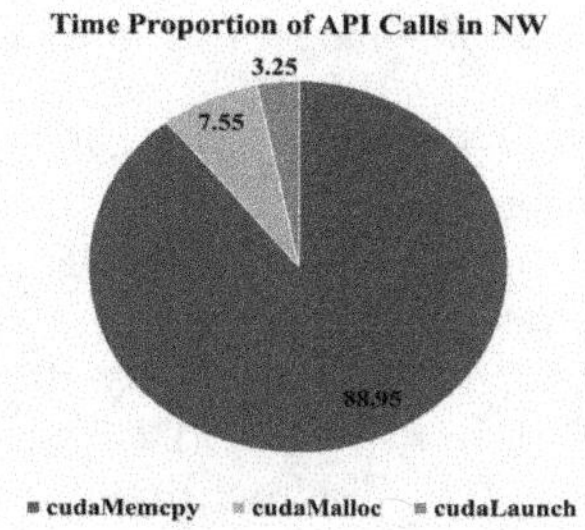

(b) API Calls

Figure 11: GPU Benchmark programs Performance Evaluation Results

5. RELATED WORK

5.1 DDS over the Cloud environment

There are several researches try to adopt the DDS middleware in the Cloud environment. Corradi, A., et al. [7] introduced Cloud monitoring and management architecture with the DDS standard. They also used an open source tool called Distributed Architecture for Resource manaGement and mOnitoring in cloudS (Dargos) [18] to implement their own management framework related to OpenStack Cloud OS. Similar to [7], An, K., et al. [3] also introduced a resource monitoring middleware in the Cloud environment with DDS. However, main purpose of [7], [3] is to introduce monitoring/management of Cloud infrastructure with DDS while our work targets to build an entire Cloud system with DDS as a data communication middleware between virtual machines.

5.2 GPU Virtualization techniques on Cloud

Performance evaluation of GPU virtualization techniques such as PCI pass-through and remote-API is done by many previous researches. Crago, S., et al. [8] introduced OpenStack Cloud platform with remote-API method called gVirtus. Younge, A., et al. [26] evaluated PCI pass-through on Xen hypervisor with SHOC [9] benchmark suite. Walters, J. P., et al. [25] evaluated performance of PCI pass-through in several hypervisors such as KVM, Xen, VMware ESXi, and LXC with SHOC benchmark suite. Jun, T., et al. [14] evaluated the performance of PCI pass-through and rCUDA remote-API on the OpenStack Cloud platform with SHOC and Rodinia benchmark suites. However, evaluation of GPU virtualization techniques on our work focuses on the performance of PCI pass-through and rCUDA on the OpenStack Cloud OS with two different high-speed networks, 10Gbps Ethernet and QDR Infiniband.

6. CONCLUSION AND FUTURE WORK

TOC for SAM system is an important platform that controls weapon systems related to the SAM in the combat situation. Previous approaches of TOC system had several limitations such as unable to support heterogeneous environments between weapon systems, inefficient computing resource management, and lack of GPGPU based system to provide high-performance decision making. In this work, we proposed a novel HPC supported mission-critical Cloud architecture as TOC for SAM system with OpenStack Cloud OS, DDS middleware, and GPU virtualization techniques. We also implemented an experimental TOC system to evaluate performance DDS, scalability of DDS, and performance of GPU virtualization techniques over two different networks, 10Gbps Ethernet and QDR Infiniband. From the evaluation result, we conclude that efficiency of DDS for communication between virtual machines highly depends on characteristics of published messages such as data length, message queue size and interval time between messages. We also observed that the number of blocked messages critically affects the increase of average latency by checking standard errors of latency results. In conclusion, we deployed an actual TOC for SAM system for Agency of Defense Development with considering evaluation results of experimental system.

In future, we plan to expand our TOC system into general purpose Cloud platform such as IoT platform. Recently, DDS middleware is used to support communication between sensors in IoT platform. Similar to the TOC system, DDS middleware handles data exchange of sensors while GPGPU system provides analysis of big data gathered from IoT sensors and actuators with machine learning algorithms.

7. ACKNOWLEDGMENTS

The authors would like to thank the Agency of Defense Development and LIG Nex1 Corporation for their support that has contributed to the research results reported within this paper.

8. REFERENCES

[1] D. Abramson. Intel virtualization technology for directed I/O. In *Intel technology journal*, 2006.

[2] Amazon. Amazon ec2 retrieved from http://aws.amazon.com/ko/ec2. 2015.

[3] K. An, S. Pradhan, F. Caglar, and A. Gokhale. A publish/subscribe middleware for dependable and real-time resource monitoring in the cloud. In *Proceedings of the Workshop on Secure and Dependable Middleware for Cloud Monitoring and Management*, 2012.

[4] Appinions. Internet of Things : An Industry Influence Study Retrieved from http://dj.appinions.com/iot-july-2014, year = 2014.

[5] S. Che, M. Boyer, J. Meng, D. Tarjan, J. Sheaffer, S.-H. Lee, and K. Skadron. Rodinia: A benchmark suite for heterogeneous computing. In *Workload Characterization, 2009. IISWC 2009. IEEE International Symposium on*, 2009.

[6] J. Chu, , and V. Kashyap. Transmission of ip over infiniband (ipoib) no. rfc 4391. 2006.

[7] A. Corradi, L. Foschini, J. Povedano-Molina, and J. Lopez-Soler. DDS-enabled Cloud management support for fast task offloading. In *Computers and Communications (ISCC), 2012 IEEE Symposium on*, 2012.

[8] S. Crago, K. Dunn, P. Eads, L. Hochstein, D.-I. Kang, M. Kang, D. Modium, K. Singh, J. Suh, and J. Walters. Heterogeneous Cloud Computing. In *Cluster Computing (CLUSTER), 2011 IEEE International Conference on*, 2011.

[9] A. Danalis, G. Marin, C. McCurdy, J. S. Meredith, P. C. Roth, K. Spafford, V. Tipparaju, and J. S. Vetter. The Scalable Heterogeneous Computing (SHOC) benchmark suite. In *Proceedings of the 3rd Workshop on General-Purpose Computation on Graphics Processing Units*, 2010.

[10] P.-C. G. Omg data-distribution service: Architectural overview. In *Distributed Computing Systems Workshops, 2003. Proceedings. 23rd International Conference on*, 2003.

[11] G. Giunta, R. Montella, G. Agrillo, and G. Coviello. A GPGPU Transparent Virtualization Component for High Performance Computing Clouds. In *Euro-Par 2010-Parallel Processing*, 2010.

[12] V. Gupta, A. Gavrilovska, K. Schwan, H. Kharche, N. Tolia, V. Talwar, and P. Ranganathan. GViM: GPU-accelerated virtual machines. In *Proceedings of the 3rd ACM Workshop on System-level Virtualization for High Performance Computing*, 2009.

[13] A. Herrera. NVIDIA GRID: Graphics Accelerated VDI with the Visual Performance of a Workstation. In *Nvidia Corp*, 2014.

[14] T. J. Jun, M. H. Y. Van Quoc Dung, D. Kim, H. Cho, and J. Hahm. GPGPU enabled HPC Cloud Platform based on OpenStack Retrieved From http://sc14.supercomputing.org/sites/all/themes/sc14/files/archive/tech_poster/poster_files/post269s2-file3.pdf. 2014.

[15] N. McKeown, T. Anderson, H. Balakrishnan, G. Parulkar, L. Peterson, J. Rexford, S. Shenker, and J. Turner. OpenFlow: enabling innovation in campus networks. In *ACM SIGCOMM Computer Communication Review*, 2008.

[16] OpenStack. OpenStack Cloud Retrieved from http://www.openstack.org. 2015.

[17] OpenStack. Pci passthrough retrieved from https://wiki.openstack.org/wiki/Pci_passthrough. 2015.

[18] J. Povedano-Molina, J. M. Lopez-Vega, J. M. Lopez-Soler, A. Corradi, and L. Foschini. DARGOS: A highly adaptable and scalable monitoring architecture for multi-tenant Clouds. In *Future Generation Computer Systems*, 2013.

[19] C. Reano, R. Mayo, E. S. Quintana-Orti, F. Silla, J. Duato, and A. J. Pena. Influence of InfiniBand FDR on the performance of remote GPU virtualization. In *Cluster Computing (CLUSTER), 2013 IEEE International Conference on*, 2013.

[20] C. Reano, F. Silla, A. Pena, G. Shainer, A. Schultz, S.and Castello, E. Quintana-Orti, and J. Duato. Boosting the performance of remote GPU virtualization using InfiniBand connect-IB and PCIe 3.0. In *Cluster Computing (CLUSTER), 2014 IEEE International Conference on*, 2014.

[21] RTI. RTI Connext DDS Combined Latency and Throughput Performance Test Getting Started Guide Retrieved from http://community.rti.com/rti-doc/510/RTI_Performance_Test_5.1.0/doc/RTI_ConnextDDS_PerformanceTest_GettingStarted_5.1.0.pdf, year = 2014.

[22] RTI. RTI Connext DDS Professional Getting Stated Guide Retrieved from http://www.rti.com/eval/rtidds510/RTI_Connext_DDS_Professional_GettingStarted.pdf. 2013.

[23] R. Russell. virtio: towards a de-facto standard for virtual I/O devices. In *ACM SIGOPS Operating Systems Review*, 2008.

[24] L. Shi, H. Chen, J. Sun, and K. Li. vCUDA: GPU-Accelerated High-Performance Computing in Virtual Machiness. In *Computers, IEEE Transactions on*, 2012.

[25] J. P. Walters, A. J. Younge, D. I. Kang, K. T. Yao, M. Kang, S. P. Crago, and G. C. Fox. GPU Passthrough Performance: A Comparison of KVM, Xen, VMWare ESXi, and LXC for CUDA and OpenCL Applications. In *Cloud Computing (CLOUD), 2014 IEEE 7th International Conference on*, 2014.

[26] A. Younge, J. Walters, S. Crago, and G. Fox. Evaluating GPU Passthrough in Xen for High Performance Cloud Computing. In *Parallel & Distributed Processing Symposium Workshops (IPDPSW), 2014 IEEE International*, 2014.

A Tool Supporting the Analytical Evaluation of Service Level Agreements

Falko Bause, Peter Buchholz, Johannes May
Department of Computer Science
TU Dortmund, 44221 Dortmund
Germany
{falko.bause, peter.buchholz, johannes.may}@tu-dortmund.de

ABSTRACT

Quantitative aspects of modern IT systems are often specified by service level agreements (SLAs) which relate the maximal load of a system with guaranteed bounds for response times and delays. These quantities are specified for single services which are combined in a service oriented architecture (SOA) to composed services offered to potential users or other service providers. To derive SLAs for composed services and to plan the required capacity to guarantee SLAs, appropriate methods and tools have to be used that compute results based on information given in SLAs. In this paper it is argued that most available approaches are not sufficient to analyze systems based on SLA information. A new method and a tool are presented that support the efficient calculation of bounds for delays in composed systems based on bounds for the load and the delay of the individual components which are specified in the SLAs of the components. Furthermore, the presented tool can be used to generate bounds for the required processing capacity which a provider has to provide in order to guarantee the quality of service defined in the SLAs.

The presented approach is in some sense a counterpart to mean value analysis for queueing networks but rather than mean values, worst case bounds for different quantities like response times or departure processes are computed. Analysis is based on min/+ algebra but the mathematical approach is hidden from the user by a graphical interface allowing a simple graphical specification and result representation for networks of composed services.

Keywords

service level agreements, analytical evaluation, performance modeling tools

1. INTRODUCTION

Quantitative aspects of current software systems are specified as part of the service level agreements (SLAs). In a service oriented world, one can distinguish between the user of a service and the provider of the service. The user requests a minimal service level which is guaranteed by the provider. An important part of the service level is the response time. Usually systems guarantee a maximal response time for a large percentage of the submitted load. The provider has to supply the requested processing capacity to process the load within the available time. However, to guarantee maximal response times, the load has to be restricted in the SLA. This implies that an SLA contains an upper bound for the load which the user can submit into the system and an upper bound for the response time to process the submitted load. Apart from these bounds an SLA defines various other quantitative and functional properties of the service, which we will not consider in our analysis. Thus, if we speak of an SLA, we explicitly consider the bounds on arrivals and response times or delays[1].

In many cases, a service is composed of sub-services. This can be the case if the provider uses third party services or if the user composes his or her service from sub-services offered by different providers. In such a case the SLA of the composed service has to be derived from the sub-services. For a provider there is additionally the need to compute the required processing capacity from the knowledge of the SLA to avoid an over- or under-loading of the available equipment.

The definition and analysis of appropriate SLAs is a capacity planning problem. Since the environment in which the problem has to be solved is highly dynamic and often extremely complex, detailed analysis approaches like simulation are not adequate, because the effort would be too high, required data is not or not completely available and some details of the system are unknown. Therefore it is important to develop analysis techniques that can work with the available information which means that the information given in the SLAs is the basis for quantitative analysis and capacity planning.

Abstract models to analyze service oriented architectures (SOAs) are usually based on results available from product form queueing networks. Often some variant of mean value analysis is applied [15–17]. In some cases hierarchical models are supported [21] but analysis is still based on product form techniques. Overview papers describing different approaches to analyze quality-of-service in service oriented architectures or cloud environments are [1, 11].

There are two disadvantages of queueing network based

[1]The terms response time and delay will be used interchangeably here although they reflect different viewpoints of the same quantity.

ICPE'17, April 22-26, 2017, L'Aquila, Italy

DOI: http://dx.doi.org/10.1145/3030207.3030215

analysis of SLAs. First, for analysis mean arrival rates and service times are input parameters and response times are outputs of the analysis. In SLAs arrival rates and response times are input parameters and service rates have to be derived. However, in the product form case, equations can be inverted such that arrival rates and response times become input parameters to compute the required service capacity [6,7]. If numerical analysis approaches or simulation are used for analysis, it is not clear how service capacities are computed from arrival rates and response times. The second disadvantage of queueing network based analysis is more critical. Product form analysis is based on the computation of mean values of result measures based on mean values of the parameters. The specification of mean values in SLAs is usually not sufficient because deviations from the mean can result in unacceptable delays or overload situations. Thus, SLAs usually contain some kind of upper bound which is unavailable in mean value analysis. Thus, a mean value based analysis approach can only over-provision the system to avoid overload situations but it is unclear how much overprovisioning is really required to meet the SLA. It should be mentioned that this also holds for variants where mean value analysis for product form queueing networks is used and it is assumed that only bounds for the parameters are available [14]. The bounds resulting from such an analysis are bounds for mean values, they do not consider the worst case which is often quantified in an SLA.

In performance analysis a calculus for computing bounds on delays and buffer spaces using bounds on arrival and service rates is known since the pioneering work of Cruz in the early nineties [9,10]. These results are the basis for the network calculus [4] and real time calculus [20]. Like queueing network based analysis approaches both calculi compute response time bounds from the knowledge of arrival and service bounds. Therefore they are not directly usable in the SLA context. However, they provide a solid basis to analyze the worst case behavior of systems which is bounded in SLAs.

The work presented in this paper has its foundations in the theory of SLA calculus [6,7] and an earlier version in [23,24]. SLA calculus uses the theory developed in [9,10] for the analysis of software architectures based on SLAs. This implies that arrival and response time bounds become input parameters to compute bounds on arrivals, departures and response times of composed services and to compute additionally bounds on the minimal service capacity. Like QN analysis, SLA calculus is a mathematical approach to compute the required results in a fairly efficient way. However, without tool support, the approach will hardly be applied because analysis algorithms have to be implemented and models have to be specified in the mathematical formalism which is quite far from the intuitive understanding of the behavior of a service.

In this paper we try to put SLA calculus to work. We introduce an approach to specify composed systems of services graphically, show how an hierarchical analysis is performed and how results are represented. The whole approach has been implemented in a tool which is also introduced here in some detail. The goal is, like in queueing network tools, to hide the details of the analysis from a user by providing an easy to use graphical interface for model specification and result representation.

The paper is structured as follows. Sect. 2 presents some basics of SLA Calculus, followed by a short introduction of input parameter estimation of our models in Sect. 3. SLA Tool is introduced in Sect. 4. Sect. 5 sketches an example of its use. The paper ends with the conclusions and a short outlook of future extensions.

2. THEORETICAL BASIS

We give a brief idea of the analysis approach for further details we refer to [6]. The approach relies on the pioneering work of Cruz [9,10] on the computation of worst case delays in computer networks. However, in contrast to the available technique we assume that information about the maximal arrival rate and the maximal response time or delay is available from an SLA. In the following subsection we briefly consider how these quantities can be specified in an SLA or can be derived from measurements.

Basically we consider services that provide some result to a user in response to a user request. For the computation of the result some time, denoted as response time or delay, is needed. We begin with the specification of the arrival stream. Service calls arrive in discrete portions and each service call delivers a portion of load to the service. The size of an arriving service call is measured in some application specific unit like the number of transactions, the number of basic operations to compute a result or the size of a data set to be stored, to mention some examples. Let $A : \mathbb{R}_{\geq 0} \rightarrow \mathbb{R}_{\geq 0}$ be the accumulated load that arrived in the interval $[0, t]$. Obviously, $A(t)$ is non-decreasing. In an SLA an upper bound for $A(t)$ is defined in form of an upper arrival curve $\alpha^U(t)$ such that $A(t) - A(s) \leq \alpha^U(t - s)$ for all $t \geq s \geq 0$. Obviously $\alpha^U(0)$ is an upper bound for the size of one service call and $\alpha^{U+} = \lim_{t\to\infty} \alpha^U(t)/t$, if it exists, is an upper bound for the average arrival rate. After a service call has been processed, it leaves the service. Let $C(t)$ be a function describing departing processed service calls. Obviously $C(t)$ is also non-decreasing and $A(t) \geq C(t)$ because service calls depart after they arrived. For convenience we sometimes define functions on the real axis, then $A(t) = C(t) = 0$ for $t < 0$.

In an SLA specification upper bounds should be defined by simple functions which can be interpreted in terms of the behavior of a software system. We use non-decreasing piecewise linear functions. A non-decreasing piecewise linear function with L segments is defined by L triplets $[x_i, y_i, s_i]$ $(i = 1, \ldots, L)$ such that $x_1 = 0$, $y_1 > 0$, $s_i \geq 0$, $x_i \leq x_{i+1}$, and $y_i + (x_{i+1} - x_i)s_i \leq y_{i+1}$. The function is continuous if $y_i + (x_{i+1} - x_i)s_i = y_{i+1}$. A continuous function is concave if $s_i \geq s_{i+1}$ and convex if $s_i \leq s_{i+1}$. The x_i specify time points, y_i the load that may have entered the system up to time x_i and s_i the slope of the load curve between x_i and x_{i+1} (i.e., the arrival rate). Thus, y_1 is the maximal size of system calls and s_L is an upper bound for the average arrival rate of the load. An example for an upper arrival curve with two segments is shown on the left side of Fig. 4.

By using more than one segment (i.e., $L > 1$) it is possible to specify arrival rates that decrease over time. Usually the arrival process is described by a concave piecewise linear function. y_1 is the amount of load which can arrive immediately and s_1 is the short term arrival rate until time x_2. In contrast to QN analysis where the arrival rate is constant, SLA calculus allows one to consider short term fluctuations in the load.

In a similar way we can define a bound for the response

time or delay induced by arriving service calls. We define a function $F : \mathbb{R}_{\geq 0} \rightarrow \mathbb{R}_{\geq 0}$ that describes the accumulated delay of service calls of size x. Obviously $F(x)$ is non-decreasing because larger calls require more effort. We define an upper delay curve $\Phi^U(x)$ such that $F(x) - F(y) \leq \Phi^U(x-y)$ for all $x \geq y \geq 0$. Again piecewise linear functions are used for the specification. For example in a system where service calls have a maximal size of 1 and the first two service calls are allowed to have a delay which is twice their size and afterwards the delay is proportional to the size of the call, $\Phi^U = \{[0,0,2],[2,4,1]\}$ would be an appropriate upper bound. The derivative of the delay bound is given by $\phi^U(x) = \left(\Phi^U\right)'(x)$. ϕ^U is piecewise constant if Φ^U is piecewise linear. An example for an upper delay curve with two segments is shown in the middle of Fig. 4.

Observe that the delay bound is a function from the load into the time domain whereas the arrival bound is a function from the time in the load domain. To combine both functions we use the pseudo-inverse of a non-decreasing function $f(t)$.

$$f^{-1}(x) = \inf\{t | f(t) \geq x\} \tag{1}$$

The pseudo-inverse can be easily computed for non-decreasing piecewise linear functions. For a strictly increasing function, the pseudo inverse corresponds to the inverse function. It should be mentioned that in SLA calculus sometimes an inverse has to be computed for more general functions such that the definition of the inverse has to be slightly extended for cases where the functions are not necessarily increasing [6,7]. We will not consider these details here and assume that f^{-1} can be computed in some way.

Additionally, we need the following operations for functions which are all available in the basic approach of Cruz [9].

$$\begin{array}{rcl} (f+g)(t) & = & f(t)+g(t) \\ (f \vee g)(t) & = & f(t) \vee g(t) \\ (f \wedge g)(t) & = & f(t) \wedge g(t) \\ (f \underline{\otimes} g)(t) & = & \inf_{0 \leq s \leq t} \left(f(t-s)+g(s)\right) \\ (f \underline{\oslash} g)(t) & = & \sup_{0 \leq u} \left(f(t+u)-g(u)\right) \end{array} \tag{2}$$

$\vee$ and $\wedge$ are the pointwise maximum and minimum and $\underline{\otimes}$, $\underline{\oslash}$ the min/plus convolution and deconvolution [4]. All operations can be easily computed for piecewise linear functions [5].

A user with load requirements that do not exceed α_0^U can immediately use a service with an SLA with arrival and delay bounds (α_1^U, Φ_1^U), if $\alpha_0^U(t) \leq \alpha_1^U(t)$. In this case, the service is analyzed under arrival bound α_0^U and the delay bound remains as defined in the SLA. If $\alpha_0^{U+} = \lim_{t \to \infty} \alpha_0^U(t)/t \leq \alpha_1^{U+} = \lim_{t \to \infty} \alpha_1^U(t)/t$ (for piecewise linear bounds this means $s_{L_0} \leq s_{L_1}$ in our setting), then the user does not overload the service in the long run, which would prohibit the use of the service. However, temporary overload situations may occur such that service calls may have to be delayed to respect the arrival bound of the SLA. An appropriate delay can be introduced by adding a smoother between user arrival process and service. A smoother is known from network calculus [4] and is realized by a leaky bucket or a set of leaky buckets such that the service of the smoother corresponds to α_1^U. An upper bound for the delay in the smoother is then given by

$$\Phi_0^U(x) = \int_0^x \left(\min\left\{\left(\alpha_0^U \underline{\oslash} \alpha_1^U\right) \underline{\otimes} \alpha_1^U, \alpha_1^U\right\}\right)^{-1}(y) - \left(\alpha_0^U\right)^{-1}(y) dy \tag{3}$$

An upper bound for the delay of the service and the smoother is $\Phi_1^{U*} = \Phi_0^U + \Phi_1^U$. In the sequel Φ_i^{U*} denotes an upper bound of the accumulated delay of service i resulting from the upper delay bound defined in the SLA plus the delay which is necessary to smooth the arrival process bounded by α_0^U to be consistent with the upper arrival bound α_1^U defined in the SLA. As long as the arrival process of the user is unknown, it is assumed to be equal to α_1^U such that $\Phi_1^{U*} = \Phi_1^U$. If the arrival stream of the user exceeds the capacity of the service, then $\Phi_1^{U*} = \{[0,\infty,\infty]\}$, i.e., the service is overloaded and in the long run response time converges to infinity. In practice this means that additional capacity is required to fulfill the requirements of the user.

The provider has to compute the required service capacity to meet the delay bound under maximal load. Under the reasonable assumption that an increasing arrival rate results in longer delays, a lower bound for the required service rate is given by

$$\sigma_1^L(t) = \left(\left(\phi_1^U + \left(\alpha_1^U\right)^{-1}\right)^{-1} \underline{\oslash} \alpha_1^U\right)(t). \tag{4}$$

The function σ_1^L resulting from piecewise linear functions α_1^U and Φ_1^L is piecewise linear and non-decreasing but not necessarily convex or concave. Thus, it might be substituted by a convex or concave upper bound to specify the minimal service requirements. On the right side of Fig. 4 the lower bound for the service curve resulting from Eq. 4 using the arrival and delay bound on the left and in the middle of the same figure is shown. It can be seen that the resulting service curve is neither concave nor convex.

It is also possible to compute the delay from a known lower bound for the service process using the following relation from [6,7] based on results from [25].

$$\Phi^U(x) = \int_0^x \left(\min\{(\alpha^U \underline{\oslash} \sigma^L) \underline{\otimes} \sigma^L, \sigma^L\}\right)^{-1}(y) - \left(\alpha^U\right)^{-1}(y) dy \tag{5}$$

Equations 3 and 5 are very similar because they both describe the delay in a component with arrival process α and service process σ under FCFS scheduling. In SOAs FCFS scheduling of service calls is usually an appropriate approximation of the real behavior.

For the presented basic relations, results for composed services can be derived. We analyze the maximal delay in a composed system. To compose services we consider three composition operations of two services numbered 1 and 2. The first is the concatenation of services, i.e., after one service the next one is called. Thus, the input process of the second service corresponds to the output process of the first service. Let γ_1^U be the upper bound for the output process of the first service under maximal delay which is given by

$$\begin{array}{l} \gamma_1^U(t+t^*) = \alpha_1^U(t) \\ \text{where } t^* = \sup_t\{t : \forall s \leq t, s + \phi^U(\alpha^U(s)) \geq t\}. \end{array} \tag{6}$$

Since Φ^U and α^U are upper arrival and delay curves, their derivatives are non-increasing. To define an upper bound for the departure process which holds in general, i.e., $C_1(t) - C_1(s) \leq \tilde{\gamma}(t-s)$ for all $t \geq s \geq 0$, the function γ^U has to be shifted by t^* to the left, resulting in

$$\tilde{\gamma}^U(t) = \begin{cases} 0 & \text{for } t < 0, \\ \gamma^U(t+t^*) & \text{for } t \geq 0. \end{cases} \tag{7}$$

Observe that the output process of a service can be more bursty than the input process because the maximal delay of an arriving call may become smaller for calls arriving later when the upper delay bound converges towards the average delay of the system.

The upper delay bound results from the upper bound for the arrival process plus the service calls that are delayed in the service as long as possible. Without knowledge of the concrete input process for the first service, the upper arrival bound for the service is used. Using $\tilde{\gamma}_1^U$ as upper bound for the input process of the second service, the delay and output process of the second service in the sequence can be computed. The delay for load x and of the composed service is

$$\Phi_{12}^{U*}(x) = \Phi_1^{U*}(x) + \Phi_2^{U*}(x). \tag{8}$$

In a parallel fork-join like composition, also denoted as &-composition, two services are called in parallel and the call terminates when both results are available. Thus, both services receive the full input and the upper bounds for delay and output process of the composed service become

$$\Phi_{12}^{U*}(x) = \int_{y=0}^{x} \phi_1^{U*}(y) \vee \phi_2^{U*}(y)dy \text{ and } \gamma_{12}^U(t) = \gamma_1^U(t) \wedge \gamma_2^U(t). \tag{9}$$

The last composition is the parallel choice, also denoted as $\|$-composition, where an arrival stream is distributed among two services. We assume that $p \in (0,1)$ is the portion of the load that is routed to the first service and $\bar{p} = 1 - p$ is the portion that is routed to the second service. Since service calls arrive as discrete portions of load that cannot be split, we have to take into account that complete calls are routed to a service. Let Ω be the maximal size of a call which often equals $\alpha_0^U(0)$ the maximal load that can arrive instantaneously. Then $p\alpha_0^U(t) + \bar{p}\Omega$ and $\bar{p}\alpha_0^U(t) + p\Omega$ are the upper bounds for the arrivals at service 1 and 2, respectively. Using (6) $\gamma_1^U(t)$ and $\gamma_2^U(t)$ can be computed and the upper bounds for delay and output process of the composed service become

$$\begin{array}{l} \Phi_{12}^{U*}(x) = \int_{y=0}^{x} \phi_{12}^{U*}(y)dy \\ \text{where } \phi_{12}^U(x) = \max\left\{\phi_1^U(p(x-\Omega)^+), \phi_2^U(\bar{p}(x-\Omega)^+)\right\} \\ \text{and } \gamma_{12}^U(t) = \min\left\{\gamma_1^U(t) + \gamma_2^U(t), \alpha_0^U\right\}. \end{array} \tag{10}$$

where $(a)^+$ stands for $\max(a, 0)$. It should be mentioned that the behavior of the parallel choice is completely different from a choice in QNs. In a QN is it always advantageous to split load since the delay grows faster than linear with the load. In SLA calculus it is better to route load to one service as long as the service is not overloaded because the delay for the first calls can be longer than the average delay that is achieved after a large number of arrivals. Splitting load and distributing it to more than one service implies then that more calls may have a long delay. A more detailed derivation and interpretation of the bounds can be found in [6, 7].

The bounds can be easily computed for piecewise linear bounds of the arrival and service process. Observe that all compositions result in a composed service with upper bound for the arrival process α_{12}^U, an upper delay bound Φ_{12}^U, and an upper bound for the departure process γ_{12}^U, which can be used in further compositions.

We have presented the whole approach here using upper bounds for arrivals and delays. The computations can be extended by also integrating lower bounds in a similar way (for details see [6, 7]). The availability of additional lower bounds often improves the behavior of a system since it becomes more predictable. Examples will be given below.

3. INPUT PARAMETER ESTIMATION

The set of parameters which is necessary to analyze networks of composed services is limited to upper bounds for arrival rates and delays. In contrast to real time systems or even computer networks the bounds need not be strict, i.e., a small percentage of violations is acceptable. However, this does not necessarily make it easier to specify appropriate bounds. The first and mainly used approach is to use the information available in SLAs. If this is not the case, then bounds have to be estimated ideally based on some data. We will briefly outline both approaches.

Even if SLAs contain information about maximal arrival and delay rates, this information has to be translated into an appropriate bounding curve. The specification of SLAs is not standardized and many different informal and semi-formal approaches to formulate SLAs in different environments exist [13, 22]. Usually an SLA contains a maximal arrival rate of service calls and a maximal size of the calls. If this is the only available information, then curves with one linear segment can be defined. For the response time usually an upper bound plus the percentage of jobs that does not exceed this bound is defined. If only the upper bound is used to define the response time bound, then the model becomes more conservative than the SLA but without knowing the distribution of response times it is impossible to define an upper bound which is met with a given probability. Often the specification of QoS parameters in SLAs is more detailed than just the definition of an upper bound for the mean arrival rate and response time. Most times an interval and an increased rate are defined such that the arrival or delay process can exceed the long time upper bound for some time. Such a specification can be immediately translated in a function with two linear segments. Usually it is sufficient to use functions with only two or three linear segments to capture the information from SLAs. Without a formal specification of SLAs, quantitative information from the SLAs has to be translated manually into appropriate arrival and delay curves.

In some cases, the SLA contains no sufficient information or no SLA is available for a service. Then the bounds have to be estimated. If measurements are available, then these measurements can be used to define an appropriate upper bound. However, in this case some statistical evaluation becomes necessary. We briefly outline the basic approach. Similar ideas have been proposed for real time and network calculus [4, 12].

If $TA(t)$ denotes the load brought into the system by an arrival event at time t, then $A(t) = \sum_{s \le t} TA(s)$. A trace from a measurement contains a finite sequence $TA(s)$ with $s \in [0, T]$ where T is the length of the measurement interval. A tight upper bound is given by

$$\alpha^U(t) = \max_{s \ge 0}\{A(s+t) - A(t)\}. \tag{11}$$

Similar bounds can be derived for delays, if departure events can be linked with corresponding arrival events. The curves for $A(t)$ and $C(t)$ resulting from traces are step functions giving also step functions for the upper bounding curves. However, curves resulting from longer traces will have an enormous number of segments and are an example for overfitting a model. Thus, we have to find an upper bound with a few linear segments. Let t_i ($i = 1, \ldots, m$, $0 \le t_1 \le t_2 \le \ldots \le t_m \le T$) be the times when system calls arrive to the system in the interval $[0, T]$ resulting from some measurement taken over the whole interval. a_i is the size of the ith arriving call. Alternatively, we can consider departure times t_i of service calls from the system and d_i is the delay of the departing call. Now assume that $[x_i, y_i, s_i]$ ($i = 1, \ldots, L$) is a bounding curve. Then the ith arrival (or departure) violates the bounding curve if and only if

$$\exists j < i : \sum_{k=j}^{i} a_k > y_l + s_l(t_i - t_j - x_l) \qquad (12)$$

where $l = \arg\max_{h \in \{1,\ldots,L\}} (x_h \le t_i - t_j)$. If d_k instead of a_k is used, a condition on delays is defined. For a given bounding curve, the number of arrivals or delays that violate the bound can be computed. Let V be the corresponding number, then V/L is the violation probability.

For a given measurement, a predefined number of segments and a predefined bound of the violation probability, a curve is better than another if the area under the curve is smaller. Thus, the finding of an appropriate curve can be formulated as a linear mixed integer program which is in most cases much too large to be solved exactly such that heuristic optimization algorithms have to be applied. Usually a small percentage of violations should be allowed for arrivals and more important delays since this helps to remove outliers resulting from very long delays. After the bounding curve is available it should be validated against some other measurement of the same system which means to evaluate Eq. 12. If the violation probability for these values is below the required threshold, then the bounding curve can be used. Other more sophisticated techniques for validation can also be applied if sufficient data from measurements is available.

In the following we describe the SLA tool and assume that appropriate bounds for the services have been determined.

4. SLA TOOL

For the analysis of systems using min/plus or max/plus algebra different tools are available. Some software systems support functions in max/plus algebra [8, 18] and can be used as building blocks for system analysis. More appropriate are tools that support modeling in a specific domain. The Real Time Calculus Toolbox [26] is a collection of Matlab functions and Java classes that support system analysis in Real Time Calculus. The specification of the system has to be made at the level of the mathematical functions. DiscoDNC [3] is a Java-based tool for network calculus. Again models are specified at a language level and the mathematical functions have to be used to compute results. The available functions for min/plus analysis cannot be used to perform the analysis of SLAs without significant modifications because it has to be switched between time and load domain several times and as shown in [6,7] the generalized inverse is not sufficient to perform this step in general. To the best of our knowledge all available tools for system analysis based on max/plus algebra are very near to the mathematical basis of the approach which means that the resulting models are very abstract and the tools are hard to use for unexperienced users from the application area.

The goal of SLA tool is to provide a simple interface to the

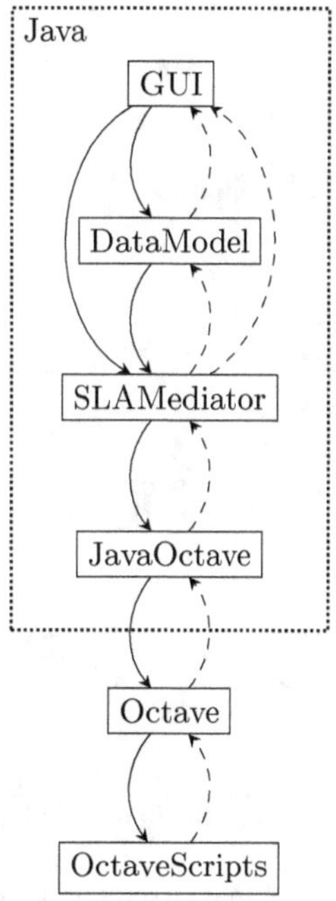

Figure 1: A block diagram showing the tool architecture. Solid lines represent function calls, dashed lines show return of results.

analysis approach which is based on the system model rather than on the mathematical functions. Such an approach is also the base of many queueing network analysis tools like JMT [2] where queueing models are specified graphically or in parameter tables and the approach becomes usable also by unexperienced users. Thus, a Service Oriented Architecture (SOA) is specified graphically as a network of services. Services are connected by the three connection operations, sequential concatenation, parallel ||-connection and parallel &-connection. In this way an acyclic graph similar to a feedforward queueing network model is generated. Before we introduce the different elements and the composition of models in some more detail, some information about the software structure of the tool will be provided.

Fig. 1 shows the part of the tool's architecture that is responsible for interacting with Octave. The OctaveScripts block represents a set of Octave functions that implement the mathematical functions as described in Sec. 2. These functions are used for all mathematical operations on curves, such as system analysis or calculating coordinates for plotting curves. As mentioned, curves in our approach are specified by piecewise linear functions and the corresponding objects in Octave are lists of three dimensional vectors $[x, y, s]$ defining a line segment.

JavaOctave provides an interface to Octave for the Java part of the application and allows the execution of strings as commands as well as providing methods to get the results back to Java. For each Octave function exists a corresponding Java method in the SLAMediator that uses parameter objects to generate a command string that can be evaluated by Octave. These commands are forwarded to Octave using JavaOctave. Afterwards the SLAMediator translates the resulting lists back to the Object oriented data model of the tool and returns the final object. The functions pro-

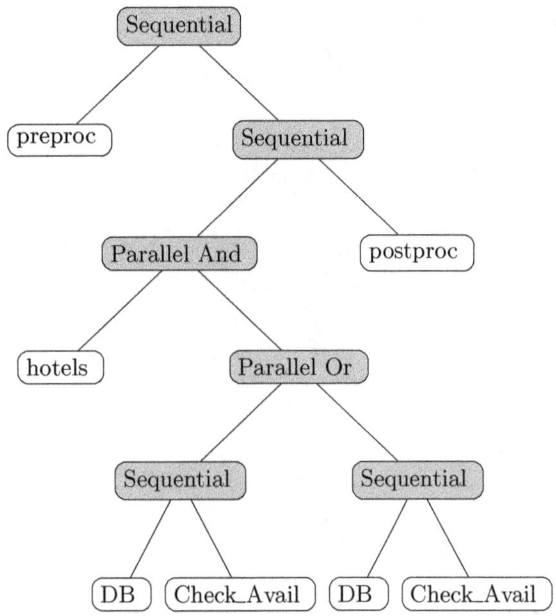

Figure 2: Structure of binary tree for travel agency example (cf. Fig. 6)

vided by the SLAMediator are called from the DataModel and the GUI of the tool. The GUI calls them to plot curves or to check input validity while the DataModel uses these functions to analyze systems. The main difference between the information about the system that is stored in the GUI and the information stored in the DataModel is as follows: While the GUI compositions are directed graphs (as shown in Fig. 5), the data model is a binary tree that can be calculated if the structure of the composition graph is valid. The system analysis uses this tree in order to calculate the resulting curves, which are then returned to the GUI for display. As an example for system analysis we consider the travel agency model of Sect. 5 (cf. Fig. 6). When the tool starts to analyze the composition it generates the corresponding binary tree (cf. Fig. 2). In order to analyze a node of the tree, all its leaves have to be analyzed first. The resulting order of nodes to be analyzed is similar to a depth-first search (see Algorithm 1).

```
<source id="id_0" x="10.5" y="110.5">
  <alphaUpper>{[0,0,1]}</alphaUpper>
  <alphaLower>{[0,0,0]}</alphaLower>
  ...
</source>
<sink id="id_1" x="310.5" y="110.5" />
<service id="id_2" x="110.5" y="110.5" name="Service">
  <alphaLower>{[0,0,0]}</alphaLower>
  <alphaUpper>{[0,1,3],[2,7,2],[3,9,1]}</alphaUpper>
  <phiLower>{[0,0,0]}</phiLower>
  <phiUpper>{[0,0,3],[1,3,2],[3,7,1]}</phiUpper>
  <dialog editDelay="true">
  ...
</service>
```

Table 1: XML description of a single service with source and sink

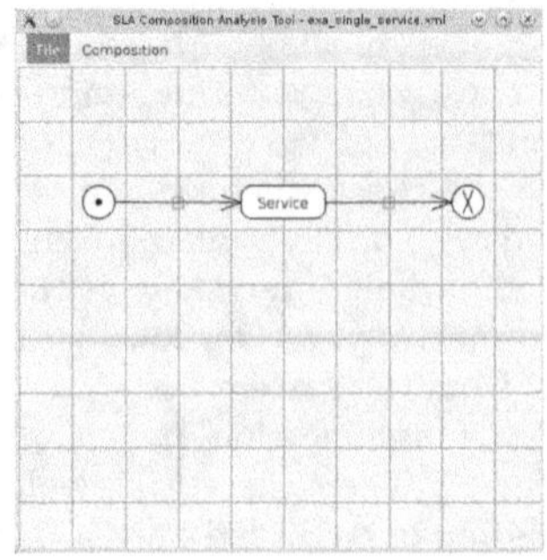

Figure 3: A model of a single service.

The graphical information of a model, the parameters (i.e., the different bounding curves) and additional information is stored in an XML format. Tab. 1 contains the XML specification of the simplest model which can be generated, consisting of a source, a service and a sink. The graphical representation, which is the interface to the user for modeling composed services, is shown in Fig. 3. The XML description includes apart from the model specification, which is shown in Tab. 1, additional graphical information which is not shown here.

For the simple model shown in Fig. 3, the user specifies the model graphically by selecting the basic elements and connecting them. Parameters of a service are the three bounding curves for arrival, delay and service, mentioned above. For the specification of a service, an upper bound for the arrivals and either an upper bound for the delay or a lower bound for the service capacity have to be available. In SLAs upper bounds on arrivals and delays are given, the service capacity is not relevant for a user. However, for a provider it could be interesting to compute a lower bound for the required service capacity. In SLA tool all three curves are associated with a service. Curves are specified by the triplets $[x_i, y_i, s_i]$ and are graphically represented as shown in Fig. 4. A triple of curves belongs to each service. The user can decide which curves are actually shown. Furthermore, the representation of a curve can be modified by choosing a color, the zoom level and the translation of the x and y axis. The graphical representations helps a user to see whether his or her curve fulfills some basic properties like being continuous, concave or convex. The curves belonging to a service are always kept consistent. If upper arrival and delay curves are defined, a lower service curve is implicitly determined and presented. One can switch to the description of the lower service curve, then the upper delay curve is computed. Apart from the upper arrival and delay curves also lower bounds can be defined. Initially lower bounds are $\{[0, 0, 0]\}$. Lower bounds are not part of SLAs but for an analysis it is sometimes useful to define a lower delay bound to make a service more predictable. From the lower delay bound an upper bound for the service capacity may be computed, although this is usually not needed since service calls that are available too early can be easily delayed, although additional space to store service calls is required in this case. Fig. 4 shows a typical scenario, the upper arrival and delay curve have been specified as concave curves with 2 segments each and the corresponding lower service curve has been computed. Observe that the resulting service curve consists of 4 segments and is neither concave nor convex. In

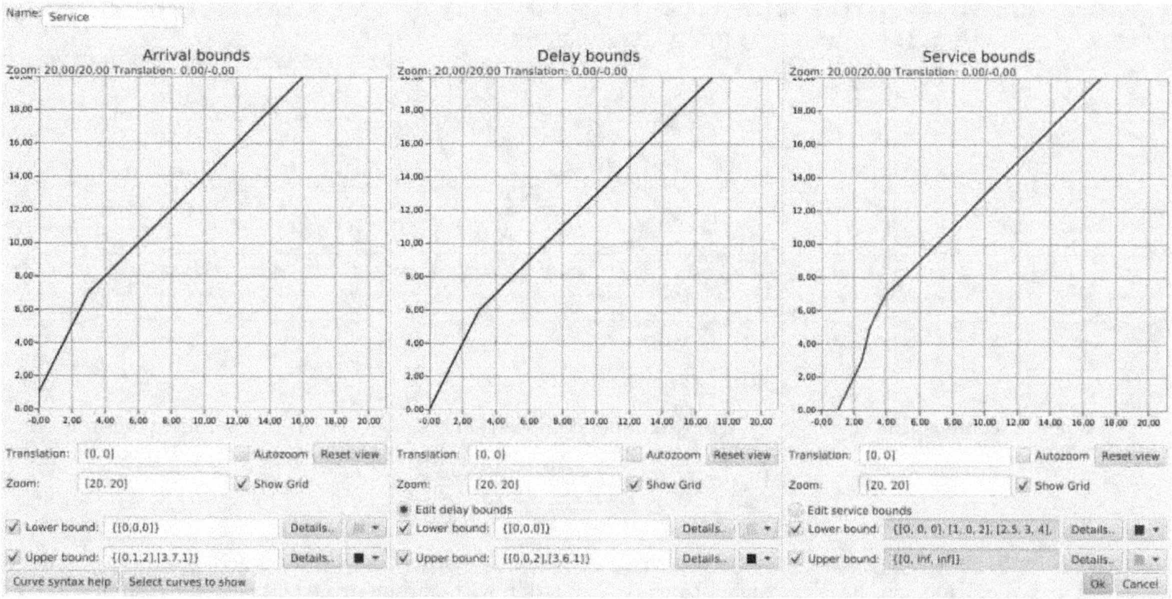

Figure 4: Bounding curves for arrival, delay and service.

the example the lower arrival and delay curve are $(0, 0, 0)$ resulting in an upper service curve $(0, \infty, \infty)$.

A source has a single parameter, the arrival curve. Again lower and upper bounds can be defined. The parameter of the source specifies bounds for the real arrival rate of the user whereas the parameter of the service describes the bound from the SLA, i.e., the maximal arrival rate the service will accept. A sink has no parameter. If the simple model is analyzed, then the delay and service bounds are computed according to the arrival bounds defined in the source. As long as the upper arrival bound from the source does not exceed the upper arrival bound of the service, the delay bound of the service, as given in the SLA, is valid. However, the lower bound for the service capacity depends on the source arrival bound. If the arrival bound of the source exceeds temporarily the arrival bound of the service, then calls have to be delayed and the upper delay bound grows. The lower bound for the service capacity is in this case the same as computed for the upper arrival bound defined in the SLA. If the mean rate of the source exceeds the mean rate of arrivals for the service, then the delay grows to infinity, as in a queueing network where the arrival rate exceeds the service rate.

We consider an example where
$\alpha_1^U = \{[0, 1, 3], [2, 7, 2], [3, 9, 1]\}$ and
$\Phi_1^U = \{[0, 0, 3], [1, 3, 2], [3, 7, 1]\}$ are the upper bounds for the arrivals and delay of the service. Furthermore, α_0^U is the upper arrival bound of the source. For $\alpha_0^U = \alpha_1^U$, the lower bound for the service process becomes
$\sigma_1^L = \{[0, 0, 0], [1, 0, 3], [3, 7, 2], [4, 9, 1]\}$.
If we choose $\alpha_0^U = \{[0, 1, 1]\}$, then Φ^U remains and
$\sigma_1^L = \{[0, 0, 0], [1, 0, 1], [3, 2, 2], [4, 4, 1]\}$.
For $\alpha_0^U = \{[0, 1, 5], [2, 11, 1]\}$, which temporarily exceeds α_1^U, σ_1^L is the same as for the arrival bound α_1^U and
$\Phi^U = \{[0, 0, 6], [1, 6, 5], [3, 16, 4]\}$ which equals the delay Φ_1^U plus the delay $\{[0, 0, 3]\}$ that is necessary to smooth the arrival stream of the source to be conform to the arrival bound of the service.

In a SOA a user can combine several services, each with a specific SLA, to build a new composed service which may then be used in further compositions. SLA tool helps to model such compositions and analyze the composed service. Analysis means that delay bounds for composed services are computed, that bounds for the arrival stream into a composed service can be determined and that the required service capacity for the whole composition or a subset of composed services can be computed.

Each composed model describes a flow through a set of services. It starts with a source, where service calls are generated and ends with a sink where processed calls leave the composed service. Basic elements are services and the three composition operators, sequential, &-parallel and ||-parallel. The graphical representations for specifying the compositions are shown in Fig. 5.

We first describe the sequential composition which can be used for an arbitrary number of services. Fig. 5a shows the composition of two services. We assume that the SLA of the first service is given by α_1^U and Φ_1^U as defined above. For the second service we have $\alpha_2^U = \{[0, 2, 2], [1, 4, 1]\}$ and $\Phi_2^U = \{[0, 0, 2]\}$. For $\alpha_0^U = \alpha_1^U$ the upper delay bound of the composed service becomes
$\Phi_{12}^U = \{[0, 0, 8.667], [1, 8.667, 7.667], [3, 24, 6.667]\}$.
For $\alpha_0^U = \alpha_2^U$ we obtain $\Phi_{12}^U =$
$\{[0, 0, 5.875], [1, 5.875, 4.875], [3, 15.625, 3.875], [4, 19.5, 3.667]\}$.

If the two services are combined by a &-parallel composition, then all calls are split and enter both services. For our example the delay curve equals $\Phi_{12}^U = \{[0, 0, 5]\}$ if arrival curve α_1^U is fed into the composed service and it is
$\Phi_{12}^U = \{[0, 0, 3.2083], [1, 3.2083, 2.2083][3, 7.625, 2]\}$ if α_2^U enters the composed service.

The last composition operator is the ||-parallel composition which needs as additional parameters the maximal size of a call b and the probability p of choosing service 1. If the two services are composed by a ||-parallel composition and $p = 0.5$, we obtain for $b = 0$ and arrival process α_1^U
$\Phi_{12}^U = \{[0, 0, 3], [2, 6, 2]\}$. A value of $b = 0$ means that ar-

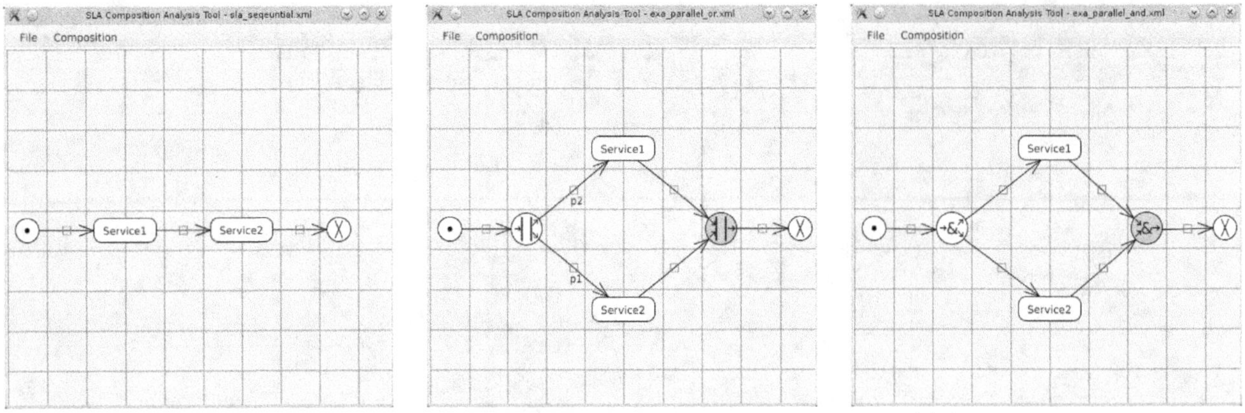

(a) Sequential composition (b) $\|$-parallel composition (c) &-parallel composition

Figure 5: Composition of services.

riving load can be split into equal parts, as it is the case for fluid. For $b = 1$ (i.e., calls can have maximal size of 1 and cannot be split), we obtain a slightly different bound $\Phi_{12}^U = \{[0,0,3],[2.5,7.5,2]\}$. In both cases the delay lies above the delay that would occur if the load is routed to the first service. The reason for this behavior have been described above, the longer delay at the beginning affects in a parallel composition more calls since it occurs in both parallel services. Of course, the delay for a service call converges to 2, the final slope of the delay curves. However, if we increase the arrival stream to $\alpha_0^U = \{[0,1,4],[3,13,1.5]\}$, then the arrival stream overloads each of the involved services if the complete load is routed to one service. The delay curve becomes

$\Phi_{12}^U = \{[0,0,3],[2,6,2.52],[22,56.47,2]\}$ for $b = 0$, $p = 0.5$ and

$\Phi_{12}^U = \{[0,0,3],[2.5,7.5,2.88],[26.5,76.61,2]\}$ for $b = 1$, $p = 0.5$.

Observe that the parallel composition operators are always used as pairs, an opening operator is followed by a closing operator of the same type. In between can be an arbitrary network of services. To specify more than two parallel services, the parallel operators have to be nested.

A complete model results from composing several subservices. The model is consistent if opening and closing parallel operators fit and the model has a single source and a single sink. Service compositions are always described by acyclic structures which is common in models using min/plus methods for analysis, although there is some work available in generalizing the approach [19]. Here we assume that loops are unwound using several $\|$-parallel connectors to define the probabilities for 1, 2, ..., n calls to the service. Of course, such an approach only works for a moderate number of loops.

The analysis of the whole system can be easily realized using a recursive data structure describing a model. Before we introduce the solution algorithm, the recursive data structure is defined. A composition of services in SLA tool is defined by the following grammar.

$$\mathcal{S} = \left(\alpha^L, \alpha^U, \Phi^L, \Phi^U\right) \mid \mathcal{S} \to \mathcal{S} \mid \mathcal{S}\&\mathcal{S} \mid \mathcal{S}\|_{b,p}\mathcal{S} \qquad (13)$$

A service is either a simple service which is specified by the arrival and delay bounds, or it is a composed service. The three composition operators $\to$ for sequential composition, & for &-parallel composition and $\|_{b,p}$ for $\|$-parallel composition with parameters b and p combine simple or composed services. A model resulting from the grammar has always a single entry and a single exit point. Models are specified graphically, are mapped implicitly to the proposed grammar that defines a recursive data structure which can be easily generated from the model specification.

In SLA tool the data structure is defined in Octave. Arrival or delay curves are vectors of triples (x, y, s). A simple service is a structure consisting of 4 curves and a composed service is a structure of two services and the composition information (i.e., the composition type and if necessary the parameters b and p). Observe that upper and lower bounds for arrivals and delays are always part of a simple service description. If lower bounds are not specified, they are implicitly set to $\{[0,0,0]\}$. In SLA tool simple services can be alternatively characterized by arrival and service capacity bounds. In this case, the delay curves are computed from the bounds for the service capacity and the arrival bounds. Similarly, if service curves are shown in the graphical interface they are always computed from arrival and delay curves. In this way a service is internally always represented by arrival and delay curves and inconsistent specifications are avoided. Computation of a service curve or a delay curve for a service is efficient as long as the number of linear segments is not too large which is usually the case.

The recursive data structure can be naturally used in a recursive algorithm to analyze a composed system. Algorithm 1 analyzes model $\mathcal{S}$ for some arrival stream with upper bound α^U. The algorithm computes upper bounds for the delay Φ and for the departure process γ which might be fed to another service. Again we describe here only the computation of upper bounds. In SLA tool also the computation of lower bounds has been implemented based on [6,7]. Computations follow the recursive structure of the model and simple services are analyzed using the basic equations introduced in Sect. 2 and in some more detail in [6,7].

Since composed services follow some hierarchical structure, SLA tool supports the building of hierarchical models by composing sub-structures to sub-services. A composition of services with a single entry and exit point can be defined as a sub-service which is a specific node in the graphical representation. Fig. 6 shows an example where the services *flights1*, *flights2* and *hotels* are composed services which in

Algorithm 1 Computation of departure and delay bounds for a composed service $\mathcal{S}$.

```
function [Φ, γ] = ANALYZE_SERVICE(α^U, S)
  if S == simple then
    if α^U ≤ S.α^U then
      Φ = S.Φ^U ;
    else
      Compute Φ_0^U via (3) ;
      Φ = Φ_0^U + S.Φ^U ;
    end if
    Compute γ via (6) ;
  else
    if S == S_1 → S_2 then
      [Φ_1, γ_1] = analyze_service(α^U, S_1) ;
      [Φ_2, γ] = analyze_service(γ_1, S_2) ;
      Φ = Φ_1 + Φ_2 ;
    else
      if S == S_1 ||_{b,p} S_2 then
        [Φ_1, γ_1] =
            analyze_service(pα^U + (1 − p)b, S_1) ;
        [Φ_2, γ_2] =
            analyze_service((1 − p)α^U + pb, S_2) ;
        Φ = Φ_1 ∨ Φ_2 ;
        γ = (γ_1 + γ_2) ∧ α^U ;
      else /* &-parallel composition */
        [Φ_1, γ_1] = analyze_service(α^U, S_1) ;
        [Φ_2, γ_2] = analyze_service(α^U, S_2) ;
        Φ = Φ_1 ∨ Φ_2 ;
        γ = γ_1 ∧ γ_2 ;
      end if
    end if
  end if
end function
```

the specific example consist of a simple sequence of two services. The hierarchical structure of the model in terms of sub-services is shown in a separate window. Composed services can be used to reduce the complexity of graphical representations. The analysis is later done using Algorithm 1 on the complete hierarchy.

5. EXAMPLE

As an example we consider an agency which sells travel packages to customers via the Internet. A package consists of a round trip by air and a reservation for a hotel at the destination. The agency's offer is based on the services provided by two flight portals and a hotel reservation system all run by external vendors. The structure of the model is shown in Fig. 6. First a preprocessing step is performed by the agency followed by calls to external services. In order to satisfy customer demands promptly requests for flights and hotels are performed in parallel. For flights two different portals are available that have different types of SLAs. The first flight portal is able to cope with jittery traffic in short time intervals, but accepts less average traffic on the long run than the second flight portal which offers an SLA with shorter long-term delays. Both flight portals offer two services, one returns all flights to the destination inspecting the flight plan via a database request (*DB*) whereas the second service checks the availability of specified flights (*Check_Avail*). The travel agency uses both services to satisfy customer demands. The portal for hotels directly checks for availability of rooms at the destination. Once all requests have been finished, the result information is finalized in a postprocessing step at the travel agency's site.

The SLA specification of all services is given in Table 2. The local services *preproc* and *postproc* as well as the service offered by the portal for hotel rooms seem to be well dimensioned. Considering the flight portals both database requests (*DB*) offer the same SLAs, whereas checking the availability of flights offers different SLAs. At first glance it seems favorable to direct requests to the first flight portal, since it is capable to handle bursty traffic better than *flights2* and guarantees similar response times. On the other hand *flights1* accepts less traffic on the long run, an arrival rate of 5 compared to an average arrival rate of 7 for *flights2*.

If we assume that customer demands are upper bounded by e.g. a bursty arrival curve of $\{[0, 20, 50], [2, 120, 8]\}$ it's obvious that the services of both flight portals need to be used to handle all traffic on the long run and the key question is to determine the portion $p_i, i = 1, 2$ of traffic which should be directed to a flight portal. The long run arrival rate of the source implies $p_1 < \frac{5}{8}$ and $p_2 < \frac{7}{8}$, since the *Check_Avail* services of both flight portals specify the most limiting upper arrival bounds. Considering moderate traffic intensities it seems favorable to use the services of *flights1*, since the upper delay bounds are lower in those situations.

Table 3 shows results of our SLA tool which are here the upper delay bounds that can be guaranteed by the agency directing different portions p_1 of the load to *flights1* by assuming that load can be split arbitrarily according to a fluid model (Note that $p_2 = 1 - p_1$ implying $0.125 < p_1 < 0.625$). It follows from the SLA specifications that it is beneficial to direct as much as possible requests to *flights1*, but only in very low traffic periods. For typical situations it is much better to select $p_1 \approx 0.52$, since the corresponding resultant upper delay bound is optimal. This means that the final de-

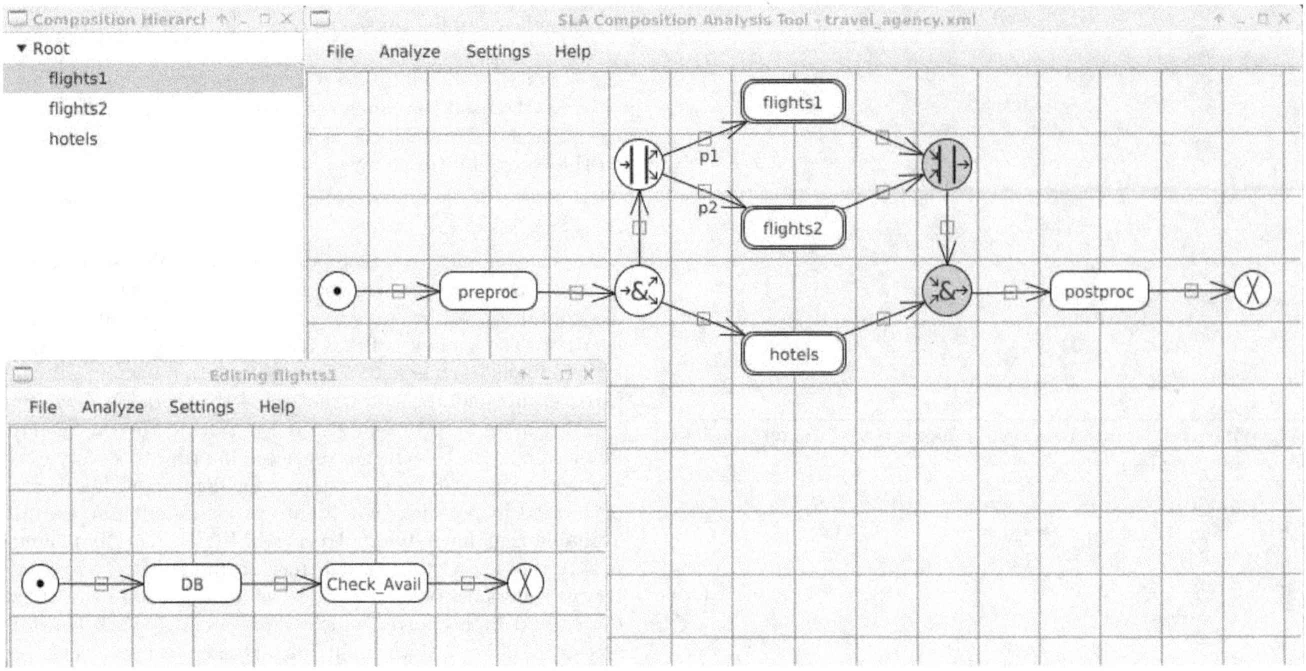

Figure 6: Model of travel agency.

Table 2: Arrival and delay curve specifications for travel agency model

Service	Upper arrival bounds	Upper delay bounds
preproc	$\{[0,6,20]\}$	$\{[0,0,2]\}$
flights1: DB	$\{[0,6,12]\}$	$\{[0,0,3]\}$
flights1: Check_Avail	$\{[0,1,20],[3,61,5]\}$	$\{[0,0,10],[3,30,8]\}$
flights2: DB	$\{[0,6,12]\}$	$\{[0,0,3]\}$
flights2: Check_Avail	$\{[0,1,8],[1,9,7]\}$	$\{[0,0,20],[1,20,6]\}$
hotels	$\{[0,10,20]\}$	$\{[0,0,3]\}$
postproc	$\{[0,6,20]\}$	$\{[0,0,2]\}$
Root source	$\{[0,20,50],[2,120,8]\}$	—

lay of 15 time units per called is reached as soon as possible and the accumulated delay at some given time is minimal.

The situation is very similar if we assume that the load can only be split in portions of size 1. the corresponding results are shown in Table 3. Again $p_1 \approx 0.52$ seems to be the best choice to distribute load among the two services.

6. CONCLUSIONS

This paper presents a new approach to analyze service oriented architectures based on the information available in service level agreements, namely bounds on the arrival stream of service calls and bounds on the response times of a service. These bounds can be adequately described by piecewise linear functions and results for composed services can then be computed using min/plus algebra. In some sense the proposed technique presents an alternative and supplement to the well established queueing network based analysis of software systems.

The proposed analysis techniques have been implemented in SLA tool. Composed services can be specified graphically using basic composition operators such that large models can be easily described and analyzed. The tool is an open source project consisting of a Java based graphical interface and a set of Octave (or Matlab) functions to perform the computations.

The current state of the solution technique and the tool describes a first step. There are several possibilities to extend the approach in future research. Models can be extended using multiple types of service calls resulting in models which are the counterpart to multi-class queueing networks. Furthermore the approach can be combined with optimization techniques to find an optimal service composition.

7. REFERENCES

[1] Danilo Ardagna, Giuliano Casale, Michele Ciavotta, Juan F. Pérez, and Weikun Wang. Quality-of-service in cloud computing: modeling techniques and their applications. *J. Internet Services and Applications*, 5(1), 2014.

[2] Marco Bertoli, Giuliano Casale, and Giuseppe Serazzi. JMT: performance engineering tools for system modeling. *SIGMETRICS Perform. Eval. Rev.*, 36(4):10–15, 2009.

[3] Steffen Bondorf and Jens B. Schmitt. The DiscoDNC v2 - A comprehensive tool for deterministic network calculus. In *8th International Conference on Performance Evaluation Methodologies and Tools, VALUETOOLS 2014, Bratislava, Slovakia, December 9-11, 2014*, 2014.

[4] Jean-Yves Le Boudec and Patrick Thiran. *Network Calculus: A Theory of Deterministic Queuing Systems for the Internet*, volume 2050 of *Lecture Notes in Computer Science*. Springer, 2001.

Table 3: Resultant upper delay bounds of travel agency model for different values of p_1 $(b = 0)$

p_1	Upper delay bound
0.13	{[0, 0, 46.96], [1.15, 53.98, 32.96], [169.33, 5597.11, 30.55], [266.67, 8570.9, 28.52], [22156.9, 632804.62, 15]}
0.2	{[0, 0, 42.55], [1.25, 53.19, 28.55], [169.33, 4852.6, 26.15], [240, 6700.36, 24.92], [1484.17, 37706.85, 15]}
0.3	{[0, 0, 38.12], [1.43, 54.46, 24.12], [169.33, 4104.93, 21.72], [210, 4988.11, 21.36], [641.43, 14201.82, 15]}
0.4	{[0, 0, 34.67], [1.67, 57.79, 20.67], [169.33, 3524.21, 18.27], [186.67, 3840.87, 18.27], [374.55, 7272.87, 15]}
0.49	{[0, 0, 32.32], [1.96, 63.37, 19.46], [6.12, 144.37, 18.32], [169.33, 3134.11, 15.91], [272.6, 4777.34, 15]}
0.50	{[0, 0, 32.1], [2, 64.2, 19.5], [6, 142.21, 18.1], [169.33, 3098.74, 15.7], [265.33, 4605.47, 15]}
0.51	{[0, 0, 31.89], [2.04, 65.08, 19.64], [5.88, 140.52, 17.89], [169.33, 3064.51, 15.48], [258.44, 4444.17, 15]}
0.52	**{[0, 0, 31.68], [2.08, 66, 19.83], [5.77, 139.1, 17.83], [169.33, 3055.69, 15.43], [252.38, 4336.73, 15]}**
0.53	{[0, 0, 31.48], [2.13, 66.98, 20.08], [5.66, 137.91, 18.08], [169.33, 3096.93, 15.67], [278.95, 4814.88, 15]}
0.54	{[0, 0, 31.28], [2.17, 68.01, 20.32], [5.56, 136.7, 18.32], [169.33, 3136.35, 15.91], [311.76, 5402.33, 15]}
0.55	{[0, 0, 31.09], [2.22, 69.09, 20.73], [5.45, 136.08, 18.73], [169.33, 3204.78, 16.32], [353.33, 6207.53, 15]}
0.56	{[0, 0, 30.9], [2.27, 70.23, 21.02], [5.36, 135.08, 19.02], [169.33, 3254.31, 16.62], [407.69, 7214.96, 15]}
0.6	{[0, 0, 30.2], [2.5, 75.51, 23.58], [5, 134.45, 21.58], [169.33, 3680.11, 19.17], [186.67, 4012.39, 19.17], [1160, 22669.94, 15]}
0.62	{[0, 0, 29.88], [2.63, 78.64, 26.11], [4.84, 136.27, 24.11], [169.33, 4101.93, 21.7], [190.91, 4570.17, 21.67], [7039.25, 152951.61, 15]}

Table 4: Resultant upper delay bounds of travel agency model for different values of p_1 $(b = 1)$

p_1	Upper delay bound
0.13	{[0, 0, 47.0], [2.02, 94.92, 33.0], [169.33, 5616.83, 30.6], [267.89, 8632.46, 28.55], [22210.07, 635153.81, 15]}
0.2	{[0, 0, 42.61], [2.05, 87.36, 28.61], [169.33, 4873.87, 26.21], [241.34, 6760.85, 24.97], [1490.8, 37960.64, 15]}
0.3	{[0, 0, 38.2], [2.13, 81.3, 24.2], [169.33, 4126.9, 21.79], [211.5, 5045.76, 21.42], [646.41, 14360.53, 15]}
0.4	{[0, 0, 34.79], [2.27, 78.85, 20.79], [169.33, 3551.99, 18.38], [188.38, 3902.08, 18.38], [381.51, 7451.96, 15]}
0.49	{[0, 0, 32.38], [2.47, 80.02, 19.48], [6.61, 160.7, 18.38], [169.33, 3152.32, 15.98], [275.42, 4847.4, 15]}
0.50	{[0, 0, 32.17], [2.5, 80.42, 19.53], [6.5, 158.55, 18.17], [169.33, 3117.12, 15.76], [268.17, 4675.04, 15]}
0.51	{[0, 0, 31.96], [2.53, 80.88, 19.67], [6.39, 156.83, 17.96], [169.33, 3083.02, 15.55], [261.3, 4513.28, 15]}
0.52	**{[0, 0, 31.75], [2.56, 81.39, 19.88], [6.29, 155.48, 17.88], [169.33, 3071.25, 15.48], [258.4, 4449.68, 15]}**
0.53	{[0, 0, 31.55], [2.6, 81.96, 20.14], [6.19, 154.31, 18.14], [169.33, 3113.52, 15.73], [285.31, 4938.16, 15]}
0.54	{[0, 0, 31.36], [2.63, 82.59, 20.44], [6.1, 153.36, 18.44], [169.33, 3164.09, 16.04], [318.56, 5557.48, 15]}
0.55	{[0, 0, 31.17], [2.67, 83.28, 20.71], [6.0, 152.29, 18.71], [169.33, 3207.9, 16.30], [360.7, 6327.63, 15]}
0.56	{[0, 0, 31.0], [2.71, 84.04, 21.19], [5.92, 151.95, 19.19], [169.33, 3288.6, 16.79], [415.81, 7426.42, 15]}
0.6	{[0, 0, 30.29], [2.9, 87.83, 23.8], [5.6, 152.1, 21.8], [169.33, 3722.17, 19.4], [188.38, 4091.6, 19.4], [1210.6, 23918.52, 15]}
0.62	{[0, 0, 29.97], [3.01, 90.26, 26.35], [5.46, 154.73, 24.35], [169.33, 4144.76, 21.94], [192.57, 4654.66, 21.89], [7269.71, 159589.96, 15]}

[5] Anne Bouillard and Eric Thierry. An algorithmic toolbox for network calculus. *Discrete Event Dynamic Systems*, 18(1):3–49, 2008.

[6] Peter Buchholz and Sebastian Vastag. An introduction to SLA calculus for the analytical validation of SLAs. Technical report, Informatik 4, TU Dortmund, 2015. http://ls4-www.cs.tu-dortmund.de/download/buchholz/sla.pdf.

[7] Peter Buchholz and Sebastian Vastag. Towards an analytical method for SLA validation. submitted for publication, 2016.

[8] G. Cohen, S. Gaubert, and J.-P. Quadrat. Maxplus algebra in Scilab and applications. In *Scilab Workshop*, 2001.

[9] Rene L. Cruz. A calculus for network delay, part I: network elements in isolation. *IEEE Transactions on Information Theory*, 37(1):114–131, 1991.

[10] Rene L. Cruz. A calculus for network delay, part II: network analysis. *IEEE Transactions on Information Theory*, 37(1):132–141, 1991.

[11] Heiko Koziolek. Performance evaluation of component-based software systems: A survey. *Perform. Eval.*, 67(8):634–658, 2010.

[12] S. Kunzli, F. Poletti, L. Benini, and L. Thiele. Combining simulation and formal methods for system-level performance analysis. In *Proceedings of the Design Automation Test in Europe Conference*, volume 1, pages 1–6, March 2006.

[13] Dimosthenis Kyriazis, editor. *Cloud Computing Service Level Agreements*. European Commission, 2013.

[14] Johannes Lüthi and Günter Haring. Mean value analysis for queueing network models with intervals as input parameters. *Perform. Eval.*, 32(3):185–215, 1998.

[15] Daniel A. Menascé. Composing Web services: A QoS view. *IEEE Internet Computing*, 8(6):88–90, 2004.

[16] Daniel A. Menascé. Mapping service-level agreements in distributed applications. *IEEE Internet Computing*, 8(5):100–102, 2004.

[17] Daniel A. Menasce and Virgilio A. F. Almeida. *Capacity Planning for Web Services: metrics, models, and methods*. Prentice Hall, 2001.

[18] Jaroslaw Stanczyk, Eckart Mayer, and Jörg Raisch. Modelling and performance evaluation of DES - A max-plus algebra toolbox for Matlab. In *ICINCO 2004, Proceedings of the First International Conference on Informatics in Control, Automation and Robotics, Setúbal, Portugal, August 25-28, 2004*, pages 270–275, 2004.

[19] David Starobinski, Mark G. Karpovsky, and Lev Zakrevski. Application of network calculus to general topologies using turn-prohibition. *IEEE/ACM Trans. Netw.*, 11(3):411–421, 2003.

[20] Lothar Thiele, Samarjit Chakraborty, and Martin Naedele. Real-time calculus for scheduling hard real-time systems. In *Proceedings. ISCAS 2000*, pages 100–104, 2000.

[21] Mirco Tribastone, Philip Mayer, and Martin Wirsing. Performance prediction of service-oriented systems with layered queueing networks. In *Leveraging Applications of Formal Methods, Verification, and Validation - 4th International Symposium on Leveraging Applications, ISoLA 2010, Heraklion, Crete, Greece, October 18-21, 2010, Proceedings, Part II*, pages 51–65, 2010.

[22] Jos J. M. Trienekens, Jacques J. Bouman, and Mark van der Zwan. Specification of service level agreements: Problems, principles and practices. *Software Quality Journal*, 12(1):43–57, 2004.

[23] Sebastian Vastag. A calculus for SLA delay properties. In *Measurement, Modelling, and Evaluation of Computing Systems and Dependability and Fault Tolerance - 16th International GI/ITG Conference, MMB & DFT 2012, Kaiserslautern, Germany, March 19-21, 2012. Proceedings*, pages 76–90, 2012.

[24] Sebastian Vastag. *SLA Calculus*. PhD thesis, Department of Computer Science, TU Dortmund, 2014.

[25] Ernesto Wandeler. *Modular Performance Analysis and Interface-Based Design for Embedded Real-TimeSystems*. PhD thesis, ETH Zürich, 2006.

[26] Ernesto Wandeler and Lothar Thiele. Real-Time Calculus (RTC) Toolbox. `http://www.mpa.ethz.ch/Rtctoolbox`, 2006.

Analytic Models of Checkpointing for Concurrent Component-Based Software Systems

Noor Bajunaid
Computer Science Department
George Mason University
Fairfax, VA 22030
nbajunai@masonlive.gmu.edu

Daniel A. Menascé
Computer Science Department
George Mason University
Fairfax, VA 22030
menasce@gmu.edu

ABSTRACT

Checkpointing and rollback is a key mechanism used to improve the reliability of software systems. The benefits of this mechanism can be offset by the overhead of checkpointing when the failure rate is low. The problem of developing analytic models of rollback and checkpointing has been continuously addressed for over four decades using different assumptions. This paper examines the problem under a more realistic angle, i.e., one in which there are several software components sharing resources (e.g., processors and I/O devices) among themselves and with the checkpointing processes. Additionally, the paper allows for different components to have different computing, rollback, and checkpointing demands, as well as different failure distributions. Our models also allow for various checkpointing processes to be executing concurrently to checkpoint the state of different software components. The analytic models developed here combine Markov Chains and Queuing Networks and allow us to compute the following metrics: (1) average time needed by a component to complete its execution, (2) average throughput of a component, (3) availability of a component, and (4) checkpointing overhead. The models were validated through extensive simulation and experimentation.

CCS Concepts

•**Software and its engineering** → **Software performance; Software reliability; Checkpoint / restart;**

Keywords

Checkpointing; concurrent components; analytic models; Markov chains; queuing networks

1. INTRODUCTION

One of the key mechanisms used to improve the reliability of software systems is checkpointing and rollback, which allows for a software component to store the state of its computation at regular intervals to reduce the amount of work to be redone in the case of a failure [27]. Without checkpointing, a software component (referred to as component hereafter) has to restart the computation from the beginning, which could be a problem for long computing tasks. With checkpointing, the computation resumes from the latest checkpoint after the computation is restored to that state.

The benefits of checkpointing can be offset by the overhead of checkpointing when the failure rate is low. The problem of developing analytic models for rollback and checkpointing has been continuously addressed for over four decades using different assumptions. This paper examines the problem under a more realistic angle, i.e., one in which there are several software components sharing resources among themselves and with the checkpointing processes. Additionally, the paper allows for different components to have different computing, rollback, and checkpointing demands as well as different failure rates. Our models also allow for various checkpointing processes to be executing concurrently to checkpoint the state of different software components. The analytic models developed here combine Markov Chains and Queuing Networks (QN) and allow us to compute the following metrics: (1) average time needed by a component to complete its execution, (2) average throughput of a component, (3) availability of a component, and (4) checkpointing overhead. The models were validated through simulation and experimentation.

As discussed in Section 4, there is a vast body of work that presents analytic models for obtaining the checkpointing interval that optimizes a variety of metrics. Some examples include: minimize total execution time, maximize availability, maximize a job's progress, and minimize the overhead generated by checkpointing and wasted work due to rollback. A comprehensive and relatively recent book by Katinka Wolter [25] contains a thorough description of many stochastic models for checkpointing, restart, and rejuvenation, including many discussed in the related work section of this paper and other novel models introduced by Wolter. However, the aforementioned models do not consider contention among components while executing or checkpointing.

Table 1 illustrates how the optimal duration of the interval between checkpoints, T_{opt}, varies for each of the metrics mentioned above and for different numbers of concurrent components ($n = 1, 4, 8$, and 16). The results in the table were obtained with the models described in this paper and assume Poisson failures at a rate of 0.005 failures per time unit. The models presented in this paper allow for

ICPE '17 April 22–26, 2017, L'Aquila, Italy

DOI: 10.1145/3030207.3030209

Table 1: Optimal checkpointing interval (T_{opt}) for different number of components (n) and $\lambda = 0.005$.

Metric	$n = 1$	$n = 4$	$n = 8$	$n = 16$
Execution time	10	7	7	7
Availability	10	8	7.5	7
Relative progress	10	7	7	7
Overhead	10	15	20	20

any failure distribution. The results in the table assume that the checkpointing time (without contention) is equal to 0.25 time units. According to a well-known result by Young [26], which does not consider contention, the value of T_{opt} that minimizes execution time is $\sqrt{2 \times 0.25/0.005} = 10$ time units. This value coincides with the value in Table 1 for $n = 1$. But, for other values of n, the value of T_{opt} is no longer the same as the one when contention is not considered. The table clearly shows that T_{opt} varies with the number of components running concurrently for the other metrics.

The main contribution of this paper is the development of analytic models based on a combination of Markov Chains and QNs to obtain the response time, throughput, and availability of *concurrent* and *heterogeneous* component-based software systems that use checkpointing. Differently from prior work, our models take into account contention for processors and storage devices by concurrent processes during their computation and checkpointing phases. Our models also allows for different software components to have different compute and I/O characteristics as well as different failure distributions.

This paper is organized as follows. Section 1 discusses some core results common to the two models described in the paper and then presents two checkpointing models: (1) a model that considers *homogeneous* components (all components have similar processing, I/O, and failure characteristics) and (2) a model for the case of *heterogeneous* components (different components may have different processing, I/O, and failure characteristics). Section 2 presents several numerical results using the models of the previous section. Section 3 discusses a validation of the models. The next section discusses related work and Section 5 presents some concluding remarks and discusses future work. Modeling Checkpointing Consider that a computing node runs n software components, $C_1, \cdots$
$, C_k, \cdots, C_n$, and that they request that their state be checkpointed every time they achieve a certain amount of computation. Thus, each component alternates between two modes: *computing* and *checkpointing*. In the former mode, a component is making forward progress towards its computational goal. In the latter, a checkpoint is being made of the component. The smaller the amount of computation before checkpoints, the faster is the recovery to the latest checkpoint at the expense of a higher checkpointing overhead. Conversely, a larger computing time before checkpointing decreases the checkpointing overhead but increases the time to return the computation to the failure point. The optimal checkpointing frequency depends on the: (1) failure rate, (2) computing time before checkpointing, and (3) time/overhead of taking checkpoints.

Checkpoint generation uses the same resources (i.e., processors and I/O devices) used by the components running at a computing node. We also assume that a component suspends its computation while checkpointing. So, each component alternates between computing and checkpointing. When a failure occurs while a component is computing, its state has to be restored to its latest checkpoint (i.e., a failure recovery) and the computation has to be restarted from that checkpointed state. In the process, all the computation since the latest checkpoint is wasted and has to be re-done.

Our models use the following assumptions:

- A1: Components can fail individually without affecting other components running on the same machine. Such failures may occur, for example, due to lack of memory, software bugs, or inability to allocate a needed resource.
- A2: One or more components may execute concurrently on the same machine.
- A3: Different components may have different processing and I/O demands. These demands are not deterministic but are expressed by their average values for each component.
- A4: Checkpoints for different components are not synchronized with those of other components and may be generated at different frequencies.
- A5: Different components may have different processing and I/O demands for generating checkpoints. These demands are not deterministic but are expressed by their average values for each component.
- A6: Different components may have different failure distributions.
- A7: Components and their checkpointing processes share resources (e.g., processors and I/O devices) on the machine they run and therefore there is *contention* for these resources by these processes.
- A8: Similarly to the vast body of literature on checkpointing modeling (see e.g. [17]) we assume:
  - failures are immediately detected,
  - no failures occur during checkpointing or during rollback, a reasonable assumption since the time to checkpoint and rollback is typically smaller than the MTTF.

Table 2 summarizes the notation used in this paper. Before we discuss in subsections 1.2 and 1.3 the *homogeneous component* and *heterogeneous component* models, we present results that are common to both.

1.1 Core Results

Figure 1 shows what can happen with a component between two checkpoints assuming two failures occur before the component is able to complete T time units of computation. In the figure, the first failure occurs after the component has processed for $W_1 < T$ time units. Then, the component spends a time equal to RT to rollback to the latest checkpoint. RT includes CPU and I/O time. The component then restarts its computation and after computing for $W_2 < T$ time units, a second failure occurs. Another period

Table 2: Notation used in the checkpointing models

Notation	Meaning
n	number of components
$C_{\text{CPU},k}$	avg. CPU time to checkpoint component k
$C_{\text{I/O},k}$	avg. I/O time to checkpoint component k
$E_{\text{CPU},k}$	avg. CPU time needed to execute component k
$E_{\text{I/O},k}$	avg. I/O time needed to execute component k
E_k	avg. time (CPU and I/O) to execute component k. $E_k = E_{\text{CPU},k} + E_{\text{I/O},k}$
$T_{\text{CPU,k}}$	CPU time between consecutive checkpoints of component k
$T_{\text{I/O,k}}$	I/O time between consecutive checkpoints of component k
T_k	total time between consecutive checkpoints of component k. This time, equal to $T_{\text{CPU,k}} + T_{\text{I/O,k}}$, determines when the next checkpoint has to occur.
$\hat{T}_k$	time to complete E_k after the last checkpoint of component k.
$\tilde{F}_k$	r.v. that represents the failure instant of component k after its last rollback or latest checkpoint when it is in computing mode
$f_{\tilde{F}_k}(x)$	pdf of $\tilde{F}_k$
q_k	probability that a failure occurs while component k is computing.
$\tilde{W}_{\text{CPU},k}$	r.v. that denotes the amount of computation to be re-done (i.e., wasted) per failure of component k
$\tilde{W}_{\text{I/O},k}$	r.v. that denotes the I/O time to be re-done (i.e., wasted) per failure of component k
$\tilde{W}_k$	r.v. that denotes the CPU and I/O time to be re-done (i.e., wasted) per failure of component k. $\tilde{W}_k = \tilde{W}_{\text{CPU},k} + \tilde{W}_{\text{I/O},k}$.
$\text{RT}_{\text{CPU},k}$	average CPU time needed to rollback component k to the latest checkpoint after a failure
$\text{RT}_{\text{I/O},k}$	average I/O time needed to rollback component k to the latest checkpoint after a failure

equal to RT ensues. The component then restarts its computation and this time it succeeds in completing the T time units of computation before the next checkpoint. It should be noted though that the time intervals C, W1, W2, RT and T in Fig. 1 represent time intervals for one component when there is no contention with other components (i.e., the case of $n = 1$). In the general case of $n \geq 1$ treated in this paper, these time intervals are elongated by the contention effect.

The number of checkpoints NX_k expected to be performed by component k is $\lfloor E_k/T_k \rfloor$, and the remaining amount of work $\hat{T}_k$ to be performed by component k after the last checkpoint is $\hat{T}_k = E - (T.NX_k)$.

The probability of exactly j failures experienced by component k between two checkpoints is $q_k^j(1 - q_k)$ assuming independence among failures, where $q_k = \int_0^{T_k -} f_{\tilde{F}_k}(x)\, dx$. If the failure model for component k is Poisson, i.e., $\tilde{F}_k$ is exponentially distributed with parameter λ_k, then $q_k = 1 - e^{-\lambda_k T_k}$. Thus, the average number of failures NF_k between consecutive checkpoints is

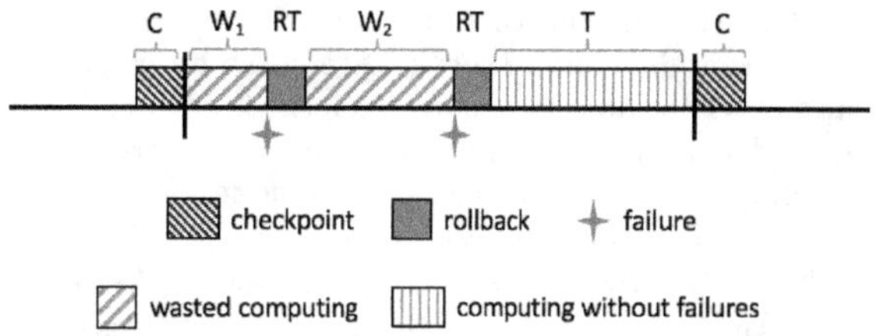

Figure 1: Timeline between two consecutive checkpoints.

$$NF_k = \sum_{j=0}^{\infty} j \times q_k^j(1 - q_k) = \frac{q_k}{1 - q_k}. \quad (1)$$

The average effective CPU time, $T^{\text{eff}}_{\text{CPU},k}$, that a component k spends computing and rolling back from failures between checkpoints is the product of the average number of failures NF_k by the sum of the average wasted CPU time, $E[\tilde{W}_{\text{CPU}}]$, and the average CPU time, $\text{RT}_{\text{CPU},k}$, needed to recover from a failure, plus the time $T_{\text{CPU,k}}$ to execute a successful computation between checkpoints.

$$T^{\text{eff}}_{\text{CPU},k} = \frac{q_k[E[\tilde{W}_{\text{CPU},k}] + \text{RT}_{\text{CPU},k}]}{1 - q_k} + T_{\text{CPU,k}} \quad k = 1, \cdots, n. \quad (2)$$

Similarly, the effective I/O time, $T^{\text{eff}}_{\text{I/O},k}$, needed by component k to recover from failures and execute a successful computation between checkpoints is given by

$$T^{\text{eff}}_{\text{I/O},k} = \frac{q_k[E[\tilde{W}_{\text{I/O},k}] + \text{RT}_{\text{I/O},k}]}{1 - q_k} + T_{\text{I/O,k}} \quad k = 1, \cdots, n. \quad (3)$$

Note that $T^{\text{eff}}_{\text{CPU},k}$ and $T^{\text{eff}}_{\text{I/O},k}$ do not include contention, which is accounted for by the models discussed in later subsections.

The average value of $\tilde{W}_k$, $E[\tilde{W}_k]$, is the average value of $\tilde{F}_k$ given that $\tilde{F}_k < T_k$ because when a failure occurs before the component completes its T_k seconds of computation, the computation up to the failure instant is wasted. The expression for $E[W_k]$ follows from the definition of conditional probability:

$$E[\tilde{W}_k] = E[\tilde{F}_k \mid \tilde{F}_k < T_k] = \frac{\int_{x=0}^{T_k -} x.f_{\tilde{F}_k}(x)dx}{\int_{x=0}^{T_k -} f_{\tilde{F}_k}(x)dx}. \quad (4)$$

For example, if $\tilde{F}_k$ is exponentially distributed (i.e., the failure model is Poisson), $f_{\tilde{F}_k}(x) = \lambda_k e^{-\lambda_k x}$ where λ_k is the failure rate. For this distribution, $E[\tilde{W}_k]$ can be computed as

$$E[\tilde{W}_k] = \frac{\int_{x=0}^{T_k -} x.\lambda_k e^{-\lambda_k x} dx}{\int_{x=0}^{T_k -} \lambda_k e^{-\lambda_k x} dx} \quad (5)$$

$$= \frac{\frac{1}{\lambda_k} - \left(\frac{1}{\lambda_k} + T_k\right) e^{-\lambda_k T_k}}{1 - e^{-\lambda_k T_k}}. \quad (6)$$

Note that the value of $E[\tilde{W}_k] \in (0, T_k)$. A value of 0 occurs when the failure occurs right at the beginning of the computing segment and there is no need to re-do any computation after the component is restored to its most recent checkpoint. The value T_k occurs when the failure takes place at the very end of the computing segment. In this case, the entire computing segment has to be re-done after the component is restored to its latest checkpoint.

To derive expressions for $E[\tilde{W}_{\text{CPU},k}]$ and $E[\tilde{W}_{\text{I/O},k}]$, we note that the fraction of $E[\tilde{W}_k]$ wasted by the CPU is $E_{\text{CPU},k}/E_k$. The same goes for wasted I/O time, as shown in Eqs. (7) and (8).

$$E[\tilde{W}_{\text{CPU},k}] = \frac{E_{\text{CPU},k}\, E[\tilde{W}_k]}{E_k}. \tag{7}$$

$$E[\tilde{W}_{\text{I/O},k}] = \frac{E_{\text{I/O},k}\, E[\tilde{W}_k]}{E_k}. \tag{8}$$

A variety of metrics can be computed using the analytic models described in the following two subsections. Of these, the following two are key because they capture the contention among the different components while computing, checkpointing, during rollback and recovery time.

- $\bar{r}_{c,k}$: average time it takes component k to complete its computation between consecutive checkpoints.
- $\bar{r}_{x,k}$: average time it takes component k to complete its checkpoint.

In order to execute T_k units of computing between checkpoints, a component needs $\bar{r}_{c,k}$ time units due to contention with other components performing computing and checkpointing, recovering from failures, and performing wasted work. And it will need $\bar{r}_{x,k}$ time units on average to perform each checkpoint. Thus, the average total time, $\bar{R}_{c,k}$, it takes a component to complete its computation taking into account contention with other components and checkpointing is

$$\bar{R}_{c,k} = [NX_k.(\bar{r}_{c,k} + \bar{r}_{x,k})] + (\hat{T}_k.\frac{\bar{r}_{c,k}}{T_k}). \tag{9}$$

where $\bar{r}_{c,k}/T_k$ is the inflation factor that must be applied to T_k due to failures and contention. We can also define the checkpointing overhead, Ov_k, of component k as the ratio between the time spent in checkpointing (including contention) and the total time (computing plus checkpointing).

$$Ov_k = \frac{NX_k.\bar{r}_{x,k}}{\bar{R}_{c,k}}. \tag{10}$$

The availability, A_k, of component k is defined as the fraction of time the component is doing useful work and is computed as the ratio between the time a component is either computing or waiting for resources divided by the total execution time. The term in square brackets in Eq. (11) represents the inflation factor that has to be applied to T_k^{eff} due to contention. This term is the ratio between the average time, $\bar{r}_{c,k}$, component k takes executing between checkpoints and the time the component would take with no contention. Note that inflation due to failures is not considered here. This definition of availability can be interpreted as the notion of achieved availability [8] where checkpointing corresponds to preventive maintenance and recovery time plus re-doing computation corresponds to corrective maintenance.

$$A_k = \frac{NX_k.T_k.[\bar{r}_{c,k}/(T^{\text{eff}}_{\text{CPU},k} + T^{\text{eff}}_{\text{I/O},k})]}{\bar{R}_{c,k}}. \tag{11}$$

We also define a metric called *relative progress* (RP_k) that indicates the relative progress of the computation, i.e., the relative amount of useful computation done by component k during a cycle:

$$RP_k = \frac{T_k}{\bar{r}_{c,k} + \bar{r}_{x,k}}. \tag{12}$$

Equations (9)-(12) require $\bar{r}_{c,k}$ and $\bar{r}_{x,k}$, which will be derived first for the case of homogeneous components and next for the case of heterogeneous components in the next two subsections, respectively.

1.2 Model for Homogeneous Components

The heterogeneous model can be used to solve systems with homogeneous components. However, the homogeneous model has a lower computational complexity. Under the homogeneous component assumption, we can drop the subscript k from the notation introduced in Table 2. All components have the same CPU and I/O demands for computing and checkpointing and the same failure distributions.

Because at any given time there may be a number of components in the computing mode and a number of components in the checkpointing mode, we model the system of components using a Markov Chain with states $0, 1, \cdots, v, \cdots, n-1, n$ where the state v indicates that there are v components performing their computation and $n - v$ components generating their checkpoints. The transition rate, μ_v, between states v and $v - 1$ is the rate at which one of the v components suspends its computation to start its checkpointing process. The transition rate, λ_v, between states v and $v + 1$ is the checkpointing completion rate for one of the components being checkpointed. The transition rates μ_v and λ_v are computed using a multiclass Queueing Network (QN) model as explained below. But first, we compute the probability p_v of being at state v of the Markov Chain. This probability is a function of λ_v, μ_v, and n.

An expression for p_v ($v = 0, \cdots, n$) is obtained by using the general birth-death equation for Markov Chains [15, 20]:

$$p_v = p_0 \prod_{i=0}^{v-1} \frac{\lambda_i}{\mu_{i+1}} \quad v = 1, \cdots, n \tag{13}$$

$$p_0 = \left[1 + \sum_{v=1}^{n} \Pi_{i=0}^{v-1} \frac{\lambda_i}{\mu_{i+1}}\right]^{-1}. \tag{14}$$

The values of p_v can be easily computed because the summation needed to compute p_0 is finite.

We now show how to compute the values of λ_v and μ_v. State v means that v components are computing and $n - v$ are checkpointing. We model this as a 2-class closed QN where the classes are: COMP and CHECK where COMP corresponds to segments of the computation between checkpoints and CHECK corresponds to the checkpointing processes. The population for the COMP class is v and for the CHECK class is $(n - v)$. Considering without loss of generality that there are two devices, CPU and I/O, the CPU and I/O service demands for the COMP class are $T^{\text{eff}}_{\text{CPU}}$ and $T^{\text{eff}}_{\text{I/O}}$, respectively, and for the CHECK class are C_{CPU} and C_{IO}, respectively.

The solution to the two-class closed QN described above can be obtained using the well-known Mean Value Analysis technique [20] and yields the following metrics:

- $X_{\text{COMP}}(v)$: average throughput of component computation segments between checkpoints when there are v components in their computing phase.

- $X_{\text{CHECK}}(n-v)$: average throughput of component checkpoints, i.e., average rate at which checkpoints complete when there are $n-v$ concurrent checkpoints in progress.

Therefore, we can write the following two relationships:

$$\lambda_v = X_{\text{CHECK}}(n-v) \quad (15)$$
$$\mu_v = X_{\text{COMP}}(v). \quad (16)$$

We can also compute the average throughput, $\bar{X}_{\text{COMP}}$, of components completing their computation before starting checkpointing, and $\bar{X}_{\text{CHECK}}$, the average checkpointing throughput, as follows:

$$\bar{X}_{\text{COMP}} = \sum_{v=1}^{n} X_{\text{COMP}}(v)\, p_v \quad (17)$$
$$\bar{X}_{\text{CHECK}} = \sum_{v=0}^{n-1} X_{\text{CHECK}}(n-v)\, p_v. \quad (18)$$

The average number of components in the computing stage, $\bar{n}_c$, and the average number of components being checkpointed, $\bar{n}_x$, are:

$$\bar{n}_c = \sum_{v=1}^{n} v\, p_v \quad (19)$$
$$\bar{n}_x = n - \bar{n}_c. \quad (20)$$

The average time, $\bar{r}_c$, spent by a component between checkpoints and the average time, $\bar{r}_x$, a component takes to generate its checkpoint is computed with the use of Little's Law [18].

$$\bar{r}_c = \frac{\bar{n}_c}{\bar{X}_{\text{COMP}}} \quad (21)$$
$$\bar{r}_x = \frac{\bar{n}_x}{\bar{X}_{\text{CHECK}}}. \quad (22)$$

Thus, the values of $\bar{r}_c$ and $\bar{r}_x$ can be used to compute the average total time, $\bar{R}_c$, it takes a component to complete its computation taking into account contention with other components and checkpointing as indicated by Equation (9). Similarly, the checkpointing overhead, Ov, the availability A, and the relative progress RP can now be computed using Equations (10)-(12), respectively.

1.3 Model for Heterogeneous Components

This section generalizes the model presented in the previous section for the case in which the n components may have totally different characteristics. At any point in time, a component is either computing or checkpointing. So, the state of the system can be represented as $(e_1, \cdots, e_k, \cdots, e_n)$ where $e_k = 1$ if component k is computing and 0 if it is checkpointing. For example, if n is 3, the set of states is $\{(0,0,0), (0,0,1), (0,1,0), (0,1,1), (1,0,0), (1,0,1), (1,1,0),$ and $(1,1,1)\}$. Clearly, there are 2^n states. For convenience, we let $N = 2^n$. We number the states from 0 to $N-1$ and the state representation is the n-bit binary number corresponding to the decimal number of the state. We denote by $b(i)$ the binary representation of state i. For example, when $n = 3$, the states would be numbered from 0 to 7 and $b(6)$ is 110. We always number the bits in $b(s)$ from left to right starting from 1. Let $\mathcal{S}$ be the set of all states.

If we assume that the events of starting a checkpoint for one component and ending a checkpoint for the same or a different component cannot occur at exactly the same time, the only possible transitions between states are the ones that change only one of the e_k's of a state from 0 to 1 or from 1 to zero. We use the notation $\odot_k(b(s))$ to represent a function that flips the k-th bit in $b(s)$ leaving and all other bits unchanged. So, $\odot_4(0011011) = 0010011$.

We can now build a Markov Chain in which the states are the N states described above. Each state in $\mathcal{S}$ has n incoming transitions and n outgoing transitions to other states because outgoing and incoming transitions are associated to "flipping" one of the n bits of the state at a time. Figure 2 shows an example of this Markov Chain for the case of $n = 2$. The state transition rates will be explained later. States are identified by their decimal numbers $(0, \cdots, 3)$ and by their binary number. Note that for clarity, we have added after the 2-bit binary number another two bits to indicate which components are checkpointing in each state. These extra two bits are not needed to represent the state because this information can be derived by flipping all the bits of the state's binary representation.

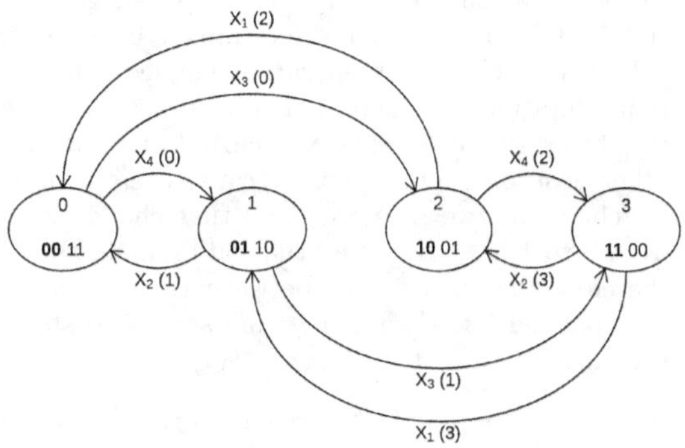

Figure 2: Example of Markov Chain for the heterogeneous case and $n = 2$.

In order to generate and solve the Markov Chain we need to write a set of balance equations and solve the resulting system of linear equations in which the variables are the probabilities $p_i, i = 0, \cdots, N-1$ of being in each state i. To find the state probabilities we need N equations, which can be obtained by applying the principle of *flow-in = flow-out* [15] to each state of the Markov Chain. This yields the following set of equations

$$\sum_{v \in \mathcal{S}_{\text{in}}(s)} p_v \times \mu_{v,s} - p_s \sum_{v \in \mathcal{S}_{out}(s)} \mu_{s,v} = 0 \quad \forall\, s \in \mathcal{S} \quad (23)$$

where $\mathcal{S}_{\text{in}}(s)$ is the set of all states from which there are transitions into state s, $\mu_{v,s}$ is the transition rate from state v into state s, $\mathcal{S}_{out}(s)$ is the set of states into which there are transitions from state s, and $\mu_{s,v}$ is transition rate from state s into state v. We can rewrite Eq. (23) using the state numbers from 0 to $N-1$. Thus, for each state i, $(i = 0, \ldots, N-1)$ we have the following equation:

$$\sum_{j=0}^{N-1} p_j \times \mu_{j,i} - p_i \sum_{j=0}^{N-1} \mu_{i,j} = 0. \quad (24)$$

The above equations are not linearly independent so we need to replace any of them with the equation that says that the sum of all probabilities is equal to 1 [15]:

$$\sum_{i=0}^{N-1} p_i = 1. \tag{25}$$

The matrix of transition probabilities, **P**, is of the form

$$\mathbf{P} = \begin{pmatrix} \mu_{0,0} & \mu_{0,1} & \cdots & \mu_{0,N-1} \\ \mu_{1,0} & \mu_{1,1} & \cdots & \mu_{1,N-1} \\ \cdots & \cdots & \cdots & \cdots \\ \mu_{N-1,0} & \mu_{N-1,1} & \cdots & \mu_{N-1,N-1} \end{pmatrix} \tag{26}$$

The Markov Chain has the following properties:

- Property 1: $\mathcal{S}_{\text{in}}(s) = \mathcal{S}_{\text{out}}(s)\ \forall s \in \mathcal{S}$. This is true because, as indicated above, transitions between states can only occur when one and only one element e_k of the state changes from one to zero or from zero to one. So, $\mathcal{S}_{\text{in}}(s) = \mathcal{S}_{\text{out}}(s) = \{\odot_1(s)\} \bigcup \{\odot_2(s)\} \bigcup \cdots \{\odot_n(s)\}$.
- Property 2: $\mid \mathcal{S}_{\text{in}}\ (s) \mid = \mid \mathcal{S}_{\text{out}}\ (s) \mid = n\ \forall s \in \mathcal{S}$. This follows immediately from property 1 above.
- Property 3: $\mu_{i,i} = 0$ for $i = 0, \cdots, N-1$.
- Property 4: the bit that changed when going from state i to state j can be determined by performing a bitwise exclusive or operation between the binary representations of i and j. The result will have a bit equal to 1 where the change occurred and a zero in all other positions. This is true because there is only one bit change between i and j and that change is either from 0 to 1 or 1 to 0. All other bits remain the same; therefore the exclusive or between them is 0. Thus, the changed bit when going from state i to state j is the only bit equal to 1 in $b(i) \oplus b(j)$.
- Property 5: $\mu_{i,j} = 0$ if $b(i)$ and $b(j)$ differ by more than one bit because transitions can only occur at the beginning or end of the checkpointing of a single component.
- Property 6: Except for Eq. (25), most of the coefficients of the unknowns on equations (24) are zero. Because of properties 3 and 4 above, only n out of 2^n transitions rates are non-zero. Thus, the matrix of transition rates (see Eq. (26)) is largely sparse, a fact we benefit from when solving the Markov Chain.

To compute the transition rates $\mu_{i,j}$ we use a multiclass QN model similarly as before with the following characteristics: (1) There are $2n$ classes. Classes 1 through n represent the n components and the population of each of these classes is either 1 or 0, depending on the status of the component (i.e., computing (1) or checkpointing (0)). Classes $n+1$ through $2n$ correspond to the checkpointing process for each of the software components. The population of each of these classes is also 1 or 0 depending whether a component is checkpointing (1) or not (0). So, the total population of this QN model is equal to the number of components n. The population of class k plus the population of class $n+k$ is equal to 1 for $k = 1, \cdots, n$ because a component cannot be computing and checkpointing at the same time. Additionally, the service demands for the component classes may be different. A state $s \in \mathcal{S}$ represents the population of classes 1 through n of the QN. The population of the remaining classes is automatically derived from the population of the first n classes. For example, the state (1, 1, 0, 1, 0) for a 5-component system indicates that components 1, 2, and 4 are computing and components 3 and 5 are checkpointing. Then, the populations for classes 1 through 5 of the QN are 1, 1, 0, 1, 0 and the populations for classes 6 through 10 are 0, 0, 1, 0, 1.

The CPU and I/O service demands for classes $k = 1, \cdots, n$ are given by equations (2) and (3), respectively. The CPU and I/O service demands for class $n+k$ $(k = 1, \cdots, n)$ are given by $C_{\text{CPU},k}$ and $C_{\text{I/O},k}$, respectively.

Appendix A provides the algorithm used to compute the transition rates $\mu_{i,j}$. These rates are used to put together the system of linear equations in Eqs. (24) and (25). Various numerical solvers can be used for that purpose. We used the solver in the R package that handles systems of linear equations with sparse matrices. The following additional notation is used in the remaining expressions.

- $v_k(b)$: value of the bit at position k (counting from the left) of binary number b. So, $v_4(000100) = 1$.
- $X_k(i)$: throughput of class k $(k = 1, \cdots, n)$ for state i.
- $X_{n+k}(i)$: throughput of class $n+k$ $(k = 1, \cdots, n)$ for state i.

With the values of p_i's we can obtain the probability P_k^c that component k is in the computing mode as the sum of all state probabilities where component k is computing. Note that P_k^c is also the average number, $\bar{n}_{c,k}$, of components of class k in the computing mode. Thus,

$$P_k^c = \bar{n}_{c,k} = \sum_{i=0}^{N-1} v_k(b(i))\ p_i. \tag{27}$$

The probability P_k^x that component k is checkpointing is simply $1 - P_k^c$ and is also equal to $\bar{n}_{x,k}$, the average number of components of class k in the checkpointing mode. Thus,

$$P_k^x = \bar{n}_{x,k} = 1 - P_k^c. \tag{28}$$

The average throughput, $\bar{X}_k$, of component k can be computed as

$$\bar{X}_k = \sum_{i=0}^{N-1} X_k(i)\ p_i. \tag{29}$$

Using the example of Fig. 2, we have that $\bar{X}_1 = X_1(3)p_3 + X_1(2)p2$. The overall average component throughput, $\bar{X}_{\text{COMP}}$, is

$$\bar{X}_{\text{COMP}} = \sum_{k=1}^{n} \bar{X}_k . P_k^c. \tag{30}$$

The average throughput, $\bar{X}_{n+k}$, of the checkpointing process for component k can be computed as

$$\bar{X}_{n+k} = \sum_{i=0}^{N-1} X_{n+k}(i)\ p_i. \tag{31}$$

In the example of Fig. 2, $\bar{X}_3 = X_3(0)p_0 + X_3(1)p_1$. The overall average throughput, $\bar{X}_{\text{CHECK}}$, of components in the checkpointing mode is

$$\bar{X}_{\text{CHECK}} = \sum_{k=1}^{n} \bar{X}_{n+k} . P_k^x. \tag{32}$$

According to Little's Law [18], the average time, $\bar{r}_{c,k}$, it takes component k to complete its computation between consecutive checkpoints is

$$\bar{r}_{c,k} = \frac{\bar{n}_{c,k}}{\bar{X}_k}. \tag{33}$$

Also according to Little's Law, the average time it takes a component k to complete its checkpoint is

$$\bar{r}_{x,k} = \frac{\bar{n}_{x,k}}{\bar{X}_{n+k}}. \tag{34}$$

The average total time, $\bar{R}_{c,k}$, it takes component k to complete its computation taking into account contention with other components and checkpointing is given by Equation (9) and the values of the overhead Ov_k, the availability A_k, and the relative progress RP_k are given by Equations (10)-(12), respectively.

When combining the individual availability of the components, one has to take into consideration how the system stakeholders view the relative importance of the different components. For example, the overall availability could be seen as the fraction of time that at least one component is available. In that case,

$$A = 1 - \prod_{k=1}^{n}(1 - A_k). \tag{35}$$

Alternatively, one could define the overall availability as a weighted average of the individual component availabilities:

$$A = \sum_{k=1}^{n} w_k.A_k \tag{36}$$

where $\sum_{k=1}^{n} w_k = 1$. Appendix B provides a discussion on the computational complexity and computation times of both models.

2. NUMERICAL EXAMPLES

We implemented both analytic models in Java and used some functions (e.g., solving systems of linear equations) provided by the R statistical package. We present here some numerical examples using the two models developed in the previous section. The time-related metrics presented in this section are normalized by the value of E, the average CPU time needed to complete the execution of a component. Thus, all normalized time-related metrics are dimensionless and have interesting interpretations. For example: R_c/E is the factor by which the average execution time of a component is elongated due to contention for resources, checkpointing, and rollback; T/E is the fraction of a component's total CPU time achieved between checkpoints; and $(1/\lambda)/E$ is the ratio between the mean time to fail and a component's total CPU time.

The top curve of Fig. 3 shows the variation of R_c/E with T/E for the case of a homogenous model with 3 components and Poisson failures with a normalized mean time to failure equal to 0.5 (i.e., two failures every execution of a component). The other normalized parameters are $E_{\text{CPU}} = 0.85, E_{\text{I/O}} = 0.15$, $C_{\text{CPU}} = 0.05$, $C_{\text{I/O}} = 0.075$, $RT_{\text{CPU}} = 0.06$ and $RT_{\text{I/O}} = 0.07$. The figure shows that R_c/E decreases with T, reaches a minimum, then starts to increase. This can be explained by looking at the change in the overhead, O_v, and the expected number of failures between consecutive checkpoints, NF, also shown on the same figure. The inflation in execution time for each component is caused by contention, failures and checkpointing overhead. The contention is constant in this example because the number of components is fixed. For smaller values of T, the checkpointing overhead is very high, however the number of expected failures in this small interval is small. After some point (the optimal T for minimum R_c), the decrease in O_v slows down while the number of failures increases fast. This increase has a bigger effect on R_c after this point.

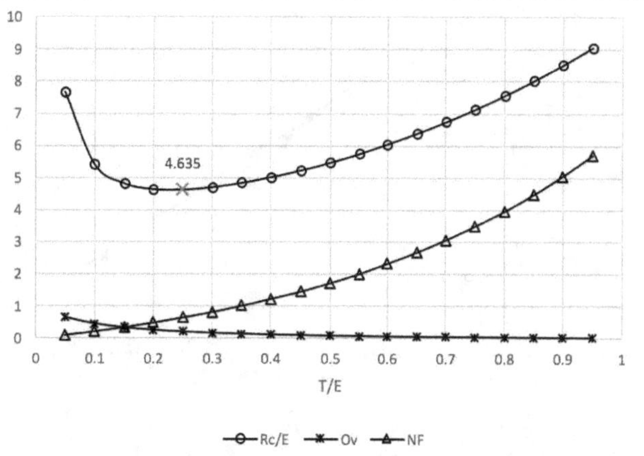

Figure 3: Normalized average execution time (R_c/E) vs. T/E for the homogeneous case and with Poisson failures. $(1/\lambda)/E = 0.5$, $n = 3$.

Figure 4 shows the normalized execution time vs. average availability for 1, 3, 5, and 7 concurrent components. The figure shows that as R_c decreases, A increases. Under constant contention, the achieved availability is affected by the same two factors as execution time: O_v (preventive maintenance), and NF (corrective maintenance). The figure shows that the optimal T value that minimizes execution time is usually the same or very close to the value that maximizes availability.

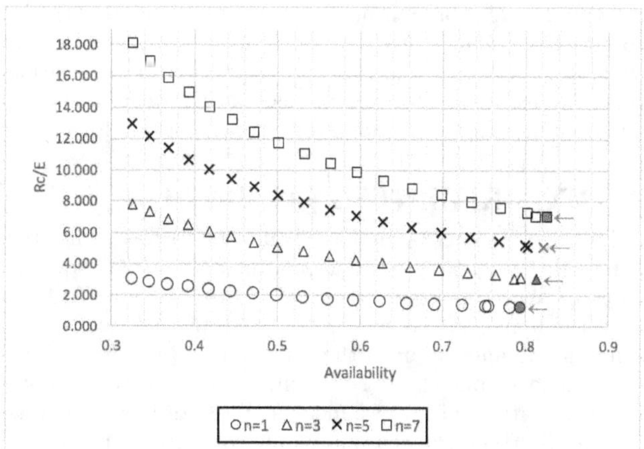

Figure 4: Normalized average execution time (R_c/E) vs. the availability A for the homogeneous case and with Poisson failures. $(1/\lambda)/E = 0.5$, $n = 1, 3, 5$, **and** 7.

Figure 5 shows the variation in availability vs. T/E for

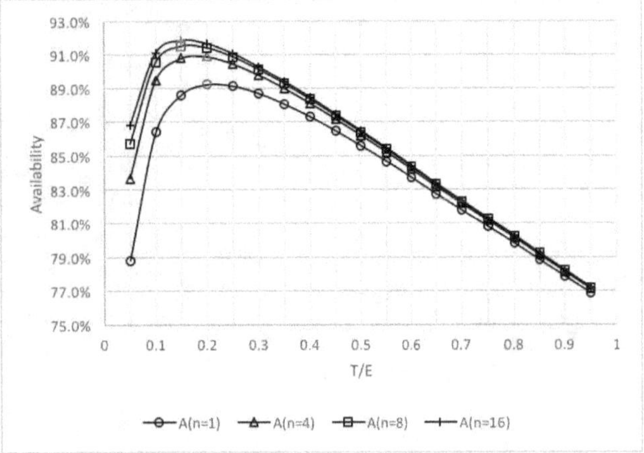

Figure 5: Availability A vs. T/E for $n = 1, 4, 8$, and 16 for the homogeneous case and with Poisson failures. $(1/\lambda)/E = 2$.

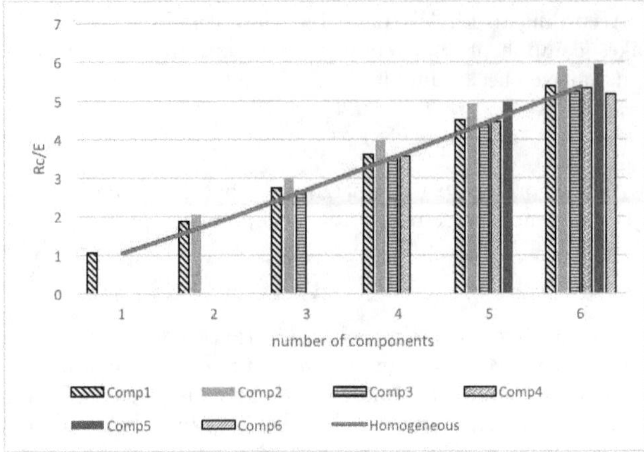

Figure 6: Normalized execution time (R_c/E) as components are incrementally added.

1, 4, 8 and 16 concurrent components and $\lambda = 1/(2E)$. In all four cases, the availability increases, reaches a maximum, and then decreases. This has the same explanation as Figs. 3 and 4. As R_c decreases, A increases, they reach their optimal values at very close values of T. After this point, R_c increases and A decreases.

Figure 6 illustrates the variation of the average normalized execution time as components are incrementally added from 1 to 6. The six components have different resource demands and different failure distributions. The characteristics of the six components vary as follows: $E = 15$ to 40 (with $E_{\text{CPU}} = 0.85E$), $T = 2$ to 4, $C_{\text{CPU}} = 0.015$ to 0.03, $C_{\text{I/O}} = 0.02$ to 0.04, $RT_{\text{CPU}} = 0.01$ to 0.028, and $RT_{\text{I/O}} = 0.002$ to 0.04. Components 1, 2, 4 and 5 have Poisson failures with failure rates equal to $0.03, 0.07, 0.02$,and 0.08, respectively. Components 3 and 6 have Weibull failure distributions with shape and scale parameters equal to (4, 50) and (3, 70), respectively. The figure also shows a red line that depicts how the normalized execution time would vary if all added components had the same characteristics as component 1. The figure also indicates how the mix of concurrent components influences on the normalized execution time. For example, R_c/E is very close to 6 for components 2 and 5 and it is close to 5 for all other components for $n = 6$.

3. EXPERIMENTAL VALIDATION

The first obvious validation of our models was to use the heterogeneous model in a situation in which the characteristics of all components were exactly the same. We then used the homogeneous model to obtain the metrics for the same inputs and obtained the same values provided by the heterogeneous model. This confirmed the correctness of our implementations of the two models. We had done unit tests previously to confirm that individual components of the implementation (e.g., QN model, Markov Chain solution) were correct. We then validated the models through both simulation and experiments as described in the next two subsections.

3.1 Validation Through Simulation

We wrote a Java program that simulates a node with a processor, a disk, and multiple software components. Each component is provided with a sequence of at least 500 jobs to execute, each representing a different execution of the component. The various properties of a component (e.g., execution time, checkpointing time, recovery time) are random variables with assigned distributions. For each task execution, values are drawn from the common distribution for that component. For example, the computation time of tasks for component k may be exponentially distributed with mean E_k, uniformly distributed checkpointing and roll back demands, and time to fail following a Weibull distribution with given shape and scale parameters. To ensure a constant level of contention during each run, the simulation run stops when one of the components finishes executing all of its tasks. At that point, the output results are averaged over all runs and 95% confidence intervals are computed over 40 runs in which each component is executed hundreds of times.. The analytic and simulation results are compared through the error $\epsilon = 100\times \mid \text{simulation} - \text{analytic} \mid /\text{simulation}$.

Table 3 compares the execution time, availability and checkpoint overhead obtained by the analytic and simulation models for 5, 10, and 15 homogeneous components. The characteristics of the components are the same as component 1 in Table 4, which shows input data for a scenario with three different components that have different values of computing demands ($E_{\text{CPU},k}$ and $E_{\text{I/O},k}$), checkpointing demands ($C_{\text{CPU},k}$ and $C_{\text{I/O},k}$), and rollback time ($\text{RT}_{\text{CPU},k}$ and $\text{RT}_{\text{I/O},k}$).

We used the values in Table 4 as input parameters (means for exponential distributions) for the heterogeneous analytic model and the simulation for three different components. Table 7 displays several results for four versions of the experiments in which the value of T_k and the failure distribution ($\tilde{F}$) vary according to Table 5. In all variations, components 1 and 3 had exponentially distributed time to fail, while component's 2 time to fail followed a Weibull distribution. Both distributions have been used in many reliability studies. We used shape parameters of 4 and 4.5 for the Weibull distributions, which means that the failure rate increases over time.

Table 7 shows the average total execution time $R_{c,k}$, the availability, and the overhead for each component k under the analytic and simulation models along with 95% confidence intervals over 40 runs of the simulation in which each component executes to completion at least 500 times in each

Table 3: Comparison between analytic and simulation results for the homogeneous case

n	R_c			A			O_v		
	simulation	analytic	ϵ	simulation	analytic	ϵ	simulation	analytic	ϵ
5	3369.3 ± 32.5	3658.5	8.6%	$44.9\% \pm 0.2\%$	42.5%	5.4%	$27.3\% \pm 0.1\%$	28.0%	2.8%
10	6390.3 ± 47.9	7245.1	13.4%	$44.8\% \pm 0.1\%$	42.5%	5.1%	$27.4\% \pm 0.1\%$	28.1%	2.3%
15	9647.2 ± 61.4	10876	12.7%	$44.5\% \pm 0.1\%$	42.5%	4.4%	$27.7\% \pm 0.1\%$	28.0%	1.1%

Table 4: Input parameters for the results on Tables 7 and 8

k	$E_{\text{CPU},k}$	$E_{\text{I/O},k}$	$C_{\text{CPU},k}$	$C_{\text{I/O},k}$	$\text{RT}_{\text{CPU},k}$	$\text{RT}_{\text{I/O},k}$
1	303.75	119.50	25.40	9.99	30.20	11.88
2	151.25	59.50	18.70	7.36	23.30	9.17
3	203.75	106.88	48.00	18.88	24.70	9.72

Table 5: Four versions of the experiments for results on Tables 7 and 8

version	T	$F_1.\lambda$	$F_2.(shape, scale)$	$F_3.\lambda$
1	25	0.009	(4.5, 115)	0.013
2	25	0.008	(4, 67)	0.011
3	50	0.009	(4.5, 115)	0.013
4	50	0.008	(4, 67)	0.011

run. In each run, each component is given a new seed to generate random samples using the means in Table 4. Note that all three components are executing concurrently during the simulation runs and sharing the CPU and I/O resources. Table 7 shows that the error of the analytic model for $R_{c,k}$ is between 9.5% and 11.4%, for exponentially distributed failures. The errors for the Weibull distribution are higher, i.e., around 14.5%, but still acceptable for execution times when queuing effects are present [16]. The lower errors for the exponential distribution may be due to its memoryless property, which is consistent with the underlying Markovian assumptions of the models presented here. But, even under non-Markovian failure assumptions, our models exhibit fairly robust prediction capabilities.

3.2 Validation Through Experimentation

A second validation was done through experimentation. We developed a micro-benchmark in C that implements software components that perform jobs repeatedly, do frequent checkpoints and fail randomly according to an exponential or Weibull distribution. Components receive as input the number of jobs, the time between consecutive checkpoints (T), and the failure rate (λ). At the beginning of each job, the component starts a timer, resets the time to checkpoint to T, and generates the next failure time using λ. During the task's execution, a component constantly checks whether it is time to fail or checkpoint. If it is time to fail, the component rollbacks to the latest checkpoint and redoes the work that was not checkpointed. If it is time to checkpoint, the components does so. After each failure or checkpoint, the component generates a new failure time, resets the time to checkpoint to T, and resets the un-checkpointed work to zero. At the end of a job, the component stops the timer and records the time taken to complete the task ($\bar{R}_c$ in our model).

Each component alternates between CPU and I/O activity by invoking the *compute*() and *doIO*() procedures (see Algorithm 1). The first performs thousands of calls to trigonometric functions and stores the results in an array. The second writes the array to a binary file. These two procedures were run thousands of times to measure the CPU and disk service demands. The CPU demand was measured using C's `clock()` function, which returns the number of clock ticks since the program was started. This value is then divided by the global variable `CLOCKS_PER_SEC` to obtain the time spent using the CPU. The disk demand was measured by running the `fs_usage` command to measure the time needed for all file system calls. Table 6 shows the CPU and disk demands of the functions *compute*() and *doIO*() averaged after 2000 runs each with 95% confidence intervals. All experiments were run on a MacBook Pro with a 2.6 GHz Intel Core i5 processor. Only one core was enabled to produce contention during experimentation with multiple concurrent components. The pseudo code for the micro-benchmark is given in Algorithms 1, 2, and 3.

Algorithm 1 Micro-benchmark Pseudo Code

```
Input: numTasks, iterations, numCompute, numIO, λ, T
for t = 1 → numTasks do
    Reset();
    START ← current_time();
    for i = 1 → iterations do
        for j = 1 → numCompute do
            Execute(compute(), compute_time, uncheckedComp);
        end for
        for j = 1 → numIO do
            Execute(doIO(), IO_time, uncheckedIO);
        end for
    end for
    END ← current_time();
    taskTimes[t] ← END − START
end for
printTaskTimes();
```

Table 6: ***compute*() and *doIO*() CPU and disk demands in msec with 95% confidence intervals**

	CPU demand	disk demand
compute()	2.66 ± 0.008	0
doIO()	0.666 ± 0.005	0.0873 ± 0.04

Similarly to the simulation, four experiments were conducted according to Tables 4 and 5. For each experiment, 40 runs were conducted. In each run, each of the concurrent components executed at least 50 jobs. The values generated using the means in Tables 4 and 5 were averaged and used as an input to the analytical model. The total execution time,

Algorithm 2 Execute Pseudo Code

```
Input: procedure, duration, counter
call(procedure);
timeToFail = timeToFail − duration;
timeToCheck = timeToCheck − duration;
if timeToFail ≤ 0 then
  Rollback();
  Redo(uncheckedComp, uncheckedIO);
  Reset();
else if timeToCheck ≤ 0 then
  Checkpoint();
  Reset();
else
  counter ← counter + 1;
end if
```

Algorithm 3 Reset Pseudo Code

```
timeToCheck ← T
timeToFail ← nextExponential(λ)
uncheckedComp ← 0
uncheckedIO ← 0
```

availability and checkpoint overhead were averaged over the jobs in each run, then over all the runs and compared to the results from the analytical model (see Table 8).

4. RELATED WORK

None of the prior work mentioned below considers, as we do, the effect of resource contention with other components or with checkpointing processes. There is a wealth of publications on analytic modeling of rollback and checkpointing since the work of Young in 1974 [26]. We highlight a few here (see [25] for an extensive bibliography). Gelenbe and colleagues developed comprehensive models for rollback and checkpointing under various assumptions regarding failure time distribution and static versus dynamic checkpointing [11, 13, 12]. Other analytic models can be found in Chandy et. al. [2] and Tantawi and Ruschitzka [23].

Nicola and Spanje [21] study and compare different checkpointing strategies and models in order to select one that adequately represents a realistic system and is yet tractable for analysis. Dimitrov et al. [6] developed analytic models to find a checkpointing schedule that optimizes a job's total processing time under implicit breakdowns, i.e., failures are not detected immediately but a special test has to be performed to detect the failure.

Kishor Trivedi has done substantial work in using performance modeling to assess software reliability and the impacts of software rejuvenation [10]. The work in [17] by Ling et al. uses variational calculus to derive a closed form expression for the optimal checkpointing frequency as a function of the failure rate with the goal of minimizing the total expected cost of checkpointing and recovery.

Daly [4] provides a high order estimate of the optimum checkpoint interval to minimize total application runtime under Poisson failures. Chen and Ren [3] analyze the relationships between checkpoint interval and system availability, task execution time, and task deadline miss probability, for soft real-time applications. Bougeret et al. [1] develop solutions for optimal checkpointing that minimize execution time for sequential and parallel jobs with Poisson failures and use a dynamic programming heuristic for the case of Weibull failures.

Lu et al. [19] derive optimal checkpointing intervals for systems with latent errors, i.e., errors that may go undetected for some time. This assumption is more realistic than that of immediate failure detection assumed by the vast majority of the checkpointing modeling work, including ours. The authors discuss the importance of multiversion checkpoints to achieve acceptable failure coverage. Di et al. [5] present a sophisticated deterministic multilevel checkpoint optimization model in the context of exascale systems with a large number of multi-core nodes. The authors consider a parallel application with many processes running on many cores. Jones et al. [14] use simulation with real workload data to demonstrate the impact of sub-optimal checkpoint intervals on application efficiency in HPC clusters. No analytic model is presented. A comprehensive survey of roll-back recovery protocols in message-passing systems was presented in [7]. Recent studies have leveraged the use of NVRAM as a replacement to disk to store checkpoints. Gao et al [9].

5. CONCLUDING REMARKS

This paper presented two analytic models for assessing the performance of software systems that use rollback and checkpointing to improve their reliability. Differently from previous work, our models allow for a compute node to run many different software components concurrently, each possibly having different resource demand and failure distribution characteristics. Our analytic models compute the average execution time per component, their availability, overhead due to checkpointing and rollback, and relative progress, while taking into account the impact of contention for shared resources such as processors and I/O devices. Simulation and experimental results used to validate the models showed very high accuracy for Poisson failures. Simulation results showed acceptable accuracy for Weibull failures. In the future, we intend to integrate our models into an autonomic controller that can dynamically tweak the various parameters of the model to maximize a utility function of execution time, availability, and overhead.

Acknowledgements

This work was partially supported by the AFOSR grant FA9550-16-1-0030.

6. REFERENCES

[1] M. Bougeret, H. Casanova, M. Rabie, Y. Robert, and F. Vivien. Checkpointing strategies for parallel jobs. In *2011 Intl. Conf. High Performance Computing, Networking, Storage and Analysis (SC)*, pages 1–11. IEEE, 2011.

[2] K. M. Chandy, J. C. Browne, C. W. Dissly, and W. R. Uhrig. Analytic models for rollback and recovery strategies in data base systems. *IEEE Tr. Software Engineering*, (1):100–110, 1975.

[3] N. Chen and S. Ren. Adaptive optimal checkpoint interval and its impact on system's overall quality in soft real-time applications. In *Proc. 2009 ACM Symp. Applied Computing*, pages 1015–1020. ACM, 2009.

Table 7: Comparison between analytic and simulation results for the heterogeneous case.

Experiment	k	R_c			A			O_v		
		simulation	analytic	ϵ	simulation	analytic	ϵ	simulation	analytic	ϵ
1	1	2525.8 ± 30.7	2766.7	9.5%	$36.6 \pm 0.1\%$	35.1%	4.1%	$46.1 \pm 0.1\%$	46.8%	1.5%
	2	857.1 ± 5.4	960.9	12.1%	$54.3 \pm 0.1\%$	50.2%	7.5%	$45.6 \pm 0.1\%$	49.7%	8.9%
	3	2712.5 ± 31.0	3009.2	10.9%	$26.0 \pm 0.1\%$	23.0%	11.3%	$58.2 \pm 0.1\%$	61.1%	5.0%
2	1	2469.9 ± 20.3	2704.1	9.5%	$37.3 \pm 0.1\%$	35.9%	3.8%	$47.2 \pm 0.1\%$	47.9%	1.6%
	2	874.5 ± 4.5	979.0	11.9%	$53.5 \pm 0.1\%$	49.4%	7.6%	$44.9 \pm 0.1\%$	48.6%	8.2%
	3	2648.8 ± 24.3	2922.5	10.3%	$26.8 \pm 0.1\%$	23.9%	10.9%	$59.7 \pm 0.2\%$	62.7%	5.0%
3	1	2078.2 ± 22.8	2295.2	10.4%	$45.9 \pm 0.2\%$	42.4%	7.8%	$26.9 \pm 0.1\%$	28.1%	4.4%
	2	642.0 ± 3.2	735.1	14.5%	$72.3 \pm 0.1\%$	65.5%	9.4%	$26.2 \pm 0.1\%$	32.3%	23.0%
	3	2074.6 ± 26.3	2310.6	11.4%	$35.9 \pm 0.2\%$	30.0%	16.5%	$35.5 \pm 0.2\%$	39.8%	12.3%
4	1	2008.0 ± 17.9	2213.7	10.2%	$47.7 \pm 0.2\%$	44.1%	7.4%	$27.9 \pm 0.1\%$	29.3%	4.8%
	2	839.2 ± 5.6	959.8	14.4%	$60.3 \pm 0.1\%$	50.3%	16.6%	$21.6 \pm 0.1\%$	24.9%	14.9%
	3	1976.9 ± 21.7	2186.7	10.6%	$37.7 \pm 0.2\%$	32.1%	14.8%	$37.9 \pm 0.2\%$	42.2%	11.4%

Table 8: Comparison between analytic and experimentation results for the heterogeneous case.

Experiment	k	R_c			A			O_v		
		experiment	analytic	ϵ	experiment	analytic	ϵ	experiment	analytic	ϵ
1	1	2688.46 ± 88.30	2727.87	1.5%	$37.5\% \pm 0.7\%$	34.3%	8.6%	$45.8\% \pm 1.0\%$	47.2%	3.2%
	2	1014.58 ± 31.51	956.58	5.7%	$51.7\% \pm 0.5\%$	50.4%	2.6%	$48.1\% \pm 0.5\%$	49.5%	2.8%
	3	2730.61 ± 156.16	2763.84	1.2%	$25.5\% \pm 0.6\%$	24.1%	5.6%	$58.8\% \pm 0.9\%$	60.3%	2.5%
2	1	2798.21 ± 139.66	2858.18	2.1%	$37.2\% \pm 0.5\%$	35.7%	4.1%	$47.6\% \pm 0.8\%$	48.0%	0.8%
	2	1011.36 ± 24.87	984.72	2.6%	$51.0\% \pm 0.6\%$	49.6%	2.7%	$47.7\% \pm 0.6\%$	48.6%	2.0%
	3	2736.92 ± 102.02	2929.27	7.0%	$25.8\% \pm 0.5\%$	23.6%	8.6%	$60.2\% \pm 0.7\%$	62.9%	4.5%
3	1	2167.65 ± 93.79	2309.34	6.5%	$47.4\% \pm 1.0\%$	42.4%	10.5%	$25.4\% \pm 0.8\%$	28.0%	10.4%
	2	754.13 ± 25.89	741.69	1.6%	$69.7\% \pm 0.7\%$	66.0%	5.2%	$28.9\% \pm 0.6\%$	31.9%	10.3%
	3	1988.79 ± 65.21	2354.04	18.4%	$38.0\% \pm 0.9\%$	30.6%	19.6%	$33.2\% \pm 1.2\%$	39.5%	18.7%
4	1	2255.41 ± 206.68	2225.69	1.3%	$48.9\% \pm 0.9\%$	44.4%	9.1%	$26.8\% \pm 1.0\%$	29.1%	8.7%
	2	924.12 ± 63.52	967.16	4.7%	$59.9\% \pm 0.7\%$	50.3%	16.0%	$21.5\% \pm 0.6\%$	24.6%	14.3%
	3	1943.90 ± 154.25	2171.24	11.7%	$39.4\% \pm 1.0\%$	31.9%	18.8%	$36.1\% \pm 0.8\%$	42.3%	17.1%

[4] J. T. Daly. A higher order estimate of the optimum checkpoint interval for restart dumps. *Future Generation Computer Systems*, 22(3):303–312, 2006.

[5] S. Di, L. Bautista-Gomez, and F. Cappello. Optimization of a multilevel checkpoint model with uncertain execution scales. In *Proc. Intl. Conf. High Performance Computing, Networking, Storage and Analysis*, pages 907–918. IEEE Press, 2014.

[6] B. Dimitrov, Z. Khalil, N. Kolev, and P. Petrov. On the optimal total processing time using checkpoints. *IEEE Tr. Software Engineering*, 17(5):436, 1991.

[7] E. N. Elnozahy, L. Alvisi, Y.-M. Wang, and D. B. Johnson. A survey of rollback-recovery protocols in message-passing systems. *ACM Computing Surveys (CSUR)*, 34(3):375–408, 2002.

[8] E. Elsayed. *Reliability Engineering*. Number v. 1 in Reliability Engineering. Addison Wesley Longman, 1996.

[9] S. Gao, B. He, and J. Xu. Real-time in-memory checkpointing for future hybrid memory systems. In *Proc. 29th ACM on Intl. Conf. Supercomputing*, pages 263–272. ACM, 2015.

[10] S. Garg, Y. Huang, C. Kintala, and K. S. Trivedi. Minimizing completion time of a program by checkpointing and rejuvenation. In *ACM SIGMETRICS Performance Evaluation Review*, volume 24, pages 252–261. ACM, 1996.

[11] E. Gelenbe. A model of roll-back recovery with multiple checkpoints. In *Proc. 2nd Intl. Conf. Software Engineering*, pages 251–255. IEEE Computer Society Press, 1976.

[12] E. Gelenbe. On the optimum checkpoint interval. *J. ACM*, 26(2):259–270, 1979.

[13] E. Gelenbe and D. Derochette. Performance of rollback recovery systems under intermittent failures. *C. ACM*, 21(6):493–499, 1978.

[14] W. M. Jones, J. T. Daly, and N. DeBardeleben. Application monitoring and checkpointing in hpc: looking towards exascale systems. In *Proc. 50th Annual Southeast Regional Conference*, pages 262–267. ACM, 2012.

[15] L. Kleinrock. *Theory, Volume 1, Queueing Systems*. Wiley-Interscience, 1975.

[16] E. Lazowska, J. Zahorjan, G. Graham, and K. Sevcik. *Quantitative System Performance: Computer System Analysis Using Queueing Network Models*. Prentice Hall, 1984.

[17] Y. Ling, J. Mi, and X. Lin. A variational calculus approach to optimal checkpoint placement. *IEEE Tr. Computers*, 50(7):699–708, 2001.

[18] J. D. Little. A proof for the queuing formula: L= λ w. *Operations Research*, 9(3):383–387, 1961.

[19] G. Lu, Z. Zheng, and A. A. Chien. When is multi-version checkpointing needed? In *Proc. 3rd Wkhp. Fault-tolerance for HPC at extreme scale*, pages 49–56. ACM, 2013.

[20] D. A. Menascé, V. A. Almeida, L. W. Dowdy, and L. Dowdy. *Performance by design: computer capacity planning by example.* Prentice Hall Professional, 2004.

[21] V. F. Nicola and J. M. Van Spanje. Comparative analysis of different models of checkpointing and recovery. *IEEE Tr. Software Engineering*, 16(8):807–821, 1990.

[22] R Core Team. *R: A Language and Environment for Statistical Computing.* R Foundation for Statistical Computing, Vienna, Austria, 2016.

[23] A. N. Tantawi and M. Ruschitzka. Performance analysis of checkpointing strategies. *ACM Tr. Computer Systems (TOCS)*, 2(2):123–144, 1984.

[24] S. Urbanek. *Rserve: Binary R server*, 2013. R package version 1.7-3.

[25] K. Wolter. *Stochastic Models for Fault Tolerance, Restart, Rejuvenation, and Checkpointing.* Springer Verlag, 2010.

[26] J. W. Young. A first order approximation to the optimum checkpoint interval. *C. ACM*, 17(9):530–531, 1974.

[27] W. Zhao. *Building dependable distributed systems.* John Wiley & Sons, 2014.

APPENDIX

A. TRANSITION RATES FOR THE HETEROGENEOUS MODEL

The following notation is used in Algorithm 4 that describes how the transition rates $\mu_{i,j}$ for $i = 0, \cdots, N-1$ and $j = 0, \cdots, N-1$ are computed.

- $n_c(i)$: number of components in the computing mode in state i. This is equal to the number of 1's in $b(i)$.
- $n_x(i)$: number of components in checkpointing mode in state i. This is equal to the number of 0's in $b(i)$.
- $f(b)$: position of the first bit 1 in a binary number b with a single 1 bit. These positions are counted from the left to the right starting at 1. So, $f(000100) = 4$. $f(b)$ can be computed as $n - \log_2 b_{10}$ where n is the number of bits in b and b_{10} is the decimal value that corresponds to b.
- $v_k(b)$: value of the bit at position k (counting from the left) of binary number b. So, $v_4(000100) = 1$.
- $n1(b)$: number of bits equal to 1 in the binary number b.
- $X_k(i)$: throughput of class k ($k = 1, \cdots, n$) for state i.
- $X_{n+k}(i)$: throughput of class $n+k$ ($k = 1, \cdots, n$) for state i.

B. MODEL COMPUTATIONAL EFFORT

The homogeneous model requires solving a 2-class closed MVA model $n+1$ times for populations $(0, n), (1, n-1), \cdots, (n, 0)$. We used exact MVA [20] but we substantially reduced the computational complexity of solving the $n+1$ QNs by storing in a hash table for further reuse the results for sub-populations as they are obtained. As Fig. 7 indicates, the

Algorithm 4 Computation of $\mu_{i,j}$'s

Input: N
for $i = 0 \to N-1$ **do**
  for $j = 0 \to N-1$ **do**
    if i=j **then**
      $\mu_{i,j} = 0$
    else
      /* find the component k that changed mode. */
      /* check different bits between states i and j */
      $bs = b(i) \oplus b(j)$;
      if $n1(bs) = 1$ **then**
        /* There is only one bit of difference */
        $k = f(bs)$;
        if $v_k(b(i)) = 1$ **then**
          $\mu_{i,j} = X_k(i)$ /* comp. k starts checkpointing */
        else
          $\mu_{i,j} = X_{n+k}(i)$ /* comp. k finished checkpointing */
        end if
      else
        $\mu_{i,j} = 0$ /* more than one bit of difference */
      end if
    end if
  end for
end for

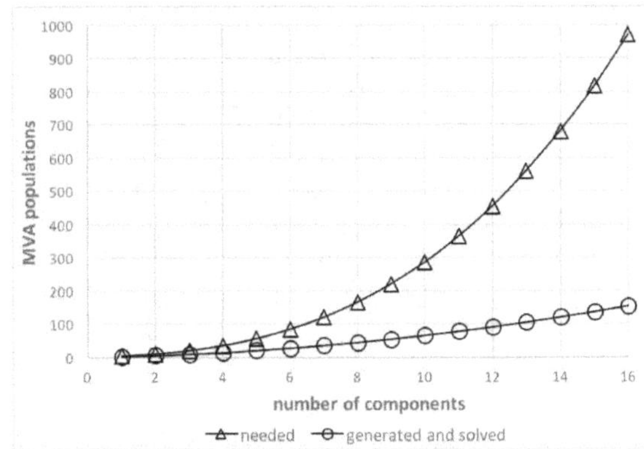

Figure 7: Number of times a QN needs to be evaluated for the homogeneous model under traditional methods and under our approach.

traditional approach requires close to 1,000 evaluations of a QN model for 16 components while the optimized method requires around 160 evaluations.

For the heterogeneous model, all n transition rates out of a given state can be obtained by solving a single multi-class QN. We use approximate MVA (AMVA) [20] instead of exact MVA to speed up the model solution. We need to solve 2^n AMVA QNs with $2n$ classes. But the population of these classes is limited to 1, which reduces the computational complexity of solving each of these QNs.

The heterogeneous model requires the solution of the system of linear equations in Eqs. (24) and (25). For a system of n components, the system of linear equations is a $2^n \times 2^n$ sparse matrix that has $(2^n - 1)(n + 1) + 2^n$ non-zero elements. We leveraged the sparseMatrix library in R [22] by sending requests to an instance of Rserve [24] running on the same machine. It took about 3.5 minutes to solve a system with 13 components on a laptop with a 2.6 GHz Intel Core i5 processor and 8 GB 1600 MHz DDR3.

Practical Implication of Analytical Models for SSD Write Amplification

Changhyun Park Seongjin Lee* Youjip Won Soohan Ahn**
Hanyang University, *Gyeongsang National University, **The University of Seoul
{pch1984|insight|yjwon}@hanyang.ac.kr, sahn@uos.ac.kr

ABSTRACT

A number of analytical models have been proposed to estimate the write amplification of the Flash storage to obtain the expected lifespan. This work is dedicated to examining the practical implication of the four existing analytical models for estimating the write amplification: Coupon Collector, Uniform Distribution, Expected Value and Markov model. Since the models assume uniform random workload in full utilization of an SSD to predict write amplification, they are not applicable in predicting write amplification in general workload. Moreover, the existing models have not been verified with the real SSD. In this work, we compare the write amplification of the models with that of a real SSD. When we use 0.147 as the overprovisioning factor of an SSD while running uniform random workload, the write amplification of Uniform Distribution, Expected Value, Markov model is 3.90, 4.08, and 4.08, respectively. However, write amplification of the real SSD shows 1.19, which is very different from that of the prediction models. Through experiment, we found that write amplification is closely related to the value of overprovisioning factor. To improve the accuracy of existing prediction models, we update the overprovisioning factor to take account of the ratio of a hot file and the utilization of the storage. We also find that by setting the overprovisioning factor to 1.15, we can obtain write amplification of 1.2 which is close to the write amplification of general workload in a real SSD.

Keywords

Solid State Drive, write amplification, overprovisioning

1. INTRODUCTIONS

The characteristics of SSDs such as low power and high performance makes the device attractive for many I/O intensive applications and workloads. However, the devices suffer from write amplification because of the intrinsic nature of the Flash memory. Write amplification pulls down the performance and reduces the life time of the devices. Thus, it is important to analyze the write amplification of an SSD for increasing its efficiency.

An append-only nature of the Flash-based storage entails that update of a Flash page invalidates the existing one. To accommodate the new updates, an SSD occasionally needs to consolidate the valid blocks and resets one or more blocks. A process to reclaim and consolidate such invalidated pages is called garbage collection (GC) [4, 5]. In the process, the garbage collection module first selects a block whose valid pages are to be migrated to a new location and which is to be erased. The selected block is a victim block. Selecting the best victim block is the crux of a successful garbage collection. A number of victim selection policies have been proposed, e.g. greedy [5], FIFO(LRU), d-choice[16], random. To effectively utilize all the Flash blocks in the storage, it is important that the number of erase/write (E/W) cycles are evenly distributed over all Flash blocks in the storage. Flash firmware levels the wear via selecting victims with smaller E/W cycle in garbage collection, *static wear-leveling* [4, 15, 6] or via occasionally switching the pages in two blocks whose difference in E/W cycle reaches a predefined threshold, *dynamic wear-leveling* [4, 7].

The write amplification describes undesirable behavior of an SSD caused by garbage collection and wear-leveling, which generates more volume of writes than the volume requested to the device. It is important to understand the effect of the write amplification of an SSD because the undesirable program operation performed on the SSD reduces the life time of the SSD. This has been the motivation for a number of works to model the write amplification of an SSD. In this work, we analyze and compare four models that are based on greedy garbage collection policy, then measure the accuracy of the models and compare them with the actual write amplification of the real SSD. Finally, we point out the limits of existing works and deduce implication, with which we address future works on the field.

2. WRITE AMPLIFICATION

Let the number of pages in a block be N. In append-only storage, the number of IOs issued to the storage from the host and the actual number of IOs occurred in the storage does not coincide because there is the garbage collection and the wear-leveling operation in the Flash storage. The actual number of IO operations can be higher than user IO requests. We call it as Write Amplification, which, denoted by

*This work has been done while the author was Post-Doctoral Fellow at Hanyang university.

ICPE'17, April 22-26, 2017, L'Aquila, Italy
© 2017 ACM. ISBN 978-1-4503-4404-3/17/04. . . $15.00
DOI: http://dx.doi.org/10.1145/3030207.3030219

Name	Description
A	Write Amplification
N	Given number of pages in a block
N_{vp} N_{ip}	Random variable representing the number of valid/invalid pages in a victim block
$\bar{N}_{vp}$ $\bar{N}_{ip}$	Expectations of N_{vp}/ N_{ip}
p_k	Probability that the victim blocks has k valid pages
T	Total number of physical blocks in an SSD
U	Number of available blocks to a user
ρ	Overprovisioning factor
s	Window size of windowed greedy GC
r	Number of free blocks to trigger greedy GC
p^*	Probability that a single page is invalidated
x^M	Minimum state number for Markov model

Table 1: Variables

A, and define as the average number of actual page programs for a single page program request from the host.

The number of the valid pages in a victim block is denoted as N_{vp}, and the number of invalid pages in a victim block is denoted as $N_{ip} = N - N_{vp}$. The garbage collection copies N_{vp} pages to a free block. The Flash storage becomes to have N_{ip} free pages. Now, we introduce existing mathematical models on the write amplification in [11, 12, 3, 14, 9]. Write amplification is described in Eq. (1), where $\bar{N}_{vp}/\bar{N}_{ip}$ denotes the additional number of programs performed in copying the valid pages.

$$A = \frac{\bar{N}_{vp} + \bar{N}_{ip}}{\bar{N}_{ip}} = \frac{N}{\bar{N}_{ip}} = 1 + \frac{\bar{N}_{vp}}{\bar{N}_{ip}} \quad (1)$$

Here, $\bar{N}_{vp}/\bar{N}_{ip}$ is referred to as the write amplification factor [11, 12], denoted by A_f. Letting T and U represent the total number of available blocks in an SSD and the available blocks visible from the host respectively, the overprovisioning factor, ρ, is defined as follows [3, 14]:

$$\rho = \frac{T - U}{U} \quad (2)$$

3. WRITE AMPLIFICATION ANALYSIS MODELS

We examine four analytical models: Coupon Collector [11], Uniform Distribution [3], Expected Value [14], and Markov [9] model. These are named based upon how they estimate the number of valid pages in the victim block.

Note that we use ρ to unify overprovisioning factor and spare factor used in all four models. The summary of variables used in this paper are described in Table 1.

3.1 Coupon Collector Model

To describe and identify the work done by Hu et al. [11], we named the work as Coupon Collector model. This model uses windowed greedy garbage collection policy with window size of s. The garbage collection process selects a victim block that has the least number of valid pages within $0 \sim (s-1)$ blocks in the occupied block queue.

The basic idea of Coupon Collector model is simple and straight forward. Let N_{vp}^{cc} and p_k^{cc} be the number of valid pages in the victim block and the probability that it has k valid pages, respectively. In Coupon Collector model, the expected number of valid pages, denoted by $\bar{N}_{vp}^{cc}$, is represented as $\bar{N}_{vp}^{cc} = \sum_{k=0}^{N} k p_k^{cc}$. For short, the write amplification in Coupon Collector model, denoted by A^{cc} can be computed as in Eq. 3.

$$A^{cc} = \frac{N}{N - \sum_{k=0}^{N} k p_k^{cc}} \quad (3)$$

The key ingredient of Coupon Collector model is p_k^{cc}. In computing the probability that the victim block contains k valid pages $p_{x_{cc}}^*$, Coupon Collector model needs to enumerate all combinations of the number of valid pages in the victim block and then find the cases where the largest number of valid pages in the blocks is k. The computational complexity to obtain A^{cc} is combinatorially increases with the number of pages in a block.

3.2 Uniform Distribution Model

Greedy Garbage Collection selects a block with the least number of valid pages as the victim block. Agarwal et al. [3] used Uniform Distribution to approximate the number of valid pages in a block and exploit them in finding the write amplification. We named the model proposed by Agarwal et al. [3] as Uniform Distribution model.

Let N_{vp}^{ud} be the number of valid pages in the victim block. By definition, the number of valid pages in the other blocks contain more than or equal to N_{vp}^{ud} number of valid pages. Let β_k be the probability that there are k valid pages in the other blocks given N_{vp}^{ud}. In Uniform distribution model, they assume that $\beta_{N_{vp}^{ud}} = \beta_{N_{vp}^{ud}+1} = \cdots = \beta_N$.

To find the probability of a valid page, it simply uses the ratio of number of pages in use and the total number of physical pages. It exploits the probability to find the distribution of valid pages, then it approximates the distribution with uniform distribution and predicts the write amplification.

$$A_{ud} = \frac{1}{2}\left(\frac{1+\rho}{\rho}\right) \quad (4)$$

As the Eq. (4) shows, the write amplification is solely dependent on ρ, which exhibits the simplest form among the four models but naturally it fails to captures the essence of the behavior because valid pages in the real SSDs do not follow uniform distribution.

3.3 Expected Value Model

Unlike the other models which are based on the valid pages in a victim block of greedy garbage collection to find the write amplification, the model proposed by Luojie et al. [14] is based on the number of invalid pages in a victim block. They use the invalid pages in a victim block as a random variable and finds the average that is the expected value of the random variable to predict the write amplification; thus, we name the model as Expected Value model.

This model assumes that all the pages in a victim block is independently invalidated with the probability of p^*. Then, the random variable N_{ip}^{ev} representing the number of invalid pages in the victim block is binomial distributed with parameters N and p^*. Then, its expectation $\bar{N}_{ip}^{ev}$ satisfies $\bar{N}_{ip}^{ev} = Np^*$. Hence, once we find p^*, we can compute $\bar{N}_{ip}^{ev}$.

We get Eq. (5) as the final equation for the write amplification, where W() denotes Lambert W function [8].

$$A_{ev} = \frac{-1-\rho}{-1-\rho-\mathrm{W}((-1-\rho)e^{-1-\rho})} \quad (5)$$

3.4 Markov Model

Desnoyers [9] further developed the earlier works and analyzed with various assumptions. Although it considers LRU cleaning and non-uniform workload, we only describe uniform workload distribution case to compare with the other models.

The model proposed by Desnoyers [9] predicts the write amplification by representing the distribution of valid pages in a block with Markov model. We used Markov model to represent the work.

The state in the model is defined as the number of valid pages in a block. It is assumed that the state i makes transition only to $i-1$ with probability of $\frac{i}{UN}$. Since this approach uses greedy garbage collection, under the assumption that x^M is the minimum value of the states of the blocks, the victim block has state $x^M - 1$. Eq. (6) is the final equation to get the write amplification.

$$A^{mar} = \frac{N}{N-(x^M-1)} \quad (6)$$

$$x^M = \frac{1}{2} - \frac{N}{\rho+1}\mathrm{W}\left(-(1+\frac{1}{2N})(\rho+1)e^{-(1+\frac{1}{2N})(\rho+1)}\right) \quad (7)$$

4. EXPERIMENTS

4.1 Experiment Setup

The environment used to compare the four models (Coupon Collector, Uniform Distribution, Expected Value, and Markov model) is described in Table 2. We first measure the write amplification using the four models, then measure the time complexity of running the model. We used MATLAB[1] running on Windows 7 64bit in Intel core i7-3820 machine with 24GB of main memory to compare the write amplification and the time complexity of analytical models.

Environment	Prediction	Measurement
CPU	Intel core i7-3820	Intel core i5-2500k
Main memory	24GB	12GB
OS	Windows 7 64bit	Ubuntu 14.04 64bit
Storage	-	Samsung 843TN

Table 2: Environments to Compare with Models and with Real SSD

Parameter	Specification
Capacity	240 GByte
Overprovisioning Capacity	23.4 GByte
Page size(read/write unit)	8 KByte
Superblock size(erase unit)	256 MByte

Table 3: SSD Specification

We compare the write amplifications of the models with the actual one of a Samsung 843TN SSD. The environment is described in the right hand side of Table 2. We modified the firmware of the device to measure the volume of requested write operations and the actual volume of data programmed on the device. We used the measurements of the real SSD to calculate the write amplification. The specification of the SSD used in this paper is described in Table 3. NAND Flash memories of the SSD used in the paper are placed in multi-channel and multi-way configuration. Unlike other SSDs, the unit of erase operation is not a block, it operates on unit of superblock which is a set blocks. The superblock is a set of a block on each NAND Flash in all channels and ways. In such configuration, channels and ways do not have any effect on write amplification because it operates as if one-channel one-way configuration.

[1]Version: 7.11.0.584(R2010b)

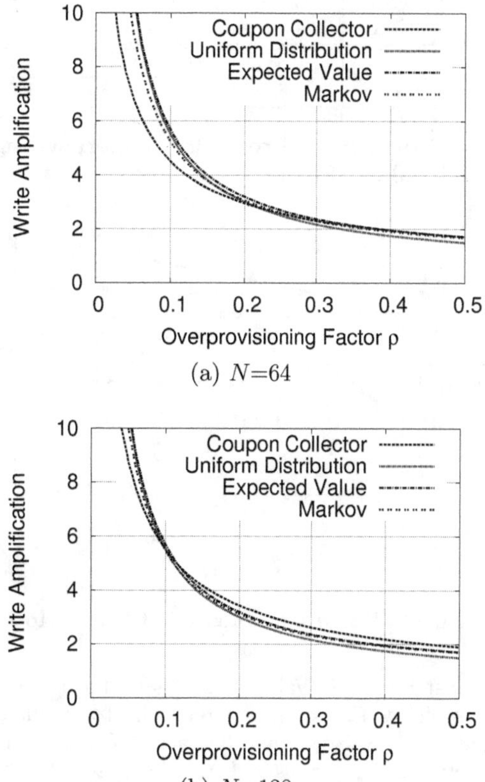

(a) N=64

(b) N=128

Figure 1: Write Amplification Prediction with Respect to Overprovisioning Factor ρ

4.2 Write Amplification

Fig. 1 illustrates the predicted write amplification with respect to overprovisioning factor ρ of Coupon Collector, Uniform Distribution, Expected Value, and Markov Model. Fig. 1(a) and Fig. 1(b) shows the predicted write amplification when the number of pages in a block N is 64 and 128, respectively.

The result shows that the total number of pages in a block is not too important in the write amplification. Uniform distribution and Expected Value model does not include N in their final model and have the same write amplification. The write amplification in Markov model increased slightly as N increased. Only the write amplification of Coupon Collector model increased noticeably as N increased.

Table 4 shows the normalized predicted write amplifica-

N	Coupon Collector	Uniform Distribution	Expected Value	Markov
64	94%	88%	100%	96%
128	105%	88%	100%	97%

Table 4: Normalized Prediction Difference against Expected Value Model

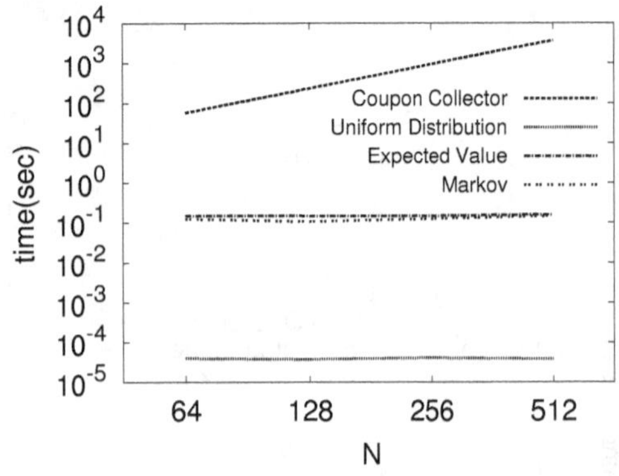

Figure 2: Time Complexity of Each Model

tion against Expected Value. It shows that Uniform distribution is off by 12% and Coupon Collector model differs by about $5 \sim 6\%$. Note the difference of Coupon Collector model between the $N = 64$ and $N = 128$ case, it is 6% lower when the total number of pages in a block is 64 and 5% larger when it has 128 pages. The result of Markov model is the closest to the result of Expected value model, it is about $3 \sim 4\%$ lower.

4.3 Time Complexity

Figure 2 shows the time spent to complete the calculation of the prediction models. We used MATLAB to measure the average time to calculate the write amplification at different overprovisioning factors. We equally divided the overprovisioning factor into 100 sections $\rho = 0.01, 0.02, ..., 0.99, 1$.

The time spent to measure the write amplification in Uniform distribution is about $4 \cdot 10^{-5}$ seconds. It shows that N has almost no effect on the time, except for Coupon Collector model. To compute the write amplification in Coupon Collector model, it takes 58 seconds, 233 seconds, 936 seconds, and 3690 seconds with $N = 64$, $N = 128$, $N = 256$, and $N = 512$, respectively. The time multiplies by factor of four every time the number of pages in a block doubles. It is because the model makes use of binomial distribution and factorial operation on N. As the number of pages in a block is increasing in SSDs, it seems Coupon Collector model is no longer feasible in practice. This is why we excluded Coupon Collector model from the comparion of this paper.

4.4 Comparison with Empirical Result

In order to have better understanding of each model and the effectiveness of the models in real life, we measured the write amplification of an SSD and compared it with the models. We format the device with EXT4 file system. We generate 8 KB write workload with direct IO to bypass the file system page cache and write immediately to the device. We also used uniform random distribution to touch all LBA addresses.

We set ρ as 0.28 which is the overprovisioning factor used

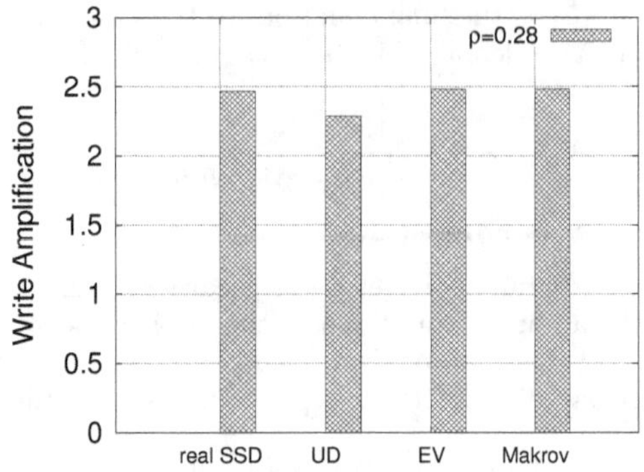

Figure 3: Write Amplification: SSD Vs. Models (N=32768)

in commercial enterprise SSDs [1, 2]. To set the overprovisioning factor on the SSD described in Table 3, we fill the device with cold data such that overprovisioning factor becomes 0.28. Note that, since models uses greedy garbage collection, the cold data are not selected as a victim block. We use this property to make overprovisioning factor to 0.28. We created cold data with the size of 102.1GB and 112.9GB of hot data. We generate 8KB uniform random writes on the hot data area. When the hot data is fully updated, we count it as one iteration, and repeated 15 iterations.

Fig. 3 compares the write amplification of the SSD, Uniform Distribution (UD), Expected Value (EV), and Markov model, when overprovisioning factor ρ is set to 0.28 and the number of pages N. in a block is set to 32768. Coupon Collector model is not shown in the graph because it took too more than a day to compute an iteration.

The result shows that write amplification of the SSD is 2.466. Note that Expected Value and Markov model shows write amplification of 2.481. The prediction based on Expected Value and Markov model is about 0.6% lower than the actual write amplification in the SSD. Uniform distribution model shows difference of about 8%.

4.5 Write Amplification of a General Case

We performed experiments on an real SSD to compare the accuracies of the models. However, the assumption of each model on the workload is not realistic. The models assume that the size of a hot file and the utilization is as large as the size of the SSD. In this section, we run set of experiments to understand limits of the models and the effect of the utilization and the size of a file on write amplification.

We created EXT4 file system on the target SSD and created a cold and hot file. We vary the utilization from 60% to 90% of the file system partition with the size of 215 GB. We used uniform random, sequential, sequential+random workload on the hot file, and measured the write amplification of each workload. The ratio of sequential and random in the sequential+random workload is set to 1:1. We vary the size of the hot file from 10% to 40%, and the cold file occupies the rest of the file system up to specified utilization ratio.

The result of the experiment is shown in Fig. 4. It shows that the measured write amplification of number of workloads are less than 1.2 which is very different from the predicted values of the models. When the size of the hot file is small with utilization of 60% and 70% the write amplification is slightly over 1. In the case of 90% of utilization and

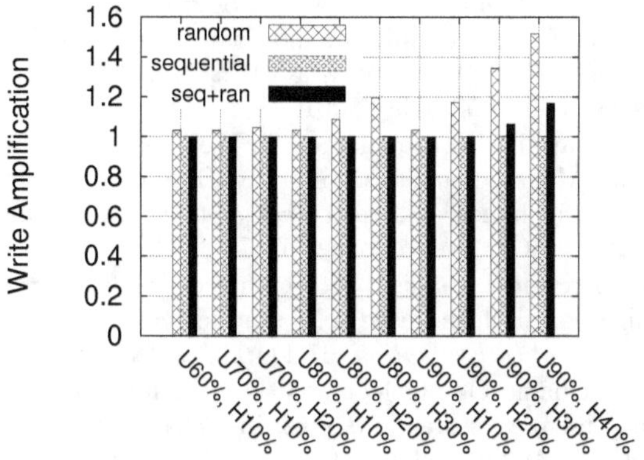

Figure 4: Write amplification by SSD utilization (U:utilization, H:hot file ratio, 10%=21.5GB)

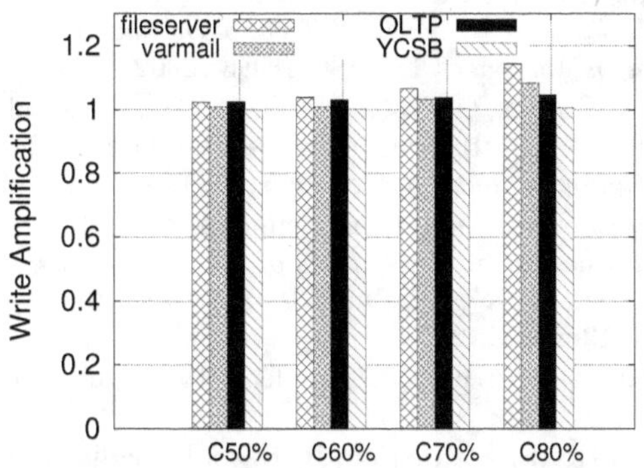

Figure 5: Write amplification of benchmarks (C:Cold file ratio, 10%=21.5GB)

the size of a hot file is set to 30% and 40% of the partition size, the write amplification of random workload is about 1.341 and 1.518, respectively.

Fig. 5 shows the write amplification of an SSD with respect to utilization. We use fileserver workload in Filebench, Varmail workload, OLTP with Sysbench, and Cassandra workload with YCSB. The configurations for the benchmarks are shown in Table 5. The result shows that the write amplification increases as the utilization increases, but the write amplification does not exceed 1.2.

The available storage capacity after formatting the SSD with EXT4 is 215GB. We counted the number of blocks U in given capacity (215GB) to and we use U to calculate the overprovisioning factor ρ and get 0.147. When $\rho = 0.147$ is used in Expected Value and Markov Model, the predicted write amplification is 4.08 showing great difference compared to the measured write amplification. The two models are limited in predicting the write amplification of an SSD when the utilization and the workload pattern varies.

		file size	files	threads
Filebench	Fileserver	256KB	80K	50
	Varmail	16KB	720K	16
		records	requests	threads
Sysbench	OLTP	45M	1M	8
YCSB	Cassandra	6M	60M	10

Table 5: Workloads of benchmarks

$$\bar{\rho} = \frac{(1 - R_{util}) + \rho}{R_{hot}} \quad (8)$$

By replacing the ρ in existing models with $\bar{\rho}$, we can more accurately predict the write amplification of an SSD while varying the utilization (R_{util}) and the ratio of the hot file (R_{hot}). For example, when the utilization and the ratio of a hot file is 90% and 30%, respectively, then we get $\bar{\rho} = \frac{(1-0.9)+0.147}{0.3} \approx 0.823$. By applying $\bar{\rho} = 0.823$ on Expected Value and Markov model, we get write amplification of 1.349 which is very close to measured write amplification of 1.341.

Utilization	80%	90%	90%	90%
Hot ratio	30%	20%	30%	40%
$\bar{\rho}$	1.16	1.24	0.82	0.62
real SSD	1.19	1.17	1.34	1.52
EV	1.19	1.17	1.35	1.53
Markov	1.19	1.17	1.35	1.53

Table 6: write amplification by $\bar{\rho}$

Except for uniform random workloads, the measured write amplification of an SSD with general workloads is less than 1.2. We can set $\rho > 1.15$ to get the write amplification of 1.2 in Expected Value and Markov Model for general workloads.

5. RELATED WORK

As SSDs are becoming more prevalent, many are trying to analyze and analytically predict the behavior of SSDs. There are some works [11, 12] that exploits windowed greedy garbage collection algorithm with assumption the workload is uniformly or non-uniformly spread across the given storage space to find the write amplification. Agarwal et al. [3] and Luojie et al. [14] uses greedy garbage collection under uniform workload to analyze the write amplification and they also investigate the relationship between the write amplification and the size of an SSD. Desnoyer [9] also provides a model to find the write amplification in greedy and LRU (FIFO) garbage collection algorithm. His work takes a step further to analyze it under non-uniform workload to find the write amplification in real-world workload.

While most works are based on greedy garbage collection, Houdt [17] set out to analyze the write amplification with an SSD running a random garbage collection algorithm. He assumed *d*-Choices garbage collection and finds the relationship between *d* and write amplification. Li et al. [13] analyzes the effect of locality of workload in garbage collection algorithm. After analyzing the cost of cleaning and wear-leveling, they show that exploiting the locality increases the efficiency of the garbage collection.

6. CONCLUSION AND FUTURE WORK

As SSDs are being widely adopted by both users and storage system vendors for performance reasons, having thorough understanding of the write amplification of SSDs are becoming more important. It is mostly because the write amplification is closely related to the life time of the SSDs. A few have analyzed the write amplification, but most of them are based on simulation or an analytical model of the behavior. A problem in understanding or building on top of the previous works is that notations, basis, and assumptions are not the same to each other. In this work, we first analyze the existing works in depth to not only address the pros and cons of the works but also to re-evaluate the models with same standards and assumptions. Secondly, we point out that the time complexity of a model is as important as the accuracy of the model. For example, Coupon Collector model cannot be used in prediction because as the number of pages in a block increases with factor of two the time complexity increases with factor four. Finally, we evaluated the write amplification of a real SSD and compared it with analytical models, which previous works have failed to show. The result shows that Expected Value and Markov model show the most closest resemblance to the actual write amplification of an SSD with difference of only 0.6% in uniform random case. The accuracy of Uniform Distribution is much lower than the two, it is off by about 8%. The experiment shows that the write amplification of models varies greatly depending on the utilization and hot file ratio in the SSD. Use of models available in the field have to be considered carefully because they are not accurate in representing the write amplification of general use cases.

All the models lack practicality in real world because they are based on the assumption that workload follows uniform distribution and exploit a form of greedy garbage collection. Two of the models, Coupon Collector and Markov model, adopts the notion of hotness in to their models to consider the case with non-uniform traffic. If their non-uniform traffic approaches are to have any practical values, wear-leveling of the SSDs must be considered, but their models do not take the wear-leveling into account. Greedy garbage collection is not the only garbage collection algorithms, yet all the models are based on the primitive garbage collection algorithms. Since the write amplification is heavily dependent on the garbage collection policy, we need more in-depth studies on the write amplification with different garbage collection algorithms. Here are suggestions for future work. Since all of the given models are based on a single storage system, uniform workload distribution, and primitive garbage collection algorithm, this field of study asks for better model that explains parallelism of SSD, wear-leveling, sophisticated garbage collection policy, and real world workload. The study of write amplification of SSDs needs to broaden its focus on addressing the life span of SSDs as a function of workload, wear-leveling, and the write amplification.

7. ACKNOWLEDGEMENT

This work is supported by IT R&D program MKE/KEIT (No. 10041608, Embedded System Software for New-memory based Smart Device), the ICT R&D program of MSIP/IITP (R7117-16-0232, Development of extreme I/O storage technology for 32Gbps data services), the BK21 plus program through the National Research Foundation (NRF) funded by the Ministry of Education of Korea, and the Basic Science Research Program of the National Research Foundation of Korea (NRF-2015R1D1A1A09059663).

8. REFERENCES

[1] Understanding over-provisioning. Technical report, Kingston Technology, 2013.

[2] Over-provisioning: Maximize the lifetime and performance of your ssd with small effect to earn more. Technical report, Samsung Electronics Co., 2014.

[3] R. Agarwal and M. Marrow. A closed-form expression for write amplification in nand flash. In *Proceedings of GLOBECOM Workshops (GC Wkshps), 2010 IEEE*, pages 1846–1850. IEEE, 2010.

[4] N. Agrawal, V. Prabhakaran, T. Wobber, J. D. Davis, M. S. Manasse, and R. Panigrahy. Design tradeoffs for ssd performance. In *Proceedings of USENIX Annual Technical Conference*, pages 57–70, 2008.

[5] W. Bux and I. Iliadis. Performance of greedy garbage collection in flash-based solid-state drives. *Performance Evaluation*, 67(11):1172–1186, 2010.

[6] L.-P. Chang. On efficient wear leveling for large-scale flash-memory storage systems. In *Proceedings of the 2007 ACM symposium on Applied computing*, pages 1126–1130. ACM, 2007.

[7] L.-P. Chang and T.-W. Kuo. An adaptive striping architecture for flash memory storage systems of embedded systems. In *Proceedings of 8th IEEE Real-Time and Embedded Technology and Applications Symposium*, pages 187–196. IEEE, 2002.

[8] R. M. Corless, G. H. Gonnet, D. E. Hare, D. J. Jeffrey, and D. E. Knuth. On the lambertw function. *Advances in Computational mathematics*, 5(1):329–359, 1996.

[9] P. Desnoyers. Analytic modeling of ssd write performance. In *Proceedings of the 5th Annual International Systems and Storage Conference*, page 12. ACM, 2012.

[10] P. Erdős. On a classical problem of probability theory. 1961.

[11] X.-Y. Hu, E. Eleftheriou, R. Haas, I. Iliadis, and R. Pletka. Write amplification analysis in flash-based solid state drives. In *Proceedings of SYSTOR 2009: The Israeli Experimental Systems Conference*, page 10. ACM, 2009.

[12] X.-Y. Hu and R. Haas. The fundamental limit of flash random write performance: Understanding, analysis and performance modelling. Technical report, IBM Research Report, 2010/3/31, 2010.

[13] Y. Li, P. P. Lee, J. Lui, and Y. Xu. Impact of data locality on garbage collection in ssds: a general analytical study. In *Proceedings of the 6th ACM/SPEC International Conference on Performance Engineering*, pages 305–315. ACM, 2015.

[14] X. Luojie and B. M. Kurkoski. An improved analytic expression for write amplification in nand flash. In *Proceedings of Computing, Networking and Communications (ICNC), 2012 International Conference on*, pages 497–501. IEEE, 2012.

[15] D. Shmidt. Trueffs wear-leveling mechanism. *Technical Note (TN-DOC-017), M-Systems Flash Disk Pioneers, May*, 20(2002):1–4, 2002.

[16] B. Van Houdt. Analysis of the d-choices garbage collection algorithm with memory in flash-based ssds. In *Proceedings of the 7th International Conference on Performance Evaluation Methodologies and Tools*, pages 11–19. ICST, 2013.

[17] B. Van Houdt. A mean field model for a class of garbage collection algorithms in flash-based solid state drives. In *Proceedings of the ACM SIGMETRICS/international conference on Measurement and modeling of computer systems*, pages 191–202. ACM, 2013.

Schedulability and Memory Interference Analysis of Multicore Preemptive Real-time Systems*

Jalil Boudjadar, Simin Nadjm-Tehrani
Department of Computer and Information Science
Linköping University, Sweden

ABSTRACT

Today's embedded systems demand increasing computing power to accommodate the ever-growing software functionality. Automotive and avionic systems aim to leverage the high performance capabilities of multicore platforms, but are faced with challenges with respect to temporal predictability. Multicore designers have achieved much progress on improvement of memory-dependent performance in caching systems and shared memories in general. However, having applications running simultaneously and requesting the access to the shared memories concurrently leads to interference. The performance unpredictability resulting from interference at any shared memory level may lead to violation of the timing properties in safety-critical real-time systems. In this paper, we introduce a formal analysis framework for the schedulability and memory interference of multicore systems with shared caches and DRAM. We build a multicore system model with a fine grained application behavior given in terms of periodic preemptible tasks, described with explicit read and write access numbers for shared caches and DRAM. We also provide a method to analyze and recommend candidates for task-to-core reallocation with the goal to find schedulable configurations if a given system is not schedulable. Our model-based framework is realized using Uppaal and has been used to analyze a case study.

Keywords

Schedulability, memory interference, processor utilization, multicore systems, task migration, model checking.

1. INTRODUCTION

Motivated by the need of high processing capacity and the decreasing cost of electronics, multicore platforms are finding their way into safety-critical embedded systems. Following the same trend as automotive industry, avionic system developers are considering the use of multicore platforms to leverage the potential for higher performance, and reduce the weight of on-board computing equipment. This is achieved by integrating different subsystems, potentially provided by different vendors, to enable incremental Design and Certification (iD&C) [29], recommended by the standard Integrated Modular Avionics (IMA) architecture [24]. In contrast to the classical federated architecture, IMA supports functions related to different subsystems to share the same computing platform with an efficient use of the hardware. Such a support is implemented using partitioning.

Partitioning [10] amounts to isolating, in space and time, the system processes to make the complexity and maintenance manageable. Moreover, it prevents propagating failure conditions from one system component to another, particularly from lower criticality to highly critical components, thereby enforcing fault containment. Multicore platforms can provide enormously larger processing capacity compared to the classical single core platforms so that more software-intensive systems can be deployed. However, the underlying complexity and interference to access shared resources may lead to lack of guarantees on schedulability and predictability.

Focusing on the temporal partitioning, in single core platforms the estimation of worst case execution time (WCET) is based on the time spent by the longest execution path of a process while assuming perfect memory access i.e. the shared memory is immediately available whenever an access request occurs. For systems with fixed priorities assigned at a global level, a separate term (blocking delay) is added for potential contention on shared resources. In multicore settings, where different applications running concurrently on different cores compete for the access to shared memories, the combination of local cache misses and interference delay for accessing a shared memory can be large and highly variable depending on the platform architecture and the number of parallel access requests. Interference represents a big challenge for the predictability of real-time embedded systems, therefore it must be considered at the design and integration stages.

In recent years, some progress on WCET and memory interference analysis of multicore systems has been achieved [15, 20, 8, 2, 7, 31]. In this paper, we provide a model-based framework for formal analysis of schedulability and memory interference of real-time applications running on multicore platforms. Our framework enables modular description of applications and platforms where models are described sep-

*This work has been supported by the NFFP6 project 2014-00917, and financed by Swedish Innovation Agency (Vinnova).

ICPE'17, April 22-26, 2017, L'Aquila, Italy
© 2017 ACM. ISBN 978-1-4503-4404-3/17/04...$15.00
DOI: http://dx.doi.org/10.1145/3030207.3030233

arately, thus different mappings of an application to different platforms can be studied as a state space exploration.

The platform consists of a set of cores each with a local scheduler and a local cache. The cores share the cache level 2 (L2) and Dynamic Random Access Memory (DRAM). We use the cache coloring policy [12] to arbitrate the concurrent access requests to L2. In addition, we adopt the policy First Ready-First Come First Serve (FR-FCFS) [22, 11] commonly used by modern COTS-based memory controllers to schedule the DRAM access requests. A schematic version of the policy is modelled in section 5.2.2 (see Algorithm 1).

The application model is given by a set of periodic preemptive tasks described with a fine grained behavior. Besides classical scheduling parameters, the description of each task includes the worst case resource access numbers (WCRA) [20, 6] stating how many times the task accesses to each shared memory for both read and write patterns. We distinguish between read and write actions to shared memories as read actions are blocking for cores, while write actions are not blocking and can be performed using dedicated buffers. To make the system behavior more realistic, we spread out the access requests to L2 and DRAM non-deterministically during tasks execution rather than using dedicated phases [25, 31]. This is motivated by the fact that a task execution, and thereby the issue time of data requests, may vary from one period to another following the changes in the computation environment.

Our model-based framework has been realized using Uppaal [3]. We use the symbolic model checker of Uppaal to analyze the system schedulability whereas interference-sensitive WCET (isWCET) and core utilization are analyzed using statistical model checking. By statistical we mean simulating different executions but not exploring the whole state space. We also propose an approach to support the distribution of tasks among cores so that the whole system becomes schedulable. This is done in two steps:

1. we analyze the system schedulability according to a given allocation of tasks to cores. If the system is not schedulable, we proceed to step (2).

2. we perform an analysis of core utilizations and average interference delay per access request to shared memories, and recommend a redistribution of the workload from overloaded cores to relatively less loaded ones by migrating tasks, then redo process (1) with the new recommended mapping.

The analysis process ends if a configuration is schedulable or system is deemed not schedulable despite some load distribution within the given constraints.

To sum up, the contributions of this paper are as follows:

- Model-based framework for modular description of multicore platforms and applications.
- Rigorous analysis of schedulability using symbolic model-checking.
- Statistical analysis of performance: core utilizations and memory interference.
- Method for reallocation of tasks to cores upon non-schedulability of a given configuration.

The rest of the paper is organized as follows: Section 2 reviews the related work. Section 3 describes the necessary background. Section 4 provides an overview of our work. Section 5 presents the Uppaal models of framework, whereas Section 6 describes schedulability, isWCET analysis and method for potential reallocation of tasks. In Section 7, a small case study is presented to show preliminary evidence of the feasibility and efficacy of the framework. Finally, Section 8 concludes the paper.

2. RELATED WORK

The analysis of schedulability and memory interference of multicore real-time systems is an active research area and can be categorized into 2 directions: computing DRAM sensitive WCETs [33, 20, 11, 2] and bounding the DRAM interference delays [17, 8, 27]. The common element of the different analysis settings is: a) measuring the WCET of each task in isolation on a single core; b) calculating the interference time caused by the access to the shared resource, e.g DRAM. The first element can be performed using dedicated measurement tools like SWEET [15] and Heptane [21], whereas the interference delays are obtained either by static analysis or using different theories (as described below).

Schranzhofer *et al.* [25] introduce an analytical approach to analyze the worst case response time of a task set running on a multicore platform. Each task runs over different dedicated phases like acquisition, execution and replication. The execution of a task takes place in a sequence of non-preemptible superblocks. The shared resource (DRAM) access requests occur only during the acquisition and replication phases of each superblock. The use of static predefined schedules among the superblocks of different tasks results in a static runtime where the analysis results are predictable.

In a similar way, Nowotsch *et al.* [20] present a theory to compute and bound interference-sensitive WCET (isWCET) of processes running on a multicore platform with a shared DRAM memory. Each process is assigned a certain share of DRAM capacity. The experiment results in [20] show that the estimated WCET values are an overestimation of the observed ones. Such an overestimation enormously affects the isWCET. In both of the above works [25, 20], the static allocation of DRAM using Time Division Multiple Access (TDMA) policy lowers the complexity but it leads to a poor utilization of DRAM.

Other authors [33, 11] introduce analytical frameworks to calculate memory interference delays in multicore systems. The interference of the request under analysis is calculated based on inter and intra-bank interference as well as *row-opening* (loading data from a row to a row-buffer) and *precharge* (moving data back from a row-buffer to a row). Each of these elements is calculated separately. According to the analysis results, the higher the number of sharing cores the longer the interference will be. Since each request is analyzed separately, a relevant question is how these analytical frameworks deal with memory-intensive systems where each process performs thousands of memory requests.

Madsen *et al.* [18] introduce a model-based framework to study the impact of execution platforms on schedulability. The platform model is given by a set of processing elements, each of which consists of a local memory (cache), a scheduler and a processor. However, not considering shared memories may lead to an underestimation of the workload because, in practice, the delays resulting from the access to shared cache and DRAM enormously impact the response time of tasks.

Lv *et al.* [17] combine the abstract interpretation of software systems running on multicore platforms with model checking to calculate the isWCET. The abstract interpretation aims to obtain the local cache behavior of a program running on a given core in order to capture the precise timing information when the program accesses DRAM (cache miss). However, characterizing each program instruction with an execution time and an access pattern (hit/miss) is not considered as feasible for a design phase of systems. The authors approach would require a rather expensive analysis of the binary code. Instead, we use a granularity at task level.

Gustavsson *et al.* [8] investigate a method based on model checking to calculate the WCETs of programs running on multicore platforms. The authors consider both local and shared caches as well as DRAM. The miss/hit of local and shared caches is non-deterministic. The WCET estimate is obtained using a binary search, which could be expensive if the initial WCET estimates are far away from the final values. Our work aligns with this but we use statistical model checking, where the analysis process runs once and performs the evaluation of thousands of different executions, rather than repeating the binary analysis process manually.

Subramanian *et al.* [27] develop a scheduling scheme (MISE-Fair) to minimize the maximum slowdown of applications running on multicore platforms. Application slowdown is the delay experienced by the application due to the wait to access shared resources compared to the case when the application runs alone on the platform. In essence, MISE-Fair estimates the slowdown of each application and redistributes the memory bandwidth to reduce the slowdown of the most slowed-down applications. However, the minimization of DRAM-related slowdown of tasks may impact the scheduling at cores level.

In some of these papers, the authors calculate the isWCET of tasks running on a given multicore platform, then apply appropriate analysis to check the schedulability. This means that the estimated isWCET cannot be used to check the schedulability if the application tasks run on a different platform. So far, for each new platform the isWCETs need to be calculated using the platform description and one needs to rerun the appropriate schedulability analysis process. In our work, we combine the analysis processes so that for a given platform we check whether the application tasks will be schedulable or not.

Compared to the state of the art, our framework enables modular description of applications and platforms with a flexible mapping. The application is given by a fine grained behavior including explicit numbers of read and write requests to each shared memory, whereas the platform includes a set of processing cores and a hierarchy of shared memories. Each of these elements is separately modeled by a template, i.e. a parameterized state-transition behavior. To make the application model more realistic, we spread out the access requests to L2 and DRAM non-deterministically during task execution rather than using dedicated phases. System configurations (consisting in an application instance, a platform instance and a mapping of the application to the platform) can be created by just providing template parameters, so that design space exploration can be performed. We use model checking to analyze schedulability and performance, in terms of memory interference and core utilization. Moreover, a novelty of our work is the introduction a method for reallocate tasks to cores upon non-schedulability based on performance metrics (core utilization, average interference delay per access request).

3. BACKGROUND

Before diving into the description of our contribution, we introduce the scheduling fundamentals of shared resources in multicore platforms: cores, shared caches and DRAM.

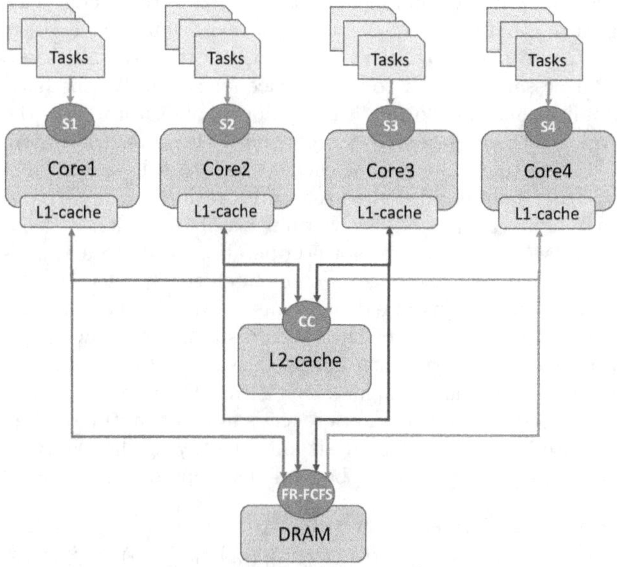

Figure 1: Simplified multicore system architecture.

The overall system architecture we consider in this paper is depicted in Figure. 1, where *cc* is the cache coloring policy and s_i are CPU scheduling policies.

3.1 Core Level Scheduling

To leverage the processing performance of a computing system, a processing unit (core in our context) can be assigned more than one task, only one task running at any point in time. The arbitration between the different task executions is performed according to a scheduling policy.

Basically, a scheduling policy determines, at any point in time, which task from the ready queue must execute first and whether a given task should be preempted by another. The most commonly used scheduling algorithms are Earliest Deadline First (EDF), Fixed Priority Scheduling (FPS) and Rate Monotonic (RM). The key factor in selecting a task from ready queue can be priority, remaining execution time, etc.

Another recent alternative to schedule memory intensive application tasks is the use of a memory-centric policy [31, 30], where tasks are sorted in the queue according to a decreasing order of their WCRA (numbers of memory accesses). In our setting, we adopt FIFO, FPS and EDF as scheduling policies for the individual cores, but the method could easily be adapted to a memory-centric one.

3.2 Shared Cache Scheduling

In order to enhance the processing performance of multicore platforms, some of modern multicore processors [1] consider a shared cache level (L2) in addition to private caches (L1). The primary goal of sharing a cache between different cores is to reduce the access requests to the main memory DRAM, and by that shorten the DRAM interference time since the interference time is strongly correlated to the number of access requests [20].

Cache coloring policy [12, 32] is an algorithm to control the access to the shared L2 cache. It has been introduced to aid performance optimization where physical memory pages are mapped to cache pages, in contrast with old caching systems where virtual memory is mapped to the cache. This means avoiding clearance of cache pages on each context switch. During execution, the algorithm frees the old pages as necessary in order to make space for currently scheduled applications (recoloring). The coloring algorithm sorts the concurrent access requests according to their release times.

Estimating the optimal cache size for each application, in order to minimize the cache miss ratio, is a non-trivial task as it requires expensive analysis of the system execution. Moreover, the recoloring operation leads to a significant overhead if the pages are not intelligently selected [12].

In our framework, we do not consider the detailed internal architecture and size of DRAM and shared cache, we focus rather on measuring the delays caused by the concurrent accesses. The reason behind this is that the impact of these characteristics on the interference is already captured when performing the static analysis and identifying the WCRAs. Accordingly, recoloring is beyond the scope of this paper.

3.3 DRAM Access Scheduling

Conventionally, a DRAM is shared by all the platform processing units. However, this increases the complexity of managing memory accesses. DRAM controllers have adopted scheduling mechanisms similarly to processor scheduling.

Naive conventional policies, like First Come First Served (FCFS) and Read-First, schedule access requests according to their arrival times with a special preference to read requests since they cause the processor to stall while write requests can normally be performed using write buffers. Another alternative to schedule accesses to DRAM, in presence of a three-dimensional structure (bank, row and column), is the Hit-First policy. The Hit-First algorithm schedules row buffer hits before misses to reduce the average memory access latency and to improve bandwidth utilization [9, 22]. This is due to the fact that requests hitting in the row buffer have shorter latency than a row buffer miss.

In Time Division Multiple Access (TDMA) policy [23], the DRAM controller allocates statically a time slot to each core to access the DRAM in a predefined manner. TDMA provides a simple and fair scheduling among all cores, however, it does not exploit the spatial locality available in memory access streams as it does not consider the demands coming from different tasks at any time point.

To maximize data throughput and minimize the DRAM latency, DRAM controllers in modern COTS-based systems use First Ready-First Come First Serve (FR-FCFS) as a DRAM policy [22, 19, 11]. FR-FCFS considers a detailed DRAM structure in terms of banks, rows and columns. The DRAM scheduler can be viewed as a 2-level filter: bank level and bus level. The access requests can target different banks separately, where they will be queued in the corresponding bank queue. Access requests will be sorted at each bank queue first according to their readiness. Then, the candidates selected from banks level will be further sorted at bus level where the earliest request gains access, i.e. the first request showing up at bus level among the requests being selected by bank schedulers. If no request hits the row-buffer, older requests are prioritized over younger ones.

[1]E.g. Intel Core i7, AMD FX, ARM Cortex and FreeScale QorIQ processors.

4. ANALYSIS OVERVIEW

This section describes the inputs required by our framework, and how they can be derived from a concrete software system designed to run on a multicore platform. It also gives a birds eye view of the analysis process.

Conventionally, task periods and deadlines (potentially also priority and criticality levels) are identifiable during the requirements analysis. Given such attributes and the architecture of the execution platform, we calculate the interference sensitive WCET (isWCET) for each task and analyze the system schedulability. isWCET is basically the sum of WCET (on a single core) and the interference delays to access shared cache and DRAM.

4.1 Flow Analysis

WCET estimation is crucial for schedulability analysis, thus providing an accurate bound on the execution time needs to be performed in a rigorous manner. Flow analysis [28, 26, 7] is a technique to estimate the WCET of a program, it consists of simulating, or concretely running, a program in isolation and measuring the time spent. Flow analysis is exercized via different analysis tools, e.g. Chronos [14], SWEET [28] and Bound-T [1]. In case of single core platforms, memory interference is not a serious challenge because the CPU triggers one access request at time.

In multicore settings, execution time estimation has become a challenge because the number of possible interleavings increases exponentially with the number of processes, number of cores and number of shared resources [7]. In practice, concurrent programs may have astronomical numbers of legal interleavings which makes the interleaving analysis not feasible. An alternative is to reuse the knowledge acquired from the single core analysis and just focus on the interference resulting from the access to shared memories.

Technically, static analysis tools use symbolic execution engines to identify potential execution paths without necessarily having to run the program. Such representations can be structured in terms of control flow graph (CFG). Similarly to compilers, a static analysis tool parses a source code of a program and converts it to an intermediate representation where each state could be a class of different program configurations. WCET is then the time spent when executing the longest path of the CFG.

4.2 Profiling

System profiling [16, 34, 11] is a measurement-based approach to estimate how many times a process accesses shared memories. The system being analyzed is run for a sufficient number of times, each of which for a long enough duration enabling the execution of most of the system functions (code). The analysis focuses on each process individually, so that for each run we track how many times a process accesses a given shared memory. However, due to technology limitations, the measurements can be performed at core level only, so that the obtained access number of a given core corresponds to the set of processes running on top of it. In order to obtain the memory access number for each process, one needs to run each process individually on one core during the analysis, so that the access number obtained corresponds only to the process being run. The number of accesses for each core can be obtained using performance monitor counters [34, 16], present in certain multicore platforms.

Profiling and static analysis techniques can both be used to measure WCET and WCRA [11, 34].

4.3 Formal Analysis

The output of flow analysis and profiling together with periods and deadlines, for a given allocation of tasks to cores, will be used as input to our framework to instantiate a system model reflecting the behavior and timing characteristics of the given software system. Such a system model can then be analyzed (using model checking) with respect to schedulability and isWCET as detailed in Section 6.

Once the system is determined to be non-schedulable for the given task-to-core allocation, we analyze what would be the utilization of cores and the interference delays if some tasks are reallocated to different cores in order to balance the workload. We will refer to such reallocations as *migration*, which should not be confused with the run-time movement of tasks. It is simply part of a pre-runtime analysis activity.

We compare different potential migration scenarios and recommend the configurations leading the system to be schedulable. In the context of IMA where tasks are encapsulated within partitions that are pre-allocated to given cores, one might need to move a whole partition instead of moving an individual task in order to satisfy both the *functional-architectural* constraints and *time composability* property of IMA. Besides, fault containment requirements must be respected when re-allocating partitions. The functional architectural constraints impose that the functionality of each architectural unit -partition- is maintained if the partition tasks do not execute on the same core. The time composability property states that the timing behavior of individual tasks will not change by the composition. In this work, since partitions are or regions are not formally modelled, we just focus on the impact of moving individual tasks. The load shedding created by moving a partition can be captured by the accumulated impact of re-allocation of its individual tasks, and the framework can be extended to model fault containment constraints.

Once a configuration is determined to be suitable, i.e. having a high probability to be schedulable according to the statistical analysis (SMC), one needs to rerun the rigorous schedulability analysis (symbolic model checking). Our framework is built to be flexible so that migrating a task from a core to another is feasible by just updating the core-Id parameter of such a task with the Id of the new core.

5. SYSTEM MODEL DESCRIPTION

Basically, an embedded system is comprised of an application mapped to a platform. The application is a parallel composition of tasks. The platform consists of a set of processing elements, a shared cache level, a shared DRAM and mechanisms to share and control the access to the platform resources like processor schedulers and DRAM connectors.

We use $\mathcal{T}$ for the set of tasks and $\mathcal{C}$ for the set of cores. The assumptions in our models are as follows:

- Tasks are periodic and preemptible during CPU execution only, i.e. a task cannot be preempted while it is performing an access to a shared memory.
- Tasks assigned to the same core are arbitrated using a local CPU scheduler.
- We consider a local cache (L1) for each core, only one shared cache (L2) and one DRAM for all cores.
- We abstract each local cache using a number stating the time taken for fetching data from it.

5.1 Application Model

An application $AP = \{T_1, .., T_n\}$ is a set of tasks each of which describes the execution model of an individual process. The process behavior is abstracted at task level using WCET and WCRA for both shared cache and DRAM[2]. WCET is the pure execution time, considered in isolation, i.e. excluding the time to fetch data. Regarding data fetching, we consider 2 attributes $WCRA_c$ and $WCRA_m$ where: $WCRA_c$ corresponds to the maximum number of successful accesses (hits) to the shared cache L2; $WCRA_m$ is the number of DRAM accesses (corresponds to L2 miss) performed by a given process. Moreover, in order to distinguish between read and write accesses to each shared memory, we denote each of the attributes with r for read and w for write, i.e. $WCRA_c^r$, $WCRA_c^w$, $WCRA_m^r$ and $WCRA_m^w$. This is because read requests make the core stalling (strong impact on isWCET) while write requests do not as they can be performed using dedicated buffers.

Accordingly, an access request to a shared memory is given by a *pattern* $\in \{L2, DRAM\}$ stating to which memory the access hits and an attribute RW indicates whether it is a read (r) or write (w) action. Moreover, as we need to keep track of when the requests are issued, so that FR-FCFS algorithm determines the priorities of requests targeting DRAM, we use *issueT*. In fact, *issueT* is initially empty and will be initialized by a core when the access request is triggered. Accordingly, an access request is formally given by $req = \langle pattern, RW, issueT \rangle$. $WCRA_c^r$ and $WCRA_c^w$, respectively $WCRA_m^r$ and $WCRA_m^w$, of a given task are then the numbers of read and write accesses to L2, respectively DRAM.

DEFINITION 1 (TASK STRUCTURE). *A task* T *is given by* $\langle$Prd, Offset, WCET, WCRA_c^r, WCRA_c^w, WCRA_m^r, WCRA_m^w, Dln, Pri$\rangle$ *where* Prd *is the task period,* Offset *is the periodic offset,* WCET *is the pure execution time,* Dln *is the relative deadline whereas* Pri *is the priority level associated to* T. WCRA_c^r, WCRA_c^w, WCRA_m^r *and* WCRA_m^w *are described above.*

In order to make the application specification flexible, we do not (statically) specify the identifier of the core to which the task is assigned. The mapping will rather be given during system instantiation. The behavior of a task is a basically a state-transition system, where states represent potential configurations of the corresponding process and transitions correspond to the execution of actions and events.

[2]thus validity of these numbers affects the validity of the outcomes

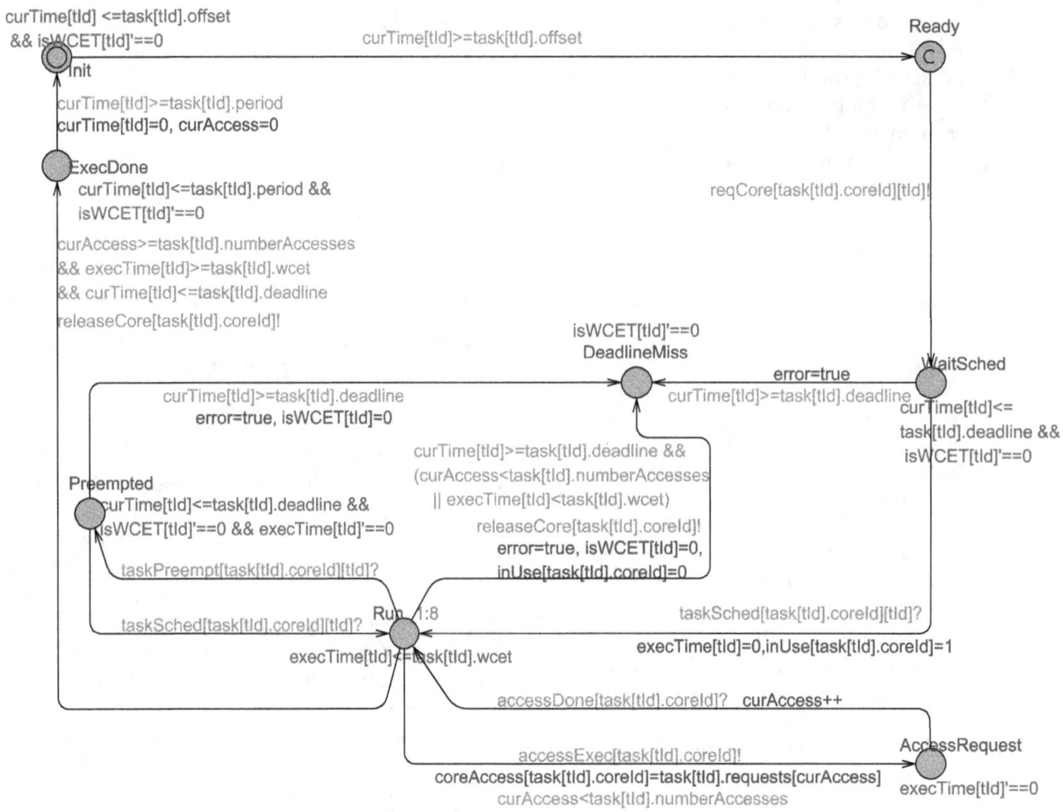

Figure 2: Task template model

Our Uppaal task template model is depicted in Figure. 2. To distinguish between different tasks, we associate to each task an identifier `tId` as a template parameter. The task starts at location Init where it initializes its variables if needed, during the offset time. Once the offset expires, the task moves to location Ready to request the core to which it is mapped, through a synchronization with the core scheduler on channel `reqCore`. The task waits to be scheduled at location WaitSched unless the deadline is reached by which it moves to location DeadlineMiss and updates a global variable *error* to true. Once a task is scheduled it updates the status of the corresponding core *inUse[]=1*, and moves to location Run where it executes. During its execution (*WCET*), a task non-deterministically triggers access requests to L2 and DRAM. For each access request, the task moves to location AccessRequest and waits until the access request is satisfied upon which it moves back to location Run. One can remark that, when a task is requesting and waiting for data the clock measuring *WCET* is stopped (*execTime[tId]'==0*) so that only the effective execution at Run consumes *WCET*. This is implemented in Uppaal by assigning rate 0 to the derivative of *execTime[tId]*. Such a clock resumes at Run. From Run, the task joins either ExecDone, if the execution *WCET* and accesses to L2 and DRAM ($numberAccesses = WCRA_c^r + WCRA_c^w + WCRA_m^r + WCRA_m^w$) are completed before deadline, or it moves to DeadlineMiss in case the execution or access requests are not achieved before deadline. Once the period expires, at location ExecDone, the task moves to Init to start a new period. The isWCET of a task is measured by clock *isWCET[tId]*. The measurement starts once a task is scheduled (location Run) and stops when the task execution is done (location ExecDone), so that it includes both *WCET* and interference. The task template can be instantiated for different tasks by just providing the aforementioned parameters.

A task can be preempted during effective core utilization only (at location Run) by the scheduler of the core to which it is currently allocated, as during memory access the task is at location AccessRequest. Once a task is preempted it moves to location Preempted. If a ready task needs to preempt a running task, the preempting task has to wait until the current memory access of the running task is finished. One can see that we do not change the core status (*inUse*) when preempting a task and moving to location Preempted as the core keeps running but with the preempting task. When a task is preempted, neither its *isWCET* nor *execTime* clocks can progress. The task can exit the preemption location Preempted by either receiving a scheduling event *taskSched[]?* or reaching its deadline.

Our preemption pattern does not allow the preemption of tasks during access requests, thus it prevents a task to wait more than once for the same access request. This aligns to an operating system policy that has a preference for a lower interference time as opposed to a greedy utilization of cores.

5.2 Platform Model

A platform is composed of a set of processing elements PE, a shared cache (L2), DRAM memory and schedulers to manage the access to L2 and DRAM. Each processing element PE consists of a computation resource (core), a local cache (L1) and a scheduler to dispatch tasks to run on that core. The access time for local caches may vary from one PE to another. Moreover, we consider the duration for an effective access (from grant to completion) to a shared memory as a platform parameter.

5.2.1 Modeling of Processing Elements

A processing element PE is given by $\langle C, sched, H\rangle$ where C is a core, *sched* is the scheduling policy (core scheduler) adopted and H is the local cache that we abstract using its access time *LocalCacheTime*. The core model is depicted in Figure. 3.

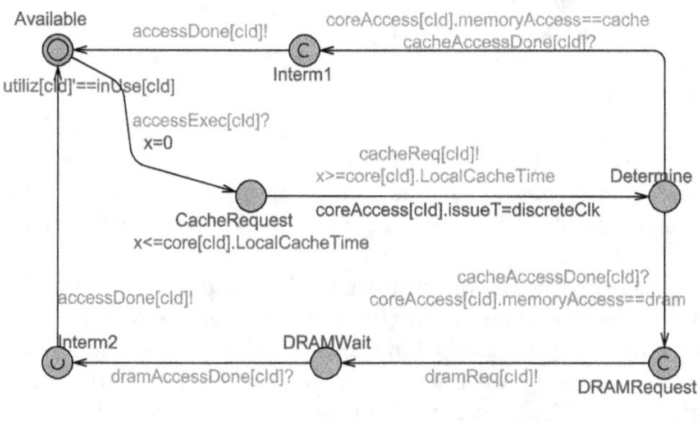

Figure 3: Core template model

Similarly to tasks, we assign to each core an identifier `cId` as a parameter to distinguish between the different platform cores. The core model is initially at location Available waiting for ready tasks. Through an allocation, the core model does not move from Available but the clock measuring its utilization *utiliz[cId]* starts counting (*utiliz[cId]'==inUse[cId]*). Such a clock can stop and resume according to the core status *inUse[cId]* manipulated at task level. Upon an access request to a shared memory (*accessExec[cId]?*), the core moves to location CacheRequest where it waits for the expiry of the local cache access time *LocalCacheTime* before performing the access request to the shared cache L2 and joins location Determine. The core updates the request issue time with the current time instant *issueT=discreteClk*.Once the access to L2 hits (*memoryAccess==cache*) and terminates, the core moves back immediately to location Available to continue executing the assigned task. Otherwise, once the L2 access terminates and misses (*memoryAccess==dram*) the core requests access to DRAM and joins immediately the location DRAMWait. The core blocking time on an access request (at locations Determine and DRAMWait) depends on the access nature. If it is a write action, the core will immediately be unlocked by the scheduler of the targeted memory, otherwise the core stalls until the read access finishes. Further details regarding how to handle read and write accesses will be provided in the description of L2 and DRAM schedulers.

The core needs to notify the running task when the current access request is done, i.e. once the core itself is notified by DRAM or L2 (according to the access pattern), so that it moves back as well from location AccessRequest to Run and accounts an access done (*curAccess++*). As it is not possible to associate two synchronization events with a transition in Uppaal, we introduce two intermediate locations Interm1 and Interm2. Thus, we create a sequence of 2 synchronizations without any delay in between. We use *urgentness* and *committedness* of Uppaal to enforce time to not elapse at a given location (locations marked with `U` and `C`).

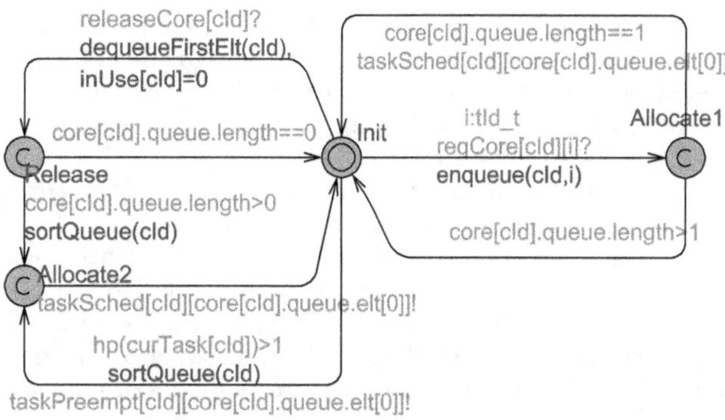

Figure 4: Scheduler template model

Figure. 4 depicts the core scheduler model. Initially at location Init waiting for a ready task, the core moves to location Allocate1 while queuing the identifier of the requesting task. If the core queue contains only one element (*queue.length==1*), which is the identifier of the newly added task, that task will immediately be scheduled otherwise the scheduler just moves back to Init, where it analyzes whether the newly added task has priority over the current running task. If so (*hp(curTask[cId])>1*), the scheduler preempts the current running task (when it is not performing an access to a shared memory) and sorts the ready queue while moving to location Allocate2. From that location, the scheduler schedules immediately the task having the highest priority in the queue. Channel *taskPreempt* is urgent, thus whenever the synchronization is available the transition from Init to Allocate2 is immediately triggered.

Once the core is released by the current running task through a signal on channel *releaseCore* due to execution termination, the scheduler moves to Release while removing the first element of the core queue. If the queue is still not empty, the scheduler calls the adopted scheduling policy *sortQueue()* of core *cId* to sort the queue and moves to location Allocate2, whereafter it schedules the task corresponding to the first element in the queue. Function *sortQueue(cId)* refers to the scheduling policy of core *cId*, which is a core parameter in our model and can be FIFO, FPS or EDF.

5.2.2 Modeling of Shared Memories

This section describes the modeling of shared memories L2 cache and DRAM as well as their schedulers. We consider both shared memories, L2 cache and DRAM, as black boxes and assume that the effective access duration[3] for fetching data is constant, regardless of the physical location in the memory. The interference delay for an access request is defined by the waiting time from the issue of the access request until the access is granted.

DRAM=$\langle$*DRAMStruct, DRAMSched, DRAMAccessTime*$\rangle$ is composed of a structure *DRAMStruct* (abstracted using the behavioral model depicted in Figure. 5), a scheduler *DRAMSched* (Figure. 6), and the length of time for an effective access *DRAMAccessTime*. The DRAM access time simulates the duration of fetching data from a physical address in DRAM once the access is scheduled. This is in fact to enable our abstraction of the DRAM internal architecture

[3]The time interval from the instant when the access is granted until the data delivery instant.

to capture the delay for accessing a DRAM bank/row. Our DRAM model can be viewed as a one-bank memory that is shared between all cores, but it can easily be extended for several banks by just duplicating the DRAM structure and assigning each to one core only [33].

The DRAM behavior model (Figure. 5) is simple. However, its allocation is complex as we will see in the description of Figure. 6. DRAM is initially waiting at location Idle for an access request, either read or write. The DRAM can be allocated, by its scheduler, to a given core i performing a read request *DRAMReqR[i]?* and moves to location Read. Similarly, DRAM can be targeted with a write request *DRAMReqW?*.

One can see that for write access requests the identifier of the involved core is missing. This is because write requests are not blocking, thus no need to keep track of which core needs to be unlocked once the access is done. At locations Read and Write, the DRAM waits for the expiry of the access time *DRAMAccessTime* then moves to location Done. From Read, once the access time expires the DRAM unlocks the involved core through a synchronization *dramAccessDone[currentCore]!*, whereas from location Write no unlock action is needed. From Done, DRAM notifies its scheduler that the current access is done.

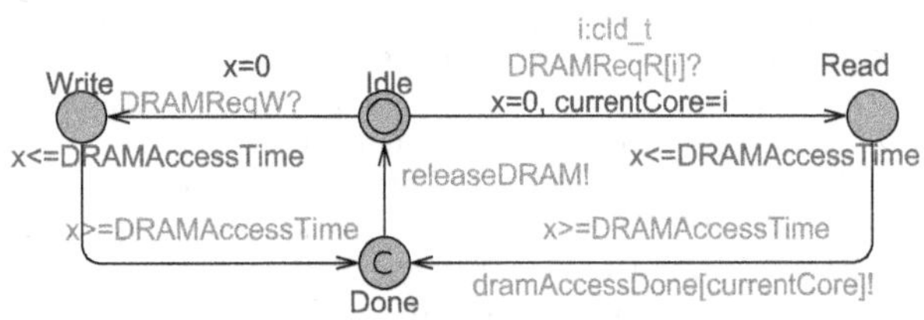

Figure 5: DRAM template model

We adopt the FR-FCFS policy to arbitrate accesses to DRAM. We assume that row opening and reload actions are instantaneous, so that we do not need to consider any preference based on the *already open row* policy [11]. This leads to considering the attribute *issueT* (issue time) of each request as a *readiness*. Hence, we characterize each request to DRAM with a new attribute *arrivalT*, besides *issueT*. In fact, *issueT* stores the time instant when the request is issued, whereas *arrivalT* stores the instant when the request reaches the corresponding bank queue. Thus, we compare requests first based on their issue times (readiness) where an earlier request has priority over later ones. If requests have the same issue time, then the request having an earlier *arrivalT* has priority over requests having later *arrivalT*. A sketch of the FR-FCFS is shown in Algorithm 1.

The DRAM scheduler is depicted in Figure. 6. Initially at location Init, upon the receive of an access request *dramReq[i]?* from any core i the DRAM scheduler inserts such a request together with the identifier of the requesting core into the queue and moves to location Allocate1. If such a request is a write (*rwAction==Write*), the requesting core will immediately be unlocked (*dramAccessDone[l]!*) as location is committed Allocate1. Moreover, if the write request is alone in the queue (*queue.length==1*) it will immediately be scheduled at location Unlocked.

In case of a read request (*rwAction==Read*), the DRAM scheduler does not unlock the requesting core after queuing the request. It just schedules the access (*DRAMReqR[DRAM.*

Algorithm 1 Sketch of the FR-FCFS algorithm

```
Int j
for each new request r do
    for i ∈ [0, q.length] do
        if (r.issueT < q[i].issueT) Or ((r.issueT = q[i].issueT) And (r.arrivalT < q[i].arrivalT)) then
            j := i
            i := q.length
        else
            j := i
        end if
    end for
    insert(r, j)
end for
```

queue.elt[0].core]!) if the current request is alone in the queue. In all of the four scenarios, the scheduler moves back to location Init.

Once an access request finishes, the scheduler is notified by the DRAM through a synchronization event *releaseDRAM?* and moves to Release while removing the head of the queue. If the queue is still not empty, the scheduler calls the algorithm FR-FCFS to sort the queue as other requests might have joined during the execution of the last access. At location Allocate2, the scheduler schedules the request in the first element of the queue *queue.elt[0]* using the appropriate channel (*DRAMReqR* or *DRAMReqW*) according to the request nature; read or write.

Due to space limitations, we omit describing the shared cache L2 and its scheduler. In essence, L2 has the same elements as DRAM , except that it uses a separate queue to store its requests. Similarly, L2 scheduler has the same behavior as that of DRAM but it operates on the L2 queue using the cache coloring policy. However, since we do not consider the internal pages of L2, the coloring policy adopted in our framework behaves in similar way to FCFS policy.

Finally, a platform P is described as $\langle\langle PE_1, .., PE_m\rangle, DRAM, L2\rangle$. One can see that updating the specification of one platform ingredient does not necessarily affect the others.

5.3 System Model

In order to make our framework flexible, the application and platform are specified separately then mapped together. A system model S is given by an application $AP = \{T_1, .., T_n\}$, a platform $P = \langle \mathcal{PE}, DRAM, L2\rangle$ and a mapping $M : AP \rightarrow \mathcal{PE}$ assigning each task to a processing element $PE_i \in \mathcal{PE}$.

6. SCHEDULABILITY AND INTERFERENCE ANALYSIS

In this section, we describe how the schedulability will be analyzed inpresence of computed interference (isWCET). Moreover, in case of non-schedulability, based on core utilization and assumed delay per access request to shared memories we recommend task migration between cores so that a new potentially schedulable configuration can be identified.

6.1 Schedulability Analysis

In our framework, system schedulability is analyzed as a reachability property using symbolic model checking [5].

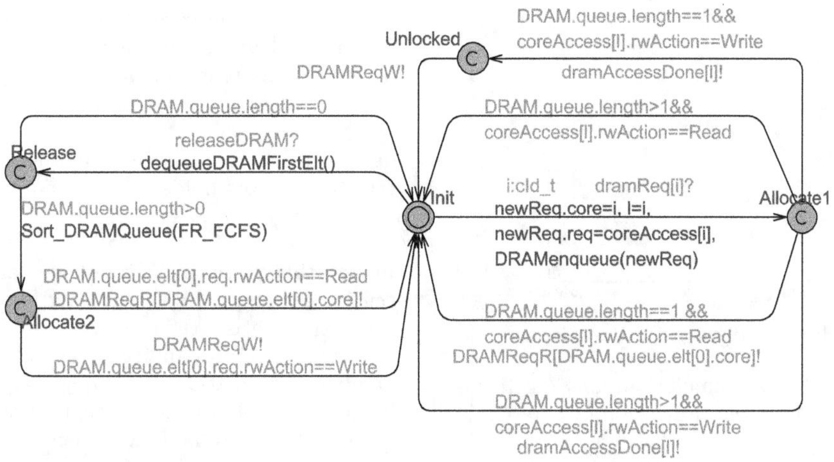

Figure 6: DRAM scheduler model

Following our task model, whenever a process misses its deadline it joins immediately the location DeadlineMiss (by which the global variable *error* is updated to true). Thus, the schedulability analysis process simply checks whether any task can reach its own DeadlineMiss location. Technically, to quantify on all tasks regardless of their identifiers we use the following CTL (Computation Tree Logic) query supported by Uppaal, where

$$\forall[]$$

denotes invariance over all reachable states, and ! denotes negation:

$$\forall[]\ !error \quad (1)$$

Using this query, the checker explores the whole state space and examines that in any state the value of variable *error* is false.

6.2 isWCET Estimation

The interference sensitive WCET (isWCET) of a task is the execution time including the effective execution (WCET), the delays caused by the interference to access shared memories as well as the effective access time to memories (L1, L2 and DRAM). Following the task model (Figure. 2), once a task is scheduled the clock *isWCET* starts measuring time until the effective execution (WCET) is finished and all the task access requests are completed (location ExecDone). To do so, we simulate the system execution for X time units, each simulation runs for Y time units and accumulate the *isWCET* values of given tasks ($T_1, .., T_n$) using the following Uppaal SMC query:

$$simulate\ X\ [<= Y]\ \{isWCET[T_1], .., isWCET[T_n]\} \quad (2)$$

The simulation time Y should be greater than the least common multiplier of the task periods. In fact, the larger X and Y are the more accurate the results will be. To display the isWCET of a task T in terms of a probability distribution, the following SMC query can be used:

$$E[clk <= Y; X](max : isWCET[T]) \quad (3)$$

where the E operator identifies the trace (given X and Y constraints) in which maximum isWCET is obtained[4].

[4]Uppaal provides different presentations of the data collected during repeated runs, e.g. cumulative density function and distribution function. As long as any run reaches a isWCET > deadline this step has served its purpose and thereby we do not do further statistical analysis.

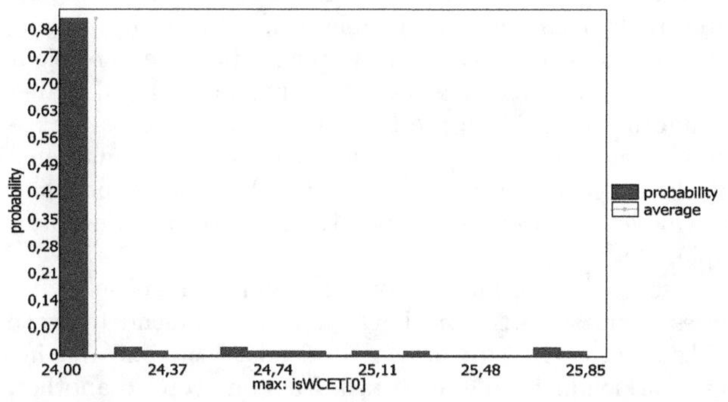

Figure 7: Probability distribution of isWCET of a given task.

Figure. 7 depicts a case where the x-axis shows the time units (simulation times) as used for all quantities below. It shows the probability distribution of the isWCET of a task T generated using query (3) where $X = 10^3$ and $Y = 10^4$. T runs in parallel with 3 other tasks mapped to 2 cores, each core serves 2 tasks. T has Prd=100, $WCET$=15, Dln=71, 13 read/write access to L2 ($WCRA_c = 13$) and 8 accesses to DRAM ($WCRA_m = 8$). Value 24 is the most likely because it has the highest probability (0.87), not far from the average isWCET 24.12.

6.3 Utilization Analysis

To estimate the utilization of cores, we need to run the execution simulation several times (X) each of which lasts for Y time units. We accumulate for each simulation the core utilization time via clock *utiliz[cId]*, and then consider the maximum value using the following SMC query:

$$simulate\ X\ [<= Y]\ utiliz[cId] \quad (4)$$

The utilization percentage of a given core is then obtained by dividing the accumulated utilization time over the total simulation time Y. Figure. 8 shows the average accumulated utilization time of 2 individual cores (C_0 and

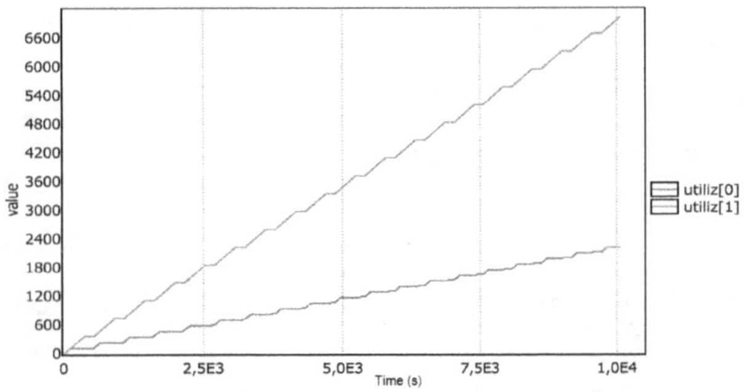

Figure 8: Simulation of cores utilization.

C_1) for 1000 simulations. Each simulation runs for 10000 clock ticks (query (4)). Thus, the utilization of core C_0 is $2223/10^4 * 100 = 22.2\%$.

6.4 Task Migration

In case a given system is not schedulable, it might be possible to find another schedulable configuration by moving some tasks between cores. However, in practice one might need to know whether a task can functionally be allocated to another core, since the IMA architecture standards assume that the system is structured in terms of functional blocks called partitions. As stated earlier, this paper does not model partitions and shows the tasks reallocation principle.

Based on the utilization of cores and average delay per access request to L2 and DRAM, we recommend to move tasks from cores with heavy workload to the ones having less workload. To migrate a task from one core to another, we estimate what would be the target core utilization given its current utilization, WCET of the task to be migrated and the workload generated by *read* accesses to L2 and DRAM ($WCRA_c^r$ and $WCRA_m^r$) of that task, i.e. number of read accesses multiplied by the average delay per request.

The fact that read requests are blocking, contributes considerably to the utilization by making the cores stall. On the other hand, write accesses are not blocking and have a smaller impact on the utilization, even though write accesses make the waiting queue longer, which some how might delay other read accesses. Currently, we ignore the workload generated by write accesses when probing migration scenarios.

Migrating a task T to a core C having a utilization U leads to a new utilization U' of C given by:

$$U' = U + \begin{array}{l}(T.WCET + T.WCRA_c^r \times a_c^r + \\ T.WCRA_m^r \times a_m^r)/T.Prd\end{array} \quad (5)$$

where a_c^r and a_m^r are the average delays per read access requests to L2 and DRAM respectively. To obtain the average delay per access request to L2 and DRAM of a task T, we use query (4) on 2 other clocks U_c^r and U_m^r to accumulate the delays spent by that task when performing all its read requests to L2 and DRAM, respectively. Namely, when a task moves to location AccessRequest to perform a read access, the delay at that location will be accumulated to either U_c^r or U_m^r according to the request pattern. The average delays a_c^r and a_m^r are then obtained by dividing the accumulated delays U_c^r and U_m^r by the number of requests $WCRA_c^r$ and $WCRA_m^r$ respectively.

We compare different potential migration scenarios and recommend the configurations leading to a more balanced workload between cores. The new configurations will first be analyzed using Uppaal SMC via query (6), so that we obtain a probability on the system schedulability, where

<>

denotes existance of some path in which the respective property (here error) holds.

$$Pr[<= Y](<> error) \quad (6)$$

In fact, this query runs a set of simulations of the system execution each for a duration Y, and checks how many (if any) simulations satisfy the property *error*, i.e. encounter a deadline miss. The probability is then obtained by dividing the number of simulations satisfying the property over the total number of simulations. Configurations having high probability to be schedulable will then be analyzed further using symbolic model checking (query (1)) to obtain deterministic evidence on the system schedulability.

As an illustration, the task T analyzed in Figure. 7 is first assigned to a core C_1 giving a high utilization 70.4% compared to core C_0 22.2% as shown in Figure. 8. We analyze what would be the utilization of C_0 if T is migrated to it, given its current utilization $U = 22.2\%$ and both $a_c^r = 0.79$ and $a_m^r = 0.97$ estimated during simulation. The utilization of C_0 if T is assigned to it would become $U' = 0.222 + 0.33 = 55.2\%$. The utilization of the original core C_1 will be reduced accordingly by 33%. The statistical analysis of schedulability for the system after migrating task T to core C_0 generates a probability $p \in [0, 0.009]$ that the system misses a deadline. We consider this probability to be low enough for further analysis of the configuration using symbolic model checking.

When analyzing this example using query (1), the analysis shows that the new configuration is actually schedulable. The idea behind using statistical analysis (SMC) first is that the analysis using SMC is cheap (in terms of resources, analysis time and memory space) compared to symbolic model checking. In this experiment, SMC consumed 8.53 seconds and 7.96MB memory space, whereas symbolic model checker consumed 46.39 seconds and 582.52MB.

7. CASE STUDY

In order to illustrate our method, we analyze a component of an autonomous vehicle system [13] presented earlier. The task functions are obtained from the PARSEC benchmark suite [4] and used to capture different components of complex real-time embedded applications such as sensor fusion and computer vision in an autonomous vehicle system.

Essentially, the application consists of 4 periodic tasks T_1 (StreamCluster), T_2 (Ferret), T_3 (Canneal) and T_4 (FluidAnimation) running on 2 identical cores (C_0 and C_1) sharing L2 and DRAM. T_1 and T_2 are assigned to C_0, whereas T_3 and T_4 execute on C_1. We calculated the WCRA by dividing the time spent by each task to fetch data over the average duration for one access from [13]. As the numbers of access requests to shared cache and DRAM are not explicitly distinguishable in [13], we rely on the analysis results obtained by Ye *et al.* [32] using the cache coloring policy, where only 22.2% of the access requests hit L2 while 77.8% of the requests need to access to DRAM.

The characteristics of the task set are shown in Table 1, where the offset is omitted since all tasks have offset equal to zero. $WCRA_c$ and $WCRA_m$ are given in terms of (reads;

writes). All time units are given in milliseconds (ms). The platform description is given in Table 2, where H is the access time for the core local cache. The time taken for effective accesses to L2 ($L2AccessTime$) and DRAM ($DRAM-AccessTime$) are $1/10^3$ and $1/10^2$ ms respectively.

Table 1: Attributes of the task set

Task	Prd	WCET	WCRA$_c$	WCRA$_m$	Dln
T_1	400	120	(40; 0)	(110; 10)	400
T_2	1200	130	(60; 60)	(136; 273)	1200
T_3	1800	500	(134; 266)	(705; 705)	1800
T_4	6000	440	(314; 626)	(1828; 1462)	6000

Each of the statistical analysis results of the case study has been calculated from 1000 simulations. Each simulation experiment runs for 1 million clock ticks. The accumulated utilization times of cores C_0 and C_1 are depicted in Figure. 9. During 1 million time units, cores accumulate 419983 and 360350 respectively. Thus, the average utilization of C_0 is 42% and the average utilization of C_1 is 36%. Schedulability analysis shows that the system is schedulable. The estimated maximum isWCETs of tasks T_1 and T_2, respectively T_3 and T_4, in terms of probability distributions, are depicted in Figure. 10 and Figure. 11, respectively. Accordingly, the most likely isWCET values of the case study tasks are 261, 262, 971 and 972 respectively. One may need to consider the maximum values for safety reasons. It is obvious that tasks performing more read requests, in particular to DRAM, produce longer isWCET.

Since the system requirements are met and the core workloads are modest and relatively comparable, there is no need to migrate any task. The longest analysis time spent by Uppaal is when running the statistical analysis to measure the core utilizations. In fact, for a simulation having 1000 runs each of which lasts for 1 million clock tick (a total of 10^9 clock ticks) Uppaal spent 3426.7 seconds. The performance and analysis results from the case study are encouraging but further studies are needed on scalability to larger systems.

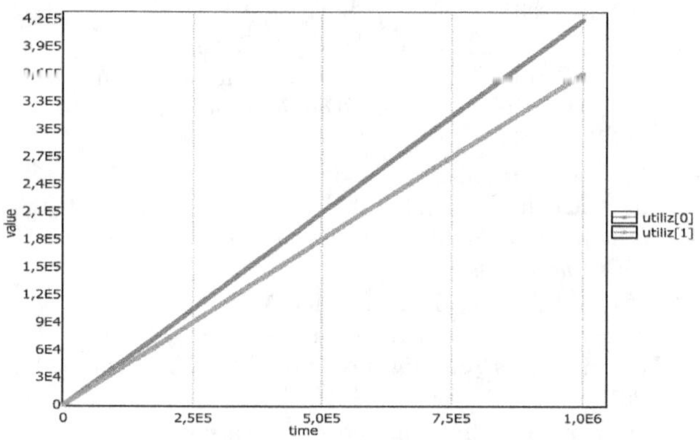

Figure 9: Accumulated core utilization.

Table 2: Platform description and mapping

Core	Sched policy	H	Mapped tasks
C_1	EDF	$1/10^3$	T_1, T_2
C_2	EDF	$1/10^3$	T_3, T_4

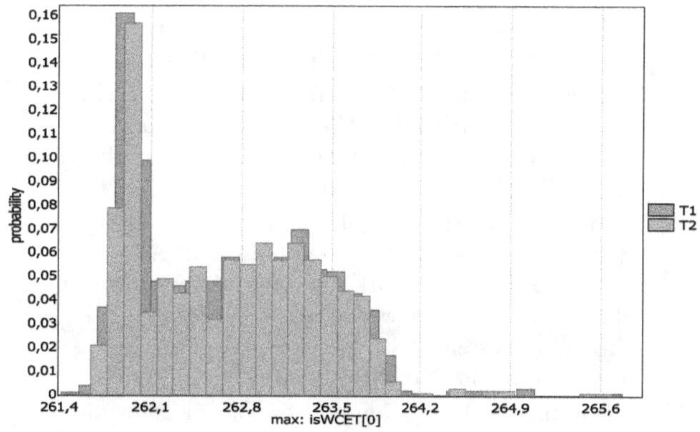

Figure 10: Probability distribution of isWCET for tasks (T_1, T_2).

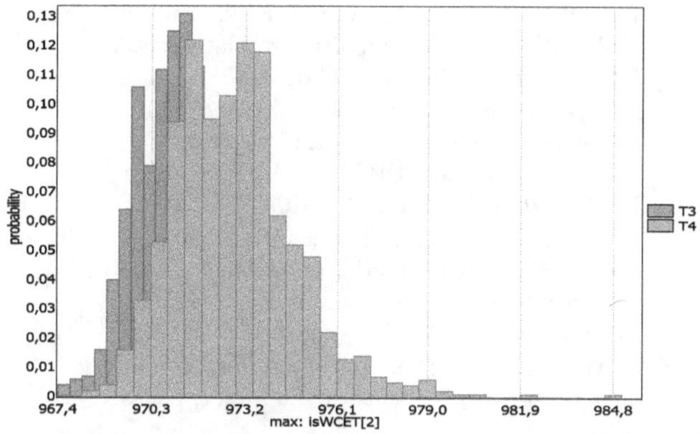

Figure 11: Probability distribution of isWCET for tasks (T_3, T_4).

8. CONCLUSION

This paper introduces a model-based framework for schedulability and memory interference analysis of multicore preemptive real-time systems. The framework captures both the multicore platform model, having a hierarchy of shared memories, and a system application given in terms of periodic preemptible tasks. In case of non-schedulability, we provide a technique to analyze the utilization of cores and study the impact of task migration with the goal to find potential mappings with which the system becomes schedulable. Our framework is realized using timed automata and stopwatch clocks of Uppaal, while the analysis of schedulability, memory interference and performance is performed using model checking technique.

As future work, interesting directions are to model and analyze more complex architectures, such as networked multiprocessor platforms and system on chips, analyze an actual avionic case study including partitions, fault containment aspects as well as cases where task re-allocation is necessary, and study the scalability of our framework.

9. REFERENCES

[1] Bound-T Execution Time Analyzer, http://www.bound-t.com/.

[2] B. Andersson, A. Easwaran, and J. Lee. Finding an upper bound on the increase in execution time due to contention on the memory bus in cots-based multicore systems. *SIGBED Rev.*, 7(1):4:1–4:4, Jan. 2010.

[3] G. Behrmann, A. David, and K. G. Larsen. *A Tutorial on Uppaal*, pages 200–236. Springer, 2004.

[4] C. Bienia, S. Kumar, J. P. Singh, and K. Li. The parsec benchmark suite: Characterization and architectural implications. In *Proceedings of PACT '08*, pages 72–81. ACM, 2008.

[5] A. Boudjadar, A. David, J. H. Kim, K. G. Larsen, M. Mikucionis, U. Nyman, and A. Skou. A reconfigurable framework for compositional schedulability and power analysis of hierarchical scheduling systems with frequency scaling. *SCP journal*, 113:236–260, 2015.

[6] J. Boudjadar, J. H. Kim, and S. Nadjm-Tehrani. Performance-aware scheduling of multicore time-critical systems. In *Proceedings of ACM/IEEE MEMOCODE*, pages 105–114, 2016.

[7] S. Chattopadhyay, C. Kee, A. Roychoudhury, T. Kelter, P. Marwedel, and H. Falk. A unified wcet analysis framework for multi-core platforms. In *RTAS'12*, pages 99–108. ACM, 2012.

[8] A. Gustavsson, A. Ermedahl, B. Lisper, and P. Pettersson. Towards WCET Analysis of Multicore Architectures Using UPPAAL. In *Proceedings of WCET'10*, pages 101–112, 2010.

[9] S. Hong, S. McKee, M. Salinas, R. Klenke, J. Aylor, and W. Wulf. Access order and effective bandwidth for streams on a direct rambus memory. In *Proceedings of HPCA'99*, pages 80–89. IEEE, 1999.

[10] H. W. Jin and S. Han. Temporal partitioning for mixed-criticality systems. In *ETFA'11*, pages 1–4. IEEE, 2011.

[11] H. Kim, D. de Niz, B. Andersson, M. H. Klein, O. Mutlu, and R. Rajkumar. Bounding memory interference delay in COTS-based multi-core systems. In *RTAS'14*, pages 145–154. IEEE, 2014.

[12] H. Kim, A. Kandhalu, and R. Rajkumar. A coordinated approach for practical OS-level cache management in multi-core real-time systems. In *ECRTS'13*, pages 80–89. IEEE, 2013.

[13] H. Kim, A. Kandhalu, and R. Rajkumar. Coordinated cache management for predictable multi-core real-time systems. Technical report, Carnegie Mellon Univ, 2014.

[14] X. Li, Y. Liang, T. Mitra, and A. Roychoudhury. Chronos: A timing analyzer for embedded software. *SCP Journal*, 69:56 – 67, 2007. Special issue on Experimental Software and Toolkits.

[15] B. Lisper. SWEET - A tool for WCET flow analysis (extended abstract). In *Proceedings of ISoLA'14*, volume 8803 of *LNCS*, pages 482–485. Springer, 2014.

[16] A. Löfwenmark and S. Nadjm-Tehrani. Experience report: Memory accesses for avionic applications and operating systems on a multi-core platform. In *Proceedings of ISSRE'15*, pages 153–160. IEEE, 2015.

[17] M. Lv, W. Yi, N. Guan, and G. Yu. Combining abstract interpretation with model checking for timing analysis of multicore software. In *Proceedings of RTSS'10*, pages 339–349. IEEE, 2010.

[18] J. Madsen, M. R. Hansen, K. S. Knudsen, J. E. Nielsen, and A. W. Brekling. System-level verification of multi-core embedded systems using timed-automata. In *IFAC'08*, pages 9302–9307, 2008.

[19] K. J. Nesbit, N. Aggarwal, J. Laudon, and J. E. Smith. Fair queuing memory systems. In *Proceedings of MICRO'06*, pages 208–222. IEEE Computer Society, 2006.

[20] J. Nowotsch, M. Paulitsch, D. Buhler, H. Theiling, S. Wegener, and M. Schmidt. Multi-core interference-sensitive WCET analysis leveraging runtime resource capacity enforcement. In *Proceedings of ECRTS'14*, pages 109–118. IEEE, 2014.

[21] A. Oliveira Maroneze, S. Blazy, D. Pichardie, and I. Puaut. A Formally Verified WCET Estimation Tool. In *Proceedings of WCET'14*. OASIcs, 2014.

[22] S. Rixner, W. J. Dally, U. J. Kapasi, P. Mattson, and J. D. Owens. Memory access scheduling. In *Proceedings ISCA'00*, pages 128–138. ACM, 2000.

[23] J. Roseen, A. Andrei, P. Eles, and Z. Peng. Bus access optimization for predictable implementation of real-time applications on multiprocessor systems-on-chip. In *Proceedings of RTSS'07*, pages 49–60. IEEE, 2007.

[24] RTCA co. DO-297/ED-124 - Integrated Modular Avionics (IMA) Development Guidance and Certification Considerations, 2005.

[25] A. Schranzhofer, J.-J. Chen, and L. Thiele. Timing analysis for TDMA arbitration in resource sharing systems. In *Proceedings of RTAS'10*, pages 215–224. IEEE, 2010.

[26] R. Sen and Y. N. Srikant. WCET estimation for executables in the presence of data caches. In *Proceedings EMSOFT '07*, pages 203–212. ACM, 2007.

[27] L. Subramanian, V. Seshadri, Y. Kim, B. Jaiyen, and O. Mutlu. Mise: Providing performance predictability and improving fairness in shared main memory systems. In *HPCA'13*, pages 639–650. IEEE, 2013.

[28] L. Tan. The worst-case execution time tool challenge. *STTT journal*, 11(2):133–152, 2009.

[29] A. Wilson and T. Preyssler. Incremental certification and integrated modular avionics. In *Digital Avionics Systems Conference. DASC'08. IEEE/AIAA 27th*, pages 1.E.3–1–1.E.3–8, 2008.

[30] G. Yao, R. Pellizzoni, S. Bak, E. Betti, and M. Caccamo. Memory-centric scheduling for multicore hard real-time systems. *Real-Time Systems*, 48(6):681–715, 2012.

[31] G. Yao, R. Pellizzoni, S. Bak, H. Yun, and M. Caccamo. Global real-time memory-centric scheduling for multicore systems. *IEEE Transaction on Computers*, 2016.

[32] Y. Ye, R. West, Z. Cheng, and Y. Li. Coloris: A dynamic cache partitioning system using page coloring. In *Proceedings of PACT'14*, pages 381–392, 2014.

[33] H. Yun, R. Pellizzoni, and P. K. Valsan. Parallelism-aware memory interference delay analysis for COTS multicore systems. In *ECRTS'15*, pages 184–195. IEEE Computer Society, 2015.

[34] H. Yun, G. Yao, R. Pellizzoni, M. Caccamo, and L. Sha. Memory access control in multiprocessor for real-time systems with mixed criticality. In *Proceedings of ECRTS'12*, pages 299–308. IEEE Computer Society, 2012.

Timeliness Evaluation of Intermittent Mobile Connectivity over Pub/Sub Systems

Georgios Bouloukakis[1] Nikolaos Georgantas[1] Ajay Kattepur[2] Valérie Issarny[1]
[1]MiMove Team, Inria Paris, France
firstname.lastname@inria.fr
[2]TCS Research & Innovation, Bangalore, India
ajay.kattepur@tcs.com

ABSTRACT

Systems deployed in mobile environments are typically characterized by intermittent connectivity and asynchronous sending/reception of data. To create effective mobile systems for such environments, it is essential to guarantee acceptable levels of timeliness between sending and receiving mobile users. In order to provide QoS guarantees in different application scenarios and contexts, it is necessary to model the system performance by incorporating the intermittent connectivity. *Queueing Network Models* (QNMs) offer a simple modeling environment, which can be used to represent various application scenarios, and provide accurate analytical solutions for performance metrics, such as system response time. In this paper, we provide an analytical solution regarding the end-to-end response time between users sending and receiving data by modeling the intermittent connectivity of mobile users with QNMs. We utilize the *publish/subscribe* (pub/sub) middleware as the underlying communication infrastructure for mobile users. To represent the user's connections/disconnections, we model and solve analytically an ON/OFF queueing system by applying a mean value approach. Finally, we validate our model using simulations with real-world workload traces. The deviations between the performance results foreseen by the analytical model and the ones provided by the simulator are shown to be less than 5% for a variety of scenarios.

Keywords

Publish/Subscribe Middleware; Mobile Connectivity; Queueing Networks; Response Time

1. INTRODUCTION

Publish/Subscribe (pub/sub) systems constitute an appealing interaction paradigm for building large-scale distributed systems. They provide a loosely coupled form of interaction that is especially useful in the case of mobile peers. Pub/sub is deemed appropriate for interaction between mobile entities and it facilitates the asynchronous and on-demand data information dissemination [1]. A large number of applications have been created and several standards have been adopted using the pub/sub interaction style, such as, web news through RSS feeds [2, 3], streaming services [4], google services [5] and real time applications [6].

To motivate our work, we provide the following illustrative use case: Metro travelers in Paris frequently utilize a transport information management system for the improvement of their travel experience. The system operates based on both authoritative and mobile crowd-sourced information from multiple heterogeneous sources. The information (i.e., events of interest) for the average user arrives with a certain rate through asynchronous pub/sub notifications. To guarantee the freshness of provided information, notifications are maintained by the system for a (limited) lifetime period. The travelers are able to access the system periodically and receive up-to-date transport information on their hand-held devices, but also publish information themselves, e.g., notifying of some incident in the transport network. They stay connected for a certain period and then disconnect, also for resource saving purposes. Moreover, actual connection/disconnection status depends on the network coverage and capacity in the metro. Under these constraints, an application designer should be able to analyze and configure certain system aspects (network and user connectivity, event lifetime period, allocated system resources) in order to guarantee the appropriate response time and delivery success rate between the sources and the mobile users. To investigate such features, it is essential to model the performance of mobile pub/sub systems by considering the above constraints.

Several existing efforts concerning the design and evaluation of mobile systems aim at guaranteeing QoS (Quality of Service) requirements under several constraints (e.g., intermittent availability, limited resources, etc). The evaluation methods used are derived mainly from the field of *Queueing Theory*. For instance, 2-Dimensional (2-D) Markov chains and quasi-birth-death (QBD) processes have been used in [7–11] to model the changing connectivity of mobile users when offloading computation or data to the cloud through either 3G or WiFi connections; the goal is to evaluate the trade-off between performance and energy consumption. However, actually applying these methods remains a complex and tedious task for system designers. On the other hand, regarding pub/sub systems, Queueing Petri Nets (QPNs) have been used in [12, 13] for accurate performance prediction. However, QPNs, while highly expressive in representing parallelism, are suited for small-to-moderate size systems and intake considerable computational resources [14].

ICPE'17, April 22 - 26, 2017, L'Aquila, Italy

ISBN 978-1-4503-4404-3/17/04...$15.00

DOI: http://dx.doi.org/10.1145/3030207.3030220

In this paper, we model the performance of a mobile pub/sub system by relying on *Queueing Network Models* (QNMs) [15, 16]. QNMs have been extensively applied to represent and analyze communication and computer systems and they have proved to be simple and at the same time powerful tools for system designers with regard to system performance evaluation and prediction. Based on QNMs, pub/sub brokers are represented as queues, called *service centers* or *queueing centers*, and the exchanged events as *jobs* served. Our performance evaluation focuses on the tradeoff between the time decoupling provided by the pub/sub paradigm and the required end-to-end timeliness in the delivery of events.

Particularly, queueing networks have simple analytical solutions and can achieve a favorable balance between accuracy and efficiency. They enable the isolation and analysis of each service center from the rest of the network. The solution of the entire network can be formed by combining these separate solutions. In this work, we analyze a service center that represents an intermittently connected mobile publisher or subscriber. This is modeled explicitly as an "ON/OFF queueing center" and relates to the publisher/subscriber being either connected (ON) or disconnected (OFF). By analyzing this queueing center, we are able to derive theoretical results relating to the expected end-to-end response time of the events. The key contributions of this work are:

1. Introducing an overall model and end-to-end event delivery model for large-scale mobile pub/sub systems as queueing networks, which provides simple and sufficiently accurate performance metrics.
2. Incorporating the "ON/OFF queueing center" into the publisher's nodes and at each broker to take into account mobile characteristics of publishers and subscribers, such as connections/disconnections.
3. Modeling the end-to-end response time from publishers to subscribers by connecting several queueing centers. This is done by following the message routing path taken via the broker overlay network and analyzing the rates and service demands at each station.
4. Providing an analytical solution to the intermittent service (ON/OFF) queueing center, which can then be used as separate component inside large queueing networks. Hence, we enrich the existing bibliography on QNMs and their solutions.
5. Validating the model using simulations based on both probability distributions and real-world workload traces. We calculate end-to-end response times from real world traces in various scenarios, subject to intermittent network connectivity or voluntary user disconnections.

As QNMs offer a simple modeling environment, this methodology can be used by system designers/developers for system tuning and capacity planning. Application developers are able to study multiple scenarios by varying parameters (i.e., arrival rates, intermittent connectivity and service demands) in our proposed model. Middleware developers are able to model middleware systems with mobile characteristics by utilizing the intermittent service center. To the best of our knowledge, our work is the first which is utilizing QNMs to model intermittently connected mobile peers as service centers and analyzing accordingly a pub/sub system. The rest of this paper is organized as follows: Section 2 introduces the system model of the pub/sub system and the parameters used to represent publishers, brokers and subscribers. In Section 3, the theoretical analysis of end-to-end response times for event delivery is provided. Comparison with simulations is considered in Section 4. Finally, related work is discussed in Section 5 followed by conclusions in Section 6.

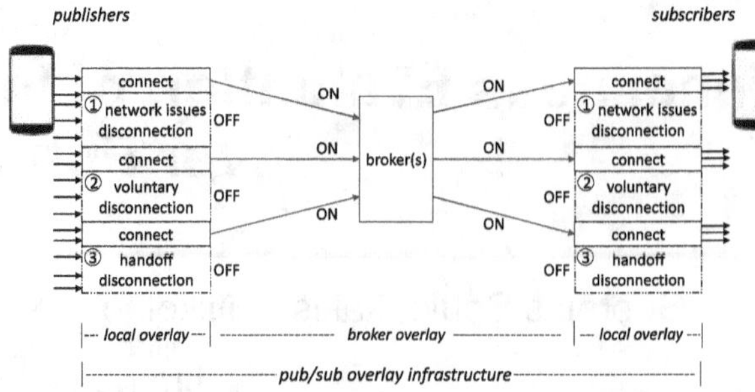

Figure 1: Peer's connectivity behaviour.

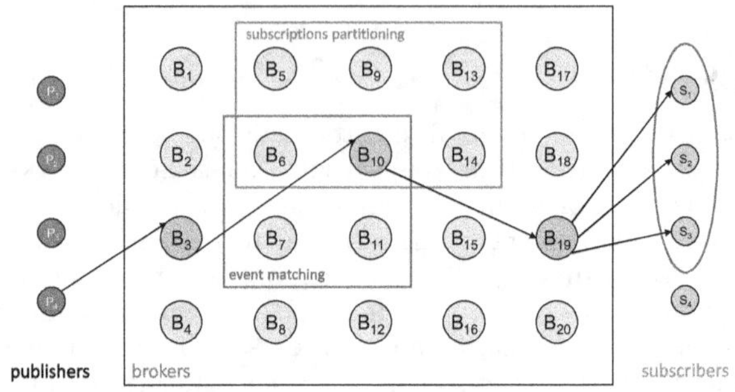

Figure 2: Network of brokers in a distributive pub/sub system.

2. SYSTEM MODEL

In this section, we first develop a model for mobile pub/sub systems. We then formulate the problem of calculating end-to-end delay for event delivery, which we call *end-to-end response time*, based on this model description.

2.1 Mobile Pub/Sub system

In this work, we assume mobile pub/sub systems, where multiple peers (publishers and subscribers) are mobile entities that interact with each other via a network of intermediate brokers. Each broker is linked to publishers/subscribers via wireless communication links and to other brokers via wired communication links. A pub/sub system generally builds upon an application-level overlay infrastructure. As depicted in Fig. 1, peers build upon the *local overlay* and they connect/disconnect to the *broker overlay* to send or receive events. More specifically, *publishers* produce events to their *local overlay*, which is occasionally connected to the *broker overlay*, to forward the published events. *Subscribers* connect occasionally (intermittent availability) to the *broker overlay* through their *local overlay* to receive new events. Both peers, connect and disconnect (state ON/OFF in Fig. 1) due to several reasons: *i)* there are network issues forcing disconnection (case ① in Fig. 1); *ii)* the peer disconnects from the broker overlay on a voluntary basis (e.g., to save energy) (case ② in Fig. 1); and *iii)* there is a peer's handoff between two brokers (case ③ in Fig. 1).

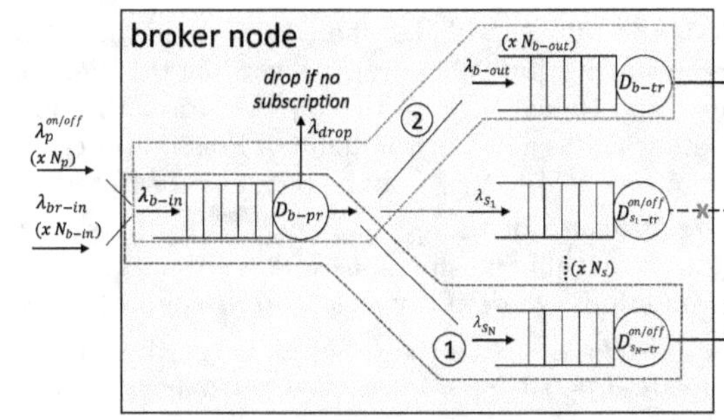

Figure 3: Pub/sub broker system model.

To support distributed applications spanning a wide-area, the pub/sub system has to be implemented as a set of independent, communicating brokers, forming the *broker overlay*. Based on [17], in such architectures, peers can access the system through any broker that becomes their *home broker*. Regardless of the subscription model (topic-based or content-based), subscribers notify interest for specific types of events (topics) to the home broker; subscriptions are spread to a subset of existing brokers (*subscription partitioning* process in Fig. 2). Such a technique of subscription partitioning provides higher scalability and improved efficiency in latency/network utilization.

On the other hand, publishers produce events characterized each by specific types (e.g., a topic) to their home broker; the subset of corresponding subscribers is determined through the *matching* process (see Fig. 2 with topic/content based filtering) which is performed by the pub/sub system. The produced events are delivered to all the determined subscribers by using the *event routing* process. This process is performed by using several algorithms, such selective routing or event gossiping. Regardless of the event routing algorithm used, produced events will pass through a specific path of brokers towards the subscribers. For example, based on Fig. 2 produced events will pass through B_3, to B_{10} and finally to B_{19}, which is the subscribers' home broker. In implementations such as Hermes [18], topic based routing of messages across brokers is carried out using a hash on the event types. Publishers wanting to publish send an advertisement message before eventual publication. A rendezvous node is set up by routing the message to a node closest to the hash of the event type name. Subscriber's subscription messages are also forwarded towards the rendezvous node. During the routing process, if an intermediary node with a particular event of interest is encountered, publications are sent using the reverse path (between the intermediary node and the subscriber), so as to prevent overloading of the rendezvous node. Such a system improves scalability and fault tolerance when compared to single broker architectures.

We model the pub/sub middleware components using simple input and output queues. An input queue is used to receive and process events and an output queue to transmit them. To tackle with mobile peer's connections and disconnections we introduce the *ON/OFF queue*. Accordingly, we model a publisher by using an *output ON/OFF queue* in its local overlay to transmit published events. If the publisher disconnects (state *OFF* in Fig. 1), events remain at the *ON/OFF queue* until its next connection (state *ON* in Fig. 1), in which are transmitted to its home broker. A subscriber is modeled as an *input queue* that receives events from the access broker. Finally, a broker (e.g., B_{19}) is modeled using a single *input queue* and multiple *output queues* as depicted in Fig. 3. Particularly, events arrive at a single input queue from generally multiple publishers/brokers with an arrival rate λ_{b_in}. Replication or dropping of events can occur at the exit of the input queue, depending on the subscriptions. If the event is not dropped is forwarded to: *i)* generally multiple continuous *output queues* for its transmission to other brokers (case ① in Fig. 3); *ii)* generally multiple *ON/OFF output queues* for its transmission to corresponding local subscribers (case ② in Fig. 3). In case a subscriber is disconnected, the event remains in its dedicated *ON/OFF output queue* until the next connection of the subscriber.

Based on the existing literature [19], every pub/sub middleware implementation (e.g., JMS [20], Gryphon [21]) offer some specific guarantees, with regard to the underlying transport protocols of the communication links. We assume that the underlying transport protocol of our system is *reliable* and offers the following guarantees: *i) Reliable message transmissions*: the underlying infrastructure guarantees that **the delivery of each message is verified** using: acks, nacks, timeouts and re-transmissions; *ii) FIFO Event ordering*: events are served in FIFO order upon arrival at any middleware component; and *iii) Persistent subscriptions*: Subscriptions are assumed to have long validity compared to the ON/OFF periods.

Thus, based on the above the broker/broker, broker/publisher, and broker/subscriber links are reliable and there are no event losses. Moreover, we assume that each broker is always up and running (e.g., deployed in a cloud [22]) and there is no broker overload and sufficient queue capacity so that no events are dropped.

The proposed pub/sub model allows representing a variety of existing mobile pub/sub systems [4, 22–24]. Events are delivered in an asynchronous way (push-based system), but our model can represent pull-based systems [25] as well. As a future direction, we intend to extend this model by applying time-to-live lifetime periods to each published event.

2.2 End-to-end Response Time Problem

With the presented mobile pub/sub system, the question that arises from a performance perspective is the following: Given the rate of published events and the availability (in terms of connectivity) of each mobile peer (publisher and subscriber), *what is the end-to-end response time of events from each publisher to each subscriber*? To estimate the end-to-end mean response time from a publisher p to a subscriber s, we define a metric called *end-to-end mean response time*, denoted by R_s^p.

In order to analytically calculate the end-to-end mean response time, we rely on queueing theory and describe formally the proposed mobile pub/sub system. To mathematically represent the arrival rates of events, we use a topic-based subscription model, since it is efficient and simple in terms of event classification. Nevertheless, our approach can be used for any model where several classification techniques are applied. Let V be the set of all topics in the system. Each *queue* or *queueing center* processes events through a dedicated *server*. Each server supports a specific *service demand* (time needed to process one event) denoted as D, which is exponentially distributed with rate $\mu > 0$. All queueing centers apply a first-come-first-served (FCFS) queueing policy. All notations can be found in Table 1.

Variable(s)	Definition/Description
$p \in P$	a publisher in the set of all publishers
V	set of all topic names in the system
V_p, V_s	sub-set of topics that p publishes events and s is subscribed
$s \in S$	a subscriber in the set of all subscribers
$\lambda_{p\_in}/\lambda_{p\_out}$, $\lambda_{b\_in}/\lambda_{b\_out}$, $\lambda_{s\_in}/\lambda_{s\_out}$	input or output rate of events at each publisher p, broker b, and subscriber s
ON, OFF	mobile peers states: ON for connected, OFF for disconnected
T_{ON}, T_{OFF}	average duration of ON (connected) and OFF (disconnected) periods
$b \in B$	a broker in the set of all brokers
$N_s \subseteq S$	number of subscribers, subscribed to b
D_{pr}, D_{tr}	the service demand for the processing and transmission of events
R_s^p	end-to-end response time from publisher p to subscriber s

Table 1: Model variables' and shorthand notation.

We model the connectivity of pub/sub peers as follows: let ON and OFF be the states where the peer is connected and disconnected, correspondingly. A given peer, is connected (ON state) for an exponentially distributed time period with parameter θ_{ON} ($\theta_{ON} = 1/T_{ON}$). Upon the expiration of this time, the peer disconnects (OFF state) and stops sending or receiving relevant events for an exponentially distributed time period with parameter θ_{OFF} ($\theta_{OFF} = 1/T_{OFF}$). To model the performance of a component that send events under the effect of the above connectivity, we introduce the "ON/OFF queueing center".

ON/OFF queueing center model : Each such component ($q_{on/off}$) is dedicated to a pub/sub peer (publisher p or subscriber s) and is responsible for the transmission of events. Its server processes events when the peer is connected. Thus, based on peers' connectivity, the $q_{on/off}$ server processes events according to the exponential distributions θ_{ON} and θ_{OFF}. A $q_{on/off}$ queueing center is defined by the tuple:

$$q_{on/off} = (\lambda_{in}, \lambda_{out}^{on/off}, D_{tr}, \theta_{ON}, \theta_{OFF})$$

where λ_{in} is the input rate of events to the queueing center, $\lambda_{out}^{on/off}$ is the output rate of events, and D_{tr} is the service demand for the transmission of events (if any) during T_{ON}. The $q_{on/off}$ accepts input rate of events according to a Poisson process λ_{in}. The output process $\lambda_{out}^{on/off}$ will be intermittent, because no event exits the queue during T_{OFF} intervals. We assume with good approximation that the output process $\lambda_{out}^{on/off}$ is Poisson during T_{ON} intervals with rate λ_{in} $*$ $(T_{ON}+T_{OFF})/T_{ON}$, so that the average output rate equals the average input rate. We call this an "intermittent Poisson process". Let $R_{p|s}^{on/off}$ be the average delay for the processing of events in $q_{on/off}$. Without loss of generality, we make the following assumption: if T_{ON} expires and there is an event currently being served, the server interrupts its processing and will continue in the next T_{ON} period.

Publisher Model : Let P be the set of all publishers in the system. Each publisher ($p \in P$) forwards the published events to its home broker when connected. For this, it maintains an "ON/OFF queueing center" to its local overlay. A publisher p is defined by the tuple:

$$p = (id_p, V_p, \lambda_{p\_in}, \lambda_{p\_out}, D_{tr}^{on/off}, T_{ON}, T_{OFF})$$

where id_p is the publisher's identifier, $V_p \subseteq V$ is the set of the topics on which p publishes events according to a Poisson process for each topic, λ_{p_in} is the input rate of the published events which is also Poisson (sum of Poisson processes for the set of topics V_p), λ_{p_out} is the output rate (intermittent Poisson because of the $q_{on/off}$), $D_{tr}^{on/off}$ is the service demand for the events transmission, and T_{ON} and T_{OFF} are the average periods where p connects and disconnects.

Subscriber Model : Let S be the set of all subscribers in the system. Each subscriber ($s \in S$) receives relevant events from its home broker when connected. A subscriber s is defined by the tuple:

$$s = (id_s, V_s, \lambda_{s\_in}, D_{pr}, T_{ON}, T_{OFF})$$

where id_s is the subscriber's identifier, $V_s \subseteq V$ is the set of the topics that s has subscribed, λ_{s_in} is the input rate which is intermittent Poisson since s receive events when connected (events match s's topics V_s), D_{pr} is the service demand for the local processing of events, and T_{ON} and T_{OFF} are the average periods where s connects and disconnects.

Broker Model : Let B be the set of all brokers in the system. Each broker ($b \in B$) receives the published events to several topics from local publishers and other brokers and forwards them to the corresponding brokers or local subscribers according to their connectivity status. A broker b is defined by the tuple:

$$b = (id_b, \lambda_{b\_in}, D_{pr}, N_s, D_s^{on/off}, \lambda_{s\_out}, N_{b\_out}, D_{b\_tr}, \lambda_{b\_out})$$

where id_b is the broker's identifier, λ_{b_in} is the broker's input rate according to a Poisson process due to the following: let $N_p \subseteq P$ be the set of publishers, and N_{b_in} be the set of brokers that publish events to b. As already defined, λ_{p_out} rate is intermittent Poisson. Accordingly, we assume that N_p randomly published λ_{p_out} rates, along with the published rates of N_{b_in} brokers, are also Poisson. Incoming events arrive at a single input queue, named "in queueing center" (q_{in}), to be processed. D_{pr} is the service demand to process the incoming events. Events without subscription are dropped. $N_s \subseteq S$ is the set of subscribers subscribed to the broker b. Depending on N_s, the broker maintains multiple output "ON/OFF queueing centers" ($q_{on/off}$) that represent subscribers connectivity. $D_s^{on/off}$ is the service demand to transmit events to s. λ_{s_out} is the intermittent Poisson output rate of events that match s's topics V_s. $N_{b\_out} \subseteq B$ is the set of brokers connected to b represented by multiple output queues, named "b_out queueing centers" (q_{b_out}). D_{b_out} is the service demand to transmit events to another broker, and λ_{b_out} is the output rate of events towards another broker (also Poisson).

End-to-end Response Time : To evaluate the average end-to-end response time from p to s, denoted by R_s^p, it is essential to consider every peer's connectivity and calculate the delay of the published events at every middleware component they pass through. For instance, considering the path of the events published from p_1 to s_3 in Fig. 2, events pass through: B_3, B_{10} and B_{19} brokers. Thus, it is essential to calculate the delay at: *i)* p_1's local overlay (p_1's $q_{on/off}$); *ii)* each intermediate broker B_3 and B_{10} (case ① in Fig. 3); *iii)* s_3's home broker B_{10} (case ② in Fig. 3); and *iv)* s_3's local overlay.

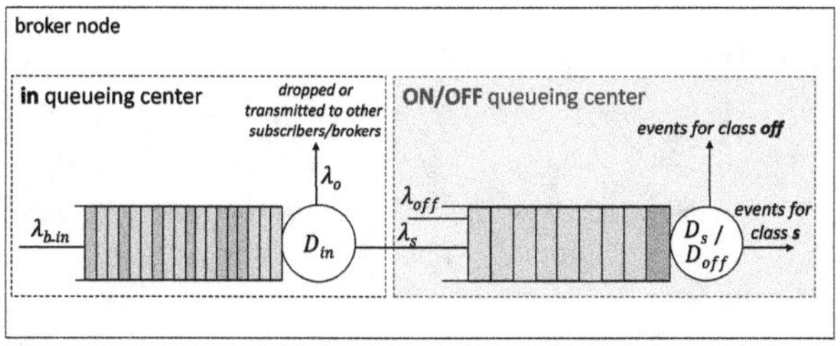

Figure 4: Queueing Network for a broker node.

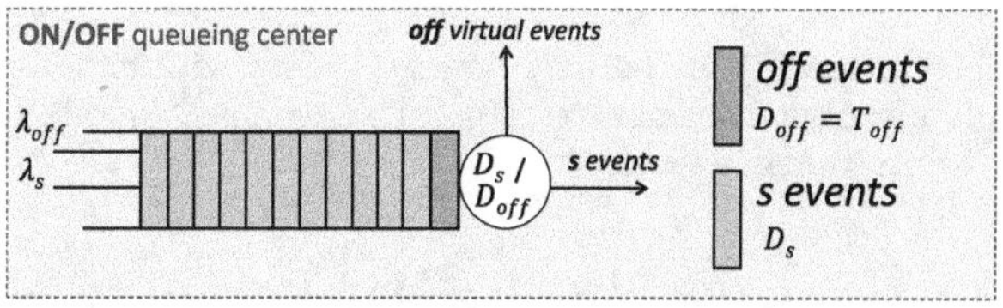

Figure 5: ON/OFF queueing center.

3. END-TO-END RESPONSE TIME

In this section, we define the properties that allow to build a queueing network. We then model the network of our system in order to calculate the *average end-to-end response time.*

3.1 Broker Queueing Network

To evaluate the end-to-end response time, we build upon *QNMs* [15, 26]. A *queueing network* is a network of connected *service centers* which provides analytical solutions for performance measures (e.g., response time). To obtain such solutions, each service center can be isolated from the rest of the network and evaluated analytically, under specific assumptions. Essentially, service centers are considered to be M/M/1 queues, i.e., featuring Poisson arrivals and exponential service times. The solution of the entire network can then be formed by combining these separate solutions. Even if these assumptions are rarely the case in real-world systems, *QNMs* have proved to provide good approximations in most such systems. In a pub/sub system, events pass through a subset of connected brokers up till the subscriber. To evaluate the performance of such a system, we model it with a network of service centers. Our main contribution lies in enhancing common QNMs with a more accurate model for the *ON/OFF queueing center.*

We evaluate our system analytically. As a first step, we focus on the subscriber's home broker. Such a broker is represented as follows: *i)* events from multiple brokers or publishers arrive at the first queue (*in queueing center*) with rate $\lambda_{\text{b\_in}}$ to be processed; *ii)* processed events are dropped if there is no subscription in the routing table by a subscriber or a another broker; *iii)* maintained events are transmitted (after possible replication) to interested subscribers and brokers; and *iv)* hence, events that match subscriber's topics are transmitted to the subscriber with rate λ_s. As already mentioned in Section 2, $\lambda_{\text{b\_in}}$ is Poisson; inside $\lambda_{\text{b\_in}}$, there is an event flow for the subscriber corresponding to a subset of topics (V_s), which is a sum of Poisson subflows, one per topic. Moreover, the service demand for the processing of events is exponential. Thus, λ_s at the output of the in queueing center is also Poisson.

3.1.1 Delay Calculation at each Service Center

We express the subscriber's home broker as a network of queueing centers (Fig. 4). Based on this queueing network, to evaluate the *average delay* (R_s^b) into the broker b for a subscriber $s \in S$, it is necessary to calculate the delay at each service center.

The *in queueing center* handles the flow of incoming events to the broker b with rate $\lambda_{\text{b\_in}}$. For each event the service demand is D_in. We model the *in queueing center* as an *M/M/1* ($q_{\text{m/m/1}}$). Based on standard solutions for M/M/1 queues [15], the response time is given by:

$$R_\text{s}^\text{in} = \frac{D_\text{in}}{1 - \lambda_{\text{b\_in}} D_\text{in}} \tag{1}$$

Regarding the *ON/OFF queueing center*, as already defined, its server is subject to an *ON/OFF* process following independent exponential T_ON/T_OFF intervals. Checking existing analytical solutions in the bibliography of QNMs, there is no solution for such a queueing center. In the following, we elaborate a solution based on the *mean value approach* [27]. This approach relies on common assumptions, such as: *i) the PASTA property*, where Poisson events encounter the mean queue upon arrival [27]; *ii) the Memoryless property of the exponential distribution*, where the expected time until completion of an event in service upon the arrival of a new event is equal to the service demand of the event in service; and *iii) Little's Law.*

To evaluate the *ON/OFF queueing center* we introduce - besides normal events - virtual *off* events that follow precisely the T_ON/T_OFF timing of the server: an (*off* event) arrives at the server exactly when the latter goes into its T_OFF interval. Moreover, we represent the server's inactivity during the T_OFF interval by the service demand of the *off* event. More precisely, we assume that an *off* event arrives at the system exactly at the beginning of a T_OFF interval and has preemptive priority over normal events. Hence, it reaches the server also at the beginning of the T_OFF interval, which corresponds to its service time.

Accordingly, we set the *off* events to have mean virtual service demand equal to T_OFF (let service demand D_off equal to T_OFF). Additionally, we assume that normal events have mean actual service demand D_s. This modeling allows mapping our *ON/OFF queueing center* to one with continuous service. Hence, as depicted in Fig. 5, we specify our model as a two-class model (normal events and *off* events) with preemptive priority [28]. As already defined, λ_s is the rate of the arriving *s* events, based on a Poisson process; events are served with service demand D_s, which is exponentially distributed. Moreover, λ_off is the rate of the arriving events of class *off*. To specify the λ_off rate, we formulate the following theorem.

THEOREM 1. *The average λ_off rate for the virtual* off *events is given by:*

$$\lambda_\text{off} = \frac{1}{T_\text{ON} + T_\text{OFF}} \tag{2}$$

PROOF. For an outside observer looking at the system an arbitrary point in time, a new *off* event arrives at the beginning of a T_OFF interval and is served for T_OFF. During T_OFF there is no other *off* event arrival. At the end of the T_OFF interval, a new *off* event will arrive after T_ON time period. Based on the above:

$$\lambda_\text{off} = \begin{cases} 0, & \text{during } T_\text{ON} \text{ intervals} \\ \frac{1}{T_\text{ON}}, & \text{during } T_\text{OFF} \text{ intervals} \end{cases} \tag{3}$$

Hence, during T_{ON}, the λ_{off} flow is Poisson with exponentially distributed parameter T_{ON}. The average λ_{off} rate for both intervals is given by:

$$\begin{aligned}\lambda_{off} &= \frac{T_{OFF}}{T_{ON}+T_{OFF}}\,0 + \frac{T_{ON}}{T_{ON}+T_{OFF}}\frac{1}{T_{ON}} \\ &= \frac{1}{T_{ON}+T_{OFF}}\end{aligned} \tag{4}$$

Note that the overall λ_{off} flow is not Poisson: during the T_{OFF} interval no new *off* event is allowed to arrive. □

The following theorem exploits the PASTA property, priority queueing, and Little's law in order to evaluate the $q_{on/off}$ queueing center.

THEOREM 2. *The average delay or response time $R_s^{on/off}$ for the $q_{on/off}$ queueing center is given by:*

$$R_s^{on/off} = \frac{\frac{T_{OFF}^2}{T_{ON}+T_{OFF}} + D_s \frac{T_{ON}+T_{OFF}}{T_{ON}}}{1 - \lambda_s D_s \frac{T_{ON}+T_{OFF}}{T_{ON}}} \tag{5}$$

PROOF. In our queueing center, the *off* class has *preemptive priority* over the class *s*. For such a model, a new arriving *off* event has to wait and be served for time:

$$R_{off} = D_{off} + Q_{off} D_{off} \tag{6}$$

where Q_{off} is the number of the *off* events present in the queue. The *off* event has priority over the *s* events and thus, it has to wait only for preceding *off* events (if any). On the other hand, a new arriving *s* event has to wait and be served for time:

$$R_s = D_s + Q_s D_s + Q_{off}^{pre} D_{off} + Q_{off}^{post} D_{off} \tag{7}$$

In this case, despite the fact that a new *s* event has arrived, there is always the possibility that an *off* event can arrive. Thus, an event *s* must wait for any *off* and *s* class events that are already in the queue when it arrives, and any *off* class events that arrive during its residence period. Let Q_{off}^{pre} be the average number of *off* events found in the queue when the *s* event arrived and Q_{off}^{post} be the average number of *off* events that arrive in the queue after the arrival of *s*.

Our model has some singularities we should take into account. More specifically, according to the the Theorem 1 λ_{off} is not Poisson. Thus, the PASTA property does not hold and Q_{off} in eq. 6, encountered by a new arriving off event, is not the average Q_{off}. Nevertheless, we have already defined that it can be only one *off* event in the system. Thus, a new arriving *off* event sees $Q_{off} = 0$, and based on the eq. 6 it has to wait for time:

$$R_{off} = D_{off} \tag{8}$$

On the other hand, *s* class arrivals are Poisson. Thus, in case of a new *s* arriving event, the PASTA property holds. Hence, by taking into account that during T_{OFF} exists only one *off* event in the system and during T_{ON} none, the average Q_{off}^{pre} number of *off* events is given by:

$$\begin{aligned}Q_{off}^{pre} &= \frac{T_{OFF}}{T_{ON}+T_{OFF}}1 + \frac{T_{ON}}{T_{ON}+T_{OFF}}0 \\ &= \frac{T_{OFF}}{T_{ON}+T_{OFF}}\end{aligned} \tag{9}$$

Furthermore, since λ_{off} is different during T_{ON} and T_{OFF} (see eq. 3), we must express the average Q_{off}^{post}, separately at each interval:

$$Q_{off}^{post} = R_s^{T_{ON}} \frac{1}{T_{ON}} + R_s^{T_{OFF}} 0 \tag{10}$$

$R_s^{T_{ON}}$ is the portion of R_s that corresponds to T_{ON} and $R_s^{T_{OFF}}$ is the portion of R_s that corresponds to T_{OFF}. Based on the eq. 7:

$$R_s^{T_{ON}} = D_s + Q_s D_s \tag{11}$$

Finally, based on Little's law:

$$Q_s = \lambda_s R_s \tag{12}$$

Thus, based on equations 9, 10, 7 and 12, we use equation 7 to derive the response time R_s, which is denoted as $R_s^{on/off}$ for the *ON/OFF queueing center.* □

Subsequently, the home broker of the subscriber is modeled by utilizing the (*in queueing center*) connected to the *ON/OFF queueing center.* Thus, we evaluate the average delay, R_s^b, for a subscriber in broker *b* by using the eq. 1 and Theorem 2 as follows:

$$R_s^b = R_s^{in} + R_s^{on/off} \tag{13}$$

Based on the above analysis, in case the published events pass through multiple brokers before reaching subscriber's home broker, they are processed at the *in queueing center* and then transmitted through the broker's *out queueing center.* Thus, such a broker is modeled using two *M/M/1 queueing centers* and the average delay R_s^b is given by:

$$R_s^b = R_s^{in} + R_s^{out} \tag{14}$$

3.2 End-to-end delay calculation from a mobile publisher to a mobile subscriber

In the previous subsection, we calculated the average delay of subscriber events into a broker *b*. Let *ps* be the class of events published from a specific mobile publisher *p* and that reach a specific mobile subscriber *s*. Let λ_{ps} be the rate of events for the class *ps*. To estimate the *average end-to-end response time* (R_s^p) regarding the events of the class *ps*, we feed the flow λ_{ps} alone through the sequence of queueing centers modeling the path between p and s while taking also into account the load of the queueing centers due to all the other flows of the pub/sub system. Thus, we create a path of queueing centers by considering the queueing centers of: *i)* the *p*'s local overlay; *ii)* the subset of brokers that the events pass through; and *iii)* the *s*'s local overlay.

Regarding *p*'s local overlay, Theorem 2 provides a simple analytical solution to calculate approximately the delay of a component that publishes events based on the peer's connectivity. Thus, the *ON/OFF queueing center* can be used to evaluate the performance of a publisher *p*. Regarding each broker *b*, if *b* is *s*'s home broker, the eq. 13 is used, otherwise the eq. 14 is used (see previous subsection). Finally, *s*'s local overlay is modeled by an output queue. Thus, the analytical solution of a simple *M/M/1 queueing center* (eq. 1) can be used to evaluate its performance.

For a given λ_{ps} flow, system designers should parameterize the above analytical solutions. Particularly they must define the T_{ON} and T_{OFF} connectivity periods of *p* and *s*, and the service demand (*D*) when *ps* events are processed at each queueing center. Additionally, they should consider the effect of other flows going through the queueing centers. Let

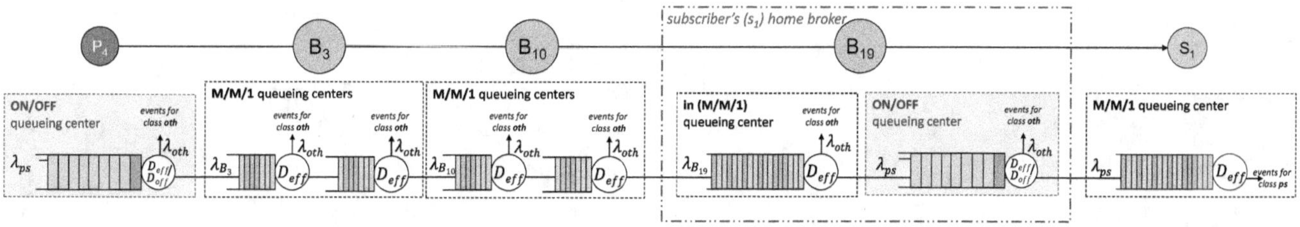

Figure 6: End-to-end queueing network from p_4 to s_1.

oth be the class of events that pass through each queueing center and are different from the events of class *ps*. Let λ_{oth} be the rate of events for the class *oth*; the service demand to serve them is D, same as for ps events. To include the effect of λ_{oth} flows going through the queueing centers, we abstract the utilization of each queueing center by its λ_{oth} flow by calculating the effective service demand D_{eff} for the λ_{ps} flow when λ_{ps} is fed alone through the queueing center. More specifically, for each queueing center, we solve:

$$R(\lambda_{\text{ps}}, D_{\text{eff}}) = R(\lambda_{\text{ps}} + \lambda_{\text{oth}}, D) \qquad (15)$$

meaning that λ_{ps} flowing alone under D_{eff} should have the same response time as when flowing together with λ_{oth} under D.

In case our queueing station is an *M/M/1 queueing center*, based on eq. 1, $D^{\text{ps}}_{\text{eff}}$ can be calculated by:

$$D^{\text{ps}}_{\text{eff}}(\lambda_{\text{oth}}, D) = \frac{D}{1 - \lambda_{\text{oth}} D} \qquad (16)$$

Similarly $D^{\text{ps}}_{\text{eff}}$ is calculated for the *ON/OFF queueing center* by using our analytical solution of Theorem 2.

Below we provide an algorithm which accepts as input the path of connected brokers $K \in B$ for the delivery of events from a mobile publisher p to a mobile subscriber s. The output of the algorithm is the network of queueing centers and can be used for the evaluation of its performance.

Algorithm 1: Composition of end-to-end queueing network publisher p to subscriber s.

Input: path of connected brokers $K \in B$ from p to s; rate of events λ_{ps}, λ_{oth}; and service demand D at p, s and each broker in K.

Output: end-to-end queueing network QN from p to s; λ_k at each queueing center; effective service demand D^k_{eff} at each queueing center.

Connect the publisher's queueing center::
$QN \leftarrow q_{\text{on/off}}$;
$\lambda_0 \leftarrow \lambda_{\text{ps}}$, $D^0_{\text{eff}} \leftarrow D^{\text{ps}}_{\text{eff}}(\lambda^{\text{p}}_{\text{oth}}, D^{\text{p}})$;
for $k \leftarrow 1$ *to* K **do**
  if $k = K$ **then**
    Connect the queueing centers of s's home broker:
    $QN \leftarrow QN + q_{\text{m/m/1}} + q_{\text{on/off}}$;
    M/M/1 queuing center;
    $\lambda_{\text{k1}} \leftarrow \lambda_{\text{ps}}$ $D^{\text{k1}}_{\text{eff}} \leftarrow D^{\text{ps}}_{\text{eff}}(\lambda^{\text{k1}}_{\text{oth}}, D^{\text{k1}})$;
    ON/OFF queuing center;
    $\lambda_{\text{k2}} \leftarrow \lambda_{\text{ps}}$, $D^{k2}_{\text{eff}} \leftarrow D^{\text{ps}}_{\text{eff}}(\lambda^{\text{k2}}_{\text{oth}}, D^{\text{k2}})$;
  else
    Connect the queueing centers of broker B_{k}:
    $QN \leftarrow QN + q_{\text{m/m/1}} + q_{\text{m/m/1}}$;
    M/M/1 queuing centers;
    $\lambda_{\text{k1}} \leftarrow \lambda_{\text{ps}}$ $D^{\text{k1}}_{\text{eff}} \leftarrow D^{\text{ps}}_{\text{eff}}(\lambda^{\text{k1}}_{\text{oth}}, D^{\text{k1}})$;
    $\lambda_{\text{k2}} \leftarrow \lambda_{\text{ps}}$, $D^{\text{k2}}_{\text{eff}} \leftarrow D^{\text{ps}}_{\text{eff}}(\lambda^{\text{k2}}_{\text{oth}}, D^{\text{k2}})$;

Connect the subscriber's queueing center:
$QN \leftarrow QN + q_{\text{m/m/1}}$;
$\lambda_{\text{k+1}} \leftarrow \lambda_{\text{ps}}$, $D^{\text{k+1}}_{eff} \leftarrow D^{\text{ps}}_{\text{eff}}(\lambda^{\text{k+1}}_{\text{oth}}, D^{\text{k+1}})$;
return QN, λ_{k} $\forall k \in \{0, K, k+1\}$, D_{k} $\forall k \subset \{0, K, k+1\}$;

For instance, in case we apply the above algorithm to the set of connected brokers from p_4 to s_1 in Fig. 2, the output of the above algorithm is the end-to-end queueing network of the Fig. 6. Thus, using our analytical solutions, the *average end-to-end response time* $R^{\text{p4}}_{\text{s1}}$ is given by:

$$R^{\text{p4}}_{\text{s1}} = R^{\text{on/off}}_{\text{p4}} + R^{\text{b3}}_{\text{s1}} + R^{\text{b10}}_{\text{s1}} + R^{\text{b19}}_{\text{s1}} + R^{\text{s1}}_{\text{s1}}$$

where $R^{\text{b3}}_{\text{s1}}$, $R^{\text{b10}}_{\text{s1}}$, $R^{\text{b19}}_{\text{s1}}$ are known by the equations 13 and 14.

In Algorithm 1, we do not deal with the actual routing protocols that are specified by the routing overlay. In actual middleware implementations (Hermes, Gryphon, Siena), the state of the overlay network (events, demand, topology, queue lengths) will determine the broker node routes used. Algorithm 1 aggregates the queue centers based on a selected topology and provides the aggregated end-to-end queuing model.

4. EVALUATION RESULTS

4.1 ON/OFF queueing center validation

To validate our model, we have developed a simulator for mobile pub/sub systems which can be parameterized using well-known probability distributions and actual data derived from a real setup (real traces).

4.1.1 Analytical vs. Simulated Response Time

Our simulator, *MobileJINQS*[1], is an open-source library for building simulations encompassing the constraints of mobile systems. *MobileJINQS* is an extension of *JINQS*, a Java simulation library for multiclass queueing networks [29].

We utilize *MobileJINQS* to implement the *ON/OFF queueing center* described in Section 2. Mobile peers connect and disconnect in the scale of seconds/minutes to send/receive events, depending on the application context. To represent such behavior, we set the ON/OFF system parameters as follows: *i)* the server remains in the *ON* and *OFF* states for exponentially distributed time periods $T_{\text{ON}} = T_{\text{OFF}} = 20/40/60$ sec, thus, the server changes its state every 20, 40 and 60 sec; *ii)* events are served with a mean service demand $D = 0.125$ sec; *iii)* there is sufficient buffer capacity so that no events are dropped; and *iv)* events arrive to the queue with a mean rate varying from 0.05 to 4 events per sec ($\lambda_{\text{max}} = 4$ events/sec). By applying λ rates greater than 4 events/sec, the system saturates. Using the above settings in our simulator, we run the system and derive the simulated curve of the mean response time for several λ rates as depicted in Fig. 7. Confidence intervals of the simulation results are found to be very small (less than two order of magnitude) and are not presented in the figures.

Subsequently, we apply the same parameters to the equation of Theorem 2 in order to analytically calculate the re-

[1]http://xsb.inria.fr/d4d#mobilejinqs

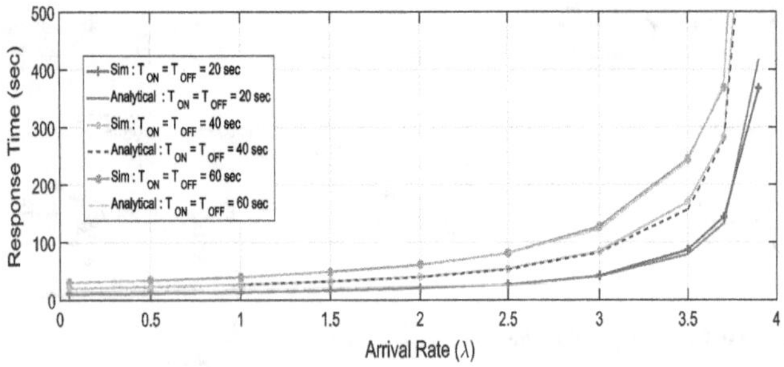

Figure 7: Analytical vs. Simulated Response Times at the *ON/OFF queueing center*.

sponse time as depicted in Fig. 7 through the analytical curve. For a service center where its server is always *ON*, the system does not saturate if $\lambda D < 1$. However, for the *ON/OFF queueing center* the system does not saturate if $\lambda D \frac{T_{ON}+T_{OFF}}{T_{ON}} < 1$ as indicated by the denominator of the Theorem 2. Thus, this confirms that $\lambda_{max} = 4$ events/sec for a system reaching a steady state. By comparing the curves for the simulated and analytical response times, we notice that results match with high accuracy for arrival rates below to 3.5 events/sec. Differences are noticed for rates equal to or higher than 3.5 events/sec. This is acceptable, since the system is close to saturation at these rates.

4.1.2 Validation using Arrival Rates from Real Traces

To further validate our model, we parameterize it using input workloads derived from real traces. The real data, named the *D4D* dataset, was provided to us by Orange Labs in the context of the *D4D* challenge[2]. The *D4D* dataset contains Call Detail Records (CDRs) of users that are subscribed to the Sonatel Telecom mobile operator in Senegal. This data was collected for the whole country over a period of 50 weeks from 7 January 2013 until 23 December 2013. More details about our analysis of the *D4D* dataset and the way we have leveraged it to model the performance of large-scale mobile pub/sub systems can be found in our recent work in [30].

For our validation we used the antenna *traces*. An antenna trace reflects the number of calls made or SMS sent by many mobile users associated to this antenna, over the period of 50 weeks. We assume homogeneity in user access patterns to mobile services (antennas) and application services. For parameterizing the *ON/OFF queueing center*, we map the number of calls or SMS per 10 min interval at the selected antenna to an equal number of events published over the same time interval. Based on [30], this mapping results in a *non-homogeneous Poisson process (or input flow)*, defined as λ_{in}, with rate parameter $\lambda_{(t)}$ piecewise constant in each interval $t \in T$:

$$\lambda_{(t)} = \frac{N_i^t}{|t|} \quad (17)$$

where T is the 50-week period, $|t|$ equals to 10 min, and N_i^t is the number of published events for each 10 min interval at a given antenna i.

Thus, in order to calculate the rate of the input flow (λ_{in}) over the 50-week period at a given antenna i, we use the eq. 17. Subsequently we use these rates to parameterize the *ON/OFF queueing center*. To perform our experiments with representative traces, we selected input flows from a

[2]http://www.d4d.orange.com/en/Accueil

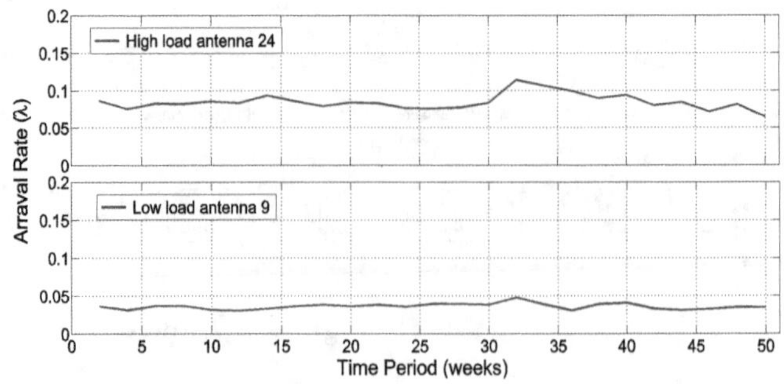

Figure 8: Low and High load Arrival Rates.

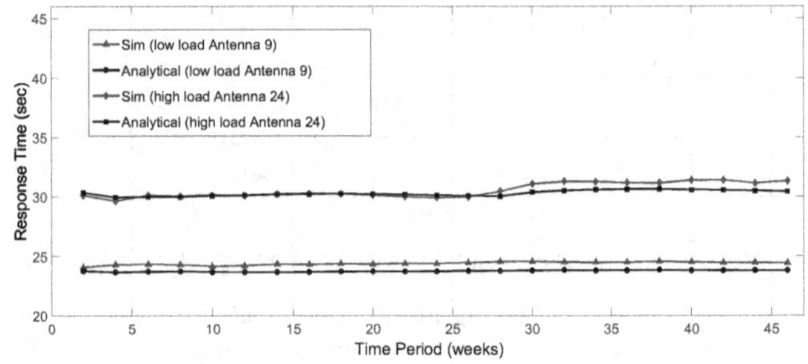

Figure 9: Analytical vs. Simulated Response Times using Arrival Rates from Real Traces.

low load antenna and a *high load antenna*. Fig. 8 depicts two antennas used for our experiments: *i)* antenna 9 has a low load input flow with overall average rate of 0.04; and *ii)* antenna 24 has a high load input flow with overall average rate of 0.075.

To perform simulations and compare the results with our analytical model, we extend the *MobileJINQS* simulator by enabling the application of non-homogeneous input flows to the *ON/OFF queueing center*. Thus, we set the system as follows: *i)* the server remains in the *ON* and *OFF* states for exponentially distributed time periods with parameters $\theta_{ON} = \theta_{OFF} = 0.025$ (i.e. $T_{ON} = T_{OFF} = 40$ sec); *ii)* events are served with a mean service demand $D = 1$ sec; and *iii)* events arrive to the queue with variable λ rate for each 10 min interval, based on the loads of antennas 9 and 24 (Fig. 8). By running the system with the above settings we derive the simulated curves of the mean response times for the input flows of antennas 9 and 24 over the 50-week period, as depicted in Fig. 9. The mean response times regarding the overall period are 24 and 31 sec, correspondingly for the two antennas.

Subsequently, we apply the same parameter values to the equation of Theorem 2 for each 10 min interval and we calculate the mean response times over the 50-week period as depicted in Fig. 9 through the analytical curves. The mean response times regarding the overall period are 23 and 30 sec, correspondingly for each antenna. Note that we selected these parameter values with respect to our condition ($\lambda_{(t)} D \frac{T_{ON}+T_{OFF}}{T_{ON}} < 1$), in order to avoid the saturation of the *ON/OFF queueing center*. By comparing the curves for the simulated and analytical response times, we notice that the absolute deviation between the two is no more than 5% (approximately 1 sec).

It is worth noting that using the load of antenna 24, the mean response time is much higher in comparison to the one of antenna 9 (7 sec difference). In this case, to get a

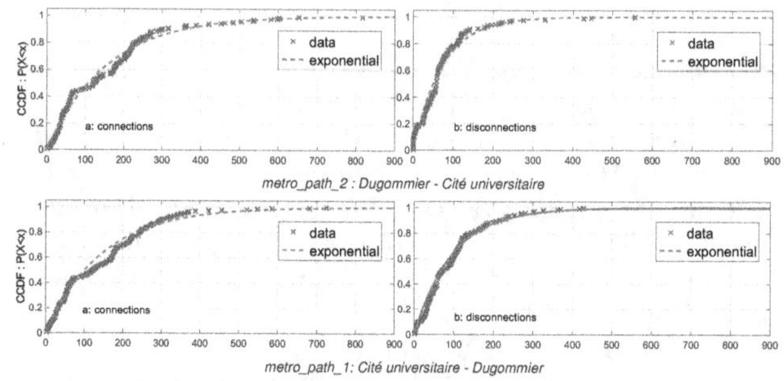

Figure 10: CCDF of connections and disconnections.

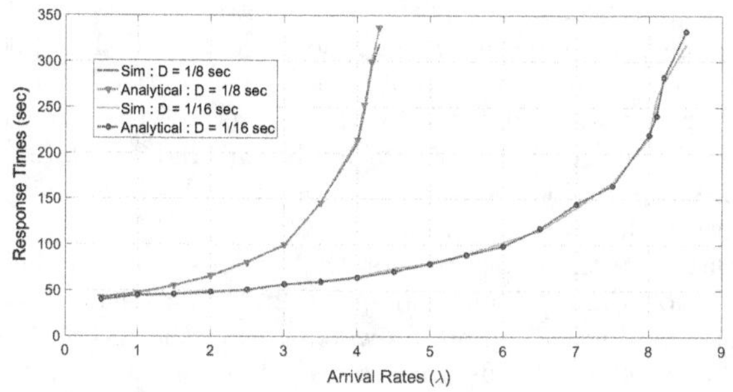

Figure 11: Response Time while traveling in metro path: Cité Universitaire - Dugommier.

lower mean response time, an application developer should set the system to process faster the published events (lower service demand D) of antenna trace 24. Assuming that user access to mobile services (or antennas) is similar to user access to application services, antenna traces can be leveraged for broker capacity planning in related areas. However, performing simulations leads to high development and computational cost in order to obtain accurate results. Therefore, our analytical model can be a useful tool for evaluating the performance of middleware systems.

4.1.3 Validation using Connectivity Rates from Real Traces

The analytical solution of our *ON/OFF queueing center* can be parameterized with parameters related to connectivity. To investigate solutions regarding issues in real life, we study the actual connections and disconnections in the metro. Towards this, we have developed an android application, named *Metro Cognition*[3], related to network connectivity data for metro passengers in Paris and Delhi.

Metro Cognition collects connectivity tuples using the Android *BroadcastReceiver* while the user is traveling. Additionally, using a background service it collects more tuples every 30 seconds for safety reasons. Let `con_tuple` be the connectivity tuple with the following 4 values: *i) ON/OFF* (depending on availability of Internet connection); *ii) timestamp* (the exact time when the connectivity status ON/OFF is captured); *iii) provider* (e.g. Vodafone) and; *vi) metro_path_id* (a unique identifier for the user's path from one metro station to another).

One `con_pattern` consists of many `con_tuple`. Each `con_pattern` is created as follows: *i)* the user starts the application and chooses the path between two metro stations; *ii)* the background connectivity service starts; *iii)* when the connectivity status changes and every 30 seconds, a tuple

[3]https://goo.gl/x6vuoB

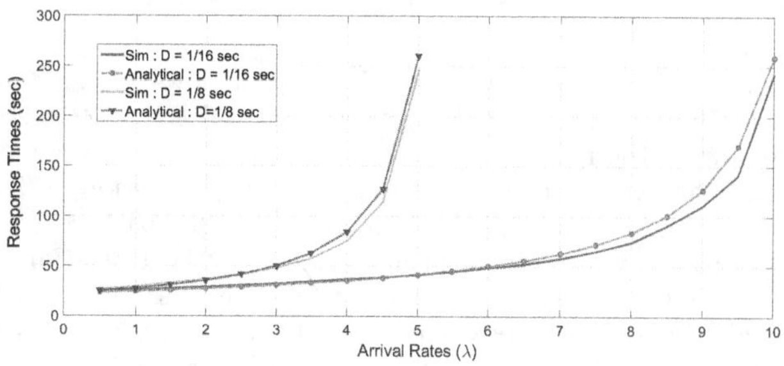

Figure 12: Response Time while traveling in metro path: Dugommier - Cité Universitaire.

(`con_tuple`) is created; *iv)* when the user's journey ends, the background service stops, the data are stored in JSON format and are sent to the cloud server *GoFlow*[4]. In [31], we initiated the creation of a dataset related to network connectivity data for metro travelers in Paris and Delhi.

To utilize our dataset for the validation of the *ON/OFF queueing center*, we concatenate all the `con_patterns` for each *metro_path_id*. So far, we have collected sufficient amount of data in the following metro paths:

-metro_path_1 : Cité Universitaire → Dugommier; *journeys* : 34; *total duration* : 15.18 hours; *average duration journey* : 26.8 min.

-metro_path_2 : Dugommier → Cité Universitaire; *journeys* : 28; *total duration* : 12.13 hours; *average duration journey* : 26 min.

Our data[5] show that metro travelers lose and recover network connection for periods equal from several seconds to 5 minutes, maximum. In average, connected periods are 1.5 times larger than the disconnected periods. As a first step, we specify the best fit of our data to existing probability distributions by applying the same method as in [9]. Fig. 10 shows the complementary cumulative distribution functions (CCDFs) of connections and disconnections at each of the above metro paths. An interesting observation from CCDFs is that our traces fit best with exponential distributions. More specifically, the measured statistics fit very well with 146.38 (i.e., T_{ON}) and 96 (i.e., T_{OFF}) seconds in average for connections and disconnections while traveling in path 1. For path 2, the average connection time is 155.88 sec (i.e., T_{ON}), and the average disconnection is 72.15 sec (i.e., T_{OFF}).

Using our simulator, we start with the 1st metro path (Cité Universitaire → Dugommier) and we generate connectivity data that follow exponential distributions with the above parameters: $T_{\mathrm{ON}} = 146.38$ sec and $T_{\mathrm{OFF}} = 96$ sec. Subsequently, we are able to calculate the delay of events when sent and received by metro travelers. Fig. 11, compares the response times between the theoretical analysis and the model-based simulation when applying the above connectivity parameters, various arrival rates, and various service times. We notice that results match with high accuracy. By applying service time, $D = 0.125$ sec, the system response time becomes too high for λ rates greater than 3.5 events/sec. To tune the system providing better response time, events should be processed faster. Thus, by applying service time, $D = 0.0625$ sec, the response time is too high for λ rates greater than 7 events/sec.

Regarding the 2nd path (Dugommier → Cité Universitaire), we confirm the correctness of the above approach as

[4]https://goflow.ambientic.mobi
[5]https://goo.gl/1SBiaU

follows: instead of generating data that follows exponential distribution, we directly apply the derived ON/OFF periods from the real traces. Using the same setup as previous and the average connected and disconnected periods (T_{ON} = 155.88 sec and T_{OFF} = 72.15 sec) in the 2nd path, Fig. 12 compares the response times between the theoretical analysis and the trace-based simulation. Results match with high accuracy for low rates. For higher rates, there is a quite good match between the two with the maximum difference of about 10%. The gap comes from the fact that our dataset is still small, and thus, simulation may not always reach mean response times. In our future work, we intend to continue the collection of data to perform experiments in several other paths of the metro in Paris.

4.2 End-to-end Response Time Evaluation

In Section 3, we provide an approach to model and evaluate the end-to-end response time over a pub/sub system by focusing on the connectivity of mobile peers. Based on several overlay infrastructures such as Jedi [32], Siena [33], Gryphon [21] and Hermes [18]; various topologies can be formed. In this paper, we are agnostic to the type of overlay topology used; and system designers are able to use Algorithm 1 to model all the queuing centers for end-to-end communication from the publisher p to the subscriber s. However, depending on the time scale of user's connectivity the response time might be significantly affected. In this subsection, we study multiple scenarios for parameterizing the queueing centers, by considering three types of connectivity and a specific overlay topology.

4.2.1 End-to-end System tuning

For our experimental setup, we use the end-to-end queueing network of the Fig. 6 to evaluate the response time from publisher p_4 to subscriber s_1. Application developers can utilize our proposed analytical solutions to study multiple application scenarios by varying the following parameters: λ, T_{ON}, T_{OFF} and D.

For all the experiments bellow we assume that the publisher p_4 transmits its events; and the subscriber s_1 process them to its local queue with service demand $D_{s_1} = 62.5$ ms. These values are set in order to evaluate if the delay introduced by the broker path significantly affects end-to-end latency. We define the peers' connectivity by considering disconnections: *i)* network issues; *ii)* voluntary reasons; *iii)* degraded network.

Network Issues

The actual connection/disconnection status of the mobile user depends on the network coverage and capacity. The average connection periods depend also on the type of user mobility. For example, there periods differ for pedestrians, vehicular, rail and metro passengers. For the present evaluation, we employ scenarios with metro passengers. In [31], we conclude that connectivity patterns of a path depend on both the network coverage and crowdedness of the metro. Thus, we evaluate the end-to-end response of the queueing network in Fig. 6 by considering the following scenarios:

Scenario 1 : p_4 travels on the path *Bastille → Cité Universitaire*. It is connected for T_{ON} = 109 sec and disconnected for T_{OFF} = 121.5 sec in average. It produces events with rate $\lambda = 1$ event/sec that reach s_1 who travels on the path *Cité Universitaire → Dugommier* and is connected and disconnected for T_{ON} = 146.3 sec and T_{OFF} = 96 sec in average. Both passengers travel during the morning.

Scenario 2 : p_4 travels on the path *Étienne Marcel → Mairie de Montrouge*. It is connected for T_{ON} = 292.1 sec and disconnected for T_{OFF} = 78.7 sec in average. It produces events with rate $\lambda = 1$ event/sec towards s_1 which travels on the path *Dugommier → Cité Universitaire* and is connected and disconnected for T_{ON} = 155.8 sec and T_{OFF} = 72.1 sec in average. Both passengers travel during the evening.

We assume that the broker network is reliable with no broker overload. Thus, the event delivery latency is in the scale of hundreds of milliseconds to 1 second. Accordingly, for each broker of the path (from p_4 to s_1), we define the service demand (D) at each queueing center equal to 0.0625 sec. The average connectivity periods are derived from the real traces of the dataset[6] in the metro of Paris. In Table 2, we compare the results of analytical and simulated response times of the above scenarios. The absolute deviation between the two is no more than 5%.

Based on the above results, the response time of the 1st scenario is much higher than the 2nd. This happens because the metro is more crowded during the morning and the connected periods are shorter. Also, since the scale of the peer's connectivity is in tenths of minutes; the transmission and processing delay in the broker path is negligible.

Voluntary Reasons

In this case, common practice of mobile subscribers is to remain disconnected for a long period, and than periodically connect to receive events that match their interests. In this way they are able to save energy resources to their smartphone or to consume their monthly data plan accordingly. For such connectivity periods, we consider the following scenarios: *i)* p_4 connects for T_{ON} = 60 sec to publish events, and disconnected for T_{OFF} = 10 min in average. Events can be produced while the user is disconnected and forwarded when is connected. The publishing rate is $\lambda = 0.5$ event/sec. s_1 connects to receive events for T_{ON} = 30 sec and disconnects for T_{OFF} = 15 min in average; *ii)* p_4 is a web server deployed on cloud always connected ($T_{\text{OFF}} = 0$) and produces events with rate $\lambda = 0.5$ event/sec towards s_1 which connects to receive events (e.g., news feeds) during T_{ON} = 30 sec and disconnects for T_{OFF} = 15 min in average.

Similarly to the previous experiment, we assume that the broker network is reliable with no broker overload. Thus, for each broker we define the service demand (D) at each queueing center equal to 0.0625 sec. Results are shown in Table 2. Similarly the absolute deviation between the analytical and the simulated response time is no more than 5% and the transmission/processing delay in the broker path is negligible (the scale of the peer's connectivity is in tenths of minutes).

Degraded network

So far, we have assumed that our broker network is reliable. In this experiment, we study situation when brokers connect through a degraded network. Network degradation refers to a decrease in connectivity and an increase in latency throughout a given network. In such a network, mobile users connect and disconnect very often (every few seconds). Published events might be re-transmitted until they reach their

[6] https://goo.gl/1SBiaU

Disconnections	p_4 (T_{ON}, T_{OFF})	s_1 (T_{ON}, T_{OFF})	Simulation	Analytical model	Deviation %
Metro Travel	109, 121.5 (sec)	146.3, 96 (sec)	118.7 (sec)	116.76 (sec)	1.63
	292.1, 78.7 (sec)	155.8, 72.1 (sec)	45.3 (sec)	43.7 (sec)	3.53
Voluntary	60 (sec), 10 (min)	30 (sec), 15 (min)	27.82 (min)	28.31 (min)	1.76
	always, 0	30 (sec), 15 (min)	17.61 (min)	18.03 (min)	2.38
Network Degradation	1 (sec), 1 (sec)	1.5 (sec), 1.5 (sec)	2.41 (sec)	2.26 (sec)	6.22

Table 2: Estimated vs Measured Response Times.

final destination. The output flows of events increases at each publisher/broker.

Based on the above, we consider the following scenario: p_4 connects for $T_{\mathrm{ON}} = 1$ sec to publish events, and disconnected for $T_{\mathrm{OFF}} = 1$ sec in average. s_1 connects to receive events for $T_{\mathrm{ON}} = 1.5$ sec and disconnects for $T_{\mathrm{OFF}} = 1.5$ sec in average. Since the broker network is degraded, we increase the publishing rate at $\lambda = 2$ event/sec (due to retransmissions) with service demand D at each queueing center equal to 0.0625 sec. Results are shown in Table 2. Note that for this scale of peers' connectivity, the transmission/processing delay in the broker path is not negligible.

5. RELATED WORK

The pub/sub interaction paradigm is increasingly being used in the design of large-scale distributed systems. Consequently, investigating evaluation techniques of such systems has become crucial. In this Section, we present our survey concerning the recent efforts in the design and evaluation of mobile systems. We divide the survey into 2 categories: the 1st is general related work in queueing theory applied to performance modeling of multiple applications, and the 2nd is literature specific to the performance of pub/sub systems.

Concerning the related work in queueing theory, we begin with the work of Mehmeti et al. [8], where *WiFi offloading* is analyzed extensively by providing performance metrics to improve the efficiency. The authors model the WiFi network availability as an ON/OFF alternating renewal process, which is similar to our mobile subscriber's availability. In order to provide performance metrics of the above models, authors investigate a queueing analytical model based on the *2-Dimensional (2-D) Markov chains.* Authors in [9], also use *2-D Markov chains* to model the WiFi offloading, however they only provide numerical solutions. Moreover, a similar approach is followed in [11, 34], concerning the offloading strategies in Mobile Cloud Computing (MCC). A birth-and-death process is a Markov chain, where transitions are allowed only to the neighboring states. Using this approach we are able to express the subscriber's intermittent connectivity [10] and derive performance metrics. However, providing solutions by following this approach will result in high computational cost since the process is solved with numerical methods [35].

Based on the above, expressing the intermittent WiFi availability for a mobile user using 2-D Markov chains, is a complex and tedious procedure. Extending this approach for expressing middleware systems, such as pub/sub, is even more complicated (2nd category). In [14], *Queueing Network (QNs)* and *Performance Petri nets (PPNs)* are compared with respect to *expressive power* and *solution efficiency.* PPNs enjoy an advantage over QNs in representing synchronization (parallel systems) and are probably best suited for design purposes. On the other hand QNs: provide convenient primitives for constructing models; guarantee that are well-formed (i.e., stable, deadlock-free, etc); and can be solved efficiently. Work done in [36] makes use of QNs to estimate performance of web applications using algorithms such as Mean Value Analysis (MVA).

For the 2nd category of related work, we begin with Pongthawornkamol et al [24]. These analytical models abstract the expressiveness of pub/sub systems under unreliable, best effort public networks. In this study, the authors apply *lifetime (or deadline) periods* for each published event, and the *intermittent availability* of each subscriber in order to estimate the subscriber's reliability. Furthermore, in [37] the authors extended the above work by providing closed form expressions of reliability as a function of the number of brokers, transmission range, area dimensions and deadline parameters. Subsequently, Gaddah et al. in [23], focus on user mobility into the pub/sub interaction paradigm to investigate a pro-active caching approach. Based on this work, to design new hand-off management solutions they consider a fixed network topology where transfer/caching of events/subscriptions between brokers occur prior to subscribers' movement. In [12], a methodology for workload characterization and performance modeling of distributed pub/sub systems is presented. In this study, authors use *Queueing Petri Nets (QPNs)* for accurate performance prediction, similar to [13]. In [38], Sachs et al. analyze the SPECjms2007 benchmark using message oriented middleware. QPNs are used to perform an analysis of the benchmark and is able to predict resource utilization, network characteristics and message latency with high accuracy. Mühl et al. [39] present an approach to stochastic analysis of pub/sub systems employing identity-based hierarchical routing. This work only considers routing table sizes and message rates as metrics. Moreover, in [40], authors study the tradeoffs between performance and QoS in pub/sub systems. Performance evaluation process algebra (PEPA) language is used to express the systems. Authors of the three above efforts, try to tackle the basic functionalities of pub/sub systems and they do not consider subscribers' mobility or events' lifetime. Finally, PEPA is used in [41] to analyze the performance of mobile applications.

Concerning the use of a network of brokers, multiple overlay topologies have been proposed for the case of event based publish-subscribe to aid in reliability, scalability and fault tolerance. Notable among these include Jedi [32], Siena [33], Gryphon [21] and Hermes [18]. The event model may be generated through pattern matching, semantic hierarchy or via object based filtering. In Jedi [32], a hierarchy of overlay servers are used wherein the events are forwarded up to parent nodes from sub trees. Siena [33] uses a more efficient peer-to-peer architecture to forward messages. Gryphon [21] makes use of a link-matching algorithm to partially filter out the most probable directions to which the event will be sent.

In this paper, we generate an analytical solution for publish/subscribe performance using queueing network models (QNMs). By using QNMs, developers have the flexibility to design their systems with the evaluation capability of these models. Moreover, developers can use our models to predict response times by taking into account realistic subscriber mobility traces. The prediction model can be further applied for system tuning and broker capacity planning. Furthermore, we are agnostic to the type of overlay topology used in the broker network – we model all the queuing stations for end-to-end communication from the publisher to the subscriber.

6. CONCLUSIONS

In this work, we model the intermittent connectivity of mobile users over Publish/Subscribe (pub/sub) middleware. *Queueing Network Models* (QNMs) are employed to provide an analytical solution for response times. We incorporate the "ON/OFF queueing center" into the overlay infrastructure of a mobile pub/sub system to model connections/disconnections of mobile publishers and subscribers. The *ON/OFF queueing center* is modeled as a separate center within QNMs, which can be isolated and analyzed within large queueing networks. We then validate the model using both simulations (including ones relying on real-world workload traces) and traces collected in field conditions (metro network coverage). Our analytical model matches simulation results within 5% deviation, proving the efficacy of our work.

In future, we intend to extend this model by applying time-to-live lifetime periods to each published event. Furthermore, we aim to take into account mobile brokers (e.g., deployed in a mobile devices), which requires the addition of further *ON/OFF queueing centers* to the pub/sub model.

Acknowledgements

This work is partially supported by the associate team ACHOR and the H2020 project CHOReVOLUTION. Furthermore, the authors would like to thank Assistant Prof. Ioannis Moscholios - Univ. of Peloponnese, for his helpful review and Dr. Rachit Agarwal - Inria, for his help in the analysis of the real traces.

7. REFERENCES

[1] Y. Sun *et al.*, "A low-delay, lightweight publish/subscribe architecture for delay-sensitive iot services," in *IEEE ICWS*, Santa Clara, CA, USA, 2013.

[2] H. Liu *et al.*, "Client behavior and feed characteristics of rss, a publish-subscribe system for web micronews," in *ACM SIGCOMM*, Berkeley, CA, USA, 2005.

[3] M. Petrovic *et al.*, "G-topss: fast filtering of graph-based metadata," in *ACM WWW*, Chiba, Japan, 2005.

[4] V. Setty *et al.*, "The hidden pub/sub of spotify:(industry article)," in *ACM DEBS*, Arlington, Texas, USA, 2013.

[5] J. Reumann, "Goops: Pub/sub at google," *Lecture & Personal Communications at EuroSys & CANOE Summer School*, 2009.

[6] "PubNub." http://www.pubnub.com, 2013.

[7] F. Mehmeti and T. Spyropoulos, "Performance analysis of "on-the-spot" mobile data offloading," in *IEEE GLOBECOM*, ATLANTA, GA, USA, 2013.

[8] F. Mehmeti and T. Spyropoulos, "Is it worth to be patient? analysis and optimization of delayed mobile data offloading," in *IEEE INFOCOM*, Toronto, Canada, 2014.

[9] K. Lee, "Mobile data offloading: how much can wifi deliver?," in *ACM, CoNEXT*, Philadelphia, Pennsylvania, 2010.

[10] T. Phung-Duc *et al.*, "A simple algorithm for the rate matrices of level-dependent qbd processes," in *ACM QTNA*, Beijing, China, 2010.

[11] H. Wu and K. Wolter, "Tradeoff analysis for mobile cloud offloading based on an additive energy-performance metric," in *VALUETOOLS*, Bratislava, Slovakia, 2014.

[12] S. Kounev *et al.*, "A methodology for performance modeling of distributed event-based systems," in *IEEE ISORC*, Orlando, FL, USA, 2008.

[13] T. Martinec *et al.*, "Constructing performance model of jms middleware platform," in *ACM/SPEC ICPE*, Dublin, Ireland, 2014.

[14] M. Vernon *et al.*, *A comparison of performance Petri nets and queueing network models*. University of Wisconsin-Madison, CSD, 1986.

[15] E. Lazowska *et al.*, *Quantitative system performance: computer system analysis using queueing network models*. Prentice-Hall, Inc., 1984.

[16] F. Baskett *et al.*, "Open, closed, and mixed networks of queues with different classes of customers," *JACM*, 1975.

[17] R. Baldoni and A. Virgillito, "Distributed event routing in publish/subscribe communication systems: a survey," *DIS, Universita di Roma La Sapienza, Tech. Rep*, 2005.

[18] P. R. Pietzuch, *Hermes: A scalable event-based middleware*. PhD thesis, University of Cambridge Cambridge, UK, 2004.

[19] L. Baresi *et al.*, "On accurate automatic verification of publish-subscribe architectures," in *IEEE ICSE*, Minneapolis, USA, 2007.

[20] "Sun Microsystems. JMS Specifications and Reference Implementation." http://www.oracle.com/technetwork/java/jms/index.html.

[21] R. Strom, "Extending a content based publish-subscribe system with relational subscriptions," tech. rep., Technical report, IBM Research, 2003.

[22] J. Gascon-Samson *et al.*, "Dynamoth: A scalable pub/sub middleware for latency-constrained applications in the cloud," in *IEEE ICDCS*, Columbus, Ohio, USA, 2015.

[23] A. Gaddah, "Extending mobility to publish/subscribe systems using a pro-active caching approach," *Journal of Mobile Information Systems*, 2010.

[24] T. Pongthawornkamol, *Reliability and timeliness analysis of content-based publish/subscribe systems*. PhD thesis, University of Illinois at Urbana-Champaign, 2011.

[25] A. Adya *et al.*, "Thialfi: a client notification service for internet-scale applications," in *ACM SOSP*, Cascais, Portugal, 2011.

[26] G. Bolch *et al.*, *Queueing networks and Markov chains: modeling and performance evaluation with computer science applications*. John Wiley & Sons, 2006.

[27] I. Adan and J. Resing, *Queueing Theory: Ivo Adan and Jacques Resing*. Eindhoven University of Technology, 2005.

[28] W. Chang, "Preemptive priority queues," *Operations research*, 1965.

[29] T. Field, "JINQS: An extensible library for simulating multiclass queueing networks, v1. 0 user guide," August 2006.

[30] G. Bouloukakis *et al.*, "Leveraging cdr datasets for context-rich performance modeling of large-scale mobile pub/sub systems," in *IEEE WiMob*, Abu Dhabi, UAE, 2015.

[31] G. Bajaj *et al.*, "Toward enabling convenient urban transit through mobile crowdsensing," in *IEEE ITSC*, Gran Canaria, Spain, 2015.

[32] G. Cugola *et al.*, "The jedi event-based infrastructure and its application to the development of the opss wfms," *Software Engineering, Transactions on*, 2001.

[33] A. Carzaniga, *Architectures for an event notification service scalable to wide-area networks*. PhD thesis, Politecnico di Milano, 1998.

[34] E. Hyytiä *et al.*, "Optimizing offloading strategies in mobile cloud computing," *Cryptanalyst*, 2013.

[35] G. Latouche and V. Ramaswami, *Introduction to matrix analytic methods in stochastic modeling*. Siam, 1999.

[36] A. Kattepur *et al.*, "Performance modeling of multi-tiered web applications with varying service demands," in *IPDPS Workshops*, Orlando, Florida USA, 2015.

[37] D. Kassa *et al.*, "Analytical models of short-message reliability in mobile wireless networks," in *ACM MSWiM*, Miami, Florida, USA, 2011.

[38] K. Sachs *et al.*, "Performance modeling and analysis of message-oriented event-driven systems," *Software & Systems Modeling*, 2013.

[39] G. Mühl *et al.*, "Stochastic analysis of hierarchical publish/subscribe systems," in *Euro-Par*, 2009.

[40] G. Singh and A. Singh, "Measuring tradeoffs between performance and qos in event based systems," 2015.

[41] N. Arijo *et al.*, "Modular performance modelling for mobile applications," in *ACM ICPE*, Karlsruhe, Germany, 2011.

Conducting Repeatable Experiments in Highly Variable Cloud Computing Environments

Ali Abedi
University of Waterloo
ali.abedi@uwaterloo.ca

Tim Brecht
University of Waterloo
brecht@cs.uwaterloo.ca

ABSTRACT

Previous work has shown that benchmark and application performance in public cloud computing environments can be highly variable. Utilizing Amazon EC2 traces that include measurements affected by CPU, memory, disk, and network performance, we study commonly used methodologies for comparing performance measurements in cloud computing environments. The results show considerable flaws in these methodologies that may lead to incorrect conclusions. For instance, these methodologies falsely report that the performance of two identical systems differ by 38% using a confidence level of 95%. We then study the efficacy of the Randomized Multiple Interleaved Trials (RMIT) methodology using the same traces. We demonstrate that RMIT could be used to conduct repeatable experiments that enable fair comparisons in this cloud computing environment despite the fact that changing conditions beyond the user's control make comparing competing alternatives highly challenging.

1. INTRODUCTION

Cloud computing environments [11] like Amazon's EC2 are attractive facilities on which to conduct an experimental performance analysis. Large numbers of machines can potentially be used to compare two or more competing alternative algorithms, designs, or implementations of a system (simply called *alternatives* for the remainder of the paper). Some example alternatives might include, comparing different applications that perform the same function or different versions of the same application. In this case, some experiments may be conducted in parallel on different systems at the same time within different portions of the cloud environment and may also be executed at different times. Additionally, some experiments may not be conducted in parallel but may be conducted by running alternatives during different periods of time.

Unfortunately, performance measurements in cloud computing environments can vary significantly. This may be due to being assigned different physical systems across different experiments at different times. Or, the performance may be impacted due to sharing, in this case variations occur due to other applications that are executing on the same physical hosts (e.g., affecting disk throughput) or elsewhere in the same cloud environment (possibly affecting network latencies or throughput).

When conducting a comparison of two or more competing alternatives, care must be taken to ensure that any differences in performance are due only to the differences in alternatives and not because, one alternative might be executing in a more favorable environment (e.g., in the absence of other applications running on the same node or on a faster node). Therefore, in this paper we examine approaches that can be used to obtain repeatable performance measurements in cloud computing environments which are a prerequisite for comparing the performance of competing alternatives.

In order to conduct a fair comparison of the performance evaluation methodologies, we employ traces collected and analyzed by an independent research group [14]. Schad et al. [14] reported high levels of variation in all studied benchmarks (i.e., for CPU, memory, disk, and network). We utilize these traces to evaluate commonly used methodologies for conducting experimental evaluations in cloud computing environments (refer to Section 4 for more details). We show that some of these techniques might lead to flawed or misleading results despite including a measures of variation such as confidence intervals. Finally, we describe and evaluate a technique called Randomized Multiple Interleaved Trials (RMIT). Although Schad et al. [14] concluded that "naive runtime measurements on the cloud will suffer from high variance and will only be repeatable to a limited extent", we show than RMIT can be used to obtain repeatable and fair comparisons between multiple alternatives for their entire 30 day traces.

The contributions in this paper are:

- We demonstrate that commonly used approaches for comparing competing alternatives have serious flaws and may lead to incorrect conclusions.
- We show that the methodology of using randomized multiple interleaved trials can be used to obtain repeatable empirical measurements in the EC2 environment and therefore is a good candidate as a methodology for comparing the performance of competing alternatives.

We focus on the challenges of conducting repeatable experiments and fair comparisons of multiple alternatives executed at different periods in time. The problem of repeatable and fair comparison of experiments conducted in parallel is discussed in Section 5 and will be the subject of future research.

2. RELATED WORK

Studies examining the variability of measured performance when using the EC2 cloud infrastructure show that the variance on EC2 performance is very high [14, 4, 11, 8]. Schad et al. [14] propose a set of guidelines to reduce the performance variation while conducting experimental evaluations on EC2. Despite the provided

ICPE'17, April 22 - 26, 2017, L'Aquila, Italy

ISBN 978-1-4503-4404-3/17/04...$15.00

DOI: http://dx.doi.org/10.1145/3030207.3030229

guidelines, the authors point out that even with such guidelines, comparing multiple alternatives and conducting repeatable experiments on EC2 might be challenging or impossible due to the high variability. In the paper, we directly examine methodologies for conducting experiments in such environments.

Despite, the high variation in the performance of cloud computing systems, a number of studies [10, 4] choose to run the experiment only once. More rigorously conducted evaluations involve running experiments multiple times and reporting the average value. For example, some studies [7, 12, 5, 6] use an evaluation technique we call multiple consecutive trials (described in Section 3). In Section 4, we show how variations in the cloud environment might lead to misleading results if these techniques are utilized for evaluation.

We recently studied methodologies for conducting repeatable experiments and fair comparisons when performing performance evaluations in WiFi networks [2]. This study [2] shows that many commonly used techniques for the experimental evaluation of WiFi networks are flawed and could result in misleading conclusions being drawn. In that work, although we propose the use of randomized multiple interleaved trials (RMIT) (described in Section 3) as a methodology for coping with changing wireless channel conditions, randomization was not necessary. In this paper, we examine commonly used approaches for measuring and comparing performance as well as the suitability of RMIT in a completely different scenario, namely cloud computing environments. We find that randomization is required, due to periodic changes in the environment, and that RMIT can be used to obtain repeatable results.

Some work [3, 4] has proposed techniques to reduce the variability of application performance when executing in cloud environments by limiting variability of network performance. Unfortunately, such work only reduces but does not eliminate variability. Other shared resources such as disks can also cause performance measurements to be highly variable. One study [9] reports that during off-peak hours disk read bandwidths would range from 100–140 MB/sec, while during peak hours it ranged from 40–70 MB/sec. Moreover, even with techniques to reduce variability, methodologies are still needed to ensure that differences in performance of different alternatives are due to the differences in those alternatives, rather than differences in the conditions under which they were executed.

3. OVERVIEW OF METHODOLOGIES

We use the term *trial* to refer to one measurement, typically obtained by running a benchmark or micro-benchmark for some period of time (the length of the trial). An *experiment* can be comprised of multiple trials executing the same benchmark, where the results of the experiment are reported over the multiple trials (e.g., the average of the measurements obtained over the trials).

Most experiments conducted in cloud computing environments utilize the single trial or multiple consecutive trials methodologies (referred to as *commonly used methodologies* in this paper). In previous work [2], we have argued for and demonstrated the use of Multiple Interleaved Trials and Randomized Multiple Interleaved Trials. We now briefly explain each of these methodologies.

- **Single Trial**: In this approach, an experiment consists of only a single trial. Figure 1-A shows an example of this approach with three alternatives. The performance results obtained from single trials are compared directly. This is the easiest methodology for running an experiment to compare multiple alternatives.
- **Multiple Consecutive Trials**: All trials for the first alternative are run, followed by the second alternative and each of the remaining alternatives. Figure 1-B shows the Multiple Consecutive Trials technique for 3 alternatives.
- **Multiple Interleaved Trials**: One trial is conducted using the first alternative, followed by one trial with the second, and so on until each alternative has been run once. When one trial has been conducted using each alternative we say that one *round* has been completed. Rounds are repeated until the appropriate number of trials has been conducted (Figure 1-C).
- **Randomized Multiple Interleaved Trials**:
If the cloud computing environment is affected at regular intervals, and the intervening period coincides with the length of each trial, it is possible that some alternatives are affected more than others. Therefore, the randomized multiple interleaved trials methodology randomly reorders alternatives for each round (Figure 1-D). In essence, a randomized block design [13] is constructed where the blocks are intervals of time (rounds) and within each block all alternatives are tested, with a new random ordering of alternatives being generated for each block.

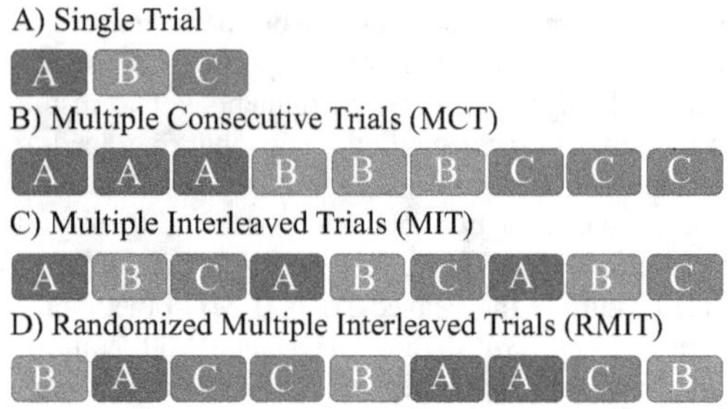

Figure 1: Different methodologies: with 3 alternatives

3.1 Methodologies used in Practice

To illustrate that these methodologies are actually used in practice, we studied the performance evaluation methodologies used in the 38 research papers published in the ACM Symposium on Cloud Computing 2016 (SoCC'16). 9 papers conduct experimental evaluations on public clouds (7 on Amazon EC2, 1 on Microsoft Azure, and 1 on Google computing engine). We found that the single trial and multiple consecutive trials (MCT) methodologies are utilized by 7 and 4 papers respectively (some papers use both techniques). No other evaluation methodology is used in these papers. Additionally, 9 other papers also use these two methodologies when conducting evaluations on research clusters.

The fundamental problem is that researchers often incorrectly assume that the characteristics of the systems and networks being used and workloads that are simultaneously executing during their experiments, do not change in ways that impact the performance of the artifacts they are evaluating. Previous work has demonstrated that performance is in fact impacted [14, 11]. In this paper, we examine methodologies commonly used for comparing performance in cloud environments and describe our RMIT methodology that is designed to handle environments in which performance measurements are variable due to circumstances which can not be controlled. To the best of our knowledge, ours is the first work that studies the (randomized) multiple interleaved trials methodologies in the context of the repeatability of experiments in cloud computing environments.

4. EVALUATION

For our evaluation, we utilize traces, collected from benchmark measurements by other researchers [14], conducted over extended period of time on Amazon EC2 servers. The authors of that paper have granted us permission to make the data publicly available [1]. We use these traces to simulate the execution of applications which are utilized by researchers to conduct performance evaluation studies. Note that although these traces were collected in 2010, they are still useful for this study because we do not perform any performance evaluation, instead we evaluate the efficacy of performance evaluation methodologies. Therefore, the age of traces is not very relevant if the performance of cloud computing environments are still variable. A recent study [11] shows that the performance of CPU, memory, and disk benchmarks are highly variable on EC2, specially for I/O-bound applications. The coefficient of variation (CV) reported for the studied benchmarks is as high or even higher (i.e., greater than 0.4) than that of the 2010 study [14].

In the original study [14] a batch of CPU, memory, disk, and network benchmarks are run every hour for one month. The benchmarks used are Unix Benchmark Utility (Ubench) for CPU and memory speed experiments and Bonnie++ for disk I/O experiments Two types of virtual machines used for collecting the measurement data, namely, small and large machine instances. The configurations of these instances are summarized in Table 1. We make use of two different traces collected on servers residing in the United States and in Europe, represented by US and EU, respectively.

Instance	Memory	Cores	Storage	32/64
Small	1.7 GB	1	160 GB	32-bit
Large	7.5 GB	2	850 GB	64-bit

Table 1: Instances configurations

Schat et al. [14] report that EC2 performance varies so much that wall clock experiments must be conducted with "considerable care". Figure 2 shows the CPU benchmark results for large instances located in the US, collected over one month from their study. Each point shows the benchmark score for a single trial (there is one trial per hour). Despite the identical configuration of the virtual machines used for this experiment, the CPU performance varies considerably. The memory and disk performance benchmarks illustrate similar behavior with large variations over the duration of the experiment.

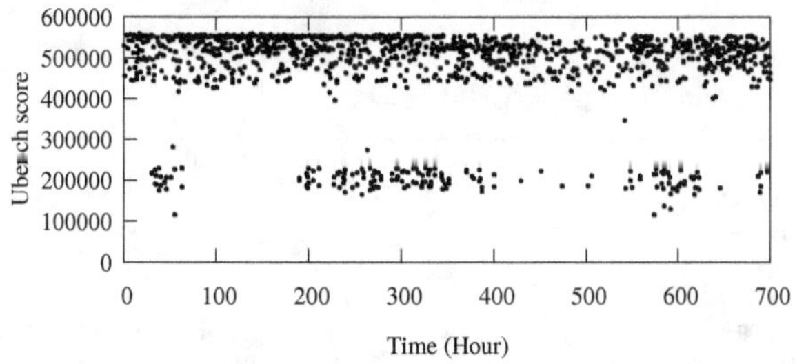

Figure 2: CPU performance, large instance, US [14].

Table 2 summaries the statistical properties of all traces we utilize in this paper. For each combination of benchmark, instance size, and region, we report minimum, maximum, mean, standard deviation (SD), and coefficient of variation (CV). These measures are presented to better understand how measured performance can vary from one experiment to another. The minimum and maximum measured values for all benchmarks show that the benchmark scores cover a wide range relative to mean. For instance, in the CPU benchmark of large instances located in the US, the benchmark score varies from 116,243 to 558,446. The mean and the standard deviation also confirm that CPU benchmark scores are highly variable in this trace. We also present the coefficient of variation (i.e., SD/mean) in order to compare the level of variation across different traces. The coefficient of variation indicates that the CPU and Memory benchmarks suffer from the most and the least variations, respectively. Interestingly, as we see in the following sections, commonly used performance evaluation methodologies (i.e., single trial and multiple consecutive trials) fail to provide valid comparisons between multiple alternatives even for the memory benchmark traces which are the most stable experiments.

Bench	Inst	Reg	Min	Max	Mean	SD	CV
CPU	S	US	55,444	122,831	103,643	23,918	0.23
		EU	55,670	123,010	108,890	19,526	0.18
	L	US	116,243	558,446	471,584	112,044	0.24
		EU	115,972	558,143	459,467	111,811	0.24
Mem	S	US	50,856	77,030	69,544	6,712	0.10
		EU	52,357	76,744	71,693	5,050	0.07
	L	US	119,696	320,642	290,211	31,345	0.11
		EU	181,566	321,758	293,390	28,472	0.10
Disk	S	US	7,972	84,267	59,551	11,875	0.20
		EU	10,489	78,693	61,757	8,388	0.14
	L	US	33,684	98,034	80,896	18,288	0.23
		EU	37,908	95,956	82,220	15,688	0.19
Net	M	US	158	836	579	117	0.20
		EU	378	886	720	88	0.12

Table 2: Traces statistical data. S: Small, L: Large, M: Mixed[1]

4.1 Single Trial

The single trial methodology is a very common approach for conducting experiments in cloud computing environments due to its simplicity. For example, 11 papers (out of 38) published in SoCC'16 utilize this technique. However, changes in the cloud environment may render this approach unreliable when comparing multiple alternatives. Figure 2 shows an example of how measured application performance can change from one trial to the next (each point is the benchmark score of a trial and should all be identical). Therefore, if comparisons are done using this methodology, it is not clear whether the observed differences are due to the difference in alternatives being studied or changes in the environment.

To better understand the performance variation between two consecutive trials, we compute the percentage difference between those trials (i.e., difference of consecutive trials divided by the minimum of these trials) for the CPU, memory, disk, and network traces collected for large instances located in the EU. In Figure 3, a value on the y-axis shows the ratio of consecutive trials that experience a difference less than or equal to the value on the x-axis for a given benchmark. For example, in the CPU benchmark, 20% of the consecutive trials experience more than a 100% change in performance. As depicted in the figure, for all traces, there are instances were the difference between two consecutive trials is more than 50%. Although the memory benchmark has the lowest variation, 17% of consecutive trials have a percentage difference of more than 20%. *As a result, a reliable comparison of multiple alternatives cannot be performed using the single trial methodology for any of the studied traces.*

4.2 Multiple Consecutive Trials

In the Multiple Consecutive Trials (MCT) methodology, experimenters often conduct all of the trials for a given alternative, before proceeding to the next. This is convenient, as there is generally some setup time involved in switching between alternatives (e.g., changing software configuration).

[1]Small and large instances use the same network interface, therefore, the instance size is irrelevant in the networking benchmarks.

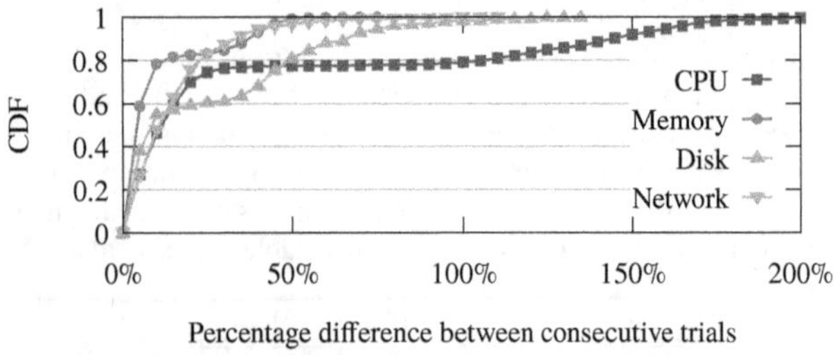

Figure 3: Single trial: falsely reported differences

To evaluate this approach, we combine 20 trials of a benchmark to constitute an experiment. For two alternatives, 20 trials for alternative *A* are run followed by 20 trials for alternative B and their results are compared. We compare results by computing the average of the 20 trials along with 95% confidence intervals. Since in each case *A* and *B* are identical benchmarks (two different labels for each alternative), a sound measurement methodology should show no statistical performance differences between them (i.e., no non-overlapping confidence intervals). However, if *any* performance difference is observed, it indicates that the measurement methodology might falsely associate the observed differences to differences in alternatives, while differences are rooted in the variable cloud computing environment. Therefore, the measurement technique can potentially lead to erroneous conclusions. When comparing the performance of alternatives *A* and *B*, we consider them statistically different if the confidence intervals *do not* overlap. On the other hand, the two alternatives are considered statistically similar if the confidence intervals *do* overlap.

Figure 4-a shows the results of applying the multiple consecutive trials technique on the CPU benchmark trace obtained in the US. The x and y axes represent the time and average of 20 benchmark scores, respectively. Note that Figures 4 and 5 are missing a few data points. There is no valid measurement score for these times in the provided trace (see [14]). The gray area highlights the time window where the non-overlapping confidence intervals are observed for one of the methodologies for a given trace. *Note that in practice only two average values are used to compare A and B. However, we continue applying MCT to obtain more points in order to observe what the outcome would be if the experiments were conducted at different times of the day.*

As seen in the figure, there are a few instances of non-overlapping confidence intervals between time 350 and 450 (highlighted with the gray box). In these cases, the alternative *A* is statistically different from the previous or next alternative *B* measurement. A similar problem is observed for the memory benchmark trace shown in Figure 5-a. Despite smaller variations in these measurements (i.e., smaller confidence intervals), there are a few non-overlapping confidence intervals for some consecutive experiments. Recall that *A* and *B* are identical, therefore, these statistically significant differences are a sign that the measurement technique is flawed. We repeated the CPU and memory speed experiments with 5 and 10 trials, instead of 20 trials, and similar results (i.e., non-overlapping confidence intervals) were observed.

The confidence intervals obtained using this technique may provide a false sense of rigor and validity when comparing different alternatives. The differences are in reality due to differences in the environment rather than the different alternatives.

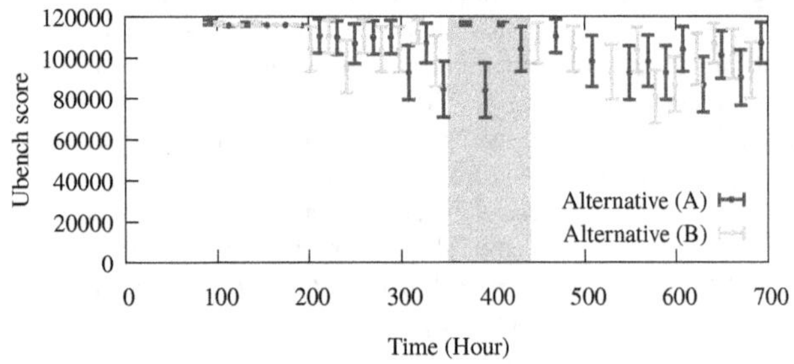

(a) MCT

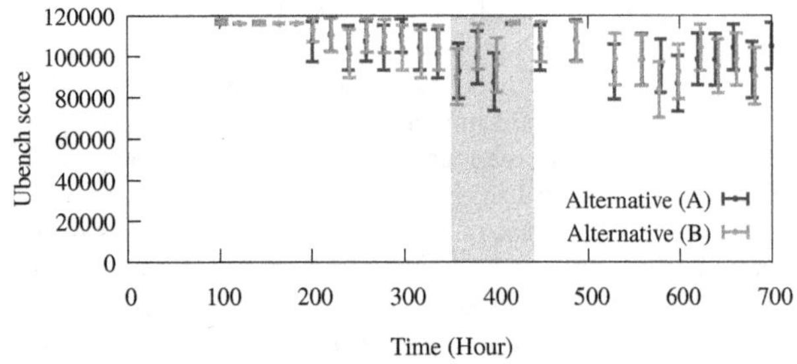

(b) MIT

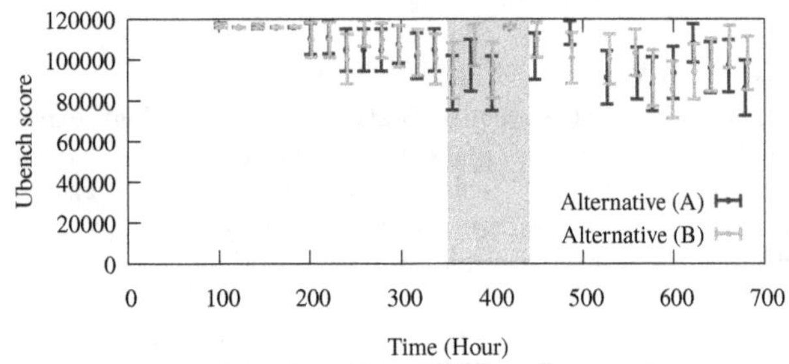

(c) RMIT

Figure 4: CPU performance, small instance, US.

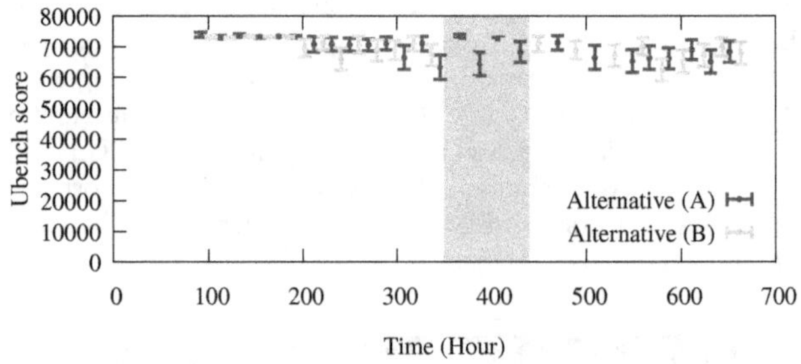

(a) MCT

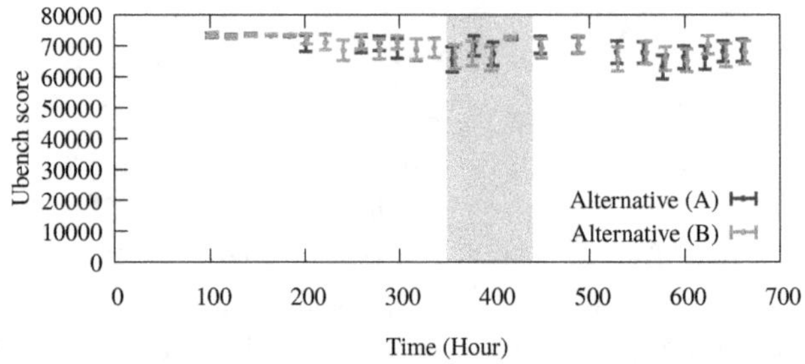

(b) MIT

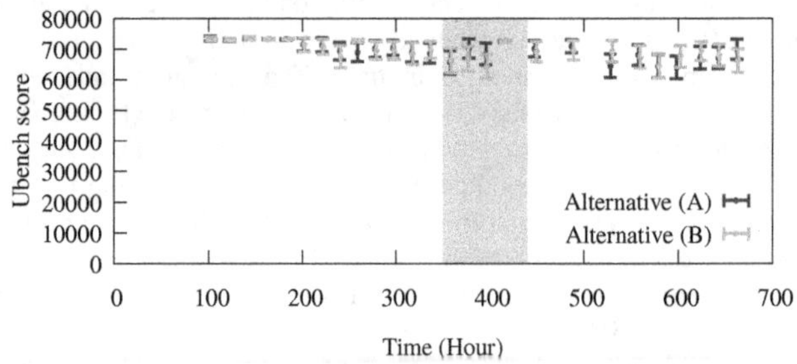

(c) RMIT

Figure 5: Memory performance, small instance, US.

We repeat the same evaluation using all traces we introduced in Table 2 and summarize the results in Table 3. For each trace, we report the Ratio of Flawed Experiments to the total number of experiments (RFE) (presented in percentage). For instance if RFE = 10%, it means that 10% of comparisons have non-overlapping confidence intervals. Note that it is not possible to tell prior to or after running experiments whether or not the measurement is flawed, as a result any non-zero value for the RFE is not acceptable for a methodology. In Table 3, we also present the maximum difference incorrectly reported by a flawed methodology. This measure is the ratio of the difference between the two mean values to the minimum of the two mean values (also presented in percentage).

Table 3 shows that, except for two disk I/O traces, the ratio of flawed experiments (RFE) is at least 4% when using the MCT methodology, rendering this technique error-prone. The maximum difference metric is also alarming. In the CPU benchmark experiments, the MCT methodology falsely reports a difference of up to 37.8% as being statistically significant (with a confidence level of 0.95) for two identical alternatives. In other words, the MCT methodology determines that a system is 37.8% better than itself! In addition to these traces, we also applied the MCT methodology on a networking trace collected using Microsoft Azure's cloud computing environment in 2013 by the authors of [14]. We found that the networking benchmark had a RFE of 14.3% and max difference of 16.6%. Our findings demonstrate that the MCT methodology must be avoided when performing any performance evaluation in cloud computing environment.

Benchmark	Instance	Region	RFE	Max Diff
CPU	Small	US	10.2	37.8
		EU	9.8	27.3
	Large	US	7.9	30.1
		EU	14.9	36.5
Memory	Small	US	9.8	15.1
		EU	6.7	8.8
	Large	US	10.2	16.8
		EU	7.0	11.1
Disk I/O	Small	US	4.0	15.3
		EU	0.0	NA
	Large	US	5.9	23.8
		EU	0.0	NA
Network	Mixed	US	6.1	19.6
		EU	5.1	12.5

Table 3: Efficacy of the MCT methodology

4.3 Multiple Interleaved Trials

The intuition behind the Multiple Interleaved Trials (MIT) methodology is that by interleaving alternatives, over time, trials of the different alternatives are closer together in time. As a result, the alternatives will be exposed to conditions that are more similar than when using multiple consecutive trials.

Figures 4-b and 5-b show the results of applying the multiple interleaved trials technique to the CPU and memory benchmark traces, in the hope of addressing the shortcomings of the MCT technique. As illustrated in these figures, the MIT methodology successfully avoids any non-overlapping confidence intervals. Therefore, based on the obtained results, alternatives A and B are statistically the same, as they should be.

As mentioned earlier, if the cloud computing environment is affected at regular intervals, it is possible that some alternatives could be affected more than others. We have found that scenarios do exist where periodic changes in the cloud computing environment adversely affect the multiple interleaved trials technique. Figure 6 shows how the multiple interleaved trials technique is unable to provide statistically similar results for alternatives A and B. A few instances of non-overlapping confidence intervals were observed between time 100 and 200.

To ensure that periodic changes cause this behavior, we plot the raw measurement data between time 100 and 180 (roughly corresponding to the shaded area). If two alternatives are compared using the MIT technique, the performance of each alternative is measured using only odd or even trials. In Figure 7, which shows the raw measurement data, we mark the odd and even trials differently in an attempt to find a particular pattern that explains the non-overlapping confidence intervals. As seen in this figure, a periodic pattern is observed for this particular time window which causes odd trials to have a lower performance score in general. As a result, 3 experiments in this time window (shaded area in Figure 6-b) obtain non-overlapping confidence intervals. The only exception is the time window between 140 and 160 where there is no obvious superior or inferior performance for the odd and even trials. In Figure 6-b, the corresponding experiments at time 160 (the second experiment from the right in the shaded area) obtains overlapping confidence intervals. *This demonstrates that trials must be randomized to avoid such problems.*

4.4 Randomized Multiple Interleaved Trials

As we saw in Section 4.3, the multiple interleaved trials methodology can not be used if the environment changes occur regularly with a period that overlaps with the length of the trials. Therefore, it is critical to randomize the order of trials to avoid this problem.

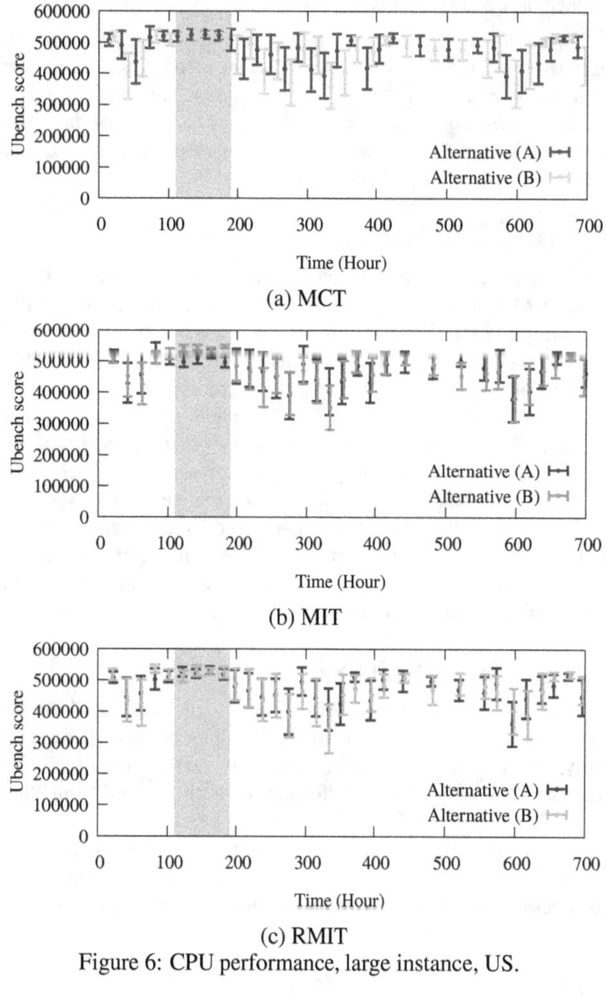

(a) MCT (b) MIT (c) RMIT

Figure 6: CPU performance, large instance, US.

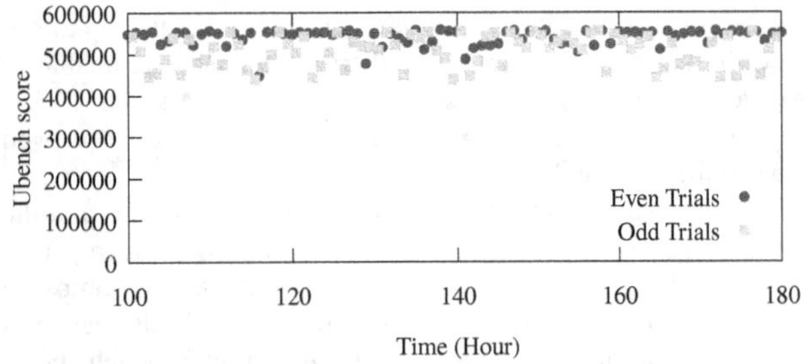

Figure 7: CPU performance, large instance, US.

The Randomized Multiple Interleaved Trials (RMIT) technique reorders the trials randomly during each round to avoid ensure that the same alternatives are not affected by periodic changes in the cloud computing environment.

We apply the RMIT methodology to the CPU performance benchmark and the results are shown in Figure 6-c. A comparisons between Figure (c) and (b) shows that the RMIT technique produces no non-overlapping confidence interval and correctly shows that there is no statistical difference between alternatives A and B. Figures 4-c and 5-c, also show that comparisons between alternatives A and B are statistically correct.

These results show that, RMIT can be used in highly variable cloud environments to compare multiple alternatives and that this methodology inherently captures the variability in performance metrics across runs. We note that if the variations are large, it may not be possible to distinguish relatively small differences between two or more alternatives. The applicability of this technique depends on the variations in the environment and the significance of the difference between alternatives.

Note that it is not possible to tell prior to or after running experiments whether or not the performance metrics may have been affected by changes in the cloud computing environment, nor if changes in the cloud computing environment may be periodic. Therefore, it is critical that randomized multiple interleaved trials be used when comparing alternatives.

5. DISCUSSION

In this work, we focus on the sequential execution of trials on a single VM. However, it is possible to run multiple trials in parallel on multiple VMs. Suppose that we compare N alternatives which require M VMs each ($M > 1$ means we are running a distributed application). All of the N alternatives are assigned to a total of $N \times M$ VMs. Because the $N \times M$ VMs might not be identical, and because some VMs might be affected by other applications that are running on the same physical hosts or on the same physical rack, one can randomly reassign the alternatives to the VMs for each trial. This procedure can be continued for the desired number of trials. As a result, different alternatives will all experience the same conditions. The complete design and evaluation of such a methodology is left for future work.

6. CONCLUSIONS

Using cloud computing environments for experimental performance evaluations is fraught with difficulties because of the possibly highly variable nature of the environment. We utilize CPU, memory, disk, and network performance traces obtained from Amazon EC2 servers and find that commonly used methodologies for conducting experiments like using single trial or multiple consecutive trials could lead to erroneous conclusions. We found that these methodologies are used by many papers published in the SoCC'16 conference. However, we do find that the randomized multiple interleaved trials methodology can be used to obtain repeatable performance metrics and should form a basis for the fair comparison of competing alternatives by appropriately randomizing the time at which trials of each alternative are conducted.

7. ACKNOWLEDGMENTS

Funding for this project was provided in part by a Natural Sciences and Engineering Research Council (NSERC) of Canada Discovery Grant and a Discovery Accelerator Supplement. We also thank Kamal Rahimi Malekshan for his careful proofreading of the paper and the anonymous reviewers for their helpful feedback. We are especially greatful to Jörg Schad, Jens Dittrich, and Jorge-Arnulfo Quiané-Ruiz for providing us with their data and allowing us to make it available to others.

8. REFERENCES

[1] http://cs.uwaterloo.ca/~brecht/data/icpe-rmit-2017.

[2] ABEDI, A., HEARD, A., AND BRECHT, T. Conducting repeatable experiments and fair comparisons using 802.11N MIMO networks. *SIGOPS Oper. Syst. Rev. 49*, 1 (2015).

[3] BALLANI, H., COSTA, P., KARAGIANNIS, T., AND ROWSTRON, A. Towards predictable datacenter networks. In *SIGCOMM* (2011).

[4] BALLANI, H., JANG, K., KARAGIANNIS, T., KIM, C., GUNAWARDENA, D., AND O'SHEA, G. Chatty tenants and the cloud network sharing problem. In *NSDI* (2013).

[5] CARDOSA, M., WANG, C., NANGIA, A., CHANDRA, A., AND WEISSMAN, J. Exploring MapReduce efficiency with highly-distributed data. In *MapReduce* (2011).

[6] FARLEY, B., JUELS, A., VARADARAJAN, V., RISTENPART, T., BOWERS, K. D., AND SWIFT, M. M. More for your money: Exploiting performance heterogeneity in public clouds. In *SoCC* (2012).

[7] IORDACHE, A., MORIN, C., PARLAVANTZAS, N., FELLER, E., AND RITEAU, P. Resilin: Elastic MapReduce over multiple clouds. In *CCGrid* (2013).

[8] IOSUP, A., YIGITBASI, N., AND EPEMA, D. On the performance variability of production cloud services. In *CCGRID* (2011).

[9] JIANG, D., OOI, B., SHI, L., AND WU, S. The performance of MapReduce: An in-depth study. *Proc. VLDB Endow. 3*, 1-2 (2010), 472–483.

[10] JUVE, G., DEELMAN, E., BERRIMAN, G. B., BERMAN, B. P., AND MAECHLING, P. An evaluation of the cost and performance of scientific workflows on Amazon EC2. *J. Grid Comput. 10*, 1 (2012).

[11] LEITNER, P., AND CITO, J. Patterns in the chaos - a study of performance variation and predictability in public iaas clouds. *ACM Trans. Internet Technol. 16*, 3 (2016).

[12] MEHROTRA, P., DJOMEHRI, J., HEISTAND, S., HOOD, R., JIN, H., LAZANOFF, A., SAINI, S., AND BISWAS, R. Performance evaluation of Amazon EC2 for NASA HPC applications. In *ScienceCloud* (2012).

[13] MONTGOMERY, D. *Design and Analysis of Experiments.* Wiley, 2012.

[14] SCHAD, J., DITTRICH, J., AND QUIANÉ-RUIZ, J.-A. Runtime Measurements in the Cloud: Observing, Analyzing, and Reducing Variance. *Proc. VLDB Endow.* (2010).

HTAPBench: Hybrid Transactional and Analytical Processing Benchmark

Fábio Coelho*
INESC TEC & U.Minho
Braga, Portugal
fabio.a.coelho@inesctec.pt

João Paulo†
INESC TEC & U.Minho
Braga, Portugal
jtpaulo@di.uminho.pt

Ricardo Vilaça
LeanXcale SL
Madrid, Spain
ricardo.vilaca@leanxcale.com

José Pereira
INESC TEC & U.Minho
Braga, Portugal
jop@di.uminho.pt

Rui Oliveira
INESC TEC & U.Minho
Braga, Portugal
rco@di.uminho.pt

ABSTRACT

The increasing demand for real-time analytics requires the fusion of Transactional (OLTP) and Analytical (OLAP) systems, eschewing ETL processes and introducing a plethora of proposals for the so-called Hybrid Analytical and Transactional Processing (HTAP) systems.

Unfortunately, current benchmarking approaches are not able to comprehensively produce a unified metric from the assessment of an HTAP system. The evaluation of both engine types is done separately, leading to the use of disjoint sets of benchmarks such as TPC-C or TPC-H.

In this paper we propose a new benchmark, HTAPBench, providing a unified metric for HTAP systems geared toward the execution of constantly increasing OLAP requests limited by an admissible impact on OLTP performance. To achieve this, a load balancer within HTAPBench regulates the coexistence of OLTP and OLAP workloads, proposing a method for the generation of both new data and requests, so that OLAP requests over freshly modified data are comparable across runs.

We demonstrate the merit of our approach by validating it with different types of systems: OLTP, OLAP and HTAP; showing that the benchmark is able to highlight the differences between them, while producing queries with comparable complexity across experiments with negligible variability.

CCS Concepts

•**Information systems → Database performance evaluation; Relational parallel and distributed DBMSs;**

*Funded by source 1 (Acknowledgments).

†Funded by source 2 (Acknowledgments).

ICPE'17, April 22-26, 2017, L'Aquila, Italy

DOI: http://dx.doi.org/10.1145/3030207.3030228

Keywords

Benchmarking; OLTP; OLAP; HTAP

1. INTRODUCTION

We are undergoing a change in database system design. Up until now, there has clearly been two main categories into which systems could be classified: operational or transactional systems (OLTP) and data warehousing or analytical systems (OLAP). For a long time, each system type lived apart from each other, as each had very distinct goals. On the one hand, transactional systems focus their operation on providing ways to enable a high throughput of rather small-sized transactions. Typically, during execution, each transaction operates under a very limited space of tuples. OLTP systems use a data schema based on reduced levels of redundancy, resulting from normalization techniques [26] across entities. On the other hand, analytical systems focus on performing aggregations over large sets of data. The query centric nature of an OLAP data schema introduces high levels of redundancy in the shape of materialized views or precomputed aggregates [19].

As pointed out by Gartner [28], a new class of engines, capable of handling mixed workloads with high levels of transactional activity and, at the same time, providing scalable business analytics directly over production data is arising. Such systems bypass the need to use the ETL [18] process and are commonly referred to as HTAP - Hybrid Analytical and Transactional Processing systems. Traditionally, both workloads are handled by separate engines, periodically feeding the OLAP with data from the OLTP engine through an ETL process. The approach seeks to ensure the best performance of each individual engine at the expense of data freshness for analytics. By eschewing the ETL process, HTAP systems are poised to reduce implementation, management and storage costs and, most importantly, enable real-time analytics over production data. Several vendors such as Oracle, SAP or PostgreSQL started to fill in this gap and proposed solutions that coined variant terminologies such as OLTAP [21](Online Transactional Analytical Processing) or OLxP [16, 22] (Online Transctional or Analytical Processing) that also aim to mix both workload types. Other companies have started to offer Hybrid solutions such as NuoDB [24], VoltDB [27] or Splice Machine [20].

Given the traditional taxonomy of OLTP and OLAP systems, the industry along with independent organizations defined benchmarking approaches specially tailored for either transactional or analytical workloads, such as TPC-C [8] and TPC-E [11] for OLTP workloads and TPC-H [9] or TPC-DS [23] for analytical workloads. Each benchmark focuses on the optimization challenges associated with each system type, defining evaluation suites with very different and contradicting goals. This is so as optimizing an OLTP targeted operation would intrinsically degrade OLAP performance and vice-versa [14]. For instance, OLTP and OLAP workloads generate specific sets of queries that require distinct storage layouts in order to be efficient. They can also accommodate different-sized datasets, employing the concept of warehouse as scaling factor. Optimizing a storage layout to support both access patterns efficiently is not a trivial task but it must be accomplished to have efficient hybrid systems. Moreover, as further discussed in the paper, storage accesses generated by OLTP workloads are mostly random while OLAP workloads are mainly sequential. Likewise, a hybrid workload will assess the ability of the system under test (SUT) to simultaneously schedule random and sequential access patterns to storage mediums and manage both light and intense operations regarding memory allocation and processor time; these are some of the reasons why these workloads have until now been evaluated independently.

Most importantly, it is not easy to combine and directly translate results from distinct benchmarks to the effectiveness of a system to handle an HTAP workload. Gartner states that an HTAP system should prioritize a sustained transactional throughput, delivering at the same time scalable analytical processing without disrupting the operational activity [28]. Consequently, even if both workloads can be run on the same engine, it is not straightforward to meaningfully and consistently reconcile the results of both workloads in a single HTAP metric. This is so as each workload is usually oblivious to the presence of the other, trying to independently reach the maximum qualified throughput in each separate workload, and therefore producing uncorrelated metrics.

In this paper, we present HTAPBench, a new benchmark suite designed to evaluate hybrid systems with mixed OLTP and OLAP workloads. HTAPBench introduces a new metric that provides a reading of the analytical capability as the system scales. The proposed benchmark introduces a hybrid workload that simultaneously exercises a workload with operational and analytical activity over the same system. It introduces a Client Balancer that controls how analytical clients are launched, ensuring that the OLTP activity stays within a configured threshold and the results are kept comparable across runs by addressing data uniformity of the workload. Throughout the paper we use *database* when referring to the stored data, *engine* when referring to the software and *SUT* or *system* when referring to the composition of software and underlying hardware.

Contributions: First, we propose a new unified metric aimed at engines with mixed workloads. Second, we present the design and implementation of HTAPBench supporting such a metric. We introduce a technique for generating realistic OLAP queries over a dynamically changing dataset resulting from concurrent OLTP, with predictable complexity. In addition, we propose a load balancer that relies on a feedback control mechanism that regulates the coexistence of the OLTP and OLAP workload execution.

Roadmap: The remainder of this paper is organized as follows: Section 2 presents an overview and the unified metric we propose. Section 3 evaluates our proposal against different systems, and Section 4 validates the results as well as discusses the properties of the system. Section 5 goes through related work and Section 6 concludes this work.

2. HTAPBench

The Hybrid Transactional and Analytical Processing Benchmark is targeted at assessing engines capable of delivering mixed workloads composed of OLTP transactions and OLAP business queries without resorting to ETL. Typically, in environments with mixed workloads, the relative weight given to OLTP and OLAP is governed by delivering a high OLTP throughput while still being able to simultaneously perform analytical business queries [28]. This goal should be met in such a way that the OLTP throughput is kept within expected intervals. Likewise, HTAPBench focuses its operation on ensuring a stable OLTP throughput and assessing the capability of the SUT to cope with an increasing demand on the OLAP counterpart. To fulfill OLTP requirements, HTAPBench requires the testing engine to grant full ACID capabilities during all stages of the benchmark. The design is composed of several modules as depicted in Figure 1. The Density Consultant, the Client Balancer and the Dynamic Query-H Generator modules provide the foundation of our approach and are discussed in this Section.

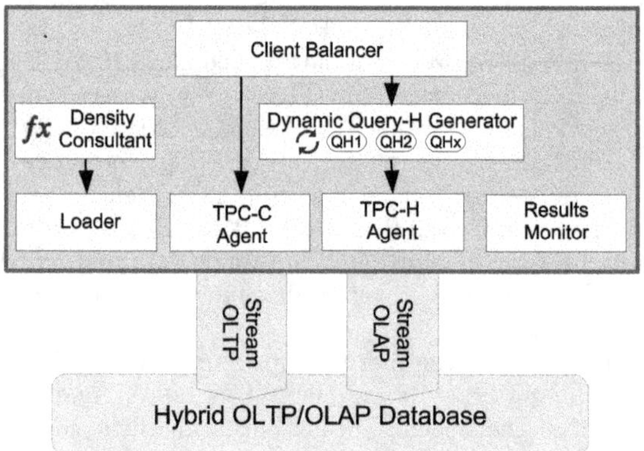

Figure 1: HTAPBench architecture.

In a nutshell, HTAPBench decomposes the execution into three main stages: (*i*) the populate stage, (*ii*) the warmup stage and (*iii*) the execution stage. Two of the modules, which we define as agents, will regulate the OLTP and OLAP activity. During system start, HTAPBench will be configured with a target OLTP throughput, triggering an OLTP workload configured with the required number of clients to meet the required throughput. Periodically, HTAPBench

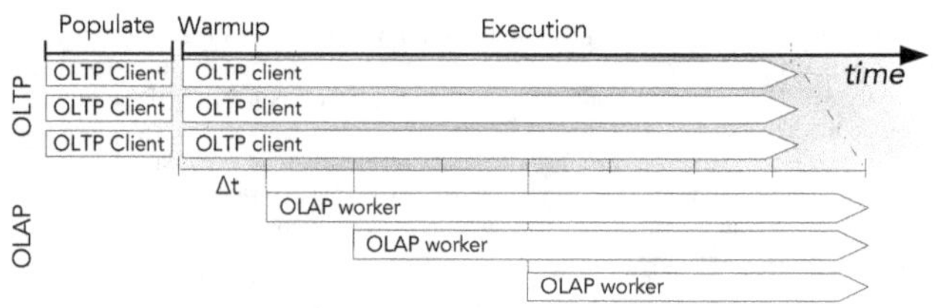

Figure 2: HTAPBench execution.

will assess the ability of the SUT to handle an increasing OLAP activity, as depicted in Figure 2, while ensuring that the transactional throughput does not decrease below a configured threshold.

The unified metric is central to our design, and its genesis is directly translated from the need of HTAP systems to scale without disturbing the OLTP activity. It mirrors the ability of a given analytical worker to complete queries, in a scenario composed of an increasing number of analytical workers and a stable transactional activity. Analyzing this behavior will enable us to identify situations where adding an additional OLAP worker degrades the OLTP/OLAP engine performance.

2.1 Workload

The mixed workload used in this benchmark is composed of a transactional agent and an analytical agent that simultaneously instruct the system to perform operations over the same dataset. We selected TPC-C and TPC-H as agents, as each is able to stress the inherent characteristics of each workload type. TPC-C was chosen as the transactional client due to its high rate of read-write operations, being one of the most used workloads for OLTP evaluation. TPC-C specification models a real-world scenario where a company, comprised of several warehouses and districts, processes orders placed by clients. The workload scales according to the number of configured warehouses.

TPC-H also specifies a real-world scenario, modeling a wholesale supplier and employing a schema that is very close in structure to TPC-C. Moreover, we selected TPC-H over TPC-DS [10] since the workload in TPC-DS is data warehouse-driven, not only relying on a star schema but also requiring the use of ETL processes to keep data updated and in conformity with such a schema. On the basis that analytical queries in a hybrid workload should exercise a dataset common to the operational workload, TPC-H better fits the requirement as it does not use a star schema, placing it closer to the workload schema in TPC-C.

The mixed workload in HTAPBench uses all the entities in TPC-C and TPC-H's `Nation`, `Region` and `Supplier`, as proposed in [5]. The remaining TPC-H entities were merged into a non-intrusive way in TPC-C's workload. The result is a workload that matches Gartner's recommendations for hybrid workloads, where data should not be moved from operational to data warehouses in order to support analytics, but live under the same schema allowing drill-down analytical operations to point toward the freshest data produced by the operational activity.

The OLTP execution in HTAPBench runs according to a target number of transactions per second (*tps*). It is thus necessary to ensure the optimal configuration regarding some TPC-C specific parameters such as the total number of warehouses and clients defining the number of transactions per second (*tpmC*).

$$target(tpmC) = target(tps) \times 60 \times \frac{\%NewOrder}{100} \qquad (1)$$

$$\#clients = \frac{target(tmpC)}{1.286} \qquad (2)$$

$$\#warehouses = \frac{\#clients}{10} \qquad (3)$$

To compute these parameters, we refer to the TPC-C specification [8] and use the characterization for the TPC-C's ideal client, considering the minimum think time for each transaction type, and provided that transactions do not fail and thus no rollback operation is required. According to TPC-C, a single client should not be able to execute more than 1.286 *tpmC*. Under these conditions, it is possible to extract the target *tpmC* from the target *tps* (expression 1), as well as the total number of *clients* (expression 2) and *warehouses* (expression 3). The required target *tps* is one of the configurable criteria in HTAPBench and directly relates with the expected scalability of the system and respective database size (further details are provided in Section 2.4).

The business queries in TPC-H are built from filtering, aggregation and grouping operations over a given result set. Filtering operations use SQL operators such as **`where`**, **`having`** or **`between`**. Their main goal is to limit the number of considered rows. Since the transactional activity will feed the analytical queries in HTAPBench, the number of rows filtered by the latter will grow over time. If not addressed, the results of these analytical queries are poised to become incomparable across runs. Data distributions regulate how the parameters for filtering operators are selected, enabling the queries to dynamically exercise several regions of the dataset while exhibiting comparable complexity. On the other hand, if the queries are not dynamically generated, the use of fixed bounds on the filters would end up traversing the full domains, preventing the query planner of the SUT to be exercised.

To verify the impact of using fixed or dynamic parameters, we conducted an experiment where we considered the execution of the 22 TPC-H queries over 2 setups. The first used a set of fixed parameters that would resemble full domain searches; the second used dynamically generated parameters without being bound to a data distribution. The configuration of dynamically generated parameters created a new set for each run, while the fixed configuration reuses the same set across runs. Each setup considers the average of 5 independent executions. Queries are computed against a column-oriented engine. In each run, the database is populated with one warehouse and the queries are executed without any of the filtering operators in their composition, establishing a baseline comparison that represents the universe of rows in each query.

The experiment observes the average difference of result set row count in consecutive executions of each run for a given setup, as a percentage of the baseline result. When using fixed parametrization, the result set cardinality did not change across consecutive runs, and in most cases, queries ended up selecting a considerably broader space of tuples. When we used dynamically generated filters in the TPC-H queries, a variation of up to 77% in result set cardinality was observed in comparison with the previous approach. This is due to not using a distribution to feed the date fields during the population stage of the benchmark. By not using a distribution to regulate how these fields are generated, it becomes likely that the items inserted during the populate stage of the benchmark present uneven time distributions when compared with the ones created during the execution stage. The next Section introduces a way to generate a workload distribution that ensures analytical queries with comparable complexity across runs.

2.2 Result Set Homogeneity

The analytical queries composing a hybrid workload are fed with data created or manipulated by the transactional agent, either during the initial populate stage, or during the transactional execution part of the hybrid workload. The engine qualifying as HTAP must operate under an isolation criterion that enables the analytical queries to observe data committed by the transactional agent at the time the analytical queries started. Likewise, a given analytical query should freely access the entire dataset, spanning from the first to the last committed transaction.

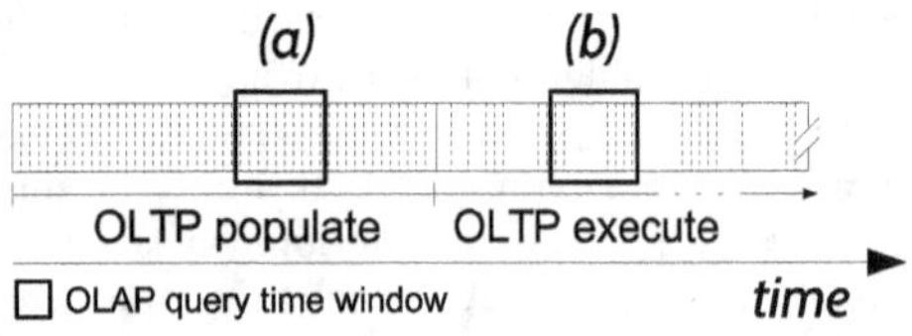

Figure 3: Timestamp density difference.

As discussed in the previous Section, the absence of a regulating mechanism would result in the use of randomized query boundaries, producing incomparable results across runs. The same may happen when analytical queries observe data generated in the populate and execution stages of the hybrid workload. Figure 3 depicts an example of the patterns that data is created or changed by the transactional agent. On the one hand, the OLTP populate stage (Figure 3a) promotes bursts of transactions inserting data, causing a high concentration of timestamps in a short time period. On the other hand, during the OTLP execution stage, the OTLP transaction rate is regulated by TPC-C.

What is desirable is that the pattern generated by the OLTP execution within TPC-C is also observed by analytical queries whenever they traverse the data loaded during the populate stage. To mitigate this issue, we introduce a density extraction mechanism that ensures the same data pattern across stages. Briefly stated, our approach observes the amount of generated date fields during the execution stage of TPC-C, allowing the system to apply the extracted density during population.

Density Function

The populate and execution stages of TPC-C generate different date densities across the whole dataset, varying according to the configured transaction mix within TPC-C. Moreover, as not all transaction types generate the same number of new timestamps, we configured our density function to reflect that behavior.

$$txnMix = \frac{\%NewOrder + \%Payment + 10 \times \%Delivery}{100} \quad (4)$$

$$d(T_S/s) = tps \times txnMix \quad (5)$$

Both the `New Order` and `Payment` transactions generate one timestamp each, while each `Delivery` transaction generates ten. The `Order Status` and the `Stock Level` transactions do not generate any timestamps. It is then possible to express density as a function between the target number of transactions per second and the ratio of `New Order`, `Payment` and `Delivery` transactions, as defined by expression 5.

In the following, we set up an experiment that allowed us to observe the expected density.

This experiment was conducted on a server with an Intel Xeon x3220 2.4 GHz QuadCore, 8GB of memory and 128GB Solid State Drive. For the purpose of this test, we relied on a Hybrid system, which we set up according to Table 1 to reflect workloads with more than 70GB in total size. In each experiment, the database was dropped and populated. Afterwards, we ran TPC-C under the standard transaction mix in runs that lasted 60 minutes.

tpmC	clients	warehouses
635	495	49
741	576	58
886	689	69

Table 1: Workload Configuration - Ideal TPC-C client.

The results depicted in Table 2 are the average of five independent runs regarding each target. The results depict an increasing amount of newly issued timestamps (T) as the defined target increases, thus reflecting a density function that also presents an increasing trend. The results also show

tpmC	Total Observed (Ts)	Expected $d(T_s/s)$	Experimental $d(T_s/s)$
635	108,051	30.24	30.01
741	125,500	35.14	34.86
886	150,114	42.02	41.69

Table 2: Density Observation Results.

that the density function provides results that are only 3% apart when comparing with the experimental observation.

The timestamp density will introduce a change in the standard TPC-C specification. It is worth noting that this modification does not introduce any change in TPC-C business logic. The individual TPC-C results are kept comparable with a same-sized TPC-C installation.

2.3 Component Design

Unified Metric

The disparity in workload complexity and structure between OLTP and OLAP workloads is a major hurdle when trying to define a unified metric for an HTAP system. So far, one of the main disadvantages of previous approaches was the fact that they would enable both OLTP and OLAP executions to grow in order to achieve the maximum throughput for each. The non-regulated growth induced by OLTP execution would inherently degrade OLAP performance since analytical queries would have to scan more data. HTAPBench removes one axis of variability by regulating the OLTP workload. The assurance of a constant transactional execution also leads to a sustained and known database growth; that is, the rate at which OLAP queries observe new data is fixed and predictable, bypassing the need to normalize the OLAP results in terms of the observed growth.

$$QpHpW = \frac{QphH}{\#OLAPworkers}@tpmC \quad (6)$$

Expression 6 defines the metric we propose, $QpHpW$ or "Queries of type H per Hour per Worker". It reads as the number of analytical queries executed per OLAP worker regarding a system that is able to sustain the configured tps.

It is defined by the ratio between TPC-H's metric and the total number of registered OLAP workers induced by the Client Balancer. A higher *QpHpW* maps a system where each OLAP worker is able to compute more queries per analytical worker, thus representing a higher overall throughput. Achieving the best configuration for a given installation becomes a multi-run optimization problem regarding a given target *tps*.

Client Balancer

The Client Balancer module is responsible for monitoring and deciding whether or not to launch additional OLAP workers. When the OLTP agent ensures that the target *tps* is stable, the Client Balancer will periodically assess whether or not the SUT is capable of handling an extra OLAP worker. This assessment relies on a proportional-integral feedback controller.

$$output = K_P \Delta tps + K_I \int \Delta t \quad (7)$$

The feedback control mechanism (expression 7) is characterized by a proportional (K_P) and an integral (K_I) gain adjustment. The gain parameters are used over the found system deviation ($\Delta tps = target\_tps - measured\_tps$) to compute the output value. The correct adjustment of either gain factor is vital to ensure that the feedback controller does not exceed too quickly the SUT's capabilities, which in turn would launch a higher number of OLAP workers, causing disruption on the throughput of the OLTP execution. We tuned the proportional-integral feedback controller by experimentation to use the gain adjustment characterized by $K_P = 0.4$ and $k_I = 0.03$. The individual study on how to reach these parameters is left out of the scope of this paper. Algorithm 1 presents the Client Balancer decision process.

Algorithm 1 Client Balancer

```
procedure
    wait(Δt)
    error ← target_tps − measured_tps
    integral ← integral + error × 1/Δt
    output ← K_P × error + K_I × integral
    previous_error ← error

    if output > (target_tps × margin) and ¬saturated then
        start OLAP worker
    else
        saturated ← true
```

The Client Balancer will periodically (Δt) poll the engine regarding the current number of transactions being delivered. This information is then fed into the feedback controller. To launch another OLAP worker, the Client Balancer ensures that the output value produced by the feedback mechanism is within a given error margin of the configured target *tps* and that the system is not saturated. The point of saturation is reached when the current number of OLTP transactions per second being delivered drops below the chosen threshold.

Density Consultant & Loader

HTAPBench follows the standard TPC-C transaction mix. The Density Consultant computes the correct density according to the chosen target *tps* and transaction mix. During the populate stage, in order to generate timestamps that follow the required density, the Loader is equipped with a clock that initiates with the system time at which the populate stage is initiated. The clock then computes how much time should elapse between clock ticks (ΔT_S) in order to fulfill the required density, as defined by expression 8.

$$\Delta T_S(ms) = \frac{1}{d(T_S/s)} \times 1000 \quad (8)$$

The HTAPBench Loader will proceed to create and load all the table entities represented in the hybrid data schema, built from merging TPC-H's schema into TPC-C's. The final installation will scale in size according to the computed number of warehouses. When loading tables with references to date items, the Load worker makes use of the clock, increasing one tick for each new date field to be loaded. After completion, applying the density function ensures that the temporal density in the date fields matches the observed density during execution of the transactional workload.

Dynamic Query-H Generator

The analytical queries within HTAPBench are constructed according to the TPC-H specification, which requires them to be built with randomized parameters within given boundaries. The Dynamic Query-H Generator module is responsible for building the SQL statements for the queries, ensuring that the random values comply with the TPC-H specification. This module integrates with the Client Balancer module that will launch the analytical workers, with its output afterwards fed into the TPC-H worker. The Dynamic Query-H Generator computes the time window frames that should be considered for query execution, and introduces a feature that enables the window frame generation to reflect a sliding window behavior. In the specification for each query, TPC-H requires static time frames. Take as an example query `Q6` that computes the total revenue for orders placed within a given period.

Listing 1: TPC-H Query 6

```
select sum(ol_amount) as revenue from
    order_line where ol_delivery_d between
[Date] and [Date + 1 year] and
ol_quantity between [Amount a] and [Amount b]
```

This particular query restricts the result set to orders placed within a one-year time frame, starting on January the first of a randomly selected year between 1993 and 1997, and ending in the following year. In TPC-H, this is attainable since it does not consider database growth. However, in HTAPBench, the database grows at the pace dictated by the OLTP execution of the benchmark. Thus, if window frames were to be kept static, the new regions on the dataset would never be queried. To produce a homogeneous result set that is representative of the whole dataset, the Dynamic Query-H Generator ensures that queries comply with the time range imposed by the specification while simultaneously leveraging the Density Consultant module to shift the starting date of the range to meet the speed at which the OLTP execution is making the database grow. Hence, the sliding window behavior not only ensures that the entire dataset is considered but also that consecutive executions of the same query are kept comparable.

Results Monitor

The Results Monitor collects the execution results produced by each worker. The final measurements are only collected after the configured execution time elapsed and all the workers finalized all procedures. The transactional activity is characterized according to TPC-C's metric (*tpmC*) while, the analytical activity is characterized by TPC-H's metric (*QphH*). Together with both metrics, this module also outputs data from the Client Balancer, characterizing each run in terms of how many OLAP workers were launched and when as well as the result set volume and latency for each analytical query executed.

Implementation

HTAPBench is available as an open source project [1]. It was implemented in Java for improved portability and includes all the aforementioned components. The current prototype was implemented as an extension of OLTPBench [13], a framework that enables the execution of several benchmarking approaches. Moreover, OLTPBench's implementation of TPC-C does not consider the think time used during transaction execution. The TPC-C specification requires a time in which each transaction simulates (by entering a sleep stage) the time required by the terminal user to insert data, as well as the terminal's processing time (TPC-C's simulation of a real-world scenario). Consequently, as part of our extension to OLTPBench to implement HTAPBench, we introduced the think time processing stage for each transaction of TPC-C.

HTAPBench relies on JDBC to establish a connection with the engine. Since JDBC defines a standard interface to connect with several engines, it is possible to use HTAPBench with a wide range of engines, provided that they support JDBC.

2.4 Benchmark Configuration

HTAPBench has several system requirements. The machine running HTAPBench should be provisioned with a Java distribution and the appropriate database engine driver.

HTAPBench requires the user to provide the engine JDBC connection URL, the fully qualified name of engine driver class and the target number of transactions per second (*tps*). The required target *tps* for a given configuration derives from an expectation regarding the performance compliance for the SUT. The user should start with a small target *tps* value and progressively increase the target *tps* until the SUT is saturated, as it happens with the warehouse scalability in TPC-C. Other configurations are allowed, enabling customization of the workload, namely: the Client Balancer Δt and `error margin`, the `TPC-C transaction mix`, the `TPC-H query mix` and the `Execution time`. Hereafter, we briefly describe the impact of the mandatory parameters on the system.

- `Client Balancer` Δt: This parameter configures the period in seconds used by the Client Balancer module to assess if further OLAP workers should be launched. Assigning the appropriate evaluation period has a direct impact on the convergence time and precision of the benchmark. Choosing a small value may cause the system to converge to quickly, but overestimate the number of admissible OLAP clients. On the other hand, choosing a large value improves the client balancer decision by exposing it to a larger number of samples, but delays the overall process. This parameter defaults to 60 seconds, configuring a trade-off between scalability and assuredness.
- `Client Balancer error margin`: This parameter configures how sensitive to change the Client Balancer should be, setting up the range of allowed *tps* computed in percentage of the target *tps*. It has a default value of 20%, which by experimentation we consider to be a reasonable trade-off of loss OLTP throughput in favor of having OLAP capability.
- `Execution time`: This parameter configures the duration of time that each run of the execution stage of the benchmark should last. This parameter defaults to 60 minutes, configuring a reasonable execution time after the warmup stage for the Client Balancer to exercise the SUT.

The execution of HTAPBench is divided into three main stages, as previously introduced. After system configuration, the user should run the populate script that generates the appropriate Comma-Separated-Values (CSV) files for the configured *tps*. Afterwards, the user should consult the documentation of the engine to be tested in order to use the correct procedure to load the CSV files (optionally, it is possible to directly populate the SUT, but this operation usually takes longer, since it does not load data in batch mode). To start the execution stage, which includes the initial warmup, the user should use the execution script, automatically deploying the required number of clients. The execution will run for the configured time and will afterwards produce result files, characterizing the OLTP and OLAP executions and computing the unified metric.

3. BENCHMARKING CAMPAIGN

The benchmarking examples presented in this Section result from an extensive study intended to evaluate the key properties of HTAPBench. As such, the main purpose of the presented scenarios is not to quantitatively compare different SUTs, but rather to demonstrate the expressiveness of the benchmark suite and its metrics.

Three different SUT were selected, namely: (*i*) an OLTP system, (*ii*) an OLAP system and (*iii*) a Hybrid system. Besides the target *tps* and the Client Balancer error margin, the same HTAPBench configuration was used across experiments. The Client Balancer was set to use an evaluation period (Δt) of 60 seconds and the OLTP activity was regulated by the standard transaction mix within TPC-C. For the OLAP activity, we set up HTAPBench so that each business query would be chosen according to a uniform distribution. Across experiments, we configured HTAPBench to inject 100 transactions per second, which according to our density extraction mechanism amounts to 2,099 active OLTP clients and 210 warehouses, a total of 117GB of data. The selected target *tps* was chosen as the number of configured warehouses generate a dataset with over 100GB, which is above the third recommended scale factor for the OLAP agent (e.g., 1GB, 10GB, 100GB). All the following experiments reflect the average of 5 independent 60 minute runs.

[1]https://github.com/faclc4/HTAPBench.git

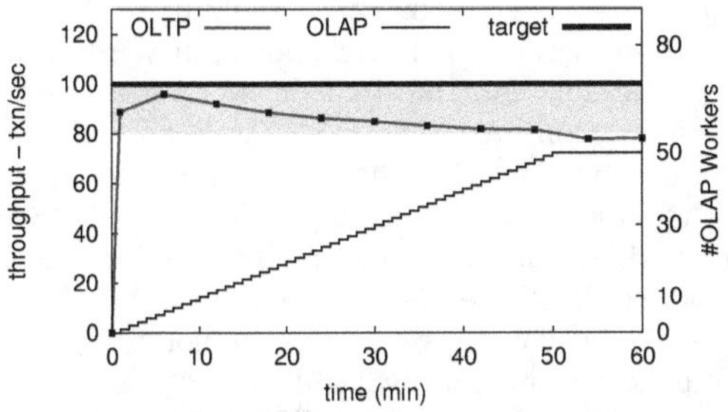

(a) OLTP SUT.

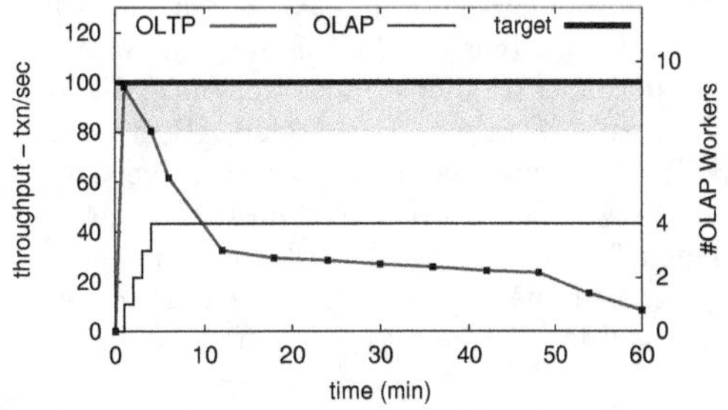

(b) OLAP SUT.

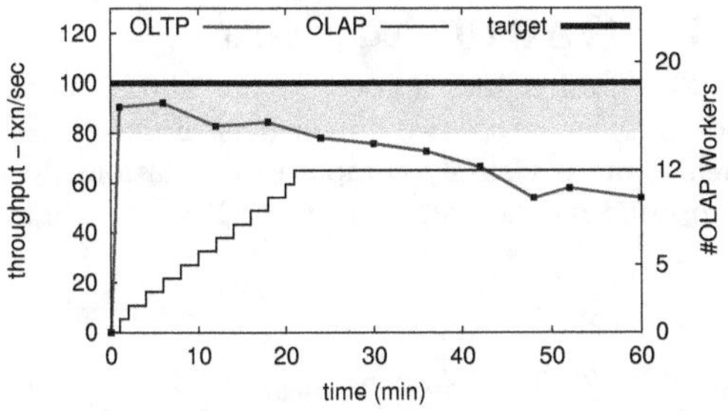

(c) Hybrid SUT.

	# OLAP workers	QpH	QpHpW
OLTP	50	7	0.14 @ 756
OLAP	4	123	30.75 @ 217
Hybrid	12	169	14.14 @ 530

(d) Overview of results for different SUT.

Figure 4: Registered progress between OLTP throughput and induced OLAP scalability. The optimal trade-off between OLTP and OLAP performance is achieved when the OLTP throughput goes below the gray area, at which point the OLAP activity is not further increased. The table in (d) summarizes the OLAP results, showing that the Hybrid SUT is more balanced for an HTAP workload.

3.1 OLTP System

The current experiment used a server with an Intel Xeon E5-2670 v3 CPU with 24 physical cores (48 virtual) at 2.3 *GHz* and 72GB of memory, running Ubuntu 12.04 LTS as the operating system. We deployed an OLTP row-oriented engine and configured the level of memory that would allow the required number of clients. The Client Balancer within HTAPBench was configured to consider the default error margin of 20%. The admissible loss of OLTP throughput induced by the configuration of the error margin is depicted as a gray area in Figures 4(a), 4(b) and 4(c). HTAPBench was launched from the same machine.

The results in Figure 4(a) depict that HTAPBench was able to launch and sustain the required target *tps* throughout the entire execution time. This is read by looking at the OLTP line that is the linear interpolation of the plotted points. The required target *tps* was reached on the first minute of execution and, from that moment on, the Client Balancer started its configuration by launching an OLAP worker at each minute. The evolution regarding when and how many OLAP workers exist is read by looking at the plotted line resembling a staircase.

With a configured error margin of 20%, the bottom *tps* barrier was only surpassed after 50 minutes, saturating the system at that point in time, and therefore not launching further OLAP workers. Please consider that by default HTAPBench's Client Balancer introduces a single OLAP worker in each evaluation period (Δt). Even though we do not present this evaluation for lack of space, it is possible to configure HTAPBench's Client Balancer to deploy more than one OLAP worker at a time.

Throughout the test, a declining trend in the OLTP throughput becomes evident. In what strictly concerns the OLAP activity, the engine under test was able to hold up to 50 OLAP clients. As previously stated, the main premise in HTAPBench's evaluation scheme is to discover how many OLAP workers are required to stress out a given SUT, while ensuring that the transactional activity does not degrade beyond a configurable threshold. In addition to providing a temporal evaluation of both OLTP and OLAP workers within the system, HTAPBench outputs the unified metric we propose, but also the standard TPC-C *tpmC* and TPC-H *QphH* metrics. Within this setup, this SUT was able to sustain 756 *tpmC* and 7 *QphH*, resulting in 0.14 QpH in each OLAP worker (7 QpH / 50 OLAP workers). As such, the unified metric, *QpHpW*, amounts to 0.14 @ 756 *tpmC*.

3.2 OLAP System

The current experiment reused the previous configuration. We deployed an OLAP column-oriented engine, only setting up the required level of clients allowed in the engine.

The results in Figure 4(b) depict that the SUT sustained the OLTP throughput for a shorter period. This behavior is not unreasonable since the focus of this engine is not on OLTP activity. From the moment the threshold was broken (6th minute), the Client Balancer stopped releasing new OLAP clients. From this time on, albeit at a lower throughput, the OLTP activity was kept stable until the end of the run time. The SUT was able to register 217 *tpmC* while sustaining 4 individual OLAP clients. Cumulatively, the OLAP activity reached a peak of 123 *QphH*. As such, the unified metric we propose, *QpHpW*, reaches 30.75@217 *tpmC*.

Compared with the previous system, we observe that the latter system can enable a larger number of analytic queries, despite the fact that this particular system was only able to launch 4 OLAP streams, compared to 50 OLAP streams with the first SUT. This may seem counter-intuitive, considering that we are working atop a column-based engine specifically designed for an analytical workload. However, the 4 OLAP streams in the current SUT are much more efficient when compared with the 50 OLAP streams in the OLTP SUT.

3.3 Hybrid System

Next, we use HTAPBench to characterize a Hybrid engine. As such systems are designed to scale out, they are usually made available over a distributed architecture.

We deployed the Hybrid system over 10 nodes, 9 of which are responsible for handling and storing data, and the remaining node provides coordination and other global services. Each node has an Intel i3-2100-3.1GHz 64 bit processor with 2 physical cores (4 virtual), 8GB of RAM memory and 1 SATA II (3.0Gbit/s) hard drive, running Ubuntu 12.04 LTS as the operating system and interconnected by a switched Gigabit Ethernet network.

The results depicted in Figure 4(c) reveal that the OLTP throughput reached the assigned target in the first minute of execution. From the first minute onward, the Client Balancer started to deploy OLAP streams until the OLTP throughput degraded beyond the considered error margin, which happened after 20 minutes, registering a grand total of 12 OLAP streams. From that moment on, the OLTP throughput slowly degraded over the remainder of the test duration. Cumulatively, the SUT was able to sustain 530 *tpmC* and 169 QphH. Therefore, our unified metric *QpHpW*, presents as 14.14@530 *tpmC*.

3.4 Discussion

The results of these three tests are summarized in the table in Figure 4(d). Although the OLTP SUT achieved the highest number of OLAP workers, the results in Figure 4(d) also show that it achieved the lowest OLAP performance (0.14). The OLAP workers in the OLTP engine spend most of their time waiting for the OLAP queries to be processed and therefore complete relatively few OLAP queries. On the other hand, the OLAP engine processes significantly more analytical queries, but fails to cope with the required OLTP throughput that is used by the Client Balancer to launch additional OLAP workers. Overall the OLTP engine completed 7 QpH and the OLAP engine completed 123 QpH. This results show that the OLAP SUT was better at handling the OLAP workload, but its inability to cope with the OLTP workload in the hybrid configuration harmed the overall scalability. The favored hardware configuration for the Hybrid SUT is significantly different from the OLTP system or the OLAP system, which undermines a direct comparison among them. Nevertheless, HTAPBench was able to evaluate the Hybrid SUT, enabling 12 OLAP streams and achieving a total of 169 OLAP queries. The results reveal that the Hybrid SUT can sustain a considerable OLTP throughput with a moderate OLAP scalability.

4. VALIDATION

In order to validate the expressiveness of our metrics, we studied the system's representativeness, workload accuracy, homogeneity, error margin variability and cost. Moreover, we discuss the benchmark portability, reproducibility and repeatability. For that matter, we used all the previous SUT configurations.

First, we show that the proposed metric can either identify systems with similar or very different goals. Second, we analyze HTAPBench's accuracy by verifying the storage traces produced in three distinct scenarios. Third, we verify that the produced query result sets are homogeneous as specified. Fourth, we conduct a variability analysis which presents the consequences of varying HTAPBench's error rate. Finally we discuss the cost of using the suite.

4.1 HTAP Unified Metric

The unified metric we propose allows us to establish a comparison across two dimensions. Figure 5 uses a quadrant field plot to visually compare the relationship between our proposed metric and the target OLTP throughput.

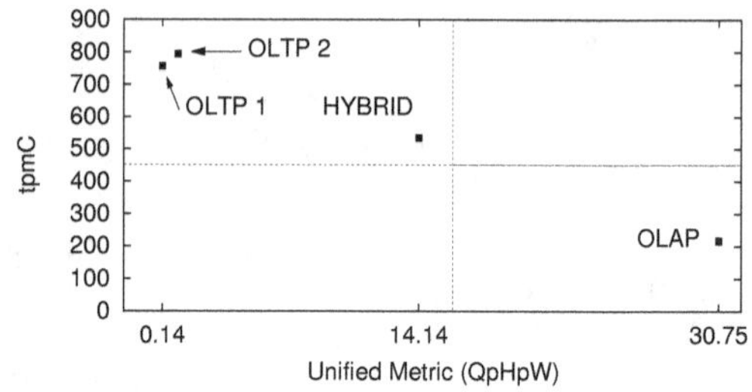

Figure 5: Quadrant field plot for the unified metric.

While an increase in the vertical axis translates into a higher OLTP throughput, the horizontal axis evaluates the capability to perform more analytical queries per OLAP worker. The best result would be a reading on the upper right quadrant. The analysis depicts that while the SUT labeled OLTP 1 registered a *QpHpW* of 0.14@756 *tpmC*, the OLAP observed 30.75@217 *tmpC* and the Hybrid 14.14@534.1 *tpmC*. Overall, we can state that the analyzed systems follow the trend in which the increase of OLTP activity diminishes the OLAP capability. The hybrid system reached a position close to the middle of the plot, indicating better support for the mixed workload with simultaneous OLTP and OLAP activity.

So far, the presented results allow us to conclude that the benchmarking suite is able to compare systems with very distinct work plans. In order to verify if the suite is able to distinguish systems designed for similar workloads, we reproduced the same experimental scenario as in Section 3.1 but changed the SUT to a different engine designed for OLTP workloads. We evaluated its performance and plotted it in Figure 5 with the label "OLTP 2". The results place OLTP system 2 very close to system OLTP 1 with enough precision so as not to overlap both results.

All of the previous experiments were integrated in a statistical study from where we were able to compute the variation coefficient of the computed metrics, pointing to a variation of 1.2%. As such, if the evaluation of 2 different systems, or system configurations produce variabilities with less than 1.2%, the systems should be considered indistinguishable.

4.2 Error Margin Variability

The Client Balancer in HTAPBench controls whether fur-

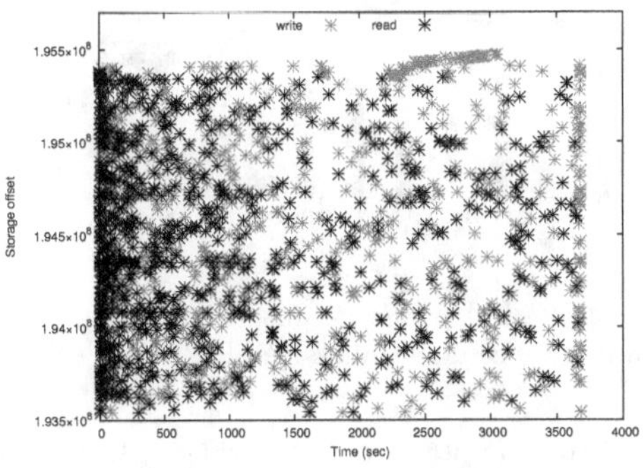

(a) OLTP access pattern.

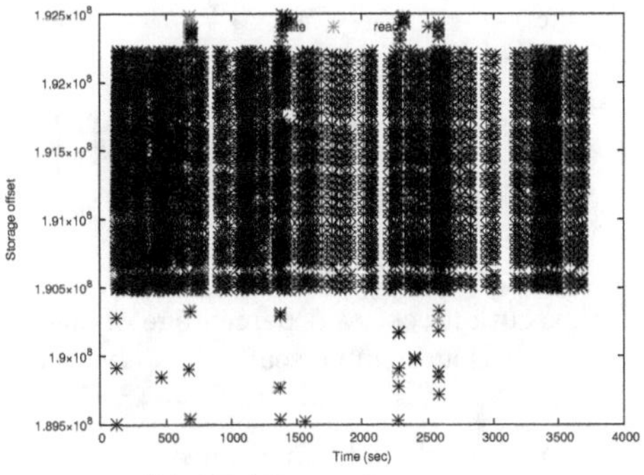

(b) OLAP access pattern.

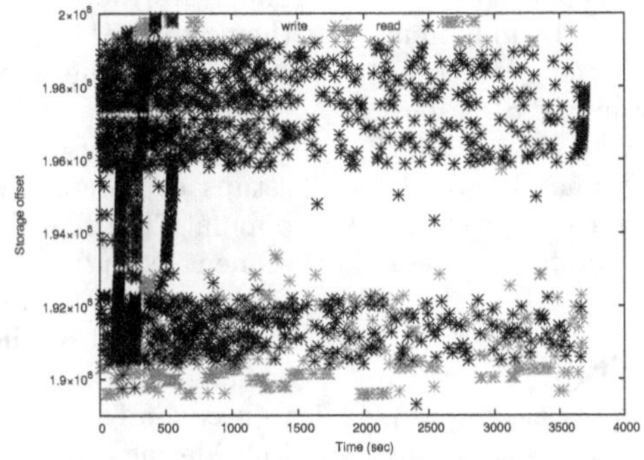

(c) HTAP access pattern.

Figure 6: Traces collected through the blktrace tool during a HTAPBench execution over an (a) OLTP, (b) OLAP and (c) HTAP SUT. The trace represents read (black marks) and write (red marks) patterns induced on the storage medium by the workload. The vertical axis represents the storage medium offset. The horizontal axis represents time in seconds.

ther OLAP streams are deployed or not, evaluating at each point in time if the current OLTP throughput does not go below a threshold defined by the error margin configuration. Intuition leads us to believe that by increasing the error margin, the Client Balancer will naturally allow more OLAP clients to be deployed, thus increasing the overall amount of analytical queries performed.

Error Rate	*QpH*	*tpmC*	*OLAP Clients*
10 %	70.99	130.64	1
20 %	168.9	131.36	5
40 %	265.99	138.30	11

Table 3: Client Balancer error rate variance.

The current experiment assesses if in fact such behavior translated into the actual behavior of the benchmark. For this purpose, we set up the OLAP SUT as in Section 3.2 but varied the error margin across runs.

First, by analyzing Table 3, the reader should be aware that the consecutive executions registered similar OLTP throughputs as expected. Moreover, as we increase the allowed error rate, we verify that more analytical queries were performed, which is a consequence of having more OLAP clients on the system, thus increasing the registered QpH and consequently the QpHpW.

4.3 Workload Representativeness

Database systems must be evaluated with representative workloads that test realistically the storage back-end capabilities. To better understand the representativeness of HTAPBench we analyzed the storage traces produced. The 3 previously tested SUT were evaluated with these workloads and the resulted storage traces were collected and analyzed with the *blktrace*[2] tool. This tool allows us to collect storage traces for a given block device. With these traces it is possible to extract useful information, such as the access patterns of storage requests, the ratio of storage reads and writes, the throughput and latency of each request, etc. Each SUT was deployed in a single machine as in Section 3.1.

Figure 6 depicts the access patterns registered by the storage medium for an HTAP SUT. The figures plot the offset of the storage medium (vertical axis) being accessed during execution time of the benchmark (horizontal axis). The analysis of the traces collected allowed us to confirm that OLTP workloads are dominated by random storage accesses (Figure 6(a)) while OLAP workloads do mostly sequential storage accesses (Figure 6(b)) dominated by read-only requests. On the other hand, mixed workloads generated by HTAPBench present a mix of these access patterns, as expected (Figure 6(c)). Moreover, the ratio of storage reads and writes is according to the specification of each workload. In summary, these results show that HTAPBench is able to simulate a realistic storage load for a hybrid SUT that pro-

[2]blktrace manual: http://linux.die.net/man/8/blktrace.

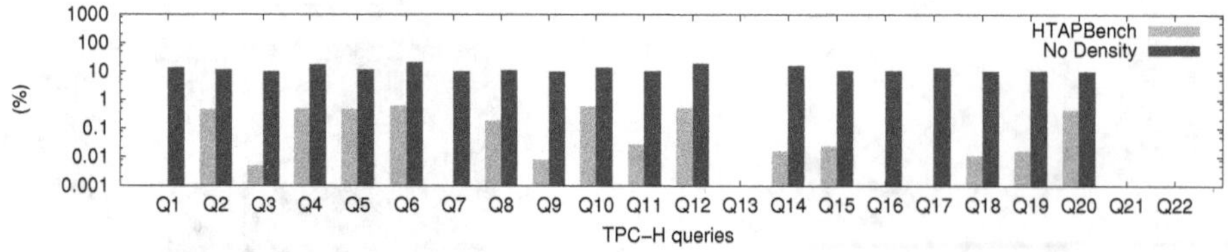

Figure 7: Result set execution cost as a percentage of the baseline across independent runs. The vertical axis is presented in logarithmic scale. The absence of columns represents null variability.

cess both OLAP and OLTP workloads simultaneously. Consequently, HTAPBench's representativeness of the analytical capability on top of a sustained transactional operation is ensured by the experimental data, but also by the individual representativeness of the TPC workloads used. Moreover, the results show that current proposals for hybrid SUT must be aware that processing simultaneously OLAP and OLTP workloads generates a mix of random and sequential storage accesses. This challenge can drive novel research proposals for both hybrid engines and the back-end storage systems supporting them.

4.4 Homogeneity and Reproducibility

The present experiment validates the effectiveness of our density mechanism. Figure 7 depicts 2 different scenarios, where we compare a distribution using random field generation with the density approach we propose. The depicted results relate to a baseline comparison where all queries were executed without any of their filtering operators, thus allowing us to extrapolate the total universe of rows considered in each analytical query. The value presented for each query is the absolute difference in produced result set rows in two consecutive executions: first, with random parameters that do not follow any distribution and, second, with the density mechanism proposed in HTAPBench.

In the first scenario, the analytical queries ran with the introduction of randomized parameters; the results show that consecutive executions of such queries produced variable result sets. The measured variability of result set lines across all query executions for this setup amounted to 12%, with a registered maximum of 20%. For the second scenario, we used HTAPBench's density mechanism to generate the random parameters to be used in all analytical queries. Queries Q13, Q21 and Q22 produce variabilities of 0% as the consecutive runs always produced the same number of result set rows.

The results show that by using our approach, we were able to produce query result sets with comparable costs. Consecutive executions of the same query registered a variability of just 0.17% on average across the different SUT and different configuration settings. These results confirm a very high level of reproducibility of results for a given configuration.

4.5 Benchmark Adoption Effort

The benchmarking suite proposed in this paper derives from two industry standard benchmarks with added functionality. The available suites offer implementations that are individually deployed to collect separate metrics, and they typically require the implementation of connector mechanisms between the benchmarking suite and the engine driver.

HTAPBench follows the trend of a few other suites, relying in the native JDBC driver of the SUT to communicate all the operations of the workload. Concerning the required time to run the benchmark, the setups considered in this paper are the result of 5 independent runs. In each one of them, the SUT had to be populated with data and then tested with the hybrid workload. The time spent during the populate stage greatly depends on the configured target of transactions per second and the SUT used. In the setups considered, we observed an average of 4 hours to populate the files for the engine. Afterwards, before subsequent executions, the engine would dump and restore the initial populate data, taking an average of 15 minutes. This technique is also valid for setups with terabytes of data. Regarding the execution stage, each setup ran for 60 minutes. Consequently, the overall cost for each SUT was 10 hours. Considering other suites, the total cost per SUT is relatively the same.

5. RELATED WORK

There are several organizations that propose benchmarking standards to assess either transactional or analytical systems, namely: the Transaction Performance Council (TPC) [12], the Standard Performance Evaluation Council (SPEC) [7] and the Storage Performance Council (SPC) [6]. We categorize several systems into OLTP, OLAP or Hybrid and we briefly present their main characteristics and shortcomings.

5.1 OLTP

Online Transactional Benchmarking systems, such as TPC-C [8], focus on assessing a system's ability to cope with a large amount of small-sized transactions. Usually, OLTP systems rely on row-oriented data stores, in which the transactions operate over a restricted space of tuples, ensuring at the same time properties such as consistency and isolation in what is commonly referred to as ACID [17].

The TPC-C specification models a real-world scenario where a company, comprised of several warehouses and districts, processes orders placed by clients. The workload is defined over 9 tables operated by a transaction mix comprised of five different transactions, namely: New Order, Payment, Order-Status, Delivery and Stock-Level. Each transaction is composed of several read and update operations, where 92% are update operations, which characterizes this as a write heavy workload. The benchmark is divided into a load and an execution stage. During the first stage, the database tables are populated and, during the second stage, the transaction mix is executed over that dataset. TPC-C defines how these tables are populated and also defines their size and scaling requirements, which is indexed to the number of configured warehouses in the system. The outcome of this benchmark is a metric defined as the maximum qualified throughput of the system, *tpmC*, or the number of New Order transactions per minute.

The TPC-E [11] benchmark builds on TPC-C, introducing a variable number of client terminals. It models a scenario where a brokerage firm receives stock purchase requests from customers, trying to acquire the correspondent stock bonds from a Stock pool. The purchase orders placed by clients are based on asynchronous transactions while stock requests between the Brokerage firm and the Stock Exchange are based on synchronous transactions. Compared with TPC-C, this benchmark builds a much wider and more complex system as it is composed of 33 tables and 10 transactions, 6 of which are read-only and the remainder are read-write transactions; the latter accounting for 23% of all requests.

Both specifications build benchmarking suites strictly intended to evaluate OLTP engines. Despite their representativity of OLTP workloads, the characteristic short operational transactions prevent the workload from exercising OLAP requirements. Engines designed to provide a high OLTP throughput are typically row oriented as the nature of a single transaction induces I/O bound operations in several attributes per transaction. This behavior translates into random access patterns to the storage medium and does not produce CPU and memory bound operations as do OLAP workloads.

5.2 OLAP

Online Analytical Systems such as TPC-H [9, 25] or TPC-DS [10] focus on assessing a system's ability to perform multi-dimensional operations, usually on top of column-oriented data stores.

TPC-H builds a workload that does not require ETL, modeling a real world-scenario where a wholesale supplier must perform deliveries worldwide. The business queries perform complex data operations (e.g., aggregations) across large sets of data. The workload defines a query mix comprised of 22 business queries that access 8 different tables. The execution is divided into three stages. The first stage loads the database. During the second stage, a single user executes all 22 business queries, while during the third stage, a multi-user setup is used in order to evaluate the system's ability to schedule concurrent operations. TPC-H does not consider any growth factor during runtime, which means that the dataset does not change in terms of its total size. The outcome of this benchmark is computed through a metric that accounts for the total number of completed queries per hour ($QphH$).

TPC-DS builds a workload that requires ETL, namely to ensure data freshness. It models a scenario where orders must be processed from physical and online stores of a wholesale supplier, mapping it into a star schema composed of 7 fact tables and 18 dimensions. The workload holds 4 different query types, namely Reporting, Iterative, Data Mining and Ad-hoc queries. The database populated for TPC-DS, as in TPC-H, does not consider any growth factor; still, the initial population is regulated in terms of a scale factor that has direct influence over the data size. The output metric is defined as the number of queries per hour at a given scale factor, $QphDS@ScaleFactor$.

TPC-DS is seen as an evolution of TPC-H, addressing oversimplifications that prevent the proper evaluation of OLAP systems. However, the need to use ETL to promote updates on the star schema prevents us from using it as an OLAP agent in our hybrid workload.

The high prevalence of read operations in these workloads mostly generate sequential accesses to storage mediums, and therefore are not able to simulate the short and cross attribute nature of OLTP workloads that also live in a hybrid workload.

5.3 Hybrid

Hybrid workloads should capture both access patterns observed in the previous individual specifications [15]. There are a few benchmarking suites that use both access patterns, namely CH-benCHmark [5] and CBTR [4, 2, 1, 3].

CH-benCHmark creates a mixed workload also based on TPC standard benchmarks, enabling two types of clients. A transactional client provides a TPC-C agent, while an analytical client provides a TPC-H agent. To allow the analytical workload across the transactional relations, CH-benCHmark merged both schema into a single one, comprising relations from TPC-C and TPC-H. The relations accessed by the OLTP execution scale according to TPC-C's specification. Relations accessed by the OLAP execution are kept unchanged. However, CH-benCHmark neglects aspects within TPC-H's specification. Namely, the analytical queries should hold random parameters in order not to constantly transverse the same regions of the dataset. It also disregards the required distributions for date fields, impacting the produced analytical results.

CBTR defines a benchmarking system aimed at mixed workloads, which does not account for any previous standardized specifications, considering them too predictable. It introduces a workload built from real enterprise data that models an order-to-cash workflow. For that matter, a new schema and the respective transactional activity is presented. By using real data, CBTR bypasses the need to use numerical distributions to populate or to generate data during benchmark execution.

The major differentiator of HTAPBench when compared with the previous approaches lies specifically in its Client Balancer module that governs how both workloads coexist. Both CH-Benchmark and CBTR use naive approaches to find the maximum qualified throughput for both the transactional and analytical workloads. The main concern that arises is that neither workload agent in each benchmarking suite is aware of the other agent, creating a dispute for resources as each agent tries to saturate the SUT. The Client Balancer in HTAPBench follows Gartner's recommendation to specify how the transactional and analytical agents coexist; instructing the transactional agent to sustain a configured throughput and allowing the analytical agent to saturate the SUT up to the point when the transactional throughput is affected. Moreover, HTAPBench also addresses the issues found in CH-Benchmark relating to non-uniform result sets by using the density mechanism to regulate that behavior.

6. CONCLUSION

This paper proposed HTAPBench, a benchmarking suite for engines that support hybrid workloads composed of high levels of transactional activity and, at the same time, provide business analytics directly over production data.

As our main contributions, we proposed a unified metric that enables the quantitative comparison of very similar systems, as well as very different systems. We also propose solutions to the key challenges of a hybrid benchmark, such as the Client Balancer.

Moreover we provide homogeneous and comparable results across executions. We validated our prototype on top of OLTP, OLAP and Hybrid systems, demonstrating the inherent expressiveness of HTAPBench's metrics to characterize such systems. We show that HTAPBench is able to distinguish different classes of systems (i.e., OLTP from OLAP), as well as distinguish systems within the same class with high precision. We ensured that HTAPBench exercised the storage layout as expected for each workload type. The results allowed us to conclude that by using the proposed approach we were able to introduce the required workload randomness while keeping the results comparable by ensuring equal query execution costs across the whole dataset.

7. ACKNOWLEDGMENTS

The authors would like to thank Marco Vieira for all the constructive reviews and comments on the final stage of this work, but also to Martin Arlitt and the anonymous reviewers for their helpful comments. This work is financed by: (1) the ERDF – European Regional Development Fund through the Operational Programme for Competitiveness and Internationalization - COMPETE 2020 Programme within project POCI-01-0145-FEDER-006961, and by National Funds through the Portuguese funding agency, FCT - Fundação para a Ciência e a Tecnologia as part of project UID/EEA/50014/2013; (2) the European Union's Horizon 2020 - The EU Framework Programme for Research and Innovation 2014-2020, under grant agreement No. 653884.

8. REFERENCES

[1] A. Bog, J. Krüger, and J. Schaffner. A composite benchmark for online transaction processing and operational reporting. In *Advanced Management of Information for Globalized Enterprises, 2008. AMIGE 2008. IEEE Symposium on*, pages 1–5. IEEE, 2008.

[2] A. Bog, H. Plattner, and A. Zeier. A mixed transaction processing and operational reporting benchmark. *Information Systems Frontiers*, 13(3):321–335, July 2011.

[3] A. Bog, K. Sachs, and H. Plattner. Interactive performance monitoring of a composite oltp and olap workload. In *Proceedings of the 2012 ACM SIGMOD International Conference on Management of Data*, SIGMOD '12, pages 645–648, New York, NY, USA, 2012. ACM.

[4] A. Bog, K. Sachs, and A. Zeier. Benchmarking database design for mixed oltp and olap workloads. In *Proceedings of the 2Nd ACM/SPEC International Conference on Performance Engineering*, ICPE '11, pages 417–418, New York, NY, USA, 2011. ACM.

[5] R. Cole, F. Funke, L. Giakoumakis, W. Guy, A. Kemper, S. Krompass, H. Kuno, R. Nambiar, T. Neumann, M. Poess, et al. The mixed workload ch-benchmark. In *Proceedings of the Fourth International Workshop on Testing Database Systems*, page 8. ACM, 2011.

[6] S. P. Council. *Storage Performance Council.* 2015.

[7] S. P. E. Council. *Standard Performance Evaluation Council.* 2015.

[8] T. P. P. Council. *TPC Benchmark C.* 2010.

[9] T. P. P. Council. *TPC Benchmark H.* 2010.

[10] T. P. P. Council. *TPC Benchmark DS.* 2012.

[11] T. P. P. Council. *TPC Benchmark E.* 2015.

[12] T. P. P. Council. *The Transaction Processing Performance Council.* 2015.

[13] D. E. Difallah, A. Pavlo, C. Curino, and P. Cudré-Mauroux. Oltp-bench: An extensible testbed for benchmarking relational databases. *PVLDB*, 7(4):277–288, 2013.

[14] C. D. French. "one size fits all" database architectures do not work for dss. In *Proceedings of the 1995 ACM SIGMOD International Conference on Management of Data*, SIGMOD '95, pages 449–450, New York, NY, USA, 1995. ACM.

[15] F. Funke, A. Kemper, and T. Neumann. Benchmarking hybrid oltp&olap database systems. In *BTW*, pages 390–409, 2011.

[16] A. K. Goel, J. Pound, N. Auch, P. Bumbulis, S. MacLean, F. Färber, F. Gropengiesser, C. Mathis, T. Bodner, and W. Lehner. Towards scalable real-time analytics: An architecture for scale-out of olxp workloads. *Proc. VLDB Endow.*, 8(12):1716–1727, Aug. 2015.

[17] T. Haerder and A. Reuter. Principles of transaction-oriented database recovery. *ACM Comput. Surv.*, 15(4):287–317, Dec. 1983.

[18] R. Kimball, M. Ross, et al. The data warehouse toolkit: the complete guide to dimensional modelling. *US: John Wiley & Sons*, 2002.

[19] S. S. Lightstone, T. J. Teorey, and T. Nadeau. *Physical Database Design: The Database Professional's Guide to Exploiting Indexes, Views, Storage, and More.* Morgan Kaufmann Publishers Inc., San Francisco, CA, USA, 2007.

[20] S. Machine. Splice machine. Technical report, Splice Macine, 2015.

[21] N. Mukherjee, S. Chavan, M. Colgan, D. Das, M. Gleeson, S. Hase, A. Holloway, H. Jin, J. Kamp, K. Kulkarni, T. Lahiri, J. Loaiza, N. Macnaughton, V. Marwah, A. Mullick, A. Witkowski, J. Yan, and M. Zait. Distributed architecture of oracle database in-memory. *Proc. VLDB Endow.*, 8(12):1630–1641, Aug. 2015.

[22] M. Nakamura, T. Tabaru, Y. Ujibashi, T. Hashida, M. Kawaba, and L. Harada. Extending postgresql to handle olxp workloads. In *Innovative Computing Technology (INTECH), 2015 Fifth International Conference on*, pages 40–44. IEEE, 2015.

[23] R. O. Nambiar and M. Poess. The making of tpc-ds. In *Proceedings of the 32Nd International Conference on Very Large Data Bases*, VLDB '06, pages 1049–1058. VLDB Endowment, 2006.

[24] NuoDB. Hybrid transaction and analytical processing with nuodb. Technical report, NuoDB, 2014.

[25] M. Poess and C. Floyd. New tpc benchmarks for decision support and web commerce. *SIGMOD Rec.*, 29(4):64–71, Dec. 2000.

[26] J. Rossberg and R. Redler. *Pro Scalable .NET 2.0 Application Designs.* Expert's Voice in .Net. Apress, 2005.

[27] VoltDB. Voltdb - whitepaper. Technical report, VoltDB, 2014.

[28] M. Waclawiczek. *HTAP - What it Is and Why it Matters.* 2015.

TARUC: A Topology-Aware Resource Usability and Contention Benchmark

Gavin Baker
Sandia National Laboratory
Livermore, California 94550
gmbaker@sandia.gov

Chris Lupo
California Polytechnic State University
San Luis Obispo, California 93407
clupo@calpoly.edu

ABSTRACT

Computer architects have increased hardware parallelism and power efficiency by integrating massively parallel hardware accelerators (coprocessors) into compute systems. Many modern HPC clusters now consist of multi-CPU nodes along with additional hardware accelerators in the form of graphics processing units (GPUs). Each CPU and GPU is integrated with system memory via communication links (QPI and PCIe) and multi-channel memory controllers. The increasing density of these heterogeneous computing systems has resulted in complex performance phenomena including non-uniform memory access (NUMA) and resource contention that make application performance hard to predict and tune. This paper presents the Topology Aware Resource Usability and Contention (TARUC) benchmark. TARUC is a modular, open-source, and highly configurable benchmark useful for profiling dense heterogeneous systems to provide insight for developers who wish to tune application codes for specific systems. Analysis of TARUC performance profiles from a multi-CPU, multi-GPU system is also presented.

1. INTRODUCTION

Non-uniform memory access (NUMA) as well as communication link bandwidth contention can reduce performance for applications used in heterogeneous computing system topologies. This paper presents *TARUC*, a new Topology Aware Resource Usability and Contention benchmark that utilizes memory and thread pinning techniques to provide detailed performance profiles of how system topology and usage patterns affect memory performance. The benchmark is tested on an x86 computing system and the results and experiences gained may be used to inform application developers about best practices for manual control of computing resources.

While parallel computational performance has improved following the trend predicted by Moore's Law, the bandwidth of memory systems and the communication links that connect peripheral coprocessor cards to main memory or network fabrics have both failed to match increasing demand for bandwidth [5, 7]. The existence of variable bandwidth and latency communication paths between CPUs, GPUs, main memory, and the network fabric has resulted in a hierarchical communication topology along with NUMA. NUMA effects can result in longer latencies for critical path operations which in turn can reduce the overall performance of the application [8]. TARUC is designed to help HPC application developers understand system topology and potentially mitigate the effects that variable topologies have on application performance.

The remainder of this paper is organized into the following sections: 2) discussion of modern system level architecture, 3) discussion of the design and implementation of the TARUC benchmark, 4) review of results acquired on a HPC test system, 5) related work on the topic of resource management of heterogeneous computing systems, 6) a summary of the most significant conclusions and topology trends and a review of continuing effort in this research area.

ICPE'17, April 22 - 26, 2017, L'Aquila, Italy

ACM ISBN 978-1-4503-4404-3/17/04 . . . $15.00
DOI: http://dx.doi.org/10.1145/3030207.3030230

2. BACKGROUND

For this paper, we focus on x86-based microprocessor computing systems that utilize coprocessor hardware to explore the architecture of densely packed computing systems. These systems comprise the majority of supercomputers [10].

2.1 NUMA

One solution for scaling beyond a single CPU is to add multiple CPU sockets to a single computing system. Separate DIMMs and corresponding memory management units (MMUs) are often provided for each CPU socket. To ensure cache and memory coherence, each CPU is connected together via a high-speed low-latency cache coherence link. One side effect is that some memory accesses require extra time/latency due to the cache coherence link. Cache coherency links are high bandwidth and low latency compared to other peripheral connections, but still fail to match either the bandwidth or latency of having a single memory bus connection between main memory and CPUs.

The effect of having memory spaces connected to cores with differing latency and bandwidth connections is called non-uniform memory access (NUMA).

2.2 Modern x86 System Architecture

Modern x86 computers typically consist of one or more CPUs, main memory, persistent storage, and a number of I/O interfaces. Each CPU integrates both memory control and high speed peripheral communication links onto a single package. Processors can contain multiple cores per package and multiple processing units per core in simultaneous multithreaded (SMT) architectures. The sharing of memory resources can be of concern in NUMA systems because of the potential for unbalanced memory usage where many cores access the memory or cache of a specific NUMA node. Figure 1 shows a basic x86 system with main memory, I/O, and multiple cores.

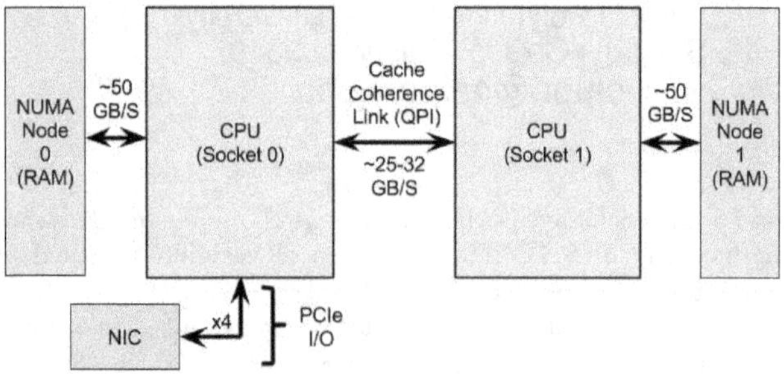

Figure 1: An x86 Cache Coherent NUMA Machine

For multiple CPU systems, cache coherency links are used to maintain the shared memory programming model guaranteed by today's symmetric multiprocessing systems. QPI is utilized on Intel processors to connect the memory subsystems of two or more CPUs within a single machine. The bidirectional bandwidth of QPI ranges from 25-32GB/s [4]. Memory access on NUMA systems may require the request to travel from one CPU over the QPI bus to the MMUs of an adjacent processor. This transaction is transparent to the application, other than the performance reduction for repeated remote access.

Peripheral devices such as NICs and GPU or Xeon Phi coprocessors may be attached via a PCIe connection. The current generation PCIe 3.0 is a point-to-point communication link that can dynamically scale between 2, 4, 8, or 16 lanes between a single device and host. Each lane can carry out 8.0GT/s (giga transfers per second) for a total bidirectional bandwidth of 32GB/s [6]. PCIe combined with integrated memory control hardware on the CPU allow for direct address (DMA) of pinned memory by PCIe devices contained on node-local PCIe slots.

2.3 Memory, Thread, and Process Management

The Linux operating system allows for the setting of memory and thread management policy to control the hardware location of allocated resources. Manual control of the location of thread or process execution can be carried out by modifying the thread's individual hardware affinity. The allocation policy of memory can be set to *firsttouch*, *bind*, *interleave*, and *nexttouch* with each policy defining where a block of memory will be placed upon allocation or use. In the TARUC benchmark, the *bind* policy is used to ensure correct memory NUMA locations during tests.

2.4 Programming Parallel Architectures

A number of software libraries allow for the use of parallel hardware through different software abstractions. Most significantly OpenMP, OpenAcc, OpenCL and CUDA provide some type of node-local software parallelism. TARUC uses OpenMP and CUDA to test heterogeneous systems for NUMA effects. This choice was made because of the flexibility and vendor support for these libraries provided on our test systems. OpenMP enjoys widespread compiler support and relatively low overhead. Compiling with OpenMP is a matter of adding relevant threading directives, the header library declaration, and linking flags. For GPU functionality, the CUDA runtime API version 7.5 is utilized. CUDA was chosen because it provides thorough functionality including a variety of host-device memory management operations and has been optimized for the NVIDIA coprocessors present on our test systems.

3. THE TARUC BENCHMARK

The Topology Aware Resource Usability and Contention (TARUC) Benchmark consists of a number of micro-benchmarks used to measure communication and memory access bandwidth within complex heterogeneous architectures.

The TARUC benchmark examines NUMA and contention effects in the context of memory transfer and operation bandwidth during single threaded and multithreaded memory migrations. Threads and memory resources are pinned to simulate specific resource utilization situations and measure performance influences. TARUC tests the effectiveness of memory types and copy methods in specific hardware allocation situations. Memory types include device memory, host pageable, host pinned, and host write-combined memories while migration methods include manual unified memory and asynchronous memory copies. In addition to built-in memory transfers, a variety of manual memory access patterns including copy assignments and triads (copy-/scale/add) are tested for throughput and latency.

TARUC examines resource contention within the memory access pipeline by profiling simultaneous memory transfers and access operations between memory resources on different computing resources. In contrast, NUMA effects and other overhead costs of utilizing different system memory types are examined in isolated, single-threaded allocations, transfers, and operations.

TARUC supports analysis of NVIDIA GPUs using the CUDA runtime along with system topology detection and control through the HWLOC library. Host multi-threading is provided by calls to OpenMP parallel tasks. HWLOC also provides memory and thread resource pinning functions through integration with pthreads and libnuma, allowing isolation of individual computing resources within benchmark test cases. Each recorded micro-benchmark data set is automatically fed into graphing scripts that iteratively generate a variety of comparative plots for performance analysis. The entire benchmark may be run with a single command and tuning is provided through a simple input parameter file. The TARUC benchmark may be downloaded from the TARUC_Bench GitHub repository located at the following URL:

https://github.com/gabaker/TARUC_Bench.git

3.1 Specification

The TARUC benchmark is defined by its feature set, software and hardware requirements, and the individual micro-benchmarks that implement the actual benchmark test cases.

3.1.1 Features

- GPU device management and control via CUDA and the NVIDIA Management Library (NVML),

- topology awareness of coprocessors, CPUs and memory systems via the portable Hardware Localitly (HWLOC) library,
- test automation of all micro-benchmark tests,
- verbose output including topology and GPU device information,
- automated graphing of micro-benchmark test cases, and
- cleanup and topology scanning scripts.

3.1.2 Non-Features

TARUC does not support the following:

- NUMA effects from distributed shared-memory programming,
- GPUs or other coprocessors that do not contain NVIDIA chipsets,
- hybrid CPU + GPU or embedded system on a chip (SoC) architectures that do not contain an NVIDIA chipset,
- systems with non-Linux operating systems, and
- NVIDIA coprocessors that do not support CUDA runtime version 7.5 or newer with compute ability 3.5+.

3.1.3 Requirements

A complete set of hardware and software requirements for building and using TARUC can be found in [1].

3.2 Micro-Benchmarks

In order to isolate resource contention and NUMA effects, TARUC is broken into four micro-benchmarks. These micro-benchmarks may be run in any combination or order. Each micro-benchmark dynamically creates a number of test cases at runtime based on the detected topology.

3.2.1 Memory Overhead

The memory overhead micro-benchmark measures allocation and deallocation cost for each memory type using various memory binding and thread pinning combinations to isolate NUMA effects caused by heterogeneous topology. A range of memory block sizes are timed if ranged test runs are enabled. All CPU socket and NUMA node combinations are tested for each of the three host memory types. Allocation and deallocations are timed consecutively for each memory type and block size step. For device memory allocations the `cudaMalloc()` function is timed for all GPU devices present within the test system after pinning the host thread to each CPU socket.

3.2.2 Memory Bandwidth

The memory transfer bandwidth micro-benchmark consists of three individual sub-tests that focus on different types of automated memory transfers (copies) and communication pipelines. Host-to-host, host-device, and device-to-device transfer bandwidth are all measured separately. For transfers involving host memory, pinned, pageable, and write-combined memory types are tested with varied memory access patterns. TARUC uses repeated, ascending and descending memory address access patterns to reduce caching effects.

Each single-threaded memory migration task is executed while pinning the executing CPU thread to a specific CPU socket/core. For transfers involving host memory, each memory type and access pattern is measured for bandwidth and transfer time. Each host memory block is bound to a specific NUMA region to test for NUMA effects while measuring pipeline bandwidth. For device-only memory transfers, additional memory copy types are considered including unified virtual addressing and direct peer-peer transfers.

3.2.3 Non-Uniform Random Memory Access (NURMA)

The NURMA micro-benchmark stresses streamed random memory access by using a large, dynamically defined stride gap to separate consecutive memory accesses. This allows the simulation of small, fixed-access strides like those present in certain stencil operations as well as larger pseudo-random memory access patterns. The main focus of this micro-benchmark is understanding how NUMA situations affect random memory access patterns.

3.2.4 Resource Contention

The resource contention micro-benchmark has one test for each of the QPI, PCIe, and integrated multi-channel memory controller communication paths. Simultaneous memory transfers to different combinations of host and device memory systems are used to isolate each communication pipeline. Threads are pinned to various combinations of CPU cores while different devices are used as sources or destinations. In this micro-benchmark host-only, device-only, and host-device transfers are measured.

3.3 Design

The TARUC benchmark suite consists of topology aware NUMA and resource contention micro-benchmarks as well as automated graphing scripts. A number of libraries are utilized for topology detection and control including HWLOC, NVML, CUDA, and OpenMP. These libraries allow for host thread and memory pinning, GPU coprocessor management and computation offload, as well as hardware affinity detection for both host and device processing units.

Figure 2 shows a block diagram of the TARUC benchmark at the software level. During benchmark initialization, the parameter values are read in from the input file and the system topology is detected via the `SystemTopo` class. A number of safety checks also occur during this phase to ensure benchmark parameters can be satisfied by system resources. These checks include a verification of the availability of NVIDIA GPUs as well as memory resources for large block allocations.

After initialization, TARUC proceeds to the benchmarking phase where each micro-benchmark is called in the order indicated by the parameter file. Each micro-benchmark reads relevant parameters from the `BenchParams` class and then generates test cases depending on the provided parameters. Ranged and multithreaded memory access tests save data for various block sizes into a multi-dimensional C++ `Vector`. This data is processed to produce either a calculated bandwidth or transfer latency value for each vector entry. These processed values are then saved to CSV files within the results folder.

Post-processing of ranged test data is carried out via Python

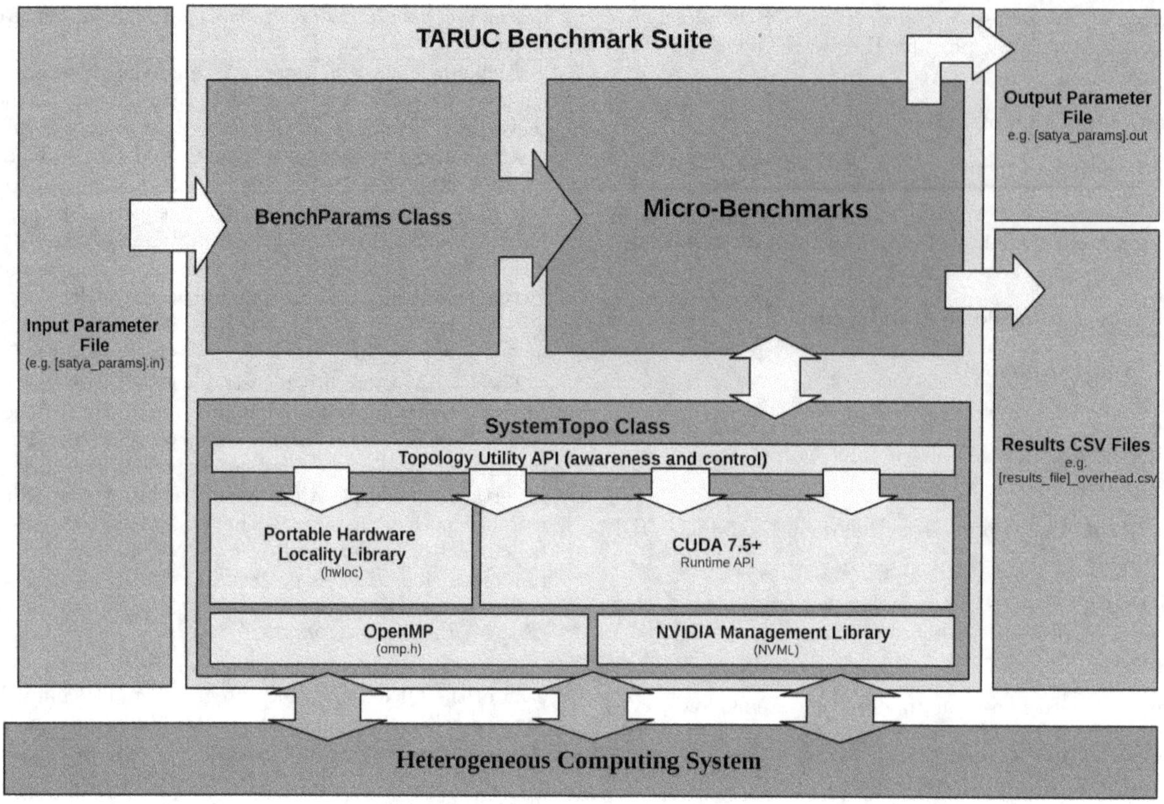

Figure 2: TARUC Benchmark Block Diagram

graphing scripts, each of which utilizes *NumPy* for data scanning/storage and *matplotlib* for plot creation. Each micro-benchmark has a separate plotting script used to graph output data. TARUC can produce a large number of graphs that the user can evaluate.

The sections below discuss the class interfaces for the `SystemTopo`, `BenchParams`, and `Timer` classes.

3.3.1 SystemTopo Class

Hardware topology detection, thread scheduling and memory policy management functionality is integrated into the `SystemTopo` C++ class. This class combines NVIDIA Management Library (NVML), CUDA runtime API, and HWLOC functionality into a single interface. At instantiation, the `SystemTopo` class parses a generalized topology object tree provided by the HWLOC API as well as device information from the NVML and CUDA libraries. All system topology information is automatically detected after instantiation of the `SystemTopo` class object. HWLOC provides detailed information about the number of CPU sockets, NUMA nodes, cores, and processing units (PUs) as well as the sizes of cache and main memory. PCIe device location information is also available. The topology information is parsed into device statistics and relational information that is later used to manage thread affinity and memory policy. The CUDA runtime API is then queried to provide basic device information including the size of memory resources and the functionality of peer-to-peer support for GPU pairs. Finally, NVML is utilized to inform the `SystemTopo` class about the proximity of GPU devices to processing units.

After the initialization phase, the class provides a number of memory, thread, and device management functions. These functions provide the ability to pin threads to execution units including CPU sockets, cores or processing units. The HWLOC library provides this functionality on Linux systems through the modification of scheduler affinity. Memory can be directly allocated on any specified NUMA node (called memory binding), or the memory policy can be modified such that memory is placed on NUMA regions after being used (such as interleaving on first touch).

3.3.2 BenchParams Class

The `BenchParams` class is a storage and utility class for keeping track of all benchmark parameters. Because of the number of class variables and intended use within the TARUC benchmark, each parameter is made publicly accessible rather than abstracted via member access functions. Each value within the parameter file corresponds to a variable within the parameter class.

Some of the available parameters include: minimum and maximum block sizes for the range tests, whether to test all GPUs in the system, whether to test all memory types, and if each socket should be included in the tests. There are many parameters available that determine the behavior of each test. Full discussion of all of TARUC's parameters is omitted from this paper due to space considerations.

3.3.3 Timer Class

The `Timer` class is a C++ class that integrates host-based timing together with a CUDA event-based device timer. The timing object is instantiated with a single `boolean` value indicating the type of timing the user wishes to use. When the value is true, the `chrono::high_resolution_clock` standard library class is utilized to provide host-based timing functionality. The `chrono` class was chosen because of its nanosecond accuracy and simple programmer interface. If the value is set to false, then the timer relies on the CUDA event interface to provide timing results. While event timings come with a lower (millisecond) accuracy than the host timer, they provide the best mechanism that is capable of timing asynchronous CUDA API calls. To prevent synchronization issues between different timers, a non-default CUDA stream is initialized and passed to event timing calls.

4. BENCHMARK RESULTS

Some of the more interesting results and insights from running TARUC on a high-performance test system are provided. These results quantify the importance of NUMA awareness and demonstrate potential uses for TARUC. Some insight based on experiences building the TARUC benchmark is also provided. The primary output from TARUC is performance profile graphs from each of the micro-benchmarks. This section presents a small subset of the graphs available. These graphs are useful for measuring the significance of NUMA effects on GPUs and host memory subsystems as well as doing comparative analysis of different GPU hardware and topologies.

4.1 Test System

The test system consists of two Intel Xeon E5-2650 Sandy Bridge CPUs that have 8 discrete 2.0 GHZ cores, and 16 processing units with hyperthreading enabled. Each CPU socket has 32 GB of attached RAM for a total of 64 GB of main memory. Cores have 32KB instruction and data L1 caches and a 256 KB L2 cache. All cores on a single socket share 20 MB of L3 cache. Attached to the PCIe slots are four discrete GPUs: two Tesla K20Xm compute-class cards, one Tesla K40c, and one GeForce GTX Titan Black graphics card. Each K20Xm and the Titan have 6GB of memory while the K40c GPU has 12 GB of memory. Each of the GPU memories have different memory clock frequencies resulting in varying memory access latency. The K20Xm, K40c and Titan GPUs have 2600 MHz, 3004 MHz, and 3500 MHz memory clock rates, respectively. The test system provides a unique testing environment because different generation GPUs allow comparison of NUMA effects on different GPU hardware. Figure 3 shows a hardware overview of the test system.

4.2 Profiling Results

The following sections contain the results of running the TARUC benchmark on the test system. These graphs are a subset of the graphs that are generated with TARUC.

The parameters have been kept consistent over all the benchmarking systems to minimize variance in graph structure. The following parameters were used for the benchmarking runs on all systems. Figure 4 below shows a simplified list of test parameters.

4.2.1 Memory Management Overhead

The graphs of memory overhead tests are log-log scale graphs showing the elapsed time in microseconds of an allocation of varied memory block sizes. Log scale graphs are useful for showing large variations in memory block sizes. However, log scale graphs can obscure overhead costs that are actually much larger than they appear.

Three types of host memory are tested within the TARUC benchmark. Pageable, pinned, and write-combined memories are measured along with device memory located on each of the on-node GPUs. Memory allocations and deallocations are measured between 100B and 1.5GB.

Figure 5 shows that allocations of non-local host memory result in a fixed overhead of 20-50%. This NUMA overhead decreases from its maximum as the block size increases past the inflection point of 1MB for non-pageable memories. This graph also shows that non-pageable memories have increased allocation overhead compared to pageable memory.

Allocations of GPU memory have no significant effect when NUMA bindings are changed. The fixed overhead associated with the allocation of GPU memory over PCIe depends more on the hardware specifications of the specific GPU device. In particular, the memory clock frequency of the GPU seems to determine the relative performance of a specific GPU for memory allocation and deallocation operations. Figure 6 shows that the GTX Titan GPU has the lowest cost for block allocations likely as a result of it having the highest memory clock frequency.

Figure 7 shows NUMA related effects in the deallocation of memory for the K20Xm GPU devices when the executing thread is pinned to the non-local CPU socket. This performance artifact can be clearly linked to NUMA as the K20Xm devices do not suffer from the performance degradation when the thread is pinned to CPU 1 as shown in Figure 8. The two K20Xm GPUs are located on PCIe connections attached to controllers on CPU 1 while the executing thread is run on CPU 0. This trend is significant, as it appears to be machine specific and only occurs for device memory deallocation events.

It is interesting that there is a very clear point where at certain memory block sizes the noise dissipates as indicated near 10MB. We do not speculate why this performance artifact occurs due to the opaqueness of the CUDA runtime system.

These graphs provide evidence that system performance can be influenced from hardware specific phenomena outside the control of the developer. It is essential that the performance profile of the memory system be benchmarked to avoid wasting time on application debugging if performance results are other than what is expected.

4.2.2 Memory Transfer Bandwidth

Host-Host Block Memory Transfers.

Host-Host memory bandwidth is measured using a single thread of execution pinned to various CPUs. This thread transfers memory from one memory block to another, each of which has an individual memory policy binding. The comparative effect of block size, memory and thread policy, and access pattern are presented. Each of the mentioned variables may change the effectiveness of caching at reducing NUMA effects. In particular, it is expected that small block sizes along with those that use repeated memory address ranges will experience less NUMA overhead due to caching.

Figure 9 shows the change in execution time associated with exceeding the available space of each level of cache. The test uses cacheable paged memory with a repeated memory

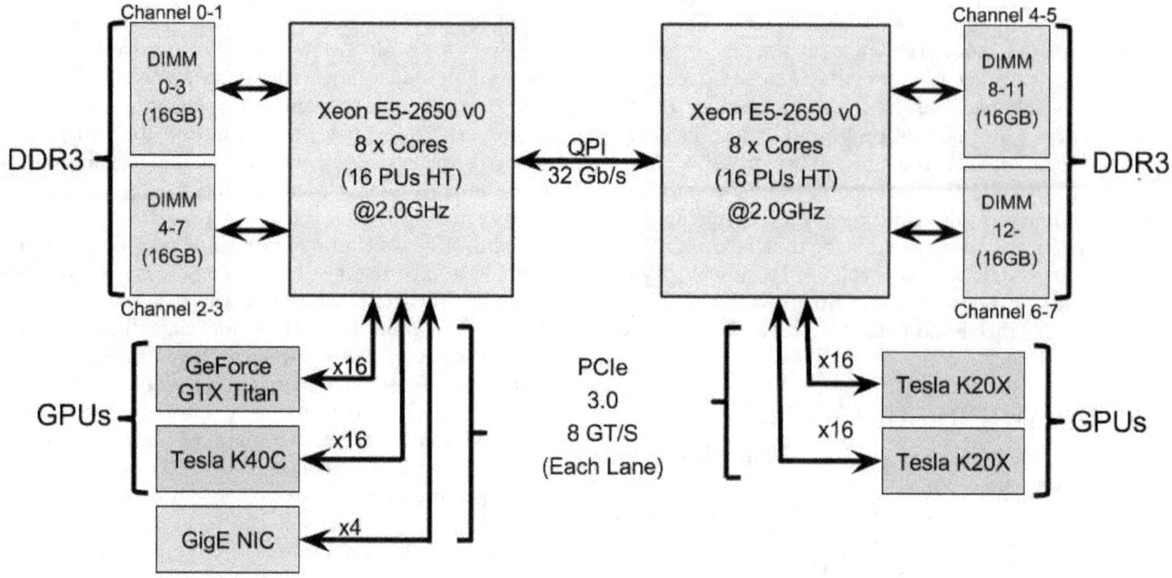

Figure 3: Test System Architecture Overview

```
Test All Sockets:                    true
Test Host Mem Types:                 true
Test all Devices:                    true
Test Access Patterns:                true
Sustained Tests:                     true
# Repeated Steps:                    20
Number Steps Per Magnitude:          10
Overhead/Bandwidth Range:            10 - 1500000000 (bytes)
NURMA Access Gap/Stride:             657 (doubles)
NURMA Host Memory Block Size:        200000000 (doubles)
NURMA Range (doubles):               10, 10000000 (min,max)
Contention Memory Block Size:        100000000 (bytes)
```

Figure 4: TARUC Test Parameters

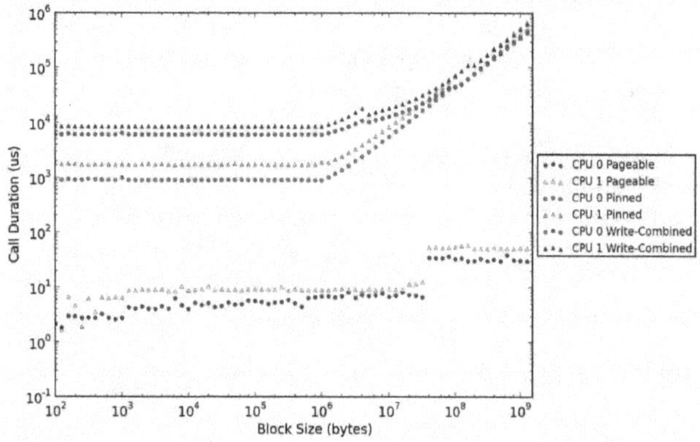

Figure 5: Memory Allocation - Memory Bound To Node Zero

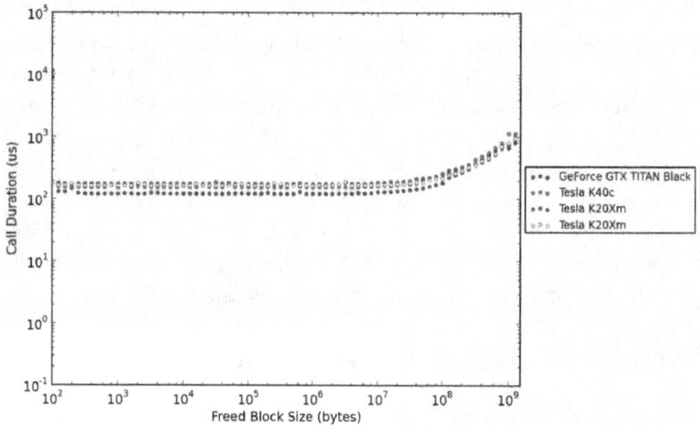

Figure 6: Memory Allocation - Thread Pinned To CPU Zero With All Devices

address. Interestingly, the local memory transfer when the executing thread is local to the memory node provides the best performance only after the size of the memory block exceeds L3 cache size.

Figure 10 shows the NUMA costs of different node bindings when the executing thread is pinned to CPU 1. The worst case for NUMA binding overhead is a 15% reduction in bandwidth when a thread executes completely non-local memory transfers. The best performance is achieved when both source and destination memory blocks remain local to the executing thread. Results also show a significant reduction in overhead if the destination memory block is on the same NUMA region as the executing thread's CPU. This indicates that cache write-back policy is slowed by having to write cache lines to non-local memory. The source block is never written which prevents it being marked as modified, and allows the cache line to be invalidated without being written back to main memory. Another result is that page-

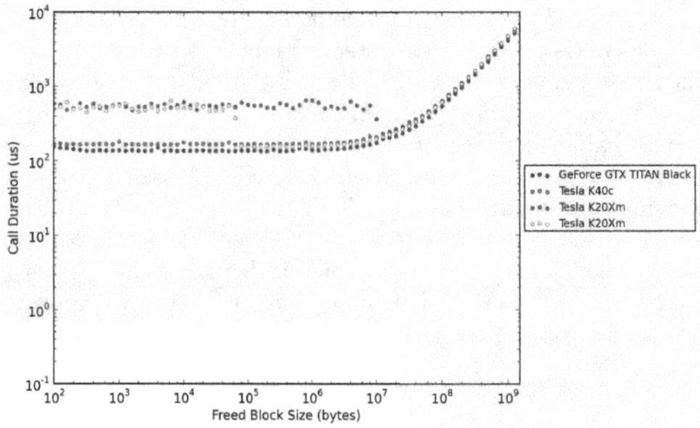

Figure 7: Memory Deallocation - Thread Pinned To CPU Zero With All Devices

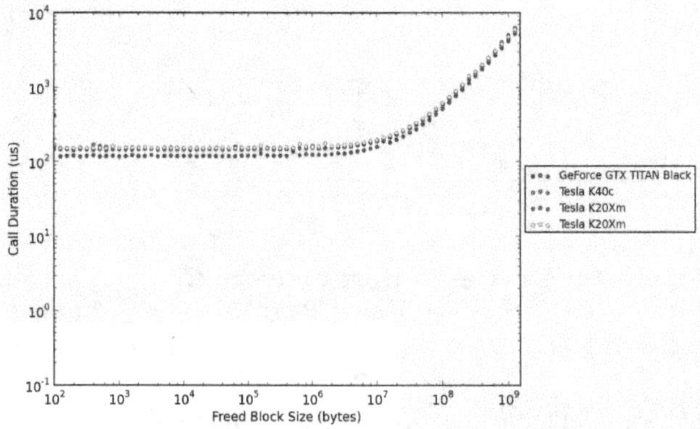

Figure 8: Memory Deallocation - Thread Pinned To CPU One With All Devices

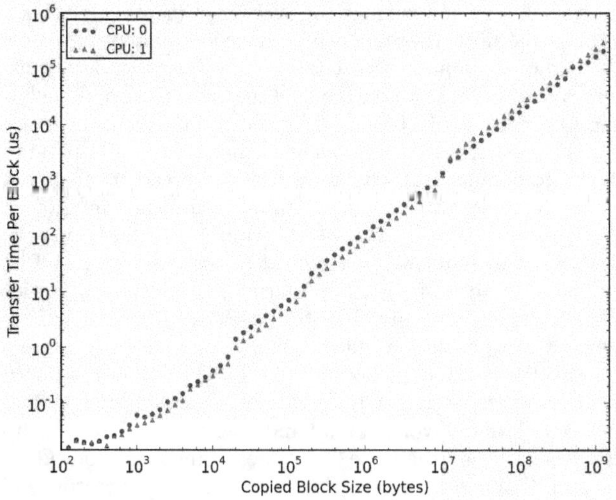

Figure 9: Host Memory Copy - Pageable Memory Bound To Node Zero With A Repeated Memory Address

able and pinned memory benefit from cache despite the use of varied access patterns.

To demonstrate that different memory address access patterns do not significantly influence the presence of NUMA

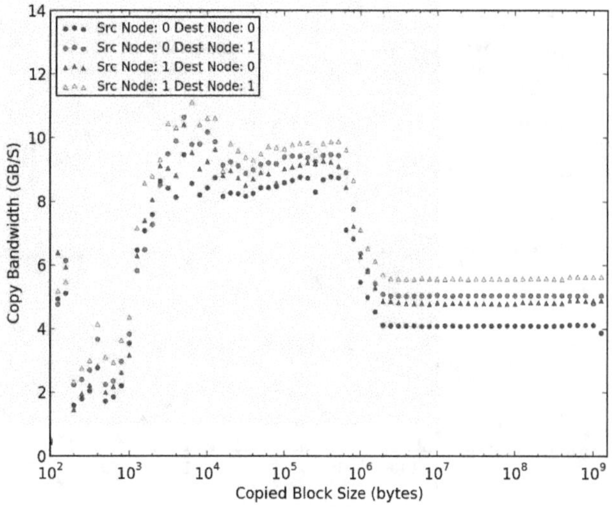

Figure 10: Host Memory Copy - Thread Pinned To CPU One And Pageable Host Memory With Linear Decreasing Memory Address

within test runs, the total transfer time of each pattern is plotted for different thread pinning combinations. Figure 11 shows that while there is a minor change in the overall execution time of a memory copy for certain patterns, this change does not outweigh NUMA performance influences.

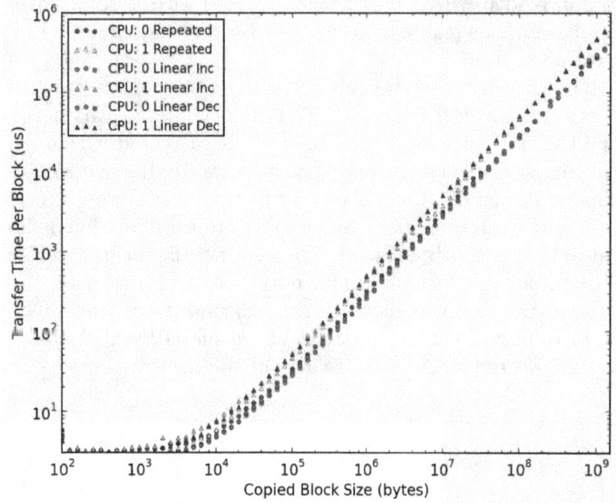

Figure 11: Host Memory Copy - Memory Bound To Node Zero, Repeated Address, And Pinned Dest Memory

Pageable memory seems to provide better performance than pinned memory on the test system. Figure 12 shows pinned memory performance and demonstrates a 50% reduction in bandwidth for non-local NUMA bindings.

Host-Device Block Memory Transfers.

Benchmarking memory copy bandwidth between GPU accelerators and host memory involves timing CUDA runtime calls for various memory types. Asynchronous and syn-

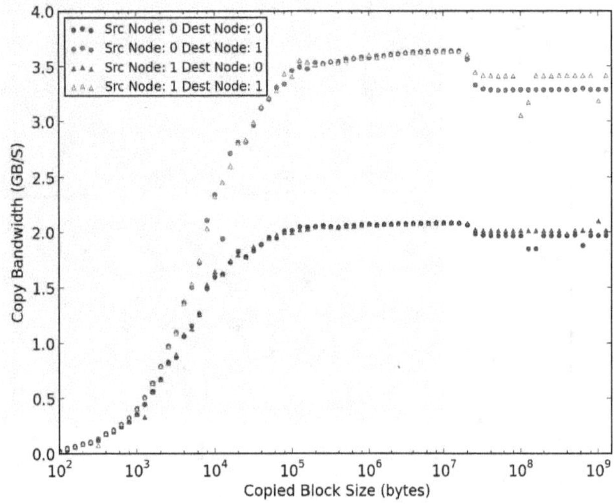

Figure 12: Host Memory Copy - Thread Pinned CPU One Using Repeated Memory Address And Pinned Memory

chronous copy types are tested depending on the host memory type. Pinned and write-combined memories allow the runtime to use asynchronous copies between host and device memory spaces. Such copies remove the need to temporarily transfer memory to a pinned buffer before copying the block to the device. The test system demonstrated a 28% increase in bandwidth when using asynchronous runtime copies over the baseline pageable memory transfer (for the largest block sizes tested).

NUMA effects on host-device memory transfers were of particular interest when the TARUC benchmark was developed. Different thread pinning and NUMA binding combinations were tested for both asynchronous and synchronous copies. Removing direct thread involvement in the copy ends the need for the memory to be copied to a buffer that is local to that executing thread. We see a significant bandwidth reduction when using pageable host memory for transfers involving non-local memory. Figure 13 illustrates this effect. Transfers involving pinned and write-combined host memory are unaffected by NUMA locality of the host memory.

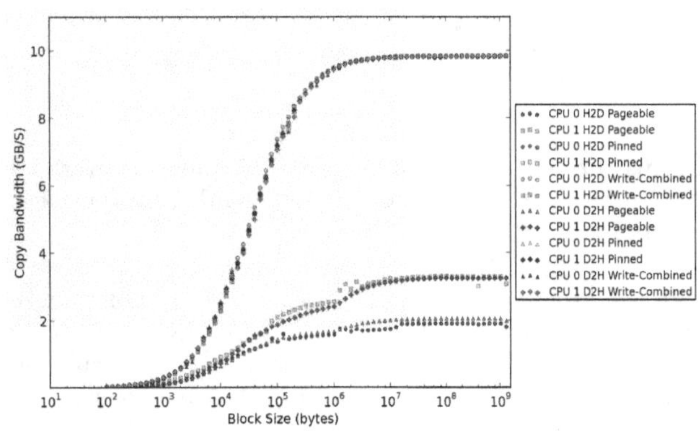

Figure 13: Host-Device Memory Copy - Host NUMA Node One And K40c GPU Using Linear Increasing Memory Address

Similar NUMA effects are demonstrated during transfers for all GPUs on the test system. Figure 14 illustrates that the most significant NUMA effect is the locality of memory to the executing host thread. When memory is non-local, the pageable host memory must be transferred before a host-device transfer can be initiated. Differing GPUs also report varying host-device bandwidth. This shows that the difference in bandwidth is a result of different device hardware rather than NUMA effects. Bandwidth rather than latency is the limiting factor when non-pageable memory transfers are concerned.

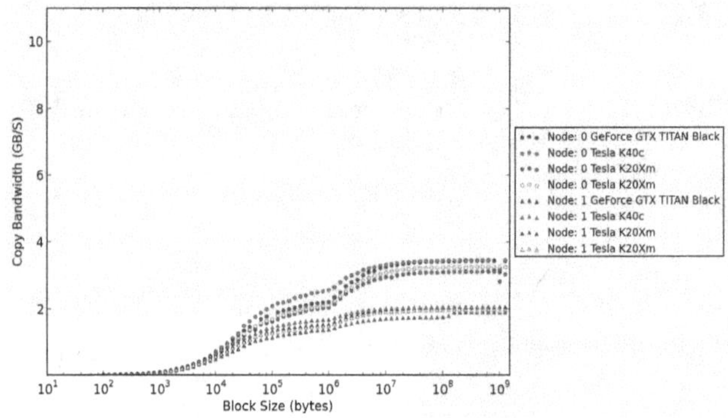

Figure 14: Device-To-Host Memory Copy - Thread Pinned To CPU Zero Using Pageable Host Memory

Device-Device Block Memory Transfers.

Direct device-device memory transfers allow the accelerators to share data during synchronization events scheduled by a host thread. Direct transfers are desirable in situations where the host does not need intermediate application data in between time steps (or other incremental steps) of a run. If the host does not need intermediate step data then GPU devices can do direct transfers. Device-device transfers reduce contention on the host memory system as well as the QPI bus. In TARUC, peer-peer and device-host-device transfers (shortened device-device) are tested. Both types of asynchronous transfers remove host thread involvement in the memory transfer. Device-device transfers involve an intermediate copy by the CUDA runtime to host memory before the memory block is copied to the destination GPU.

The first test of device performance is internal device memory transfer bandwidth. In the case of Figure 15, intra-device transfers are profiled. The actual memory system bandwidth is doubled because the bandwidth is measured from the perspective of the block being transferred. Intra-device transfers involve a read and a write to different memory blocks within the same GPU. Measuring intra-node GPU memory bandwidth shows the difference in accelerator generation and type (consumer or compute class).

Figures 16 and 17 show that peer transfers provide higher bandwidth for small to medium memory block transfer sizes, but underperform for some transfers of large device memory blocks. This result is contrary to expectation since peer transfers should allow for lower latency and higher bandwidth when enabled. Instead, we see that For large block sizes there can be an advantage to using device-device memory transfers. The direction of the transfer can also influence the bandwidth. Transferring memory between the con-

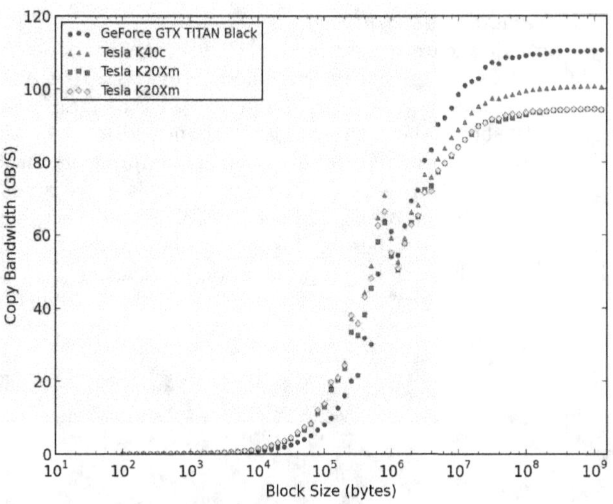

Figure 15: Intra-Device Memory Transfer - Thread Pinned To CPU Zero

sumer class GTX Titan GPU and the compute class K40c is a clear demonstration of this effect. Something relating to hardware generation or optimization levels between the two cards reduces the performance when transferring from the K40c to the Titan GPU. This is consistent no matter which CPU core is pinned for the host thread. Bandwidth decreases are more significant during peer transfers (than device-device) for certain transfer directions when copying memory between different GPU models.

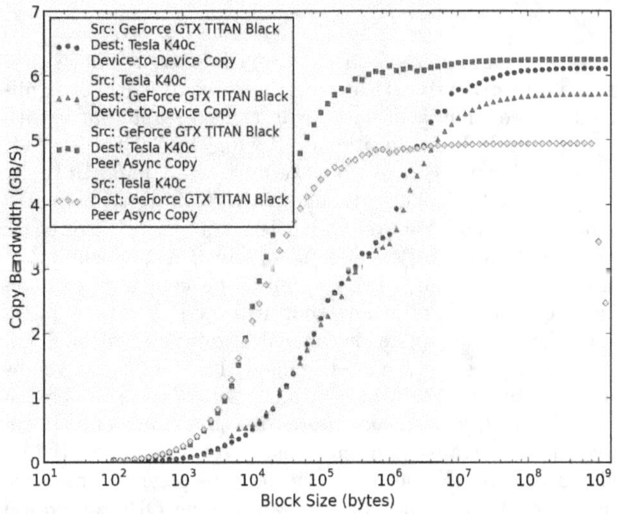

Figure 16: Device-Device Memory Copy - Titan And K40c GPUs With Thread Pinned To CPU Zero

The K20Xm GPUs consistently show almost identical bandwidth no matter the transfer direction. They also show the premature maxing of peer transfer bandwidth when compared to device-device transfers of large enough block sizes.

4.2.3 NURMA Latency

The NURMA micro-benchmark is useful for understanding how different memory access patterns are affected by

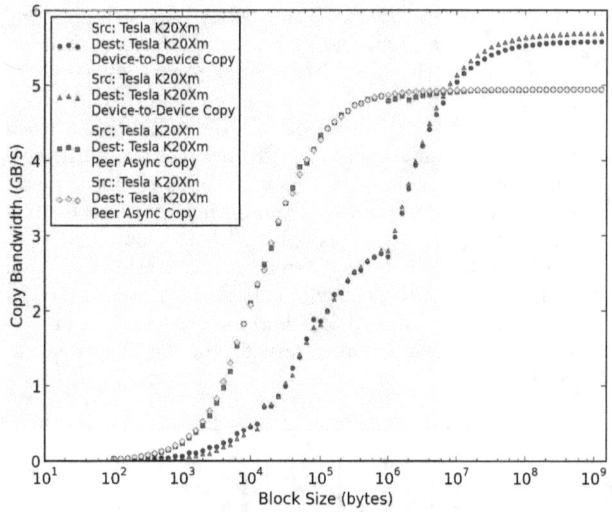

Figure 17: Device-Device Memory Copy - Both K20Xm GPUs With Thread Pinned To CPU Zero

NUMA. Small memory gap sizes mimic strided memory access while larger gap sizes that exceed cache line width and page size mimic random memory access. If the gap size is reduced to zero, streamed memory transfer is simulated.

Figure 18 illustrates that there is no significant difference in performance or NUMA impact on pinned versus pageable memory for streamed random access. Both types of memory demonstrate differences in performance for local and non-local memory access.

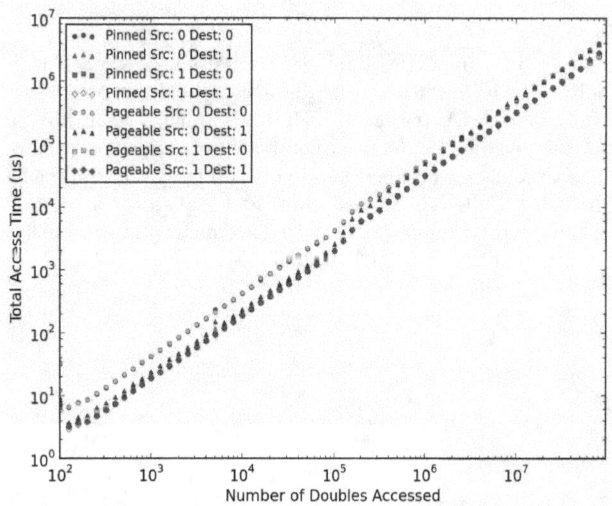

Figure 18: NURMA Test - Thread Pinned to CPU One With All Memory Types And NUMA Bindings

4.2.4 Resource Contention

Local Memory Aggregate Bandwidth.

In general, ideal real-world memory bandwidth will be achieved when the locality of memory access is maximized. To achieve ideal memory locality, threads should be pinned to execution spaces where NUMA policy allocates memory. In the case of the local memory bandwidth test, memory is accessed from the local NUMA node for all executing threads. Figure 19 shows bandwidth scaling for single-node or multi-node memory situations. Bandwidth peaks when the number of simultaneous threads matches the number of memory channels connecting each CPU to its local memory space. This graph shows a bump in performance when oversubscribing threads to cores by 1.5x. This could be a result of the OS scheduling threads that are bottlenecked by memory transfers more efficiently. Once thread-to-core oversubscription exceeds 1.5x, there is a decrease in performance to slightly below the bandwidth of the one thread to one core ratio.

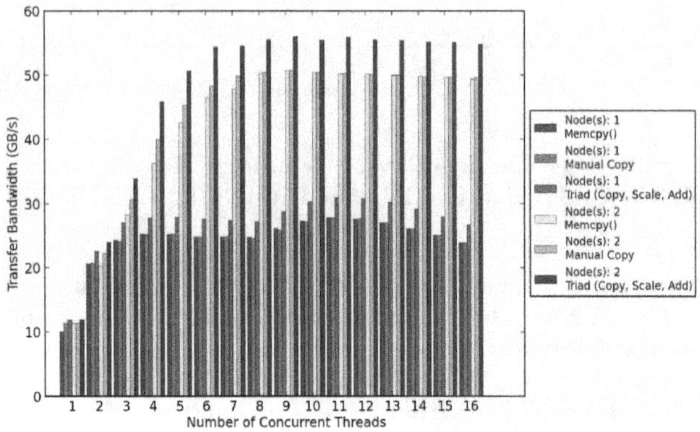

Figure 19: Local Memory Bandwidth - All NUMA Bindings And Memory Operation Types

Inter-Socket QPI Contention.

The worst case NUMA related contention occurs when simultaneously executing threads access host memory from adjacent NUMA regions. QPI links quickly saturate on the test system for inter-socket transfers. since they have a maximum bidirectional bandwidth roughly the same as a single 16x PCIe 3.0 connection. Figure 20 shows a roughly 50% drop in bandwidth compared to maximum host memory bandwidth when QPI is saturated.

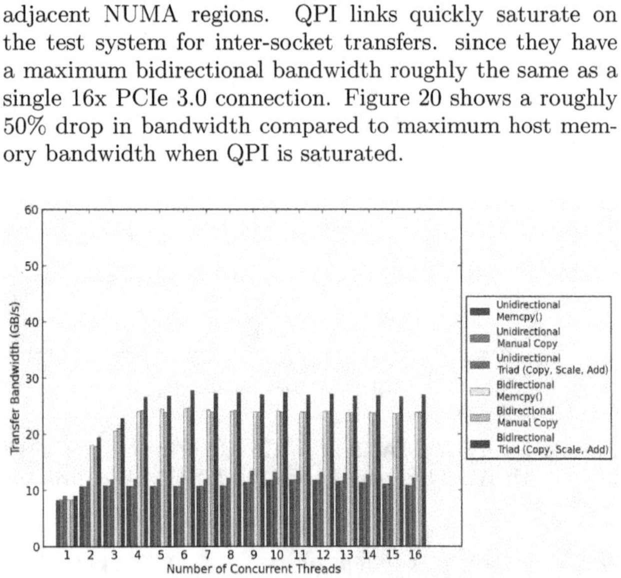

Figure 20: Inter-Socket Host Memory Access Bandwidth - All Directions And Memory Operation Types

Host-Device PCIe Contention.

To provide accurate assessment of PCIe contention, a system-wide baseline of aggregate performance provides a reference for realistic bandwidth scaling of different GPU assignments. Figure 21 shows the aggregate PCIe bandwidth when all GPUs are copying memory simultaneously to and from local CPU memory. Bidirectional memory copies are measured to ensure pipeline saturation. Each GPU has two execution and memory copy engines, so this test is an oversubscription of 4x since each thread does a bidirectional transfer.

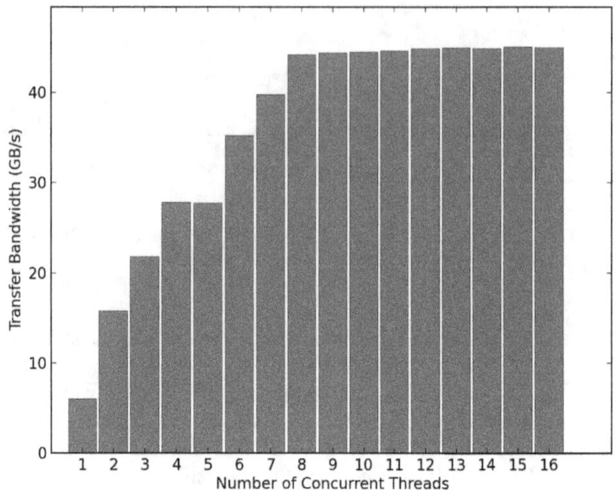

Figure 21: Baseline PCIe Bandwidth - Four Threads Per GPU With Bidirectional Transfers, All Threads On Local CPUs

Local assignment of GPUs to CPU memory is critical to maximize bandwidth because QPI bandwidth is significantly lower than host memory or the aggregate bandwidth of multiple PCIe connections. Moving half of the threads to a non-local CPU reduces the aggregate bandwidth by roughly 6 GB/S. This amounts to a 13% drop in overall bandwidth. For a system with less contention, aggregate bandwidth might be less affected making this test somewhat less valid. However, pipeline contention certainly does occur in balanced applications that utilize GPUs for computation when kernel operations synchronize with host memory. In previous tests it was determined that for asynchronous pinned memory host-device transfers, little in the way of NUMA effects exist when contention is not present. Pageable memory transfers do not benefit from a lack of NUMA effects due to the need to transfer the pageable memory block to a local pinned buffer. Minimizing QPI contention is essential for maximizing bandwidth during synchronization events.

Figure 22 displays the per node host-device bandwidth of the test system when up to four threads per GPU are executing simultaneous transfers. Results show that node 1 has slightly lower bandwidth than node 0, which verifies that that the GTX Titan and K40c have higher aggregate bandwidth than the two K20Xm GPUs. Because the K40c and the Titan are local to CPU 0, they have a direct higher bandwidth connection that does not travel over QPI. Allocating GPUs based on the locality of CPU resources is a viable option assuming memory is local to the executing thread. Otherwise, allocating GPU resources based on the locality of memory the thread is using should be preferred. It is important to note that the per node transfer bandwidth graph shows roughly the same performance reduction as partially non-local baseline bandwidth test. The performance of both local memory bandwidth and aggregate PCIe bandwidth appears to be limited by the host memory system for the test system rather than PCIe bandwidth. This is true for contended systems when all GPUs simultaneously execute bidirectional memory transfers.

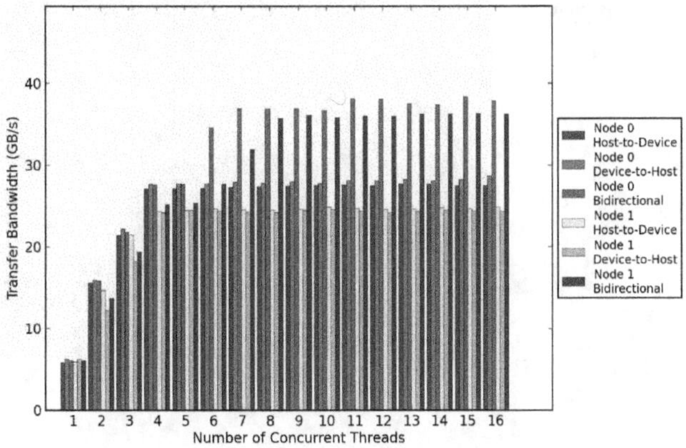

Figure 22: Per NUMA Node Aggregate PCIe Bandwidth

These results show that the TARUC benchmark can be used to profile a target hardware system to find the inflection points in bandwidth and execution time or possible hardware specific performance artifacts.

5. RELATED WORK

The existence of NUMA effects and the necessity of designing NUMA aware schedulers and algorithms has been well documented by a number of researchers. Research related to the material covered in this paper has mainly benchmarked host memory contention via either synthetic memory kernels [2] or real applications [8].

The synthetic benchmarks addressed specific instances of NUMA effects in much the same way the host-based TARUC tests do by carrying out memory operations over a number of NUMA pinning situations. Application performance benchmark tests on NUMA systems generally utilize application codes along with command line memory policy tools (such as *hwloc-bind*) to test poorly scheduled thread and memory binding combinations on overall application performance. Some new architectural enhancements like large virtual page sizes have been demonstrated to negatively impact the performance of certain applications on NUMA machines [3]. Additionally, some work has been carried out to develop a NUMA aware thread scheduler with knowledge of critical path operations. This type of scheduler has been shown to allow the deployment of near ideal thread scheduling algorithms for NUMA machines [9].

Most of the previous research has not dealt with the effect NUMA has on coprocessor enabled systems. Previous NVIDIA conference presentations allude to NUMA effects on GPUs with the solution being to statically define GPU locality based on initial problem partitioning. Based on TARUC benchmark results on x86 systems, we observe that NUMA effects result in more complicated performance phenomenon than simple bandwidth or latency reductions. Both load balancing and NUMA awareness are required along with a system specific understanding of NUMA and contention effects. In addition, few benchmarking tools have been developed to test the significance of on-node NUMA effects on differing systems.

To the best of our knowledge, no publicly available tools that benchmark NUMA effects also take into account the significance of PCIe based coprocessors in addition to measuring memory contention.

6. CONCLUSIONS AND FUTURE WORK

This paper presents the Topology Aware Resource Usability and Contention (TARUC) benchmark that allows performance profiling of heterogeneous computing systems. TARUC consists of micro-benchmarks that demonstrate how NUMA and contention influence performance. These benchmark subtests address memory allocation and deallocation performance for a number of host and device memory types. Tests of host-host, host-device, and device-device pipeline bandwidth can be measured over various thread, memory type and memory binding combinations. In addition to streamed consecutive memory access, the non-uniform random memory access (NURMA) micro-benchmark addresses other possible memory access patterns on memory performance on NUMA machines. Contention micro-benchmark tests seek to stress system communication pipelines including main memory, I/O links like PCIe and cache-coherence links like QPI.

TARUC performance profiles were acquired from a test system containing four NVIDIA GPU devices. Our results show NUMA effects can have a significant impact on achieved memory performance, and that TARUC can be used as a guide for application developers who wish to tune the performance of their application on a specific system. It is our hope that the TARUC benchmark will be useful for HPC application developers for improving performance on complex heterogeneous NUMA systems.

For future work we plan to measure communication and resource contention on Intel Xeon Phi Knights Landing systems, as they will present a new NUMA region in the form of High-Bandwidth Memory.

7. REFERENCES

[1] G. Baker. An emperical study of contention and NUMA effects on heterogeneous computing systems. Master's thesis, California Polytechnic State University, June 2016.

[2] L. Bergstrom. Measuring NUMA Effects With the STREAM Benchmark. *arXiv preprint arXiv:1103.3225*, 2011.

[3] F. Gaud, B. Lepers, J. Decouchant, J. Funston, A. Fedorova, and V. Quéma. Large Pages May be Harmful on NUMA Systems. In *2014 USENIX Annual Technical Conference (USENIX ATC 14)*, pages 231–242, 2014.

[4] Intel. White paper: An Introduction to the IntelÂő QuickPath Interconnect. Technical report, Intel Corporation, January 2009.

[5] P. Jacob, A. Zia, O. Erdogan, P. M. Belemjian, J.-W. Kim, M. Chu, R. P. Kraft, J. F. McDonald, and K. Bernstein. Mitigating Memory Wall Effects in High-Clock-Rate and Multicore CMOS 3-D Processor Memory Stacks. *Proceedings of the IEEE*, 97(1):108–122, 2009.

[6] J. Lawley. White paper: Understanding Performance of PCI Express Systems. Technical report, XILINX, October 2014.

[7] S. A. McKee. Reflections on the Memory Wall. In *Proceedings of the 1st conference on Computing frontiers*, page 162. ACM, 2004.

[8] K. Spafford, J. S. Meredith, and J. S. Vetter. Quantifying NUMA and Contention Effects in Multi-GPU Systems. In *Proceedings of the Fourth Workshop on General Purpose Processing on Graphics Processing Units*, page 11. ACM, 2011.

[9] C. Su, D. Li, D. S. Nikolopoulos, M. Grove, K. Cameron, and B. R. De Supinski. Critical Path-Based Thread Placement for NUMA Systems. *ACM SIGMETRICS Performance Evaluation Review*, 40(2):106–112, 2012.

[10] The Top500 List of Supercomputers. http://www.top500.org. Accessed: 2016-4-14.

Cloning IO Intensive Workloads Using Synthetic Benchmark

Dheeraj Chahal Manoj Nambiar

{d.chahal|m.nambiar}@tcs.com
TCS Innovation Labs
Mumbai, India

ABSTRACT

Performance evaluation of an enterprise application on multiple storage systems of interest called target systems, is a time consuming and costly process. Moreover, it is increasingly challenging to predict the performance at higher concurrencies (no. of users) on target systems when the application is migrated from the low performance source system where the application is currently deployed.

In this paper, we present a methodology to generate equivalent synthetic benchmark workloads for IO intensive applications. These synthetic benchmarks are easy to deploy and recreate the application behavior faithfully. We essentially extract the temporal and spatial characteristics of the application workload traces on the source system and replay those characteristics using synthetic benchmark on the target system. Also, we extrapolate these characteristics to predict the performance at higher concurrencies using synthetic benchmark without generating traces for those concurrencies.

To verify the efficacy of our methodology, we have tested our approach successfully using two different types of workloads namely TPCC and JPetStore. We present our extrapolation results on the target storage system with an error bound of less than 20% for concurrencies up to an order of the magnitude of the source system.

Keywords

Performance prediction; IO traces; extrapolation

1. INTRODUCTION

When the resource utilization or latency of an IO intensive application increases, enterprises are interested in migrating their data from a system using slow performing storage devices (e.g. low-end HDDs) to a system with low latency devices like high-end hard disk drives (HDDs) or solid-state-drives (SSDs). SSDs are becoming commonplace and practitioner in academia and industry are giving more emphasis on their performance studies [6] as SSDs offer dual advantage of better performance and energy efficiency.

Unfortunately, studying the performance of an application with multiple types of storage devices and varying number of cores is a time consuming and daunting task. It either requires deploying the application and migrating the data to each target system or a priori knowledge of the system with different concurrency levels (no. of users). IO trace replay is one technique that can be used to reproduce the application characteristics without deploying the application on the target system. Trace collection at large workload results in time dilation and replaying such traces results in incorrect performance estimation. Hence, trace replay based techniques are not advisable for large workloads.

Synthetic benchmarks like IOZone [3], IOmeter [8] overcome many drawbacks of trace and replay when configured appropriately for representing the application workloads.

Our scheme presented in this paper allows system administrators to experiment easily with multiple systems with minimal efforts. We capture IO traces of the application of interest at low concurrencies and extract important properties. We feed these properties to synthetic benchmark and play them on the target system and thus accurately creating the same behavior of the application. Also, we use statistical methods to extrapolate these features to predict the performance at higher concurrency levels without generating the traces at those concurrency levels.

This approach does not require deploying real database on the target system because performance of the system is dependent on the access pattern instead of the actual data. We are recreating the same access pattern using only replica of database files of the same size as in the real database. Also, our approach is independent of operating systems or schedulers as we capture application characteristics in the traces which does not change across operating systems or schedulers.

The objective of this research work is two-fold:

1) Generate representative workloads for IO intensive enterprise applications using synthetic benchmarks that can be used with ease across multiple platforms with different storage systems.

2) Extrapolate features of the application that represent the workload of the application at higher concurrency levels.

We make an assumption that there are no software bottlenecks present in the application and bottlenecks are resulted only due to hardware resources at higher concurrencies.

The rest of the paper is structured as follows: Section 2 describes related work and state of the art. In section 3, we

ICPE'17, April 22-26, 2017, L'Aquila, Italy

DOI: http://dx.doi.org/10.1145/3030207.3030238

discuss our approach and implementation in detail. We discuss experimental setup in section 4. Results are discussed in section 5 followed by conclusion in section 6.

2. RELATED WORK

Trace and replay is a well known technique used for debugging and profiling applications. There is a large body of work available for trace replay based mechanisms for storage system evaluation[5][10]. Tak et al. developed a trace based technique called PseudoApp[9] to estimate the performance and resource consumption of the application. ROOT[11] is similar work in this area to capture the traces at each resource and replay them in the same order on the target system. These methods either replay traces as it is on the potential target systems or develop representative workloads using traces without extracting application features.

In another work, Carrington et al. [4] used statistical methods for extrapolating the trace characteristic of the application for inferring the large scale computation behavior of an application. While this work is applied to compute intensive applications, our research is focused on IO intensive applications where application features differ from compute-intensive applications.

We extend the recent work of Carrington et al. for IO intensive applications by introducing novel method for extrapolating the application features and predict the scaling behavior. To the best of our knowledge there is no work available for extrapolating the IO workloads using application features from IO traces.

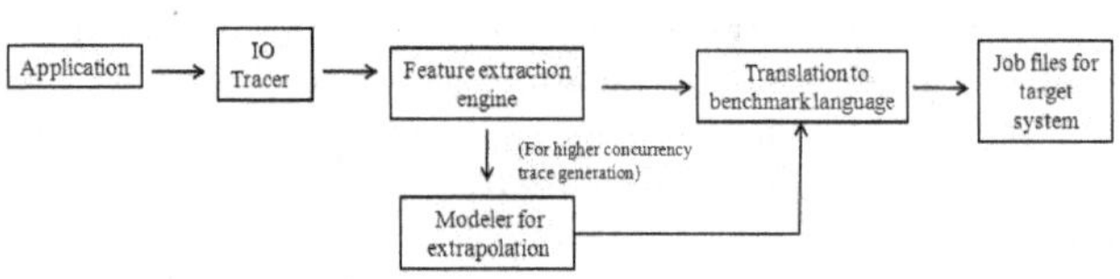

Figure 1: Framework

3. OUR APPROACH

The framework we developed is as shown in Figure 1. Our approach requires running the application workload at different levels of concurrencies and recording the IO traces at the system call level of the database server. All significant features are extracted from the traces by the feature extraction engine. These features are extrapolated by modeler using the statistical models. Extrapolated feature values are translated into job file for synthetic benchmarks. Synthetic benchmark is run with the extrapolated values to study the performance of the new device at larger concurrencies. Detailed description of each component is as below:

3.1 IO Trace Recording

Two popular tools for tracing I/O activity of an application are *strace* and *blktrace*. *strace* records system calls of the application and blktrace records I/O activity of the device. We choose *strace* as it is a better representation of application behavior which can be easily reproduced unlike blktrace which captures kernel activity related to a device. To capture the trace at database server we first track all the threads spawned by MySQL and then attach *strace* to each of those threads. The *strace* induces some overhead, which increases with an increase in workload due to the fact that *strace* pauses application twice for each system call, i.e. when a system call begins and when system call is stopped. We capture only IO related system calls to mitigate the strace overhead and size of the trace file as well. Moreover, we collect traces at low concurrencies only and extrapolate for higher. The IO calls that we capture are *read()*, *write()*, *pread()*, *pwrite()*, *lseek()*, *fsync()*, *open()*, *close()*. Our trace file contains system calls with thread ids, timestamp value, size of data read or written, offset address and system call execution time.

3.2 Feature Extraction

Feature extraction is the most important step in this work. The challenge lies in selecting all the important features that represent the temporal and spatial characteristics of an application and then extracting judiciously from the traces. We observe that there is a *n:m* relationship between threads and database files, i.e. a thread can access multiple files in the database and multiple threads can access the same file as well. In a worst case scenario, a thread can access all *m* files in the database. Hence, for an application running *n* threads would require $n*m$ jobs in the benchmark. We overcome this limitation by grouping threads in the trace file based on file descriptor (FD) such that for each FD we create two trace files,one containing read IO threads and other containing write IO operations threads. All features are extracted from read and write files of each FD. There are two benchmark jobs created (read and write ops) for each FD representing all features corresponding to that FD. Since all database files are not opened in RW mode i.e. some are read only and others write only, hence total number of benchmark jobs created is equal to or less than twice the number of unique FDs (Figure 2).

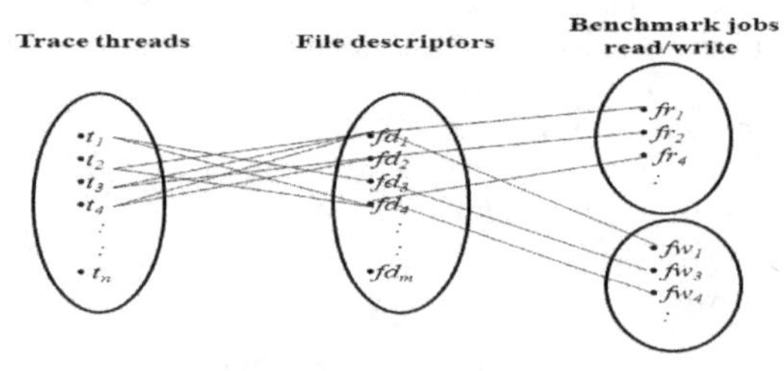

Figure 2: Thread (tn), file descriptor(fd) and benchmark jobs mapping

The important features we captured that represent the application characteristics and also affect the device performance significantly are as follows [7]:

Randomness:The performance of a storage device is significantly affected by the retrieval and the storage patterns. The sequential read and write operations are performed faster as compared to random read and write operations.

Thinktime: Time duration for which a job is stalled after an IO has completed and before next IO operation is issued.

Blocksize: The distribution of chunk sizes to issue IO.

IOPS: Total number of IO (read and write) operations performed per second.

3.3 Feature Extrapolation

In this work we propose use of a statistical method based approach to predict the performance of the application at

No.of Users	iops(writes/s)							
	customer.ibd (fd1)	orders.ibd (fd2)	stock.ibd (fd3)	order_line.ibd (fd4)	ibdata1.ibd (fd4)	ib_logfile0(fd5)	....	10.ibd
10	1.67	2.2	8.1	2.6	1.7	2	....	1.8
15	2.5	3.1	12.14	3.3	1.6	3.5	....	2.5
20	3.2	4.1	16	4.7	2.2	5.4	....	3.3
.....	.....	.....	.....	.....	.....	.....	.....	.....
200(extrapolated)	**30.70 (linear)**	**31.9(power)**	**154(power)**	**42.3(linear)**	**4.4(linear)**	**64.7(power)**	**........**	**24.23(power)**

Table 1: Extrapolation of TPCC feature iops (writes/s) for each file descriptor

higher concurrency on the target system by extrapolating the application features.

Each feature might exhibit a different scaling behavior. Some features scale linearly as the workload or concurrency increases while others might scale differently (e.g. power or logarithmic). Various canonical functions can be fitted in to different features [4]. We used four canonical forms in this study namely linear, logarithmic, power and exponential. In order to decide the right statistical method for extrapolating each feature for each FD, we take traces at three different workloads and extract all features corresponding to each FD. We fit all four statistical methods in each feature for all FDs and then choose the one that has largest coefficient of determination (R^2) value. In Table 1 we show extrapolation of one application feature (iops). Using the feature data for 10,15,20 user workloads we extrapolate the write iops for 200 users for each FD. Likewise, we can extrapolate read iops for each FD. Other features described in section 3.2 are also extrapolated from both read and write trace files for required concurrencies.

3.4 Trace Feature Replay

In addition to defining all the features that are mentioned in the section 3.2, we also define some additional application and system configuration specific parameters as below:

ioengine: Defines how IO is delivered to the kernel.
buffered: Set for buffered IO.
fsync: Set to sync dirty data when writing to a file.
time_based: Time based criterion for a benchmark run.
runtime: Duration of the job run.
filesize: File size for each job to perform r/w ops.
filename: Name of the database file.

Benchmark jobfile is prepared by defining all the parameters or features defined above and in section 3.2 for each FD. This file can be migrated to any storage system where benchmark is installed and run with ease.

4. EXPERIMENTAL SETUP

We have validated our approach using a well know TPC-C benchmark and web based application JPetStore [1]. TPC-C is a benchmark for comparing online transaction processing (OLTP) performance on various software and hardware configuration. IO intensive TPC-C has a complex database and consists of five concurrent complex instructions. JPetStore is an eCommerce J2EE application benchmark which emulates an online pet store. For replaying the application characteristics on target systems we use flexible IO (FIO) [2] tester synthetic benchmark due to flexibilty it provides for detailed workload setup. MySQL is used as a back-end for both the benchmarks. The storage systems used in this study are HDD and SSD (Table 2). IO traces are captured at multiple concurrency levels on the database server for 20 minutes including 3 minutes warm-up time.

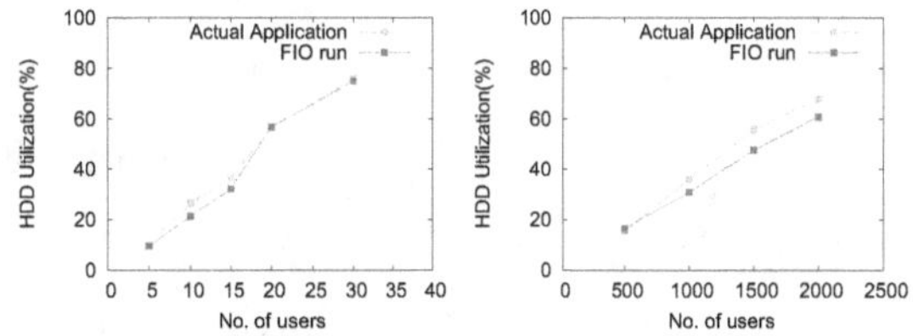

(a) (b)

Figure 3: FIO vs application run on HDD for (a) TPCC and (b) JPetStore

5. RESULTS

We performed tests to validate our thesis for replicating the application behavior using synthetic benchmark FIO and also extrapolating the features for higher concurrency levels. The resemblance in storage device utilization is used as an evaluation criterion.

5.1 Feature Replay on HDD

Our first objective is to generate representative workloads for IO intensive applications. We show that using application feature with the FIO synthetic benchmark, we are able to recreate the application behavior. Results for two applications that we used are as below:

5.1.1 TPCC on HDD

We run TPCC at multiple concurrency levels 5, 10, 15, 20 and 30. Trace files are captured for all these concurrencies. We also record the disk utilization for each of these concurrencies when strace is not running. These trace files are supplied to feature extraction component. The output of feature extraction component is a jobfile for FIO. We run FIO with each of these files on the same storage device and record resource utilization. As shown in Figure 3a, the FIO run results in resource utilization comparable to actual application run for most of the concurrencies.

5.1.2 JPetStore on HDD

Similar behavior is seen with the JPetStore application as well. We collect traces for 500, 1K, 1500 and 2K users. After extracting features from these traces, we feed in FIO jobfile and run for same duration (Figure 3b). We see some difference in the device utilization only at higher concurrency i.e. 1500 and 2K. This can be attributed to the *strace* overhead while collecting traces as discussed earlier.

5.2 HDD to SSD Migration and Extrapolation

Another objective of this work is to predict the performance across platforms and extrapolate for higher concurrency levels. We run our applications on HDD first and replay the features using FIO on SSD. Since SSD shows significant improvement in resource utilization over HDD, we

Storage type	Disk Model	RPM	No. of Disks	IO Schedular	File System	Interface	System Config	Linux Kernel
High-end HDD	HP	10000	1	CGQ	ext4	Dual Port,SAS 6GB/s	16 Core Xeon CPU @ 2.4 GHz,12MB L2 cache	CentOS 6.6,2.6.32
SSD	Virident Systems Inc. FlashMAX Drive Micron-slc-32	-	1PCIe	Default	ext3	-	16 Core Xeon CPU @ 2.4 GHz,,12MB L2 cache	CentOS 6.6,2.6.32

Table 2: Storage systems used in our study

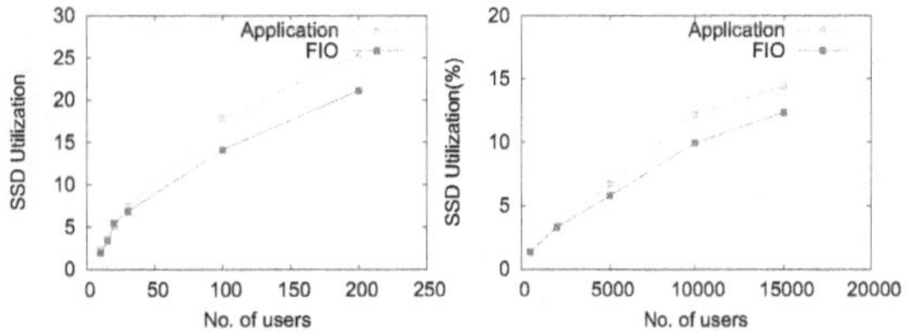

(a) (b)

Figure 4: FIO vs application run on SSD for (a) TPCC and (b) JPetStore

should be able to extrapolate for larger concurrencies.

5.2.1 TPCC on SSD

We take traces of TPCC application for three concurrency levels i.e. 10, 15, 20 on HDD. Features are extracted and extrapolated for 30, 100 and 200 and run with FIO on SSD. For concurrencies 10,15,20 (no extrapolation), we see same resource utilization by FIO and actual application (Figure 4a). There is some deviation from the actual resource utilization due to strace overhead amplification but within 20% error bound at large concurrencies.

5.2.2 JPetStore on SSD

For JPetStore application we collect IO traces for 1K,1500 and 2K users on HDD. All significant features are extrapolated for higher concurrencies 5K,10K and 15K. These features are replayed with FIO on SSD and results are as shown in Figure 4b. We observe a small difference in resource utilization only at large concurrencies due to strace overhead amplification.

6. CONCLUSION AND FUTURE WORK

We have presented a method that can be used for generating representative workloads for IO intensive applications by extracting features from IO traces. We also proposed a methodology for extrapolating the application features using canonical functions. Using synthetic benchmark FIO, we have faithfully replayed the representative workload of two applications on HDD. Also, we have successfully tested the application behavior on SSD for higher concurrencies using extrapolated features.

We have seen that the trace closely matches the application utilization behavior w.r.t concurrency. This means that the trace can be trusted to emulate the real application I/O behavior. The trace can then be used on any server with a different storage device without having to install the application or generate concurrent user workload. The utilization generated by the trace at a certain concurrency level can be divided by the throughput to derive the service demand of the application on the new storage device. Also, throughput(IOPS) can be easily converted to application transactions per second metric by comparing the application performance and trace data at the source system. This a can be fed along with other resource demands into an analytical or simulation model to predict performance of the application on the target system with a different storage device than the source while other things being the same. We intend to validate with experiments few more accuracy metrics (e.g. response time) using resource utilization and IOPS data.

7. REFERENCES

[1] iBATIS JPetStore. http://sourceforge.net/projects/ibatisjpetstore/.

[2] J. Axboe. FIO-Flexible I/O Tester. http://freshmeat.net/projects/fio/.

[3] D. Capps. Iozone file system benchmark. www.iozone.org.

[4] L. Carrington, M. A. Laurenzano, and A. Tiwari. Inferring large-scale computation behavior via trace extrapolation. In *Parallel and Distributed Processing Symposium Workshops & PhD Forum (IPDPSW), 2013 IEEE 27th International*, pages 1667–1674. IEEE, 2013.

[5] C. Delimitrou, S. Sankar, K. Vaid, and C. Kozyrakis. Accurate modeling and generation of storage i/o for datacenter workloads. In *Proceedings of the 2nd Workshop on Exascale Evaluation and Research Techniques, EXERT, Newport Beach, CA (March 2011)*, 2011.

[6] I. Jo, D.-H. Bae, A. S. Yoon, J.-U. Kang, S. Cho, D. D. G. Lee, and J. Jeong. Yoursql: A high-performance database system leveraging in-storage computing. *Proc. VLDB Endow.*, 9(12):924–935, Aug. 2016.

[7] Q. Noorshams, R. Reeb, A. Rentschler, S. Kounev, and R. Reussner. Enriching software architecture models with statistical models for performance prediction in modern storage environments. In *Proceedings of the 17th international ACM Sigsoft symposium on Component-based software engineering*, pages 45–54. ACM, 2014.

[8] OSDL. Iometer project. www.iometer.org.

[9] B. C. Tak, C. Tang, H. Huang, and L. Wang. Pseudoapp: Performance prediction for application migration to cloud. In *Integrated Network Management (IM 2013), 2013 IFIP/IEEE International Symposium on*, pages 303–310, May 2013.

[10] M. Tarihi, H. Asadi, and H. Sarbazi-Azad. Diskaccel: Accelerating disk-based experiments by representative sampling. In *ACM SIGMETRICS Performance Evaluation Review*, volume 43, pages 297–308. ACM, 2015.

[11] Z. Weiss, T. Harter, A. C. Arpaci-Dusseau, and R. H. Arpaci-Dusseau. Root: Replaying multithreaded traces with resource-oriented ordering. In *Proceedings of the Twenty-Fourth ACM Symposium on Operating Systems Principles*, SOSP '13, pages 373–387, New York, NY, USA, 2013. ACM.

Autonomic Storage Management at Scale

Arif Merchant
Google, Inc.
aamerchant@google.com

ABSTRACT

Cloud data centers use enormous amounts of storage, and it is critical to monitor, manage, and optimize the storage autonomically. Optimally configuring storage is difficult because storage workloads are very diverse and change over time. Data centers measure running workloads, but this measurement data stream is itself quite large. We present some real world case studies in the use of big data techniques, sampling, and optimization to manage storage in data centers.

CCS Concepts/ACM Classifiers

• Information systems~Storage management • Information systems~Data centers

Author Keywords

Data center management; Monitoring; Sampling

BIOGRAPHY

Arif Merchant is a Research Scientist at Google and leads the Storage Analytics group, which studies interactions between components of the storage stack. His interests include distributed storage systems, storage management, and stochastic modeling. He holds a B.Tech. from IIT Bombay and a Ph.D. in Computer Science from Stanford University. He is an ACM Distinguished Scientist.

REFERENCES

1. C. Albrecht et al. Janus: Optimal flash provisioning for cloud storage workloads. Proc. USENIX Annual Technical Conference, pages 91–102, June 2013, San Jose, CA.
2. A. Sharov et al. Take me to your leader!: Online optimization of distributed storage configurations. Proc. VLDB Endow., 8(12):1490–1501, Aug. 2015.
3. M Möstl et al. Self-aware systems for the internet-of-things Proc. Eleventh IEEE/ACM/IFIP International Conference on Hardware/Software Codesign and System Synthesis (CODES), October 2016.

ICPE'17, April 22–26, 2017, L'Aquila, Italy.
ACM ISBN 978-1-4503-4404-3/17/04.
http://dx.doi.org/10.1145/3030207.3030247

An Efficient Performance-Driven Approach for HW/SW Co-Design

(Vision Paper)

Daniele Di Pompeo
DISIM
Via Vetoio, 1
L'Aquila, Italy
daniele.dipompeo@graduate.univaq.it

Emilio Incerto
GSSI
Viale F. Crispi, 7
L'Aquila, Italy
emilio.incerto@gssi.infn.it

Vittoriano Muttillo
DEWS
Via Vetoio, 1
L'Aquila, Italy
vittoriano.muttillo@graduate.univaq.it

Luigi Pomante
DEWS
Via Vetoio, 1
L'Aquila, Italy
luigi.pomante@univaq.it

Giacomo Valente
DEWS
Via Vetoio, 1
L'Aquila, Italy
giacomo.valente@graduate.univaq.it

ABSTRACT

Nowadays embedded systems are powerful and everywhere. They implement complex functionality relying on a huge set of different hardware and software (HW/SW) architectures. In order to reduce their development effort, HW/SW Co-Design techniques are used during the entire development cycle. These techniques aim at helping designers to define a feasible hardware and software partitioning for the system in such a way that functional and non-functional requirements are fulfilled. In this context Design Space Exploration is a challenging activity since a huge number of different implementation alternatives need to be evaluated.

By exploiting some intrinsic properties of the embedded system domain, in this paper we propose our vision for a novel Performance-Driven HW/SW Co-Design methodology. It combines: (i) the "design for verifiability" concept, suitable to model the system behaviour avoiding the state space explosion problem, and (ii) model-driven techniques to address performance issues. For this goal, we introduce the concepts underlying: (i) a novel formal modeling language and, (ii) a performance-driven verification/transformation chain.

CCS Concepts

•Hardware → Emerging technologies; •Software and its engineering → *Correctness; Formal methods; Software performance;*

ICPE'17, April 22-26, 2017, L'Aquila, Italy

DOI: http://dx.doi.org/10.1145/3030207.3030239

Keywords

HW/SW Co-Design, Performance awareness, Model-Driven Engineering, Design for verifiability

1. INTRODUCTION

Nowadays embedded systems are powerful and everywhere, as they are widely used in industries for different kinds of applications (e.g., aircraft autopilots, telecommunication products, medical devices) with different criticality and requirements. As a consequence, the design of such systems is becoming an increasingly complex process since several implementation alternatives with different hardware constraints (e.g., CPU speed, memory limitation, battery life) need to be considered.

In such a context, heterogeneous multi-processor architectures have been introduced with the aim of developing heterogeneous multi-processor systems (HMPS), which are exploited for a wide range of application domains (e.g. [3, 4]). In particular, they are often used to implement digital electronic systems with an application-specific HW/SW architecture aimed at satisfying functional and non-functional requirements.

In order to cope with the growing complexity of those systems, it is fundamental to exploit a design flow that allows an entry point at a high level of abstraction. In view of these considerations, HW/SW Co-Design has been recognized as the mainstream technology for the rapid development of complex HMPS [17]. Basically it aims at helping designers in choosing the right hardware and software partition for the system functionality in such a way that the requirements are fulfilled.

Unfortunately, to the best of our knowledge, despite the proliferation of works in this research field, none of them addresses the problem of providing an automated and efficient Co-Design methodology, in that they usually require several user interactions with considerable timing overhead. In this paper we propose our vision of a novel multi-staged approach that combines the *design for verifiability* concept [6] with *performance model-driven* techniques suitable to reduce the complexity of the Design Space Exploration (DSE) process. We intend to automatically and efficiently derive an optimal hardware and software partitioning for the system's capabilities by improving an existent DSE approach [14]

The main idea underling our proposal is that, by exploiting some properties of the embedded system domain (such as the real-time scheduling and the few number of user interactions), we aim to build a novel modeling language whose formal semantic is equipped only with those constructs leading to a compact state space representation. Then, by leveraging on it, we intend to realize a model-driven verification/transformation chain where, at each step, the initial high-level system behavioral specification is refined in a more concrete version that is verified against user-defined properties. The goal of the step-wise verification is to identify the HW/SW configurations that do not meet functional and non-functional requirements, so as to reduce the size of the feasible solutions set that is evaluated during the design space exploration phase of our approach. By doing so, we aim to reduce both the user intervention and the timing overhead in the design and implementation activities of complex and heterogeneous multi-processor embedded systems. Fig 1 depicts the conceptual structure of our vision.

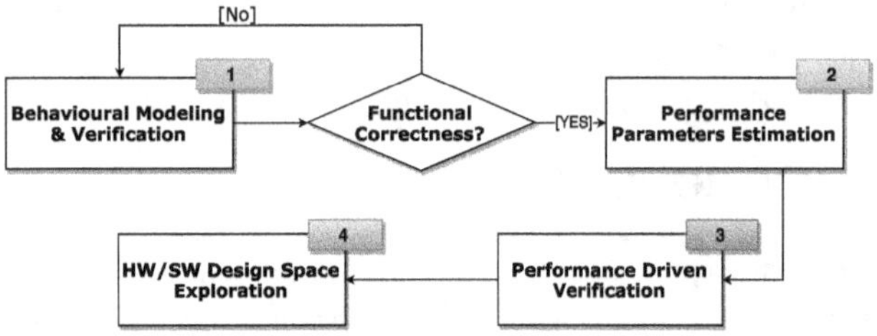

Figure 1: Overview of the reference Co-Design approach

In the *Behavioral Modeling & Verification* stage the high-level behavior representation of the system is modeled. As described before, the syntax and semantic of the envisaged modeling language, i.e. HW/SW Modeling Language (HML), are based on the "design for verifiability" concept that enables an efficient functional verification. Goal of this stage is to identify and eliminate all the system configurations for which functional requirements are certainly not fulfilled, hence useless to be considered in the following stages of the process. In the *Performance Parameters Estimation* stage the initial behavioral specification is simulated in order to estimate some performance attributes. Then, the outcome of this stage is used as the input for the *Performance Driven Verification* one in which a performance evaluation of the system is conducted, aimed at generating a set of constraints that identify the architectural elements that have not to be considered in the last step. Finally in the *HW/SW Design Space Exploration* stage, by exploiting and improving the existed DSE approach defined in [14], an optimal HW/SW partitioning of the system is identified on the basis of by the architectural constraints derived in the previous steps.

2. THE VISION OF PERFORMANCE-DRIVEN CO-DESIGN

In the following we provide a detailed description of the blocks introduced in Figure 1 that have been expanded as in Figure 2. We use square boxes for denoting artifacts (i.e., models and constraints) and the elliptic boxes for actions (i.e., transformations and verification).

Behavioral Modeling and Verification

The starting point of this stage is a *Behavioral Model* representing the behavioral view of the system written in HML. It can be seen as an extension of the well-known Communication Sequential Processes (CSP) [8] formalism equipped with a novel semantic suitable to associate a compact state space representation to each HML model, hence enabling an efficient functional verification. Our vision, at this stage, is to exploit some intrinsic properties of the embedded systems domains (e.g., real time scheduler or synchronous communication channels) for reducing the non-determinism and the parallelism of the model. Moreover, it is worth to notice how a reduced complexity allows to move the assessment of some critical functional properties, such as input-output relation, from the testing to the verification stage. Once the HML model is defined, it can be used as an input for a Model to Model (M2M) transformation whose outcome is a new model (i.e., Verifiable Model) on which the user-defined functional requirements can be efficiently verified using off the shelf model checkers ([7, 9, 13]).

Performance Parameters Estimation

Goal of this stage is to estimate the timing information for the system's behaviors so as to produce a quantitative annotated version of the original behavioral specification. For doing so, the behavioral model is given as input to a Model to Text (M2T) transformation aimed to generate a SystemC [2] platform-independent executable representation. Our vision here is to make an early lightweight estimation of the performance of each behavioral block by focusing only on their execution time. To this goal, we map each SystemC subsystem on elements of a Technology Library (TL) representing basic hardware components, whose assembly can model different execution platforms could be composed. In particular, it contains all the available processors, memories and interconnection links that can be used for generating the HW platform on which the system will be executed. As a result, the simulation of this technology-dependent representation enables to build a performance-profile for each of the HML process, later used to drive the Design Space Exploration aimed at timing requirements fulfillment.

Our vision here relies on the assumption that the timing estimation produced in this stage can be considered as a kind of *best case scenario*, since the estimated performance will be worse with an increased simulation accuracy (e.g., scheduling and communication overhead, interaction with sensors and peripherals, etc.). This is the key factor that makes the simulation results as necessary conditions with respect to the timing requirements fulfillment, thus allowing us to eliminate all basic hardware components that certainly lead to unfeasible system configurations.

Performance Driven Verification

The objective of this stage is to explore the possible system HW/SW partitions and mappings, in order to identify those that surely do not fulfill timing requirements. For doing that, both the Quantitative Annotated Model and Technology Library are given as inputs to a M2M transformation aimed to produce a *Performance Super Model* (PSM) that,

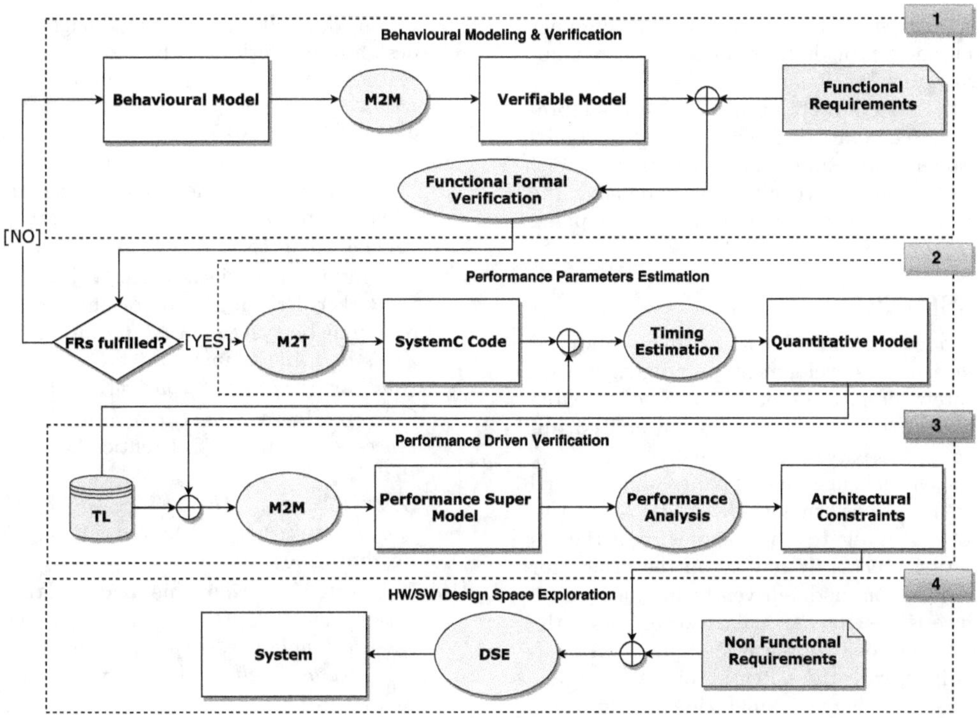

Figure 2: The reference Co-Design flow

similarly to what presented in [12], is suitable to encode all the system variability (i.e., software to hardware mapping) in one single model. Our vision here, analogously to what presented in [10], is to exploit the Satisfiability Modulo Theory (SMT) for encoding both PSM and the chosen performance model (e.g., Queueing Networks, Petri Nets, Markov Chains) in such a way that the exploration process can be conducted in a performance-driven fashion. Basically, the idea of the Performance Analysis phase is to ask an SMT solver for the architectural elements that do not belong to any correct system configuration (i.e., satisfying the performance requirements), that are thus worthless to be considered in the Design Space Exploration step. Then, the result of this analysis is encoded in a set of Architectural Constraints used as input for the last stage of the proposed approach.

HW/SW Design Space Exploration

The last stage of this vision is the *HW/SW Design Space Exploration*, in which we ntend to exploit the power of genetic algorithms for searching the optimal HW/SW mapping and partitioning driven by non-functional requirements. Our *DSE* approach builds on the idea presented in [14], which enables the optimization of the system with respect to a richer set of non-functional requirements than those used in the previous stage (e.g., production costs, load-balancing of the whole system, and communication overhead).

We want to emphasize that the key feature of our approach is to make a multi-staged filtering in order to reduce the solution space. Hence, we automatically generate an optimal set of solutions (see *System* in Figure 2), which the designer can refer to in order to find look her solution.

3. RELATED WORK

In the past years, a remarkable number of research projects focused on the system-level HW/SW Co-Design embedded systems following the "Y" structure [11]. To the best of our knowledge, none of them fully addresses the problem of both "automatically suggest an HW/SW partitioning" and "map the partitioned entities into an automatically defined heterogeneous multi-processor architecture". Beside this we provide the opportunity to perform an early formal functional verification. In this section we consider only those works that respect the "Y" structure.

The Essyn project [15] requires the definition of three submodels. The first UML/MARTE sub-model is specifically used to design software applications; the second one is used to represent hardware platforms, and both are connected by a third model, namely Platform Specific Model, which defines the mapping among software applications and hardware platforms. With respect to it, our vision provides an higher level of abstraction of the system behaviour, and it intend to provide an automated generation of optimal mapping among functionality and basic hardware components.

Another related project is Contrex [5]. In order to allow both a system synthesis and an analysis, with respect to non-functional requirements (e.g., temperature), it provides an environment suite, based on Papyrus[1], that is augmented with a specific extension for DSE. Our methodology is quite different, because it aims to suggest, other than a HW/SW partitioning and mapping, an hardware platform by composing basic elements from a Technology Library.

Art2kitekt [16] is aimed at modeling and analyzing systems with respect to both hardware and software representation and, additionally, it provides set of integrity checks and DSE algorithms that help to perform offline real-time

[1]https://eclipse.org/papyrus/

and schedulability analysis. In our approach the designer would not be required to provide as input an explicit mapping between hardware and software.

Finally, it is worth to cited Intel CoFluent [1]. It is a representative SystemC-based commercial product, as a promising system-level modeling and simulation environment. With respect to our methodology it requires, by exploiting the hardware configuration given as input, a manual mapping among hardware and behavioral models.

4. CONCLUSIONS

Nowadays embedded systems are increasingly powerful and complex, hence novel development paradigms are required. Unfortunately, despite the proliferation of research works in this area, no efficient and fully automated approaches have been proposed yet.

In order to face such challenge, in this paper we presented our vision for an efficient performance-driven HW/SW Co-Design methodology. It mitigates the complexity of the design space exploration process by relying on the design for verifiability concept and on model-driven techniques for removing performance issues. In particular, we provided the high level architecture of our approach for building an efficiently automated flow, with the potential of requiring few user interactions and introducing a small timing overhead.

As future work, our research agenda includes the following tasks: (i) choosing the right trade-off between the expressiveness of the envisaged modeling language and the efficiency of its semantic, we plan to infer it by analyzing several real-world embedded systems applications; (ii) identifying the suitable granularity (e.g., varying from the instruction level to process level) of the timing simulation for the estimation of performance parameters; (iii) choosing the most appropriate modeling formalism for encoding a Performance Super Model and Architectural Constraints, and the proper analysis technique; (iv) improving the used algorithm for the HW/SW Design Space Exploration stage.

The big challenge that appears in our vision is the integration among the four stages. In fact, we intend to use a multi-representation, which might bring to the incompatibility among the outcome of a stage and the input of the subsequent one.

Finally we plan to validate the proposed approach on HW/SW Co-Design case studies coming from real industrial applications.

5. REFERENCES

[1] Intel co-fluent. http://www.intel.com/content/www/us/en/cofluent/overview.html. Accessed: 2016-25-11.

[2] Systemc. http://www.accellera.org. Accessed: 2016-25-11.

[3] L. H. Crockett, R. A. Elliot, M. A. Enderwitz, and R. W. Stewart. *The Zynq Book: Embedded Processing with the Arm Cortex-A9 on the Xilinx Zynq-7000 All Programmable Soc*. Strathclyde Academic Media, 2014.

[4] P. Cumming. The ti omap^{TM}platform approach to soc. In *Winning the SOC Revolution*, pages 97–118. Springer, 2003.

[5] E. Ebeid, F. Fummi, and D. Quaglia. Model-driven design of network aspects of distributed embedded systems. *IEEE Transactions on Computer-Aided Design of Integrated Circuits and Systems*, 34(4):603–614, 2015.

[6] J. F. Groote, T. W. D. M. Kouters, and A. Osaiweran. Specification guidelines to avoid the state space explosion problem. *Softw. Test., Verif. Reliab.*, 25(1):4–33, 2015.

[7] A. Hinton, M. Kwiatkowska, G. Norman, and D. Parker. Prism: A tool for automatic verification of probabilistic systems. In *International Conference on Tools and Algorithms for the Construction and Analysis of Systems*, pages 441–444. Springer, 2006.

[8] C. A. R. Hoare et al. *Communicating sequential processes*, volume 178. Prentice-hall Englewood Cliffs, 1985.

[9] G. J. Holzmann. *The SPIN model checker: Primer and reference manual*, volume 1003. Addison-Wesley Reading, 2004.

[10] E. Incerto, M. Tribastone, and C. Trubiani. Symbolic performance adaptation. In *Proceedings of the 11th International Workshop on Software Engineering for Adaptive and Self-Managing Systems*, pages 140–150. ACM, 2016.

[11] K. Keutzer, S. Malik, A. Newton, J. Rabaey, and A. S. Vincentelli. System level design: Orthogonalization of concerns and platform-based designh. *IEEE Trans. Comput.-Aided Des. Integ. Circ. Syst.*, 19(12):1523–1543, 2000.

[12] M. Kowal, M. Tschaikowski, M. Tribastone, and I. Schaefer. Scaling size and parameter spaces in variability-aware software performance models (t). In *Automated Software Engineering (ASE), 2015 30th IEEE/ACM International Conference on*, pages 407–417. IEEE, 2015.

[13] K. G. Larsen, P. Pettersson, and W. Yi. Uppaal in a nutshell. *International Journal on Software Tools for Technology Transfer (STTT)*, 1(1):134–152, 1997.

[14] L. Pomante. Hw/sw co-design of dedicated heterogeneous parallel systems: an extended design space exploration approach. *IET Computers Digital Techniques*, 7(6):246–254, November 2013.

[15] H. Posadas, P. Peñil, A. Nicolás, and E. Villar. Automatic synthesis of communication and concurrency for exploring component-based system implementations considering uml channel semantics. *Journal of Systems Architecture*, 61(8):341–360, 2015.

[16] W. Weber, A. Hoess, J. van Deventer, F. Oppenheimer, R. Ernst, A. Kostrzewa, P. DorÃÍ, T. Goubier, H. Isakovic, N. Druml, et al. The emc2 project on embedded microcontrollers technical progress after two years. In *Eur. Conf. on Digit. Syst. Des. (DSD)*, pages 524–531, 2016.

[17] W. Wolf. A decade of hardware/software codesign. *Computer*, 36(4):38–43, 2003.

DuckTracks: Path-based Object Allocation Tracking

[Work in Progress]

Stefan Fitzek[1] Philipp Lengauer[2] Hanspeter Mössenböck[2]

[1]Christian Doppler Laboratory MEVSS
Johannes Kepler University Linz, Austria
stefan.fitzek@jku.at

[2]Institute for System Software
Johannes Kepler University Linz, Austria
philipp.lengauer@jku.at

ABSTRACT

Efficiently tracking an application's object allocations is of interest for areas such as memory leak detection or memory usage optimization. The state-of-the-art approach of instrumenting every allocation site with a counter introduces considerable overhead. This makes allocation tracking in a production environment unattractive. Our approach reduces this overhead by instrumenting control flow paths instead of allocation sites and dynamically determining the hot path through a method. Our ultimate goal is to reduce the amount of required counter increments by such a degree that using it in production environments becomes feasible. We present an implementation of our approach for the Java HotSpot Virtual Machine. First measurements already show a reduction of required increments of up to 30% compared to the state of the art.

Keywords

Allocation Tracking; Allocation Site; Hot Path; Memory Monitoring; Path; Control Flow

1. INTRODUCTION

Detecting and localizing memory leaks, reducing the amount of required garbage collections, or identifying possible code optimizations regarding memory behavior count among the areas that require, or benefit from, allocation tracking. The general approach used by state-of-the-art allocation trackers is to instrument every allocation site with a counter. The drawback of this approach is that the counter overheads ruin the advantage of Java's fast allocations. Although it provides accurate results, the introduced run-time overhead makes this approach infeasible in a production environment. State-of-the-art memory monitoring software such as ElephantTracks sometimes introduces run-time overhead exceeding 1000% [7], although it has to be said that they track some additional events like object deaths, too.

We introduce DuckTracks, an allocation tracking approach that uses path information to reduce the amount of counter increments, and, therefore, the introduced overhead required to track allocations. We define a path as a sequence of connected blocks in the control flow graph of a method. All blocks and edges in the control flow graph belong to exactly one path.

Every method usually has multiple paths which the control flow can take during execution. One of these paths will be taken more often than the others. We call this the *hot path*. By identifying this path and by instrumenting it with a counter representing its allocations we can track the allocations of a method with just a single counter increment in most cases. To correctly track allocations during executions that diverge from the hot path, we have to instrument all diverging paths as well. Their counters may add additional allocations or remove allocations which were already counted, but will not happen due to the control flow diverging from the expected path.

Correctly identifying the hot path is best done by analyzing the path usage of a method while it is executed, which can be done by gathering a path profile during a data gathering run and then basing the instrumentation on this profile during the actual run. This, however, assumes that the data gathering run is representative for the actual method usage and would require tailoring data gathering runs to profiled applications. We therefore chose a more dynamic approach. By initially choosing paths based on heuristics, DuckTracks gathers hot path information during the actual run. It then reinstruments methods based on this information, if necessary.

To the best of our knowledge, DuckTracks is the first monitoring tool that tracks allocations pathwise in order to reduce the amount of required counter increments. Furthermore, these paths are not statically determined and fixed, but dynamically adjusted based on data derived from our allocation counters. This enables DuckTracks to adapt itself to the behavior of the monitored application.

2. APPROACH

Our approach dynamically instruments the methods of every class at load time, using functionality provided by the Java Virtual Machine Tool Interface (*JVMTI*) and the Java Native Interface (*JNI*). The instrumentation process is divided into six steps, as shown in Figure 1.

The first step is acquiring the method's bytecode which is trivial due to existing JVMTI functionality. We then construct the bytecode's control flow graph.

ICPE'17, April 22-26, 2017, L'Aquila, Italy

DOI: http://dx.doi.org/10.1145/3030207.3030235

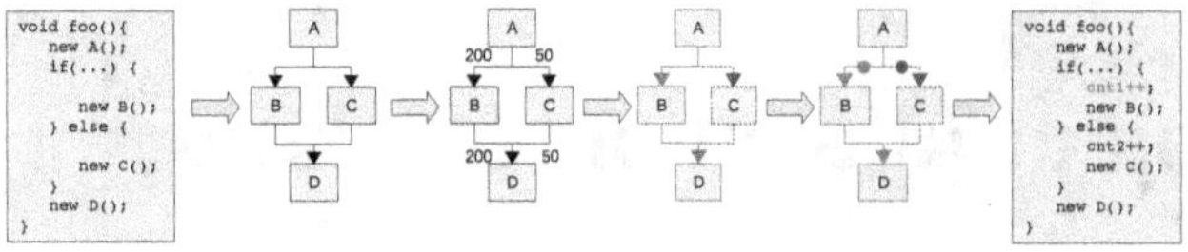

Figure 1: From original to instrumented bytecode

In the next step, we mark every edge of this control flow graph with its execution frequency. Naturally, when a class is initially loaded no edge frequency data exists. Therefore, we additionally instrument every method with an entry counter. These entry counters trigger a reload of the class after a certain number of method calls, which allows us to re-instrument its methods. During reinstrumentation we have access to the counter values of the previous instrumentation, which gives us the traversal frequencies of all instrumented edges. We then propagate these values through the control flow graph. This propagation is currently rather rudimentary, and improving it will be part of our future work.

The frequency-marked control flow graph is then used to create the paths through the method. We continue by determining the ideal counter position for each of these paths and then calculate the counter semantics, i.e., which allocations are measured by a specific counter and which other allocations have to be corrected. Finally, the method's bytecode is instrumented with these counters and the instrumented class is loaded.

Although constructing the control flow graph and instrumenting the bytecode are comprehensive topics by themselves, the path building and counter calculation steps constitute the core of our contributions. We will therefore cover these two aspects in more detail, starting with how paths are built.

2.1 Path Building

We define a path as a sequence of connected blocks in the control flow graph of a method. The left side of Figure 2 shows a trivial method with two such paths and purely sequential control flow. A path can either start at a block without predecessors, such as the continuous (red) path at the method entry block A, or by branching off from another path, as the dashed (blue) path. The block from which a path branches off is called its *branching block*, e.g., block A is the dashed path's *branching block*. Similarly, a path can end by leaving the method, indicated by ending with a block without successors, such as block E, or by joining another path, i.e., the path's last block is connected to a block that belongs to another path. The block at which the path joins is called its *joining block*, e.g., block E is the dashed path's *joining block*.

2.1.1 Handling Sequential Paths

Path building starts with the hot path, which starts at the method entry block. We build it by incrementally appending the most likely successor of the current tail block. If the control flow graph is not frequency marked, e.g., when the class is initially loaded, the most likely successor is picked based on static heuristics. Otherwise, we pick the successor with the highest edge frequency. The picked successor becomes the path's new tail block. This process repeats until we reach a method exit, which ends the path.

The resulting path may contain several *branching points*,

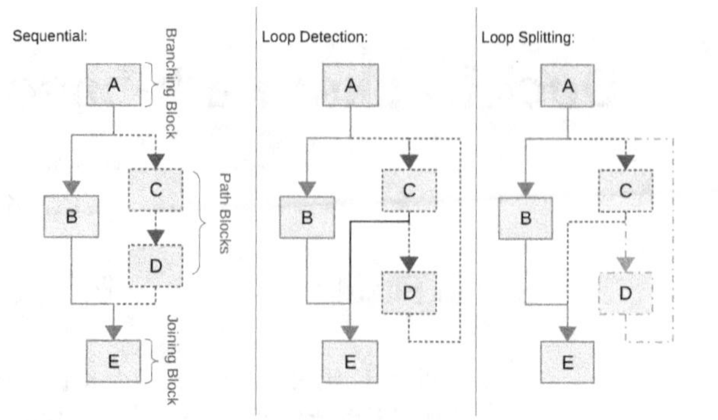

Figure 2: Sequential and looping path structure

i.e., blocks with more than one successor where additional paths branch off. We now create each of these side paths. Unlike the initial path, these paths may select successors that already belong to other paths. This leads to a join: The path's *joining block* is set accordingly, which ends the path. The result of this process can be seen on the left side of Figure 2, with the dashed path branching off from block A and rejoining at block E.

2.1.2 Handling Loops

Loops are detected during path building when a path under construction, called the *current path*, tries to append a block that is already part of this path. We call this block the *header block*. Figure 2 shows this situation in the middle graph: the dashed (blue) path tries to append block C as the successor of block D, but block C is already part of the dashed path. Therefore, block C is identified as the *header block* of a loop.

We handle loops by splitting off the path segment after the *header block* and turning it into a separate path. The resulting path's *branching block* and its *joining block* are identical, i.e., the *header block*. This has been done in the rightmost graph of Figure 2, resulting in the dashed-dotted (green) path which branches off from block C. Construction of the dashed path then continues at the *header block* by picking another successor, which leads to the dashed path joining the continuous (red) path at block E in our example.

If the *header block* has no other successors, then the *current path* ends with the *header block*. As a rule, the *current path* cannot join any loop path that has been split off from the *current path* itself. After the *current path* has been constructed, the *branching points* in any of the split off loop paths are handled in addition to the path's own *branching points*.

No further knowledge of loop structure or specialized handling is required. Loops are therefore simply paths that branch off from some block and rejoin at the same block.

2.2 Counter Construction

We now construct a counter for each path. These counters are defined by two attributes: their location and their semantics, i.e., the set of allocation sites that are affected by a specific counter. A counter's semantics is influenced by its own location as well as by the locations of other counters. We therefore determine the locations of all counters before calculating their semantics.

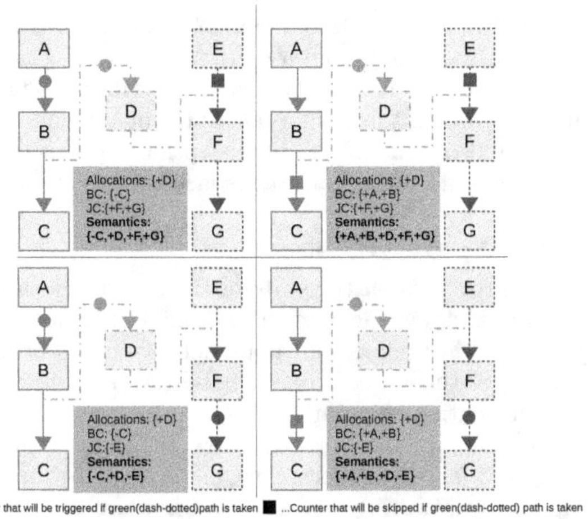

Figure 3: Counter semantics as dictated by location

2.2.1 *Counter Locations*

Counters are placed on edges in the control flow graph. We want to place counters such that as few of them as possible are triggered during any given method execution. To achieve this, we introduce the terms *flow* and *share count.* A *flow* is a sequence of blocks from the method entry to the method exit, i.e., a complete control flow through the method during a particular execution. The *share count* of an edge specifies how many *flows* share this edge. Since every edge is owned by exactly one path, the *share count* is at least one. It is increased by every path that branches off after the edge's end block and every path that joins before the edge's start block.

The chance of incrementing multiple counters during a method execution rises for every counter placed on an edge with a *share count* greater than one. We therefore aim to place counters at the least shared edge of every path.

2.2.2 *Counter Semantics*

A counter's semantics is the set of allocation sites that the counter represents. It consists of three components: the *allocations*, the *branching correction* and the *joining correction.*

A path's *allocations* represent the allocation sites of the path itself and are therefore the set of all allocation sites in its blocks. The *branching correction* and the *joining correction* represent allocations before and after the path. Their values depend on the counter placement in the path from which the *current path* branches off and the counter placement in the path that the *current path* joins. Figure 3 shows the four possible counter placement scenarios and their effect on the *branching correction* and the *joining correction.* In this example, we are interested in the value of the dash-dotted (green) path, which branches off from the continuous (red) path and joins the dashed (blue) path.

If the continuous path's counter is placed before the *branching block B*, it will have been incremented already when the dash-dotted path is entered. The dash-dotted path therefore requires a *branching correction* (*BC*) that subtracts the allocations on the continuous path after the *branching block B* since they have been counted but will not be traversed. This is the case in the two graphs on the left side of Figure 3.

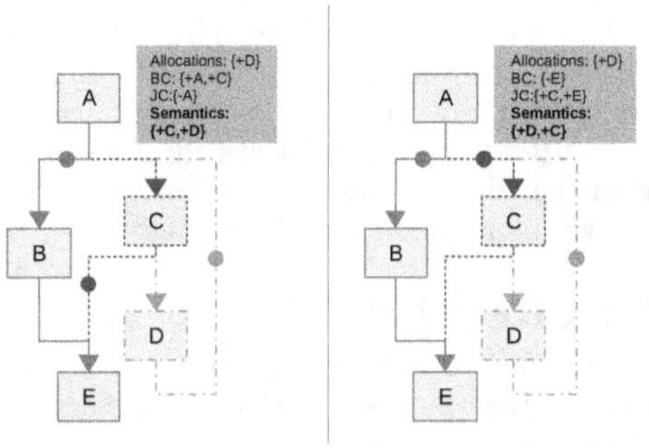

Figure 4: Loop counter semantics as dictated by location

On the other hand, if the continuous counter is placed after the *branching block B*, it will not have been incremented yet when the dash-dotted path is entered. The dash-dotted path's *branching correction* therefore needs to add all allocations that happen before and in the *branching block B* since they have been traversed but were not counted. This can be seen in the two graphs on the right side of Figure 3.

The same principle applies when calculating the *joining correction* (*JC*) of the dash-dotted path. If the dashed path's counter will be skipped, i.e., if it is placed before the *joining block F* the *joining correction* needs to add all allocations of the dashed path after and in the *joining block F*. This case holds in the two upper graphs in Figure 3. If the dashed path's counter will be incremented, i.e., if it is placed after the *joining block F*, the *joining correction* needs to subtract all allocations of the dashed path that happen before the *joining block F*. This is the case in the two lower graphs in Figure 3.

This example assumes, for simplicity's sake, that both the continuous path and the dashed path do not branch off from, or join, another path. If, for example, the dashed or continuous path were to join a fourth path, then this fourth path would also affect the dash-dotted path's corrections, as would every other path in this join chain until a path is reached that exits the method. The dashed and continuous paths' branching chains affect the dash-dotted path's corrections in the same way. This will be explained in more detail in future work.

The actual counter semantics is the sum of these three components. Consequently, parts of the *branching correction* and the *joining correction* may cancel each other out. Loops are a good example of this. Since a loop's *branching block* and *joining block* are the same, namely the *header block*, both corrections will be calculated based on the same path segment. The result will be that the parts of the corrections that handle blocks before and after the *header block* cancel each other out, leaving only the allocations of the *header block* itself. The resulting counter semantics for the loop will therefore include the loop's *allocations* and the allocations of the *header block*, which together represents a single loop iteration. This is shown in Figure 4: the placement of the dashed (blue) path's counter changes the dash-dotted (green) path's *branch correction* and *join correction*, but the resulting counter semantics remains the same.

When this step is completed, we know the location and semantics of every path's counter. A path's counter semantics may be empty, meaning that traversing the path has no effect on the allocation total. We eliminate such counters.

After placing the counters into the bytecode, they will accurately count the number of allocations caused by every method execution. Since we identified the hot path and constructed the counters based on it, only a single counter increment will be needed most of the time.

3. FIRST RESULTS

We tested our prototype implementation on various benchmarks of the DaCapo, DaCapo Scala and SPECjvm suites. These preliminary tests showed a reduction of required counter increments of up to 30% compared to counting allocations individually. We measured a run-time overhead of 20-30%. Section 5 will present some of our ideas to further improve these first results.

4. RELATED WORK

There is ample work on tracking allocations, resulting in varying levels of overhead and precision. Some approaches, such as AntTracks [6], modify a VM and thus benefit from having full access to VM functionality. This allows for low overhead as well as for tracking events that cannot be accessed from outside the VM. The price for this level of access is a lack of portability due to the required VM modifications.

Agent-based approaches such as ElephantTracks [7] implement tracking through instrumentation. These approaches cause significantly more overhead and have less access to VM events. They are, however, not restricted to a single VM. DuckTracks falls into this category and attempts to reduce the overhead penalty to a level that makes its usage feasible in a production environment.

Creating and utilizing path information is a well-researched area, too. The seminal work of Ball and Larus [1, 2] describes an algorithm for creating path traces in purely sequential programs. It has been built upon in a variety of subsequent work, including additions for loop handling such as D'Elia et al. [4], or selective profiling such as Vaswanie et al. [8]. The main difference between the Ball/Larus algorithm and our approach is that they consider paths as complete sequences of blocks from method entry to method exit, which requires counters that ensure that every such sequence is correctly tracked. Since we are only interested in tracking allocations, we can omit all counters for path sequences that do not change the number of allocated objects. Also, their counter placement is optimized to reduce the number of placed counters while still delivering a complete path trace. The goal of our counter placement is to minimize the number of counter increments during execution.

Hot path information is extensively used in areas such as compilation and code optimization, as shown in the work of, e.g., Bebenita et.al [3] or Gupta et al. [5]. However, to the best of our knowledge, we are the first to use hot path information to achieve more efficient allocation tracking.

5. FUTURE WORK

We currently work on improving edge frequency propagation by exploiting dominance relationships between blocks as well as marking edges with frequency ranges if precise marking is not possible. Since it would by trivial to extend DuckTracks to allow tracking of other attributes such as method calls, eventually adding such attributes remains a possibility for future work. A more immediate improvement is the addition of counter inlining. This involves removing the hot path counter from a method and adding its semantics to the counters of every calling method. This would reduce the amount of required counter increments even further. We also plan to handle exceptions by instrumenting catch blocks and using the stack trace to correct allocations.

6. CONCLUSIONS

We improved upon the state-of-the-art approach for allocation tracking by tracking per path instead of per allocation site. We further refined our approach by constructing paths according to their execution probabilities, thereby using hot path information to great effect.

Preliminary results already show that our approach reduces the amount of necessary increments by up to 30% compared to counting allocations individually, with further optimizations under way.

Reducing the amount of required increments brings us one step closer to realizing an allocation tracker that is suited for production use. This is achieved without the need for extra runs to gather profiling information due to DuckTrack's self-optimizing, adaptive nature.

7. ACKNOWLEDGMENTS

This work was supported by the Christian Doppler Forschungsgesellschaft and by Dynatrace Austria.

8. REFERENCES

[1] T. Ball and J. R. Larus. Optimally profiling and tracing programs. *ACM Trans. Program. Lang. Syst.*, 16(4), July 1994.

[2] T. Ball and J. R. Larus. Efficient path profiling. In *Proc. of the 29th Annual ACM/IEEE Int'l. Symposium on Microarchitecture*, Washington, DC, USA, 1996.

[3] M. Bebenita, M. Chang, G. Wagner, A. Gal, C. Wimmer, and M. Franz. Trace-based compilation in execution environments without interpreters. In *Proc. of the 8th Int'l. Conf. on the Principles and Practice of Programming in Java*, New York, NY, USA, 2010.

[4] D. C. D'Elia and C. Demetrescu. Ball-larus path profiling across multiple loop iterations. In *Proc. of the 2013 ACM SIGPLAN Int'l. Conf. on Object Oriented Programming Systems Languages & Applications*, New York, NY, USA, 2013.

[5] R. Gupta, D. A. Berson, and J. Z. Fang. Resource-sensitive profile-directed data flow analysis for code optimization. In *Proc. of the 30th Annual ACM/IEEE Int'l. Symp. on Microarchitecture*, Washington, DC, USA, 1997.

[6] P. Lengauer, V. Bitto, and H. Mössenböck. Accurate and efficient object tracing for java applications. In *Proc. of the 6th ACM/SPEC Int'l. Conf. on Performance Engineering*, New York, NY, USA, 2015.

[7] N. P. Ricci, S. Z. Guyer, and J. E. B. Moss. Elephant tracks: Portable production of complete and precise gc traces. In *Proc. of the 2013 Int'l. Symp. on Memory Management*, New York, NY, USA, 2013.

[8] K. Vaswani, A. V. Nori, and T. M. Chilimbi. Preferential path profiling: Compactly numbering interesting paths. In *Proc. of the 34th Annual ACM SIGPLAN-SIGACT Symp. on Principles of Programming Languages*, New York, NY, USA, 2007.

Efficient Sampling-based Lock Contention Profiling for Java

Andreas Schörgenhumer
andreas.schoergenhumer@jku.at

Peter Hofer
peter.hofer@jku.at

David Gnedt
david.gnedt@jku.at

Christian Doppler Laboratory on Monitoring and Evolution of Very-Large-Scale Software Systems
Johannes Kepler University Linz, Austria

Hanspeter Mössenböck
hanspeter.moessenboeck@jku.at
Institute for System Software
Johannes Kepler University Linz, Austria

ABSTRACT

Concurrent code commonly uses locks. Choosing between simpler but less scalable and more sophisticated but error-prone locking mechanisms is difficult during development. Therefore, lock contention analysis at run-time is crucial to aid such decisions.

We present a novel sampling-based approach for collecting detailed information on lock contention in Java applications by using the Java Virtual Machine Tool Interface (JVMTI) and bytecode instrumentation. We support both intrinsic locks as well as java.util.concurrent locks. Moreover, we can determine not only where contention *occurs* but also where it is *caused*. With a mean run-time overhead of about 5%, we consider our approach suitable for use in production environments.

Keywords

Locking, Contention, Java, Concurrency, Parallelism, Threading, Synchronization, Profiling, Monitoring

1. INTRODUCTION

Multi-core hardware has become widely available and offers a considerable performance improvement over single-core systems. However, developers have to explicitly write concurrent software to make use of these capabilities. With concurrent programming, synchronization is necessary to safely access shared resources, which is commonly achieved with locks. When using locks incorrectly, anomalies and bugs can occur that are difficult to detect, locate and fix. Coarse-grained locking is simpler and less error-prone, but it can lead to higher lock contention, which is when multiple threads try to acquire the same lock at the same time. Fine-grained locking can alleviate this problem, but it may be more difficult to implement correctly. Deciding on an appropriate locking mechanism when developing concurrent software is not an easy task. Lock contention analysis at run-time is crucial to reveal performance bottlenecks. These can then be resolved by opting for a more complex but also more scalable locking mechanism.

In earlier work, we presented an efficient lock contention profiler directly in the OpenJDK HotSpot Virtual Machine (VM) that provides detailed information on lock contention in Java applications while imposing only a small performance overhead [5]. However, this approach relies on specific capabilities of the VM, which might not be available in an existing environment. In this paper, we describe an approach to lock contention analysis which relies only on the commonly available Java VM Tool Interface (JVMTI) and on bytecode instrumentation.

The main contributions of this work in progress paper are:

1. We describe a novel approach for collecting lock contention information at run-time by only using JVMTI and bytecode instrumentation. Our approach is capable of recording similar information as our previous VM-internal approach that we described in [5]. The collected data shows both where lock contention occurs and where it is caused.

2. We provide a preliminary evaluation of the run-time overhead as well as the amount of generated data of our implementation. The results demonstrate that both of these metrics are low enough so that we consider our approach to be feasible for the use in production environments.

The rest of this paper is organized as follows: Section 2 characterizes locking in Java. Section 3 presents our novel approach and describes how we collect and record information on lock contention. Section 4 evaluates the run-time overhead and the amount of generated data with our approach. In Section 5, we discuss related work and Section 6 concludes this paper.

2. LOCKING IN JAVA

Every object in Java has exactly one intrinsic lock (also known as the monitor of the object) which can be used for mutual exclusion of threads in *synchronized* code blocks. The

ICPE'17, April 22-26, 2017, L'Aquila, Italy

DOI: http://dx.doi.org/10.1145/3030207.3030234

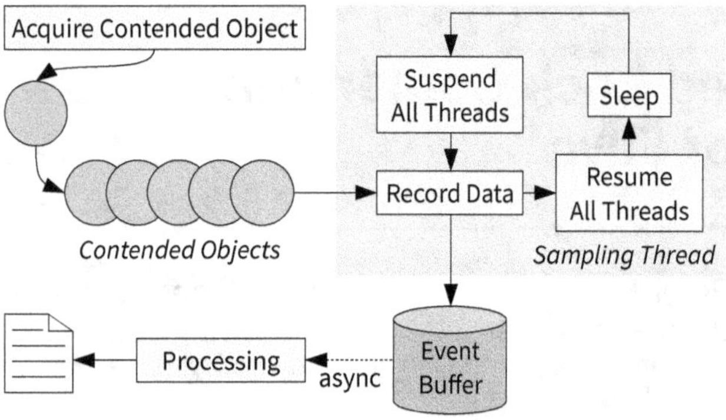

Figure 1: Overview of the sampling approach.

synchronized keyword can also be used for entire methods. Every time a thread wants to enter such a synchronized block, it must first acquire the object's monitor. All other threads that also want to enter the same block or a block protected with the same synchronization object have to wait until the lock is released again by the thread currently holding it. Intrinsic locks are always automatically released upon exiting the synchronized block, whether it is due to the normal program execution or due to an exception. Their implementation in the VM typically imposes a significant overhead only when there is actually lock contention [1, 10].

The java.util.concurrent package of Java 5 offers another way of implementing synchronization. The *LockSupport* class provides the methods *park* and *unpark* for the current thread and a given blocker object. In contrast to intrinsic locks, which are implemented in the VM, *park* and *unpark* can be used together with compare-and-set operations to implement synchronization directly in Java. The *AbstractQueuedSynchronizer* (AQS) class provides a framework for lock implementations relying on wait queues on which many ready-to-use *synchronizers* in Java are based. The main goal of synchronizers is to minimize performance overhead, most notably under contention and especially in heavily multi-threaded applications, where the overhead of intrinsic locks would be high [7]. An example for an implementation based on AQS is the *ReentrantLock* class which provides similar semantics as intrinsic locks.

3. APPROACH

Initially, we attempted to recreate our VM-internal profiler [5]. We used JVMTI callbacks for recording lock contentions and combined them with Java bytecode instrumentation to signal when a monitor is released. However, this required instrumenting every possible monitor exit, regardless of whether actual contention occurred. As a result, the overhead was infeasible and we decided to implement a sampling-based approach. We will use the phrase *contended objects* throughout this paper to conveniently address objects for which there is contention.

Figure 1 shows an overview of our sampling-based approach. We manage a list of possibly contended objects for both intrinsic locks as well as for java.util.concurrent locks. For intrinsic locks the contended objects are the lock objects used in the synchronized blocks, for java.util.concurrent they are the blocker objects. In the loop of the sampling thread, we periodically inspect each of the objects in this list. If an object is still contended at that time, we record contention data which consists of the object itself, the owner thread, all threads that are currently waiting on this object and the stack traces of these threads. While taking the sample we suspend all threads in order to guarantee that the recorded stack traces correspond to the locations where the contentions occurred. The collected data is stored in events that are written into a buffer. This buffer is asynchronously processed and the results are written to a file which can then be analyzed with the same visualization tool as described in [5]. The processing includes an optional online analysis which can be viewed in the visualization tool at run-time.

Our analysis not only reveals which threads were blocked (where and how long) but also which threads were responsible for the blocking. This is possible because our samples record the contended object and its owner thread for all waiting threads. A description of this analysis can be found in [5].

3.1 Intrinsic Locks

For intrinsic locks we get currently contended objects from the JVMTI callback *MonitorContendedEnter* (MCE). This callback is invoked whenever a thread cannot acquire an object's lock and must wait because another thread currently holds this lock. We add every newly encountered object to a list of intrinsic lock objects and assign an additional data structure to it using JVMTI's object tagging capability. The data structure contains a unique identifier (see Section 3.4) and a contention flag which indicates whether the object is contended. The flag is initially set. The sampling loop periodically inspects each object in the list by calling JVMTI's *GetObjectMonitorUsage* (GOMU). This function returns the object's owner thread as well as all threads that are currently waiting for this object's lock. Since we do not capture when a contention is resolved, the list can contain objects which are no longer contended, in which case GOMU returns no waiting threads. If an object is no longer contended, we clear its contention flag and remove it from the list. In case the MCE callback is invoked again for this object, we simply set the contention flag and reinsert it into the list. We could also track uncontended objects with the *MonitorContendedEntered* callback which signals when a waiting thread finally acquires the lock. However, we decided against this because executing code in this callback would increase the duration of holding the lock which could cause more lock contention and affect our analysis results.

3.2 java.util.concurrent

The java.util.concurrent part requires bytecode instrumentation to get the list of contended objects since JVMTI does not provide the means. As explained in Section 2, AQS provides a basis for locking implementations. Hence, we modified its method *parkAndCheckInterrupt*, which invokes the *LockSupport.park* method. In the method, we introduced additional bytecode that inserts the blocker object into a list (separate from the list used for intrinsic locks). The blocker object is always the *this* object, that is, an instance of AQS. Each object in the list is inspected in the sampling loop by retrieving its owner thread and all waiting threads via the AQS interface. If an object is no longer contended, it is removed from the list.

3.3 Sampling

Using JVMTI we record stack traces of the owner thread and all waiting threads for every contended object used in intrinsic locks and java.util.concurrent locks. After recording the stack traces all data is packed into a so-called *contention event* which is inserted in a global event buffer. An asynchronous Java thread periodically retrieves all events in this buffer, processes them and writes the result into a file, optionally using compression.

3.4 Metadata

In order to efficiently create the contention event mentioned above, we do not include information like the thread name, the class signature or the stack trace data in this event itself but rather use unique identifiers that refer to additional metadata events. This way we significantly reduce the amount of output data because we need to write the actual metadata only once and not repeatedly in every contention event. Each time a thread is started, we are notified via the corresponding JVMTI callback and record a *thread start event* with the name of the thread. When we encounter a contended object for the first time, we create a *new object event*, both for intrinsic locks and for java.util.concurrent locks. This event consists of the identity hash code and the class signature of the object. The *new stack event* stores the method signature as well as the class signature of every stack frame. It is only created once for every newly encountered stack trace, because previously recorded stack traces are already stored in a stack trace cache. All events are written to the same global buffer.

4. EVALUATION

We evaluated the run-time overhead and the amount of generated data using OpenJDK version 8u45 on a set of real-world benchmarks. We also looked at the accuracy of our approach using a synthetic benchmark.

4.1 Overhead

For simulating real-world tasks, we decided to use the multi-threaded benchmarks from both the DaCapo 9.12 [2] benchmark suite[1] and the Scala Benchmarking Project 0.1.0 [11]. Each benchmark was run with 45 iterations of which we only used the last ten iterations for our evaluation to exclude the VM's startup phase. We repeated this process 40 times to avoid other biases in the results.

All benchmarks were executed on a hyper-threaded quad-core processor Intel Core i7-4770 with 16 GB of main memory and operating under Ubuntu Linux 15.10. Dynamic frequency scaling and turbo boost were disabled for more stable and reliable results. The benchmark suite was started while no processes other than essential system services were running. We chose sampling frequencies of 20 samples/s and 100 samples/s, which we consider a reasonable trade-off between overhead and accuracy. We measured the run-time overhead by comparing the execution times of the individual benchmarks with and without our profiler.

Figure 2 shows the median execution times for all multi-threaded benchmarks. The first and third quartiles are represented by the error bars. The *G.Mean* shows the geometric mean over all benchmarks with a 50% confidence interval displayed as its error bars. The mean run-time overhead is 1.5% when sampling with 20 samples/s and 5.1% when sampling with 100 samples/s.

[1]We excluded *batik* and *eclipse* (do not work on OpenJDK 8) and *tradesoap* which constantly timed out on our system.

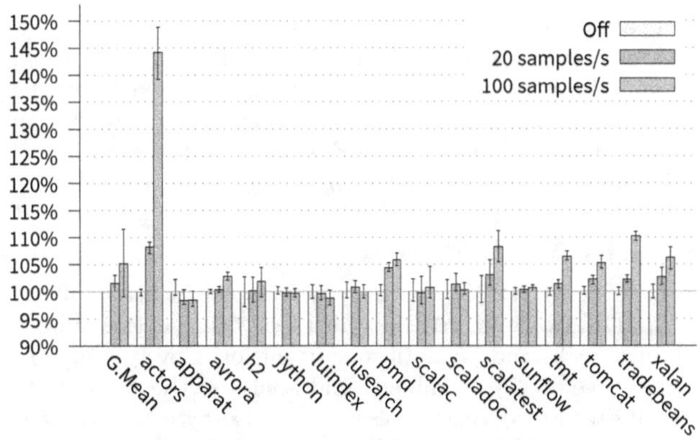

Figure 2: Run-time overhead with different sampling frequencies compared to using no profiler.

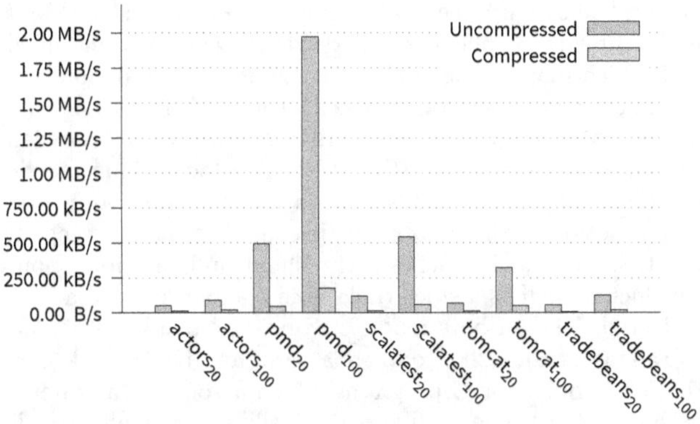

Figure 3: Output data written per second. The subscripts show the sampling frequency in samples/s.

As expected, the higher sampling frequency has a greater impact on performance. The highest overhead is caused by *actors* with 44% at 100 samples/sec. This is because the number of possibly contented objects to inspect in the sampling loop is four to 20 times larger than in all other benchmarks. On the other hand, some benchmarks like *apparat* or *luindex* even slightly gain performance. This can be attributed to small influences on thread scheduling and on garbage collection.

Figure 3 shows the average amount of data written per second for the benchmarks that yield the highest values. The largest output when sampling with 100 samples/s is produced by *pmd* with slightly below 2 MB/s, followed by *scalatest* with about 540 KB/s. For 20 samples/s the same benchmarks drop to 500 KB/s and 120 KB/s, respectively. All other benchmarks produce significantly less output, especially those that are not part of Figure 3 for which we recorded less than 50 KB/s. Enabling compression substantially decreases the amount of generated data by typically 70% to 90% and reduces it to under 200 KB/s in all cases. Moreover, the difference in run-time overhead is negligible (below 0.1%).

4.2 Accuracy

For determining the accuracy, we built a test suite using the Java Microbench Harness [8]. Our suite creates lock contention in a predefined way by varying the number of threads, lock sites and the duration of lock holding times (ranging from very short to very long contentions). This means that we can predict which threads are waiting for how long at what lock site. We found that our sampling approach yielded the predicted results. Moreover, we executed the test suite with our VM-internal profiler which resulted in similar output. A more detailed analysis of the accuracy of our sampling approach will be part of our future work.

5. RELATED WORK

In earlier work [5], we proposed a modification of the OpenJDK HotSpot VM to record lock contention for both intrinsic locks and java.util.concurrent locks by tracing contention events. We combined and analyzed these events to identify where contention occurs and also by which threads it is caused, including detailed information on the contending object, its owner thread, all waiting threads and their call chains. Contrary to our sampling-based approach, our previous profiler records all contention with high accuracy and still causes an acceptable mean overhead of just 7.8% for multi-threaded applications. However, it relies on a modified VM which may be unsuitable for existing environments.

Another modification of the HotSpot VM is described by David et al. [3]. Their profiler monitors the so-called *critical section pressure* (CSP) for each lock. This metric represents the time threads have to wait for lock acquisition as a function of the number of threads that are running. If the CSP of a lock reaches a threshold, information about this lock as well as a stack trace from one blocked thread are collected. The authors report a worst-case overhead of 6%.

Tallent et al. [12] proposed a sampling-based lock contention profiler for C programs which associates a counter with each lock. The profiler periodically inspects all threads and for each thread that is blocked on a lock, it increases the lock's counter. When the lock is later released by its owner thread and the lock's counter is non-zero, the owner thread records the contention and its call chain. While this approach has an overhead of only 5%, it does neither record which threads had to wait nor their call chains.

Using hardware performance counters can result in even less overhead. Inoue and Nakatami [6] presented a sampling profiler that utilized such counters in a Java VM to collect information on where locks are acquired and where blocking occurs. They use a technique to record call chains using the stack depth and achieve an overhead of typically below 2.2%. However, they cannot determine the cause of contention and java.util.concurrent locks are not supported.

Another approach is used in the Java Flight Recorder (JFR) [4], a commercial tool built into the Oracle JDK. It mostly imposes only about 1% run-time overhead and provides data on the objects used in locking, which threads were blocked and their call chains. However, only contentions longer than 10 ms are recorded by default. Furthermore, JFR blames the last thread that owned the lock for the contention. This thread's call chain, however, is not recorded and threads that held the same lock before this last thread are not taken into account. java.util.concurrent locks are not supported.

Research investigating java.util.concurrent locks was conducted by Patros et al. [9]. They modified the IBM Java VM to record park contention data whenever threads are parked. The records include class data of the blocker object, thread names and stack traces. They measured where locks are held for how long and how many threads have to park. The modifications result in a overhead below 0.5%. However, they collect no information about where contention is caused.

6. CONCLUSIONS AND FUTURE WORK

In this paper, we presented a sampling-based lock contention profiler for Java applications that works outside the VM. Using only JVMTI and Java bytecode instrumentation, we can collect detailed contention data for both intrinsic locks as well as for locks of the java.util.concurrent framework. This data does not only show where contention occurs but also where it is caused. Our novel approach incurs only 1.5% overhead when running with a sampling frequency of 20 samples/s and 5.1% with 100 samples/s. Therefore, we consider this approach to be feasible for the use in production environments.

Future work includes a statistical evaluation of accuracy of our new profiler by comparing its contention output against the results of our VM-internal approach [5]. Furthermore, we intend to add capabilities to determine the actual lock site of java.util.concurrent locks which we currently cannot obtain from the stack traces.

7. ACKNOWLEDGEMENTS

This work was supported by the Christian Doppler Forschungsgesellschaft and by Dynatrace Austria.

8. REFERENCES

[1] D. F. Bacon, R. Konuru, C. Murthy, and M. Serrano. Thin locks: featherweight synchronization for Java. In *ACM SIGPLAN Not.*, volume 33, pages 258–268, 1998.

[2] S. M. Blackburn et al. The DaCapo benchmarks: Java benchmarking development and analysis. OOPSLA '06, pages 169–190, 2006.

[3] F. David, G. Thomas, J. Lawall, and G. Muller. Continuously measuring critical section pressure with the free-lunch profiler. OOPSLA '14, pages 291–307, 2014.

[4] M. Hirt and M. Lagergren. *Oracle JRockit: The Definitive Guide*. Packt Publishing Ltd, 2010.

[5] P. Hofer et al. Efficient tracing and versatile analysis of lock contention in Java applications on the virtual machine level. ICPE '16, pages 263–274, 2016.

[6] H. Inoue and T. Nakatani. How a Java VM can get more from a hardware performance monitor. OOPSLA '09, pages 137–154, 2009.

[7] D. Lea. The java.util.concurrent synchronizer framework. *Sci. Comput. Program.*, 58(3):293–309, Dec. 2005.

[8] Oracle. OpenJDK Code Tools: Java Microbench Harness (JMH). http://openjdk.java.net/projects/code-tools/jmh/.

[9] P. Patros, E. Aubanel, D. Bremner, and M. Dawson. A java util concurrent park contention tool. PMAM '15, pages 106–111, 2015.

[10] T. Pool. Lock optimizations on the HotSpot VM. Technical report, 2014.

[11] A. Sewe, M. Mezini, A. Sarimbekov, and W. Binder. Da capo con scala: Design and analysis of a scala benchmark suite for the java virtual machine. OOPSLA '11, pages 657–676, 2011.

[12] N. Tallent, J. Mellor-Crummey, and A. Porterfield. Analyzing lock contention in multithreaded applications. PPoPP '10, pages 269–280, 2010.

Identifying Derived Performance Requirements of System Components from Explicit Customer- and Application-Facing Performance Requirements

André B. Bondi
Software Performance and Scalability Consulting LLC
Red Bank, New Jersey 07701 USA
andrebbondi@gmail.com

ABSTRACT

Explicitly stated response time, throughput, and other performance requirements of an application implicitly impose other performance requirements on the system components that implement it. We call these *derived* performance requirements. The explicit performance requirements cannot be met if the derived performance requirements are not met. Explicit performance requirements naturally give rise to corresponding derived performance requirements expressed in terms of the same metrics. Derived performance requirements may also be identified that specify the sizes of object pools or the amount of memory needed to meet explicit and other derived requirements. Moreover, derived requirements may be identified that depend on the implementation of the components. We explore how derived requirements arise and present a methodology for identifying and specifying them.

Categories and Subject Descriptors

• **General and reference~Performance** • General and reference~Measurement • **Software and its engineering~Software performance** • **Software and its engineering~Requirements analysis**

Keywords

Performance requirements engineering, software engineering, software life cycle, performance analysis.

1. INTRODUCTION

The specification of an average response time requirement for a transaction inherently imposes upper limits on the acceptable values for the times taken to support the various actions that must occur to complete it .Similarly, the specification of a transaction completion rate inherently imposes throughput requirements on those actions and on those system components that must be traversed to carry those actions out. In addition to derived throughput and response time requirements, we must consider space/time requirements that arise indirectly, such as those for object pools needed to avoid queueing and buffer sizes needed to sustain low probabilities of message loss.

We shall examine the performance requirements that must be derived from the end-to-end performance requirements to determine the suitability of these components for inclusion in the system. A performance model would be used to determine whether a component is suitable from a performance standpoint. The outputs of the model would be the parameters of the derived performance requirements. Examining, testing, and validating the performance requirements of components in the architectural phase of the lifecycle reduce the risk of rework close to the intended delivery date. Omission of these steps increases the risk of performance failure on delivery [9]. The identification of derived requirements cannot occur until the components have been specified in the architectural or design phases of the software life cycle. The derived performance requirements must conform to the same guidelines as the external performance requirements [3], [4].

Space/time considerations engender performance requirements on discrete software resources such as page frames, object pools, locks, and logical connectors like JDBCs. Their pool sizes must be large enough to keep the probability of transaction failure due to pool exhaustion below a very low value. The sizes of the resource pools needed to support the performance of the hosted applications are performance requirements that must be derived from the frequency with which their members are requested and the probability distribution of how long they are held.

Here, we explore ways to derive implied performance requirements about system components from specifications about performance requirements as seen from the standpoint of the sources of one or more requests for specified actions, or, in the case of a computer-controlled system, from the standpoints of components that are receiving commands from the control system and issuing stimuli or sending data to it. Examples of specified actions include initiating batch jobs, responding to transaction requests, triggering an activity within a system in response to a browser click, activating an alarm, delivering a message, or failing over to a standby machine. If the machine of interest is a communications switch or some other mission-critical component, there may be a requirement that a boot or failover be completed within a short amount of time. If several machines need to synchronously shake hands with a central server while booting, there will of necessity be both throughput and delay requirements on it that must be formulated and met to support the timing requirements of the booting procedure. The minimum achievable handshaking delay to the application of interest will be a lower bound on the achievable boot time. If the consequent lower bound is greater than the desired boot time, improvements must be made.

ICPE'17, April 22 - 26, 2017, L'Aquila, Italy.

ACM 978-1-4503-4404-3/17/04 $15.00
DOI: http://dx.doi.org/10.1145/3030207.3030246

The architecture of a large-scale data analytics and storage system may be influenced by the volume of historical and recent data used as input to an analysis algorithm. The tradeoff between the cost of moving and storing that data and the location and cost of computing power may determine whether the computation of the analysis is done where the data are stored or if the data are moved to where the computation is done. That decision induces requirements for bandwidth and storage at each of the nodes involved.

Derived requirements can impact the configuration in a system that already exists or in an architecture that has already been chosen. For instance, in a multitier web system, the number of Java database connections (JDBCs) needed to prevent queuing for them is determined by the rate at which transactions occur between the application server and the backend database and the duration of those transactions. While one can observe whether packet loss, call loss, or queueing for a JDBC occurs orders of magnitude more often than it should, e.g., with relative frequency 10^{-3} instead of 10^{-9}, a long test time and a large number of transactions are needed to determine whether the relative frequencies of these events are 10^{-7} instead of 10^{-9}. If we can collect data to estimate throughputs and the means and variances of resource holding times, and buffer or object pool sizes, we can combine approximate modeling with tests that verify the configured object sizes to help us ensure that the frequencies with which undesired events occur are likely to be in the required range. Instrumentation of the object pool is needed to ensure that performance needs are met and to enable the measurement of object holding times and throughputs.

As with performance requirements that are formulated from the perspective of an end user or from the perspective of a software-controlled industrial system, derived performance requirements on software and hardware components provide a basis for defining the parameters of performance test plans. These test plans may be executed whenever the components are available. Testing of components should be conducted as early as possible so that one can identify unsatisfactory performance characteristics and choose alternative components well before release.

The remainder of this paper is organized as follows. After discussing related work, we consider how derived requirements arise, how they might be identified, and the metrics in which they might be expressed. These metrics may differ from those of the external performance requirements. For example, while a buffer pool exhaustion probability is not explicitly stated in end-to-end throughput and response time requirements, it may be necessary to specify one to sustain them. We then go on to describe a process for obtaining derived requirements, and possible impacts of explicit and derived requirements. Finally, we discuss the relationship between derived requirements and performance testing.

2. RELATED WORK

Hierarchical models can sometimes be formulated to determine the drivers of performance requirements, even if this was not the original intent [6], [13], [8].

In [14], Smith uses queueing network models and execution graphs to predict the effect of component throughputs and response times on the performance of an overall system. Smith illustrates heuristics for determining the extent to which components must be sped up to provide the required performance characteristics of components under a given workload. A response time requirement is more easily achieved when a component has a lower anticipated offered load. The Processing vs. Frequency Tradeoff Principle [14] states that one should minimize the processing times frequency product of each component. The implication is that a higher response time requirement might be tolerated if the frequency of execution of the component is smaller. The Centering Principle states that the dominant workload functions should be identified and their processing minimized. In the context of performance requirements, this means that the most frequently visited components should have more stringent response time requirements than those that are visited less often. In [15], it is suggested that performance budgets be allocated to collaborating components to ensure that an end-to-end response time requirement is met. Argent-Katwala *et al* [1] use process algebra models to show how end-to-end performance might be predicted for complex interactions of concurrently executing processes and threads, but they do not describe the derivation of performance requirements based on these predictions. Grassi and Mirandola describe how performance models of components can be composed to yield performance models of the system as a whole [7], but they do not attempt to use their framework to derive performance requirements on the components. Bondi briefly discusses and gives examples of derived performance requirements in [3] and [4]. He explains how performance requirements could be derived from other requirements or from the values of performance measures prescribed in domain-related specifications such as fire codes, but he does not show how they might be derived from queueing network models or execution graphs.

3. OCCURRENCE OF DERIVED PERFORMANCE REQUIREMENTS

From the standpoint of the stakeholders of a system component, such as architects, developers, and owners, the response time and throughput requirements appear to be externally driven. These requirements may have arisen from the needs of the system components that use the component of interest, or they may be domain-specific. For instance, the routing of parcels in a conveyor system may be determined by queries to a database [5]. The query and the response must be delivered before a parcel arrives at the next junction in the system. The time allowed for the response to be delivered depends on the conveyor speed. This imposes a response time requirement on the combined database query response time and the latency of the network and programmable logic controllers that run the belt. The frequency with which queries occur depends on the rate at which parcels pass a bar code scanner. That rate in turn depends on routing patterns, the speed of the belt, and the distance between parcels on each segment of the belt. A model is needed to determine the peak database query rate as a function of the number of parcel movements and of the parcel volume combined. The calculated query rate constitutes a throughput requirement of the parcel routing database.

A driver of the required object pool size is the number of discrete objects needed to sustain the throughput of the units of work that need them to proceed through the system. For an analogy, consider a physical system such as an airport security checkpoint. The mechanism by which objects such as trays for passengers' belongings are returned to the free pool plays a crucial role in determining the necessary object pool size, i.e., the number of trays, to sustain throughput, because it affects the object holding time. To see this, let us compare the mechanisms by which recently emptied trays are moved from the secured side of the checkpoint to the unsecured side so that they can be reused. At Newark Airport, the released trays are stacked up on dollies and returned to the unsecured side of the checkpoint according to rules that are unknown to this author. At Gatwick Airport, released trays are placed one at a time on a conveyor positioned under the roller table used to move the trays and luggage towards the X ray machine, and are thus continuously returned to unsecured side. Little's Law tells us that the number of trays (and in the case of Newark, the number of dollies) needed to sustain a given level of passenger throughput depends in part on the tray return procedure, and that the achievable passenger throughput will be degraded if trays are only returned when very large stacks of them accumulate before they are made available. At Gatwick, the throughput and latency of the returning belt are factors that only limit passenger throughput and increase the holding times for trays to the extent that the latency exceeds the time for a passenger to traverse a check point once the trays have been filled. The Gatwick system is analogous to bytewise acknowledgement of messages in a sliding window protocol, while the Newark system is somewhat analogous to intermittently acknowledging the delivery of large packets before more data can be sent. The architecture of each tray return system engenders its own set of derived requirements. At Newark, the use of dollies to return stacks of trays engenders requirements on the number of trays needed at each checkpoint, the number of dollies needed at the passenger entry and exit points at each baggage X ray machine, and the frequency with which the dollies are returned to the passenger entry point at the approach to each baggage X ray machine. At Gatwick, the use of a conveyor mounted under the table of rollers at the approach to each X ray machine engenders requirements for tray throughput, the number trays needed to retain that throughput, the travel time of each tray on return, and the numbers of dollies to hold stacks of trays at the conveyor entry and exit points, even if the trays are not moved on them. The average time to inspect each piece of luggage and each tray as they pass through the X ray machine is independent of tray movements from the exit to the entry point. It depends on the capabilities of the human inspector and perhaps on any automated intelligence that is used to interpret the X ray images.

The airport security example is a metaphor for what might happen in a control system. If each tray is equipped with an RFID, there must be a corresponding record for it in the associated computerized tracking system. This illustrates how domain-specific requirements can arise from physical situations. Domain-specific requirements such as those for computer-controlled systems induce performance requirements on the software systems that provide the control and on the services that support them. Similarly, Software as a Service (SaaS) and Service-Oriented Architectures (SOAs) have performance requirements imposed upon them by the demands and transaction rates of the applications.

4. OBTAINING DERIVED PERFORMANCE REQUIREMENTS

In our experience, derived requirements arise while identifying a top-down hierarchy of non-functional requirements or quality attributes, including performance requirements, starting with external, explicitly specified performance requirements. These correspond to a top down view of both the architecture and of the implementation. There is a need to iterate between architecture choices and performance requirements on the architectural components to eliminate bottlenecks, foci of overload. Then one must respond to tradeoffs between architectures due to the cost of processing, the cost of replication, and the cost of data movement, as well as to constraints imposed by the need to incorporate legacy components or components from a designated supplier. This is especially important if modeling to derive requirements shows that a component cannot meet performance requirements. The predicted or measured inability for a component to meet performance requirements may necessitate its replacement with something else, a performance improvement, or even a change to the envisioned deployment scenario or other architectural aspect.

Our proposed process of deriving performance requirements is closely related to the execution graph methodology proposed in [14] for predicting the demands on various components and modeling their response times. Performance modeling and deriving performance requirements both require that information flows be captured. The required sizes of discrete pools should be explored based on the derived understanding of throughputs and delays. Traversing the execution graphs enables one to identify where performance requirements need to be derived and where the sizing of discrete object pools is needed. A single tool and data representation of the system could be used for both activities. The process is top-down recursive in the sense that each component may in turn consist of other components for which derived performance requirements are needed..

We can use a process to derive performance requirements that is analogous to modeling the performance of complex systems via hierarchical decomposition. This entails decomposing the system into different parts, modeling them separately (perhaps approximately), and then iteratively plugging the outputs of component models into a model of the entire system. This process of hierarchical decomposition allows the modeler to approximately capture the interactions between the components. The global or higher level system model predicts the loads that will be offered to the components. The models of the components are used to predict response times and maximum attainable throughputs. These predictions are fed into the higher-level model. The process is repeated until convergence is achieved.

We can use a similar process to derive performance requirements. The higher-level model predicts the throughput requirements of the subcomponents. We can also use the higher-level model to approximately predict whether the achievable response times of the subcomponents at the offered loads are low enough to achieve the required response time of the entire system, and, if not, to determine how low the response times of the subcomponents must be to achieve the overall response time. Sufficiently low values for the response times of the subcomponents at the predicted offered throughputs constitute the performance requirements for the respective measures of the components of interest. Performance improvements must be made to subcomponents that cannot meet those requirements, or else alternative components or even a different architecture must be used instead.

We may identify the following steps to derive performance requirements for components.

The first step is to ensure that a baseline set of end-to-end performance requirements exists. If the system is a platform for service-oriented architectures (SOA) [11] and for software as a service (SaaS), a baseline set of performance requirements may be obtained by first identifying current use cases and then computing reference workloads from them. The reference workloads will constitute the baseline for performance requirements. Like all performance requirements, the baseline requirements must be traceable, testable, verifiable, and unambiguous. They must be expressed in measurable terms [4]. It is important that the baseline performance requirements include specifications regarding peak traffic and the anticipated durations of the peaks, because the onset of peaks will tax discrete object pools most heavily. If the workload has not yet been defined or is in dispute, a reference workload and a set of corresponding performance requirements should be devised as a basis for system design and testing [12].

The second step is a review of the information flow through the system for frequently occurring and computationally intensive use cases. This step should be carried out whether the system already exists or whether it is in the early stages of a software development life cycle. It is also the first step in a performance-oriented architecture review. A welcome side benefit of this step is that it may uncover performance bottlenecks that had not been thought of before, and thus trigger a modification of the architecture before any implementation or procurement is done. The links between functional requirements, end-to-end performance requirements, security, and other non-functional requirements can be explored at this time. The development of execution graphs to identify performance bottlenecks could be part of this step [14].

The third step is to develop a top-down recursive hierarchy of throughput, response time, and supporting requirements such as buffer sizes and object pool sizes for the various model components. These can be mapped to external transactions. The method is top-down because we are using end-to-end requirements to identify derived requirements. The method is recursive in the sense that we are identifying derived requirements as we proceed from one layer of components to the next. Performance requirements and resource usage demands for background activity such as database maintenance, archiving, batch jobs, or backups should be considered in this step as well. A framework for doing so could be developed using the principles in [14] as starting points. For systems in which two or more activities are launched simultaneously that must all be concluded before work can proceed to the next processing step, one must use the time to complete the longest activity to compute the holding times of any resources that are used.

5. ARCHITECTURAL IMPACTS

An architecture may have to be changed if one or more of its components cannot meet the derived performance requirements imposed upon it by traffic or by architectural characteristics. This can occur in different contexts. For example, domain-specific requirements such as those for computer-controlled systems induce performance requirements on the software systems that provide the control and on the services that support them. The combined effects of stringent response time requirements and bandwidth requirements for status information may necessitate a decentralized architecture in which control logic is deployed close to the system being controlled, while voluminous status data is moved upstream for storage and subsequent analysis. This is one of the concerns related to Fog Computing and the architecture of the Internet of Things [2]. As an architecture is formulated and the data flows between its components are modeled, a hierarchy of functional and nonfunctional requirements, including performance and security requirements, will emerge to reveal that saturation of some components is unavoidable unless the deployment scenario is changed [10]. This means that it will be necessary to iterate between (a) architectural specifications, (b) modeling to understand the performance requirements on system components, and (c) the formulation of models and new performance requirements as proposed changes the architecture are evaluated.

6. IMPACTS ON PERFORMANCE TESTING

End-to-end performance requirements are useful for planning performance tests over suitable ranges of load parameters and configurations [4]. The same holds for the derived performance requirements of software and hardware components, such as networks, object pools, and even of third party services whose function and performance are outside the control of the system owner. A third-party service might be essential to a transaction when a functional requirement or regulation demands that it be invoked before a transaction can be completed. Yet, the attainable throughputs and response times of these services might be outside the control of the owners of primary application web site, while affecting its end-to-end performance.

One element of a process for identifying derived performance requirements is somewhat similar to the process of hierarchical decomposition used to model components and their interactions with one another. It also has much in common with the combination of execution graphs and queueing models used to predict the performance of complex systems [14]. Performance test plans can be derived for system components that can be tested in environments one controls just as they would be for the whole system. Once a set of performance requirements has been derived for a system component, it should be subjected to performance tests structured in the same manner as for end-to-end performance tests. A component whose load is driven by transactions would be tested for a range of offered throughputs above and below the targets predicted by a high-level model described in [14]. Similarly, software platforms such as a messaging environment would also be tested over a variety of loads before it is incorporated into the architecture and before a commitment is made to development decisions that assume its presence [8]. Where it is not possible to verify a performance requirement that an event occur rarely, such as packet loss or the exhaustion of an object pool, tests should be conducted to ensure that the preconditions for the event to occur rarely as predicted by a model are satisfied given assumptions about the nature of the traffic and resource holding times. For example, a test would verify that the pool size is configured to N if, according to the model, N is the number needed to keep the exhaustion probability below a set level.

7. CONCLUSIONS

External performance requirements inherently impose performance requirements upon system components. The components may have structural characteristics, such as object pool sizes, that necessitate the formulation of performance requirements for loss and blocking probabilities. When these requirements cannot easily be validated by testing, because they refer to events that are intended to occur very rarely, it may be useful to verify instead that the configuration parameters correspond to those used to make a performance prediction with a model, such as a pool size or buffer size. In the foregoing, we have outlined how a hierarchical decomposition of the system could be used to model the parameters of performance requirements on components. This method is analogous to that used for approximate performance modeling. Finally, we discussed how performance test plans could be written to verify that the derived performance requirements on the components are met.

8. ACKNOWLEDGMENTS

This paper was completed while the author was a visiting professor at the University of L'Aquila.

9. REFERENCES

[1] Argent-Katwala, A., J. T. Bradley, and N.J. Dingle. Expressing performance requirements using regular expressions to specify stochastic probes over process algebra models. Proc. ACM WOSP 2004Workshop on Software and Performance) Redwood Shores, California, 49-58, 2004.

[2] Bonomi, F., R. Milito, J. Zhu, S. Addeppelli. Fog computing and its role in the internet of things. MCC'12, Proceedings of the First Edition of the MCC Workshop on Mobile Cloud Computing, 13-16, 2012.

[3] Bondi, A. B. "Best practices for writing and managing performance requirements: a tutorial." *Proc. ICPE 2012*, 2012.

[4] Bondi, A. B. Foundations of Software and System Performance Engineering: Process, Performance Modeling, Requirements, Testing, Scalability, and Practice. Addison-Wesley, 2014.

[5] Bondi, A.B., C. S. Simon, and K. A. Anderson. Bandwidth usage and network latency in a conveyor system with Ethernet-based communication between controllers. Proc. IEEE PACRIM 2005, 9-12, 2005.

[6] Chandy, K.M., U. Herzog, and L. Woo. Parametric Analysis of Queuing Networks. IBM J. of R.&D. 19 (1), 36-42, 1975.

[7] Grassi, V., and R. Mirandola. Toward automatic compositional performance analysis of component-based systems. Proc. ACM WOSP 2004Workshop on Software and Performance) Redwood Shores, California, 59-63, 2004.

[8] Lazowska, E. J., J. Zahorjan, G. S. Graham, and K. C. Sevcik. *Quantitative System Performance.* Prentice Hall, 1984. Also available online at www.cs.washington.edu/homes/lazowska/qsp .

[9] Masticola, S., A. B. Bondi, and M. Hettish. "Model-based scalability estimation in inception-phase software architecture." In *ACM/IEEE 8th International Conference on Model-Driven Engineering Languages and Systems, 2005. Lecture Notes in Computer Science* 3713, 355–366. Springer, 2005.

[10] Mylopoulos, J., L. Chung, and B. Nixon. Representing and using nonfunctional requirements: a process-oriented approach. IEEE Transactions on Software Engineering 18 (6), 483 – 497, 1992.

[11] O'Brien P. P. Merson, and L. Bass. Quality Attributes for Service-Oriented Architectures. SDSOA '07 Proceedings of the International Workshop on Systems Development in SOA Environments, 2007.

[12] Rempel, G. Defining Standards for Web Page Performance in Business Applications, Proc ICPE2015 (International Conference on Performance Engineering), 245-252, 2015.

[13] Sauer, C. and K. M. Chandy. Computer Performance Modeling. Prentice Hall, 1981.

[14] Smith, C.U. Independent General Principles for Constructing Responsive Software Systems. ACM TOCS 4(1), 1-31, 1986.

[15] Smith, Connie U., and Lloyd G. Williams. *Performance Solutions: A Practical Guide to Creating Responsive, Scalable Software*. Addison-Wesley, 2002.

Many Flies in One Swat: Automated Categorization of Performance Problem Diagnosis Results

Tobias Angerstein
University of Stuttgart
Universitätsstraße 38
Stuttgart
Germany

Dušan Okanović
University of Stuttgart
Universitätsstraße 38
Stuttgart
Germany

Christoph Heger
NovaTec Consulting GmbH
Dieselstraße 18
Leinfelden-Echterdingen,
Germany

André van Hoorn
University of Stuttgart
Universitätsstraße 38
Stuttgart
Germany

Aleksandar Kovačević
University of Novi Sad
Trg Dositeja Obradovića 6
Novi Sad
Serbia

Thomas Kluge
NovaTec Consulting GmbH
Dieselstraße 18
Leinfelden-Echterdingen,
Germany

ABSTRACT

As the importance of application performance grows in modern enterprise systems, many organizations employ application performance management (APM) tools to help them deal with potential performance problems during production. In addition to monitoring capabilities, these tools provide problem detection and alerting. In large enterprise systems these tools can report a very large number of performance problems. They have to be dealt with individually, in a time-consuming and error-prone manual process, even though many of them have a common root cause.

In this vision paper, we propose using automatic categorization for dealing with large numbers of performance problems reported by APM tools. This leads to the aggregation of reported problems, reducing the work required for resolving them. Additionally, our approach opens the possibility of extending the analysis approaches to use this information for a more efficient diagnosis of performance problems.

1. INTRODUCTION

Large enterprise systems are usually composed of a large number of services running on many computing nodes. Any performance degradation in these systems results in significant losses. There are many approaches for dealing with performance problems by performing diagnosis and root cause analysis, both before [10, 15] and after [5] the software enters production.

ICPE'17, April 22-26, 2017, L'Aquila, Italy

© 2017 ACM. ISBN 978-1-4503-4404-3/17/04...$15.00

DOI: http://dx.doi.org/10.1145/3030207.3030242

In large enterprise systems, application performance monitoring (APM) tools can report a large number of performance incidents, such as slow response times or increased resource consumption. However, the capabilities of these tools are limited to alerting and reporting performance problems [3], while only few approaches deal with diagnosing them [5]. In both cases, all performance problems are reported separately, again leaving the performance expert to deal with one problem at the time.

We propose to use well-known automatic categorization approaches [6] with the goal of reducing the number of performance problems that have to be analyzed. Problems that are similar to each other are categorized and dealt with together, reducing the effort required from the performance expert. We also propose to use optimization approaches, to improve the quality of the categorization result. The main goal of the preliminary work presented in this vision paper is the assessment of different clustering and optimization approaches in categorization of performance problems.

The remainder of this paper is organized as follows. Section 2 emphasizes the addressed problem and states our vision. Section 3 outlines our approach and shows preliminary findings. In Section 4 we discuss related work, while in Section 5 we draw the conclusions and outline the future work.

2. PROBLEM STATEMENT

In our previous work [5], we presented *diagnoseIT*—an approach for automated diagnosis of performance problems. The motivation for our work was the fact that APM practice requires enormous manual effort and expertise. As stated before, APM tools provide very little support in identifying root causes of performance problems. The manual process is often problematic for performance analysts, as most of the tasks are recurring, time-consuming, and error-prone. The goal of our work was to address this issue by formalizing APM expert knowledge. This knowledge is further used to automatically execute recurring APM tasks, such as the proper configuration of APM tools and diagnosis of performance problems, to isolate their root causes.

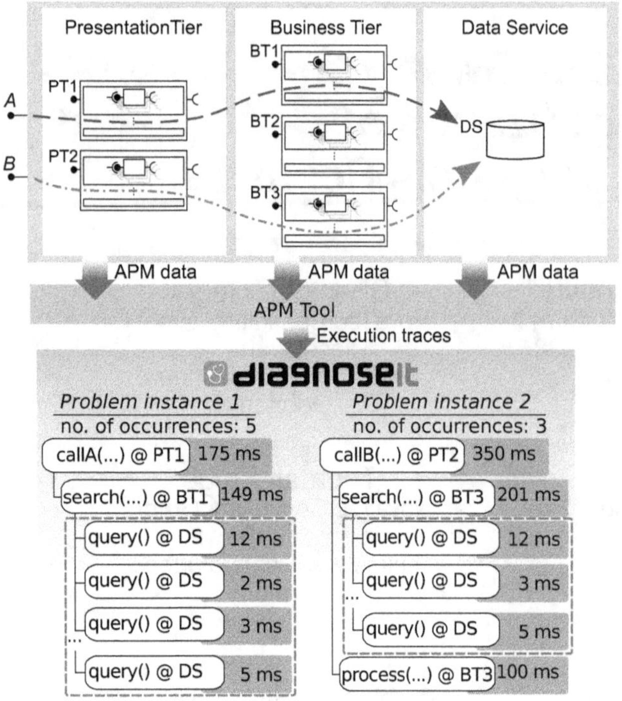

Figure 1: Example of diagnosis results in the system that provides different services.

This automation of the diagnosis process reduces the number of performance problems reported by APM tools, that usually have to be manually dealt with. The *diagnoseIT* approach will report where the problem occurred, provide an explanation why is this a problem, and recommend how it can be fixed. In the context of *diagnoseIT*, *problem instances* represent a concrete atomic performance problem, and are extracted from an execution trace [11]. They are described using the following attributes. *Entry point* is a point in the system from which the execution of the trace started. *Root cause* is a method in the execution trace that causes a performance problem. *Problem context* is a method which takes the largest amount of time in the execution trace, for example 80 % of a trace's execution time. *Node type* is a type of the node in the system, where the problem appears, e.g., *presentation tier*, *business tier*. *Exclusive duration* represents the time that was consumed by the affected method.

However, although there are many problem instances, they often have the same or a similar root cause. For example, consider a three-tiered system as shown in Fig. 1. This system provides two services—*Service A* and *Service B*. To process requests from clients to these two services, different components are used. While processing the requests to the *Service A*, the execution goes over the component *PT1* in the presentation tier to the component *BT1* in the business tier. In the end, *BT1* obtains the data from the service *DS*. Requests to *Service B* are processed in a similar fashion, this time using the components *PT2*, *BT3*, and *DS*.

Now consider that the component *DS* is improperly configured, e.g., the database connection pool is to small, causing the well-known N-Lane Bridge problem [13]. This results in slow response times of this component. This additional delay will cause the response times of *Service A* and *Service B* to increase. The APM tool that monitors the system will register this increase in response times as a performance problem, and it will pass it to *diagnoseIT*. The diagnosis for both performance problems is the same: "slow access to service *DS* due to an N-lane bridge". However, as they come from two different business transactions, these problems will be reported as separate problem instances. The basic implementation of *diagnoseIT* groups problem instances only if all of the attributes, except for the exclusive duration, are equal. As a consequence, in large enterprise systems, where the number of services and components is often very large, the number of reported problem instances can be extremely high. They would all have to be dealt with separately by the expert, although they all have the same root cause.

To tackle this issue, we propose a categorization of similar performance problems. This will reduce the amount of work performance experts have, as the problems with similar root causes become members of the same group. This will allow the performance expert to deal with them as one problem—"killing multiple flies with one swat."

In this vision paper, we present preliminary research on the choice of the automatic categorization approach. We perform a sensitivity analysis to evaluate the influence of problem instance attributes on the categorization result. The results of this evaluation are used for an optimization of the process. During the optimization, weights are assigned to problem instance attributes, which aims to improve the quality of the result.

3. CATEGORIZATION OF PROBLEM INSTANCES

An overview of our approach is presented in Fig. 2. *diagnoseIT* analyzes the data from the APM tool and generates problem instances (*PIs*). Problem instances, each represented as a vector whose features correspond to attributes of problem instances, e.g., root cause and exclusive duration, are then automatically categorized, using an unsupervised approach (Section 3.1). In this case, the resulting categories are *Category 1*, *Category 2*, and *Category n*. Along with the process of categorization, optimization is performed (Section 3.2). The initial categorization of problem instances is performed using default weights. The role of weights is to define the influence of each problem instance attribute on the categorization result. The goal of the optimization is to generate a better set of parameters for categorization by as-

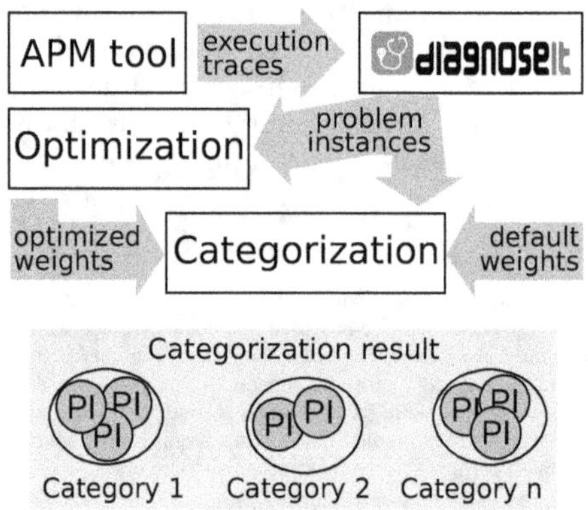

Figure 2: An overview of the approach.

signing different weights to attributes of problem instances, as these weights can be specific for each case.

Section 3.1 provides an overview of the considered automatic categorization approaches. Section 3.2 provides an overview of the optimization approaches. Preliminary findings are presented in Section 3.3.

3.1 Categorization of Problem Instances

Cluster analysis is an unsupervised approach to organizing data elements into clusters based on their proximity [6]. Contrary to supervised approaches, unsupervised approaches do not require pre-classified training data. In our case, since we want to perform the analysis automatically and do not have prior information about the data, we opt to use an unsupervised approach.

According to Jain et al. [6], there are several steps in the clustering activity. The first step is pattern representation. A problem instance can be represented as a vector $\vec{P} = (p_1, p_2, ..., p_n)$, where p_1, p_2,..., p_n are the values of the problem instance's attributes (as described in Section 2).

In the second step, proximity of patterns is defined. Our approach uses Euclidean distance because of its simplicity. However, Euclidean distance can be very sensitive to distortion, e.g., when data does not consist of compact and isolated clusters. A solution for this is to assign weights to features, so that the vector $\vec{P}$ becomes $\vec{P'} = (w_1 \cdot p_1, w_2 \cdot p_2, ..., w_n \cdot p_n)$.

The third step is the choice of the most appropriate approach for grouping of patterns, and in our case, it is dictated by the following assumptions.

Uniqueness Each problem instance represents one performance problem, so each problem instance should belong to one category only.

Independence The algorithm should be independent of the number of categories, as the potential number of categories is not known at the beginning of the process.

Performance The algorithm should be able to handle large numbers of instances in a reasonable amount of time.

We found that, among different clustering approaches [1, 6, 16], *hierarchical clustering* and *k-means algorithm* satisfy our requirements. Other approaches are not suitable because they provide multiple solutions, e.g., evolutionary clustering, or require some sort of training set, e.g., artificial neural networks.

Hierarchical clustering provides the result as a hierarchical structure. It is independent of any initial choice of clusters, and provides one solution. However, the drawback of this approach is that it can be very slow because of its high complexity.

k-means algorithm is faster than hierarchical clustering, as it has fairly low complexity. Although the number of clusters has to be known in advance, there are ways to perform the estimation [14].

The obvious advantage of using the k-means approach is its speed. On the other hand, the hierarchical approach provides results that can be useful in the diagnosis of performance problems, as problem instances can be categorized by symptoms [15].

Assessing the quality of clustering result can be done in two general ways [12]. Using the *internal quality criteria*, the clustering result is evaluated based on the data about clusters themselves, such as the distances between instances in the cluster (*Sum of Squared Errors*) and the distances between clusters (*Standard Deviation of Cluster Center Distances*). *External quality criteria* use external data, such as separately created reference clusters.

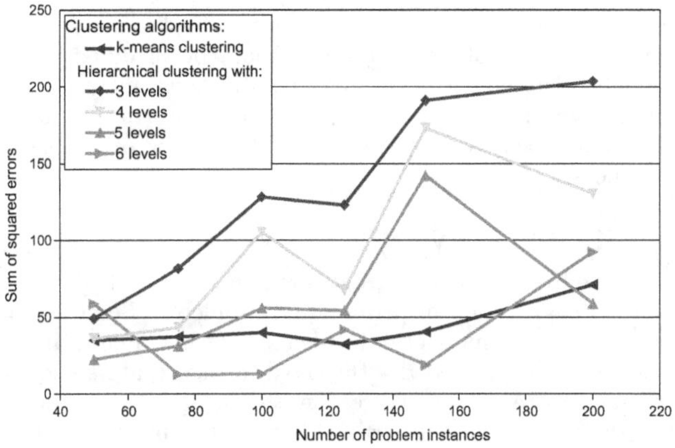

Figure 3: Sum of squared errors for k-means and hierarchical clustering algorithms, for different number of problem instances.

3.2 Optimization of Categorization

As stated before, not all problem instance attributes contribute equally to the clustering result. To assess the influence of each attribute, a calibration of parameters is needed to assign them weights.

We evaluated three approaches for optimization. The *evolutionary approach* uses standard evolutionary operators to create variations in weights. After clustering is performed with each set of weights, results are compared with a fitness function. The *hill-climbing* constantly modifies weights as long as the result is improving. The *human-in-the-loop* approach requires manual effort, instead of the fitness function, to pick the optimal result.

3.3 Preliminary Evaluation of Approaches

A preliminary evaluation of the selected approaches was performed using the data obtained by monitoring the DVD Store application and the inspectIT APM tool,[1] which was then analyzed with *diagnoseIT*. The problem instance categorization and optimization was performed using the Weka framework [4]. The experimental setup and a runnable example can be found in the supplementary material.[2]

An evaluation of the clustering results using internal quality criteria shows that the results of the k-means algorithm are better, although, in some rare cases, hierarchical clustering has some advantage (Figure 3). Similar results are obtained when analyzing the standard deviation of cluster center distances. Additionally, results show that, as expected, k-means performs faster. Although these results are as expected, hierarchical clustering proves valuable for the diagnosis of performance problems, because of the hierarchical structure of the result.

A comparison of optimization approaches has shown that the results of automatic optimization approaches almost do not bring any improvement of clustering results. However, improvement was present with the human-in-the-loop ap-

[1]http://www.inspectit.rocks/

[2]https://doi.org/10.5281/zenodo.321383

proach, which leads us to the conclusion that some knowledge about the observed system should be included. Although this seems contrary to our initial idea, inclusion of humans in this case is justified, as the performance analyst would deal with a much smaller number of problem instances.

4. RELATED WORK

To the best of our knowledge, modern APM tools [3] provide no aggregation of performance problems. Some tools report the total number of incidents, e.g., how many times response times exceeded a threshold, or aggregate some of the metrics, e.g., average response time of some method, but the correlation between incidents has to be established manually.

There are some approaches to dealing with the large number of results in load testing. Malik et al. [9] use Principal Component Analysis to reduce the performance counter data, e.g., CPU utilization, disk I/O, queues and network traffic, and identify performance gains and losses. The same group of authors [8] proposes the use of performance signatures, which aggregate the data from performance counters into smaller, more manageable sets. Further, to deal with these sets, they propose both supervised and unsupervised approaches (including k-means) to detect possible performance deviations. The reduction of data is a topic of Foo [2], where performance metrics are converted into discrete levels. However, this results in loss of information about small deviations between these levels. The approach proposed by Jiang [7] uses execution logs and performs mining of the load test data. The drawback of the approach is that it relies on the log formats, which are platform-specific.

5. CONCLUSIONS

In this paper we presented an approach to categorization of problem instances for more efficient problem diagnosis. The goal is to group similar problem instances, and reduce the effort of manually inspecting every single problem instance that is required by performance experts. Our preliminary results are promising, as the use of k-means provides a manageable number of clusters. The use of hierarchical clustering, although slower, provides results that are particularly useful for performance problem diagnosis.

Future work will deal with the extending of the problem instances, so that they include more data from the execution trace, e.g., which classes and components were involved, on which nodes the execution took place, and timing information about all segments of the execution. We think that this would allow us to detect more complex performance antipatterns that cannot be detected from a single trace. Also, we plan to investigate the influence of problem instance attributes. Furthermore, we plan to investigate other categorization approaches.

6. ACKNOWLEDGMENTS

This work is being supported by the German Federal Ministry of Education and Research (grant no. 01IS15004, *diagnoseIT*), the Research Group of the Standard Performance Evaluation Corporation (SPEC), and by the Serbian Ministry of Education (project "Infrastructure for Technology Enhanced Learning in Serbia (III47003)").

7. REFERENCES

[1] V. L. Brailovsky. A probabilistic approach to clustering. *Pattern Recogn. Lett.*, 12(4):193–198, 1991.

[2] K. C. Foo. Automated discovery of performance regressions in enterprise applications, 2011.

[3] C. Haight and F. D. Silva. Gartner's magic quadrant for application performance monitoring suites, 2016.

[4] M. Hall, E. Frank, G. Holmes, B. Pfahringer, P. Reutemann, and I. H. Witten. The weka data mining software: An update. *SIGKDD Explor. Newsl.*, 11(1):10–18, 2009.

[5] C. Heger, A. van Hoorn, D. Okanović, S. Siegl, and A. Wert. Expert-guided automatic diagnosis of performance problems in enterprise applications. In *Proc. 12th Europ. Dependable Computing Conf. (EDCC '16)*, 2016.

[6] A. K. Jain, M. N. Murty, and P. J. Flynn. Data clustering: A review. *ACM Comput. Surv.*, 31(3):264–323, 1999.

[7] Z. M. Jiang. Automated analysis of load testing results. In *Proc. 19th Int. Symposium on Soft. Testing and Analysis (ISSTA '10)*, pages 143–146, 2010.

[8] H. Malik, H. Hemmati, and A. E. Hassan. Automatic detection of performance deviations in the load testing of large scale systems. In *Proc. 35th Int. Conf. on Soft. Eng. (ICSE '13)*, pages 1012–1021, 2013.

[9] H. Malik, Z. M. Jiang, B. Adams, A. E. Hassan, P. Flora, and G. Hamann. Automatic comparison of load tests to support the performance analysis of large enterprise systems. In *Proc. 14th European Conf. on Soft. Maintenance and Reengineering (CSMR '10)*, pages 222–231, 2010.

[10] A. Nistor, P.-C. Chang, C. Radoi, and S. Lu. Caramel: Detecting and fixing performance problems that have non-intrusive fixes. In *37th Int. Conf. on Soft. Engineering (ICSE '15)*, pages 902–912, 2015.

[11] D. Okanović, A. van Hoorn, C. Heger, A. Wert, and S. Siegl. Towards performance tooling interoperability: An open format for representing execution traces. In *Proc. of the 13th European Workshop on Perf. Engineering (EPEW '16)*, pages 94–108, 2016.

[12] L. Rokach and O. Maimon. Clustering methods. In *Data Mining and Knowledge Discovery Handbook*, pages 321–352. Springer, 2005.

[13] C. U. Smith and L. G. Williams. Software performance antipatterns. In *Proc. 2nd Int. Workshop on Soft. and Performance (WOSP '00)*, pages 127–136, 2000.

[14] R. Tibshirani, G. Walther, and T. Hastie. Estimating the number of clusters in a dataset via the gap statistic. *Journal of the Royal Statistical Society Series B (Statistical Methodology)*, 63:411–423, 2000.

[15] A. Wert, J. Happe, and L. Happe. Supporting swift reaction: Automatically uncovering performance problems by systematic experiments. In *Proc. 2013 Int. Conf.on Soft. Engineering (ICSE '13)*, pages 552–561, 2013.

[16] C. T. Zahn. Graph-theoretical methods for detecting and describing gestalt clusters. *IEEE Trans. Comput.*, 20(1):68–86, 1971.

Performance Analysis of Applications in the Context of Architectural Rooflines

Boyana Norris
University of Oregon
norris@cs.uoregon.edu

Wyatt Spear
University of Oregon
wspear@cs.uoregon.edu

Allen Malony
University of Oregon
malony@cs.uoregon.edu

ABSTRACT

Intuitive visual representations of architecture capabilities and the performance of applications are critical to enabling effective performance analysis, which in turn guides optimizations. The Roofline Model and its derivatives provide such an intuitive representation of the best achievable performance on a given architecture. The Roofline Toolkit project is a collaboration among researchers at Argonne National Laboratory, Lawrence Berkeley National Laboratory, and the University of Oregon and consists of three principal components: hardware characterization, software characterization, and data manipulation, which includes a visualization interface. These components address the different aspects of performance data acquisition and manipulation required for performance analysis, modeling and optimization of applications. In this paper we introduce an implementation of the third component, a system for visualizing roofline charts and managing roofline performance analysis data. We demonstrate analysis of an application use case within this framework and outline future directions for this type of performance analysis and visualization.

Categories and Subject Descriptors

H.4 [**Information Systems Applications**]: Miscellaneous; D.2.8 [**Software Engineering**]: Metrics—*complexity measures, performance measures*

Keywords

performance, analysis, visualization

1. INTRODUCTION

The Roofline model [17] enables programmers to visualize the performance potential of algorithms by introducing a simple way to quantify the computation's locality and parallelism and present them in the context of a given architecture's capabilities. Until recently Roofline models were typically laboriously created through (1) collection of hardware performance data, e.g., with micro benchmarks; (2) manual code analysis to determine the arithmetic intensity of the algorithm(s) being studied; and (3) visualizing both the architectural rooflines and the kernel's expected performance under different optimization assumptions. Automating most of this process has been the goal of the Roofline Toolkit Project. The development of portable microbenchmarks that automate the first step is discussed in [13]. In this paper we first introduce the current state of the data representation and visualization infrastructure required to automate the third step. The main contribution is a *usable software framework* for generating and visualizing architectural rooflines. We also discuss future research on automation performance bottleneck analysis and the generation of *accurate, fine-grained, understandable* performance models that can significantly improve the current state of the art in terms of precision, usability, and efficiency.

ICPE'17, April 22-26, 2017, L'Aquila, Italy
© 2017 ACM. ISBN 978-1-4503-4404-3/17/04...$15.00
DOI: http://dx.doi.org/10.1145/3030207.3030232

2. BACKGROUND

We briefly overview the roofline model and the tools that were leveraged in our research and implementations to date.

2.1 Roofline Analysis

For any machine model, we can evaluate the upper bound on performance by using the roofline model introduced by Williams et al [17]. Given the arithmetic intensity of an algorithm, the roofline model defines an upper limit on kernel performance P_k with the equation, $P_k = minP_f, BA_i$ where P_f is the peak hardware floating-point performance, B is peak bandwidth, and A_i is the arithmetic intensity, typically expressed as the ratio of floating-point operations to bytes transferred to/from memory.

The Roofline model and its extensions (e.g., for energy [9]) provide a compact representation of the *architectural* capabilities as a context that enables visualization of the current and *potential* performance of a computational kernel within its algorithmic and architectural constraints. As operational intensity increases memory bandwidth's limiting influence decreases until the flat, peak bound of processor GFLOPS is reached. Placement of compute kernels on the graph indicates their relationship with the system's theoretical peak performance given their operational intensity.

2.2 Eclipse

Eclipse [1] is a popular and extensible software development platform. The default set of plugins is designed for Java development, but the Eclipse community has provided support for other languages including C/C++ and Fortran. Support for high performance computing has also been provided via the Parallel Tools Platform (PTP) [2]. The portability and extensibility of the Eclipse platform motivated our choice to use it as the basis of the Roofline visualization framework.

3. CURRENT STATE

In this section we discuss the current state of the ongoing efforts to automate performance analysis and modeling in the context of architectural rooflines.

3.1 Visualization Implementation

The initial roofline visualizations were implemented using general-purpose scientific charting tools such as Gnuplot [18]. This was adequate for developing and testing the roofline system and and for the performance analysis activities of experts. It was clear, however, that general adoption of the roofline system would benefit greatly from a simpler automated means of visualizing the performance data. Moreover, given the intended major use case of comparing the performance of multiple applications or functions to establish best-case performance behavior with respect to the roofline model, a framework that allows rapid and easy analysis would be of benefit even to experts with other visualization techniques at their disposal.

We implemented the roofline visualization system using JavaFX [3]. The new graphing functionality provided in the JavaFX API allows reasonably sophisticated visualizations without relying on external libraries as long as a relatively recent version of Java is available.

The data for visualizing Roofline architectural profiles is generated by a collection of portable micro benchmarks [13]. By default, a single set of architectural roofline data is displayed. Multiple roofline datasets may be loaded simultaneously, either from the local filesystem or from a remote repository enabling rapid switching of views or overlaying rooflines for comparison. The intersection points and the inflection points on the roofline chart may be selected to display the specific recorded metric values.

Figure 1 shows the rooflines generated for the NERSC Cray XC30 Edison supercomputer[1]. The left side of Figure 1 shows just the non-interactive architectural roofline plot generated by the ERT [13]. The top GFLOP/s rate achieved by the micro-benchmark data is indicated with the top orange line. The right side of Figure 1 is a screenshot of the interactive roofline visualization Eclipse-based tool we developed, showing the arithmetic intensity of the functions in the MiniFE proxy application [12] that take a significant portion of the execution time. In some cases lines corresponding to different hardware components overlap. Different rooflines reflect peak capabilities of different hardware components with respect to the operational intensity (x-axis) of the computation. We can also visualize different versions of the same functions in a single plot, which enables study of the effects of optimizations on the operational intensity and performance.

At present application developers can evaluate their application performance at the level of individual routines with respect to the architectural roofline models of systems where it is being or will be run. This will provide valuable insight into the question of attainable performance gains. Application performance profiles stored in TAUdb databases are searchable from the Eclipse interface and plotted on the chart of the selected roofline. The Eclipse UI supports selection of code elements from the project source tree which will facilitate examination of the performance of specific routines with respect to the architecture roofline. This requires accurate measurement of GFLOPS/byte when generating application profiles. Collecting this data is not trivial, as shown in [16], but a capability we hope will be provided in future releases of TAU and other performance analysis systems and then integrated into the Roofline visualization framework.

3.2 Roofline Data Management

There are two primary elements to roofline visualization data. The systems where the roofline is being modeled are typified by the benchmarked upper bounds on memory throughput and computational intensity. These values and metric names are stored as name-value pairs. Memory throughput values are typically subdivided into the FLOPs per byte capacity supported by the different cache layers. Additional metrics representing the technical specifications may be included along with the empirically collected data. The simplicity of these data accommodate a wide range of data presentation options. We have selected JSON [4] for roofline data storage because it is simple to work with and there is strong support for it in Java and Python.

In addition to the core metrics of the architectural and application performance data, the data format must allow integration of metadata for systems and experimental trials. This is necessary to establish the provenance of collected data, to avoid duplicate trials and to allow searching and comparison of task specific data from what may be a very large general collection of system models. A robust metadata system also supports more advanced analytical features under development, such as comparison between rooflines of different systems or between the same system with altered software or hardware parameters.

The nature of roofline analysis lends itself to central, publicly available data repositories. Because the system benchmarks are useful to all developers working in the same environment it makes sense to make these a common resource. Motivated by this community oriented use case, the roofline visualization system supports accessing roofline data from a remote repository. A roofline data library is being assembled, hosted by the University of Oregon. As of this writing it is organized using simple name based selection of rooflines from the available systems. It is also possible to use metadata values as criteria to search the repository.

4. FUTURE DIRECTIONS

While viewing arithmetic intensity at the level of function and loop granularity is a useful capability, all current tools *do not* provide a comprehensive and usable modeling infrastructure. In this section we discuss outstanding research and implementation challenges.

4.1 Performance Experiments, Analysis, and Model Generation

Generating fine-grain performance models automatically is essential for fast and accurate identification of sources of

[1]Edison has 5576 nodes, each with two 12-core Intel "Ivy Bridge" processor at 2.4 GHz and 64 GB DDR3 1866 MHz memory, 460.8 Gflops/node peak per node.

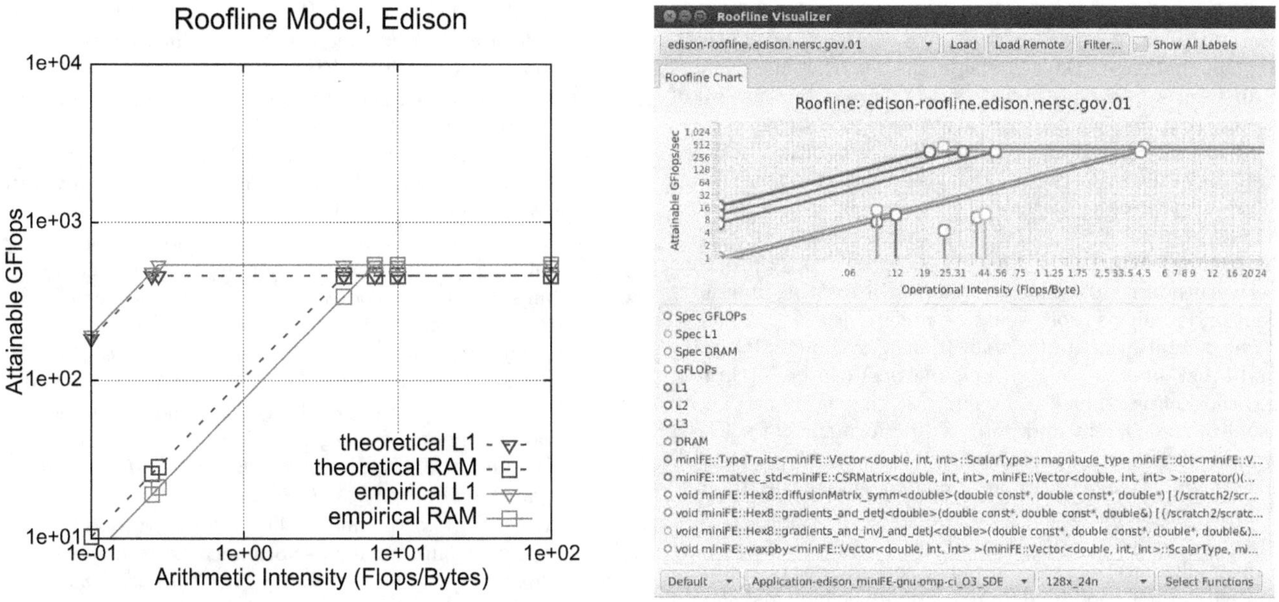

Figure 1: Left: Architectural roofline plot for Edison, a Cray XC30 supercomputer. Nodes are 12-core Intel "Ivy Bridge" processors (2.4 GHz) with 64 GB memory. Right: Application analysis for the MiniFE mini-app [12].

performance degradation and strategies to optimize the corresponding computations. For example, Calotoiu et al. [8, 7] show that it is possible to generate scalability models from empirical data. These models require only wall-clock time but even this relatively simple measurement involves running an application at varying scales. Selecting problem sizes for each experiment are typically user-defined tasks, which can be both error-prone (because of lack of complete knowledge on how to scale problem sizes in complex codes) and potentially wasteful (e.g., running too many large-scale experiments that are not necessary for constructing the model).

When modeling single-node performance, a number of additional complications arise. Consider estimating arithmetic intensity as defined in the roofline model, which requires measurement of floating-point operations and main memory traffic. Even homogeneous platforms do not provide consistent interfaces for obtaining accurate measurements of these quantities. On each platform, the user must learn how to install and use a mix of tools with different interfaces and information granularities. In some cases, there are no hardware counters for the quantity of interest (e.g., floating-point operations on Intel Haswell servers). The alternatives are manual estimates for time-intensive portions of the application (an approach taken by some HPC numerical packages such as PETSc [5, 6], or using static source code analysis to estimate such quantities [15, 11]. The static approach allows the generation of more abstract models, which can then be modified by the user to reflect planned or necessary optimizations, with the resulting performance visualized in the context of architectural rooflines.

Arithmetic intensity is just one way of viewing the efficiency of computations. Other metrics of interest include energy, or domain-specific quantities such as number of vertices or edges processed per second in graph computations. When used in the context of the architectural roofline, arithmetic intensity or a similar measure of *useful work* is a good first step in identifying functions that should be targeted for optimizations. Arithmetic intensity by itself, however, does not provide information to inform the optimization decisions, e.g., are the GFLOP/s lower because a significant loop was not vectorized or because of conflict misses in a multithreaded computation? To identify root causes, more detailed (automated) measurements are required. Again, the lack of common interfaces and tool infrastructure across platforms makes this a challenging and time-consuming task. Increasing heterogeneity at node level is also not addressed by existing measurement approaches – users are expected to use separate tools for CPUs and GPUs. Merging data from different tools is also non-trivial because of differences in sampling rates or types of measurements available. Our Autoperf framework [10] implements some initial steps toward automating complete performance modeling (and eventually optimization) workflows. Much remains to be done before performance experiment automation is widely available in support of performance analysis and model generation on modern heterogeneous platforms.

So far we have considered mostly empirical performance analysis and modeling. Because of the challenges in obtaining accurate measurements across platforms, we believe that static program analysis will play an increasingly important role in the analysis and model generation process. For example, we are pursuing static approaches that consider both source code and binary analysis (on both CPUs and GPUs) to generate models for metrics such as arithmetic intensity.

4.1.1 Visualization

The roofline visualization system remains under development and there are a number of features we anticipate adding as the project proceeds. These will dovetail with the continuing development of the roofline data collection and analytical utilities also under development.

Comparison between systems and between multiple sets of application trial data within a single chart will be useful in performance engineering operations that incorporate roofline data. Devising good visual representations that are informative rather than cluttered and confusing has been an ongoing challenge. Beyond single metrics, the effectiveness of different approaches to 2-D or 3-D representations [14] of multidimensional data merit future investigation.

We are also planning to increase the integration between the Eclipse framework and the visualization system. Enabling control of performance measurements, analysis and models from within the IDE is a natural next step. Rather than reimplementing existing tools, leveraging approaches (e.g., Autoperf [10]) that interface with existing measurement and analysis tools would be preferable.

The computation and visualization of arithmetic intensity (and other emerging algorithmic metrics) can be integrated into the Eclipse source code views, so that users can easily visualize the current and potential performance of selected computations as they are developing them. To accomplish this we will implement two main components of the Roofline Toolkit—developer-aided static model generation and empirical performance data integration.

In its ultimate form the visualization system, in conjunction with other roofline data collection mechanisms, should enable system designers to easily compare and typify fundamental performance characteristics for proposed and existing hardware, help software developers to explain and tune the performance of their computational kernels in a hardware-aware fashion and encourage sharing and use of system and application level performance data.

5. CONCLUSION

We have introduced a new Eclipse-based performance visualization system that shows loop-level performance information in the context of architectural rooflines. The generation of the hardware roofline profiles is fully automated. Most of the application performance data gathering on Intel architectures is also automated, as is the computation of the derived metrics required for displaying performance in the context of the rooflines. We then discuss the ways in which this framework can be extended to enable more complete automation of performance measurement, analysis, and model generation on modern heterogeneous platforms.

Acknowledgments

This work was supported in part by DOE Grant DE-SC0004510.

6. REFERENCES

[1] Eclipse IDE. http://www.eclipse.org. Accessed: 2014-10-20.

[2] Eclipse Parallel Tools Platform. http://www.eclipse.org/ptp/. Accessed: 2014-10-20.

[3] JavaFX. http://www.oracle.com/technetwork/java/javase/overview/javafx-overview-2158620.html. Accessed: 2014-10-20.

[4] JSON. http://www.json.org. Accessed: 2014-10-20.

[5] S. Balay, J. Brown, K. Buschelman, W. D. Gropp, D. Kaushik, M. G. Knepley, L. C. McInnes, B. F. Smith, and H. Zhang. PETSc Web page. http://www.mcs.anl.gov/petsc, 2016.

[6] S. Balay, W. D. Gropp, L. C. McInnes, and B. F. Smith. Efficient management of parallelism in object oriented numerical software libraries. In E. Arge, A. M. Bruaset, and H. P. Langtangen, editors, *Modern Software Tools in Scientific Computing*, pages 163–202. Birkhäuser Press, 1997.

[7] A. Calotoiu, D. Beckingsale, C. W. Earl, T. Hoefler, I. Karlin, M. Schulz, and F. Wolf. Fast Multi-Parameter Performance Modeling. Oct. 2016. Accepted at IEEE International Conference on Cluster Computing (Cluster'16).

[8] A. Calotoiu, T. Hoefler, M. Poke, and F. Wolf. Using automated performance modeling to find scalability bugs in complex codes. In *Proceedings of the International Conference on High Performance Computing, Networking, Storage and Analysis*, SC '13, pages 45:1–45:12, New York, NY, USA, 2013. ACM.

[9] J. W. Choi, D. Bedard, R. Fowler, and R. Vuduc. A roofline model of energy. In *Parallel Distributed Processing (IPDPS), 2013 IEEE 27th International Symposium on*, pages 661–672, May 2013.

[10] X. Dai, B. Norris, and A. D. Malony. Autoperf: Workflow support for performance experiments. In *Proceedings of the Workshop on Challenges in Performance Methods for Software Development (WOSP-C'15), Austin, Texas*, 1 2015.

[11] L. Djoudi, D. Barthou, P. Carribault, C. Lemuet, J.-T. Acquaviva, , and W. Jalby. MAQAO: Modular assembler quality analyzer and optimizer for Itanium 2. In *Proceedings of the Workshop on Explicitly Parallel Instruction Computing Techniques, Santa Jose, California, March*, 2005.

[12] M. A. Heroux, D. W. Doerer, P. S. Crozier, J. M. Willenbring, H. C. Edwards, A. Williams, M. Rajan, E. R. Keiter, H. K. Thornquist, and R. W. Numrich. Improving performance via mini-applications. Technical Report SAND2009-5574, Sandia National Laboratories, Sept. 2009.

[13] Y. Lo, S. Williams, B. Van Straalen, T. Ligocki, M. Cordery, N. Wright, M. Hall, and L. Oliker. *Roofline Model Toolkit: A practical tool for architectural and program analysis*, volume 8966 of *Lecture Notes in Computer Science*, pages 129–148. Springer Verlag, 2015.

[14] O. G. Lorenzo, T. F. Pena, J. C. Cabaleiro, J. C. Pichel, and F. F. Rivera. 3dyrm: a dynamic roofline model including memory latency information. *The Journal of Supercomputing*, 70(2):696–708, 2014.

[15] S. H. K. Narayanan, B. Norris, and P. D. Hovland. Generating performance bounds from source code. In *Proceedings of the First International Workshop on Parallel Software Tools and Tool Infrastructures (PSTI 2010)*, 9 2010.

[16] G. Ofenbeck, R. Steinmann, V. C. Cabezas, D. G. Spampinato, and M. PÃijschel. Applying the roofline model. In *Proceedings of the IEEE International Symposium on Performance Analysis of Systems and Software (ISPASS)*, pages 76–85, 2014.

[17] S. Williams, A. Waterman, and D. Patterson. Roofline: An insightful visual performance model for multicore architectures. *Commun. ACM*, 52(4):65–76, 2009.

[18] T. Williams, C. Kelley, and many others. Gnuplot 4.4: an interactive plotting program. http://gnuplot.sourceforge.net/, March 2010.

Performance and Dependability Evaluation of Distributed Event-based Systems: A Dynamic Code-injection Approach

[Work-in-Progress Paper]

Saleh Mohamed, Matthew Forshaw, Nigel Thomas
School of Computing Science, Newcastle University, Newcastle upon Tyne, UK
{s.mohamed,matthew.forshaw,nigel.thomas}@ncl.ac.uk

Andrew Dinn
Red Hat UK Ltd, UK
a.dinn@redhat.com

ABSTRACT

Distributed stream processing and event-based systems are an increasingly critical component in contemporary large-scale data processing applications, and are often subject to strict latency and reliability requirements. However, to achieve scalability demands, they are often deployed on distributed clusters of heterogeneous nodes, causing unpredictable runtime performance and complex fault characteristics.

The behaviour of these systems is poorly understood, and existing performance and dependability evaluation techniques are ill-equipped to handle the challenges introduced by the complex and distributed nature of event-based systems.

We develop a dynamic code-injection approach to evaluate the performance and dependability of stream processing and event-based systems. Our approach supports fine-grained instrumentation of applications and their runtime infrastructure, and the dynamic injection of code mutations and faults into a production system at runtime. We demonstrate the proposed approach by performing instrumentation and code injection on a distributed Apache Spark cluster.

Keywords

Event-based systems; performance; dependability

1. INTRODUCTION

Event-based systems and complex event processing (CEP) engines are an increasingly critical component in modern large-scale software deployments, e.g., Internet of Things (IoT). In order to make optimal deployment and resource management decisions, it is necessary to gain an understanding of the performance of systems. However, the performance and dependability characteristics of these systems are not well understood [6]. Furthermore, there are compelling scenarios to motivate autonomic operation and fault recovery of event-based systems [13, 3], but there is a reluctance – particularly within industrial applications – to add complexity to fault resolution scenarios. There is the belief that software will be buggy, especially under error cases and code which is executed infrequently.

Existing approaches to evaluate event-based systems have focused on the instrumentation of applications or infrastructure, but few have the ability to capture the interactions between the software deployment and its runtime environment [16]. Benchmarks for stream processing systems are emerging, but these generally only consider application-level metrics [7], and not infrastructure issues such as resource utilisation and energy consumption. Preliminary efforts are emerging to apply code injection techniques within stream processing systems [17], though these focus on instrumentation only, rather than code and fault injection.

Our work was motivated by the limitations of existing fault injection approaches, limiting their usefulness to evaluate the dependability of distributed event-based systems. Firstly, many approaches require the re-compilation of application code. Secondly, there is limited flexibility in when faults can be injected in the application lifecycle. Finally, coordinating complex test scenarios enacted across multiple nodes in distributed clusters is an open challenge.

We present an approach which addresses these key challenges to evaluate the performance and dependability, using our non-invasive dynamic code injection tool, Byteman [4]. Our approach allows a practitioner to instrument an application, and develop code injection rules with only the knowledge of the public interface of the application, and without the need to adapt or re-compile the application. We can *'attach'* our tool to a deployment at runtime, and dynamically load and unload our rules during the execution of the system under evaluation. Our system facilitates greater test coverage. Finally, our approach allows programmatic specification of complex fault scenarios, across distributed nodes.

The remainder of this paper is organised as follows. In Section 2 we present our architecture, and describe how code and fault injection rules are specified in the Byteman language. In Section 3 we demonstrate the applicability of our approach in performance evaluation and dependability as-

ICPE'17, April 22 - 26, 2017, L'Aquila, Italy

ISBN 978-1-4503-4404-3/17/04...$15.00

DOI: http://dx.doi.org/10.1145/3030207.3030245

sessment of an Apache Spark cluster. We present related work in Section 4. Finally, in Section 5 we provide concluding remarks and present future challenges and research directions.

2. ARCHITECTURE

We present our system architecture in Figure 1. This shows a typical deployment of our approach to add dynamic code injection to an Apache Spark cluster distributed across remotely running Java Virtual Machines (JVMs). We evaluate this representative use case in Section 3.

Fault Load: We adopt a fault load which describes the types of faults experienced on the system under test [9] and runtime environment [16]. We can also use metrics obtained from production deployments to inform our fault load through workload characterisation.

Byteman Rules: The defined 'Fault Load' acts as the basis when developing a Byteman ruleset which captures these failure types, targeting components of the runtime system to recreate these faults.

Test Scenario: One or more rules may be then composed, alongside timing information and other required metadata, to construct a test scenario.

Test Coordinator: Our tool is capable of ingesting a test scenario definition, automatically deploying the test infrastructure [?] and enacting code injection through the Thermostat Client, which communicates over a Command Channel with Thermostat agents on each node.

On each compute node we instrument, we run two *'agents'*, the *'Thermostat agent'* and *'Byteman agent'*.

Byteman Agent: Byteman [4] is an open-source dynamic Java bytecode manipulation tool, facilitating code injection into running JVM processes.

Thermostat Agent: Thermostat [2] is an open-source instrumentation and monitoring tool, facilitating performance monitoring covering various aspects of the operating system and fine-grained JVM behaviour. Thermostat is responsible for instructing Byteman to perform code injection into a JVM, specified by a *'rule'* (Section 2.1).

Storage Layer: Logging data and metrics – whether emitted by Byteman rules or obtained from OS/JVM processes – are aggregated via the Thermostat agent and saved to a MongoDB persistent store.

2.1 Code injection with Byteman Rules

Byteman rules are expressed as Event-Condition-Action rules (ECA-rules) [5], describing ***where*** during application execution a side-effect should occur, ***whether*** the side-effect should happen or not, and ***what*** the side effect should be.

Events: A rule specifies the `CLASS` and `METHOD` the rule targets, as well as the stage in the method call lifecyle the rule applies (e.g. `ON EXIT, AT INVOKE`). A location specifier (e.g. `AT ENTRY`, `AT EXIT` or `AT LINE`) specifies the trigger point within the target method call.

Condition: Rules can be enacted conditionally, based on boolean rule expressions.

Action: POJO code and/or Byteman built-in calls supporting complex thread coordination, exception raising.

We explore each aspect of an ECA-rule, with respect to a representative example of a Byteman rule in Listing 1. This rule instruments Spark batches. The rule is enacted `AT EXIT` for the `onBatchCompleted` method within the `spark.JobListener` class, and uses `BIND` to access a number of instance variables within the class. Each time the rule is triggered, the rule dispatches these bound values – in JSON format to the MongoDB persistent store – using the `send(...)` method of the Thermostat `HELPER` class.

Listing 1: Exemplar Byteman Rule

```
RULE Instrumentation of Spark job batches
CLASS spark.JobListener
METHOD onBatchCompleted
AT EXIT
HELPER org.jboss.byteman.thermostat.helper.ThermostatHelper
BIND timestamp = $time,
     input_size = $inputSize,
     processing_time = $processingTime,
     scheduling_delay = $schedulingDelay,
     total_delay = $totalDelay
IF TRUE
DO
   debug("Sending batch metrics to thermostat");
   send("map", new Object[] { "timestamp", timestamp,
                         "batch_size", input_size,
                         "processing_time", processing_time,
                         "scheduling_delay", scheduling_delay,
                         "total delay", total_delay});
ENDRULE
```

2.2 Rule classification

Byteman rules may be written to target components at different levels of the applications and infrastructure.

1) Operating system (OS) and environment issues can be targeted, e.g. node crash, network connectivity, resource contention, launching of external processes leading to interference, etc.

2) We can explore the impact of JVM-specific issues e.g. Stop-the-World (STW) garbage collection, memory leaks, thread deadlocks, etc.

3) Issues arising related to the particular event-based system under test, e.g. Spark-specific exceptions and faults.

4) Finally, we consider domain-specific faults concerning the user's application, e.g. performance degradation. At each level, we consider two broad classes of *rule*:.

Instrumentation: Collection of metrics not otherwise exposed by the system. We can optionally share state between Byteman rules at runtime, such that the enactment of a rule be conditional on global system state; e.g. a rule could be triggered when a tuple arrives to a worker node with high CPU load.

Fault Injection: A class of rule to bring about a failure of a component, representative of a real-world fault. For example, one may trigger node crashes, deadlocks, or impose probabilistic delays to processing (based on models derived from empirical evaluation of production systems, e.g. [11]).

2.3 Coordinated failure scenarios

Many previous works focus on *'independent'* failures, namely those affecting an individual node. In the context of distributed event-based systems, we must consider scenarios exhibiting inter-cluster fault propagation, where a fault on a particular node has a knock-on impact across the cluster.

A significant contribution of our approach is to offer programmatic specification of distributed test scenarios. These scenarios control the automatic provisioning of runtime infrastructure, automated code injection allowing multiple Byteman rules to be injected across nodes in a cluster. This allows us to enact complex test scenarios to evaluate emergent

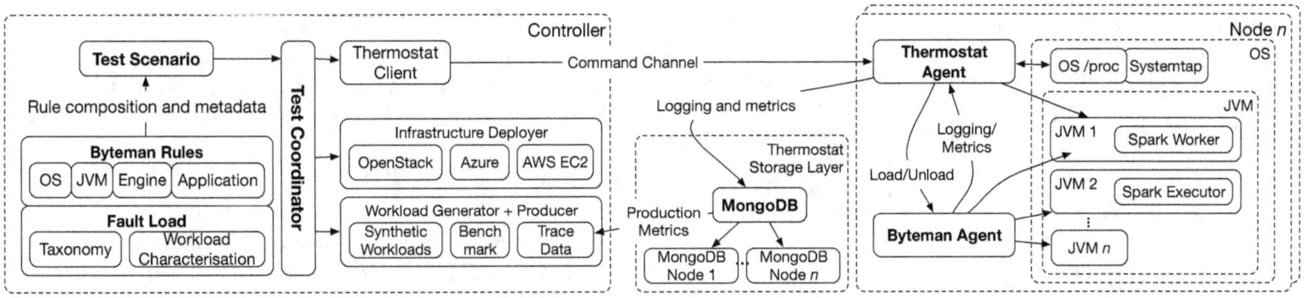

Figure 1: System architecture to support code-injection of event-based and stream processing systems.

behaviours across distributed clusters, e.g. fault propagation. This work is closely aligned with our related research concerning the automated deployment of distributed event-based infrastructure to support IoT applications [14].

3. EVALUATION

Fault-injection approaches are often evaluated in the literature according to the tradeoff between three key requirements; *representativeness*, *usability* and *efficiency* [15]. Here we demonstrate our approach satisfies each of these, and is a suitable option for evaluating event-based systems.

Representativeness: The representativeness of a fault injection approach describes the realism of the tests, in relation to the types of faults encountered by the system and its environment. Our ability to compose rules together allows us to explore sophisticated test scenarios representative of those specified in *fault loads* for stream based systems.

Usability: Our developed tool is portable, and can be used with any stream processing system with little modification. Our simple rule specification, as highlighted in Section 2.1, allows rules to be written for any application whose Java public interface is known. In Section 3.2 we show our tool to be minimally intrusive, with the loading and unloading of our rulesets having negligible impact on the target workload and its underlying runtime infrastructure.

Efficiency: We lower experimental effort by offering automated test infrastructure deployment and tooling support for runtime injection, and we offer highly targeted fault injection through expressive rule language (Section 2.1).

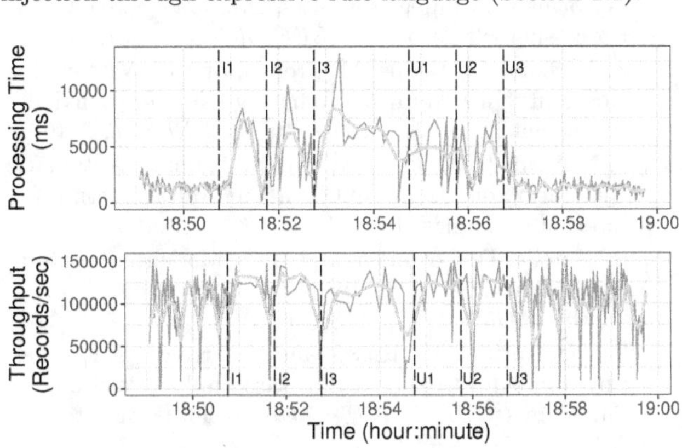

Figure 2: Code injection of probabilistic processing delays in a distributed Apache Spark cluster.

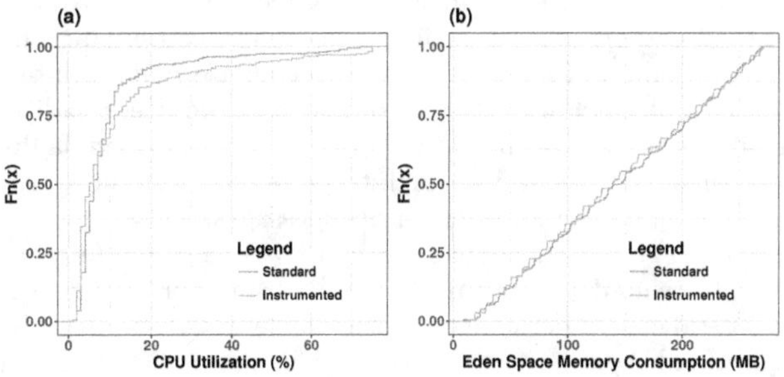

Figure 3: Injection overhead (a) CPU, (b) Memory

3.1 Example scenario

We demonstrate the effectiveness of our approach in experiments using Apache Spark [1]. We use a cluster of Microsoft Azure `DS1_V2 standard` virtual machines (1 core, 3.5GB disk space and 7GB of RAM) running Ubuntu 14.04. The cluster consists of one single-node Kafka server, one Spark master, and three Spark workers.

The workload is a Spark streaming word count application where a Kafka producer publishes lines of text into a Kafka server. The streaming application consumes the lines of text using the Spark-Kafka connector and performs a series of Spark built-in RDD transformations (`map`, `mapToPair` and `reduceBykey`) to generate the word counts.

Due to limiting space, we evaluate a single use case; injection and removal of tuple processing delays on our three Spark workers. Figure 2 shows the results of our experimentation on application throughput and processing time, where the red lines are the actual time series and the green lines represent the moving averages. The annotation lines mark the time when delaying faults were introduced to the system. At points *I1*, *I2* and *I3* we inject a 10ms processing delay on every 1000th message processed, for worker node one, two and three respectively. We see this leads to increased processing time, and degraded throughput. At points *U1*, *U2* and *U3* we unload the rules from worker node one, two and three respectively. It can be seen that processing time and throughput recover to their original level.

3.2 Performance Evaluation

In order for performance and dependability measurements to be meaningful, we must demonstrate that the presence of our instrumentation does not perturb the normal operation of the system under evaluation.

Here we evaluate the impact of the dynamic loading and

unloading of Byteman rules into a production Apache Spark cluster. We collect two ten-minute performance traces from a node in a Spark cluster, with and without code injection. Figure 3(a) shows the empirical CDF plot of CPU load, while Figure 3(b) shows JVM Eden Space Memory Consumption. In both cases, we observe that our code-injection approach has negligible impact on host resource utilisation, giving us confidence our approach is non-intrusive.

4. RELATED WORK

Lopez *et al.* [12] explore the performance of Apache Storm, Apache Flink, and Apache Spark Streaming, with respect to message processing performance in the presence of node failures. The authors provide experimental results from a testbed comprising eight virtual machines, comprising one master node and eight workers. To emulate node failures, one virtual machine is turned off. Meanwhile, Heorhiadi *et al.* [8] propose Gremlin, an approach to evaluating fault-tolerance of microservice architectures, through network-level manipulation of inter-service messages.

Vögler *et al.* [17] demonstrate the use of the AspectJ aspect-oriented programming (AOP) framework to instrument and collect performance measurements from an Apache Spark and Apache Storm cluster. This research focuses on the instrumentation of production stream processing systems, while our research furthers the application of fault injection in event-based systems, by supporting dynamic injection of faults and automated management of the testing lifecycle, including infrastructure provisioning.

Hummer *et al.* [9] present a taxonomy of classes of faults encountered in event-based systems such as, event stream processing (ESP) and complex event processing (CEP) systems. Pietrantuono *et al.* [16] present a characterisation of software faults arising from the runtime environment. Both of these efforts are complementary to ours. Their findings can inform our *'Fault load'* and our derived Byteman rules.

Gupta *et al.* [7] present BFT-Bench for evaluating Byzantine Fault Tolerance algorithms using fault injection. Jacques-Silva *et al.* [10] consider a fault-injection approach to evaluate the viability of Partial Fault Tolerance (PFT) for a financial application running within IBM System S. Their approach involves developing a fault injection operator (FIOP) which emulates a particular faulty operator behaviour. The application is then recompiled, with these faulty operators placed directly infront of the *'target'* operator.

5. CONCLUSION

In this paper we have shown how a dynamic code injection approach can be used to instrument distributed event-based systems for performance and dependability evaluation. Our approach provides practitioners with a usable set of tools which address many common issues inhibiting automated and holistic performance and dependability evaluation of event-based systems. We contribute our source code to the community as open-source through Github[1].

Our future work will focus on a full-scale evaluation of our approach, developing further tooling support, enabling practitioners to model more sophisticated failure scenarios.

[1]https://github.com/ncl-IoT/Fault-Injection

6. ACKNOWLEDGMENTS

This work was supported by the Engineering and Physical Sciences Research Council, Centre for Doctoral Training in Cloud Computing for Big Data [grant number EP/L015358/1].

7. REFERENCES

[1] Apache Spark. http://spark.apache.org/.

[2] Thermostat. http://icedtea.classpath.org/thermostat/.

[3] T. Cooper. Proactive Scaling of Distributed Stream Processing Work Flows Using Workload Modelling: Doctoral Symposium. In *DEBS'16*, pages 410–413. ACM, 2016.

[4] A. E. Dinn. Flexible, Dynamic Injection of Structured Advice Using Byteman. In *Proceedings of the Tenth International Conference on Aspect-Oriented software Development companion*, pages 41–50. ACM, 2011.

[5] K. R. Dittrich, S. Gatziu, and A. Geppert. The Active Database Management System Manifesto: A Rulebase of ADBMS Features. In *RIDS*. Springer, 1995.

[6] M. Forshaw, N. Thomas, and A. S. McGough. The Case for Energy-Aware Simulation and Modelling of Internet of Things (IoT). In *ENERGY-SIM*, 2016.

[7] D. Gupta, L. Perronne, and S. Bouchenak. BFT-Bench: A Framework to Evaluate BFT Protocols. In *ACM/SPEC ICPE '16*, 2016.

[8] V. Heorhiadi, S. Rajagopalan, H. Jamjoom, M. K. Reiter, and V. Sekar. Gremlin: Systematic Resilience Testing of Microservices. In *IEEE ICDCS*, 2016.

[9] W. Hummer, C. Inzinger, P. Leitner, B. Satzger, and S. Dustdar. Deriving a Unified Fault Taxonomy for Event-Based Systems. In *ACM DEBS*, 2012.

[10] G. Jacques-Silva, B. Gedik, H. Andrade, K.-L. Wu, and R. K. Iyer. Fault Injection-Based Assessment of Partial Fault Tolerance in Stream Processing Applications. In *Proceedings of the 5th ACM International Conference on Distributed Event-Based system*, pages 231–242. ACM, 2011.

[11] A. Khoshkbarforoushha and R. Ranjan. Resource and Performance Distribution Prediction for Large Scale Analytics Queries. In *ACM/SPEC ICPE*. ACM, 2016.

[12] M. A. Lopez, A. Lobato, and O. Duarte. A Performance Comparison of Open-Source Stream Processing Platforms. In *IEEE Globecom*, 2016.

[13] P. Michalák, S. Heaps, M. Trenell, and P. Watson. Doctoral Symposium: Automating Computational Placement in IoT Environments. In *DEBS'16*, 2016.

[14] S. Mohamed, M. Forshaw, and N. Thomas. Automatic Generation of Distributed Run-time Infrastructure for Internet of Things (IoT). In *ICSAW'17*, 2017.

[15] R. Natella, D. Cotroneo, and H. S. Madeira. Assessing Dependability With Software Fault Injection: A Survey. *ACM CSUR*, 48(3):44, 2016.

[16] R. Pietrantuono, S. Russo, and K. Trivedi. Emulating Environment-Dependent Software Faults: Position Paper. In *COUFLESS'15*, pages 34–40. IEEE Press, 2015.

[17] M. Vögler, J. M. Schleicher, C. Inzinger, B. Nickel, and S. Dustdar. Non-Intrusive Monitoring of Stream Processing Applications. In *2016 IEEE SOSE'16*, pages 162–171, March 2016.

Predicting Power Consumption of High-Memory-Bandwidth Workloads

Norbert Schmitt
University of Würzburg
norbert.schmitt@uni-wuerzburg.de

Jóakim von Kistowski
University of Würzburg
joakim.kistowski@uni-wuerzburg.de

Samuel Kounev
University of Würzburg
samuel.kounev@uni-wuerzburg.de

ABSTRACT

High performance workloads with high bandwidth memory utilization are among the most power consuming software applications [15]. When writing such applications, developers can directly influence power consumption of the final software through their choice of data size and traversal method, mostly due to caching characteristics. Explicit knowledge on how choices influence power consumption can thus lead to greater overall energy efficiency. In existing work, power prediction for memory accesses and high bandwidth applications requires either detailed measurement information on the system on which the software is executed or it is too generic, not taking significant aspects, such as caching and data size into account. In this paper, we propose a power model that bridges this gap by modeling power consumption based on concrete software properties, while considering hardware characteristics on a more abstract level, characterizing it primarily using publicly available data. The model is designed to enable developers to compare power consumption of implementation alternatives for high memory bandwidth software components. We validate our model by measuring modified versions of the high bandwidth benchmark stream [11]. We show that our model can predict the relative change of power consumption due to implementation changes and the power consumption of a concrete system under test with an average error of 19 percent.

Keywords

Cache, SPEC, Performance Counter, Workloads, Energy Efficiency, CPU, Load level, Utilization

1. INTRODUCTION

Energy efficiency of computing systems has become a significant issue over the past decades. In 2010, the U.S. Environmental Protection Agency (U.S. EPA) estimated that 3% of the entire energy consumption in the U.S. is caused by data center power draw [8]. High performance workloads with high bandwidth memory utilization are among the most power consuming software applications. Especially when comparing high performance CPU workloads, workloads with additional high-bandwidth memory usage draw more power than their less memory intensive counterparts [15].

Software developers can directly influence the power consumption of high-bandwidth software components through their implementation and design decisions. Especially, characteristics such as data type and data traversal methods can have a significant impact both on performance, as well as power consumption. Explicit knowledge on the relationship between power consumption and implementation details can help developers to make conscientious choices regarding energy efficiency during development and may lead to more efficient software.

Existing power models are either too generic or too specific for use in such a context. Simple full-system power models, such as [4, 13] do not consider memory access sufficiently. In stark contrast, models intended for hardware design [12, 10, 9] are too specific, requiring detailed information about target hardware. Similarly, some more general purpose models which consider memory accesses, such as [5] also require very specific hardware information. More generic models that consider memory accesses are mostly intended to be used for system management and thus still require some concrete hardware descriptions. [2] features a processor power model, whereas [3] and [14] focus on management of virtual machines.

In this paper, we propose a power model that bridges this gap of models being either too generic or too specific by modeling power consumption based on concrete software properties. Specifically, model parameters that characterize hardware may be set to default values, in which case the model's power prediction is proportional to actually consumed power on a concrete system. This way, the model enables developers to compare power consumption of implementation alternatives for high memory bandwidth software components. The model may also be used with system-specific hardware parameters, in which case model results absolute accuracy increases.

The major contributions of this paper are as follows:

1. We classify the differences in power consumption that can be achieved by high-memory-bandwidth workloads.
2. We propose a model that allows for comparison of implementation options, based on data type and data traversal method.

We evaluate our model using measurements of nine modified versions of the stream benchmark [11]. We predict power consumption for memory operations using different

ICPE'17, April 22 - 26, 2017, L'Aquila, Italy

ISBN 978-1-4503-4404-3/17/04...$15.00

DOI: http://dx.doi.org/10.1145/3030207.3030241

data types and strides. We define stride as the step size for each iteration over a contiguous block of memory. We show that our model can accurately predict the relative change in power consumption between the different versions without calibration to the specific hardware. We also show that the model can predict CPU and Memory power consumption with a mean error of 32 and 54 percent, if calibrated to a specific system.

The remainder of this paper is structured as follows: We describe our model and its parameters in Section 2, followed by an evaluation of both relative and absolute prediction accuracy in Section 3. Finally, we conclude the paper in Section 4.

2. POWER PREDICTION MODEL

The goal of the power prediction model is modeling power consumption of *(1)* CPU and *(2)* full-system power. We are also able to estimate memory power. For each of these predictions, we predict either relative changes in power depending on workload characteristics or absolute power, which requires additional information on the hardware.

CPU power ($pwr(CPU)$) and full-system power ($pwr(sys)$) are the results of our workload model, whereas memory power ($pwr(mem)$) can be derived from the former two. To derive memory power, we assume that the high-memory-bandwidth workload exercises a negligible amount of I/O. If so, pwr_{mem} can be derived as follows (Eq. 1):

$$pwr(mem) = pwr(sys) - pwr(CPU) - pwr(idle) \quad (1)$$

pwr_{idle} is a constant that can be read from manufacturer sheets or standard benchmark results, such as SPECpower-ssj2008 [7] or the SPEC SERT [8].

The power models for full-system and CPU power are based on the hypothesis that larger data types and bigger steps in data traversal cause lower CPU power consumption. This behavior is expected due to the way in which execution and power consumption depend on the CPU cache. The general rationale is as follows: Every memory access instruction reads data either from cache (cache hit) or directly from memory (cache miss), each direct memory access (caused by cache miss) causes the CPU to wait, reducing its power consumption, while at the same time, causing memory to perform work, increasing its power consumption. Consequently, the CPU power consumption decreases with the cache miss probability up to the minimum power consumption $pwr_{min}(CPU)$ and $pwr_{min}(sys)$. The memory power consumption increases with the cache miss probability. However, as memory consumes far less power than CPU overall full-system power consumption scales with the CPU power consumption factor p (Eq. 4) to $pwr_{max}(CPU)$ as well as $pwr_{max}(sys)$, as shown in Eq. 2 and Eq. 3.

$$\begin{aligned} pwr(CPU) = {} & pwr_{min}(CPU) \\ & + (pwr_{max}(CPU) - pwr_{min}(CPU)) * p \end{aligned} \quad (2)$$

$$\begin{aligned} pwr(sys) = {} & pwr_{min}(sys) \\ & + (pwr_{max}(sys) - pwr_{min}(sys)) * p \end{aligned} \quad (3)$$

CPU and full-system power values are either system specific or default values. Full-system power values can be read from standard benchmark results, such results from the SPEC SERT [8]. However, the cache miss probability also depends on the workload. We calculate cache hit probability (Eq. 4) based on the data type size, stride, and cache size of the last level cache (LLC). Cache size can also be set using a default value. However, cache sizes of existing processors are public information and available from the manufacturer's data sheets.

$$p = \frac{datasize * stride}{cachesize} * inverseprefetcheraccuracy \quad (4)$$

The $inverseprefetcheraccuracy$ in Eq. 4 is the only hardware parameter that can not be pulled from a manufacturer data sheet or standard benchmark result. Fortunately, it does not affect the ranking of relative results, which means that it can be omitted for relative comparisons. It models the hardware cache prefetcher's ability (or rather inverse ability, as we are modeling cache misses) to pre-fetch data for the cache that would normally not be in the cache according to naive caching algorithms. To keep the model simple, the cache miss probability is the only modeled hardware parameter. This enables the model to compare relative results if neglected as described, and predict the power consumption with reasonable accuracy.

Note that the model's absolute prediction accuracy is expected to strongly depend on the accuracy of the pwr_{max} and pwr_{min} parameters. If these do not correlate for a full-system and a corresponding CPU power model it may be prudent to use different cache miss probabilities for these models, even though this is semantically unintuitive.

The data types are selected which we see as the most commonly used data types in C programming. We do not distinguish between floating point and integer types. Therefore longer strides for integers are not evaluated.

3. EVALUATION

We evaluate the relative and absolute prediction accuracy of our model. To this end, we modify the stream benchmark [11] to iterate over 16 arrays in parallel. We compare the accuracy of comparative predictions (relative accuracy) using default hardware parameters and absolute prediction accuracy using hardware parameters for a specific system.

3.1 Workloads and Measurement

We use modified versions of the stream benchmark [11] to evaluate our model. Stream is a high-memory-bandwidth intensive benchmark that performs sequential memory accesses for scalar multiplication and copy operations on three large arrays. We modify stream to be used according to the SPEC power measurement methodology [1]. To this end, we execute stream in parallel using 16 system processes, each with separate arrays. The array iterations are repeated with the number of iterations per second serving as a throughput metric. Iterations are repeated for the entire measurement duration. In adherence to the SPEC methodology [1], we run the workload for 15 seconds before beginning the measurement phase, which lasts for 120 seconds, collecting throughput, system power (using an external power meter) and CPU performance counters each second. CPU performance counters are monitored using the IntelPCM tool [6]. We measure CPU Power, Memory Power, and memory bytes read and written.

We modify the workload by changing the data type of the stream array (`char`, `int`, `double`, and `long`) and the stride of the array iteration (1, 2, 4, 8, 16, and 24).

To determine the *inverseprefetcheraccuracy*, we select the

	pwr_{min}	pwr_{max}	$inverseprefetcheraccuracy$
Full system power	$104.7W$	$140.6W$	$151,518$
CPU power	$63.81W$	$89.37W$	$189,552$

Table 1: Benchmark results for the machine specific configuration of power consumption

Data Type	Stride	Power Measured	Power Estimated	Ordering
`char`	1	$120.8W$	$140.31W$	8
`int`	1	$109.9W$	$139.43W$	32
`long`	1	$108.7W$	$138.26W$	64
`double`	1	$109.6W$	$138.26W$	64
`double`	2	$110.0W$	$135.26W$	128
`double`	4	$110.4W$	$131.26W$	256
`double`	8	$109.6W$	$121.92W$	512
`double`	16	$107.4W$	$103.23W$	1024
`double`	24	$105.8W$	$84.55W$	1536

Table 2: Measured full system power compared to configured model and predicted ordering

stream workload using its standard data type `double` together with a stride of 16. We select a stride of 16 to accommodate for normal software with a mixture of data with good spatial memory locality, benefiting from the hardware prefetcher, and random access to main memory. The `double` data type with stride 16 is used as a training value and is therefore excluded from the evaluation. The machine onto which the model is trained is a HP DL160 Gen9 with a Xeon E5-2640 v3 (2.6Ghz) processor with 20MiB L3 cache (LLC) and 32GiB (2133Mhz) memory. The machine specific *inverseprefetcheraccuracy* as the mean of both training values, full system power and CPU power, is 170,535. *inverseprefetcheraccuracy* for the trained model is obtained by measuring the L3 cache miss rate with IntelPCM.

As $pwr_{min}(CPU)$ we use the LU benchmark from the SERT and SOR for $pwr_{max}(CPU)$, also from the SERT. They are designed to specifically stress the CPU with a negligible amount of memory access of 0.18KiB/s (LU) and 0.24KiB/s (SOR). The low memory access makes both benchmarks well suited to determine the maximum and minimum CPU power. All benchmarks are executed on the same machine used for the *inverseprefetcheraccuracy* shown in Table 1.

3.2 Prediction Accuracy

We use our model to predict the relative changes in power consumption. To only show the relative changes, we remove all machine specific values from the model. $pwr_{min}(CPU)$ and $pwr_{max}(CPU)$ are set 0 and 1 respectively. The value for *cachesize* and *inverseprefetcheraccuracy* are set to 1, removing all machine specific impacts on our model. The resulting power consumption values therefore only rely on the data type and stride. Results together with the measured full system power as well as the predicted ordering for comparison are shown in Table 2.

As can be seen from our results, the model can keep the ordering in cases the $datasize * stride$ exceeds the cache line size or the size of the data type is small. Comparing the predicted ordering with the measurement results shows that the model can predict the ordering correctly, if the difference

Data Type	Stride	Power Measured	Power Estimated
`char`	1	$69.04W$	$89.14W$
`int`	1	$60.36W$	$88.44W$
`long`	1	$60.30W$	$87.52W$
`double`	1	$60.79W$	$87.52W$
`double`	2	$60.66W$	$85.67W$
`double`	4	$61.04W$	$81.95W$
`double`	8	$60.72W$	$75.58W$
`double`	16	$59.80W$	$59.80W$
`double`	24	$58.24W$	$45.02W$

Table 3: CPU power measured compared to configured model estimation

Data Type	Stride	Power Measured	Power Estimated
`char`	1	$9.13W$	$14.75W$
`int`	1	$9.11W$	$14.50W$
`long`	1	$9.12W$	$14.16W$
`double`	1	$9.14W$	$14.16W$
`double`	2	$9.10W$	$13.49W$
`double`	4	$9.12W$	$12.14W$
`double`	8	$9.09W$	$9.45W$
`double`	16	$9.04W$	$4.070W$
`double`	24	$8.99W$	$-1.32W$

Table 4: Measured and estimated memory power consumption with an idle full system power of $36.4W$

in $datasize * stride$ is large. The model results also show a minor discrepancy between `long` and `double` stemming form different data types. Our model does not take different data types into account that might use different execution units of the CPU resulting in different power consumptions.

To evaluate the prediction accuracy of our model, we measure the CPU power with IntelPCM while executing modified versions of the stream benchmark. The full system power consumption is measured concurrently with an external power meter. Both, CPU and full system power consumption are estimated with the aforementionend *inverseprefetcheraccuracy* and compared to the measurement results.

The results presented in Table 3 shows that the model can predict the CPU power consumption with an average deviation of $21.7W$ / 32.02%. As with the ordering, the best results are achieved if $datasize*stride$ exceeds the cache line size, with a deviation of −15.1%. For the full system power shown in Table 2, an average deviation of $23.5W$ / 19.34% could be achieved, with the lowest deviation using `double` together with a step size of 8.

The measured and estimated memory power are shown in Table 4. As idle power for the configured system, the IDLE workload from the SERT benchmark run is used with a full system power consumption of $36.4W$. The average memory power deviation is $0.36W$ / 3.97% with the lowest deviation at a step size of 8 with `double`. This coincides with the CPU power estimation. With deviations from both, the full system power and CPU power estimate propagating, a higher deviation than for other estimates is expected. The estimated memory power deviates with an average of $4.90W$ or 53.98% from the measurement.

Promising results at the edge cases with a high step size

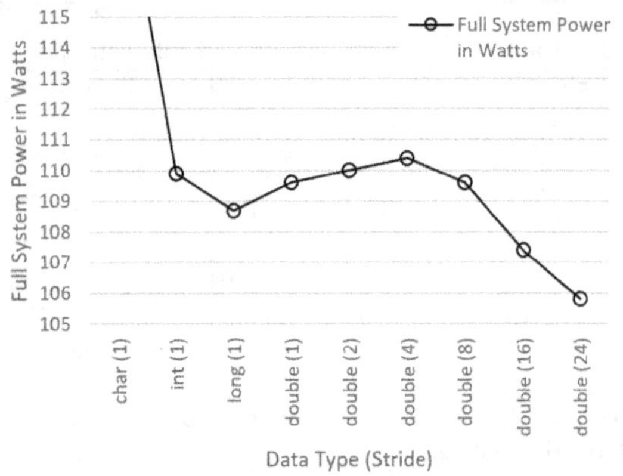

Figure 1: Measured full system power in watts for data types and strides

or low data type size stems from irregularities within our measurement results. While slight divergence from a linear model is expected, power consumption behaves non-linearly for small differences in step size or data type size, shown in Figure 1, which subsequently can lead to the observed misordering and deviations in the estimation.

The figure also shows that further measurements are necessary to improve our model. Also additional research for suitable reference benchmarks, more closely related to high-bandwidth memory workloads, is necessary to achieve better accuracy determining pwr_{min} and pwr_{max} for the CPU and full system power. Future work should also include a guideline for determining the $inverseprefetcheraccuracy$ for predictions. Higher accuracy for the $inverseprefetcheraccuracy$ parameter would also aid in avoiding mispredictions as seen in Table 4 for `double` with a step size of 24.

4. CONCLUSIONS

This paper introduces a model for prediction of power consumption of high-memory-bandwidth workloads. The model bridges the gap between system specific prediction models that require extensive system information, including measurements, and more generic models that do not consider memory specific workloads and their properties.

The model can help developers to compare power consumption of different implementation options by specifying their workload and using publicly available hardware information and/or default values for hardware specification. As a result, the model may lead to implementation choices with less power consumption.

We show that the model is able to predict a system's power consumption accurately with a mean deviation of 19 percent and ranks implementation options correctly if used with abstract default hardware parameters, enabling implementation comparisons.

5. REFERENCES

[1] SPEC Power and Performance Benchmark Methodology. http://spec.org/power/docs/SPEC-Power_and_Performance_Methodology.pdf.

[2] R. Basmadjian and H. De Meer. Evaluating and modeling power consumption of multi-core processors. In *Future Energy Systems: Where Energy, Computing and Communication Meet (e-Energy), 2012 Third International Conference on*, pages 1–10, May 2012.

[3] A. Bohra and V. Chaudhary. Vmeter: Power modelling for virtualized clouds. In *Parallel Distributed Processing, Workshops and Phd Forum (IPDPSW), 2010 IEEE International Symposium on*, pages 1–8, April 2010.

[4] X. Fan, W.-D. Weber, and L. A. Barroso. Power provisioning for a warehouse-sized computer. In *The 34th ACM International Symposium on Computer Architecture*, 2007.

[5] S. Gurumurthi, A. Sivasubramaniam, M. J. Irwin, N. Vijaykrishnan, M. Kandemir, T. Li, and L. K. John. Using complete machine simulation for software power estimation: The softwatt approach. In *Proceedings of the 8th International Symposium on High-Performance Computer Architecture*, HPCA '02, pages 141–, Washington, DC, USA, 2002. IEEE Computer Society.

[6] Intel. Intel Performance Counter Monitor. https://software.intel.com/en-us/articles/intel-performance-counter-monitor.

[7] K.-D. Lange. Identifying Shades of Green: The SPECpower Benchmarks. *Computer*, 42(3):95–97, March 2009.

[8] K.-D. Lange and M. G. Tricker. The Design and Development of the Server Efficiency Rating Tool (SERT). In *Proceedings of the 2nd ACM/SPEC International Conference on Performance Engineering*, ICPE '11, pages 145–150, New York, NY, USA, 2011. ACM.

[9] S. Li, J. H. Ahn, R. D. Strong, J. B. Brockman, D. M. Tullsen, and N. P. Jouppi. McPAT: An Integrated Power, Area, and Timing Modeling Framework for Multicore and Manycore Architectures. In *Proceedings of the 42Nd Annual IEEE/ACM International Symposium on Microarchitecture*, MICRO 42, pages 469–480, New York, NY, USA, 2009. ACM.

[10] M. Mamidipaka and N. Dutt. eCACTI: An enhanced power estimation model for on-chip caches. *Center for Embedded Computer Systems, Technical Report TR*, pages 04–28, 2004.

[11] J. D. McCalpin. STREAM benchmark. *Link: www. cs. virginia. edu/stream/ref. html# what*, 22, 1995.

[12] G. Reinman and N. P. Jouppi. CACTI 2.0: An integrated cache timing and power model. *Western Research Lab Research Report*, 7, 2000.

[13] S. Rivoire, P. Ranganathan, and C. Kozyrakis. A comparison of high-level full-system power models. In *Proceedings of the 2008 Conference on Power Aware Computing and Systems*, HotPower'08, pages 3–3, Berkeley, CA, USA, 2008. USENIX Association.

[14] A. Verma, P. Ahuja, and A. Neogi. Power-aware dynamic placement of hpc applications. In *Proceedings of the 22Nd Annual International Conference on Supercomputing*, ICS '08, pages 175–184, New York, NY, USA, 2008. ACM.

[15] J. von Kistowski, H. Block, J. Beckett, K.-D. Lange, J. A. Arnold, and S. Kounev. Analysis of the Influences on Server Power Consumption and Energy Efficiency for CPU-Intensive Workloads. In *Proceedings of the 6th ACM/SPEC International Conference on Performance Engineering (ICPE 2015)*, ICPE '15, New York, NY, USA, February 2015. ACM.

User-centered Offline Analysis of Memory Monitoring Data

[Work in Progress]

Markus Weninger[1] Philipp Lengauer[2] Hanspeter Mössenböck[2]

[1]Christian Doppler Laboratory MEVSS
Johannes Kepler University Linz, Austria
markus.weninger@jku.at

[2]Institute for System Software
Johannes Kepler University Linz, Austria
philipp.lengauer@jku.at

ABSTRACT

State-of-the-art memory monitoring tools collect lots of raw data. Yet, the analysis of this data is often not well supported. Existing tools restrict the user in the way how to analyze the underlying data, how to process it, and how to visualize it. This results in the dilemma that the raw data often contains more information than what can be exploited. We present a novel user-centric approach, allowing custom offline analysis and visualization of memory monitoring data by employing user-defined classification on heap objects. Putting the user in the center of the analysis process and providing flexible query and classification interfaces can change the way how we monitor memory usage. Our goal is to turn special-purpose memory monitoring tools into more general and customizable tools.

Keywords

Java, Memory Monitoring, Analysis Tool, User-centered, Classification, Grouping

1. INTRODUCTION

Modern programming languages, such as Java or C#, relieve the programmer from the error-prone task of freeing memory manually by relying on automatic garbage collection. Nevertheless, poor data structure implementation and usage may result in performance problems and memory leaks. Performance problems often root in known software performance anti-patterns (Smith and Williams [9]), e.g., *excessive dynamic memory allocations* (Peiris and Hill [7]). Memory leaks occur if an object references objects which are not needed anymore. This results in allocated memory that would be released otherwise. Since it is hard to manually detect and prevent such defects, advanced analysis tools are required.

A multitude of memory monitoring and analysis tools exist, all serving a specific purpose. They range from heap health metrics derived from the heap structure, as done in Mitchell and Sevitsky [6], object death time estimation, as done in Ricci et al. [8], to graph mining tools to detect reoccurring subgraphs, as done in Maxwell [5]. While serving their specific purpose well, they ignore the fact that much more information could be derived from the underlying data, and that this information is lost.

The data structures employed by these approaches are designed to provide fast access and processing only for the given purpose, but miss features to derive further information which lies outside their focus. Minimalistic user interfaces, which are often not even graphical, further increase the gap between available data and retrievable information. To reduce this information loss, tools have to support two fundamental concepts: (1) a general-purpose data structure with a flexible yet efficient data access layer and (2) a user interface to this data access layer, both graphically and via an programming interface.

In this paper, we present a novel approach on how to achieve flexible, user-centered information retrieval in memory monitoring and analysis tools using *user-defined object classifiers*. An object classifier is used to classify heap objects, i.e., objects that existed in the monitored application's heap, based on certain properties. New custom classifiers can easily be defined by the user as small dynamically-loaded code segments.

Instead of providing a non-extendable, predefined set of classifiers (e.g., the object's *type* or its *allocation site*), as done in conventional tools, *user-defined object classifiers* allow versatile object classification based on the user's needs, which puts the user in the center of the data analysis process. This enables retrieving information without the mentioned restrictions in a user-centered way.

Our heap processing framework encompasses various features based on object classifiers, such as filtering or grouping the objects on the heap. It is also possible to group heap objects based on multiple classifiers, e.g., to first group them by *type* and then by *allocation site*. This results in a classification tree that allows for step-wise, fine-grained data analysis. We call this *multi-level grouping*, a novel approach that is not available in other tools.

User-defined object classifiers do not have to be defined at load-time. They can be added at run-time utilizing Java Service Provider Interfaces (SPI) and in-memory on-the-fly compilation.

As a proof of concept, we implemented *user-defined object classifiers* in AntTracks (Lengauer et al. [4]), a memory monitoring tool based on a modified JVM (Java Virtual Machine) that was derived from the Java Hotspot^{TM} VM.

ICPE'17, April 22-26, 2017, L'Aquila, Italy

 ISBN 978-1-4503-4404-3/17/04...$15.00

DOI: http://dx.doi.org/10.1145/3030207.3030236

2. BACKGROUND

This section encompasses a short overview on AntTracks's workflow and heap reconstruction architecture.

2.1 Trace Recording And Reconstruction

As described in Lengauer et al. [4, 3], AntTracks' JVM records memory events throughout an application's execution and write them into trace files. These events include object allocations, object movements, and pointer updates during garbage collection. The heap's state can be reconstructed for the beginning and the end of every garbage collection cycle by incrementally processing the events in the trace.

2.2 Data Structure

The work in Bitto et al. [1] shows that a naïve approach, representing each heap object by a Java object in the analysis tool, results in unacceptable memory overhead. Therefore, the data structure shown in Figure 1 has been developed. It separates the heap into multiple spaces (e.g., the ParallelOldGC's heap consists of one eden space, two survivor spaces, and one old space). Each of these spaces encompasses various fields such as the starting address, the size, or the kind of the space (i.e., *eden*, *survivor* or *old*). Additionally, each space contains an address-to-LAB map. A LAB (local allocation buffer) represents a set of objects that have been processed together during garbage collection (e.g., objects that have been allocated by the same thread within the same thread-local allocation buffer (TLAB)). The LAB's object array contains pointers to the global cache of object representations, called `ObjectInfo`. `ObjectInfo`s are cached structures that contain information about objects, namely the event which created the object (e.g., an allocation by the interpreter), the object's allocation site, its type and its size. For arrays, also the array-length is stored. Furthermore, for each entry in the LAB's object array, a corresponding pointer entry exists.

3. APPROACH

To allow user-centric analysis within AntTracks, the underlying data structures and the user interface have been refactored and extended. The heap data structure supports heap traversal, filtering, mapping, and (multi-)grouping operations. Most of these operations rely on *object classifiers*, which are guidelines on how to classify heap objects based on their properties. In addition to a set of ready-to-use pre-

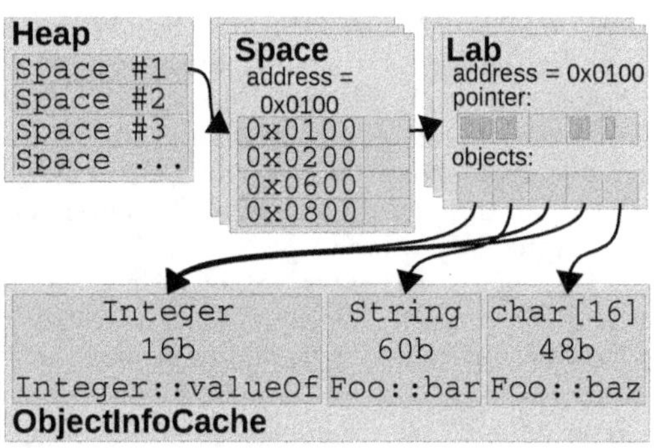

Figure 1: Reconstructed heap structure, splitted into spaces and LABs, in conjunction with a cache for `ObjectInfo` objects

defined classifiers, new classifiers and filters (a special kind of classifiers) can be defined by the user, either before or at run-time. Based on all the available classifiers and filters, the user can select a set of classifiers and filters which should be used to process, filter and group the heap. The resulting classification tree is then shown to the user in an expandable tree view control and an experimental visualization view, which allow step-wise and user-controlled analysis and data exploration.

The following sections will give details on the *heap analysis framework*, the different kinds of *object classifiers* and the resulting *classification tree*.

3.1 Heap Analysis Framework

As explained in the previous section, heap objects are not stored as distinct Java objects, but each LAB contains a map of addresses that refer to `ObjectInfo`s. Furthermore, the containing space and the object's pointers are available, therefore the information known about every heap object can be expressed as the set

$$Object = \{Space, Address, PointsTo, ObjectInfo\}$$

Constructing temporary objects for this set of information, which would be needed to support Java 8's streaming functionality, would introduce too much overhead (cf. Bitto et al. [1]), in terms of memory (i.e., object headers) as well as increased GC frequency. Therefore, a performant, user-extendable framework has been developed for heap analysis. It encompasses the following functions: (1) **Filter** allows restricting further functions to only process heap objects which match the defined `ObjectFilter`. (2) **ForEach** allows method execution on every filtered heap object. (3) **Mapping** allows mapping a filtered heap object's properties to an object of type `T`, which allows further processing as a Java `Stream<T>`. (4) **Grouping** applies (multiple) object classifiers to group all filtered objects based on their classification keys into a classification tree.

3.2 Object Classifiers

Object classifiers are objects that provide a `classify` function, which takes the heap object's properties as parameter and returns one ore more classification keys. If a classifier cannot classify an object, it is expected to return null.

To support user-defined classifiers, we provide a `ObjectClassifier` *service provider interface (SPI)* which can be seen in Figure 2. Classifiers implementing this interface can either be included as precompiled jar files or can be compiled on-the-fly from source code within AntTracks.

```
interface ObjectClassifier<T> {
  T classify(Space space, long address,
  long[] pointsTo, ObjectInfo obj);
}
```

Figure 2: ObjectClassifier interface

To provide a name, a description and a type for the classifier, classes which override this interface are also expected to be annotated with the following Java annotation: `@Classifier(name = "<name>", desc = "<description>", type = ClassifierType.<type>`

Classifiers can differ in their multiplicity of classification: (1) One-to-one classifier (`ClassifierType.ONE`), (2) One-to-many classifier (`ClassifierType.MANY`) and (3) One-to-hierarchy classifier (`ClassifierType.HIERARCHY`).

3.2.1 One-to-one Classifier

A *one-to-one classifier* classifies a heap object by exactly one key. An example for such a classifier is the predefined *type* classifier within AntTracks, which identifies a heap object based on its type's name. Figure 3 shows how this classifier would look like if it were implemented by the user.

```
public String classify(Space space, long address,
  long[] pointsTo, ObjectInfo obj) {
  return obj.type.name;
}
```

Figure 3: A one-to-one classifier that classifies objects based on their *type*

`ObjectFilters` are a special kind of *one-to-one classifiers*, which classify each heap object by a `boolean` value. This defines whether a heap object should be further processed.

3.2.2 One-to-many Classifier

A *one-to-many classifier* classifies a heap object by multiple keys. An example for such a classifier is the predefined *feature* classifier within AntTracks. By using a feature-to-code mapping tool, a mapping between object allocations and 0...* features may be created (e.g., allocations at code location x belong to feature #1, #4 and #7). The *feature* classifier processes this mapping for every heap object and returns an unordered list of features to which its allocation site belongs. Another example for a *one-to-many classifier* is the one that can be seen in Figure 4, which classifies objects based on the *authors of the package* in which their type was declared. Note that an unordered `String` *array* is returned, instead of a single object as in the case of a one-to-one classifier.

```
public String[] classify(Space space, long address,
  String[] pointsTo, ObjectInfo obj) {
    Type type = obj.type;
    if(type.package.startsWith("foo"))
      return new String[] {"mw", "pl"};
    if(type.package.startsWith("bar"))
      return new String[] {"pl", "hm"};
    return new String[] {"mw", "pl" , "hm"};
}
```

Figure 4: One-to-many classifier that classifies objects based on their *package's authors*

3.2.3 One-to-hierarchy Classifier

A *one-to-hierachy classifier* is typically used if a heap object is classified by multiple keys in a hierarchical fashion (i.e., keys with a parent-child relation). Such a classifier returns an ordered array, where the object at index 0 is the root, and for all $n > 0$ the object at index $n - 1$ is the parent of the object at index n. An example for a *one-to-hierarchy classifier* is the predefined *allocation site* classifier within AntTracks, which classifies an object by its allocation site and the allocation's call sites. The root object (at index 0) is the code location where the object was allocated, the object at index 1 the code location from where the allocating method was called, and so on. For each object, AntTracks collects a partial call stack, containing the first few call frames. An example implementation for the *allocation site* object classifier can be seen in Figure 5. Note that an ordered `String` *array* is returned.

```
public String[] classify(Space space, long address,
  long[] pointsTo, ObjectInfo obj) {
  AllocationSite as = obj.allocationSite;
  return as.toString() +
         Arrays.stream(as.callSites)
         .map(cs -> cs.toString())
         .toArray(String[]::new);
}
```

Figure 5: One-to-hierarchy classifier that classifies objects based on their *allocation sites*

3.3 Classification Tree

Grouping based on multiple classifiers results in a classification tree. The tree's root has a child node for ever distinct classification key returned by the first classifier, while each of this nodes has a child node for every distinct classification key returned by the second classifier, and so on. Therefore, for each $n > 0$, each node on level n represents a group of objects that have been classified with the same keys by the classifiers on all levels $< n$. An exception are *one-to-hierarchy classifiers*, which may add multiple levels at once within the tree.

For example, assuming a list of n objects, i.e., $O(1)$, $O(2)$, ..., $O(n)$, the user chooses to multi-group based on three classifiers, i.e., age, author and allocation site (AS) including call sites. The grouping algorithm classifies one object after another based on the selected classifiers and merges the result into the classification tree. Processing the following list of objects yields the classification tree in Figure 6.

Object (Input): Classification keys (Result)
O(1): Age(1), Author("mw", "pl"), AS(add:4, A:480)
O(2): Age(1), Author("mw", "pl"), AS(add:4, B:110, D:88)
O(3): Age(3), Author("mw"), AS(main:44, C:520, A:100)
O(4): Age(3), Author("mw"), AS(clone:16, D:172)
O(5): Age(3), Author("mw"), AS(main:44, C:520, A:100)
O(6): Age(1), Author("mw", "pl"), AS(add:4, A:480)

Rectangles (yellow) represent tree nodes and smoothed rectangles (blue) represent the data a node is holding. This tree can then be visualized hierarchically, first grouping by age, then by author, and finally by allocation site, showing information such as the number of objects, the number of bytes and the average object size for each node.

3.4 Dynamic loading

Since classifiers are instances of Java classes, their classes have to be loaded before the classifiers can be applied. We

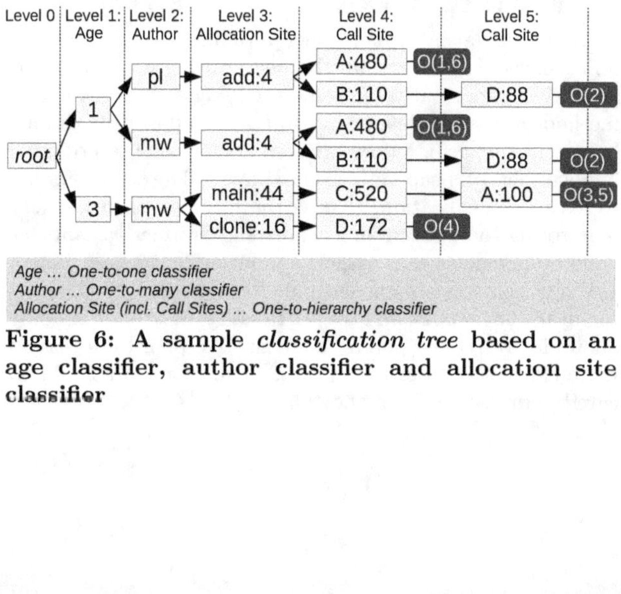

Figure 6: A sample *classification tree* based on an age classifier, author classifier and allocation site classifier

implemented two ways to dynamically load user-defined classifier classes at run-time: (1) Utilizing Java Service Provider Interfaces (SPI), and (2) in-memory on-the-fly compilation.

Java SPI defines a way how to provide services and how to look for them in the environment. First, a service interface has to be provided, i.e., the `ObjectClassifier` interface. Based on this interface, concrete services, i.e., user-defined classifiers, can be developed by the user and third-party developers. These services can then be detected and loaded at runtime using Java's `ServiceLoader` class.

For on-the-fly compilation, we take advantage of the `JavaCompiler` class, which allows compilation of code at runtime. To prevent the generation of class files (the default behavior), we implemented a custom `JavaFileManager` and a `ClassLoader` that manage the compilation of user-defined classifier in-memory at runtime.

4. USE CASES

Use cases for user-defined classifiers include all tasks where memory classification and analysis is needed. For memory leak detection, classifiers based on various metrics could be implemented, such as the number of objects reachable via a classified object or the GC size (i.e., the number of bytes that will be released if the object is reclaimed by the garbage collector). Moreover, user-defined classifiers may also be used for tasks outside the area of memory leak detection, such as change impact analysis. Classifiers are so versatile that one could think of a classifier that groups objects based on the source code repository change history (e.g., to detect if changes at certain code locations had an impact on the memory behavior).

5. RELATED WORK

The *Object Query Language (OQL)*, developed by the Object Data Management Group, is a SQL-like query language used to query objects from object-oriented databases. The downside of OQL is its complexity, which results in the problem that no vendor implements the whole standard. For example, the Eclipse Memory Analyzer (MAT) as well as VisualVM, two popular memory analysis tools, only allow queries in the form of `SELECT <select clause> FROM <from clause> WHERE <where clause>`, without further grouping. *Where clauses* can be represented in our approach using filters, while *select clauses* can be represented using an object classifier. Multi-grouping, as supported in our approach, is neither possible in MAT nor in VisualVM.

6. FUTURE WORK

AntTracks also supports heap diffing, e.g., analyzing object-level changes within the heap during a certain time span. While currently the same grouping and classification methods are available for heap states as well as heap diffing, heap-diffing-specific information may increase the potential applications of heap diffing classifiers. The same applies to feature classification, to ease the integration in memory monitoring tools based on features and product variants, as done by Lengauer et al. [2].

While pointers are currently included as `long[]` parameter in an `ObjectClassifier`'s `classify` method, this only allows for restricted pointer analysis. We plan to develop a more efficient data structure that allows for more sophisticated pointer-based classification.

Finally, all heap query features may be combined in a DSL for memory object querying.

Detailed evaluation is also part of future work. The performance can be compared to a *Java Stream-based* approach. To analyze AntTracks's applicability and effectiveness in memory leak detections compared to other tools, technical metrics such as *task completion time* or *number of found memory leaks* and subjective metrics such as *user satisfaction* can be collected during a user study, based on faulty benchmark implementations or industry applications.

7. CONCLUSIONS

In this paper we presented a user-centered memory analysis technique that builds up on *user-defined classifiers*, a novel way to classify heap objects.

This versatile classification method, in combination with heap filtering and multi-level grouping, results in a classification tree, representing matching groups of heap objects, that allows stepwise data analysis, from a coarse overview to in-detail information. This allows more flexible and user friendly analysis of an application's memory behavior.

Beside broadening the field of memory monitoring to allow classification of heap objects on arbitrary properties, even those that are untypical or not supported in state-of-the-art tools, user-centric memory analysis may change the way how memory monitoring tools are designed. It opens new possibilities on how to visualize the recorded information, allowing for new visual exploration and analysis techniques to be applied.

8. ACKNOWLEDGMENTS

This work was supported by the Christian Doppler Forschungsgesellschaft and by Dynatrace Austria.

9. REFERENCES

[1] V. Bitto, P. Lengauer, and H. Mössenböck. Efficient rebuilding of large java heaps from event traces. PPPJ '15.

[2] P. Lengauer, V. Bitto, F. Angerer, P. Grünbacher, and H. Mössenböck. Where has all my memory gone?: Determining memory characteristics of product variants using virtual-machine-level monitoring. VaMoS '14.

[3] P. Lengauer, V. Bitto, S. Fitzek, M. Weninger, and H. Mössenböck. Efficient memory traces with full pointer information. PPPJ '16.

[4] P. Lengauer, V. Bitto, and H. Mössenböck. Accurate and efficient object tracing for java applications. ICPE '15.

[5] E. K. Maxwell, G. Back, and N. Ramakrishnan. Diagnosing memory leaks using graph mining on heap dumps. KDD '10.

[6] N. Mitchell and G. Sevitsky. The causes of bloat, the limits of health. OOPSLA '07.

[7] M. Peiris and J. H. Hill. Automatically detecting "excessive dynamic memory allocations" software performance anti-pattern. ICPE '16.

[8] N. P. Ricci, S. Z. Guyer, and J. E. B. Moss. Elephant tracks: Portable production of complete and precise gc traces. ISMM '13.

[9] C. U. Smith and L. G. Williams. Software performance antipatterns. WOSP '00.

An Empirical Study of Computation-Intensive Loops for Identifying and Classifying Loop Kernels

[Full Research Paper]

Masatomo Hashimoto
RIKEN Advanced Institute for Computational Science
Kobe, Hyogo 650-0047, Japan
m.hashimoto@riken.jp

Masaaki Terai
RIKEN Advanced Institute for Computational Science
Kobe, Hyogo 650-0047, Japan
teraim@riken.jp

Toshiyuki Maeda
RIKEN Advanced Institute for Computational Science
Kobe, Hyogo 650-0047, Japan
tosh@riken.jp

STAIR Lab
Chiba Institute of Technology
Narashino, Chiba 275-0016, Japan
tosh@stair.center

Kazuo Minami
RIKEN Advanced Institute for Computational Science
Kobe, Hyogo 650-0047, Japan
minami_kaz@riken.jp

ABSTRACT

The process of performance tuning is time consuming and costly even if it is carried out automatically. It is crucial to learn from the experience of experts. Our long-term goal is to construct a database of facts extracted from specific performance tuning histories of computation-intensive applications such that we can search the database for promising optimization patterns that fit a given kernel.

In this study, as a significant step toward our goal, we explored a thousand computation-intensive applications in terms of the distribution of kernel classes, each of which is related to expected efficiency and specific tuning patterns. To statistically estimate the distribution of the kernel classes, 100 loops were randomly sampled and then manually classified by experienced performance engineers. The result indicates that 50–70% of the kernels are memory-bound and hence difficult to run efficiently on modern scalar processors. In addition, based on the classification results, we constructed experimental classifiers for identifying loop kernels and for predicting kernel classes, which achieved cross-validated classification accuracy of 81% and 65%, respectively.

Keywords

Software performance tuning; computation-intensive application; kernel classification; kernel prediction; Fortran parser

1. INTRODUCTION

For scientists that conduct large-scale computations on supercomputers, application performance tuning is essential to maximizing their scientific results. To improve the performance of an application, we have to identify its computational kernels, each of which is typically composed of one or more loops. Then various empirical attempts are made to achieve a high percentage of the theoretical peak performance of the given computing system; attempts to change compiler options, to adjust program parameters, or even to transform the programs in a semantics-preserving manner are repeated until sufficient simulated time/resolution and sufficient accuracy of the physical models/algorithms are achieved [3].

While performance tuning is still a demanding manual task relying on experience and intuition in general, a number of studies on auto-tuning systems are conducted for some specific kernels such as stencil code, linear algebra solvers, and matrix multiplications [4], or even full applications [21]. However, the process of performance tuning is time consuming and costly even if it is carried out automatically. Since auto-tuning systems rely on empirical techniques that evaluate possible parameters and/or implementations of a computational kernel to spot the best one in an automated manner, combinatorial explosion of the search space is inevitable. For example, approximately a hundred of flags for performance tuning are available in the GNU compiler collection (GCC) [11], which forces us to explore an extremely large search space of possible candidates.

Thus, it is crucial to learn from the experience of performance tuning experts in a way that enables us to improve the performance of an application based on how they improved the performance of similar applications. In our previous work [14], we addressed the problem of extracting facts from performance tuning histories of computational kernels. As a proof-of-concept, we have created a database of facts, or *factbase*, extracted from performance tuning histories of several kernels of a few real world scientific applications. We extracted facts about loop transformations performed on an original kernel by comparing it with its variants made by experts, and stored the facts into a factbase together with a set of source code metrics and performance profiling data as the evidence.

Our long-term goal is to create a sufficient factbase that

ICPE'17, April 22-26, 2017, L'Aquila, Italy

 ISBN 978-1-4503-4404-3/17/04...$15.00

DOI: http://dx.doi.org/10.1145/3030207.3030217

can be searched for promising optimization patterns, or even for patches, that match a given kernel. However, it is not an easy task to collect performance tuning examples suitable for factbase construction. In general, detailed histories of performance tuning of a large-scale scientific application tend to be lost, since the tuning process is temporary and independent of the development of the application. We should select tuning examples according to some criteria in order to efficiently expand a factbase.

Classifying kernels into several classes and examining the distribution of the classes over computation-intensive applications would guide us in seeking out performance tuning instances that should be supplied to the factbase preferentially. HPC Challenge Benchmark [8] characterizes computational kernels based on spatial and temporal locality in memory access streams and provides 7 representative benchmarks for high-performance computing (HPC) systems. Instead of traditional benchmarks, Asanovíc and others [1] introduced 13 *Dwarfs*, each of which is an algorithmic method that captures a pattern of computation and communication. However, to the best of the authors' knowledge, there is no large-scale survey in terms of the distribution of such classes over computation-intensive applications.

In this study, we introduce another set of kernel classes and explore a thousand computation-intensive applications in terms of the distribution of the kernel classes. The set of classes was proposed to estimate expected efficiency of kernels and has been used for drawing up plans of the performance tuning of scientific applications running on the K computer [23].

In order to statistically estimate the distribution of the kernel classes, 100 loops were randomly sampled from the 1000 applications and then manually classified by experienced performance engineers. The experts rely on static information extracted from the source code in addition to their experience and intuition. To support the classification task, we developed a web application that shows static features obtained by analyzing the source code.

In addition to the loop classification, we also discuss the correlation between static features of a kernel and its class by making use of the source code features and the manual classification results. We make an attempt to construct a binary classifier for predicting kernels and a multi-class classifier for predicting kernel classes by means of a supervised machine learning algorithm.

In summary, the aim of the study is two-fold:

- to reveal the distribution of the kernel classes over a thousand compute-intensive applications, and
- to examine the possibility of determining the class of a kernel only from static source code features of the kernel.

The remainder of the paper is organized as follows. Section 2 introduces the set of kernel classes. Then, static source code features that give supplementary information for manual kernel classification are presented in Section 3. After an overview of the analysis we carried out for extracting the source code features is given in Section 4, Section 5 details experiments conducted for a large-scale exploration of computation-intensive applications and for an examination of kernel and kernel class prediction. After related work and a few limitations are reviewed in Sections 6 and 7, Section 8 concludes the work.

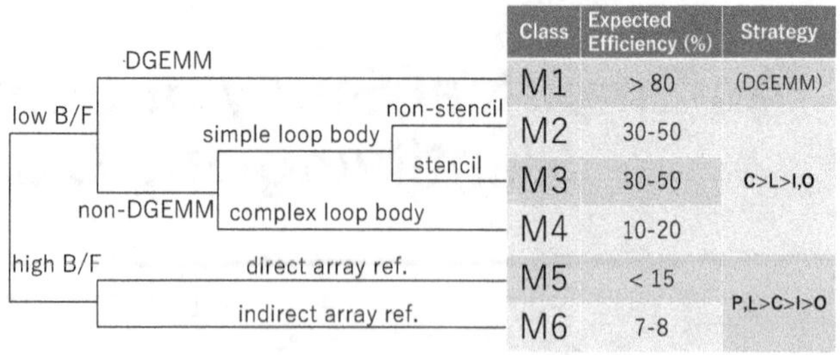

Figure 1: Kernel classes

2. CLASSIFYING LOOP KERNELS

To improve the performance of a scientific application, particular pieces of code, called *computational kernels*, or *kernels* for short, are extracted from it first. Kernels are identified by inspecting source code and/or by finding performance bottlenecks [20]. In this study, we focus on single-processor performance of a *loop kernel*, or a code region composed of one or several nested loops. We focus on the following in particular:

1. setting a performance target for each kernel, and
2. developing an optimization strategy for each kernel.

Once kernels are identified, a performance target is set and plans of optimization are drawn up for each kernel.

2.1 Classes of Computational Kernels

For the purpose of facilitating the steps above, we consider the *kernel classes* M1 through M6 shown in Figure 1. Each of the classes is related to expected efficiency, or a percentage of the theoretical peak performance (floating-point operations per second), and a typical tuning strategy. In the figure, the classes are arranged in descending order of expected efficiency, where rough estimates (%) for SPARC64VIIIfx, used in the K computer, are shown. Although efficiency percentages of M5/M6 kernels can be estimated based on the roofline model [22], typical values are shown in the figure. Note that the order of the classes should be similar for other modern scalar processors, although individual percentages may vary.

A tuning strategy is composed of the following basic steps, where examples of the relevant optimization techniques are shown in brackets for each step.

P Hiding memory access latency. [enabling prefetching]

L Exploiting data in cache lines. [array merging, data reordering]

C Improving temporal locality of memory accesses. [loop blocking]

I Improving instruction scheduling. [loop fission (to simplify loop bodies)]

O Utilizing fused multiply-add (FMA) and single instruction multiple data (SIMD) operations. [loop interchange (to place SIMD vectorizable loops innermost)]

Note that Figure 1 also shows the priority of these steps for each class except M1 in the figure. For example, "P,L>C" means that data prefetching and exploitation of cache lines have priority over improving temporal locality. For further details on performing these steps, see the book [2] by Bailey and others for instance. The strategy for M1 is simply using DGEMM library as explained later in the next section.

2.2 Classification of Kernels

A computation that a piece of kernel code describes can be characterized primarily by the amount of bytes of memory (RAM) accesses relative to floating-point operations, *B/F* for short, essentially required by the computation regardless of individual implementations. Note that we can also use multiplicative inverse of B/F, or *operational intensity*, used in the roofline model as long as it is used consistently.

In general, computations that require low B/F can be executed more efficiently than those that require high B/F, since the former can take advantage of cache memories. Thus, kernels are roughly divided into two classes: low-B/F kernels and high-B/F kernels. Then, each class is further divided into 4 (M1–4) or 2 (M5–6) classes based on the expected efficiency and the relevant optimization strategy.

We distinguish throughout the rest of the paper abstract B/F, denoted by $\mathcal{B}/\mathcal{F}$, essentially required by the computation that a kernel describes, from concrete B/F, denoted by B/F, calculated by syntactically counting memory references and floating-point operations in kernel source code. As a rule of thumb, we expect less than 0.5 for low $\mathcal{B}/\mathcal{F}$ and more than 1.5 for high $\mathcal{B}/\mathcal{F}$.

2.2.1 *Low $\mathcal{B}/\mathcal{F}$ Kernels*

Some kernels that require low $\mathcal{B}/\mathcal{F}$ are essentially matrix-matrix multiplication and hence can be replaced with calls to an efficient matrix-matrix multiplication subroutine like DGEMM. They are classified as M1, where typical applications include first principles calculations based on density functional theory (DFT).

Otherwise, instead of DGEMM, cache blocking techniques may be effective in reducing the volume of memory traffic. If this is the case, the bodies of the loop kernels tend to be relatively simple in terms of size, the number of branching statements, and so on. They belong to M3 if they are stencil code and to M2 otherwise. M3 kernels have been rarely seen, while they can be executed relatively efficiently. Some particular high-order accuracy stencil computations are typical applications of M3 kernels. M2 kernels are used in, for example, classical molecular dynamics (MD) simulations of Coulomb interaction and n-body simulations of gravitational interaction.

If cache blocking is not effective, loop kernels tend to have relatively complex loop bodies and are considered to be in M4, where complex memory access patterns hinder efficient instruction scheduling and SIMD. Typical applications of M4 kernels include physical components of climate model simulations and plasma simulations based on particle-in-cell method.

2.2.2 *High $\mathcal{B}/\mathcal{F}$ Kernels*

Kernels that require high $\mathcal{B}/\mathcal{F}$ are simply divided into two classes depending on whether they have indirect array references or not. If a kernel does not contain indirect array references, it is in M5. M5 kernels are often seen in standard stencil computations. Typical applications include dynamical components of climate model simulations, fluid dynamics simulations, and earthquake simulations.

	Feature	Judgment
1	AR (Array References)	M1–4 | M5–6
2	FOp (Floating-point Ops)	(by B/F)
3	St (Statements)	
4	Br (Branches)	
5	Ca (Procedure Calls)	M2–3 | M4
6	MAR (Max. Array Rank)	(by complexity)
7	MLD (Max. Loop Depth)	
8	IAR (Indirect Array References)	M5 | M6
9	MLL (Max. Loop Nest Level)	
10	MFL (Max. Fusible Loops)	kernel | non-kernel
11	MMA (Max. Mergeable Arrays)	

Table 1: Syntactic features of a loop

Kernels in the last class, M6, use indirect array references. Typical applications include structural simulations and fluid dynamics simulations based on finite element method (FEM).

3. STATIC FEATURES OF LOOPS

3.1 Loop Features

As explained in Section 2, we set a performance target for each kernel at an early stage of performance tuning. This is done by inferring the kernel class; we rely in part on syntactic features extracted from the source code for the inference. Table 1 presents our proposal for a set of source code features we consult to narrow down the candidate classes.

The first two features are for estimating B/F of a kernel and hence used for distinguishing M1–4 from M5–6. Note that B/F of a loop may differ from its $\mathcal{B}/\mathcal{F}$, since multiple implementations are possible for a computation. A kernel classification task requires comprehensive interpretation of data including B/F values, comment lines, and supplemental documents. The third through seventh are for measuring the complexity of a loop body. They are used to distinguish M2–3 and M4. The eighth feature distinguishes M5 and M6. The last three are mainly used for judging whether a loop is a kernel or not. MLL represents maximum loop nest level where a loop is placed in the call tree, which reflects the order of the number of potential iterations. MFL and MMA are from the perspective of specific code optimization patterns: loop fusion and array merging. Both patterns in a loop are easily identified syntactically and can be an indication of a kernel.

Loop fusion is a loop transformation which combines two adjacent loops that have the same iteration range into a single loop. It can improve temporal and spatial localities of data references. Array merging is a data layout optimization technique that merges two or more arrays of the same size into a single array. It can improve the spatial locality between elements of different arrays.

3.2 Estimation Schemes for B/F

As mentioned above, B/F plays a primary role in the kernel class identification. Actual B/F of a specific code region is usually measured dynamically by profiling or tracing. Although we cannot statically obtain cache miss rate and hence actual B/F in general, we statically estimate B/F based on heuristics that are derived from the experience of performance tuning.

While syntactically counting floating-point operations is relatively straightforward, estimating the volume of memory traffic is far from easy, as it would require cache behavior prediction. Instead of employing complex cache models, we simply count the unique signatures of array references found in a loop. We provide three estimation schemes, ES0–2, each of which has its own method of calculating the signature of an array reference. All of the schemes assume that the *abstract syntax tree (AST)* of an array reference is available.

ES0 For the signature of an array reference $a(x)$, the scheme calculates hash value of the AST of $a(x)$.

ES1 For the signature of an array reference $a(x_1...)$, the scheme calculates hash value of the AST of $a(\bullet...)$ derived from the original by anonymizing the first dimension.

ES2 In addition to ES1, for the signature of an array reference $a(x_1, \mathsf{op}(x_2, c)...)$, the scheme calculates hash value of the AST of $a(\bullet, x_2...)$ derived from the original by modifying it in a way that the addition or subtraction (op) of constant c are ignored at the second dimension.

ES0 only assumes that data is shared in cache among syntactically identical array references. ES1 assumes that the data referenced by the array references that differ only by the first dimension are located in the same cache block. ES2 assumes that the data referenced by the array references that differ only by the first dimension and by additions/subtractions of constants at the second dimension are located in the same cache block. For example, we assume by ES2 that a(i1,j,k) and a(i2,j+1,k) are located in the same cache block.

```
1  integer m
2  integer n1,n2,n3
3  double precision u(n1,n2,n3),v(n1,n2,n3),r(n1,n2,n3),a(0:3)
4  integer i3,i2,i1
5  double precision u1(m), u2(m)
6  do i3=2,n3-1
7     do i2=2,n2-1
8        do i1=1,n1
9           u1(i1) = u(i1,i2-1,i3) + u(i1,i2+1,i3)&
10                 + u(i1,i2,i3-1) + u(i1,i2,i3+1)
11          u2(i1) = u(i1,i2-1,i3-1) + u(i1,i2+1,i3-1)&
12                 + u(i1,i2-1,i3+1) + u(i1,i2+1,i3+1)
13       enddo
14       do i1=2,n1-1
15          r(i1,i2,i3) = v(i1,i2,i3)&
16                      - a(0) * u(i1,i2,i3)&
17                      - a(2) * ( u2(i1) + u1(i1-1) + u1(i1+1) )&
18                      - a(3) * ( u2(i1-1) + u2(i1+1) )
19       enddo
20    enddo
21 enddo
```

Listing 1: A loop kernel

Suppose that we are estimating B/F's for a loop kernel shown in Listing 1 taken from MG (Multi-Grid), which is a component of NPB[1]. The kernel has 15 floating-point operations. The volume of memory accesses is different according to estimation scheme. By ES0, we count all occurrences of the array references, that is, 3 stores and $18 + 3$ loads (in the case of SPARC64VIIIfx, also a load is issued for an array reference at the left hand side of an assignment). Thus, the B/F (ES0) is estimated to be $8 * 21/15 = 11.2$. We count by ES1 a store at line 15 as well as 2, 2, 2, 2, 2, and 1 loads at lines 9, 10, 11, 12, 15, and 16, respectively. Thus, the B/F (ES1) is estimated to be $8 * 12/15 = 6.4$. By ES2, we count a store at line 15 as well as 1, 2, and 2 loads at lines 9, 10, and 15, respectively. Thus, B/F (ES2) is estimated to be $8 * 6/15 = 3.2$.

[1]http://www.nas.nasa.gov/publications/npb.html

4. ANALYZING THOUSANDS OF FORTRAN APPLICATIONS

For the purpose of investigating the distribution of kernel classes across thousands of computation-intensive applications, we have developed a tool that is composed of a Fortran parser and a *factbase*. A factbase is filled with facts about the ASTs and the semantic information extracted by the parser. Source code features are obtained by querying the factbase.

4.1 Parsing for Source Code Survey

Extracting features of loop kernels from source code requires an understanding of the code's semantics instead of simple string pattern matching. The most basic requirement is to *parse* it [5] to obtain its AST. If we employ ordinary compiler frontends for parsing source code, we have to *build* applications. In order to parse tens of million lines of source code from thousands of Fortran applications in reasonable time, we would have to overcome the following obstacles that hinder the development of automated analysis.

Building applications By searching the root directories of 2000 repositories tagged with "language:FORTRAN" hosted on GitHub, we found that approximately 800 of the root directories contain `Makefile` or its variation which suggests the use of "make" command. We also found that other 100 root directories contain `CMakeLists.txt` which suggests the use of "cmake" command, while we could not identify how to build for the rest of the repositories.

Specifying configuration options By observing several of the repositories in more detail, we have noticed that quite a few of the applications use preprocessor directives such as `#ifdef` for adapting to different compilation/computing environments. For example, WRF (the Weather Research & Forecasting model)[2] has hundreds of `#ifdef` variables. Obviously, it is not practical to handle the whole possible combinations of such variables.

Covering language variants Since Fortran is one of the longest-lived programming languages, there exist several standards incompatible with each other. Moreover, some applications depend on vendor-specific language extensions or dialects, which would require us to purchase a number of commercial compilers.

Preparing external libraries Without the help of a package management system, we have to manually install the required external libraries.

To cope with the situation, we employ a dedicated Fortran parser that we have developed for the previous work [14]. The parser is based on the following major standards: FORTRAN77, Fortran90, Fortran95, Fortran2003, and Fortran2008. It is also capable of handling the following.

Varieties of dialects and language extensions The parser is capable of parsing dialects and language extensions made locally by compiler vendors such as IBM, PGI, and Intel.

[2]http://www.wrf-model.org/

Directives It can also directly parse directives/constructs of the C preprocessor, OpenMP[3], OpenACC[4], OCL (Fujitsu), XLF (IBM), and DIR/DEC (Intel).

Partial failure It provides keep-on-parsing mode since we made use of Menhir[5], a LR(1) parser generator, with error recovery function enabled to build the core of the parser.

Incomplete program fragments It is also capable of parsing incomplete program fragments such as sequences of statements, which are typically included in other source files.

By virtue of the unusual features explained above, we can parse application programs without hooking the build process of the applications, which means that we can parse source files in any order without taking care of the dependencies among them. Instead, some dependencies caused by INCLUDE lines, `#include` directives, and USE statements may hinder the parser from determining types of some syntactic entities. As a result, AST nodes such as array elements, substrings, function references, or structure constructors may be left ambiguous. For example, since both an array access and a function reference are written in the same form like a(x), the type of a is required to disambiguate a(x).

The parser has been intensively tested for numerous applications. The number of tested source files amount to more than 20,000, the source lines of code (blank lines and comment lines excluded) more than 6,600,000, and the number of AST nodes more than 62,000,000. Although about 6% of the AST nodes are left ambiguous by our parser, we could disambiguate them later by resolving dangling references in a factbase.

4.2 Source Code Facts and Ontologies

As mentioned in Section 4.1, our parser requires deferred resolution of dangling references or ambiguous symbols. Moreover, a loop classification task requires call trees to obtain maximum loop nest level (MLL) as seen in Section 3. Thus, we need a database for storing facts extracted from multiple source files by the parser. Feature extraction is performed later by querying the database.

As the database queries may contain syntactic AST patterns and/or call graph patterns, it is natural to use tree/graph databases rather than conventional relational databases. We use RDF (Resource Description Framework)[6] store for the databases. Instead of rigid database schemas, RDF stores require more flexible vocabularies, or *ontologies*. An ontology defines hierarchies of concepts such as "a *do-stmt* is a statement" and allows us to describe database queries concisely. We do not have to describe all kinds of statements when referring to "statement" in a query, for example.

A fact about AST and semantic information extracted by the parser is described as a triple of *subject*, *predicate* (also called *property*), and *object* following RDF. Both subject and object may be source code entities such as files, functions/subroutines, and statements. A predicate denotes a binary relation between a pair of entities or between an entity and its attribute. In the latter case, objects may be literals. For example, (e, name, "foo") represents a fact that an entity e has a name `foo`. Conceptual classes of entities and predicates such as "name" above are specified by ontologies. Ontologies define concepts and relationships used for describing facts. We have designed the following ontologies in the OWL ontology language[7].

SRC A core ontology for source code entities independent of specific programming languages.

FORTRAN An ontology for Fortran languages that defines the classes of Fortran entities based on specifications such as FORTRAN77, Fortran90, and other dialects.

In OWL, a class is defined as a subclass of owl:Thing. We disambiguate the names of conceptual classes by prefixing namespaces to the names like owl:Thing or src:Entity. We use namespaces listed in the following table throughout the rest of the paper.

Prefix	Meaning
xsd:	XML Schema Datatypes
rdf:	Resource Description Framework
rdfs:	RDF Schema
owl:	OWL Web Ontology Language
src:	Core source code entity
f:	Fortran source code entity

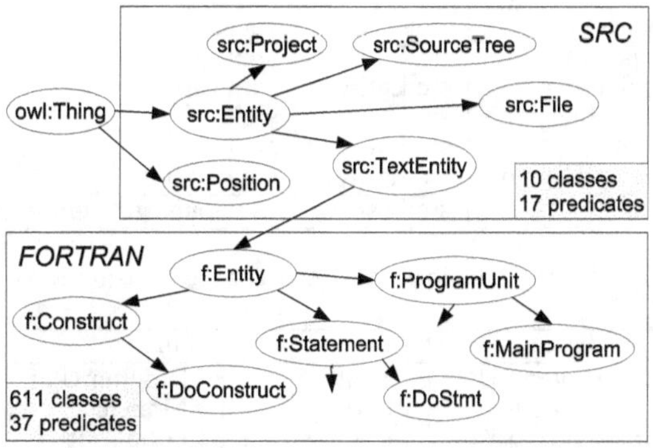

Figure 2: Classes in ontologies (excerpts)

Figure 2 illustrates the hierarchy of conceptual classes in the ontologies. *SRC* defines classes including src:TextEntity for source code entities represented as texts. *FORTRAN* defines classes for Fortran entities as subclasses of f:Entity, which in turn is a subclass of src:TextEntity.

In addition to the classes above, we also have defined predicates for each ontology. There exist two types of predicates in OWL: *object property*, which is a relation between instances of conceptual classes, and *datatype property*, which is a relation between instances and RDF literals or possibly values of XML schema datatypes[8]. A predicate is defined as a subproperty of owl:ObjectProperty or owl:DatatypeProperty.

Excerpts of the predicates in *SRC* are listed in Table 2. The first five predicates are object properties and the rest is a datatype property. A predicate src:inFile is a subproperty of src:containedIn. The domain and the range of a predicate are also specified. Note that the predicates in *SRC* include

[3]http://openmp.org/
[4]http://openacc.org/
[5]http://cristal.inria.fr/~fpottier/menhir/
[6]http://www.w3.org/RDF/
[7]http://www.w3.org/standards/techs/owl#w3c_all
[8]http://www.w3.org/XML/Schema/

Predicate	Domain	Range
src:parent	src:Entity	src:Entity
src:children	src:Entity	rdf:List
src:containedIn	src:Entity	src:Entity
⊢ src:inFile	src:Entity	src:File
src:startPosition	src:Entity	src:Position
src:line	src:Position	xsd:nonNegativeInteger

Table 2: Predicates in source code ontology

Predicate	Domain	Range
f:inProgramUnit	f:Entity	f:ProgramUnit
⊢ f:inModule	f:Entity	f:Module
f:loopControl	f:DoConstruct	f:LoopControl
f:name	f:Entity	rdfs:Literal

Table 3: Predicates in Fortran ontology (excerpts)

src:parent and src:children. They define parent-children relationships in terms of hierarchical structures such as directory trees and ASTs. Table 3 gives excerpts from the predicates defined in *FORTRAN*. The first three predicates are object properties and the last one is a datatype property. A predicate f:inModule is a subproperty of f:inProgramUnit. The domain and the range of a predicate are also specified. Since f:Module is a subclass of f:ProgramUnit, a fact $(e, \text{f:inModule}, p)$ entails $(e, \text{f:inProgramUnit}, p)$.

4.3 Factbase Query for Feature Extraction

In order to search factbases for loop features, we write queries for the patterns in SPARQL[9]. SPARQL is a standard query language for RDF. Roughly speaking, SPARQL is an extension of SQL with graph patterns described by a set of triples with *query variables*. For example, consider the following query that will enumerate names of all main programs in the factbase, where identifiers prefixed by "?" denote query variables.

```
SELECT DISTINCT ?name WHERE {
  ?prog a f:MainProgram ;
        f:name ?name .
}
```

This query instructs the RDF store to find fact graphs matching the pattern

$$\text{f:MainProgram} \xleftarrow{\text{rdf:type}} \text{?prog} \xrightarrow{\text{f:name}} \text{?name}$$

and report values for specified variables. The query contains a graph pattern in the WHERE clause. A graph pattern is essentially a set of triples written in the format

subject predicate object .

that may contain abbreviation symbol "a" for rdf:type that is used to specify a conceptual class of an entity. Consecutive triples that share a subject can also be written as

subject predicate object ;
⋮ ⋮
predicate object .

Note that predicates and ontology classes are prefixed. Prefix bindings that are placed in the head of a query are omitted for brevity.

[9]http://www.w3.org/TR/sparql11-query/

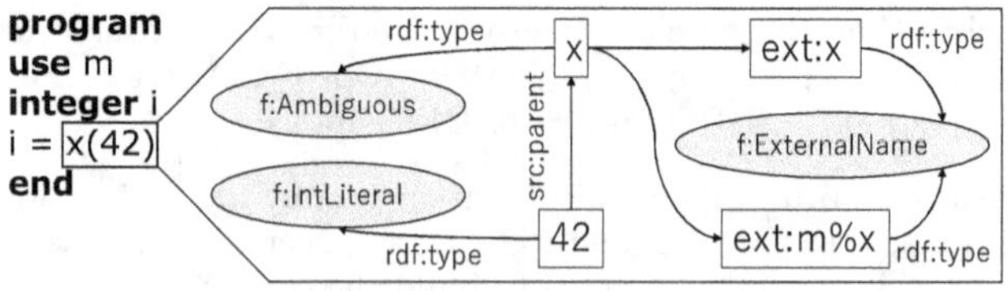

Figure 3: Fact graph for ambiguous reference x(42)

4.3.1 *Deferred Reference Resolution*

As mentioned in Section 4.1, our parser may yield ambiguous AST nodes due to dangling references. The dangling references are however easily resolved by querying the factbase augmented by inserting f:refersTo facts. This is achieved by the following SPARQL Update[10] snippet

```
INSERT {
  ?ent f:refersTo ?provider .
}
WHERE {
  ?provider f:provides ?ext .
  ?ent f:requires ?ext .
}
```

that adds f:refersTo facts that link f:provides facts to f:requires facts, which are also generated by the parser. Suppose that we have a program shown in Figure 3 that contains ambiguous reference x(42). According to the RDF data model, a set of facts form a directed graph, where each triple (s, p, o) is represented by a graph fragment $s \xrightarrow{p} o$. By parsing the fragment, we obtain a set of facts that corresponds to the fact graph illustrated in Figure 3, where ext:x and ext:m%x denote possible external names that may be required by x. Then the ambiguous x(42) will be resolved to an array element if module m provides array x, or to a function reference if m provides function x. Otherwise, x may be defined elsewhere at the top level. If both of the external names are defined, ext:m%x should precede based on the scoping rule.

4.3.2 *Feature Extraction*

The loop features explained in Section 3 are obtained by querying the factbase. As an example, we consider the number of floating-point operations (FOp). The query shown in Listing 2 counts distinct (sub-)expressions in a loop relying on hash values of the sub-ASTs.

OPTIONAL clause at lines 5 through 26 specifies optional parts of the graph pattern. In the optional match, either the optional graph pattern matches a graph, thereby variables ?loop and ?nfop in the pattern are bound to solutions, or the variables are left null. The subquery at lines 6 through 25 calculate aggregate value COUNT(DISTINCT ?h) for each ?loop specified by **GROUP BY**. Each **FILTER** clause limits solutions to the ones satisfying the condition: logical and concatenation operators are filtered out at line 13, and the solutions are further limited at lines 18 through 24 to the ones that the operands are *real-literal-constant* or expressions containing variables of floating-point type such as REAL. A SPARQL property path src:parent+ is used at line 16 for specifying a path of one or more occurrences of src:parent.

[10]https://www.w3.org/TR/sparql11-update/

```
SELECT DISTINCT ?loop ?nfop WHERE {
?loop a f:DoConstruct ;
      f:inProgramUnit ?pu .

 OPTIONAL {
  SELECT ?loop (COUNT(DISTINCT ?h) AS ?nfop)
  WHERE {
   ?fop a f: IntrinsicOperator ;
        src: treeDigest ?h ;
        a ?fop_cat ;
        f:inDoConstruct ?loop .

   FILTER (?fop_cat NOT IN (f:Not, f:And, f:Or, f:Concat))

   ?opr a f:Expr ;
        src: parent+ ?fop .

   FILTER (EXISTS { ?opr a f:RealLiteralConstant } ||
           EXISTS {
             ?opr f: declarator ?dtor .
             ?dtor a f: Declarator ;
                   f:declarationTypeSpec ?tspec .
             ?tspec a f: FloatingPointType .
           })
  } GROUP BY ?loop
 }
}
```

Listing 2: Query for counting floating-point ops

5. EXPERIMENTS

In this section, we report on our experiment conducted on loops in a thousand Fortran applications. All experiments described in the rest of this section were performed on a workstation with an 8-core Intel Xeon processor (3.0 GHz) with 64GB RAM.

5.1 Surveying Loops Across Applications

5.1.1 Analyzing Fortran Applications on GitHub

We have cloned approximately 2000 popular repositories tagged with "language:FORTRAN" hosted on GitHub. We evaluated the popularity of repositories based on the number of "stars" they have. Among the cloned repositories, 1180 were selected based on the occurrence of keywords such as "simulation" or those indicating the use of OpenMP, OpenACC, MPI to filter out irrelevant applications. Then by parsing the source code contained in the repositories, we extracted facts about the loops that are reachable from main programs and then finally selected 175 963 loops from 1020 repositories based on the occurrences of non-trivial arrays and floating-point operations. More precisely, we selected the loops that have non-zero B/F by ES2. It took approximately 10 hours to extract the source code facts from 1,180 repositories (58M source lines of code, 220K files), 24 hours to create a factbase of the facts, and 37 hours to extract the loop features.

Table 4 gives the statistics of the loop features: the quartiles, the means, and the standard deviations, where the suffixes 0, 1, and 2 for AR, IAR, and BF indicate the estimation schemes ES0, ES1, and ES2, respectively. The histograms of the features over the 175,963 loops are shown in Figure 4. The values of St, AR0, FOp, IAR0, Br, and Ca are shown up to 100 to magnify the distribution. Nevertheless, they still cover more than 95% of the samples. Similarly, those of BF0, BF1, and BF2 are shown up to 60.0. We omit AR1, AR2, IAR1, and IAR2 since they are quite similar to AR0 or IAR0.

Feat.	Min.	25%	Med.	75%	Max.	Mean ± S.D.
AR0	1	5	8	16	1199	15.49 ± 30.01
AR1	1	2	4	7	739	6.33 ± 12.15
AR2	1	2	3	6	739	6.04 ± 11.72
FOp	1	2	6	16	5326	21.87 ± 65.26
St	2	5	9	20	2820	22.67 ± 52.72
Br	0	0	0	2	794	2.30 ± 7.96
Ca	0	0	1	4	1550	4.32 ± 14.64
MAR	1	2	2	2	7	2.29 ± 0.74
MLD	1	1	2	3	18	2.12 ± 1.19
IAR0	0	0	0	0	463	0.45 ± 4.05
IAR1	0	0	0	0	150	0.22 ± 2.11
IAR2	0	0	0	0	232	0.21 ± 1.80
MLL	0	0	2	4	29	2.92 ± 3.26
MFL	0	0	1	1	109	1.06 ± 1.86
MMA	1	2	2	4	162	3.71 ± 4.59
BF0	0.05	5.65	11.64	24.00	2856.0	18.92 ± 29.24
BF1	0.01	2.00	5.33	12.00	1248.0	9.60 ± 15.04
BF2	0.01	2.00	4.80	12.00	1248.0	9.34 ± 14.67

Table 4: Statistics of loop features (quartiles, mean, and standard deviation)

The distributions look like skew-normal distributions except those of BF0, BF1, and BF2 in that they have strange spikes at regular intervals of 4 or 8. We can observe similar spikes at a cycle of 1.0 in the distribution of the quotients of two positive integers as shown in Figure 5. Note that B/F ratio is the quotient of integers, that is, the number of transferred bytes and the number of floating-point operations. Since the number of the bytes depends on the type of transferred data, the cycle is multiplied by 4 or 8, which are the sizes for REAL or DOUBLE PRECISION, respectively.

5.1.2 Manual Classification of Sampled Loops

From the set of loops, 100 loops were randomly sampled and then manually classified into the six classes by Terai (junior performance engineer, 5 years of experience) and Minami (expert performance engineer, 30 years of experience). In addition to knowledge of computer architectures, compilers, programming languages and numerical algorithms, the task requires the ability to understand what kind of computation (e.g. stencil code) a given loop implements by inspecting the source code and by consulting reference materials if needed.

In order to support classifying the loops, we developed a web application that shows them the sampled loops and receives the classification results. A snapshot of the web application is shown in Figure 6, where a sampled loop decorated with loop features such as estimated B/F is highlighted over the outline of the AST and the call tree of the entire application. The experts performed the classification task based on the criteria explained in Section 2.1 consulting the feature values and the source code. The results were submitted to another database through the class selection menu.

5.1.3 Results

Table 5 and Figure 7 show the distribution of kernel classes and 95% confidence intervals (in parentheses and by error bars, respectively) for each expert. They indicate that M5 kernels are in the majority, accounting for approximately 60% (95% confidence interval: 50%–70%) of the sampled *kernels*. It should be also noted that "OtherKernel" is second to M5 and accounts for a relatively large fraction. Some

	Terai	Minami
Nonkernel	0.36 (0.27–0.45)	0.23 (0.15–0.31)
M1	0.05 (0.01–0.09)	0.05 (0.01–0.09)
M2	0.01 (0.0–0.03)	0.09 (0.03–0.15)
M3	0.01 (0.0–0.03)	0.00 (n/a)
M4	0.03 (0.0–0.06)	0.02 (0.0–0.05)
M5	0.39 (0.29–0.49)	0.44 (0.34–0.54)
M6	0.03 (0.0–0.06)	0.03 (0.0–0.06)
OtherKernel	0.12 (0.06–0.18)	0.14 (0.07–0.21)

Table 5: Classification results

kernels were judged to be OtherKernel due to the lack of information such as source code of external libraries, while others since they are (part of) test programs.

As mentioned in Section 3, our classes of computational kernels are closely related to B/F, that is, M1–4 kernels require low $\mathcal{B}/\mathcal{F}$, while M5–6 kernels high. Figure 8 shows how average B/F's are distributed over classes identified by the junior expert, Terai (left) and the senior expert, Minami (right). We can see that average B/F's for M5 and M6 are higher than those of M3 and M4. It should be noted that average B/F's for M1 and M2 are relatively high, though both classes require low $\mathcal{B}/\mathcal{F}$ by definition. This is because both experts inspected the loops qualitatively regardless of the B/F relying on the comment lines or their expertise in numerical algorithms.

5.2 Predicting Loop Kernels

This section explains how we can predict loop kernels for a given application by means of the classification results and statistical classification techniques. We rely on *supervised learning* to classify a loop according to whether it is a kernel or not. Supervised learning is a machine learning technique that requires a set of examples called *training set* to construct predictive models. In this case, an example is composed of a set of loop features and a kernel class. We employ the Minami's classification results for the training set. We represent a set of source code features as an n-dimensional vector of numerical values, called *feature vector*. This means that we characterize a code fragment simply by n attributes.

A training set is a set of examples

$$\{(\mathbf{x}, c) | \mathbf{x} \in \mathbb{R}^n, c \in \{\text{NonKernel}, \text{Kernel}\}\},$$

where $\mathbf{x}$ and c are a feature vector and a binomial class, respectively. For example, $(\mathbf{x}, \text{NonKernel})$ means a loop characterized by $\mathbf{x}$ is not a kernel. By applying a classification algorithm we obtain a classification function $p \in \mathcal{P} : \mathbb{R}^n \rightarrow \{\text{NonKernel}, \text{Kernel}\}$ that predicts c from $\mathbf{x}$.

From the features mentioned in Section 3, we selected the following seven attributes by analyzing their correlation with the class (kernel or not) in order to maximize the classification accuracy: MLL, MLD, MMA, MFL, IAR0, Ca, and BF0, where IAR0 and BF0 denote the number of indirect array references and B/F both of which are calculated by ES0, respectively.

We employed C-SVC (C-Support Vector Classification) in LIBSVM [6] from a data mining library called scikit-learn[11] to construct a predictive model from the training set. The parameters were chosen following a cookbook [15], that is, $C = 32$, kernel=RBF (Radial Basis Function), and $\gamma = 8$. It took 0.4 seconds to construct the model.

[11] http://scikit-learn.org/

Classification Accuracy: 81.00% (100 examples)

	True Kernel	True NonKernel	Prec.
Pred. Kernel	73	16	82.02%
Pred. NonKernel	3	8	72.73%
Recall	96.05%	33.33%	

Table 6: Evaluation of loop kernel prediction

5.2.1 *Evaluation of Loop Kernel Prediction Model*

The result of 20-fold cross validation of the model is summarized in Table 6, where precision (abbreviated by prec.) means the proportion of true positives among instances classified as positive, recall means the proportion of true positives among all positive instances, and classification accuracy means the proportion of correctly classified examples.

Except for disappointing recall of non-kernel prediction, all scores look promising. The result indicates the correlation between static features of a loop and the likelihood that it is a kernel, although it does not immediately entail that the classifier predicts kernels with 80% accuracy for unknown applications.

5.2.2 *Predicting Kernel Classes*

Although our training set does not have sufficient examples for each kernel class other than M5, we made an attempt to construct a model for predicting the class of a given kernel. We employed again LIBSVM as it supports *multi-class classification.* A training set is a set of examples $\{(\mathbf{x}, c) | \mathbf{x} \in \mathbb{R}^n, c \in \{\text{M1}, \text{M2}, \text{M4}, \text{M5}, \text{M6}, \text{OtherKernel}\}\}$, where $\mathbf{x}$ and c are a feature vector and a polynomial class, respectively. Note that M3 is omitted since the training set is taken from the Minami's classification result and also that the training set is shrunk by filtering out the examples each of which were classified as non-kernel, hence the size becomes 76. For constructing a classifier, we selected three attributes St, Br, and Ca in the same way as the binomial classifier above. The result of leave-one-out cross validation of a model by means of C-SVC with $C = 16$, kernel=RBF, and $\gamma = 0$ is summarized in Table 7. We adopted leave-one-out since the number of examples are significantly decreased. It took less than 1 second to create and to evaluate the model.

As expected, we could not construct a classifier for distinguishing kernel classes since the training set does not have sufficient examples of kernel classes except M5. Nevertheless, the result suggests that a classifier for distinguishing M5 kernels from the others would be promising and again indicates the correlation between static features and the likelihood of being an M5 kernel.

6. RELATED WORK

There is a large body of empirical studies that surveyed a considerable amount of source code [17, 7, 12, 13, 18, 10, 9, 19]. We discuss only a few of them due to space limitations.

An empirical study conducted by Knuth [17] is one of the earliest studies that analyze a number of Fortran programs. He and his collaborators performed source code analysis on over 440 programs consist of 250 000 punched cards, each of which corresponds to a line of code. They counted the statements in the programs for each statement type (e.g., assignment, IF, DO, etc.), calculated the length and the depth of nesting of 7933 DO-loops, rated the complexity of 83 304 assignment statements by counting operators ('+'

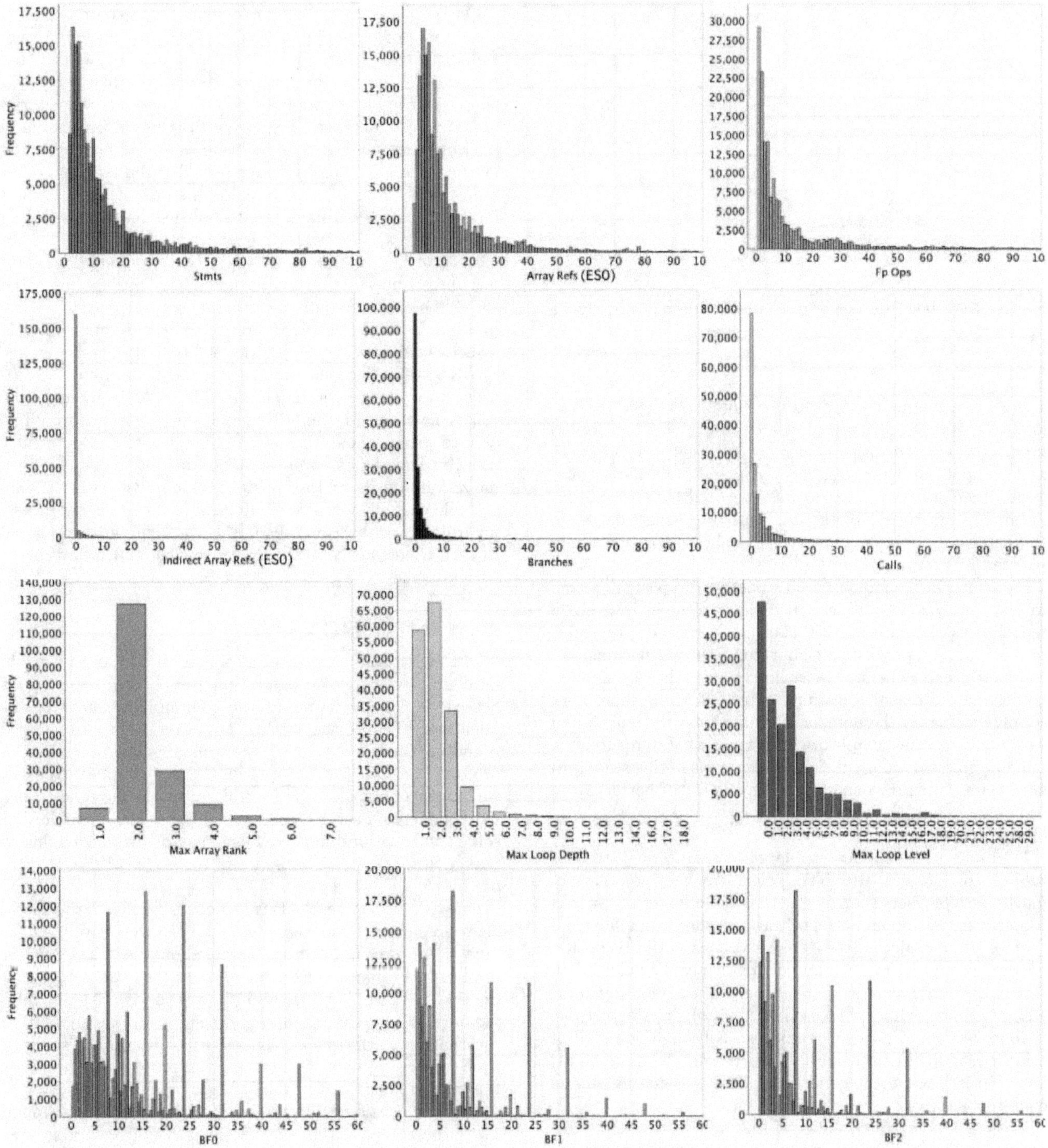

Figure 4: Distribution of loop features

Classification Accuracy: 65.79% (76 examples)

	True M1	True M2	True M4	True M5	True M6	True OtherKernel	Prec.
Pred. M1	2	0	0	0	0	0	100.00%
Pred. M2	0	1	0	0	0	1	50.00%
Pred. M4	0	0	0	0	0	0	0.00%
Pred. M5	3	6	0	40	2	5	71.43%
Pred. M6	0	0	0	0	0	0	0.00%
Pred. OtherKernel	0	2	2	4	1	7	43.75%
Recall	40.00%	11.11%	0.00%	90.91%	0.00%	53.85%	

Table 7: Evaluation of kernel class prediction

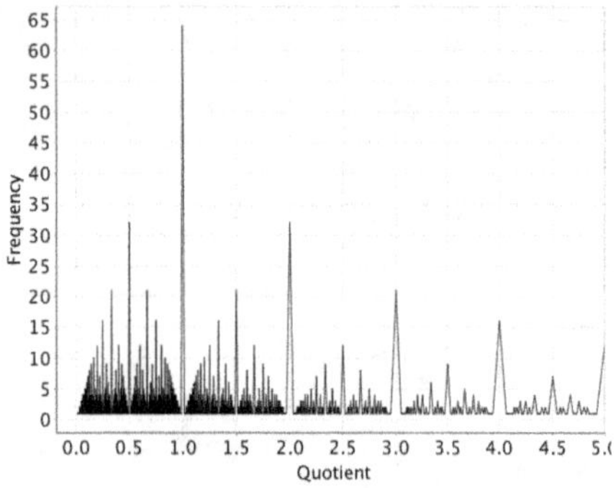

Figure 5: Distribution of quotients (positive integers up to 64)

and '−' were counted as 1, '∗' was counted as 5, etc.), and so forth. In addition, they performed run-time analysis on 25 programs randomly selected out of the target programs. To find hotspots in a program, they counted how many times each statement in a program was executed by inserting instrumentation code into the program. Moreover, based on the run-time analysis, they identified kernels of randomly selected 17 programs.

By virtue of technological advances in the past 45 years, we can analyze 58 million source lines of code from 1020 repositories compared to 250 000 lines from 440 programs. In addition, we performed elaborated B/F calculations and conducted experiments in predicting and classifying loop kernels with a machine learning approach, while their work simply calculated the number of statements, the length and depth of loops, the complexity of assignment statements. We did not, however, conduct run-time analysis in this study unlike theirs. Our previous work [14] made use of performance profiling though the number of analyzed projects was very limited like theirs.

Dyer and others conducted a large-scale empirical study of 31,432 Java projects [10]. The reason why they could study much more projects than ours is that the number of Fortran projects found in public repositories is much smaller than that of Java projects (they analyzed Java projects hosted on SourceForge, while we used Fortran projects hosted in GitHub). They focused on analyzing the usage of Java language features, while we focused on analyzing characteristics of loop kernels of Fortran programs. Although the goal of their work differs from ours, there is one common point; both works implemented infrastructures for mining source code repositories.

With the increase of the size of the target and of the complexity of the properties to be analyzed, it becomes harder to write analysis programs that directly accesses the target source code repositories. Dyer and others designed and implemented a domain-specific language (DSL) and its infrastructure called Boa [9] for mining source code. With Boa, users can write analysis programs concisely and efficiently because it automatically obtains data from source code repositories and prepares data structures that are necessary for simple description of mining tasks. In addition, Boa is capable of distributing specified mining tasks to a cluster system automatically, thus users can enjoy the benefit of the cluster without worrying about the details of task distribution.

On the other hand, we implemented a factbase, which is a database of facts about ASTs and the semantic information obtained by parsing Fortran programs. By writing and running queries on the factbase, users are able to analyze simple to complex properties of the source code repositories stored in the factbase. Regarding distributed processing of queries, since the database software we utilized in this study (Virtuoso) is capable of running on a distributed cluster system, users should be able to enjoy the benefit of the cluster for free, though we have not tested distributed processing on a cluster system yet.

Both of DSL approach and factbase approach have their own pros and cons. For example, our factbase approach should be able to handle more complex properties with simpler queries than their DSL approach because our approach utilizes RDF database with the elaborated query language SPARQL and rich vocabularies, while their approach utilizes simple data structures derived from ASTs by using the visitor-pattern. On the other hand, their approach would be able to process analysis tasks more efficiently than our approach because Boa employs map-reduce style data processing and its infrastructure utilized Hadoop, which is a highly scalable and efficient distributed data storage and processing framework. Fortunately, both approaches are orthogonal to each other, hence it should be feasible and promising to integrate them.

7. LIMITATIONS

In this study, all repositories are taken only from GitHub. Of course, we cannot assume that the Fortran applications hosted on GitHub represent the computation-intensive applications all over the world. Moreover, there are several potential perils such as "*A repository is not necessarily a project*" in mining repositories on GitHub [16]. Nevertheless, we have avoided those by carefully filtering the repositories as explained in Section 5.1. Note that it is also possible that some computation-intensive loops may be overlooked due to parsing errors or to the absence of the use of MPI, OpenMP, or OpenACC.

Due to lack of time, the kernel identification and the kernel class prediction functions have not been extensively evaluated on loops other than the sampled ones yet. They might have to be evaluated based on whether they can detect bottlenecks in an application, even though they were made relying only on manual classification results without measuring the runtime performance. In general, however, it is a very time-consuming task. Even preparing proper input data for the measurement is far from straightforward.

Another consideration is about test programs. Although 11 of the sampled 100 loops were parts of test programs, we did not exclude them since it is not trivial to identify test programs. Actually, 7 of the 11 loops were located in files whose path names did not contain "test" regardless of capitalization.

8. CONCLUSION

The process of performance tuning is time consuming and costly even if it is carried out automatically. It is crucial to share the experience in optimizing similar computational kernels. In this study, we explored a thousand computation-intensive applications written in Fortran to reveal the distribution of kernel classes, each of which is related to expected

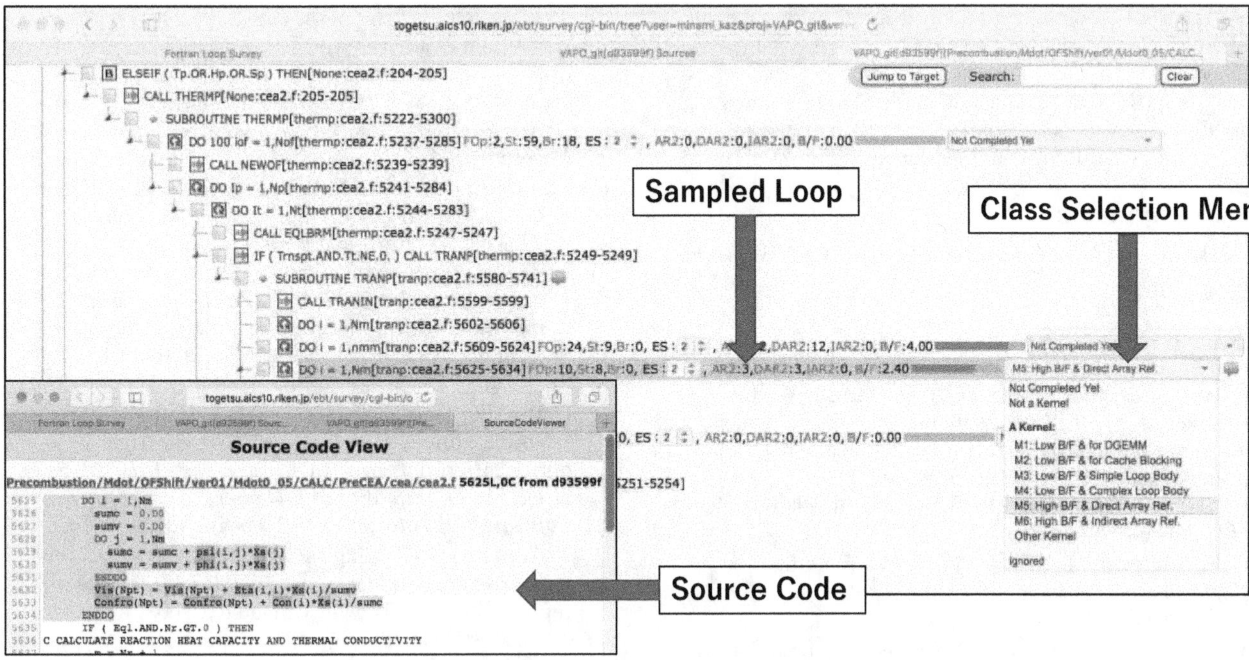

Figure 6: A web application supporting manual loop classification

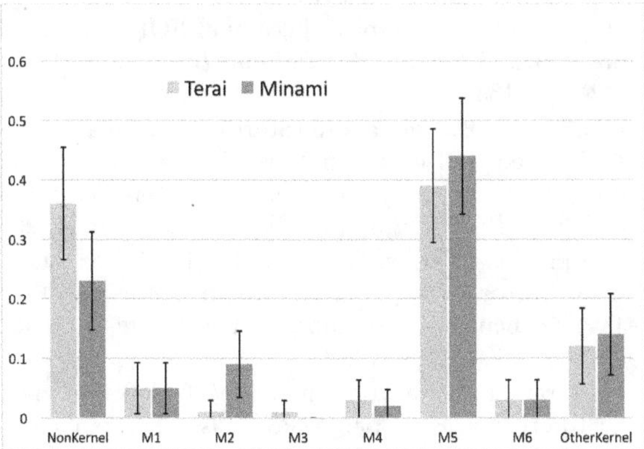

Figure 7: Classification results

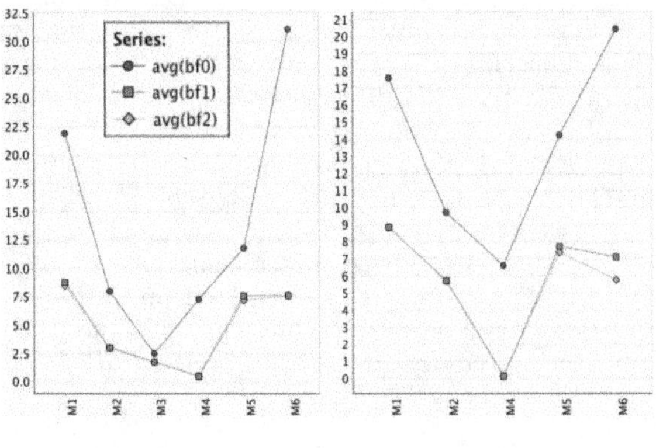

Figure 8: Average B/F over kernel classes (left:Terai, right:Minami)

efficiency and specific tuning patterns. Such exploration is a significant step toward the development of computational kernel identification as well as tuning pattern prediction to facilitate evidence-based performance tuning.

We constructed a factbase, or a database of source code facts obtained by parsing the whole source code contained in the applications. Then we extracted static features of the loops from the factbase and selected 175 963 of them based on the occurrence of non-trivial array references and floating-point operations. To estimate the distribution of the kernel classes, 100 loops were randomly sampled and then manually classified by experienced performance engineers[12].

The result indicates that 15–45% of the 175 963 loops are non-kernel loops and that 30–50% belong to a class of memory-bound kernels such as standard stencil computations, which require a high ratio of memory accesses to floating-point operations and hence are difficult to execute efficiently on modern scalar processors.

In addition to the loop classification, we discussed the correlation between the static features and the likelihood of belonging to a kernel class by constructing a binary classifier for identifying loop kernels and a multi-class classifier for predicting kernel classes, based on the manual classification data and a machine learning algorithm. The results of cross-validation of the classifiers indicate the correlation between static features of a loop and the likelihood of being a kernel, although the experts inspected the loops qualitatively depending on the information including comment lines as well as the static features.

Last but not least, the framework we employed for the experiment is not limited to a single programming language, a single classification scheme, nor a single repository hosting

[12]The results of the experimentation with supplementary information are publicly available at https://github.com/ebt-hpc/icpe2017

service. It would be possible to analyze applications written in more popular languages such as Java and C, since we have parsers for them and can make use of external static analyzers to extract call graphs. It would also be interesting to roughly estimate the cost of a given loop based on the profiling data of randomly sampled loops.

Acknowledgments

This work was supported in part by JSPS KAKENHI Grant Number JP26540031.

9. REFERENCES

[1] K. Asanović, R. Bodik, B. C. Catanzaro, J. J. Gebis, P. Husbands, K. Keutzer, D. A. Patterson, W. L. Plishker, J. Shalf, S. W. Williams, and K. A. Yelick. The landscape of parallel computing research: A view from berkeley. Technical Report UCB/EECS-2006-183, EECS Department, University of California, Berkeley, 2006.

[2] D. H. Bailey, R. F. Lucas, and S. W. Williams. *Performance Tuning of Scientific Applications*. CRC Press, 2011.

[3] V. R. Basili, J. C. Carver, D. Cruzes, L. M. Hochstein, J. K. Hollingsworth, F. Shull, and M. V. Zelkowitz. Understanding the high-performance-computing community: A software engineer's perspective. *IEEE Software*, 25(4):29–36, 2008.

[4] P. Basu, M. Hall, M. Khan, S. Maindola, S. Muralidharan, S. Ramalingam, A. Rivera, M. Shantharam, and A. Venkat. Towards making autotuning mainstream. *International Journal of High Performance Computing Applications*, 27(4):379–393, 2013.

[5] A. Bessey, K. Block, B. Chelf, A. Chou, B. Fulton, S. Hallem, C. Henri-Gros, A. Kamsky, S. McPeak, and D. Engler. A few billion lines of code later: Using static analysis to find bugs in the real world. *Commun. ACM*, 53(2):66–75, 2010.

[6] C.-C. Chang and C.-J. Lin. Libsvm: A library for support vector machines. *ACM Trans. Intell. Syst. Technol.*, 2(3):27:1–27:27, 2011.

[7] C. Collberg, G. Myles, and M. Stepp. An empirical study of java bytecode programs. *Softw. Pract. Exper.*, 37(6):581–641, 2007.

[8] J. Dongarra and P. Luszczek. HPC challenge benchmark. http://icl.cs.utk.edu/hpcc/.

[9] R. Dyer, H. A. Nguyen, H. Rajan, and T. N. Nguyen. Boa: Ultra-large-scale software repository and source-code mining. *ACM Trans. Softw. Eng. Methodol.*, 25(1):7:1–7:34, 2015.

[10] R. Dyer, H. Rajan, H. A. Nguyen, and T. N. Nguyen. Mining billions of ast nodes to study actual and potential usage of Java language features. In *Proceedings of the 36th International Conference on Software Engineering (ICSE)*, pages 779–790, 2014.

[11] G. Fursin, Y. Kashnikov, A. W. Memon, Z. Chamski, O. Temam, M. Namolaru, E. Yom-Tov, B. Mendelson, A. Zaks, E. Courtois, F. Bodin, P. Barnard, E. Ashton, E. V. Bonilla, J. Thomson, C. K. I. Williams, and M. F. P. O'Boyle. Milepost GCC: machine learning enabled self-tuning compiler. *International Journal of Parallel Programming*, 39(3):296–327, 2011.

[12] T. Gorschek, E. Tempero, and L. Angelis. A large-scale empirical study of practitioners' use of object-oriented concepts. In *Proceedings of the 2010 ACM/IEEE 32nd International Conference on Software Engineering (ICSE)*, volume 1, pages 115–124, 2010.

[13] M. Grechanik, C. McMillan, L. DeFerrari, M. Comi, S. Crespi, D. Poshyvanyk, C. Fu, Q. Xie, and C. Ghezzi. An empirical investigation into a large-scale Java open source code repository. In *Proceedings of the 2010 ACM-IEEE International Symposium on Empirical Software Engineering and Measurement (ESEM)*, pages 11:1–11:10, 2010.

[14] M. Hashimoto, M. Terai, T. Maeda, and K. Minami. Extracting facts from performance tuning history of scientific applications for predicting effective optimization patterns. In *Proceedings of the 2015 IEEE/ACM 12th Working Conference on Mining Software Repositories (MSR)*, pages 13–23, 2015.

[15] C.-W. Hsu, C.-C. Chang, and C.-J. Lin. A practical guide to support vector classification. Technical report, National Taiwan University, 2003. http://www.csie.ntu.edu.tw/~cjlin/papers/guide/guide.pdf.

[16] E. Kalliamvakou, G. Gousios, K. Blincoe, L. Singer, D. M. German, and D. Damian. The promises and perils of mining github. In *Proceedings of the 11th Working Conference on Mining Software Repositories (MSR)*, pages 92–101, 2014.

[17] D. E. Knuth. An empirical study of FORTRAN programs. *Software: Practice and Experience*, 1(2):105–133, 1971.

[18] R. Lämmel, E. Pek, and J. Starek. Large-scale, AST-based API-usage analysis of open-source Java projects. In *Proceedings of the 2011 ACM Symposium on Applied Computing (SAC)*, pages 1317–1324, 2011.

[19] G. Pinto, W. Torres, B. Fernandes, F. Castor, and R. S. Barros. A large-scale study on the usage of Java's concurrent programming constructs. *J. Syst. Softw.*, 106(C):59–81, 2015.

[20] M. Terai, H. Murai, K. Minami, M. Yokokawa, and E. Tomiyama. K-scope: A Java-based Fortran source code analyzer with graphical user interface for performance improvement. In *Proceedings of the 41st International Conference on Parallel Processing Workshops (ICPPW)*, pages 434–443, 2012.

[21] A. Tiwari, J. K. Hollingsworth, C. Chen, M. Hall, C. Liao, D. J. Quinlan, and J. Chame. Auto-tuning full applications: A case study. *Int. J. High Perform. Comput. Appl.*, 25(3):286–294, 2011.

[22] S. Williams, A. Waterman, and D. Patterson. Roofline: An insightful visual performance model for multicore architectures. *Commun. ACM*, 52(4):65–76, 2009.

[23] M. Yokokawa, F. Shoji, A. Uno, M. Kurokawa, and T. Watanabe. The K computer: Japanese next-generation supercomputer development project. In *Proceedings of the 2011 International Symposium on Low Power Electronics and Design (ISLPED)*, pages 371–372, 2011.

An Exploratory Study of the State of Practice of Performance Testing in Java-Based Open Source Projects

Philipp Leitner
Department of Informatics
University of Zurich
Switzerland
leitner@ifi.uzh.ch

Cor-Paul Bezemer
Software Analysis and Intelligence Lab (SAIL)
Queen's University
Canada
bezemer@cs.queensu.ca

ABSTRACT

The usage of open source (OS) software is wide-spread across many industries. While the functional quality of OS projects is considered to be similar to closed-source software, much is unknown about the quality in terms of performance. One challenge for OS developers is that, unlike for functional testing, there is a lack of accepted best practices for performance testing. To reveal the state of practice of performance testing in OS projects, we conduct an exploratory study on 111 Java-based OS projects from GitHub. We study the performance tests of these projects from five perspectives: (1) developers, (2) size, (3) test organization, (4) types of performance tests and (5) used tooling. We show that writing performance tests is not a popular task in OS projects: performance tests form only a small portion of the test suite, are rarely updated, and are usually maintained by a small group of core project developers. Further, even though many projects are aware that they need performance tests, developers appear to struggle implementing them. We argue that future performance testing frameworks should provider better support for low-friction testing, for instance via non-parameterized methods or performance test generation, as well as focus on a tight integration with standard continuous integration tooling.

Keywords

performance testing; performance engineering; open source; mining software repositories; empirical software engineering

1. INTRODUCTION

The usage of open source (OS) software libraries and components is by now widely spread across many, if not all, industries and domains. Studies claim that, from a functional perspective, the quality of OS software is on par with comparable closed-source software [1]. OS projects have largely converged against accepted best practices [5] (e.g., unit testing) and widespread standard tooling for functional testing, such as JUnit in the Java ecosystem.

ICPE'17, April 22 - 26, 2017, L'Aquila, Italy

ISBN 978-1-4503-4404-3/17/04... $15.00

DOI: http://dx.doi.org/10.1145/3030207.3030213

However, the quality of OS software in terms of non-functional attributes, such as reliability, scalability, or performance, is less well-understood. For example, Heger et al. [10] state that performance bugs in OS software go undiscovered for a longer time than functional bugs, and fixing them takes longer. One reason for the longer fixing time may be that performance bugs are notoriously hard to reproduce [26].

As many OS software libraries (such as `apache/log4j` or the `apache/commons` collection of libraries) are used almost ubiquitously across a large span of other OS or industrial applications, a performance bug in such a library can lead to widespread slowdowns. Hence, it is of utmost importance that the performance of OS software is well-tested.

Despite this importance of performance testing for OS software, our current understanding of how developers are conducting performance, stress, or scalability tests is lacking. There is currently no study that analyzes whether and how real projects conduct performance testing, which tools they use, and what OS software developers struggle with. As such, there exist no guidelines for how OS developers should test the performance of their projects.

In this paper, we conduct an exploratory study on the state of practice of performance testing in Java-based OS software. We study 111 Java-based projects from GitHub that contain performance tests. We focus on five perspectives:

1. **The developers who are involved in performance testing.** In most studied OS projects, a small group of core developers creates and maintains the performance tests. Our findings suggest that in general, there are no developers in the studied OS projects that focus solely on performance testing.
2. **The extent of performance testing.** In most studied OS projects, the performance tests are small in terms of lines of code, and do not change often. We did not observe a statistically significant difference in the size of the performance tests of projects that make claims about their performance (e.g., "fastest implementation of X") and projects that do not make such claims.
3. **The organization of performance tests.** The Java OS software community has not yet converged against a common understanding of how to conduct and organize performance tests. Developers freely mix performance tests with unit tests and code comments are used to describe how a performance test should be executed.

4. **The types of performance tests.** Half of the studied OS projects have one or two performance smoke tests for testing the performance of the main functionality of a project. 36% of the studied projects use microbenchmarks for performance testing. Less popular types of performance tests are one-shot performance tests (i.e., tests that focus on one very specific performance issue), performance assertions and implicit performance tests (i.e., measurements that are done during the execution of functional tests).
5. **The tooling and frameworks used for performance tests.** While there exist dedicated tools and frameworks for performance tests, the adoption of these tools and frameworks is not widespread in the Java OS software community. Only 16% of the studied projects uses a dedicated framework such as `JMH` or `Caliper`.

Our findings imply that practitioners who use OS software in their projects must thoroughly test the consequences of doing so on the performance of their own projects, as developers should not assume that OS software necessarily follows stringent performance testing practices. From our exploratory study follows that writing performance tests is not a popular task in OS projects. Performance tests form only a small portion of the test suite, are rarely updated, and are usually maintained by a small group of core project developers. Further, we argue that future performance testing frameworks should provider better support for low-friction testing, for instance via non-parameterized methods or performance test generation, as well as focus on a tight integration with standard continuous integration (CI) tooling.

The remainder of this paper is structured as follows. In Section 2, we summarize related work. In Section 3, we describe our exploratory study setup and research methodology. Section 4 contains our study results, followed by a discussion of the main implications resulting from our work in Section 5. Section 6 discusses the main threats to the validity of our study. Finally, Section 7 concludes the paper.

2. BACKGROUND AND RELATED WORK

In this section, we will discuss work that is related to our exploratory study. The overall body of research on performance testing is too broad to cover here in its entirety. Therefore, we focus on work that has informed our study or is particularly related to it.

Empirical Studies. As a non-functional quality attribute, performance is often equally critical to the perceived value of a program as functional correctness is. For instance, in a cloud computing context, writing inefficient, low-performance code often directly translates to higher operations costs, as more cloud resources need to be used to deliver the same end-user perceived quality (e.g., response time) [7]. Consequently, (at least) two decades of research have led to great insights into how to design and construct performance-optimal systems [22]. A number of empirical studies have recently analyzed the anatomy of reported performance problems [9, 15, 26], arguing that these problems take longer to get reported and fixed than functional problems. Further, recent research on performance regression mining (a research method inspired by software repository mining that repeatedly benchmarks different revisions of a software system to discover historical, unreported, performance bugs) has shown that performance problems can originate from a wide range of code changes, including simple updates of dependencies [2, 21]. A system following a similar basic operating principle is `PerfImpact` [17], which aims to find changes and input combinations that lead to performance regressions. PRA (performance risk analysis) is an approach used to narow down commits that led to a (previously detected) performance regression [13]. Baltes et al. [4] study how developers locate performance problems, and conclude that standard tools do not provide sufficient support for understanding the runtime behavior of software.

Problems of Performance Testing. Early on, studies have reported that industrial practice in performance testing is not on the same level as functional testing [25], even for large, performance-sensitive enterprise applications. Similar results have also recently been presented for performance testing and debugging for Android applications [24]. Historically, performance testing has been made difficult by two peculiarities. Firstly, performance testing of higher-level programming languages, including interpreted languages or those running in a virtual machine as in the case of Java, is difficult due to the high number of confounding factors introduced by features of the program runtime environment. For instance, in the case of Java, just-in-time compilation, hardware platforms, virtual machine implementations, or garbage collection runs can all significantly impact test results [8]. Secondly, performance test results often depend strongly on the used benchmarking workload, such as the load patterns used for testing. Hence, writing expressive performance tests requires careful identification and modeling of representative workloads or production usage patterns [3,14]. Unfortunately, representative workloads tend to not be as stable as functional unit interfaces. Consequently, workloads need continuous validation and maintenance [23].

Industrial Approaches. Besides these more academic research attempts, there are also a number of industrial-strength tools available in the domain of software performance testing. For instance, `Caliper`, an older Java-based framework from Google, allows developers to write performance tests using a `JUnit`-like API, and provides some built-in support for metric collection and aggregation. However, many of the problems of benchmarking Java-based software still exist when using `Caliper`. For this reason, `OpenJDK` contains since version 7 a proprietary extension called the Java Microbenchmarking Harness (`JMH`). Not unlike `Caliper`, `JMH` allows developers to build performance tests using a simple annotation-based syntax. However, given that `JMH` is part of the Java virtual machine rather than a library, `JMH` is able to control for some of the problems of Java benchmarking. For instance, `JMH` is able to control for Just-in-Time compilation or garbage collection runs. Both, `Caliper` and `JMH`, are largely intended for low-level code benchmarking. For performance testing at the system-level (especially for Web-based systems), a number of additional tools are available that foster the definition and execution of workloads, such as HTTP sessions. Arguably, the two most prevalent OS representatives of this class of tools are Apache `JMeter`[1] and `Faban`[2]. Both allow the definition and execution of complex workloads, and also contain facilities to collect performance test results. `JMeter`, for instance, exports detailed performance test outcomes in an XML or CSV file, which can then be used in other tools, such as dashboards (e.g., the Perfor-

[1]http://jmeter.apache.org
[2]http://faban.org

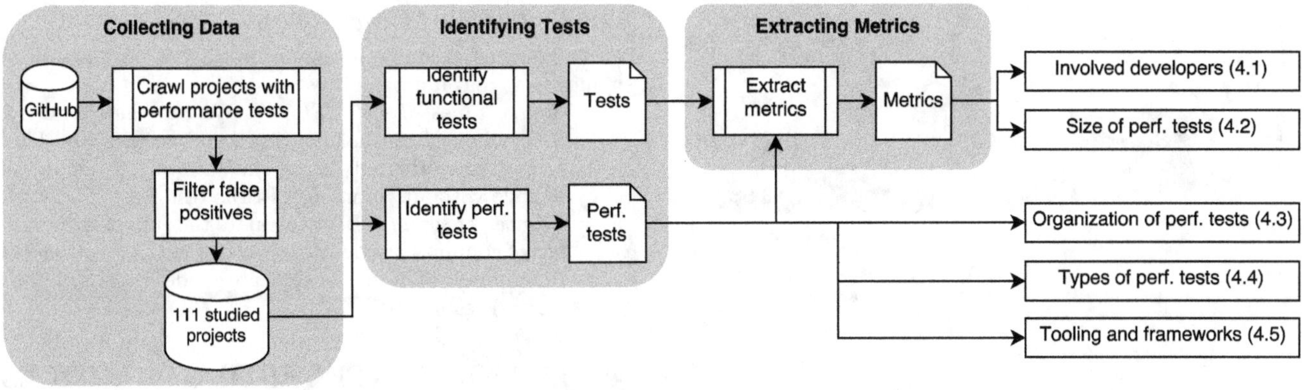

Figure 1: Overview of our exploratory study approach.

mance plugin for the Jenkins CI system[3] or for statistical analysis.

In our research, we contribute to the state of the art via an exploratory study that establishes to what extent these industrial tools, as well as the concepts and ideas originating from earlier research on performance testing, have been adopted in Java-based OS software. Hence, our study serves as a reality check and can guide future research directions.

3. EXPLORATORY STUDY SETUP

In this section, we describe the setup of our exploratory study and our methodology for collecting data and identifying performance tests. Figure 1 depicts the steps of our methodology, which are detailed below.

3.1 Collecting Data

We aim to generate a data set of OS projects that conduct performance testing. We build a custom crawler for GitHub which uses the GitHub search engine to search for OS projects using a combination of search heuristics. Our crawler searches for Java projects with tests in the path `src/test`, which use one or more terms in the test file name or source code (i.e., "bench" or "perf") or which imports known performance testing frameworks, such as `JMH` or `Caliper`. We have identified these search heuristics to be simple yet reasonably robust ways to identify projects with performance tests as part of a pre-study, where we manually inspected known projects with performance tests, e.g., `apache/log4j` or `ReactiveX/RxJava`. Our crawler extracts an initial data set of 1697 candidate projects. From those candidate projects, we filter forked projects and projects with less than 10 "stars" or less than 50 commits on GitHub, resulting in a data set of 154 projects.

Finally, we manually identify and discard false positives, i.e., projects that match our search heuristics but, upon manual inspection, turn out to not contain performance tests after all. Examples for false positives include projects that have domain objects containing the word "bench", or projects that themselves implement performance testing frameworks (surprisingly, these projects often do not provide performance tests themselves). To foster the exploratory nature of our study, we are inclusive in our manual filtering and use a broad definition of "performance test". For example, we include projects in this step which simply report on runtime performance as part of regular unit testing. After discarding false positives, our data set finally consists of 111 Java-based OS projects that actually contain performance tests.

In addition, we manually study the GitHub description of the projects to classify them as performance-sensitive (PS) or not performance sensitive (not PS). We categorize projects as PS if they self-identify as the fastest implementation of a given functionality, or stress having high performance in their project description. For example, the project `nativelibs4java/BridJ` describes itself as "blazing fast" (PS). Our expectation is that PS projects dedicate more effort to performance testing than non-PS projects to support the claims that PS projects make about their performance. Using this metric, we classify 26 of our projects (14%) as PS, and 85 projects (76%) as "not PS".

Projects in the data set include a healthy mix of well-known large projects (e.g., `apache/hadoop`) and smaller, lesser-known ones (e.g., `TridentSDK/Trident`, a Java-based Minecraft server). A summary of statistics about the projects in the data set is provided in Figure 2. Data is reported as available via GitHub at the time of collection, i.e., in July 2016. Furthermore, the entire data set is available online, on GitHub[4] as well as on the Zenodo artefact repository[5].

3.2 Identifying Tests

We manually identify which files contain performance tests in the studied projects. First, we manually identify the test suite of the project, which is `src/test` in most cases by construction. However, in some projects, the `src/test` directory contains resource files that we manually exclude from our study. We search the test files for Java source code files that contain the terms "perf" or "bench" and we manually validate that the tests are indeed performance tests. Further, we sample the remaining test and source code in an exploratory manner for additional performance tests not identified via our heuristics. The set of identified test files and performance test files is available in the online appendix.

3.3 Extracting Metrics

We extract several metrics that describe the effort that is dedicated to the performance and functional test suites.

[3]https://wiki.jenkins-ci.org/display/JENKINS/Performance+Plugin

[4]https://xleitix.github.io/appendix_perf_tests/

[5]https://doi.org/10.5281/zenodo.167895

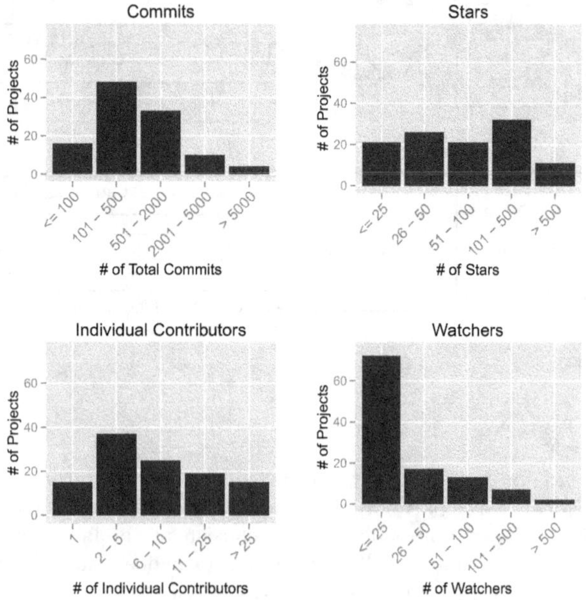

Figure 2: Summary statistics of the 111 OS projects in the data set. The subfigures show the age of the projects in number of total commits, the popularity of the projects as measured by the number of stars on GitHub and the number of subscribers ("watchers"), and the number of individual contributors.

In the remainder of this section, we explain how we extract these metrics. Our scripts for extracting and analyzing these metrics are available in the online appendix.

3.3.1 Developer Metrics

We extract the names and number of commits of the developers who work on the performance tests, tests and project. In addition, we compute the proportion of performance test developers who are core (test) developers of the project.

- *Names and number of commits of developers:* We run the command `git shortlog -s -n HEAD %FILES%` for each studied project to get a list of developers of files `%FILES%` that is ordered by the number of commits that a developer made to those files. Table 1 shows examples of these lists for **SoftInstigate/restheart**.
- *Proportion of performance test developers who are core (test) developers:* We calculate the number of performance test developers who are in the top-n project developers by the number of commits. We define n as the number of performance test developers in the project. Table 1 shows the performance test developers, test developers and project developers in **SoftInstigate/restheart**. The three performance test developers are *Andrea di Cesare*, *Maurizio Turatti* and *gokrokvertskhov*. However, only *Andrea di Cesare* and *Maurizio Turatti* are in the top-3 of project developers, hence the proportion of performance test developers who are core developers is 0.67. The proportion of test developers who are core developers is 0.5, as *Stephan Windmuller* and *gokrokvertskhovh* are not in the top-4 of project developers.

3.3.2 Test Size Metrics

We extract the source lines of code (SLOC) of the performance tests and functional tests.

- *Source Lines of code (SLOC):* We run the command line tool `cloc`[6] on the identified (performance) test files and we `grep` the output for the Java SLOC, i.e., lines of code without comments, in the test files.
- *Number of commits:* We calculate the sum of the number of commits per developer as described above to get the number of commits that are made to the (performance) tests.

4. PERFORMANCE TESTING PRACTICES IN OPEN SOURCE SOFTWARE

We report on the results of our exploratory study on performance testing in Java-based OS software from five perspectives: (1) the developers that are involved in performance testing, (2) the extent of performance testing, including the size of the performance test suite, (3) the organization of the performance test suite, (4) the types of performance tests and (5) the tooling and frameworks used. In this section, we discuss the motivation for and the results of studying each of these five perspectives.

4.1 The Involved Developers

Motivation: Large-scale industrial projects may be able to commit one or more dedicated engineers to performance testing, who are experts in software performance engineering [19] (SPE). Contrary, even for many well-known OS projects, such as the Apache web server [18], the team of core developers who contribute the most to the project is small. Hence, it seems unlikely that there are developers who specialize in performance in most OS projects.

Approach: We conduct a quantitative study on the developers of the 111 studied OS projects using the developer metrics that are described in Section 3.3.1 to investigate whether OS projects have developers who specialize in performance.

We use the Wilcoxon signed-rank test to compare distributions of observations. The Wilcoxon signed-ranked test is a non-parametrical statistical test of which the null hypothesis is that two input distributions are identical. If the p-value of the Wilcoxon test is smaller than 0.05, we conclude that the distributions are significantly different.

In addition, we calculate Cliff's delta d [16] effect size to quantify the difference in the distributions of observations. A large value for d implies that the distributions differ at a large scale. We use the following threshold for interpreting d, as suggested by Romano et al. [20]:

$$\text{Effect size} = \begin{cases} \textit{negligible}, & \text{if } |d| \leq 0.147. \\ \textit{small}, & \text{if } 0.147 < |d| \leq 0.33. \\ \textit{medium}, & \text{if } 0.33 < |d| \leq 0.474. \\ \textit{large}, & \text{if } 0.474 < |d| \leq 1. \end{cases}$$

Results: **Performance test developers are usually the core developers of the project.** Figure 3 shows the proportion of (performance) test developers who are in the top-n list of developers based on the number of commits.

[6]http://cloc.sourceforge.net/

Table 1: Developers of the `SoftInstigate/restheart` project.

Performance test developers	
Name	# of Commits
Andrea di Cesare	27
Maurizio Turatti	9
gokrokvertskhov	1

Test developers	
Name	# of Commits
Andrea di Cesare	113
Maurizio Turatti	49
Stephan Windmuller	1
gokrokvertskhovh	1

Project developers	
Name	# of Commits
Andrea di Cesare	743
Maurizio Turatti	261
Michal Suchecki	4
Ayman Abdel Ghany	2
Srdjan Grubor	2
Bence Erls	1
Blake Mitchell	1
Stephan Windmuller	1
The Gitter Badger	1
gokrokvertskhov	1

Figure 3 shows that in 50% of the studied projects, all performance test developers are core developers of the project. Figure 3 shows that the median proportion of test developers who are core developers is slightly lower. However, the Wilcoxon signed-rank test shows that the two distributions are not significantly different.

Performance tests are created and maintained by one or two developers in most of the studied projects. Figure 4 shows the number of performance test developers, test developers and project developers in each of the studied projects. 50% of the studied projects have 2 or less performance test developers, while the median number of developers in a project in our data set is 9. The projects with the highest number of performance test developers are `aseldawy/spatialhadoop` (13 performance test developers), `alibaba/druid` and `franzinc/agraph-java-client` (7 each), `apache/commons-ognl` (6), and finally `jasonrutherglen/HBASE-SEARCH` (5).

In 53 of 111 studied projects (48%) the performance tests are created and maintained by a single developer. This is particularly interesting for 13 of these 53 projects, which have 10 or more developers in total. In 43 of the 53 projects, the performance tests are created by the core developer of the project.

1 of 6 project developers work on the performance tests at least once in 50% of the studied projects. Figure 5 shows the proportion of performance test developers compared to the total number of developers and test developers in the project. We observe that test developers are not necessarily also responsible for performance testing. In 50% of the studied projects, only 44% of the test developers worked on the performance tests as well. The Wilcoxon signed-rank test shows that the distributions in Figure 5 are significantly different with a large effect size.

In most studied OS projects, performance tests are created and maintained by a single person or a small group of core developers.

4.2 The Extent of Performance Testing

Motivation: The size of the performance test suite of a project is an indication of the effort that the project dedicates to performance testing. While there exist no guidelines for the ideal size of a performance test suite, intuitively, we expect that projects that care about their performance have a larger performance test suite than other projects.

Approach: We conduct a quantitative study on the source

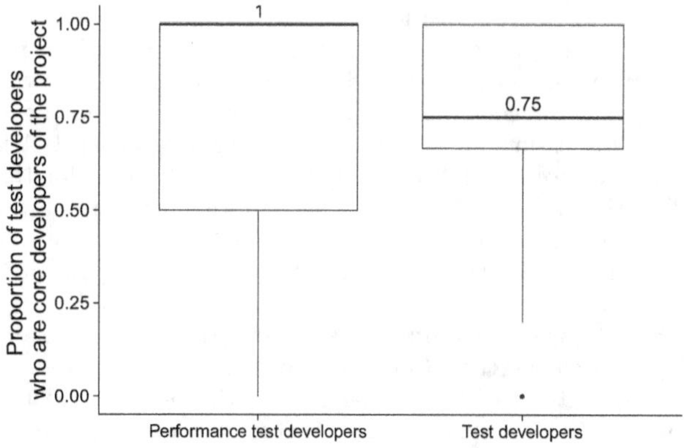

Figure 3: The proportion of (performance) test developers per project who are core developers. The number displayed within/above the boxplot is the median.

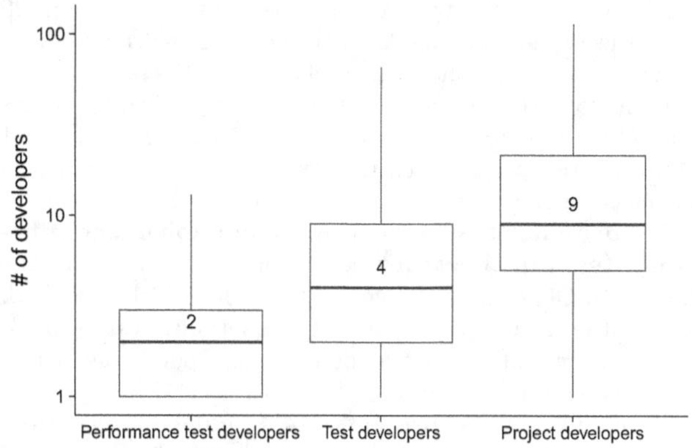

Figure 4: The number of developers per project. The number displayed within the boxplot is the median. Note that the axis is in logarithmic scale.

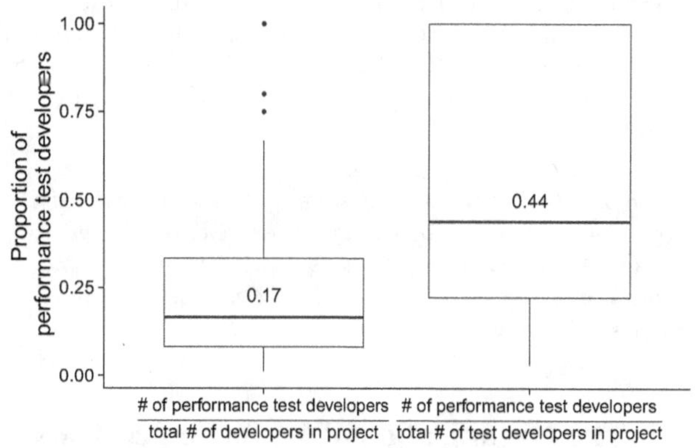

Figure 5: The proportion of performance test developers per project. The number displayed within the boxplot is the median.

lines of code (SLOC) of the performance tests and functional tests in the studied 111 OS projects using the SLOC metric that is described in Section 3.3.2.

Note that we decide against using the cyclomatic complexity as an indication of development effort. Over the last years, the contribution of complexity metrics has been under discussion in software engineering research [11, 27]. Therefore, we decide to use SLOC as an indication for the effort that a project dedicates to performance testing and additionally, we conduct a qualitative study on the contents of the performance tests to study their complexity in Section 4.4.

Results: **Performance tests are small in most projects.** Figure 6 shows the SLOC for the performance tests and functional tests. The two outliers in the boxplot are the `DeuceSTM/DeuceSTM` and `madiator/HadoopUSC` projects, which have 9460 and 6802 SLOC in their performance tests. The `DeuceSTM/DeuceSTM` description on GitHub[7] mentions that the included performance tests are known benchmarks, and not specific to this project.

There is no significant difference between the performance test suite size of PS and non-PS projects. Figure 6 shows the SLOC for the (performance) tests in 26 PS projects and 85 non-PS projects. The Wilcoxon rank-sum test shows that the number of SLOC in the performance tests in PS and non-PS projects are not significantly different. Our data does not show evidence that projects that claim superior performance take extra measures in their performance testing suites to justify these claims.

Performance tests form a small portion of the functional tests in most projects. Figure 6 shows that the median SLOC of performance tests is 246, which is a small part of the median SLOC used for functional tests (3980). We calculate that the median percentage of performance test SLOC is only around 8%.

16 of 111 studied projects (14%) have a single performance test commit. Figure 7 shows the number of performance and functional test commits for each project. In 16 projects, the performance tests are committed once and never maintained after, which suggests that the performance tests do not evolve together with the code in these projects. The median number of commits for the performance tests is 7, which indicates that many projects do not actively maintain performance tests. The outlier in our study is `h2oai/h2o-2` with 242 performance test commits, which is 18% of the total commits of this project at the time of study.

> *In most studied OS projects, the performance test suite is small and does not change often. While the mean SLOC of performance tests is larger in projects that claim high performance (PS), these results are not statisically significant.*

4.3 The Organization of Performance Tests

Motivation: By construction, all 111 projects have at least one performance test in place. However, we observe during our quantitative study on the developers involved and the size of performance tests that the extent and rigor of performance testing varies immensely between projects. To investigate whether OS software developers follow specific guidelines for organizing their performance tests, for example, as is the case with unit tests for functional testing, we study the organization of performance tests in OS projects.

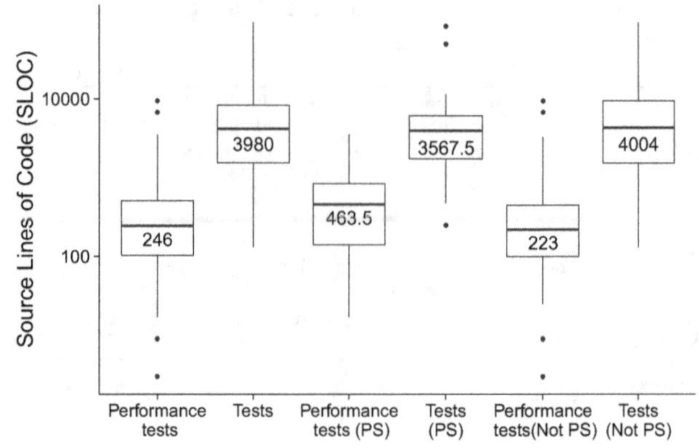

Figure 6: The number of (performance) test source lines of code (SLOC) per project. PS stands for performance-sensitive. The number displayed within the boxplot is the median. Note that the axis is in logarithmic scale.

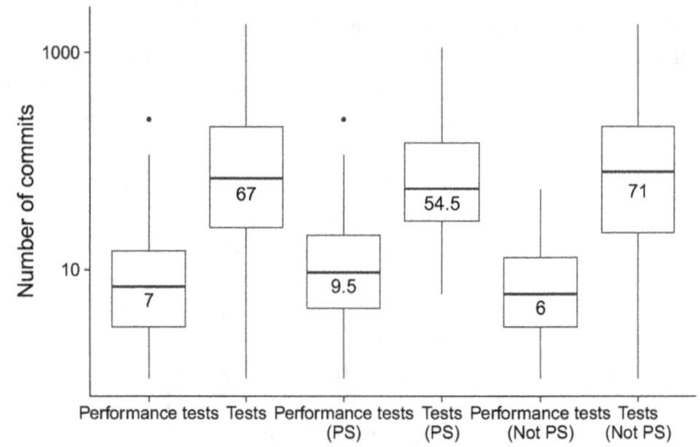

Figure 7: The number of (performance) test commits per project. PS stands for performance-sensitive. The number displayed within the boxplot is the median. Note that the axis is in logarithmic scale.

Approach: We conduct a qualitative, exploratory study on the organization of the performance tests of the 111 studied OS projects. The first author of this paper studies the performance tests with regards to their file structure and infrastructure. The results are independently verified by the second author. Both authors have more than five years of experience in doing research on software performance. The exploratory methodology that is used to conduct the qualitative study is as follows:

1. Scan the performance tests of a project for remarkable observations, or for characteristics that are observed in other projects.
2. For each observation, count the number of projects for which this observation holds.
3. Continue with the next project until all projects are studied.

Results: **The Java open source community has not yet converged against a common understanding of**

[7]https://github.com/DeuceSTM/DeuceSTM

how to conduct performance tests. While there are projects that appear to have a well-defined strategy for conducting performance tests, most projects in our study lack an evident performance testing vision, instead selecting what to write performance tests for and how to write those tests on a case-by-base basis. An example is **crosswire/jsword**, which has a single performance test for an isolated implementation issue mixed with the project's functional test suite, and two more end-to-end benchmarks that are implemented as stand-alone Java programs.

Generally, the vast majority of projects in our study are not treating performance testing as a matter of similar importance to functional testing, which is confirmed by the results of our quantitative study in Section 4.1 and 4.2. While we observe that 103 projects in our study include unit testing, usually following rather standardized best practices, the performance testing approach of the same projects often appears less extensive and less standardized.

58 of 111 (52%) studied projects scatter performance tests throughout their functional test suite. Another problem that projects seem to struggle with is how to organize and classify performance tests. 58 of the studied 111 (52%) projects, e.g., **alibaba/simpleel**, mix performance tests freely with their functional test suite (i.e., performance tests are in the same package, or even the same test file, as functional tests). 48 of 111 (43%) projects have separate test packages or categories that are related to performance, load, or stress testing. Finally, in 6 projects, performance tests are implemented as usage examples, and are delivered along with other example applications. This is the case for instance in the **apache/commons-math** project.

10 of 111 (9%) studied projects use code comments to communicate how a performance test should be executed. We also observe that some developers struggle with how to communicate to other project stakeholders how to run performance tests, what good or healthy results for specific tests are, and what environment these tests have been run in previously. 10 projects, including the **nbronson/snaptree** project, use code comments to communicate run configurations, as illustrated in Listing 1.

```
/*
 * This is not a regression test, but a micro-benchmark.
 *
 * I have run this as follows:
 *
 * repeat 5 for f in -client -server;
 * do mergeBench dolphin . jr -dsa\
 *     -da f RangeCheckMicroBenchmark.java;
 * done
 */
public class RangeCheckMicroBenchmark {
  ...
}
```

Listing 1: nbronson/snaptree/../RangeCheckMicroBenchmark.java

In 4 projects, we even observe that they use code comments to communicate previous benchmarking results. For instance, performance tests in **maxcom/lorsource** list a selection of previous run results in the footer of the source code files, as shown in Listing 2.

5 of the 111 (5%) studied projects include empty stubs for performance testing. These projects, including the **graphaware/neo4j-reco** project, apparently planned to write performance tests, but never actually finished implementing them, leaving stubs in the project source code, as in Listing 3.

```
public class ImageUtilBenchTest {
  ...
}

/**
 * #1
 Running ru.org.linux.util.image.ImageInfoBenchTest
 Tests run: 1, Failures: 0, Errors: 0, Skipped: 0,
   Time elapsed: 0.228 sec
 Running ru.org.linux.util.image.ImageUtilBenchTest
 Tests run: 1, Failures: 0, Errors: 0, Skipped: 0,
   Time elapsed: 0.637 sec
 * #2
 Running ru.org.linux.util.image.ImageInfoBenchTest
 Tests run: 2, Failures: 0, Errors: 0, Skipped: 0,
   Time elapsed: 0.374 sec
 Running ru.org.linux.util.image.ImageUtilBenchTest
 Tests run: 2, Failures: 0, Errors: 0, Skipped: 0,
   Time elapsed: 1.152 sec
 * #3
 */
```

Listing 2: maxcom/lorsource/../ImageUtilBenchTest.java

```
package com.graphaware.reco.perf;

public class EnginePerfTest {
}
```

Listing 3: graphaware/neo4j-reco/../EnginePerfTest.java

> *There appears to be no common understanding of how to conduct performance tests in Java OS software. Developers have no standardized way of organizing, executing, and reporting on the results of performance tests.*

4.4 The Types of Performance Tests

Motivation: The types of performance tests in a project represent different mind sets and goals that developers have when writing them. Hence, by studying the types of performance tests that a project uses, we get an insight into the developer's mind regarding performance testing.

Approach: We conduct a qualitative study on the types of performance tests used in each of the studied project following the same approach as described in Section 4.3. We extract five types of performance tests, which are discussed below. Note that none of the types represent "optimal performance testing" per se. Instead, all types exhibit their own advantages and disadvantages, upon which we comment in our discussion.

Results: **Type 1 – Performance Smoke Tests.** We use the term *performance smoke tests* for tests that are written with a high level of abstraction, and typically measure the end-to-end execution time of the most important end-user features for a limited number of example workloads. This type of test was the most common performance testing approach that we observed in our study, and was used by 55 of 111 (50%) projects. These projects typically implement a rather limited number of performance smoke tests, most commonly one or two. For example, **lbehnke/hierarchical-clustering-java** implements a single performance test case with a randomized clustering workload, as in Listing 4.

```
public class ClusterPerfTest {
  ...
  private Long timeN(int n) {
    Long t0 = System.currentTimeMillis();
    Cluster cluster = randomCluster(n);
    return System.currentTimeMillis() - t0;
  }

  @Test
  public void testn() throws Exception {
    for (int n = 2; n < 513; n = n * 2) {
      Long t = timeN(n);
      System.out.println("" + n + "\t" + t);
    }
  }
  ...
}
```

Listing 4: `lbehnke/hierarchical-clustering-java/../ClusterPerfTest.java`

A similar example is ↗ **`kennycason/kumo`**, a library to produce word clouds, which implements just two performance tests, one per major rendering strategy implemented in the library. These smoke tests allow developers to quickly identify large, end-user visible performance regressions. Another advantage of performance smoke tests is that they require little maintenance, as the end-user facing interfaces that these tests are written against change rarely. This is consistent with our quantitative results discussed in Section 4.2, where we have shown that many projects rarely or never change their performance tests. However, performance smoke tests provide little support for detailed debugging and metering of an application. Further, given that these high-level tests can be expected to exhibit substantial natural variability, small regressions cannot be detected with statistical confidence.

Type 2 – Microbenchmarks. 36 of 111 (32%) studied projects use performance testing that is more in line with unit testing, and strive to measure performance on a detailed level for smaller units of program code, i.e., using *microbenchmarks*. The microbenchmarking approach naturally requires more extensive performance test suites. An example of the microbenchmarking approach is the ↗ **`TridentSDK/Trident`** project, as shown in Listing 5.

In this project, performance testing is implemented in around 2500 SLOC using `JMH` and encompasses 49 separate performance tests, which are each configured with more than 10 different workloads. Unlike performance smoke tests, microbenchmarks allow developers to identify less severe performance regressions, before they have a noticeable impact on end-users. However, because microbenchmark suites are often larger than performance smoke tests, they require more time to develop and maintain, and typically take longer to execute.

Type 3 – One-Shot Performance Tests. 17 (15%) studied projects use what we dub *one-shot performance tests*. These tests usually benchmark very detailed performance issues, and appear to have been written primarily to support development-time decision making or to debug a specific issue. Such tests often compare different implementation alternatives or multiple external libraries with similar functionality, and appear to not be intended to be part of the regression test suite of the project. Consequently, such tests are often either implemented as stand-alone tests with their own main-method, or, if they are implemented as unit tests, set to `@Ignore`. An example snippet from the ↗ **`jenkinsci/remoting`** project that compares different regular expression pattern matching strategies is shown in Listing 6.

```
@State(Scope.Benchmark)
public class LatchTest {
  private static final HeldValueLatch<HeldValueLatch<?>> LATCH
        = HeldValueLatch.create();
  @Param({ "1", "2", "4", "8", "16", "32", "64",
        "128", "256", "512", "1024" })
  private int cpuTokens;

  ...

  @Benchmark
  public void down() {
    Blackhole.consumeCPU(cpuTokens);
    LATCH.countDown(LATCH);
  }

  @Benchmark
  public void wait(Blackhole blackhole) {
    Blackhole.consumeCPU(cpuTokens);
    try {
      blackhole.consume(LATCH.await());
    } catch (InterruptedException e) {
      e.printStackTrace();
    }
  }
}
```

Listing 5: `TridentSDK/Trident/../LatchTest.java`

```
@Ignore("This is not a test just a benchmark"+
  "and is here for ease of running")
public class RegExpBenchmark {

  final Pattern p1 =
    Pattern.compile("^org\\.codehaus\\.groovy\\.runtime\\..*");
  final Pattern p2 =
    Pattern.compile(
      "^org\\.apache\\.commons\\.collections\\.functors\\..*");
  final Pattern p3 =
    Pattern.compile("^.*org\\.apache\\.xalan\\..*");

  ...
}
```

Listing 6: `jenkinsci/remoting/../RegExpBenchmark.java`

Many examples of one-shot performance tests in our study appear to be source code artifacts of previous debugging sessions or discussions, rather than tests that provide continuing value to the project.

Type 4 – Performance Assertions. A fourth variation of performance test that is used by 6 (5%) projects in our study is the performance assertion. These tests are the result of developers striving to align performance testing with their functional test suite. Consequently, such tests are exclusively written in conjunction with unit testing frameworks such as `JUnit`, and often mixed with functional tests. An example of this approach comes from ↗ **`anthonyu/Kept-Collections`** in Listing 7. This example compares the performance of two bytecode deserializers, and asserts that one implementation is at least 4 times as fast as the alternative. The same test file also contains similar tests for converters of other data types, with assertions that are different but seem similarly arbitrary

Presumably, the appeal of such performance assertions is that they integrate naturally with the unit testing frameworks that most OS projects already use (and with which developers are comfortable). Unfortunately, performance assertions are also relatively inflexible, require constant maintenance to ensure assertions remain useful, and are in dan-

```
@Test
public void testSerDeserIntPerf() throws Exception {
  long startNanos = System.nanoTime();
  for (int i = 0; i < 10000; i++)
    Assert.assertEquals(i, Transformer.bytesToObject(
      Transformer.objectToBytes(i, int.class), int.class));
  final long elapsed1 = System.nanoTime() - startNanos;

  Transformer.STRINGIFIABLE_PRIMITIVES.remove(int.class);

  startNanos = System.nanoTime();
  for (int i = 0; i < 10000; i++)
    Assert.assertEquals(i, Transformer.bytesToObject(
      Transformer.objectToBytes(i, int.class), int.class));
  final long elapsed2 = System.nanoTime() - startNanos;
  Assert.assertTrue(elapsed2 > elapsed1);
  Assert.assertTrue(elapsed2 > 4 * elapsed1);
}
```

Listing 7: anthonyu/KeptCollections/../TransformerTest.java

ger of producing volatile failures due to external factors. Further, parameterizing performance assertions (e.g., deciding that the "right" speedup factor in the above example is 4) is fickle, as defining assertions conservatively means that smaller regressions can easily slip through, while aggressive assertions lead to many arbitrary test failures.

Type 5 – Implicit Performance Tests. 5 (5%) projects in our study choose to not have dedicated performance testing at all, but instead provide execution-time metrics as part of primarily functional tests. Such metrics are often as simple as writing performance data to `System.out` within a subset or all unit tests. This low-friction approach to performance testing has the advantage of exceedingly low additional development effort. However, systematically using the resulting data to track the performance of a project over multiple builds or versions is difficult. Further, functional tests are not necessarily optimized for performance measurement (e.g., they often do not use representative workloads, but rather workloads that implement the edge cases that are most important for functional testing). Hence, the expressiveness of such implicit performance tests is arguably low as compared to well-written dedicated performance tests.

> *Most studied OS projects use one or two performance smoke tests, to test the performance of the main functionality of the project, or a suite of microbenchmarks, to test the performance of smaller parts of the project.*

4.5 The Tooling and Frameworks

Motivation: There exist several widely-spread tools and frameworks, such as `JUnit`, for functional testing. In this section, we investigate whether there are performance testing tools that are similarly dominating in OS projects.

Approach: We conduct a qualitative study using the approach described before. We extract three general approaches that Java-based OS software uses for performance testing.

Results: **Approach 1 – Performance Unit Testing.** 57 (51%) projects in our study use their unit testing framework, typically `JUnit`, to write and run performance tests. These tests are unusual in that they typically do not actually "assert" anything (except in the case of performance assertions, as discussed above). Instead, such performance-related unit tests often just run an example workload and print metrics, either to `System.out` or to a file. An example from ↗ `fasseg/exp4j`, a simple Math calculator, is shown in Listing 8.

```
public class PerformanceTest {

  private static final long BENCH_TIME = 2l;
  private static final String EXPRESSION =
    "log(x) - y * (sqrt(x^cos(y)))";

  @Test
  public void testBenches() throws Exception {
    StringBuffer sb = new StringBuffer();
      ...
    int math = benchJavaMath();
    double mathRate = (double) math / (double) BENCH_TIME;
    fmt.format(
      "| %-22s | %25.2f | %22.2f %% |%n",
      "Java Math", mathRate, 100f
    );
    System.out.print(sb.toString());
      ...
  }
}
```

Listing 8: fasseg/exp4j/../PerformanceTest.java

The main advantage of using a unit testing framework to run performance tests is that this approach requires little to no changes to the project build configuration, including configuration of the CI server. Furthermore, developers do not need to learn additional tools such as `JMH`.

However, unlike dedicated frameworks, unit testing frameworks are not optimized for performance testing. Hence, the intricacies of benchmarking modern virtual machine code [6] (e.g., just-in-time compilation and garbage collection) can easily influence performance testing results. Another problem is that performance tests often take substantial time to execute. As a result, performance tests slow down the build considerably if these tests are part of the regular unit test suite of the project. Solutions to this issue include putting performance unit tests into a different test category that is excluded from standard builds, or setting performance tests to `@Ignore` by default and only running them on-demand.

Given the apparent popularity of performance unit testing in practice, it is unsurprising that some performance testing frameworks actually extend `JUnit` to ease integration. One example of such a tool is the `JUnitBenchmarks` framework[8]. However, the authors have by now discontinued the project and suggest using `JMH` instead.

Approach 2 – Stand-alone Performance Testing. In 55 (50%) projects in our study, performance tests are written as stand-alone Java programs. These projects eschew using any support framework for writing and executing tests. Instead, benchmark workloads, performance tests, and data reporting are implemented from scratch and customized for the project. These customizations can take the form of a large number of programs intended to be run independently (i.e., each with their own main method), simple bash scripts that launch a benchmark run, or sophisticated testing frameworks that appear to have required non-trivial development effort. An example is ↗ `rabbitmq/rabbitmq-java-client`, which built a dedicated command-line tool for launching performance tests, implementing various scenarios and workloads, and supporting more than 25 command line options.

Writing performance tests as stand-alone Java programs offers the advantage of great flexibility, and naturally avoids

[8] https://labs.carrotsearch.com/junit-benchmarks.html

"polluting" the project's unit tests. However, stand-alone performance tests need specific tooling or more complex setup should they be integrated into the project build, e.g., on the CI server. Furthermore, building and maintaining a sophisticated custom performance testing framework on a per-project basis arguably leads to considerable additional development effort. Some developers building such stand-alone performance tests seem to be at least aware of the problems of naïvely benchmarking Java code. Attempted workarounds that these developers employ include excessively invoking `System.gc()`, or finding workloads using trial-and-error that avoid just-in-time compilation for their specific system and used JVM. Furthermore, some developers use code comments or strings of test data to indicate doubt about the expressiveness of their performance tests. The example in Listing 9 shows this from the **dustin/java-memcached-client** project.

```
String object =
  "This is a test of an object blah blah es, "
  + "serialization does not seem to slow things down so much. "
  + "The gzip compression is horrible horrible performance, "
  + "so we only use it for very large objects. "
  + "I have not done any heavy benchmarking recently";
```

Listing 9:
`dustin/java-memcached-client/../MemcachedThreadBench.java`

Approach 3 – Using Specific Performance Testing Frameworks. Finally, only 18 (16%) projects in the study use dedicated performance testing frameworks. More detailedly, `JMH` is used by 10 projects, and Google `Caliper` by 4. An additional 4 projects are using lesser-known or more specialized frameworks, such as `JUnitBenchmarks`, `Contiperf`, or `Faban`. However, not all of these projects use dedicated performance testing frameworks for all their performance tests. Some projects, for instance **apache/commons-csv**, have some newer performance tests written in `JMH` in addition to their `JUnit`-based legacy tests.

An interesting question is why, even among projects that are per se interested in performance testing, so few elect to use a dedicated performance testing framework (even going through the pain of manually building a custom performance testing framework from scratch instead, as discussed above). One potential explanation is that performance testing frameworks may not be widely-known among developers. Another explanation is that dedicated frameworks may be perceived as too difficult to set up or to write tests with, or that the benefits of a dedicated framework do no outweigh the disadvantages of writing tests in `JUnit`. Finally, a possible explanation is that dedicated frameworks do not integrate easily with standard build systems, such as Jenkins. More research is needed to address the question of why OS software developers do not use a dedicated performance testing framework.

> *Most studied OS projects use either JUnit or simple standalone programs for performance testing in lieu of a dedicated performance testing framework.*

5. IMPLICATIONS

In this section, we give an overview of the lessons that we learned from our study, and we provide an interpretation of what our results imply for practitioners, OS developers, and academics who are working on topics that are related to performance testing.

There is a lack of a "killer app" for performance testing. First and foremost, a recurring observation in our study is that performance testing in Java-based OS software is neither as extensive nor as standardized as it is the case for functional testing. While the lack of standardization was already observed by Weyuker et al. in 2000 [25], our study results indicate that even at the time of writing there is still a long way to go before performance engineering truly becomes an integral part of the software development lifecycle for OS software. We speculate that one reason for this evident lack of standardization is that there currently is no "killer app" to conduct performance tests with in an easy, yet powerful, way, similar to how `JUnit` has standardised unit testing for Java.

Writing performance tests may not be a popular task in OS projects. In 48% of the studied projects, performance tests are written by a single developer, who usually is a core developer of the project. In addition, performance tests are often written once and rarely or never updated after. These observations suggest that performance testing may be a daunting and unpopular task in open source projects which does not attract many external contributors. Potential reasons for the small number of external contributors may include a perceived difficulty of writing performance tests or a lack of awareness in OS projects that performance tests are a potential contribution to the project. However, our data does not allow us to provide an answer to this question, requiring further research.

OS developers require better support for quick-and-dirty performance testing. In performance testing research, emphasis is typically put on providing the most accurate and statistically rigorous performance results possible (e.g., controlling for as many confounding factors as possible). Contrarily, in our study we observe that developers are often willing to write "quick-and-dirty" performance tests, trading off accuracy of measurement for lower implementation effort. For instance, many projects are either not aware of or knowingly ignore the influence of the Java virtual machine on their performance tests, or report only arithmetic mean values, ignoring standard deviations or outliers. The apparent mismatch between what OS developers want and what performance testing research is delivering may be an explanation for the low adoption of existing performance testing tools. We feel that there is unexplored potential for future research on performance testing approaches that particularly focus on being low-friction for developers, for instance, through easy-to-use and non-parameterized methods, reusing existing code (e.g., existing unit tests) for performance testing, or through automated performance test generation.

Performance testing is multi-faceted. One potential reason why no universal performance testing framework has emerged yet is that performance testing is inherently multi-faceted. We identify five different types of performance tests, which are usually conducted with vastly different goals in mind, consequently leading to different implementation and tool selection choices. However, note that this is not different to functional testing, where the difference between unit testing, integration testing, or user acceptance testing is well-understood in research and practice. We hope that our study will serve as a first step towards a similar understanding of performance testing, ultimately leading to more targeted tool support.

Integration into standard CI frameworks is key. 51% of the projects in our study are piggy-backing on their unit testing frameworks to also conduct performance testing, despite not actually using any assertions. The usage of unit testing frameworks for performance testing indicates that a straight-forward integration into standard build and CI tooling, as provided by unit testing frameworks, is a key real-world feature which current industrial performance testing tools as well as research approaches do not sufficiently value. Recent work by Horký et al. [12] on declarative performance testing that integrates well with unit testing is a promising direction for addressing this integration challenge.

6. THREATS TO VALIDITY

In this section, we discuss the most relevant threats to the validity of our study.

External Validity. One of the external threats to our results is generalization. While the goal of our exploratory study is not to be exhaustive, we aimed at studying a wide range of representative Java-based OS projects that conduct performance testing. However, it is possible that our results do not extend to projects that are written in different languages or industrial projects. In order to address this threat, additional research on industrial projects and projects that are written in different languages is necessary.

Our project selection may be biased by assuming that the test code of a project is stored inside the `src/test` directory, following the conventions introduced by Apache `Maven`. While this assumption seems reasonable for Java-based OS projects, more research is needed for identifying an exhaustive list of projects that have performance tests.

Construct Validity. There are several threats to the construct validity of our study. First, we assume that the performance tests of a project are stored as part of the GitHub repository. We are aware that some OS projects have externalized their benchmarking and performance testing code to external projects. These projects are not considered by our research design.

Further, we use a manual identification process to identify the performance tests in a project, which may in some cases have led us to miss performance tests, especially if those are stored in a non-standard location. To mitigate this threat, the process was conducted by the two authors of the paper, who both have more than five years of experience in performance testing research.

In addition, in several projects, developers appear to be using multiple GitHub profiles. As it is difficult to decide whether these profiles are actually owned by the same developer, we treat them as owned by different developers. As a result, our observations may be slightly overestimating the number of developers that are engaged in performance testing.

Finally, we count only the SLOC in Java files. If a project uses a different language for its performance tests, the code is not included in our study. We observed that only one of the projects uses Scala for its performance tests.

7. CONCLUSION

In this paper, we have presented an exploratory study of performance testing in OS Java projects. We have extracted a data set of 111 projects from GitHub which conduct performance testing. We used a combination of quantitative and qualitative research methods to investigate the performance tests used by these projects. We find that that the current state of performance testing in Java-based OS projects is not overly reassuring. Most projects contain few performance tests, which are also hardly maintained. Projects do not appear to receive many source code contributions related to performance testing. Instead, performance tests are often written as a one-time activity by a core developer. Further, we note that projects approach performance testing from different angles – while most projects focus particularly on high-level performance smoke tests, others conduct more extensive microbenchmarking or even define a small number of performance assertations using `JUnit`. While performance testing frameworks exist, they are not used by most projects. Instead, projects often either build more or less sophisticated standalone test suites from ground up, or repurpose their unit testing framework for performance testing.

Our study results imply that developers are currently missing a "killer app" for performance testing, which would likely standarize how performance tests are conducted similar to how `JUnit` has standardized unit testing. An ubiquitious performance testing tool will need to support performance tests on different levels of abstraction (smoke tests versus detailed microbenchmarking), provide strong integration into existing build and CI tools, and support both, extensive testing with rigorous methods as well as quick-and-dirty tests that pair reasonable expressiveness with being fast to write and maintain even by developers who are not experts in software performance engineering.

The main limitation of our work is that we have focused exclusively on OS projects written in the Java programming language. Hence, it is unclear to what extent our results generalize to other communities. This question should be answered in a follow-up study. Further, more research will be needed to investigate whether existing performance testing tools such as `JMH` are indeed missing important functionality as indicated above, or simply not well-known enough in the OS community.

Acknowledgements

The research leading to these results has received funding from the Swiss National Science Foundation (SNF) under project name "MINCA" (Models to Increase the Cost Awareness of Cloud Developers).

8. REFERENCES

[1] M. Aberdour. Achieving quality in open-source software. *IEEE Software*, 24(1):58–64, Jan 2007.

[2] J. P. S. Alcocer and A. Bergel. Tracking down performance variation against source code evolution. In *Proceedings of the 11th Symposium on Dynamic Languages (DLS)*, pages 129–139. ACM, 2015.

[3] A. Avritzer, J. Kondek, D. Liu, and E. J. Weyuker. Software performance testing based on workload characterization. In *Proceedings of the 3rd International Workshop on Software and Performance (WOSP)*, pages 17–24. ACM, 2002.

[4] S. Baltes, O. Moseler, F. Beck, and S. Diehl. Navigate, understand, communicate: How developers locate performance bugs. In *2015 ACM/IEEE International Symposium on Empirical Software Engineering and Measurement (ESEM)*, pages 1–10, Oct 2015.

[5] M. Beller, G. Gousios, A. Panichella, and A. Zaidman. When, how, and why developers (do not) test in their IDEs. In *Proceedings of the 10th Joint Meeting on Foundations of Software Engineering (ESEC/FSE)*, pages 179–190. ACM, 2015.

[6] S. M. Blackburn, R. Garner, C. Hoffmann, A. M. Khang, K. S. McKinley, R. Bentzur, A. Diwan, D. Feinberg, D. Frampton, S. Z. Guyer, M. Hirzel, A. Hosking, M. Jump, H. Lee, J. E. B. Moss, A. Phansalkar, D. Stefanović, T. VanDrunen, D. von Dincklage, and B. Wiedermann. The DaCapo benchmarks: Java benchmarking development and analysis. In *Proceedings of the 21st ACM SIGPLAN Conference on Object-oriented Programming Systems, Languages, and Applications (OOPSLA)*, pages 169–190. ACM, 2006.

[7] J. Cito, P. Leitner, T. Fritz, and H. C. Gall. The making of cloud applications: An empirical study on software development for the cloud. In *Proceedings of the 10th Joint Meeting on Foundations of Software Engineering (ESEC/FSE)*, pages 393–403. ACM, 2015.

[8] A. Georges, D. Buytaert, and L. Eeckhout. Statistically rigorous java performance evaluation. In *Proceedings of the 22nd ACM SIGPLAN Conference on Object-oriented Programming Systems and Applications (OOPSLA)*, pages 57–76. ACM, 2007.

[9] X. Han and T. Yu. An empirical study on performance bugs for highly configurable software systems. In *Proceedings of the 10th ACM/IEEE International Symposium on Empirical Software Engineering and Measurement (ESEM)*, pages 23:1–23:10, 2016.

[10] C. Heger, J. Happe, and R. Farahbod. Automated Root Cause Isolation of Performance Regressions During Software Development. In *Proceedings of the 4th ACM/SPEC International Conference on Performance Engineering (ICPE)*, pages 27–38, 2013.

[11] I. Herraiz and A. E. Hassan. Beyond lines of code: Do we need more complexity metrics? *Making software: what really works, and why we believe it*, pages 125–141, 2010.

[12] V. Horký, P. Libič, L. Marek, A. Steinhauser, and P. Tůma. Utilizing performance unit tests to increase performance awareness. In *Proceedings of the 6th ACM/SPEC International Conference on Performance Engineering (ICPE)*, pages 289–300. ACM, 2015.

[13] P. Huang, X. Ma, D. Shen, and Y. Zhou. Performance regression testing target prioritization via performance risk analysis. In *Proceedings of the 36th International Conference on Software Engineering (ICSE)*, pages 60–71. ACM, 2014.

[14] Z. M. Jiang and A. E. Hassan. A survey on load testing of large-scale software systems. *IEEE Transactions on Software Engineering (TSE)*, 41(11):1091–1118, 2015.

[15] G. Jin, L. Song, X. Shi, J. Scherpelz, and S. Lu. Understanding and detecting real-world performance bugs. In *Proceedings of the 33rd ACM SIGPLAN Conference on Programming Language Design and Implementation (PLDI)*, pages 77–88. ACM, 2012.

[16] J. D. Long, D. Feng, and N. Cliff. Ordinal analysis of behavioral data. *Handbook of psychology*, 2003.

[17] Q. Luo, D. Poshyvanyk, and M. Grechanik. Mining performance regression inducing code changes in evolving software. In *Proceedings of the 13th International Conference on Mining Software Repositories (MSR)*, pages 25–36. ACM, 2016.

[18] A. Mockus, R. T. Fielding, and J. Herbsleb. A case study of open source software development: The apache server. In *Proceedings of the 22nd International Conference on Software Engineering (ICSE)*, pages 263–272. ACM, 2000.

[19] R. Pooley. Software engineering and performance: A roadmap. In *Proceedings of the Conference on The Future of Software Engineering (ICSE)*, pages 189–199. ACM, 2000.

[20] J. Romano, J. D. Kromrey, J. Coraggio, J. Skowronek, and L. Devine. Exploring methods for evaluating group differences on the NSSE and other surveys: Are the t-test and Cohen's d indices the most appropriate choices. In *Annual meeting of the Southern Association for Institutional Research*, 2006.

[21] J. P. Sandoval Alcocer, A. Bergel, and M. T. Valente. Learning from source code history to identify performance failures. In *Proceedings of the 7th ACM/SPEC on International Conference on Performance Engineering (ICPE)*, pages 37–48, 2016.

[22] C. U. Smith and L. G. Williams. Software performance engineering: A case study including performance comparison with design alternatives. *IEEE Transactions on Software Engineering (TSE)*, 19(7):720–741, July 1993.

[23] M. D. Syer, Z. M. Jiang, M. Nagappan, A. E. Hassan, M. Nasser, and P. Flora. Continuous validation of load test suites. In *Proceedings of the 5th ACM/SPEC International Conference on Performance Engineering (ICPE)*, pages 259–270. ACM, 2014.

[24] M. L. Vasquez, C. Vendome, Q. Luo, and D. Poshyvanyk. How developers detect and fix performance bottlenecks in Android apps. In R. Koschke, J. Krinke, and M. P. Robillard, editors, *Proceedings of the International Conference on Software Maintenance and Evolution (ICSME)*, pages 352–361. IEEE Computer Society, 2015.

[25] E. J. Weyuker and F. I. Vokolos. Experience with performance testing of software systems: Issues, an approach, and case study. *IEEE Transactions on Software Engineering (TSE)*, 26(12):1147–1156, 2000.

[26] S. Zaman, B. Adams, and A. E. Hassan. A Qualitative Study on Performance Bugs. In *Proceedings of the 9th IEEE Working Conference on Mining Software Repositories (MSR)*, pages 199–208. IEEE Press, 2012.

[27] F. Zhang, A. E. Hassan, S. McIntosh, and Y. Zou. The use of summation to aggregate software metrics hinders the performance of defect prediction models. *IEEE Transactions on Software Engineering (TSE)*, (1):1–16, 2016.

Collaborative Computing for Heterogeneous Integrated Systems

Li-Wen Chang†, Juan Gómez-Luna*, Izzat El Hajj†, Sitao Huang†, Deming Chen†, Wen-mei Hwu†

†University of Illinois at Urbana-Champaign, *Universidad de Córdoba
lchang20@illinois.edu, el1goluj@uco.es, {elhajj2, shuang91, dchen, w-hwu}@illinois.edu

ABSTRACT

Computing systems today typically employ, in addition to powerful CPUs, various types of specialized devices such as Graphics Processing Units (GPUs) and Field-Programmable Gate Arrays (FPGAs). Such heterogeneous systems are evolving towards tighter integration of CPUs and devices for improved performance and reduced energy consumption. Compared to traditional use of GPUs and FPGAs as offload accelerators, this tight integration enables close collaboration between processors and devices, which is important for better utilization of system resources and higher performance. Programming interfaces are also adapting rapidly to these tightly integrated heterogeneous platforms by introducing features such as shared virtual memory, memory coherence, and system-wide atomics, making collaborative computing even more practical.

In this paper, we survey current integrated heterogeneous systems and corresponding collaboration techniques. We evaluate the impact of collaborative computing on two heterogeneous integrated systems, CPU-GPU and CPU-FPGA, using OpenCL. Finally, we discuss the limitation of OpenCL and envision what suitable programming languages for collaborative computing will look like.

1. INTRODUCTION

While GPUs have been a central part of computing systems due to their ability to provide high performance at low energy costs while being programmable, FPGAs have also been integrated into computing systems by industry vendors such as Microsoft [19, 5], Intel/Altera [18, 2], Xilinx [22], and IBM [4] due to their extremely high power efficiency. The continuous demand for higher performance under constrained power and energy budgets is driving tighter system-level integration of CPUs with other coprocessors or accelerators, such as GPUs or FPGAs.

With such tight integration, fine-grain collaboration between processors becomes a practical approach to improving resource utilization and system performance [12]. For this reason, programming interfaces such as OpenCL 2.0 and CUDA 8.0 have introduced features such as shared virtual memory and system-wide atomics to productively express fine-grain collaboration. Among existing programming interfaces, OpenCL is perhaps the most suitable interface for programming these heterogeneous architectures because it is supported by a wide range of processors, including CPUs and GPUs, as well as FPGAs via high-level synthesis (HLS). Although OpenCL FPGA stacks [13] currently support only OpenCL 1.2 which does not support the new features, it is expected to support OpenCL 2.0 in the near future.

Multiple studies [8, 14] have investigated characteristics of and optimization for heterogeneous systems with CPUs, GPUs, and FPGAs. Recent literature [21, 15, 16, 11, 10] has focused on fine-grain collaboration in the context of system-level CPU-GPU integration. A variety of general collaboration patterns have been investigated [21, 11], which can be mainly classified into data or task partitioning. However, similar collaborative computing techniques have not been studied for CPU-FPGA systems.

We envision future integrated heterogeneous system including CPUs, GPUs, and FPGAs. Features such as shared virtual memory and system-wide atomics will be widely adopted in most programming models. Coherence will be supported, which can either be achieved via unified physical memory or via coherence protocols over various interconnect technologies. These features are a step forward in programmability, simplifying fine-grain collaboration which will become ubiquitous, instead of traditional use of GPUs and FPGAs as offload accelerators.

Although OpenCL and other existing programming models support expressing fine-grain collaboration in applications for specific integrated systems, these programming models show limited support for automatically converting a program from one collaboration pattern to another pattern across systems. We envision new high-level programming languages that are capable of synthesizing kernels with different collaboration patterns from generic representations of the program. These languages will replace OpenCL as a programming interface for end users.

The rest of this paper is organized as follows. Section 2 describes our envisioned heterogeneous integrated system, and surveys existing techniques to realize these systems. Section 3 describes collaborative computing, its patterns, and provides a preliminary evaluation using current integrated systems as proxies. Section 4 describes the limitation of current programming models and our envisioned model. Section 5 concludes this paper and outlines future work.

ICPE'17, April 22-26, 2017, L'Aquila, Italy

DOI: http://dx.doi.org/10.1145/3030207.3030244

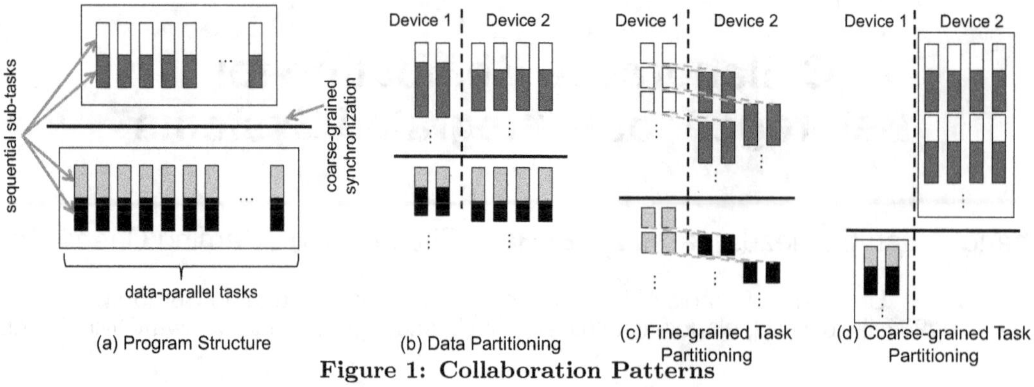

Figure 1: Collaboration Patterns

2. INTEGRATED HETEROGENEOUS SYSTEMS

Traditionally, accelerators such as GPUs and FPGAs have been connected to CPUs through PCIe or similar interfaces, which provide efficient large-block data transfer through Direct Memory Access (DMA) engines between devices. However, DMA overhead is a burden on performance for smaller data transfers due to non-uniform data accesses in many contemporary workloads (e.g., graph-based algorithms, machine learning inference, etc.). For this reason, heterogeneous systems need shared memory between CPUs and accelerators. There have been several recent efforts led by industry vendors in this direction for both CPU-GPU and CPU-FPGA systems. They all provide shared coherent memory in a similar way, but differ in CPU architecture, processor implementation, and silicon fabrication.

For CPU-GPU systems, NVIDIA has launched the Pascal architecture [17] which implements coherence over PCIe and NVlink. AMD APUs provide even closer integration by coupling devices on the same die, and using specialized memory buses. The CPU-FPGA counterparts are Intel QPI [18], Hyper Transport, Front Side Bus (FSB), AXI Coherency Extension (ACE) [22], Acceleration Coherency Port (ACP), ARM Core Link Interconnect, IBM CAPI [4], and CCIX [1].

We envision that future heterogeneous systems will contain CPU cores with one or multiple GPUs and/or FPGAs. The three devices have access to coherent memory through specific interfaces. Additional non-coherent interfaces might also be included for data not shared across devices, or not simultaneously accessed. The system could include a shared last-level cache (LLC) that can help accelerate collaborative workloads [10]. The three devices might be integrated at either chip-level or realized as separate chips. As mentioned above, current trends integrate CPU and GPU or CPU and FPGA [2] in the same die. However, systems with the three devices in the same die are already available, though the GPU is not OpenCL-programmable yet [22].

3. COLLABORATIVE COMPUTING

3.1 Collaboration Patterns

Multiple collaboration patterns have been studied for integrated heterogeneous architectures [11, 21]. These patterns can be classified into two major types based on work partitioning strategies: data partitioning and task partitioning. Task partitioning can be further refined into fine-grain and coarse-grain, based on partitioning points in the code.

Figures 1(b)-(d) illustrate different patterns for an example program in Figure 1(a) containing two sets of data-parallel tasks, each with two sequential sub-tasks (white/dark gray, and light gray/black). We provide a few key insights behind the collaboration patterns, while referring to [11] for more detailed explanations. First, given an application, different devices might prefer different sub-tasks due to different device characteristics (such as parallelism and resources), making collaborative computing non-trivial. Second, while fine-grain task partitioning (Figure 1(c)) improves utilization of parallelism across devices via pipeline execution, it may require coherent memory and system-wide atomic support which may introduce some communication overhead. Third, traditional accelerator models with CPUs and accelerators are special cases of coarse-grain task partitioning (Figure 1(d)). Last, coarse-grain task partitioning may utilize all devices in a pipeline fashion if multiple independent data sets are processed independently.

Multiple factors may impact the choice of collaboration pattern. These factors include: the diversity of sub-tasks, the cost of communication between devices (latency and bandwidth), the relative metrics (such as performance, power, energy, etc.) among devices for a specific workload, and hardware resource constraints. Moreover, collaborative computing can be considered with multiple objectives such as maximizing performance, minimizing latency, minimizing power, or minimizing energy. In this paper, we mainly focus on performance.

3.2 Preliminary Evaluation

We evaluate the performance benefits of collaborative execution in two current heterogeneous integrated systems: CPU-GPU and CPU-FPGA. Our CPU-GPU system is an AMD Kaveri A10-7850K APU, while our CPU-FPGA system is an Intel Xeon E3-1240 v3 connected through PCIe 3.0 x8 with an Altera Stratix V GX FPGA on a Terasic DE5-Net board. The AMD APP SDK 3.0 with OpenCL 2.0 is used for Kaveri, and Intel OpenCL FPGA SDK 16.0 with OpenCL 1.2 is used for Stratix V, since OpenCL 2.0 is not supported. Two OpenCL benchmarks, Canny Edge Detection (CED) and Random Sample Consensus (RSC) from the Chai benchmark suite [11] are used for evaluation. CED is evaluated for both data partitioning and coarse-grain task partitioning, while RSC is evaluated for both data partitioning and fine-grain task partitioning.

CPU-GPU. Figure 2 presents the speedups of CED and RSC over CPU-only on the CPU-GPU system. For CED, while GPU-only delivers 9.30× more performance than CPU only, collaboration with data partitioning does

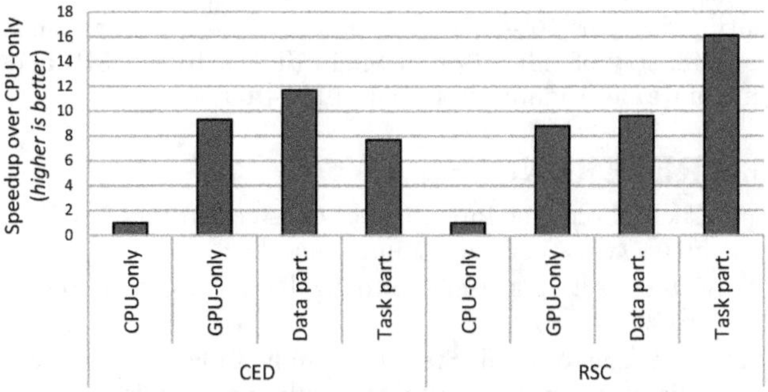

Figure 2: Speedup on CPU-GPU

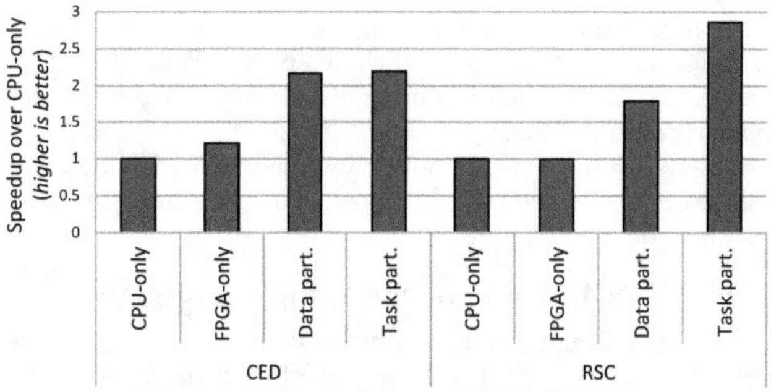

Figure 3: Speedup on CPU-FPGA

even better with 11.67× and 1.26× over CPU-only and GPU-only respectively. However, unlike data partitioning, coarse-grain task partitioning is only 0.83× of GPU-only performance. One reason is that by assigning tasks to the CPU, the performance of the entire flow is hampered, since in CED the GPU performance dominates the CPU. Another reason is that task partitioning introduces cache coherence cost for data sharing between the CPU and the GPU.

For RSC, while GPU-only achieves an 8.80× speedup over CPU-only, collaboration with fine-grain task partitioning outperforms CPU-only and GPU-only by 16.14× and 1.83× respectively. The main reason is that one sub-task in RSC is inherently sequential so its efficiency is improved by moving it to the CPU. However, data partitioning is only slightly better than GPU-only by 1.09×, and significantly worse than fine-grain task partitioning by 0.59×, because the GPU efficiency in data partitioning still suffers from that inherently sequential sub-task.

These two examples show that the best collaborative execution pattern highly depends on application characteristics.

CPU-FPGA. Figure 3 shows speedups for CED and RSC over CPU-only on the CPU-FPGA system. The best CED collaboration pattern is coarse-grain task partitioning which is 2.25× and 1.85× faster than CPU-only and FPGA-only respectively. Data partitioning is just slightly slower than coarse-grain task partitioning by a factor of 0.96×. The best RSC collaboration pattern is fine-grain task partitioning, with 2.57×, 2.36×, and 1.38× speedup over CPU-only, FPGA-only, and data partitioning respectively. The reason is similar to CPU-GPU collaboration.

An important consideration for improving performance on FPGAs is the OpenCL HLS *kernel duplication* factor. Performance typically improves with more duplication, but then saturates when a limit on one of the resources is reached. Different applications, or the same application with a different collaboration pattern, may saturate for different resources. In our evaluation, the performance of CED with data partitioning and task partitioning both saturate the memory bandwidth. However, for RSC, while task partitioning saturates the memory bandwidth, data partitioning saturates the DSP resource on FPGAs before the memory bandwidth limit is reached. This explains why the disparity between collaboration patterns differs across applications.

Comparison. In our evaluation for both systems, collaborative execution seems beneficial for performance if applied correctly. We observe that different applications favor different collaboration patterns. For example, CED performs better with data partitioning, while RSC favors task partitioning. We also observe that different devices may favor different collaboration patterns. For example, for CED, data partitioning is better on CPU-GPU, but task partitioning is slightly better on CPU-FPGA.

Note that the collaboration had more performance benefit in the CPU-GPU platform than in the CPU-FPGA platform. One reason is that in the CPU in our CPU-FPGA platform is more powerful than the CPU in our CPU-GPU platform, diminishing the speedups gained from using FPGA. Another reason is the difference in OpenCL support. OpenCL 2.0, which is used for CPU-GPU execution, comes with heterogeneous features such as shared virtual memory and system-wide atomics that enable more practical collaboration than OpenCL 1.2 which is used for CPU-FPGA execution. Moreover, OpenCL stacks for FPGAs based on HLS might be less mature than OpenCL stacks for GPUs.

4. PROGRAMMING INTERFACE

4.1 Limitation of Current Practice

Different collaboration strategies can be seen as different choices of program optimizations. In this sense, conversion between collaboration strategies is a code transformation between specific optimizations. Finding the best collaboration strategy for a given program is an optimization-space exploration problem, while adapting across different integrated systems is a performance portability problem. Current practices of programming languages, such as OpenCL, require programmers to explicitly express collaboration strategies. Doing so limits the potential for automatic code transformation for collaboration in multiple ways.

First, it is challenging to automatically apply fine grain task partitioning to a generic OpenCL kernel. Sub-tasks can only be partitioned at specific points of the code. More precisely, it requires kernel fission at specific points of the code and introduces extra queue objects for communication among those new kernels. Therefore, while coarse-grain task partitioning is commonly adopted in adaptive runtimes [9, 3] and data partitioning can be achieved through parameter tuning or dynamic fetching [11], fine-grain task partitioning, to the best of our knowledge, has not yet been automated by existing OpenCL frameworks for general purpose applications.

Second, it is even more challenging to automate conversion from one collaboration strategy to another in OpenCL. Conversion from data partitioning or coarse-grain task partitioning to fine-grain task partitioning is at least as difficult as automation of fine-grain task partitioning, which requires kernel fission. On the other hand, conversion from fine-grain task partitioning into data partitioning or coarse-grain task partitioning requires kernel fusion. Considering two subtask kernels might not have identical work-item/work-group mapping, kernel fusion requires sophisticated analyses and transformations to harmonize the mapping. Even though it is possible, the introduced branch divergence might tax the benefits of kernel fusion.

Lastly, to the best of our knowledge, OpenCL delivers limited performance portability when used as one source for different devices [7, 6].

4.2 High-Level Programming Language

High-level languages such as TANGRAM [6] and Halide [20] provide generic unified programming interfaces for applications, and deliver promising performance portability across devices. By introducing collaboration strategies as optimizations, kernels with collaborative computing can be directly synthesized in these high-level languages. Therefore, compared to OpenCL, we envision these high-level languages will be more suitable programming interfaces for collaborative execution.

For example, TANGRAM is able to synthesize kernels with various granularities. For fine-grain task partitioning, atomic codelets in TANGRAM can be considered the most fine-grain sub-tasks, thus defining sub-task boundaries. Doing so avoids having to identify fission points in an OpenCL kernel, and significantly simplifies the automation of fine-grain task partitioning. Coarse-grain task partitioning can be achieved by simply synthesizing each kernel to the target device it will be mapped to. Data partitioning can be achieved by extending TANGRAM's containers such as `map` and `partition` for adjusting work-item/work-group mapping. While TANGRAM currently supports only CPUs and GPUs, introducing HLS as a backend can extend TANGRAM to support FPGAs.

While these high-level languages have promising potential to automatically synthesize kernels with various collaboration patterns, there remains the step of searching for the optimal collaboration strategy for a given integrated system. This emphasizes the need for performance modeling, effective heuristics, offline tuning, or adaptive runtime for collaborative computing on heterogeneous integrated systems.

5. CONCLUSION AND FUTURE WORK

In this paper, we have explored collaborative computing for heterogeneous integrated systems. We surveyed techniques in integrated architectures for enabling effective collaboration. We demonstrated the benefits of collaborative computing by evaluating both CPU-GPU and CPU-FPGA systems. We also discussed the limitation of current programming interfaces, such as OpenCL. Finally, we envision that multiple high-level languages, such as TANGRAM and Halide, will be more suitable programming interfaces for collaborative computing than OpenCL.

For future work, we will study more heterogeneous implementations of collaborative workloads in order to find generic optimization techniques which can be automatically applied by compilers of high-level languages.

Acknowledgment

This material is based upon work supported by the DoE National Nuclear Security Administration (DE-NA0002374), Hewlett-Packard Enterprise Labs, the Starnet Center for Future Architecture Research (C-FAR), the Huawei Project (YB2015120003), and the IBM Center for Cognitive Computing Systems Research Center at UIUC. We also thank the Ministry of Education of Spain (TIN2013-42253P) and the Junta de Andalucía of Spain (TIC-1692).

6. REFERENCES

[1] Cache Coherent Interconnect for Accelerators (CCIX). http://www.ccixconsortium.com, 2016.

[2] Altera. Altera's User-Customizable ARM-Based SoC, 2015.

[3] C. Augonnet et al. StarPU: a unified platform for task scheduling on heterogeneous multicore architectures. *CCPE*, 23(2):187–198, 2011.

[4] Bruce Wile. IBM Systems and Technology Group. Coherent Accelerator Processor Interface (CAPI) for POWER8 systems. White paper, September 2014.

[5] A. M. Caulfield et al. A cloud-scale acceleration architecture. In *ISCA*, 2016.

[6] L.-W. Chang et al. Efficient kernel synthesis for performance portable programming. In *MICRO*, 2016.

[7] L.-W. Chang et al. A programming system for future proofing performance critical libraries. In *PPoPP*, 2016.

[8] E. S. Chung et al. Single-chip heterogeneous computing: Does the future include custom logic, FPGAs, and GPGPUs? In *MICRO*, 2010.

[9] A. Duran et al. OmpSs: a proposal for programming heterogeneous multi-core architectures. *PPL*, 21(02):173–193, 2011.

[10] V. Garcia-Flores et al. Evaluating the effect of last-level cache sharing on integrated GPU-CPU systems with heterogeneous applications. In *IISWC*, 2016.

[11] J. Gómez-Luna et al. Chai: Collaborative heterogeneous applications for integrated-architectures. In *ISPASS*, 2017 (in press).

[12] W.-m. W. Hwu. *Heterogeneous System Architecture: A New Compute Platform Infrastructure.* Morgan Kaufman, 2015.

[13] Intel. Intel FPGA SDK for OpenCL. Programming Guide, October 2016.

[14] A. Morad et al. Generalized multiAmdahl: Optimization of heterogeneous multi-accelerator SoC. *IEEE CAL*, 13(1):37–40, Jan. 2014.

[15] S. Mukherjee et al. Exploring the features of OpenCL 2.0. In *IWOCL*, 2015.

[16] S. Mukherjee et al. A comprehensive performance analysis of HSA and OpenCL 2.0. In *ISPASS*, 2016.

[17] NVIDIA. NVIDIA Tesla P100. White paper, 2016.

[18] PK Gupta. Intel. Xeon+FPGA Platform for the Data Center, June 2015.

[19] A. Putnam et al. A reconfigurable fabric for accelerating large-scale datacenter services. In *ISCA*, 2014.

[20] J. Ragan-Kelley et al. Halide: A language and compiler for optimizing parallelism, locality, and recomputation in image processing pipelines. In *PLDI*, 2013.

[21] Y. Sun et al. Hetero-Mark, a benchmark suite for CPU-GPU collaborative computing. In *IISWC*, 2016.

[22] Xilinx. Zynq UltraScale+ MPSoCs. White Paper, June 2016.

Empirical Study of Usage and Performance of Java Collections

Diego Costa
Institute of Computer Science
Heidelberg University,
Germany
diego.costa@informatik.uni-heidelberg.de

Artur Andrzejak
Institute of Computer Science
Heidelberg University,
Germany
artur@uni-hd.de

Janos Seboek
Institute of Computer Science
Heidelberg University,
Germany
seboek@cl.uni-heidelberg.de

David Lo
School of Information Systems
Singapore Management
University, Singapore
davidlo@smu.edu.sg

ABSTRACT

Collection data structures have a major impact on the performance of applications, especially in languages such as Java, C#, or C++. This requires a developer to select an appropriate collection from a large set of possibilities, including different abstractions (e.g. list, map, set, queue), and multiple implementations. In Java, the default implementation of collections is provided by the standard Java Collection Framework (JCF). However, there exist a large variety of less known third-party collection libraries which can provide substantial performance benefits with minimal code changes.

In this paper, we first study the popularity and usage patterns of collection implementations by mining a code corpus comprised of 10,986 Java projects. We use the results to evaluate and compare the performance of the six most popular alternative collection libraries in a large variety of scenarios. We found that for almost every scenario and JCF collection type there is an alternative implementation that greatly decreases memory consumption while offering comparable or even better execution time. Memory savings range from 60% to 88% thanks to reduced overhead and some operations execute 1.5x to 50x faster.

We present our results as a comprehensive guideline to help developers in identifying the scenarios in which an alternative implementation can provide a substantial performance improvement. Finally, we discuss how some coding patterns result in substantial performance differences of collections.

ICPE'17, April 22-26, 2017, L'Aquila, Italy

DOI: http://dx.doi.org/10.1145/3030207.3030221

Keywords

empirical study, collections, performance, memory, execution time, java

1. INTRODUCTION

Collection libraries and frameworks offer programmers data structures for handling groups of objects in an abstract and potentially efficient way. The popularity and importance of such libraries and frameworks is indicated by the fact that programming languages such as Java, C#, Python, Ruby, or C++ include them as a part of the core language environment (STL is a de facto standard in case of C++.)

Typically in such libraries each of the major abstract collection types (e.g., lists, sets and maps) has multiple implementations adhering to the same API. Each implementation attempts to fulfill the requirements of different execution scenarios and thus provides different trade-offs. For example, Java's ArrayList has a smaller memory footprint than a Java LinkedList, yet it has a higher asymptotic complexity when it comes to inserting or deleting elements at random positions.

Given that modern programs use collections in thousands of program locations [23], selecting appropriate type and implementation is a crucial aspect of developing efficient applications. Choosing a wrong collection may result in performance bloat - the excessive use of memory and computational time for accomplishing simple tasks. Numerous studies have identified the inappropriate use of collections as the main cause of runtime bloat [5, 16, 27, 28]. Even in production systems, the memory overhead of individual collections can be as high as 90% [16].

The problem of selecting an appropriate collection becomes more complex when accounting for third party libraries. These allow for many more choices compared to the standard Java Collection Framework (JCF), from simple alternatives to existing JCF implementations to collections with extra features such as immutability and primitive-type support.

Despite its importance, we found a gap in experimental studies comparing execution and memory performance of non-JCF collections. Partial benchmarks, especially on the websites of the libraries, are common enough; they, however, do not give a performance comparison for different libraries, nor do they provide an evaluation under a large set of scenarios. This paper attempts to fill this gap in experimental studies and derive a set of guidelines for developers on how can they improve performance with little code refactoring.

To this aim (i) we study the usage of collections in real Java code via repository mining and (ii) evaluate the memory consumption and execution performance of collection classes offered by six most popular collection libraries. The key question to be answered by our study is: *"Can we improve performance of applications in typical scenarios by simply replacing collection implementations, and if yes, to which degree?"*. In particular, we explore alternatives to JCF implementations under the same collection abstraction.

Our results show a considerable variance in performance in different implementations of the same data structure. Moreover, the best alternative implementations outperform the collections provided by the standard JCF library across many workload profiles, making them a better choice in terms of memory consumption and runtime for most applications in many circumstances. Improvements range from 20% to 50 times in execution time, and saving up to 88% in memory.

The contributions of this paper are as follows:

- We analyze the popularity and usage patterns of collection libraries based on mining a dataset with 10,986 Java projects (Section 3).
- We propose a framework for systematic evaluation of collection performance. This framework can be further extended to cover new libraries, scenarios and implementations (Section 4).
- We evaluate the performance of JCF and six major alternative libraries in terms of execution and memory under a variety of scenarios. As a part of the study, we investigate the performance of primitive collections (Section 5).
- We provide a guideline for developers on replacing standard JCF collections by alternative implementations based on performance characteristics (Section 6).
- We explain the causes of performance differences of collection implementations by analyzing the source-code and benchmark indicators for some relevant scenarios (Section 6).

2. BACKGROUND

Collections are data structures that group multiple elements into a single unit. A collection uses metadata to track, access and manipulate its elements via specified APIs. Naturally, the metadata incurs extra memory consumption (*collection overhead*) in addition to the memory used by its elements (*element footprint*). Collections come in several *abstraction types*, primarily list, map, set, and queue.

The standard implementation of the collections in Java is the *Java Collections Framework*, or *JCF*. It provides implementations of all major abstraction types in several variants, e.g. ArrayList, HashMap, HashSet and others. JCF is implemented purely as *object collection*, i.e. the metadata contains only references to Java objects, but no data itself (Figure 1).

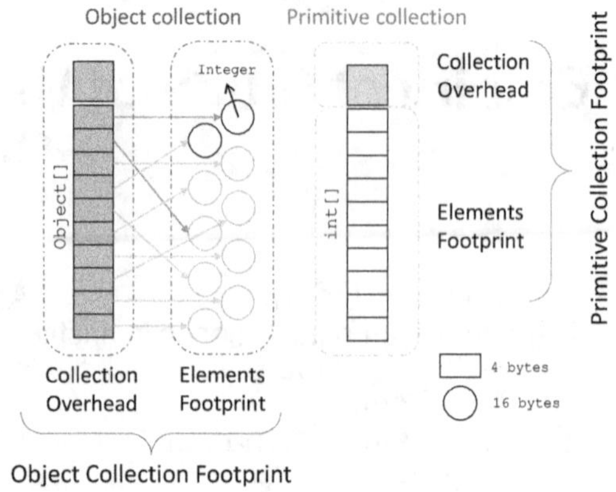

Figure 1: Conceptual view of object collections vs. primitive collections with the example of ArrayList, and terms related to memory usage.

The JCF offers programmers a stable and reliable collections framework. However, there exist many alternative collection libraries that can outperform standard JCF abstraction types, and additionally target features not supported by the JCF, such as immutable collections, multisets and multimaps.

If a collection contains simple objects like Integer, Long, Double, Character, etc., *primitive collections* can be used to reduce the memory footprint. The key difference is that a primitive collection stores data directly in an array of primitives (int, long, double, char), instead of using an array of references to data objects. Figure 1 illustrates an ArrayList of integers as an object collection (left) and a primitive collection (right). The primitive variant reduces the collection footprint in two ways. First, the primitive collection needs only a single reference to an array of primitives instead of an array of references. Second, each primitive data element (type int) requires only 4 bytes instead of 16 bytes of an object Integer. This example indicates that alternative collections can slash memory footprint of collections by a large factor.

3. ANALYSIS OF COLLECTION USAGE

In this section we describe the usage patterns of collections found in a large code corpus. Understanding such patterns helps us to identify the most popular collection types and implementations. This study will help us devise a benchmark presented later in the paper.

3.1 Data and Static Analysis

For our analysis we use the GitHub Java Corpus [1], a dataset from GitHub containing 10,986 Java projects, in total more than 268 millions lines of code. This corpus consists only of projects with more than one fork to eliminate small or inactive projects, which prevail at GitHub [12]. In addition, the creators of GitHub Java Corpus analyzed and pruned this dataset manually in order to eliminate project clones.

We categorize the whole data into two sets of repositories, namely all projects provided by Java GitHub Corpus (*FullSet*) and a subset of the 50 most popular projects (*Top50*). The popularity of the latter set is based on ranking of projects provided by GitHub corpus [1], and it is illustrated by the fact that *Top50* contains projects like Eclipse IDE[1], Clojure[2], and Elastic Search[3]. By analyzing both sets we can investigate whether there is an impact of project maturity (approximated by popularity) on the patterns of collection usage.

We need to extract from the code every declaration of a collection and every site of a collection instantiation. This is needed to count the usages of collection classes, record the types of held elements, and count how often the initial capacity is specified. We use JavaParser[4] to extract each variable declaration and instantiation site in the code. We then filter the collection instances by applying a heuristic as defined by the following regular expression:

.*List|.*Map|.*Set|.*Queue|.*Vector| .

This pattern finds all collection implementations of interest but also retrieves some false positives, e.g., `java.util.BitSet` is not a general purpose collection but is retrieved by our heuristic regardless. We rank the retrieved types and manually inspect and filter out false positive for the top 99% of the retrieved data, ranked by occurrence.

3.2 Collections Usage in Real Code

Collection Types. We analyze the instantiations sites and extract the most used collections in the code (see Figure 2). Unsurprisingly, list is the most commonly used collection abstraction, followed by map and finally by set. Our ranking is dominated by JCF as developers only rarely opted for others, not nearly often enough to make it into our charts.

Among the abstraction types, lists are the most common ($\approx$ 56%), followed by maps ($\approx$ 28%) and sets ($\approx$ 15%). Contrary to this, queues are rather rare (1.23% of usages). Among lists, ArrayList makes up the bulk of all collections usages, namely 47%. The LinkedList is surprisingly common, with $\approx$ 5% and is ranked as the fourth most common implementation. In maps, HashMap is most commonly used, representing $\approx$ 23% of all collections instantiation, followed by LinkedHashMap ($\approx$ 2%) and the TreeMap ($\approx$ 1%). Set instances follow a similar pattern to maps, HashSet is most used ($\approx$ 10%), followed by TreeSet and LinkedHashSet with both $\approx$ 1% of occurrences.

In summary, the top four most frequently used collections are JCF implementations: ArrayList, HashMap, HashSet and LinkedList. Together they account for approximately 83% of all collections declared in the repository. We found a similar distribution in *Top50*, which have a slightly higher usage of concurrent collections and a lower variety of types.

Element Types. By *element type* we mean the object types held by collections. Understanding their distribution helps us to cover in our benchmark the most frequent real scenarios. To simplify, we group the element types into four categories:

- Strings: String, String[], and String[][].
- Primitives: The primitive-wrappers such as Double, Float, Long, Short, Integer, as well as Boolean, Character, and their respective arrays.
- Collections: Collection types that can be identified by our heuristic from Section 3.1.
- Other: All the classes and data types not fitting any of the mentioned categories.

The result of our analysis, presented in Figure 3, shows a clear similarity between the results in *FullSet* and *Top50*. A pattern that emerges is the similar usage of primitive wrappers throughout the categories, always ranging from $\approx$ 5% to $\approx$ 8% of the declarations. This category is particularly interesting because it contains the collections that can be replaced by primitive collections with simple code refactoring.

The remaining categories show a distinct pattern for each of lists, maps and sets. Lists have a higher variability of element types, but hold strings $\approx$ 20% of the time. Sets hold strings more often than lists, $\approx$ 31% of the time. Maps also hold strings very often: $\approx$ 70% of all declared maps use the String as a key and $\approx$ 28% as a value. Map values are often a collection ($\approx$ 15%) pointing to a common usage of maps as a collection holder.

Initial Capacity Specification. Defining an appropriate initial capacity of a collection is a simple but effective method for optimizing runtime and memory. We sample 400 of the instantiation sites of ArrayList, HashSet and HashMap, which give us 5% confidence interval. Then we manually categorize whether a developer specifies an initial capacity, copies this instance from another collection, or uses default constructor values.

Figure 4 shows that programmers specify initial capacities for ArrayList only in $\approx$ 19% of the declarations. HashMap and HashSet have their capacity specified in $\approx$ 7% and $\approx$ 8% of collection declarations, respectively. Our analysis with the *Top50* provides very similar results, with a slightly higher percentage of initial capacity in ArrayList declarations. Interestingly, HashSet is the category more commonly created through copy instruction (in $\approx$ 11% of cases in *FullSet* and $\approx$ 14% in *Top50*).

Project Maturity and Collections Usage. We found similar results in our analysis of *FullSet* and *Top50*. This indicates that, regardless of the project maturity, programmers instantiate collections in a similar fashion. They mostly select standard collections types, and rarely specify the initial capacity in a collection instantiation.

4. EXPERIMENTAL DESIGN

In this section we describe the design of experiments for evaluating performance of collection implementations in terms of execution time and memory usage. In particular:

1. We identify a suitable set of collection libraries for this evaluation through ranking of libraries in terms of their popularity.
2. We describe a benchmark framework capable of measuring the steady-state performance of collections with high precision.
3. We design an experimental plan which covers a large set of usage scenarios based on the findings of usage patterns reported in Section 3.

[1] https://github.com/eclipse/eclipse.jdt/
[2] https://github.com/clojure/clojure
[3] https://github.com/elastic/elasticsearch
[4] https://github.com/javaparser/javaparser

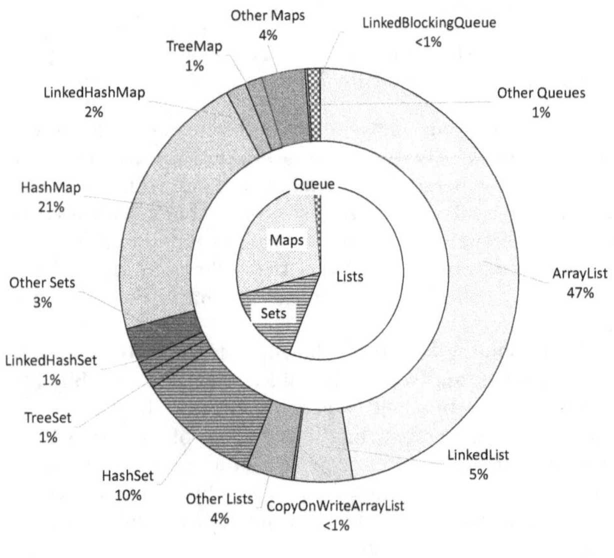

Figure 2: Distribution of instantiated collection types in *FullSet*. Every specific collection in this chart is from JCF, as standard implementations are the most prominent ones.

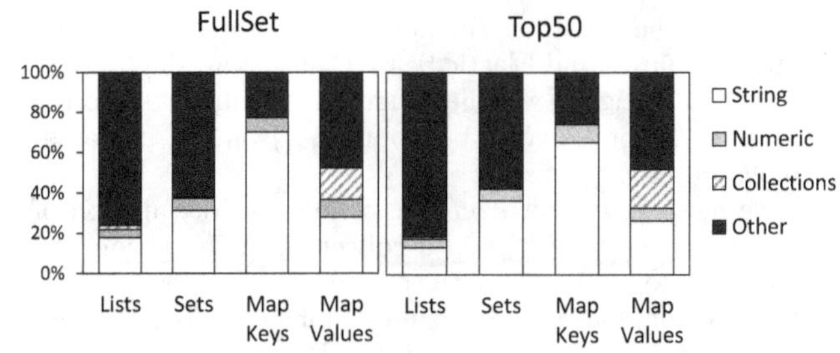

Figure 3: Distribution of element types by collection for both the *FullSet* and the *Top50* set.

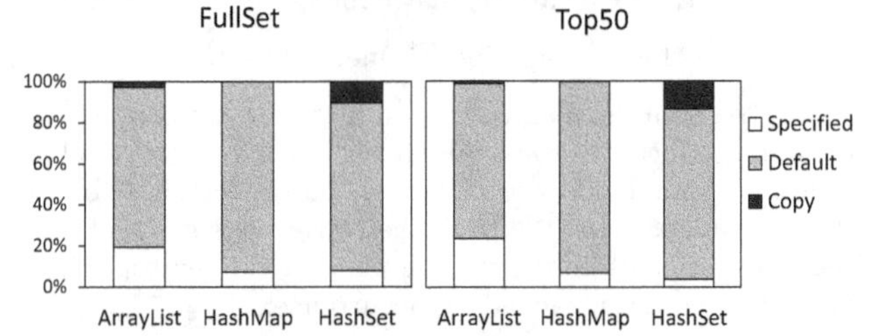

Figure 4: Statistics on the style of specifying initial capacity of collections for *FullSet* and *Top50*. "Specified" denotes that the developer explicitly set the initial capacity, and "Copy" that a copy constructor was used.

The results of rigorous statistical analysis of each evaluated scenario are presented then in Section 5.

Note that we compare the performance within the same abstraction type (i.e. list, map, set). Our experimental parameters include the number of elements held in a collection, and a particular usage scenario (Section 4.2).

4.1 Selection of Collection Libraries

We search the Web for alternative collection libraries implemented in Java and find a total of 14 libraries. From these, we use two different approaches to extract a suitable set for our experimental evaluation. First, we rank them by popularity of their project in GitHub, see Table 1. Second, we analyze how many times they have been included in existing benchmarks (Table 2).

The GitHub metrics such as number of stars and number of watches provide a simple but effective method for ranking software projects. Such metrics have also been used as a criterion in other studies [19, 22]. To account for libraries that are not on GitHub, we retrieve a set of collection benchmarksfrom the web, and count for each collection library in how many benchmarks it was evaluated.

Furthermore, we filter libraries that do not provide implementations that can serve as a replacement to JCF collections. This excludes Javaslang as it provides only immutable collections for lambda function usage. In the final step we select the top five libraries from each ranking and merge them into a single list. This yields seven unique libraries (three of them occur in both rankings) to be included in our experimental evaluation. For this study we use the JCF of Java 8 (jdk1.8.0_65.)

4.2 Benchmark Design

A managed runtime environment such as the Java Virtual Machine poses a challenge for performance measurement. Numerous factors can affect performance: the effects of the garbage collector, the Just in Time compilation (JIT), the heap size, the method sampling optimization, and many other unpredictable system effects [3, 4, 18]. To reduce the impact of these factors we follow the suggestions by Georges et al. [4] and implement a four-step methodology for evaluating a steady state performance of collection implementations:

Table 1: Ranking of collection libraries by GitHub popularity. We select the top 5 collections from this ranking. Data was obtained on 28 September 2015.

Rank	Library	# Stars	# Watches
1	Guava	5067	641
2	GS-Collection	1293	196
3	Koloboke	369	69
*	Javaslang	309	31
4	HPPC	189	31
5	Fastutil	69	6
6	HPPC-RT	8	3

S1 For each scenario we execute ten warm-up iterations to achieve a steady performance [5].

S2 We execute 30 iterations while measuring our response variables. Each iteration executes the same operation (sample) in an uninterrupted fashion for five seconds. After reaching the timeout, we calculate the average of all samples as a result. Each result also contains

[5]Our preliminary analysis showed that the execution time of the experiment converges after seven warm-up iterations

Table 2: Ranking of collection libraries by number of occurrences in benchmarks. We select the top 5 collections from this ranking.

Rank	Library	# Occurrences
1	JCF	13
2	Trove	10
3	HPPC	6
4	Koloboke	5
5	Fastutil	4
6	GS-Collection	4
7	Javolution	4
8	Guava	3
9	Mahout	3
10	Commons	2
11	Brownies	1
12	Colt	1
13	Javaslang	0
13	HPPC-RT	0

the experimental error of the iterations at a 99% confidence interval.

S3 We execute steps S1 and S2 twice to avoid circumstantial external influence.

S4 We analyze the results of 2 x 30 iterations using rigorous statistical methods. In detail, we analyze the variance with ANOVA [17] and compare multiple means accounting for their experimental errors.

We perform this experimental methodology on our benchmark suite called *CollectionsBench*. CollectionsBench is built upon JMH[6], a Java harness framework for building, running and pre-analyzing benchmarks. JMH provides support for benchmark forks, warm-up iterations, and can give the benchmark results with nanosecond precision.

To reliably measure performance using CollectionsBench, we perform the following steps: First, we guarantee a homogeneous benchmark behavior throughout different collection implementations. The Template design pattern helps us reuse the same test code in all JCF compliant libraries (see Table 3) and to delegate the collection creation to the library specific code. Second, we consume every non-void return to avoid undesired dead-code optimization. All these steps help to minimize sources of non-determinism in the JVM.

Finally, to only measure time and memory on the collections operations, we divide our experiment into two distinct *setup* and *benchmark* phases: In the *setup* phase we allocate all the elements and insert them into an instance of the evaluated collection. The values of each element are generated randomly through a uniform distribution, and we then reuse the random seed to ensure the same conditions in all tests. In the *benchmark* phase we execute the collection operations and measure the following response variables:

- *Execution time*: Time spent executing the benchmark in nanoseconds, using JMH native support.
- *Memory allocation*: The sum of memory requested during the benchmark execution. Since we allocate the elements in the *setup* phase, this variable shows only the memory requested for the collection overhead (including the collection object header and eventual memory padding), but does not consider the element footprint. We extract this information through the JMH GC profiler.

We also collect some performance indicators through the Perf[7] profiler, such as the number of instructions executed, cache miss rate and branch misprediction rate. In Section 6 we analyze those indicators along with the source-code to understand the reasons for performance differences of implementations.

The memory allocated during the benchmark is sensitive to buffers and temporarily allocated objects. For instance, when expanding the ArrayList allocates a new and larger buffer to accommodate more elements. The previously allocated buffer and the new one will be measured by the *memory allocation* variable. Therefore, the memory allocation alone cannot provide an accurate view of the memory usage of a collection.

To account for this problem, we evaluate the memory usage of a collection by computing their collection overhead. We use the tool Java Object Layout (JOL)[8] to retrieve the collection overhead of each implementation. We then analyze both memory allocation and overhead together, to give a detailed perspective of a collection's memory consumption.CollectionsBench is open-source and is fully available online[9].

4.3 Experimental Planning

Our experimental plan takes into consideration the findings on collections usage presented in Section 3. First, we focus on the most frequently used collection types while investigating possible alternatives (from third-party libraries) to the JCF collections. Therefore we select the four most used collection types, ArrayList (AL), LinkedList (LL), HashMap (HM), HashSet (HS), which accounts for more than 84% of all declared collections.

Most of the libraries do not implement an alternative to LinkedList, so we opted to compare JCF LinkedList implementations against ArrayList alternatives, as they are interchangeable. We also profile primitive alternatives to the top three collection types, as they provide a small-footprint option to collections that hold primitive wrappers (see Table 3).

Second, we pay a special attention to collections holding the element type String. Strings are particularly interesting in Java due to their extensive use, and have been studied by various authors [13]. To expand on the results, we evaluate the collection implementations for Integer and Long objects as well. We opt for these two numeric objects as they are representative: primitive-wrappers are the second most common category identified. Moreover, they mainly represent objects with 32 bytes and 64 bytes respectively, a common object size.

Third, we do not specify the initial capacity in our benchmark because from our static analysis results, specifying the initial capacity is done rarely in real code. Since we aim to provide results that are useful to the widest range of programmers, we evaluate collections with their default initial capacity.

Fourth, given C as a collection populated with N elements

[6]http://openjdk.java.net/projects/code-tools/jmh/

[7]https://perf.wiki.kernel.org/index.php/Main_Page

[8]http://openjdk.java.net/projects/code-tools/jol/

[9]https://gitlab.com/DiegoCosta/collections-bench

Table 3: **The evaluated collection implementations. The primitive implementations are marked with (p). The column JCF indicates whether the libraries provide implementations compatible with the Java Collection Framework (only for object collections). In total we evaluate 33 implementations.**

Library	Version	JCF	List(AL/LL)	HashMap (HM)	HashSet (HS)
JCF [20]	8.0_65	yes	ArrayList LinkedList	HashMap	HashSet
Guava (Gu) [8]	18.0	no		HashMultimap	HashMultiset
Fastutil (Fu) [24]	7.0.10	yes –	ObjectArrayList IntArrayList(p)	Object2ObjectOpenHashMap Int2IntOpenHashMap(p)	ObjectOpenHashSet IntOpenHashSet(p)
Koloboke (Ko) [2]	0.6.8	yes –		HashObjObjMap HashIntIntMap(p)	HashObjSet HashIntSet(p)
HPPC (HP) [21]	0.7.1	no –	ObjectArrayList IntArrayList(p)	ObjectObjectHashMap IntIntHashMap(p)	ObjectHashSet IntHashSet(p)
GSCollections (GS) [7]	6.2.0	yes –	FastList IntArrayList(p)	UnifiedMap IntIntHashMap(p)	UnifiedSet IntHashSet(p)
Trove (Tr) [6]	3.0.3	yes –	 TIntArrayList(p)	THashMap TIntIntHashMap(p)	THashSet TIntHashSet(p)

in the *setup* phase, we evaluate the collections under the following scenarios:

- *populate*: add N random elements into an empty collection.
- *iterate*: iterate through all elements of C.
- *contains*: check whether C contains an existing random element.
- *add*: add a random element to C. To keep C with the same size throughout the experiment, we remove the added element at the end of the scenario.
- *get*: get a random existing element from C.
- *remove:* find and remove a random element from C. Analogously to *add*, we add the removed element in C at the end of the scenario.
- *copy*: copy C into an empty collection using the copy constructor.

We could not obtain the size of collections through static code analysis. To compensate for this fact and to account for various scenarios, we run our benchmarks with multiple values for N ranging from 100 to 1M, with the interval set as a power of ten (five categories of size).

In summary, we perform a *factorial experiment* [17] with three element types and five collection sizes, in a total of 15 different configurations. This 15-configuration experiment is run through the seven scenarios for each of the 33 collection types (see Table 3). We execute a total of 3,465 experiments, where each experiment lasts five minutes including replications and forks. Running the full benchmark takes 12 days to finish.

We conduct our experiments on a machine with a E5-1660 3.3GHz CPU, 64GB RAM using Linux 3.16.0-53. We use 64-bits JVM HotSpot, and the jdk1.8.0_65 as our Java version. All tests were executed in a single-threaded environment, as our target collections were built for such settings.

5. RESULTS

Our goal is to find a *superior alternative* that can outperform JCF in terms of execution time and/or memory consumption in several scenarios, while introducing no or minimal penalties in others. To achieve this, we ask the following research questions:

RQ1. Does the type of elements stored in collections influence execution time?

RQ2. Are there superior alternatives to the most used JCF collections with regard to execution time?

RQ3. Do primitive collections perform better than JCF collections with regard to execution time?

RQ4. Are there superior alternatives to the most used JCF collections with regard to memory consumption?

RQ1 addresses the impact of element type in the execution time of collections; RQ2 and RQ3 show the analysis of alternative object and primitive-collections on execution time; RQ4 reports superior object-collection alternatives on memory consumption. We omit the analysis of primitive-collections on memory consumption, as this question is rather well-explored and exemplified in Section 2.

RQ1. Does the type of elements stored in collections influence execution time?

> **Key result:** The element type has a significant influence in the execution time in all major collection abstractions. For lists, however, this impact is homogeneous throughout all implementations.

We analyze the impact of the element type in the object-collections execution time to verify whether our results can be generalized beyond the types evaluated. We use the ANOVA method [17], with a 95% confidence interval and analyze the influence of element type on lists, sets and maps.

The element type influences execution time significantly in our three main categories ($p < 0.05$). For lists, however, the element type factor does not interact with the list implementation ($p = 0.76$), indicating that it influences the performance regardless of the list type. Thus, we expect that our results for lists can be generalized beyond the type used. We report the results for sets and maps only for the String element type as it represents the largest amount of collection instantiations.

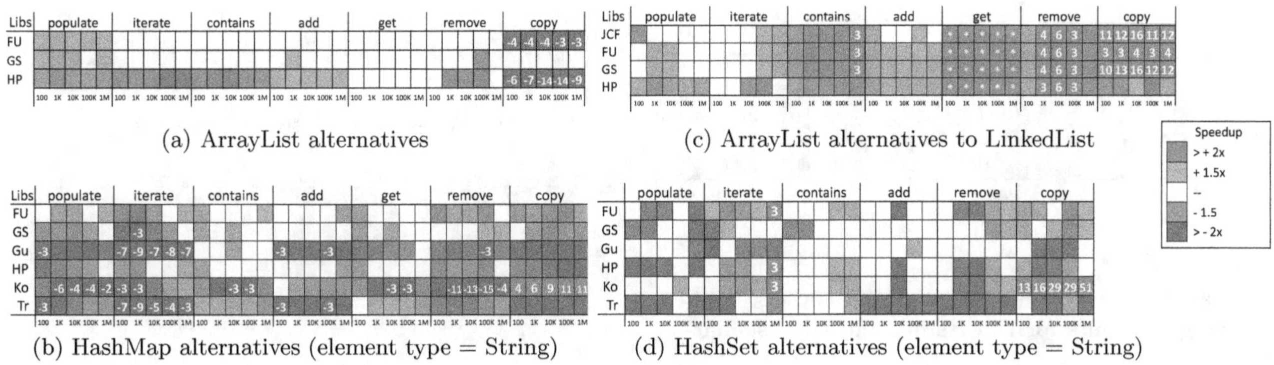

(a) ArrayList alternatives

(c) ArrayList alternatives to LinkedList

(b) HashMap alternatives (element type = String)

(d) HashSet alternatives (element type = String)

Figure 5: Heatmap showing speedup/slowdown (as defined in Equation 1) of alternative collections compared to JCF, per scenario and size. Green cells indicate a speedup, red cells represent a slowdown. Performance ratios larger than factor 2x are rounded to the nearest integer and printed inside the cell. LinkedList *get* ratios are substantially higher and not shown.

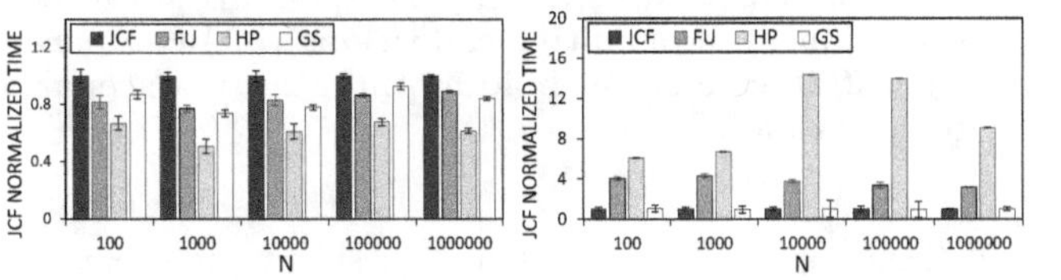

(a) populate

(b) copy

Figure 6: Execution time profiles of Array Lists for the *populate* and *copy* scenarios.

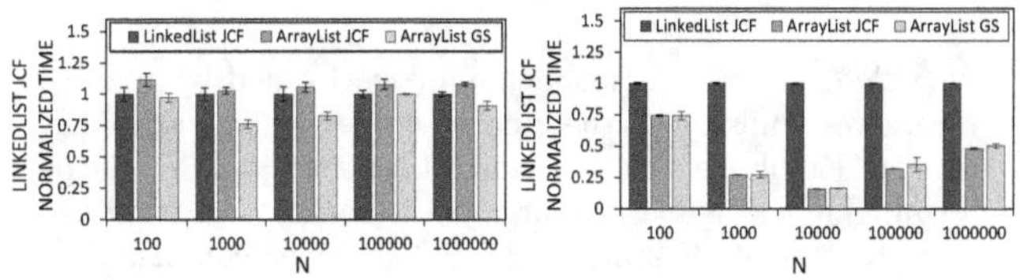

(a) populate

(b) remove

Figure 7: Execution time profiles of LinkedList for *populate* and *remove* scenarios.

RQ2. Are there superior alternatives to the most used JCF collections with regard to execution time?

> **Key result:** GSCollections provides a superior alternative to JCF ArrayList. LinkedList is outperformed by any other ArrayList implementation, and both the HashSet of Koloboke and Fastutil are a solid improvement over the standard one. We found no superior alternative to the JCF HashMap, which provides a stable and fast implementation throughout all the scenarios.

We report our results as a comparison to the JCF implementation instead of the absolute performance. First, we extract only comparisons where the errors (99% confidence interval) do not overlap. Then we calculate the impact of an alternative collection over JCF using the following speedup/slowdown S definitions:

$$S = \begin{cases} \dfrac{T_{jcf}}{T_{alt}}, & \text{if } T_{jcf} > T_{alt} \\ -\dfrac{T_{alt}}{T_{jcf}}, & \text{otherwise} \end{cases} \quad (1)$$

where T_{jcf} and T_{alt} are the time obtained with using the JCF implementation and the time using an alternative implementation respectively.

We present our results in a broad heatmap analysis in Figure 5, labeled by color. We make an in-depth analysis for each category in the remainder of the section.

ArrayList. In the *populate* scenario occurrences of JCF ArrayList can be replaced by the implementation from GSCollections to achieve faster population without compromising the speed of any other operation. In fact, all evaluated alternatives are faster than JCF when populating the list (see Figure 6.) The HPPC implementation is, however, slower when iterating the elements in both the *iterate* and the *contains* scenario. In addition, both Fastutil and HPPC copy their lists from 3 to 14 times more slowly.

LinkedList. JCF LinkedList is outperformed by all ArrayList implementations by a large margin, even in scenarios where LinkedList has a theoretical advantage (Figure 7). This is the case for the *remove* scenario, where we search and remove the element through the `remove(Object)` method. Despite the asymptotic advantage, LinkedList was outperformed by a large margin for $N \geq 1k$. Furthermore, LinkedList has a comparable performance in the *populate* scenario, even without having to reallocate its buffer (as ArrayList does). The LinkedList is up to three times slower when searching for a random element ($N = 1M$), and it was also outperformed in the *iteration* scenario by some ArrayList variants, but only for $N > 10k$. Note that in our benchmark design the LinkedList is unfragmented as the elements are inserted without any removal. Hence, we consider these results a best-case scenario for LinkedList.

HashMap. JCF HashMap provides solid performance and cannot be easily replaced by any alternative in terms of ex-

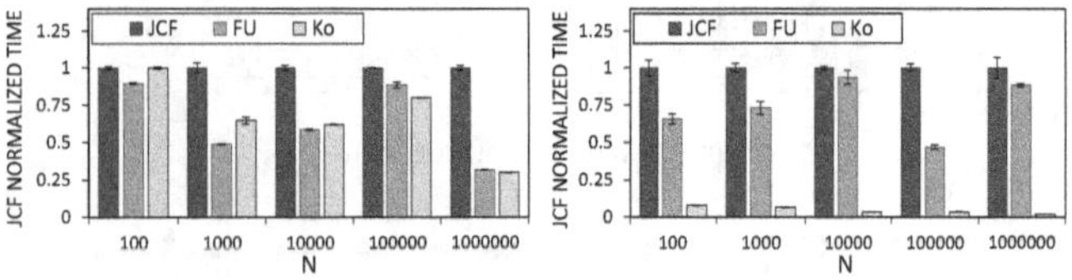

(a) iterate (b) copy

Figure 8: Execution time profiles of HashSets holding String elements for the *iterate* and *copy* scenarios.

ecution time improvement. As shown in Figure 5, some implementations have a comparable performance, like Fastutil, GSCollections and HPPC. Standard HashMap is outperformed only in the *copy* scenario, where Koloboke is able to copy up to 11x faster. However, Koloboke is substantially slower in most of the other remaining scenarios.

HashSet. Standard HashSet is outperformed by many alternatives, mostly in the *iterate* and *copy* scenarios (Figure 8). Koloboke is a superior alternative to JCF, outperforming JCF HashSet for large set iteration, and copying at least 10x faster. Fastutil and GSCollections can also be selected as good alternatives: both are slower when populating but faster in the *copy* and and *iterate* scenarios. The JCF implementation is faster than the majority of alternatives when adding elements to the set, but is often outperformed in the remaining scenarios for large workloads ($N > 100k$).

RQ3. Do primitive collections perform better than JCF collections with regard to execution time?

Key Result: For all three abstraction types (list, map, set) we found a set of primitive implementations that are superior to JCF implementations. GSCollections and Koloboke provide the fastest primitive-based alternatives, followed by Fastutil and HPPC. Trove is often outperformed by JCF implementations in this context.

Our results for analyzing the experiments are summarized in a colored heatmap in Figure 9.

Primitive ArrayList. Primitive lists provide a superior alternative to JCF ArrayList (Figure 9a). The speedup in some cases reaches four times better than the baseline when checking or removing an element from the list. GSCollections consistently outperforms the JCF, followed by Fastutil, which is slightly slower when iterating through the list. HPPC and Trove are much slower when copying their lists, and should be avoided if the workload demands this operation often.

Primitive HashMap. As a consequence of the standard JCF HashMap's good performance, in some scenarios there is no underlying benefit gained from changing to a primitive-type map implementation (Figure 9b). Iterations are especially good with the standard HashMap, up to five times faster than the alternatives. For the *contains*, *add*, *get* and *remove* scenarios, most primitive implementations can provide an improvement. When also considering the *copy* scenario, GSCollections and Koloboke provide the highest performance gain among the alternatives.

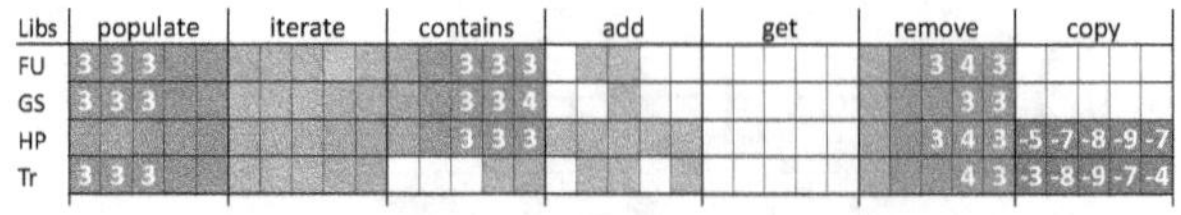

(a) ArrayList primitive alternatives

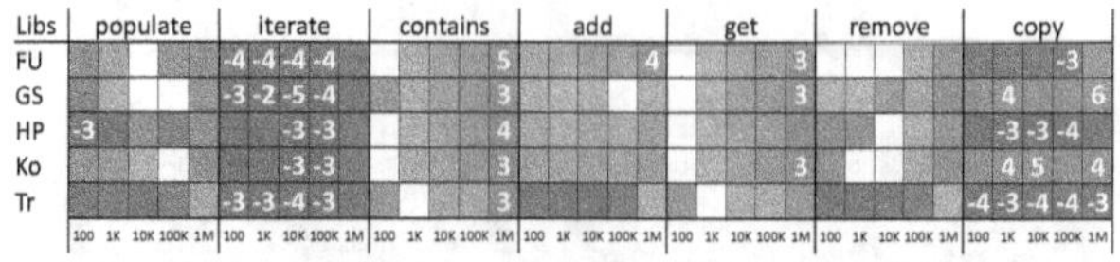

(b) HashMap primitive alternatives

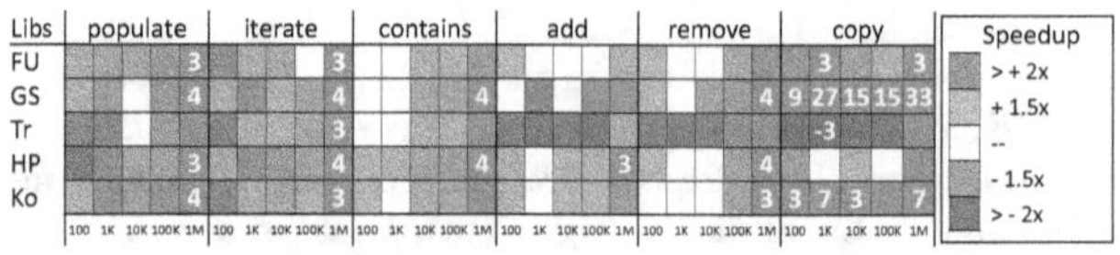

(c) HashSet primitive alternatives

Figure 9: Heatmap showing the speedup/slowdown (Equation 1) of primitive collections (int) compared to the JCF collections holding Integers, per scenario and workload.

Primitive HashSet. Primitive-based sets can be beneficial for the application's performance when it comes to a large number of elements (Figure 9c). In fact, the speedup commonly reaches four times as fast across many scenarios with $N = 1M$. GSCollections, Fastutil and Koloboke provide superior alternatives and can copy their instances up to 27 times faster. HPPC is also a good alternative but it does not provide the same copy operation speed gain as the other mentioned libraries. Trove's implementation was the only primitive-based HashSet outperformed by the standard HashSet in the *add*, *remove* and *copy* scenarios.

RQ4. Are there superior alternatives to the most used JCF collections with regard to memory consumption?

Key result: We found no superior alternative to the JCF ArrayList in terms of memory overhead, but Fastutil allocates less memory when populating its own list implementation. Numerous alternatives offer a superior alternative to the JCF HashMap and HashSet. LinkedList has a higher overhead than any considered ArrayList alternative.

In this section, we analyze the difference in the overhead of collections as the main goal for a superior collection replacement. As a supplementary analysis, we also looked at an aspect often neglected by micro-benchmarks: memory allocation. A collection that allocates more memory than indicated by its overhead requests memory for two reasons: (i) allocation as a buffer for future operations, (ii) allocation for temporary objects. The latter reason has a negative impact on performance and can be used as an indicator of how often a collection implementation can trigger the action

Table 4: **Comparison of collection overhead and memory allocation of various implementations. The overhead is given in bytes in the form $\alpha \times N + \beta$, where N is the number of elements in the collection, and α and β are implementation-specific factors. The average allocated is given in bytes per element.**

Category	Libs	Collection Overhead	Avg Allocated populate	Avg Allocated copy
Array Lists	JCF	$4 \times N + 24$	14.83	4.01
	Fu	$4 \times N + 24$	10.07	4.02
	GS	$4 \times N + 24$	13.56	4.01
	HP	$4 \times N + 48$	15.10	4.01
Linked List	JCF	$24 \times N + 32$	24.07	28.11
Hash Maps	JCF	$36 \times N + 48$	49.93	41.05
	Fu	$8 \times N + 64$	35.52	42.18
	GS	$8 \times N + 64$	59.87	24.62
	Gu	$96 \times N + 64$	96.90	132.36
	HP	$8 \times N + 96$	36.41	18.16
	Ko	$8 \times N + 232$	35.47	17.96
	Tr	$8 \times N + 72$	47.23	18.37
Hash Sets	JCF	$36 \times N + 80$	48.85	40.43
	Fu	$4 \times N + 40$	24.43	8.43
	GS	$4 \times N + 32$	34.44	14.21
	Gu	$52 \times N + 112$	64.77	58.25
	HP	$4 \times N + 88$	16.88	8.43
	Ko	$4 \times N + 208$	16.84	8.43
	Tr	$4 \times N + 64$	22.25	8.35

of the Garbage Collector (GC). Collections that require frequent intervention of the GC can reduce the performance of an application in a long run, a behavior difficult to observe with micro-benchmarks.

Since the elements are pre-allocated in the setup phase, memory allocation only comes into play when elements are added to the collection, namely by *populate* and *copy* operations.

ArrayList. All implementations have a similar overhead (see Table 4). Due to its buffer reallocation, each implementation allocates on average three times its own overhead in the *populate* scenario. Regarding only memory allocation, Fastutil can be a good alternative, saving 30% of allocations in the *populate* scenario.

LinkedList. We show in Table 4 that the standard LinkedList implementation has an overhead of 24 bytes per element, as opposed to the 4 bytes required in each ArrayList implementation. This is a consequence of the pointers to neighbor elements for each LinkedList entry. Essentially, an ArrayList saves 83% of the memory overhead. Despite the buffer expansion of ArrayList, LinkedList still allocates twice as much memory in the *populate* scenario, and it allocates five times more memory when copying from a previous instance.

HashMap. We can observe in Table 4 that the JCF implementation has a considerably higher overhead. Standard HashMap has an overhead of 36 bytes per each entry in the map while almost every other alternative consumes only 8 bytes. This difference occurs because JCF uses a Node object for each entry, a structure that contains three references (12 bytes) and a primitive (4 bytes), but, being an object, also has an overhead of 12 bytes of header and 4 bytes lost due to alignment. The alternatives do not define each entry as an object and instead use two arrays where each key and value pair are stored. As a consequence, they save 77% of memory overhead. Regarding allocations however, the difference of JCF and the alternatives are not quite as drastic as in the collection overhead. This means that even though the alternatives have five times less overhead, the memory involved in the map operations is of a similar size.

HashSet. Similarly to Maps, JCF HashSet is implemented with a larger overhead than almost any of the potential alternatives. In fact, it uses a HashMap internally to store the elements, causing the same additional overhead of 36 bytes per element, due to the HashMap's Node object. The alternatives, on the other hand, implement the HashSet as a simple single array. This allows them to save 88% of memory overhead compared to the JCF HashSet. Unlike HashMap, this difference holds in the memory allocation as well, where JCF allocates twice as much memory in the *populate* and five times as much memory in the *copy* scenario.

6. DISCUSSION

6.1 Guideline for Collection Replacement

Each additional alternative collection implementation used in a software project increases its complexity and maintenance effort. Consequently, developers should consider replacing collection implementations only if such a change will result in a significant benefit. In order to support programmers in such decisions, we present a guideline (Table 5) showing the potential benefits and drawbacks of using alternative implementations for several relevant scenarios and/or optimization objectives.

We illustrate the effect of JCF collection replacement on execution time for collections with one thousand (small) and one million elements (large). Note that in case of object collections the memory savings come solely from a reduced overhead as the elements themselves are not modified. In case of the primitive collections the programmer must replace the object element type by its respective primitive. However, the impact on memory savings is higher as the memory footprint of elements is reduced as well.

Table 5 presents seven recommendations for replacements leading to a substantial improvements. Recommendation R1 describes the replacement of a LinkedList by an ArrayList from one of three libraries, each offering a consistent improvement in time and memory. In R2 we recommend Koloboke's alternative to JCF HashSet, as it provides a substantial improvement on execution time and memory overhead. For HashMaps it is possible to aim for a memory overhead reduction with a small execution time penalty (R3), or to reduce memory and improve the execution time of copy operations (R4).

An important result is the universal superiority of primitive collections. It is possible to considerably improve both memory footprint (overhead + elements) and execution time for all three major collections: ArrayList (R5), HashSet (R6) and HashMap (R7). Note that in all cases the replacement is particularly beneficial for large collections as the savings of memory and execution time are, in general, bigger.

6.2 Reasons for Performance Differences

Our investigation of the source code of collections revealed some implementation patterns responsible for performance

Table 5: **A guideline showing the impact of replacing JCF collections with alternative collection implementations for some relevant scenarios/optimization objectives. For primitive collections, the memory savings include overhead reduction as well as smaller element footprint (results assume replacing Integer objects by the primitive int).**

	Overhead Savings	Speedup/Slowdown 1k elements	Speedup/Slowdown 1M elements
To reduce JCF LinkedList overhead and improve time performance			
R1) Replace it by JCF/Fasutils/GSCollections ArrayList	84%	+2x contains +4x remove +12x/+3x/+13x copy	+3x contains +2x remove +4x/+2x+4x copy
To reduce JCF HashSet overhead and improve time performance			
R2) Replace it by Koloboke HashSet	88%	+1.5x iterate -1.5x remove +16x copy	+3x iterate +1.5x contains +51x copy
To reduce JCF HashMap overhead with smallest time penalty			
R3) Replace it by GSCollections/Fastutils HashMap	78%	-1.5x populate -1.5x/-3x iterate -1.5x copy	-1.5x copy
To reduce JCF HashMap overhead and improve copy performance			
R4) Replace it by Koloboke HashMap	78%	+6x copy -6x populate -11x remove	+11x copy -2x populate -4x remove

	Footprint Savings	Speedup/Slowdown 1k elements	Speedup/Slowdown 1M elements
To reduce JCF collections footprint and improve time performance			
R5) Replace ArrayList by GSCollections primitive-collection	60%	+3x populate +2x contains +2x remove	+2x populate +4x contains +2x remove
R6) Replace HashMap by GSCollections/Koloboke primitive-collection	76%	+1.5x/2x populate -2x iterate +2x remove	+2x populate -2x iterate +6x/+4x copy
R7) Replace HashSet by GSCollections/Koloboke primitive-collection	84%	+2x populate +2x/+1.5x iterate +27x/7x copy	+4x populate +4x/+3x iterate +33x/+7x copy

differences in collections. We discuss these in the following.

Distinct API calls. The implementations often differ in usage of the API call for copying an array. Here two methods are used: `System.arraycopy()` and `Arrays.copyOf()`. The latter is just a wrapper for `System.arraycopy()` which requires only the original array, as opposed to the System version, where the target must be passed as a parameter. Our experiments showed that `System.arraycopy()` is 25% faster than `Arrays.copyOf()` for arrays up to 1 million elements. This is one of the reasons why GSCollections ArrayList (which calls `System.arraycopy()`) is faster than JCF counterpart, since *populate* scenario is dominated by the buffer expansion cost.

Add copy versus Memory Copy. Collections copy is the scenario with the largest discrepancy in performance of our experiments. We found that libraries implement two main approaches: they either add all elements one by one to a new created collection instance, or they perform a memory copy. Needless to say, the memory copy is faster as adding elements one by one has the burden of manipulating objects individually. This explains why Koloboke executes up to 50x faster than JCF when copying a set with 1 million elements.

Nevertheless, libraries often opt for adding the elements into the new instance for the simplicity of the workflow. The copy constructor receives a collection reference as a parameter and must be able to polymorphically handle all kinds of collection types. A memory copy is restricted only to copies from the same type. GSCollections and JCF use memory copy for ArrayLists but rely on addAll for HashSet and HashMap. Koloboke is the only library that use memory copy for HashSet/HashMap. It is important to address that copy is called 11% of the HashSet instantiations. Therefore applications can strongly benefit from memory copy implementation.

Sub-optimal primitive API. Iterating elements of FastList's ArrayList primitive collection is slower than JCF ArrayList, and far more time-consuming than any other primitive implementation. To understand this, note that each primitive library provides a `forEach(IntProcedure)` method to iterate and process the list. However, FastList provides a `forEach()` method defined by JCF `AbstractCollection`, which accepts an `Object` and implicitly converts each primitive to its wrapper, degrading the performance by a factor of 5x. This case illustrates the complexity of a collection API, which often provides multiple ways of performing the same task, but with distinct performance costs.

Sub-optimal loop implementation. The `contains()` method of Trove primitive ArrayList is 3 times slower than any other primitive implementation (see Fig 9a). The code inspection reveals that contrary to other primitive alternatives, Trove defined the array loop using an unconventional for loop, namely `for ( int i = offset; i-- > 0; )`. This loop, albeit correct, produces three times more branches and 30% more branch misses than a backwards loop defined with the decrement in third position of the `for`-statement. In fact, after refactoring the `contains()`-method in an obvious way in our own extension of Trove's primitive ArrayList the performance bottleneck was fixed.

6.3 Threats to Validity

There are several issues that may affect the validity of our work. As a benchmark study, our results are subject to a number of external factors. Even though we mitigate their influence with our methodology (see Section 4), the hardware specs may have an impact on collections time performance [11]. In particular, the speedup/slowdown indicators might be biased towards our test machine configuration. The memory footprint results, however, can be generalized beyond the hardware specification.

We try to reuse the same code to provide a homogeneous benchmark for the different collection libraries. Some implementations are not JCF compliant though, e.g. HPPC implementations and most primitive collections. For those cases we carefully adapt our code to their respective API, introducing only subtle code differences. Still, this may impact time performance of evaluated collections.

Lastly, we do not consider workloads with a convoluted set of operations. For such workloads, the memory overhead and execution time can be impacted by complex interactions among operations. Such workloads are harder to generalize though. That is why we based our micro-benchmark on single operations so that a useful guideline can be derived from the results.

7. RELATED WORK

There is a substantial body of research devoted to understanding the impact of collections on code performance.

Empirical Studies of Java Collections. To the best of our knowledge our evaluation is the most comprehensive study of the space and time profiles of alternative collection implementations in Java. However, the benchmarks we evaluated partially cover some aspects featured in our experiments. In [25] the author evaluates different HashMaps libraries in more convoluted scenarios. Lewis [15] compares JCF implementations and suggests a new collection for a specific GUI update scenario. Another interesting paper [14] exemplifies the time and memory trade-offs of HashMaps. Our work differs from these in some key aspects. First, we evaluate a wider range of implementations, presenting the performance profile of lists, sets and maps, including primitive alternatives, while those works focus more commonly on HashMap alternatives. Second, we based our experimental planning on patterns found on real code (Section 3). This allows us to evaluate scenarios more commonly adopted by developers in real applications, and provide more representative results. Lastly, we investigate and report some patterns in real code that explain some performance differences, an aspect rarely explored in the benchmarks we have found.

More recently, some works have studied the collections selection problem in relation to energy consumption of applications [10]. In particular, Hasam [9] presented an inspiring work which experimentally explores the impact of collections on energy consumption and concludes that some implementations can increase the energy usage of an application up to 300%. Their work does not consider time/memory profile as we do, and we believe that time, memory and energy consumption profiles can be combined to give programmers a more complete view of collections performance.

Collection inefficiencies. Several authors have designed methods to detect collection inefficiencies. Xu et al, [28] use both static and dynamic analysis to detect overpopulated and underutilized collections. Yang et al, [29] tracks and records the containers and the flow of its elements, and uses an offline analysis to pinpoint some inefficiencies. Those works target performance problems related to collection without exploring the effect of different collection types. Thus the authors attempt to solve an orthogonal problem to collection selection.

Performance optimization by collection replacement. Recently, several studies have attempted to advise developers on selecting collection abstraction type which improves the performance in a context-dependent way. Shacham et al., [23] optimizes applications by monitoring and replacing the collections types using a user-defined model. Coco [26] also utilizes a user defined model to replace the collections at runtime. Both works differ from our approach as they deploy solely asymptotic analysis to select the most suitable collection type, without accounting for the real performance profile. Consequently, the authors do not consider alternative collection libraries, and focus only on JCF.

The approach of Brainy [11] is most closely related to our work. Brainy is a C++ framework which generates a large amount of synthetic applications, models their performance via machine learning, and suggests appropriate collection replacements. This framework does not consider alternative implementations, but rather, focuses on a set of specific cross-abstraction transformations which might be difficult to apply to real code. Our work targets understanding the performance of alternative libraries, and we provide a guideline for replacing collection implementations for scenarios with a high impact on performance.

8. CONCLUSIONS AND FUTURE WORK

We analyzed usage patterns of collections by mining a code corpus of 10,986 Java projects and found that even in high-quality code, the usage of alternative collections libraries is rare. To investigate the potential for performance improvement in Java applications with only moderate programming effort, we have conducted a rigorous performance evaluation study of the standard Java Collection Framework and six most popular alternative collection libraries. We found that such alternative libraries can offer a programmer a significant reduction of both execution time and memory consumption.

We summarized the impact of collection replacement on runtime improvements and memory savings for some relevant scenarios. The resulting guideline assists programmers in deciding whether in a given setting an alternative implementation can offer a substantial performance improvement, and if so, which implementation should be used. Some of these replacements are easy to automate and can improve the performance profile of collections through simple code refactoring.

As future work, we target implementation of such automated refactoring tools. We also intend to evaluate our recommendations in more complex scenarios, including a study of their performance impact in large, mature software projects.

9. REFERENCES

[1] M. Allamanis and C. Sutton. Mining source code repositories at massive scale using language modeling. In *Proceedings of the 10th Working Conference on Mining Software Repositories*, MSR '13, pages 207–216, Piscataway, NJ, USA, 2013. IEEE Press.

[2] Chronicle. Koloboke. http://chronicle.software/products/koloboke-collections/, Oct. 2015.

[3] A. Georges, D. Buytaert, and L. Eeckhout. Statistically rigorous java performance evaluation. *SIGPLAN Not.*, 42(10):57–76, Oct. 2007.

[4] A. Georges, L. Eeckhout, and D. Buytaert. Java performance evaluation through rigorous replay compilation. *SIGPLAN Not.*, 43(10):367–384, Oct. 2008.

[5] J. Y. Gil and Y. Shimron. Smaller footprint for java collections. In *Proceedings of the ACM International Conference Companion on Object Oriented Programming Systems Languages and Applications Companion*, OOPSLA '11, pages 191–192, New York, NY, USA, 2011. ACM.

[6] GNU Trove. Trove. http://trove.starlight-systems.com/, May 2015.

[7] Goldman Sachs Group, Inc. GS Collections. https://github.com/goldmansachs/gs-collections, June 2015.

[8] Google. Guava. https://github.com/google/guava, Aug. 2014.

[9] S. Hasan, Z. King, M. Hafiz, M. Sayagh, B. Adams, and A. Hindle. Energy profiles of java collections classes. In *Proceedings of the 38th International Conference on Software Engineering*, ICSE '16, pages 225–236, New York, NY, USA, 2016. ACM.

[10] N. Hunt, P. S. Sandhu, and L. Ceze. Characterizing the performance and energy efficiency of lock-free data structures. In *2011 15th Workshop on Interaction between Compilers and Computer Architectures*, pages 63–70, Feb 2011.

[11] C. Jung, S. Rus, B. P. Railing, N. Clark, and S. Pande. Brainy: Effective selection of data structures. *SIGPLAN Not.*, 46(6):86–97, June 2011.

[12] E. Kalliamvakou, G. Gousios, K. Blincoe, L. Singer, D. M. German, and D. Damian. The promises and perils of mining github. In *Proceedings of the 11th Working Conference on Mining Software Repositories*, MSR 2014, pages 92–101, New York, NY, USA, 2014. ACM.

[13] K. Kawachiya, K. Ogata, and T. Onodera. Analysis and reduction of memory inefficiencies in java strings. *SIGPLAN Not.*, 43(10):385–402, Oct. 2008.

[14] R. Leventov. Time - Memory Tradeoff With the Example of Java Maps. https://dzone.com/articles/time-memory-tradeoff-example.

[15] L. Lewis. Java Collection Performance. https://dzone.com/articles/java-collection-performance, July 2011.

[16] N. Mitchell and G. Sevitsky. The causes of bloat, the limits of health. In *Proceedings of the 22Nd Annual ACM SIGPLAN Conference on Object-oriented Programming Systems and Applications*, OOPSLA '07, pages 245–260, New York, NY, USA, 2007. ACM.

[17] D. C. Montgomery. *Design and Analysis of Experiments*. Wiley, Hoboken, NJ, 8 edition edition, Apr. 2012.

[18] T. Mytkowicz, A. Diwan, M. Hauswirth, and P. F. Sweeney. Evaluating the accuracy of java profilers. In *Proceedings of the 31st ACM SIGPLAN Conference on Programming Language Design and Implementation*, PLDI '10, pages 187–197, New York, NY, USA, 2010. ACM.

[19] H. A. Nguyen, R. Dyer, T. N. Nguyen, and H. Rajan. Mining preconditions of apis in large-scale code corpus. In *Proceedings of the 22Nd ACM SIGSOFT International Symposium on Foundations of Software Engineering*, FSE 2014, pages 166–177, New York, NY, USA, 2014. ACM.

[20] Oracle. Java development kit. https://www.oracle.com/java/index.html, Sept. 2015.

[21] S. Osiński and D. Weiss. HPPC: High Performance Primitive Collections for Java. http://labs.carrotsearch.com/hppc.html, Jan. 2015.

[22] B. Ray, D. Posnett, V. Filkov, and P. Devanbu. A large scale study of programming languages and code quality in github. In *Proceedings of the 22Nd ACM SIGSOFT International Symposium on Foundations of Software Engineering*, FSE 2014, pages 155–165, New York, NY, USA, 2014. ACM.

[23] O. Shacham, M. Vechev, and E. Yahav. Chameleon: Adaptive selection of collections. In *Proceedings of the 30th ACM SIGPLAN Conference on Programming Language Design and Implementation*, PLDI '09, pages 408–418, New York, NY, USA, 2009. ACM.

[24] S. Vigna. Fastutil. http://fastutil.di.unimi.it/l, Jan. 2016.

[25] M. Vorontsov. Large HashMap Overview. http://java-performance.info/hashmap-overview-jdk-fastutil-goldman-sachs-hppc-koloboke-trove-january-2015/, Feb. 2015.

[26] G. Xu. Coco: Sound and adaptive replacement of java collections. In *Proceedings of the 27th European Conference on Object-Oriented Programming*, ECOOP'13, pages 1–26, Berlin, Heidelberg, 2013. Springer-Verlag.

[27] G. Xu and A. Rountev. Precise memory leak detection for java software using container profiling. In *Proceedings of the 30th International Conference on Software Engineering*, ICSE '08, pages 151–160, New York, NY, USA, 2008. ACM.

[28] G. Xu and A. Rountev. Detecting inefficiently-used containers to avoid bloat. In *Proceedings of the 31st ACM SIGPLAN Conference on Programming Language Design and Implementation*, PLDI '10, pages 160–173, New York, NY, USA, 2010. ACM.

[29] S. Yang, D. Yan, G. Xu, and A. Rountev. Dynamic analysis of inefficiently-used containers. In *Proceedings of the Ninth International Workshop on Dynamic Analysis*, WODA 2012, pages 30–35, New York, NY, USA, 2012. ACM.

Unit Testing Performance in Java Projects: Are We There Yet?

Petr Stefan[1], Vojtěch Horký[1], Lubomír Bulej[1,2], Petr Tůma[1]

[1] Department of Distributed and Dependable Systems
Faculty of Mathematics and Physics,
Charles University
Prague, Czech Republic
first.last@d3s.mff.cuni.cz

[2] Faculty of Informatics,
Università della Svizzera italiana
Lugano, Switzerland
bulejl@usi.ch

ABSTRACT

Although methods and tools for unit testing of performance exist for over a decade, anecdotal evidence suggests unit testing of performance is not nearly as common as unit testing of functionality. We examine this situation in a study of GitHub projects written in Java, looking for occurrences of performance evaluation code in common performance testing frameworks. We quantify the use of such frameworks, identifying the most relevant performance testing approaches, and describe how we adjust the design of our SPL performance testing framework to follow these conclusions.

Keywords

Performance Unit Testing; Open Source; Survey; JMH; SPL

1. INTRODUCTION

This paper is motivated by two observations, one related to performance testing and one to software testing activities in general:

- Software performance testing is widely recognized as an essential software quality assurance tool. Reports of major companies practicing systematic performance testing [11], as well as analyses of project failures associated with insufficient performance testing [4], make performance testing a common wisdom activity.
- Another common wisdom argument in software testing activities, associated especially with test driven development, is that the earlier a test is done, the cheaper it is to remove the discovered defects [24].

Combining the two points naturally leads to work on early performance testing, such as performance evaluation through architectural performance models [1]. Here, we focus on unit testing of performance, which is situated roughly between architectural performance modeling and system performance testing.

ICPE'17, Apr. 22–26, 2017, L'Aquila, Italy
© 2017 ACM. ISBN 978-1-4503-4404-3/17/04...$15.00
DOI: http://dx.doi.org/10.1145/3030207.3030226

Much of the existing work on unit testing of performance is situated in the Java ecosystem. Java is a major software platform for performance sensitive applications, including server side containers such as Glassfish or Tomcat or distributed computing frameworks such as Flink or Hadoop, but also a software platform whose performance related behavior is often more complex than that of traditional languages like C.

The Java ecosystem offers multiple frameworks potentially suitable for unit testing of performance, including Caliper [19], ContiPerf [2], Japex [28], JMH [27], or JUnitPerf [7]. Some of these frameworks exist for over a decade, however, anecdotal evidence suggests that unit testing of performance is still not as established as unit testing of functionality or system performance testing. In this paper, we replace the anecdotal evidence with more rigorous data on the actual practice of unit testing of performance, and propose modifications to our performance testing framework, SPL [6], to reflect this data.

The main contributions of this paper are:

- We analyze 99019 open source software projects on GitHub, totaling nearly 3 TB of data, and provide both current and historical statistics on the use of performance testing frameworks in these projects.
- We collect and summarize positions on unit testing of performance from 111 open source software developers who use the JMH performance testing framework, and use these to supplement the GitHub analysis results.
- We identify those projects that implement performance tests potentially suitable for unit testing of performance, and provide statistics on the test time and measurement accuracy.
- We explain how we adjust the design of our SPL performance testing framework to reflect these results.

The paper is structured as follows. In Section 2, we point to the motivating context and introduce the performance testing frameworks whose use is analyzed in later sections. Section 3 formulates the research questions for our survey and discusses threats to internal validity. Section 4 presents and discusses measurements that answer the research questions. Section 5 focuses on the adjustments of our own performance testing framework. Finally, Section 6 concludes the paper.

2. RELATED WORK

Taken separately, both unit testing and performance testing are well established quality control activities. At the unit testing side, studies such as [12] and [25] report successful defect reduction in industrial settings. At the performance testing side, studies such as [35] provide an early summary of the issues, and papers such as [36] contain a broader overview of the software performance engineering challenges.

Moving beyond the established principles of unit testing, multiple studies summarize developer opinions on the testing practice and identify open research issues. Runeson [29] remarks that multiple companies report issues with the effort of testing automation, Engstrom and Runeson [10] repeat the same concern in the context of regression testing. Greiler et al. [14] examine unit testing in the context of component systems, pointing out both a strong developer preference for testing automation and a need for reasonable setup effort and test time. Our work contributes to the existing unit testing studies by focusing specifically on unit testing of performance – where, interestingly, some of the listed concerns are emphasized due to more demanding test automation and more expensive test execution.

A unit testing survey by Daka and Fraser [8] observes that some developer responses are not necessarily accurate. As an alternative to surveying developers, source code repositories are mined in an open source software testing study by Kochhar et al. [20]. Our work provides more detailed information by combining repository mining with surveying developers for supplementary information. Also, our focus on the Java ecosystem permits us to process the repository content much more accurately – for example we identify tests by searching for specific code constructs rather than for file name patterns.

A related line of research surveys the performance testing practices. Nistor et al. [26] look at the difference between performance bugs and functional bugs. The authors point out that compared to reasoning about functionality, developers have little support for reasoning about performance. From the testing perspective, better oracles for evaluating test conditions are called for.

Jit et al. [17] and Liu et al. [23] focus on characterizing real world performance bugs, as opposed to performance bugs discovered in possibly artificial testing conditions. Their work, one experimenting with Linux and one with Android, identifies typical features of existing performance bugs and applies this knowledge to look for new bugs. Again, the need for automated evaluation of measurement data is listed as one open issue.

Linares-Vásquez et al. [22] investigate the current practices of locating and fixing performance issues in mobile applications. Among other results, the conclusions of the study most related to testing show that 73 % of developers rely on manual testing and 51 % on user feedback to locate performance issues, expressing preference for observation based analysis rather than automation.

Overall, the conclusions of the existing studies reveal definite gap between testing of functionality and performance. In functional testing, automation at unit test level works reasonably well, even if the setup effort and test time are not necessarily trivial. In performance testing, manual approaches appear dominant and automation is asked for. Our study investigates this gap.

Combined together, unit testing and performance testing are also particularly close to the increasingly popular DevOps movement. Acceptance of DevOps principles can not only lead to increased performance awareness [13, 21, 34], but also provide direct software process benefits – for example a retroactive case study by Waller et al. [33] shows how integrating Kieker (performance monitoring tool) with Jenkins (continuous integration tool) can lead to earlier detection of performance regressions.

On the technical side, both unit testing and performance testing rely on established tool support. Among tools relevant to the platform context and testing scale of this work, we have:

- unit testing tools such as JUnit [18] or TestNG [31], which simplify unit test implementation by providing standard constructs for marking test methods, expressing test conditions and managing test fixtures, together with an environment that automatically executes the tests and reports the results, and
- performance testing tools such as JMH [27], which provide constructs for marking measured workload, defining measurement conditions and controlling potentially disruptive optimizations, together with an environment that automatically executes the measurements and collects the results.

For the purpose of this work, we are interested in tools that support unit testing of performance. Table 1 provides a list of the relevant frameworks. While common unit testing tools have no performance testing support, special purpose extensions exist. The table includes ContiPerf [2] and JUnitPerf [7] as two extensions of JUnit, both support specifying absolute limits on test execution time as the test condition. For performance testing tools, the table lists Caliper [19], Japex [28] and JMH [27], three frameworks that target microbenchmark implementation.

Somewhat separately, Table 1 also lists SPL [6]. SPL is our performance testing framework and formalism for specifying test conditions. Although SPL can be used in real open source projects [16], the framework is still subject to frequent

Framework	Metrics	Asserts	Output	Maintained
SPL	Time	Yes	CSV, charts[a]	2012 –
JMH	`perf`[b]	No	Text[c], JSON	2013 –
Caliper	Time	No	Text[c]	2008 –
JUnitPerf	Time[d]	Yes	Text[c]	2009 – 2010
ContiPerf	Time[d]	Yes	CSV, charts[a]	2010 – 2014
Japex	Time[d]	No	XML, charts[a]	2005 – 2011

Table 1: *Comparison summary of Java benchmarking frameworks. SPL is a research project on performance unit testing; JMH, Caliper and Japex are microbenchmarking frameworks; JUnitPerf and ContiPerf are performance related extensions of the JUnit testing framework.*

[a] Charts embedded in an HTML report.
[b] Linux perf counters and throughput available.
[c] For human reader, machine processing possible.
[d] Throughput also available.

large scale modifications and therefore not a part of our usage survey – instead, we use the survey to collect feedback that motivates modifications described in Section 5.

From the broader context of automated performance testing, we want to mention the performance monitoring frameworks that collect data through instrumentation, such as Kieker [32]. With performance monitoring, unit test execution time can be observed and possibly used for performance testing, however, such practice is complicated by the need for repeated test execution with stable test fixtures and other issues.

Also related is the issue of robust measurement environment. For performance testing to deliver meaningful results, the measurement environment must be sufficiently representative. In performance sensitive applications, unit test execution may benefit from environments such as DataMill [9] to guard against the accidental measurement bias due to platform configuration and to provide platform variability.

3. SURVEY DESIGN

To assess whether unit testing of performance is as well established as unit testing of functionality, we formulate multiple research questions with measurable answers. We aim for answers that can be measured by analyzing source code repositories – such repositories are available for many software projects and we can therefore achieve reasonable project coverage. We start with the key question:

Q1: How much is unit testing of performance used?

An answer to Q1 can be expressed as the share of software projects that use unit testing of performance. To recognize whether a software project uses unit testing of performance, we look for statements that import packages or declare annotations distinctive for particular performance testing frameworks. This approach can be reasonably automated, however, it requires careful discussion of threats to validity on two levels – at the implementation level, it is not necessarily true that recognizing packages or annotations equates to using a performance testing framework, and, at the process level, it is not necessarily true that using a performance testing framework equates to practicing the unit testing of performance.

At the implementation level, we detect usage patterns associated with all the performance testing frameworks surveyed in Section 2. In these frameworks, importing distinct packages or declaring distinct annotations are reliably established usage patterns. Table 2 lists the base packages and the test markers – we consider a reference to the base package anywhere in code as an indicator that the associated framework is used, and we count the uses of test markers to determine the number of tests. Our detection tool uses source code parser to properly resolve imports and distinguish ambiguous textual identifiers.

Although it is technically possible to avoid the listed usage patterns and still invoke particular framework features, such practice would be obscure. We therefore classify the threat of failing to detect a framework that is actually used as low.

Inversely, we can detect a framework that is present but not used. Performance testing frameworks implement packages and annotations that software projects are unlikely to use

Framework	Base package Test marker
Caliper	`com.google.caliper` `@Benchmark`
ContiPerf	`org.databene.contiperf` `@PerfTest`
Japex	`com.sun.japex` `JapexDriverBase`
JMH	`org.openjdk.jmh` `@Benchmark, @GenerateMicroBenchmark`
JUnitPerf	`com.clarkware.junitperf` `TimedTest, LoadTest`
JUnit	`org.junit` `@Test`
TestNG	`org.testng` `@Test`

Table 2: *Packages and annotations used to detect particular frameworks. Presence of any type from the base package indicates framework use. One use of any test marker counts as one test.*

for purposes other than performance testing, the threat is therefore most likely manifested with abandoned performance testing attempts. Because we execute all the recognized performance tests to answer some of the further research questions, we avoid this threat entirely.

A software project can also implement performance tests in a proprietary manner, not relying on any performance testing framework. This threat needs to be considered especially because our initial premise is that performance testing frameworks are not well established and proprietary test implementations are therefore likely. To identify such software projects, we rely on the assumption that a performance test must query the clock to determine performance. Any code that uses standard system interface to query the clock is identified as a potential performance test, further manual classification is used to determine the purpose for which the clock is queried.

At the process level, an answer to Q1 requires making a distinction between projects whose code contains performance tests and projects whose development process involves unit testing of performance. The existence of performance tests is a necessary but not sufficient condition for unit testing of performance, which also requires that the tests execute with unit granularity and that the test conditions are specified and evaluated.

To address the issue of granularity, we attempt to execute all recognized performance tests. Tests that fail to run due to missing external dependencies (network services to connect to, external data to read, etc.) are not considered unit tests (unit tests should mock or do without dependencies). Similarly, tests that run too long are not considered unit tests (unit tests should be small enough to execute during regular builds). The remaining performance tests, which execute without dependencies and within reasonable time, are considered candidates for unit testing.

Given only project code, it is not possible to reliably check whether the candidate tests specify and evaluate test conditions. Simple assertion statements, typical for unit testing of functionality, are not suitable for unit testing of performance, where performance measurements can seldom be compared using classical test conditions [5, 6]. More complex evaluation approaches can escape detection when implemented in the build infrastructure rather than the project code [15, 3]. In the answer to Q1, we therefore include all the candidate tests, assuming they could be easily used as unit tests of performance if they are not already. Further research questions evaluate the accuracy of such tests.

To interpret the answer to Q1, we also need a baseline. We therefore measure the share of projects that implement unit tests of functionality, and compare that to the share of projects that implement unit tests of performance. The technical implementation is similar, but we detect the use of general testing frameworks rather than performance testing frameworks.

Q2: How much does unit testing of performance change with time?

Source code repositories permit examining not only the current state of a software project, but also the development history. By measuring the answers to Q1 at different points in time, we therefore provide an answer to Q2. Again, we use measurements for unit testing of functionality as a baseline to interpret the measurements for unit testing of performance.

Q3: What kind of software projects are measuring performance?

Unit testing of performance is likely to differ depending on the kind of software project involved. This has important repercussions – the general project domain may determine what the unit tests need in terms of environment, configuration, mock dependency injection and other features, while parameters such as code size and commit frequency determine requirements on the scalability of the testing infrastructure.

To provide an answer to Q3, we measure the project size in lines of code both now and at the time a performance test first appeared in the project. We also collect the average commit frequency across the project. Finally, we manually classify the general project domain.

Q4: How long does unit testing of performance take?

Unit tests of functionality typically take a fixed amount of time to arrive at the pass or fail decision. Due to the variability inherent to performance measurements, this is not the case with unit tests of performance – instead, the test can collect measurements continuously and the longer it runs, the higher confidence or sensitivity it provides. Furthermore, modern execution environments need some minimum execution time to reach stable performance, making short test runs less representative.

To answer Q4, we give the time needed to execute all the candidate performance tests. However, this time depends on factors such as measurement framework configuration options, which are often set in the build infrastructure rather than the project code. When the real options differ from the defaults, so will the time reported. We therefore also report the accuracy obtained after one hour of measurement, as a metric that is connected with the test time and reflects what results to expect when testing with one hour period (one hour was picked to resemble testing after each commit).

Q5: Does unit testing of performance reveal actual performance changes?

With unit tests in place, the obvious remaining question is, do their results reveal actual performance changes? To answer Q5, we simply look at the differences in measured performance at chosen points in project lifetime. Such differences can arise due to real change in project performance, but also due to changes in test code. To avoid mixing the two, we compare current performance with performance measured after last test code modification, thus excluding differences due to changes in test code.

Developer Survey

Repository mining readily provides aggregate statistics but does not explain the results. To avoid speculation when discussing the results of the formulated research questions, we have asked the developers who use the dominant performance testing framework to answer a short survey on the following topics:

- reasons for choosing a particular framework,
- degree of integration into the development process,
- degree of automation in processing the results,
- perceived usefulness of performance testing,
- perceived obstacles to performance testing.

We present selected results of the developer survey when discussing answers to the research questions. Exact wording of the survey questions and complete results are available at [30].

4. SURVEY RESULTS

To answer the formulated research questions, we analyze source code repositories from GitHub. GitHub is likely the most popular open source software hosting facility, claiming over 15 million users and 38 million projects[1], compared for example to SourceForge with 3.7 million users and 430 thousand projects[2] (these and other presented numbers on repository sizes and project counts were collected in the period of August to October 2016). Our use of an open source repository can naturally introduce bias, however, it is not likely that we would succeed in getting information on a similar number of closed source software projects and the associated development processes from the software industry.

GitHub provides a code search API with functions essential to our survey – in particular, we can list projects that meet particular language criteria. As a complication, the API is limited to returning at most 1000 entries matching a query, plus an information on the total number of matching entries. Also, answers to queries whose processing exceeds preset timeout are incomplete. To sidestep these limitations, we split each query that returns more than 1000 entries into multiple smaller queries whose answers together form the answer to the original query. This is done by adding interval filters on attributes such as repository size and fork count and recursively splitting the intervals until the queries are satisfied. We note this approach can introduce races because the individual queries observe GitHub at slightly different moments in time (the processing time for the central query that lists all surveyed projects was almost 7 hours), however,

[1] http://github.com/about
[2] http://sourceforge.net/about

we submit the individual queries in the order of growing repository sizes and growing fork counts, making it less likely that we miss a project (it would have to shrink in size or fork count just between the relevant queries).

We use the API to identify Java projects, getting approximately 2.4 million entries excluding forks. Because these contain a high number of obviously invalid projects (for example, we get approximately 314 thousand entries for projects whose repository size is below 16 kB and over 94 thousand of those are empty), we restrict our survey to projects that have been forked at least twice (a non zero fork count is a liberal filter for projects that receive some attention, established projects collect up to thousands of forks). There are approximately 100 thousand such projects, for our analysis we have successfully cloned and processed exactly 99019 repositories totaling almost 3 TB of data.

A1: How much is unit testing of performance used ...

Table 3 gives the share of projects whose source code uses one of the surveyed performance testing frameworks (Caliper, ContiPerf, Japex, JMH, JUnitPerf). As a baseline, the table also gives the share of projects whose source code uses either JUnit 4 or TestNG, two dominant unit testing frameworks.

The table indicates that unit testing of performance using the surveyed performance testing frameworks is extremely rare. The most used framework, JMH, is found on average less than three times in thousand projects, the other frameworks are used an order of magnitude less often. Because subsequent analysis steps further reduce this number, we will only consider projects that use JMH and refrain from drawing conclusions on projects with other frameworks (generalizing from what are basically singular use cases is not possible).

With JMH identified as the dominant framework, we have also sent the developer survey to the developers who use it – specifically, those developers who have updated any performance test in any commit of the 278 relevant projects. We have sent out a total of 483 invitations to fill in the survey and received 111 completed forms (78 with permission to publish results, 26 with permission to publish summary, 7 with no permission to publish).

The developer survey lists trust in results as the top reason for choosing JMH at 72 %. Other reasons include active maintenance at 60 % and good documentation at 40 %. Build system integration is rated comparatively low at 33 %. These results emphasize the difficulty of writing correct performance tests and suggest few frameworks are considered mature.

Framework	Repositories	Relative usage
Caliper	12	0.012 %
ContiPerf	17	0.017 %
Japex	52	0.053 %
JMH	278	0.281 %
JUnitPerf	11	0.011 %
JUnit 4	30871	31.177 %
TestNG	2053	2.073 %
Total	99019	100 %

Table 3: *Java test framework usage on GitHub.*

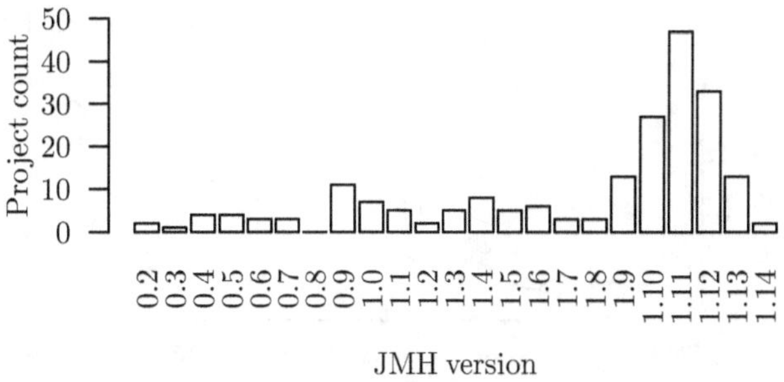

Figure 1: *JMH versions used by projects. Versions 1.11, 1.12, 1.13 and 1.14 were released on January, April, July and September 2016, respectively.*

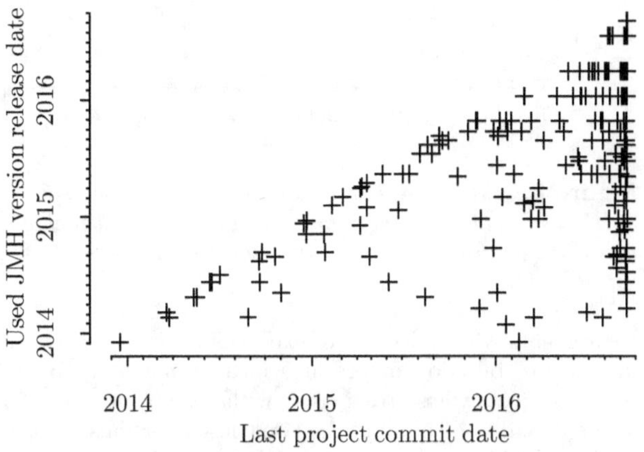

Figure 2: *JMH version adoption delay. Each project is represented by one point, projects near the diagonal use the most current JMH version, the further from the diagonal, the more obsolete the JMH version used.*

Subsequent analysis steps require building and executing all the recognized performance tests. For this, we use Fedora Linux 24 with OpenJDK 1.8.0 in the latest update, software dependencies resolved through build configuration, running on a dual Intel Xeon E5-2660 machine (20 MB cache, 2.2 GHz clock, 8 cores) with 48 GB RAM. For measurements, we disable hardware threads, frequency scaling and boosting, and constrain the execution to single NUMA node for both memory and processor allocation.

As a technical complication, JMH outputs only summary measurement information but for accurate statistical processing we need individual measurements. Before building the projects, we therefore created a modified JMH version and inserted it among project dependencies. For that, we need projects with standard dependency specification – among the projects that use JMH, these are 223 projects built with Maven and 52 projects built with Gradle. Figure 1 lists the JMH versions originally used in the projects, Figure 2 illustrates the JMH adoption speed by plotting the release date of the used JMH version against the last commit date for each project. We note that our modifications are included in standard JMH starting with version 1.14.

After inserting the modified JMH version, we attempt to build two versions of each project. One is the HEAD commit, one is the last commit which modified any recognized performance test. This yields 29 projects whose tests produce

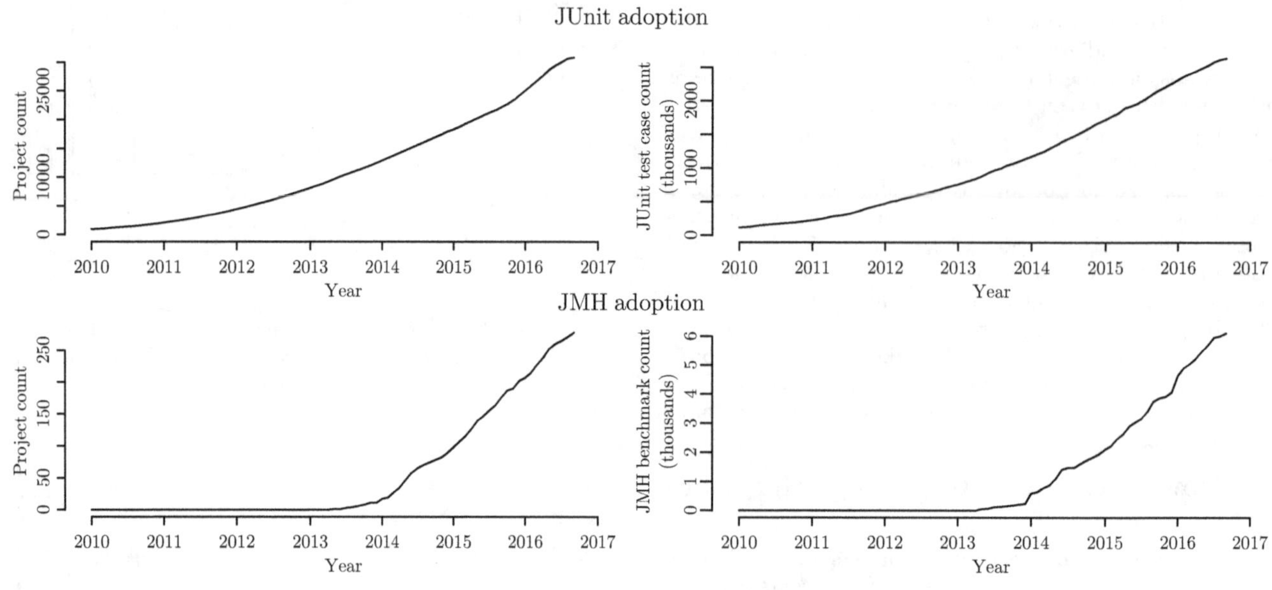

Figure 3: *JMH and JUnit adoption rate comparison. The plots show how the number of projects that use JUnit 4 or JMH (left) and the total number of test cases or benchmark methods in these projects (right) changes with time. The data was collected for each day in the plot range.*

measurements within 4 hours of execution, 9 projects whose tests execute but do not produce measurements within 4 hours, 9 projects whose tests crash without output, and 235 projects that do not build in the two chosen versions. In the following, the 29 projects whose tests produce measurements within 4 hours are referred to as the measured projects and the two versions as the measured versions.

To summarize the answer to Q1 where the use of performance testing frameworks is concerned: use of the surveyed performance testing frameworks is extremely rare, at most 0.37 % of the analyzed projects use any performance testing framework and at least 62 % of those projects whose tests readily build and execute produce measurements within 4 hours. Although the analysis suffers from high attrition rate, these numbers should represent reasonable upper and lower bounds.

To analyze projects that implement performance tests without any performance testing framework, we look for the use of three clock query functions available in Java – **System.nanoTime()**, **System.currentTimeMillis()** and **ThreadMXBean.get*Time()**. Because manual classification of all 99019 projects is not practical, we pick 1000 projects at random. Of those, 332 projects did query the clock, their classification is in Table 4.

The classification is based on manual exploration of the call site and the immediately surrounding code. To reduce classification error, the exploration was done independently by two researchers and keywords were assigned to each project. Afterwards, similar keywords were gradually merged into clusters as in hierarchical clustering. To provide some estimate of the classification error involved, we note that 70 % of the time there was overlap between keywords assigned by the two researchers to a project.

The classification contains several categories where unit test use is not likely – timeout handling in caches and sockets, calendar, scheduling, randomization. In some categories, unit

Usage	Count	99 % CI
Timeout handling	125	99 – 154
Logging of durations	133	107 – 163
Querying calendar time	122	97 – 151
Event scheduling, GUI	89	67 – 115
Randomization, unique naming	65	47 – 88
Proprietary benchmarking	34	21 – 52
Custom timer infrastructure	29	17 – 46

Table 4: *Usage of System.nanoTime and System.currentTimeMillis. Projects that span multiple categories are counted multiple times.*

test use is possible – information from logs or benchmarks can be used for testing, but the free form of the output and the lack of established benchmark culture (warmup, repetitions, randomization) often suggests otherwise. The custom timer infrastructure category groups situations where the collected time samples are wrapped and propagated beyond reach of the immediately surrounding code with no hint on use.

To summarize the answer to Q1 with proprietary performance tests: no more than 33.2 % of the randomly selected projects query clock using the most common function calls, and no less than 3.4 % of the randomly selected projects query clock in direct relation to testing or benchmarking. The confidence intervals in Table 4 help extrapolate the ratios to general project population.

A2: How much does unit testing of performance change with time ...

Figure 3 shows how the number of projects that use JMH and the number of JMH benchmark methods in those projects changed over time, contrasted with the number of projects that use JUnit 4 and the number of JUnit 4 test cases in those projects. The gradually rising shape is similar in both cases,

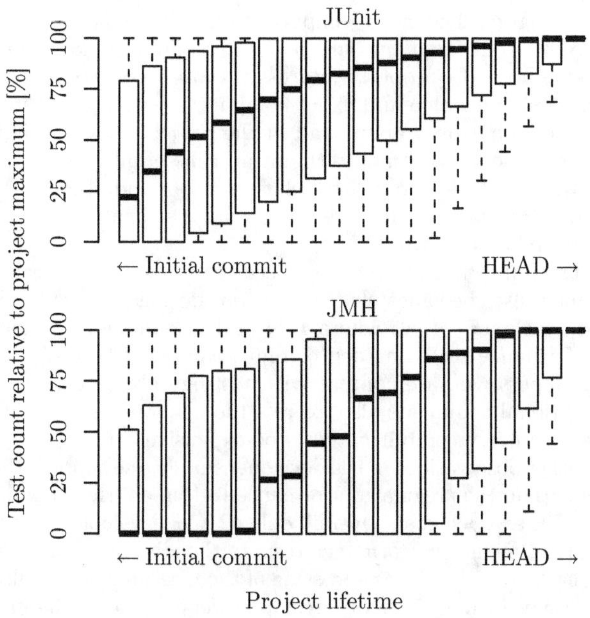

Figure 4: *Test count during project lifetime. Both axes are normalized, the project lifetime (X axis) stretches from the initial commit to the HEAD commit of each project, the test count (Y axis) ranges from zero to maximum number of test cases across the history of each project. Outliers are not shown, whiskers are at 1.5 IQR.*

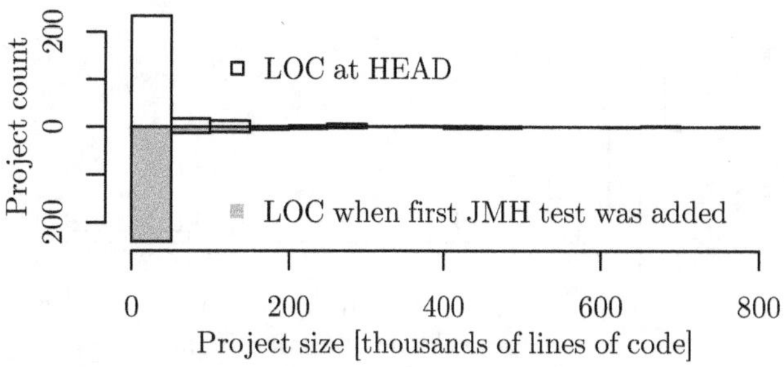

Figure 5: *Source code size for projects that use JMH.*

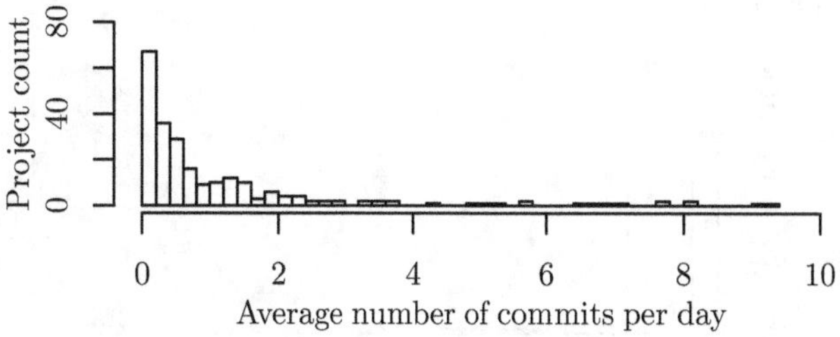

Figure 6: *Commit frequency for projects that use JMH. We show only projects with at least five commits and history longer than two weeks. One project with over 30 commits per day was omitted to preserve readable scale.*

the absolute numbers are naturally very different. Results for other performance testing frameworks are not given due to low use count, which makes it impossible to distinguish stagnating trends reliably.

To provide individual project perspective, Figure 4 shows how the number of benchmark methods or test cases changes over time within each project. Project data is aggregated by normalizing the time (X axis) to stretch from the initial commit to the HEAD commit, and the count (Y axis) from 0 % to 100 % of the maximum count observed. Again, results for other performance testing frameworks are not given due to low use count.

Figure 4 suggests that although both the benchmark method count and the test case count tend to increase across project lifetime, the first benchmark methods tend to appear later than the first test cases. There are several possible explanations. For one, the test first approach to implementation may be easier to do with functional testing than performance testing, because the test conditions are more obvious. Performance tests may also require more complete implementation than functional tests. The developer survey provides another insight – 64 % of developers touch performance test implementation only when addressing performance issues, only 28 % of developers maintains performance tests as often as other code.

A3: What kind of software projects are measuring performance …

Figures 5 and 6 show the size and commit frequency of projects that use JMH, measured between the first commit that introduced any recognized performance test and the HEAD commit. We note that although some large projects are included, most projects that use JMH have less than 50 kLOC.

Table 5 provides rough classification for projects that use JMH. The table was constructed by labeling each project with information from the project documentation and then clustering similar labels until reasonable granularity was reached (each project is counted only once). Not listed are 66 analyzed projects whose clusters were smaller than 10 projects and 30 analyzed projects whose only purpose was to compare other projects against each other. Complete information is available in [30].

The developer survey provides additional information on the use of performance tests across categories – 80 % of developers report measuring their own code, 37 % of developers report measuring external code such as libraries. Also, 64 % of developers measure performance to compare alternatives. This can help explain the prominent position of tutorials and examples – obviously, explorative performance measurements provide important information during development.

Category	Count
Database (ORM, SQL …)	33
Tutorials and examples	30
Networking and distributed systems	29
Algorithms	27
Data structures	22
Object serialization, parsers (XML, JSON, …)	22
Web frameworks or plugins	18

Table 5: *JMH benchmark classification. Categories created through hierarchical clustering, small categories not shown, complete information in [30].*

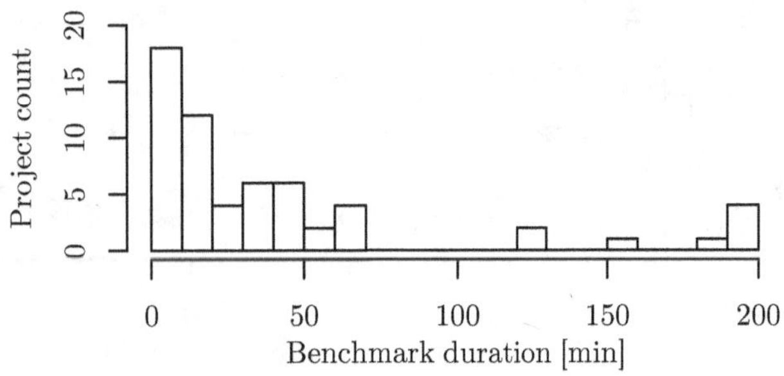

Figure 7: *Benchmark durations. Distribution of total benchmark execution time for all projects, measured with default settings.*

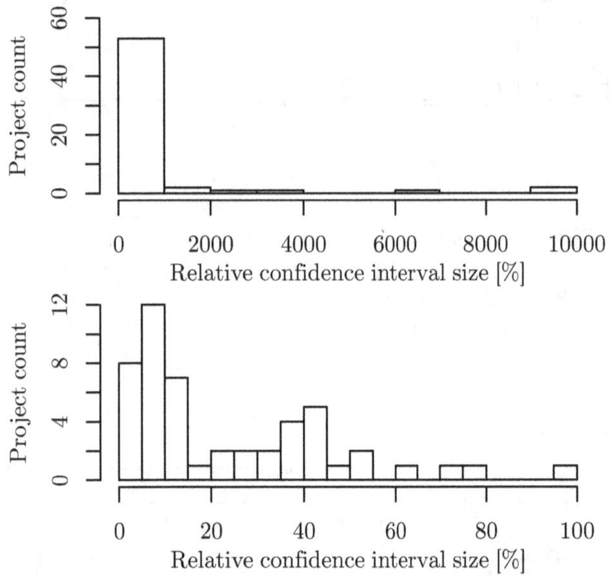

Figure 8: *Benchmark accuracy. Distribution of the worst relative confidence interval sizes of the mean for all projects. Relative confidence intervals of the mean were computed for each benchmark from one hour of measurements, each project is represented by the widest interval. The bottom graph is a zoom of the top one.*

A4: How long does unit testing of performance take . . .

Figure 7 shows the distribution of the time needed to execute the performance tests with the default configuration for the measured projects, with each project counted in two measured versions. We note that the default configuration uses a small number of test executions (forks in JMH parlance), here median 3 and maximum 10, but still only about one third of the tests finishes within one hour, suggesting that collecting enough measurements for sensitive performance change detection can be an issue.

Figure 8 shows the accuracy obtained after one hour of measurement, expressed as the distribution of the relative confidence interval sizes for the mean. Specifically, we compute the relative 99 % confidence interval width (99 % confidence interval width divided by mean) for each benchmark method in each project using a bootstrap procedure, and then select the least accurate width to represent the project in the figure. The mean computation in the bootstrap procedure uses only as many samples as there are test executions in one hour, to properly address variation between executions (for rationale and exact computation we refer to [6]). We note that only about half of the projects have enough measurements to estimate the mean time of all benchmark methods with at most 20 % relative width, and about 20 % of the projects provides the least accurate estimate with over 100 % relative width.

The importance of the time needed to execute the performance tests becomes clear when considering the results of the developer survey, where 47 % of developers want to run performance tests on each commit, as opposed to 37 % of developers who are content with testing only each release. Additional comments also express the opinion that running tests on every commit may be too expensive.

Other observations in the developer survey also support the conclusion that regular performance testing on each commit remains an open goal. Overall, only 42 % of developers report running regular performance tests (although not necessarily on each commit). The processing of the measurements is also an issue – whole 77 % of developers report mostly manual processing, only 13 % mention automated plotting and only 6 % further automated evaluation.

A5: Does unit testing of performance reveal actual performance changes . . .

Figure 9 shows the distribution of performance changes across individual benchmark methods, expressed as the ratio of the mean times from the two measured versions (new over old). Due to the large relative confidence interval widths in one hour of measurement, almost no change is statistically significant (99 % confidence intervals overlap).

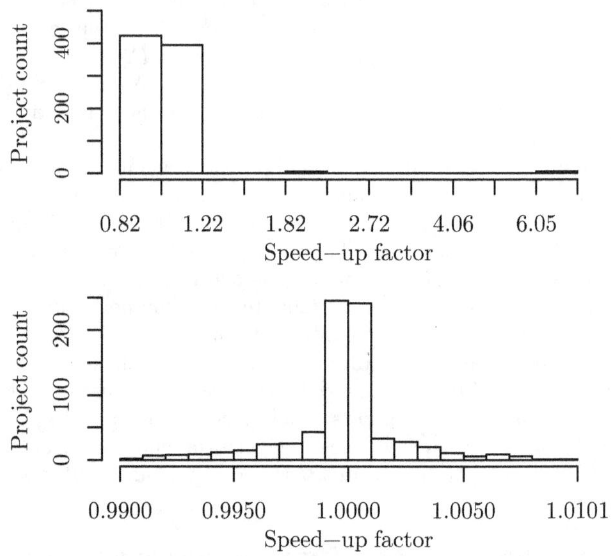

Figure 9: *Distribution of performance changes. A performance change is a ratio of mean execution times of each benchmark in the two measured versions. Logarithmic scale used for symmetry around 1. The bottom graph is a zoom of the top one.*

The developer survey offers additional explanation to the small changes in performance on Figure 9. Overall, 80 % of developers report acting on performance testing results in the past, however, less than one third of those report finding performance improvements or regressions – the remaining majority used the results to guide design decisions. Also, 13 % of developers mention seeing interesting results only rarely. This may suggest that performance testing is perceived as more useful during initial development stages, where it helps guide design.

To conclude, we summarize the remaining results of the developer survey, which concerns perceived obstacles to performance testing. These are in line with the previous findings – 61 % of developers believe automated evaluation would encourage more performance testing, 50 % of developers also want better build integration. Whole 31 % of developers feel the environment for implementing performance tests should be simpler, and 27 % mention budget issues.

4.1 Threats To Validity

Most threats to internal validity of our analysis were discussed together with the research questions. Where the recognition of performance testing frameworks is concerned, we classify the threat of false positives as low (we use source code parsing rather than mere text pattern searching), the threat of false negatives is limited to obscure usage patterns and unknown performance testing frameworks. For proprietary performance tests, the threats include possible classification mistakes due to manual processing and no support for native code implementation outside Java.

For building and executing the recognized performance tests, we avoid attributing specific causes to failures. Some projects may be broken from the very start, some projects may be correct but fail due to mismatch in platform requirements or dependencies. While some failures may be amenable to manual correction, some may be beyond fixing. Our survey does not have data to distinguish these cases.

Threats to external validity are tied to the high attrition rate. While we believe it is connected mostly to the general shape of open source projects and common backward compatibility issues, it still prevents most generalizations.

5. SPL INTEGRATION DESIGN

We want to reflect the results of the survey from Section 4 in the design of our SPL performance testing framework. In general, we strive to integrate SPL-based performance testing into the software development process in a manner similar to that of commonly used unit testing frameworks, with the goal of supporting three basic use cases: identifying performance regressions, capturing performance assumptions about (third-party) code, and providing performance documentation [6].

Briefly, in the case of a functional unit test, the test result depends on evaluating program state. A test is responsible for setting up the initial state, executing the test operations, and checking whether the resulting program state meets the expectations. Each test is the sole arbiter of the correctness of the tested behavior, and the testing framework just orchestrates test execution and provides the tests with means to indicate test results.

In contrast, in the case of a performance unit test, the test results depends on performance data collected during program execution. A test needs to provide a way to induce (representative) workload on a performance sensitive part of the program code, and a test condition in form of a hypothesis over performance measurements collected during test execution. The test itself does not determine the test result, because the workload may need to be executed many times to obtain data suitable for statistical analysis, and because the test condition may actually involve more than one version of the program code. Here the role of a testing framework is much more involved, because it needs to direct the collection of performance data from test executions (possibly for different versions), and then evaluate the test conditions on the collected data.

The specific requirements of performance unit tests have led our work on integrating SPL into development process towards a complex framework that supports different version control systems and build systems, performs measurements on demand and controls the amount of measured data to evaluate SPL-based test conditions, keeps a history of the measured data, and integrates with IDEs such as Eclipse and continuous integration tools such as Hudson. However, the results of the survey from Section 4 suggest that a different design direction may be needed to make SPL-based performance unit testing attractive to developers.

What we find interesting is that practically the only framework that is being used to conduct some form of performance evaluation or testing is JMH. Apparently, JMH is considered more useful or easier to use by the developers who have adopted some kind of performance testing into their project. Consequently, when it comes to integrating SPL-based performance testing into project development, we should consider the needs of these developers. We therefore turn to JMH for usability cues, and adapt the design of our SPL evaluation framework so that we can provide loosely-coupled building blocks that the developers can integrate into their projects as they see fit, without having to face the steep learning curve of a huge integrated framework. Before discussing the adjustments to the design of our performance testing framework, we first briefly review the typical usage of JMH in projects analyzed in our survey.

5.1 Overview of Typical JMH Usage

JMH provides developers with a simple way to implement and execute microbenchmarks correctly. Microbenchmarks typically execute operations that take very short time, but because they may be executed very often in many programs, they have the potential to influence the overall performance. Unsurprisingly, there are many pitfalls related to microbenchmarking – especially on a managed platform with a just-in-time compiler such as Java. JMH goes to great lengths to avoid them.

With JMH, the developer is responsible for providing the workload (i.e. the operation to be measured), while JMH takes care of benchmark execution and data collection. When finished, JMH typically reports aggregate statistics concerning the durations of the measured operations. From the developer's perspective, the usage of JMH is rather simple, as shown in Listing 1. Similar to using a testing framework such as JUnit, the developer only needs to create a class containing the operations to be measured in form of methods annotated with the `@Benchmark` annotation. Unlike JUnit, JMH does not evaluate the results in any way (apart from providing aggregate statistics), and leaves the responsibility for interpreting the results to the developer.

```
public class SimpleBenchmark {
    @Benchmark
    public void measuredOperation() {
        // Implementation of the
        // operation to be measured.
    }
}
```

Listing 1: *Minimal JMH-based benchmark*

JMH supports additional annotations that provide more fine-grained control over microbenchmark execution, including benchmarking mode, output time units, output format, the number of warmup iterations, and many others. While they may require deeper understanding on the side of the developer, this does not really change the fact that a basic microbenchmark is very simple to write.

The microbenchmarks are also executed using JMH, which locates all the benchmark methods, generates benchmarking harness around those methods and executes the microbenchmarks in separate virtual machines configured to disable inlining of the benchmark method. While JMH can run the benchmarks directly (from an IDE or a command line), it is typically used to build a self-contained JAR file with the benchmark, which can then be simply executed on a dedicated machine. In contrast to functional unit testing, this is an important prerequisite for obtaining measurements that are not influenced by interference that may be present on the developer's machine.

With respect to build system integration, JMH officially supports Maven through a plugin which provides a JMH benchmark project archetype. Community-supported bindings enable integration with other build systems and IDEs. The typical (and endorsed) way using JMH is to create a standalone Maven-based project which contains benchmark code and depends on the application JAR files. The artifact produced by the project is the benchmark JAR file, which can then be used to execute the benchmarks as needed.

5.2 Catering to the Use Case that Matters

Given that performance unit testing is not yet a common practice and its benefits are not as immediate as in the case of functional unit testing, we need to support the adoption of SPL-based performance unit testing in a lightweight and gradual fashion. Considering that the role of JMH is to produce performance data which the developers have to process and analyze themselves to determine whether there has been a performance regression, we believe that the next useful step would be to automate the detection of performance regressions based on the data collected by JMH.

Recall that SPL is a simple language that allows capturing performance assumptions as formulas evaluated using statistical tests applied to performance data. An SPL formula that captures the essence of performance regression testing can be actually as simple as $last \leq 1.05 \times base$. Attached to something that can produce performance data (e.g. a microbenchmark), this formula captures the assertion that the measured operation in the last software version is not more than 5% slower than in some base (e.g. previous) version. In a project using JMH, performance regression testing would mean subjecting the results of all microbenchmarks to such tests, with the corresponding SPL formulas adjusted to the nature of the tested operation.

While the SPL formula representing the performance assumption for this particular use case is trivial, evaluating the formula is not. To remove this burden from the developer, we provide a tool for evaluating given SPL formulas with given data. Just like JMH allows the developer to implement microbenchmarks correctly, the SPL evaluator allows the same developer to compare microbenchmark results between versions correctly and with confidence. Also like JMH, the SPL evaluator is a standalone tool, leaving the developer free to integrate it into a project in any way desired.

To automate performance unit testing, the developer has to ensure that benchmarks will be automatically executed to collect performance data for new software versions, and that the SPL evaluator will be executed with data representing the performance of the last and the base versions of the software. The specifics of the automation and performance data storage remain at the discretion of the developer.

Because JMH officially supports integration with the Maven build system, we also provide a Maven plugin intended to ease adoption of SPL and to simplify integration. We present the SPL evaluator and the Maven plugin in more detail.

5.3 SPL Evaluator Tool

The SPL evaluator provides a command-line interface to the SPL evaluation engine originally developed for our much heavier-weight SPL-based performance unit testing framework. Decoupling the evaluator from the framework provides more opportunities for reuse and integration in existing build systems.

To illustrate the operation of the evaluator, let us again consider the simple SPL formula that can be used for performance regression testing: $last \leq 1.05 \times base$. An SPL formula is one of the evaluator inputs, and the evaluator expects to find it in a text file within the `META-INF` directory of a JAR file, in an external text file, or on the command line, in that order.

In the formula, the relation operator ($\leq$) represents a statistical test, the symbols *last* and *base* identify the data sets on which to perform the test, and the constant represents a scaling factor for the values from the *base* data set.

Conceptually, the symbols *last* and *base* denote the software versions that are the subjects of the performance test. However, the SPL evaluator is not tied to any particular version control system, and has no notion of the concept of a version – all it cares about is whether it can find data associated with the names used in an SPL formula. The evaluator looks for the data sets in directories corresponding to the identifiers used in the formula, relative to a base directory that can be specified on the command line.

In addition, the evaluator can read external files providing custom mapping between the names used in SPL formulas and the names to look for in the base directory of benchmark results. Using this mechanism, the developer can associate the symbols used in SPL formulas with version identifiers specific to a particular version control system, such as commit identifiers in Git. It should be possible to configure most version control systems to update the mapping file automatically, thus keeping a name such as *last* always mapped to the latest commit in a particular branch.

Finally, provided with all the required information, the evaluator performs the statistical tests necessary to evaluate the given formula, and returns the result. If the result cannot be computed, for example because there is not enough data, the evaluator will return an alternative result specifying the reason. The developer is then responsible for providing more data for the software versions being tested.

5.4 JMH SPL Maven Plugin

It is important to note that the SPL evaluator presented in the previous section is not tied to JMH in any way, except that it can use data produced by JMH.[3] The actual integration of SPL and JMH occurs at the level of the build system and only affects the project containing JMH benchmarks.

To make adoption of SPL-based performance unit testing as non-intrusive as possible, we have created a Maven plugin to aid with basic integration tasks. The plugin provides three execution goals bound to different phases of the JMH benchmark project's build cycle.

The first goal, `spl_annotation`, is bound to the `generate-sources` build phase, and its purpose is to generate a single source file with the definition of the `@SPLFormula` annotation. The annotation can then be used to attach SPL formulas to JMH benchmark methods. This goal serves to avoid introducing additional compile dependencies into the JMH benchmark project – instead, the necessary file is simply injected into it.

The second goal, `formula_extractor`, is bound to the `compile` build phase, and its purpose is to scan the compiled benchmark classes for annotations containing SPL formulas. All SPL formulas are then stored into a text file within the `META-INF` directory of the benchmark JAR file produced by JMH in the subsequent `package` build phase.

The third goal, `data_saver`, is bound to the `verify` build phase, and its purpose is to execute the JMH benchmarks and store the collected performance data for later use with the SPL evaluator. This goal is important because the JMH benchmarks need to be run with specific options to store the results into a revision-specific directory, and to output raw data needed for SPL formula evaluation. By providing this goal, we avoid requiring the developer to change the JMH execution options when adopting SPL-based performance unit testing.

In summary, through the plugin we provide a thin, non-intrusive layer on top of a JMH benchmark project. This layer enables annotating JMH benchmarks with SPL-formulas and using JMH as a provider of performance data. To facilitate SPL-based performance unit testing based on the collected performance data, we provide a standalone SPL formula evaluator. As a result, developers can introduce SPL-based performance unit testing into their software project gradually, without having to adopt a heavy-weight approach imposed by a fully integrated testing framework. However, they are left with the responsibility for automating the performance testing process and integrating it into their development process.

6. CONCLUSION

Coming back to the question posed in the title of this paper, we have to conclude that as far as Java open source projects from the GitHub repository are concerned, we are not there yet.

[3]It requires JMH with support for reporting raw measurement data, which was introduced in version 1.14.

Of the 99019 projects that we have analyzed, only 0.37 % (370) actually use any performance testing framework. Of those projects whose performance tests we have executed, only 62 % produce performance measurements within 4 hours. Considering a broader class of projects that query clock using functions available in Java, only 3.4 % of sampled projects (using a random sample of 1000 projects) obviously implement performance tests or benchmarks.

Focusing on the usage of the JMH framework, performance tests are usually introduced later in the lifetime of a project (compared to functional unit tests), and can be mostly found in projects with less than 50 kLOC. Using the default settings, only about one third of the tests finishes within one hour, but more importantly, only half of the projects using JMH has enough measurements to estimate the mean time of all benchmark methods at 99 % confidence level with at most 20 % relative confidence interval width. About 20 % of projects using JMH can only estimate the mean execution time with a relative confidence interval width exceeding 100 %. Consequently, in one hour of execution, almost none of the tests can provide enough data to detect other than very obvious changes in performance. Collecting enough data to achieve higher sensitivity would prevent such tests from being executed on every commit. Observations on the relationship between accuracy and execution time suggest that careful measurement scheduling, rather than simple execution of all tests on all commits, is needed to achieve reasonable sensitivity at reasonable cost.

Survey responses from 111 developers who use the JMH performance testing framework indicate automation of performance testing is a major issue – 77 % of developers report processing results manually, automated evaluation and build integration are listed by 61 % and 50 % of developers, respectively, as needed features. The developers also recognize that correct test implementation is important – 72 % report trust in results as their reason for choosing the JMH framework, and 31 % mention need for simpler test implementation.

The issue of test execution time is further highlighted by 47 % of developers preferring to run performance tests at commit time, contrasted with 37 % of developers preferring to run performance tests only before each release.

Also interesting is the role of performance tests in enabling reasoning about performance. Only 23 % of developers report regularly acting on performance improvements or regressions, as opposed to 57 % of developers who report using performance tests for design decisions.

Our own effort in the area of performance unit testing is centered around SPL, a performance testing framework and formalism to express performance assumptions that can be validated through statistical testing. The results of our survey indicate that, contrary to our previous development, SPL should consider a light and flexible design to make it easier to introduce performance testing into a software project. Inspired by JMH as the most popular framework among projects that do any performance testing, we have focused on providing the essential building blocks of SPL while reusing tools such as JMH that the developers have already adopted, and otherwise leaving much of the responsibility for the actual implementation of the performance testing process with the developers.

Additional resources to complement our submission are available at [30].

Acknowledgments

We gratefully acknowledge the help of developers who have completed our survey. This work was partially supported by Charles University Institutional Funding (SVV) and by the Research Group of the Standard Performance Evaluation Corporation (SPEC).

7. REFERENCES

[1] S. Balsamo, A. D. Marco, P. Inverardi, and M. Simeoni. Model-based performance prediction in software development: a survey. *IEEE Transactions on Software Engineering*, 30(5), 2004.

[2] V. Bergmann. ContiPerf. http://databene.org/contiperf, 2012.

[3] C. Bezemer, E. Milon, A. Zaidman, and J. Pouwelse. Detecting and analyzing I/O performance regressions. *Journal of Software: Evolution and Process*, 26(12), 2014.

[4] P. Brebner. Thoughts on the ABS Census website crash on census night (9 August 2016). http://www.performance-assurance.com.au/thoughts-on-the-abs-census-website-crash-on-census-night-9-august-2016/, 2016.

[5] L. Bulej et al. Capturing Performance Assumptions Using Stochastic Performance Logic. In *Proc. of ICPE '12.* ACM, 2012.

[6] L. Bulej et al. Unit testing performance with Stochastic Performance Logic. *Accepted for Automated Software Engineering*, 2016.

[7] Clarkware Consulting, Inc. JUnitPerf. http://clarkware.com/software/JUnitPerf.html, 2009.

[8] E. Daka and G. Fraser. A Survey on Unit Testing Practices and Problems. In *Proc. of ISSRE '14.* IEEE Computer Society, 2014.

[9] A. B. de Oliveira, J.-C. Petkovich, T. Reidemeister, and S. Fischmeister. DataMill: Rigorous Performance Evaluation Made Easy. In *Proce. of ICPE '13.* ACM, 2013.

[10] E. Engström and P. Runeson. A Qualitative Survey of Regression Testing Practices. In *Product-Focused Software Process Improvement.* Springer, Berlin, Heidelberg, 2010.

[11] D. G. Feitelson, E. Frachtenberg, and K. L. Beck. Development and Deployment at Facebook. *IEEE Internet Computing*, 17(4), 2013.

[12] B. George and L. Williams. An Initial Investigation of Test Driven Development in Industry. In *Proc. of SAC '03.* ACM, 2003.

[13] W. Gottesheim. Challenges, Benefits and Best Practices of Performance Focused DevOps. In *Proc. of LT '15.* ACM, 2015.

[14] M. Greiler, A. v. Deursen, and M.-A. Storey. Test Confessions: A Study of Testing Practices for Plug-in Systems. In *Proc. of ICSE '12.* IEEE Press, 2012.

[15] C. Heger, J. Happe, and R. Farahbod. Automated Root Cause Isolation of Performance Regressions During Software Development. In *Proc. of ICPE '13.* ACM, 2013.

[16] V. Horký et al. Performance Regression Unit Testing: A Case Study. In *Computer Performance Engineering*, 8168 in LNCS. Springer Berlin Heidelberg, 2013.

[17] G. Jin, L. Song, X. Shi, J. Scherpelz, and S. Lu. Understanding and Detecting Real-world Performance Bugs. In *Proc. of PLDI '12.* ACM, 2012.

[18] JUnit. JUnit. http://junit.org/, 2006.

[19] G. Kick, C. Decker, P. Duffin, et al. Caliper. https://github.com/google/caliper, 2015.

[20] P. S. Kochhar, T. F. Bissyandé, D. Lo, and L. Jiang. Adoption of Software Testing in Open Source Projects–A Preliminary Study on 50,000 Projects. In *Proc. of CSMR '13*, 2013.

[21] J. Kroß, F. Willnecker, T. Zwickl, and H. Krcmar. PET: Continuous Performance Evaluation Tool. In *Proc. of QUDOS '16.* ACM, 2016.

[22] M. Linares-Vásquez, C. Vendome, Q. Luo, and D. Poshyvanyk. How developers detect and fix performance bottlenecks in Android apps. In *Proc. of ICSME '15*, 2015.

[23] Y. Liu, C. Xu, and S.-C. Cheung. Characterizing and Detecting Performance Bugs for Smartphone Applications. In *Proc. of ICSE '14.* ACM, 2014.

[24] J. D. McGregor. Test early, test often. *The Journal of Object Technology*, 6(4), 2007.

[25] N. Nagappan, E. M. Maximilien, T. Bhat, and L. Williams. Realizing quality improvement through test driven development: results and experiences of four industrial teams. *Empirical Software Engineering*, 13(3), 2008.

[26] A. Nistor, T. Jiang, and L. Tan. Discovering, Reporting, and Fixing Performance Bugs. In *Proc. of MSR '13.* IEEE Press, 2013.

[27] Oracle Corporation. Java Microbenchmarking Harness (JMH). http://openjdk.java.net/projects/code-tools/jmh/, 2016.

[28] Oracle Corporation, Project Kenai, and Cognisync. Japex Micro-benchmark Framework. https://japex.java.net/, 2014.

[29] P. Runeson. A Survey of Unit Testing Practices. *IEEE Softw.*, 23(4), 2006.

[30] P. Stefan, V. Horký, L. Bulej, and P. Tůma. Supplementary Material. http://d3s.mff.cuni.cz/resources/icpe2017, 2017.

[31] TestNG. TestNG. http://testng.org/, 2006.

[32] A. van Hoorn, J. Waller, and W. Hasselbring. Kieker: A Framework for Application Performance Monitoring and Dynamic Software Analysis. In *Proc. of ICPE '12.* ACM, 2012.

[33] J. Waller, N. C. Ehmke, and W. Hasselbring. Including Performance Benchmarks into Continuous Integration to Enable DevOps. *SIGSOFT Softw. Eng. Notes*, 40(2), 2015.

[34] J. Walter, A. van Hoorn, H. Koziolek, D. Okanovic, and S. Kounev. Asking "What"?, Automating the "How"?: The Vision of Declarative Performance Engineering. In *Proc. of ICPE '16.* ACM, 2016.

[35] E. J. Weyuker and F. I. Vokolos. Experience with Performance Testing of Software Systems: Issues, an Approach, and Case Study. *IEEE Trans. Softw. Eng.*, 26(12), 2000.

[36] M. Woodside, G. Franks, and D. C. Petriu. The Future of Software Performance Engineering. In *Proc. of FOSE '07.* IEEE Computer Society, 2007.

Agile Scalability Requirements

Gunnar Brataas and Tor Erlend Fægri
SINTEF Digital
Trondheim, Norway

ABSTRACT

Many software organisations struggle to provide appropriate levels of scalability in their software systems. Agile development rests on pragmatic and value-centred approaches to requirement capture that allows customers and vendors to interact in the process of producing the software system that best mets the real needs of the customers. In collaboration with Norwegian software organisations we have observed that setting scalability requirements is hard. Organisations struggle because they lack a conceptually sound language for expressing scalability requirements. To improve current practice, we propose a light-weight and flexible approach to specifying scalability requirements. Flexibility ensures that a more extensive characterisation can be used if higher precision is required, and more information becomes available.

CCS Concepts

•**Software and its engineering** → **Agile software development;** *Requirements analysis;* •**General and reference** → *Performance;*

Keywords

Agile development; Requirements engineering; Metrics

1. INTRODUCTION

In this paper we refer to *scalability* as the ability of a service to increase its capacity by consuming more hardware and software resources [5]. Software resources are lower-level software services like DBMSs, and with hardware, we mean CPUs, disks and networks. These resources all have a cost, which may be expressed as dollars per hour.

Capacity is the maximum workload a service can handle as bound by its SLA (Service Level Agreement) [5]. Together, work and load constitute the workload of a service. A scalable software service can satisfy more customers (load) or more demanding customers (work) by consuming more software and hardware resources. In their interaction with software-based services, people have little patience – regardless of the number of users of a service or service complexity. Software vendors must provide appropriate scalability despite rapid innovation cycles or requirement volatility.

We have established a research project named ScrumScale [1] who's objective is to reduce the total cost of handling scalability using a tailored, agile development approach. ScrumScale involves the collaboration with three Norwegian software organisations: 1) EVRY is a leading Nordic supplier of software-based solutions and services within the financial and other sectors. 2) Powel is a provider of software solutions for the energy, public and contracting sectors 3) Altinn is the largest Norwegian public portal, for example used by the tax authority to deliver digitised public services.

ScrumScale is now in the initial phase, and our work has so far focused on understanding how these organisations address the scalability challenge when developing software-based services. All three organisations have extensive scalability knowledge, but nonetheless, suffer from expensive re-engineering because of unaddressed scalability requirements. Like many other organisations, they often end up with significant accumulation of technical debt with the costly consequence that scalability must be retrofitted at the end of the project. Why does this happen? We have identified vague and unclear scalability requirements as one potential root cause.

Agile development is fuelled by rapid feedback loops and accepts simplicity in written documents as a trade-off for more 'live' understanding of the system under development. Agile development encourage collaboration among stakeholders to bridge understanding from both the problem-space and the solution-space. To support a more collaborative approach to scalability engineering, we need a light-weight, yet reasonably accurate approach to capture scalability requirements.

In this paper, we describe a conceptual model for scalability. The model constitutes a language for expressing scalability requirements. We deliberately keep the number of scalability parameters low. We also describe granularity trade-offs so that the scalability requirements can accommodate different contexts yet remain conceptually consistent.

In Section 2, we will summarise some early findings from our three Norwegian software organisations. Our initial approach for describing scalability requirements is outlined in Section 3. In this section, we also describe important granularity trade-offs. State of the art is described in Section 4. Conclusions and further work are offered in Section 5.

ICPE'17 April 22-26, 2017, L'Aquila, Italy

ACM ISBN 978-1-4503-4404-3/17/04

DOI: http://dx.doi.org/10.1145/3030207.3030240

2. EARLY FINDINGS

We have collected data at all three organisations using semi-structured interviews, observation of regular performance review meetings, project retrospectives, available documentation and meetings with participants from the organisations. The following is a brief summary of the findings.

We have learned that software organisations often choose to emphasise functional requirements that provide visible and tangible value to their customers. Non-functional requirements, such as scalability, receive less attention. The ownership of scalability requirements is frequently unclear. Limited collaboration when defining scalability requirements leads to vague scalability requirements, e.g. "our solutions shall scale vertically and horizontally." Vagueness in scalability requirements imply that they rarely need revision, and they therefore remain outside the center of attention.

Because scalability requirements are vague and ownership is unclear, testers must sometimes guess and make their own proposal for testable scalability requirements. Architects and developers may then be working on new projects and subsequently become less accessible. Valuable insights from testers and operations personnel are also easily lost when designing new services. We speculate that misplaced and diffuse ownership of scalability requirements is a fundamental explanation why scalability requirements are subjected to such ad-hoc treatment.

However, we observed an interesting paradox. There is a large gap between theory and practice. Several of the people we interviewed commented that the scalability concepts we propose are valuable and even obvious. On the other hand, these concepts are not used in practice. Project after project fails to deliver sufficient levels of scalability.

We conclude that managing scalability is difficult in our three case organisations. We believe that the complexity is probably not buried in the individual concepts, but in the lack of a systematic approach to apply *the set of concepts* relevant for scalability. To achieve this, we need a lightweight and flexible approach to define scalability requirements based on a conceptually sound model of scalability. Moreover, actors with clear ownership of scalability requirements need to be involved early in development.

3. SCALABILITY REQUIREMENTS

Our method for capturing scalability requirements focuses on the concepts shown in Figure 1. A service delivers one or more operations, each offering a unique way of interacting with the service. Stakeholders are responsible for formulating critical operations with quality metrics and quality thresholds. They have to decide on projected maximum load for these critical operations, where operation mixes play an important part, as they describe the probability of each of the operations. Work parameters describe the amount of data used by the critical operations. All these information is part of scalability requirements.

According to our scalability definition in Section: 1, (theoretical) scalability is about the ability to increase capacity. This ability is vital. However, if the cost of achieving a certain capacity is too high, this may severely limit the *practical* scalability. We will first consider the important theoretical scalability requirement concepts. Afterwards, we will also introduce cost so that practical scalability can be explored.

Scalability focuses on steady-state behaviour. In practice, especially open load varies heavily. Cost efficiency is about the total cost also when fluctuations in work and load are taken into account, but is outside of our scope in this paper.

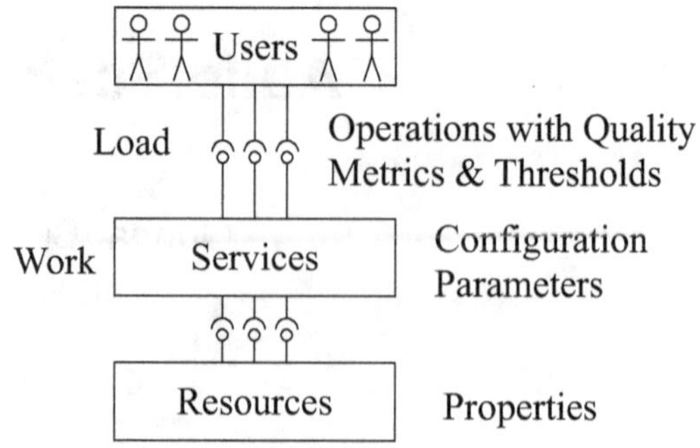

Figure 1: Scalability concepts.

3.1 Maximum Values in Planning Horizon

According to our scalability definition, we should investigate how our service responds to increasing workloads as well as stricter SLAs. To simplify this task, we focus on capturing the toughest values for work, load and SLAs, during a given planning horizon. A planning horizon of less than three years will seldom be meaningful when developing new software. A simple scalability analysis uses the maximum values for work, load and SLAs. A more complex scalability analysis may also consider even tougher requirements.

3.2 Quality Metrics and Thresholds

A quality metric defines how we measure a certain quality and is a key part of an SLA (Service Level Agreement). Generally, all the operations will share the same quality metrics for each operation, e.g., average response times or 90 percentile response times. However, with many operations, they we may of course also use several quality metrics.

Quality thresholds (QTs) describe the border between acceptable and non-acceptable quality for a given metric, e.g., 2 seconds. For each quality metric for each operation, there must be one quality threshold.

3.3 Critical Operations

In the ideal case, we should carefully consider the scalability implications of *all* operations for a service. However, there may be several hundred relevant operations. We must therefore simplify, and focus on the critical operations. The critical operations are the operation that from a scalability point of view poses the largest risks for SLA violations.

This poses a difficult dilemma, however. Critical operations are those operations that are most influential in determining the scalability of the service. Unfortunately, their influence can only be determined accurately after the service is developed and is deployed in operation. As a result, we cannot know with confidence which operations will be critical, but must select critical operations from careful reasoning. Confidence will increase by expanding the number of critical operations, but at the expense of the human effort involved in formulating the scalability requirements.

We must at least implicitly know the quality metrics and thresholds to determine the critical operations. With a long enough response time, an operation will never be critical.

3.4 Load and Operation Mix

Load describes how often the operations in a service are invoked. A closed system has a constant number of users. Load for a closed system is specified by think time (Z) and simultaneous number of users (N). An open system has a variable number of users and is characterised by the arrival rate λ. Based on the number of simultaneous users, we can derive the number of concurrent users actually using the same lower-level software service at the same time. Today closed systems are generally more challenging compared to online systems, simply because a system only becomes a batch system if it is too heavy for being an online system.

For simplicity, let us first assume that we have an open system with only one operation. Load is now characterised by the arrival rate for this operation. We are typically interested in the maximum load, but often more investigations are required to find this maximum load. To think about how the arrival rate fluctuates according to seasonal and trend variations may be helpful; not because of all the details, but to find the maximum load.

Seasonal variations can be yearly, monthly, weekly or daily. During one typical day, load may be highest immediately after people arrive at work at 9AM. In a week, load may be highest on Wednesdays. For a month, load may reach its maximum near the end of the month. During one year, load may be highest just before Christmas. A trend may be a linear or exponential growth with, for example, 10 % every year. Assuming a three year planning horizon, we can expect the highest load to be just after 9AM on a Monday around December 20 in the third year.

With more operations, load can be specified for each operation individually, or we may specify the load on the average operation. An operation mix describes the probability of each of the operations. We define the operation mix for the critical operations to sum to 1. As a result, the probability of one operation depends on which operations are included in the set of critical operations.

If some of the critical operations refer to an open system, and others to a closed system, we get a group of critical open operations and a group of critical closed operations. Both these groups have a corresponding operation mix. For the open operation mix, when a new user arrives, the operation mix represents the probability of the different operations. A heavy operation will last longer than a light operation. Therefore, the number of simultaneous operations will not reflect the operation mix. In a closed system, when one operation is completed, the closed operation mix represents the probability of the new operations.

3.5 Work Parameters

Work characterises the amount of data to be processed, stored, or communicated by the operations in a service, e.g., the average size of a document or the number of documents. A service may have anything from none to several work parameters.

We are interested in the maximum values for each work parameter, e.g. the highest number of documents or the highest average size of documents. For work parameters, we have tree assumptions: 1) Seasonal variations are not relevant. 2) Trends are relevant. 3) Work parameters grow so that we get the highest work values towards the end of the planning horizon.

3.6 Practical Scalability

Ideally, we should not focus on implementation when describing requirements. However, if we are interested in cost, we have to consider lower-level software resources as well as amount of and cost of hardware. We also have to consider the mapping between our service and the lower-level software and hardware resources. Will this mapping be linear, and if not, which form will it take? Moreover, scalability will also be determined by the configuration parameters for the lower-level software services and hardware, but this is very detailed information, and may therefore be ignored.

3.7 Feedback Loops

For hard challenges such as scalability, it is often necessary to cycle extensively between working in the problem space and the solution space. Collaborative practice involving stakeholders from both domains can support this, for example, guided by techniques such as proof of concepts, prototyping and incremental demoes. Agile development methods embrace such cycling. For example, to formulate quality thresholds, the critical operations must be known. To determine the critical operations the quality thresholds are required. Hence, this information must be developed in close collaboration driven by feedback between the parties. Information from operations from similar services can help.

3.8 Granularity

By granularity, we mean level of detail. It is common practice in agile development to ensure mutual understanding of requirements in dialogue between the product owner and the development team taking responsibility of implementation. In this dialogue, pending implementation, we expect that the level of detail in scalability requirements can be a core topic. As we have mentioned before, there are inherent cyclic dependencies between the problem- and the solution-space in complex development tasks. The scalability requirements will evolve together with the understanding of both the solution- and the problem-space. Our scalability requirements will therefore themselves be agile, as well as support an agile development method.

Our suggested prioritised list of dimensions of granularity can be a useful conceptual origin for such dialogue:

- **Decomposed operations:** One operation may be decomposed into several lower-level operations. As a result, load and quality thresholds must also be detailed.
- **Lower level services:** We may also have scalability requirements for lower-level services, which may be formulated in the same way as the service scalability requirements. For example, a certain operation from a lower-level service has a quality threshold with a quality metric guaranteed for a maximum load and for a given value of work parameters.
- **More work parameters:** Initially, only a few work parameters may be relevant, but gradually more can be introduced, e.g. we may start with number of documents (one work parameter) and afterwards add average as well as maximum document size (two more work parameters).
- **Richer quality metrics:** The quality metric may be implicit, e.g. an organisation will always assume

the average response times metric, unless otherwise is clearly stated. By explicitly detailing the quality metrics, the level of granularity as well as the accuracy of our requirements will increase.

- **Detailed quality thresholds:** Instead of the same quality thresholds for all operations, we can specify individual quality thresholds for each operation. There may also be more quality thresholds for each operation, e.g. good, fair, bad or contract violation (with corresponding penalty fees).

We also assume that there will be context-specific demands to the level of precision that the scalability requirement will be specified to. Secondly, there will be variations in the amount of information that is available. For development projects using agile methods, flexibility in precision can allow requirements with sufficient levels of precision for the specific context. The following list of aspects can be adjusted according to specific needs:

- **Can we cope with one critical operation?** Quality threshold, implicit quality metric (e.g. average response times) and maximum load required. No work parameters specified.
- **Can we cope with several critical operations as well as critical work?** Above plus: Individual quality thresholds for all critical operations, operation mix and work parameters.
- **What is the resulting cost of the critical operations?** Above plus: mapping from workload to amount of lower-level services (a coarse model or based on measuring a running system — both options may require considerable manual effort in practise). Hardware costs (bare metal or IaaS) and costs of lower level software resources (licences or costs for PaaS/SaaS). We may be satisfied if the cost grows approximately linear with the load and work, assuming the cost of the initial configuration is acceptable.

4. STATE OF THE ART

Among our Norwegian partners, use of reactive performance tools is widespread. The tools are predominantly supporting application load testing and performance monitoring. Prolonged stress testing is also used to identify memory leaks, etc. that potentially could create performance problems during use. When testing scalability, load generation tools (JMeter, LoadRunner etc.) are heavily used. Load generators depend on precise specifications of work, load, quality metrics and quality thresholds. Profiling tools are used, but less frequently. Our partners do not make models of software and hardware.

Still, there are fundamental problems with this reactive approach. Scalability is a quality that transcends the concerns of the individual user. It is an aggregate quality that can best be observed at high workloads when many users compete for resources.

There has been significant research interest in the ability of agile methods to accommodate 'technical requirements' in a balanced manner to avoid the accumulation of technical debt [3]. However, to our knowledge, scalability has not yet been addressed specifically by researchers in agile methods. Nevertheless, relevant insight from this field suggests that agile practises are able to accommodate non-functional requirements as long as certain considerations are taken seriously [2]. Nord et al. [6] suggested the merging of both functional and architectural requirements incrementally during development. This was coined 'the zipper model' to agile architecting.

Duboc et al. [4] describe a general framework for scalability requirements, while we focus only on scalability related to software and hardware resources. We make our scalability assumptions *explicit* by describing them as operations, load profile, work, load and quality thresholds. In contrast to Duboc, we make the granularity trade-off explicit and focus on the usefulness of our approach in a practical, industrial setting.

5. CONCLUSIONS AND FURTHER WORK

In this paper, we have outlined a conceptual framework for capturing scalability requirements. Going forward, we seek to address the following research questions: (1) Is the presented conceptual model of scalability requirements useful for software organisations in practice? (2) What processes are necessary to effectively support the generation of scalability requirements? (3) To which extent are our scalability requirements testable? (4) How do we manage the evolution of scalability requirements for long-lived systems?

Much work remains to be done. Agile developers are accustomed to capture requirements in user stories. We need worked out examples where we apply our concepts and describe the challenges met and how we deal with them, for example, by detailing our scalability requirement concepts. If our conceptual model of scalability requirements is effective, tailored tools should be developed further to streamline an agile development process.

6. ACKNOWLEDGMENTS

The research leading to these results has received funding from the Norwegian Research Council under grant #256669 (ScrumScale).

7. REFERENCES

[1] ScrumScale. www.scrumscale.com. Visited: 20 February 2017.

[2] M. A. Babar. *Agile Software Architecture.* Morgan Kaufmann, 2014.

[3] W. N. Behutiye, P. Rodriguez, M. Oivo, and A. Tosun. Analyzing the Concept of Technical Debt in the Context of Agile Software Development: A Systematic Literature Review. *Information and Software Technology*, 82:139–158, 2017.

[4] L. Duboc, E. Letier, and D. Rosenblum. Systematic Elaboration of Scalability Requirements through Goal-Obstacle Analysis. *Transactions on Software Engineering*, 39(1):119 – 140, 2013.

[5] S. Lehrig, H. Eikerling, and S. Becker. Scalability, Elasticity and Efficiency in Cloud Computing: a Systematic Literature Review of Definitions and Metrics. In *Conf. on Quality of Software Architectures.* ACM, 2015.

[6] R. L. Nord, I. Ozkaya, and P. Kruchten. Agile in Distress: Architecture to the Rescue. In *XP Workshops.* Springer, 2014.

ICPE 2017 Tutorials Chair's Welcome

It is our pleasure to welcome you to the ICPE 2017 Tutorial Track, through which ICPE enhances the experience of attending researchers and industry professionals by proposing tutorials led by renowned scientists and practitioners in the fields of relevance for the ICPE community.

We are looking forward to the five tutorials that will be presented on Saturday 22 and Sunday 23, April 2017 in L'Aquila, Italy. The tutorials will run concurrently in two tracks on both days. The topics of the tutorials cover a spectrum of areas that we expect to be of significant interest to a large number of ICPE 2017 attendees.

The tutorial by Christoph Heger, André van Hoorn, Mario Mann, and Dušan Okanović will focus on application performance management (APM) in industrial practice and academic research. The speakers will present the ways to collect data and perform analysis using available commercial and open-source APM tools.

Salman Baset, Marcio Silva, and Nicholas Wakou will present an overview of the SPEC Cloud IaaS 2016 benchmark, which is the first industry standard benchmark that measures the performance of infrastructure-as-a service clouds.

The tutorial by Kingsum Chow and Wanyi Zhu will focus on software performance analytics in the cloud. The speakers will address the challenges of measuring software performance in the data center and optimizing software for resource management by bringing the knowledge of software performance monitoring in the data center to the world of applying performance analytics.

Alberto Leva will introduce in his tutorial the basics of system and control theory so as to foster their utilization for the management, but most important for the design, of computing systems. The tutorial focus will be set on the systems and control theory as a forma mentis rather than a source of algorithms.

The tutorial by André Bauer, Nikolas Herbst, and Samuel Kounev will guide the attendants step-by-step through the design and evaluation of a proactive and application-aware auto-scaling mechanism. Throughout the tutorial, the speakers will also present the related tools that are available online for the construction of the auto-scaler building blocks and their evaluation.

A total of eight tutorial proposals were submitted to the ICPE 2017 Tutorials track from which five were finally accepted. All the proposals were reviewed by the chair and the final selection was approved by the ICPE 2017 General Chairs. We are grateful to the ICPE community for the diverse and high-quality proposals we received. This guarantees a strong Tutorials Track program at ICPE 2017 and we hope you will it interesting, thought-provoking, and useful for your work. In this volume, you will find the companion papers that provide a commented outline of the tutorials.

Valeria Cardellini
ICPE 2017 Tutorial Chair
University of Rome Tor Vergata, Italy

Software Performance Analytics in the Cloud

Kingsum Chow and Wanyi Zhu
Alibaba Inc
Hangzhou, China
kingsum.chow@gmail.com, wanyi.wyz@alibaba-inc.com

ABSTRACT

The emergence of large-scale software deployments in the cloud has led to several challenges: (1) measuring software performance in the data center, and (2) optimizing software for resource management. This tutorial addresses the two challenges by bringing the knowledge of software performance monitoring in the data center to the world of applying performance analytics. It introduces data transformations for software performance metrics. The transformations enable effective applications of analytics. This tutorial starts with software performance in the small and ends with applying analytics to software performance in the large. In software performance in the small, it summarizes performance tools, data collection and manual analysis. Then it describes monitoring tools that are helpful in performance analysis in the large. The tutorial will guide the audience in applying analytics to performance data obtained by common tools. This tutorial describes how to select analytical methods and what precautions should be taken to get effective results.

CCS Concepts

• Computer systems organization □ Architectures □ Distributed architectures • Software and its engineering □ Software organization and properties □ Extra-functional properties □ Software performance.

Keywords

Datacenter efficiency; software performance; capacity planning; analytics.

1. INTRODUCTION

The tutorial will guide the audience in applying analytics to performance data obtained by using mostly freely downloadable tools. This tutorial describes how to select analytical methods and what precautions should be taken to get effective results. The following is the outline of the tutorial.

(1) Software Performance Analytics: Past, Present and Future

ICPE'17, April 22 - 26, 2017, L'Aquila, Italy

ACM 978 1 4503-4404-3/17/04...$15.00
DOI: http://dx.doi.org/10.1145/3030207.3053676

(2) Software Performance 101

(3) Introduction to Analytics

(4) Putting it together: Applying analytics to software performance in the cloud and data centers

We started with a brief overview of the classic text on Introduction to Algorithms [9]. Then we moved on to a set of common systems performance tools [12]. To put them together on computer servers running nowadays, we applied knowledge gain from the classic text on Computer Architecture: A Quantitative Approach [11]. We put together the knowledge of software performance analysis [4]. We also coached performance engineers 0 in using a set of mostly freely available tools and a massive amount of data that need to be analyzed [6][8] together on a modern computer server running multiple processes. We applied design of experiments [7] to aid computer performance analysis. We used a collection of scripts to process and analyze the data. Among them, R becomes a cornerstone of our analysis process. R is a great statistics tool. But to deal with the vastly different computer performance data sources, we found Advanced R [10] comes in handy in bring analytics together. As this tutorial is targeting software performance engineers, this paper will cover some details of analytics. The full tutorial will cover details of putting software performance and analytics together.

2. ANALYTICS

Statistical techniques have been applied in many areas of computer performance measurement, such as designing experiments and simulation, analyzing, predicting and optimizing performance. Owing to the stochastic nature of computer systems, measuring performance is prone to noise and experimental errors. The field of statistics provides a rich set of tools and techniques to effectively deal with such noise and errors, allowing one to obtain meaningful measurements. This section will focus on one key application of statistical analysis the anomaly detection, and two methodologies (univariate and multivariate analysis), which have been deployed in many data center management.

2.1 Univariate Analysis

The selection of anomaly detection methods depends on different data situations such as the distribution, degree of skewness and sample sizes. This section reviews several univariate methods.

3.1.1 Parametric Method. One simple classical approach to screen outlier is to use the Standard Deviation (SD) method. It is defined as any observations beyond two or three SD above and below the mean of the observations may be considered as outliers. This is based on the assumption that the data follows a parametric distribution. According to Chebyshev inequality, if a random variable X with mean u and variance exists, no more than $1/k^2$ of the distribution's values can be more than k standard deviations away from the mean- $P(|x-\mu| >= k\sigma) <= 1/k^2$ .The inequality has great utility because it can be applied to any probability distribution in which the mean and variance are defined, and enable us to determine the likelihood of having extreme values in the data. It is limited in that it only gives the smallest proportion of our data within k standard deviations of the mean. For instance, at least 75%, 89% and 94% of the data are within 2, 3, 4 standard deviations of the mean, respectively.

Another similar univariate method that can be used to screen data for outliers is the Z-Score, using the mean and standard deviation. $Z_i = \frac{x_i - \bar{x}}{sd}, where\ x_i \sim N(\mu, \sigma^2)$ and sd is the standard deviation of data. When X follows a normal distribution, Z-scores that exceed 3 in absolute value are generally considered as outliers. It presents a reasonable criterion for identification of the outlier when the sample size is larger than 10. However, this method can be affected by extreme values and cause a masking problem, i.e., the less extreme outlier go undetected because of the most extreme outliers, and vice versa. To avoid this problem, the median and the median of the absolute deviation of the median (MAD) are employed in modified Z-Score ($M_i = \frac{0.6745\,(x_i - \bar{x})}{MAD}$) where $\text{MAD} = \text{median}\{|X_i - \bar{x}|\}, \bar{x}\ is\ the\ sample\ median.$ The observations are suggested to be labeled as outliers when |Mi| > 3.5 through the simulation based on pseudo-normal observations for sample size larger than 10.

3.1.2 Non-parametric Method – Tukey's univariate boxplot. In parallel with robust statistics, practical methods for analyzing data evolved known as Exploratory Data Analysis (EDA). It is common to consider Tukey's schematic boxplot as an informal test for flagging the existence of outliers. A significant feature of this method is that it does not assume an underlying probability distribution for the data and therefore is flexible in practical settings. The Tukey univariate boxplot is specified by five parameters: the two extremes, the upper Q3 (75th percentile) and lower Q1 (25th percentile) quartiles and median. Data outside the outer fences (Q1 – 3 IQR, Q3 + 3 IQR) are considered to be extreme outliers. Tukey's boxplot method is quite effective for large data set without any prior assumption of data distribution.

2.2 Multivariate Analysis

Even though statistical tests are quite powerful under well-behaving statistical assumptions such as distribution assumption, most distributions of real-world data may be unknown, or may not follow specific distributions, or include correlated features.

The common multivariate anomaly detection has been deployed in many data centers management to offline fixed threshold using training data- such as Multivariate adaptive statistical filtering (MASF) maintain a separate threshold for data segmented and aggregated by time [1]. With the increasing complexity of performance data, real-time detection have been proposed as opposed to traditional methods that rely on static profiling or limited sets of historical data.

These online algorithms can be categorized into three groups. 1) Time series analysis. This becomes quite popular for continuous performance monitoring system used widely in cloud data centers, such as monitoring spikes in user engagement on the data platform, and detecting anomalies in system metrics after a new software release [2]. 2) Statistical learning: This includes a combination of Tukey method and the multinomial goodness-of-fit test using the Relative Entropy statistic. This approach has demonstrated sufficient accuracy and effectiveness for monitoring and detecting the 'anomaly' in performance data from production environment to data captured from multi-tier web applications running on server class machines [3]. 3) Cluster analysis: Outliers can be detected using distance/density measures where objects that are at a substantial distance from any other cluster are considered as outliers. Many clustering algorithms- KMeans, Hierarchical clustering algorithm, and Density-Based Clustering have been utilized in anomaly detection of cloud data center.

With the data center environment increasing in scale and complexity, these machine-learning algorithms enable automating the detection of suspicious anomalies in a responsive and accurate manner.

ACKNOWLEDGMENTS

We thank multiple teams in Alibaba that has developed multiple data collectors, storage and analysis portals for multiple projects.

REFERENCES

[1] J.P. Buzen and A.W. Shum, "MASF: multivariate adaptive statistical filtering," in Int. Computer Measurement Group (CMG) Conf., Nashville, TN, USA, Dec. 4-8, pp. 1-10, 1995.

[2] Owen Vallis , Jordan Hochenbaum , Arun Kejariwal, A novel technique for long-term anomaly detection in the cloud, Proceedings of the 6th USENIX conference on Hot Topics in Cloud Computing, p.15-15, June 17-18, 2014, Philadelphia, PA

[3] Chengwei Wang, Krishnamurthy Viswanathan, Lakshminarayan Choudur, Vanish Talwar, Wade Satterfield, and Karsten Schwan. 2011. Statistical techniques for online anomaly detection in data centers. In Proceedings of the IFIP/IEEE International Symposium on Integrated Network Management (IM'11). IEEE, 385--392.

[4] Kingsum Chow, Pooja Jain and Khun Ban, "Tutorial: Java Application Performance in the Data Center, Data Collection and Analysis" CMG imPACt 2016 Conference. November 7-10, 2016 in La Jolla, California.

[5] Kingsum Chow, Li Chen and Colin Cunningham, "How We Coach Performance Engineers to Adopt Data Science in Reproducible Analytics", Intel Analytics Summit, March 22-24, 2016, Santa Clara, California.

[6] Kingsum Chow and Pranita Maldikar "Applying Analytics to Workload Optimized Systems" [best paper award] presented at the FastPath workshop, held in conjunction with the IEEE International Symposium on Performance Analysis of Systems and Software (ISPASS), March 23-25, 2014.

[7] Keerthi Palanivel, Kingsum Chow, Khun Ban and David Lilja, "A Stepwise Approach to Software-Hardware Performance Co-Optimization Using Design of Experiments", Computer Measurement Group Performance and Capacity 2013, Nov 5th to 7th, La Jolla, California, USA.

[8] Shruthi Deshpande, Kingsum Chow, Peng-fei Chuang and Latifur Khan, "Big Data Analysis to Characterize Workload using Machine Learning Algorithms for High Dimensional Performance Data", Computer Measurement Group Performance and Capacity 2013, Nov 5th to 7th, La Jolla, California, USA.

[9] Cormen, Thomas H., Charles Eric. Leiserson, and Ronald L. Rivest. *Introduction to Algorithms DC*. Cambridge, MA: MIT, 1989. Print.

[10] Wickham, Hadley. *Advanced R*. Boca Raton, Fla.: Chapman & Hall, 2015. Print.

[11] Hennessy, John L., David A. Patterson, and Krste Asanovicÿ . *Computer Architecture: A Quantitative Approach*. Amsterdam: Elsevier, 2012. Print.

[12] Gregg, Brendan. *Systems Performance: Enterprise and the Cloud*. Upper Saddle River, NJ: Prentice Hall, 2014. Print

SPEC Cloud^{TM} IaaS 2016 Benchmark

Salman Baset
IBM Research
sabaset@us.ibm.com

Marcio Silva
IBM Research
marcios@us.ibm.com

Nicholas Wakou
Dell
nicholas_wakou@dell.com

1. INTRODUCTION

The SPEC Cloud^{TM} IaaS 2016 benchmark [1] is the Standard Performance Evaluation Corporation's (SPEC) first benchmark suite to measure cloud performance. The benchmark suite's use is targeted at cloud providers, cloud consumers, hardware vendors, virtualization software vendors, application software vendors, and academic researchers.

The SPEC Cloud^{TM} IaaS 2016 Benchmark addresses the performance of infrastructure-as-a-service (IaaS) cloud platforms. IaaS cloud platforms can either be public or private.

The benchmark is designed to stress provisioning as well as runtime aspects of a cloud using I/O and CPU intensive cloud computing workloads. SPEC selected the social media NoSQL database transaction and K-Means clustering using map/reduce as two significant and representative workload types within cloud computing.

Each workload runs in multiple instances, referred to as an application instance. The benchmark instantiates multiple application instances during a run. The application instances and the load they generate stress the provisioning as well as run-time aspects of a cloud. The run-time aspects include CPU, memory, disk I/O, and network I/O of these instances running in a cloud. The benchmark runs the workloads until quality of service (QoS) conditions are reached. The tester can also limit the maximum number of application instances that are instantiated during a run.

ICPE'17, April 22-26, 2017, L'Aquila, Italy

DOI: http://dx.doi.org/10.1145/3030207.3053675

The key benchmark metrics are:

- Scalability measures the total amount of work performed by application instances running in a cloud. The aggregate work performed by one or more application instances should linearly scale in an ideal cloud. Scalability is reported for the number of compliant application instances (AIs) completed and is an aggregate of workloads metrics for those AIs normalized against a set of reference metrics.
- Elasticity measures whether the work performed by application instances scales linearly in a cloud when compared to the performance of application instances during baseline phase. Elasticity is expressed as a percentage.
- Mean Instance Provisioning Time measures the time interval between the instance provisioning request and connectivity to port 22 on the instance. This metric is an average across all instances in valid application instances.

2. ACKNOWLEDGEMENTS

The authors were actively involved in the development of SPEC Cloud^{TM} IaaS 2016 benchmark and acknowledge the work of all participants.

3. REFERENCES

[1] SPEC Cloud^{TM} IaaS 2016 Benchmark. https://www.spec.org/cloud_iaas2016/, May 2003.

Design and Evaluation of a Proactive, Application-Aware Auto-Scaler

Tutorial Paper

André Bauer
University of Würzburg, Germany
andre.bauer@uni-wuerzburg.de

Nikolas Herbst
University of Würzburg, Germany
nikolas.herbst@uni-wuerzburg.de

Samuel Kounev
University of Würzburg, Germany
samuel.kounev@uni-wuerzburg.de

ABSTRACT

Simple, threshold-based auto-scaling mechanisms as mainly used in practice bring no features to overcome resource provisioning delays and non-linear scalability of a software service. In this tutorial paper, we guide the reader step-by-step through the design and evaluation of a proactive and application-aware auto-scaling mechanism.

First, we introduce the building blocks for such an auto-scaling mechanism: (i) an on-demand arrival rate forecasting method, (ii) resource demand estimates at run-time, (iii) a descriptive and continuously updated performance model of the deployed software and (iv) an intelligent adaptation planner that incorporates a threshold-based mechanism as fall-back.

Second, we cover auto-scaler evaluation steps: (i) the preparation steps are an application scenario and workload profile definition and (ii) an automated scalability analysis. In step (iii), we show how representative and repeatable auto-scaler experiments can be conducted and (iv) the results analyzed with the help of elasticity and end-user metrics for a detailed and fair comparison of alternative auto-scaler mechanisms and their respective configurations even across platforms.

For the individual steps of the construction of the auto-scaler building blocks and for their evaluation, we shortly introduce open-source tools available online[1].

CCS Concepts

•General and reference → Cross-computing tools and techniques; •Networks → Cloud computing; •Computer systems organization → Self-organizing autonomic computing; •Software and its engineering → Virtual machines;

Keywords

Elasticity, IaaS, Cloud, Auto-Scaler, Benchmark, Metric, Load Profile, Resource Demand, Forecasting, Descriptive Performance Model

1. INTRODUCTION

In practice, threshold-based controllers are commonly applied to dynamically add or remove computing resources of a service in an elastic cloud environment. Numerous proactive approaches based on control theory, queuing theory, machine learning, and time series analysis have been proposed in literature. In general, a proactive auto-scaler aims to overcome resource provisioning delays. We understand application-aware as features to learn non-linear scalability and inter-dependencies between different layers of a service.

In the first part, this tutorial paper presents an ensemble of open-source tools available online[1] that enable the composition of a proactive, and application-aware auto-scaler with the following components:

Forecasting of Arrival Rates:
Forecasting the next request arrival rates of incoming requests is an essential requirement for proactive auto-scaling. Hence, we use a self-adaptive forecasting technique with combinations of time series analysis methods and forecast accuracy feedback. We select as solution for this issue the WCF (Workload Classification and Forecasting Framework, see Section 2) [2].

Online Resource Demand Estimation:
Resource demand estimates per request class are crucial information for good auto-scaling decisions. In this part of the tutorial, we cover a library of methods that estimate the resource demand per request class based on basic performance metrics. For us, the library LibReDE (Library for Resource Demand Estimation, see Section 3) [5] offers the demanded features.

Descriptive Software Performance Model:
In the case, multiple layers of a service are elastically scalable, the next required information is at which layer and how many resources should be added or removed. Thus, we discuss about a descriptive and continuously updated performance model of the deployed application. We base on the Descartes Modeling Language (DML, see Section 4) [4]).

Proactive, Application-Aware Auto-Scaler:
After the required components are introduced, we cover

[1]Descartes Tools: http://descartes.tools/

ICPE'17, April 22 - 26, 2017, L'Aquila, Italy

ISBN 978-1-4503-4404-3/17/04...$15.00

DOI: http://dx.doi.org/10.1145/3030207.3053678

a possible integration of these tools and the associated logic behind the scaling decisions. We call our proactive, and application-aware elasticity mechanism Chameleon (see Section 5) [1].

In the second part, we cover the methodology for evaluating the elasticity achieved by the auto-scaler:

Modelling of Load Profiles:
In order to trigger and benchmark automated scaling events, a variable, representative, and reproducible load intensity profile is required. We show how to automatically a extract load intensity model from a given trace including how adapt such a load profile for their needs. We use for our workload scenario definition the load intensity modeling tool called LIMBO (see Section 6) [6].

Benchmarking of Elasticity:
The performance measurement and the comparison with other auto-scalers or different configurations is an important step in the development of such an auto-scaler. Hence, we discuss elasticity metrics to rate and rank the designed auto-scaler. For our elasticity measurements, we use the BUNGEE Cloud Elasticity Benchmarking Framework (see Section 7) [3].

2. WCF FORECASTING

As forecasting component of our proactive auto-scaler, we use the Workload Classification and Forecasting Tool [2]. It provides a set of automated forecasting methods based on time series analysis such as auto-regressive integrated moving averages with seasonality (sARIMA), extended exponential smoothing (ETS) or its extension tBATS for complex seasonal patterns, and a machine learning based-forecaster that leverages neural nets. For achieving a good forecast accuracy, WCF uses a decision tree for selecting dynamically a set of suitable methods. WCF allows the user to define objectives based on parameters such like forecast time horizon, confidence level and processing overhead limitation. Forecast results come with an accuracy estimate based the mean absolute scaled error (MASE) metric that helps to drop and repeat or trust a forecast result.

3. LIBREDE ESTIMATION

In order to estimate during run-time the amount of time that an individual request requires on a resource given the application and the current mix of request classes, the Library for Resource Demand Estimation [5] is used. Usually, for obtaining accurate resource demands, a fine-grained instrumentation of the software would be necessary. However, this instrumentation is likely to introduce high overheads and can distort their own measurement. Therefore, LibReDE supplies offline and online resource demand estimation techniques based on basic, aggregate monitoring data (e.g., utilization, number of request arrivals and average response times) with different state-of-the-art techniques based on the service demand law, linear regressions or Kalman filters. Also concepts from queuing theory are used.

4. DML MODEL

The Descartes Modeling Language (DML) [4] belongs to the architecture-level modeling languages for performance, quality-of-service, and resource management. It provides information about the performance behaviour and system properties. In addition, the configuration space and adaptation processes can be modelled. The structure and the four meshing models (resource landscape, application architecture, adaption points and adaption process) are depicted in Figure 1. Leveraging simulative what-if-analyses, DML allows to find an appropriate system configuration without changing the system. I.e., Chameleon uses a DML model instance of the controlled application continuously parameterized with the latest resource demand estimates to determine where and how to adapt the system resource configuration.

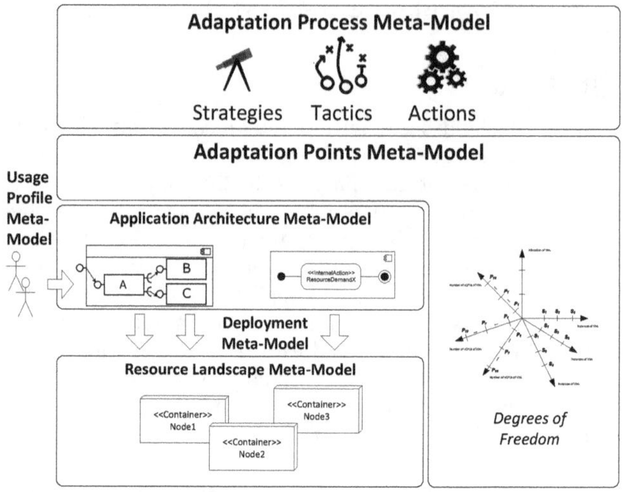

Figure 1: Structure of DML.

5. CHAMELEON AUTO-SCALER

Our proactive and application-aware auto-scaler consists of four components: (i) the controller, (ii) a performance data repository, (iii) the forecast component (here a modified version of WCF) and (iv) the resource demand estimation component (here LibReDE). The design and the flow of information is depicted in Figure 2. The central part of Chameleon is the controller. It communicates with the three remaining components and the managed cloud. The functionality of the controller is divided into two sub-tasks: monitoring and reconfiguration.

During the monitoring task, the controller communicates with the cloud and the performance data repository. This repository contains a time series storage and the DML descriptive performance model instance of the application. The controller periodically polls (e.g., every minute) information on the current state of the application from message queues. The collected information includes CPU utilization averages per node, average request residence times at the nodes, and the number of request arrivals. The new information is stored in the performance data repository for the recent time window. If the CPU utilization exceeds configurable thresholds, Chameleon scales the system reactively according to a standard threshold-based rule approach that is implemented as a fallback.

The reconfiguration of the system is planed proactively in longer intervals, e.g., 4 minutes, for a set of future scaling

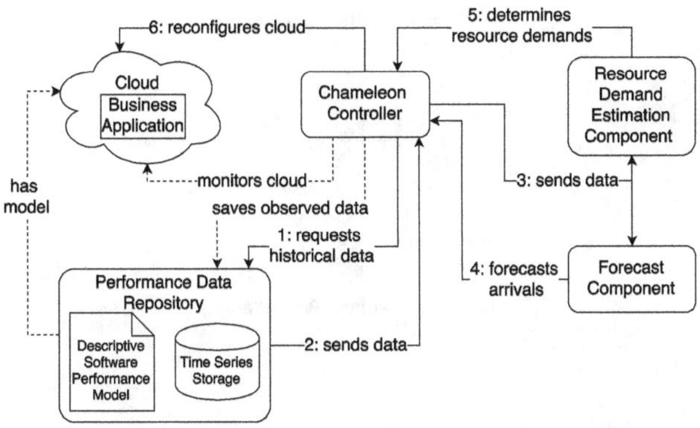

Figure 2: Design overview of Chameleon.

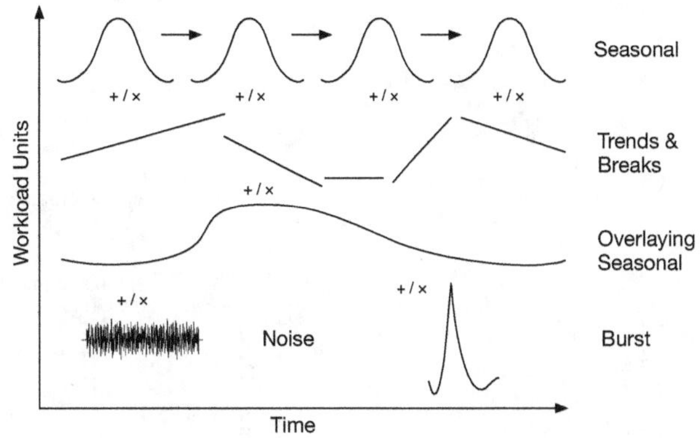

Figure 3: Elements of a load profile model.

intervals. It involves six tasks: (1) at first, the controller queries the performance data repository for the available historical data. (2) Then, the available time series data is send to the controller. (3) Afterwards, the time series of request arrival rates is forwarded to the forecast component and data about the CPU utilization and average request residence times per node is send to the resource estimation component. The forecast component predicts the arrival rates for the next reconfiguration intervals. If an earlier forecast result still contains predicted values for requested future arrival rates, no new time series forecast is computed. In case, a drift between the forecast and the recent monitoring data is detected, a new forecast is executed. (4) Then, the new forecast values are sent to the controller. (5) The resource demand estimation component estimates the time a single request needs to be served on the CPU of a node and sends the estimated value to the controller. (6) Finally, the controller scales the application deployment based on the estimated resource demands, the forecast arrivals and knowledge from the descriptive software performance model in case multiple tiers are scaled.

6. LIMBO LOAD MODELING

The LIMBO tool is capable to automatically extract from a given workload trace (that contains the amount of request arrivals per interval over a given period) a Descartes Load Intensity Model (DLIM) instance [6]. A DLIM model instance can be used to define any load intensity profile as it represents a tree of mathematical functions that are combined over the modeled time. Each instance captures the characteristics of the trace (e.g., trends, seasons, bursts, and noise, see Figure 3) that can be modified for creating a target dynamic work load scenario.

7. BUNGEE EXPERIMENT CONTROLLER

The BUNGEE Cloud Elasticity Benchmarking Framework measures the elasticity independently of the given platform performance. Therefore, it observes the given application under stress via a given load profile that is provided by LIMBO or as plain arrival rate data. The resulting workflow of BUNGEE is depicted in Figure 4 and is split into four phases:

1. SYSTEM ANALYSIS: BUNGEE constructs a mapping function for the relationship between a given load intensity and the associated demand for resources. The demand for resources is the minimal amount of resources that is required for handling the intensity without violating a predefined response-time SLO. This is done via a binary search per possible resource configuration.
2. BENCHMARK CALIBRATION: BUNGEE creates based on the given load profile and the mapping function an identical set of demand changes on every platform under comparison.
3. MEASUREMENT: BUNGEE starts with a warm-up period and then runs the measurement with the predefined workload intensity profile, in which the maximum intensity and the experiment time can be adjusted. During the run, BUNGEE coordinates, times and monitors each request and gathers additional information on resource supply from the platform. At the end, a measurement sanity check is conducted.
4. ELASTICITY EVALUATION: In this last step, BUNGEE calculates elasticity metrics and a score based on the observed supply changes and the generated demand changes:
    - UNDER-PROVISIONING ACCURACY
      This metric describes the relative amount of resources that is under provisioned during the measurement interval. I.e., acc_U is the number of resources that the system has too less in relation to the current demand divided by the experiment time.
    - OVER-PROVISIONING ACCURACY
      Analogous to the under-provisioning accuracy, this metric represents the relative amount of resources that are over-provisioned during the measurement interval. In other words, acc_O is the number of resources that the system has in excess in relation to the current demand divided by the experiment time.
    - UNDER-PROVISIONING TIME SHARE
      This metric captures the time in percentage, in which the system is under-provisioned during the experiment interval. I.e., ts_U is the time relative to the measurement duration, in which the system has to less resources.
    - OVER-PROVISIONING TIME SHARE
      Analogous to the under-provisioning time share,

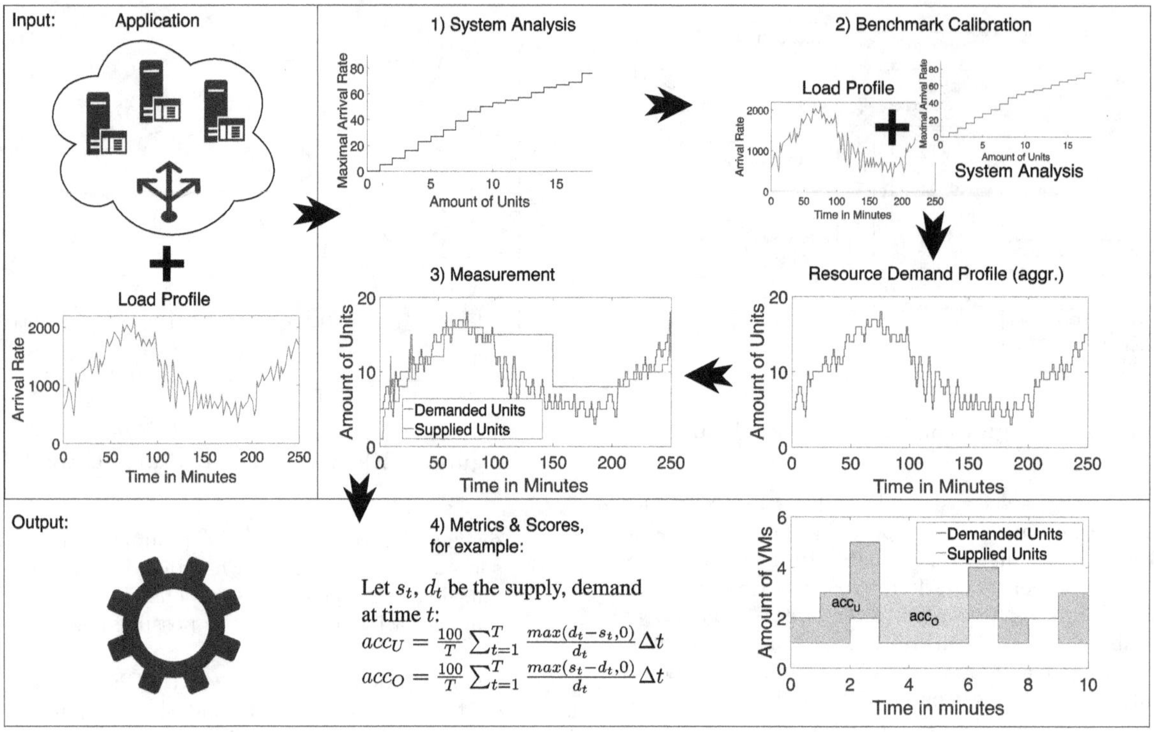

Figure 4: Operation principle of the BUNGEE elasticity benchmarking methodology.

this metric describes the time in percentage, in that the system is over-provisioned during the measurement interval. In other words, ts_O is the time relative to the measurement duration, in that the system has more resources than required.

- INSTABILITY
  The instability metric describes the percentage of time in which the supply and the demand curves are not changing in the same direction. I.e., in measures the fraction of time in which the demand change and the resource change have different signs.

The elasticity score of a cloud platform with a deployed elasticity mechanism is then computed via a weighted geometric mean of the aforementioned metrics normalized by a baseline for the given scenario. Further metrics, like the average/median response time, SLO violation percentage, average resources and the amount of adaptions are reported.

8. CONCLUSION

The tutorial addresses topics of central interest to the ICPE community such as run-time performance management using software performance models and estimation techniques. We demonstrate how theory in these disciplines can be brought into practice. The system properties of elasticity and scalability play a central role when designing and evaluating an auto-scaling mechanism. We touch new aspects of a benchmarking methodology to enable the rating of elastic properties.

Acknowledgments

This research is supported by the Research Group[2] of the Standard Performance Evaluation Corporation (SPEC)[3]. This work was co-funded by the German Research Foundation (DFG) under grant No. KO 3445/11-1.

9. REFERENCES

[1] A. Bauer. Design and Evaluation of a Proactive, Application-Aware Elasticity Mechanism. Master Thesis, University of Würzburg, September 2016. [Online] http://descartes.tools/chameleon.

[2] N. Herbst, N. Huber, S. Kounev, and E. Amrehn. Self-Adaptive Workload Classification and Forecasting for Proactive Resource Provisioning. *Wiley CCPE*, 26(12):2053–2078, March 2014.

[3] N. Herbst, S. Kounev, A. Weber, and H. Groenda. BUNGEE: An Elasticity Benchmark for Self-adaptive IaaS Cloud Environments. In *SEAMS 2015*, pages 46–56, Piscataway, NJ, USA, 2015. IEEE Press.

[4] S. Kounev, N. Huber, F. Brosig, and X. Zhu. A Model-Based Approach to Designing Self-Aware IT Systems and Infrastructures. *IEEE Computer*, 49(7):53–61, July 2016.

[5] S. Spinner, G. Casale, X. Zhu, and S. Kounev. LibReDE: A Library for Resource Demand Estimation. In *ACM/SPEC ICPE 2014*, pages 227–228, New York, NY, USA, March 2014. ACM Press.

[6] J. von Kistowski, N. Herbst, S. Kounev, and more. Modeling and Extracting Load Intensity Profiles. *ACM TAAS*, 11(4):23:1–23:28, January 2017.

[2]SPEC Research: http://research.spec.org
[3]SPEC: http://www.spec.org

Application Performance Management: State of the Art and Challenges for the Future

Christoph Heger,[1] André van Hoorn,[2] Mario Mann,[1] Dušan Okanović[2]
[1]NovaTec Consulting GmbH, Competence Area APM, Leinfelden-Echterdingen, Germany
[2]University of Stuttgart, Institute of Software Technology, Stuttgart, Germany

ABSTRACT

The performance of application systems has a direct impact on business metrics. For example, companies lose customers and revenue in case of poor performance such as high response times. Application performance management (APM) aims to provide the required processes and tools to have a continuous and up-to-date picture of relevant performance measures during operations, as well as to support the detection and resolution of performance-related incidents.

In this tutorial paper, we provide an overview of the state of the art in APM in industrial practice and academic research, highlight current challenges, and outline future research directions.

1. INTRODUCTION

Business success is directly influenced by the performance of the enterprise application systems that support it. Any performance issue that may arise during the production use of such applications may bring losses in revenue, and even cause customers to turn away. Examples of these losses and their impact are well documented. Google loses 20% traffic if their web sites respond 500 ms slower [9]. Amazon loses 1% of revenue for every 100 ms in latency [8]. Mozilla's study showed that if the page is not loaded within one to five seconds, users will leave the web site [4].

Application performance management (APM), as a core IT operations discipline, aims to achieve an adequate level of performance during operations. To achieve this, APM comprises methods, techniques, and tools for *i)* continuously monitoring the state of an applications system and its usage, as well as for *ii)* detecting, diagnosing, and resolving performance-related problems using the monitored data.

In this paper, we provide a state-of-the-art overview of the common APM activities (Section 2) and tools (Section 3), and highlight selected challenges and future directions (Section 4).

ICPE'17, April 22-26, 2017, L'Aquila, Italy
© 2017 ACM. ISBN 978-1-4503-4404-3/17/04. . . $15.00
DOI: http://dx.doi.org/10.1145/3030207.3053674

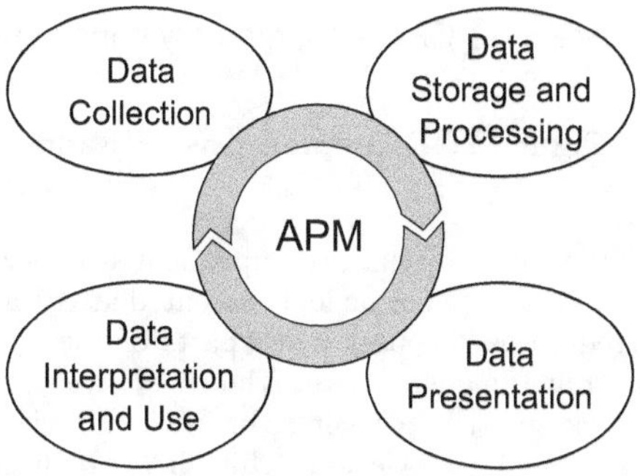

Figure 1: Continuous APM activities

2. APM ACTIVITIES

Regardless of the actual technical realization, APM involves the following four—concurrently conducted and interrelated—activities (Figure 1):

1. *Data collection.* Performance measures are collected from the different system tiers, layers, and locations by a combination of complementary techniques and technologies.
2. *Data storage and processing.* The collected data is combined into higher-level data structures, such as time series or execution traces.
3. *Data presentation.* Data is made available for visual inspection on different levels of abstraction and detail.
4. *Data interpretation and use.* The data is used to manually or automatically reason about and act upon the current state.

The remainder of this section details these activities.

2.1 Data Collection

Various types of performance-relevant measures can and need to be collected from a system and its clients. A core decision of APM regarding data collection is *where*, *what*, and *how* to collect, as detailed in the remainder of this section and depicted in Figure 2.

2.1.1 *Where to Collect Data?*

Modern application systems are multi-tiered, highly distributed, multi-layered, and accessed via different types of clients and devices (e.g., third-party systems and humans using desktop or mobile devices).

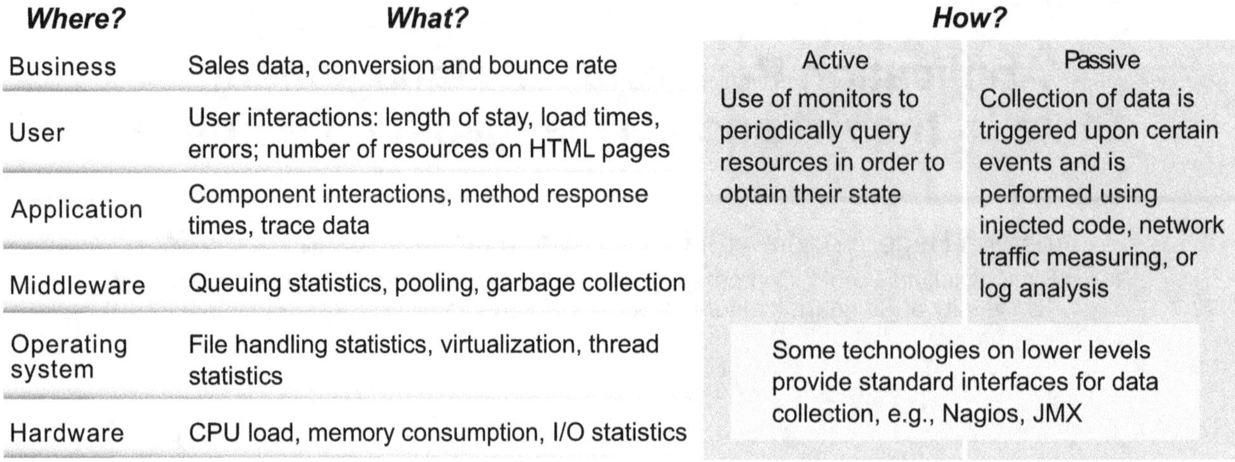

Figure 2: Example measures and techniques for data collection on different system levels

Most application systems are implemented in a way that, in addition to the application logic executed at the provider's site (referred to as the back-end), parts of the application are executed at the client's site. The client site usually constitutes a system tier accessing the back-end via (graphical) interfaces such as fat-clients, thin clients realized in web browsers, or native apps on mobile devices. Communication between clients and the back-end may be conducted by networked, wireless, and/or cellular connections. The back-end involves multiple tiers, for instance concerned with functionality regarding presentation, business, and persistence. The different application tiers and services are usually deployed to a heterogeneous infrastructure of distributed physical and virtual computing resources, each involving stacked layers from hardware to the application.

To provide an end-to-end view on application performance, APM requires the collection of relevant performance measures from all of the mentioned locations.

2.1.2 What Data to Collect?

The types of measures that can and should be collected depends on the previously mentioned locations, but also on the architectural style used by the application system.

As mentioned previously, the primary goal of any application system is to provide support for business processes. Hence, following a top-down perspective of APM, measures related to business and end-user experience are of primary interest. On a business level, these measures include data about completed and uncompleted conversions (e.g., statistics about client sessions with and without buy transactions). Measures about the end-user experience obtained on the client site include end-to-end response times of interactions, (page) load times, errors, and data about the UI usage. On the application level, measures about the application-internal behavior can be collected, including executions of methods, occurrences of exceptions, calls to remote services or databases, etc. On the system level, i.e., middleware, operating system, and hardware, measures about the state of hardware and software resources are collected in particular. Additional example measures for the different levels are included in Figure 2.

2.1.3 How to Collect Data?

There are many approaches for collecting the data, which can be categorized into two main groups: active and passive.

Active data collection is performed by periodic sampling of system services or resources. This includes the emulation of customers using synthetic requests. *Passive data collection*, on the other hand, is performed by collecting the data when certain events, such as method executions, occur. The data can be gathered by, e.g., injecting the measurement logic into the application source or byte code, stack trace sampling, capturing application logs, or mirroring network traffic. Additionally, for some system levels, there are standard interfaces that allow accessing and collecting data.

2.2 Data Storage and Processing

In order to have a central view on the collected data, it is usually transferred by the agents to a data storage for further processing and analysis. Proprietary or standard technologies (e.g., database management systems) can be and are being used. APM usually results in very large data sets that need to be handled efficiently [14].

Two data representations are commonly used: time series and execution traces. While time series represent summary statistics (e.g., counts, percentile, etc.) over time, execution traces [3] provide a detailed representation of the application-internal control flow that results from individual system requests. From this data, architectural information, including logical and physical deployments and interactions (topology), can be extracted.

2.3 Data Presentation

Due to the high quantity, APM information needs to be presented in a meaningful and comprehensible way using different interrelated and navigable views. These views can be categorized using two dimensions: the scope (business vs. technology) and the level of abstraction. Views can contain detailed business information such as the status of user devices, geolocations, as well as the health of the available services. On the other hand, data can be presented in the form of traces, time series, page flows, underlying topologies, server health, etc. These views vary from more abstract to more detailed, depending on what is required to answer the respective concern.

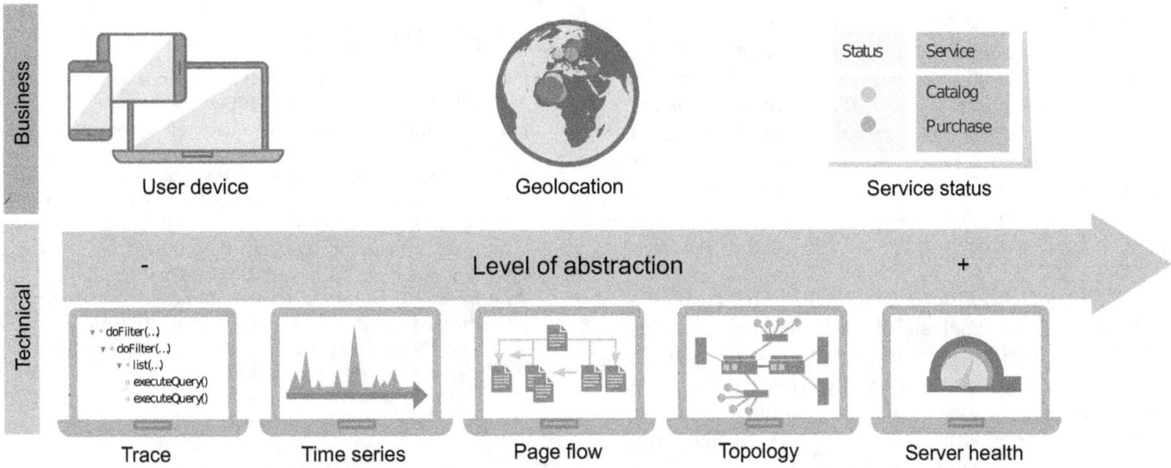

Figure 3: Example views on APM data with different scope and level of abstraction

An example use of the different views is as follows. A service status view shows that all services are healthy. As soon as a service is indicated not to be healthy any more, the incident needs to be analyzed. This is achieved by navigating to the other, more detailed views.

2.4 Data Interpretation and Use

The available data—comprising time series, execution traces, and topology information—can be interpreted and used with different goals, e.g.:

- *Problem detection and alerting.* Statistical techniques can be applied to the data to detect anomalies, which can indicate problems. Particularly time series data is used to detect violations of thresholds, which are either specified manually (e.g., based on service level agreement—SLAs) or learned from the historic data (baselines). In case an anomaly is detected, alerts can be sent out to system operators. To retain trust in the automatic detection and alerting, a high classification quality (e.g., in terms of precision, recall, and related measures) is desired.
- *Problem diagnosis and root cause isolation.* In case a problem occurred, the goal is to isolate its root cause during problem diagnosis—again manually or automatically. Manual analysis is usually conducted by employing the previously mentioned data representations, e.g., by navigating from status lights, via application topologies, to component drill downs, execution traces, and time series. There are also approaches to automatically detect root causes of typical performance problems, also known as performance antipatterns [15]. These approaches usually use trace data [6], but may also add other information, e.g., configuration data [12].
- *System refactoring and adaptation.* Other approaches use the data for automatic reaction in order to minimize the impact of performance issues. In cloud environments, auto-scaling approaches [10] can compare the data with SLAs [7], to determine further actions.

The aforementioned approaches can be conducted in a reactive or proactive manner, i.e., after a problem occurred or to predict that a problem will occur [13].

3. TOOLING SUPPORT

Tooling support is at the core of realizing the previously described APM activities. An ever increasing number of APM-supporting tools exist, ranging from fully-fledged APM tool suites covering the whole process, to specialized tools focusing on specific smaller problems, e.g., collection of certain measures, tailored database management systems, analytics, and visualization.

Most APM tools provide some basic functions, such as resource monitoring, architecture discovery, component deep-dive, end-user experience monitoring. In addition, they can provide data visualization and some form of analytics, e.g., baseline calculation and anomaly detection. Modern APM tools usually support monitoring in complex environments, that can consist of different platforms, different programming languages, etc. Tools usually consist of two components: *i)* a monitoring agent that collects the data, and *ii)* a storage and analysis component. Depending on the requirements, the analysis component can be further divided. Two usual modes of installation are available [2], *on-premise* and *SaaS-based* (software as a service).

The most mature and feature-rich APM tools are commercial products such as AppDynamics, CA APM, Dynatrace, and New Relic, regularly reviewed by Gartner [5]. As an alternative to commercial solutions, open-source tools are often used to implement the technical APM infrastructure. Mature open-source tools for monitoring on system-level have been around for many years (e.g., Nagios[1]). Open-source application-level monitoring tools (e.g., Kieker [17] and inspectIT[2]) are available. Other tools are available for collecting distributed execution traces (e.g., Zipkin[3]) and are being used together with emerging technologies for data storage and analytics (e.g., logging infrastructure, NoSQL databases, big data).

4. CHALLENGES AND DIRECTIONS

In this section, we share our view on what selected challenges and promising future research directions are.

[1] http://www.nagios.org/
[2] http://www.inspectit.eu/
[3] http://zipkin.io/

Automation of Supporting Activities. APM practice requires expertise and effort. For instance, expertise is required for setting up and maintaining APM configurations (e.g., deciding which parts of the software to instrument), as well as for the analysis and visualization of the data. Even for experts, manual tasks can be error-prone, costly, and frustrating because various tasks and problems are recurring. Automation of these tasks could be performed by formalizing the expert knowledge, and using it to solve these tasks.

Problem Detection, Diagnosis, and Prediction. Regarding the root cause analysis of performance problems, today's tools give little or no support. They are usually limited to alerting and visualization, but the diagnosis and root-cause analysis of performance issues, still has to be performed manually. Systematization of expert knowledge and machine learning approaches could provide key support here.

Interoperability. Currently, all of the tools store the data in their own format. As a consequence, it is a common practice that the same analysis approach has to be re-implemented for different APM tools. Some tools allow export of data in some machine readable format, such as XML, and this data can than be parsed with more or less effort [11]. However there are ongoing works on developing APIs and formats for APM tool interoperability [1, 11].

Development Paradigms and Architectural Styles. Modern development paradigms such as *DevOps* aim for frequent releases— posing additional APM challenges, e.g. how to calculate new baselines when the time span between new releases is extremely short. On the other hand, in these kind of environments, APM data from production can be made available to developers, e.g., for use in IDEs and extracted performance models. Emerging architectural styles and new cloud-based delivery models, e.g., microservice and serverless architectures, further extend the task of cross-platform monitoring and require the tools to cope with new measures and uncertainty in results.

5. CONCLUSIONS

APM allows to provide deep insights into the run-time behavior of application systems, supporting the detection, diagnosis, and resolution of incidents. In this paper, we covered the core APM activities and tooling support, and identified current limitations.

Modern development paradigms and architectural styles provide challenges to which APM practice and research will have to provide solutions. APM is not a purely technical topic anymore, as there is also a need for support of business activities and vice versa. We see promising future research directions in automation of supporting activities and analysis of data. In our current research, we try to tackle selected challenges by including expert knowledge and analyzing performance concerns by a declarative approach [6, 18]. Technology transfer of new APM approaches developed in research would benefit from the availability of real-world APM data for the evaluation of the approaches.

6. ACKNOWLEDGMENTS

This work is being supported by the German Federal Ministry of Education and Research (grant no. 01IS15004, *diagnoseIT*). The authors and this paper have benefited from frequent discussions with Stefan Siegl—including joint work on our APM poster [16] that served as a basis for this paper.

7. REFERENCES

[1] OpenTracing: A vendor-neutral open standard for distributed tracing. http://opentracing.io/, 2016.

[2] T. M. Ahmed, C.-P. Bezemer, T.-H. Chen, A. E. Hassan, and W. Shang. Studying the effectiveness of application performance management (APM) tools for detecting performance regressions for web applications: An experience report. In *Proc. 13th Int. Conf. on Mining Software Repositories (MSR '16)*, pages 1–12, 2016.

[3] G. Ammons, T. Ball, and J. R. Larus. Exploiting hardware performance counters with flow and context sensitive profiling. In *Proc. ACM SIGPLAN '97 Conf. on Programming Language Design and Implementation (PLDI '97)*, pages 85–96, 1997.

[4] B. Cutler. Firefox and page load speed (part I). https://blog.mozilla.org/metrics/2010/03/31/firefox-page-load-speed-part-i/, 2010.

[5] C. Haight and F. D. Silva. Gartner's magic quadrant for application performance monitoring suites, 2016.

[6] C. Heger, A. van Hoorn, D. Okanović, S. Siegl, and A. Wert. Expert-guided automatic diagnosis of performance problems in enterprise applications. In *Proc. 12th Europ. Dependable Computing Conf. (EDCC '16)*. IEEE, 2016.

[7] Y. Kouki and T. Ledoux. CSLA: A Language for improving Cloud SLA Management. In *Proc. Int. Conf. on Cloud Computing and Services Science (CLOSER 2012)*, pages 586–591, 2012.

[8] J. Liddle. Amazon Found Every 100ms of Latency Cost Them 1% in sales. http://blog.gigaspaces.com/amazon-found-every-100ms-of-latency-cost-them-1-in-sales/, 2008.

[9] G. Linden. Marissa Mayer at Web 2.0. http://glinden.blogspot.de/2006/11/marissa-mayer-at-web-20.html, 2006.

[10] T. Lorido-Botran, J. Miguel-Alonso, and J. A. Lozano. A review of auto-scaling techniques for elastic applications in cloud environments. *Journal of Grid Computing*, 12(4):559–592, 2014.

[11] D. Okanovic, A. van Hoorn, C. Heger, A. Wert, and S. Siegl. Towards performance tooling interoperability: An open format for representing execution traces. In *Proc. 13th Europ. Workshop on Computer Performance Engineering EPEW '16*, pages 94–108, 2016.

[12] T. Parsons and J. Murphy. Detecting performance antipatterns in component based enterprise systems. *Journal of Object Technology*, 7(3):55–91, 2008.

[13] T. Pitakrat, D. Okanovic, A. van Hoorn, and L. Grunske. An architecture-aware approach to hierarchical online failure prediction. In *12th Int. ACM SIGSOFT Conf. on Quality of Soft. Architectures*, pages 60–69, 2016.

[14] T. Rabl, S. Gómez-Villamor, M. Sadoghi, V. Muntés-Mulero, H.-A. Jacobsen, and S. Mankovskii. Solving big data challenges for enterprise application performance management. *Proc. VLDB Endow.*, 5(12):1724–1735, 2012.

[15] C. U. Smith and L. G. Williams. Software performance antipatterns. In *Proc. 2nd Int. Workshop on Software and Performance (WOSP '00)*, pages 127–136, 2000.

[16] A. van Hoorn and S. Siegl. Application performance management (APM): Continuous monitoring of application performance (OBJEKTspektrum poster, in german). https://www.sigs-datacom.de/wissen/fachposter/.

[17] A. van Hoorn, J. Waller, and W. Hasselbring. Kieker: A framework for application performance monitoring and dynamic software analysis. In *Proc. 3rd ACM/SPEC Int. Conf. on Perf. Eng. (ICPE '12)*, pages 247–248, 2012.

[18] J. Walter, A. van Hoorn, H. Koziolek, D. Okanovic, and S. Kounev. Asking "what"?, automating the "how"?: The vision of declarative performance engineering. In *Proc. 7th ACM/SPEC on Int. Conf. on Perf. Eng.*, ICPE '16, pages 91–94, 2016.

An Introduction to Systems and Control Theory for Computer Scientists and Engineers

[Tutorial paper]

Alberto Leva
Politecnico di Milano
Dipartimento di Elettronica, Informazione e Bioingegneria
Piazza Leonardo da Vinci 32
20133 Milano, Italy
alberto.leva@polimi.it

ABSTRACT

This paper accompanies a tutorial aimed at introducing the basics of system and control theory so as to foster their utilisation for the management, but most important for the *design*, of computing systems. The tutorial is divided into three parts. The first one introduces the fundamental concepts of dynamic system and feedback and gives an overview of the properties that a control system has to enjoy, together with the main techniques to prescribe and assess these properties formally. The second part discusses a few computer-related application examples, revisiting the addressed problems from scratch with a system-centric viewpoint, and comparing the solutions - and most important, the way the system is viewed and designed - with state-of-the-art alternatives. This leads to envisage the potentialities of control-based computing systems design, but at the same time to identify open problems, both technological and methodological: an overview of these aspects is the subject of the third part. This companion paper motivates the tutorial, illustrates its *rationale*, and provides a commented outline.

CCS Concepts

•General and reference → **Design;** **•Computing methodologies** → *Modeling and simulation;* **•Software and its engineering** → *Software performance;*

Keywords

Systems and control theory, control-based computing system design.

ICPE'17, April 22-26, 2017, L'Aquila, Italy

DOI: http://dx.doi.org/10.1145/3030207.3053677

1. WHY TEACH SYSTEMS AND CONTROL TO COMPUTER SCIENTISTS AND ENGINEERS

Control theory has been applied since a long time to manage computing systems for best performance [Abdelzaher et al. 2003]. This has given rise to a wealth of works on "computing systems control"—see e.g. the two books [Hellerstein et al. 2004] and [Janert 2013], spanning almost a decade, and their bibliographies.

The main *rationale* of computing systems control is to close feedback loops around a system, dynamically acting on some tuning parameters in such a way to optimise some measured metrics. Note that in doing so one implicitly assumes that in the absence of those control loops the system can operate, albeit not optimally. In a nutshell, therefore, the role of control theory in this setting is to provide a mathematical foundation to complement or replace heuristics in frameworks like the MAPE(-K) [IBM 2003].

The *scenario* just sketched is very well summarised in [Diao et al. 2005]. This paper, originating from an IBM research report, aims at exploring "the extent to which control theory can provide an architectural and analytic [notice the first adjective] foundation for building [notice the verb] self-managing systems" and showing the usefulness of establishing a "correspondence between the elements of autonomic systems and those in control systems", because "control theory provides a rich set of methodologies for building automated self-diagnosis and self-repair systems with properties such as stability, short settling times, and accurate regulation"—in one word, to ensure good and guaranteed performance.

If this viewpoint is taken, the main control skills required to use the control theory in computing systems are

1. model an existing and functional system, most frequently based on input/output measurements given the internal complexity of computing systems, and
2. design a control law to enforce the required properties.

Both these skills can be achieved with a quite basic and partial comprehension of the underlying theory – significantly more basic and partial than this proposal, to be explicit – and since the theory is well established and widely used in other domains, its application should be straightforward and successful.

As a literature and technology review too long to fit therein would reveal, however, things seldom go this way, and heuristics still plays a dominant role in the management of computing systems.

Heuristics is not evil by itself, of course, but if not properly confined, it can easily turn into "local problem by local problem" design, contrary to the systemic view that is typical of control theory. Sometimes, the complexity of systems designed by superimposing heuristic layers, reveals detrimental effects that a lack of systemic analysis allowed to stay concealed for a long time—a recent, impressing such story can be found in [Lozi et al. 2016]. Apparently, therefore, something is preventing control from fully unleashing its potential.

The main problem with the approach described so far is that *first* the system is designed, and *then* control moves in—this is another way to say that control loops are closed around *functional* systems, or from a slightly different standpoint, that design is not control-aware.

Indeed, if design is not carried out having control in mind, as is most frequently the case according to the story mentioned above and many others, or if the system is obtained by combining components designed previously with no awareness of their possible role in a control system, then a number of problems can – and do – arise: the available tuning knobs may be adequate for a human administrator sizing the system but not for controlling the required metrics online, components may reveal inadequate – if not unpredictably variable – timing properties, compounds can behave in ways unexpected by observing their components one by one, and so forth.

It has been recognised years ago that "software engineers need to use control concepts to master the ever-increasing complexity of computing systems" [Sanz and Årzen 2003, p. 14]. The author believes that this must also mean *designing* systems, or at least their critical parts, with control in mind, making the systems and control theory a means not only to manage complexity, but also and most important, to not create it unduly.

In this respect, recall the adjective "architectural" and the verb "building" evidenced in the quote from [Diao et al. 2005] above. Taking them in their full significance calls for much more than the mainstream "control of computing systems": it naturally leads to control-based computing system *design* [Leva et al. 2013]—an idea that has numerous declinations and can be applied to different depths, from instrumenting the system to make it easier to control with quite mainstream methods [Brun et al. 2009, Maggio et al. 2011, Patikirikorala et al. 2012], through the insertion of control-based specific active components [Hoffmann et al. 2013, Arcelli et al. 2015], down to a complete re-design of parts identified as critical [Terraneo et al. 2014, Al-Areqi et al. 2015].

Summing up, the author believes that the real potential of systems and control theory in the computing systems domain, is to formalise and set up management layers and loops, but also to help designing systems that are easily and well governed by those layers and loops.

In process control, the community has been talking for decades about "process/control co-design", see e.g. the historical paper [Ziegler and Nichols 1943], which is basically the same idea of building process and cotnrol together. Of course realising this in "industrial" domains in the strictest and somehow old sense of the term can be extremely difficult, because there the "process" can be something as heavy as a chemical plant. But in computers, where most objects to be controlled are software themselves, the idea of co-design should find a domain of election.

It has to be noted, however, that control-based design requires a deeper knowledge of systems and control than the basic one sketched above: in particular, it requires to master the subject not just as "yet another source of algorithms", but rather as a theoretical *corpus* to induce a *forma mentis* in analysing and designing the addressed systems. In the opinion of the author, for a proper use of control and an effective cooperation with control specialists when needed, computer scientists and engineers should be taught systems and control with the objective just outlined.

The problem is how so ambitious an objective can be achieved, and in the following a proposal is formulated. In detail, Section 2 talks basically about principles without necessarily thinking of a specific didactic form, while Section 3 specialises to the tutorial that this paper accompanies.

2. HOW TO TEACH (SOME IDEAS ON)

When teaching a subject new to a community, and that can affect their design habits significantly, quite often the best way to go is top down.

Specialising to the subject at hand, first one has to master the key ideas of *dynamic system* and *feedback* without thinking of any specific computer-related application. Otherwise, the temptation of classifying the presented control-based solutions against one's previous ideas – i.e., against a taxonomy that is inherently unfit to comprehend them – is irresistible, and if this temptation prevails, the pernicious idea of "control theory as a source of algorithms" is sowed.

On the contrary, first one has to be led to view dynamic systems as a formalism to describe the world, and perceive the generality of this description independently of its various flavours (continuous-time, discrete-time, event-based, and so forth); then, and in some sense as a consequence, one has to realise that feedback is already present in nature, simply as the way for systems to govern themselves and operate.

Once these two ideas are mastered, a conclusion quite naturally arises to guide the use of control in computers. In nature, systems start out with their feedback loops already installed—or, better, as a primary ingredient of their design. In computing systems one "creates one's physics", and wherever possible has to view feedback control as an ingredient of that physics, not a subsequent add-on.

More specifically, in computing systems one designs a "virtual physics" – think for example of the way jobs are created, accumulated and served in a queue network – employing resources from "real physics" like CPUs, disks, network transceivers, power supplies, and the like. The dynamic model of such a system entails unmodifiable parts – the laws of real physics – plus modifiable ones (referring again to the queue network case, all the queues', routers' and servers' management layers).

If the latter parts are designed in such a way to be well described by dynamic system, which is certainly and somehow naturally true for the former, then control moves in straightforwardly and successfully. If on the contrary the created physics is not keen to be modelled that way, for example because it was conceived directly as algorithms instead of dynamic systems generating algorithms, then control may find so hard an obstacle that the only feasible solution is to close loops around the system *as is*—with the known and already mentioned limitations.

Indeed, and of course once again in the opinion of the author, teaching systems and control to computer people is primarily attaining the goals above. One may object that in so doing hardly any recipe to solve a problem is taught, but the author bears to state that attempting to proceed by recipes is exactly the reason why introducing control in the computer community seems so difficult (when seen from the control side, at least).

In fact, a computer scientist or engineer is not required to learn and apply the huge variety of control techniques – control people are there to do that – but rather and most important, to help create control-friendly systems (analogous, in some sense symmetrical considerations hold about teaching computer concepts to control people, but the matter is outside the scope of this paper).

Of course, once the cultural result just sketched out is gained, one can also illustrate some recipes for specific problems of if this is deemed convenient and interesting for the audience, but at this point the said specific applications cannot blur the mastered general ideas.

3. THE TUTORIAL – A MOTIVATED STRUCTURE OVERVIEW

As anticipated, the tutorial is divided into three main parts, that are briefly described in this final section.

The first part introduces dynamic systems as a mathematical object, defines their properties, and provides some engineering interpretations, avoiding the computer domain for the reasons outlined above in Section 2.

Then, the fundamental idea of feedback is introduced, concentrating on its role as a means to prescribe relevant properties like stability and performance, and some examples are worked out. Only at this point parallels are introduced with analogous ideas in computer-related works, such as the SASO properties [Hellerstein et al. 2004]. This first part of the tutorial hence provides the tools—but most important, the concepts and the viewpoint.

The second part works out a few design examples. The addressed problems are revisited from scratch, compatibly with the available time, so as to to show that the key point is not to apply another type of algorithm, but to change the design perspective.

In this part, the occasion is taken on one hand to structure the treatise distinguishing problem, model, solution and algorithm, and on the other hand also to organise the system design along the control-theoretical structuring into sensor, controller and actuator. Besides streamlining the matter, this facilitates future interactions of the audience with control people. In particular, for example, the focus is set on when a system is control-friendly and when it is not.

The second part also stresses the importance of system-level simulation, with synthetic models that not only provide the (model of) the controller, but at the same time can be suitable to assess formal properties without requiring too much detail on the system, nor information that should strictly pertain to downstream design phases.

The third and final part re-visits the previous two in a view to generalising and abstracting the proposed ideas, and foster a discussion on the audience concerning their interest, expectations, and impressions.

On one hand, the purpose is here to point out the potential benefits yielded by control-based computing systems design, as proven by the shown examples and as perceivable by the sketched problem characterisation in control terms. On the other hand, a number of open problems, from both the technological and the methodological standpoints. To date, systems appear far less control-friendly than they could and should be, and to fill this gap, both new theoretical elaborations and design practices are needed. The ultimate hope of the author is that the tutorial can give a contribution to the establishment of collaborations toward this important goal.

4. REFERENCES

[Abdelzaher et al. 2003] T.F. Abdelzaher, J.A. Stankovic, C. Lu, R. Zhang, and Y. Lu. 2003. Feedback performance control in software services. *IEEE Control Systems Magazine* 23, 3 (2003), 74–90.

[Al-Areqi et al. 2015] S. Al-Areqi, D. Görges, and S. Liu. 2015. Event-based networked control and scheduling codesign with guaranteed performance. *Automatica* 57, 7 (2015), 128–134.

[Arcelli et al. 2015] D. Arcelli, V. Cortellessa, A. Filieri, and A. Leva. 2015. Control theory for model-based performance-driven software adaptation. In *Proc. 11th International ACM SIGSOFT Conference on Quality of Software Architectures.* New York, NY, USA, 11–20.

[Brun et al. 2009] Y. Brun, G. Di Marzo Serugendo, C. Gacek, H. Giese, H. Kienle, M. Litoiu, H. Müller, M. Pezzè, and M. Shaw. 2009. Engineering self-adaptive systems through feedback loops. In *Software engineering for self-adaptive systems*, B.H.C. Cheng, R. de Lemos, H. Giese, P. Inverardi, and J. Magee (Eds.). Springer, Berlin, Germany, 48–70.

[Diao et al. 2005] Y. Diao, J.L. Hellerstein, S. Parekh, R. Griffith, G.E. Kaiser, and D. Phung. 2005. A control theory foundation for self-managing computing systems. *IEEE journal on selected areas in communications* 23, 12 (2005), 2213–2222.

[Hellerstein et al. 2004] J. Hellerstein, Y. Diao, S. Parekh, and D.M. Tilbury. 2004. *Feedback control of computing systems.* John Wiley & Sons, New York, NY, USA.

[Hoffmann et al. 2013] H. Hoffmann, M. Maggio, M.D. Santambrogio, A. Leva, and A. Agarwal. 2013. A generalized software framework for accurate and efficient management of performance goals. In *Proc. 2013 International Conference on Embedded Software.* Montréal, Canada, Article No. 6658597.

[IBM 2003] IBM. 2003. An architectural blueprint for autonomic computing. *IBM White paper* (2003).

[Janert 2013] P.K. Janert. 2013. *Feedback control for computer systems.* O'Reilly Media, Sebastopol, CA, USA.

[Leva et al. 2013] A. Leva, M. Maggio, A.V. Papadopoulos, and F. Terraneo. 2013. *Control-based operating system design.* IET, London, UK.

[Lozi et al. 2016] J.P. Lozi, B. Lepers, J. Funston, F. Gaud, V. Quéma, and A. Fedorova. 2016. The Linux scheduler: a decade of wasted cores. In *Proc. 11th European Conference on Computer Systems.* London, UK, 1–16.

[Maggio et al. 2011] M. Maggio, H. Hoffmann, M.D. Santambrogio, A. Agarwal, and A. Leva. 2011. Decision making in autonomic computing systems: Comparison of approaches and techniques. In *Proc. 8th ACM International Conference on Autonomic Computing*. Karlsruhe, Germany, 201–204.

[Patikirikorala et al. 2012] T. Patikirikorala, A. Colman, J. Han, and L. Wang. 2012. A systematic survey on the design of self-adaptive software systems using control engineering approaches. In *Proc. 2012 ICSE Workshop on Software Engineering for Adaptive and Self-Managing Systems*. Zürich, Switzerland, 33–42.

[Sanz and Årzen 2003] R. Sanz and K.E. Årzen. 2003. Trends in software and control. *IEEE Control Systems Magazine* 23, 3 (2003), 12–15.

[Terraneo et al. 2014] F. Terraneo, L. Rinaldi, M. Maggio, A.V. Papadopoulos, and A. Leva. 2014. FLOPSYNC-2: sub-microsecond, sub-μA clock synchronisation for wireless sensor networks. In *Proc. IEEE Real-Time Systems Symposium RTSS 2014*. Roma, Italy, 11–20.

[Ziegler and Nichols 1943] J.G. Ziegler and N.B. Nichols. 1943. Process lags in automatic control circuits. *Transactions of the ASME* 65, 5 (1943), 433–443.

Author Index

Abad, Andres G. 87
Abad, Cristina L. 87
Abedi, Ali 287
Ahn, Soohan 257
Ali-Eldin, Ahmed 75
Andrzejak, Artur 389
Angerstein, Tobias 341
Apte, Varsha 115
Arlitt, Martin 143
Arnold, Jeremy A. 155
Awad, Mahmoud 127
Bajunaid, Noor 245
Baker, Gavin 305
Bast, Salman 423
Bauer, André 425
Bause, Falko 233
Beckett, John 155
Bezemer, Cor-Paul 373
Binder, Walter 0
Bitto, Verena 3
Bondi, André B. 335
Boudjadar, Jalil 263
Bouloukakis, Georgios 275
Brataas, Gunnar 413
Brecht, Tim 51, 287
Buchholz, Peter 233
Bulej, Lubomír 401
Cardellini, Valeria 417
Carlsson, Niklas 143
Casale, Giuliano 169
Cassell, Benjamin 51
Cazzoli, Mattia 169
Chahal, Dheeraj 171, 173, 317
Chang, Li-Wen 385
Chen, Deming 385
Chen, Yao-Min 157
Cho, Kyu Tae 223
Chow, Kingsum 419
Coelho, Fábio 293
Cortellessa, Vittorio 0
Costa, Diego 389
Czarnecki, Krzysztof 39
Dayarathna, Miyuru 91
Deffner, Maximilian 155
Demertzi, Melina 157
Di Pompeo, Daniele 323
Dinn, Andrew 349
Eager, Derek 51
El Hajj, Izzat 385
Epema, Dick 75
Fægri, Tor Erlend 413
Fischmeister, Sebastian 39
Fitzek, Stefan 327
Forshaw, Matthew 349
Ganesan, Karthik 157
Gawali, Devidas 115
Georgantas, Nikolaos 275
Ghit, Bogdan 75
Gnedt, David 331
Gómez-Luna, Juan 385
Guo, Jianmei 39
Gupta, Anshul 115
Hackenberg, Daniel 27
Hashemian, Raoufehsadat 143
Hashimoto, Masatomo 361
Hauser, Frederik 103, 175
Heger, Christoph 341, 429
Herbst, Nikolas 75, 425
Hofer, Peter 331
Horký, Vojtěch 401
Huang, Sitao 385
Hwu, Wen-mei 385
Ilyushkin, Alexey 75
Incerto, Emilio 323
Iosup, Alexandru 75
Issarny, Valérie 275
Jalby, William 15
Jayasena, Sanath 91
Jiang, Shuai 169
Joshi, Shrinivas 157
Jun, Tae Joon 223
Kattepur, Ajay 275
Kaur, Arvinder 213
Khawaja, Ahmed 157
Kim, Daeyoung 223
Kluge, Thomas 341
Kommireddy, Akhilesh 115
Kounev, Samuel 155, 353, 425
Kovačević, Aleksandar 341
Koziolek, Anne 0
Krishnamurthy, Diwakar 143
Kuck, David 15
Kumar, Mukund 171
Kunde, Shruti 159
Laaber, Christoph 167
Lange, Klaus-Dieter 155
Lee, Seongjin 257
Lee, Seung Young 223
Leitner, Philipp 167, 373
Lengauer, Philipp 3, 327, 357
Leva, Alberto 433
Liang, Qianlin 63
Lo, David 389
Lopes, Vitor S. 169
Lucio, Luis E. 87
Lupo, Chris 305
Maeda, Toshiyuki 361
Malony, Allen 345
Mann, Mario 429
Mathew, Beeny 173
May, Johannes 233
Mazouz, Abdelhafid 15
Menascé, Daniel A. 127, 245
Meng, Tianhui 139
Menth, Michael 103, 175
Merchant, Arif 321
Michael, Nicolas 189
Minami, Kazuo 361
Mohamed, Saleh 349
Molka, Daniel 27
Mössenböck, Hanspeter 3, 327, 331, 357
Muttillo, Vittoriano 161, 323
Nadjm-Tehrani, Simin 263
Nagel, Wolfgang E. 27
Nambiar, Manoj Karunakaran 171, 317

Nasser, Rabee 163
Norris, Boyana 345
Odeh, Feras 163
Okanović, Dušan 341, 429
Oliveira, Rui 293
Papadopoulos, Alessandro V. 75
Park, Changhyun 257
Patil, Sheetal 189
Paulo, João 293
Pavlin, Gregor 179
Penders, Ate 179
Pereira, José 293
Petkovich, Jean-Christophe 39
Phalak, Chetan 165
Poess, Meikel 0
Pomante, Luigi 323
Quaglia, Francesco 177
Ramakrishnan, Raghu 213
Ramannavar, Nitin 189
Ravindra, Sajith 91
Rotondi, Marco 161
Salhi, Haytham 163
Schmitt, Norbert 353
Schöne, Robert 27
Schörgenhumer, Andreas 331
Seboek, Janos 389
Serazzi, Giuseppe 169
Shang, Zhihao 139
Shen, Yixiao 189
Silva, Marcio 423
Singhal, Rekha 159, 165
Sips, Henk 179
Smirni, Evgenia 0
Spear, Wyatt 345
Stefan, Petr 401
Summers, Jim 51
Sung, Jan-Lung 189
Szepesi, Tyler 51
Szucs, Michelle 157
Taweel, Adel 163
Terai, Masaaki 361
Thomas, Nigel 349
Tůma, Petr 401
Urgaonkar, Bhuvan 63
Valenete, Giacomo 323, 161
Valov, Pavel 39
van Hoorn, André 341, 429
Varbanescu, Ana Lucia 179
Vilaça, Ricardo 293
Viswanath, T.V.S. 115
von Kistowski, Jóakim 155, 353
Wakou, Nicholas 423
Wang, Cheng 63
Wang, Luyang 157
Weninger, Markus 3, 357
Wolter, Katinka 139
Won, Youjip 257
Wong, Bernard 51
Wong, David C. 15
Wuerthinger, Thomas 1
Yeun, Kyuoke 223
Yoo, Myong Hwan 223
Zagieboylo, Drew 201
Zaman, Kazi A. 201
Zhu, Lulai 169
Zhu, Wanyi 419

www.ingramcontent.com/pod-product-compliance
Lightning Source LLC
LaVergne TN
LVHW080007210926
848481LV00011B/2965